MANAGING HUMAN RESOURCES

SIXTH EDITION

RANDALL S. SCHULER
NEW YORK UNIVERSITY

SOUTH-WESTERN College Publishing
An International Thomson Publishing Company

Publishing Team Director: John Szilagyi
Developmental Editor: Alice Denny
Production Editor: Kelly Keeler
Internal Design: Lou Ann Thiesing
Internal Illustrations: Sam Sisco
Cover Design: Barb Matulionis Design
Cover Illustration: © James Yang/SIS
Production House: settingPace
Marketing Manager: Steve Scoble

ISBN 0-538-87745-6

Library of Congress Cataloging-in-Publication Data:
Schuler, Randall S.
Managing human resouces/Randall S. Schuler—6th ed.

p. cm.
Includes bibliographical references and index.
ISBN 0-538-87745-6
1. Personnel management. 2. Personnel management—case studies.
I. Title
HF5549 .S24895 1997 97-
CIP

Printed in the United States of America
2 3 WST 0 9 8

I(T)P®

International Thomson Publishing
South-Western College Publishing is an ITP Company.
The ITP trademark is used under license.

To Wilson and Mary Schuler, who by their own actions have instilled in me the belief that working hard, doing one's best, and continuous improvement are satisfying and rewarding.

CONTENTS

PREFACE

Managing Human Resources, sixth edition identifies the opportunities and challenges facing human resource management. The book will give you an understanding of the fundamental ways that organizations and their HR departments go about managing their people. No two people are the same. The same can be said of organizations and HR departments. In this textbook, you will learn from the examples of the organizations that have been recognized as effective managers of human resources. These organizations include: Aetna, Au Bon Pain, Avon, Chaparral Steel, Chrysler, Cisco, Coca-Cola, Disney, Federal Express, General Electric, Hallmark Cards, Intel, Levi Strauss, Lincoln Electric, Microsoft, Nordstrom, PepsiCo, Saturn, Southwest Airlines, Starbuck's, Sun, Texas Instruments, Unilever, UPS, Wal-Mart, Weyerhaeuser, and WMX Technologies. These firms are typically effective year after year and are considered to be innovators in HR management.

Several important themes run throughout the textbook: ethics, partnership, multiple stakeholders, change, diversity, teamwork, and globalization. Each of these themes greatly impacts HR management. In fact, these themes have become broad societal concerns as we reach the 21st century. Devote some energy and thought to these themes as you will encounter them in one form or another throughout your working life.

The textbook also provides opportunities to increase your skills in managing human resources. Analyzing the end-of-chapter cases will increase your critical thinking, problem-solving, and oral presentation skills. The end-of-text projects and field projects will increase your analytical skills and your ability to relate HR activities to the needs of the business. The Career Management Exercises, such as the one at the end of Chapter 6, will increase your self-diagnostic skills. Awareness of your career goals, desires, strengths, and weaknesses can help you choose a career in which you will be satisfied and productive. Company examples found on the Internet and end-of-section Internet exercises will further strengthen your skills in managing human resources.

Particular emphasis is placed on HR management in the international arena. The text acquaints you with various aspects of global HR management. Comparisons are made between HR management practices in the United States and in other countries. Issues related to HR management of a global workforce by U.S. firms are presented throughout the text. In addition, selected Career Management Exercises encourage you to explore your interest in being an expatriate employee.

This text will enable you to view HR management issues and challenges from the viewpoints of the employee, employer, customer, supplier, the organization, and society. Each of these stakeholders has a different viewpoint and agenda. HR professionals must identify each stakeholder's perspective and manage in such a way that the goals and concerns of each stakeholder group are considered. Today, effective HR management involves everyone in the organization. The 1990s have witnessed an increased partnership among top management, HR professionals, line managers, and employees. This partnership trend will continue to grow.

The new edition of *Managing Human Resources* also conveys the importance of managing human resources in an increasingly complex legal and regulatory environment. As U.S. employment law becomes more complex and as firms grow into global operations, HR professionals must carefully consider the legal ramifications of their human resource decisions.

New to the Sixth Edition

Every chapter has been extensively rewritten and reorganized to incorporate the most current ideas, research results, and real company examples of human resource practices in action. More emphasis is placed on developing the student's HR management skills. Other new materials include:

- An additional case has been added to selected chapters. One of the end-of-text cases is entirely new, Nordstrom, while the other, Lincoln Electric, has been updated. These cases allow students to explore HR management issues in a service and a manufacturing company.
- Chapter 5, "Managing Organizational Change and HR Planning," is entirely new. It explores three major changes in organizations: downsizing and layoffs, workforce diversity, and mergers and alliances. Clearly, these changes will continue to affect the ways in which human resources are managed well into the 21st century.
- The emphasis placed on the themes of multiple stakeholders, change, and teamwork are new to this edition. They join with and enhance the previous key themes of ethics, partnership, diversity, and globalization.
- Internet exercises are included at the end of most chapters. These exercises are structured to provide a starting point for identifying what companies are doing to manage their human resources. Web addresses are provided where appropriate and a list of current web addresses is included in Appendix B. The web addresses were current at the time of publication. We also limited the sites listed to those that should be fairly stable over time.

Features

All important features from the successful fifth edition have been retained. These include:

- Four types of margin notes: Learning objectives, Did You Know? items, review notes, and definitions of key terms
- Managing Human Resources features in each chapter that provide real world examples of HR management in practice
- HR Advice and Application features in each chapter that provide insight about important HR and career management decisions
- End-of-chapter materials: Key Concepts, Review and Discussion Questions, Cases, Projects and Exercises, and extensive endnotes
- Glossary
- Two end-of-text cases (Lincoln Electric and Nordstrom), which are integrated throughout the text with end-of-chapter questions
- Appendices summarizing relevant laws, court decisions, and regulations

Since ethics, partnership, multiple stakeholders, change, diversity, teamwork, and globalization are recurring themes in HR management today, each is featured throughout the text. Small icons identify significant discussions of selected topics. Specific treatment of these issues includes:

Ethics. This edition contains many examples of how firms deal with ethical issues. For example, Chapter 3 includes "Managing Human Resources at WMX Technologies: Building an Ethical Culture" feature. As a follow-up, Chapter 11 includes a discussion of the WMX ethics training program. In addition, most chapters include discussions on ethics as it relates to the HR management topic.

Partnership. Near the beginning of every chapter is a Partnership feature. This feature reflects an important theme in HR today: effective HR management requires the involvement of everyone. Involvement assures that those affected by HR management activities have a say in what happens. Partnership also ensures that HR activities are clearly linked to the nature and needs of the business.

Multiple Stakeholders. Consistent with the theme of partnership, multiple stakeholders are extensively described in Chapter 1. Stakeholders are groups or individuals interested in and affected by the quality of a firm's HR management activities. The major stakeholders for any company include employees, investors, customers, suppliers, the company itself, and society. The real challenge for the HR professional is to coordinate and attain the many and varied objectives and goals of these stakeholders.

Change. The environment for business is in a state of constant change. The rate of change appears to be building as the century comes to a close. Although change is a recurring theme, Chapter 5 extensively discusses the role the HR department plays in assisting firms manage the change process and adapt to changes in the environment.

Diversity. Firms have always had diversity in their workforce in terms of age, work functions, level in the organization, manager/nonmanager distinctions, and educational levels. The workforce of the 1990s has grown in diversity of ethnic groups, gender, religion, nationality, culture, and disabilities. Firms now realize that to manage human resources effectively means learning how to manage and motivate in new and different ways. This textbook considers the impact of a diverse workforce on the various aspects of HR management. Chapter 5 includes a thorough discussion of diversity as an example of a significant environmental change that has major HR management implications.

Teamwork. Increasingly, companies are depending on teamwork to accomplish their strategic goals. Technology, market conditions, competitive requirements, and change make teamwork vital for organizational success. Consequently, more HR management activities need to be designed for individuals working as part of a team. Chapter 7 includes an extensive discussion of teamwork as it relates to job design.

Globalization. Because we live in an increasingly global environment, the new edition includes more descriptions of HR practices in other countries. Emphasis is given to comparative information among the U.S., Mexico, and Canada. This edition also has increased discussion about U.S. multinational corporations. For example, Chapter 11 includes a feature that describes how the Gillette Company develops global managers.

Organization of the Book

The guiding principle in presenting this exciting material is a flow model for a complex and ever-changing environment.

- Section 1 provides an overview of HR management and the HR department. We then describe the environment of HR management.
- Section 2 provides understanding of the environment that is critically important to all other topics developed in the text.
- Section 3 explores the management of organizational and human resource changes. It includes the new Chapter 5 that discusses the three major changes in organizations. This section also includes an important chapter on

career planning and management. This chapter will help you begin to identify the important issues you will face as you enter the workforce.

- Section 4 describes the activities that occur as organizations plan for the number and types of employees they need. This includes assessing present and future employee needs in light of fairness and legal issues, labor market demand, competition, and the nature and needs of the organization.

- Sections 5 and 6 explore the human resource activities that relate to training, appraising, and compensating employees. Training and retraining are critical issues in an information era. With rapid changes in job requirements, existing employees must learn new sets of skills. Once trained, employees need fair and clearly stated performance standards. The book describes effective appraisal systems that give feedback at the right time and that allow performance deficiencies to be identified and corrected. Finally, compensation issues are fully explored. Various systems of direct and indirect pay are considered, including methods that connect pay to performance.

- Section 7 examines ways to improve work environments and relationships with selected stakeholders. The ever-evolving role of unions is considered, including their participation in the globalization of business. Safety and health and collective bargaining are important issues for employees and organizations. The role of HR management in these issues is discussed. The last chapter of the text explores the management and storage of the vast amount of human resource data gathered by businesses. Legal and security issues are addressed. In addition, the ways in which the human resource information system can be utilized for strategic purposes is investigated.

Ancillaries

Supplementary materials for *Managing Human Resources*, sixth edition, were prepared by Paul Buller and Randall Schuler. Contact ITP's Academic Resource Center at 1-800-423-0563 for information about any of the ancillary items.

Instructor ancillaries for the sixth edition of *Managing Human Resources* include:

- An *Instructor's Manual* (ISBN: 0-538-87746-4) that contains chapter outlines and lecture enhancements including experimental and skill building exercises, end-of chapter case notes, and additional cases related to the major text themes

- A *Test Bank* (ISBN: 0-538-87079-6) that includes multiple choice, true/false, and short essay questions with answers page-referenced to the text

- WesTest™ (ISBN: 0-538-87749-9), a computerized version of the *Test Bank*

- PowerPoint presentation screens (ISBN: 0-538-87083-4) that contain elements of each chapter

- Video Examples (ISBN: 0-538-87083-4) that include short segments of companies illustrating topics discussed in various chapters.

To further enhance HR management skills and classroom activities, South-Western College Publishing has several supplemental texts that may be bundled with the main text for student purchase:

- *Applications in Human Resource Management: Cases, Exercises, and Skill Builders*, 3e by Stella M. Nkomo, Myron D. Fottler, and R. Bruce McAfee (ISBN: 0-538-85337-9). This text supplement includes seventy-five new and updated cases, experiential exercises, skill builders, and term projects.

- *Internet Guide to Human Resources* by Georganna Hall and Gemmy Allen (ISBN: 0-538-87620-4). The Guide identifies many relevant HR web sites with interesting learning activities.
- *Case Problems in Management, Organizational Behavior and Human Resource Management*, by R. S. Schuler and P. Buller (ISBN: 0-314-07140-7).
- *Personal Computer Projects for Human Resource Management* by N. J. Beutell (ISBN: 0-314-07135-0).

Acknowledgements

Special appreciation goes to several reviewers who provided extremely helpful comments and suggestions. They include:

- John Griffen, Northeastern University
- Fred Heidrich, Black Hills State University
- Natalie Hunter, Portland State University
- Sallie Johnson, Embry Riddle
- Brian Klass, University of South Carolina
- Machelle Schroeder, University of Wisconsin-Platteville
- Jusanne Vest, University of Southern Mississippi

As with previous editions, many fine individuals were of critical importance in the completion of the final product. They include Paul Buller, Gonzaga University; Peter Cappelli, Wharton School; Clifford Jay and David Yu-Chia Kuo, Stern School of Business; Susan Jackson, New York University; Stuart Youngblood, Texas Christian University; Gary Florkowski, University of Pittsburgh; Bill Todor, Ohio State University; Nancy Napier, Idaho State University; Vandra Huber, University of Washington; John Slocum, Southern Methodist University; Lynn Shore, Georgia State University; Mary Ahmed, Grand Forks; Ed Lawler, Gerry Leford, and Susan Mohrman, Center for Effective Organizations, University of Southern California; Hrach Bedrosian and Richie Freedman, New York University; Stewart Black and David Ricks, Thunderbird; Mark Mendenhall, University of Tennessee at Chattanooga; Vladimir Pucik, Cornell University; Moshe Banai, Baruch College; Steve Korbin, Wharton School; Mickey Kavanaugh, SUNY, Albany; and Mark Huselid, Rutgers University.

International associates involved include Ed van Sluijs, University of Limberg; Hugh Scullion, University of Newcastle in England; Paul Sparrow, Manchester Business School in England; Shimon Dolan, University of Montreal; Peter Dowling, University of Tasmania in Australia; Lynda Gratton and Nigel Nicholson, London Business School; Chris Brewster and Shaun Tyson, Cranfield Management School; Michael Poole, Cardiff Business School; Paul Stonham, European School of Management, Oxford; Jan Krulis-Randa and Bruno Staffelbach, University of Zurich; Albert Stahli, GSBA in Zurich; Per Jenster and Jean Marie Hiltrop, IMD; Paul Evans, INSEAD; Jason Sedine, ISA/HEC; Christian Scholz, University of Saarlandes; Pay Joynt, Henley Management College; Reijo Luostarinen, Helsinki School of Economics & Business; Steve Barnett, York University; Carol Somers, Lowell University; Yoram Zeira, Tel-Aviv University; Dan Ordrack, University of Toronto; and Cal Reynolds, ORC.

Several human resource managers and practicing line managers also contributed in many important ways to this edition, particularly with examples and insights from their work experiences. The include Mike Mitchell, Judith Miller, Tom Kroeger, Patricia Ryan, Margaret Magnus, Allan Halcrow, Barbara Heckman, Don Bohl, Bob Kenny, Rose Cervino, Steve Marcus, Paul Beddia, Mark Saxer,

Franz Gerny, John Fulkerson, Cal Reynolds, Joan Kelly, Michael Losey, Jo Mattern, Price Pritchett, Lyle Steele, Rowland Stichweh, Bill Maki, Rick Sabo, Bruce Cable, Gil Fry, Bill Reffett, Jerry Laubenstein, Richard Hagan, and Horace Parker.

The following individuals graciously provided case and exercise materials: George Colley, Bruce Evans, Mitchell W. Fields, Hugh L. French, Jr., Susan E. Jackson, Stuart Youngblood, Ed Lawler, John Slocum, Jeff Lenn, Hrach Bedrosian, George Biles, Kay Stratton, Bruce Kiene, Martin R. Moser, and James W. Thacker. A special note of thanks goes to Pamela Lewis, Stephen Goodman, Patricia Fandt for their materials on IBAX; Arthur Sharplin for Lincoln Electric; and Richard Freedman for Nordstrom.

The support, encouragement, and assistance of many individuals were absolutely critical in the completion of the total project. They include Paul Buller of Gonzaga University who prepared the *Instructor's Manual* and other ancillaries; Lou DeCaro, who worked extensively and carefully in the preparation of the final chapter drafts; and Dave Rogers, Chair of the Management Department and George Daly, Dean of the Stern School of Business. Also, Kelly Keeler, production editor at South-Western College Publishing deserves special thanks for her help and competence.

RANDALL S. SCHULER
New York

SECTION 1

Managing Human Resources

To be effective in the highly competitive environments of today, American business needs to devote a significant amount of skill, knowledge, and attention to managing human resources. Chief executive officers, managers, and people at all levels of an organization need to be involved in this process: all the people in an organization need to see themselves as actually sharing the human resource (HR) function, in partnership with each other. At the same time, the HR department leader needs to be part of the senior management team making vital business decisions.

Chapter 1 describes the reasons why effective management of the HR function is growing in importance. In part, it is because managing people well influences so many outcomes, such as profitability, productivity, employee involvement, and investor return, that are important to the stakeholders of HR management, including the organization itself, its employees, stockholders, customers, and the entire society. It also is being seen as a way to gain competitive advantage and to be successful in the global marketplace. But gaining this advantage through the effective management of human resources is very challenging. Increasingly it requires partnership among everyone in the organization—line managers, HR professionals, and employees. This partnership is described in Chapter 1.

Chapter 1 also describes some major trends in managing human resources: globalization; diversity; teams and teamwork; the growth of small business and entrepreneurial firms; and the use of technical expertise and systematic analysis. These trends are having a major impact on how companies manage their human resources today and likely will do so in the foreseeable future.

Chapter 2 details the roles and activities of the formal HR department. These roles include performing activities that assist an organization in improving its bottom-line results, being more creative and adaptive to change, and continuously evaluating and improving HR activities. The various roles of the HR leader and staff are described. You will see that there are many roles to be played and many jobs to be done—in short, there are many opportunities to find a niche that suits your mix of skills and abilities if you wish to work in the HR department.

Chapter 2 also discusses how HR departments organize and "customerize" themselves to better serve the needs of line managers, employees, and the organization. Here we revisit the theme of partnership. There is also a discussion of several major trends within HR departments: becoming world-class; re-engineering and outsourcing; the greening of HR; and the development of HR mission statements. Such statements tell everyone what the HR department is doing, what its values are, and how important it is to the rest of the organization. Mission statements have become an important avenue for change and a way to focus direction and implement strategies. The first of several discussions on the impact of globalization takes place in Chapter 2. We begin to look at the HR issues facing American firms doing business abroad and at how cultural differences can impact the way a firm manages its human resources in another country. Of vital importance to businesses today, globalization will be revisited in future chapters.

CHAPTER 1

Human Resource Management

Learning Objectives

When you have finished studying this chapter, you should be able to:

1. Explain why managing human resources effectively has become so important.
2. Identify the stakeholders of human resource management and their objectives.
3. Describe major activities of human resource management.
4. Describe who is responsible for managing human resources.
5. Describe the meaning of partnership in managing human resources.
6. Discuss some current trends in human resource management.

> *"We owe our success to our people."*
>
> *Herb Kelleher*
> *Chief Executive Officer*
> *Southwest Airlines*[1]

Chapter Outline

MANAGING HUMAN RESOURCES

at Southwest Airlines

"The real difference is the effort that Herb gets out of the people who work for him. That is very, very hard to duplicate."[2] Of course, the Herb being referred to is Herbert D. Kelleher, president and chief executive officer (CEO) of Southwest Airlines. Headquartered in Dallas, Texas, Southwest Airlines has over 18,000 employees, and holds the airline industry record for most consecutive years of profitability: 25! Its history of 25 percent yearly earnings increases has made it a favorite stock among the analysts on Wall Street since its beginnings in the early 1970s. Today it is the sixth largest U. S. airline.

The secret? Although Southwest Airlines' employees, 80 percent of whom belong to unions, are paid about average for the industry, they are far more productive than those at rival airlines, allowing Kelleher to fly more planes and serve more passengers with fewer employees than the other airlines. Southwest Airlines has a generous profit-sharing plan (about 15 percent of net profits are shared with the employees), and it matches 100 percent of an employee's contribution to his/her retirement plan. In part because the hourly compensation rate (which begins at around $6.50) is tied to seniority, few employees leave the company. (There never has been a layoff and voluntary turnover is only four percent per year.) Employees have a great deal of flexibility in the number of hours worked: "You can work as much or as little as you want, because you can trade shifts with people," says Libby Sartain, vice president of people.[3]

A big part of what motivates the people at Southwest Airlines to work so productively is Herb Kelleher himself. Kelleher wants his employees to have fun. He even hires them on this basis: "What we are looking for, first and foremost, is a sense of humor."[4] Once people are hired, Kelleher allows, even encourages, outrageous behavior. As a result, Southwest Airlines recruits and retains employees who can flourish in a friendly work environment and foster good customer service. Kelleher's style and philosophy of managing not only have resulted in a highly productive airline with highly satisfied employees, the airline has achieved the highest on-time flight record, highest customer satisfaction, and best baggage handling distinctions—in other words, the Service Triple Crown—from the U. S. Department of Transportation. Herb Kelleher has been named by Fortune as one of the best CEOs in America. And because of its record of earnings and profit growth, Business Week named Southwest Airlines one of its "Go-Go Goliaths" along with the likes of Microsoft, Hewlett-Packard, Wal-Mart, Intel, Nucor, and Motorola.[5]

If Southwest is so successful in an industry that has lost billions of dollars over the past 20 years, why haven't other airlines tried to copy Southwest? They have, but it is very hard to copy the way a company manages its employees; it is also very hard to duplicate the efforts of a great leader like Herb Kelleher. Consequently, Southwest retains its competitive advantage over its rivals and would-be rivals thanks to its employees and its leader.[6]

The preceding discussion illustrates three important themes in human resource (HR) management. One is the link that exists between the success of a firm and the quality of its people. At Southwest Airlines, Herb Kelleher believes and acts in ways that demonstrate the company's belief in the importance of people (associates) to the business. This gives associates reason to believe and trust the company. In return, the associates deliver high-quality, friendly, and knowledgeable service—the essence of airlines according to Herb Kelleher.

Another theme is the conscious attempt to actively link the employees to the success of the business. Southwest joins its business and people management philosophies through great recruitment and selection, performance appraisal and compensation, extensive training, and excellent leadership. Leadership is critical in making the other HR activities work effectively. Southwest's leadership is basi-

In Southwest Airlines, human resource management is

- **Effective**
- **Linked to business decisions**
- **Done in partnership with everyone**
- **Key to its success**
- **Key to customer satisfaction**

"We feel this fun atmosphere builds a strong sense of community. It also counterbalances the stress of hard work and competition."

Elizabeth Pedrick Sartain
Vice President of the People Department
Southwest Airlines

cally humble leadership: it is the manager catering to the associates and putting them first, not putting management first. Then there is the team spirit, the hearty enthusiasm and willingness to celebrate and have fun. Together these practices contribute to the success of the firm and make it very difficult for other firms to do the same thing. And HR management is central to this unbeatable combination.

The third theme is related to the first two. It involves sharing the responsibility for this important activity—people management. Top management is responsible for managing human resources. And, of course, the people under the leadership of Libby Sartain are responsible as well. This kind of partnership, a recent development in American business, is gaining widespread acceptance. Some organizations are taking this idea even further: they are actively encouraging the involvement of the employees themselves in HR management! Southwest Airlines has been involving employees in HR management since 1971, when it was not a prevalent business practice. Today, employee involvement is happening in many other companies including Wal-Mart, Nordstrom, Chrysler, Lincoln Electric System, Coca-Cola, Harley-Davidson, Au Bon Pain, Disney, L. L. Bean, Deere & Co., Levi Strauss, General Electric, Weyerhaeuser, Campbell Soup, US West, Microsoft, Texas Instruments, First Chicago, AT&T, Ben and Jerry's Homemade, Inc., Johnson & Johnson, and Merck. Many businesses, giant *and* small, are joining the ranks.

"At other places, managers say that people are their most important resource, but nobody acts on it. At Southwest, they have never lost sight of the fact."

Alan S. Boyd
Retired Chairman
Airbus North America

The two other themes suggested by this feature are that managing human resources effectively results in Southwest's success (productivity, profits, and stock price) and its high levels of customer satisfaction. Kelleher recognized a long time ago that in this customer-service intense industry, customer satisfaction is a result of employee satisfaction. He also recognized that because gaining customer satisfaction is not easy, when Southwest gained it, they would have an advantage over their competitors.

Because these developments in managing human resources are so pervasive in organizations today and are likely to be important for the foreseeable future, they influence everything we will discuss in this book, beginning here with the definition of the central topic of this book.

Human Resource Management

Human Resource Management is about managing people in organizations for the good of the employees, the company, and society.

Human resource management is about managing people in organizations as effectively as possible for the good of the employees, the company, and society. As companies like Southwest Airlines practice HR management effectively, they draw upon the skills and knowledge of line managers, HR professionals, and all other employees. Managing human resources effectively requires that the special expertise of HR professionals in the HR department be used by, and in cooperation with, line managers and other employees.

Managing human resources is a vital function in organizations. It engages everyone and it takes time. It involves attending to the concerns of the moment while keeping a longer-term perspective in mind. It also involves continuously improving and changing, activities that take time to put in place and produce results. Consequently, the expression *managing human resources* includes (a) the people management activities, policies, and practices that organizations can use to compete effectively now, and (b) the many changing forces (e.g., new competitors, new technology, business restructuring, legal and societal concerns) that organizations need to understand and respond to today in order to ensure they are positioned to compete effectively.

LEARNING OBJECTIVE 1

Explain why managing human resources has become important.

Why is Human Resource Management Important?

Today, organizations, large and small, face an environment characterized by:

- Extremely high levels of competition
- Hundreds of thousands of small and entrepreneurial firms
- Many nations with low wages and highly skilled workers
- Rapid technological advances
- Dynamic legal, political, and social realities
- Changing values and educational standards
- Demands for high-quality products and services at low prices

Successful firms in today's competitive environment resemble the profile given in Exhibit 1.1. The implications for HR management are enormous.

EXHIBIT 1.1

Characteristics of Successful Organizations

- Global
- Flatter
- Populated by teams
- Oriented toward differentiation, producing high value-added goods and services, creating niche markets
- Totally quality conscious
- Cost conscious
- More responsive, concerned about speed
- Faster to innovate
- Reliant on highly trained and flexible people
- Dependent on networks of competencies and partnerships
- Continually evolving strategies, structures, and practices
- Customer-focused
- Concerned about ethics and environment
- Concerned about managing diversity
- Successful in adjusting to change
- Engaged in mergers and acquisitions

Chief Executive Officers Say It Is

In addition to Herb Kelleher, many CEOs attest to the importance of managing human resources:

> *I am the ultimate believer in people first, strategies second. To me, strategy starts with the person you hire. If a business lacks a good strategy, then put in charge of the business someone who will develop one.*
>
> *Jack Welch, CEO*
> *General Electric*[7]

> *People are the number one asset in every organization. If you do not have the people in place that are tuned to the goals and objectives of your business, and if you're not involved in that process, you're failing in your job.*
>
> *John W. Teets, CEO and Chairman*
> *Dial Corporation*[8]

If you take a look at the sources of sustainable, competitive advantage during the last decade, the only one that has endured has been the quality of the people who work for you.

Jim Alef, Executive Vice President and Head of HR
First Chicago Corporation[9]

Limited human resources—not unreliable capital—are the biggest constraint when companies globalize.

Floris Maljers, CEO
Unilever[10]

Jack Welch's belief in the value of managing human resources effectively goes far beyond just hiring the right person. For a great discussion of just how far, see the feature, "Managing Human Resources at General Electric."

Surveys Indicate the Importance

While these statements from the CEOs are substantive, there is more. According to Korn Ferry, the international consulting firm who conducted a worldwide survey of 1,500 CEOs on what expertise they need to run their businesses, the response was:

Management of people is an indispensable component of sustained corporate performance and competitive advantage. Accordingly, human resource management as an area of CEO expertise rises from the third most important ranking in 1988 to the number two position in 2000.[11]

In a related study of CEO styles, five types of leadership styles emerged: a) strategic, b) human asset, c) expertise, d) box, and e) change. Of these, the human asset style is the most popular; it is used by over 30 percent of the CEOs. This style means these leaders

- Accept change
- Listen to customers
- Decentralize authority
- Hire carefully
- Teach continuously
- Control costs[12]

These actions and attitudes are the same ones followed by the companies described as "Go-Go Goliaths" in the opening story on Southwest Airlines.

What are the financial investment results of managing human resources effectively?

Financial Investment Measure	Bottom 25 Percent of HR Effectiveness	Top 25 Percent of HR Effectiveness
Annual Shareholder Return	6.5%	9.4%

In an extensive national survey, the top 25 percent of the firms—those managing their people most effectively—had an annual shareholder return of 9.4 percent versus 6.5 percent for the firms in the bottom 25 percent. People who bought

MANAGING HUMAN RESOURCES

at General Electric

General Electric Company's dramatic changes in the 1980s and early 1990s reflect a company adjusting to an increasingly competitive environment in innovative and successful ways. The firm management of human resources during the period offers an example of how the firm successfully meshed its human resource policies and the needs and strategy of the business.

During the 1970s, GE's chief executive, the highly regarded "financial wizard" Reginald H. Jones, built the firm into one of the strongest financial performers in the United States.

In 1981, at age 45, Jack Welch assumed the post of GE's chief executive officer. In picking Welch as his successor, Jones supported Welch's objective of making the $27-billion GE a "world class competitor," able to thrive in an increasingly global marketplace. In taking the helm of a strong yet somewhat complacent firm, one of Welch's key challenges was to "instill in... managers a sense of urgency when there is no emergency."[13] When Welch took over the top job at GE in 1981, his first goal was to prepare the company to meet the challenges of the 1980s and 1990s. Welch saw the world marketplace as a tough and increasingly competitive playing field that would eventually be dominated by a few large firms. To compete in such a world, Welch believed GE had to identify and operate only in markets in which it could be the first or second player worldwide. Such a move led to major restructuring: GE exited all but about 14 businesses, reducing its labor force by 25 percent. During the 1980s, about 100,000 employees left GE through layoff, attrition, or divestiture of businesses.

Welch views effective human resource management as part of the solution to making GE a firm well-positioned for the next century. He argues that the company needs new ways of doing business, and that includes human resource management. In planning and staffing business units for the future, for example, Welch says the company must seek managers who are "business leaders," able to "create a vision, articulate the vision, passionately own the vision, and... relentlessly drive it to completion."[14] Also extremely important is for business leaders to be open and willing to change. Welch considers the process of identifying and preparing future leaders to be so important that he regularly reviews files of selected employees from the time they join the firm, to get a sense of their potential for future positions.

Training and communication are also among Welch's top priorities for the firm. He takes his message directly to employees during training sessions at GE's in-house university in Crotonville, New York, which trains 5,000 employees annually. To improve the work environment and further reduce bureaucracy, GE initiated a program called "Work-Out" in late 1989. The heads of the 14 business units meet regularly with subordinates to identify and eliminate unnecessary activities—meetings, reports, any unproductive work. The process also seeks to identify better ways to evaluate and reward managers.

Finally, Welch has tried to bring GE's labor unions into the new way of thinking and managing as well. He wants labor, as well as white-collar managers, to gain a sense of "ownership" of the company and its direction.

During the 1980s and early 1990s, GE overhauled its strategy, streamlined business lines to compete for the future, and used human resource management to achieve its massive change. As the company moves toward the year 2000, managing human resources effectively will play an important role in the success of the firm's strategy.

stock in the companies that manage their people effectively saw their investments grow in value almost 50 percent faster than those who invested in companies that manage their people ineffectively![15]

Business Analysts Say It Is

Because people are important to short- and long-term competitiveness and survival, business analysts pay attention to whether companies are effective in the area of managing their human resources domestically and globally.[16] For example, the *Fortune* ratings of America's most admired corporations, published early each year, considers the ability to attract, develop, and keep talented people as one of its primary performance dimensions, along with long-term investment value, financial soundness, use of corporate assets, quality of products and services, innovation, quality of management, and community and environmental responsibility.[17] In addition to *Fortune,* other business magazines such as *Inc., Business Week,* and *Money* include among their criteria of successful businesses the ability to attract, develop, and keep talented people, in other words, great HR management.

Thus, while we have in the past thought of this activity as "personnel" and something to be done by those in the HR department, it is a different story today and will continue to be so for the foreseeable future. Management is more interested than ever before and more willing to participate in this activity.

> *There is a saying at Merck that goes like this, "Human resources are too important to be left to the HR department." Fully one-third of the performance evaluation of the managers is related to people management.*[18]

All of this interest and involvement in HR management by CEOs and other managers stems from their recognition that to be competitive in the world today, they need their people to be as effective as possible. And "effective people" means people who are

- Adaptable
- Committed
- Motivated
- Skilled/reskilled
- Possessing high energy levels
- Good performers in diverse employee groups
- Good team players

With the recognition by management of the importance of this endeavor comes the recognition that the HR department cannot do it alone. Managers are now embracing the responsibility for people management more than ever before. For managers to succeed in today's competitive environment, they need some knowledge of people management. We begin with an understanding of the goals of HR management and the stakeholders.

LEARNING OBJECTIVE 2

Identify the stakeholders of human resource management and their objectives.

The Goals of Human Resource Management: Serving Multiple Stakeholders

> *At Harley-Davidson, we are committed to a corporate Vision that mandates how we run our businesses. Our Vision says: "Harley-Davidson, Inc. is an action-oriented, international company—a leader in its commitment to continuously improve the quality of profitable relationships with stakeholders.... Harley-Davidson believes the key to success is to balance stakeholders' inter-*

ests through the empowerment of all employees to focus on value-added activities.[19]

Stakeholders are the institutions and people who influence and are influenced by how well human resources are managed.[20] They include the organization itself, stockholders and investors, customers, employees, society, and the strategic partners of the business (e.g., suppliers). These stakeholders and their objectives are illustrated in Exhibit 1.2. When success is defined as effectively serving the objectives of these groups, their needs define a firm's central HR goal.

Stakeholders are those institutions and people who influence and are influenced by how well human resources are managed.

For Mobil Corporation, this means measuring customer satisfaction, quality, innovation, employee development, and financial soundness.

EXHIBIT 1.2

Stakeholders of Human Resource Management

THE ORGANIZATION
- Productivity
- Profits
- Survival
- Adaptability
- Competitive advantage

CUSTOMERS
- Quality service
- Quality products
- Speed and responsiveness
- Low cost
- Innovation

SHAREHOLDERS/INVESTORS
- Shareholder return
- Return on sales
- Return on assets
- Return on investments

EMPLOYEES
- Fair treatment
- Satisfaction/morale
- Empowerment
- Employability
- Safety and health
- Flexibility

STRATEGIC PARTNERS
- Suppliers; joint venture partners
- Unions
- Customers

SOCIETY
- Legal compliance
- Social responsibility
- Ethical management practices
- Concern for the environment

Adapted from R. S. Schuler and S. E. Jackson, *Human Resource Management: Positioning for the 21st Century* (St. Paul: West Publishing Co.: 1996).

The Organization

Productivity—the value of goods and services produced by each employee—is an important goal of all business organizations. As a nation, our ability to earn more money and enjoy a higher standard of living depends on productivity improvement. After experiencing meager productivity increases of less than one percent during the 1980s and early 1990s, by the mid-1990s, U.S. companies were registering rather strong productivity growth rates of more than three percent. Particularly outstanding increases were seen in the automobile, machinery, chemical, food processing, and computer sectors.[21] For example, in the automobile industry, productivity, measured as thousands of dollars of output per employee, increased more than 30 percent between 1988 and 1994. In several industries today, the productivity of U.S. companies exceeds that of firms in any other nation, including Japan and Germany.[22] This rather dramatic change in the overall rate of productivity growth has come about for several reasons, including improvement in how companies manage their human resources. As we move into the 21st centu-

Productivity means the amount of quality output for the amount of input.

Did You KNOW?

Our rate of productivity growth actually fell in the 1970s and 1980s. Recently it has been going up, and U. S. workers are still the most productive in the world.

"The company views each employee's performance strategically as a means to help Chaparral gain competitive advantage."

Gordon E. Forward
President
Chaparral Steel Company

ry, productivity improvement through better management of human resources, such as Southwest Airlines' employee satisfaction orientation, Ford's total quality program ("Quality Is Job One"), and Chrysler's team-based management system, will continue to be important.[23] Although not always the case, this increased productivity is likely to result in increased profitability and greater chances for survival.

Because competition is the name of the game, especially for firms in highly competitive environments such as Southwest Airlines, General Electric (GE), Lincoln Electric, Coca-Cola, and Nordstrom, companies seek ways to compete that can last a long time and cannot easily be imitated by competitors. Harvard's Michael Porter refers to this as the desire of firms to gain competitive advantage.[24]

"We must have people who use facts and knowledge to add something... to add value to our customers' businesses. In an age where everyone has basically the same information at the same time, the advantage goes to people who can take information and quickly put it to effective and profitable use. It means having people with what can be called the 'mind of the strategist...' people who can create a competitive advantage...out of common knowledge."

Roberto C. Goizueta
CEO
Coca-Cola Company

Firms also gain competitive advantage through their wise and innovative use of human resources. In fact, according to auto industry expert Maryann N. Keller, the "enduring advantages will come from making better use of people."[25] She nominates Saturn Industries' dealers and Toyota Motor Corporation's Georgetown, Kentucky, plant workers as examples of the kind of competitive advantage that will last: whole groups of carefully picked, highly motivated people determined to make customers happy.[26]

Stockholders and Investors

According to the U.S. Department of Labor report "High Performance Work Practices and Firm Performance," firms with great HR management practices have substantially higher annual sales, market value, profits, and earnings-per-share growth. Further support comes from an analysis of the firms that are recognized as having some of the most effective HR practices. From firms listed in *The One Hundred Best Companies to Work for in America*, those with the most effective pay and benefits, availability of opportunities, job security, pride taken in work and company, level of openness and fairness, and friendliness and camaraderie, were also likely to be strong economic performers according to a variety of indicators.[27]

- In terms of total shareholder return (the sum of stock price appreciation and dividends paid), the annual return for the one hundred best firms in 1993 was 19.5 percent over that in the previous eight years, compared with a 12 percent annual return for the three thousand largest companies in America.
- The financial performance of firms after they have been chosen as one of the one hundred best is also illuminating. Firms among the one hundred best in 1984 had an annual total return of 15 percent in the eight subsequent years, also above the average 12 percent for the three thousand largest companies.
- About two-thirds of the firms in 1993's one hundred best ranked in the top half of their industry in return on sales and in return on assets.[28]

Did You KNOW?

Southwest Airlines has been named as one of the ten best places to work in America.

It pays companies to utilize their human resources effectively.

Another study focused on companies that had gone through major changes and transformed their corporate culture from a traditional top-down one to a more participatory culture. Companies that made a change to greater employee involvement and participation reaped rewards such as higher returns on sales and investments in subsequent years.[29]

Satisfying Customers

Without customers, there is no business.

As Southwest Airlines and other companies have found, improving customer satisfaction is a primary means through which HR management practices affect success. We typically think that reducing costs and improving product quality are two ways of improving customer satisfaction, but as many companies have now learned, customers react to more than just these.[30] Good service is also important. Satisfied customers usually return to purchase more products and services in the future. Because repeat business can cost less than new business, improving customer retention by as little as five percent has been shown to improve profits by

28 percent for auto service, 35 percent for business banking, and 125 percent for credit card service.[31]

Service companies can win or lose during the moments of contact between employees and customers. This point was not lost on one famous CEO:

> *"As I was putting on paper some of my reflections on managing a service company, I realized that it was actually during the instant of contact between customer and staff that the future of the company hung in the balance. I call it the 'moment of truth'."*
>
> *Jan Carlzon, CEO and Chairman (Retired)*
> *Scandinavian Airlines System*[32]

This moment of truth, it turns out, is often the moment when customers get a glimpse of how a firm manages its human resources. When the internal climate of the organization is positive, with employees generally getting along well and not leaving the company at too rapid a pace, customers report they are more satisfied and intend to return.[33] For example, using a 60-second customer survey to study 771 stores, Sears, Roebuck and Company learned that the stores where customer service was best also had lower turnover rates of employees.[34] Herb Kelleher at Southwest Airlines strongly acts on the belief, "If you don't treat your own people well, they won't treat other people well."[35]

"Total customer satisfaction is fundamental to our survival."

George Fisher
CEO
Kodak

Because frontline employees—such as the FedEx delivery people, the attendants at Disney theme parks, the sales clerks at Nordstrom, or the flight attendants at Southwest Airlines—are critical to service delivery, some experts have argued that service companies should literally be turned upside down.[36] These frontline employees should control important decisions, and everyone else should provide secondary support. Marketing campaigns, operations management systems, and practices for managing human resources should all be coordinated with customers' needs in mind. The objective? To create a *passion* for service by everyone in the company.

Frontline employees are those customers see every day in companies.

Approaches to managing human resources appear to play a significant role in creating a passion for service, which is ultimately experienced by customers. For example, in financial services, passion for service appears to be strongest when employees are carefully selected for their service orientation, are trained extensively, receive plenty of performance feedback, and get paid fairly.[37]

Regardless of *how* they seek to satisfy customers, most companies recognize customers as primary stakeholders who wield considerable power, which is felt throughout the organization. To meet customers' demands for higher quality, for instance, companies such as Southwest Airlines and FedEx are organizing to maintain an environment for quality excellence conducive to full participation and personal and organizational growth for their employees.

Did You KNOW?

Au Bon Pain, the bakery café noted for being an outstanding customer service business, attributes its success to:

- **Hiring people who care**
- **Offering a variety of choices**
- **Offering good food fast, not fast food**

Responding to Employees

To be effective, businesses must increase productivity, satisfy stockholders and investors by increasing share value, and respond to customers' demands for quality, speed, innovation, low prices, and so on. Furthermore, we have argued that businesses cannot fully satisfy their major stakeholders without managing their employees effectively. Organizations that recognize and respond to the needs of employees and provide opportunities for development and involvement provide a higher quality of working life, thereby increasing their ability to attract and retain the best talent. Many aspects of HR management contribute to a good quality of working life: training and development to improve employees' skills and knowledge; job designs that allow employees to really use their knowledge and skills; management practices that give employees responsibility for important decisions; selection and promotion systems that ensure fair and equitable treatment; safe and

Did You KNOW?

CEO Fred Smith's philosophy, active since day one of Federal Express, is "People, Service, and Profit."

Highly skilled and motivated employees are invaluable to companies.

"If we treat employees the right way, they'll naturally treat our customers the right way."

Elizabeth Pedrick Sartain
VP of the People Department
Southwest Airlines

healthy physical and psychological environments; and work organized around teams. Such practices increase employee commitment, satisfaction, morale, and feelings of empowerment.[38]

The feature "HR Advice and Application" describes in more detail just how organizations are increasing employee commitment, satisfaction, morale, and empowerment in order to be more effective. Notice how the organizations described by Edward E. Lawler III, using HR practices, now sometimes referred to as high-performance work practices, are able to manage in ways that benefit both employees as individuals and the business. An illustration of this is managing to ensure that employees are flexible and adaptable.

HR ADVICE & APPLICATION

Getting Everyone Involved: Principles for Effective Organizations

"The enormous changes in corporate structures and needs over the past decade have necessitated a refocusing of management approaches," according to Ed Lawler, Director of the Center for Organizational Effectiveness at the University of Southern California. Professor Lawler's research has focused on exactly what it means when organizations adapt new management approaches. He summarized that the following principles of management apply to any product of service organization, large or small, wanting to be highly effective and successful. He generally defines effectiveness in terms of *high-quality, customer-driven organizations* that survive and flourish by staying ahead of their competitors with new and better products and services.

Based on extensive research that he and his colleagues have done over the years, Professor Lawler suggests that there are several governing ideas that effective organizations share today. One is an organization design that makes extensive use of *self-managing teams* and a relatively *limited number of hierarchical levels of management.* This enables employees to feel a sense of ownership in what they are doing and therefore a heightened sense of responsibility and accountability. Teams in effective organizations have direct contact with suppliers. For example, at the Digital Equipment plant at Enfield, Connecticut, the teams producing electronic boards deal directly with both suppliers and costumers.

Today's effective organizations do not restrict the use of teams to the production floor only, but *extend the team concept to all areas of the company.* This broader use of self-managed teams further "flattens" the organization by reducing the number of supervisors and managers.

Teamwork can be extended to allow cross-functional teams to work together. This *cross-functional integration* might combine manufacturing, product engineering, and product design. Not only can a better product be produced, but the employees involved will have a better understanding of the needs of the business. The extensive use of information technology can enhance this understanding; such technology allows workers in the manufacturing area to have *direct access to marketing and sales* and even to answer questions from customers.

In today's effective organizations, *reward systems compensate* individuals for successful teamwork, for gaining more skill-based competencies, for continuous improvement, and for business and organizational performance. Of course, the teams themselves have a significant input in compensation decisions, such as deciding when employees have attained mastery of needed skills. Some of these skills relate to the use of information and data technology. The effective organization today is networked with computers, relies extensively upon videos for training, and uses television screens to link employees in various parts of the firms.

No less important than the above aspects of effective organizations are the following: a)[the use of total quality management tools and principles in problem-solving approaches and in] a continuous commitment to process and product improvement; b) continuous and widely available training for all employees on topics ranging from technical job details to business strategy; and c) employee commitment to participation, continuous learning, and constant improvement.[39]

Flexible and Adaptable Employees. Firms in highly competitive environments must move quickly and often. Doing so requires a workforce that rapidly adjusts to new technologies, strategies, and competitors' practices. Thus, being responsive to employees' concerns also involves preparing employees for inevitable change. When employees are not prepared for and capable of change, their employability decreases and their economic livelihood is threatened. HR management practices play a major role in meeting employees' concerns about their long-term **employability**. For example, continuous training prepares the workforce for change and develops employees' confidence in their own ability to continuously learn new ways of working. Regular employee assessments, feedback, and career management activities provide the information employees need to understand their strengths and weaknesses and to prepare for the future. Ultimately, by developing their employees, employers help ensure that the workforce is employable in good jobs that pay well enough to maintain the high standard of living to which Americans have grown accustomed.[40]

Workforce flexibility and adaptability means that workers are ready and able to change.

Employability means that employees have the skills to work in several different companies.

Responding to Society

Legal Regulations. To be effective, businesses must also be responsive to broader societal concerns and comply with an extensive set of legal regulations regarding human resources. By doing so, firms establish their legitimacy and gain acceptance and support from the community; ultimately, they increase their chances for long-term survival. Codes of conduct for some aspects of business behavior take the form of formal laws, and many of these have implications for managing human resources. In addition, businesses are subject to regulation through several federal agencies, including the Occupational Safety and Health Administration, the Equal Employment Opportunity Commission, the Office of Federal Contract Compliance Programs, and the Immigration and Naturalization Service. They also must attend to the actions of various state and city equal employment commissions, and human rights and civil rights commissions. Finally, multinational corporations (MNCs) must be aware of the employment laws in other countries. Because they affect virtually all HR management activities, many different laws, regulations, and court decisions are described throughout this book, beginning with an overview in Chapter 4.

Social Responsibility and Ethics. Formal laws and regulations establish relatively clear guidelines for how society expects a company to behave, but effective companies respond to more than simply the formal statements of a community's expectations.[41] The most effective companies understand that the enactment of formal laws and regulations often lags behind public opinion by several years. Indeed, unless a community's most strongly held values are being violated, legal restrictions are unnecessary. Long before legislation is agreed to, communities communicate their expectations and attempt to hold organizations accountable for violations of those expectations. In turn, proactive organizations stay attuned to public opinion and use it as one source of information that may shape their own management practices. As described in "Managing Human Resources for the 21st Century at WMX Technologies," WMX Technologies (formerly Waste Management) of Oak Brook, Illinois, is building an ethical culture that demonstrates the firm's commitment to encouraging and supporting behavior consistent with the norms and values of society.

In addition to ensuring that their internal functioning is consistent with society's expectations, some companies interpret social responsibility to include active involvement in the external community. Ben and Jerry's Homemade Incorporated, the Vermont ice cream company, is a great example. It prints its "social performance report" right after the president's letter in its annual report. The company's credo, "Turning Values into Value," reflects a philosophy that centers on creating a socially responsible firm, which means giving back to the community. When asked to describe what would make him happiest, former president and founder

MANAGING HUMAN RESOURCES

at WMX Technologies

WMX Technologies Corporation (Oak Brook, IL), the largest U. S. waste services company, with over $10 billion in sales, is taking a leading role in building ethics awareness into the company culture for its 60,000 employees. Under the impetus of Chairman and CEO Dean Buntrock and an Executive Environmental Committee, WMX is seeking to gain employee commitment and leadership awareness through a number of management systems.

Overall responsibility for the effort belongs to Jodie Bernstein, vice president of environmental policy and ethical standards, also general counsel for Chemical Waste Management and a former general counsel for the Environmental Protection Agency and the Department of Health and Human Services in Washington. She believes that explicit and active management of ethical issues is vital to WMX because of the nature of its business, but it's also becoming increasingly important to other businesses as well. "Increasingly, we are seeing a breakdown in government's ability to regulate environmental and other ethical issues, and there is a growing public distrust of government interference in these matters. Moreover, on the individual level, we just can't make the assumptions we used to about our shared value systems. The diverse workforce and our increased globalization mean we have to recognize that people have different ideas about what is and isn't ethical. Rather than leave things up to chance, we're going to spell it out for people.

RULES VS. CLIMATE

"In some areas, like compliance with EPA regulations, for example, we tell people exactly what the rules and expectations are. Falsifying information on a regulatory filing, for example, means immediate dismissal. But we think it has to go beyond that. Ethics is more than following the rules. You can't make enough rules to cover all the things that can come up, so it's important that all employees have a general level of ethical awareness, so that they will at least be asking the right questions. And you have to create a climate in which it's possible—easier, even—for employees to do the right thing. Most of the programs we are developing focus on this latter area: increasing awareness of ethical issues and building an ethical climate throughout the company."

ETHICS COMMUNICATION

To do that, the company is adapting many of its existing human resource and communication systems. Under Jodie Bernstein's direction, explicit business conduct guidelines are being written, and she is considering the establishment of a regular ethics column in the employee publication. Ethics goals are also being developed for the performance appraisal system, which already includes factors related to environmental compliance and health and safety. The company also is trying to rejuvenate an existing employee hotline program to encourage more use. Established in 1984, the hotline may be used by employees who wish to call attention to a situation they find disturbing or to ask questions on ethical, environmental, or safety issues.

The bottom line, according to Bernstein, is ethical leadership: "This is the lifeblood of our company. We are an environmental services company. How we handle these issues is critical to our success."[42]

Bennett R. Cohen replied, "I'd like to see Ben & Jerry's act as a force for social change in trying to help deal with some of the root causes of poverty and starvation and disease and illiteracy."[43] The firm's Partnerships—subsidized franchises located in areas of high unemployment, like Harlem, with all profits returned to the community—reflect this vision.[44] Respect and concern for people permeates the company, which pays employees well above the average in Vermont, offers generous benefits, and aggressively strives to make business decisions that are consistent with the concerns of employees.[45]

Working with Strategic Business Partners

In the U.S., we tend to think of firms as autonomous organizations, with clear boundaries separating one from another. However, such an image is overly simplistic. A more realistic image portrays firms as nodes in a web of relationships. Other firms in the web might include suppliers, joint venture partners, potential merger partners, and partners in coalitions formed for community service and political action. In some cases, even customers are viewed as strategic business partners, especially when they are other businesses rather than individual consumers. All of these inter-firm relationships potentially involve issues of HR management.

Suppliers. A company's suppliers include the organizations that provide the company with resources needed to conduct business. The resources needed by most companies include capital, material, information, and people. Suppliers of people might include schools, employment agencies, and other firms. It is easy to understand why suppliers of people should be considered important strategic partners for managing human resources. What about other types of suppliers?

Firms that supply raw materials or component parts clearly are strategic partners, especially for companies competing on the basis of quality. To improve quality, improvements in raw materials or component parts can and must always be found. As organizations such as Xerox Corporation, the National Aeronautics and Space Administration (NASA), and Ford have learned, eventually a stage is reached where the quality of the product cannot be improved without improving the quality of the materials coming in. That is, the organization has to work with its suppliers to improve their total quality.[46] The Baldrige Award for quality essentially requires companies to demonstrate that their suppliers also have **total quality management (TQM)** programs in place. And because much of TQM involves managing human resources, the supplier becomes a key stakeholder for HR management. AT&T's total quality approach specifically includes a partnership with the firm's suppliers, as shown in Exhibit 1.3.

The Baldrige Award is named for Malcolm Baldrige, who served as Secretary of Commerce from 1981 until his tragic death in a rodeo accident in 1987. His managerial excellence contributed to long-term improvement in efficiency and effectiveness of government.

Total quality management is a systematic and coordinated effort to continuously improve the quality of the firm's products and services.

EXHIBIT 1.3

AT&T's Total Quality Approach

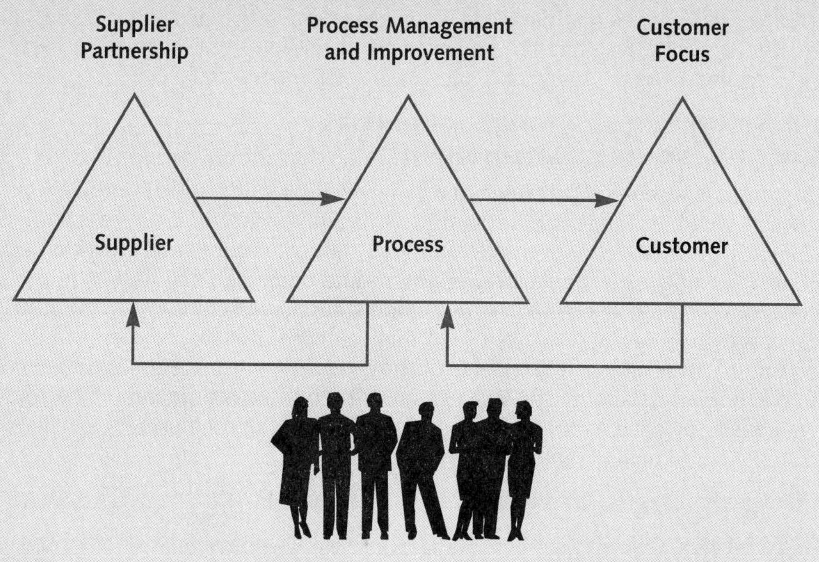

Supplier firms are also of special importance to companies because of their mutual interest in legal compliance. For example, companies that sell to the federal government, called federal contractors, develop affirmative action plans and in turn ask their suppliers to do the same. Compliance with the *Americans with Disabilities Act of 1990* requires that companies obligate their suppliers to also adhere to the mandates of the act.

Unions. A special supplier is the union that represents workers and potential workers. Firms such as GE, AT&T, Xerox, and the three U.S. auto makers look to the unions for joint discussion on issues such as improving productivity, the quality of working life, and outsourcing. In these firms, the union leadership and members have moved from a traditional adversarial relationship to a collaborative, problem-solving relationship. Thus, although the proportion of union membership shrank from the mid-1980s to the mid-1990s, it still plays a vital role in supplying the ideas and motivated workers necessary for companies seeking to be globally competitive and profitable.

Customers. On occasion, the firm also may treat customers as strategic partners and help them improve their quality. If a dealership (customer) that sells Ford cars improves its service orientation, then it might sell more cars. The more it sells, the more Ford will benefit. Therefore, it is to Ford's advantage to help its dealers with their own TQM programs. Similarly, insurance companies recognize that both they and their corporate customers benefit by managing human resources in ways that ensure the safety and health of employees. Thus, it is in the best interests of both the suppliers of insurance and the buyers of their policies to collaborate in the area of health and safety.

In summary, the objectives of HR management are many. Managing human resources effectively is beneficial for a multitude of stakeholders: employees, society, the company itself, partners, stockholders, investors, and customers. And we now have a great deal of evidence that suggests that when companies manage their people better, the companies perform better. We now will examine what companies do to manage their human resources.

LEARNING OBJECTIVE 3

Describe major activities of human resource management.

Activities in Human Resource Management

The activities that companies use to manage their human resources include (1) understanding the environment of HR management, (2) managing organizational and HR changes, (3) staffing the organization, (4) training and appraising, (5) compensating, and (6) establishing and improving work environments and relationships.

Understanding the Environment of Human Resource Management

Understanding the environment and meeting its demands entails:

- **Knowing the external environment**
- **Knowing the internal environment**
- **Managing change**
- **Planning and forecasting**
- **Career management**
- **Designing jobs**
- **Analyzing jobs**

Increasingly, successful HR management depends on understanding the organization's external and internal environment. Important aspects of the external environment include levels of domestic and international competition, workforce and demographic changes, and general economic and organizational trends. Important aspects of the internal environment include the business strategy of the firm, its technology, the goals and values of top management, the size of the firm, its culture, and its structure. These aspects of the internal environment are discussed in Chapter 3. Understanding the external and internal environments and scanning them constantly ensures that the needs and objectives of the business and all of its stakeholders are being identified.

Managing Organizational and Human Resource Changes

Helping to serve the needs and objectives of the business and its stakeholders are initiatives to manage major organizational changes. Such changes include blending the cultures of two newly merged companies, successfully managing a downsizing effort, and managing diversity in the workplace. Also central to meeting the demands of the business environment is effective HR planning. This activity involves 1) planning and forecasting short- and long-term requirements, 2) developing or implementing career management programs, 3) analyzing jobs, and 4) designing jobs throughout the organization. In fact, HR planning can be viewed as the major factor influencing the staffing and development functions of the entire organization. An HR plan must indicate 1) what types of employees and how many of them are needed both today and in the future, 2) how employees will be obtained (for example, from outside recruiting or by internal transfers and promotions), and 3) any training programs the organization may need. It enables the organization to accommodate an increasingly diverse workforce. Increasingly, jobs are designed to encourage diversity, to enhance levels of employee motivation, and to provide attractive and flexible work schedules.

> **"Best Management Decision: Appointing the right people. Biggest Management Mistake: Appointing the wrong people."**
>
> **Richard Goldstein**
> **CEO**
> **Unilever, United States**

Staffing the Organization

Once the organization's people needs have been determined, staffing can take place. This includes 1) analyzing the jobs that are to be staffed, 2) recruiting job candidates, and 3) selecting the most appropriate job applicants for the available jobs. All of these activities must be done in accordance with legally mandated fair employment practices and with attention to the effect they will have on the overall direction of the firm. Doubtless, they will have a significant impact on the firm's success:

> *Ask Bill Gates, Chairman of Microsoft, what the most important thing he did last year was and he will answer: "I hired a lot of smart people."*[47]

The organization must cast a wide net in its recruitment of employees to ensure a full and fair search for job candidates. After the candidates have been identified, final selections must be made. Common selection procedures include obtaining completed application forms or resumes; interviewing the candidates; checking education, background, experience, and references; and administering various forms of tests.

> **"If a company depends on employees for a competitive advantage, you've got to create an environment to attract people from all segments of the population."**
>
> **Jim Porter**
> **Vice President**
> **for Human Resources**
> **Honeywell**

Training and Appraising

Activities related to training and development include 1) orienting new employees to the company and its values, mission, and objectives; 2) determining, designing, and implementing programs to increase employee ability and performance; and 3) creating a culture that values and rewards continuous learning and growth.

Increasingly, companies claim that it is difficult to hire well-trained employees, particularly at the entry level. Many companies have responded to this by providing orientation and training to new employees. Firms that provide summer jobs and internships, such as public accounting firms, hire new employees who are more able to "hit the ground running."

> **"There's no magic. What will make all the difference in business will be how well you train your workforce, how well you motivate—and how well you empower."**
>
> **Robert Eaton**
> **CEO**
> **Chrysler Corporation**

The best firms today, such as Intel, Microsoft, Motorola, GE, Coca-Cola, and Procter & Gamble, also spend a great deal of time and money training and developing current employees, especially technical, professional, and managerial employees.

Once on the job, employees' performances must be evaluated. If they are not doing well, it is necessary to find out why. Employee training may be necessary, or some type of motivation such as more rewards, feedback, or a redesigned job may be in order. The HR department cooperates with line managers to gather and utilize performance appraisal information.

> **"We have to upgrade the math, reading, and deductive capabilities of the people coming into our plants."**
>
> **Alexander Trotman**
> **Chairman**
> **Ford Motor Company**

Although conducting performance appraisals can be painful to both manager and employee, it is a critical activity. Legal considerations necessitate that employee decisions be made on the basis of performance. This is a sound employment practice, with or without legal requirements. Many companies have embraced a performance appraisal process that involves the employees themselves, a process called self-management. Because you are likely to encounter this process, several self-management career exercises and a questionnaire on career planning are included in this book.

Did You KNOW?

While the average company spends approximately 1.5 percent of revenues on training, the best firms spend up to 4 percent.

Compensating

Employees are generally rewarded on the basis of the value of the job, their personal contributions, and their performance. Although rewarding performance can increase motivation, rewards are often given only according to the value of the job. Other rewards, known as indirect benefits, are provided just for being a member of the organization. The role of the HR department in the compensating activity includes administering 1) monetary compensation, 2) performance-based pay, and 3) indirect compensation benefits.

Because of the rising medical costs over the past decade, cost containment in the benefits area became a major concern for many firms. It resulted in more cost-sharing with employees and even the reduction of some benefits. The challenge has been to manage costs while keeping employee commitment high.

Did You KNOW?

Hourly wage rates for high school graduates have gone up only 10 percent since 1973, while the same rates for college graduates have gone up more than 15 percent.

Establishing and Improving Work Environments and Relationships

This activity is composed of the following sets of activities: 1) creating a safe and healthy work environment; 2) understanding the reasons and methods used by employees in organizing; 3) bargaining and settling grievances with employees and the groups representing them; and (4) monitoring and assessing how well HR activities are being performed.

The crucial activity here is establishing and improving the physical and sociopsychological workplace to maximize employee safety and health. The federal regulations specified in the *Occupational Safety and Health Act of 1970* have had a direct influence on the physical safety and security of employees and their well-being. Failure to improve work conditions for health and safety is illegal and can be very costly.

The work relationship is particularly important for organizations that have unionized employees. Unions can be instrumental in developing new programs for the improvement of HR management. As the experiences at Southwest Airlines have shown, cooperation between unions and management can result in a very successful company.

Did You KNOW?

Without rapidly available data and information, companies are unable to respond, improve, and succeed.

Another crucial activity involves assessing and improving. Management data and information systems must be created and then used to ensure that decisions are made with timely and accurate information. This requires conducting organizational surveys, developing valid tests for selection, and in general, assessing all the HR activities.

Who Is Responsible for Managing Human Resources?

LEARNING OBJECTIVE 4

Describe who is responsible for managing human resources.

Clearly, managing human resources is not just something to be done by those in the HR department. Managers are the ones responsible for the management of people. No department alone can effectively manage a company's human resources. So, regardless of whether a line manager ever holds a formal position in human resources management, he or she will be accountable for the task of managing people. In the long run, every manager's portfolio of knowledge and skills must reflect this reality.

The Human Resource Professional

HR management is the task of individuals who work in this field—that is, **HR professionals**. These professionals have acquired the specialized and generalized knowledge and skills necessary for managing human resources. These professionals and the HR department are described in detail in the next chapter.

HR professionals are those who have specialized or general knowledge in managing human resources.

The Line Manager

While HR professionals have the special knowledge and skills, it is the **line manager** who must ultimately manage the employees. To be effective in this endeavor, line managers need to work hand-in-hand with HR professionals. Today, all managers from the CEO on down are teaming with HR professionals to effectively manage their employees. Even the HR leader is seeking input from the professionals in the HR department.

Line managers are those directly responsible for producing products or services through and with employees.

In small businesses, the owner must have HR expertise because he or she will be building the company from the ground up. This reality is clearly reflected in the various popular magazines targeted to small-business owners—for example, *Inc.*, *Money*, *Success*, and *Entrepreneurship*. These publications devote a great deal of space to discussing issues related to managing the people in small companies. Eventually, as a company grows, the owner may contract out some of the administrative aspects related to managing people (e.g., payroll), or delegate some of the responsibilities to a specialist, or both.

As the company grows even larger, more specialists may be hired—either as permanent staff or on a contract basis to work on special projects, such as designing a new pay system. But, as with other business activities, these specialists will not bear all responsibility for the project. For example, many companies have a marketing department; nevertheless, they employ people outside that department to conduct marketing activities. Similarly, most companies have a few people with special expertise in accounting; nevertheless, employees throughout the company perform accounting activities. The same is true for HR management activities.

Did You KNOW?

At Nordstrom, managers are encouraged to have a feeling of ownership about their department. They are responsible for hiring, firing, scheduling, training, coaching, nurturing, encouraging, and evaluating their sales team.

Thus CEOs, HR managers, and all levels of senior management need to be involved in managing their human resources. While this *is* happening, both CEOs and senior HR managers in the IBM/Towers Perrin survey agreed that co-involvement should become much more prevalent by the year 2000. Exhibit 1.4 indicates the type of involvement most favored. In this scenario, the HR department's leader will be counted among senior executives and will play significant roles in attracting, retaining, and motivating the firm's most vital resources.

The HR leader will be indistinguishable from other senior executives in the concern for, and understanding of, the needs of the business. Likewise, the HR staff will appear indistinguishable from their counterparts in the firm. Sharing this function together, line managers, HR staff, and nonmanagerial employees will forge and implement all of the activities entailed in the human resources discipline.

Did You KNOW?

Jack Welch, CEO of GE, believes that CEOs are in essence personnel directors because "If we get the right people in the jobs, we've won the game."

The Employee

Employees, the nonmanagers, are taking an ever more active role in HR management. For example, employees are now often asked to appraise their own performance or that of their colleagues. It is no longer uncommon for employees to write their own job descriptions, select team members, and evaluate their own performance. Perhaps most significantly, employees are actively managing their careers and assessing their own needs and values. However, the HR department is often asked to assist in this process. To these ends, the HR department must be staffed with qualified individuals; staffing is discussed in Chapter 2.

LEARNING OBJECTIVE 5

Describe the meaning of partnership in managing human resources.

Thus a Partnership

This book treats managing human resources as a responsibility shared by everyone in the company—line managers and professionals in the HR department, top-level executives, and entry-level new hires. Consistent with the stakeholder model in Exhibit 1.2, this partnership can even extend to human resources working with managers in supplier firms, with customers, and even with members of community organizations. Yet, for the most part, on a day-to-day basis, the firm's line managers have responsibility for actually managing most people in an organization.

EXHIBIT 1.4

An Emerging Role for Line Management

PERCENTAGE AGREEING THAT LINE MANAGEMENT SHOULD SHARE RESPONSIBILITY WITH THE HR DEPARTMENT

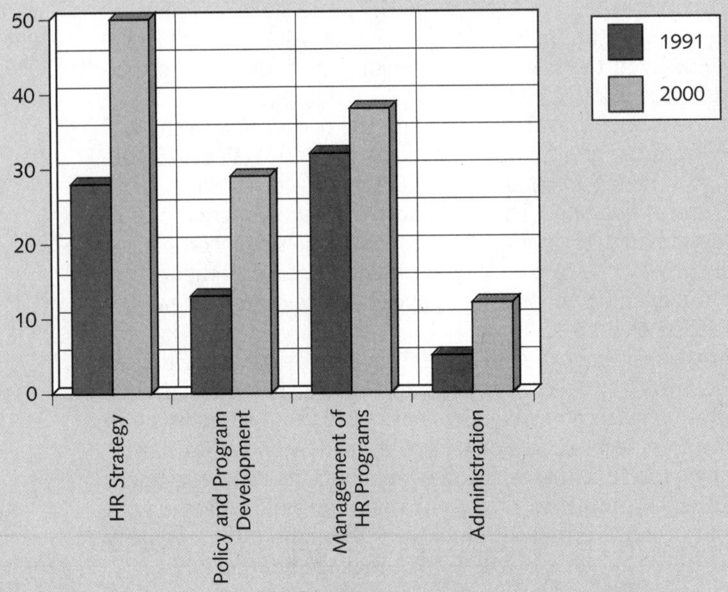

Source: Adapted from "Priorities for Competitive Advantages: A Worldwide Human Resource Study" (IBM and Towers, Perrin, 1992), 26.

Those managers who recognize the importance of this responsibility work in partnership with HR professionals who have specialized knowledge and skills, as described more extensively in Chapter 2.

Partnership is the cooperation of everyone in the organization in managing human resources.

This theme of **partnership**, or working together to manage human resources, is present throughout this book. Because it is so important, it is highlighted in a feature called "Partnership: Working Together In Managing Human Resources," which appears in most of the chapters, beginning with this one. These features present a list of HR activities that can be done by line managers, HR professionals, and the other employees in companies today. The greater the partnership, the more success a company is likely to have. Consequently, there is little doubt that you will be actively involved in managing human resources in your career, even if you do not become an HR professional.

Historical Perspective

As with many aspects of the way businesses operate, the way they approach managing people has changed rather dramatically during the 20th century. Throughout this book, we will discuss the approaches being taken today by many successful companies. Because companies are different, their approaches to managing human resources differ. We can, however, learn from them all. We also can learn by describing sophisticated approaches honed through decades of research and analysis.

To fully appreciate current approaches, you need some understanding of their historical evolution. Exhibit 1.5 presents a thumbnail sketch of the changing concerns of HR management within the United States. At the beginning of the 20th

PARTNERSHIP: WORKING TOGETHER IN MANAGING HUMAN RESOURCES

LINE MANAGERS

- Include HR professionals in the formulation and implementation of business strategy.
- Work closely with HR professionals and employees to develop and implement HR activities.
- Accept shared responsibility for managing the human resources of the company.
- Set policies that are supportive of ethical behavior.

HR PROFESSIONALS

- Work closely with line managers and employees to develop and implement HR activities.
- Work with line managers to link HR activities to the business.
- Work with employees to help them voice their concerns to management.
- Develop policies and practices to support ethical conduct.

EMPLOYEES

- Work closely with line managers and HR professionals to develop and implement HR activities.
- Accept responsibility for managing their own behavior and careers in organizations.
- Recognize the need for flexibility and adaptability.
- Realize their impact on the success of the company.

century, Frederick W. Taylor helped shape management practices. Trained as an engineer, Taylor emphasized the importance of developing precise analytical schemes to select, train, evaluate, and reward production workers for the purposes of motivating them, controlling their behaviors, and improving productivity.

Taylor had a major impact on how firms manage human resources.

During the second quarter of the century, the focus shifted somewhat to acknowledging the importance of the work group's influence on employees. Elton Mayo and his work at the Hawthorne plant (the "Hawthorne studies") focused on improving individual productivity by experimenting with changing the work group's composition and incentive schemes, in addition to its environmental conditions, such as the lighting and physical arrangements.[48] Knowledge of groups and the effect of groups on individuals advanced during the 1930s and into the 1940s. World War II refocused attention on the importance of improving selection procedures for people doing more complex jobs (e.g., for fighter pilots and secret service agents).

Did You KNOW?

During the early 1900s, 85 percent of our workers were in agriculture. Now agriculture involves less than 3 percent of the workforce.

During the 1950s and 1960s, practices developed in the military, such as assessment centers, spread into the private sector. From the 1920s on, a bureaucratic view of personnel activities predominated. The use of practices such as formal performance appraisals, selection testing, and centralized employment decisions; the presence of a full-time personnel director; and the presence of rule books and extensive record-keeping became increasingly common throughout most sectors of the economy, often with the support of industrial unions.

The terms "personnel management" and "human resource management" present different pictures of how companies value employees.

During the 1970s, the term "human resource management" emerged and began to replace the older term, "personnel management." The new term reflected a broader perspective, which included issues such as safety and health, stress, employee satisfaction, and industrial relations. As the century is drawing to a close, "human resource management" is used to acknowledge the importance of employees as corporate assets. The skills, knowledge, and experiences of employees have economic value to an organization because they enable it to be productive and adaptable.[49] Like other assets, employees have value in the marketplace; but unlike other assets, they have a potential value that can be fully realized only with their cooperation. Furthermore, human resources now are recognized as sources of potential competitive advantage.[50] Competitive advantage is gained by implementing a value-creating strategy that competitors cannot easily copy and sustain.

EXHIBIT 1.5

Changing Concerns of Human Resource Management

TIME PERIOD	PRIMARY CONCERNS	EMPLOYEE PERCEPTIONS	TECHNIQUES OF INTEREST
Before 1900	Production technologies	Indifference to needs	Discipline systems
1900–1910	Employee welfare	Employees need safe conditions and opportunity	Safety programs, English language classes, inspirational programs
1910–1920	Task efficiency	Need high earnings made possible with higher productivity	Motion and time study
1920–1930	Individual differences	Employees' individual differences considered	Psychological testing, employee counseling
1930–1940	Unionization	Employees as adversaries	Employee communication programs, anti-unionization techniques
	Productivity	Group performance	Improving conditions for groups
1940–1950	Economic security	Employees need economic protection	Employee pension plans, health plans, fringe benefits (pensions, etc.)
1950–1960	Human relations	Employees need considerate supervision	Foremen training (role playing, sensitivity training)
1960–1970	Participation	Employees need involvement in task decision	Participative management techniques
	Employment laws		
1970–1980	Task challenge and quality of working life	Employees from different groups should be treated equally	Affirmative Action, Equal Opportunity
1980–1990	Employee displacement; Quality, Cost, and Customers	Employees need work that is challenging and congruent with abilities	Job enrichment, integrated task teams
1990–2000	Productivity Competitiveness Globalization Change	Employees need jobs—lost through economic downturns, international competition, and technological changes	Outplacement, retraining; total quality management
		Employees need to balance work and nonwork and make contributions; need to be flexible	Linking the needs of the business, training, ethics, diversity, and workplace accommodation

Adapted from S. J. Carroll and R. S. Schuler, "Professional HRM: Changing Functions and Problems," in *Human Resources Management in the 1980s*, edited by S. J. Carroll and R. S. Schuler (Washington D. C.: Bureau of National Affairs, 1983): 8–10.

Creating and re-creating such strategies is now recognized as a primary objective for human resources management. Frank Calamita, an executive at Sony Music Entertainment, describes the changing importance of people this way:

> *The only aspect of the people aspect used to be, "What is the head count?" Now they say, "Let's take each one of these strategic issues and look through the lens of human resources."*[51]

As in the GE feature, current approaches to managing people within any particular company reflect both the past and the process of letting go of the past in order to prepare for the future. As environmental change quickens, more and more companies are concluding that some of the traditional approaches to managing human resources, which are rooted in the organizations of the past, must be modified. Intense international and domestic competition is forcing major companies to reassess themselves. Reassessment often culminates in fundamental changes in technologies, organizational structures, business strategies, and HR management philosophies and practices. Thus, the decade of the 1990s has emerged as a period of experimentation in new approaches to managing human resources within the context of new organization and work designs. Organizations are rapidly learning from this experimentation in order to be very competitive in the global economy.

Current Trends

LEARNING OBJECTIVE 6

Discuss some current trends in human resource management.

What is happening today in the field of HR management is nothing short of revolutionary. This organizational function is more important than ever. Line managers are getting involved in the process and HR managers are becoming members of the management team. Also, because this endeavor is seen as critical to the success of organizations, it is recognized that virtually everyone in an organization can make a contribution to the management of people and the success of the organization at the same time. Five trends accompany this excitement and challenge.

Trends in human resource management:

- **Globalization**
- **Workforce diversity**
- **Teams and teamwork**
- **Small business and entrepreneurial firms**
- **Technical expertise and systematic analysis**

Globalization

Within the U. S. there are many variations in how companies manage human resources. However, the variations that appear around the world are often even more dramatic. As more and more U. S. companies are reaching out to take advantage of the resources and markets available in other countries, managers are discovering that they cannot ignore the many variations of managing human resources in the international arena. Indeed, they will benefit from welcoming them:

> *As companies' global ambitions grow, many fast-track executives now see foreign tours as necessary for career advancement. Gerber Products Company's CEO Al Piergallini, who is building markets in Latin America and Central and Eastern Europe, says foreign assignments will be "emphasized" in the future as part of normal career development for his executives. As a result, Gerber's country manager in Poland feels he has an edge over many of his colleagues. "My overseas experience sets me apart from the rest of the MBA bunch," says Jan Lower. "I'm not just one of hundreds of thousands."*[52]

"As managers deal with global competitiveness, they will see that human resources are the core of a company's strategic competence and organizational capabilities."

Christopher Bartlett
Professor
Harvard Business School

Therefore, throughout this book we return repeatedly to comparisons of how managing human resources differs among countries, especially the countries in Europe, Asia, and the members of the North American Free Trade Agreement (NAFTA). These particular countries include the United States' largest trading partners, the locations of many joint ventures and strategic alliances involving U.S. companies, and the locations of many of the major competitors of U.S. companies. Readers who are particularly interested in cross-cultural and international HR management should consult the sources referenced throughout the chapters.

Managing a diverse workforce well can result in a competitive advantage.

Workforce Diversity

Increased awareness of global diversity is accompanied by increased awareness of the diversity present within the domestic workforce. Successful organizations recognize diversity as an issue that demands attention.[53] According to Stona J. Fitch, vice president of manufacturing for Procter and Gamble Company, the first companies that achieve a true multicultural environment will gain a competitive advantage. Diversity provides a much richer environment, a variety of viewpoints, and greater productivity.[54] And, importantly, it can make work much more fun and interesting.

As organizations develop effective domestic multiculturalism, they appear to expand their appreciation of the many other dimensions of diversity that characterize their workforce. For example, organizations develop initiatives to encourage the understanding and appreciation of differences in age, language, background, and physical capabilities. Throughout this book, diversity initiatives at companies are described to illustrate how paying attention to this aspect of the environment shapes HR management practices.

The U. S. workforce has, of course, always been diverse. And diversity within organizations is certainly increasing. But changes in the composition of the workforce alone cannot account for the attention this issue has drawn in the 1990s. The importance of workforce diversity and the consequences of ignoring it have been highlighted by other changes, especially the increased use of teams.

Working in teams is the reality for many people today!

Teams and Teamwork

Many firms now use teams and teamwork.[55] Team-based approaches to work can increase innovation, improve quality, serve customers better, and shorten the time it takes to transform an idea into a product that is available in the marketplace. To create and orchestrate teams, people need to be selected, appraised, compensated, and trained in ways that reflect the unique relationships that develop between employees who work together. Most companies know—or at least believe—that people working in teams should not be managed in the same manner as people who work more or less independently. Nevertheless, teamwork really is a somewhat new phenomenon in the American workplace, so considerable experimentation in how best to manage teams is still taking place around the country. Some practices now viewed as experimental will undoubtedly become commonplace within the next decade. Therefore, preparing for the 21st century requires understanding how teamwork is changing HR management in leading companies. Accordingly, illustrative examples and suggestions appear throughout the remaining chapters of this book.

Great management of human resources is vital to the success of small businesses and entrepreneurial firms.

Small Business and Entrepreneurial Firms

While many large firms have been downsizing and creating fewer jobs, small businesses and entrepreneurial firms have been creating hundreds and thousands of jobs. Because these firms have only a few employees, the quality and contribution of each individual is extremely important. Consequently, it is important to be aware of the HR management challenges and issues they face and how they manage them.

In discussing these smaller firms, it is important to distinguish between them. Small businesses have relatively few employees and expect to stay that way. Entrepreneurial firms start small, but then add employees as they expand and grow.

We could further distinguish these firms a bit more: small firms can be family-owned or not. Family-owned firms have the added HR challenges of managing one's relatives! Entrepreneurial firms can be distinguished by those that are started and managed independently and those that are a part of a larger network of firms, typically called franchises. Dunkin' Donuts, Subway, and McDonald's are well-known franchises. Thus we actually have four types of small businesses and entrepreneurial firms that are highlighted throughout the book. You may begin your career in one of these firms, move into one later in your career, or decide to become an entrepreneur and start your own business. In any case, you'll want to know as much as possible to help ensure your success.

Combining Technical Expertise and Systematic Analysis

What distinguishes firms that are relatively successful in achieving their HR objectives is their capacity to choose and implement the appropriate HR activities, policies, and practices. This requires both technical expertise, based on much research and practice, and systematic analysis, based on the experiences and circumstances facing each company.

Technical expertise is necessary to perform the HR activities effectively.

Technical Expertise. Firms can distinguish themselves by being more technically competent than other firms. Technical knowledge about how to manage human resources accumulated through most of the 20th century, and was established from the early 1970s to the mid-1990s. As a result of thousands of research studies, we know a great deal about how to design effective methods of selecting people, how to assess performance, how to design training programs, how to design pay systems, and so on. Like any body of technical knowledge, however, our understanding of how to manage people effectively is based on what has worked in the past. As conditions change, some of our knowledge may become obsolete. In addition, much of the technical knowledge we have was developed by experts working in narrowly defined subareas of HR management—for example, compensation specialists and training specialists. Specialists in each area often have been guided by the desire to answer the question: "*In general,* what are some basic principles (e.g., of compensation, training) that seem to apply?" Technical specialists often do not consider questions such as: "How do the training activities within a specific organization affect the way employees will react to a particular type of compensation plan?"

Because of constantly changing conditions and because our technical knowledge has been created by specialists, technical knowledge alone will not be sufficient for effective HR management. Managing people effectively requires using the available technical knowledge in a thoughtful and systematic way.[56]

A Systematic Approach. Throughout this book, we describe several examples of how companies are using a systematic approach to manage for high productivity while respecting the needs of individual employees and the larger society in which the company operates. We started with Southwest Airlines and GE. Other companies include Disney, Wal-Mart, Chrysler, Lincoln Electric, Coca-Cola, Harley-Davidson, L.L. Bean, Levi Strauss, Aid Association for Lutherans, UPS, FedEx, U.S. West, Microsoft, Intel, Cisco Systems, Texas Instruments, First Chicago, AT&T, Ben and Jerry's Homemade, Inc., Johnson & Johnson, Nordstrom, and Sears.

A systematic approach involves:

- **Considering how HR management practices affect employees' attitudes and behaviors**
- **Considering the unique characteristics of the company**
- **Examining the constantly changing aspects of the environment**

These effective companies take advantage of the power of HR policies and practices by using them systematically. A **systematic approach** has three defining characteristics. *First,* a systematic approach involves considering how all the specific practices for managing people affect the attitudes and behaviors of employees working in various jobs. HR philosophies, policies, and practices that are consistent with each other and coordinated with each other communicate the same message to employees.[57] A performance appraisal system that evaluates employees on the basis of the attainment of long-term goals, coupled with a compensation system that rewards employees on the same basis, sends a clear message to employees. On the other hand, an HR policy that describes employees as the most valuable resource, coupled with constant layoffs and little training, sends conflicting messages. Consistency across all HR policies and practices results in consistency and clarity about what is expected, what is rewarded, and what is important.

Second, a systematic approach also involves taking into account the unique characteristics of the company, including the company's history, top management's goals and the strategies they intend to pursue, the corporate culture, the size of the company and the way it is structured, and the technologies people use. As a consequence of their unique characteristics, we find that successful firms, even in the same industry, can have rather different HR activities and use different competitive strategies.

Firms can be equally effective in managing human resources with different philosophies and practices, but it must be done systematically to be successful.

The strategy pursued by a company is related to what customer satisfaction means in the context of that particular company. Companies competing through innovation seek to satisfy customers by creating something totally new and different. In contrast, those competing on quality seek to satisfy customers by offering products or services that predictably meet rigid specifications at a low cost. For example, Nordstrom is a retail department store that competes on the basis of customer service, whereas Sears, which is in the same industry, competes largely on the basis of low cost and brand names. Although both are fine organizations in the same industry, they have substantially different HR practices and philosophies. These differences reflect their different approaches to retailing and the needs that result from these.[58]

In firms that manage their employees systematically, managers know why they lead their people the way they do: their entire set of HR practices has been explicitly developed to match the needs of their employees and customers, and the strategies of their businesses. In this way, they all fit each other and fit the qualities of the company.

Third, a systematic approach also involves looking at the constantly changing aspects of the environment. HR practices must be sensitive to changes in the labor market and the economy; the actions of competitors and strategic partners; man laws and regulations, both current and proposed; and even political processes. Chapters 3 and 4 examine these considerations.

Summary

HR management is about managing people in organizations as effectively as possible for the good of the employees, the company, and society. As such, HR management is becoming more and more important to organizations in their efforts to manage people as effectively as possible.

Managing human resources is critical to the success of all companies, large and small, regardless of industry. The more effectively a firm manages its human resources, the more successful the firm will be. Using the stakeholder framework, companies define success by how well they serve their stakeholders. Stakeholders include those who have a claim on the resources, services, and products of the companies. Although stakeholders influence all parts of an organization, they affect some aspects more than others, and some aspects are affected by several stakeholders. The stakeholders who make a significant claim on HR management, and thus define a firm's general HR objectives, include—but are not limited to—the organization itself, the employees, the stockholders and investors, the customers, the suppliers, and society. Because the claims of stakeholders sometimes conflict, managing human resources is a challenging and important task.

As the environment around us is changing rapidly, organizations are re-examining all aspects of managing the business. As a result, companies are discovering new ways to effectively manage human resources. Successful firms in today's highly competitive environments have found that it pays to have everyone involved in the effort. Employees, line managers, and HR professionals have to work together if their firm is to be effective in managing their human resources. Because you will be in one or more of these categories during your career, we will discuss the activities of HR management from each of these viewpoints.

In the next several chapters, you also will see a particular emphasis is given to certain themes: ethics, partnership, multiple stakeholders, change, diversity, teamwork, and globalization.

Although you may never work in an HR department, or at least think you will not do so in your career, it is important for you to be familiar with these themes because they are changing the way organizations conduct business. This book is written to help you prepare for a future that is becoming more dependent on its human resources than ever before. The key terms used in this book are defined in Exhibit 1.6.

Major themes throughout this book are:

- Ethics
- Partnership
- Multiple stakeholders
- Change
- Diversity
- Teamwork
- Globalization

EXHIBIT 1.6

What Is Human Resource Management?

A GLOSSARY OF KEY TERMS

Recognizing that some variations exist within and across organizations in the use of words in HR management, this book uses the following definitions:

Employees All those in the company who are nonmanagers. They work with HR professionals and line managers in managing human resources.

Human resource management Managing people in organizations as effectively as possible for the good of the employees the company, and society.

HR activities Understanding the business environment and planning; staffing; appraising; compensating; improving; establishing and maintaining effective work relationships, and monitoring and assessing.

HR administration Performing day-to-day operations such as writing job descriptions and preparing recruiting ads.

HR department/leader/staff (HR professionals) A formal unit and individual(s) designated to be in charge of the HR function and, therefore, responsible and accountable for the organization's HR management activities.

HR function A set of activities, practices, roles, responsibilities, and structures in an organization concerned with HR management that may be carried out by any and all employees (managers and nonmanagers).

HR issues/concerns Those topics, areas, and thoughts related to HR management.

HR philosophy A general statement about the value of employees to the firm that in turn shapes the content of HR policies.

HR policies General guidelines, based on the HR philosophy, that are referred to in the development of the HR practices and activities to be used by the firm.

HR practices Specific HR actions used to attract, motivate, retain, and retrain employees.

HR professionals The HR leaders and staff, generalists and specialists.

HR programs Action plans that direct and implement a set of HR practices and that are consistent with HR policies and philosophy.

Human resources The people being attracted, motivated, retained, or retrained by an organization.

HR strategy Developing and implementing overall plans that effectively link HR management activities with the business.

Line manager The person responsible for managing people in order to attain the business objectives of the company. Line managers are in all areas of the company.

Partnership The cooperative relationship among the HR department and staff, line managers, and employees in managing human resources.

In the next chapter we will discuss issues associated with the HR department. Again, even if you never work in such a department, it is important to know what the department does and how it can help you in your efforts to manage human resources. If you do accept a job in an HR department, you will understand more clearly the issues and challenges faced by HR professionals. Throughout the text we will use examples of what some of the best companies are doing. They will show that the job of HR management can be done well in a highly competitive, global environment!

Key Concepts

employability
human resource management
HR professionals
line manager
partnership
productivity
systematic approach
stakeholders
total quality management (TQM)

Review and Discussion Questions

1. What has Southwest Airlines been doing that demonstrates the value of managing human resources?
2. Why do organizations place great importance on managing human resources?
3. What are common characteristics of today's effective organizations?
4. Using the stakeholder framework, outline the objectives that HR needs to be concerned with from all its major stakeholders.
5. Describe the relationships among managing human resources, the objectives of the organization, and the stockholders and investors.
6. Describe the relationships between managing human resources and the objectives of the customers.
7. Describe the relationships between managing human resources and the objectives of the employees.
8. Describe the relationships between managing human resources and the objectives of society.
9. Describe the relationships between managing human resources and the the objectives of strategic business partners (e.g., suppliers, joint venture partners).
10. Briefly summarize the major activities of HR management.
11. Who is responsible for managing human resources?
12. Who are HR professionals and line managers?
13. Describe the theme of "Partnership in Managing Human Resources."
14. Describe the importance of being systematic in managing human resources.

PROJECTS, EXERCISES & CASES

Projects: Application of the Stakeholder Framework

Read the two cases at the end of this textbook, entitled "Lincoln Electric Company" and "Nordstrom." Then, using the stakeholder framework illustrated in Exhibit 1.2, make an illustration that identifies the stakeholders of each company and shows the relative importance of each stakeholder to each company.

Here, as in the chapters to follow, you can gather your information from materials in the chapter, the cases at the end of the text, and from other sources including newspapers, magazines, the Internet, and your experience. Make your best judgments if you are unable to find the precise information.

Field Project

Look at the most recent issues (say, the last five issues) of *Fortune, Business Week, Inc., The Wall Street Journal, Workforce*, and any other pertinent journals or papers including your local newspaper. Select two companies and focus on these questions:

1. What are the prime issues faced by HR management and its responsibility in the organization?
2. What is the role of people and line managers, respectively, in dealing with those issues?
3. How does the involvement of HR management help the company grow and develop?
4. Is the company a large corporation or small proprietorship? What do you think is the difference between those two in managing human resources? Compare your results with others who had read about companies of different sizes than yours.

Case: What Makes Southwest Airlines So Successful?

For several years Southwest Airlines' successful low-cost, on-time, no-frills, no-allocated seats, no-meals approach to air travel has helped the company fly high above its competitors with hefty profit gains. In contrast with the industry as a whole, which has lost billions of dollars, Southwest's lean, mean flying machine has carved out 25 consecutive years of profits and has risen to become the eighth largest U. S. airline.[1]

This profitability has fueled Southwest's tremendous stock success over the years. Since Southwest began selling stock to the public in 1972, its value has increased more than 21,000 percent! Yes, hard to believe. It is even better than Wal-Mart, which gained an equally impressive 19,000 percent in that same time period.[2]

Early Days

Texas businessman Rollin King and lawyer Herb Kelleher founded Air Southwest Company in 1967 as an intrastate airline, linking Dallas, Houston, and San Antonio. Braniff and Texas International sued the company, questioning whether the region needed another airline, but the Texas Supreme Court ruled in Southwest's favor. In 1971 the company (renamed Southwest Airlines) made its first scheduled flight, from Dallas Love Field (its home base) to San Antonio.[3]

When other airlines moved to the Dallas-Fort Worth (DFW) airport in 1974, Southwest stayed at Love Field, gaining a virtual monopoly at the airfield. This monopoly proved to be limiting, however, with adoption of the Wright Amendment in 1979. This federal law prevents airlines operating out of Love Field from providing direct service to states other than those neighboring Texas. Southwest's customers can fly from Love Field to New Mexico, Oklahoma, Arkansas, and Louisiana but must buy new tickets and board different Southwest flights to points beyond.

When Lamar Muse, Southwest's president, resigned in 1978 because of differences with King, Kelleher became president. Regarded as something of an industry maverick, Kelleher went on to introduce advance-purchase "Fun Fares" in 1986 and a frequent-flyer program based on the number of flights, rather than mileage, in 1987. He often stars in Southwest's unconventional TV commercials, and when Southwest became the official airline of Sea World (Texas) in 1988, Kelleher had a 737 painted to resemble Shamu, the park's killer whale.

All in the Same Boat

Today, Kelleher continues to lead Southwest Airlines in its success as a low-cost, no frills, regional airline. To help keep costs low, it uses only fuel-efficient Boeing 737s. Since any airline can buy these planes, competitors have tried to muscle into this low-frills, short-haul market. For example, United Airlines introduced its shuttle service on the West Coast in October 1994. Starting with 184 flights, United increased its daily flights to 304 by the end of the year. United soon found out, however, that "it's one thing to imitate a winner—and quite another to beat him at his own game."[4] Here's how industry analysts described United's efforts:

Shuttle by United, launched with hope and fanfare in 1994, calculatedly resembled Southwest. It boasted a 45-plane fleet of Boeing 737s—the same plane Southwest flies. It was able to effect looser union work rules than those in force at its parent. And it aimed to approach the low operating costs that are a key factor in Southwest's success.

The result: After 16 months, Shuttle by United has retreated from many Southwest routes and admits it hasn't gotten as close as it had hoped to Southwest's low costs. And Southwest has not only regained traffic lost initially to the Shuttle, but also increased its California business.[5]

Although analysts cite many factors for United's retreat, two major factors do stand out: cost and its workforce. While the "cost per available seat mile" (the standard measure in the industry for cost) is around 9.1 cents for the major U.S. airlines, Southwest's is 7.1 cents. United's Shuttle got down to 8 cents.

Making it possible to have these significantly lower costs is Southwest's workforce. Its workforce is probably the most productive and most motivated in the business. By an accepted standard in the industry to measure employee productivity, Southwest has 81 employees per airplane and the major airlines have up to 157.[6] The number of passengers per Southwest employee is nearly double that of the industry average. It also provides excellent service. It has won the industry's triple crown, 1) best on-time performance, 2) fewest lost bags, and 3) fewest passenger complaints in the same month, nine times. No competitor has achieved that even once!

These outstanding productivity and service figures result from a well-managed and highly motivated workforce, starting with Herb Kelleher as president and CEO and Elizabeth Pedrick Sartain, vice president of the people department, through to every single Southwest employee.[7] Herb Kelleher is famous for his strong belief that people make the difference, and it's in how you manage that makes that difference. His managers are the same. "At other places, managers say that people are their most important resource, but nobody acts on it. At Southwest, they have never lost sight of the fact."[8] Not surprisingly then, industry observers say that Southwest Airlines has a competitive advantage over its rivals, and this advantage comes from managing its human resources.

Case Questions

1. What evidence do you have to say that there is a real partnership in managing human resources at Southwest Airlines?
2. What is the relationship between winning the industry's triple crown and how Southwest manages its workforce?
3. What is the relationship between Southwest's productivity numbers and how Southwest manages its workforce?
4. Why do the other airlines sit back and let Southwest continue to beat them largely on the basis of how well it manages its people? Why don't these other airlines try to do the same?

Case Endnotes

1. Compiled by industry analysts and reported on the Internet at pathfinder.com.

2. Figures reported in J. Pfeffer, *Competitive Advantage Through People* (Boston: Harvard Business School Press, 1995): 4.

3. This section on Southwest's early days was compiled by industry analysts and reported on "The Hoover 100." *Hoover's Company Profile Database* (Austin, TX: The Reference Press, Inc., 1996).

4. S. McCartney and M. J. McCarthy, "Southwest Flies Circles Around United's Shuttle," *The Wall Street Journal* (February 20, 1996): Bl, 9; F. E. Whittlesey, "CEO Herb Kelleher Discusses Southwest Airlines' People Culture: How the Company Achieves Competitive Advantage from the Ground Up," *ACA Journal* (Winter 1995): 8–25.

5. McCartney and McCarthy, "Southwest Flies Circles Around United's Shuttle."

6. K. Labich, "Is Herb Kelleher America's Best CEO?" *Fortune* (May 2, 1994): 50.

7. B. Paik Sunoo, "How Fun Flies At Southwest Airlines," *Personnel Journal* (June 1995): 62–73.

8. Labich, "Is Herb Kelleher America's Best CEO?" p. 50.

Chapter 1 Endnotes

1. B. Paik Sunoo, "How Fun Flies At Southwest Airlines," *Personnel Journal* (June 1995): 62–73; K. Labich, "Is Herb Kelleher America's Best CEO?" *Fortune* (May 2, 1994): 44–52; P. Sellers, "What Exactly is Charisma?" *Fortune* (January 15, 1996): 68–75.

2. Sunoo, "How Fun Flies At Southwest Airlines"; Labich, "Is Herb Kelleher America's Best CEO?"; Sellers, "What Exactly is Charisma?"; F. E. Whittlesey, "CEO Herb Kelleher Discusses Southwest Airlines' People Culture: How the Company Achieves Competitive Advantage from the Ground Up," *ACA Journal* (Winter 1995): 8–25.

3. "Southwest Airlines Won't Be Grounded by a Strict Compensation Structure," *Personnel Journal* (March 1995): 23.

4. Sunoo, "How Fun Flies At Southwest Airlines."

5. W. Zellner et al., "Go-Go Goliaths," *Business Week* (February 13, 1995): 64–70.

6. W.G. Lee, "A Conversation with Herb Kelleher," *Organizational Dynamics* (Autumn 1994): 64–74.

7. J. Welch, quoted in J. W. Peters, "Strategic Staffing: A Key Link in Business and Human Resource Planning," *Human Resource Planning* 11, No. 2, 1988: 155.

8. "Teets Reminds HR Executives That People are Top Asset in Business," *HR Reporter* (October 1994): 1–2.

9. S. Caudron, "HR Leaders Brainstorm," *Personnel Journal* (August 1994): 54.

10. C. A. Bartlett and S. Ghosal, "What Is a Global Manager?" *Harvard Business Review* (September—October 1992): 131.

11. *Reinventing the CEO* (New York: Korn/Ferry International and Columbia University, 1989): 1.

12. C. M. Farkas and P. DeBacker, "There Are Only Five Ways to Lead" (excerpt from *Maximum Leadership*), *Fortune* (January 15, 1996): 109–112.

13. L. Landro, "GE's Wizards Turning from the Bottom Line to Share of the Market," *The Wall Street Journal* (July 12, 1982): 1; N. Tichy and R. Charan, "Speed, Simplicity, and Self-Confidence: An Interview with Jack Welch," *Harvard Business Review* (Sept.–Oct. 1989): 116.

14. Ibid., p. 113. Also from material in GE Annual Reports 1992 and 1993; and T. Smart, "GE's Money Machine," *Business Week* (March 8, 1993): 62–68; T. S. Fiske, "HR Issues Drive Production Offshore," *Personnel Journal* (January 1991): 84–88; N. Tichy and S. Sherman, *Control Your Destiny or Someone Else Will* (New York: Currency/Doubleday, 1993).

15. *High Performance Work Practices and Firm Performance* (Washington, D.C.: U.S. Department of Labor, 1993).

16. "Change in the Global Economy: An Interview with Rosabeth Moss Kanter," *European Management Journal* (March 1994): 1–9; J. Pfeffer, *Competitive Advantage through People: Unleashing the Power of the Work Force* (Boston: Harvard Business School Press, 1994); T. A. Stewart, "Your Company's Most Valuable Asset: Intellectual Capital," *Fortune* (October 3, 1994): 68–74.

17. R. Jacob, "Corporate Reputations," *Fortune* (March 6, 1995): 54–56; A. Farnham, "America's Most Admired Company," *Fortune* (February 7, 1994): 50–87; M. Galen, D. Greising, and S. Anderson, "How Business Is Linking Hands in the Inner Cities," *Business Week* (September 26, 1994): 81, 83.

18. R. S. Schuler, "World Class HR Departments: Six Critical Issues, " *Accounting and Business Review* (January 1994): 43–72.

19. Harley-Davidson, Inc., *Annual Report*, 1992: 10.

20. L. D. Lerner and G. E. Fryzell, "CEO Stakeholder Attitudes and Corporate Social Activity in the Fortune 500," *Business and Society* (April 1994): 58–81; R. E. Freeman, *Strategic Management: A Stakeholder Approach* (Boston: Pitman, 1984); D. J. Wood, "Corporate Social Performance Revisited," *Academy of Management Review* 16 (1991): 691–718; J. H. Dobrzynski, "Tales from the Boardroom Wars," *Business Week* (June 6, 1994): 71–72; G. T. Savage et al., "Strategies for Assessing and Managing Organizational Stakeholders," *Academy of Management Executives* 2 (1991): 61–75.

21. L. Therrien, "Plumper Profits Ahead," *Business Week* (January 10, 1994): 78; Z. Schiller, "No Rust on This Market,"*Business Week* (January 10, 1994): 73; K. Kerwin, "Value Will Keep Detroit Moving," *Business Week* (January 10, 1994): 71; J. Weber, "Lean, Mean, And... Healthier?" *Business Week* (January 10, 1994): 76; C. Arnst. "The End of the End for 'Big Iron," *Business Week* (January 10, 1994): 81.

22. C. Farrell, "Is the Japanese Dynamo Losing Juice?" *Business Week* (June 27, 1994): 44.

23. S. Nasar, "The American Economy, Back on Top," *New York Times* (February 27, 1994): p. F1, col. 6; Kerwin, "Value Will Keep Detroit Moving," *Business Week* (January 10, 1994): 71–108.

24. See M. E. Porter, *Competitive Strategy* (New York: Free Press, 1985); M. E. Porter, *Competitive Advantage* (New York: Free Press, 1985).

25. S. Sherman, "Are You as Good as the Best in the World?" *Fortune* (December 13, 1993): 95–96.

26. Ibid.

27. R. Levering and M. Moskowitz, *The One Hundred Best Companies to Work for in America* (New York: Doubleday, 1993); annual return data on publicly traded companies in the *1993 One Hundred Best* (sixty-three firms), the *1994 One Hundred Best* (sixty-two firms), and the Frank Russell 3,000—the three thousand largest companies in America (with each firm weighed equally, not by capital) was provided by Oliver Buckley of BARRA; Cascio, *Costing Human Resource: The Financial Impact of Behavior in Organizations*; G. R. Jones and P. M. Wright, "An Economic Approach to Conceptualizing the Utility of Human Resource Management Practices," in *Research in Personnel and Human Resource Management*, ed. K. Rowland and G. Ferris (1992).

28. M. Huselid, "The Impact of Human Resource Management Practices on Turnover, Productivity and Corporate Financial Performance," *Academy of Management Journal* (1995): 635–672. See also D. Dravetz, *The Human Resources Revolution* (San Francisco: Jossey-Bass, 1988); C. Ichniowski, "Human Resource Management Systems and the Performance of U.S. Manufacturing Businesses" (NBER working paper no. 3449, September 1990).

29. D. Denison, *Corporate Culture and Organizational Effectiveness* (New York: John Wiley & Sons, 1990); E. E. Lawler III et al., *Employee Involvement and Total Quality Management* (San Francisco: Jossey-Bass, 1992).

30. R. Jacob, "Why Some Customers Are More Equal Than Others," *Fortune* (Sept. 19, 1994): 215–224; J. D. Olian and S. L. Rynes, "Making Total Quality Work: Aligning Organizational Processes, Performance Measures, and

Stakeholders," *Human Resource Management* (Fall 1991): 303–334; A. Parasuraman, L. L. Berry, and V. A. Zeithaml, "Perceived Service Quality as a Customer-Based Performance Measure: An Empirical Examination of Organizational Barriers Using an Extended Service Quality Model," *Human Resource Management* (Fall 1991): 335–364.

31. Source: Heskett, Sasser & Hart (1990) .

32. J. Carlzon, *Moments of Truth* (Cambridge, Mass.: Ballinger, 1987).

33. J. W. Wiley, "Customer Satisfaction: A Supportive Work Environment and Its Financial Cost," *Human Resource Planning* (1991): 117–28.

34. R. Berner, "Sears' Softer Side Paid Off in Hard Cash This Christmas," *The Wall Street Journal* (December 29, 1995): B3; D. Ulrich, "Strategic and Human Resource Planning: Linking Customers and Employees," *Human Resource Planning* (1992): 47–62; M.A. Verespej, "How the Best Got Better," *Industry Week* (March 7, 1994): 27–28.

35. R. S. Teitelbaum, "Southwest Airlines: Where Service Flies Right," *Fortune* (August 24, 1994): 115–16; K. Labich, "Is Herb Kelleher America's Best CEO?" *Fortune* (May 2, 1994): 44–52; W. G. Lee, "A Conversation with Herb Kelleher," *Organizational Dynamics* (Autumn 1994): 64–74.

36. C. Gronroos, *Service Management and Marketing* (Lexington, MA: D. C. Heath, 1990); J. Campbell Quick, "Crafting an Organizational Culture: Herb's Hand at Southwest Airlines," *Organizational Dynamics* (Autumn 1992): 45–56; L. L. Berry and A. Parasuraman, "Prescriptions for a Service Quality Revolution in America," *Organizational Dynamics* (Spring 1992): 5–15.

37. B. Schneider and D. E. Bowen, "The Service Organization: Human Resources Management Is Crucial," *Organizational Dynamics* (Fall 1992): 39–52; D. E. Bowen and E. E. Lawler III, "Total Quality-Oriented Human Resources Management," *Organizational Dynamics* (Spring 1992): 29–43.

38. E. E. Lawler III, *The Ultimate Advantage: Creating the High Involvement Organization* (San Francisco: Jossey-Bass, 1992); E. E. Lawler III, S. A. Mohrman, and G. E. Ledford, *Employee Involvement in America: An Assessment of Practices and Results* (San Francisco: Jossey-Bass, 1992).

39. Adapted from E. E. Lawler, "The New Plant Approach: A Second Generation Approach," *Organizational Dynamics* (Summer 1991): 5–14.

40. N. Alster, "What Flexible Workers Can Do," *Fortune* (May 4, 1992): 50; L. C. Thurow, *Head to Head* (New York: William Morrow & Co., 1992): 45; R. B. Freeman, *Working Under Different Rules* (New York: Russell Sage Foundation, 1994).

41. B. Cohen, "Corporate Responsibility for Social Change," interview in *Prevention: The Critical Need,* ed. J. Pransky (Springfield, MO: Burrell Foundation, 1991); J. J. Laabs, "Ben & Jerry's Caring Capitalism," *Personnel Journal* (November 1992): 50–57. See also S. Caudron, "Volunteer Efforts Offer Low-Cost Training Options," *Personnel Journal* (June 1994): 38–44.

42. "Training at Waste Management," *HR Reporter* (April 1991): 1–3. Reprinted with the permission of the publisher, Buraff Publications, 1350 Connecticut Ave. NW, Washington, DC 20036.

43. Ben and Jerry's Homemade, Inc., *Annual Report,* 1992.

44. L. L. Drey, "Making a Difference: Ice Cream Meets Charity in Harlem," *New York Times* (February 21, 1993): F13.

45. P. C. Judge, "Is It Rainforest Crunch Time?" *Business Week* (July 15, 1996): 70–71; A. Halcrow, "Ben and Jerry's," *Personnel Journal* (January 1992): 59.

46. "NASA: Supplier Teamwork, " *HR Reporter* (January 1992): 1–3; W. Zellner, E. Schine, and J. E. Ellis, "Turning Rivals into Teams," *Business Week Enterprise 1993*: 222–224.

47. "Microsoft: Bill Gates' Baby is on Top of the World. Can It Stay There?" *Business Week* (February 24, 1992): 60–65.

48. B. Rice, "The Hawthorne Defect: Persistence of a Flawed Theory," Psychology Today (February 1982): 70–74; F. J. Roethlisberger, *The Elusive Phenomena* (Cambridge: Harvard University Press, 1977); F. J. Roethlisberger, W. J. Dickson, and H. A. Wright, *Management and the Worker* (Cambridge: Harvard University Press, 1939); E. Mayo, *The Human Problems of an Industrial Civilization* (Cambridge: Harvard University Press, 1933); I. C. Barnard, *The Functions of the Executive* (Cambridge: Harvard University Press, 1938); A. Bolton, "The Hawthorne Studies: Relay Assembly Participants Remember" (unpublished dissertation, Nova University, 1985); G. Greenwood, A. Bolton, and A. Greenwood, "Hawthorne a Half Century Later: Relay Assembly Participants Remember," *Journal of Management* (1983): 217–31; S. J. Carroll and R. S. Schuler, "Professional HRM: Changing Functions and Problems," in *Human Resource Management in the 1980s*, ed. Carroll and Schuler (Washington, D. C.: Bureau of National Affairs, 1983).

49. G. S. Becker, *Human Capital* (New York: National Bureau for Economic Research, 1964).

50. R. S. Schuler and I. C. MacMillan, "Gaining a Competitive Advantage through Human Resource Management Practices," *Human Resource Management* (Fall 1984): 241–256; P. M. Wright and G. C. McMahan, "Theoretical Perspectives for Strategic Human Resource Management," *Journal of Management* 18, No. 2: 295–320.

51. B. Presley Noble, "Retooling the 'People Skills' of Corporate America," *New York Times* (May 22, 1994): F8.

52. P. Oster et al., "The Fast Track Leads Overseas," *Business Week* (November 1993): 64–68; J. A. Byrne et al., "Borderless Management: Companies Strive to Become Truly Stateless," *Business Week* (May 23, 1994): 26–28; P. Dowling, R. S. Schuler, and D. Welch, *International Dimensions of Human Resource Management,* 2nd ed. (Belmont, CA: Wadsworth, 1994); C. M. Solomon, "Transplanting Corporate Cultures Globally," *Personnel Journal* (October 1993): 78–88.

53. S. E. Jackson et al., *Diversity in the Workplace: Human Resource Initiatives* (New York: Guilford Press, 1992).

54. L. Copeland, "Valuing Diversity, Part 2: Pioneers and Champions of Change," *Personnel Journal* (July 1988): 48–49.

55. M. R. Weisbord, *Productive Workplaces* (San Francisco: Jossey-Bass, 1987); R. S. Wellins, W. C. Byham, and J. M. Wilson, *Empowered Teams* (San Francisco: Jossey-Bass, 1991).

56. S. E. Jackson and R. S. Schuler, "Understanding Human Resource Management in the Context of Organizations and Their Environments," *Annual Review of Psychology* (1995); P. Osterman, "How Common Is Workplace Transformation and How Can We Explain Who Adopts It? Results from a National Survey," *Industrial and Labor Relations Review* (1994).

57. R. S. Schuler, "Strategic Human Resources Management: Linking the People with the Strategic Needs of the Business," *Organizational Dynamics* (1992): 18–32; R. S. Schuler and S. E. Jackson, "Linking Competitive Strategies with Human Resource Management Practices," *Academy of Management Executive* (August 1987): 207–219; G. E. Ledford, Jr., J. R. Wendenhof, and J. T. Strahley, "Realizing a Corporate Philosophy," *Organizational Dynamics* (Winter 1995): 5–19.

58. P. Cappelli and A. Crocker-Hefter, *Distinctive Human Resources* Are *the Core Competencies of Firms*, Report no. R117Q00011-91 (Washington, D. C.: U.S. Department of Education, 1994); M. Hequet, "Worker Involvement Lights up Neon," *Training* (June 1994): 23–29.

2

CHAPTER

The Human Resource Department

Learning Objectives

1. Discuss why the HR department is so important.
2. Describe the roles that the HR department plays in organizations.
3. Describe the various HR professionals in the HR department.
4. Discuss the ethical issues dealt with by HR departments.
5. Tell how an HR department changes when the organization becomes international.

Chapter Outline

The Human Resource Department

Why is the Human Resource Department Important?

The Many Roles of the Department

Roles for the Leader

Roles for the Staff

Staffing the Department

Professionalism in Human Resource Management

Organizing the Department

Current Trends

Globalization

Summary

"HR no longer is sitting on the sidelines. We're trying to figure out how to put together a catalog better. We're trying to figure out how to improve the turnaround time to our customers. We're right in there with line people as opposed to playing a more secondary support role."

Robert Peixotto
Vice President, Quality and Human Resources
L. L. Bean[1]

MANAGING HUMAN RESOURCES

at Levi Strauss & Co.

Over the past few years, the Levi Strauss organization has linked its HR department and practices closely to the business:

> *HR participates in every major business decision, and every HR program directly supports a business goal. The payoff is enormous.*
>
> *Donna Goya*
> *Senior Vice President of Human Resources*[2]

Instrumental in this approach has been the chairman and CEO Robert D. Haas. Working with the employees, Haas and Goya have crafted a mission statement for human resources that emphasizes the importance of people and that guides the management of the firm's human resources. As a result, according to Goya:

> *I really think that our senior directors do understand now that people can give you the competitive edge.*[3]

For the employees at Levi Strauss, this has meant empowerment. It is essential, says Goya, that all employees know where they fit into the organization and how they contribute to the broader vision and goals of the company. Sounds easy, but try doing it with more than 36,000 employees in 75 production, distribution, and finishing facilities throughout the world!

This insistence on linking their people to the business has also made the HR department more aware of the issues that line managers face daily: keeping employees excited about what they are doing and keeping their productivity high—so high that Levi Strauss continues to be one of the most competitive manufacturers in the world. This awareness has resulted in the development of several programs, including:

- Management and awareness training organization-wide, to communicate the company's commitment to creating a comfortable work-and-family environment
- Flexible work hours to accommodate plant employees' needs to address family responsibilities
- A new time-off-with-pay program, to replace separate vacation, sick leave, and floating holiday plans
- Child-care leave, expanded to cover care for other family members, including elders and significant others
- Corporate child-care fund, to enhance the existing community services, ranging from infant day care to after-school programs, based on worker needs
- Child-care voucher system for hourly employees working in field locations
- Elder-care programs
- Expansion of employee assistance program services in the field[4]

Developing and running these programs successfully is the work of a partnership of HR professionals, line managers, and staff. This takes time and energy—and money—and is indicative of the company's level of commitment. At the San Francisco headquarters alone, there are 100 employees in human resources with another 200 in various facilities around the United States and overseas!

This feature on Levi Strauss highlights several things about HR management: 1) it is very important in making organizations successful; 2) it means developing a mission statement supported by effective policies and programs, aspiration statements, and HR practices; and 3) it can be very effective in coordinating and operating all the parts of the company.

Of course, Levi Strauss & Co. is doing much more in HR management, and we will discuss other aspects throughout this chapter. In the meantime, what is your impression of Levi Strauss? Do you think it is a good company? Do you think that

Did You KNOW?

Levi Strauss has operations in 75 countries and more than 36,000 employees. Its revenue is about $7 billion yearly.

The HR department is the group formally established by the firm to assist in managing the organization's people as effectively as possible for the good of the employees, the company, and society.

your opinion is due in part to how well the firm manages its people? It appears that many people think so; Levi Strauss gets thousands of student resumes annually. Its reputation is partially due to its HR department. This department is not only important at Levi Strauss, it is very important in many organizations. Let's see what is going on inside HR departments today; you may identify an ideal job for you.

The Human Resource Department

The **human resource department** is the group formally established by an organization to assist in managing the organization's people as effectively as possible for the good of the employees, the company, and society. As indicated in Chapter 1, the working partnership of HR professionals, line managers, and employees is a major trend in business today. At times, this partnership extends outside the organization to include strategic business partners such as suppliers. The partnership may even venture into local education facilities as the HR staff works with schools to prepare students for internships in the firm.

Today HR departments, in both small and large organizations, are playing an integral role in improving the firm's competitiveness, profitability, and thus "survivability"! They are also playing a key role in addressing the multiple objectives of the organization's many stakeholders.

LEARNING OBJECTIVE 1

Discuss why the HR department is so important.

Why Is the Human Resource Department Important?

In 1991, IBM and Towers Perrin, the internationally recognized HR consulting firm, conducted a study of nearly 3,000 senior HR leaders and line managers worldwide. Results indicate that about 70 percent of HR managers see the HR department as critical to the success of organizations. By the year 2000, more than 90 percent expect this department to be critical. While the HR respondents naturally expect this trend to continue, line managers also recognize the growing importance of HR departments. These results are illustrated in Exhibit 2.1.

EXHIBIT 2.1

Expectations of Greater Impact for HR Department on Business Success

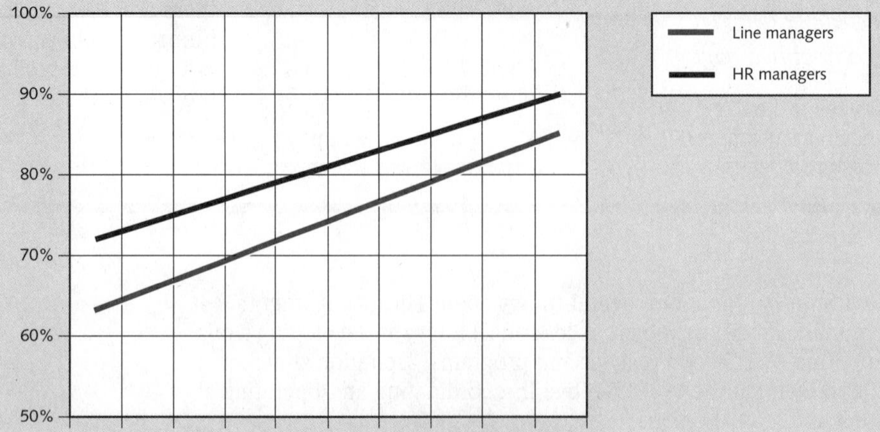

Adapted from R. S. Schuler and S. E. Jackson, *Human Resource Management: Positioning for the 21st Century* (St. Paul: West Publishing Co.: 1996).

The HR department is critical to the success of companies because human resources are the essence, the life-blood, of most companies. Richard Seithi, manager of executive education at AT&T, describes this and how this view has changed over time:

> *For a long time, American business focused on "hard" issues. We thought if we could fix that we'd be O.K. Now we know that no matter how grand the strategy is, if you don't have people skills, it's not worth the paper it's written on.*[5]

By the year 2000, 90% of HR managers think their department will be critical to the success of the business.

Yes, people and people skills in companies are fundamental to their success. Donna Goya's description of how the managers at Levi Strauss think about people confirms this. Our discussion in Chapter 1 identified the five major stakeholders of HR management; serving them and their objectives are major goals of HR. Although departments or functions within organizations serve the interests of one or more of these major stakeholders, the HR department is often the only one that serves all the stakeholders. Not surprisingly then, HR departments perform a broad range of activities (described in Chapter 1) and they play many roles. We will discuss these here, along with issues associated with staffing and globalization.

There was a time when the HR department was the last to know. "Now, the first thing you do is call human resources and say 'Can you help me do things properly'."

Richard Zimmerman
CEO
Hershey Food Corporation

The Many Roles of the Department

LEARNING OBJECTIVE 2

Describe the roles that the human resource department plays in organizations.

Effective firms in today's highly competitive environments encourage their HR departments to play many roles in the organization. And, the more roles they play well, the more likely they will be effective in improving the organization's productivity, enhancing the quality of work life in the organization, complying with all the necessary laws and regulations related to managing human resources effectively, gaining competitive advantage, and enhancing workforce flexibility.

The Business Role

Traditionally, HR departments had a relatively limited involvement in the total organization's affairs and goals. "Personnel" managers were often only concerned with making staffing plans, providing specific job training programs, or running annual performance appraisal programs (the results of which were sometimes put in the files, never to be used). They focused on the short-term—perhaps day-to-day—needs of personnel.

Roles of the HR department:

- **Business**
- **Enabler**
- **Monitoring**
- **Innovator**
- **Adapter**

With the growing importance of human resources to the success of the firm, as seen in Exhibit 2.1, HR managers and their departments are becoming more involved in the organization. They are getting to know the needs of the business—where it's going, where it should be going—and are helping it to get there. More typical today then is the comment by Jim Alef, Executive Vice President and Head, Human Resources, First Chicago Corporation:

> *"All of our HR programs serve the bank's mission. If they didn't, we wouldn't have them. In the last five years, we've become increasingly a part of the decision-making process at the bank," he says. "We assist with business strategy development by defining the HR implications of those strategies."*
>
> *"It's much more rewarding," he adds, "to be a thinking participant on the front end of a decision, rather than someone who undoes the damage created by those decisions."*[6]

Did You KNOW?

66% of senior HR managers are members of a senior policy-making committee and more than half attend board meetings, 40% frequently

Managing human resources is done on three levels:

- **Strategic**
- **Managerial**
- **Operational**

Linking HR to the business is the newest role played by the HR department, and it may be the most important one. One consequence of this role is the increased involvement in the longer-term, strategic directions of the organization. A second consequence is the new emphasis on long-term activities in addition to the more typical medium- and short-term activities. Within these three distinct time horizons, HR departments are really contributing to company success at three levels: strategic, managerial, and operational.

Strategic level means doing HR activities that focus on long-term needs of the business.

Strategic Level. At the strategic (longer-term) level, HR departments get involved in broader decisions—those that provide overall direction and vision for the organization. For example, according to Kathryn Connors, Vice President of HR at Liz Claiborne,

> *Human resources is part of the strategic planning process. It's part of policy development, line extension planning, and the merger and acquisition processes. Little is done in the company that doesn't involve us in the planning, policy, or finalization stages of any deal.*[7]

This process of linking HR to the broader, longer-term needs of firms is the essence of strategic HR management.[8]

At Bank One in Columbus, Ohio, HR executive Mike Hagar defines his HR objectives using the company's business objectives.

Typically, strategic business needs arise from decisions organizations make, such as the business objectives, what products and services to offer, and on what basis to compete—quality, cost, or innovation, or for purposes of survival, growth, adaptability, and profitability.[9] These decisions are associated with the formulation and implementation of the organization's strategy, so they are likely to reflect characteristics of the external and internal environments.

The internal environment includes the nature of the business (i.e., manufacturing or service), top management's goals and values, organizational size, technology, structure, and the life cycle of the business. Characteristics in the external environment that have an impact on organizational strategy include the types of competitive battles being waged in the industry (e.g., cost, quality, innovation); social, legal, political, and cultural factors; economic conditions; scope and degree of competition; labor pool attributes; and customers.

Together these aspects of the environment influence an organization's broader, longer-term, strategic needs and even its mission statement. Notice how the mission statement for Levi Strauss takes this longer-term view and also mentions the objectives of several stakeholders:

> *The mission of Levi Strauss & Co. is to sustain profitable and responsible commercial success by marketing jeans and selected casual apparel under the Levi's brand.*
>
> *We must balance goals of superior profitability and return on investment, leadership market positions, and superior products and service. We will conduct our business ethically and demonstrate leadership in satisfying our responsibilities to our communities and to society. Our work environment will be safe and productive and characterized by fair treatment, teamwork, open communications, personal accountability, and opportunities for growth and development.*

Levi Strauss's Aspiration Statement is its HR philosophy, showing how important human resources are to the company.

This mission statement at Levi Strauss, which indicates how the firm will manage its human resources, is closely linked with the firm's aspiration statement shown in Exhibit 2.2.

Thus, as HR departments begin to link their activities to the business, they must become knowledgeable in all these aspects of the environment; they must become strategic players. This not only helps link HR to the strategic level, but it also provides the necessary knowledge and confidence that allows this role to be played in a proactive manner, rather than in a reactive manner.

EXHIBIT 2.2

Aspiration Statement

We all want a Company that our people are proud of and committed to, where all employees have an opportunity to contribute, learn, grow and advance based on merit, not politics or background. We want our people to feel respected, treated fairly, listened to and involved. Above all, we want satisfaction from accomplishments and friendships, balanced personal and professional lives, and to have fun in our endeavors.

When we describe the kind of LS&CO. we want in the future, what we are talking about is building the foundation we have inherited: affirming the best of our Company's traditions, closing gaps that may exist between principles and practices, and updating some of our values to reflect contemporary circumstances.

Source: J. L. Laabs, "HR's Vital Role at Levi Strauss," *Personnel Journal* (Dec. 1992): 38. Used by permission.

Managerial Level. At the managerial (medium-term) level, HR departments validate personnel selection criteria, develop recruitment marketing plans, establish new recruiting markets, set up five-year compensation plans for individuals, and set up benefits packages. They also develop systems that relate current employment conditions and future business potential. They set up assessment centers, establish general management development programs, participate in organizational development, foster self-development, identify career paths, and provide career development services. While these activities could be done in any HR department, when done in a department that is linked with the business, they take on two specific characteristics. For one, the formulating process is different—here the department begins with an assessment of what is needed by the business. The types of leaders and managers needed to successfully drive the business are then identified before the assessment center is set up. For another, the content of the HR activities begins to represent the views of all employees—the managers and nonmanagers, inside and outside the HR department.

Managerial level **means doing medium-term HR activities to help managers and employees.**

Operational Level. At the operational (short-term) level, HR departments make staffing and recruitment plans, set up day-to-day monitoring systems, administer wage and salary programs, administer benefits packages, set up annual or less frequent appraisal systems, and set up day-to-day control systems. They also provide for specific job skill training and on-the-job training, fit individuals to specific jobs, and plan career moves.

As the department begins to perform within the business role, these operational-level HR activities also get linked to the business. For example, training programs are explicitly designed to fill specific employee skills needed by the business.

Operational level **means doing short-term, administrative HR activities.**

The Enabler Role

In reality, HR programs succeed because line managers make them succeed. The department's bread-and-butter job, therefore, is to enable line managers to make things happen. Thus, in the more traditional activities—such as selecting, interviewing, training, evaluating, rewarding, counseling, promoting, and firing—the HR department basically provides a service to line managers. In addition, the department administers direct and indirect compensation programs. It also assists line managers by providing information about, and interpretation of, equal employment opportunity legislation and safety and health standards.

In the enabler role, HR helps line managers fulfill their people responsibilities.

To fulfill these responsibilities, the HR department must be accessible, or it will lose touch with the line managers' needs. The HR staff should be as close as possible to the employees. Being accessible and providing services and products to others (customers) is a trend called customerization.

Customerization means viewing everybody, whether internal or external to the organization, as a customer and then putting that customer first.

"We exist because of customers. They are our raison d'etre."

Michael Mitchell
Vice-President of
Human Resources
Swiss Bank Corporation

Benchmarking is a structured approach for looking outside an organization and adapting the best practices to complement internal operations with creative, new ideas.

Customerization. Adding to the HR department's ability to gain strategic involvement are its knowledge of the business, its creative insights into how the organization can be more effective, and its familiarity with, and acceptance by, top management. More and more, these qualities are being found in departments that practice customerization. **Customerization** means viewing everybody, whether internal or external to the organization, as a customer and then putting that customer first. For HR departments, customers are typically other line managers but increasingly include other organizations and the nonmanagerial employees.

Essential to this philosophy is the realization that HR departments produce and deliver products and have "customers."[10] So too is the realization that the products provided to satisfy the customer are determined with the customer. Together, in partnership, both the customers and the HR representatives determine what is best for the situation. Levi Strauss & Co. exemplifies this philosophy under the leadership of Donna Goya.

Another important part of customerization is benchmarking. **Benchmarking** is a structured approach for looking outside an organization to study and adapt the best outside practices to complement internal operations with creative, new ideas. Learning about the practices used by competitors and other companies is of great value. As such, benchmarking usually challenges "business as usual" methods.[11]

The Monitoring Role

In the monitoring role, HR tries to ensure a fair and consistent management of the firm's people.

Although the HR department may delegate much of the implementation of its activities to line managers, it is still responsible for seeing them implemented fairly and consistently—that is, monitoring the outcomes of its programs. This is especially true today because of fair employment legislation. Various state and federal regulations are making increasingly sophisticated demands on organizations. Responses to these regulations are best made by a central group supplied with accurate information, the needed expertise, and the support of top management.

Expertise is also needed for implementing HR activities such as employee benefit administration. Since HR management experts are costly, organizations hire as few as possible and centralize them as well. Their expertise then filters to other areas of the organization.

In organizations with several locations and several divisions or units, tension often exists between the need to decentralize—or "flatten"—and the need to centralize expertise. (More on this later.) A major trend in this role of monitoring and coordinating development is the use of computer technology and HR information systems described in Chapter 20.

The Innovator Role

Important and ever-expanding roles for the HR department include providing up-to-date application of current techniques and developing and exploring innovative approaches to personnel problems and concerns. Benchmarking certainly helps in this role.

In the innovator role, HR identifies and develops new practices and methods for managing people.

Today, organizations are asking their HR departments for innovative approaches and solutions to improve productivity and the quality of work life while complying with the law in an environment of high uncertainty, energy conservation, and intense international competition. These approaches and solutions must be justified in dollars and cents. Past approaches don't always make the cut in this environment; innovation is no longer a luxury—it's a necessity.

The Adapter Role

Organizations implement new technologies, structures, processes, cultures, and procedures to meet the demands of stiffer competition. Organizations look to the HR department for the skills to facilitate organizational change and to maintain organizational flexibility and adaptability. One consequence of this adapter role is the need to be more future-oriented. For example, as external environments and organizational strategies change, new skills and competencies are needed. To ensure that the right skills and competencies are available at the appropriate time, HR departments must anticipate change. Having a mind-set of continuous change and continuous education, as Motorola has, fosters a flexible and adaptable workforce. The HR department can be the role model of change and adaptability.

Flexible Role Model. HR departments face the same demands as their organizations. They must continually streamline their operations. Not waiting for mandated cutbacks, they review and evaluate expenses and implement incremental changes to become, and stay, lean. Flexible HR departments aggressively seek to be perceived as "bureaucracy busters," setting an example for other staff functions and line organizations.[12]

To be competitive, HR departments have to be flexible and adaptable.

How effective the HR department is in playing all these roles depends on 1) how effective the leader is, 2) how well the department is staffed, and 3) how the department is organized.

Roles for the Leader

For the HR department to perform all these roles effectively, it needs to have a very special leader. The leader must not only be knowledgeable in HR activities, but must also be familiar with the needs of the business and be able to work as a partner with line management. The leader must be well versed in topics such as mergers and acquisitions, productivity, and total quality efforts. Being part of the management team means the HR leader must assume some new key roles. These roles and their criteria for success are illustrated in Exhibit 2.3.

Roles for the Staff

As the HR leader begins to play many of the roles listed in Exhibit 2.3, staff members must recognize this and adapt accordingly. After all, the leader is playing the roles in Exhibit 2.3 because of the need to better link to the business, to be more effective, and to establish a partnership with the employees and the line managers. Just as the department and its leader must change, so must the staff members. While they may not play the roles listed in Exhibit 2.3 to the same depth as their leader, the staff members still need to know the business, facilitate change, be conscious of costs and benefits, and work with line managers (though this is probably more true for the generalist than the specialist). The HR staff is active at the operational level and the managerial level, while the majority of the leader's time is spent at the strategic level with some time spent at the managerial level.

Staffing the Department

LEARNING OBJECTIVE 3

Describe the various HR professionals in the HR department.

The top HR leaders and staff members are often expected to be functional experts, capable administrators, business consultants, and problem solvers with global awareness. Management expects the HR staff "to have it all." Administrative skills are also essential for efficiency. Specialized expertise is also important, but particularly in combination with business knowledge and perspective. In flexible organizations, problem-solving and consulting skills are vital in guiding and supporting new management practices.

In effective organizations, the HR staff works closely with managers to solve people-related business challenges. While line managers may best understand their own people, many desire the more distant perspective of HR staff in handling problems. As the HR staff actively builds working relationships with line management, the managers will find it easier to work with them as partners.

EXHIBIT 2.3

Key Roles for the HR Leader

KEY ROLE	WHAT'S EXPECTED ON THE JOB
1. Businessperson	• Shows concern for bottom line • Understands how money gets made, lost, and spent • Knows the market and what the business is • Has long-term vision of where business is headed
2. Shaper of change in accordance with the business	• Can execute change in strategy • Can create sense of urgency • Can think conceptually and articulate thoughts • Has sense of purpose—a steadfast focus, a definite value system
3. Consultant to organization/partner to line management	• Has ability to build commitment into action • Responds to organizational needs • Recognizes importance of teamwork • Is capable of relationship building
4. Strategy/business planner	• Knows plan of top executives • Is involved in strategy formulation of executive committee—is not an afterthought • Develops and sells own plans and ideas—able to get needed resources • Has three- to five-year focus
5. Talent manager	• Sees the movement from an emphasis on strictly numbers or bodies needed to the type of talent and skills needed in the organization • Sees the emphasis on talent needed for executing future strategies as opposed to today's needs • Is capable of educating line managers • Knows high-potential people and anticipates their concerns—for example, who is bright but bored?
6. People manager	• Initiates—does not wait for others to call attention to need for action • Can educate and sell line managers • Can creatively measure effectiveness in own areas of responsibility and other areas of organization • Can use technology effectively

Source: Adapted from "How to Develop HR Professionals for Today's Business Environment," *HR Reporter* (Aug. 1987), 6–7. Used by permission.

The effective management of an organization's human resources depends in large part upon the knowledge, skills, and abilities of the people in the HR department, particularly the HR leader, the HR generalists, and the HR specialists (collectively referred to as HR professionals).

The Human Resource Leader

Of course, the most effective person who can head the department is an outstanding performer in the organization with both HR management expertise and line management experience:

> *In essence, to be a true professional in many areas of HR management, individuals virtually have to have an advanced degree in the subject and spend full time in that field. Areas like compensation have become incredibly complicated because of their close connection to strategic, legal, financial, and tax matters... [But] with the exception of technical specialists, HR managers need to spend a significant amount of time in line management positions. It is not enough for senior HR managers to have worked in different areas of the HR function; they must have had some line business experience so that they have a first-hand familiarity with the business operations.*[13]

"My boss, as the CEO, views my job as equivalent in value to the CFO, to the VP of engineering, to the VP of manufacturing, and expects me to deliver the same amount of value. I don't think people will last long in senior HR jobs here who don't have this perspective."

David Lietzke
VP of HR
Bay Networks

Line experience gives the HR leader an understanding of the needs of the business and the needs of the department's customers. To prepare potential leaders for this, the department's staff could rotate through various line positions over the course of several years. Short of actually serving as a line manager, such individuals could serve as special assistants to line managers or head up a special task force for a companywide project.

To be effective in playing the roles described in Exhibit 2.3, the leader needs the following knowledge, skills, and abilities (competencies):[14]

- problem-solving skills
- business knowledge/organization sensitivity
- information technology skills
- knowledge of compensation techniques that reinforce business plans
- strategic and conceptual skills
- knowledge of succession planning/career planning systems
- acknowledged leadership skills
- ability to analyze data and plan from it
- organizational change skills
- global awareness
- diversity management skills
- computer literacy
- competence in HR functional areas
- awareness of financial impacts, particularly in areas such as pension costs, health care, and compensation

Did You KNOW?

The Seven Essential Skills for HR Leaders in the Future

1. **Global operating skills**
2. **Business and financial savvy**
3. **Strategic visioning and critical thinking and problem-solving skills**
4. **Ability to use information technology**
5. **Deep HR technology savvy**
6. **Change management skills**
7. **Organization effectiveness**

This rather extensive list of competencies describes the ones that effective HR leaders in firms in highly competitive environments will need. Some firms are now adopting procedures to identify competencies for their HR staff:

> *At Weyerhaeuser each major division, led by its human resources director, is responsible for developing a list of specific, required competencies. Of course, overlaps occur among major divisions. The HR directors help generate a slate of competencies based on their interviews with the "cus-*

tomers"—others in the organization—and HR professionals, and on their own requirements. The corporation is also aiming to predict future HR issues as a basis for updating human resources strategies and developing future competency requirements for HR staff.[15]

Some ways companies train their HR professionals to gain these competencies are shown in Chapter 11 (See Exhibit 11.10).

Human Resource Generalists

Human resource generalists are those who know a little about many HR practices.

Line management positions are one important source for **human resource generalists**. A brief tour by a line supervisor in an HR staff position, usually as a generalist, conveys the knowledge, language, needs, and requirements of the line in a particularly relevant way. As a result, the HR department can more effectively fill its roles. Another source of generalist talent is the nonmanagerial employee. Like line managers, these people bring with them information about employee needs and attitudes.

These results are consistent with the survey results showing that a "human asset management" approach is the most common CEO leader style already.

Some companies assign line managers to work in the corporate HR department for two or three years as a part of their career development. Indeed, in the IBM/Towers Perrin survey, having experience in HR is seen as critical for the careers of line managers—at least, this is what the results indicate for the year 2000. In 1991 the story was a bit different. As shown in Exhibit 2.4, only 25 percent of the CEOs and line managers identify the HR experience as critical for a line manager. However, fully 55 percent said it would be critical in the year 2000. This latter result certainly fits the criteria for potential CEOs in the year 2000, also. According to a major worldwide survey conducted by the Korn Ferry consulting firm and the Columbia Business School and referred to in Chapter 1, knowledge and skill in HR management is seen as second in importance for CEOs, right behind skill and knowledge in strategy formulation. A position as a generalist is a good place to gain such expertise.

EXHIBIT 2.4

A Position in the HR Department Is Critical Experience for Line Managers

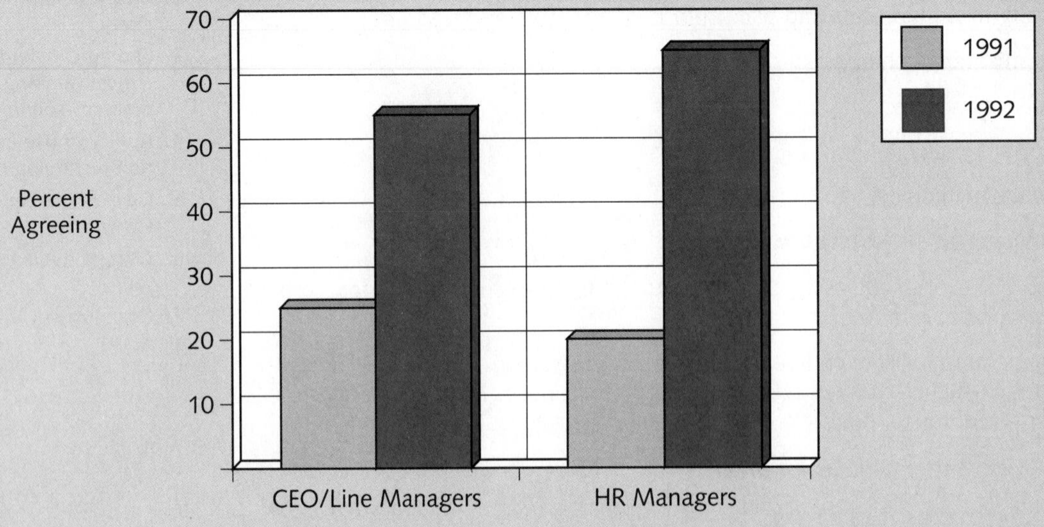

Source: Adapted from "Priorities for Competitive Advantage: A Worldwide Human Resources Study," (IBM/Towers Perrin, 1992): 26. Used by permission.

Generalists should possess many of the same qualities as HR specialists, but the generalist's level of expertise in an HR specialty will usually not be as great. After serving as a nonmanagerial generalist, the next job might be to manage an HR activity or even one of the firm's field locations. Whereas the former may result in specialization, fieldwork is likely to result in a broadening of one's experience.

Human Resource Specialists

Human resource specialists should have skills related to a particular specialty, an awareness of the relationship of that specialty to other HR activities, and a knowledge of where the specialized activity fits in the organization. Since specialists may work at almost any HR activity, qualified applicants can come from specialized programs in law, organizational and industrial psychology, labor and industrial relations, HR management, counseling, organizational development, and medical and health science. In addition, specialists are needed in the newer areas of total quality management, service technologies, behavioral performance improvement systems, and organizational change and design.

Human resource specialists are those who know a lot about one or two HR practices.

With the increases in regulatory requirements and the levels of expertise needed to deal with complex HR activities, some organizations have moved away from generalists and now rely more on specialists. However, under pressure to better serve the customer, other organizations are finding they still need generalists. Both are valuable, and both reflect this profession's drive to ever-increasing standards of excellence.[16]

Professionalism in Human Resource Management

Like any profession, HR management follows a code of professional **ethics** and has an accreditation institute and certification procedures. All professions share the code of ethics that HR management follows.

Ethics is a set of guiding principles for interaction with others.

1. Practitioners must regard the obligation to implement public objectives and protect the public interest as more important than blind loyalty to an employer's preferences.
2. In daily practice, professionals must thoroughly understand the problems assigned and must undertake whatever study and research are required to assure continuing competence and the best of professional attention.
3. Practitioners must maintain a high standard of personal honesty and integrity in every phase of daily practice.
4. Professionals must give thoughtful consideration to the personal interest, welfare, and dignity of all employees who are affected by their prescriptions, recommendations, and actions.
5. Professionals must make sure that the organizations that represent them maintain a high regard and respect for the public interest and that they never overlook the importance of the personal interests and dignity of employees.[17]

HR professionalism entails maintaining:

- **Public interest**
- **Competence**
- **Integrity**
- **Humanity**
- **Responsibility**

Ethical Issues

Increasingly, HR professionals are becoming involved in ethical issues. Some of the most serious issues center around differences in the way people are treated because of favoritism or a relationship to top management. In a survey conducted by the Society for Human Resource Management (SHRM) and the Commerce Case Clearing House (CCCH), HR professionals identified more than 40 ethical inci-

LEARNING OBJECTIVE 4

Discuss the ethical issues with which the HR department must deal.

Ethical behavior is behavior that society considers right. Illegal behavior is behavior that violates a law in a particular jurisdiction or area.

dents, events, and situations relevant to HR activities. The ten most serious ethical situations are shown in Exhibit 2.5

In the SHRM/CCCH study, the professionals surveyed agreed that workplace ethics require people to be judged solely on job performance.

> *Ethics requires managers to eliminate such things as favoritism, friendship, sex bias, race bias, or age bias from promotion and pay decisions (it is, of course, also* unlawful *to take sex, race, or age into account).*
>
> *Is ethics a "bottom line" issue? It becomes one when we consider that by acting in an ethical manner, companies will, in fact, hire, reward, and retain the best people. This will, in turn, help assure that the company has the best workforce possible to achieve its business goals.*

There are few other ethical issues that impact the bottom line in the way favoritism versus employee performance does. By adopting a definition of workplace ethics that centers on job performance, HR professionals will be in a better position to persuade others in the organization that making ethical behavior a priority will produce beneficial results.[18]

How to encourage ethical behavior:

- **Ensure that the reward system and other management policies do not create pressure for unethical behavior**
- **Have top management set a good example**
- **Establish a code of ethics**
- **Conduct internal audits**
- **Enforce laws more thoroughly**

Encouraging Ethical Behavior

To assume, however, that a single policy can be devised to ensure that everyone in an organization behaves ethically and legally all the time is unrealistic. Nevertheless, there are a number of ways in which business ethics can be improved. A good starting point is for top management to examine such management practices as reward systems, managerial style, and decision-making processes. In some organizations, the reward system promotes unethical behavior by

EXHIBIT 2.5

The Ten "Most Serious" Ethical Situations Reported by HR Managers

SITUATION	PERCENT
Hiring, training, or promotion based on favoritism (friendships or relatives)	30.7
Allowing differences in pay, discipline, promotion, etc., due to friendships with top management	30.7
Sex harassment	28.4
Sex discrimination in promotion	26.9
Using discipline for managerial and nonmanagerial personnel inconsistently	26.9
Not maintaining confidentiality	26.4
Sex discrimination in compensation	25.8
Nonperformance factors used in appraisals	23.5
Arrangements with vendors or consulting agencies leading to personal gain	23.1
Sex discrimination in recruitment or hiring	22.6

"Percent" is the percent responding which 4 or 5 on 5-point scale measuring "degree of seriousness" (5 = "very great").

Source: *1991 SHRM/CCCH Survey* (Chicago: Commerce Case Clearinghouse, June 26, 1991): 1.

encouraging the achievement of organizational goals at almost any cost. Clearly then, HR professionals can play a major role in influencing ethical behavior in organizations. Accordingly, in the following chapters we present relevant ethical issues. For more discussion on what ethical behavior is and how it differs from illegal behavior, see the feature "HR Advice and Application: Ethical Behavior."

Professional Certification

The SHRM has established the Human Resource Certification Institute to certify HR professionals. The institute has the following purposes:

1. To recognize individuals who have demonstrated expertise in particular fields
2. To raise and maintain professional standards
3. To identify a body of knowledge as a guide to practitioners, consultants, educators, and researchers
4. To aid employers in identifying qualified applicants
5. To provide an overview of the field as a guide to self-development[19]

The certification institute has two levels of accreditation: basic and senior. The basic accreditation is the Professional in Human Resources. This designation requires an examination covering the general body of knowledge and four years of professional experience. A bachelor's degree in HR management or social sciences counts for two years of professional experience.

Did You KNOW?

Approximately 50,000 HR professionals are members of SHRM.

HR ADVICE & APPLICATION

Ethical Behavior

What is ethical and unethical behavior? How does it differ from legal or illegal behavior? Many instances of ethical and unethical behavior do not make headlines. Consider the purchasing agent who repeatedly refuses gifts of any kind from suppliers and the manager who always charges personal calls made from the office to his home number. A large number of managers turn in scrupulously honest expense accounts. And many managers believe that acting only in the interest of shareholders, without considering employees and consumers, is unethical behavior.

The term ethics is a slippery one. For example, an early study on ethics found that all the people surveyed believed they were behaving ethically, according to their own standards. Furthermore, society's ideas about laws and ethics keep changing. Almost everyone would agree that child labor in factories is not only illegal but unethical. Yet when the U. S. Congress passed the *Fair Labor Standards Act* in 1938 in which child-labor provisions were established, the act was bitterly contested.

Laws and ethics are related but not identical. **Illegal behavior** is behavior that violates a law in a particular jurisdiction or area. Ethical behavior stems from values and gives rise to laws. Thus, behavior can be legal but unethical. Lavish entertainment of, and gifts to, customers is an accepted business practice in the United States. At what point, however, does the practice remain legal but become unethical?

While values influence a person's beliefs and behavior, ethics is concerned with moral rights and wrongs and with the individual's moral obligations to society. From the viewpoint of the manager, **ethics** is "the rules or standards governing the moral conduct of the organization management profession." In simple terms, **ethical behavior** is behavior that society considers right. But determining specific rights and wrongs is complicated since moral concepts, like other ideas, change over time and differ from individual to individual. Thus ethics is also a set of guiding principles that helps individuals retain their self-respect while behaving justly toward others. Ethics, then, is a personal responsibility for each individual.[20]

The senior level accreditation is the Senior Professional in Human Resources. This accreditation requires a minimum of eight years of experience, with the three most recent years including policy-development responsibilities. All professionals receiving accreditation will be listed in the *Register of Accredited Personnel and Human Resource Professionals.*[21]

Careers in Human Resource Management

Did You KNOW?

Most U. S. firms see growth coming from abroad, thereby, having overseas assignments may be a typical part of any manager's career.

Numerous career possibilities in human resources exist. HR specialists can pursue their fields of specialization within a company and still sell some of their time to external organizations as consultants. Generalists in this field can remain in human resources and also occasionally serve on company-wide task forces for special issues such as downsizing or capital improvement projects.

Generalists are likely to be from three ranks: career HR professionals with degrees in business or psychology, former line managers who have switched fields, and line managers on a required tour of duty. As human resources becomes an activity more heavily valued by organizations, required tours of duty by line managers will become more frequent. Finally, as U. S. organizations become more global, there will be increased opportunities for careers in international HR management.

Careers in International HR. A thorough description of these opportunities is provided in the feature, "Managing Human Resources: Careers at the International Level." More on careers and career management is provided in Chapter 6.

Organizing the Department

In organizing the HR department, two major questions need to be addressed: 1) Where are the HR decisions made? and 2) What alternatives does the company have?

The first question has to do with the advantages and disadvantages of centralized and decentralized organizations. The second question has to do with the issue of budgets and compensation.

Centralization Versus Decentralization

Centralization means that essential decision making and policy formulation are organized and done at one location. Decentralization means that these activities are organized and done at several locations.

Centralization means that essential decision making and policy formulation are conducted at one location (at headquarters); **decentralization** means that the essential decision making and policy formulation are conducted at several locations (in various divisions or departments of the organization).

The organization of HR departments varies widely from one company to another, not only because of the differing requirements of various industries, but also because of differing philosophies, cultures, and strategic plans of individual organizations. For purposes of illustration, let us compare the centralized structure of Merck with the decentralized structure of TRW.

In the centralized HR structure of Merck, large specialized corporate staffs formulate and design HR strategies and activities. These are then communicated to the small HR staffs of operating units for implementation. High consistency and congruence with corporate goals are thus attained. In the decentralized model of TRW, small corporate staffs only manage the HR systems for executives and only act as advisors to operating units. Here there tends to be wider divergence in practices and a greater flexibility in addressing local concerns.

Looking at the nature of the businesses of Merck and TRW, it is apparent that the organizational structures they use are very appropriate for their respective types of business. TRW, a high-technology company with a diverse array of businesses, cannot use the consistent, stable approach to HR that Merck, with a more singular product focus, is able to use.[22]

Because of the rapidly changing and highly competitive environment, the trend seems to be toward greater decentralization. Responsibilities are delegated

MANAGING HUMAN RESOURCES

Careers at the International Level

The globalization of business is occurring at a much faster pace than American economic growth. According to the U. S. Department of Commerce, the gross national product increased by 15 percent between 1985 and 1990. During that same period, U. S. exports grew by 72 percent; nearly five times as fast. Exports now constitute 15 percent of GNP. In the late 1980s, U. S. foreign direct investment climbed by 34 percent. Even much faster at 105 percent was the growth of direct investment by foreigners in the United States. Every indication is that globalization will continue and in all probability accelerate.

All this suggests that from a career perspective, international business is a good place to be. If corporations are to succeed in the global arena, they must manage human resources effectively. International human resource management (IHR) should be one of the great growth functions of the 1990s and beyond.

How can you break into the field? What is the potential for growth?

In a survey of 35 major U. S. multinationals, it was found that over 90 percent of senior IHR executives have experience in other HR functions. Nearly half have held line positions and managed a business; 60 percent have had overseas assignments.

Those aspiring to upper levels of HR management (global, international, or domestic) will have a much better chance of success if they have a degree in human resources and/or international business and enter the field through one of the domestic functions, such as planning, management development, executive compensation, or industrial relations. Solid experience in two or more domestic HR areas will vastly improve the opportunities for transfer into the international arena at a significant management level.

However, a major problem for those whose experience is limited to human resources is the difficulty of obtaining an overseas assignment. There are very few Americans overseas with a primary responsibility for HR management. It is easier to gain overseas experience in other functions such as marketing, finance, and engineering. Indeed, many senior IHR executives got their overseas experience in other functions.

Is overseas experience necessary for IHR executives? Perhaps not, but it is interesting to note that the 40 percent of senior HR executives who have not worked abroad cited their lack of overseas experience as their greatest weakness.

In all probability, there will be dramatic changes in IHR management over the next decade, including much more emphasis on strategic issues and support for business objectives. IHR will become a more vital management function, and greater emphasis will be placed on staffing the function with executives possessing overseas and line experience, as well as having a solid grounding in general human resources.

In the meantime, it is important to know how to pick your way through the career maze. Those who desire careers as functional specialists may find expatriate compensation and benefits fascinating and challenging. Those who aspire to higher IHR management would be well advised to acquire a solid domestic base and experience in a line function before seeking an overseas assignment. Clearly there are other options: working for a foreign multinational or consulting firm, for example. Regardless, those who will be managing IHR in the major multinationals of the future will find the challenges exciting.

Mr. Reynolds is Senior Counselor, Organization Resources Counselors, Inc.[23]

to lower HR levels and to the operating units and line managers themselves. There is also a trend toward less formalization of policies—that is, fewer rules that are seen as bureaucratic hurdles. HR departments and their organizations thus have greater flexibility to cope with the continually changing environment. Diminished bureaucracy can also lead to greater openness in addressing problems. Of course, some activities such as fair employment issues and compensation matters may have to be centralized because of legal requirements and the need for consistency. Nevertheless, the general trend is for less formalization and less centralization. Thus, we see firms such as Levi Strauss & Co. developing broad policy statements. Local units then develop HR practices that are tailored to specific needs, yet consistent with overall company philosophy.

The Budget as an Organizational Force

The amount of money that organizations allocate to their HR departments rises yearly. In 1995, the average per-employee cost allocated to the HR department was $823. The median 1995 expenditure per employee was lower among manufacturing companies ($894) than nonmanufacturing companies ($936). Not surprisingly, department expenditures per employee decrease steadily with company size. Firms with fewer than 250 employees recorded a median expenditure of $1,162 per employee in 1995, compared with $1,031 per employee in companies with 250 to 499 employees; $650 per employee among employers with 500 to 999 employees; $542 per employee in organizations with 1,000 to 2,499 workers; and over $323 per employee among firms with 2,500 or more employees.[24]

For all firms, the median ratio of HR department staff to the workforce currently is 1.1 staff member for every 100 workers. In banking and finance, the ratio is 1.5. Among firms with fewer than 250 employees, the median ratio is 1.7 staff per 100 workers, and among companies with 250 to 499 employees, it is 1.2 per 100 employees. Ratios of HR staff to total employment are substantially lower in organizations with 500 to 2,499 employees (0.8 per 100), and lowest among employers with 2,500 or more workers (0.6 per 100).[25]

Compensation as an Organizational Force

HR management is becoming very attractive as a field of employment. Salaries tend to be generally higher for those individuals in larger organizations, for those with more experience, and for those with more education. In addition, salaries are higher in the Northeast, where the cost-of-living is higher. The corporate HR director (sometimes called senior vice president) is the most highly paid, of course, earning an average of more than $350,000, including salary, cash bonuses, and profit sharing).[26]

Current Trends

Trends in the HR department include:

- **Striving to become world-class**
- **Re-engineering and outsourcing**
- **Creating HR mission statements**

Becoming a World-Class Department

HR departments and professionals alike are striving for world-class competency. Many of the firms mentioned in this book certainly have world-class HR departments, and this basically means that they are:

- Relating HR to the needs of the business
- Seen as a business unit within the firm (operating in the same way as other units—having customers, doing benchmarking, etc.)
- Organized in a way that brings maximum service to the customer and maximum motivation to the HR staff
- Making the best HR products available for the customers
- Implementing HR programs that fulfill the agendas of the HR group and its customers
- Actively sharing an HR vision with the entire group
- Managing change and diversity
- Involved in key business discussions

"Our No. 1 priority is getting our people strategies to where they're business-based—to where business managers don't talk about a business strategy on one hand and a people strategy that has people components to it—not separate paths, but integrated paths."

Chuck Nielson
VP, HR
Texas Instruments (TI)

- Seen as a great place to work and as a model of a great organization
- Serving all the stakeholders
- Being effective internationally

Because doing all these things is not necessarily easy, many firms choose not to do them; some departments may say their companies are not big enough or global enough. Since the world is the playing field for all companies, those firms that do strive for world-class competency usually capture the competitive advantage and increase their ability to survive, grow, and adapt.

Re-engineering and Outsourcing

Re-engineering the HR department basically means taking a look at what the department is doing to see whether it can be done better and more effectively.[27] Customerization is certainly consistent with re-engineering because it asks, "What are we doing for our customers, what do they want, and how can we fill in the gaps between what they get and what they want?" Re-engineering, however, goes much further. It seeks to examine all the parts of the department with these questions in mind: "What is the purpose of this group, what jobs does it do, how does it do these jobs, and can they be done better, more effectively?" As in customerization, benchmarking can be used to ensure that, in the interest of continual improvement, the best available HR practices and activities are obtained. Partnership, mentioned in Chapter 1, is often a result of re-engineering. The end product of such an endeavor is often a more effective department that better serves and involves the employees. Consequently, re-engineering is likely to grow in significance during the remainder of the 1990s.

Another result of re-engineering may be the decision to outsource some HR activities. The re-engineering process should identify what counts, what adds values, and what can best be done by someone else (i.e., another firm specializing in one or more HR activities such as pension-plan administration.)[28]

Novell, like many other companies, decided that adding value through pension plan administration was better left to an outside vendor. According to Theresa Dadone, Director of Compensation and Benefits for Novell:

> *It wasn't long ago that employees had to come to HR and request a loan from their 401(k) plan. They had to talk to an HR person and fill out papers. A committee then had to review the request and decide whether or not to grant the loan. Well, that's not in keeping with customer service. That's treating our employees like children. So, we outsourced that responsibility. There's now a toll-free number for employees to call so they don't have to involve HR in their personal finances. We're out of the loop... that isn't where our value is. Our value is in helping employees understand the plan.*
>
> *Educational assistance is another responsibility that's been outsourced. HR used to approve all course request and process reimbursement requests. Today, an outside agency takes care of it. Employees don't have to come begging to HR, hat in hand, to process something. We now spend our time helping employees understand the benefits of educational assistance and how it can serve them in their personal and professional lives.*[29]

One implication of this **outsourcing** of HR department activities is that the HR department will never be the same! And as it outsources, typically to consulting firms, it spends time on activities that add more value to the company. It also helps employees and line managers more. Outsourcing should result in a smaller but more effective HR department. Consequently, if you plan a career in HR, you may

Did You KNOW?

HR's Concerns 2005:

- **Skill level of the workforce**
- **Managing change**
- **Aging of the workforce**
- **Management issues**
- **Quality of education**
- **Work ethic, values, and attitudes**
- **Managing diversity**
- **Improving productivity**
- **Employee communications**

"The optimist says the glass is half full, the pessimist says the glass is half empty, the re-engineer says the glass is too big."

Michael Hammer
Coauthor
Re-engineering the Corporation

Re-engineering means taking a look at what the HR department is doing to see whether it can be done better.

Did You KNOW?

TI's HR re-engineering effort was a total redesign of its HR systems so that it now has a distributed, decentralized system, rather than a mainframe system, throughout its global operations.

Outsourcing means that the company decides to have an outside company perform an activity, for example, administer the pension plan or run the cafeteria.

Did You KNOW?

Twenty-five percent of firms will outsource all or part of the HR department by 1998. HR departments will never be the same!

An HR mission statement describes the values, objectives, and goals of the HR department.

work in the HR department of a company or in a consulting firm that provides HR activities to many companies.

Creating Mission Statements

Firms that have HR departments dedicated to doing the best job possible create an HR philosophy indicating how important people are to the firm (there is more discussion on the HR philosophy in Chapter 3 under Corporate Culture). Then the HR departments take the next step: they create an HR mission statement for the department, similar to the aspiration statement of Levi Strauss & Co. (Exhibit 2.2). An **HR mission statement** is a general statement, developed with the participation of all concerned, that describes the values, objectives, and goals of the HR department. While HR mission statements may seem to the outsider to be mere platitudes, they are anything but. Often the significance of the mission statement lies in the process by which it was created. If an HR mission statement is created in a highly participatory process—that is, where all the employees, line managers, and HR staff are involved, and where the public discussion brings clarity, understanding, and commitment—then the result is not merely a piece of paper, but a new atmosphere of partnership within the company. Everyone has a basis that they have created together upon which they can evaluate the nature and quality of the practices that are developed. These types of HR mission statements become beacons of understanding and cooperation. They enable firms to develop a crucial consistency in HR philosophies, policies, and practices as discussed in Chapter 1. It is this consistency that in turn enables HR management to positively influence all the stakeholders of HR. Another example of an HR mission statement, this one developed by Mike Mitchell and his HR team at the Swiss Bank Corporation, is shown in Exhibit 2.6.

The Greening of This Discipline

HR management is increasingly concerned with ethics and ethical behavior, with linking the environment to the needs of the company, and in being more systematic and more global in orientation. It is much more externally focused than ever before, and it subscribes to the values of the baby-buster generation:

> *The consciousness of the generation right now is that they're very environmentally aware. That's something that's a concern of theirs, and if they can get involved with a company that's environmentally aware, it's more in tune with their own ethics.*

Terri Wolfe
Director of Personnel
Patagonia[30]

EXHIBIT 2.6

The Swiss Bank Corporation HR Mission Statement

OUR MISSION IS TO

- Provide quality, innovative, and sensitive human resource products and services that meaningfully support the needs and vitality of our organization and its employees.
- Create a business strategy for our function that challenges the limitations of the HR practice and provides the potential for us to become a successful business enterprise in our own right.
- Be the best at who we are and what we do.

MANAGING HUMAN RESOURCES

How HR Managers Help Companies Become Green

As interest in the environment has increased in the United States, companies are recognizing and responding to the environmental push from management and employees. Often, an in-house recycling program results.

"Recycling is one activity that allows people to express their environmental commitment in a tangible way," says Ralph Earle, a senior consultant for Arthur D. Little, a Cambridge, Massachusetts-based environmental consulting firm. "if you recycle that aluminum can you're drinking out of—something that you can touch, feel, and see—it helps the environment."

Earle also explains that companies are differentiating themselves from their competition through their environmental posture and actions. "One of the things that we preach is that, for an environmental strategy to work, it can't be viewed as a separate issue. It *has* to permeate the corporation," he says. Everybody must be involved.

There are two objectives in starting an in-house recycling program. "The first is to reclaim the material and prevent it from being disposed of," says Earle. "But the second, from an HR standpoint, is to provide programs that enable workers to feel proud about their workplace and to feel that they're making a contribution during working hours. People tend to separate their personal beliefs from what they do at the office— recycling is a way of bringing the two together."

Earle says he's noticed a direct trend linking employee interest and the growth of recycling programs in business. Why? "Recycling is extremely motivational for employees and therefore generates high participation because it's so tangible and it's so personal."

HR departments can get involved in communicating the environmental message by setting up payroll deduction programs for workers to donate money to such environmental causes as the National Resources Defense Council or the World Wildlife Fund.

What if no one on staff can spare the time to organize the recycling project? "I've seen a number of companies hiring groups of individuals who have disabilities or are learning-disadvantaged to run their in-house recycling programs," says Earle.

Another way to get involved is to become a facilitator between departments. "An objective party, such as HR, can get such groups as office workers and facilities personnel working together to make a recycling project happen," suggests Earle.

Perhaps the most important way to get the environmental message out is through constant communication. In addition to such media as company newsletters, bulletin boards, and posters, employees can learn about recycling through an in-house video on the subject.

The environmental department at Federal Express in Memphis, Tennessee, for example, is producing such a video and is even considering using the company's own television station, called FX/TV, to update employees on current environmental policies and guidelines. "It's a superb method, because it gives us instantaneous access to all of our employees," says Louis Lechleiter, the company's environmental manager.

"Our objective is employee empowerment," says Lechleiter. Already, employees throughout the organization are participating in recycling efforts, which range from recycling the batteries used in the hand-held Cosmos tracking devices to collecting cans.

A partnership is developing at Federal Express between the environmental and HR departments. An environmental module may be developed jointly and incorporated into management-development training courses.

For HR professionals, it all starts with studying the issues. "This isn't a criticism, it's just a reality: most HR people aren't really aware of this kind of visceral-level environmental issue," says Earle, "So I think there's some training and awareness that can go on."[31]

Thus, issues of the ecological environment are becoming a concern of HR management! While this may seem a bit far-fetched at first, consider the issues raised in the feature, "Managing Human Resources: How HR Managers Help Companies Become Green." Again, this concern of HR is really a stakeholder objective of society.

LEARNING OBJECTIVE 5

Tell how an HR department changes when it becomes international.

"For all practical purposes, all business today is global. Those individual businesses, firms, and industries, and whole societies that clearly understand the new rules in a world economy will prosper; those that do not will perish."

Ian Mitroff
Professor of Management
University of
Southern California

Did You KNOW?

The trend is accelerating. Overseas U. S. executives are increasing by:

- **101% at Nynex from 5 years ago**
- **15% at General Motors from 1991**
- **300% at Gerber Products by 1995**
- **10% at Motorola in 1993, 10% again in 1994**

Globalization

The globalization of world markets is inevitable.[32] More and more firms are moving operations outside their domestic borders. The last two decades in particular have seen dramatic changes in international trade and business. Once-safe markets are now fierce battlegrounds where firms aggressively fight for market share against both foreign and domestic competitors. It is, therefore, not surprising to find that, in an increasing number of firms, a large proportion of the workforce is located in other countries.

These trends are likely to continue throughout the 1990s as employers increasingly reach across borders to find the skills they need. The multicultural workforce is beginning to slowly percolate to the top echelons of the management of multinationals as well: Unilever headquarters staff includes 30 different nationalities, and DuPont appointed its first non-American president in 1991.

Globalization is forcing managers to grapple with complex issues as they seek to gain or sustain a competitive advantage. Faced with unprecedented levels of foreign competition at home and abroad, firms are beginning to recognize that not only is international business high on the list of priorities for top management, but finding and nurturing the human resources required to implement an international or global strategy is also of critical importance. Thus, effective HR management is essential, especially for small- and medium-sized firms, where international expansion places extra stress on the limited pool of people.

Across Countries

The complexities of operating in different countries and of employing different nationalities are the main factors that differentiate domestic and international HR management, rather than differences between the functions performed. Many companies underestimate the complexities involved in international operations, and there is some evidence to suggest that business failures in the international arena are often linked to poor management of human resources.

> *The primary causes of failure in multinational ventures stem from a lack of understanding of the essential differences in managing human resources, at all levels, in foreign environments. Certain management philosophies and techniques have proved successful in the domestic environment: their application in a foreign environment too often leads to frustration, failure, and underachievement. These "human" considerations are as important as the financial and marketing criteria upon which so many decisions to undertake multinational ventures depend.*[33]

Increasingly, domestic HR is taking on an international flavor as the workforce becomes more and more diverse. But there *are* differences. The following issues differentiate international HR from domestic HR.

More Functions and Activities. To operate in an international environment, the HR department must engage in a number of activities that would not be necessary in a domestic environment: international taxation, international relocation and orientation, administrative services for expatriates, host government relations, and language translation services.

Broader Perspective. Domestic managers generally administer programs for a single national group of employees who are covered by a uniform compensation policy and who are taxed by one government. International managers face the problem of designing and administering programs for more than one national group of employees, and they must therefore take on a more global view of issues. This is exactly what is being done at Baxter International, an international pharmaceutical company. Its activities are described in the feature "Managing Human Resources at Baxter International: Managing Global Diversity."

More Involvement in Employees' Lives. A greater degree of involvement in employees' personal lives is necessary for the selection, training, and effective management of expatriate employees. The international HR department needs to ensure that expatriate employees understand housing arrangements, health care, and all aspects of the compensation package provided for assignments abroad.

Risk Exposure. Frequently, the human and financial consequences of failure in the international arena are more severe than in domestic business. For example, expatriate failure (the premature return of an expatriate from an international assignment) is a persistent, high-cost problem for international companies. Another aspect of risk exposure that is relevant to international HR is terrorism. Major multinational companies must now routinely consider this factor when planning international meetings and assignments.

More External Influences. Other factors that influence the international arena are the type of host government, the state of its economy, and business practices that may differ substantially from those of the originating country. A host government can, for example, dictate hiring procedures, as was the case in the late 1970s in Malaysia. The government required that foreign firms comply with what became known as the "30:30:30 Rule,"—that is, that 30 percent of employees be indigenous Malay, 30 percent Chinese Malays, and 30 percent Indian Malays, at all levels of the organization, with monthly statistics required to corroborate this.

Across Cultures

Another variable that heavily impacts HR activities in the international arena is the widely differing cultural mores of the world—the cultural environment.

The Cultural Environment. There are many definitions of **culture**, but they all in some way describe a "shaping" process. That is, members of a group or society share a distinct way of life with common values, attitudes, and behaviors that are transmitted over time in a gradual, yet dynamic, process.

Culture here means that members of a group share a distinct way of life with common values, attitudes, and behaviors that are transmitted over time in a gradual, yet dynamic, process.

> *A person is not born with a given culture; rather she or he acquires it through the socialization process that begins at birth. An American is not born with a liking for hot dogs, or a German with a natural preference for beer; these behavioral attributes are culturally transmitted.*[34]

Culture is so subtle a process that we are not always conscious of its effect on values, attitudes, and behaviors. We usually have to be confronted with a different culture in order to fully appreciate this effect. Anyone traveling abroad, either as a tourist or businessperson, experiences situations that demonstrate cultural differences in language, food, dress, hygiene, and attitude to time. While the traveler can perceive these differences as novel, even enjoyable, for people required to live and work in a new country, such differences can prove difficult. They experience **culture shock**—a phenomenon experienced by people who move across cultures. The new environment requires many adjustments in a relatively short period of time, challenging the person's frame of reference to such an extent that his or her sense of self, especially in terms of nationality, comes into question. The person, in effect, reacts with shock to new cultural experiences. This causes psychological disorientation because he or she misunderstands or does not recognize the cues. Culture shock can lead to negative feelings about the host country and its people and a longing to return home.[35]

Culture shock is the reaction to new cultural experiences that causes psychological disorientation.

MANAGING HUMAN RESOURCES

at Baxter International
Managing Global Diversity

Baxter International is approaching its growing international business with the same people-awareness that it used to successfully manage its merger with American Hospital Supply Corp. "We do business in 100 countries, and over one-third of our revenue comes from overseas," said Tony Rucci, senior vice president of human resources." And that percentage is growing. As a result, we've made managing diversity a long-range corporate goal.

"We define 'diversity' differently than most companies," said Rucci. "We look at it as 'what does it mean to do business in different countries around the world,' not just as 'how will we work with women and minorities?'

"As global marketers, we need to be sensitive to different cultural values around the world. As an example, we often think of Germany's culture as not that different from ours. But when we marketed our disposable surgical drapes and gowns in Germany, they just didn't sell. Why? Because in Germany there's a cultural norm against throwing things away. So a concept that made a lot of sense in the U. S. couldn't be translated there. We've learned from these experiences that we can't anticipate everything. To function well globally we are going to have to have a diverse range of opinion within our own company.

"We are approaching this with the same seriousness we used to implement our merger, and with many of the same values and techniques. We have established three corporate task forces to work on the diversity issue. Each addresses one of these issues:

- How should senior management send a visible commitment to this issue?
- Awareness and training: How can we broaden our company's perspective? How extensive and how deep should the training be?
- How do we identify, promote, and develop a more diverse pool of talent globally?

"Each of the top 27 officers of the company serves on one of these task forces—9 staff officers and 18 line officers. I'm on the third one myself. What we're looking for is five or six actionable things to do so that five years from now we really do have a more diverse work force. One of the things we're starting to do now is rotate managers in our foreign subsidiaries more actively with our U. S. people. We're bringing more European managers here, as well as rotating them within Europe. And we're sending more U. S. people overseas. With the European market opening up in 1992, we think this is even more important.

"Aside from the task force activities, we're giving the process an extra push by building diversity goals into our compensation and performance appraisal systems. Like everything else, we've made sure there's commitment from the top. One of the CEO's major objectives (one of four or five) is to promote work force diversity. Each of the top 100 officers, including the CEO, has a major portion of his or her bonus dependent on meeting diversity objectives. These objectives vary depending on the person's job, but every manager has at least one.

"We're not where we want to be yet. But we are making progress. As our people get more experience with diverse cultures, they are gaining more awareness. I think we've progressed to the point where at least people 'know they don't know.' They know that in another culture, they have to challenge everything they think is the right way to get something done. They know they can't rely on their intuition the way they used to be able to do at home."[36]

The Importance of Cultural Awareness. It is now generally recognized that culturally insensitive attitudes and behaviors stemming from ignorance or from misguided beliefs ("my way is best," or "what works at home will work here") not only are inappropriate, but often cause international business failure.

Therefore, an awareness of cultural differences is essential for the HR manager. Activities such as hiring, ethical behavior, promoting, rewarding, and dismissal will be determined by the practices of the host country and are often based on a value system peculiar to that country's culture.[37] A firm may decide to head up a new overseas operation with an expatriate general manager, but appoint a local, a person who is familiar with the host country's HR practices, as the department manager. This practice can cause problems, though, for the expatriate general manager, as happened to an Australian who was in charge of a new mining venture in Indonesia. The local responsible for recruitment could not understand why the Australian was upset to find that he had hired most of his extended family rather than staff with the required technical competence. The Indonesian was simply ensuring that his duty to his family was fulfilled—since he was in a position to employ most of them, he was obligated to do so. The Australian, however, interpreted the Indonesian's actions as nepotism, a negative practice according to his own value system.[38]

Here is an example of the fallacy of assuming "what works at home will work here" when dealing with work situations in another culture.[39] The HR staff of a large organization in Papua New Guinea was concerned over a number of accidents involving operators of very large, expensive, earth-moving vehicles. The expatriate managers investigating the accidents found that local drivers involved in the accidents were chewing betel nut, a common habit for most of the coastal peoples of Papua New Guinea and other Pacific islands. Associating the betel nut with depressants such as alcohol, the expatriate managers banned the chewing of betel nut during work hours. In another move to reduce the number of accidents, free coffee was provided at loading points, and drivers were forced to alight from their vehicles at these locations. What the managers did not realize was that betel nut, like their culturally acceptable coffee, is, in fact a stimulant, though some of the drivers were chewing it to cover up the fact that they had had a few beers before commencing work. Many indigenous workers used betel nut as a pick-me-up in much the same way as the expatriates used coffee!

Adjusting to a new cultural environment can also cause problems not only for the expatriate employee, but also for the accompanying spouse and family members. Coping with cultural differences is a constant challenge for the international manager. Preparing expatriates and their families for the cultural environment they will encounter is now a key activity for HR departments in those international firms that appreciate (or have been forced, through experience, to appreciate) the impact that the cultural environment can have on staff performance and wellbeing.

Did You KNOW?

Prudential Relocation, an arm of Prudential Insurance, asked 72 HR managers working at multinationals to name the best trait for overseas success. Nearly 35% said cultural adaptability: patience, flexibility, and tolerance for others' beliefs. Only 22% of them listed technical and management skills.

Did You KNOW?

Helping expatriate families adjust to a new culture helps make the expatriate employees more successful.

Summary

Because of the increasing complexity of HR management, nearly all organizations have established an HR department. Not all of these departments, however, perform all the activities discussed in Chapter 1. A department's activities—and the way it performs them—depend greatly on the roles the department plays in the organization. Organizations that are most concerned with HR management allow their departments to perform the business role as well as the roles of enabler, monitor, innovator, and adapter. When this occurs, HR departments are able to link their activities to the business and perform activities that influence productivity, employee safety and empowerment, competitive advantage, adaptability, and legal compliance—all goals associated with stakeholders of HR.

For each of the HR activities described in Chapter 1, departments can choose from many HR practices. For example, in performance-based pay, HR departments may choose to use a merit pay plan or profit-sharing plan. In addition to being familiar with all the HR practices, HR departments need to know which ones to use depending upon the needs of the business. Thus, departments need to be staffed with individuals who are aware of all the HR activities and practices and have a knowledge and appreciation of the business. They should also be knowledgeable about the goals and roles of HR management in organizations.

HR professionals also need to be knowledgeable about the issues of globalization. By going global, companies create many additional challenges for the HR department, including radically differing employment laws around the world and subtle and opaque cultural differences that affect HR management. The knowledge needed to deal with these challenges can be gained through understanding the environment in which firms operate today. Thus, this is the focus of Chapter 3.

Key Concepts

benchmarking
centralization
culture
culture shock
customerization
decentralization
ethics
ethical behavior
HR mission statements
human resource department
human resource generalists
human resource specialists
illegal behavior
managerial level
operational level
outsourcing
re-engineering
strategic level

Review and Discussion Questions

1. How does Levi Strauss & Co. link its HR department to the needs of the business?
2. Why is the HR department seen as critical to the success of organizations? Do line managers and HR managers agree on this?
3. What roles can the HR department play in an organization? How are the basic activities related to these roles?
4. What types of HR issues are faced at the operational, managerial and strategic levels?
5. What can HR departments gain from customerization?
6. Describe the process of benchmarking and how it can be used by HR departments.
7. What are the roles for the HR leader and the staff?
8. Distinguish between generalists and specialists.
9. What are ethical HR issues in organizations?
10. What is the Society of Human Resource Management? If you plan to pursue a career in HR management, where could you go for more information?
11. Briefly describe the professional certification process for HR managers. Why is professional certification important in HR management?
12. Why are some HR departments centralized while others are decentralized?
13. What is the purpose of HR mission statements?
14. Explain why organizations outsource some HR activities.
15. How does going international impact the HR department?

PROJECTS, EXERCISES & CASES

End-of-Text Project

Lincoln

1. Describe how well you think Lincoln Electric is managing its human resources. How is it done?
2. Describe the partnership in managing human resources at Lincoln Electric.
3. What roles do you think the HR department plays at Lincoln Electric?

Nordstrom

1. Describe how well you think Nordstrom is managing its human resources. How is it done?
2. Describe the partnership in managing human resources at Nordstrom.
3. What roles do you think the HR department plays at Nordstrom?

Field Project

Make appointments and visit local companies (even the college) to interview a line manager and the HR manager about their views of the HR department in the organization. It is best if these interviews are done separately. The HR manager can probably arrange the interview with a line manager. Interview your working parents to solicit their opinions of HR management and its role in the companies in which they work.

Case: Bringing the Human Resource Department to the Business

Mike Mitchell left the Bank of Montreal to become vice president of human resources at the North American branch of the Swiss Bank Corporation (SBC) in the autumn of 1993. It was a move up for him in terms of status, responsibility, monetary compensation, and challenge. Of these, it was the challenge that was most intriguing to Mitchell. In his mid 30s, he saw this as perfect time to take a risk in his career. He realized that if he succeeded he would establish a prototype that could be marketed to other firms. In addition, success could lead to further career opportunities and challenges. While he had a general idea of what he wanted to do and had gotten verbal support from his superiors, the senior vice president of human resources and the president of SBC, North America, the details of exactly what he was going to do and how he was going to do it remained to unfold.

In 1992 the parent company of SBC (a $110 billion universal bank) headquartered in Basel, Switzerland decided it needed a clearer statement of its intentions to focus its energies and resources in light of the growing international competition. Accordingly, it crafted a vision statement to the effect that the bank was going to better serve its customers with high-quality products that met their needs rather than just those of the institution. While the North American operation was relatively autonomous, it was still expected to embrace this vision. The details of its implementation, however, were in local hands. For the human resource side, the hands became those of Mitchell.

While Mitchell had spent some time in human resources at the Bank of Montreal in New York, the bulk of his work experience was as an entrepreneur in Montreal, Canada. It was this experience that impacted his thinking the most. Thus when he came to the SBC, his self-image was a businessperson who happened to be working in human resources. It was in part because of this image that his stay at the Bank of Montreal was brief: the idea of human resources was still a bit too conservative for his style. Too many of his ideas "just couldn't be done." In interviewing with the top managers at SBC, they warned him of the same general environment. Thus, he knew change would be slow among the 1000 employees, including his own department of 10 employees. He knew, however, that he wanted to reposition and "customerize" the HR department at SBC. He also understood the importance of connecting the HR department to the business.

He identified the four major aspects for his program to reposition and customerize the HR department. The four aspects included: gathering information; developing action agendas; implementing those agendas; and then evaluating and revising those agendas.

Gathering Information

To gather information about the current environment, Mitchell asked the customers, diagnosed the environment, and asked the HR department itself. From the customers, Mitchell learned the nature of the business strategy and how

HR currently fits with or helps that strategy. Customers discussed what they now get from the HR department, what their ideal would be, and how the ideal could best be delivered. Each HR activity, as well as the entire department and the staff, were discussed. From the environment, Mitchell learned what other companies are doing with their HR departments and HR practices. He examined competitors and those in other industries in order to gather ideas for the entire department and for each HR activity. From the HR department he learned how they see themselves in relation to servicing their customers, their knowledge of strategy, how they think the customers perceive the department, and their desire to improve and change.

Developing Agendas

Making agendas based upon this information was the second aspect of Mitchell's plan. As the HR staff analyzed the information, they were asked to develop plans (agendas) for resolving any discrepancies between what they are currently doing and what their customers want. As the staff worked, they began to recognize a need to determine a vision of themselves; to formulate a statement of who they are and how they interact with the rest of the organization. They also began to examine if their current ways of operating and the department's current structure were sufficient to move ahead. The need to reorganize began to become apparent. Once the vision began to take shape and the agendas were developed, the HR department established a game plan to get their agendas implemented. Approval by top management and line managers immediately impacted was seen as critical to successful implementation.

Implementing the Agendas

To begin the implementation phase, the HR staff met with the customers to discuss the agendas. In addition to responding to the specific needs of the line managers, it also involved selling the line managers on other activities. With a new focus to be more strategic and customer-oriented, the HR department began to develop programs that went beyond the regular administrative activities and services that it had provided to the line managers. Because these services were new, they had to be sold to their customers, at least at first. So in addition to implementing the specifically agreed upon agendas and contracts, this aspect included developing, selling, and implementing new programs.

Evaluating and Revising

Developed along with the agendas were contracts, specifying what will be delivered to the customer. The customer was given the right to appraise the work delivered. Based on these appraisals by the customers (line managers), the agendas are evaluated. Revisions and adjustments can then be made for continual improvement. In addition to these contracts, the work of the HR department is reviewed internally using such criteria as the reduction in turnover resulting from better selection procedures or an increase in the number of new ideas or innovations resulting from a change in the HR practices to facilitate the innovative strategy of the business.

Implications for the HR Department

There are several implications for the HR department (Mitchell and his staff) in their efforts to reposition and customerize:

1. The HR department has been re-oriented to be strategic and customer-oriented.
2. The HR department is becoming a constant gatherer of information from the internal and external environments. By knowing the competition, the business strategy, and the current assets of the company, the HR staff can develop new HR activities, implement new ideas, and work to maintain the company's competitive advantage.
3. The HR department has identified the level of excellence it wants to attain. The staff is working to become a strategic player while fulfilling their managerial and operational roles.
4. HR managers and staff are working closely with the line managers to design systems to gather the needed services and information. They also work with the line managers to develop contracts by which the HR department will be evaluated by the line managers.
5. The HR department is changing so that there is more of a generalist rather than a specialist orientation. A greater team orientation is also being built.
6. Things will never be the same. The HR professionals in the department will be gathering, servicing, evaluating, revising, and most of all listening. And because the business is always changing, the HR department will continue to evolve and change.

Implications for the Line Managers

There are also several implications in the repositioning and customerization program for the line managers.

1. The line managers need to cooperate with Mitchell and his staff as they gather information and implement new ideas and practices. Together, they are becoming partners in the business. The line managers must accept the new role being played by Mitchell and his HR staff.
2. The line managers need to work closely with the HR staff in developing the action agendas.
3. The line managers must continue to work with the HR staff in appraising the success of the HR efforts.

The Benefits from the Partnership

From Mitchell's perspective, there are several products from a repositioning and customerization program. They include:

- enhancing the quality and responsiveness of the HR department

- developing the HR department in terms of new jobs (skill-wise), providing new excitement, and building commitment to the company's mission, goals, and strategies
- linking HR with the business
- integrating HR with the corporate strategy
- becoming market or customer-oriented with flexibility to respond to and anticipate changes
- developing criteria by which the behaviors of the HR department can be evaluated and changed
- gaining an ability to develop and use HR practices to gain competitive advantage
- gaining an awareness of the potential ways different HR practices can be done by constantly monitoring what other successful companies are doing
- becoming more keenly aware of the internal and external environment
- providing standard HR products more efficiently
- developing new products and services
- developing technology to deliver the new products
- selling new services and products outside the company
- changing the HR department dramatically and consequently becoming a catalyst for change with the company
- becoming a department where everyone wants to work

Case Questions

1. Who are the customers of Mitchell and his HR staff?
2. What must Mitchell do in order for his staff to be able to do the things necessary to reposition and customerize?
3. Do you think that the line managers will cooperate with Mitchell and his staff? What will it take to see that they do? What would be their reasons for resisting a partnership with the HR department?
4. Develop a matrix with projects, dates, milestones and people involved (i.e., HR, line managers and employees) for Mitchell and his staff.

Source: This case was prepared by Randall S. Schuler, who expresses his appreciation for the cooperation of Michael Mitchell.

Case: A Broader View Seizes More Opportunities

Don English, corporate vice president of human resources, is now finally able to take a pause from the ongoing stream of "fire fighting" he has been engaged in since he came to Bancroft ten years ago! Like many of his colleagues in other firms, Don's knowledge of HR management came as much from doing it as from formal education.

Because of his workload, Don tended to keep pretty narrowly focused, and he rarely read HR journals or attended professional conferences. However, recently, things have been easing up. He has been able to recruit and train almost all the division managers in charge of human resources. It is Don's intention that the newly trained division managers will put out most of the company's "fires," and he will be freed to look at the "big picture." And he has been doing more reading than ever before. Of course, Don has not been totally out of touch with the rest of the world or the growing importance of HR management planning. When he started filling the slots for division HR managers, he made sure that it was a learning experience for him. Don always required job candidates to prepare a one-hour talk on the state of research and practice in different areas of personnel—for example, selection, appraisal, compensation, or training. He would even invite MBA candidates who had no course work in HR and ask them to relate their field of interest to HR management.

Don is planning to become the chief executive officer of Bancroft or some other firm of similar or larger size within the next five to seven years. He thinks he can achieve this if he remains in human resources and does an outstanding job. He will have to be outstanding by all standards, both internal and external to the firm. From his interviews during the past three years, Don knows that it is imperative to move human resources in a strategic direction while at the same time doing the best possible job with the "nuts and bolts" operational activities.

During a moment of reflection, Don begins to scribble some notes on his large white desk pad. In the middle is Bancroft, a well-established clothing manufacturer. To its left are its suppliers and to its right are its customers. In his head are all the HR practices he is so familiar with. He has a hunch that there must be a way to use the firm's expertise in performance appraisal and training to help Bancroft be more effective. Bancroft has been learning tremendously from its five-year drive to improve quality, but during the past year, quality gains have slowed. Bancroft must continue to improve its quality to gain and sustain competitive advantage, but large internal quality gains are becoming more and more difficult as Bancroft climbs the learning curve. Don wonders, "How can he help Bancroft experience the excitement of seeing large gains in quality improvement again?" Don circles the list of suppliers and begins to formulate a plan that will improve his chances of becoming CEO. He now seeks your advice in exactly what to do and how to go about doing it.

Case Questions

1. Is it reasonable for Don and the rest of Bancroft management to think about the suppliers of Bancroft as a source of competitive advantage? Refer to Chapter 1.

2. Should Don go directly to Bancroft's suppliers and talk to them or should he work with others in his company such as the person in charge of purchasing or even the CEO?

3. Is there really a place here for the corporate vice president of human resources to help his company gain competitive advantage by working with the suppliers?

4. Can Don become a CEO by being effective in human resources?

Introduction to Internet Exercises

Each section of this book will include one or more exercises requiring you to use the Internet. The purpose of these exercises is to familiarize you with HR sites on the Internet, and with searching the Internet in general. The Internet is an excellent resource for finding information about HR management, and for keeping up with new developments in the field.

The Visit the Internet Library exercises were designed with the assumption that not all readers have used the Internet extensively. For this reason, exercises for the first couple of sections will be very basic and will include detailed instructions, while later exercises will be more open-ended and complex. For those readers already familiar with the Internet, addresses will be provided for each HR site that you will access.

Internet Basics

This section will explain some basics of searching the Internet. Further information will be provided later in the book, as it is needed for other exercises. Readers who are already familiar with the Internet and its various features may move directly to the Visit the Internet Library exercise.

World Wide Web

The World Wide Web is the primary means of searching the Internet, and will be used for all exercises in this book. The World Wide Web consists of Hypertext Transfer Protocol (HTTP) sites. HTTP sites are documents that can include text, sound, and words. HTTP sites are linked to each other by special keywords (which are usually referred to as links), such that when a keyword is clicked in one site, the user is transferred to another related site.

HTTP sites can be accessed through keywords in other sites, or directly through the site's Internet address. All Web browsers (the program you will be using to access the World Wide Web) have an address field that specifies the address of the current site, and into which addresses for other sites can be keyed. All HTTP addresses begin with the prefix http://. For example, the following is a World Wide Web HTTP address: http://www.shrm.org

It is important to note that the Internet is not a completely stable environment, and both site addresses and the sites themselves are subject to change. When a site's address is changed, the old address will usually include a link that you can click in order to get to the site's current address. Since the sites themselves are subject to change, in some instances you may need to click on a slightly different set of commands than those listed within the exercise, once you are within a given site. This should not be difficult, since the sites you will be accessing are menu-driven and very user-friendly.

Connecting to the Internet and the World Wide Web

Use of the World Wide Web requires a Web browser program, such as Microsoft Explorer or Netscape. There are several ways of gaining access to the World Wide Web (and to a Web browser). For students, the easiest (and cheapest way) may be through an on-campus computer. Most colleges and universities have Internet-accessible computers that are available to students.

In addition, some colleges offer special computer accounts that allow students free access to the Internet through their own computers. This requires that the user have a modem connected to his/her computer.

Finally, several commercial programs (such as America Online and Compuserve) are available through computer stores. These programs provide many user services, but require users to pay a variety of fees.

Gopher Files

Gopher sites allow you to access information through a series of fixed menus. Gopher sites are easy to navigate, but are not as flexible as HTTP sites. Many Web browsers also include specialized gopher browsers. However, gopher sites can also be accessed directly though any Web browser, simply by typing the prefix gopher:// before the address. For example, to access the gopher for New York University through the World Wide Web, use the following address: gopher://gopher.nyu.edu

User Newsgroups

User newsgroups are often referred to as electronic "bulletin boards." They are Internet sites allowing the user to read and post messages concerning a specific topic of interest. Newsgroups for many topics can be found on the Internet, and they are excellent resources for obtaining (and disseminating) information that might not be available through other Internet resources.

VISIT THE LIBRARY

End-of-Section Exercises

This exercise is written to give you an introduction to HR sites on the web. Please follow the instructions below very carefully. For this and all other Visit the Internet Library exercises, remember to key the Internet addresses EXACTLY as they appear.

1. To begin this exercise, enter your Web browser.
2. In the address field, delete the current address and key the following address in its place:

   http://www.shrm.org/docsotherlnk.html

   After you have keyed the address exactly as it appears, hit the ENTER key. You will now be transferred to the address you just typed. It may take a while for all of the information in this document to appear on the screen, due to the fact that the information is being downloaded to your computer from a remote location.
3. You should now be see a screen with the title "HR Links." This is a free and useful resource provided by the Society for Human Resource Management. This site provides links to a plethora of HR sites on the Internet. Also included is the powerful Yahoo search engine, which can be used to locate specific information on HR topics. Yahoo will be used for other Visit the Internet Library exercises.
4. Click on the link labeled "HR Headquarters," under the heading "General Resources." (The address for HR Headquarters is **http://www.hrhq.com**)
5. Click on "Preview HR Headquarters" to get a description of HR Headquarters. As the preview states, HR Headquarters is a free service. However, in order to use HR Headquarters (and in order to complete this exercise), you will need to sign onto HR Headquarters. To sign on, click on "Sign Me Up" at the bottom of the Preview screen.
6. After you have submitted your information to sign on, click "HR HQ." After entering your user name and password, you will be at the site's main screen.
7. Click on "Library," and then on "HR Library."
8. From the HR Library, click on "Human Resource Management."
9. Click on an article titled "How HR Keeps Current in Century-Old Companies," and read it.
10. You have now completed the Visit the Internet Library exercise. Exit the HR Headquarters by clicking on the Home icon in your Web browser.

Chapter 2 Endnotes

1. S. Caudron, "HR Leaders Brainstorm," *Personnel Journal* (August 1994): 54.

2. Excerpt from "HR's Vital Role at Levi Strauss," by J. J. Laabs, copyright December 1992. Used by permission, *Personnel Journal.* Also see R. Mitchell and M. Oneal, "Managing By Values," *Business Week* (August 1, 1994): 46–52.

3. Ibid., 35.

4. Ibid., 43. Also read A. Halcrow, "A Day in the Life of Levi Strauss," *Personnel Journal* (November 1988): 14–15; and J. Sterngold, "Levi Strauss Makes Buyback Bid Valuing Company at $14 Billion," *New York Times* (February 9, 1996): 1, D4; R. Howard, "Values Make the Company: An Interview with Robert Haas," *Harvard Business Review* (September–October 1990): 134–144.

5. B. Presley Noble, "Retooling the 'People Skills' of Corporate America," *New York Times* (May 22, 1994): F8.

6. S. Caudron, "Strategic HR at First Chicago," *Personnel Journal* (November 1991): 56. Also see P. Stuart, "HR and Operations Work Together at Texas Instruments," *Personnel Journal* (April 1992): 64–68; T. Stewart, "Human Resources Bites Back," *Fortune* (May 13, 1996): 175–176; "Report Stresses Importance of Human Resources," *Bulletin to Management* (May 5, 1994): 138, 143; "Present and Future Human Resources Challenges: American Management

Association's 65th Annual HR Conference," *Bulletin to Management* (May 26, 1994): 1.

7. S. Lawrence, "Voice of HR Experience," *Personnel Journal* (April 1989): 64.

8. Ibid.

9. J. R. Schultz, "Align HR to Serve the Customer," *Personnel Journal* (January 1995): 61–64; R. Zemke and S. Zemke, "Partnering: A New Slant on Serving the Internal Customer," *Training* (September 1994): 37–43.

10. "Customers for Keeps: Training Strategies," *Bulletin to Management* (March 31, 1988): 8. See also R. L. Desatnik, *Managing to Keep the Customers* (San Francisco: Jossey Bass, 1987).

11. S. Greengard, "Discover Best Practices Through Benchmarking," *Personnel Journal* (November 1995): 62–73; P. Hawken, "The Employee as Customer," *Inc.* (November 1987): 21–22; A. Halcrow, "Operation Phoenix: The Business of Human Resources," *Personnel Journal* (September 1987): 92–109; R. S. Schuler and S. E. Jackson, "Customerizing the HR Department," *Personnel Journal* (June 1988): 36–44; R. N. Bramson, "The Secret Weapon in the War for Customers," *HR Magazine* (January 1991): 65–68.

12. J. J. Laabs, "HR for Profit: Selling Expertise," *Personnel Journal* (May 1995): 84–92; T. A. Stewart, "Taking on the Last Bureaucracy," *Fortune* (January 15, 1996): 105–108; J. Walker, "Managing Human Resources in Flat, Lean and Flexible Organizations: Trends for the 1990s," *Human Resource Planning,* 11 (1988): 129.

13. E. E. Lawler, III, "Human Resources Management: Meeting the Challenge," *Personnel* (January 1988): 25.

14. "Special PPF Survey Report: A Profile of Human Resource Executives," *Bulletin to Management* (June 22, 1995): 1–7; K. Ludeman, "Motorola's HR Learns the Value of Teams Firsthand," *Personnel Journal* (June 1995): 117–123; "Roundtable Report," *HR Reporter* (December 1988): 3–6.

15. J. Walker, "What's New in HR Development?" *Personnel* (July 1990): 41.

16. T. Stewart, "Human Resources Bites Back," *Fortune* (May 13, 1996): 175–176; C. Marmer Solomon, "Managing the HR Function," *Personnel Journal* (June 1994): 62–76; J. Fasqualetto, "New Competencies Define the HRIS Manager's Future Role," *Personnel Journal* (January 1993): 91–99; J. Walker, "Human Resources Roles for the '90s," *Human Resource Planning,* 12 (1989): 55.

17. S. H. Applebaum, APD, "The Personnel Professional and Organization Development: Conflict and Synthesis," *Personnel Administrator* (July 1980): 57–61; F. R. Edney, "The Greening of the Profession," *Personnel Administrator* (July 1980): 27–30, 42; F. R. Edney, "Playing on the Team," *Personnel Journal* (August 1981): 598–600; L. B. Prewitt, "The Emerging Field of Human Resources Management," *Personnel Administrator* (May 1982): 81–87.

18. R. R. Ladenson, *Ethics in the American Workplace: Policies and Decisions* (Horsham, Penn.: LRP Publications, 1996); B. Geber, "The Right and Wrong of Ethics Offices," *Training* (October 1995): 103–109; F. H. Applebaum, APD, 1991 SHRM/CCH Survey (June 26, 1991); M. T. Brown, *Working Ethics: Strategies for Decision Making and Organizational Responsibility* (San Francisco: Jossey-Bass, 1990); L. L. Nash, *Good Intentions Aside: A Manager's Guide to Resolving Ethical Problems* (Boston, Mass.: Harvard Business School Press, 1990); L. Tone Hosmer, *The Ethics of Management* (Homewood, Ill.: Irwin, 1991).

19. Certification Information Handbook, (Alexandria, VA: HR Certification Institute, 1994); D. Yoder and H. Heneman, Jr., *PAIR Jobs, Qualifications, and Careers, ASPA Handbook of Personnel and Industrial Relations* (Washington, D.C.: The Bureau of National Affairs, 1978): 18; W. M. Hoffman, R. Frederick, and E. W. Petry, Jr., eds., *The Ethics of Organizational Transformation: Mergers, Takeovers and Corporate Restructuring* (New York: Quorum Books, 1989).

20. Adapted from E. F. Huse, *Management,* 2nd ed. (St. Paul, Minn.: West, 1982); and P. F. Buller, J. J. Kohls, and K. S. Anderson, "The Challenge of Global Ethics," *Journal of Business Ethics* Vol. 10 (1991): 767–775.

21. W. W. Turnow, "The Codifications Project and Its Importance to Professionalism," *Personnel Administrator* (June 1984): 84–100; C. Haigley, "Professionalism in Personnel," *Personnel Administrator* (June 1984): 103–106. Also contact the Institute directly by calling the Society for Human Resource Management at 1-800-331-2772.

22. S. Carroll, "HRM Roles and Structures in the Information Age," in R. S. Schuler, ed., *HRM in the Information Age* (Washington, D.C.: SHRM/BNA, 1991).

23. C. Reynolds, "Careers in International Human Resources," *The SHRM Student Newsletter* (January–February 1992): 1.

24. "SHRM-BNA Survey No. 61 Human Resources Activities, Budgets, and Staffs: 1995–96," *Bulletin to Management* (June 27, 1996): 1–18; "SHRM-BNA Survey No. 60 Human Resources Activities, Budgets, and Staffs: 1994–95," *Bulletin to Management* (June 29, 1995): 1–16; "HR Activities and Expenses Explored," *Bulletin to Management* (July 27, 1995): 240; Human Resource Compensation Survey (Dearfield, Ill.: William M. Mercer, Inc., 1993); "Human Resource Compensation Survey," *Bulletin to Management* (July 22, 1993): 228–229.

25. "SHRM-BNA Survey No. 61 Human Resources Activities, Budgets, and Staffs: 1995–96"; "SHRM-BNA Survey No. 60 Human Resources Activities, Budgets, and Staffs: 1994–95"; "HR Activities and Expenses Explored."

26. "The Benefits Department: Salaries and Structures," *Bulletin to Management* (January 18, 1996): 18; "Human Resource Compensation Survey," *Bulletin to Management* (July 18, 1996): 22. "The $350,000 HR Director," *Personnel Journal* (June 1993): 18.

27. J. A. Byrne, "Has Outsourcing Gone Too Far?" *Business Week* (April 1, 1996): 26–28; "Outsourcing Offers Strategic

Advantage," *Bulletin to Management* (June 29, 1995): 208; "HR's Advances in Reengineering and Restructuring," *Personnel Journal* (January 1996): 60; G. Flynn, "Optimas Awards Celebrate Exemplary HR," *Personnel Journal* (January 1996): 50; T. A. Stewart, "Re-engineering: The Hot New Management Tool," *Fortune* (August 23, 1994): 41–48; M. Hammer and J. Charnpy, *Re-engineering the Corporation* (New York: Harper-Collins, 1993); C. Marmer Solomon, "Working Smarter: How HR Can Help," *Personnel Journal* (June 1993): 54–64.

28. "Shrinkage of HR Examined," *Bulletin to Management* (August 3, 1995): 248.

29. Caudron, "HR Leaders Brainstorm": 59–60.

30. C. M. Solomon, "Managing the Baby-Busters," *Personnel Journal* (March 1992): 56.

31. Excerpt from "The Greening of HR," by J. J. Laabs, copyright August 1992. See also F. Rice, "Who Scores Best on the Environment," *Fortune* (July 26, 1993): 114–122.

32. R. Henson, "Globalization: A Human Resource Mandate," *Solutions* (January 1994): 62–63.

33. P. J. Dowling, R. S. Schuler, and D. Welch, *International Dimensions of Human Resource Management*, 2nd ed. (Belmont, CA: Wadsworth, 1994).

34. Dowling, Schuler & Welch, *International Dimensions of Human Resources Management*; C. M. Solomon, "Transplanting Corporate Cultures Globally," *Personnel Journal* (October 1993): 78–87.

35. P. R. Harris and R. T. Moran, *Managing Cultural Differences* (Houston, Texas: Gulf, 1979); R. S. Bhagat and S. J. McQuaid, "Role of Subjective Culture in Organization: A Review and Directions for Future Research," *Journal of Applied Psychology* 67 (1982): 653–685.

36. "Giving and Getting Respect at Baxter," *HR Reporter* (April 1992): 7. Used by permission.

37. C. Marmer Solomon, "Put Your Ethics to a Global Test," *Personnel Journal* (January 1996): 66–74.

38. P. J. Dowling, D. E. Welch, and H. DeCieri, "International Joint Ventures: A New Challenge for Human Resource Management," in *Proceedings of the 15th Conference of the European International Business Association*, ed. R. Luostarinen (Helsinki, Finland, Dec. 1989).

39. T. Wyatt, "Understanding Unfamiliar Personnel Problems in Cross-Cultural Work Encounters," *Asia Pacific HRM 27* (1989): 5–18.

SECTION 2

Understanding the Environment of Human Resource Management

Increasingly, successful management of organizations and their human resources depends on understanding the existing environment and anticipating changes to the environment. To do a great job with your career planning, you have to know what types of jobs may be available in the future and what skills and abilities they will require. Similarly, organizations must be looking ahead to deal effectively with critical HR issues.

In the external environment, organizations gather and analyze information about: the events and trends in domestic and international competition; the sizes of, and projections for, the global and domestic population and workforce; economic and organizational changes; and legal and social considerations relating to human resources. Organizations also assess their internal environment including the organization's strategy, culture, technology, size, and the goals and values of top management. Aspects of both the internal and external environments are described in detail in Chapter 3.

Chapter 4 examines the fair and legal treatment of employees. People want to be treated with respect and dignity, and they are actively asserting this desire in the workplace as they lobby to have more and more rights recognized by their employers. In addition to the numerous laws that impact workplace rights, employees today think they have many rights that employers should recognize and honor. As more employee rights gain legal protection, decisions such as discharges, layoffs, and demotions must be made with care and supported by evidence.

The legal qualities of American society can make failure to be in legal compliance—and the courts here often mean more than the letter of the law, they mean the spirit of the law—a costly mistake. A single settlement can damage an organization's image and result in financial hardship. Hence, it is imperative that organizations carefully formulate employee rights policies; that the HR department continually scan the legal environment for shifts in public and legal opinion; and that the entire workforce be informed and possibly retrained in appropriate behaviors. These legal issues are also discussed in Chapter 4.

Understanding External and Internal Environments

CHAPTER 3

> *At Wal-Mart, our philosophy is that the best ideas come from associates—employees—on the firing line.*
>
> *David Glass*
> *Chief Executive Officer*
> *Wal-Mart Stores*[1]

Learning Objectives

1. Indicate the nature of domestic and international competition and its impact on managing human resources.
2. Describe the workforce conditions and their impact on managing human resources.
3. Describe the demographic conditions and expected changes and their impact on managing human resources.
4. Describe how economic, technological, and organizational conditions are affecting the way firms manage their human resources.
5. Explain the impact on managing human resources from: a) company vision, business objectives, and values; b) CEO's leadership style and assumptions about people; c) corporate culture; d) organizational structure; e) organizational size; f) organizational life cycle; g) type of business (manufacturing vs. service); and h) competitive strategies.

Chapter Outline

MANAGING HUMAN RESOURCES

at BMW-Spartanburg, South Carolina

On June 23, 1992, the Bavarian Motor Works (BMW) of Munich, Germany announced that it was building a plant in Spartanburg, South Carolina. This was the first time a German auto company decided to build a manufacturing plant in the U.S. In 1993, Mercedes-Benz announced plans to build a manufacturing plant in Alabama. In both cases, some of the factors convincing these firms to move to the U.S. were the combined costs of labor, shipping, and components. At that time, the hourly costs of the German auto worker were about $42 versus $24 in the U.S. Devaluation of the dollar in 1994 and 1995 amplified those differences; however, currency values fluctuate. After lengthy investigation and negotiations, both companies selected rural areas in the South as the locations for their plants.

While BMW officials wanted to locate near a deep water port, many locations would have met this condition. What factors swayed the decision in favor of Spartanburg? The $35 million dollars in incentives offered certainly helped the case. The work climate and perceived work ethic of the people in South Carolina were important also. The HR representative from BMW in Germany insisted on the availability of training and funding for training. As a result, the state provides up to 400 hours of on-the job training for each employee at BMW. According to Susan Crocker, vice president of HR at the plant, it was the entire package offered by the state and the area that made the difference.

Interestingly, the BMW officials were not concerned with the fact that the workers in the area had never worked in an automobile factory. Says Crocker:

> *We're of the philosophy that people don't have to know how to make cars before they come to work for us. We'll train them to do that. We need people who are flexible, who can think, who can use their brains and are willing to work in a team environment.*[2]

Thus BMW was interested in workers who were able and willing to adapt to the BMW way of operating. In Spartanburg, the company has found workers who are very capable and willing to train, to adapt, and to learn. They are also willing to work for wages that are substantially below their counterparts in Munich. In fact, BMW has found that workers in South Carolina are much more flexible and adaptable than the workers in Munich. In Germany, tradition and independence prevail: workers can still enjoy a beer on the job and they refuse to wear standard blue uniforms with their names on them.[3]

In this feature, HR concerns were very important to BMW in locating and operating their plant. The HR professionals were involved from the beginning in the process of site selection and in the earliest stages of long-term business planning. Who else would be better prepared to gather environmental information on education, the quality of the workforce, and training facilities in the local area?

The experience at BMW is an example of a successful link between HR management and the business as described in the first two chapters. The values and goals of top management are actively influencing the HR management philosophy and HR practices that BMW is becoming known for worldwide.[4] It is obviously very important for HR professionals to know the values and goals of top management and how to translate them into the appropriate HR practices.

Understanding the external and internal environments means knowing what's going on out there and determining what it means for HR management.

BMW's experience reminds us that the HR department needs to be attuned to the environment—it needs to know what is happening, and what is likely to happen, in the environment and then to identify the implications for HR management. Understanding the external and internal environments means knowing what is going on out there—that is, continuously scanning the environment—and then determining what this means for managing human resources.

The process of gaining an environmental understanding can be divided into these general categories: a) gather data about current issues and conditions; b) gather data, expectations, and predictions about future issues and conditions; c) define the implications of these conditions for the organization and its management of human resources; and d) learn what other companies are doing to manage or are preparing to do to manage these implications.

Why Is an Understanding of Environments Important?

Understanding the environment prevents surprises and aids in preparing for and making organizational changes in HR planning.

HR activities do not exist in a vacuum; HR professionals increase their effectiveness when they scan many aspects of the environment. They can thus link people management to the needs of the business and the demands of the external environment. While input is useful for all HR activities, it is particularly critical for organizational changes and HR planning.

Without understanding internal and external environments, organizations are likely to be unpleasantly surprised by events that could imperil their long-run success. Meaningful and timely responses to major events take time to develop and implement. Continuous scanning and analysis can give an organization the time it needs. Even in the short run, though, organizations must understand the environment in which they operate. For example, a solid understanding of employment laws is critical to avoiding substantial fines and penalties levied for their violation.

Before continuing, study Exhibit 3.1 carefully. What aspects of the environment do you think have the greatest impact on business and HR management today, and will have the greatest impact in the year 2000? Now, for the items that will have the greatest change between today and the year 2000, describe the implications of your responses on managing human resources. Exhibit 3.2 illustrates possible implications for managing human resources of increased national and international competition. The business realities column represents the possible actions that companies will need to take because of this increased competition. The implications for managing human resources result because of these possible actions. You can see that the implications for managing human resources are significant and take time to address. Thus, the earlier you know about them, the faster you can adapt.

Did You KNOW?

Going, if not yet gone, are the 9–5 workdays, lifetime jobs, predictable, hierarchical relationships, corporate culture security blankets, and, for a large and growing sector of the workforce, the workplace itself (replaced by a cybernetics "workspace").

The External Environment

While many characteristics of the **external environment** have an impact on a firm's efforts to manage its human resources effectively, we will consider the following:

The external environment is the major aspects outside companies that have a big impact on the company's human resource management.

- Domestic and international competition
- The emerging workforce
- Demographics
- Economic, technological, and organizational trends

The impact of these characteristics is, literally, changing the face of business and in the process, the importance of managing human resources effectively.

LEARNING OBJECTIVE 1

Indicate the nature of domestic and international competition and its impact on managing human resources.

Domestic and International Competition

Given the worldwide business climate, "the most important characteristic of today's business environment—and therefore the yardstick against which

EXHIBIT 3.1

Implications of Changes in the Environment

Many observers have predicted significant changes in the environment for the 21st century. Some of these changes are listed below. Please choose and rank the five changes that you think currently have the most impact on business and HR management, and the five that you think will have the most impact in the future: "1" indicates the highest impact, "2" indicates the next highest impact, etc.

TODAY	ENVIRONMENT	2000+
________	a. Increased national/international competition	________
________	b. Increased governmental regulation	________
________	c. Globalization of corporate business structure	________
________	d. Growth in nontraditional business structure (e.g., business alliances, joint ventures)	________
________	e. Globalization of the economy/breakdown of trade barriers	________
________	f. Increased energy costs	________
________	g. Increased reliance on automation/technology to produce goods and services	________
________	h. More sophisticated information/communication technology	________
________	i. Changing attitudes of society toward business	________
________	j. Heightened concern about pollution and natural resources	________
________	k. Heightened focus on total quality/customer satisfaction	________
________	l. Changing employee values, goals, and expectations (e.g., less loyalty to current employer)	________
________	m. Fewer entrants into the workforce	________
________	n. Inadequate skills of entrants into the workforce	________
________	o. Cross-border application of employee rights	________
________	p. Changing composition of the workforce with respect to gender, age, and/or ethnicity	________
________	q. Greater concerns about the confidentiality of personal information	________

Source: Adapted from Priorities for Competitive Advantage (IBM/Towers Perrin, 1992). Used by permission.

Did You KNOW?

In 1975, it took U.S. steel firms 12.5 hours to produce a ton of cold-rolled sheet steel. Today it takes fewer than 4.5 hours, fewer than Japan, Germany, France, and Britain.

managerial techniques must be measured—is the new competition."[5] This competition comes both from abroad and from within the U.S. The U.S. is a vast and highly competitive marketplace. Almost no industry is excluded from intense competition. Even electric utilities, once thought of as essential natural monopolies that had to be regulated by the government, are facing less regulation and more open environments where consumers can have a choice in purchasing their power supplies. The telecommunications industry is literally changing every day. Semiconductors continue to gain power at ever-lower prices; thus, the domestic environment is not only intense (filled with many competitors) but also rapidly changing. This environment, of course, has resulted in the emergence and success of many small and entrepreneurial firms.[6]

Domestic competition from imports of shoes, textiles, and electronics continues to increase. Less than ten years ago, U.S. companies dominated the office copier business here and abroad. Today their domestic share is approximately 50 percent. Similar situations are occurring throughout American business because of

EXHIBIT 3.2

Human Resource Management: Implications of Increased National and International Competition

BUSINESS REALITIES	POSSIBLE IMPLICATIONS FOR MANAGING HUMAN RESOURCES
1. Need for more productivity	**Increase employee motivation** a. Empowerment and teamwork b. Incentive pay c. Better selection and training
2. Need to reduce costs	**Better utilize employees** a. Better assignment of employees b. Downsizing
3. Need to develop new products	**Faster creativity** a. Encourage employees to change b. Develop new skills and abilities
4. Need to operate around the world	**Develop a global workforce** a. Select and develop expatriates b. Select and develop local nationals c. Develop global cultures

lower-priced products or inventive marketing techniques, or both. An analysis of U.S. performance between 1970 and 1996 indicates that U.S. share of markets in several other industries declined.

Wage disparities and fluctuating currency values make it challenging for U.S. businesses to compete in markets with products requiring a great deal of labor, and make it harder for U.S. companies to maintain employees abroad. The successes of large U.S. multinationals such as Gillette, Hewlett-Packard, and Pepsi-Cola International, however, show it is possible; it simply takes a lot of hard work and a global perspective.[7]

In other industries, U.S. businesses thrive. For some companies, foreign sales account for between one-third and two-thirds of their total sales. These industries include:

- Computers and office equipment (59 percent foreign sales)
- Machinery (51 percent foreign sales)
- Autos and auto parts (44 percent foreign sales)
- Chemical products (39 percent foreign sales)
- Transportation equipment (34 percent foreign sales)[8]

Huge markets for products and services are not the only things enticing companies to enter the global arena. Foreign labor markets also attract interest. At 1994 growth rates, the labor force in developing nations alone will expand by about 700 million people by the year 2010, while the U.S. labor force will grow by only 75 million.[9] Furthermore, opportunities for productivity growth are much greater in developing countries.[10] Between 1988 and 1992, for example, U.S. productivity increased by about three percent and Mexico's by more than six percent.[11] The rea-

Did You KNOW?

Computer power is now 8,000 times less expensive than it was 30 years ago. "If we had similar progress in automotive technology, today you could buy a Lexus for about $2. It would travel at the speed of sound, and go about 600 miles on a thimble of gas."

John Naisbitt
Global Paradox

sons for these differences in productivity potential are many, but simple demographics tell much of the story. The workforce is generally older in developed countries and younger in developing countries. Furthermore, education levels are rising more rapidly in developing countries. For example, in 1970, less than 25 percent of all college students were from developing countries. By 1990, about 50 percent of all college students were from developing countries.[12]

For employers seeking flexible and adaptable workers, the young and newly educated workforces in developing countries are particularly attractive. Thus, it is not surprising that many firms headquartered in developed countries now have a large proportion of their workforce located elsewhere. For example:

- The Ford Motor Company has half its employees outside the United States.
- Philips Electronics, N.V., has three-fourths of its employees working outside The Netherlands.
- More than half of Matsushita Electric's employees are outside Japan.
- Just over half of L. M. Ericsson's staff work outside Sweden.[13]

The same is happening in Germany but at an increasing rate. This is due in large part to the huge wage cost disparities that exist between Germany and the world. Some of these disparities are shown in Exhibit 3.3. The figures support the estimate made by BMW that labor costs are between 30 and 40 percent less in Spartanburg, S.C. than in Munich, Germany.[14] Clearly then, for many firms, developing a global perspective is no longer an option. Consequently, organizational structures with global functions are becoming a necessity, and the workforce to staff them mandatory. HR managers can aid their organization's transition into the arena of more intense domestic and worldwide competition.

Implications For Managing Human Resources

To empower employees means to give them freedom and responsibility to make job-related decisions.

Empowered employees make companies more competitive.

Empowerment and Teamwork. Intense levels of domestic and international competition are forcing organizations to be more productive; more effective management of human resources is seen as a way to improve productivity. The nature of workforce demographics means that efforts to improve productivity must include employees in the decision-making process. Greater employee involvement in workplace decisions is a growing trend. Organizations seeking to improve product and service quality actively seek employee involvement. Many **empower employees**— that is, give them the freedom and responsibility to make job-related decisions. They recognize employee empowerment results in quality gains. Many firms such as Corning Glass and Ford have found that empowerment is often the best way to reduce costs and improve profitability:

> *Officials at Ford Motor Company believe in empowerment. After watching profits and quality drop sharply in the late 1970s, management knew something had to be done. By using employee involvement and participative management programs, Ford not only listened and responded to employee problem-solving ideas, but management also encouraged employees to take the lead. As a result of these efforts, Ford experienced one of the most dramatic turnarounds of the past decade.*[15]

Many firms now use teams and teamwork. Team-based approaches to work can increase innovation, improve quality, and shorten the time it takes to transform an idea into a product that is available in the marketplace. To create and orchestrate teams, people need to be selected, appraised, compensated, and trained in ways that reflect the unique relationships that develop between employees who work together. Teamwork is a somewhat new phenomenon in the American workplace. Yet its power is hard to deny. Some of the outstanding success of Wal-Mart is due

EXHIBIT 3.3

Germany's Cost Disadvantage

Total hourly cost for auto workers, in German marks
On September 13, 1995, a dollar was worth 1.4737 marks

	1980	1995		1980	1995
Germany	27	58	Holland	24	33
Japan	14	46	France	19.5	30
U.S.	25	39.5	Italy	18	27
Belgium	28	38.5	Britain	15	26.5
Sweden	28.5	36	Spain	13	26.5

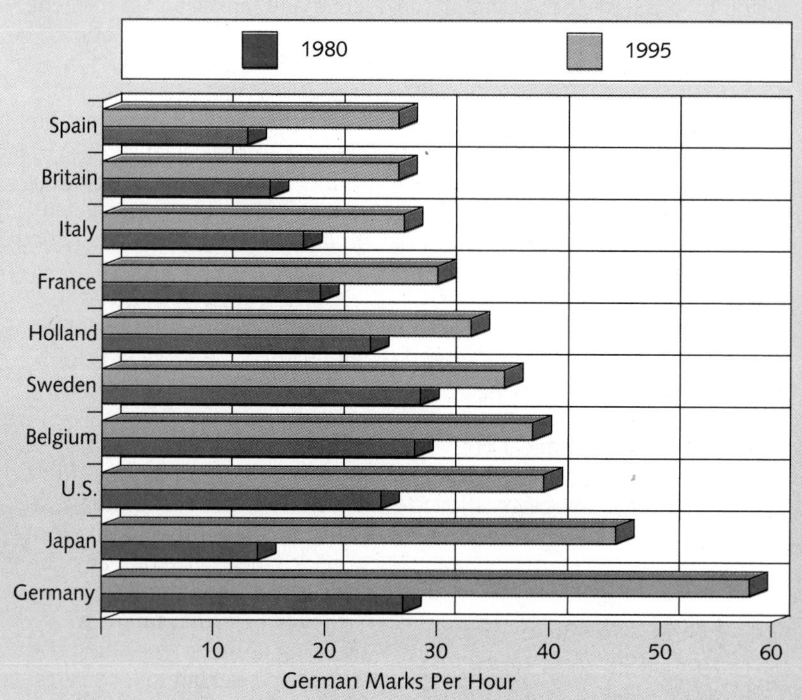

Source: *The New York Times*, Sept. 13, 1995, D1. Used by permission.

to teams and the team spirit as described in the feature, "Managing Human Resources at Wal-Mart."

Developing a Global Workforce. Faced with unprecedented levels of foreign competition at home and abroad, firms are seeking and nurturing the human resources required to implement global strategies. As we move into the 21st century, more and more companies will see opportunities that can be seized only by adopting a global perspective, and the question of how best to staff and manage such organizations will become more pressing. The situation has been described like this: "Virtually any type of international problem, in the final analysis, is either created by people or must be solved by people. Hence, having the right people in the right place at the right time emerges as the key to a company's international growth. If we are successful in solving that problem... we can cope with all others."[16] Apparently, many companies underestimate the complexities involved in international operations, and poor management of human resources is responsible for many business failures in the international arena:

MANAGING HUMAN RESOURCES

at Wal-Mart

What do people have to do with the success of the world's largest retailer? The answer is, EVERYTHING!

The founder of Wal-Mart, Sam Walton, believed that the essence of successful retailing lay in giving the customers what they want. Yes, customers want a great selection at the lowest possible prices. But they also want friendly and knowledgeable service that is accessible. In today's highly competitive environment, most customers can easily get great selection at low prices. What they can't get as easily is the friendly and knowledgeable service!

Yes, people—associates—are an integral part of Wal-Mart's success. Sam Walton knew that people are important—his motto (and the company's motto today):

> *It takes a team, and we're a team and we are together!*

In his golden rules of retail competition, the majority are about people—for example: share your profits; motivate your associates; communicate everything to your associates; appreciate everything your associates do for the company; celebrate your successes; and listen to everyone. By the way, the other rules are: commit and be passionate about the business; control costs; exceed customers' expectations; and ignore conventional wisdom.

But just how much has this attention to people paid off for Sam Walton and Wal-Mart? The first Wal-Mart store opened in Bentonville, Arkansas, in 1962. About fifteen years later, the market value of Wal-Mart stock was $135 million. Today, it is over $50 billion! If you had bought 100 shares of the company in 1962 at a cost of $1,650, you would have (because of 2-for-1 splits) more than 60,000 shares today valued at more than $3 million! The number of associates has gone from fewer than 50 to more than 675,000. Only General Motors has more employees in the United States. Wal-Mart's profits and revenues have seen double-digit growth every year, and there are now about 2,000 stores.

Sam Walton created a great deal of wealth—not only for himself and his family, but also for many others. Typical of the people who have worked for the company for many years is Joyce McMurray:

> *One Arkansas worker, Joyce McMurray, said that since she joined the company as a high school graduate in 1969, her profit-sharing account had grown to $492,230, including an increase of $175,000 in one year.*

Joyce's good fortune is due to one of Sam's golden rules of retailing: share the profits with your associates.

With results like these, you would think everyone would be doing the same thing, right? Yes, but then why aren't they? Is it really that hard to manage people? This is the key, isn't it?

Well, let's see what Wal-Mart does. First, Wal-Mart's philosophy is that it is easier to take care of the associates you have than to replace them and train someone else. Therefore, the company makes a commitment to do a great job in selection, recruitment, and motivation of associates. Wal-Mart's generous profit-sharing plan, which is tied directly to performance outcomes, has a way of motivating associates, and it has attracted many who want to make a good living.

The company believes in giving customers friendly and knowledgeable service. It follows then that the associates need to be trained and retrained, extensively and often. But what makes them friendly? Ah, here is the part that is difficult for competitors to duplicate! This is where the company culture comes in. Sam Walton believed in management by walking around, by visiting the stores and talking to associates and customers, and his legacy remains strong. Typical is Andy Wilson, one of 15 regional vice presidents, who continually takes Sam Walton's message to associates in stores around the country:

> *My job isn't important. You're the people who make it happen.*

For a vice president to say this is one thing; for associates to truly believe it is another. The associates at Wal-Mart believe it. They have heard the same thing for years, and they have seen the behavior: the managers at Wal-Mart "walk the talk." Related to this humble profile assumed by managers is the role they play to support the importance and value of the associates. Managers constantly ask the associates, "Is there anything we can do for you?"

The team spirit of Wal-Mart is apparent throughout the company. They remember: "it takes a team, and we're a team." The team at Wal-Mart believes that it is important to have fun: team rallies and other spirit-building activities are common. Combining this team spirit with the profit sharing and the down-to-earth management style sustains a company in which the associates truly care about the customer. Needless to say, these qualities have contributed greatly to Wal-Mart's astonishing success. And because many of these qualities are seemingly so hard for others to do, the firm has a formula that is hard to beat.

One more thing, remember that one of Sam's golden rules was doing things not usually done by others? Well, the HR department at Wal-Mart is called the "people division." All these people components add up to a real success story in which HR management really makes a big contribution.[17]

> *The primary causes of failure in multinational ventures stem from a lack of understanding of the essential differences in managing human resources, at all levels, in foreign environments. Certain management philosophies and techniques have proven successful in the domestic environment: their application in a foreign environment too often leads to frustration, failure, and underachievement. These "human" considerations are as important as the financial and marketing criteria upon which so many decisions to undertake multinational ventures depend.*[18]

Many international business failures result from ineffective people management.

To reduce this frustration, failure, and underachievement firms are: a) selecting and developing expatriates, and b) developing their awareness of different cultures. The number of U.S. expatriates was estimated to be around 125,000 in 1994. As we enter the 21st century, this number is expected to move upward, perhaps to 130,000.[19] This rate of growth does not mirror that of global trade because many U.S. multinational companies are staffing their international operations with nationals (residents of the country in which the firm is operating). Although the number of U.S. expatriates is modest, the positions occupied are extremely important to the companies.

Many U.S. workers, like BMW's employees in Spartanburg, work for non-U.S. firms operating in the U.S. Increasingly, non-U.S. companies are sending their executives to the U.S., so more and more American workers have non-American bosses. For example, about 400,000 Americans work in U.S. subsidiaries of Japanese firms, usually with Japanese bosses.[20] Issues associated with staffing international operations, including the selection of local nationals, are discussed in detail in Chapter 10 on Selection and Placement. Career issues for you are discussed in Chapter 6 on Career Planning and Management.

Developing Global Corporate Cultures. Perhaps the greatest challenge to managing human resources in a global economy is transporting a corporate culture successfully around the world. When a company's operations are flung across great distances and many national cultures, corporate culture glues the pieces together. According to Calvin Reynolds, senior counselor with Organization Resources Counselors, "If you don't have a strong set of cultural principles from which to function, when people get overseas, they're so lacking in clarity that no one knows where they're going."[21] Here are two examples to illustrate how this works:

Global corporate culture gives common meaning and serves as social glue.

ABB. The Swiss-Swedish firm Asea Brown Boveri (ABB) is one global firm with a strong corporate culture. "We think of ABB as a company without regard to national boundaries....We just operate on a global basis," explains Richard Randazzo, vice president of human resources. The corporate culture—focused on making money, taking action, using a hands-on approach, and traveling to wherever business opportunities arise—is not insensitive to national cultures, however. Indeed, the firm insists that its 213,000 employees working in 1,300 national companies adapt the corporate culture to blend with the local cultural scene. Local activities, in turn, influence the ABB corporate culture because local learning is shared across borders. For example, ABB's approach to equal employment opportunity in Europe will reflect its U.S. experience. This is because European countries have become actively concerned with issues of equal employment opportunity only recently, whereas the United States has many years of experience addressing these concerns.[22]

PCI. Pepsi-Cola International (PCI), the international bottling division of PepsiCo, is another company with a strong corporate culture that is now being successfully transported across national borders. But this was not always true:

> *"In 1985, there was some confusion about what it took to be individually successful in Pepsi-Cola International. There was no shared value system or vocabulary for describing individual performance. For example, in the socialist countries the concept of individual performance was practically nonexistent, whereas in Germany it carried the same meaning as it does in the United States. The business was beginning to develop and grow at a rapid rate, and the pressures on individual managers were considerable."*[23]

Since then, PCI, which operates in over 150 countries, has worked hard to establish a common understanding of its business objectives and values, which are shown in Exhibit 3.4. PCI made many changes in the way it managed its managers, some of which are described in "Managing Human Resources at Pepsi-Cola

EXHIBIT 3.4

Business Objectives and Values at Pepsi-Cola International

BUSINESS VISION

To be the world's leading soft drink company

HR PHILOSOPHY

To be a world-class company where business results and career satisfaction are synonymous

HR VALUES

- Leadership
- High standards of personal performance
- Career/skill development
- Balancing teamwork and individual achievement

BUSINESS OBJECTIVES

- Committed bottling organization
- Uncompromising dedication to quality
- Development of talented people
- Focus on growth
- Quality business plans

Source: Pepsi-Cola International company material provided by J.R. Fulkerson for J.R. Fulkerson & R.S. Schuler (1992), "Managing Worldwide Diversity at Pepsi-Cola International," in S.E. Jackson (ed.), *Diversity in the Workplace: Human Resources Initiatives* (New York: Guilford Press).

MANAGING HUMAN RESOURCES

Around the World
at Pepsi-Cola International

Pepsi-Cola International (PCI) always knew it needed a certain kind of savvy, intelligent manager to succeed in the complex world of international production and marketing. But just to be sure, the international division quantified its values and expectations, says John Fulkerson, HR director for Pepsi-Cola International (Somers, New York).

"We recently studied 100 successful managers and 100 unsuccessful managers, with the help of the Center for Creative Leadership, and came up with eleven qualities that seem to make a difference in success at Pepsi-Cola International. We looked at very junior to very senior managers over a three-year period.

"We were not surprised by any of the qualities— especially the top three:

- The ability to handle business complexities
- The ability to lead and manage people
- Drive and a results orientation

"All these qualities support our company's success and results orientation, which lies at the heart of our corporate culture. It sounds hard to maintain a workable corporate culture when doing business across cultures. However, Pepsi-Cola International has built a set of values that transcend petty differences and apply to everyone, everywhere.

"What's important is how you treat people. We operate on the principles of telling people what we expect, showing them how to develop, and helping them reach the goals. Those ideas work in any of the 150 countries we do business in.

"People are more similar than we think; they want the same things. They want to be successful. That even applies in the Communist bloc countries. After all, they invited us in. They just want to be successful, too.

"Our 1,200 international employees help us sell 40 billion 8-ounce servings of Pepsi annually in 145 countries through 16 regional offices. Our people need to be mature and savvy. They must be able to handle complex business and understand global issues.

"We need these kinds of people to do business in the complex international arena, and Pepsi-Cola needs people like this to operate in the result-oriented culture that (former Pepsi chairman) Don Kendall pioneered here. We key on results because, especially in international, you quickly learn there are 100 ways to do anything....

"Our culture centers around clear communication of the expected results, and risk taking with no punishment for making mistakes. Along with this expectation that our mature, savvy people will know what to do is another expectation that they'll know when it's time to ask for help. We emphasize the criticality of communication. We make it known that we expect, for example, a manager in Spain to know when it's appropriate to check with New York to see what Australia is doing in a certain circumstance. If you talk to others, you lessen the chance of making a mistake.

"Our culture also tells managers that being defensive will get you nowhere and that you are not viewed as being mature if you just complain. Things are very open and above board here, and that is even reflected in a formalized personnel program we call 'Instant Feedback.' It's a system for reinforcing our desire to have constant quick communication.

"Some cultures don't like this, and we are flexible. For example, in the Far East, you can't give feedback in front of peers, you wait until you're alone. In Latin America, on the other hand, people are much more vocal in discussing performance issues. They throw it out on the table and it's a jump ball.

"Though we try to emphasize similarities in our culture, and hope that most of our values cut across cultures, we are not unmindful of varying customs in different cultures and regions. We're willing to modify our practices to get results, because wanting results is at the heart of our culture."[24]

International." As the PCI experience reveals, the evolution of multinational enterprises is increasing the importance of effectively managing human resources. It is also increasing the need for firms to recognize and incorporate cultural differences in the ways they manage their human resources.

In summary, there are several implications for managing human resources from the current and projected conditions associated with increased domestic and international competition. You and your career are likely to be in the center of them. Another set of conditions affecting you and companies is associated with the qualities and characteristics of the workforce.

LEARNING OBJECTIVE 2

Describe the workforce conditions and their impact on managing human resources.

The Workforce

Ongoing changes in the workforce in the U.S. and the world contribute to several new and major concerns for companies and for managing human resources.

Workforce Educational Attainment. After installing millions of dollars worth of computers in its Burlington, Vermont factories, the IBM Corporation discovered, much to its dismay, that it had to teach high school algebra to thousands of workers before they could run the computers. David Kearns, Xerox's former chairman and CEO, has said:

> *... [T]he American workforce is running out of qualified people. If current demographic and economic trends continue, American business will have to hire a million new workers a year who can't read, write, or count. Teaching them how, and absorbing the lost productivity while they're learning, will cost the industry $25 billion a year for as long as it takes.*[25]

Illiteracy is but one symptom of a much larger problem afflicting the U.S. economy. The $100 billion plus yearly trade deficit and a foreign debt of nearly a trillion dollars reflect the inability of a large percentage of the American workforce to compete effectively in an integrated world economy. "Much of the success of Japan stems from the fact that its blue collar workers can interpret advanced mathematics, read complex engineering blueprints, and perform sophisticated tasks on the factory floor far better than blue collar workers in the United States," says Merry I. White, professor of comparative sociology at Boston University and author of *The Japanese Education Challenge.*[26] Becoming more typical is:

> *Andre Miles has applied for a job at Lincoln Electric Co. three times in the past three years, but he never got past a screening interview.*
>
> *"It is frustrating that I don't even have a chance," says the 22-year-old construction worker. He isn't alone. More than 20,000 applications have been submitted to Lincoln in the past 18 months, and most were rejected. Yet the maker of motors and welding products says it still has positions to fill and can't find the workers it needs.*
>
> *Lincoln currently has about 200 openings, with hourly pay ranging from $8.39 to $20. While some openings are at the lowest rung of the plant, the company also needs many skilled tool-and-die makers, mold makers and machinists.*
>
> *But few of the thousands of applicants who applied for jobs at Lincoln could do high school trigonometry or read technical drawings, and most didn't show an aptitude for learning how to operate computer-controlled machines—skills that Lincoln says even entry-level workers need.*[27]

As a consequence of this general situation:

Employees with certain skills are hot commodities. "A journeyman welder is like a free agent in baseball," says Walt Elish, executive director of the Economic Development Corp. of Waukesha County, Wisconsin. "We can't find welders, we can't find [computer controlled] machine operators." He says such workers can earn from $35,000 to $50,000 a year, and it isn't uncommon for a good toolmaker to pull down $60,000 with overtime.[28]

Values. This is a common business complaint: the need to compete globally is occurring while the work ethic is disappearing. According to some commentators, however, the work ethic has not disappeared. People today are willing to work hard at "good" jobs, providing they have the freedom to influence the nature of their jobs and to pursue their own lifestyles. People value work, but the type of work that interests them has changed. They want challenging jobs that allow them the freedom to make decisions. Increasingly, people may not seek or desire rapid promotions, especially when they involve geographic transfers, but they do seek influence and control.[29] **Values**, then, are the ideals and principles people hold as most important.

Values are the ideas and principles people hold most important for themselves.

In today's workforce, there are three distinct age groups that tend to have different values. The **baby boomers** (born between 1946 and 1964) tend to value and trust authority, see work as a duty and vehicle to financial wealth, and expect that performance will be rewarded more than years of experience. Their parents, the **traditionalists** (born between 1925 and 1945), value job security, employment security, and income security. Because the traditionalists tend to be less mobile, organizations need to be concerned with targeting training and retraining, not just at the entry-level worker but at older workers as well.[30]

- **Traditionalists: born between 1925 and 1945**
- **Baby boomers: born between 1946 and 1964**
- **Baby busters: born between 1965 and 1985**

As organizations begin to look at the values of their employees in the workplace, however, they realize the need to make room for another age category—those individuals born between 1965 and 1985, the **baby busters**. According to a recent study, this group values recognition and praise; time with their managers; opportunity to learn new things; fun at work; unstructured, flexible time; and small, unexpected rewards for jobs well done. Increasingly, companies recognize that these values are different from the other groups and must be accommodated. For example, at Patagonia, the Ventura, California-based manufacturer of products for outdoor enthusiasts, 40 percent of 700 employees are in their twenties. Patagonia has nontraditional open offices, flexible work schedules, and flexible personal leave times for up to four months each year.

The baby busters are also known as Generation X because they are the tenth generation of Americans.

The upshot of these value differences in the workplace is that companies with a mix of workers (young to older) may have to consider managing and motivating them differently. It appears, however, that all workers seem to have one important value in common.

Ownership. The one value that seems to cut across employee age groups is the desire for ownership. The new buzzword in employee motivation is **ownership**, which can mean either an equity share or just a worker's sense that [s]he counts. Says Harvard business school professor J. Richard Hackman: "If you want me to care, then I want to be treated like an owner and have some real voice in where we are going." The concept grows out of the "employee involvement" of the 1980s, which got off to a shaky start with quality circles that never amounted to much, then grew stronger as workers were brought into decision making.[31]

Ownership can mean either an equity share (stock ownership) or just a worker's sense that (s)he counts.

Giving workers an equity share in the business is a growing practice. As we discuss in Chapter 14, Performance-Based Pay, many firms are giving stock and stock options to all their employees. They give these based upon the employees' performance and/or willingness to take a reduction in pay for a chance to get more equity in the company. The result seems to be a more motivated and committed workforce.

Did You KNOW?

Constant training, retraining, job-hopping, and even career-hopping, will become the norm.

Mary O'Hara-Devereaux and Robert Johansen
GlobalWork: Bridging Distance, Culture and Time

Implications for Managing Human Resources

Major implications of the change occurring in the workforce include: a) more extensive recruiting activities, b) more training, c) providing a more entrepreneurial feeling, and d) tapping Generation X's potential.

More Recruiting. The situation at Lincoln Electric has forced this 100-year-old company to adopt some unusual tactics to find employees. Along with advertising on local radio stations, managers have met with local ROTC units and the Interchurch Council of Greater Cleveland to discover candidates. Lincoln won't specify how much it spends on recruiting, but says it has spent more in the past two years than it has in the previous 98 years put together.

The HR staff holds frequent open houses for high-school teachers, career counselors, and students and has sent recruiting teams to neighboring counties in Ohio and Pennsylvania. When Lincoln asked the Ohio Bureau of Employment Services to search its databases for candidates for the tool-and-die openings, the bureau couldn't come up with a single candidate in the entire state—even though Ohio has one of the highest numbers of machine-tool companies in the U.S.[32]

More Training. In addition to more extensive recruiting, firms are energetically training and retraining their workforces. At the same time, more managers and executives are exposed to new and sometimes eccentric methods and styles of training, aimed at shaping their behavior toward more effective leadership and greater productivity. In the name of leaner, meaner, and more efficient management, corporate educators are forging ahead with no evidence beyond the promise that these emerging techniques will produce long-term results.

There is, however, a solid base for all the technical training and retraining that needs to be done in factories and offices. In the next five years, four out of five people in the industrial world will be doing jobs differently from the way they have been done in the last 50 years. Most people will have to learn new skills. By the year 2000, 75 percent of all employees will need to be retrained in new jobs or taught new skills. Corporate trainers, in the interest of saving time, will explore alternative and faster methods of delivering new skills and learning, including interactive video, audiotapes, take-home videodiscs, computer-based instruction, and expert systems.[33] An excellent example of what one business in Ohio is doing to train and educate its workforce is detailed in the feature "Managing Human Resources at Will-Burt."

Providing the Entrepreneurial Feeling. Building on the common value of ownership, some firms are providing conditions for that "entrepreneurial feeling," that feeling of being in charge as if you owned the place. Companies are giving workers more input into decision-making and empowering workers to act on their best ideas. In addition, companies like Xerox, 3M, and Honeywell help finance startups by employees who have promising ideas in return for a minority share. Alfred West, founder and chairman of SEI Corp., a large financial services company in Wayne, Pennsylvania, is planning a more radical experiment with his 1,100 workers. He intends to divide his company into entrepreneurial units, each led by a so-called champion who has been particularly effective in promoting whatever the unit does. West will give each group of employees a 20 percent interest in their unit. After a suitable period, he will invite an investment bank to put a price on the unit. Then West will pay members their 20 percent . If the unit flops, the members get nothing more than their salaries. Says West: "I'm an entrepreneur, and I want more people like that here."[34]

Managing Generation X. Due to generational differences and media-driven stereotypes, members of "Generation X"—those people between the ages of 20 and 35—are often misunderstood and underutilized by employers, says Bruce

MANAGING HUMAN RESOURCES

at Will-Burt

One Plus One Equals a Thriving Business

Dennis Donahue, president of Will-Burt, Inc., a $20 million machine parts manufacturer in Orrville, Ohio, confesses that when the company started a remedial training program for employees in 1985, it wasn't just for the benefit of the employees. "The company had to save itself," he says. "The reasons weren't altruistic, to be honest with you"

With 2,000 hours of rework a month and a 35 percent product-rejection rate, Will-Burt teetered on the brink of bankruptcy. The company hired professors from nearby University of Akron and set up classrooms in the factory. Classes were mandatory and included basic math courses, as well as reading and other subjects.

Now, eight years later, the company has not only saved itself, it is thriving. According to Donahue, Will-Burt spends less than 1 percent of annual sales on remedial training. But as a result, defective products have fallen from 8 percent of sales to 2 percent. Employee tardiness has dropped, as well—from 70 late employees a day to 2 in seven months. Disability costs also have been cut.

Central to the program was math instruction. "If the worker does the math wrong in making a product, the quality is bad," says Donahue. "They have to have a certain level of math skills, especially with the computers we're using now." But some employees weren't eager to learn the new math, especially when they felt they were being held up for ridicule. "The employees didn't react very well to the program at first," admits Donahue. "When we started getting publicity for it, they thought management was telling people we had dumb employees.

"Now they understand there is a nationwide problem of employees not being able to do calculations on new machinery. It's being received better. Part of that has to do with everyone in the plant—secretaries, purchasing people, as well as lathe operators—taking the courses."

Will-Burt is now held up as a shining example. The Department of Labor endorsed the program, and the National Association of Manufacturers will include it in a remedial training package it plans to offer its 13,000 members.[35]

Tulgan, author of *Managing Generation X: How to Bring Out the Best in Young Talent.* Tulgan offers the following guidelines to motivate young workers and tap their unique talents:

- Support their quest for new skills. Recognize that their careers will not be limited to any one employer.
- Emphasize goals, not processes. Generation Xers tend to have an independent spirit, and managers often interpret this nonconformist attitude as a liability.
- Provide constant feedback. Because Xers are engaged in a skills-enhancement process, they expect and need more feedback from management than other employees do.
- Discourage a "dues paying" culture. At one time, it could be expected that new employees would perform grunt work as a rite of initiation, but this practice only makes sense when employees and employers have formed long-term relationships.[36]

Learning Objective 3

Describe the demographic conditions and expected changes and their impact on managing human resources.

Demographics

The World. Currently there are slightly more than 5.5 billion people on this planet. By the year 2000 the worldwide population is projected to be around 6 billion. At current growth rates, over the next 20 years the workforce in the industrializing nations alone will expand by about 700 million. Between 1995 and 2000, Asia's workforce is projected to grow by 240 million, while Europe's is projected to grow by only 6 million.[37] What this means for many firms is the existence of a huge labor market worldwide. With an apparent worldwide labor surplus, a downward pressure on wages is likely to persist for some time.

United States. With a population of more than 250 million today, projections indicate that this figure will slowly swell into the 21st century. By the year 2000, the U.S. population will reach 275 million, an increase of 15 percent over the 240 million U.S. residents in 1985. Population is expected to hit 383 million by 2050. These figures are significant because they make the U.S. even more unusual than Europe and Japan; for a comparison, see the "HR Advice and Application" feature. Study this feature, and discuss three trends and their implications resulting from these population projections for the U.S., Japan, and Europe.

Women in the Workforce. During the 1990s, women are expected to continue to join the workforce in substantial numbers. By the year 2000, approximately 50 percent of the workforce will be women, and 61 percent of all U.S. women will be working. Women will have comprised almost three-fifths of the new entrants into the labor force between 1985 and 2000.[38] By contrast, of new entrants into the labor force in this same period of time, only 15 percent will be native white males. This figure and others illustrating the increasing heterogeneity of the U.S. labor force are shown in Exhibit 3.5.

Currently, the occupational makeup of the civilian labor force reflects much higher percentages of women in clerical positions and higher percentages of men in managerial and administrative jobs and employed as crafts workers.

About 25 percent of women occupy professional and technical positions; most of those are in the nursing and teaching professions. Thus, many working females are in service, clerical (secretarial), nursing, and teaching jobs. Women are now

EXHIBIT 3.5

New Entrants into the Labor Force

CATEGORY	LABOR FORCE (%), 1985	NET NEW WORKERS (%), 1985–2000
Native white men	47	15
Native white women	36	42
Native nonwhite men	5	7
Native nonwhite women	5	13
Immigrant men	4	13
Immigrant women	3	9
Total workers	115,461,000	25,000,000

Source: *Workforce 2000* (Washington D.C.: U.S. Government Printing Office, Department of Labor, 1987).

HR ADVICE & APPLICATION

The Upside of America's Population Upsurge

If demography is destiny, then America's economy in the next century may be very different from that of its chief trading rivals. Almost alone among industrial nations, the U.S. now looks forward to sizable population growth through 2050 and beyond.

This picture is in sharp contrast to other industrial nations, where growth is now grinding to a halt. While the world is adding a record 90 million people a year, almost all of that growth is in developing nations. "The only major exception is the U.S.," says Carl Haub of the Population Reference Bureau. (Canada and Australia are also growing, but their populations are only 17 percent of the U.S. total.)

Why is America the exception out in the industrial world? Haub notes that the U.S. fertility rate, which had dipped below the population-replacement level of 2.1 children per woman in the 1970s, has moved back close to that level. By contrast, the fertility rate averages only 1.5 to 1.6 in Japan and Europe.

At the same time, U.S. immigration, enhanced by liberalized legislation a few years ago and by a sizable influx of illegal immigrants, is now on a par with the great migrations of the early 20th century. The U.S. now absorbs 1 million immigrants a year, which amounts to 1 out of every 100 people added to the world population. Meanwhile, other industrial countries are in the process of closing their doors to both legal and illegal immigrants.

The growing opposition among Europeans—and among more and more Americans—to further immigration reflects tensions spawned by the high unemployment plaguing the industrial world. But the more liberal U.S. policy could turn out to be advantageous in the long run.

For one thing, other industrial nations must cope with static or declining labor forces. By 2025, for example, Japan will lose 12.2 million people aged 15-64, Germany 4.5 million, and Italy 4 million. But the U.S. will actually add some 38 million.

More important, all advanced nations face rapidly aging populations and a sharp drop in the ratio of working-age people to the elderly early in the next century. Because the U.S. baby boom generation is now entirely in the labor force, there are more than five Americans 15-64 years old for each older person, compared with an average ratio of only 4.3 to 1 in Western Europe.

Although most of America's baby boomers will be age 65 and older by the year 2025, current projections indicate that the U.S. ratio will still be higher than that of most other advanced nations—holding at about 3.3 to 1 in the U.S., compared with 2.9 to 1 in Britain, 2.1 in France, 2.5 in Germany, and just 2.3 in Japan, where 30 percent of the population will be elderly. "America's high fertility and immigration could prove to be a big plus in the decades ahead," says economist Philip Suttle of Morgan Guaranty Trust Co.[39]

moving into managerial jobs. The majority of men, on the other hand, are in semiskilled (operative), skilled (crafts workers), managerial and administrative, and professional and technical jobs.

This distribution has, in part, resulted from the notion of **job sex-typing**. That is, a job takes the image of being appropriate only for the sex that dominates the job. Consequently, once a job becomes sex-typed, it attracts only persons of that sex. Job sex-typing, combined with sex-role stereotyping, has traditionally restricted perceived job choices and preferences for both men and women. Whereas job sex-typing refers to the labeling of jobs as either "men's" jobs or "women's" jobs, **sex-role stereotyping** refers to labels, characteristics, or attributes that become attached to men and women solely because they are members of their respective sexes.

Job sex-typing means a job takes on an image of being appropriate for only the gender that dominates the job.

Sex-role stereotyping refers to labels, characteristics, or attributes that become attached to men and women solely because they are members of their respective sexes.

Evidence now indicates that the range of perceived job choices and preferences is expanding for both men and women. This trend has been facilitated in part by the gradual reduction of sex-role stereotyping in our society. In addition, some of the job sex-typing has been reduced through sex-neutral job titles (often crafted by HR departments) and because of the increased number of women graduating from professional schools, especially business schools.[40]

These changes, however, definitely appear to be gradual. Furthermore, the real choices of women and minorities in the top levels of management still seem to be limited. In 1978, *Fortune* counted ten women among the 6,400 highest paid officers and directors of major publicly held firms. The comparable figures for 1990 were 19 of 4,012.[41] This surprisingly slow progress is due in part to the phenomenon called the **glass ceiling**—an invisible but seemingly unbreakable barrier. In today's progressive atmosphere, it may seem hard to believe glass ceilings still exist in corporate America. However, according to "Women and Minorities in Management," a recent study by researchers Mary Ann Von Glinow and Ann Morrison, women and minorities are still prevented from entering top executive ranks. This is discussed further in Chapter 5.

The glass ceiling is the invisible but seemingly unbreakable barrier women and minorities face in climbing the organizational ladder.

Clearly, although women have made significant inroads into management, they have fallen short of the top.[42] Consequently, many women have decided to start their own businesses. More discussion of job choices for you are in Chapter 6 on Career Planning and Management.

Minority Groups in the Workforce. In recent years, a minority group that has become increasingly vocal is the group comprised of disabled people. When the Americans with Disabilities Act was passed in 1990, supporters argued that (1) there are almost 45 million disabled Americans; and (2) the rest of the Americans might think of themselves as "temporarily abled." According to this way of looking at it, almost everyone could at some point be disabled. This is a new way of looking at disabilities with some important implications for HR management practices.

Over the next decade, the racial profile of the American workforce will change dramatically. African-Americans, Native Americans, Asians, and Hispanics will make up a larger share of the workforce than ever before. Between 1990 and 2000, they will contribute 20 percent to the new workforce. By the way, "Hispanic" identifies a group comprised of a number of nationalities and ethnicities of Hispanic origin—including persons from Mexico, Cuba, Puerto Rico, and the countries of Central and South America. By far the largest nationality in this category hails from Mexico, which accounts for 63 percent of all Hispanics in the U.S. labor force.

While America has always been a land of immigrants, it was also thought to be a "melting pot," where differences in background gradually disappeared. Today, many individual differences are recognized by law and society as being very important. Consequently, many employment laws deal with diversity. Understanding and managing diversity is a major HR theme throughout this book.

Immigrants in the Workforce. The number of immigrants in the workforce is expected to increase dramatically over the next 10 years. The *Immigration Act* of 1990 allocates 750,000 visas annually, up from the previous limit of 500,000. While most of these visas are granted to reunite family members, job-based immigration is now at 150,000, up from 54,000. The Census Bureau predicts that during the 1990s California will add almost two million immigrants. Other states with large numbers of immigrants include: New York, Texas, Illinois, and Florida. The majority of working-age immigrants will join the labor force.

Implications for Managing Human Resources

There are two major responses from companies regarding these demographic changes: a) programs for **managing diversity,** and b) utilization of immigrants and foreign workers.

Managing diversity means effectively utilizing the talents of all members of a diverse workforce.

Managing Diversity. The radical demographic transformation in the workforce means organizations must learn to manage a very diverse workforce—

African-Americans, Hispanics, Asians, males, females, young, old, and much more.[43] Workforce diversity means having workers with many different characteristics. For Northern States Power (NSP) in Minneapolis, it means all the groups identified in the "HR Advice and Application: Diversity is Valuing Differences at NSP." NSP sees the emerging workforce diversity not only as a reality, but also as an opportunity. To support this philosophy, NSP has many human resource programs that enable it to "capitalize on diversity."

In general, successful organizations implement proactive, strategic HR planning to manage diversity. Short-term strategies designed to circumvent the situation prevent an organization from effectively positioning itself in tomorrow's world of cultural, gender, and lifestyle diversity. Top management in corporations, then, needs to emphasize to line managers two goals of "diversity competence": productivity growth and market-share expansion, both domestically and internationally.

HR managers typically need to focus on nine key areas in managing diversity.

- *Recruitment:* Mount a concerted effort to find quality minority employees by improved college relations programs and other recruitment strategies.
- *Career development:* Expose those minority employees with high potential to the same key developmental jobs that traditionally have led to senior positions for their white, male, U.S.-born counterparts.
- *Diversity training for managers:* Address stereotypes and cultural differences that interfere with the full participation of all employees in the workplace.
- *Upward mobility:* Break the "glass ceiling" and increase the number of minorities in upper management through mentors and executive appointment.
- *Diverse input and feedback:* Ask minority employees themselves what they need versus asking managers what they think minorities need.
- *Self-help:* Encourage networking and support groups among minorities.
- *Accountability:* Hold managers accountable for developing their diverse workforces.
- *Systems accommodation:* Develop respect and support for cultural diversity through recognition of different cultural and religious holidays, diet restrictions, and so forth.[44]

HR ADVICE & APPLICATION

Diversity is Valuing Differences at NSP

Race	Religion	Economic Status
Minnesotan	Language	Marital Status
Non-Minnesotan	Height	Nationality
Weight	Gender Preference	Appearance
Traditional Thinker	Age	White-Collar
Nontraditional Thinker	I.Q.	Blue-Collar
Nontraditional Job	Smoking Preference	Single Parent
Education	Differently Abled	Affectional

- *Outreach:* Support minority organizations and programs, thus developing a reputation as a multicultural leader.

Utilization of Immigrants and Foreign Workers. For U.S. companies that require high skill levels in areas such as science and engineering, adopting an international approach is no longer questioned. Declining test scores and lack of interest among U.S. students mean these companies must seek needed talent in other countries.[45] Because of the skills shortage at home and the resulting high wages demanded by skilled Americans, each year some 35,000 U.S. companies request visas, especially for physical therapists, civil engineers, and people in computer-related jobs.[46] And if companies can't move needed workers to the U.S., they move the jobs abroad. In many cases this solves the skill shortage and reduces payroll costs:

> *U.S. companies are increasingly hiring highly skilled workers in Asia, the former Soviet bloc, and Europe to perform jobs once reserved for American professionals. Texas Instruments Inc., Chase Manhattan Corp., International Business Machines Corp., and scores of other companies have contracted with Indians, Israelis, and other foreigners to write computer programs. Film and TV producers increasingly bring in foreign film professionals to keep costs down. And American Telephone & Telegraph Co., DuPont Co., Hewlett-Packard Co., and others have moved business units abroad, along with hundreds of high-paying managerial and research jobs.*[47]

Solving the skills shortage in this manner helps companies keep their overall costs down and earnings up.[48]

LEARNING OBJECTIVE 4

Describe how economic, technological, and organizational conditions are affecting the way firms manage their human resources.

Economic, Technological, and Organizational Conditions

National, state, and local economies can have a significant impact on business and on managing human resources. So can the international economy, whose recent impact has increased the level of competition and has forced U.S. corporations to become more flexible, competitive, and bottom-line oriented.

Executives looking at the business environment realize that the 1990s are tougher than the 1980s. They see companies being forced to make decisions faster. Consequently, they are adopting more fluid structures that can be altered as conditions change. More than before, companies are living by computers, shaping strategy and structure to fit information technology. They are engaging in more mergers, joint ventures, acquisitions, downsizing, and development in order to become and stay competitive, and they are coping with a more demanding workforce, increasingly characterized by its overall diversity.

Best cities worldwide in which to run a business:

1. **Singapore**
2. **San Francisco Bay Area**
3. **London**
4. **New York**
5. **Frankfurt**
6. **Hong Kong**
7. **Atlanta**
8. **Toronto**
9. **Paris**
10. **Tokyo**

Changing Jobs and Skills Needed. What will the workforce of 2000 be doing? The changes projected for the nation's industries will restructure U.S. occupational patterns. According to the Bureau of Labor Statistics, between 23.4 and 28.6 million new wage and salary jobs will be created by 2000. Most of the job growth will be in the service-producing and not the goods-producing arenas. Of these, between 1.0 and 4.6 million will be in high-technology industries. Thus, a substantial number of new jobs will be in industries other than high technology.[49]

The largest job growth in the first half of this decade occurred in these industries:

Temp and full-time employment agencies

Restaurants and bars

Local government administration

Hospitals

Recreation (health clubs, casinos, etc.)

Home health care

Nursing and personal care

Medical and doctors' offices

Computer software

State government administration

Trucking and parcel delivery

Business services (security, drafting, etc.)

Residential care (rehab centers, etc.)

Management consulting and public relations

Social services

Offices of optometrists, podiatrists, etc.

Child care

Grocery stores

Motion picture production

Elementary and secondary schools[50]

Did You KNOW?

In 1990, government jobs surpassed manufacturing jobs when there were 18.6 million government jobs and 18.2 million manufacturing jobs!

Exhibit 3.6 shows the occupations that will have the greatest number of new jobs by 2005. A number of jobs in the least-skilled job classes will disappear, while high-skilled professions will grow rapidly. Overall, the skill mix of the economy is moving rapidly upscale, with most new jobs demanding more education and higher levels of language, math, and reasoning skills.

> *Skills critical to the future of the workplace are emerging, but some are or will be in short supply. Several factors are driving the shift toward new skills for work: greater use of information technologies, the move away from craft and assembly manufacture and toward computer-mediated processes, the larger amount of knowledge work in almost every occupation, new requirements for education and the ability to manage complexity, and the redesign of many jobs to include computer-based work. Frequently, several skills will be folded into one job, often with a new title and greater individual responsibility.*[51]

These changes are occurring because future jobs require substantially more education than the current jobs. This is why an estimated 25 percent functional illiteracy rate among U.S. adults is especially critical[52] and why companies are reaching into the educational system with a variety of incentives, new ideas, and cooperative agreements. In Minneapolis, for example, corporate contributions underwrote extensive participatory planning, which was used in the successful restructuring of the city's school system, particularly its inner-city high schools. In Peking, Illinois, IBM's "Writing to Read" program helped first graders, cutting the number who needed remedial teaching from 11 percent to 2 percent.[53]

EXHIBIT 3.6

Current Jobs and Projected Growth for Selected Categories of Work (in thousands)

	1990	GROWTH BY 2005
Executive, Administrative, and Managerial		
General managers/top executives	3,100	14 to 24%
Accountants/auditors	985	25 to 34%
Financial managers	701	25 to 34%
Restaurant/food service managers	557	25 to 34%
Personnel/labor relations managers	456	25 to 34%
Marketing/advertising/PR managers	427	35% or more
Wholesale/retail buyers	361	14 to 24%
Engineering/data-processing managers	315	25 to 34%
Health services managers	257	35% or more
Marketing and Sales		
Retail sales workers	4,754	25 to 34%
Cashiers	2,633	25 to 34%
Manufacturers'/wholesale sales reps	1,944	14 to 24%
Service sales representatives	588	35% or more
Insurance agents/brokers	439	11 to 24%
Real estate agents/brokers/appraisers	413	14 to 24%
Securities/financial services sales reps	191	35% or more
Administrative Support		
Record clerks	3,761	5 to 13%
Traffic/shipping/stock clerks	3,755	5 to 13%
Secretaries	3,576	14 to 24%
General office clerks	2,737	14 to 24%
Word processors/data-entry keyers	1,448	–4 to 4%
Information clerks	1,400	35% or more
Transportation and Material Moving		
Truck drivers	2,700	14 to 24%
Other transportation workers	698	5 to 13%
Bus drivers	561	25 to 34%
Agriculture and Forestry		
Farm operators/managers	1,223	–5% or more
Farm workers	837	–5% or more
Construction Trades		
Carpenters	1,077	14 to 24%
Electricians	548	25 to 34%
Highway maintenance workers	151	14 to 24%

	1990	GROWTH BY 2005
Technical Support		
Engineering technicians	755	25 to 34%
Licensed practical nurses	644	35% or more
Computer programmers	565	35% or more
Medical technologists/technicians	258	14 to 25%
Science technicians	246	14 to 25%
Production		
Miscellaneous production workers	1,997	5 to 13%
Supervisors	1,800	5 to 13%
Metal-/plastic-working machine ops.	1,473	–4 to 4%
Apparel workers	1,037	–5% or more
Welders/cutters/welding machine ops.	427	–4 to 4%
Repairs and Installation		
General maintenance mechanics	1,128	14 to 24%
Automotive mechanics	757	14 to 24%
Electronic equipment repairers	444	5 to 13%
Unskilled Labor		
Miscellaneous unskilled workers	2,082	5 to 13%
Freight/stock/material movers	881	5 to 13%
Construction trades helpers	549	5 to 13%
Miscellaneous Service		
Food/beverage service workers	4,400	25 to 34%
Chefs/cooks/kitchen workers	3,100	25 to 34%
Janitors/cleaners	3,000	14 to 24%
Nursing/psychiatric aides	1,374	35% or more
Professional		
Registered nurses	1,727	35% or more
Kindergarten/elementary teachers	1,520	14 to 24%
Engineers	1,519	25 to 34%
Secondary-school teachers	1,280	25 to 34%
College/university faculty	712	14 to 24%
Lawyers/judges	633	25 to 34%
Physicians	580	25 to 34%
Computer systems analysts	463	35% or more

Source: Adapted from W. Woods (1993). The Jobs Americans Hold. *Fortune*, July 12, 1993, pp. 54–55.

Flexible Production Systems and Telematics Technologies. Technology generally refers to the equipment and knowledge used to produce goods and services. Today's organizations are discarding yesterday's technologies and replacing them with new technologies.[54] For example, old technology such as Henry Ford's mass production are ending up in the junkyard. In their place are new technologies, such as the "lean" production systems of Eiji Toyoda of Toyota and his production genius, Taiichi Ohno:

> *Just as the mass-production principles pioneered by Henry Ford and General Motors' Alfred Sloan swept away the age of craft production after World War I, so the ideas of Toyoda and Ohno are today chipping away at the foundations of mass production. We call their system "lean" production because it uses less of everything than a comparable mass production operation: half the human effort in the factory, half the manufacturing space, half the investment in tools, half the engineering hours to develop a new product. Lean production is built not simply on technical insight but on a precisely defined set of relationships that extends far beyond the factory floor to encompass designers, suppliers, and customers.*[55]

Did You KNOW?

Henry Ford's moving assembly line in 1913 helped cut the Model T's production time from 12 hours to 1.5 hours.

The new production systems are not just leaner—they are also more flexible. Mass production was used to produce standardized goods at low cost, using special purpose, product-specific machines and semi-skilled labor. But now consumers are demanding more specialized products. Flexible specialization is a modern form of production that shares some of the features of the craft modes of production that were common prior to the industrial revolution.[56]

With this newer technology, jobs are more complex so both production and managerial employees need more skills and higher levels of skill.[57] Paying for these skills is costly. This fact is not lost on organizations using flexible production technologies. To reap the highest returns from the money they spend on compensation, firms using the more modern technologies more often link pay to performance. Until recently, performance-based pay was rare for American production workers, due in part to the nature of assembly lines and in part to union opposition to such plans. But the modern technologies, combined with statistical process control techniques like those used for total quality management, may fit well with some types of performance-based compensation as discussed in Chapter 15.

Did You KNOW?

As recently as the 1960s, almost one-half of all workers in the industrialized countries were involved in making (or helping to make) things.

Information technology, data communications, voice mail, and information systems are revolutionizing the ways we perform work and organize our companies. These so-called **telematics technologies** encompass:

Telematics technologies enable organizations to respond more quickly, operate faster, and be more flexible.

- Mainframe computers and associated information systems
- Microcomputers and word processors
- Networking technologies
- Telecommunications technologies
- Reprography and printing
- Peripherals[58]

Telematics technologies are enabling organizations to shape themselves into winners. They facilitate speed, flexibility, decentralization, and communication with the customer. For example:

> *How fast is fast enough? The Limited (an upscale retail store with headquarters in Columbus, Ohio) tracks consumer preferences every day through point-of-sale computers. Orders, with facsimile illustrations, are sent by satellite to suppliers around the U.S. and in Hong Kong, South Korea, Singapore, and Sri Lanka. Within days, clothing from distant points begins to collect in Hong Kong. About four times a week, a chartered 747 brings it to the com-*

pany's distribution center in Ohio, where goods are priced and shipped to stores within 48 hours. Says Chairman Leslie Wexner: "That's not fast enough for the 90s."[59]

Computers also allow customers to look inside an organization. The trucking firm Pacific Intermountain Express gives customers access to its computers so they can check the status of their shipments. Banks and brokerage firms use computers to enable customers to conduct business from their homes and offices.

These technologies enhance quality by ensuring better parts and services from suppliers. Already retail chains are linked with their suppliers so that they know the timing and the nature of needed shipments. Telematics will also facilitate R&D capabilities and give managers more free time to get to know their companies better.

Automation, whether in the factory or the office, will continue to change organizational structures and culture. Because information is instantaneously available, there is little need for layers of management between the top and first line management. Top management can bypass middle managers on their way to the first-line management, and this breaks the chain of command and can lead to ambiguity in reporting relationships.[60]

Did You KNOW?

Machines on the assembly line today are built for organizational flexibility. Power is moving away from managers and into the hands of workers. All of this is made possible by information technologies.

Thus, as the telematics technologies produce better products and faster and leaner organizations, so will they undermine traditional authority structures. At advanced plants, blue-collar workers will become information managers by becoming computer operators. Traditional managers may no longer be needed.

A few observers believe the computers in the workplace will lead to far more than better information and better products. Shoshana Zuboff, an associate professor at the Harvard Business School and author of In the Age of the Smart Machine, *argues that computerization undermines traditional forms of authority and breaks down barriers between job categories and functions. "You have people doing work that is more abstract, more analytical," says Zuboff. "People not considered managerial in the past are managing information." Zuboff concludes that the role of the managers will have to be redefined in the 90s. Says she: "Since managers are no longer the guardians of the knowledge base, we do not need the command-control type of executive."*[61]

Did You KNOW?

The first practical industrial robot was introduced during the 1960s. By 1982 there were approximately 32,000 robots being used in the U.S. Today there are over 20,000,000.

In summary, more telematics implementation will provide organizations with opportunities to downsize, decentralize, and make their organizations more flexible and responsible. However, organizations must also be prepared to retrain workers, out-place workers (especially managers), and redesign jobs.

Changing Organizations. Phrases heard frequently include multinational alliances and joint ventures, mergers and acquisitions, virtual organization and horizontal corporations.[62] Even if a company is not itself multinational, multinational interdependencies may affect the business. To understand how complex these global interdependencies can become, consider the following factual example:

Natural gas owned by Indonesia's oil agency, Pertamina, flows out of a well discovered by Royal Dutch Shell into a liquification plant designed by French engineers and built by a Korean construction company. The liquified gas is loaded onto U.S.-flagged tankers, built in U.S. shipyards after a Norwegian design. The ships shuttle to Japan and deliver the liquid gas to a Japanese public utility, which uses it to provide electricity that powers an electronics factory making television sets that are shipped aboard a Hong Kong-owned container ship to California for sale to American farmers in Louisiana who grow rice that is sold to Indonesia and shipped there aboard Greek bulk carriers. All of the various facilities, ships, products, and services involved in the complex series of events are financed by U.S., European, and Japanese commercial banks, working in some cases with international and local government agencies. These facilities, ships, products, and services are insured and reinsured by U. S., European, and Japanese insurance companies. Investors in these facilities, ships, products, and services are located throughout the world.[63]

To get in on the action, companies will need a reputation as a desirable partner. Of course, they will also need a core competency in an area such as technology or marketing. But in addition, they will need people who are both able and motivated to cross organizational boundaries easily and be productive in a "temporary" job, yet remain loyal to the home base.

Instead of entering into alliances and joint ventures with others, companies are choosing to engage in mergers and acquisitions (M&As). Here either two companies combine to form a new one or one acquires and absorbs the other, usually smaller, firm. During the 1980s, U.S. firms restructured through M&As at a dizzying pace. M&As subsequently slowed somewhat, but they remained popular as a strategy for improving organization effectiveness. Novell Incorporated, which sells computer networking software, uses M&As aggressively to penetrate markets and diversify its offerings. In 1993, for example, Novell worked on five acquisition deals.[64]

For Novell, a major objective of M&As is to acquire the skills and talents of people employed by another company. According to Ernest J. ("Tim") Harris, Novell's senior vice president of HR:

The reason a company will buy another company many times is not only because of the technology but definitely because of the people that developed that technology and make it successful in the marketplace. You need to ensure that you can continue to operate the company and develop the technology on an ongoing basis, and the best way to do that is by having an integration that's successful enough to maintain continuity and continued employment for the people who are part of that entity.[65]

To ensure that executives think through all the HR issues when merging companies, Novell developed the *Merger Book*. Its two-thousand questions pertaining to HR serve as a road map for all Novell's M&A activities. The book helps the company keep the best talent, by facilitating smooth integration between companies. Information gathering and analysis are the heart of the process.[66]

In addition to alliances, joint ventures, and M&As, some companies are transforming themselves into the so-called **"virtual corporation."** What is it? In the minds of a few future-oriented executives, it is a temporary network of companies with diverse core competencies who quickly form a collaboration to take advantage of fleeting opportunities. Having exploited an opportunity, the "corporation" may disband as quickly as it formed. There will be no hierarchy, no central office, and no organizational chart in these corporations.[67]

The virtual corporation is a temporary network of companies brought together by a unique opportunity.

Implications for Managing Human Resources

The implications here for managing human resources are many. Overall, a strong economy tends to lower the unemployment rate, increase wage rates, make recruitment more necessary and more difficult, and increase the desirability of training current employees. In contrast, a weak economy tends to increase the unemployment rate, diminish demands for wage increases (and even result in wage concessions), make recruitment less necessary and easier, and reduce the need for training and developing current employees.[68]

Downsizing means reducing the number of employees.

Contingent workers are those hired on a limited-time basis.

Outsourcing is the process of transferring to another company work that was previously done inside the company.

Downsizing, Contingent Workers, and Outsourcing. Eliminating layers of employees, **downsizing**, continues to be an important aspect in shaping the organization. The typical target is middle management. The elimination of this group facilitates the process of decentralizing, the process so necessary to enhance the speed with which decisions can be made. Along with this trend is the use of more contingent workers. **Contingent workers** are individuals hired on a limited-time basis. They are subject to dismissal on short notice and typically do not receive as many benefits as regular employees.[69] Companies are increasingly **outsourcing** some HR activities like payroll activities to payroll processing firms such as Automatic Data Processing (ADP). Again, these activities are occurring in concert as new lean and trim organizations form in the 1990s.

Flexible and Adaptable Workers. While downsizing, outsourcing, and the use of contingent workers may be ways of getting flexibility and adaptability for the organization, companies also seek to get it by developing flexible and adaptable workers. This is done through continuous training programs and the use of teams. Teams can do some jobs better than individuals, and they can also encourage and support the training and adapting of team members.[70]

New Social Contract. All the realities we have been describing are having a significant impact on the relationship between the individual and the corporation.[71] According to Richard Belous, senior economist at the National Planning Association in Washington, D.C., labor policies attuned to life-time employment at a megacorporation will change. Workers will need to carry their own social-welfare system as they move from job to job. You, not your employer, will be responsible for amassing your retirement funds and providing your health coverage; when you switch jobs, your benefits will move with you."[72]

Workers are assuming responsibility for their own careers, no longer assuming the company will take care of them. What impact has this had on employee loyalty? Louis Csoka, research director of human resources at The Conference Board in New York City, summarizes the situation:

Loyalty? Job security? They are nearly dead. But employers that deliver honesty and satisfying work can expect a new form of commitment from workers.

> *The new relationship between employers and employees centers more around immediate work than long-term careers at an organization. Employers may not be able to assure continued employment, but they can try to retain qualified employees by offering challenging work, performance-based pay, greater flexibility and employee participation, family-supportive policies, and the training and experience needed to enhance employability both inside and outside the organization. Employees, in return, are expected to give their commitment to tasks and work teams, and take responsibility for their organization's success.*[73]

Transformation of the HR Department. Perhaps one of the biggest implications on managing human resources from all these external environmental factors is the change in the HR department itself. Because the change is so significant, it is more appropriate to refer to the "transformation of the HR department." The details of this transformation are described in the feature, "Managing Human Resources Around the World." You can now compare your responses to Exhibit 3.1 with those in Exhibit 3.7. How can you explain your differences? How can you explain the differences across the countries listed in Exhibit 3.7?

MANAGING HUMAN RESOURCES

Around the World
The Environment Is Transforming the HR Department

A study was released in 1992. International Business Machines Corporation and the HR consulting firm of Towers Perrin surveyed almost 3,000 CEOs and HR managers of firms in 20 countries. The firms were selected because they are effective and operate in highly competitive environments. Translated into eight languages, the survey was based on the premise that characteristics of the environment have been having a major impact on events in HR management. A major objective of the study was to test this premise and to explore what characteristics are having the most impact today and are predicted to have the most impact in the year 2000. Of course, the researchers were also interested in knowing whether characteristics with the most impact would vary depending on the country of the survey respondents.

The results of the study strongly supported the premise that the environment plays a major role in shaping personnel and HR management around the world. While several characteristics of the environment impact this role, some are regarded as more significant than others, and significance varies country by country. The results are shown in Exhibit 3.7. (Compare this exhibit against the evaluations you made using Exhibit 3.1.) Certain factors were more important to some countries than others. For example, respondents in the U.S. and Japan indicated changing workforce demographics as relatively high in importance, while respondents in Korea and Australia indicated them as comparatively low in importance (but still high in the overall results).

Increased levels of national and international competition refer to more commerce and competition from firms in countries all over the world. Globalization of the economy refers to what a firm must do in order to compete on a global basis—for example, to operate in all countries of the world or just in some.

Notice that results are presented with no indication of the present or the year 2000; regarding the impact of the environment, respondents said "the future is today." They said the same thing when it came to identifying the most important goals. Here, worldwide, the two most important goals selected were productivity/quality/customer satisfaction and linkage of human resources to the business.

In addition to indicating the most significant aspects of the environment, respondents were asked how these aspects were specifically affecting HR management. Basically, respondents saw the HR department literally being transformed from a functional specialist to a business partner. The impact of this transformation on four areas of HR management is shown in Exhibit 3.8.

EXHIBIT 3.7

Geographic Differences for the Six Most Important Environmental Factors

ENVIRONMENTAL FACTORS FOR HR	RELATIVELY HIGH RATINGS IN...	SOMEWHAT LOWER RATINGS IN...
1. Increased national/international competition	Mexico, Brazil	Japan, U.S.
2. Focus on quality/customer satisfaction	Latin America, Australia	Japan, Korea
3. Changing employee values	Korea, Japan, Germany	Latin America, Italy
4. Globalization of the economy	Latin America, Italy	Japan, U.S.
5. Fewer entrants to the workforce	Japan	Latin America, Korea, Australia
6. Changing workforce demographics	Japan, U.S.	Latin America, Korea, Australia

Source: *Priorities for Competitive Advantage* (IBM/Towers Perrin, 1992), 13. Used by permission.

EXHIBIT 3.8

A Model of the HR Department's Transformation

	FUNCTIONAL SPECIALIST		BUSINESS PARTNER
Nature of HR programs and functions	Responsive	→	Proactive
	Operational	→	Strategic
	Internal	→	Societal
Creation of HR strategy and policy	HR department has full responsibility.	→	HR department and line management share responsibility.
Organization of HR department	Employee advocate	→	Business partner
	Functional structure	→	Flexible structure
	Reporting to staff	→	Reporting to line
Profile of HR professionals	Career in HR	→	Rotation
	Specialist	→	Generalist
	Limited financial skills	→	Financial expertise
	Current focus	→	Focus on future
	Monolingual	→	Multilingual
	National perspective	→	Global perspective

Source: Adapted from *Priorities for Competitive Advantage* (IBM/Towers Perrin, 1992), 6. Used by permission.

LEARNING OBJECTIVE 5

Explain the impact on managing human resources from: a) company vision, business objectives, and values; b) CEO's leadership style and assumptions about people; c) corporate culture; d) organizational structure; e) organizational size; f) organizational life cycle; g) type of business (manufacturing vs. service); and h) competitive strategies.

Internal environment is those aspects of companies themselves that impart human resource management.

Vision is what the company strives to be.

The Internal Environment

Several aspects within organizations influence how effectively a firm manages its human resources. They include: the company's vision, business objectives, and values; the CEO's leadership style and assumptions about people; corporate culture; organizational structure; organizational size; organizational life cycle; type of business (manufacturing or service); and competitive strategies. These aspects often influence each other—for example, business objectives shape competitive strategy, which in turn influences various HR management activities. The implications of these internal environmental factors on HR management are described in the following sections.

Company Vision, Business Objectives, and Values

Vision. A company's **vision** states what it wants to be. At the 35,000 employee, Tacoma, Washington-based Weyerhaeuser lumber and paper company, the vision is to be:

The best forest products company in the world

At Southwest Airlines, the vision is to be:

The Airline of Choice

While a company's vision statement may seem very general to outsiders, if formulated with the deliberation and input of many employees, it can take on great meaning. Southwest Airlines is one company where these dynamics are clearly visible to employees and passengers alike. From the beginning, CEO Herb Kelleher has tried to establish a unique vision. He wants his company to overflow with "an insouciance, an effervescence." Counterbalancing this light-hearted aspect of

Kelleher's vision is a tough-minded pursuit of high productivity, which allows Southwest to serve two to three times as many passengers per employee as other major airlines.[74]

Business Objectives. In order to give more specific direction to employees than just a vision, companies develop **business objectives.** These objectives generally reflect what is particularly important for the company to be focusing on in a given time period, for example, one year or five years. They indicate what the company needs to be doing in order to be successful. An illustration of possible business objectives for companies is shown in Exhibit 3.9. This exhibit also shows possible **HR objectives** that give direction and content for managing human resources.

Business objectives are those objectives that are most important for the company to attain.

HR objectives are those objectives that are most important for managing human resources.

Values. **Business values** communicate how the employees should go about performing their jobs and attaining the company's vision and business objectives. They also communicate how the company feels about all its stakeholders.[75] The business values, or values of Weyerhaeuser Company are:

Business values are the ideals and principles held by the company that tell employees how they and the company should behave.

Customers

We listen to our customers and improve our products and services to meet their present and future needs.

People

Our success depends upon high-performing people working together in a safe and healthy workplace where diversity, development, and teamwork are valued and recognized.

EXHIBIT 3.9

Sample of Business Objectives and HR Objectives

BUSINESS OBJECTIVES	HR OBJECTIVES
Increase marketshare	Attracting new applicants
Increase shareholder value	Retaining desirable employees
Improve efficiencies	Motivating the workforce
Improve customer service	Participation (decision and profit) and empowerment (lean organization)
Improve staff development	Fairness
Grow revenue by developing new business	Serve the business to gain and sustain competitive advantage
Execute with a sense of urgency	Secure all employees continuous employment and a share of success commensurate with their achievement
Teamwork	Add value for the individual, company, and society by an effective and efficient HRM
Grow via acquisitions and alliances	Recognition of personnel
Force divisions to become #1 or #2	Employment of highly organized, motivated, and supportive employees
Cut costs	Achieve business objectives with the same number of employees
Maximize profits	Encourage employees to pursue increasing job-requirements (job enrichment and enlargement)
Increase stock value	In-house recruiting
Increase sales by 15 percent	
Expand customer and products into Europe and Asia	
Reduce costs as percentage of revenues	

> ***Accountability***
> *We expect superior performance and are accountable for our actions and results. Our leaders set clear goals and expectations, are supportive, and provide and seek frequent feedback.*
>
> ***Citizenship***
> *We support the communities where we do business, hold ourselves to the higher standards of ethical conduct and environmental responsibility, and communicate openly with Weyerhaeuser people and the public.*
>
> ***Financial Responsibility***
> *We are prudent and effective in the use of the resources entrusted to us.*

Bill Hewlett and David Packard, founders of Hewlett-Packard, believe "that people want to do a good job and that it is important for them to enjoy their work."

These values are typically expanded upon and clearly communicated to employees. Top management shares responsibility in setting the stage for employee rights and ethical conduct because they set policy, with input from the HR department, on the treatment of employees and on the definition of ethical behavior. Top management's policy and actions regarding ethics and employee rights are important in shaping the way the organization treats its employees and the conduct of employees with respect to each other and to customers.

For an excellent description of the role of top management regarding ethics, reread the feature, "Managing Human Resources at WMX Technologies: Building an Ethical Culture" in Chapter 1. Note the role the HR department plays in the communication process.[76] Its role in the training process is described in Chapter 11.

CEO's Leadership Style

Sherwin-Williams HR philosophy: "To get profitable growth through HR policies and programs to attract and retain highly skilled and productive employees and develop organizational capability to get competitive advantage."

As Herb Kelleher at Southwest Airlines shows, the leadership style of the CEO has a big impact on what the employees in a company do, think, and value. The style also affects how employees are managed. Introduced in Chapter 1 were the five leadership styles of CEOs, with the human assets style being the most popular. Compare and contrast this style with the box style:

> *Human assets style:* The chief executive manages for success through people policies, programs, and principles.
>
> *Box style:* The chief executive builds a set of rules, systems, procedures, and values that essentially control behavior and outcomes within well-defined boundaries.[77]

Needless to say, these two styles would create sizable differences in the way employees are managed. In addition to the CEO style, assumptions about people at work are more specific and can have a far-reaching impact if widely shared.

Assumptions About People At Work

If you owned your own business, what assumptions would you make about the employees you hire? Would you assume money or an interesting job is their biggest motivator? What would the impact be if you assumed money? It would probably mean that you would develop innovative payment programs so that people could earn as much as possible. Take a moment to rank the assumptions of people at work shown in Exhibit 3.10. Compare your rankings with others in your team or members of the class. What are the differences? What is the impact or differences in your rankings?

Corporate Culture

Corporate culture describes what is important, what should be done, and what should be avoided.

Organizational or **corporate culture** represents the organization's values.[78] It gives meaning and life to the values. As such, it becomes a more widely shared perspective

EXHIBIT 3.10

Assumptions About People At Work

Rank these from 1 to 16, with 1 being your most certain assumption about the motivations of people at work.

1. People like to be compensated fairly. ____
2. People with high self-esteem are more likely to be satisfied with their job. ____
3. People like to have interesting jobs. ____
4. Money alone cannot make a job satisfying. ____
5. People want mutual respect. ____
6. People have different interests from their employers. ____
7. People are opportunistic to some degree. ____
8. People want to be in an environment where they like their co-workers. ____
9. People want their company to look after their best interests. ____
10. People want to feel that their job is important. People want recognition. ____
11. People want to know their organization's mission and goals. ____
12. People like to learn. ____
13. People want to have a life outside work. ____
14. People want to be proud of the company for which they work. ____
15. People want job security. ____
16. People want to be accountable for what they do. ____

on how things should be done, what's important, and what should be avoided. For example, at Southwest Airlines, humor is important. Passengers are treated to little amusements such as the following announcement heard over the intercom: "Good morning, ladies and gentlemen. Those of you who wish to smoke will please file out to our lounge on the wing, where you can enjoy our feature film."[79]

HR Philosophy. One aspect of corporate (or organizational) culture is a company's **HR philosophy**. To understand the HR philosophy at Southwest, consider Kelleher's description of how top management selects employees:

HR philosophy is a statement of how the organization regards its employees.

> *"What we are looking for, first and foremost, is a sense of humor.... Then we look for people who excel to satisfy themselves and who work well in a collegial environment. We don't care that much about education and expertise, because we can train people to do whatever they have to do. We hire attitudes."*[80]

In some companies, the HR philosophy is a formal statement describing how people are to be treated and managed. Weyerhaeuser Company uses its HR philosophy statement to describe what employees mean to the company. The following is an excerpt:

- People are mature, responsible individuals who want to contribute.
- People hold themselves to high standards of integrity and business ethics; they are responsible stewards of the land and environment.
- Our work environment is based on mutual respect, personal satisfaction, and growth opportunities for everyone.
- People recognize that teamwork, cooperation, and a clean, safe, well-maintained workplace are essential to fulfilling our customer commitments.
- Continuing education is an ongoing commitment that involves everyone.[81]

At BMW, the HR philosophy is that:

- The qualified employee will become a self-confident entrepreneur of his own labor potential.
- The central key to efficiency and productivity lies in corporate and leadership culture.
- Qualification will become the key factor relevant to success for both the employees and the company.
- The time for revolutionary changes in production is over. In the future, one will face evolutionary developments in structures of labor and organization.
- The older employee will become a central challenge for HRM.
- The attractiveness of BMW as employer depends more and more on its role as leader in the field of ecological-oriented innovation in the car industry.[82]

Instead of using the term "HR philosophy" to describe how employees are regarded and how they are to be treated and managed, some organizations just use the word *culture*—that is, "We will create a culture that recognizes how important we feel people are and how we are going to treat them." Culture is always reflected in the company's HR activities. For example, companies such as Levi Strauss that have a culture of caring for and respecting the individual are likely to offer employment security and provide for a variety of employee needs. Many employees learn the culture and the HR philosophy of the organization through HR activities—how it selects employees, what performance is evaluated, and what behaviors it compensates most highly.

Corporate culture is very important for companies doing business worldwide. For example, as Pepsi-Cola (PepsiCo) expands its global business, it still wants to retain a certain image and a certain way of doing business. Having a culture that is shared worldwide helps PepsiCo and its international division, Pepsi-Cola International (PCI), achieve a consistent image, as described in the feature, "Managing Human Resources Around the World: Pepsi-Cola International."

Organizational structure describes the allocation of tasks and responsibilities among individuals and departments.

Organizational structure alternatives:

- **Department**
- **Division**
- **Matrix**
- **Cross-countries**

Organizational Structure

Organizational structure describes the allocation of tasks and responsibilities among individuals and departments; they designate the nature and means of formal reporting relationships as well as the groupings of individuals within the organization.[83] The structural forms generally recognized for domestic firms include functional departmentalization, product-based divisionalization, geographic divisionalization, matrix organization with dual reporting relationships, and several network arrangements. Different structures arise in response to a variety of internal and external forces, including technological demands, organizational growth, environmental turbulence, size, and business strategy. Each structural form creates unique implications and challenges for managing human resources.

Departmental. Businesses with a single product or service often have a **departmental structure.** Careers in these types of companies generally focus narrowly on developing single-function, "silo-like" expertise. Departmentalization can easily engender feelings of commitment and loyalty to functional groups (accounting, marketing, R&D), and turn organizational decision-making into a competitive sport in which departments battle over turf and resources.[84] Customers are almost always the losers of these battles. According to Richard C. Palermo, a vice president for quality and transition at Xerox, "If a problem has been bothering your company and your customers for years and won't yield, that problem is the result of a cross-functional dispute." He calls this Palermo's law. And Palermo's corollary is "People who work in different functions hate each other."[85]

Departmental structure refers to an organization that is divided into specialized areas such as finance, marketing, manufacturing, and human resources.

Divisional. Multiproduct or multiservice firms often take a **divisionalized structure,** with each division serving a different customer need (product-based divisions) or a different customer base (geographic divisions). Divisionalized firms tend to be more externally focused than are firms structured around functional departments, and they emphasize bottom-line results over process. To support their results focus, divisionalized firms are more likely to offer stock ownership and bonuses for companywide performance.

Divisional structure refers to an organization that has several units, each with its own departmental structure serving its own customers.

In divisionalized companies, each division, sometimes called a strategic business unit (SBU), usually operates autonomously; coordination between divisions may be modest, at best. However, too little coordination among divisions can create problems for the total corporation. To offset this problem, many large companies began to adopt matrix structures during the 1970s and 1980s.

Matrix. In a **matrix structure,** employees report to more than one boss, with each boss responsible for a different aspect of the organization.[86] For example, a clothes designer artist might report to the vice president of marketing *and* the vice president of outerwear. These vice presidents, in turn, might report to a general manager for manufacturing *and* a general manager for the North American region. In this type of structure, managers must coordinate with each other in assigning work to their subordinates, evaluating employee performance, and so on. The vast majority of medium and large companies in the U.S. are structured around functional departments, divisions, or some hybrid of these in a matrix form. Increasingly, firms such as GE, Eaton Corporation, and Weyerhaeuser are using common corporate visions, missions, values, and principles to help provide some unity and means of coordination.

Matrix structure refers to an organization whose employees report to more than one boss, each in a different unit of the company.

Structures that Cross Country Borders. The effect of structure is particularly evident in multinational companies and international joint ventures. Many terms can be used to describe global organizational structures, including *multinational*, *transnational*, and *multi-domestic.*[87] Briefly, **multinational structure** refers to an organization that has operations in more than one country and whose major business decisions are made at the headquarters. **Transnational structure** refers to an organization that also has operations in more than one country but whose major business decisions are likely made throughout the world. This structure often results from the growth of companies and the nature of the business. As companies grow, they may set up major operations in different countries. These operations may become so large, or local conditions may require, that they almost operate as independent companies, each responsible for its own major business decisions. If this structure arises as a result of the type of product—for example, restaurants—it may also be called a **multidomestic structure**.

Multinational structure refers to an organization that has operations in more than one country and whose decisions are made at headquarters.

Transnational structure refers to international organizations whose decisions are made throughout the world.

Multidomestic structure refers to international organizations whose major operations operate as independent companies.

All these global organizational structures represent alternatives. Each structure has unique implications for how people are managed, with the fundamental challenge being how to use HR activities to link globally dispersed units while also adapting to the societal requirements of host societies. Thus, the phrase "Think globally, act locally" has many HR implications. Similar challenges and implications also accompany multinational companies from different countries when they seek to collaborate in an international joint venture.

Organizational Size

Top U.S. Private Employers*

1. **General Motors** *(709,000)*
2. **Wal-Mart Stores** *(675,000)*
3. **PepsiCo** *(480,000)*
4. **Ford Motor** *(346,990)*
5. **United Parcel Service** *(337,000)*
6. **AT&T** *(299,300)*
7. **Sears Roebuck** *(275,000)*
8. **INTL Business Machines** *(252,215)*
9. **Kmart** *(250,000)*
10. **Columbia/HCA Healthcare** *(240,000)*

***Number of employees listed in parentheses.**

When the size of firms is discussed, several measures can be used. The federal government typically defines small organizations as having fewer than 500 employees. Others define small to mean fewer than 100 employees. In either case, firms over 500 employees are then labeled as large organizations. The median size of firms in the U.S. is 20 employees.

Consequence of Size. HR departments in smaller organizations tend to be small. As mentioned in Chapter 2, the number of HR professionals per 100 employees is about 1. If an organization has 50 employees, it may not even have an HR department. Such firms often outsource such items as payroll and benefits administration, but most issues relating to HR will fall to the line managers. Line managers usually have full responsibilities for designing and carrying out all the activities related to recruitment, interviewing, selection, compensation, training, performance measurement, and so on. As firms get larger, HR professionals are hired to share in the partnership between line managers and employees. When this occurs, it is important that line managers stay in the partnership equation.

Firm size is important because legal considerations impact large and small firms differently. Federal legislation generally applies to firms with 15 or more employees. State and city employment legislation, however, can apply to firms of all sizes. Firms must know which laws apply to them.

Organizational size is also an important factor in HR activities. Although exceptions exist, generally the larger the organization, the more developed its internal labor market and the less its reliance on the external labor market. In contrast, the smaller the organization, the less developed its internal labor market and the greater its reliance on the external labor market.

Internal labor market exists inside the company and it determines rates of pay, promotion, and training.

External labor market exists outside the company and it determines rate of pay, promotion, and training.

The organization that relies more on an **internal labor market** is itself the critical factor in deciding how much to pay people and what type job evaluation, job classifications, and equity will be used. For the organization that relies mostly on the **external labor market,** the determining factor in such issues as pay rates and equity will be what other organizations are doing in these areas.

Larger companies attract more attention from the media and from government regulators, and this puts more pressure on them to be socially responsive. Also, sufficient economies of scale mean that larger companies are better able to implement more costly HR technologies. In addition, larger firms are more likely to:

- Have narrowly defined jobs that use less variety of skills
- Manage for "high involvement" of employees
- Rely less on temporary staff
- Use more sophisticated procedures to recruit and select employees
- Include self-ratings and peer ratings as input for performance appraisals
- Pay employees more
- Put more pay at risk through the use of bonuses and long-term incentives
- Test employees for drugs
- Use due process procedures to handle grievances

Although larger companies generally develop more sophisticated and coordinated HR philosophy and HR practices, size alone is a great predictor of the quality of a company's HR activities.

Organizational Life Cycle

The choice of specific HR activities is also constrained by an organization's life cycle. The concept of organizational life cycle is adapted from the concept of product life cycle developed in marketing. It relates growth in sales revenues to the age of the organization, and states that organizations, like products, go through different stages of development: start-up, growth, maturity, and decline. Changing managerial priorities characterize organizations in these various developmental stages.[88] These changing priorities, in turn, have implications for HR management. For example, they have been used to argue that selection criteria and assessment methods for top-level executives need to be matched to life cycle stages.[89] The role requirements of CEOs in a rapidly growing firm are quite different from those encountered by founding CEOs when the company was in its start-up phase. Often CEOs find it difficult to switch roles, and outsider CEOs are likely to be hired when firms enter a growth phase. Similarly, the roles of the CEOs and top-level executives change again as the firm moves out of a period of rapid growth and into a stage of maturity or perhaps decline. These changes in the needs of the organization, in turn, influence staffing decisions. The life cycle concept is useful for planning how an organization may need to change its activities as it evolves. Its use is illustrated in more detail in Chapter 12, where life cycle stages are related to compensation practices.

Type of Business (Manufacturing Vs. Service Sectors)

The U.S. and global economies can be carved up into many different industry sectors, commonly classified by Standard Industrial Classification (SIC) numbers. Two of these sectors are manufacturing and service.[90] During the 19th century, the U.S. economy was based on agriculture, trades, and crafts. Henry Ford's assembly line quickly changed all that, and for most of the 20th century, mass manufacturing industries dominated the U.S. economy. During the industrial era, most of the U.S. workforce moved off the farm and out of small shops into large, formal business organizations. Their work focused on producing, distributing, and selling standardized goods. Formal approaches to managing human resources were developed in this context.

As we approach and move into the 21st century, the U.S. economy is completing yet another transformation, this time from a manufacturing to a service economy. The second half of the 20th century saw the number of blue-collar production jobs cut in half, while white-collar administrative and service jobs tripled.

As the transformation of our economy unfolds, it is becoming clear that managing human resources in the service sector demands a new approach. A service company that manages its employees the same way big manufacturing firms do will probably not be successful.

Three characteristics distinguish services from manufacturing, and they all have implications for managing human resources. First, most services involve something intangible. Second, the customer and employee usually collaborate in the production-and-delivery process for services. Third, production and consumption of services are usually simultaneous; that is, as soon as a service is produced, it is being received and "consumed" by the customer.[91] In theory, these distinctions are sometimes sharply drawn, but in reality, many firms cannot be easily classified as service versus manufacturing because their activities include both components. Furthermore, some types of services are more intangible and simultaneous than others. The dinner at a nice restaurant evidently has some tangible product (the food), as well as some intangibles (the ambiance, the server's manner, etc.).

For supervisors, the intangible nature of services makes it difficult to monitor employee performance directly, so traditional means of quality control—the inspect-and-reject model—are useless. The imperative for service employees is getting the job done right the first time. This means employees must be fully capable

Did You KNOW?

"The factory of the future will have only two employees, a man and a dog. The man will be there to feed the dog. The dog will be there to keep the man from touching the equipment."

Warren Bennis
Author and Distinguished Professor of Business Administration
University of Southern California

of monitoring their own performance. It also means supervisors must trust employees to monitor themselves.[92]

In services, the customer plays a unique role. Because they are essential to service delivery, customers may be thought of as partial employees. This means they are subject to being managed by the company, and they can be expected to participate in the process of managing regular employees.[93] For example, employers in the service sector often ask customers for input in the performance appraisals of regular employees.[94]

Differences in the nature of manufacturing and service also have implications for other HR practices, including recruitment, compensation, the employment of temporary workers, the development and maintenance of appropriate organizational climates and cultures, and stress management. For example, more employee training and socialization occur in services than in the manufacturing sector. Also, service firms can benefit more by attending carefully to the personal characteristics of employees, such as friendliness and a pleasant smile, instead of focusing solely on skills and abilities. However, some evidence suggests that manufacturing firms that are pursuing total quality and continuous improvement goals are also seeking employees with technical skills *and* a willingness to work cooperatively with others in teams.

Competitive Strategies

Organizations continually develop strategies to beat their competitors. These strategies include:

- Quality improvement
- Cost reduction
- Innovation
- Speed and responsiveness

These are significant for HR management because they determine needed employee behaviors. That is, for competitive strategies to be successfully implemented, employees have to behave in certain ways. Keep in mind the general model shown in Exhibit 3.11 as you read the following text.

Quality Improvement. Organizations are continually confronted and challenged with the need to deliver quality goods and services. As consumers, we continue to demand high-quality products and are willing to buy from whomever offers such products. In the international arena, the standards of quality keep going up: what was acceptable quality yesterday is unacceptable today. Thus, organizations must continue to pursue quality improvement with a vengeance; HR management is central to quality improvement.

Do you think the quality of service you get from a bank has anything to do with the treatment you get from the bank's tellers? Do you think the quality of products such as a stereo, VCR, CD player, or car has anything to do with level of motivation, dedication, training, and commitment of the individuals making these products? Of course. In both cases, product quality depends on the people we are dealing with as well as on the people behind the scenes who make the products. Total quality depends on all parts of the organization working together. Consequently, organizations are bound to give increasing attention to their human resources as they seek to enhance their product quality. Further implications of quality improvement are described in detail in Chapter 10, Performance Appraisal.

Cost Reduction. We all want quality; but, if there are two products with equal quality, which will you buy? Even as organizations enhance quality, they also seek to reduce costs. Consequently, we are likely to see large organizations continue workforce reductions throughout this decade.

EXHIBIT 3.11

Competitive Strategies and Managing Human Resources

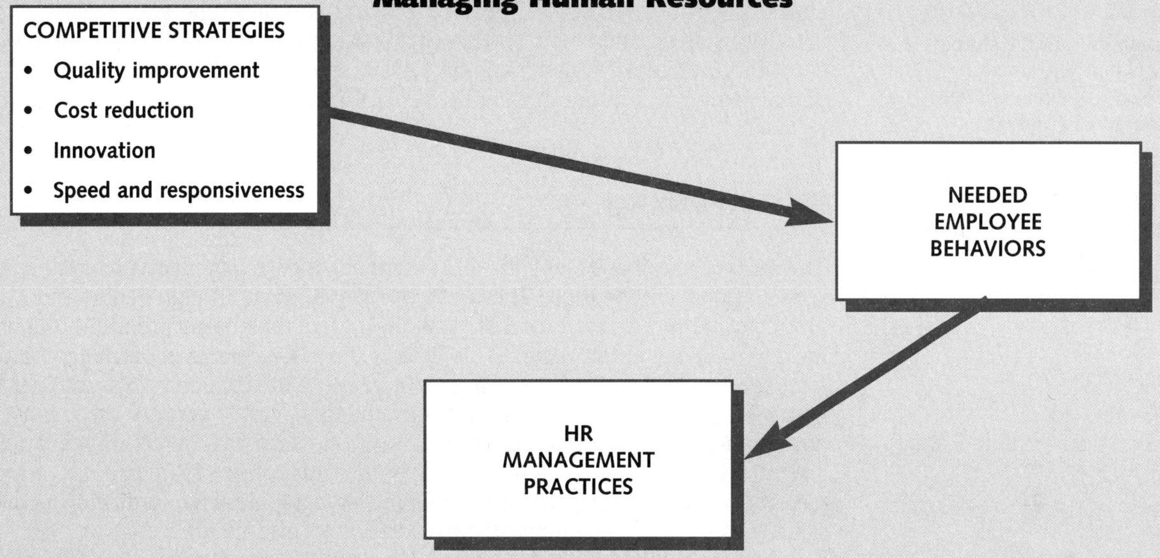

Source: Adapted from R. S. Schuler and S. E. Jackson, "Linking Competitive Strategies with Human Resource Practices," *Academy of Management Executive* (August 1987): 207–219.

We are also likely to see organizations take advantage of substantial wage disparities by shifting some production outside the U.S. Workers will also be asked to hold down wage demands and to become more flexible in job assignments, or both, as organizations try to reduce their costs of operation. This is especially true in service-oriented organizations, where the cost of labor is a relatively large percentage of the total operations cost.

Innovation. A third competitive strategy is the continued need to develop new products and offer new services. The same environment that necessitates quality improvement and cost reduction also necessitates innovation. Some observers believe this is where the U.S. should concentrate its efforts. If we cannot make the cheapest or the highest-quality products, we can at least develop products no one else has and get them to market faster once we have developed them. Innovation requires careful HR management; it takes highly talented people managed very effectively to develop new products and ideas. Some U.S. firms such as Motorola have shown that they can do this rather well. The challenge in the future is for more firms to do this and for those doing it to stay ahead of domestic and international competitors.

Speed and responsiveness mean satisfying the customer quickly and correctly.

Speed and Responsiveness. Concern about quality, cost, and innovation reflects the general issue of being responsive to the environment. The world order is changing and will continue to change. Although some trends are somewhat predictable, increasingly, changes are becoming unpredictable and are having a greater effect on managing human resources. Speed and responsiveness, as well as accuracy, have become critical. Decentralized decision-making helps companies make decisions faster, and with more knowledge of the customer. But it requires companies to empower their employees—that is, to give their employees the power and ability to make organizational decisions.

Did You KNOW?

Communication technology is radically changing the speed, direction, and amount of information flow, even as it alters work roles all across organizations. As a case in point, the number of secretaries is down 521,000 just since 1987.

The changing market may also require organizations to be able to quickly reduce, expand, or fundamentally change their workforce. A contingent workforce allows a company to reduce output in line with market demand. Longer term, in anticipation of major market changes, companies can train their employees to enable them to serve different customers, use new machinery, or sell new products. With speed and responsiveness growing in importance as we approach and enter the 21st century, many companies are experimenting with new approaches to managing human resources with the goal of increasing workforce flexibility.

Summary

The rest of the 1990s will be filled with change, challenge, uncertainty, and intense global competition. The marketplace will demand high-quality innovative products and services at low cost. There is a higher-than-ever premium on obtaining and utilizing information. This means the HR department must continually scan the external environment to stay abreast of international and national economic activity, social and demographic changes, and technological trends and developments. Using this information, the HR department can create scenarios on how these external environmental forces will impact the organization. For example, an environmental scan of workforce demographics may indicate upcoming skilled labor shortages among U.S. workers, but also indicate that any shortfalls may be made up by new immigrants. Keeping abreast of external environmental changes allows the HR department to craft effective organizational responses.

Given the current external environment, organizational success results when organizations are:

- Capable of rapid response
- Flexible
- Adaptable
- Focused
- Lean and cost-oriented
- Quality-oriented
- Customer-oriented
- Innovative

For responses to be effective, they must be sufficiently anticipated, discussed, and shared with all employees, then implemented with full support of the organization.

The HR department must also scan the internal environment to stay attuned to changes in organizational strategies and directions, the needs of the workforce and line managers as they seek to make their organizations more competitive, flexible, adaptable, and focused. Combining these internal characteristics with the external conditions, HR professionals will help their companies recruit and develop employees who are:

- Adaptable
- Committed
- Motivated
- Skilled/reskilled
- Highly energetic
- Good performers in diverse employee groups
- Good team players

Key Concepts

baby boomers
baby busters
business objectives
business values
contingent workers
corporate culture
departmental structure
divisional structure
downsizing
empower
external environment
external labor market
glass ceiling
HR objectives
HR philosophy
internal environment
internal labor market
job sex-typing
matrix structure
multidomestic structure
multinational structure
organizational life cycle
organizational size
organizational strategy
organizational structure
outsourcing
ownership
sex-role stereotyping
telematics technologies
traditionalists
transnational structure
values
virtual corporation
vision
workforce diversity

Review and Discussion Questions

1. Why did BMW locate in Spartanburg, South Carolina?
2. What is the impact of domestic and international competition on managing human resources?
3. What workforce and demographic changes are likely to significantly affect HR management? Describe the nature of the effects.
4. What can U.S. firms do to manage diversity in the workforce?
5. Do you expect that by the year 2000 jobs will no longer be sex-role stereotyped?
6. Should U.S. employers encourage a greater influx of immigrants? What are the HR implications of this issue?
7. How are the economic, technological, and organizational trends discussed in this chapter impacting HR management?
8. Explain the impact on managing human resources from: company vision, business objectives and values, CEO's leadership style, assumptions about the way people work, corporate culture, organizational structure, organizational size, organizational life cycle, type of business, and competitive strategies.
9. What are your assumptions about people at work?
10. How can assumptions about people at work influence how companies manage their human resources?

PROJECTS, EXERCISES & CASES

End-of-Text Project

Lincoln

1. Using the Lincoln Electric case at the end of the text, describe the impact/relevance of the following environmental factors on the company's HR objectives and practices:
   a. the global economy
   b. its current technology
   c. the size of Lincoln Electric (primarily by number of employees, but also by sales)
   d. its form of organization, particularly its use of teams vs. individuals

e. its competitive strategy
f. top management's philosophies, visions, and values
g. its business objectives

2. What are the business objectives and the HR objectives of Lincoln Electric?

Nordstrom

1. Using the Nordstrom case at the end of the text, describe the impact/relevance of the following environmental factors on the company's HR objectives and practices:
   a. the global economy
   b. its current technology
   c. the size of Nordstrom (primarily by number of employees, but also by sales)
   d. its form of organization, particularly its use of teams vs. individuals
   e. its competitive strategy
   f. top management's philosophies, visions, and values
   g. its business objectives
2. What are the business objectives and the HR objectives of Nordstrom?

Field Projects

1. Select an organization, large or small, with which you are familiar. Identify and describe the characteristics of its environment and their impact on how the organization manages its human resources.
2. Interview four people, two from a large organization and two from a small organization. Ask them to describe their organization's culture, particularly as it relates to managing people. Report to the class the differences and your explanation for them.
3. Analyze the labor force in your local area. Report on the number employed, what type of work they perform, their pay levels, the number unemployed, etc. How are the characteristics of the local labor force viewed by companies in the area? Are the characteristics of the labor force an attraction for companies? Is the labor force more attractive for some types of companies and less attractive for other types of companies? Explain.

VISIT THE LIBRARY

Workforce Online: An Introduction

For more in-depth reading about HR activities in companies you know, visit the Internet Library.

1. Enter your Web browser.
2. Enter "Workforce Online." To do this, follow the directions provided in the Visit the Internet Library in Chapter 2 exercise (steps 2 through 4). Alternatively, you can simply type the following address into the address field: **http://www.workforceonline.com**
3. Select "Winning Ideas." In the process of doing this, you may be asked to enter your username and password.
4. Find and review the following articles within "Winning Ideas":

   Colgate's Global HR Unites Under One Strategy

   Strategic HR at First Chicago

   HR's Vital Role at Levi Strauss

   Hewlett-Packard's Core Values Drive HR Strategy

   Community Service Helps UPS Develop Managers

6. Find and review the following articles under the keyword "Research Center":

   Customer Service Drives Reengineering Effort

   New Technology is HR's Route to Engineering

   HR Leaders Brainstorm the Profession's Future

   HR Unites the World of Coca-Cola

7. Return to "Workforce Online" homepage.

Case: Business and HR Objectives at the Barden Corporation

Background

The largest segment of the Barden Corporation is the Precision Bearings Division. It manufactures high-precision ball bearings for machine tools, aircraft instruments and accessories, aircraft engines, computer peripherals, textile spindles, and medical and dental equipment. Currently, the division employs about 1,000 people and includes a marketing department and a small corporate staff. It was founded during World War II to manufacture the special bearings needed for the Norden bombsight and has been nonunion since the beginning (which gives you a hint about the culture). Mr. Donald Brush, vice president and general manager of the Precision Bearings Division, gives the following description of his division.

Reporting directly to me is a small staff comprising a manufacturing manager, a quality manager, an engineering manager, a director of manufacturing planning, and a manager of human resources (Exhibit 1). We meet several times a week to discuss current problems, as well as short and long-range opportunities and needs. On alternate weeks, we augment this group by including the supervisory personnel who report to the senior managers listed above. I might interject here that all supervisors meet with hourly employees on either a weekly or biweekly basis to review specific departmental successes and failures, and to otherwise keep employees informed about the business and to encourage ownership of their jobs. The managers themselves meet on call as the Employee Relations Committee to discuss and recommend approval of a wide range of issues that include the evaluation and audit of hourly and salaried positions, as well as the creation and modification of all divisional personnel policies.

A few words about our Human Resource Department: There are six employees who together provide the basic services of employment, affirmative action, employee activity support, labor relations, interpretation of the federal and state laws, benefits administration, wage and salary administration, records preparation and maintenance, cafeteria supervision, and so on. There are, in addition, two people who coordinate our rather extensive training activities.

As currently organized, the Medical Department comes under the supervision of the manager of human resources. Its authorized staff includes a medical director, the manager of employee health and safety (who is an occupational health nurse), a staff nurse, a safety specialist, and secretary/clerk.

The development and execution of plans and programs, including those of a strategic nature, almost invariably involve the active participation of HR. And that's how we want it to

CASE EXHIBIT 1

Precision Bearings Division

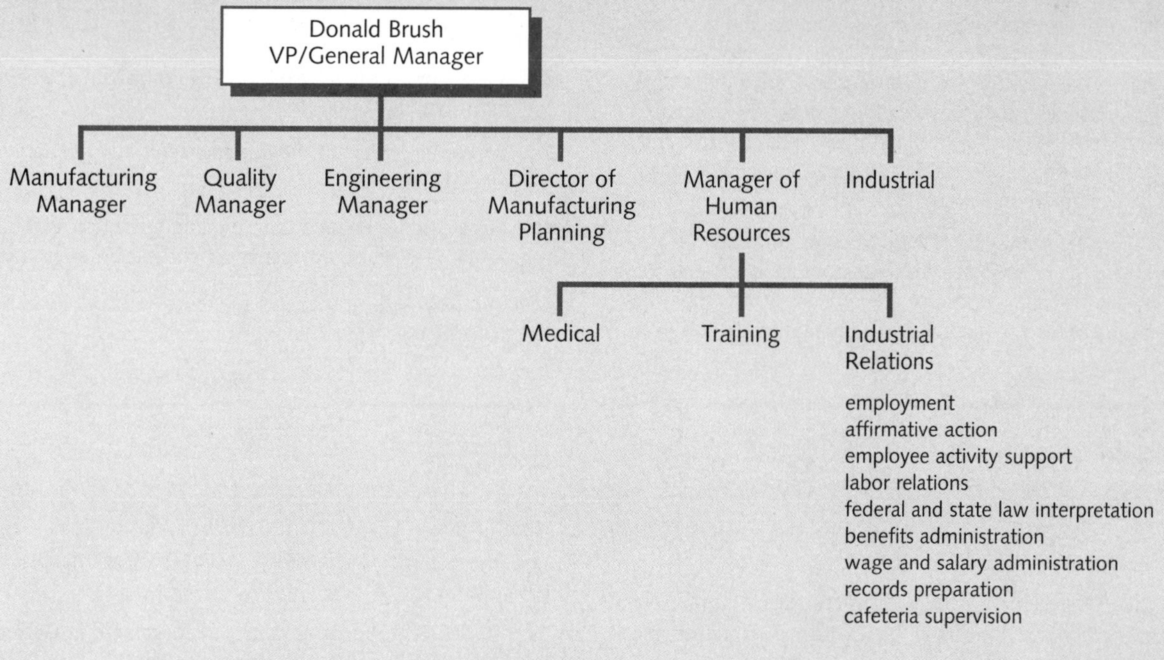

be. On the other hand, the HR Department doesn't run the business. By this I mean they don't hire or fire, promote or demote. They don't write job descriptions or determine salaries or wages. All these things are done by the line managers with the HR Department providing a framework to ensure consistency and that all actions are appropriate to company goals. You might say that HR is our "Jiminy cricket"—they are there for advice, consent, and, importantly, as a conscience.

Business Objectives Impact HR Objectives

During the past several months, we have been running into many issues that affect the very essence of our business objectives: growth, profits, survival, and competitiveness. Because the issues involve our human resources, these must be our major HR objectives. Would you please give us your experience, expertise, and suggestions as to how we can solve them? Thanks! The following briefly describes the nature of each of the four HR objectives.

HR Objective: Recruiting and Training New Hourly Employees. The need to recruit and train approximately 125 new hourly workers to respond to a surge in business is very challenging. By mid-year, it became evident that we had an opportunity to significantly increase our business. In order to achieve otherwise attainable goals, we need to increase our hourly work force by a net of about 125 employees (that is, in addition to normal turnover, retirements, etc.) in one year. I have asked HR to test the waters, recognizing the unemployment in the Danbury labor market for skilled workers has reached an unprecedented low of about 2.5%.

HR Objective: Safety and Occupational Health Improvement. The need to create a heightened awareness by the workforce for safety and occupational health considerations is very important. This is an evolving mission born of a dissatisfaction on our part about "safety as usual." Over the years, Barden employees have assumed that, because we are a metalworking shop, people were just going to get hurt. But we cannot afford to have people get hurt and miss work anymore. Yet, as our workforce ages, the employees seem to get out of shape and become more injury and illness prone.

HR Objective: Managing Health Costs of an Aging Workforce. The spiraling health costs of an aging and, sometimes, out-of-shape work force are very costly. All employers face this. Barden's problem is a little unique in that hourly employees tend to stay with the company and retire from the company. For example, we still have several employees whose careers began with us 45 years ago, shortly after the company was founded. Our average age approaches 45 for employees and their dependent spouses. Generally, our jobs do not require much physical effort, and it's easy to become out of shape. As a consequence, employees get sick, use hospitals, and have accidents.

HR Objective: New Machines and the Development of Qualified Workers. The technological evolution of increasingly complex machinery and related manufacturing equipment, and the development of trained workers to operate and maintain this equipment, are important facts of life. This process is unceasing and requires a good deal of planning for both the short- and the long-run. For example, what should we do in the next year, or five years out, in order to remain competitive in terms of cost, quality, and service? Buying and rebuilding machines is part of the story. Running them efficiently is quite another. As you know, modern equipment of this sort requires operational people who are not only knowledgeable about the turning or grinding of metals, but also conversant with computerized numerical controls. The employee who sets up and operates a $500,000 machine must be well trained. Yet finding trained people is getting more difficult.

Summary

Mr. Brush knows that these HR objectives all reflect the increasing diversity of the workforce. Because of this, he knows these issues will be around for a long time. Therefore, he requests that you provide him with your general ideas and suggestions. He doesn't want details at this time.

Case Questions

1. Are these HR objectives facing Mr. Brush really very important?
2. On which HR objectives is the HR department able to be most helpful?
3. At Barden, who are the line managers and who are the employees?
4. How can the HR manager, the line managers, and the employees work together to meet these HR objectives?

Source: This case was prepared by Randall S. Schuler, who expresses his appreciation for the cooperation of Donald Brush.

Chapter 3 Endnotes

1. P. Sellers, "Can Wal-Mart Get Back the Magic?" *Fortune* (April 29, 1996): 130–136.

2. M. Tennesen, "HR Faces Distinct Issues in Rural Areas," *Personnel Journal* (June 1994): 112–120; D. Woodruff and J. Templeman, "Why Mercedes is Alabama Bound," *Business Week* (October 11, 1993): 138–139; B. Vlasic, "In Alabama, The Soul of a New Mercedes?" *Business Week* (March 31, 1997): 70–71.

3. C. Scholz, "Human Resource Management in Germany," Universitat des Saarlandes, November 1994.

4. Ibid.

5. I. Morrison, *The Second Curve: Managing the Velocity of Change* (New York: Ballentine Books, 1996); L. C. Thurow, *How Today's Economic Forces Shape Tomorrow's World* (New York: William Morrow & Company, 1996); D. Q. Mills, *The New Competitors* (New York: Wiley, 1985): 19; and J. C. Grayson and C. O'Dell, *Two Minute Warning* (New York: The Free Press, 1988).

6. R. Maynard, "Trade Tide Rises Across the Pacific," *Nation's Business* (November 1995): 52–55; R. Maynard, "Hot Markets Overseas," *Nation's Business* (June 1995): 42–44.

7. J. Aley, "New Lift for the U.S. Export Boom," *Fortune* (November 13, 1995): 73–78; L. Uchitelle, "U.S. Corporations Expanding Abroad at a Quicker Pace: Creating Jobs Overseas," *New York Times* (July 25, 1994): A1, D2; R. Norton, "Strategies for the New Export Boom," *Fortune* (August 22, 1994): 125–30; "Top Fifty U.S. Industrial Exporters," *Fortune* (August 22, 1994): 132; "The Year of Mixed Results," *Fortune* (August 22, 1994): 181–82; "The One Hundred Largest Diversified Service Companies," *Fortune* (August 22, 1994): 183–207.

8. C. Farrell et al., "It Won't Take Your Breath Away, but... the Economy Is Posed for Modest, Steady Growth This Year," *Business Week* (January 10, 1994): 60–66.

9. W. B. Johnston, "Global Workforce 2000: The New World Labor Market," *Harvard Business Review* (March–April 1991): 115–127.

10. Johnston, "Global Workforce 2000."

11. D. Harbrecht, G. Smith, and S. Baker, "The Mexican Worker, " *Business Week* (April 19, 1993): 84–130.

12. U.S. Department of Education, National Center for Education Statistics, *Digest of Education Statistics* (Washington, D.C., 1989): Table 341, pp. 386–387.

13. P. J. Dowling, R. S. Schuler, and D. Welch, *International Dimensions of Human Resource Management, 2nd ed.* (Belmont, CA: Wadsworth, 1994).

14. N. C. Nash, "Luxuries They Can't Afford," *New York Times* (September 13, 1995): D1, 22; D. Foust and M. Mallory, "The Boom Belt," *Business Week* (September 27, 1993): 98–102; J. Templeman, "A Serious Blow to German Competitiveness," *Business Week* (March 27, 1995): 60.

15. K. Matthes, *HR Focus* (March 1992): 1.

16. M. G. Duerr, "International Business Management: Its Four Tasks," *Conference Board Record* (1986): 43.

17. Materials here on Wal-Mart and Sam Walton were compiled from several sources including: P. Sellers, "Can Wal-Mart Get Back the Magic?" *Fortune* (April 29, 1996): 130–136; M. Kuntz et al., "Reinventing the Store," *Business Week* (November 27, 1995): 84–96; C. Rapoport, "Retailers Go Global," *Fortune* (February 20, 1995): 102–108; S. Walton, "Sam Walton in His Own Words," *Fortune* (June 29, 1992): 98–106; B. Saporito, "A Week Aboard the Wal-Mart Express," *Fortune* (August 24, 1993): 77–84; V. Johnston and H. Moore, "Pride Drives Wal-Mart to Service Excellence," *HR Magazine* (October 1991): 79–82; J. Huey, "America's Most Successful Merchant, "*Fortune* (September 23, 1991): 46–59; T. C. Hayes, "Wal-Mart's Late Founder Still Stirs Stockholders," *New York Times* (June 6, 1992): 39. By no means is Wal-Mart without fault or criticism. For some commentary on this, particularly in their alleged use of low-wage Chinese workers for products made in China (at a time when the firm was known for its "Made in America" campaign), see T. C. Hayes, "Wal-Mart Disputes Report on Labor," *New York Times* (December 24, 1992): D1, D4. For some discussion on its movements into areas that bring competition to towns, see B. J. Feder, "Message for Mom & Pop: There's Life After Wal-Mart," *New York Times* (October 24, 1993): F4; J. Steinberg, "One Town's Stores Plot Survival As Wal-Mart Grows in Northeast," *New York Times* (November 28, 1993): A1; 4.

18. P. Dowling, R. S. Schuler, and D. Welch, *International Dimensions of Human Resource Management, 2nd ed.* (Belmont, CA: Wadsworth, 1994).

19. P. Oster et al., "The Fast Track Leads Overseas," *Business Week* (November 1, 1993): 64–68.

20. R. L. Tung, "Managing Cross-National and Intra-National Diversity," *Human Resource Management* (Winter 1993): 461–477.

21. C. M. Solomon, "Transplanting Corporate Cultures Globally," *Personnel Journal* (October 1993): 80–88.

22. Ibid.

23. J. R. Fulkerson and R. S. Schuler, "Managing Worldwide Diversity at Pepsi-Cola International," in S. E. Jackson, ed., *Diversity in the Workplace: Human Resource Initiatives* (New York: Guilford Press, 1992).

24. Source: "Pepsi's Expectations," *HR Reporter* (July 1987): 4–5. Used by permission of HR Reporter, copyright 1987.

25. W. H. Miller, "Employers Wrestle with 'Dumb' Kids," *Industry Week* (July 4, 1988): 47.

26. B. Nussbaum, "Needed: Human Capital," *Business Week* (Sept. 19, 1988): 100; A. P. Carnevale, L.J. Gainer, and A. S. Meltzer, *Workplace Basics: The Essential Skills Employers Want* (San Francisco: Jossey-Bass, 1990); A. P. Carnevale, L. J. Gainer, and E. Schulz, *Training the Technical Workforce* (San Francisco: Jossey-Bass, 1990).

27. R. Narisetti, "Job Paradox: Manufacturers Decry A Shortage of Workers While Rejecting Many," *The Wall Street Journal* (September 8, 1995): A1, 4; K. Miller, "Dwindling Supply of Engineers Brings a Sense of Desperation to Auto Makers," *The Wall Street Journal* (June 7, 1994): B3.

28. Narisetti, "Job Paradox: Manufacturers Decry a Shortage of Workers While Rejecting Many"; Miller, "Dwindling Supply of Engineers Brings a Sense of Desperation to Auto Makers."

29. C . M. Solomon, "Managing the Baby Busters," *Personnel Journal* (March 1992): 54–60.

30. "Managing Generation X," *Bulletin to Management* (November 30, 1995): 384; B. Tulgan, *Managing Generation*

X: How to Bring Out the Best in Young Talent (New York, NY: American Management Association, 1995); B. Paik Sunoo, "How to Manage Generation X," *Personnel Journal* (December 1995): 118; L. Carleton, "Vacationing, Generation X Style," *Training* (September 1995): 17; J. Spiers, "The Baby Boomlet is for Real," *Fortune* (February 10, 1992): 101–104; "Downward Mobility," *Business Week* (March 23, 1992): 56–63; N. Hale, *The Older Worker* (San Francisco: Jossey-Bass, 1990); also see S. Ratan, "Why Busters Hate Boomers," *Fortune* (October 4, 1993): 56–70. L. Zinn, "Teens," *Business Week* (April 11, 1994): 76–86.

31. N. Perry, "Saving the School: How Business Can Help, " *Fortune* (November 7, 1988): 45.

32. Ibid.

33. J. F. Coates, J. Jarratt, and J. B. Mahaffie, "Future Work," *The Futurist* (May–June 1991); J. F. Coates, J. Jarratt, and J. B. Mahaffie, *Future Work: Seven Critical Forces Reshaping Work and the Workforce in North America* (San Francisco: Jossey-Bass, 1990).

34. E. T. Smith, "The Baby Boom That Has to End," *Business Week* (April 11, 1994): 73; L. Zinn et al., "Teens: Here Comes the Biggest Wave Yet," *Business Week* (April 11, 1994): 76–86; W. B. Johnston, *Workforce 2000* (Indianapolis: Hudson Institute, 1987); G. Gallup, Forecast 2000 (New York: Simon and Schuster, 1988); C. D. Fyock, *America's Workforce Is Coming of Age* (Lexington, Mass.: Heath/Lexington Books, 1990).

35. R. Glier, "The Math Gap," *Profiles* (August 1993): 58.

36. Tulgan, *Managing Generation X: How to Bring Out the Best in Young Talent.*

37. Sunoo, "How to Manage Generation X"; Carleton, "Vacationing, Generation X Style."

38. G. Koretz, "The Upside of America's Population Surge," *Business Week* (August 9, 1993): 20.

39. G. Koretz, "The Good News About Fertility," *Business Week* (June 12, 1995): 28.

40. "U.S. Department of Labor Women's Bureau: Facts on Women Workers," *Bulletin to Management* (April 14, 1994): 118; J. F. Coates, J. Jarratt, and J. B. Mahaffie, "Future Work," *The Futurist* (May–June 1991): 11.

41. *Personnel* (December 1990): 17. For a discussion of these data and issues, see Johnston, *Workforce 2000*; P.T. Kilborn, "More Women Take Low-Wage Jobs Just So Their Families Can Get By," *New York Times* (March 13, 1994): 23; R. R. Thomas, Jr., "From Affirmative Action to Affirming Diversity," *Harvard Business Review* (March–April 1990): 107–117; C. M. Solomon, "Careers Under Glass," *Personnel Journal* (April 1990): 96–105; J. Fierman, "Why Women Still Don't Hit the Top," *Fortune* (July 30, 1990): 41–62; W. Konrad, "Welcome to the Woman-Friendly Company," *Business Week* (August 6, 1990): 48–52; J. Nelson Horchler, "Derailing the Mommy Track," *Industry Week* (August 6, 1990): 22–26.

42. R. Sharpe, "Family Friendly Firms Don't Always Promote Females," *The Wall Street Journal* (March 29, 1994): B1, 5; R. Sharpe, "The Waiting Game: Women Make Strides, But Men Stay Firmly in Top Company Jobs," *The Wall Street Journal* (March 29, 1994): A1; D. L. Jacobs, "Back From the Mommy Track," *New York Times* (October 9, 1994): Sec. 3, 1–2; "Glass Ceiling Report," *Bulletin to Management* (April 6, 1995): 108; F. Schwartz, "Don't Write Women Off As Leaders," *Fortune* (June 8, 1987): 185; C. Cockburn, *In the Way of Women: Men's Resistance to Sex Equality in Organizations* (Ithaca, NY: ILR Press, School of Industrial and Labor Relations, Cornell University, 1991); K. A. Matthews and J. Rodin, "Women's Changing Work Roles: Impact on Health, Family, and Public Policy," *American Psychologist* (November 1989): 1389–1393. But also see E. Riley, "More Women Are Executive VPs," *Fortune* (July 12, 1993): 16; "Women, Sex and Power" *Fortune* (August 5, 1996): 42–56.

43. J. J. Laabs, "Diversity Training Is a Business Strategy," *Personnel Journal* (September 1993): 25–26; S. E. Jackson and Associates, *Diversity in the Workplace: Human Resource Initiatives* (New York: The Guilford Press, 1992); J. D. Goodchilds (ed.), *Psychological Perspectives on Human Diversity in America: Master Lectures* (Washington, D.C.: American Psychological Association, 1991); J. P. Fernandez, *Managing a Diverse Workforce: Regaining the Competitive Edge* (Lexington, Mass.: Lexington Books, 1991); D. Jamieson and J. O'Mara, *Managing Workforce 2000: Gaining the Diversity Advantage* (San Francisco: Jossey Bass, 1991); L. I. Kessler, *Managing Diversity in an Equal Opportunity Workplace* (Washington, D.C.: National Foundation for the Study of Employment Policy, 1990); S. B. Thiederman, *Bridging Cultural Barriers for Corporate Success* (Lexington, Mass.: Lexington Books, 1991); R. R. Thomas, Jr., *Beyond Race and Gender: Unleashing the Power of Your Total Workforce by Managing Diversity* (New York: AMACOM, 1991); P. Stuart, "What Does the Glass Ceiling Cost You?" *Personnel Journal* (November 1992): 70–79.

44. M. Galen and A. Palmer, "White, Male, and Worried," *Business Week* (January 31, 1994): 50–56; L. Copeland, "Valuing Diversity, Part 2: Pioneers and Champions of Change," *Personnel* (1988): 48; H. Jain, B. M. Pitts, and G. De Santis (eds.), *Equality for All: National Conference on Racial Equality in the Workplace—Retrospect and Prospect* (Hamilton, Ontario, Canada: McMaster University and IRRA, Hamilton and District Chapter, 1991); A. Dastmalchian, P. Blyton, and R. Adamson, *The Climate of Workplace Relations* (New York: Rutledge, a Division of Rutledge, Chapman and Hall, 1991).

45. J. Greenberg, "The Social Side of Fairness: Interpersonal and Informational Classes of Organizational Justice," in R. Cropanzano, ed., *Justice in the Workplace Approaching Fairness in Human Resource Management* (Hillsdale, NJ: Lawrence Erlbaum Associates, Publishers, 1993).

46. "Arbitration Provisions in Union Agreements in 1949," *Monthly Labor Review 70* (1950): 160–165.

47. G. P. Zachary, "White-Collar Blues," *The Wall Street Journal* (March 17, 1993): A1, 8; "The Economics of Aging," *Business Week* (September 12, 1994): 60–66.

48. K. N. Gilpin, "Corporate Profits Are Robust, Despite Slowing Growth," *New York Times* (August 4, 1995): D3; J. C. Cooper and K. Madigan, "More Jobs + Productivity = A Free Lunch," *Business Week* (March 21, 1994): 31.

49. J. E. Ellis and C. Del Valle, "Tall Order for Small Businesses," *Business Week* (April 19, 1993): 114–118; J. Gordon, "Into the Dark," *Training* (July 1993): 21–30; W. Woods, "The Jobs Americans Hold," *Fortune* (July 12, 1993): 33–41; L. S. Richman, "Jobs That Are Growing and Slowing," *Fortune* (July 12, 1993): 52–55.

50. J. Aley, "Where the Jobs Are," *Fortune* (September 18, 1995): 53.

51. J. F. Coates, J. Jarratt, and J. B. Mahaffie, "Future Work," *The Futurist* (May–June 1991).

52. K. Hube, "Where the Jobs Will Be in '96 (Hint: Think Healthy)," *Money Forecast 1996*: 21–24; J. Gilbert, "The Best Jobs in America," *Money* (March 1994): 70–79; A. Cortese, "Manhattan Turns into 'Silicon Valley'," *Business Week* (January 30, 1996): 82–83; "Rethinking Work," *Business Week* (October 17, 1994): 80–81; *Training America: Learning to Work for the 21st Century* (Alexandria, Va.: American Society for Training and Development, 1990); "The American Workforce, 1994–2005," *Bulletin to Management* (January 4, 1996): 4–5.

53. Coates, Jarratt, and Mahaffie, "Future Work."

54. O. Port, "The Responsive Factory," *Business Week/Enterprise 1993*: 48; P. S. Adler, *Technology and the Future of Work* (New York: Oxford University Press, 1992).

55. J. P. Womack, D. T. Jones, and D. Roos, "How Lean Production Can Change the World," *New York Times Magazine* (September 23, 1990): 20–24, 34, 38; A. Taylor III, "New Lessons From Japan's Carmakers," *Fortune* (October 22, 1990): 165–166.

56. S. Zuboff, *In the Age of the Smart Machine: The Future of Work and Power* (New York: Basic Books, 1988). See also B. Garson, *The Electronic Sweatshop* (New York: Simon and Schuster, 1988).

57. M. J. Piore and C. F. Sabel, *The Second Industrial Divide: Possibilities for Prosperity* (New York: Basic Books, 1984).

58. Coates, "An Environmental Scan: Projecting Future Human Resources Trends," *Human Resource Planning* (December 1987): 219.

59. A. Kupfer, "Managing Now for the 1990's," *Fortune* (September 26, 1988): 44–47.

60. J. Main, "The Winning Organization," *Fortune* (September 26, 1988): 50–56; J. A. Byrne, "The Horizontal Corporation," *Business Week* (December 20, 1993): 76–81.

61. Kupfer, "Managing Now for the 1990's," 47.

62. R. Jacob, "The Struggle to Create an Organization for the 21st Century," *Fortune* (April 3, 1995): 90–99.

63. T. Peters, *Thriving on Chaos* (New York: Alfred Knopf, 1987): 123.

64. D. Anfuso, "Novell Idea: A Map for Mergers," *Personnel Journal* (March 1994): 48–55.

65. "Doing Mergers by the Book Aids Growth," *Personnel Journal* (January 1994): 59.

66. A. F. Buono and J. L. Bowditch, *The Human Side of Mergers and Acquisitions: Managing Collisions between People, Cultures, and Organizations* (San Francisco: Jossey-Bass, 1989).

67. J. A. Byrne, R. Brandt, and O. Port, "The Virtual Corporation," *Business Week* (February 8, 1993): 98–103; S. Tully, "The Modular Corporation," *Fortune* (February 8, 1993): 106; W. H. Davidow and M. S. Malone, *The Virtual Corporation* (1992); A. Taylor III, "The New Golden Age of Autos," *Fortune* (April 4, 1994): 51–66.

68. P. B. Doeringer and M. J. Piore, *Internal Labor Markets and Manpower Analysis* (Lexington, Mass.: Heath, 1971); P. Osterman, ed., *Internal Labor Markets* (Cambridge, Mass.: London, 1984).

69. J. Aley, "The Temp Biz Boom: Why It's Good," *Fortune* (October 16, 1995): 53–55; R. Kuttner, "Talking Marriage and Thinking One-Night Stand," *Business Week* (October 18, 1993): 16; S. Bing, "Outsource This, You Turkeys!" *Fortune* (December 11, 1995): 43; J. Fierman, "The Contingency Workforce," *Fortune* (January 24, 1994): 30–36; B. Paik Sunoo and J. J. Laabs, "Winning Strategies for Outsourcing Contracts," *Personnel Journal* (March 1994): 71–78; J. Scott Lord, "Contract Recruiting: Coming of Age," *Personnel Administrator* (November 1987): 49–53. See also L. Carroll, "Strategies to Make Outplacement an INHOUSE Program," *HR Focus* (September 1993): 12–13; R. Henkoff, "Getting Beyond Downsizing," *Fortune* (January 10, 1994): 58–64; S. Caudron, "Calculating the Cost of Contingent Workers," *Personnel Journal* (November 1994): 48a–c.

70. J. Holusha, "Industry Is Learning to Love Agility," *New York Times* (May 25, 1994): D1, 5; B. Geber, "The Flexible Workforce," *Training* (December 1993): 23–27.

71. R. Kuttner, "Needed: A Two-Way Social Contract in the Workplace," *Business Week* (July 10, 1995): 22; "Rethinking Work," *Business Week* (October 17, 1994): 102; H. Gleckman et al., "Rewriting the Social Contract," *Business Week* (November 20, 1995): 120–138; J-M. Hiltrop, "The Changing Psychological Contract: The Human Resource Challenge of the 1990s," *European Management Journal* (September 1995): 286–294.

72. K. Labic, "Four Possible Futures," *Fortune* (January 25, 1993): 43.

73. "The Changing Employment Relationship," *Bulletin to Management* (February 9, 1995): 48.

74. K. Labich, "Is Herb Kelleher America's Best CEO?" *Fortune* (May 2, 1994): 44–52.

75. D. Jones Yang, "The New Growth at Weyerhaeuser," *Business Week* (June 19, 1993): 63–64.

76. "Waste Management: Building an Ethical Culture," *HR Reporter* (April 1991): 1, 3.

77. C. M. Farkas and P. De Backer, "There Are Only Five Ways to Lead: Book Excerpt from Maximum Leadership, " *Fortune* (January 15, 1996): 109–112.

78. T. E. Deal and A. A. Kennedy, *Corporate Cultures* (Reading, Mass.: Addison-Wesley, 1982); R. Pascale, "Fitting New Employees into the Company Culture," *Fortune* (May 28, 1984): 28–40.

79. K. Labich, "Is Herb Kelleher America's Best CEO?" *Fortune* (May 2, 1994): 44–52.

80. Labich, "Is Herb Kelleher America's Best CEO?" See also R. Mitchell and M. Oneal, "Managing by Values," *Business Week* (August 1, 1994): 46–52.

81. R. S. Schuler, "Strategic Human Resource Management: Linking People with the Strategic Needs of the Business," *Organizational Dynamics* (Summer 1992): 32.

82. C. Scholz, "HRM in Germany," monograph, Universitat des Saarlandes (1993): 119–127.

83. W. A. Randolph and G. G. Dess, "The Congruence Perspective of Organization Design: A Conceptual Model and Multivariate Research Approach," *Academy of Management Review 9* (1984): 114–127.

84. P. Cappelli and A. Crocker-Hefter, "Distinctive Human Resources *Are* the Core Competencies of Firms," report no. R117 Q00011–91 (Washington, D.C.: U.S. Department of Education, 1994).

85. R. Jacob, "The Search for the Organization of Tomorrow," *Fortune* (May 18, 1992): 95.

86. S. M. Davis and P. R. Lawrence, *Matrix* (Reading, MA: Addison-Wesley, 1977).

87. S. Ghoshal and C. A. Bartlett, "The Multinational Corporation as an Interorganizational Network, " *Academy of Management Review 15* (1990): 603–625; A.V. Phatak, *International Dimensions of Management* (Boston: PWS-Kent, 1992).

88. J. H. Eggers and K. T. Leahy, "Entrepreneurial Leadership," *Business Quarterly* (Summer 1995): 71–76.

89. L. Baird and I. Meshoulam, "Managing the Two Fits of Strategic Human Resource Management," *Academy of Management Review 13* (1988): 116–128.

90. M. Gerstein and H. Reisman, "Strategic Selection: Matching Executives to Business Conditions," *Sloan Management Review 24* (1983): 33–49.

91. See J. A. Chatman and K. A. Jehn, "Assessing the Relationship between Industry Characteristics and Organizational Culture: How Different Can You Be?" *Academy of Management Journal 37* (1994): 522–553.

92. B. Schneider, J. K. Wheeler, and J. F. Cox, "A Passion for Service: Using Content Analysis to Explicate Service Climate Themes," *Journal of Applied Psychology 777* (1992): 705–716.

93. D. E. Bowen, "Managing Customers as Human Resources in Service Organizations," *Human Resource Management 23* (1986): 371–383; P. K. Mills and J. H. Morris, "Clients as 'Partial' Employees of Service Organizations: Role Development in Client Participation," *Academy of Management Review 11* (1986): 726–735.

94. S. E. Jackson, R. S. Schuler, and J. C. Rivero, "Organizational Characteristics as Predictors of Personnel Practices," *Personnel Psychology 42* (1989): 727.

An Environment of Fair and Legal Treatment

4

CHAPTER

> *"We weren't sure what we were getting into [in setting up their peer review process]. We just felt it was the right thing to do."*
>
> *Richard Kellogg, Human Resource Director, Coors Brewing Company*[1]

Learning Objectives

1. Explain the purposes and importance of managing employees fairly.
2. Describe procedural and distributive justice.
3. Explain how grievance procedures in companies are carried out.
4. Describe legalities impacting managing employees fairly.
5. Discuss managers' responsibilities for ensuring fairness in the workplace.

Chapter Outline

MANAGING HUMAN RESOURCES

at Hallmark Cards

If the measure of employees' job satisfaction is the length of time they stay with a company, Kansas City, Missouri-based Hallmark Cards Inc. has some seriously satisfied people. Once a year, the company hosts a celebration for *Quarter-century Club* members—those who've put in 25 years or more with Hallmark. In 1995, more than 25 percent of the workforce—3,600 employees—received an invitation.

In these days, when job-hopping is the norm for most employees, Hallmark keeps its workforce safely snuggled in its fold. The key is the way it treats employees: the company just does right by them. In 1993, it even earned the prestigious honor of a top-10 ranking in Robert Levering and Milton Moskowitz's book, "The 100 Best Companies To Work For In America."

So just what's so wonderful about Hallmark? Start with its work-life approach. Perhaps Hallmark has a little more insight into the work-family balance, being a family-run business itself (founding family the Halls still own about two-thirds of the stock). Whatever the reason, the company devotes a lot of time and energy to the issue. New parents can take advantage of a six-month leave; adopting parents receive reimbursement of up to $5,000—one of the most generous in the country. In addition, sick children get a little TLC through a partnership Hallmark forged with six area hospitals—the first day of care is free; every day after costs only $3 to $3.50 an hour.

But Hallmark also wants to treat employees themselves to a little extra. To start with, the company does its best to alleviate worries over continued employment. It has basically a spotless history as far as layoffs go. Even with terminations, employees know they'll get a fair shake: The director of employee relations must sign off on any termination of an employee who's been at Hallmark two to five years; for those with five or more years' service, two vice presidents must approve the termination.

Hallmark also shares. Since 1956, employees have received an average of 9 percent to 10 percent of their pay a year in profit sharing. The profit-sharing plan is worth 1.4 billion; Hallmark stock comprises 67 percent of the plan, making employees one-third owners.

But Hallmark doesn't just share money. It shares information through a variety of communications, including an employee newsletter, "Noon News," published daily since 1957. In addition, a monthly CEO forum allows groups of employees to speak their mind with no managers present. Diversity also enjoys dialogue through the *Multicultural Exchange*, of which CEO Irvine O. Hockaday is a member.

Perhaps most importantly, though, Hallmark just has a friendly, energetic environment. "There's something about this place I felt the first day I walked in here," says Jerry Kenefake, director of compensation and benefits. "People genuinely mean it when they say, 'Have a good day.' People work hard, but they have a good time doing it. The management of this company for years has encouraged that kind of feeling, and I think it's resulted in deep-seated loyalty. I think people, by and large, enjoy coming here every day."[2]

Hallmark gets great job applicants because it is a great place to work!

This feature on Hallmark Cards shows that an outstanding company treats employees fairly, legally, and with respect. Such treatment is a result of Hallmark's values, culture, and top management. To its 35,000 employees worldwide, Hallmark provides an attractive, energetic environment in which many job applicants would like to work; low turnover among employees; an excitement and dedication to working hard; and a sense of loyalty among the employees. Yes, loyalty. Loyalty isn't dead everywhere. Hallmark Cards fosters it, and uses it as a competitive advantage to attract and retain the best employees. The basic element of treating employees fairly, legally, and with respect include: a) giving employees policies and procedures for appeal of grievances, b) eliminating all forms of harassment, c) handling terminations effectively and with consideration, and d) respecting employee privacy.

While these issues are the focus of this chapter, other chapters also discuss HR practices that can be designed to demonstrate a concern for fairness, respect, and legal considerations. For example, in Chapter 7 we discuss how companies can design jobs to accommodate the needs and capabilities of individuals. In Chapters 8, 9, and 10 we discuss how companies can make their recruitment and selection procedures fair for all applicants. Throughout all remaining chapters, legal considerations are discussed as relevant.

The chapter begins by explaining how employees evaluate whether they have been treated fairly and how this affects their behavior at work. Next, we describe workplace policies, procedures, and practices that employers use to ensure fair treatment of employees. As you will see, some approaches to workplace fairness mirror the procedures used in the U.S. courts. In the U.S., the legal system plays an important role in defining and interpreting for society the meaning of fair treatment within employment settings. Thus, this chapter concludes with an overview of the legal rights and responsibilities of employers and employees.

Managing Employees Fairly

LEARNING OBJECTIVE 1

Explain the purposes and importance of managing employees fairly.

What does it mean to be treated fairly? Do we automatically feel that we have been treated unfairly when things do not turn out in our favor? What do people do when they have been treated unfairly? We address these and related questions in this chapter.

Managers, HR professionals, and employees all play important roles in their partnership in ensuring that human resources are managed fairly. **Managing employees fairly** means working together to establish workplace policies, procedures, and practices to help ensure that significant employment decisions are made with fairness and due process, respect for the rights and responsibilities of employees and employers, justice, and as much information as possible.

Managing employees fairly means establishing workplace policies, procedures, and practices to help ensure that significant employment decisions are made with fairness and due process, respect for the rights and responsibilities of employees and employers, justice, and as much information as possible.

PARTNERSHIP:

WORKING TOGETHER MANAGING EMPLOYEES FAIRLY

LINE MANAGERS	HR PROFESSIONALS	EMPLOYEES
Set policy for treatment of employees in workplace issues Accept responsibility for their behavior in dealing with employees Show concern for due process and fair treatment Be proactive in attempts to understand employees' views about fairness	Ensure line managers set policy in accordance with legal considerations Develop policies, procedures, and practices that support and are consistent with fair and ethical behavior by everyone in the organization Help keep employer and employee rights and responsibilities in balance	Accept responsibility to respect the rights of other employees Work with HR professionals in establishing policies, procedures, and practices for dealing fairly with workplace issues Accept responsibility for behaving fairly and ethically toward one's employing organization

Societal Concerns About Fairness

Chapter 3 described the many economic and business forces that help to shape the approaches companies use to manage their human resources. Much of our discussion in Chapter 3 reflected the importance to American companies of profit-making. In a pure capitalistic economic system, managers on behalf of shareholders would seek to maximize profits free of noneconomic external constraints—that is, without constraints other than those imposed by consumers and competitors. As explained in Chapter 1, however, companies are addressing the concerns of many stakeholders. Today, businesses and consumers do not make decisions based solely on economic self-interests; they also acknowledge the interests of the broader society.

Managing employees fairly is an important objective of society.

At the societal level, a fundamental concern is that employees be treated fairly. As employees, most people believe that fairness is a desirable social condition—we want to be treated fairly, and we want others to view us as being fair.[3] Companies that rank high as the best places to work, such as Hallmark Cards, Ben & Jerry's Homemade Inc., and Marriott Corporation, generally emphasize fairness as part of their corporate culture because fairness creates the feeling of trust that is needed to "hold a good workplace together."[4] As at Hallmark Cards, a corporate culture emphasizing fairness can result in a workforce that is energetic, talented, dedicated, and gives a competitive advantage to the company. Sounds like a real win-win situation.

Fairness is about the relative distribution of outcomes and the quality of the procedures used in determining these outcomes.

The concept of **fairness** has many connotations, so ensuring fair treatment can be a major challenge for employers. Furthermore, society's view of what constitutes fair treatment of employees is in constant flux, so companies must continually readjust. Many practices that were considered fair at the beginning of the 20th century had become illegal by the middle of the 20th century. Similarly, practices considered fair today may no longer be legal in five or ten years. Consequently, companies must constantly scan and interpret the environment to see what does constitute fairness. Two parts of the environment very relevant here are the workforce and our legal institutions.

The Workforce and Legal Institutions as Key Stakeholders

The concerns of our broader society about what's fair and what's legal are communicated through, and supported by, the actions of two primary stakeholders: the labor force and legal institutions.

The Workforce

Members of the workforce communicate their concerns in both direct and indirect ways. As free agents (before they are employees of companies), they communicate their concerns to employers directly. For example, when deciding which company to work for, a potential employee evaluates whether a company pays a fair wage, whether it offers desirable benefits, whether the corporate culture is appealing, and so on. When making these evaluations, perceptions of what is "fair," "desirable," and "appealing" reflect the potential employee's concerns. The free agency of job applicants, combined with the diversity of the U.S. workforce, means that companies must consider a broad array of workforce concerns in order to attract and hire the best talent.

Once hired, employees continue to express their concerns and they also evaluate whether their employer is addressing those concerns. Indirectly, or informally, employees may voice their concerns in daily conversations at work. Many companies also offer formal channels of expression, such as employee surveys and employee grievance systems. Finally, union members voice their concerns directly when they collectively bargain with employers over working conditions and compensation.

Legal Institutions

Legal institutions provide indirect channels for the workforce to use in communicating their concerns to employers. Through elected government representatives, members of the workforce initiate and ultimately create federal and state laws. Through their tax payments, employees pay for the operations of a vast array of government agencies and courts, which are responsible for interpreting and enforcing the laws. Thus, employment laws should be thought of not only as legal constraints; they are also sources of information about the issues that potential employees are likely thinking about as they decide whether to join or leave an organization.

Legal institutions codify what is fair.

What Fairness Means to Employees

LEARNING OBJECTIVE 1

Describe procedural and distributive justice.

Employees' perceptions of fairness reflect at least two features of the situations they find themselves in: the actual *outcomes* and the *procedures* used in arriving at these outcomes. These two features are referred to as distributive justice and procedural justice, respectively.[5]

Distributive Justice

Distributive justice refers to the allocation of outcomes.

Distributive justice is the actual outcome or resolution of a situation. Distribution of justice is one important aspect that affects fairness perceptions. Not surprisingly, employees prefer favorable outcomes for themselves. Consider the following two situations and imagine that you are the employees involved. How do you feel? And what will you do?

A Missed Promotion. Michelle Chang graduated with her BA in business five years ago. Since then, she has worked for a large financial services company as an industry analyst. Her performance reviews have always been positive. She and her peers assumed she was on the company's informal fast track. But recently, she has begun to wonder. After the manager of her unit left last month for a better opportunity at another firm, Michelle applied for the job. She did not get the promotion. To her surprise, the person chosen to manage the unit was Jim Johnson, a twenty-year veteran of the firm who was transferred in from Chicago. After three weeks at his new job, it is obvious that Jim's previous experiences have not provided him with the knowledge he needs. Michelle feels that the company's decision to give Jim the job is a signal that her future may not be as bright as everyone thought. Perhaps it is time to look into possibilities at other companies.

Let's look at Michelle's situation. To her, any promotion is better than no promotion. However, in evaluating the fairness of her situation, Michelle may compare her outcome to that of Jim Johnson. If Michelle felt that the outcomes she and Jim experienced reflected their relative qualifications, then Michelle probably would accept the situation as fair even though she did not get promoted. However, since Jim does not seem to be qualified for the job, Michelle and her co-workers may perceive that she has been unfairly treated, and they may also conclude that their employer generally treats employees unfairly.

Fair Pay. When evaluating whether people are paid fairly, two factors are relevant: 1) the level of pay people receive; and 2) changes in pay over time (e.g., due to raises). Generally, people see pay as fair when they believe that the distribution of pay across a group corresponds to the relative value of the work being done by each person. Similarly, when the relative sizes of raises correspond to the relative performance levels of people in the unit, people are likely to feel fairly treated. In the workplace, distributive fairness is perceived under conditions of *equity*, or merit-based decision making.[6]

What is the impact of the trend in CEO pay in the U.S.?

In the early 1990s, issues of equity (distributive justice) were salient in the ongoing public discussion about CEO compensation. Exhibit 4.1 shows CEO pay

EXHIBIT 4.1

CEO Compensation

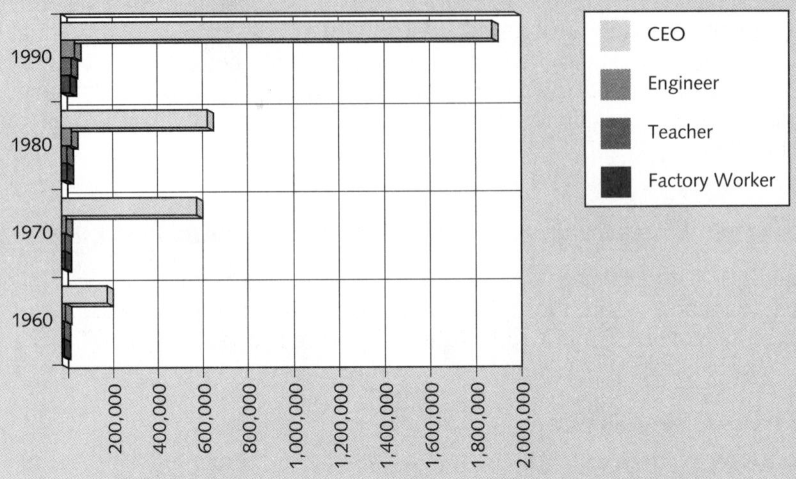

Source: Adapted from B. H. Sheppard, R. J. Lewicki, and J. W. Minton, *Organizational Justice: The Search for Fairness in the Workplace* (New York: Lexington Books, 1992).

in comparison to the pay of engineers, teachers, and factory workers over a 30-year period. Is it fair that CEO pay has been growing at a pace that is twice the rate of growth in pay for these other workers? What arguments would convince you that this distribution of outcomes is fair?

Did You KNOW?

The difference in pay between the lowest paid worker and the CEO in Japan is less than 10 times!

Typical American employees generally consider "equity" when evaluating fairness at work; employees from other countries and cultures may see things quite differently. American culture is individualistic; many other cultures are more collectivistic. In collectivistic cultures, concern for social cohesion is greater than in the U.S. Going along with a perspective that focuses more on groups, people from collectivistic cultures value *equality* of treatment and treatment is based on *need*,[7] and they allocate rewards accordingly.[8] Thus, from a collectivistic perspective, Michelle might be viewed as having been treated fairly. Michelle was treated the same as her coworkers (equally), and perhaps Jim needed the job more than did Michelle. Not surprisingly, income differences between the highest paid workers and the lowest paid workers in almost all other countries are substantially less than in the U.S.

Procedural Justice

Procedural justice refers to perceptions about fairness of the process.

Perceptions of justice depend on more than the relative distribution of outcomes: beliefs about the entire process used to determine outcomes are also important. The term **procedural justice** refers to perceptions about fairness of the process. For example, Michelle and Jim might wonder how their company made its decision described earlier. In American culture, a procedure is considered fair if:

- The information used to make the decision is appropriate and accurate.
- The basis for making the decision is clearly explained.
- All legitimately interested parties are given the opportunity to have input into the decision process.
- Attention is paid to ensuring that the less powerful parties are protected from abuse by the more powerful parties.

- All interested parties have equal and open access to the system.
- The system is relatively stable and consistent over time.
- The system is flexible enough to be responsive to changing conditions and unique circumstances.[9]

Most employees think of an open and honest process as fair.

With these criteria in mind, how would you design a procedure for detecting harassment and disciplining those involved? For deciding who to fire or lay off? How would you design drug-testing procedures? Before addressing such issues, it is useful to consider how employees react when they feel they have been treated unfairly, and to consider possible legal constraints.

Reactions to Fair and Unfair Treatment

When employees feel they have been treated unfairly, they can react in many different ways. Consider again the situation of Michelle. If you were Michelle, you would probably consider actions that fall into one of the following categories:

Which of these actions would you choose?

a. Leave the organization and put the incident behind you

b. Stay and simply accept the situation as something you must tolerate

c. Stay but engage in negative behaviors that help you restore your sense of fairness (e.g., shorten your hours a bit; stop attending unnecessary meetings and functions)

d. Voice your concern to people inside the organization (e.g., discuss the situation with your colleagues; talk about it with a mentor; talk to someone in the HR department)

e. Voice your concern to external authorities (e.g., explore possible legal action; talk to the press)[10]

For high performers like Michelle, choice a., quitting, may be the best alternative. From the company's perspective, however, having Michelle leave and perhaps join the competition may be the least desirable alternative. From society's perspective, turnover caused by feelings of injustice is undesirable because it tends to reduce productivity.[11] Alternative b. would be better for Michelle's employer, but it is probably not very common because few people easily shrug off injustices suffered at the hands of their employers. Instead, their outlook sours. Employees who stay in situations that they believe are unfair lose confidence in the competence and trustworthiness of management.[12] Employees who feel unfairly treated also report feeling dissatisfied and uncommitted to both their employers and the goals their employers set for them.[13]

Feelings of injustice affect behavior, not just attitudes, even for employees who decide not to quit because of unfair treatment. Therefore, reactions that fall into categories c. and e. are possible. Employees attempt to maintain a sense of balance in their relationship with employers. If a legal issue is involved, employees may seek legal solutions.

Often, however, feelings of unfairness arise in response to perfectly legal management behavior. This was illustrated quite dramatically in a company that temporarily cut employees' pay. The company was a large manufacturer of aerospace and automotive parts. Due to the loss of two contracts, temporary pay cuts were required at two of the company's three plants. Everyone at the two plants, including management, took a 15 percent pay cut for ten weeks. These two plants, however, were treated differently. In one plant, the company tried to convey how much it regretted the pay cuts, explained that the pay cuts would eliminate the need for layoffs, and assured employees that no favoritism would occur. At a full meeting with the employees, top management spent an hour answering employees' questions. At the second plant, the pay cut was announced at a brief fifteen-minute meeting with no apology and very little explanation. Employees' reactions were assessed in terms of theft rates, turnover, and responses to a survey. At both the plants taking pay cuts, theft rates went up during the weeks the cuts were in effect and then went back down again when full pay was restored, particularly at the plant where the inadequate explanation was given (see Exhibit 4.2).

Turnover at the plant with inadequate explanation of the pay cuts also soared from 5 percent to 23 percent. Survey results confirmed that employees at this plant did not understand how their pay cut was determined and felt they were treated unfairly.[14] As this company found out, people are sensitive to changes that disturb their sense of equity, and will seek ways to rebalance the scales if they are tipped.[15]

Giving employees a voice in the process increases acceptance.

The way companies manage situations can greatly influence how employees react.[16] One aspect of managing situations effectively involves using formal organizational systems to deal with conflicts and disputes. By fully explaining *how* decisions are made (the process of decision-making) and by offering employees opportunities to voice their concerns and have their questions answered, employers can minimize negative employee reactions. In well-managed companies such as Hallmark Cards, employees' feelings of dissatisfaction are intentionally surfaced and used to stimulate positive changes that actually benefit both employees and employers. This is the reason why many companies are installing grievance procedures for employees.

Managing to Ensure Fair Treatment

LEARNING OBJECTIVE 3

Explain how grievance procedures in companies are carried out.

Grievance Procedures

Formal grievance procedures are one way to encourage employees to voice their concerns and seek constructive resolutions. In unionized settings, the presence of such procedures had already become nearly universal by 1950.[17] Almost all

EXHIBIT 4.2

Pay Cuts and Employee Theft

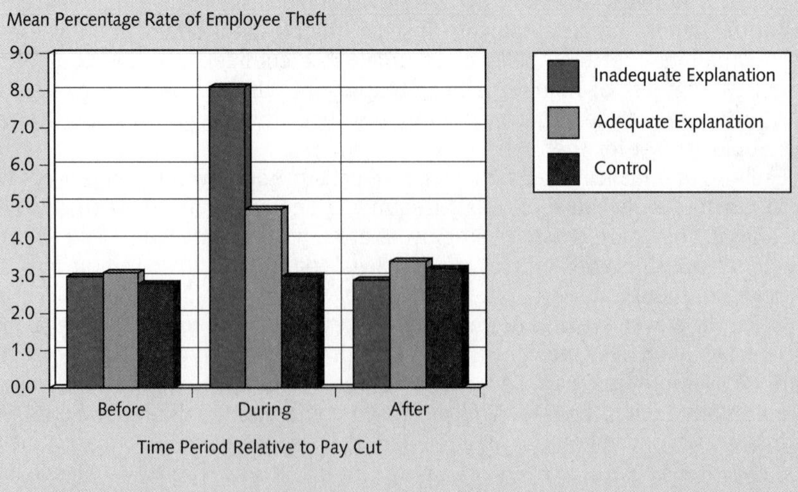

Source: J. Greenberg, "Employee Theft as a Reaction to Underpayment Inequity: The Hidden Cost of Pay Cuts," *Journal of Applied Psychology* 75 (1990): 565.

public and private unionized employees are covered by contracts that specify formal written grievance procedures, and most of these result in final and binding arbitration by a third-party arbitrator.[18] Historically, the picture has been quite different for nonunion employees. In 1950, formal procedures were almost never available to these employees. Today, more than half of America's largest corporations have some type of formal grievance resolution system. This reflects managers' belief that employees have a right to fair treatment.[19] When they work well, grievance systems may also help lower the legal costs associated with resolving disputes in the courts.

Fair Treatment at Coors. Fairness systems like the one at Coors are particularly helpful in environments where employees lack the representation and negotiating power of a union.[20] Coors's appeal process gives employees a voice in how they are treated. This voice, combined with peer review, ensures a better balance of power. Over time, employees learn to trust and use the procedures. The inclusion of an appeal process helps to allay employees' concerns about fairness.[21] Details of just how this process works at Coors are presented in the feature, "Managing Human Resources at Coors."

Did You KNOW?

Coors has approximately 7,000 employees in Colorado, Tennessee, and Virginia.

Proactive Policies and Practices

Is the absence of a formal system for processing employees' complaints necessarily bad business? It may seem so at first, but some companies may choose not to support such systems for good reasons. Grievance systems are reactive. They focus the attention and energy of disputants on the past, and formalize a process for *naming* an injured party, *blaming* someone or something for the injury, and *claiming* a remedy.[22]

Given limited resources, some companies choose to develop and promote proactive policies and practices designed to prevent the need for formal grievance procedures.[23] Proactive approaches to ensuring fair treatment might include, for example, formal performance appraisals, frequent informal feedback, progressive discipline policies, annual surveys to monitor employees' attitudes and perceptions, benefits packages designed to meet the diverse needs of employees, employee involvement in managerial decision-making, management training in how to treat employees fairly, and frequent use of communication channels.

Some companies choose to be more proactive to ensure fair treatment.

Legal Regulations to Ensure Fair Treatment

LEARNING OBJECTIVE 4

Describe legalities impacting managing employees fairly.

American society is perhaps the most litigious in the world. In the past ten years, the number of lawsuits filed has increased more than 50 percent. No wonder we have so many lawyers—more than twice as many per capita as England, three times as many as Japan, and six times as many as Switzerland.[24] Legal activity regarding employment issues is a significant portion of this general picture.[25] In 1994, 88,000 charges of employment discrimination were filed with the federal agencies that handle most such lawsuits.[26] Exhibit 4.3 shows in more detail the growth in these lawsuits in just five years.

The legal environment communicates society's concerns through state and federal laws, regulations, and court decisions. Failure to comply with societal expectations as defined by this environment may result in monetary fines, imprisonment, and court orders that constrain future activities. In general, the legal system is designed to encourage socially responsible behavior.[27]

To understand how the legal environment affects the way companies manage human resources, it is helpful to understand the U.S. legal system in general. U.S. companies must act in accordance with several different types of laws, including constitutional laws, statutory laws, administrative regulations, executive orders, and common laws.

MANAGING HUMAN RESOURCES

at Coors

The Coors Brewing Company, headquartered in Golden, Colorado, is famous for its beer and for its procedures for managing employees fairly. Headed by the family heir, Peter Coors, Coors Brewing Company realized in 1978 that they had to develop better relations with employees. A bitter confrontation between the union that had represented the employees for nearly fifty years and the management preceded a failed strike against the company. Furthermore, the employees voted to decertify the union representation. Naturally, this left the employees without protection from what they saw were the "potential abuses of management."

Employees were afraid that management would take control from them and give them no recourse in such matters as employee discipline. To their way of thinking, "if management wants to get us out of here, they'll do it and do it without a fair hearing." According to Richard Kellogg, who was involved in the grievance process at that time and later became Coors HR director, representatives for the workers told Bill Coors, who was head of the company: "Our employees are frightened because they've had this union here that was taking care of our needs and making sure that discipline was meted out fairly. Now we don't have that and we've got to either find a way to provide it or ultimately the employees will bring in another union."

The company, specifically the HR department, acted swiftly. Borrowing from a Coors subsidiary, Coors Container Company, the HR department set up a peer review system designed to give employees a chance to air their complaints and have their peers take part in evaluating whether their complaints were legitimate. HR believed that such a system would benefit employees and management alike. Others in senior management, including the Coors family members, were not so positive. They feared that every disciplinary action would be considered unfair. So disciplinary actions would always be reviewed by the peer review system. This, in turn, would mean that the disciplinary action would always be reversed. Despite their concerns, they agreed to put the system in place. To appease senior management's fears, HR said it would use the system only for debates over termination actions. According to Kellogg: "We found out early on, however, that some employees get very upset about a first written warning." As a result, the company expanded the system to include hearings for all forms of discipline including first warnings, final warnings, suspensions without pay, and terminations.

Coors' Peer Review system works like this: An employee who's unsatisfied with the application of a company policy—but not the policy itself—may file an appeal with his or her employee relations representative within seven working days. The employee relations representative then sets up an appeal board by randomly selecting two members of management and three employees from the same job category as the appellant.

A hearing is held, orchestrated by the employee relations representative. At the hearing, the supervisor describes the circumstances surrounding the discipline. The employee then explains why the supervisor's action was unfair. Board members may ask questions of both parties during the proceedings and also may request testimony from witnesses.

When the board members are satisfied that they have all the information that they need, they privately discuss the case. They decide by majority vote on one of three outcomes: to uphold the action; to reduce the severity; or to overturn the action completely. The board's decision is final. The employee-relations representative notifies both the supervisor

Continued

and the appellant of the decision through a brief, written summary, signed by all the board members.

The results thus far indicate that management's fears were unfounded: for the past ten years, an average of only nine percent of management's decisions have been overturned by the review boards.

Management now recognizes an added value of the review board: Coors has never lost a wrongful termination case in court. According to Ed Cruth, employee relations manager for the company: "If we can't substantiate or uphold a termination internally with an appeal board, we can almost guarantee it wouldn't be upheld in front of a jury. And if it is upheld internally, then we feel comfortable that it's going to be upheld in front of a jury." Cruth goes on to add that the peer review system is also consistent with the *Civil Rights Act of 1991* that specifically provides for and encourages the use of alternative dispute resolutions. Over time, employees learn to accept, trust, and use a grievance and appeal system even when the majority of decisions are not made in their favor! The experience of Coors, as well as a great deal of research on the topic, shows that the process and procedures used to make decisions are as important to employees as are the decisions themselves.[28]

EXHIBIT 4.3

A Staggering Civil-Rights Backlog

The EEOC's backlog of complaints at the end of each year has been increasing because of the rising number of federal civil-rights charges (numbers in parentheses indicate percentage change from the previous fiscal year).

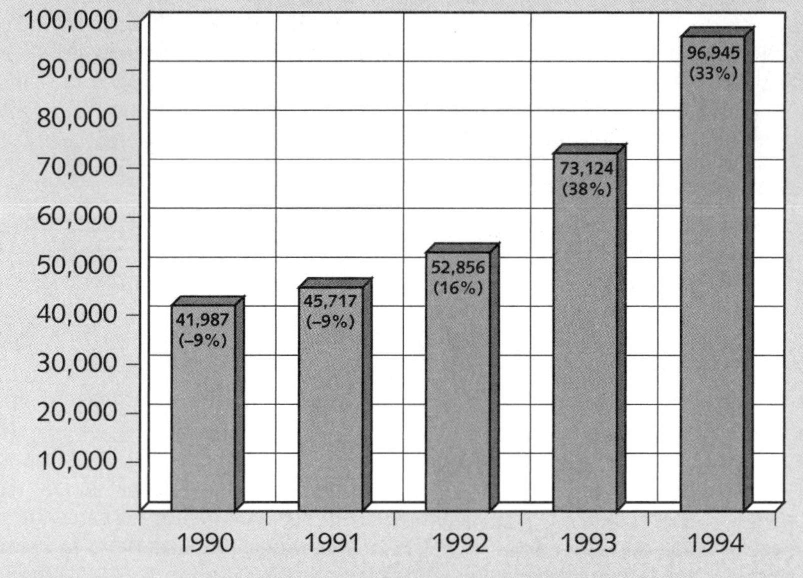

Source: U.S. Equal Employment Opportunity Commission

Constitutional Laws

In countries that have one, the constitution is the fundamental law of the land. The U.S. Constitution is the oldest written constitution still in force in the world. It defines the structure and limits of the federal government and allocates power among the federal government and the states. All 50 states also have written constitutions. State and federal laws must be consistent with the U.S. Constitution.

In the area of employment, one section of the U.S. Constitution that is particularly important is the 14th Amendment, which guarantees due process and equal protection. This amendment also prohibits state actions that are inconsistent with federal law. Because of its equal protection clause, the 14th Amendment often plays a role in cases involving reverse discrimination.

Statutory Laws

The U.S. Constitution gives Congress all power to make laws on behalf of the federal government. Paralleling the federal constitution, state constitutions give lawmaking power to state-level governmental bodies. The resulting federal and state laws are called *statutes.*

Key statutory laws include:

- *Fair Labor Standards Act*
- *Civil Rights Act* **of 1964**
- *Americans with Disabilities Act* **of 1990**
- *Civil Rights Act* **of 1991**
- *Family and Medical Act* **of 1993**

One especially important federal employment statute has been Title VII of the *Civil Rights Act.* As originally enacted in 1964, Title VII prohibited discrimination by employers, employment agencies, and unions on the basis of race, color, religion, gender, or national origin. A 1978 amendment prohibited discrimination against pregnant women. In 1991, a new version of the *Civil Rights Act* went into effect. The new law reinforces the intent of the *Civil Rights Acts* of 1964, but states more specifically how cases brought under the act should proceed. The *Civil Rights Acts* and other key federal statutes are summarized in Appendix A.

State laws must be consistent with federal law, but this does not imply that they are the same. Two important differences between state and federal laws are common. First, state laws often cover companies that are not covered by federal laws. For example, federal employment laws such as Title VII often apply only to businesses with 15 or more employees, but similar state laws often apply to even smaller businesses.[29] Second, state laws are often predecessors to federal law, and in this sense, tell us what to expect in the future at the federal level. For example, Massachusetts passed the first minimum wage legislation in 1912, which was a predecessor to the federal *Fair Labor Standards Act* of 1938 (FLSA). New York adopted a fair employment law in 1945 and about half the states had similar laws by the time the *Civil Rights Act* of 1964 was passed at the federal level. Florida, Maine, and the District of Columbia had each adopted family leave legislation before the federal *Family and Medical Leave Act* of 1993 was enacted.

Administrative Regulations

Key federal enforcement agencies are:

- EEOC
- OSHA

At both the federal and state levels, the legislative and executive branches of government can delegate authority for rule making and enforcement to an administrative agency. For example, the federal *Equal Employment Opportunity Act* of 1972 gave power to enforce Title VII of the *Civil Rights Act* to the Equal Employment Opportunity Commission (EEOC). The EEOC also administers the *Equal Pay Act* of 1963 and the *Age Discrimination in Employment Act* of 1967. In carrying out their duties, agencies such as these make rules—often called standards, guidelines, or decisions; conduct investigations; make judgments about guilt; and impose sanctions. In practice, this means these federal agencies have the responsibility and authority to prosecute companies they believe are in violation of the law. Furthermore, they generally require companies to monitor their own behavior and file reports, either at preset time intervals or following particular types of events. For example, the Occupational Safety and Health Administration (OSHA) conducts safety and health inspections, investigates accidents and alleged hazardous conditions, issues citations for violations, levies fines, collects mandatory reports prepared by employers, and compiles statistics on work injuries and illnesses.

Executive Orders

U.S. presidents shape the legal environment by approving and vetoing bills passed by Congress and by influencing how vigorously administrative agencies carry out their duties and responsibilities. In addition, the President can create law by issuing executive orders that specify rules and conditions for government business. Businesses that do work for the federal government are referred to as federal contractors. In the area of employment, the actions of federal contractors are most affected by *Executive Order 11246*, issued in 1965 by President Lyndon B. Johnson. Like Title VII, *Executive Order 11246* prohibits discrimination on the basis of race, color, religion, or national origin. It applies to federal agencies and to federal contractors and subcontractors. In 1966, *Executive Order 11375* was issued to prohibit discrimination based on gender.

There are about 70,000 federal contractors in the U.S.

Whereas *Executive Orders 11246* and *11375* parallel federal law that applies to all employers, *Executive Order 11478*, issued in 1969, has no parallel in federal statutory law. *Executive Order 11478* requires that employment policies of the federal government be based on merit.

Common Laws

Common laws are rules made by judges as they resolve disputes between parties. The U.S. system of common law is rooted in English common law, which was established after the Normans conquered England in 1066. To help unify the country, William the Conqueror established the King's Court. Its purpose was to develop a common set of rules and apply them uniformly throughout the kingdom. Decisions were based on the opinions of judges. Important decisions were recorded and subsequently referred back to as *precedents* (examples) for making future decisions. When new types of disputes arose, judges created new law to resolve them. This system is still in effect today in England.

Unlike English judges, U.S. judges do not make laws, they only interpret and apply them. But their interpretations continue in the tradition of setting precedent to decide new cases. The use of precedent to decide cases, referred to as the doctrine of *stare decisis*, helps employers anticipate how the courts might rule should they find themselves involved in a similar case.

Consider the 1971 decision of the U.S. Supreme Court in *Griggs v. Duke Power Company*. Griggs was an African-American male who applied for a job at the Duke Power Company but was not accepted because he lacked a high school diploma. The lawsuit charged that Duke Power Company had engaged in racial discrimination. By requiring a high school diploma, the firm deemed that fewer African-American applicants would be qualified for available jobs. Furthermore, given the work performed in these jobs, mandating a high school diploma seemed questionable.

In its decision in favor of Griggs, the Supreme Court argued that Title VII prohibited not only overt racial discrimination but also practices that are fair in form, but discriminatory in operation. This meant that *direct* evidence of intentional discrimination would not be necessary to pursue cases under Title VII. Cases of discrimination could also be brought using statistics showing a disproportionate rate of rejection for members of groups protected by Title VII. Disproportionately high rejection rates would be considered evidence of illegal discrimination if the practice leading to these rates (e.g., requiring a high school diploma) could not be shown to be related to job performance.

In writing their decision, the justices of the Supreme Court made it clear that employers were to accept responsibility for ensuring that the criteria they used in making employment decisions were fair. But over time, other Supreme Court decisions indicated a shift to a different point of view. In particular, the 1989 decision in *Wards Cove Packing Company v. Atonio* appeared to suggest that: a) plaintiffs would have more responsibility for proving that a particular practice resulted in discrimination, and b) employers accused of illegal discrimination would have less responsibility for proving that an apparently discriminatory employment practice was justified by business necessity.

This apparent shift in the Supreme Court's interpretations of the *Civil Rights Act* of 1964 generated considerable debate among some segments of our society,

Did You KNOW?

The U.S.-Japanese Treaty of Friendship states that foreign corporations are allowed to discriminate in favor of citizens from their own country in filling specified high-level positions within the U.S.

including legal scholars, social scientists, and employers. This debate culminated in the passage of the *Civil Rights Act* of 1991. In establishing this new law, Congress sought to clarify and reassert its view of what constitutes fair employment practices; this and other new laws make clear that the intent of Congress was consistent with earlier court decisions and was misconstrued in later decisions such as *Wards Cove*. The feature "HR Advice and Application: The Burden of Proof Grows Heavier" explains how this shift affects HR management.

As the preceding discussion of the *Civil Rights Act* illustrates, court rulings indicate how laws have been interpreted when applied to specific employment disputes. When interpreting the implications of court decisions, keep in mind that rulings made by the Supreme Court carry the most weight because the decisions of all other federal and state courts are subject to review by the Supreme Court. Appendix A lists several Supreme Court rulings of particular importance for managing human resources. As you read this appendix, remember also that even a ruling by the Supreme Court can be reversed, should Congress decide that it is not consistent with society's view of socially responsible behavior.

Remedies to Disputes in Civil Litigation

Although we read about some cases in the newspapers, most civil suits never actually reach the stage of a formal trial. Instead, they are resolved privately. These are referred to as "out-of-court settlements." For cases that are resolved in court, monetary damages are a common remedy.

Monetary Damages

If a legal right has been violated and has resulted in injury, the defendant may be required to pay monetary damages to the plaintiff. Compensatory monetary damages are intended to help victims retrieve what they have lost; for example, back pay and attorneys fees. Punitive damages are intended specifically to punish wrongdoers and deter future wrongdoing. A 1993 case illustrates how these remedies work:

> *Firing employees and making examples out of them can prove costly for employers if such actions are not based on clear facts. This point is illustrated starkly in a Texas case, where damages in excess of $15 million were awarded a former Procter & Gamble employee who was fired after being accused of stealing a $35 telephone.*
>
> *The employee had worked for P&G for 41 years and, according to his attorney, had an unblemished record. He had purchased the phone with his own money and was not reimbursed because he had lost the receipt. Later, a security guard stopped the employee as he was leaving work and discovered the phone in his belongings. After an internal investigation, P&G fired the employee and announced through internal notices that he had committed a theft. The employee sued for libel, saying P&G used him as an example to prevent other thefts.*
>
> *Procter & Gamble committed actual malice in falsely accusing the employee of stealing the phone, the jury in the case decided. The jury awarded the employee $14 million in punitive damages and more than $1 million for actual damages to the employee's character and damages to his mental and physical well-being (*Hagler v. Procter & Gamble Manufacturing Co., *1993).*[30]

HR ADVICE & APPLICATION

The Burden of Proof Grows Heavier

The 1991 *Civil Rights Act* has redefined discrimination and exposed employers to greater financial liability. The law now in effect reversed several Supreme Court rulings and shifted the burden of proof for cases of intentional discrimination from the employee to the employer. In addition, workers who successfully prove they were discriminated against now can receive compensatory and punitive damages that previously were not allowed. Under the original civil rights legislation, employees could only receive reinstatement, back pay, and attorneys' fees.

The total amount of compensatory and punitive damages allowed by the law is determined by the number of employees at the company and cannot exceed the following limits:

- $50,000 for companies with 15 to 100 employees
- $100,000 for employers with 101 to 200 employees
- $200,000 for companies with 201 to 500 employees
- $300,000 for employers with over 501 employees

These damages would be added to attorneys' fees, which can range anywhere between $40,000 and $150,000, according to professionals in the employment law field. Companies also may be responsible for paying the fees of expert witnesses called by the plaintiffs, which often range between $10,000 and $15,000.

Legal experts agree that damages will be awarded more easily now because an employee can have his or her case heard before a jury. Previously, discrimination cases were tried before judges, many of whom were considered more sympathetic to employers. Juries, on the other hand, historically have decided against businesses and awarded plaintiffs huge sums of money for damages.

"*The Civil Rights Act*, on top of the *Americans with Disabilities Act* (ADA), is the final kick in the pants for managers," said attorney Fred Sullivan of the Springfield, Mass., firm Sullivan & Hayes. "Managers have to think differently."

This new way of thinking represents a radical departure for businesses, according to Sullivan. Companies must approach their employment practices from the perspective of a jury, rather than from a managerial viewpoint. The underlying question employers need to consider regarding any potentially liable action is, "How can this be perceived differently than the way we perceive it?" Sullivan added.

"The *Civil Rights Act* and the ADA place more limitations on recruiting as well as discharging employees," said Howard Flaxman, an attorney with the Philadelphia firm Blank, Rome, Comisky & McCauley. "The stakes are very high right now."

THE BURDEN IS SHIFTED

The stakes are higher because any employer brought before a court on a "disparate impact" discrimination case today must prove that the challenged employment practice was a result of a business necessity. In the past, companies only had to submit evidence of a business justification, and the employee was responsible for persuading the court against the employer's evidence.

The act also shifts the burden of proof to employers in dual motive cases, that is, cases in which both lawful and unlawful factors were involved. Before, a company that used an illegal factor, such as race or gender, to make an employment decision could prevail if it proved that the same decision would be made even if that factor were not considered. Now an employer must show that only lawful factors were used to make the employment decision. The employee only has to prove that his or her protected status, such as race, gender or disability, was a "motivating factor" in the decision regardless of other factors involved.

Flaxman said that such changes in the law, in addition to increased monetary awards, will provoke more litigation, particularly for marginal cases that would not have gone to court in the past. Attorneys also may be more likely to use the law as a bargaining tool to negotiate better out-of-court settlements for their clients.

AN EMPLOYER'S DEFENSE

Companies now must review all of their personnel policies to protect themselves against any litigation that could result from the new law. As part of the

Continued

review process, Flaxman advised employers to make sure they have established a sexual harassment policy. Businesses also need to study their disciplinary policies to ensure that every problem is dealt with through progressive and corrective actions that are thoroughly documented.

"With juries, the issue is more of fairness, not discrimination. That's the issue, even though it's not supposed to be," Flaxman said. "Juries are punishing employers who appear to be almost cavalier in their attitude."

"You want to show to the jury that efforts went beyond what was normally expected," Sullivan added. "Go beyond the final warning; issue a second warning."

Hiring practices also must be reviewed to comply with the new law. Employers must make sure that the people conducting the screening process ask the proper questions and conduct the proper investigations.

Although the law encourages both parties to seek an alternative method to resolve disputes, such as arbitration, its effectiveness remains questionable. Unless the employee is legally bound by an arbitration agreement, the matter still can go to court.

Sullivan, however, said the use of a third party can be helpful in settling disputes. Many employers have resisted arbitration, believing they did not need a third party to tell them how to manage their business. "But today there is a third party—the jury."[31]

Settlement Agreements

Court proceedings can be lengthy and costly. When the objective is correcting employer wrongdoing, court procedures often are not expedient. The U.S. Justice Department and administrative agencies can speed the process of ensuring that employers engage in responsible behavior by negotiating a settlement. When lawsuits are resolved by a settlement agreement, the defendant (employer) usually does not admit to wrongdoing. Nevertheless, it may agree to pay money to the plaintiff or plaintiffs. And it may agree to conduct itself according to the court's specific directives. The first settlement agreement regarding unfair employment practices was negotiated with AT&T and its 24 operating companies. In 1973, the firm agreed to: a) pay $15 million to 13,000 women and 2000 men of color who had been denied pay and promotion opportunities, and b) develop goals for employing women and people of color in all jobs in all of its 700 establishments. In a more recent settlement, the courts recognized that the circle of victims in organizations that engage in unfair employment practices can be surprisingly large. In 1993, Shoney's Incorporated's restaurant chain agreed to pay $105 million to victims of the company's blatant racial discrimination. Most of the plaintiffs were African-American employees, but some settlement money also was awarded to white managers and supervisors who were dismissed because they refused to follow orders to terminate African-American employees.[32]

Alternative Dispute Resolution

Alternative dispute resolution (ADR) is an agreement to resolve disputes either by internal mediation or arbitration.

A growing number of businesses are using **alternative dispute resolution (ADR)** to resolve charges of employment discrimination or wrongful termination. Working out a dispute before it reaches litigation can promote goodwill between management and employees and reduce the adverse publicity often associated with legal disputes.[33] It can also reduce legal costs to both employers and society.

Mediation and arbitration are the two most common forms of alternative dispute resolution. Internal review procedures, such as those used at Coors, can also be thought of as alternative dispute resolution systems.

Mediation

Mediation is the most popular form of ADR, partly because its format is more flexible than that of other proceedings. All concerned parties come before a neutral third party (the mediator), who may be appointed by a judge or selected by the parties or their attorneys. Parties to a civil dispute may be ordered into mediation by the court, or they may volunteer to submit to the process in an effort to settle the dispute without litigation. The role of the mediator is to have the parties resolve their differences through mutual understanding and agreement.

Arbitration

Arbitration is also a popular method of alternative dispute resolution.[34] It can be included in the employment contract or it may be court ordered. Here are some key ways that arbitration differs from mediation:

- Arbitration is more formal and often more expensive. Attorneys must actually present their cases in a formal manner.
- The neutral third party might be an expert in the industry involved. The third-party neutral may be a single arbitrator or a panel of three. Arbitrators are selected by national organizations, by a judge, or by the parties themselves.
- Arbitrators have some powers in that they may make an award after hearing both sides of the case.
- Arbitration often is specified long before any actual dispute arises. Arbitration clauses are frequently written into employment contracts or collective bargaining agreements.
- Arbitration may be binding or nonbinding. Employment or labor contracts that call for arbitration in the event of a dispute should specify whether the arbitration will be binding. If the award is nonbinding, the process could lead to a trial. If it is binding, the arbitrator's decision is final, subject to a very limited right of appeal.

Managers' Responsibilities for Ensuring Fairness in the Workplace

LEARNING OBJECTIVE 5

Discuss managers' responsibilities for ensuring fairness in the workplace.

The task of managing to ensure fairness in the workplace is complex. To succeed, line managers and HR managers must behave in ways that are consistent with societal expectations regarding employee and employer rights and responsibilities.[35] Failure to do so jeopardizes the success of their companies.

During the 20th century, society's expectations gradually shifted from the doctrine of *employment-at-will,* which seemed to give employers the right to treat employees in almost any way they wished, to a more balanced approach to employment relations. Early in the century, the rights of most concern to employees were basic working conditions. Both the rhetoric of union organizers and early workplace legislation reflected these concerns. In comparison, from the mid-1970s to the mid-1990s, much attention focused on the right to equal opportunities in employment: women's opportunities should equal men's, and members of minority groups should have the same opportunities as members of the majority.[36]

A new *USA Today*/CNN/Gallup poll, one of the most extensive in the 30-year history of affirmative action, finds 55 percent support the broad concept of expanding opportunities for minorities and women.

Only a third, 37 percent, want such programs cut back; 31 percent want efforts increased; 26 percent want them kept at the same level.

Most people favor affirmative action, but not the actual remedies.

But support drops sharply when people are asked about specific efforts to combat past discrimination and improve chances of women and minorities in hiring, promotion, contracting, and schooling:

- 67 percent oppose setting aside scholarships at public universities for women and minorities.
- 63 percent oppose hiring quotas.
- 84 percent oppose hiring a less qualified minority over a white applicant at a business that has few minority workers. Resistance to such favoritism includes 68 percent of blacks.

White men are the strongest opponents of affirmative action, though most say they have not personally been affected.

- Only 15 percent of white men say they've lost a job because of affirmative action; 42 percent of black men say they lost a job because of discrimination.[37]

Fairness for All Groups

We now recognize that unfair discrimination can take many forms. Eliminating discrimination on the basis of race, age, and gender has been the focus of most attention in the recent past. As we move into the 21st century, and as the workforce becomes more diverse, however, it is increasingly evident that members of other groups, for example those with disabilities, sometimes are victims of unfair discrimination.[38] Gradually, legal protection has been extended to prohibit more and more types of discrimination.[39]

Recently, the U.S. Supreme Court ruled that state and local governments must justify their preference programs on the basis of narrowly defined past discrimination.[40] This action may cause a re-evaluation of other equal opportunity and affirmative action laws; however, it appears unlikely to cause a shift in the employment practices of many companies. If a company depends on employees for a competitive advantage, "you've got to create an environment to attract people from all segments of the population," proclaims Jim Porter, Honeywell Inc.'s vice-president for human resources.[41]

Programs to reverse past discrimination need to be narrowly and specifically focused.

Nevertheless, for members of some groups, no legal protection is currently available, and it is probably safe to predict that regardless of how broadly the reach of legal protection eventually extends, some groups of employees will always remain vulnerable to legal unfair treatment. In other words, legal compliance will likely never guarantee total workplace fairness. Ensuring workplace fairness requires attending to the fabric of the organization's culture.

Fairness in All Aspects of Employment Relations

A second shift in perspective has been the recognition that concerns about fairness and equal opportunity are relevant to many aspects of managing people. For many years, the term *equal opportunity* had been interpreted to mean equal hiring opportunities for entry-level jobs. In other words, attention focused most often on assessing whether unfair discrimination was occurring when hiring new organizational members, especially for jobs that had very large numbers of applicants, that is, entry-level jobs. As we move into the 21st century, this type of fairness is recognized as only a small piece of a much larger pie. Concerns about fairness permeate all aspects of managing human resources and are as relevant to people at the top of the company as to people at lower levels of the company.

"To fully capture the competitive advantages of diversity, Salomon Brothers is striving to become the 'employer of choice' by creating an environment where every individual is respected, valued, and encouraged..."

Deryck Maughan
Chairman and CEO
Salomon Brothers

Fairness and Ethics

It is easy to emphasize the responsibility of employers to treat employees fairly. Fairness is a two-sided coin, however, and the other side is the responsibility of employees to treat their employers fairly. This side of the coin is often referred to as ethics. The feature "Managing Human Resources at J. P. Morgan" illustrates the point that fairness and ethics depend upon mutual respect and concern. In many firms, the responsibilities of employees are spelled out in policy statements on conflicts of interest.

Both employer and employee have a responsibility for fair and ethical behavior.

MANAGING HUMAN RESOURCES

at J. P. Morgan

A guiding philosophy of J.P. Morgan's approach to managing human resources is that the contract between the firm and its employees should be based on mutual commitment. From the firm's perspective, a fair situation requires that both employees and the firm live up to each other's expectations. The expectations the firm has for employees, and the firm's statement of how they will reciprocate in their relationships with employees, is spelled out in a company document titled, *Mutual Commitment: Guiding Principles of the Relationship Between Morgan and You.* The excerpt below addresses the area of ethics:

Ethics: We insist on the highest standards of personal and professional conduct so that we will be deserving of our clients' and colleagues' trust.

The firm expects you to:

- Act with personal and professional integrity
- Understand and comply fully with the letter and spirit of laws and regulations, as well as the firm's rules and policies
- Safeguard the firm's reputation
- Preserve the confidentiality of information about our clients, colleagues, and the firm

You can expect the firm to:

- Engage in business activities that are consistent with its reputation for integrity
- Articulate its standards and rules clearly
- Provide you with support in making legal and ethical decisions
- Refuse to tolerate illegal, unethical, or unprofessional conduct

Source: Adapted from "Mutual Commitment: Guiding Principles of the Relationship Between Morgan and You," *JP Morgan* (1994).

Conflict-of-interest policies are often implemented by employers to ensure ethical business conduct and high standards of integrity. Generally, such policies specify that the best interests of the company must be employees' foremost concern in all business dealings.

Typical conflict-of-interest policies prohibit employees from serving, in any capacity, a competitor of a company with which the employer does business. Such policies also may require employees to:

- Disqualify themselves from involvement in transactions that could lead to personal financial gain or other benefits for the employees
- Refuse gifts or entertainment offered by anyone who has a business relationship with the employer
- Refrain from using company information for personal gain or divulging proprietary information to anyone who would use it in a manner detrimental to the employer.[42]

By developing and using these policies, the employers essentially define unethical and ethical behavior. Thus, what is fair is defined not so much by the larger society, but by the specific organization. Often, organizational and societal definitions may overlap. For example, the company may say that departing employees cannot take company secrets. It would justify such a policy in the courts on the basis that taking company secrets and documents is stealing.

Harassment in the Workplace

HR and line managers always need to be alert to employees' concerns about fairness. In today's workplaces three concerns are particularly salient: harassment, employment-at-will, and privacy.

Three major fairness concerns today include:

- **Harassment**
- **Employment-at-will**
- **Privacy**

Harassment is offensive and hostile behavior in a work environment that prohibits effective performance; leads to expensive financial settlements and negative publicity that tarnishes the company's image; and, ultimately, interferes with the ability of the company to attract and retain the best talent.[43]

What Is Harassment? In 1980, the EEOC issued guidelines stating that sexual harassment is a form of gender discrimination. This view was consistent with several earlier court decisions (*Tomkins v. Public Service Electric and Gas Company*, 1977; *William v. Saxbe*, 1976; *Barnes v. Costle*, 1977; *Heelen v. Johns-Manville Corporation*, 1978). According to the guidelines, verbal and physical conduct of a sexual nature is harassment when the following conditions are present:

- Submission to such conduct is either explicitly or implicitly made a term or condition of an individual's employment
- Submission to, or rejection of, such conduct by an individual is used as the basis for employment decisions affecting that individual
- Such conduct has the purpose or effect of substantially interfering with an individual's work performance or creating an intimidating, hostile, or offensive working environment

In 1993, the EEOC issued regulations that broadened the types of harassment considered illegal.[44] Under the new regulations, employers have a duty to maintain a working environment free of harassment based on race, color, religion, gender, national origin, age, or disability. Furthermore, conduct is harassment if it creates a hostile, intimidating, or offensive work environment; unreasonably interferes with the individual's work; or adversely affects the individual's employment opportunities. Harassing conduct includes such things as racist epithets, raunchy jokes, and ethnic slurs, and usually, though not always, it is systematic.

The 1993 regulations clarify that the standard for evaluating harassment is whether a "reasonable person" in the same or similar circumstances would find the conduct intimidating, hostile, or abusive. The perspective of the victim—her or his race, gender, age, place of origin, and so forth—has an important place in the evaluation. This is an expansion of the "reasonable-woman" standard articulated in *Ellison v. Brady* (1991). There the court said that "unsolicited love letters and unwanted attention. . . might appear inoffensive to the average man, but might be so offensive to the average woman as to create a hostile working environment." The "average woman" in this case became the "reasonable woman," and this standard was reaffirmed later in *Harris v. Forklift Systems* (1993).[45]

Did You KNOW?

If an outside contractor sends into a workplace employees who sexually harass the on-site workers, those workers can sue their employer who hired the outside contractor.

Finally, the 1993 EEOC guidelines clearly state that employers are liable for the acts of those who work for them if they knew or should have known about the conduct and took no immediate, appropriate corrective action. Employers who fail to draw up explicit, detailed antiharassment policies and grievance procedures may put themselves at particular risk.[46]

Preventing Harassment. Strategies to prevent harassment begin with a clear policy statement describing the management philosophy. At Northern States Power, a letter from CEO James J. Howard to employees reads, in part: "All of us have the right to be treated fairly, with dignity and respect. Any violation of this right simply will not be tolerated. We will continue to enforce a 'Zero Tolerance' approach to all forms of discrimination and harassment. Inappropriate behavior will result in the strict use of our Positive Discipline program with the possibility of termination. . . . Join me in making this a company that respects men and women of all ages, races, backgrounds, affectional orientations, and physical abilities."[47]

Discrimination and harassment are not tolerated at Northern States Power Co.

To support such policy statements, effective strategies include the following:[48]

- Raise affirmatively the issue of harassment. Acknowledge that it may be present in the company, and make all employees aware of the company's position on harassment.
- Build in checkpoints designed to detect harassment. For example, review all discharges to ensure that the employee was clearly performing poorly and had been given adequate opportunity to improve.
- Set up reporting procedures for harassed employees to use. Employers are responsible for taking immediate and appropriate corrective action when harassment occurs. To do so, they must first be aware of its happening. In designing reporting procedures, protections are needed to assure harassed employees that they will not experience retaliation for reporting the situation.
- Establish procedures for corroborating a harassment charge, and give the person accused of harassment opportunity to respond immediately after charges are made. Due process must be provided the alleged perpetrator as well as the alleged victim.
- Specify a set of steps in a framework of progressive discipline for perpetrators of harassment. These could be the same steps used by the organization in treating any violation of company policies.

Implementing these strategies does not guarantee elimination of harassment, but it does help communicate the company's expectations and provides a fair means for enforcing appropriate behavior. Training programs further support efforts to prevent harassment. Awareness-training programs can help employees understand the pain and indignity of harassment. If they are comprehensive and used aggressively, such programs can be highly effective. According to one study, the estimated cost for training ranges from $5,000 for a small company to $200,000 for a large one. These rates compare favorably against the costs of losing key employees, incurring negative publicity, and handling expensive lawsuits. According to one attorney who specializes in defending companies against sexual harassment lawsuits, employers spend an average of $200,000 on each complaint that is investigated in-house and found not to be valid. For claims that are valid and end up in court, you can add the cost of the average court verdict for sexual harassment, which is $225,000. Up to 90 percent of the *Fortune* 500 companies have dealt with sexual harassment complaints and 25 percent have been sued repeatedly. It is easy then to see why one labor lawyer estimates the total cost of harassment in the $1 billion range.[49]

While this training may seem costly, the alternatives are even more costly.

Employment-at-Will

As the industrial era was beginning, near the end of the 19th century, employers managed their businesses under the assumption that they had the right to terminate employees for any reason. This right is known as the **employment-at-will** doctrine. It is a common-law rule with historical roots in medieval England. In the United States, one Tennessee court explained it as follows: "All may dismiss their employee(s) at will, be they many or few, for good cause, for no cause, or even for cause morally wrong without being thereby guilty of legal wrong" (*Payne v. Western and A.R.R Company*, 1884).

Employment-at-will means that the employer can fire you at any time for no reason.

Limits to the Employment-at-Will Doctrine. The courts still recognize the force of at-will employment, but during the 20th century, numerous regulations and court decisions acknowledged that employers should not have absolute autonomy to end a person's employment. Giving employers too much self-government would be harmful to employees and essentially nullify all employee rights. Thus, the *Civil Rights Act*, the *Age Discrimination in Employment Act*, and the

Americans with Disabilities Act each curtail employers' use of the employment-at-will doctrine by stating that certain personal characteristics (race, sex, age, etc.) cannot be used as justification for employment decisions of any kind, including termination. In addition, the *National Labor Relations Act* prohibits discharge for union-organizing activities or for asserting rights under a union contract, even if the employee in question had a record of poor performance (*National Labor Relations Board v. Transportation Management*, 1983).[50] When employees are represented by a union, the union contract replaces the employment-at-will doctrine and specifies the conditions under which an employee may be fired.

Did You KNOW?

A statement about job security in an employee handbook can become an enforceable legal contract that protects the employees.

Individual employees are not the only beneficiaries of changing views about employment-at-will; society also has a stake in this issue. For example, it is clearly to the benefit of society in general to have employees who are willing to expose the unethical and illegal behaviors of their employers. To encourage employees to "blow the whistle," society protects employees from losing their jobs for blowing the whistle.[51]

Today, fair employment practices prohibit employers from terminating employees for many reasons including the following:

- Whistle-blowing (for example, opposing and publicizing employer policies or practices that violate laws such as the antitrust, consumer protection, or environmental protection laws)
- Being garnished for any one indebtedness
- Complaining or testifying about violations of equal pay, wage, or hour laws
- Complaining or testifying about safety hazards or refusing an assignment because of the belief that it is dangerous
- Engaging in union activities, provided there is no violence or unlawful behavior
- Engaging in concerted activity to protest wages, working conditions, or safety hazards
- Filing a workers' compensation claim
- Filing unfair labor practice charges with the National Labor Relations Board (NLRB) or a state agency
- Filing discrimination charges with the EEOC or a state or municipal fair employment agency
- Reporting OSHA violations
- Cooperating in the investigation of a charge against the company[52]

Permissible Termination. In union settings, employers often agree to contracts that include clauses stating that employees will be terminated only for good cause. Although this doctrine is not an explicitly stated condition of employment for most nonunion workers, these workers may implicitly expect it to apply to them. Few employees expect their jobs to be guaranteed for life regardless of their own behavior. Nevertheless, employers and employees do not always agree on what constitutes "good cause" for termination, and many disputes on this issue have been resolved in the courts. The decisions of the courts suggest that termination is fair and legal when it occurs for the following reasons:

Companies can fire employees legally for many reasons.

- Incompetence in performance that does not respond to training or to accommodation
- Gross or repeated insubordination
- Civil rights violations such as engaging in harassment

- Too many unexcused absences
- Illegal behavior such as theft
- Repeated lateness
- Drug activity on the job
- Verbal abuse
- Physical violence
- Falsification of records
- Drunkenness on the job[53]

At the federal level and for most states, the law does not currently require employers to have good cause for terminating employees. Currently, Montana is the only state which has adopted a just-cause standard for dismissal, preempting the at-will doctrine. This is contained in the *Montana Wrongful Discharge from Employment Act*, which was passed in 1987. This legislation was enacted at the urging of employers who were being besieged by wrongful discharge lawsuits which frequently resulted in exorbitant damage awards for plaintiffs. Violations of the statute are punishable by damage awards of up to four years wages or salary, plus attorneys' fees. The Montana statute also encourages employers to develop and use grievance procedures to resolve disputes internally. Following Montana's lead, the Uniform Law Commissioners developed the *Model Employment Termination Act* for other states to adopt, so continued changes can be expected at the state level. As we move into the 21st century, it seems likely that fewer and fewer employees will accept the 1884 view of what constitutes fair termination, and more employees will expect employers to adopt procedurally fair practices.

Similarly, the courts are expressing new views about acceptable reasons and procedures for terminating employees. Decisions of the past 10 years emphasize the value of procedural justice. That is, termination of employment should be the last step in a series of documented steps designed to ensure that an employee understood that performance problems existed and had opportunity to improve. Furthermore, all evidence and material relevant to each step should be documented and filed. Even though an employer may have the right to discharge an employee, the employer may be required to show evidence indicating that none of the protections against wrongful termination were violated. In the next chapter, there is more discussion of terminations and layoffs as related to entire plant and office closings.

Employee Privacy

Simply stated, the **right to privacy** is the right to keep information about ourselves to ourselves. Nowhere in the Bill of Rights are private-sector employees directly guaranteed a right to privacy. Perhaps this is why Henry Ford faced no resistance from the government when he sent social workers to the homes of employees to investigate their personal habits and family finances. He and other early industrialists were free to monitor whether employees went to church and to check up on the dating habits of their young female employees. Such invasions of privacy went hand-in-hand with the doctrine of employment-at-will.

Right to privacy is the right to keep information about ourselves to ourselves.

Although the U.S. Constitution does not guarantee us the right to privacy, in 1965, the U.S. Supreme Court concluded that various guarantees stated in the Constitution (e.g., the Fourth Amendment's protection against illegal search and seizure) have the effect of creating zones of privacy.[54] Since then, new state and federal legislation has begun to address employee privacy rights more explicitly. The best example of this at the federal level is the *Family Education Rights and Privacy Act* of 1974, also known as the Buckley Amendment. It allows students to

Employees have more privacy rights in the public sector than the private sector.

inspect their educational records and prevents educational institutions from supplying information without students' consent. Employee rights to control private information were also a consideration in the passage of the *Employment Polygraph Protection Act* of 1988, which gives individuals the right to refuse to take a polygraph test as a condition of employment for most jobs.

Other privacy legislation is of a much weaker form. Rather than giving individuals control over who gets what information, most statutes simply give individuals a right to access and verify the information others already have.

The Privacy Act of 1974 was the first major statute to address issues of privacy directly. This act, which applies only to federal agencies, gives individuals the right to verify information collected about them and used in selection and employment decisions. It allows individuals to determine which records pertaining to them are collected, used, and maintained; to review and amend such records; to prevent unspecified use of such records; and to bring civil suit for damages against those intentionally violating the rights specified in the act. The Privacy Act is consistent with the *Freedom of Information Act* of 1974, which allows individuals to see all the material a federal agency uses in its decision-making processes.

In contrast to federal employees and citizens affected by the decisions of federal agencies, private-sector employees are relatively unprotected against employers who have the ability to access and use information, often without the knowledge or consent of employees or job applicants. Two laws establish exceptions to this generalization:

- The *Fair Credit and Reporting Act* of 1970 permits job applicants to know the nature and content of credit files, which can easily be obtained by potential employers and used for employment or other legitimate business purposes.
- The *Employee Exposure and Medical Records Regulation* of 1980 gives employees the right to access their on-the-job medical records and records that document their exposure to toxic substances.

Concerns about privacy also are addressed by state-level legislation. Several state laws—for example, in California, Connecticut, Maine, Michigan, Oregon, and Pennsylvania—give employees access to their HR files and define what information employees are and are not entitled to see, as well as where, when, and under what circumstances employees may view their files.[55]

There are many questions about privacy yet to be answered.

Issues of privacy will continue to be debated into the 21st century. Questions to be answered include: How much access should employers have to medical records? Is there any nonmedical information that employers should not have the right to obtain, and are all methods of monitoring employees acceptable? Should employers have the right to use information about employees' behavior off the job when making employment decisions?[56] The feature "HR Advice and Application: Opinions About Privacy," shows how U.S. workers and HR executives feel about some such questions.

Do you believe companies should have the right to refuse to hire an overweight job applicant?

Access to Medical Information. Health insurance costs grew so dramatically from the mid-1980s to the mid-1990s that many employers now feel pressure to do whatever is necessary to contain healthcare costs. One way to lower these costs is to employ people who make little use of health care services, because insurance for such employees is less expensive. Like insurance companies, employers can predict how much health care a person is likely to need if they have information about variables that put people into high-health-risk categories: Does she smoke? Is he overweight? Does she abuse alcohol or use other drugs? Does he exercise regularly? Does she like to bungee jump or drive too fast?

A study of 4000 employees by DuPont documented the following additional annual costs associated with several personal behaviors and conditions:[57]

HR ADVICE & APPLICATION

Options About Privacy

In 1993, Louis Harris and Associates, a firm that specializes in opinion polls, surveyed a national cross-section of 1,000 private-sector employers.

% WHO SAY EMPLOYERS SHOULD NOT BE ABLE TO DO IT:	
Verify education levels attained	81%
Forbid employees from engaging in dangerous sports and hobbies	90%
Forbid alcohol consumption off the job	93%
Forbid tobacco consumption off the job	88%
Require overweight employees to lose weight	80%
Require genetic testing	88%
Require AIDS testing	73%
Test job applicants for drugs	30%

Source: Adapted from "Employer Intrusions Shunned," *Bulletin to Management* (September 1, 1994): 280.

Average smoking habit	$960
Excessive weight	$401
Alcohol abuse	$369
Elevated cholesterol	$370
High blood pressure	$343

Data like these support General Mills' policy of lowering workers' insurance premiums if they lead healthy lives, as measured by behaviors such as not smoking, drinking little or no alcohol, controlling blood pressure and cholesterol, and wearing seat belts. They also support Turner Broadcasting System's policy of not hiring people who smoke and help explain why drug testing has quickly gone from a rare to a routine practice.[58]

It appears that employers can penalize or even terminate employees because of some types of conditions associated with high health care costs. But other employee conditions are clearly protected. The *Americans with Disabilities Act* (ADA) protects anyone with a history of drug use who has successfully completed or is currently engaged in rehabilitation. Certain exceptions exist, especially when public safety may be at risk. The ADA also states that a medical exam may be given only after a conditional job offer has been made. Then, the offer may be rescinded only if the exam reveals a condition that would prevent the applicant from performing the job, and cannot be accommodated. Under the ADA, medical records are supposed to be kept separate from other human resource records and treated as confidential.[59]

The ADA protects primarily people with disabilities. It does not address directly the question of how employers might use information about genetic makeup. Advances in our understanding of the link between genetics and disease susceptibility raise new concerns about medical privacy. Should a 25-year-old applicant for a sales job be required to undergo genetic screening for diseases that he or she may experience in middle age? Is it fair to penalize workers with high cholesterol, given that genes as well as diet affect cholesterol levels?

Advances in medicine may introduce new frontiers in privacy.

Access to Nonmedical Information. Employers who seek medical information usually do so for good reasons. They may be concerned about keeping health insurance costs as low as possible or about protecting employees and customers from contagious diseases or unsafe behavior.[60] Medical information seems to be directly relevant to such concerns.

What about other concerns? For example, research suggests linkages between watching violent TV and movies and engaging in violent behavior.[61] With violence in the workplace becoming a major issue in our society, should employers be allowed, perhaps even expected, to attempt to screen out employees whose viewing behaviors suggest they are likely to be violent?[62] Suppose an employer wants to ensure that employees do not engage in illegal behaviors, such as industrial espionage, drug dealing, or insider trading: Does this give the employer the right to listen in on employees' telephone calls? Do employers have the right to access and use all computer files on employees' office PCs? May employers monitor all employee mail and e-mail communications?[63] These types of ethical dilemmas are unresolved, although many HR departments are actively working to craft appropriate practices and procedures to address these issues.

International Considerations

When operating abroad, as when operating at home, complying with legal regulations is one step toward managing fairly. To be truly effective, however, managers need to realize that perceptions of fairness reflect cultural assumptions and values—not just legal realities. Managers who are insensitive to the broader social fabric will find it difficult to anticipate employees' reactions to how they are treated. Unenlightened managers run the risk of triggering negative employee reactions.

Termination Liabilities

In many countries, termination of employment is viewed as a harsh action that is potentially harmful to employees. Consequently, in fairness to employees, employers are held responsible for minimizing its negative consequences. Most countries have some traditional or legally required practices take effect in the event of a plant closing or a substantial reduction of the workforce.[64] In general, these practices create costlier and more extensive employer obligations than do layoffs in the United States and Canada. One such obligation is the individual termination payment required by law, collective bargaining agreements, or individual contracts.

Furthermore, in many countries, a company that wishes to close down or curtail operations also must develop a "social plan" or its equivalent, typically in concert with unions and other interested stakeholders. The plan may cover continuation of pay, benefit plan coverage, retraining allowances, relocation expenses, and supplementation of statutory unemployment compensation. Frequently, a company planning a partial or total plant closing must present its case to a government agency. In the Netherlands, for example, authorities may deny permission for a substantial workforce reduction unless management is able to demonstrate that the cutback is absolutely necessary for economic reasons and that the company has an approved social plan.

Employee-Employer Expectations in Mexico

Mexico's social structure is similar to its family structure, and its institutions—whether government, business, or church—resemble an authoritarian, paternalistic family. A plant manager, like the president of Mexico, fills a fatherly role, rather than a mere organizational function.

Mexican law and history reflect the Mexican view that the employer has a moral and paternal responsibility for all its employees, even when the workers have a union. Mexican employees are not just working for a paycheck: they tend to expect to be treated as the "extended family" of the boss; they expect to receive a wide range of services, including food baskets and medical attention for themselves and their families, apart from social security. Medical benefits are not considered "an extra" or discretionary; they simply fulfill the employer's role and responsibilities. Corresponding to these expectations, employees have a reciprocal obligation to be loyal, to work hard, and to be willing to do whatever is requested of them. American managers who accept the Mexican sense that a job is more than a paycheck and who try to fulfill the expectations of their employees can reap the benefits of these reciprocal expectations.

Summary

Workplace fairness is a complex issue that touches all employees and all employers. When managing human resources, the question "What is fair?" may be difficult to answer. Historically, the power to determine workplace conditions rested largely in employers' hands. Gradually, society recognized that this was unfair and a shift in the power balance was needed. Numerous laws now sanction employer actions. Some practices that employers once considered fair are now illegal.

A first step toward ensuring workplace fairness, therefore, is legal compliance. Legal compliance is expected of employers, and HR professionals are often responsible for ensuring compliance. By following the laws, employers should at least be able to protect themselves from losing lawsuits alleging unfair employment practices. However, workplace fairness is more than an issue of legal compliance. Even legal employer actions may be considered unfair by employees. For example, drug-testing practices are becoming routine. They are accepted as legal by the courts. Does this mean employees agree that drug testing is fair? Not necessarily. Employees tend to evaluate whether drug testing is fair on a case-by-case basis. They weigh issues of invasion of privacy, threats to safety and health, the specific procedures used to conduct the drug tests, and the penalties associated with failing a drug test.[65] Even the American Medical Association prefers to see employers use other means for detecting drug use, such as simple eye-hand coordination tests.[66]

Managing human resources fairly requires an understanding of how employees evaluate fairness. Managing in ways that meet the principles of distributive and procedural justice is one approach to creating fair employment conditions. In addition, because perceptions of fairness constantly change, employees' attitudes about fairness should be determined and taken into account when establishing policies. Finally, managers need to understand that the same policy and the same outcome can be perceived as relatively fair or unfair depending on the attitudes they display and the amount of respect they show for the concerns of employees.

Key Concepts

- alternative dispute resolution (ADR)
- distributive justice
- employee rights
- employment-at-will doctrine
- fairness
- harassment
- managing employees fairly
- procedural justice
- right to privacy

Review and Discussion Questions

1. What does Hallmark Cards do that makes it such a great place to work?
2. Why should companies be concerned about managing employees fairly?

3. What are procedural justice and distributive justice? Why are they important?
4. Describe possible employee reactions to unfair treatment.
5. How does the grievance procedure work at Coors?
6. Describe the legal regulations ensuring fair treatment.
7. What is the employment-at-will doctrine? Why do you suppose courts in the late 1880s were more willing to uphold the doctrine than courts are today?
8. How would you distinguish a just from an unjust dismissal? Is this distinction easier to make for lower-level jobs than for upper-level or managerial jobs? Explain.
9. What kinds of behaviors might constitute sexual harassment? How does an organization prevent those behaviors from occurring?
10. What are the major issues involved in privacy rights of employees?

PROJECTS, EXERCISES & CASES

End-of-Text Projects

Lincoln Electric

1. What is the evidence that Lincoln Electric manages employees fairly? Are there are any aspects of Lincoln's practices that you would consider unfair? Why?
2. Describe what Lincoln's management appears to expect from employees. What does Lincoln agree to give employees in return? How do the expectations and responsibilities of Lincoln's management relate to notions of distributive and procedural justice?

Nordstrom

1. What is the evidence that Nordstrom manages employees fairly? Are there are any aspects of Nordstrom's practices that you would consider unfair? Why?
2. Describe what Nordstrom's management appears to expect from employees. What does Nordstrom agree to give employees in return? How do the expectations and responsibilities of Nordstrom's management relate to notions of distributive and procedural justice?

Field Project

1. Interview five people who work in different companies. Ask them if they are treated fairly. Ask them how they could be managed more fairly.
2. Consult BNA's Fair Employment Practices manual, Labor Relations Reporter, or Labor Arbitration Reports to find a recent case that involves a charge of unjust dismissal. Address the following issues: What type of job was involved? Describe the discharged employee (age, gender, prior history with company). Did the company have a grievance procedure? On what basis did the employee contest the discharge? What did the judge or arbitrator rule? Why? State whether you agree with the outcome of the case, and why.
3. Interview an individual who has experienced harassment on the job. Report to the class on the content of the interview, including such things as:
   a. Where did the harassment take place?
   b. Who was involved?
   c. How long did it last?
   d. What did the person(s) do?
   e. How did the person feel?
   f. What was the resolution or what is the person trying to do now to resolve the situation?

VISIT THE LIBRARY

Workforce Online

Because you are now familiar with getting onto the Internet and using the Workforce Online, the following steps are abbreviated.

1. Enter your Web browser.
2. Enter Workforce Online.
3. Enter the Research Center.
4. Find and review the following article: "The Possible Legal Entanglements of Motivating Temps"
5. Return to your homepage.

Career Management Exercise: What Will You Do To Protect Your Rights?

After graduation, you get a great job. Your employer has certain rights and responsibilities. Likewise, you, as an employee, have various rights and responsibilities. We have discussed some of these in the chapter. From your knowledge, answer the following questions.

1. Would you sign an ADR? Briefly explain.
2. What would you do if your first supervisor harassed you several times in your first few months on the job? (Alternatively, what would you advise a friend in this same situation?)
3. You have been employed at the company for six months. If you saw illegal activities occurring in the company, what would you do? Explain why you would or wouldn't blow the whistle.

Case: What's Wrong With What's Right?

Stuart Campbell, now 35, moved slowly down the front steps of the courthouse and squinted as the last rays of sunlight pierced through downtown Cleveland. It had been a long day in the life of Stuart Campbell, who had spent the entire day in court recalling the details of his past employment with Nako Electronics, a major marketer of audio tapes in the U.S. Nako Electronics had—and still has—a considerable stake in Stuart Campbell. The arbitrator's decision and the award of $500,000 plus interest of $82,083.50 was a bitter pill for Nako to swallow for having terminated their Midwest sales representative.

Stuart had agreed to meet his attorney, Jim Baldwin, for a couple of drinks and to unwind from the courtroom tension. His spirits began to pick up as he maneuvered through the city traffic, but he couldn't help thinking how, within a year's time, his good job had soured.

Five years ago, Stuart Campbell was riding high as the Midwest representative for Nako covering Ohio, West Virginia, and Pennsylvania. Stuart, a hard worker, contracted with Nako Electronics and then boosted the sluggish sales of Nako audio tapes from less than $300,000 to a $2 million business in about 14 months. In fact, business was going so well for Stuart that he began driving a Mercedes-Benz 450 SEL. But that's when Mike Hammond, vice-president of marketing at Nako Electronics, took notice of Campbell. On one of his visits to Campbell's territory, Hammond commented to Stuart that he really liked his car. Mike remarked that he was making a trip to California soon. "I distinctly remember Mike saying he would like to have a Buick," Stuart testified. "He didn't want anything as fancy as I had, because a new Buick would be adequate and, after all, he wanted me to bear the expense!"

Mike Hammond unfortunately couldn't be in court that day to defend himself; Hammond died unexpectedly last year of a heart attack. During the trial, though, Nako Electronics had to defend a number of allegations made against Mike Hammond. It seems that some of Stuart Campbell's co-workers suffered a similar fate. Not only had Stuart refused to go along with Hammond's car scheme, but he also refused to invest in a cartridge business begun by Hammond, which Stuart believed was a phony. Hammond, in fact, had approached all the sales representatives of Nako Electronics to invest in the cartridge company at $1,250 a share, a company for which Hammond and two other associates paid $1 a share for 80 percent of the stock. Stuart's attorney, Jim Baldwin, made sure that two of Stuart's former fellow sales representatives testified at the court proceedings that they were mysteriously fired after refusing Mike Hammond's demands to invest in his side company.

In the year following Stuart's successful boost in the sales of Nako audio tapes and Hammond's thwarted attempts at commercial shakedown, Nako increased Campbell's sales quota by more than 75 percent. As Campbell further testified, Nako sabotaged a substantial proportion of his sales by refusing to give his large customers promotional assistance. In the fall of that year, Nako fired Stuart without explanation. Nako argued in court that it didn't need a reason to fire Campbell and, besides, Campbell wasn't meeting his new, increased sales quota. Moreover, the company argued, Mr. Hammond could not defend himself against the charges of Campbell and others.

Stuart rehashed these details many times with his attorney, both during the private arbitrator hearing and during numerous rehearsals for the trial. As he arrived at the restaurant, he hoped he could put these memories behind him. As they talked, Jim summarized the day's proceedings and expressed cautious optimism for the final outcome. "But you know, Stuart," mused Jim, "If you would have kicked in the $10 or $15K that Hammond demanded, you would have outlived him, you'd have a business worth over $4 million in sales today, and we wouldn't be having this drink!"

Case Questions

1. Why did the arbitrator award Stuart so much money?
2. Was the arbitrator's decision a just and fair one?
3. Did Nako have to give Stuart a reason for firing him?
4. If his firing was due to his failure to invest in Hammond's side company, could this be defended in court?
5. Do you think there was anything Stuart could have done, legally, to avoid being fired?
6. How do you think Stuart's old co-workers at Nako would react to what happened to Stuart?

Source: Stuart A. Youngblood, Texas Christian University

Case: The Payback

Lucy Pascal was hired by ABC Jobbers, Inc., two months ago. ABC had wooed Lucy away from her previous employer because of her outstanding sales record. Enticed by a substantial boost in pay, commissions. and perks. Lucy was looking forward to widened professional contacts and increased income. Also, she was thrilled at having been one of the first women to be directly hired for sales work at ABC.

Lucy liked working for her new company even though she was certainly a rarity there. Virtually all of the other professionals and salespeople were male. Most were macho types, often joking and talking about their latest exploits with "a little number" met while on the road. When Lucy was around, they enjoyed teasing her to see what her reaction would be. She would change the subject pleasantly, but their conversations bothered her, and then there were all the centerfold pictures prominently displayed in a lot of the offices, which Lucy did her best to ignore. Yet, even with all this, she was still pleased she had made the job move because of its growth potential.

On one of her initial sales calls in her newly assigned district, Lucy visited Frank Grumman, a major client who was responsible for signing off on all sales contracts for his company. Lucy gave Frank Grumman a sales pitch in her typically persuasive and professional manner. Frank responded that he was most impressed not only with the product. but also with Lucy herself. He cajoled her to go out with him so they "could get to know each other better." Lucy began feeling increasingly uncomfortable with Frank's comments. It was obvious he was more interested in her as a woman than as ABC's sales representative.

Finally, in response to his insistent urgings that they take off together for the evening, Lucy, as nicely as she could, gave him a firm no. She, with a forced smile, advised him she had to catch an early flight.

Frank, feeling rejected, testily replied that Lucy really must not want the contract very much if she wasn't going to "entertain" him. Angered, Lucy told him in no uncertain terms what he could do with the contract if "entertaining" was part of the price she had to pay in order to get it. She stormed out of Frank's office.

Upon returning to her district office, Lucy related to James Roberts, her first-line supervisor and the district sales manager, what had happened on her sales call. James reacted with laughter. He said to Lucy, "There are certain things we all have to do to keep our clients happy.

If you knew all the rounds of golf I've played with some real creeps for business purposes, then you'd realize what I was talking about." Lucy said "James, I'm not talking about playing golf. That's not the type of game he wanted me to play." James grew chilly. He told Lucy "By God, you better not lose that contract. You do, and you'll lose your district and all its fat commissions!"

Lucy had been placed in a no-win situation by both her client and her boss. As she pondered over her dilemma, the chief executive officer of ABC saw her in the hall. "Lucy," said Donald Stubbs, "what's my favorite new sales gal looking so worried about?"

"Come on into my office and tell me how things are going." The grandfatherly Mr. Stubbs gently ushered Lucy into his office. After only a few moments, Lucy blurted out her situation. Losing control, and to her great embarrassment, she broke into tears. Concerned, Mr. Stubbs placed his arms around Lucy to console her. Lucy soon calmed down enough to apologize for her behavior. Mr. Stubbs advised her he would place some phone calls and try to smooth things over. As he led her to the door, he admonished her. "You have to realize, Lucy, that men will be men. You'll just have to get used to these things in this business."

Lucy wandered down the hall wondering what was going to happen to her now. Samuel Kindel, a fellow salesperson, spotted Lucy and asked her if she'd like to have some coffee. Lucy replied she needed to talk to someone about the things that were happening to her. In the cafeteria, she told Samuel the entire story and the frustration she felt. Samuel became furious. He told her that "those guys are all no-good skunks." Lucy was relieved to have such a sympathetic ear to bend. As they continued their talk, Samuel said, "You know, I've been wanting to get to know you better ever since you got here, Lucy. What do you say we take in a movie tonight and forget this place?"

Case Questions

1. What sorts of measures could ABC Jobbers take with its clients to prevent this situation?
2. Samuel Kindel asked Lucy for a date. Was she being sexually harassed by him? How do you think she should have responded?
3. Could Lucy have dealt with the situation differently?
4. What type of company policies would you recommend that ABC Jobbers institute for its employees to forestall sexually harassing behaviors?

VISIT THE LIBRARY

End-of-Section Exercises

EXERCISE 1

Many companies have Web pages on the Internet, and some recruit employees using the Internet. Web pages of such organizations usually include some information about company culture and may provide insight as to how the organization deals with specific HRM issues, such as workforce diversity. A visit to Microsoft's Web page will illustrate this.

1. After entering your Web browser, go to the following Internet address:

   http://www.microsoft.com

   Alternatively, you can find Microsoft's address (and addresses of many other organizations) by going to the address:

   http://www.directory.web.

   This Web page is an alphabetical listing of organizations with Internet sites, and includes an option to search for a specific organization.
2. Click on "About Microsoft."
3. Click on "Employment."
4. Click on "Microsoft Culture," under the heading "Information."
5. Click on "Diversity" to read about Microsoft's policy on diversity.
6. Click on "Diversity and Social Groups" to read about social groups within Microsoft that help to promote diversity and cultural awareness within the organization.
7. Return to your homepage.

EXERCISE 2

The purpose of this section is simply to introduce you to Cornell University's Law Documents, an Internet site that provides information on laws relevant to employment. This site will be used in later exercises.

1. Use your Web browser to go to the following address:

   http://www.law.cornell.edu/topics/topic2.html
2. After browsing through the topics on this Web page, return to your homepage.

Chapter 4 Endnotes

1. D. Aufuso, "Coors Taps Employee Judgment," *Personnel Journal* (February 1994): 56.

2. G. Flynn, "A Satisfied Work Force Is in Hallmark's Cards," January 1996. "Optimas Awards Celebrate Exemplary HR," *Personnel Journal* (January 1996): 50.

3. J. Greenberg, "Looking Fair vs. Being Fair: Managing Impressions of Organizational Justice," in B. M. Staw and L. L. Cummings, eds., *Research in Organizational Behavior*, vol. 12 (Greenwich, CT: JM Press, 1990), 111–157.

4. R. Levering, *A Great Place to Work* (New York: Random House, 1988).

5. For good reviews of research on these topics, see T. R. Tyler and E. A. Lind, "A Relational Model of Authority in Groups," *Advances in Experimental Social Psychology* 25 (1992): 115–191; R. Cropanzano, ed., *Justice in the Workplace: Approaching Fairness in Human Resource Management* (Hillsdale, NJ: Lawrence Erlbaum Associates, Publishers, 1993); B. H. Sheppard, R. J. Lewicki, and J. W. Minton, *Organizational Justice: The Search for Fairness in the Workplace* (New York: Lexington Books, 1992).

6. M. P. Miceli, "Justice and Pay System Satisfaction," in Cropanzano, *Justice in the Workplace*; R. L. Heneman, D. B. Greenberger, and S. Strasser, "The Relationship between Pay-for-Performance Perceptions and Pay Satisfaction," *Personnel Psychology* 41 (1988): 745–761; M. P. Miceli et al., "Predictors and Outcomes of Reactions to Pay-for-Performance Plans," *Journal of Applied Psychology* 76 (1991): 508–521.

7. K. James, "The Social Context of Organizational Justice: Cultural, Intergroup, and Structural Effects on Justice Behaviors and Perceptions," in Cropanzano, *Justice in the Workplace*; H. C. Triandis, "Cross-Cultural Industrial and Organizational Psychology," in H. C. Triandis, M. D. Dunnette, and L. M. Hough, eds., *Handbook of Industrial and Organizational Psychology*, 4 (Palo Alto, CA: Consulting Psychologists Press, 1994), 103–172.

8. See for example, H. C. Triandis, "The Self and Social Behavior in Differing Cultural Contexts," *Psychological Review* 96 (1989): 506–520.

9. Cropanzano, *Justice in the Workplace*; Sheppard, Lewicki, and Minton, *Organizational Justice*; Tyler and Lind, "A Relational Model of Authority in Groups."

10. See C. E. Rusbult et al., "Impact of Exchange Variables on Exit, Voice, Loyalty and Neglect: An Integrative Model of Responses to Declining Job Satisfaction," *Academy of Management Journal* 31 (1988): 599–627.

11. R. B. Freeman and J. L. Medoff, *What Do Unions Do?* (New York: Basic Books, 1984).

12. T. R. Tyler and R. Schuler, "A Relational Model of Authority in Work Organizations: The Psychology of Procedural Justice" (manuscript, American Bar Foundation, 1990).

13. D. B. McFarlin and P. D. Sweeney, "Distributive and Procedural Justice as Predictors of Satisfaction with Personal and Organizational Outcomes," *Academy of Management Journal* 35 (1992): 626–637.

14. J. Greenberg, "Employee Theft as a Reaction to Underpayment Inequity: The Hidden Cost of Pay Cuts," *Journal of Applied Psychology* 75 (1990): 561–568.

15. R. B. Freeman and J. L. Medoff, *What Do Unions Do?* (New York: Basic Books, 1984); D. G. Spencer, "Employee Voice and Employee Retention," *Academy of Management Journal* 29 (1986): 488–502.

16. R. H. Moorman, "Relationship between Organizational Justice and Organizational Citizenship Behaviors: Do Fairness Perceptions Influence Employee Citizenship?" *Journal of Applied Psychology* 76, no. 6 (1991): 845–855.

17. "Arbitration Provisions in Union Agreements in 1949," *Monthly Labor Review* 70 (1950): 160–165.

18. See M. E. Gordon and G. E. Fryxell, "The Role of Interpersonal Justice in Organizational Grievance Systems," in Cropanzano, *Justice in the Workplace*.

19. D. W. Ewing, "Who Wants Employee Rights?" *Harvard Business Review* 49 (November-December 1971): 22–35.

20. B. S. Klaas and A. DeNisi, "Managerial Reactions to Employee Dissent: The Impact of Grievance Activity on Performance Ratings," *Academy of Management Journal* 32 (1989):445–458.

21. M. P. Miceli and J. P. Near, *Blowing the Whistle: The Organizational and Legal Implications for Companies and Employees* (New York: Lexington Books, 1992).

22. W. L. F. Felstiner, R. L. Abel, and A. Sarat, "The Emergence and Transformation of Disputes: Naming, Blaming, Claiming. . . ," *Law and Society Review* 15 (1980): 631–654.

23. P. Feujile and J. T. Delaney, "The Individual Pursuit of Organizational Justice: Grievance Procedures in Nonunion Workplaces," *Research in Personnel and Human Resources Management* 10 (1992): 187–232.

24. Institute for Legal Studies, University of Wisconsin, cited in A. H. Ringleb, R. E. Meiners, and F. L. Edwards, *Managing in the Legal Environment* (St. Paul, MN: West Publishing Co., 1993).

25. A. F. Westin and A. G. Felin, *Resolving Employment Disputes without Litigation* (Washington, DC: Bureau of National Affairs, 1988).

26. C. Yang, "The EEOC: Too Swamped to Shoot Straight," *Business Week* (May 1, 1995): 155; P. Eisler, "Overloaded System Tests New Strategies, *USA Today* (August 16, 1995): B6; "Record Number of EEOC Charges Filed in Fiscal Year 1993," *Fair Employment Practices Guidelines* (January 27, 1994): 9.

27. R. D. Arvey and R. H. Faley, *Fairness in Selecting Employees*, 2nd ed. (Reading, MA: Addison-Wesley Publishing Co., 1988).

28. D. Anfuso, "Coors Taps Employee Judgment," *Personnel Journal* (February 1994): 56.

29. F. S. Steingold, *The Legal Guide for Starting & Running a Small Business* (Berkeley, CA.: Nolo Press, 1995); W. E. Barlow, "From Act of Congress to Federal Law: Making Sense of the Regulatory Maze," *Personnel Journal* (February 1995): 100–102.

30. "Firing Proves Costly," *Bulletin to Management* (May 13, 1993): 145.

31. B. Smith, *HR Focus* (February 1992): 1, 6. Used by permission.

32. R. Smothers, "$105 Million Poorer Now, Chain Mends Race Policies," *New York Times* (January 31, 1993): L16.

33. Adapted from "Alternative Ways to Resolve Disputes," *Fair Employment Practices Guidelines* (August 26, 1992): 4–5. See also B. Presley Noble, "Attacking Compulsory Arbitration," *New York Times* (January 15, 1996): F21.

34. "Arbitration Called 'Wave of the Future'," *Bulletin to Management* (November 17, 1994); 368.

35. "Are Supervisors Personally Liable for Bias Under Title VII?" *Fair Employment Practices* (October 6, 1994): 117; "Supervisor Liable Under ADEA," *Fair Employment Practices* (February 9, 1995): 17; "Special Survey Report: Legal Oversight of the HR Department," *Bulletin to Management* (February 2, 1995): 1.

36. C. Marmer-Solomon, "Affirmative Action: What You Need to Know," *Personnel Journal* (August 1995): 57–67; C. Yang et al., "A 'Race-Neutral' Helping Hand?" *Business Week* (February 27, 1995): 120–121; J. P. Pinkerton, "Why Affirmative Action Won't Die," *Fortune* (November 13, 1995): 191–198; J. Kaufman, "How Workplaces May Look Without Affirmative Action," *The Wall Street Journal* (March 20, 1995): B1, 6.

37. A. Stone and J. Norman, "Affirmative Action: Fairness Key to Support," *USA Today* (March 24, 1995): 1.

38. C. Yang and S. Anderson, "Business Has to Find a New Meaning for 'Fairness'," *Business Week* (April 12, 1993): 72; C. Yang and M. McNamee, "A Hand Up, But Not a Handout," *Business Week* (March 27, 1995): 70–72.

39. For more information, see M. E. Gold, *An Introduction to the Law of Employment Discrimination* (Ithaca, NY: ILR Press and Cornell University, 1993); M. D. Levin-Epstein, *Primer of Equal Employment Opportunity* (Washington, DC: Bureau of National Affairs, 1987); J. Ledvinka and V. G. Scarpello, *Federal Regulation of Personnel and Human Resource Management,* 2nd ed. (Boston: PWS Kent, 1991).

40. S. Crock and M. Galen, "Affirmative Action: 'A Thunderous Impact' on Equal Opportunity," *Business Week* (June 26, 1995): 37.

41. Ibid.; M. Galen and A. T. Palmer, "Diversity: Beyond the Numbers Game," *Business Week* (August 14, 1995): 60–61.

42. "A Question of Ethics," *Bulletin to Management* (July 9, 1992): 211.

43. L. Nathans Spiro, "The Angry Voices at Kidder," *Business Week* (February 1, 1994): 60–63.

44. "Employment Agency and Sex Harassment," *Fair Employment Practices Guidelines* (January 12, 1995): 5; "EEOC Proposes Harassment Guidelines," *Fair Employment Practices Guidelines* (July 29, 1993): 87.

45. "Reasonable Woman Standard Gains Ground," *Fair Employment Practices Guidelines* (June 25, 1993): 4.

46. "Harassment Costs Chevron $2 Million; Discrimination Suit Still Pending," *HR Reporter* (March 1995): 6; F. R. Lee, "A Sexual Harasser? His Friends Don't Recognize the Description," *New York Times* (August 5, 1995): 23.

47. *What Is Harassment?* Brochure of the Northern States Power Co.(St. Paul, MN: Company Publication, 1993): 1.

48. J. J. Laabs, "What to Do When Sexual Harassment Comes Calling," *Personnel Journal* (July 1995): 42–53; J. J. Laabs, "HR Put its Questions on the Line: Sexual Harassment," *Personnel Journal* (February 1995): 36–45; "How Employers Can Avoid Liability for Civil Rights Law Violations," *Fair Employment Practices* (August 11, 1994): 93.

49. A. B. Fisher, "Sexual Harassment: What to Do," *Fortune* (August 23, 1993): 84–88.

50. J. D. Aram and P. F. Salipante, "An Evaluation of Organizational Due Process in the Resolution of Employee/Employer Conflict," *Academy of Management Review* 2 (1977): 197–204; B. H. Sheppard, R. J. Lewicki, and J. W. Minton, *Organizational Justice: The Search for Fairness in the Workplace* (New York: Lexington/Macmillan, 1992).

51. C. Sims, "GE Whistle-Blower Is Awarded $13.4 Million," *New York Times* (December 5, 1992): 35. See also B. Ettorre, "Whistleblowers: Who's the Real Bad Guy?" *Management Review* (May 1994): 18–23; S. Antilla, "Whistle-Blowers and Layoffs," *New York Times* (October 9, 1994): 11.

52. "Firing," Fair Employment Practices Guidelines 241 (1985): 3. See also "Discrimination Denied," *Bulletin to Management* (June 13, 1985): 3.

53. "Employment Law Basics: Employees' Rights vs. Employers' Rights," *Fair Employment Practices* (October 5, 1995): 117; C. Roberson, *Hire Right/Fire Right: A Manager's Guide to Employment Practices that Avoid Lawsuits* (New York: McGraw-Hill, 1992).

54. T. J. Wiencek, "Privacy in the Workplace: A Guide for Human Resource Professionals," *Fair Employment Practices Guidelines* (December 10, 1993): 4.

55. "Impose Restrictions on Your Employees' Access to Their Personnel Files," *HR Reporter* (June 1995): 1; J. E. Jackson and W. T. Schantz, "A New Frontier in Wrongful Discharge," *Personnel Journal* (January 1991): 101–104.

56. E. Alderman and C. Kennedy, "Privacy," *Across the Board* (March 1996): 32–35; "Be Careful What Your Employees Think You'll Never Find Out About," *HR Reporter* (May 1994): 1–2; R. Naylor, Jr., "Survey: Many Fear Employers Too Nosey," *Saginaw News* (August 18, 1994): D8; "Right-to-Privacy Lawsuits: A Growing Threat," *Fair Employment Guidelines* (August 10, 1994): 6–8.

57. P. T. Kilborn, "The Boss Only Wants What's Best for You," *New York Times* (May 8, 1994): E3; L. Smith "What the Boss Knows about You," *Fortune* (August 9, 1993): 88–93.

58. I. A. Lipman, "Fight Drugs With Workplace Tests," *New York Times* (July 18, 1993): F15.

59. "Discrimination Charges Filed Under ADA," *Bulletin to Management* (June 2, 1994): 172–173. For a full discussion, see T. L. Jones, *The Americans with Disabilities Act: A Review of Best Practices* (New York: American Management Association, 1993).

60. For a comprehensive discussion of the difficult issues raised by AIDS in the workplace, see W. F. Banta, *AIDS in the Workplace: Legal Questions and Practical Answers* (New York: Lexington Books, 1992).

61. W. Wood, F. Y. Wong, and J. G. Chachere, "Effects of Media Violence on Viewers' Aggression in Unconstrained Social Interaction," *Psychological Bulletin* 109 (1991): 371–383.

62. H. F. Bensimon, "Violence in the Workplace," *Training and Development Journal* (January 1994): 27–32; M. Braverman, "Violence: The Newest Worry on the Job," *New York Times* (December 12, 1993): 11; O. M. Kurland, "Workplace Violence," *Risk Management* 40 (1993): 76–77.

63. "E-Mail Raises Privacy Questions," *Bulletin to Management* (February 25, 1993): 64.

64. P. R. Sparrow and J-M. Hiltrop, *European Human Resource Management in Transition* (New York: Prentice Hall, 1994).

65. B. J. Tepper, "Investigation of General and Program-Specific Attitudes Toward Corporate Drug-Testing Policies," *Journal of Applied Psychology* 79 (1994): 392–401.

66. J. Schaubroeck, D. R. May and F. W. Brown, "Procedural Justice Explanations and Employee Reactions to Economic Hardship: A Field Experiment," *Journal of Applied Psychology* 79 (1994): 455–460; "Two Legal Challenges to Drug Testing," *Fair Employment Practices Guidelines* (February 1993): 2.

SECTION 3

Managing Organizational and Human Resource Changes

All of the forces in the environment of HR management described in Chapters 3 and 4 are not only extensive, they are also changing rapidly! Companies today must be constantly aware of what is happening in the environment and then develop strategies to effectively deal with the changes. Many of these changes involve the management of human resources as described in Chapter 5. For example, the growing global competition is causing many companies to reduce costs. The strategy of many companies to reduce costs is to reduce the workforce, to downsize. When this major HR management issue is handled effectively, the better it will be for the companies and the employees. Other changes that require effective HR management include the growing diversity in the population and the trend of mergers and acquisitions. Companies need to systematically identify these changes and develop HR actions that address them. The greater the partnership in managing these HR issues, the more effective companies will be in managing them.

In the process of identifying changes, understanding their implications on the company, and developing the needed HR actions, companies themselves must change. HR departments can serve companies by helping them facilitate the change process. They can develop programs that help managers change their behaviors to make the new strategies work. They can implement programs and practices that increase the flexibility and adaptability of employees. HR departments can also facilitate change by helping organizations do a better job of planning.

Planning involves two major activities: 1) planning and forecasting short- and long-term HR requirements, and 2) developing and offering career planning and management activities. Both activities are important for the organization and its employees. Today, many organizations, small and large, are relating HR planning to their business objectives and the changing environment. HR planning offers companies a systematic approach to scanning the environment for significant changes, to interpreting their impact on their business objectives, to identifying the HR implications, and in developing HR actions. To complement this discussion of what HR planning does for companies, Chapter 6 is devoted to your individual career planning and management activities. The sooner you start your own HR planning, the more effective your career is likely to be.

In order to make planning activities as effective as possible, organizations must look closely at the jobs they have—that is, at the design of their jobs. Jobs can be designed around individuals or teams. Increasingly, teams are being used, so we discuss them in greater detail in Chapter 7. Companies also need to see how jobs can be made more interesting and challenging so employees will be motivated and how jobs can accommodate individual needs such as alternative work schedules. These topics are also addressed in Chapter 7.

5

CHAPTER

Managing Organizational Changes and Human Resource Planning

Learning Objectives

1. Use the framework for analyzing the HR implications of organizational changes.
2. Describe the implications for managing human resources from: a) downsizing and layoffs, b) workforce diversity, and c) mergers and alliances.
3. Describe the role of top management in: a) downsizing and layoffs, b) workforce diversity, and c) mergers and alliances.
4. Explain the current state of human resource planning.
5. Describe how organizations can be "learning organizations."

People always ask, "Is the change over? Can we stop now?" You've got to tell them, "No, it's just begun." They must come to understand that it is never ending. Leaders must create an atmosphere where people understand that change is a continuing process, not an event.

Jack Welch
CEO
General Electric Company[1]

Chapter Outline

MANAGING HUMAN RESOURCES

at IBAX

IBAX is a provider of information services software to the health care industry. The company, created in 1989, is a joint venture alliance between IBM and Baxter Healthcare. For IBM, the venture provided entry into the software side of the computer business. For Baxter, the alliance with IBM provided much-needed credibility in a computer-related business.

From an organizational and employee perspective, IBAX was in a very poor position. The company had developed through the acquisition of a number of small information systems software companies. As a result, it was geographically dispersed. Corporate headquarters was in Long Island, New York. There was a big operating facility in Orlando, Florida, a service center in Ohio, another business unit in Rhode Island, one in Illinois, and a major project staff in California. Employees in these various locations felt little need to cooperate with employees elsewhere in the organization.

Even more detrimental than IBAX's geographic fragmentation was the fact that there was no homogenous culture within the company. Employee commitment to the company was very weak and there were no evolved corporate values.

Morale was extremely low and the employees were described as "generally miserable." They were, as one IBAX employee said, "being hammered by customers, the IBM and Baxter partners, and the trade press." The customers were perpetually unhappy because the products did not meet their expectations and did not perform as promised. The management style at IBAX was authoritative and directive.

Intra-organizational communication at IBAX was so poor that the employees didn't even know how badly the company was performing (it posted losses of millions of dollars in its two years of existence). Some described their relationship with customers as "adversarial," and many employees didn't seem to understand why such a relationship was detrimental. The company had few performance standards and made little effort to hold employees accountable for their efforts.

The market for healthcare information systems was extremely competitive, and gaining market share proved more difficult than originally thought. In addition, the healthcare industry was experiencing significant change due to a continuing stream of technological improvements and an uncertain regulatory environment.

Operationally, the company was very inefficient. The company had 750 employees and was well on its way to growing to 800. In an industry where labor costs represent a high proportion of total costs (60 percent), IBAX was heavily over-staffed.

Finally, and perhaps most importantly, IBAX lacked strong leadership and, as a result, couldn't seem to correct its problems. That was the situation when Jeff Goodman assumed the role of chief executive officer of IBAX in early 1991. Within two months of his arrival, the only senior staff at IBAX were Goodman, an attorney, and a human resource executive. Although the deficiency presented an immediate problem in that many functions were devoid of leadership, Goodman would have an opportunity to build an entirely new management team. Goodman knew that he faced many challenges in turning IBAX around, but he was committed to doing whatever was necessary to make this venture a success.

The situation Jeff Goodman faced was not an enviable one. How could he take a company that was struggling to survive to a position of leadership? Improving technology, escalating demands for quality and value, and growing pressures from government regulation had created a business environment characterized by rapid and dramatic change. IBAX's ability to survive and prosper would depend upon the abilities of Jeff Goodman and his management team to adapt to this environment. Employees would also need to change their skills, abilities, attitudes, and even relationships with each other. For Goodman, his ability to manage human resources effectively was going to be a key to his success in turning around IBAX. Clearly there was a need for major organizational changes, ones that would influence all departments, especially human resources and its vice president, Meigann Putnam.[2]

Managing Organizational Changes and Human Resource Planning

Through the 21st century, companies such as IBAX will need to respond to many events associated with changes in the environmental factors described in Chapter 3. Because many of these changes involve people and will affect people, they have major implications for managing human resources and they raise significant issues for the stakeholders of human resources. To address these implications effectively, organizations need to understand the changes themselves and understand the process of change. As Jack Welch suggests in the quote introducing this chapter, managers must accept and get their employees to accept the idea that change is both necessary and a continuous process. The environmental forces necessitating organizational change vary over time and across different businesses, but the process of change does not change. Once the environmental forces are known and the process of change understood, the company can act on the HR implications by developing specific HR actions.

Three major changes for companies today include:

- **Downsizing and layoffs**
- **Workforce diversity**
- **Mergers and alliances**

This chapter looks at three examples of organizational changes that have major implications for managing human resources and that are likely to remain into the 21st century: a) the continued activities of companies to de-layer, downsize, and lay off employees; b) increased diversity in the workforce; and c) the continued number of mergers and alliances such as IBAX. This chapter also describes the process of change and the role of HR professionals in that process. Because addressing these three organizational changes requires that future HR requirements be anticipated and fulfilled, the chapter then discusses systematic HR planning tools and techniques. The relationships between these changes and activities are shown in Exhibit 5.1.

Managing organizational changes takes time in part because realigning HR capabilities with new organizational conditions takes time. Furthermore, the

EXHIBIT 5.1

Major Organizational Changes and Their Implications for Managing Human Resources

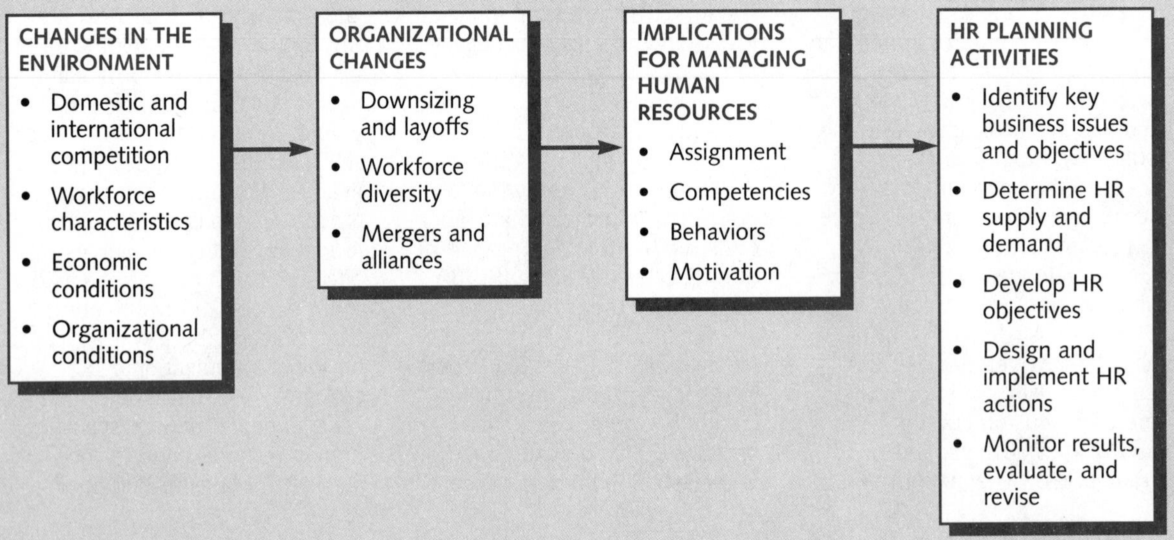

PARTNERSHIP: WORKING TOGETHER MANAGING ORGANIZATIONAL CHANGE AND HR PLANNING

LINE MANAGERS

- Be aware of the HR implications of managing organizational changes like downsizing, diversity, and mergers and acquisitions
- Work with employees to become comfortable with change
- Make the decisions on which employees need to be outplaced
- Describe their business plans and HR needs

HR PROFESSIONALS

- Identify the implications of business changes on the targets of HR
- Help establish policies and procedures for downsizings and diversity
- Facilitate change
- Identify supply of human resources to help match needs of line managers
- Develop HR programs relevant for each target of HR action

EMPLOYEES

- Participate in training programs to prepare for downsizing and layoffs
- Enhance skills and abilities for flexibility and change
- Respond to empowerment programs and actively participate in teamwork
- Learn to work with diversity in organizations
- Anticipate being asked to change behaviors, assignments, competencies, and motivation

process of change itself takes time: because organizations are complex systems with multiple interdependencies, bringing about change involves collaboration and partnerships between line managers, HR professionals, and all employees. Possible activities of these three groups are shown in the feature "Partnership: Working Together in Managing Organizational Changes and HR Planning." Ideally, this collaboration occurs during all phases of change, beginning with an understanding of the nature of the organizational changes and continuing through HR planning, implementation, reassessment, and readjustment.

The key to success of organizational changes is effectively managing human resources.

The phrase "organizational changes and HR planning" refers to the activities and processes related to aligning, redesigning, and repositioning an organization's human resources to align with the realities and objectives of the business. We illustrate the activities and processes involved in organizational changes and HR planning with three examples. First we begin by describing a framework for analyzing the HR implications of organizational changes.

Framework for Analysis

LEARNING OBJECTIVE 1

Use the framework for analyzing the HR implications of organizational changes.

Exhibit 5.2 depicts a framework we can use to understand the possible implications of major organizational changes on managing human resources. The three major changes shown in Exhibit 5.2 are: a) downsizings and layoffs, b) workforce diversity, and c) mergers and alliances. These are just a few of the major organizational changes resulting from the environmental forces described in Chapter 3.

Other major changes facing many companies include:

- **New technology**
- **Skill shortages**
- **Global competition**

Targets of HR Actions

HR management in organizations has four primary targets. Because we use a multiple stakeholder model of HR management, social and legal aspects are respected, as are employee concerns for health and safety, when analyzing the targets. In

EXHIBIT 5.2

Framework for Analyzing the Implications of Organizational Changes for Managing Human Resources

TARGETS OF HR ACTIONS	ORGANIZATIONAL CHANGES AND POSSIBLE HR ACTIONS		
	DOWNSIZING AND LAYOFFS	WORKFORCE DIVERSITY	MERGERS AND ALLIANCES
EMPLOYEE ASSIGNMENT • Right numbers? • Right place?	• Provide outplacement • Offer early retirement • Offer severance packages	• Make sure workforce diversity is represented throughout the firm	• Reduce duplication • Offer outplacement
EMPLOYEE COMPETENCIES • Now available? • Needed?	• Select those to stay on basis of performance	• Train about dimensions of diversity • Institutionalize new learning	• Select those to stay on basis of performance
EMPLOYEE BEHAVIORS • Now rewarded? • Needed?	• Define the behaviors needed for success in the new smaller firm	• Change corporate culture • Change top management style and assumptions	• Communicate behaviors to new employees
EMPLOYEE MOTIVATION • Productivity • Retention • Attraction	• Help survivors stay focused • Ensure fairness in process	• Motivate diverse employees to work together in teams	• Ensure fairness in process • Ensure high motivation for those who stay

The four primary targets of HR management are employee:

- **assignments**
- **competencies**
- **behaviors**
- **motivation**

using this framework, the analysis of the targets serves to help us detail the implications for managing human resources and develop HR action plans to address those implications.[3]

Employee Assignments. The key questions here are: a) Do we have the right number of people? and b) Are they in the right place? For companies that are downsizing, they typically have too many people. Companies that are merging often have too many people and people who need to be reassigned to different jobs in the new organization, offered early retirement, or offered other forms of severance.

Employee Competencies. The key questions here are: a) What knowledge, skills, and abilities do the employees now have? and b) What knowledge, skills, and abilities are needed? If an organization is changing its products or technologies, the employees may not have the necessary knowledge, skills, and abilities to perform adequately.

Employee Behaviors. The key questions here are: a) What behaviors do the employees now use in the company? and b) What behaviors are needed from the employees? If the firm is adapting a competitive strategy of quality improvement and customer focus, the behaviors of the employees may need to change substantially. In the new environment, they may need to be friendly with customers, answer detailed questions, and solve problems for the customers.

Employee Motivation. The key questions here are: a) How productive are the employees? b) How can we increase the retention rates of those we need to keep? and c) How can we become more attractive to the "best and the brightest?" If a company merges with another, duplication is likely to result. For the person remaining, the resulting job is bigger, yet the firm needs to motivate this person to perform this larger job at a salary that may be only slightly greater than the previous smaller one.

As you read the rest of this chapter, use this framework to analyze the implications of managing human resources during major organizational changes. Also use it to understand the impact of HR practices on managing human resources.

Analyze the implications of organizational changes on managing human resources using Exhibit 5.2.

Managing Downsizing and Layoffs

LEARNING OBJECTIVE 2

Describe the implications for managing human resources from a) downsizing and layoffs; b) workforce diversity; and c) mergers and alliances.

In their quest for efficiency, survival, global competitiveness, and profitability, many firms are undergoing major organizational change: they are restructuring, re-engineering, and de-layering their operations. Almost without exception, this means lost jobs and layoffs.[4] For example, IBAX had to lay off 200 employees, almost 25 percent of its total workforce. Exhibit 5.3 shows some conservative estimates of the number of jobs lost in major firms during the mid-1990s.[5]

Given numbers like those in Exhibit 5.3, it is easy to understand why people are feeling insecure. In the early 1980s, about 75 to 80 percent of employees described their job security as good or very good, but by the mid-1990s, only 50 or 55 percent did so.[6] These feelings of insecurity are likely to continue into the 21st century, particularly in larger organizations. Fortunately, many firms recognize that restructuring, downsizing, and layoffs significantly affect the lives of employees.

Feelings of insecurity and uncertainty make it hard for employees to feel committed.

Analysis for HR Actions

Using the framework in Exhibit 5.2, how would you analyze the implications on HR management of downsizing and layoffs? Let's look at the targets of HR action. It appears as if employee assignments are a key target: the company no longer has

EXHIBIT 5.3

Major Job Loss During Mid-1990s

COMPANY	JOBS CUT	SHARE OF WORKFORCE
AT&T	123,000	30%
IBM	122,000	35
General Motors	99,400	29
Boeing	61,000	37
Sears, Roebuck	50,000	15
Digital Equipment	29,800	26
Lockheed Martin	29,100	17
Bell South	21,200	23
McDonnell Douglas	21,000	20
Pacific Telesis	19,000	19
Delta Airlines	18,800	26
GTE	18,400	14
Nynex	17,400	33
Eastman Kodak	16,800	13
Baxter International	16,000	28

Source: L. Uchitelle and N.R. Kleinfield, "On the Battlefields of Business, Millions of Casualties," *New York Times* (March 3, 1996): 26.

Did You KNOW?

The number of hourly workers at the big three automakers, GM, Ford, and Chrysler, went from 623,133 in 1985 to 422,708 in 1995. Production levels are nearly the same.

the right number of employees. HR actions could include the provision for outplacement services and early retirement opportunities. Employee motivation may be another key target: the remaining employees, "the survivors," may need help to stay focused on performing well.

Did You KNOW?

Back in the old Ma Bell days, AT&T employed a little more than 950,000 people. Today it employs roughly 130,000. Yet the industry still employs around 950,000. In other words, industrywide there's been virtually no job loss despite AT&T's downsizing.

The Survivors' Side of Downsizing and Layoffs

The employees who remain in the company—the survivors—are also affected by layoffs.[7] Facing the threat of job loss and seeing others lose their jobs can be a traumatic and bitter experience.[8] It appears, however, that the process by which jobs are eliminated can make a difference. In summarizing the effect of job loss resulting from an acquisition, one study concluded that loss of attachment, lack of information, and a perception of "apparent managerial capriciousness" as the basis for decisions about who will be terminated, cause anxiety and an obsession with personal survival.[9] The negative cycle of reactions may not be inevitable. If survivors feel that the process used to decide who to let go was fair, their productivity and the quality of their job performance may not suffer as much. The same study found that "it was apparently not the terminations *per se* that created...bitterness but the manner in which the terminations were handled. Those who remained... expressed feelings of disgust and anger that their friends and colleagues were fired [and] felt guilty that they were not the ones who were let go because they believed their coworkers performed at least as well or better than they did."[10] Thus, in developing HR policies, procedures, and practices for effective downsizing and layoffs, even the needs of survivors require attention.

Did You KNOW?

Only 57% of workers in downsized companies are satisfied with their jobs, compared to 72% of workers in expanding companies.

A process model that recognizes all employees and their desire for fairness in downsizing and layoffs is shown in Exhibit 5.4.

Managerial Responsibilities during Downsizing

Line managers need to accept the responsibility for dealing with downsizing.

As with any major organizational change, the steps of diagnosing the current situation and developing a careful plan to implement change are essential. But even the best plan is little guarantee that chaos will not break out. The process of carrying out change is not just about strategies and plans; it is also about relationships between the people in a company and it is about personal character. Perhaps the greatest challenge to managers is maintaining employee morale while the actions of the company seem to say, "You are not valuable." A manager who had the challenge of maintaining the morale and performance of employees until the closing of more than six General Motors auto plants offers the following tips for how to be effective in such situations:

Communicate. *Give notice as far in advance as possible—certainly before workers read it in the paper. Be thorough and repetitious, because they may not be able to absorb everything the first time.*

Be visible. *Take personal responsibility for guiding people through the change. Don't just have an "open door" policy; wander around outside your office.*

Be honest. *False hope isn't helpful for anyone. Be blunt about the plant closing, even if you don't know the exact date.*

Be positive. *Reward top performers and implement worker ideas for improvements. Also, encourage plant tours by schoolchildren and customers. They imply that workers are worth showing off.*

Demand more. *Remind workers that improving skills will help the plant today and make them more marketable later.*

EXHIBIT 5.4

Final Proposed Process Model for Developing and Implementing Downsizing Plans

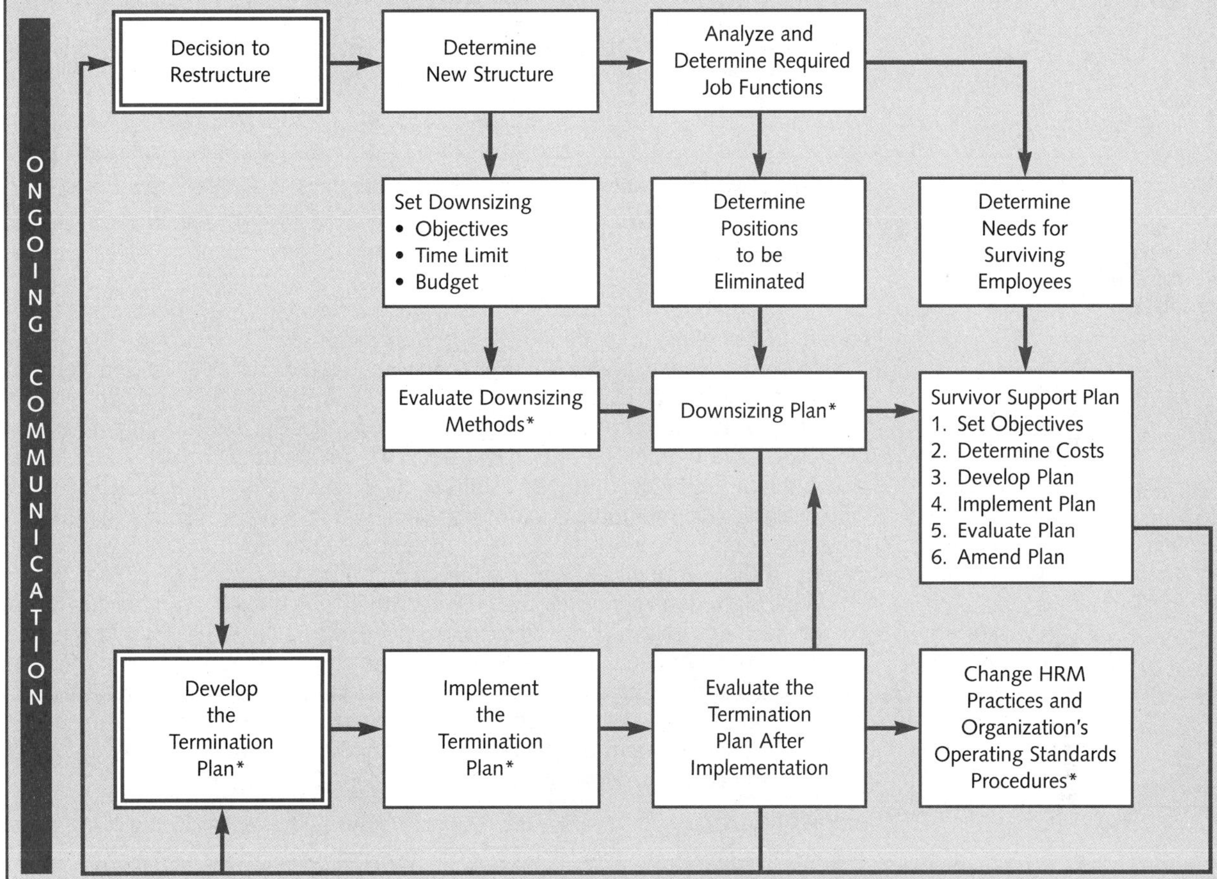

Components of the Downsizing Plan
- Methods of Employee Terminations (Voluntary/Involuntary, Termination/Retirement, Redeployment)
- Phases of the Plan and Time Schedule
- The Termination Plan
- The Survivor support plan (Before, During and After Downsizing)
- The Communication Plan (What information will be given to whom and when)

Components of the Termination Plan
- Management/supervisor training re termination interviews
- The severance package: determine key variables: age, years of service, employability, etc.
- Type and extent of employee assistance given: outplacement services, retraining, referrals, extended benefits
- Notice of Termination: lead time allowed, work or pay
- Method of termination: the termination interview and by whom, method of exit
- The Communication Program: what information will be given to whom, when, by whom, and how program

Components of Survivor Support Plan
- Management/supervisor training - re addressing survivor concerns and morale problems
- The Communication Program: what information will be given to whom, when, by whom, and how
- Wrap sessions to address group concerns and hotline to address individual concerns
- Stress counseling
- Information sessions: objectives, roles, performance requirements, career opportunities
- Employee Development Program: Retraining for increasing survivor skills, and career planning independent of the organization.

Other HR and Organizational Components
- Restructuring jobs and supporting compensation packages
- Employee development program: career paths, redefining security, career planning, development of required KSAs
- Changes in operating standards and procedures

*Denotes activities that require consideration of legal issues.

Source: N. Labib and S.H. Applebaum, "Strategic Downsizing: The Human Resource Perspective," *Human Resource Planning* 4 (1993).

Keep the plant looking good. *Clean it, paint it. Don't let the equipment deteriorate. Morale is iffy enough already.*

Craig B. Parr
Manager
General Motors' Pontiac-West Assembly Plant[11]

Additional recommendations are provided in "HR Advice and Application: Laying Off Employees in a Dignified Way," which illustrates the partnership between HR professionals and line managers.[12]

Legal Considerations in Downsizing and Layoffs

The law requires that employees receive warning about closings and layoffs.

Closing Notification. The stress imposed by a loss of employment can be severe. Indeed, the suicide rate among displaced workers is almost thirty times the national average. Clearly, society has a legitimate interest in minimizing the harm to workers, their families, and their communities. Several states now recognize the importance of plant or office closings and relocations and are considering legislation to control them. Maine and Wisconsin require pre-notification and penalize employers who move plants or offices without it. At the federal level, the *Worker Adjustment and Retraining Notification Act* took effect in 1989. It mandates that employers give employees sixty days' notice of layoffs of 50 or more employees where the number constitutes one-third or more of the workforce. It also requires employers to give pre-notification of layoffs of 500 or more workers, regardless of the total number of workers at the company. The act covers all businesses that employ 100 or more employees, excluding part-timers.[13]

"I will be laid off in seven days. It's an interesting concept. I think that corporate America is letting the people who work for them down."

Debra Vasishth, 38
Bank Vice-President
West Windsor, NJ

Where a union represents the workers, the right of employers to move production facilities is greatly affected by the *National Labor Relations Act* (NLRA), section 8(a). It has been clearly established that employers must bargain over the effects of a plant closing and relocation in most situations. Companies must negotiate with the union before they make a decision to move if the nature of the employer's operation at the new location does not change in any basic way (*NLRB v. Dubuque Packing Company*, 1991).

Layoff Notification. Under the *Worker Adjustment and Retraining Notification Act*, layoffs that are temporary in nature or downsizings that are permanent but do not involve a complete shutdown do not require advance notification. HR needs to ensure that the entire process is not in violation of the *Age Discrimination in Employment Act* (ADEA), which covers workers aged forty and above. This is true whether organizations downsize by layoffs or early retirements, with or without incentives. It appears that downsizing programs that are specifically directed at easing out older workers are in violation of ADEA. However, in attempts to survive and reduce expenses, employers are able to reduce their overall head count including workers over age forty (*Schibursky v. IBM Corporation*, 1993).

Alternatives to Layoffs

Regardless of the cause, the loss of a job can be traumatic for employees. Providing outplacement services and severance pay may help to reduce this trauma.[14] But given the evidence that downsizings may not always lead to better productivity anyway, some companies seek alternatives to layoffs.[15]

Job sharing enables two employees to share one job.

Job Sharing. Rather than terminating those with less seniority or poor performance, some companies have initiated job-sharing programs. **Job sharing** involves reducing an individual employee's work week and pay. This helps the company cut labor costs and may actually lead to higher overall productivity because each employee is working more concentrated hours. One apparent cost-related

HR ADVICE & APPLICATION

How HR Can Help Managers Lay Off Employees In a Dignified Way

Now that downsizings and reorganizations have become a necessary part of business for most U.S. companies, there are many workers who wouldn't be surprised if they received a layoff notice at some time in their careers. This doesn't mean, however, that employees relish the idea of being laid off. What they want most is to be treated with dignity during the process. Here are 10 basic principles that HR professionals can use to help managers lay off or eliminate employees in a respectful way. These principles include:

1. Conduct the meeting in private. A terminated employee has the right to a private severance meeting conducted by the employee's supervisor, not someone from the HR department. Because termination is a personal issue, employees want to hear the news from their supervisors, not from someone they don't know.

2. Keep the meeting short and to the point. The meeting should last no more than 10 to 15 minutes. Employees want to know the facts. They don't want nuances and indirect language. As soon as the employee is seated, explain why you called him or her in: "Fred, I'm sorry, but your position has been eliminated." Repeat the statement if necessary, and ask if he or she understands it.

3. Offer support and compassion, but don't give hope of reversing the decision. For example, tell the employee that this decision has been reviewed at the highest levels, and there's no possibility for appeal. Tell him or her that efforts have already been made, without success, to find him or her another assignment.

4. Explain why the company made the decision. Tell the employee why he or she is being laid off: a change in the company's strategic direction, or whatever is the reason for the decision. Don't argue about issues that should have been resolved long ago. Be firm in telling the employee that the decision is made, and it's final.

5. Don't make discriminatory statements. Be aware of the many U.S. laws on discrimination and wrongful termination. The HR department should be involved in giving managers advice on what they can and can't say to employees.

6. Control your emotions. Don't try to keep the employee from leaving the room (you could be accused of false imprisonment); don't touch (you could be prosecuted for assault and battery); don't yell (you could be accused of intentional infliction of emotional abuse).

7. Give the severance package in writing. When doing this, explain that the company wishes to make the employee's transition as painless as possible. Express confidence in the employee and his or her prospects. Remind the person that this termination was a business decision, and that you'll do all you can to help him or her.

8. Encourage the employee to take positive, rather than destructive, actions. Tell the person to follow the advice of the outplacement consultant who will help him or her move in a positive career direction.

9. Plan a graceful exit. Walk the employee to the door or bring the outplacement consultant to him or her.

10. Inform other employees, customers, and suppliers of the decision. Don't criticize the employee. Make the statement simple and non-blaming, such as, "Joe left the company to pursue other interests."

There should be no winners and losers in a termination. All parties should come out as whole as possible with a promise for a better future.[16]

> **In job sharing all employees share in the need to reduce costs.**

> **Nucor Steel manages downturns by gearing down to four-day work weeks; employees lose pay but keep their jobs.**

disadvantage is that expenses per employee may increase because benefits costs are usually a function of the number of employees, not the number of hours worked or amount of pay. On the other hand, cost savings are realized by reduced severance pay, unemployment insurance, outplacement and employee assistance expenses, and so on.

Early Retirement. Age-based mandatory retirement is illegal for most employees because it is considered a form of unfair discrimination under the ADEA. This means employers cannot rely on attrition due to forced retirement as a planned form of downsizing. Early retirement programs, however, can attempt to create voluntary attrition. The key to a successful early retirement program is understanding the needs of targeted employees and providing incentives that meet those needs. Incentives may include pension payments before and after age 62, when Social Security payments start, and company-paid health and life insurance. Alternatively, a company may maintain its current retirement program but lower the qualifying age in order to increase the pool of potential retirees. This, of course, is expensive and accounts for some of the "restructuring charges" companies take when they downsize. Giving employees severance pay, essentially bonus pay for leaving, also adds to the expenses.

> **L. L. Bean is using a voluntary sabbatical program. During this time they receive no pay but they do receive their usual benefits. The sabbatical can last between 6 months and 2 years.**

> **Did You KNOW?**
>
> **In 95% of downsizings, severance pay is offered, but in only 4% of terminations is severance pay offered.**

Workforce Diversity

The publication in 1987 of the U.S. Department of Labor monograph *Workforce 2000* created a widespread awareness of the need for business to develop competence in managing a workforce filled with diversity of many types. One chart from *Workforce 2000* dramatically shows that the entry-level workforce in the year 2000 will be much more diverse than the 1985 workforce in general (see Chapter 3, Exhibit 3.6). After reading and digesting *Workforce 2000*, many managers realized that successful companies would react to diversity as an important business issue by implementing proactive, strategic HR planning. Today, this view is very widely shared.[17]

> **Managing workforce diversity is a major change facing almost all companies.**

Analysis of HR Actions

Using the framework in Exhibit 5.2, how would you analyze the implications of workforce diversity on HR management? As you see in Exhibit 5.2, there are some suggestions under each of the four targets of HR action: employee assignment, employee competencies, employee behaviors, and employee motivation. As you read this discussion on workforce diversity, develop and extend the entries made in Exhibit 5.2.

> **The entries in Exhibit 5.2 are only samples. Your challenge is to add two items to each target box.**

The Importance of Managing Diversity

Surveys of business leaders confirm the perception that interest in managing diversity successfully is widespread. For example, in one study of 645 firms, 74 percent of the respondents were concerned about increased diversity, and of these, about one-third felt that diversity affected their corporate strategy. Why are companies so concerned? The two primary reasons cited were a belief that supervisors did not know how to motivate their diverse work groups, and uncertainty about how to handle the challenge of communicating with employees whose cultural backgrounds result in differing assumptions, values, and even language skills.[18]

> **"The Coca-Cola Company has aspired to diligently incorporate diversity as a daily responsibility. We have done it because not only is it the right thing to do for our business, it is the right thing to do, period."**
>
> **M. Douglas Ivester**
> **President and CEO**
> **The Coca-Cola Company**

As the term **managing diversity** implies, the organizational interventions that fall within the realm of this label focus on ensuring that the variety of talents and perspectives that already exist within an organization are well-utilized. Organizations that attack the diversity issue with full force do so because they believe that taking action is a strategic imperative.[19] For most organizations, simply knowing the facts about workforce diversity—which are now parading as headlines in our daily newspapers—does not stimulate major changes in management practices. The facts are most significant when they are considered in the con-

> **Managing diversity means managing employees who differ on dimensions such as age, religion, gender, culture, and ethnicity.**

text of the changing business environment: increased emphasis on the highly interpersonal task of providing quality service, globalization of markets and businesses, and the increasing use of work teams are all making diversity management a high priority. These changes are bringing more and more people from diverse backgrounds into contact with each another, and, at the same time, mean that businesses are becoming more reliant on person-to-person contact as a way to get things done. Add to these trends the changing demographics of both consumers and the workforce, and the stage is set for diversity to emerge as a strategic business issue.

Every competitive advantage begins with people. People are different. Differences create opportunity. That's Diversity. That's Quaker.

Quaker Oats Company
Chicago, IL

Dimensions of Diversity

Many companies, such as Northern States Power, understand and value many dimensions of diversity, including gender, ethnicity, culture, age, functional areas of expertise, religion, lifestyle, and so on. By considering just three aspects of diversity, you may begin to understand the bigger picture.

Dimensions of diversity include:

- **gender**
- **ethnicity**
- **culture**
- **age**
- **functional expertise**
- **lifestyle**

Gender Diversity. In the late 1950s, when many of today's CEOs were entering the labor force, the professional and managerial ranks were almost exclusively male. Back then, men were receiving 95 percent of the MBA degrees awarded and 90 percent of the BBA degrees. As these men are finishing their careers, 40 years later, the picture is dramatically different. In 1990, women received approximately 31 percent of the MBA degrees awarded, as well as 39 percent of the law degrees, 13 percent of the engineering degrees, and half of all undergraduate degrees.[20]

Today, females are better educated than ever before, and more are choosing to be in the active labor force. Furthermore, gender-based segregation within organizations is gradually decreasing, although in 1990, women held fewer than 0.5 percent of the top jobs in major corporations.[21]

Maximizing the productivity of women is essential to achieving competitiveness. This often requires attacking the artificial barrier of a male-dominated corporate culture. As the CEO of Avon Products has noted:

> *Cultural discrepancies can come out in little ways. We used to have a lot of white male traditions at Avon. We bought season tickets to sporting events, and we called the annual management outing President's Golf Day. Our first two women officers complained.... We realized these activities were no longer appropriate. They were too male-oriented and unwittingly made others feel like outsiders.*[22]

According to one survey, 60 percent of women executives in large firms feel that their organization's male-dominated corporate culture is an obstacle to the success—that is, productivity—of women.[23] These women may be underestimating the problem. In a poll of 241 *Fortune* 1000 CEOs, nearly 80 percent of the respondents said women face barriers that keep them from reaching the top. And of those who admitted that barriers exist, 81 percent identified stereotypes and preconceptions as problems women face.[24]

Cultural and Ethnic Diversity. After gender diversity, cultural and ethnic diversity is the second most frequently noted change in the workforce. Cultures have consequences that are easily experienced but more difficult to describe. For many people, the concept of culture conjures up images of the exotic customs, religions, foods, clothing, and lifestyles that make foreign travel—as well as trips into the ethnic enclaves in our local cities—both stimulating and enjoyable. These aspects of a foreign culture can be experienced without ever engaging in conversation with someone from that culture.

"Driving our workforce diversity is our fundamental belief that valuing differences—among employees, customers, shareowners, suppliers and the communities in which we live and work—is a business and moral imperative."

Donald R. Beall
Chairman and CEO
Rockwell

The deeper consequences of culture—such as values and ways of interpreting the world—cannot be handled merely by changing menus and policies. When people with different habits and world views come together in the workplace, misunderstandings and conflicts inevitably occur as a result of dissimilar expectations and norms. Employees who behave according to the cultural adage that "the squeaky wheel gets the grease" may be viewed as offensive and undesirable teammates by employees who were taught that "the nail that sticks out gets hammered down." Employees behaving according to the latter adage may be viewed as ineffective by those following the former.

"The economic opportunities for generations to come—in America and, yes, even around the world—depend upon the continuing success of the United States in advancing diversity throughout the business and corporate sector."

John Bryan
Chairman and CEO
Sara Lee

Several circumstances seem to account for employers' current recognition that cultural diversity requires active management:

1. Although the proportion of African-Americans in the United States has remained stable, their employment patterns have changed considerably during the affirmative action era, with substantial integration occurring for clerical, technical, and skilled crafts jobs.[25] Also, although often overlooked, educational levels of African-Americans have risen during this time, providing another stimulant for workplace integration.

2. Although the number of immigrants entering this country each year is relatively small, over the years, the number of employees with strong ties to another national culture grows due to the continuing effect of nationality on second- and third-generation citizens.[26]

3. The variety of the immigrant population has itself increased, as Asians and Latins from dozens of countries join European immigrants.

4. Insightful business leaders recognize that they can use their multicultural domestic workforce as an educational resource and training ground for learning some of the tough lessons associated with conducting business internationally.

Age Diversity. In developed countries such as the United States, the median population age has been increasing. Along with this comes the bulging ranks of "older" employees trying to climb the corporate ladder, which creates havoc for traditional, hierarchical organizations. The distribution of population by age categories in the U.S. is shown in Exhibit 5.5. Traditional organizations are structured to accommodate large cohorts of entry-level employees and smaller cohorts of employees at more advanced career stages. These organizations tend to segregate employees by age. Organizational elders supervise the cohorts who will soon replace them, who in turn supervise their own replacements.

A part of the challenge in managing age diversity is to recognize the different values held by different age groups.

But these old hierarchies are a dying breed. As layers of hierarchy are removed, previously segregated generations of employees find themselves working together and even rotating jobs among themselves. Often, the result is an unfamiliar reversal of roles. As one restaurant manager put it, giving orders to older workers "is sort of like telling your grandma to clean the table." If younger generations find this uncomfortable, so do older generations. As one working retiree explained: "For 30 years I was a supervisor, and then one night I step out of one role and into another....When you're being supervised by someone younger, you see a lot of things that aren't going to work, but you have to bite your tongue."[27]

The combination of changes in the age distribution of employees and new, flatter organizational structures means that three generations of workers can find themselves working side-by-side. Even if employees from these generations were all born and raised in the U.S., they will differ in their values and attitudes about work, their physical and mental functioning, and the everyday concerns that reflect their stages in the life cycle. Of course, within each generation, gender and cultural variety also abound, yielding a workforce that reflects the complete palette of human potential.[28]

Diversity Managers

Businesses are taking the diversity issue very seriously—so seriously, in fact, that many large corporations have followed Digital Equipment Corporation's early lead

EXHIBIT 5.5

Distribution of Population by Age

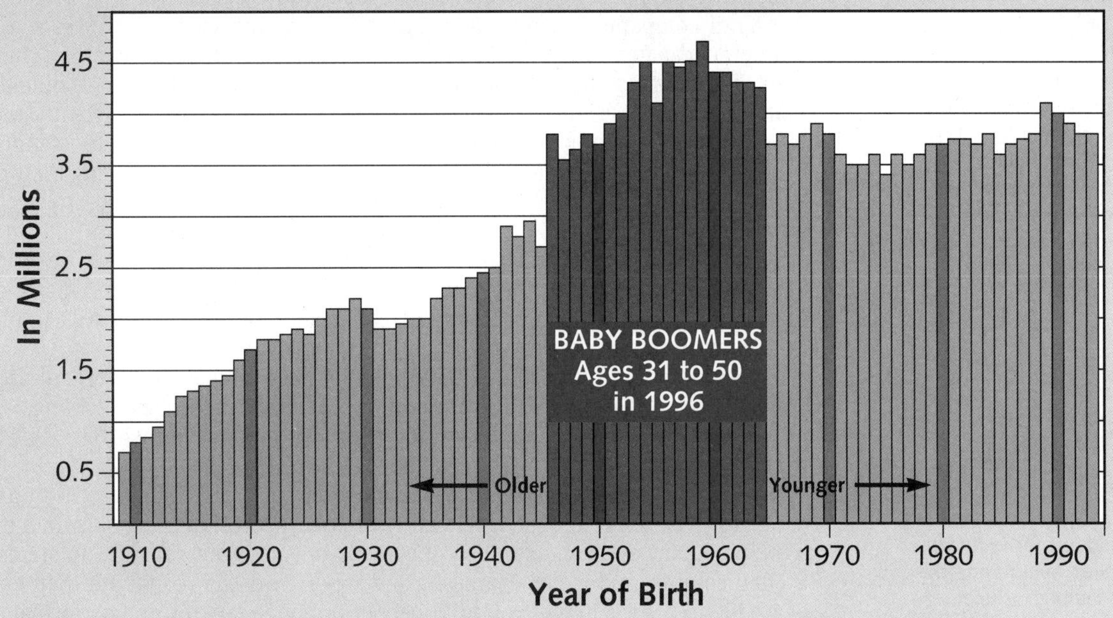

Source: U.S. Census Bureau, 1995 (Washington, D.C.)

by adding a diversity manager to their team. For example, Honeywell Incorporated has a director of workforce diversity, and Avon Products has a director of multicultural planning and design.[29] What do the people with such titles do? Fundamentally, their jobs are about creating change in organizations. Long-term goals include changing corporate cultures. Short-term goals include changing the behaviors of individuals and ensuring that all employees fulfill their potential.

To achieve these goals, managers of diversity engage their organizations in many types of activities designed to create change. For example, Hewlett-Packard Company conducts training sessions for managers to teach them about different cultures and ethnic groups and about their own gender biases and training needs.[30] Procter and Gamble has implemented "valuing diversity" programs throughout the company. A mentor program designed to retain black and female managers has been developed at one plant, and one-day workshops on diversity are given to all new employees.[31] Equitable Life Assurance encourages minority group members to form support groups that periodically meet with the CEO to discuss problems in the company pertaining to them. At Avon, women have made significant inroads into management; however, more remains to be done. To help improve the progress of women and minority group members, the company uses councils that represent various groups, each having a senior manager present at meetings. These councils inform and advise top management.[32]

Breaking the Glass Ceiling. The glass ceiling is a barrier that, although hard to see, nevertheless prevents women and people of color from gaining access to senior management positions. Until recently, the dominant approach has been to focus on helping non-majority individuals develop a "winning style" to succeed in a "white man's" world. This has worked to some extent, but it is not enough. The

Did You KNOW?

The *Miami Herald* wins the federal government's highest award honoring corporate workplace diversity programs for 1995, the Frances Perkins/ Elizabeth Hanford Dole National Award for Diversity and Excellence in American Executive Management.

Did You KNOW?

Companies that have been singled out for reducing and even eliminating the glass ceiling include:

- **Allstate Insurance**
- **Kraft Foods**
- **Motorola**
- **Xerox**
- **Northern Trust Bank**
- **IBM**
- **Proctor & Gamble**

Did You KNOW?

Only 3.9% of all managers at Japanese companies are women. This is up from the 2.5% of ten years ago.

more long-term approach to helping break the glass ceiling, and the one that might determine whether businesses will survive in the future, is to ensure that the workplace has no artificial barriers to performance in day-to-day activities or to advancement. That way, everyone can offer their individual talents to a company, rather than suppress them to conform to deep-rooted prejudices.

Until companies change their culture to become truly merit-based, a short-term practical approach is for women and people of color to be aware of the kinds of behavior management prefers and to respond to those preferences. Some believe that "[t]o be successful in upper management, women must constantly monitor their behavior, making sure they are neither too masculine nor too feminine.[33] Some women in upper management have achieved success by altering their behavior to what is desirable to the male management hierarchy already in place. Nevertheless, simply expecting everyone to change themselves to "fit" into the existing culture of upper management is not the long-term solution. The long-term objective is to increase an organization's effectiveness by improving management practices. Changing organizational norms, policies, and structures that inhibit full utilization of the workforce is the goal.[34]

Because organizations have so little experience in changing their culture to fit a more diverse workforce, it is too soon to say what approaches to change are the most effective. Nevertheless, an examination of some of the many strategies companies are experimenting with may prove helpful.[35]

Several activities focus on increasing awareness of discriminatory attitudes and practices. For example, managers can be trained to work and manage in a diverse workforce, and everyone can be educated about how our reliance on stereotypes is often counterproductive. Managers and supervisors can work with their employees to identify ways in which traditional performance-ranking and performance-rating systems can be improved so that they do not perpetuate disadvantage. Task forces can be formed to plan new programs and make recommendations for change based on problems discovered in the workplace. These task forces could also review and monitor such programs on a continuing basis.

Other programs can be implemented that will benefit a diverse workforce by helping everyone reach their potential. For example, career planning can be used to ensure that everyone has the opportunity to gain experience, knowledge, and exposure, as well as to provide career guidance. Mentorship programs can be encouraged as a means of giving everyone access to advice from the upper ranks. Companies can address the need to balance work and family by offering more generous adoption- and pregnancy-related leaves of absence and flexible hours (some even provide on-site child care, flexible projects, and opportunities to work at home).[36]

Companies that have taken action to remove the glass ceiling are already seeing results. For example, Merck reports that about 25 percent of its middle managers were women in 1990, versus approximately 10 percent in 1980,[37] and the Prudential Insurance Company of America had 50 percent women managers in 1990 versus 30 percent in 1980.[38]

These are just a few of the interventions that can chip away at the glass ceiling in organizations. In the best companies, such activities fit within a larger strategic plan focused on improving organizational effectiveness. These companies tend to follow several basic principles.

Basic Principles

Many options and choices must be made when introducing initiatives for working through diversity. There are a few basic principles that can guide change processes related to initiatives for managing diversity:

1. Develop a comprehensive understanding of the many types of diversity in the organization and decide which to address.
2. Stay close to the customers.

3. Anticipate possible problems and be prepared to deal with them.
4. Institutionalize new learning.[39]

Although these principles could easily apply to any organizational change efforts, they are particularly relevant when considering new initiatives for managing diversity.[40]

> **"We are beginning to truly understand what being 'global' means, and this understanding is making us all the more sensitive to the unique differences we, as individuals, possess."**
>
> **Earl Washington**
> **Senior Vice President**
> **of Communications**
> **Rockwell**

Mergers and Alliances

IBAX represents a major trend in business today: alliances between companies. Even big companies with vast resources need to form alliances. Baxter Healthcare and IBM thought that an alliance, a joint venture, that pools their unique strengths, made sense. In this case the result of their alliance was a new, third, company: IBAX.

In other cases, companies are joining to form a new, single company. The Chemical Bank and the Chase Manhattan Bank in New York City merged their operations into one: in this case the new bank is called Chase. It was decided to use this name, even though Chase Manhattan was the smaller bank, because of its greater worldwide name recognition. Although the merger of these two banks was really an acquisition by Chemical of Chase, in many respects the new company represents a merger of the two companies, their cultures, their businesses, and their ways of managing human resources. IBAX represented a combination of two small parts of IBM and Baxter. IBAX then had to forge a new identity and develop its own approaches to business and ways of managing human resources. This was a significant change in itself, but then this new joint venture required new leadership and major organizational change to survive and grow. Thus, IBAX is both an example of what's happening as far as mergers and alliances go, and an example of a company that needed to change its leadership and approach to doing its business and managing its human resources. An excellent example of a joint venture in an international context, its challenges, and the role of the HR department is featured in "Managing Human Resources at Merck & Co." Such challenges include merging different cultures, compensation structures, and business strategies. While these are challenging enough when two U.S. companies are involved, they get more challenging when a U.S. company and a French company are involved.

Did You KNOW?

There are almost 6,000 mergers each year. One of the biggest was Walt Disney and Capital Cities/ABC.

Did You KNOW?

IBAX had products for small, medium, and large hospitals. Each had problems that needed to be solved.

Analysis for HR Actions

Using the framework in Exhibit 5.2, how would you analyze the implications of HR management of mergers and alliances?

Employee Assignments. Especially in mergers, the challenge is often to reduce duplication. There are literally two people for each job after a merger. If the merger is between companies of different sizes, the larger one can often call the shots in deciding who stays. This is especially true if the larger firm actually buys or acquires the smaller firm. In this situation, often called a takeover, the HR practices of the new firm are frequently those of the dominant, acquiring firm.

Employee Competencies. Often the two firms in a merger agree that keeping the "best people" is the best business strategy. In this case, the two firms analyze what competencies are needed in the new company and what competencies the employees of both companies currently have. Once these matches are determined, a downsizing occurs.

Employee Behaviors. If two firms are merging and each is remaining in their same business, new employee behaviors may not be necessary for many employees. However, if one of them has been more successful at achieving the needed employee behaviors, the employees in the other company may be asked to adopt

MANAGING HUMAN RESOURCES

for the 21st Century
at Merck & Co.

Whitehouse Station, New Jersey-based Merck & Company Inc. is the world's largest maker of prescription drugs, with 37,000 employees worldwide and revenues of more than $8.5 billion. Despite having all of these resources on hand, Merck has improved particular elements of its business by using resources of other companies more capable than itself in specific areas. In turn, Merck has offered its resources to those companies for their growth.

In 1990, Merck teamed up with Wilmington, Delaware-based E.I. DuPont. DuPont had a $700 million pharmaceutical business. Because the chemical producer's area of expertise was not the pharmaceutical business, however, it lacked the development capability for these products that Merck had. It did have approximately 300 scientists and a substantial research budget, however. By forming a joint venture. Merck could help develop and bring to market DuPont's experimental compounds.

The partnership was successful. Today, DuPont Merck Pharmaceutical Company—the company created from the joint-venture—is a Fortune 500 business worth more than a billion dollars.

The success of that alliance has prompted several others. Johnson & Johnson • Merck Consumer Pharmaceuticals Co. was formed when several of Merck's overseas patents were expiring and Merck wanted to modify the products for over-the-counter sales—in which Johnson & Johnson had expertise. Two of Merck's other large enterprises have been formed overseas: The Astra-Merck Group is a strategic alliance between Merck and the Swedish company AB Astra, and Pasteur Merieux, Serums, et Vaccins is an alliance in France. Although each of these businesses was formed for different strategies, all were pursued so that the companies involved could accomplish a desired result more rapidly and at a lower cost than each could do on its own.

From the beginning of each of these joint enterprises, HR was involved. HR resolved most of the issues surrounding the melding of two companies: issues such as the blending of two corporate cultures, two different compensation strategies, and two different business strategies. "There's a real challenge in the alliances in merging cultures and strategies and I think HR plays a key role in helping the companies resolve the issues," says Eric Marquardt, director of executive compensation for Merck. For example. when Merck teamed up with its French alliance, one of HR's greatest challenges was developing a reward system for employees. Merck promotes ownership of the company and has profit-sharing pay programs. Because these concepts aren't part of the French culture, a system had to be developed to satisfy both parties.

Other challenges that HR undertakes for these alliances deal with staffing. It has been involved in determining who will head the joint ventures—whether the CEOs will come from one of the parent companies or from the outside—and in developing packages to attract these people, as well as employees from the two parent companies, to the new assignments. The service HR offers to the company in these strategic alliances makes an important element for their success.[41]

the behaviors of the other firm. Use of the HR practices of the more successful firm will aid all the employees in adopting and maintaining the needed behaviors.

Employee Motivation. After a merger or alliance that has involved a reduction in the workforce, an essential HR challenge is to motivate the employees who remain to perform at even higher levels. The process of merging usually eliminates position duplication, for example, two HR managers, but it increases the amount of work and responsibility. While compensation for this new, larger position may increase, it will not be equal to the salaries of the two former positions. So the remaining employees will need to be motivated with other things besides money. The thrill of the new job is certainly one way. The chance to have the job and the security it brings is often another key motivator.

In summary, there are substantial HR implications resulting from a merger or alliance, and as with all major organizational changes, the challenge rests with top management. The next section will examine the special implications of organizational changes on top management leadership.

Top Management Leadership and the Process of Change

LEARNING OBJECTIVE 3

Describe the role of top management in a) downsizing and layoffs; b) workforce diversity; and c) mergers and alliances.

It is now widely recognized that for change to occur in organizations, leaders must change and must get others to change.[42] All the changes we have described thus far—downsizings and layoffs, managing diversity, and mergers and alliances—start at the very top and cascade down. Jeff Goodman at IBAX is an excellent example. He is what current leaders need to be, or what companies need to search for in their selection of a new leader: one who exhibits new leader behaviors.

New Leadership Behaviors

Like Jeff Goodman, CEOs and all other managers must change before other employees will. Managers have to move from the command-and-control style to empowering, visioning, cooperating, and supporting. They must also change the way they behave with respect to suppliers and customers outside the organization, the environment, social and ethical issues of business and society, and the strategy and direction of the organization. The new leader behaviors at Levi Strauss are shown in Exhibit 5.6. Top management at Levi Strauss believes and acts as if these behaviors are necessary for it to reach its aspirations (shown in Exhibit 2.2).

Did You KNOW?

Many large firms believe that the quality of leadership comes from specific behaviors.

EXHIBIT 5.6

Leader Behavior at Levi Strauss

WHAT TYPE OF LEADERSHIP IS NECESSARY TO MAKE OUR ASPIRATIONS A REALITY?

New Behaviors: Leadership that exemplifies directness, openness to influence, commitment to the success of others, willingness to acknowledge our own contributions to problems, personal accountability, teamwork and trust. Not only must we model these behaviors, but we must coach others to adopt them.

Diversity: Leadership that values a diverse work force (age, sex, ethnic group, etc.) at all levels of the organization, diversity in experience, and a diversity in perspectives. We have committed to taking full advantage of the rich backgrounds and abilities of all our people and to promote a greater diversity in positions of influence. Differing points of view will be sought: diversity will be valued and honesty rewarded, not suppressed.

Recognition: Leadership that provides greater recognition—both financial and psychic—for individuals and teams that contribute to our success. Recognition must be given to all who contribute: those who create and innovate and also those who continually support the day-to-day business requirements.

Ethical Management Practices: Leadership that epitomizes the stated standards of ethical behavior. We must provide clarity about our expectations and must enforce these standards through the corporation.

Communications: Leadership that is clear about Company, unit, and individual goals and performance. People must know what is expected of them and receive timely, honest feedback on their performance and career aspirations.

Empowerment: Leadership that increases the authority and responsibility of those closest to our products and customers. By actively pushing responsibility, trust and recognition into the organization, we can harness and release the capabilities of all our people.

Source: Excerpt from "HR's Vital Role at Levi Strauss," by J. J. Laabs, copyright December 1992. Used by permission.

"Big changes to big things is the way you build a business. The CEO's role is to articulate that message."

Roger Enrico
CEO
PepsiCo

These changes in leadership are seen as vital to many companies today, but they are not likely to occur unless systematic strategies are in place to help managers make them. Companies like IBAX, McDonald's, General Electric, Levi Strauss, Federal Express, and Weyerhaeuser are systematically linking specific on-the-job experiences and training and development programs to the new behavioral competencies required in the new organizational forms. Some companies are even establishing leadership institutes.

Leadership Institutes. In the late 1980s, Weyerhaeuser's Forest Products Company (FPC) established its own leadership institute to help its managers change their behaviors. This was during the time when the firm was repositioning strategically from a functionally organized company to a divisional one with strategic business units, just like IBAX. Within FPC, Chief Executive Charles W. Bingham, his executive team, and the director of strategic education, Horace Parker, concluded that a major strategic repositioning called for upgrading the firm's human capabilities through executive development:

> *How the organization was sold on the worth of an executive development program is an important lesson. The trump card used in closing the deal was to involve the executives at various levels of the organization in the planning stages. During those stages, they came to see, as did the executive team, that an intensive development program such as the Leadership Institute was not an expensive frill but a prerequisite for survival. The Leadership Institute, top management was convinced, would be a powerful catalyst that could accelerate the normal process of change—of everything from a corporate culture to how a salesperson deals with customers.*[43]

Working with others in HR management and with the top management team, FPC created a leadership institute where managers could come to discuss the new strategy and its implications for them. In addition, the institute offered training to help managers acquire needed skills, knowledge, and leadership styles. A success, this institute grew into a total quality company program. By 1994, the entire Weyerhaeuser Company used the institute to help managers learn new leadership behaviors. The new leadership behaviors identified as critical for total quality management flow directly from what leadership means to the company:

Weyerhaeuser is an excellent example of how organizational change has to start with top management changing its behaviors.

> *We are committed to leadership behavior that empowers people to fully contribute to company goals. This means that:*
>
> - *Leadership behavior and standards are well defined and understood throughout the organization and are linked with company values.*
> - *The criteria for selecting leaders include demonstrated commitment to company values and leadership skills.*
> - *Leaders set clear goals and expectations and inspire others to meet them.*
> - *Development is provided for existing and current leaders.*
> - *Leaders seek and use feedback to improve their leadership skills.*
> - *A key measure of leadership success is the development of others.*

Management Development On-the-Job. When systematically developed and coordinated by the HR department, education and job experiences can go a long way toward helping managers change themselves and, in the process, change their organizations.

Today's environment calls for unceasing change.

The Weyerhaeuser Company went from a centralized structure to a decentralized structure; then later to a decentralized structure coordinated through shared vision, values, and leadership philosophy. At the same time, it has moved from a maker of undifferentiated commodity products to one of customer-focused, total quality products. Continuous management development helps to ensure that all these changes last and continue to filter down in the company. Frequent meetings between top managers are one type of activity facilitating on-the-job development. Working as a team develops, shares, and coordinates efforts to help each individual manager learn more about the company as a whole. A deeper understanding of the business puts each manager in a better position to lead in ways that are consistent with the several separate businesses, yet coordinated to reflect the functions of these businesses as part of one larger company.

Did You KNOW?

As much as 80% of all training and development occurs on the job.

IBAX: Change Through Team Building, Culture, Communication, and Motivation

The three areas that Goodman thought were essential to IBAX's survival were team building. communications, and employee motivation. Goodman knew that successful change would require strong leadership throughout the organization. He felt strongly that "leading by example" would be critical in getting employees to deal more effectively with each other, the customers, the partners, and other stakeholders of the organization.[44]

Key actions at IBAX:

- **Team Building**
- **Communications**
- **Employee Motivation**

His goal was to change the culture of IBAX. Goodman knew from the outset that developing a strong and healthy corporate culture at IBAX, which had no homogeneous culture, would be a prerequisite to all the other changes that needed to take place. From the beginning, Goodman was open with the employees about his concerns, goals, and plans. He involved them in both the assessment of the business and the development of the plan to turn it around. Employees started to believe that Goodman was committed to involving the employees in decision-making. Further, he promised to reward organizational commitment, creativity, and hard work, and he followed through. Trust began to build within the ranks. As one person put it, "for the first time, the words and the music started to match." As trust continued to grow, the culture began to change. Morale began to improve, and employees started to feel empowered to make a difference at IBAX.

Team Building. Upon his arrival, Goodman assessed the individuals who occupied managerial positions in the company, as well as those who appeared capable of assuming such roles. His challenge was to turn this group of individuals into a team that would be committed to the company, as well as to each other. He began by taking the senior management group through an intensive off-site team-building program that involved everything from classroom lectures to scaling walls and swinging on ropes. The program was intended to build the trust and commitment of the team.

Goodman's challenge was to ensure that the team-building training was transferred back into the workplace. He continued to stress the importance of the concepts within the work environment, and eventually, the team philosophy became part of the organizational culture at IBAX. The ongoing behavior of the employees began to reflect their dedication to the company and their teams. This was evidenced by a growing commitment to deliver better-quality products and services to the customers.

Did You KNOW?

Firms such as Whirlpool and General Electric use outdoor training programs to help build trust and cooperation amongst their management team.

Communication. As was mentioned previously, communication at IBAX prior to Goodman's arrival had been limited and primarily one-way—from the bottom up. Top management rarely communicated with the employees at the lower levels of the organization. As a result, the employees were literally unaware of the severity of the problems facing the company in early 1991. Therefore, one of Goodman's primary challenges was to inform the employees of the reality of the situation at IBAX and then develop the communication infrastructure to ensure that they had the information they needed to do their jobs effectively.

Change requires open, honest, factual, and free-flowing communications.

Once Goodman knew that he had successfully communicated the need for change, he began to build a communication infrastructure that kept everyone apprised of the condition of the company and provided open access to the information they needed to do their jobs well. Everyone in each business unit had open access to revenues, expense, statistics, and other decisional information that was relevant for their business.

Motivation. Goodman also needed to establish methods for motivating employees to do what was necessary to improve product quality, customer service, and customer satisfaction. This required an understanding of what motivates people and the development of a reward system that was based on realistic, but aggressive, performance goals.

Goodman's assumption about people at work: They want to be involved and to "buy-in."

Goodman's philosophy of motivation was simple. He believed that people are motivated by the ability to be involved, make decisions, and make a difference. They want to "buy in" to their company and its products, and they want to reap the rewards associated with doing a good job. With this philosophy in mind, Goodman knew that he had to encourage the employees of IBAX to take ownership in the turnaround—to feel responsible for the company's success.

Much of the success of Goodman's change at IBAX can be attributed to the organizational changes described above. The move to a product-based structure put the focus of the company on the products it marketed and the customers it served. Responsibility and authority were delegated to those who could make a difference in product quality and customer service. Decision-making was in the hands of self-managed teams who understood their performance objectives clearly and knew they were accountable for achieving those objectives. The overall effect of these changes was improved product quality, greater productivity, better customer satisfaction, and strong bottom-line profitability for all of IBAX's product lines.

The Role of the Human Resource Department in Organizational Change

From hiring and firing to training and performance management, every HR activity influences human resources and, thus, the success or failure of most efforts for organizational change and competition.[45] Keeping HR systems aligned with business strategies, such as the changes at IBAX for total quality and customer focus, will be a major HR challenge going into the 21st century. IBAX's organizational change provides specific illustration of how the HR department can facilitate strategic business goals. In general, however, the HR department can:

- Help formulate the firm's strategic business principles and strategies
- Identify an HR mission or culture consistent with the business needs
- Identify the key strategic HR imperatives that result from the business principles and strategies
- Develop and implement HR initiatives and activities consistent with the HR culture

The HR Department at IBAX

The HR department went from being centralized to being decentralized within the new decentralized business units.

The HR department at IBAX changed dramatically as part of the retrenchment strategy. While the HR department had been structured traditionally in the past, Goodman and the vice president of human resources, Meigann Putnam, designed more creative and innovative methods to better accomplish HR objectives.

Rather than providing the traditional services of recruitment, selection, compensation, training and development, and employee relations centrally, the HR function was decentralized. An HR adviser was assigned to each business unit at

IBAX. This adviser worked within the business so he or she could better understand the products and markets of the business and, therefore, better assess its HR needs. The adviser would involve the team members in the business in all elements of the HR management process. For example, the teams assumed responsibility for hiring their own people based on the assessed needs of their business. What had once been a top-down approach to HR management was transformed into an integrated, team-based process.[46]

Reducing Resistance to Change

An HR department can be very helpful in reducing resistance to change. Often individuals resist change for reasons such as:

- More work
- Concerns about ability to perform
- Loss of control
- Excess of uncertainty
- Threats to power and influence
- Resource limitations
- Habit
- Fear of new social relationships
- Uncertainty about a new boss[47]

Most dissenters won't stand up and shout at you that they hate what you're doing to them and to their comfortable old ways. Instead they will nod and smile and agree with everything you say—and then behave as they always have.

Dale Gambill
Vice-President, Customer Care
Jaguar of North America

The HR department can reduce these concerns by:

- Generating excitement about the "new way"
- Lowering perception of personal risk
- Communicating potential rewards
- Involving employees in planning and implementation
- Training the employees

These can be done more effectively, however, with the active partnership and involvement of the line managers.

Partnership Between HR and Line Managers

Line managers play a critical role in managing change. They contribute by providing answers to questions such as:

1. What are the implications of the business strategy on the four HR targets of action (see Exhibit 5.2)? Implications will vary, of course, by the degree of change in the business strategy.
2. What types of key behaviors/skills are currently rewarded?
3. What types of key behaviors/skills not presently available are needed?
4. What action steps are you taking to ensure these behaviors/skills are available?
5. What types of key behaviors/skills presently available are no longer used/needed?
6. What action steps are you taking to ensure that there is a minimum of redundant skills? Retraining? Transfer? Promotion? Termination?
7. What action steps are you taking to ensure you get the key employee behaviors?

8. What are the right numbers of employees really needed to ensure success? What plans are in place to deal with excess numbers? With shortages?
9. How much more productive will employees need to be to ensure success? Can reductions in absenteeism and turnover be helpful here? Do new people need to be attracted?
10. What specific objectives do you have for each of the nine items above?
11. Who is responsible for meeting these objectives?
12. What measures of success vis-a-vis the objectives are you using?
13. What constraints exist in moving ahead?
14. What do you need from the HR department to help you be successful?

LEARNING OBJECTIVE 4

Explain the current state of HR planning.

Human Resource Planning

In general, today the term **HR planning** refers to the efforts of firms to systematically identify the HR implications resulting from environmental and organizational changes, in order to align their human resources with needs resulting from those changes and issues.[48] Earlier, in times of environmental stability, HR planning was essentially focused on matching HR demand with HR supply, and the target of HR action was employee assignment (Exhibit 5.2). At that time, forecasting HR needs and planning the steps necessary to meet those needs was largely a numbers game. This process typically consisted of developing and implementing plans and programs to ensure that the right number and type of people were available at the right time and place to serve relatively predictable business needs. For example, if business was growing at 10 percent, top management would continue to add to the workforce by 10 percent: it worked before, it would work again.

HR planning refers to the efforts of firms to identify the HR implications of organizational changes.

From Numbers to Issues

Today, because the environment is changing organizations so dramatically, HR planning has become more of a dynamic, volatile issues game.[49] Key questions include: What are major changes in the environment? What are the issues of most importance to our business: Downsizing, workforce diversity, mergers and alliances, other issues? What are the HR implications? How can we orchestrate the way people are managed, in order to address the issues successfully? Of course, HR planning still involves numbers, but as illustrated by the feature on IBAX, it often involves much more, including:

1. Crafting mission and value statements consistent with the business
2. Ensuring that employees understand and buy into the process of change
3. Systematically crafting the appropriate HR actions based upon an analysis of the HR targets of action and an explicit understanding of the company
4. Creating a dynamic HR planning process that mirrors the business planning process and that identifies key changes and implications for managing human resources

The HR planning process must consider both the long-term and short-term HR implications of organizational changes. In fact, firms might typically go out five years in their planning and then work back to the present. Exhibit 5.7 shows the integration between business and HR planning across several time horizons. This process can be used in dealing with the three major organizational changes already discussed in this chapter, or any other changes or key business issues specific to a particular company. Using HR planning helps ensure that the HR implications of organizational changes and key business issues are dealt with systematically and thoroughly.

EXHIBIT 5.7

Dynamic Linkages Between Components of a Fully Integrated System of Business and Human Resource Planning

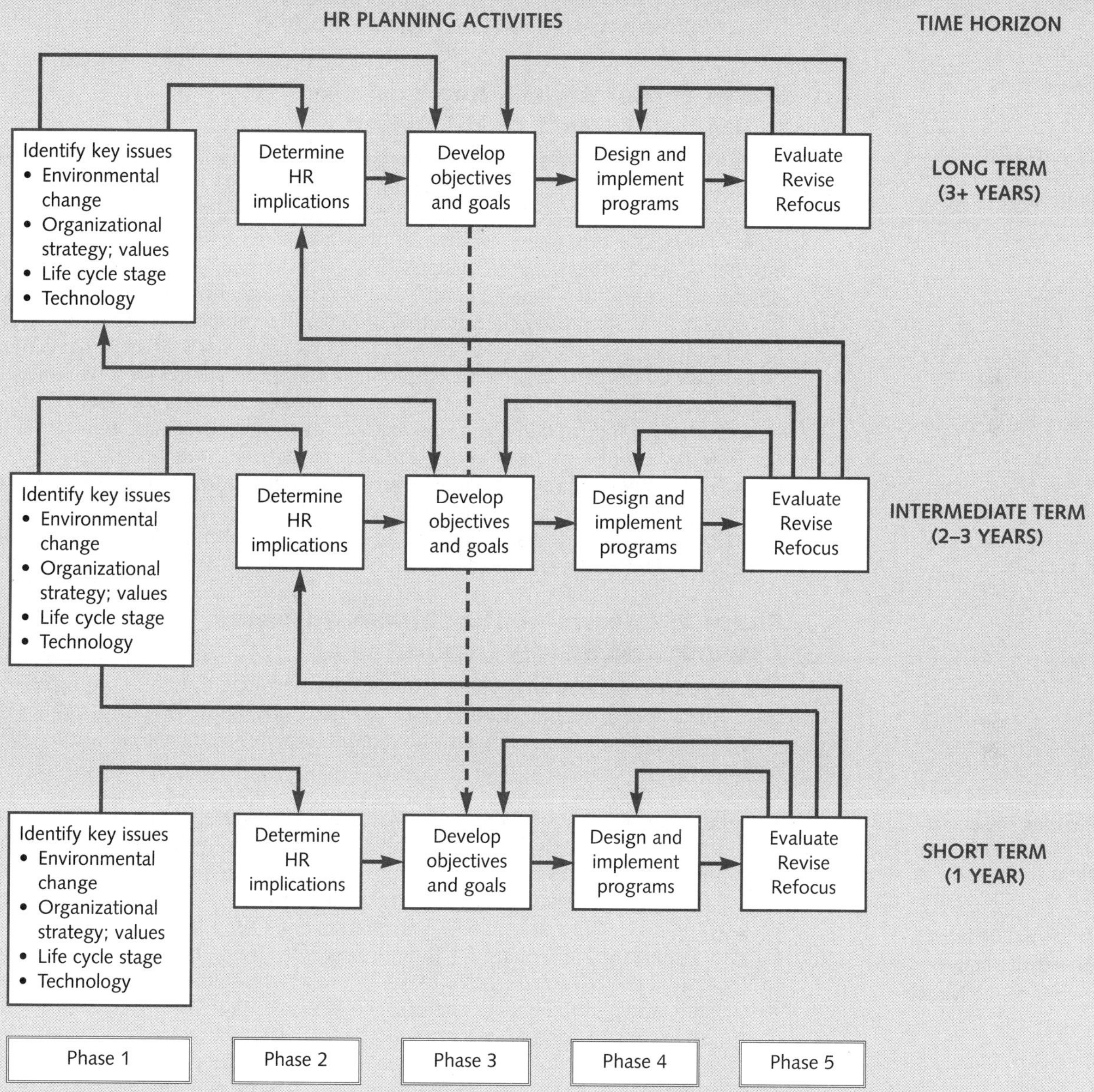

Source: Adapted from S. E. Jackson and R. S. Schuler, "Human Resource Planning: Challenges for Industrial/Organizational Psychologists," *American Psychologist* (February 1990): 225.

Five Phases of the Human Resource Planning Process

Regardless of the time horizon or the issues, the HR planning process has five phases.[50]

1. Assess key business issues and their impact on targets of HR action.
2. Determine the HR demand and supply implications.
3. Develop HR objectives and goals for addressing the issues and actions.
4. Design and implement HR actions: policies, programs, and practices.
5. Monitor results, evaluate, revise, and refocus.[51]

Phase 1: Identify the Key Business Issues and Targets of HR Action

HR planning depends on a thorough scanning of the environments.

The first phase of HR planning involves gathering data to learn about and understand all aspects of the organization's environment. This helps the organization anticipate and plan for issues arising from both stable and dynamic conditions. In other words, the first phase of HR planning involves understanding how all the environmental factors we have discussed so far in this book (see Exhibit 3.2 and Exhibit 5.2) relate to a specific company, its business realities and objectives, and the implications for managing human resources. If a company is going to expand its revenue by 10 percent over each of the next five years, it may need more employees. Or perhaps improved technologies will mean a need for fewer employees. The organizational structure may need to be examined: Is the distribution of positions at the top, middle, and lower levels of the organization appropriate for the organization of tomorrow? Which specific activities or functional areas can be expected to experience particularly severe growth or contraction? Where will the work and workers be located in the future: in the United States or abroad? In a central location, in regional offices, or in employees' homes? At IBAX, divisions were created with decentralized power.

Phase 2: Determine the Human Resource Demand and Supply Implications

The objectives of the second phase are: a) to develop a clear understanding of how the information generated during Phase 1 affects the future HR *demands* of the organization, and b) to develop an accurate picture of the current HR *supply* available internally.

Forecasting the demand and supply of human resources is traditional HR planning. Now added to this is analysis of:

- **Employee behaviors**
- **Employee competencies**
- **Employee motivation**

Forecasting Human Resource Demands. A variety of forecasting methods—some simple, some complex—can be used to determine an organization's demand for human resources. The type of forecast used depends on the time frame, the type of organization, the organization's size and dispersion, and the accuracy and certainty of available information. The time frame used in forecasting the organization's demand for human resources frequently parallels that used in forecasting the potential supply of human resources and the needs of the business. Comparing the demand and supply forecasts then determines the firm's short-, intermediate-, and long-term needs.

Forecasting involves approximations—not absolutes or certainties. The forecast quality depends on the accuracy of information and the predictability of events. The shorter the time horizon, the more predictable the events and the more accurate the information. For example, organizations are generally able to predict how many graduates they need for the coming year, but they are less able to predict how many they will need for the next five years.

A study indicates that 60 percent of major firms conduct some form of HR forecast. More than half of these firms prepare both the short-term (one year) and the long-term (five years) forecasts. The emphasis is generally on predicting HR demand rather than supply, perhaps because firms believe they have more control over demand than supply. In fact, more than half of the firms predict only demand, and only one-third formally forecast both supply and demand.[52]

Two classes of techniques that HR planners and line managers can use to determine their company's projected demand for human resources are **judgmental forecasts** and **conventional statistical projections**.

Judgmental forecasting employs experts and includes the most common method of predicting HR demand, **managerial estimates**.[53] These estimates, based upon experience and familiarity with the employee productivity rates, can be made by top managers. Alternatively, the review process can begin at lower levels of management, with the results sent to higher levels for refinement. Useful information can include data on current and projected productivity levels, market demand, and sales, as well as current staffing levels and mobility information.

Another way to make judgments about HR demand is the **Delphi technique**. At a Delphi meeting, experts take turns presenting their forecasts and assumptions to the others, who then make revisions in their own forecasts. This combination process continues until a viable composite forecast emerges. The composite may represent specific projections or a range of projections, depending on the experts' positions.

A related method is the **nominal group technique**. Several people sit at a conference table and independently list their ideas on a sheet of paper.[54] The ideas presented are recorded on larger sheets of paper so that everyone can see all the ideas and refer to them in later parts of the session.

The Delphi and nominal group techniques are similar in process, but the Delphi technique is more frequently used to generate predictions, and the nominal group technique is more frequently used to identify current organizational problems and solutions to those problems. Although all these judgmental forecasts rely on less data than those based on statistical methods such as linear and multiple linear regressions, they tend to dominate in practice.[55]

Forecasting HR Supplies. Forecasted supply can be derived from both internal and external sources of information. Internal sources of supply are generally the focus at this stage of planning. External sources are considered in later phases, as part of the process of designing the practices needed to prepare for the future.

As with forecasting demand, two basic techniques help forecast internal labor supply: judgmental and statistical. Once made, the supply forecast can be compared with the HR demand forecast to help determine, among other things, action programming for identifying HR talent and balancing supply and demand forecasts. More often, however, the forecasting of labor supply is short range, with the focus often on budgeting and controlling costs.

Forecasts for periods of five or more years, if made, usually address the company's need to plan for managerial replacements.[56] Two judgmental techniques used by organizations to make supply forecasts are replacement planning and succession planning. **Replacement planning** involves developing replacement charts to show the names of the current and potential occupants of positions. Potential promotions can be estimated by the performance levels of employees currently in jobs, and their development needs. Incumbents are listed directly under the job title. Individuals likely to fill potential vacancies are listed directly under the incumbent.

Succession planning is similar to replacement planning except that it is usually longer-term and more developmental. Companies are practicing succession planning now more than ever, as they recognize that great leadership is needed to be effective in today's business environment.

Renewed attention is focused on Human Resources and the strategic role it plays in securing our future success. Emphasis will grow on conducting meaningful interactive performance reviews linked to career development, training and education, and, very importantly, succession planning.

Lincoln Krochmal, MD
President and CEO
Unilever Research, U.S.[57]

Judgmental forecasts are predictions about the future based upon one's personal judgment.

Conventional statistical projections are predictions about the future based upon exploration of past statistics and data.

Managerial estimates are predictions about the future made by judgments of managers.

The Delphi technique is a method used to predict the future based upon the judgments of many experts.

The nominal group technique is a method to predict the future using a conference-style format of discussion.

Did You KNOW?

"There is clearly a supply and demand problem for many manufacturers," says Michael Cantwell, national director of manufacturing at Grant Thornton, a management consulting firm. A recent survey of 919 small businesses by Arthur Andersen's Enterprise Group found 25% worried that a lack of qualified workers will hamper their growth.

Replacement planning involves describing who's where and who could be there.

Succession planning identifies and grooms candidates for top management jobs.

These same companies realize that what makes a good manager today may not be what makes a good manager in the future. Consequently, companies such as AT&T, Unilever, and Allstate Insurance Company are trying to identify what will make a good manager in the years ahead and to design developmental activities to make sure the right people will be available with the right skills at the right time. As we see in Chapter 9, succession and replacement planning are also important in a firm's internal promotion policy.

Phase 3: Develop Human Resource Objectives and Goals

After phase 2 is completed, a great deal of descriptive information about current and future conditions is available. The next phase involves interpreting this information and using it to establish priorities and set objectives and goals.

With a short time horizon, which is often the time frame adopted for downsizing efforts, objectives are often easy to state in quantifiable terms. Examples of short-term HR objectives include increasing the number of people who are attracted to the organization and apply for jobs (the applicant pool), attracting a different mix of applicants (with different skills, in different locations, etc.), improving the qualifications of new hires, increasing the length of time that desirable employees stay with the organization, decreasing the length of time that undesirable employees stay with the organization, and helping current and newly hired employees quickly develop the skills needed by the organization. Such objectives can generally be achieved in a straightforward way by applying state-of-the-art HR management techniques and working with line managers to ensure agreement with and understanding of the program objectives.

The issues of downsizing and diversity management usually involve adopting intermediate- and long-term time frames for setting objectives. Differences in the types of objectives established for the shorter and longer term reflect differences in the types of changes that are feasible with two to five additional years of time. Thus, whereas short-term objectives include attracting, assessing, and assigning employees to jobs, intermediate-term objectives are more likely to include readjusting employees' skills, attitudes, and behaviors to fit major changes in the needs of the business, as well as adjusting HR practices to fit changes in the needs of employees. Longer-term objectives might include creating a major change in the corporate culture as in IBAX, or positioning the firm to compete in totally new businesses.

Phase 4: Design and Implement Human Resource Policies, Programs, and Practices

Whereas the focus of phase 3 was establishing *what* to accomplish, phase 4 addresses *how* to accomplish it. What specific HR actions will help the organization achieve its stated objectives? A great variety of actions can be designed during this phase. These include diversity programs to make organizations more attractive to a broader array of applicants; programs to improve socialization efforts so that good employees want to remain with the organization; and programs to downsize or rightsize the organization, such as early retirement incentives and generous severance packages to complement the normal attrition process. Exhibit 5.2 illustrates more of these for the three major changes described in the first half of this chapter.

Did You KNOW?

The Marriott Company develops great HR programs so potential employees will regard it as a great place to work, thus helping to ensure a good supply of job applicants.

Phase 5: Evaluate, Revise, and Refocus

When a company offers a product to the external marketplace, it will evaluate the success of that product using some type of objective indicator. Likewise, the success of products and services offered in the company's internal marketplace should be monitored closely. In this phase, the objectives set during phase 3 again come into play, for these define the criteria to be used in evaluating whether a program or initiative is successful or is in need of revision. For example, if personal self-development is the only objective one hopes to achieve from holding diversity awareness workshops, then asking employees whether the workshop experience was valuable may be the only data that should be collected. However, when large investments are made for the purposes of reducing turnover, attracting new or different employees to the firm, or improving team functioning, then data relevant to these objectives should be examined. Chapter 20 will address how an HR information system facilitates evaluation by allowing for more thorough, rapid, and frequent collection of data.[58]

Evaluation of HR plans and programs is an important process, not only for determining the effectiveness of HR planning, but also for demonstrating the significance of both HR activities and the HR department in the organization as a whole. Without this phase, the improvement process can slow down significantly.

Current Trends

LEARNING OBJECTIVE 5

Describe how organizations can be "learning organizations."

Two major trends today are: a) learning organizations and b) aligning human resources with the business.

Creating Learning Organizations

A learning organization is one that shares and distributes information and knowledge to continually improve.

Creating **learning organizations** means making a company capable of learning: learning from its mistakes; learning from other parts of the same company; and learning from other companies.

If companies are changing for the purpose of getting better, they should know what they used to do. But knowing is not always easy for a company to do. You might remember what you did last year, but a company or a department in a company may not remember! In this age of downsizing, as companies lose employees, they lose knowledge of what used to happen: walking out the door with the employees is the knowledge and wisdom they have accumulated during their time with the company. With the greater use of teams, more employees know more about what is happening, so the loss of one does not necessarily mean the loss of knowledge. But organizations still need to be systematic in recording and gathering information about what it is doing to help prevent them from repeating mistakes and "re-inventing the wheel."

Companies can also learn by making it easier for employees in different parts of the organization to share their knowledge and experiences with each other. Many times employees in different parts of an organization are working on the same challenge, but are completely unaware of each other. The use of cross-functional teams, those from different departments such as marketing and human resources, helps to reduce this isolationism. The use of information-transfer technology, such as e-mail, also helps individuals in different departments and different parts of the business learn from each other.

Companies also learn from their willingness to learn from other companies. This practice is now very common in many of the very best companies, such as GE, Wal-Mart, Hewlett-Packard, and Nordstrom.[59] In fact, GE claims that it learned from Wal-Mart about the importance of a speedy distribution system and the importance of rapid inventory turnover. Many companies have visited Lincoln Electric in Cleveland, Ohio in order to hear and see first-hand how their famous incentive system works. This practice, referred to as benchmarking, enables companies to learn from other companies how things might be done differently, even from companies that are in different industries.

Companies in the same industry, however, might also learn from each other. Porsche, the German auto maker famous for its fast sports car, learned from

Even the best companies are willing to learn from each other.

employees at Toyota. Through extensive training and teaching by the Japanese, Porsche has reduced the time it takes to produce a car from 120 hours to 72 hours and manufacturing flaws from six per car to three per car. But according to Wendelin Wiedeking, Porsche's chief executive officer, what is ultimately revolutionary about what the Japanese have done is redefine craftsmanship for the Germans:

Porsche learned from the Japanese the meaning of craftsmanship!

> *"The traditional craftsmanship for which Germany became famous was filing and fitting parts so that they fit perfectly. But that was wasted time. The parts should have been made right the first time. So the new craftsmanship is the craftsmanship of thinking up clever ways of making things simpler and easier to assemble. It is the craft of creating an uninterrupted flow of manufacturing."*[60]

Aligning Human Resources with the Needs of the Business

All of our HR programs serve the bank's mission. If they didn't, we wouldn't have them.

Jim Alef
Corporate Senior Vice-President and Head, Human Resources
First Chicago Corporation

Ensuring that business needs are met by human resources will be a significant issue through the 21st century. In particular, human resources must be a strategic partner to the line manager, international needs must be addressed, and sufficient programs must be put in place to ensure cost efficiency. Success in all these areas will depend on the organization's HR planning skills and programs.

Planning at organizational and individual levels will continue to change. At the organizational level, there will be a greater focus on shaping and managing change. Planning, as an identifier of needs and mobilizer of human resources, will increasingly be used to identify business needs and the ways in which employees can meet those needs. To deal with the rapidly changing environment, planning will become more tentative and short-term focused. At the same time, long-term needs will still be important because some organizational change efforts—such as quality improvement—take time.

HR planning will also be done with demographics in mind. As skilled labor shortages develop, there will be more concern both for retaining and retraining good employees. As employee commitment and empowerment are causally linked to quality improvement, there will be even stronger emphasis on this area.

However, there will be a corresponding need to link HR planning and business planning so that excess supply of personnel is not created. As the external environment changes, so may the strategy and business needs of the firm. Therefore, HR planning must cultivate workforce flexibility, diversity, and adaptability Planning professionals will assume the responsibility for systematically orchestrating all the HR practices to stimulate and reinforce these issues. This orchestration will become more important as the need to link business strategies with labor supply grows.

Finally, businesses must ensure that the most effective HR practices are being used. To that end, continuous and extensive environment scanning will be an important feature of successful firms in highly competitive environments as described in Chapter 3.

Summary

Change is everywhere, and as the 21st century approaches and unfolds, change becomes more pervasive and intense. This chapter highlighted some of the key issues facing companies today, including: a) downsizing and layoffs, b) managing diversity, and c) mergers and alliances. When major business issues such as these are involved, the cycle of anticipating change, planning and carrying out change, and evaluating and readjusting becomes continuous. Change becomes the constant in managing human resources effectively.

Common to all these major issues are the necessary involvement of top management, the necessary involvement of the HR department, and the necessary use of HR planning. Without the leadership and support, and even change, of top management, these three major issues are not likely to be effectively managed. As Jeff Goodman and his team at IBAX realized, before they could expect the rest of the company to embrace total quality management, they had to change first. So change they did, and then the rest of the organization followed. The HR department helped the organization determine the content of the needed changes (e.g., what skills the employees needed), and the process of change (e.g., who should change first and how fast the changes should be made). Like any effort that affects the entire company, change requires a great deal of business and HR planning. Selecting, designing, and implementing the appropriate HR policies and practices in response to change requires a great deal of information, wise judgment, and managerial skills.

Key Concepts

conventional statistical projections
Delphi technique
job sharing
judgmental forecast
human resource planning
learning organization
managing diversity
managerial estimate
nominal group technique
replacement planning
succession planning

Review and Discussion Questions

1. Describe the organizational change facing IBAX and Jerry Goodman.
2. Using the framework in Exhibit 5.2, describe the implications for managing human resources from: a) downsizing and layoffs, b) workforce diversity, and c) mergers and alliances.
3. What aspects of downsizing and layoffs make some of these efforts more effective than others?
4. What are the legal considerations in downsizing and layoffs?
5. Describe the meaning of managing diversity.
6. What must the top management in most organizations do in order to manage total quality, downsizing and layoffs, workforce diversity, and mergers and alliances successfully?
7. Describe the role of the HR department and its partnership with line managers and employees in making major organizational changes.
8. Describe how HR planning is different today than in earlier days when conditions were more stable and predictable.
9. Describe the phases of HR planning.
10. In what ways can companies create themselves as "learning organizations"?

PROJECTS, EXERCISES & CASES

End-of-Text Projects

Lincoln Electric

1. Describe the major environmental and organizational changes facing Lincoln.
2. Develop a framework for analyzing the implications of organizational changes for managing Lincoln Electric's human resources. (Use Exhibit 5.2 as a guide.)
3. Next, describe what HR actions Lincoln Electric could be taking to address these implications.
4. Predict the environmental and organizational changes Lincoln Electric will experience in the 21st century.

Nordstrom

1. Describe the major environmental and organizational changes facing Nordstrom.
2. Develop a framework for analyzing the implications of organizational changes for managing Nordstrom's human resources. (Use Exhibit 5.2 as a guide.)
3. Next, describe what HR actions Nordstrom could be taking to address these implications.
4. Predict the environmental and organizational changes Nordstrom will experience in the 21st century.

Field Projects

1. Choose a company, either through a personal visit or by reading about it, and identify major organizational changes it is experiencing. Describe the implications for managing the organization's human resources. Then describe how these implications will affect the firm's HR activities.
2. Interview an HR manager from both a large and a small company to learn about the strategy and planning of their company. How is HR planning related to the mission, goals, and objectives of the company? In relation to the industry the company is in, what period of planning is the company focusing on: Long-term or short-term? Are there any differences based upon the size of the companies? Does the small firm plan less or more than the big firm?

VISIT THE LIBRARY

Workforce Online

1. Enter your Web browser.
2. Enter "Workforce Online."
3. Review the following articles within the "Winning Ideas":

   U.S. West Finds Strength in Diversity

   Diversity Keeps Newspaper Up With the Times

   3M's Staffing Strategy Promotes Productivity and Pride
4. Return to the homepage.
5. Enter the "Research Center."
6. Find and review the following articles:

   Merck's Prescription for Joint Ventures

   Novell Idea: A Map for Mergers.

   Contingent Workforce Spurs HR Planning

   HR Facilitates the Learning Organization Concept

   How HR Keeps Current In Century-Old Companies

   Global Operations Demand that HR Rethink Diversity
7. Return to your homepage.

Case: Seeing the Forest and the Trees

The current face of domestic and global competition that the leaders of the Forest Products Company (FPC) and its parent, the Weyerhaeuser Corporation, saw as they surveyed an industry on its knees in the early 1980s was a far different face than the one Weyerhaeuser and its subsidiaries had successfully competed against for so long. They knew how to compete—and win—against a large-firm, commodity lumber business. But that business was in its death throes, and what was emerging from the ashes presented an entirely new set of challenges, one that would require a radical change in Weyerhaeuser's strategy. The new competitors were not the old monolithic organizations but were instead small mills, lean and mean, configured so they could tailor their products to customer demand and change their product lines rapidly if the need arose. They were nonunion, owner-operated, and entrepreneurial and, in this configuration, were running the lowest-cost, most market-oriented operations around.

Going out of business was not an alternative anyone cared to think about, but if things didn't change it was a definite possibility. So Charley Bingham, the CEO of the Forest Products Company, knew that something had to be done—and sooner, not later. He gathered his top dozen managers, and together they decided that a massive reorganization was called for, accompanied by a radical change in strategy. According to Bingham, the change in strategy went something like this:

> *Approximately 80 percent of our sales dollars in 1982 represented products sold as commodities. By 1995, we resolved that we must reverse the proportions.*

The massive reorganization at FPC mirrored that occurring at its parent company. The Weyerhaeuser Corporation decided to drastically decentralize. The three operating units, of which FPC was one, were given free reign on how to do their business. Given this scenario, Bingham and his team decided they needed to create an organization capable of acting and responding just like their competitors. Thus, they created 200 profit centers with each center largely responsible for its own bottom line.

This restructuring soon proved to be only a first step in the right direction. FPC's ability to implement its new strategy was being undermined by low morale, which was pervasive. In addition, many middle managers, those needed to actually carry out the change, were pessimistic about the possibility of sustained future success. Silently, they even questioned their own ability to operate the profit centers.

With insights from Horace Parker, director of executive development at FPC, the rest of the top team came to realize that there would have to be a total transformation of the organization: the corporate culture, knowledge base, skill levels, style of leadership, and team orientation would all have to change, for all employees. With 18,000 employees across the United States, Parker wasn't sure where to start. The others said they would help, but Horace had to tell them what to do. Horace, of course, is waiting to hear what you have to tell him.

Case Questions

1. Where does Horace start? What programs does he put in place to deal with the needs of corporate culture, knowledge, skills, leadership, and team orientation?
2. How does he go about developing the programs that he needs to put in place? Does he do it by himself? Can he buy off-the-shelf programs?
3. What time frame does Horace need to implement the programs to make the change successful? If he deals only with the executive development programs, does he need to be concerned with programs for middle managers and below? How does he do this?

Chapter 5 Endnotes

1. J. F. Welch, "A Master Class in Radical Change," *Fortune* (December 13, 1993): 83.

2. IBAX materials adapted from P. S. Lewis, S. H. Goodman, and P. M. Fandt, *Management: Challenges in the 21st Century* (St. Paul: West Publishing, 1995).

3. This framework has been developed from the basic ideas described by Professor Lee Dyer, Cornell University, personal communications, August 1994.

4. J. Nocera, "Living With Layoffs," *Fortune* (April 1, 1996): 69–108; J. A. Byrne, "The Pain of Downsizing," *Business Week* (May 9, 1994): 60–69.

5. L. Uchitelle and N. R. Kleinfield, "On the Battlefields of Business, Millions of Casualties," *New York Times* (March 3, 1996): 26. See the entire week from March 3–9 for stories on downsizing.

6. C. Arnst, "The Bloodletting at AT&T Is Just the Beginning," *Business Week* (January 15, 1996): 30; C. Arnst, "Out One Door and In Another," *Business Week* (January 22, 1996): 41; J. J. Keller, "AT&T Will Eliminate 40,000 Jobs and Take a Charge of $4 Billion," *The Wall Street Journal* (January 3, 1996): A3, 4; O'Reilly, "The New Deal: What Companies and Employees Owe One Another," *Fortune* (June 13, 1994): 44–52.

7. D. Stamps, "Corporate Anorexia," *Training* (February 1996): 24–30; P. Stuart, "New Internal Jobs Found for Displaced Employees," *Personnel Journal* (August 1992): 50–56; E. Faltermayer, "Is This Layoff Necessary?" *Fortune* (June 1, 1992): 71–86.

8. S. Caudron, "Teach Downsizing Survivors How to Thrive," *Personnel Journal* (January 1996): 38–48; R. L. Knowdell, E. Branstead, and M. Moravec, *From Downsizing to Recovery—Strategic Transition Options for Organizations and Individuals* (Palo Alto, CA: CPP Books, 1994); D. Stamps, "Corporate Anorexia" *Training* (February 1996): 24–30.

9. C. R. Leana and D.C. Feldman, "When Mergers Force Layoffs: Some Lessons about Managing the Human Resource Problems," *Human Resource Planning* 12, no. 2 (1989): 123–140; K. S. Cameron, S. J. Freeman, and A. K. Mishra, "Best Practices in White Collar Downsizing: Managing Contradictions," *Academy of Management Executive* 5, no. 3 (1991): 57–73; W. F. Cascio, "Downsizing: What Do We Know? What Have We Learned?" *Academy of Management Executive* 7, no. 1 (1993): 95–104.

10. D. M. Schweiger, J. M. Ivancevich, and F. R. Power, "Executive Actions for Managing Human Resources Before and After Acquisition," *Academy of Management Executive* 1, no. 2 (1986): 127–138.

11. J. B. Treece, "Doing It Right, Till the Last Whistle," *Business Week* (April 6, 1992): 58–59.

12. R. I. Schiff, "Linking Systems Eases Layoffs," *Personnel Journal* (July 1994): 22–23; M. Messmer, "Strategies to Calm Those Restructuring 'Jitters'," *Personnel Journal* (October 1993): 18.

13. "Employers Seldom Warn Workers about Layoffs," *Bulletin to Management* (August 26, 1993): 265; B. P. Noble, "Straddling the Law on Layoffs," *New York Times* (February 28, 1993): F37.

14. L. Moser Illes, "Site Shutdown: One HR Leader Tells Her Story," *Personnel Journal* (March 1996): 95–107; G. Flynn, "Does Your Severance Plan Make the Cut?" *Personnel Journal* (August 1995): 32–40; "Use of Outplacement Services," *Bulletin to Management* (February 10, 1994): 44–45.

15. "Severance Practices," *Bulletin to Management* (January 11, 1996): 12–13; "Staff Cuts Scrutinized," *Bulletin to Management* (November 9, 1995): 360; G. Koretz, "America's Trade Ace in the Hole," *Business Week* (February 20, 1995): 26; B. Presley Noble, "Questioning Productivity Beliefs," *New York Times* (July 10, 1994): F21; F. Rose, "Job-Cutting Medicine Fails to Remedy Productivity Ills at Many Companies," *The Wall Street Journal* (June 7, 1994): A5.

16. "How HR Can Help Lay Off Employees in a Dignified Way," by J. Meissner, copyright November 1993.

17. B. P. Foster, "Workforce Diversity and Business," *Training and Development Journal* (April 1988): 59.

18. Towers, Perrin, and Hudson Institute, *Workforce 2000: Competing in a Seller's Market: Is Corporate America Prepared?* (Valhalla, NY: Towers, Perrin, 1990); S. Caudron, "Sexual Politics," *Personnel Journal* (May 1995): 50–61.

19. D. Anfuso, "Diversity Keeps Newspaper Up With the Times," *Personnel Journal* (July 1995): 30–41; G. Flynn, "Do You Have the Right Approach to Diversity," *Personnel Journal* (October 1995): 68–75.

20. S. G. Butruille, "Corporate Caretaking," *Training and Development Journal* (April 1990): 49–55.

21. J. Fierman, "Why Women Still Don't Hit the Top," *Fortune* (July 30, 1990): 40–62. See also J. M. Brett and A. H. Reilly, "All the Right Stuff: A Comparison of Female and Male Managers' Career Progression," *Journal of Applied Psychology* 77 (1992): 251–260; E. A. Fagenson, ed., *Women in Management,* vol. 4, *Women and Work* (Newbury Park, CA: Sage, 1993).

22. A. Edwards, "Special Report: Cultural Diversity in Today's Corporation," *Working Woman* (January 1991): 60.

23. "Welcome to the Woman-Friendly Company Where Talent Is Valued and Rewarded," *Business Week* (August 6, 1990): 48–50.

24. Edwards, "Special Report: Cultural Diversity in Today's Corporation."

25. "Race in the Workplace: Is Affirmative Action Working?" *Business Week* (July 8, 1991): 50–63.

26. S. S. Fugita and D. J. O'Brien, *Japanese American Ethnicity: The Persistence of the Community* (Seattle: University of Washington Press, 1991).

27. J. S. Hirsch, "Older Workers Chafe under Young Managers," *The Wall Street Journal* (February 26, 1990): B1, 6.

28. G. H. Elder, Jr., "Age Differentiation and the Life Course," *Annual Review of Sociology* 1(1975): 165–190; S. R. Rhodes, "Age-Related Differences in Work Attitudes and Behavior: A Review and Conceptual Analysis," *Psychological Bulletin* 93 (1983): 328–367; "Work Attitudes: Study Reveals Generation Gap," *Bulletin to Management* (October 2, 1986): 326.

29. Anfuso, "Diversity Keeps Newspaper Up With the Times"; Flynn, "Do You Have the Right Approach to Diversity."

30. J. Nelson-Horchler, "Demographics Deliver a Warning," *Industry Week* (April 18, 1988): 58.

31. L. Copeland, "Valuing Diversity, Part 2: Pioneers and Champions of Change," *Personnel* (July, 1988): 48.

32. Ibid.

33. A. Morrison, R. P. White, and E. Van Velsnor, "Executive Women: Substance Plus Style," *Psychology Today* (August 1987): 18–21, 24–26.

34. S. E. Jackson, ed., *Diversity in the Workplace: Human Resource Initiatives* (New York: Guilford Press, 1993); J. D.

Goodchilds, ed., *Psychological Perspectives on Human Diversity in America: Master Lectures* (Washington, D.C.: American Psychological Association, 1991); J. P. Fernandez, *Managing a Diverse Workforce: Regaining the Competitive Edge* (Lexington, MA: Lexington Books, 1991).

35. T. Cox, Jr., *Cultural Diversity in Organizations: Theory, Research, and Practice* (San Francisco: Berrett-Koehler Publishers, 1993): 216–218.

36. K. Myers, "Cracking the Glass Ceiling," *Information Week* (August 27, 1990): 38–41; G.N. Powell, "Upgrading Management Opportunities for Women," *HR Magazine* (November 1990): 67–70; D. T. Hall, "Moving Beyond the 'Mommy Track': An Organization Change Approach," *Personnel* (December 1989): 23–29; E. Ehrlich, "The Mommy Track," *Business Week* (March 20, 1989): 126–134: F. N. Schwartz, "Management Women and the New Facts of Life," *Harvard Business Review* (January-February 1989): 65–76.

37. Information provided by J. Hunt, Merck and Company, as part of an MBA project, New York University, Fall 1990.

38. Information provided by M. Penso, Prudential Insurance Company.

39. This discussion is based on S. E. Jackson, "Stepping into the Future: Guidelines for Action," in Jackson, *Diversity in the Workplace.*

40. For more information, see Fernandez, *Managing a Diverse Workforce*; C. D. Fyock, *America's Workforce Is Coming of Age* (Lexington, MA: Lexington Books, 1990); M. Loden and J. B. Rosener, *Workforce America! Managing Employee Diversity as a Vital Resource* (Homewood, IL: Business One Irwin, 1991); A. M. Morrison, *The New Leaders: Guidelines on Leadership Diversity in America* (San Francisco: Jossey-Bass, 1992).

41. "Helping Two Companies Form a Third," by D. Anfuso, copyright January 1994, *Personnel Journal.*

42. J. P. Kotter, "Leading Change: Why Transformation Efforts Fail," *Harvard Business Review* (March-April 1995): 59–67; L. D. Goodstein and W. W. Burke, "Creating Successful Organization Change," *Organizational Dynamics* (Spring 1991): 5–12; N. M. Tichy, "Managing Change Strategically: The Technical, Political, and Cultural Keys," *Organizational Dynamics* (Autumn 1982): 59–80; G. Hamel and C. K. Prahalad, *Competing for the Future* (Boston: Harvard Business School Press, 1994); J. Huey, "The New Post-Heroic Leadership," *Fortune* (February 21, 1994): 42–50.

43. Based on J. Bolt, *Executive Development* (New York: Harper & Row, 1989).

44. Based on Lewis, Goodman, and Fandt, *Management: Challenge in the 21st Century* (St. Paul, MN: West Publishing, 1995).

45. For a full discussion, see A. Howard, ed., *Diagnosis for Organizational Change: Methods and Models* (New York: Guilford, 1994).

46. Based on Lewis, Goodman, and Fandt, *Management: Challenge in the 21st Century* (St. Paul, MN: West Publishing, 1995).

47. A. B. Fisher, "Making Change Stick," *Fortune* (April 17, 1995): 121–127; T. A. Stewart, "Rate Your Readiness to Change," *Fortune* (February 7, 1994): 106–110.

48. B. J. Smith, J. W. Boroski, and G. E. Davis, "Human Resource Planning," *Human Resource Management* (Spring-Summer 1992): 81–94; J. W. Walker, "The Ultimate Human Resource Planning: Integrating the Human Resource Function with the Business," in *Handbook of Human Resource Management,* ed. G. R. Ferris (Oxford, England: Blackwell, 1995); K. S. McKinlay and A. McKinlay, *Strategy and the Human Resource* (Oxford, England: Blackwell, 1993); S. E. Jackson and R. S. Schuler, "Human Resource Planning: Challenges for Industrial/Organizational Psychologists," *American Psychologist* (February 1990): 223–239.

49. R. S. Schuler and J. W. Walker, "Human Resources Strategy: Focusing on Issues and Actions," *Organizational Dynamics* (Summer 1990): 5–19.

50. D. E. Ripley, "How To Determine Future Workforce Needs," *Personnel Journal* (January 1995): 83–89; C. Mackey, "Human Resource Planning: A Four-Phased Approach," *Management Review* (May 1981): 17–22.

51. For an extensive description of each of these phases, see B. J. Smith, J. W. Boroski, and G. E. Davis, "Human Resource Planning," *Human Resource Management* (Spring-Summer 1992): 81–93; S. Caudron, "Contingent Work Force Spurs HR Planning," *Personnel Journal* (July 1994): 52–59; E. H. Burack, "A Strategic Planning Operational Agenda for Human Resources," *Human Resource Planning* 11, no. 2 (1988): 63–68.

52. M. J. Feuer, R. J. Niehaus, and J. A. Sheridan, "Human Resource Forecasting: A Survey of Practice and Potential," *Human Resource Planning* (1988): 85–97.

53. For a description of managerial estimates, see J. W. Walker, *Human Resource Planning* (New York: McGraw-Hill, 1980).

54. For a more extensive discussion of group techniques, including the nominal group technique, see A. C. Delbecq, A. H. Van de Ven, and D. H. Gustafson, *Group Technique for Program Planning* (Glenview, IL: Scot, Foresman, 1977).

55. H. Kahalas et al., "Human Resource Planning Activities in U.S. Firms," *Human Resource Planning* 3 (1980): 53–66.

56. M. London, E. S. Bassman, and J. P. Fernandez, eds., *Human Resource Forecasting and Strategy Development: Guidelines for Analyzing and Fulfilling Organizational Needs* (Westport, CT: Quorum Books, 1990); S. E. Forrer and Z. B. Leibowitz, *Using Computers in Human Resources: How to Select and Make the Best Use of Automated HR Systems* (San Francisco: Jossey-Bass, 1991).

57. Unilever, *Innovator* (Winter 1994); R. J. Sahl, "Succession Planning Drives Plant Turnaround," *Personnel Journal* (September 1992): 67–70.

58. M. London, E. S. Bassman, and J. P. Fernandez, eds., *Human Resource Forecasting and Strategy Development: Guidelines for Analyzing and Fulfilling Organizational Needs* (Westport, Conn.: Quorum Books, 1990); S. E. Forrer and Z. B. Leibowitz, *Using Computers in Human Resources: How to Select and Make the Best Use of Automated HR Systems* (San Francisco: Jossey-Bass, 1991).

59. L. B. Ward, "In the Executive Alphabet, You Call Them C.L.O.'s," *New York Times* (February 4, 1996): F12. See also J. W. Slocum, M. McGill and D. Lei, "The New Learning Strategy: Anytime, Anything, Anywhere," *Organizational Dynamics* (Autumn 1994): 33–48.

60. N. C. Nash, "Putting Porsche in the Pink: German Craftsmanship Gets Japanese Fine-Tuning," *New York Times* (January 20, 1996): 35, 38.

Career Planning and Management

CHAPTER 6

> *"Some people are very clever at figuring out what lake has a lot of fish in it and then knowing how to get the boat out there at the right time of day.*
>
> *John Kotter*
> *Professor*
> *Harvard Business School*[1]

Learning Objectives

1. Explain why companies offer career planning and management programs.
2. Discuss the problems and issues that arise during organizational entry, midcareer, and late career.
3. Tell what companies are doing for their employees in career planning and management.
4. Describe what you can do to prevent career obsolescence and ensure your employability.

Chapter Outline

Career Planning and Management

Why Is Career Planning and Management Important?

Career Development: Stages and Issues

Career Management Programs in the Organization

Sharing the Responsibility: Your Career Activities

Summary

MANAGING HUMAN RESOURCES

for Greater Employability

A year ago, Terri Welk, a 37-year-old airline worker with a new bachelor's degree in the emerging field of computer-based information systems sent out a single resume. After an interview two weeks later, she landed a job paying close to $40,000 a year.

Behind these prosaic facts is an adventure story of one woman's escape from the trap doors and falling pillars of the economy of the 1990s. Mrs. Welk may not have struck gold, but she had seen disaster coming and stayed one step ahead. She is a winner in a world of work that for so many has become a world turned upside down.

A NIGHT SCHOOL ROUTE

Working as a telephone operations manager for Trans World Airlines in the late 1980s, she watched as the airline began reducing its workforce and reorganizing its reservations business. "I started wondering how secure my job really was," she said.

So she took classes at night and on Saturdays to earn her degree, and now she helps manage the telecommunications system of Twentieth Century Services, a rising company that manages mutual funds.

Some of her day is spent scrolling through data on her computer, troubleshooting the company's telephone circuits and its answering system, which directs thousands of customers each day to account managers. She programs the telephones and computers that make the company's telecommunications network run.

"Telecommunications is everywhere," she said. "In some capacity, I think I can find a job anywhere."

Mrs. Welk has worked hard to insure her survival. She first peered into the future of the job market in 1979, when she barely escaped a furlough from her first job as a clerk at TWA's administrative offices and she was shifted to another clerical job. "I thought I should go to night school," said Mrs. Welk, who dropped out of college after her sophomore year to get married.

She noticed that TWA was hiring more and more people with data processing skills, so she took noncredit courses at a community college and was quickly promoted to positions installing software in the company's mainframe computers and managing its voice-mail system.

Then, four years ago, she sensed greater changes afoot as the troubled airline desperately looked for ways to consolidate its operations and save money.

"This is the best thing that ever happened to me," she said. "I like doing this, and I think I'll like it for a long, long time."

Her husband, Cary Welk, 39, cannot say the same thing for his job on the assembly line at the Ford Motor Company plant, where he has worked since 1977.

In these days of booming automobile sales, Mr. Welk is making a lot of money: $18.23 an hour for 40 hours, plus high overtime pay. Each hour on the line, Mr. Welk installs 50 Ford Tempo headliners, the interior fabric on the roof, the visors and the bracket for the map light. "You can go almost into a trance," he said. "I can go to the Caribbean for 20 minutes."

But it's the uncertainty of the work, not the routine, that gets to him. Robots or lower wage workers in Mexico, where Ford has a similar plant, could take his job some day. Laid-off, unskilled auto workers here can still find jobs, he said, but they pay only $6 or $7 an hour.

LIVING WELL

Still, he looks at the $1,000 a week he is earning now and at the travails his wife has been through, and says he is willing to run the risk that he and Ford will stay together. From a peak of 5,400 workers at the end of the 1970s, the plant cut back to about 3,000 during the last recession. With his lengthening seniority, Mr. Welk has survived the cuts, and with sales surging again the plant now has more than 4,000 workers.[2]

Career Planning and Management

The feature, "Managing Human Resources for Greater Employability," illustrates two aspects of career planning and management. The first is that times are changing and people need to take charge of their own lives and careers. This is the essence of the new social contract we discussed in Chapter 3. This means managing change, taking risks, working hard at one job and trying to learn at the same time, and a willingness to do this continuously![3] Some people like Terri Welk are willing to do this; others, like Cary Welk are not. In part these differences are based upon personality, how people perceive their environment, and how much assistance and support they receive from their employers. This relates to the second aspect of career planning and management in the opening feature.

The new social contract makes it important for you to take charge of your career.

The feature also presents an opportunity for organizations to update policies and procedures to encourage employees to learn new skills and to become more responsible for the management of their own careers. Companies must also monitor policies and procedures to ensure fairness in access to promotion opportunities and upward mobility.

Key to success is the development of systematic programs of career support, top management involvement, the leadership of the women and minorities themselves, all in partnership with HR. Issues such as the glass ceiling, diversity, family considerations, and demographic trends require new and different policies and programs. While current efforts appear promising, firms will also have to reach out and involve the larger community. The discussions later in the chapter showcase efforts being made by companies today.

Who's Responsible for Career Planning and Management?

Both individuals and organizations (line managers and HR managers) are responsible for career planning and management, each for a different component, as shown in "Partnership: Working Together Managing Career Planning." Organizations can provide career management programs for employees to help them match their needs, goals, and abilities with organizational job demands and rewards. Such programs include:

- Career pathing
- Career counseling
- Career planning workshops
- Continuous learning opportunities
- Training and development programs
- Work-family interface programs
- Outplacement
- Stress management
- Retirement planning
- Glass ceiling programs

"If people want to change functions or they want to go get different experiences, that's not frowned on at all. There's a lot of movement internally and laterally. Employees drive their own development, and we need to design all of our management and our training programs to support, augment, and facilitate that development."

Mike Canizales
Human Resource Manager
Microsoft

Individuals should undertake career planning activities to ensure their own career success, job security, self-esteem, growth, and comfort. Such activities you can do now include:

- Prepare resume
- Plan for job type

- Get interview
- Have interview
- Negotiate salary
- Do well
- Get promoted
- Manage boss

A Historical Perspective. Traditionally, an individual's career was decided by the organization. If the organization needed someone in another location, an individual was transferred. The success of one's career was often measured by the number of moves that were made, since these moves were generally rewarded by promotions to more important and better-paying jobs. The organization was rarely concerned with whether the new job was what the individual wanted, and the individual had limited control over his or her career.[4]

Few companies promise job security. Lincoln Electric is an exception.

Careers Today. Companies such as Intel, Motorola, and Hewlett-Packard (HP) are concerned about their employees staying current. This is a significant concern: "The skills of some HP engineers have a half-life of only 18 months, meaning that half of their knowledge becomes obsolete in the space of less than two years.[5] They are also concerned about getting the commitment from employees without promising in return lifetime job security. By providing learning opportunities and a chance to utilize skills and abilities, companies hope that employees will be excited about their work, if not the company itself. Further efforts by firms to obtain employee commitment include recognition of nontraditional career tracks, work-life accommodation and balance, and diversity management programs.

Career management is the assistance provided by organizations to aid their employees in their careers.

Career planning is the process of identifying career goals and establishing activities that must be accomplished to retain these goals.

Most **career management** programs are based on the premise that both the employee and the organization are responsible for these activities. Of course, some companies say that the individuals are entirely responsible! That is, you, as an individual, must evaluate your personal strengths and weaknesses, preferences, values, interests, and motivations and be responsible for seeking out and taking advantage of opportunities afforded by an organization's career management programs. You must be ready and able to undertake **career planning** activities.[6]

LEARNING OBJECTIVE 1

Explain why companies offer career planning and management programs.

Why Is Career Planning and Management Important?

It is both costly and time-consuming for organizations to offer career management programs and for individuals to plan their careers. The investments of money and

PARTNERSHIP:

WORKING TOGETHER MANAGING CAREER PLANNING

LINE MANAGERS	HR PROFESSIONALS	EMPLOYEES
Share knowledge with and train employees	Develop career planning and management programs	Assume responsibility for career planning and work with HR professionals and line managers in career development programs.
Support career planning and management programs	Help develop a culture of continuous learning and self-management	Engage in continuous learning
Demonstrate continuous learning		Plan your career

time, however, are worthwhile because career management fulfills many important purposes for both employer and employee.

To the Employee

Individuals feel pressure to engage in career management because the current work environment is highly competitive. Indeed, employees today are willing to assert themselves to achieve control over work and nonwork pursuits. In addition, the meaning of success has been broadened to encompass not only salary and status, but also personal contribution and the realization of one's potential. Employees today feel that they are entitled to such things as enriched tasks, participation in decision making, job security, and equitable treatment. Finally, employees are increasingly concerned with balancing the demands of work, family, and leisure activities.[7]

To the Organization

The general purpose of career management programs is to match employees' needs, abilities, and goals with current and future opportunities and challenges within the organization. In other words, these programs are designed to increase the chances that the organization places the right people in the right place at the right time. Thus, these programs aim at matching skills, knowledge, ability, and job demands with personality, interests, and preferences and job rewards.

Employers don't necessarily expect loyalty, but they do expect commitment.

Effective career management means effective utilization of human resources and equal employment opportunity, both of which are important to an organization. If people are an organization's most important asset, then employees whose skills are underutilized or misutilized and who become disillusioned and dissatisfied are wasted assets. Since the image of the "organization man" has eroded, companies can no longer assume blind loyalty and automatic acceptance of promotions and relocations.[8]

Equal employment opportunity concerns initially focused on recruitment and selection. During the next decades, however, equal employment emphasis is likely to shift to individuals who are already employed by the organization. Providing career opportunities for women and ethnic minorities is particularly important. Various protected groups (for example, women, ethnic minorities, disabled workers, older workers) are seeking assistance in career development. Already companies are realizing that in order to help women and minorities advance they must develop programs to break the "glass ceiling" (as discussed in Chapter 3), and some companies are working hard on this issue. Mentoring programs are a promising development. For example, according to Gordon Smyth, senior vice-president of employee relations, at DuPont:

> *Mentoring is informal. We urge people who are good at it to do it. We have tried to encourage other people to get good at it. One of the best things you can do is know your people; they'll tell you whether they are getting any help.*
>
> *One of the most helpful things that we are working on lately in addressing the glass ceiling problem is to define it as a corporate and not a departmental or divisional problem. Most units say they have a management position candidate, but chances are the candidate is a white male. We come in now and say that there may be other candidates somewhere else that are minorities or female. It is in the corporate interest to place those people in that position. It has to be done carefully. You have to have a good person who can do the job.*[9]

LEARNING OBJECTIVE 2

Discuss the problems and issues that arise during organizational entry, midcareer, and late career.

Career is a patterned sequence of attitudes and behaviors associated with work experiences that span a person's life.

Career Development: Stages and Issues

As organizations seek to help employees by establishing specific career management programs, they find that it is useful to think in terms of the stages in a career. Employees have different needs at different stages. Thus, by understanding the stages in a career, firms can more effectively design career management programs.

A **career** is a dynamic process that spans an individual's life. In this section, we will discuss the stages of career development and some of the major issues during three critical career stages (that is, organizational entry, midcareer, and late career).

The Stages of a Career

Most career development models suggest that careers include various stages with predictable sequences of events that apply to most people independent of the specific type of job they have. A knowledge of career stages can help individuals and organizations understand the "typical" issues and events across a career's life span. We will briefly examine five stages: (1) preparation for work, (2) organizational entry, (3) early career, (4) midcareer, and (5) late career (see Exhibit 6.1). The feature "HR Advice and Application: The Meaning of Career" gives a thought-provoking definition.

EXHIBIT 6.1

Five Stages of Career Development

STAGE 1: PREPARATION FOR WORK

Typical age range:	0–25
Major tasks:	Develop occupational self-image, assess alternative occupations, develop initial occupational choice, pursue necessary education.

STAGE 2: ORGANIZATIONAL ENTRY

Typical age range:	18–25
Major tasks:	Obtain job offer(s) from desired organization(s), select appropriate job based on accurate information, prepare for the possibility of having many jobs.

STAGE 3: EARLY CAREER

Typical age range:	25–40
Major tasks:	Learn job, learn organizational rules and norms, fit into chosen occupation and organization, increase competence, pursue goals, build networks, be flexible, stay aware of other opportunities.

STAGE 4: MIDCAREER

Typical age range:	40–55
Major tasks:	Reappraise early career and early adulthood, reaffirm or modify goals, make choices appropriate to middle adult years, remain productive in work. Continually learn, stay current, and be flexible.

STAGE 5: LATE CAREER

Typical age range:	55–Retirement
Major tasks:	Remain productive in work, maintain self-esteem, prepare for effective retirement.

Source: Adapted From J. H. Greenhaus, *Career Management* (Hinsdale, IL.: The Dryden Press, 1987).

HR ADVICE & APPLICATION

The Meaning of Career

What is a career? The work career has many different meanings. A career can be a sequence of related or unrelated jobs. For example, an individual's career may include seventeen different jobs with four organizations. In a different vein, many people think of a career with reference to "the professions" (for example, law or medicine). Perhaps the most common connotation of career is the idea of advancement or "climbing the company ladder." According to this view, career success is measured in promotions and salary. Although all of these views are reasonable, a more formal definition of a career is required. For our purposes, a *career* is a patterned sequence of attitudes and behaviors associated with work-related experiences that span a person's life. According to this definition, each of us has a career.

Several things should be noted about this definition. First, the notion of a patterned sequence suggests that there is order in the career planning and management process. Second, neither success nor failure is implied; note that research has attempted to understand the processes involved in career management and to avoid value judgments about what constitutes success. Third, careers span a long period of time from an individual's earliest jobs through retirement. Various career stages have been identified, and we discuss them in this chapter. Fourth, a career includes both attitudes and behaviors. Attitudes include feelings, thoughts, and anticipated actions, whereas behaviors are things that individuals actually do. Thus, a career has both subjective aspects (for example, feelings of success and pride) and objective aspects (a job offer, a promotion). Fifth, virtually any type of work (paid or unpaid) performed over a long period of time constitutes a career. And lastly, there are many things individuals can do to manage their careers and that companies can do to help them.[10]

Stage 1: Preparation for Work. This stage extends from birth to approximately 25 years of age. The major tasks during this stage are developing an initial occupational choice and following an educational curriculum that will assist in implementing that choice. Overall, an occupational self-image is developed during childhood, adolescence, and early adulthood.

Stage 2: Organizational Entry. Selecting a job and an organization are the major focus here. A major issue during this stage is **reality shock**. Individuals usually have unrealistically high expectations and find that many entry-level jobs are not particularly challenging, at least initially. This stage usually occurs between the ages of 18 and 25. It is important to prepare for the possibility of working in several different companies.

Reality shock is the gap between one's expectations and the reality of the new job and organization.

Stage 3: The Early Career. The essential task at this stage is establishing oneself in a career and organization. Two periods are encompassed by this stage: fitting into the adult world and struggling for success in one's chosen field. This usually occurs between 25 and 40 years of age. It is important to build a wide network of colleagues who may be helpful later.

Stage 4: The Midcareer. The midcareer stage (age 40–55) begins with the midlife transition—the link between early and middle adulthood. Characteristic of the midcareer is the reassessment of the lifestyle that governed the early career. A new life structure is forged that may or may not be in keeping with the previous structure. Employees typically review the goals that they have attained and consider how many additional goals they can achieve in the future. Possible career stage issues include obsolescence and plateauing. There is a need to continually learn and remain adaptable.

Stage 5: The Late Career. The final career stage, the late career, involves continued productivity and eventual preparation for disengagement from work life. Although very little research has been directed toward the late career, it is known that a negative bias against older individuals exists.[11]

In addition, successfully disengaging from the work role is a major challenge, and organizations are attempting to assist older workers with this life transition. Retirement can also be an opportunity to pursue activities that could not be enjoyed during employment.

Critical Issues

Of the career stages, three raise particularly critical career management issues and problems for organizations and individuals: organizational entry, midcareer, and late career (retirement). In the following sections, we discuss these issues in greater detail.

Organizational Entry Issues. Although organizational entry always involves moving inside an organization from outside, it also frequently entails moving from an educational environment to an organizational environment. Newcomers (especially those coming from college) generally have inflated expectations even if they have engaged in self-assessment activities aimed at awareness of self and work environment. Inflated expectations may lead to disappointments (reality shock).

Organizational entry issues include:

- **expectations**
- **disappointments (reality shock)**
- **self management**

Organizations can use realistic job previews to counteract the effects of reality shock. Unrealistically high expectations can stem from the educational process, the recruitment process, and organizational stereotypes. Realistic previews attempt to present both the positive and negative aspects of the job and organization. Such realistic previews have been shown to reduce voluntary turnover among new employees.[12]

Self-management teaches people to exercise control over their own behavior.

Self management teaches people to exercise control over their own behavior.[13] Self-management begins by having people assess their own aspirations and set specific concrete goals in relation to those aspirations. Once goals are set, the employees can discuss ways in which the environment facilitates or hinders goal attainment. The challenge here is to develop strategies that eliminate blocks to performance success. Put another way, self-management teaches people to observe their own behavior, compare their outputs to their goals, and administer their own reinforcement to sustain goal commitment and performance.

The concept of self-management is important in programs of empowerment. For employees to work effectively in a firm that delegates power and responsibility, they need to have the basic skills of self-management. Also, as organizations move from individual-based systems to team-based systems of management, the concept of self-management extends to self-managed work groups, described in Chapter 7.

Midcareer Issues. Two critical issues facing employees in the midcareer years are the midlife transition and the career plateau. Many employees experience a crisis between the ages of 40 and 55. This crisis, which has been called the **midlife transition,** entails a reexamination of one's accomplishments relative to one's initial career goals. Feelings of restlessness and insecurity are common. Individuals in this transition become aware of advancing age and death, the signs of aging, a growing sense of obsolescence, and changes in family relationships. All of these factors can create stress.

Midlife transition involves reexamining one's accomplishments relative to one's initial career goals.

Organizations can help employees cope with this crisis by encouraging them to develop new skills and to serve as mentors for younger employees. Individuals can also engage in **self-assessment** activities. Self-assessment during the midlife transition should focus on the individual's feelings about middle age and determining the relative priority of work, family, leisure, and self-development.[14]

Self-assessment activities involve stating one's feelings about events and stating their importance.

Career plateau occurs when career prospects for promotion slow or stop.

At some point, nearly every employee reaches a **career plateau**, a situation in which the career slows and the prospects for promotion dramatically decrease.

Plateaus can be personal or organizational. Personal plateauing means that the employee has decided not to accept additional promotions in the organization. Organizational plateauing occurs when the employee desires advancement but no opportunities exist, or the organization does not consider the employee promotable. Since fewer opportunities exist at each higher level in companies, plateauing is natural and may not be indicative of success or failure.[15] But plateauing may also reflect **career obsolescence**.

Career obsolescence means no longer having the skills to perform the job.

This means that the employee has reached a state where his/her skills are no longer relevant to the job. Perhaps the technology has changed or the intensity of the competition has changed the way business is done. Regardless of the cause, the employee who can no longer perform successfully under these new conditions is obsolete. Employees in this condition may need help in dealing with plateauing (or obsolescence) because our culture views advancement as a yardstick of success, and many employees feel like failures when they are no longer promotable.[16]

Managers can take a number of steps to help employees cope with career plateauing and obsolescence. These steps include making the facts visible, being realistic about the strengths and weaknesses of others, counseling people, eliminating skill obsolescence, letting people know they are appreciated, creating new rewards, encouraging initiative, discouraging employees from leading a "workaholic" life, giving honest appraisals, and managing by "walking around" and being available when needed.[17]

Companies can help employees avoid career plateauing by keeping them flexible and adaptable. This can be done by emphasizing the reality of continuous change and the need for **continuous learning.** Frequent job rotations and international assignments are ways to help develop an attitude of and skills for adaptability. While not ensuring that employees will stay with the company forever, it does help ensure that the employees will be more employable, regardless of the company.[18]

Continuous learning means always finding new ideas, new ways of doing things, and being willing to change.

Late Career Issues. Individuals in the late career stage must continue to be productive and eventually prepare for retirement. Retirement is a major career transition for many employees because it represents the culmination of 40 or more years of work involvement. Moreover, older individuals may be viewed as less productive, less versatile, closed to new ideas, and less adaptable.[19] Such stereotyping can make continued effective performance even more difficult.

Late career issues include:

- **Remaining productive**
- **Preparing for retirement**

Organizations can help employees in the late career stage in a number of ways by:

- Carefully examining HR policies and procedures affecting older workers
- Surveying the needs of older workers
- Providing realistic retirement previews
- Developing retirement programs
- Implementing flexible work patterns and options[20]

Organizations must also consider the legal issues that affect the treatment of older workers. The *Age Discrimination in Employment Act* forbids discrimination in hiring, placement, compensation, promotion, and termination for individuals aged 40 and over. Treating these workers fairly makes good business sense and also helps to avoid costly litigation.

Late-career individuals should actively manage their careers just as employees do at earlier career stages. Successful late-career management may help to dispel some myths and stereotypes about older workers. Late-career employees can also help themselves by actively planning for their retirement, whether the organization provides retirement programs or not. The retirement transition can raise many fears, but it also contains many opportunities. We will discuss retirement programs later in this chapter.

We have sketched what organizations and individuals can do in these career stages, and we are now ready to go into more detail. First we begin with specific things organizations can do and then we list specific things individuals like you can do in your own career planning.

LEARNING OBJECTIVE 3

Tell what companies are doing for their employees in career planning and management.

Career Management Programs in the Organization

Career management programs are offered by organizations to assist employees in career planning and management. A number of programs will be examined here to illustrate the diversity of needs filled by these programs and the wide range of concerns that organizations consider important in career management.

Career Pathing

Career Planning. The career planning activity aids an individual in his or her personal appraisal or self-assessment. When an organization provides this service, however, it is likely to be related as much to the organization's needs as to the individual's. An individual's personal appraisal, however, need not be related to a specific organization. An example of a career planning guide from a large organization appears in Exhibit 6.2.

Career pathing **consists of career ladders, career planning, and job progression.**

Career pathing programs consist of three major activities: career ladders, career planning, and job progression. Career ladders address the issues of opportunity. Career planning activities help employees identify their abilities, values and goals, and strengths and weaknesses. Job progression provides a set of job experiences that helps employees: 1) satisfy some of their values or goals, 2) utilize some of their strengths and abilities, and 3) improve upon some of their weaknesses identified in the career planning activity.

Career ladders **are guidelines and policies that help employees progress in their careers in a company.**

Career Ladders. Providing career ladders involves several decisions on the part of an organization. First, should there be an active policy of promotion from within? Second, should there be a training and development program to provide sufficient candidates for internal promotion? If the answers to these questions are yes, then the organization must identify career ladders consistent with organizational and job requirements and employee skills and preferences. This may result in wide career ladders where employees can move across many areas and functions within the company, or it may result in narrow career ladders where employees only move within a few areas and functions.

An organization may identify several career paths for different groups or types of employees—for example, fast-track or slow-track. Such an approach is based on the premise that an organization cannot afford to place applicants in jobs at the lower rungs of the ladder when they already possess the skills necessary for jobs at the higher rungs. This actually occurs, however, with many people recruited from college. Although new recruits may be essentially overqualified for their first jobs, the organization hires them for more difficult "future" jobs. This approach is partially to blame for the higher turnover rate among new college graduates and also has implications regarding legal compliance. Employers may claim that a college degree is necessary for an entry-level job when they may actually consider the degree necessary only for the second- or third-level job. Such a policy can lead to discriminatory barriers in recruitment and promotion.

One way to reduce potential discriminatory barriers is through career ladders and paths. When career ladders and paths are in place with clearly specified requirements anchored in sound job-content analyses, organizations can present better legal defenses for their recruitment policies. In essence, sound HR planning establishes a case for long-term job relatedness. Organizations with clearly defined career ladders may also have an easier time attracting and recruiting qualified job applicants and a better chance of keeping them.

EXHIBIT 6.2

Organizational Career Planning Guide

1. My job satisfaction on my present job is (circle) Very Low Low Average High Very High

2. I would like to progress in my work by	Yes	No
A. Developing improved performances and results on my present job	—	—
B. Qualifying for the next logical higher position above my present one	—	—
C. Qualifying for a different type of work within another department	—	—
D. Qualifying for several positions above my present one	—	—
3. I consider myself best suited to		
A. Supervision	—	—
B. Supporting staff work	—	—
C. Production of operation management	—	—

4. Goals

   A suitable job goal for me is ______________________________

   ____

   ____

5. Qualifications

   Evaluate your own qualifications based on current standing and what is needed for your job goal.*

6. My Development Balance Sheet

   A. My strong points are ______________________________

   B. I like to do work that is ______________________________

   C. My limiting factors are ______________________________

   D. I dislike work that is ______________________________

7. Development

   If I want to develop either on my present job or to qualify for a different job, I need the following:

   A. More job knowledge in ______________________________

   B. I like to do work that is ______________________________

   C. A better attitude or outlook concerning ______________________________

8. Taking Action to Reach Your Job Goal

   List how you can develop greater knowledge, job skills, or personal abilities that will help you reach your career goals.

   A. Formal study of a subject (list seminars, night school, company training program, or correspondence courses that will increase your knowledge of a subject): ______________________________

   ____

   ____

   ____

   B. Informal study (list activities outside of school or work that might be helpful in gaining new skills):

   ____

   ____

   ____

*When this form is used within the company, space is provided so an individual is able to write a lengthy response. This is true for items 5–8.

Career Alternatives. As firms "restructure" and cut back on positions, making corporate structures flatter, there are fewer opportunities for upward mobility. Reducing corporate layers to cut costs means outplacing middle management. The work-life-cycle bulge of the baby boomers will create problems as they retire and even now as they are followed by a smaller workforce. More women in the workforce brings a whole other set of issues. Firms and individuals are therefore increasingly forced to rethink notions of career planning and management.

In such an environment, Quaker Oats Company has been a leader in addressing career issues from both organizational and employee perspectives. In the fast-paced world of product brand management, Quaker Oats is experimenting with the idea of a "part-time brand manager." Rather than lose a valuable brand manager after the birth of her son, the company agreed to let her work three days per week, an unprecedented move in such a position. The program has been quite successful.

A career-management system at Amoco is helping managers and employees balance rapidly changing business needs with individual development.

With the full force of baby boomers now in the labor force, Quaker Oats and its employees have come to view careers in new ways. The company's "pyramid" has flattened to the point where one manager, after six promotions in nine years, has remained in the same job for three years. While his initial reaction at staying in one place was one of frustration that he was not being viewed as successful, the advantages of staying in one job have changed his mind. He gets to see the results (both good and bad) of earlier decisions, whereas before he often moved on before the results were in. In addition, he has been able to take the time to create a team and develop his subordinates more thoroughly. Quaker Oats has actually begun to encourage lateral moves as a way to broaden manager experience, allowing people to become knowledgeable about many aspects of the company, which can have benefits when and if those managers do move into senior management positions.[21]

Organizations are beginning to accept the fact that not all people want to be promoted. The new attitude is one can have a successful career without climbing to the top.

Work–Family Interface Programs

Balancing work and family demands has become an increasingly important organizational issue. The "traditional" family with a husband who is the bread-winner, a wife who is a full-time homemaker, and two children is coming to constitute a minority of U.S. households. With the dramatic influx of women into the workforce and the growing number of dual-career and two-wage couples, individuals are finding it difficult to avoid conflict between work and family areas. Since work and family have been treated as "separate worlds" in the past, many people feel that conflict is not supposed to happen, that they are the only people experiencing such problems and that the organization will not be impressed if family problems are causing poor job performance. Perhaps the most significant aspect of **work–family interface programs** is the recognition that work and family life are interdependent, that it is important to our society and to business that they be interdependent, and that family issues can affect work performance and career development.[22]

Work–family interface programs are meant to help employees balance the demands of work and family.

In fact, career development can now be viewed as a family affair. Family-friendly organizations provide a setting for employees to discuss work-family issues and to identify coping strategies that can reduce the conflict. In a more direct way, organizations can provide child-care assistance, flexible work schedules, and career and life-planning activities. Securing new jobs for working spouses of employees being relocated or transferred is a service provided by a growing number of firms, according to The Conference Board in New York:

> *More than one-half of American corporations currently offer some sort of reemployment assistance to spouses of transferred employees. Nearly 500,000 employees are transferred annually, with an average cost per transfer of $41,000. Aid to spouses adds $500 to $2,000 to that figure. Much of this largesse is impelled by changes in the U.S. family and emerging trends in the workforce, the report says, pointing out that "about 70 percent of all American couples represented in the work force are dual earners."*[23]

Typically, companies providing job-information materials to spouses use such materials in addition to other approaches; for example:

- US West gives working partners a choice of either a self-guided workbook with audio tapes or up to $2,500 to apply to job search costs such as employment agency fees, interview trips, and job counseling. While the printed information is aimed at satisfying the needs of most spouses, the reimbursement option can be used by those facing more difficult job transitions.
- Compaq Computer Corporation supplements its information package with a "Career Corner" at the company's relocation resource center. The company also participates in a consortium of Houston employees who cooperate in circulating spouse resume's. Compaq provides the materials to all its married transferees, even if not requested.
- Johnson & Johnson offers personal counseling to relocating families to supplement its package of in-depth information on job-search techniques.[24]

Childcare Assistance. Between 1960 and 1990, the percentage of married women with children under six years of age who work outside the home jumped from 19 percent to 55 percent. Today more than one child in five lives with a single parent. More companies are providing some kind of childcare services for their employees. Because childcare services is such a critical employee benefit, we will discuss them in detail in Chapter 15.

Small firms as well as large firms are developing innovative family-assistance programs. And employees appreciate their efforts. In a recent *Inc.* magazine survey of the "best small companies" to work for, many had highly creative programs for child- and familycare assistance. Some of the programs are described in the feature "Managing Human Resources at the Best Small Companies."

Firms large and small are helping employees with children by complying with the *Family and Medical Leave Act* (FMLA) of 1993. This not only helps employees with children, but those planning to have children. The FMLA requires private sector employers of 50 or more employees to grant employees as many as 12 work weeks of unpaid leave during any 12-month period at the time of the birth or adoption of a child, or when a serious health condition affects the employee or a family member. In addition, FMLA requires employers to maintain employees' existing group health insurance coverage during periods of FMLA leave, and to restore employees to their same or equivalent positions, including employment benefits, pay, and other terms and conditions of employment upon the employee's return from FMLA leave.[25]

Outplacement Programs

Being terminated for any reason can be a very traumatic career transition. Unfortunately for many individuals, outplacement has become very common in recent years because of cuts in middle management, mergers and acquisitions, shifts in corporate goals, and the general business climate.

When it occurs, job loss can threaten self-esteem and confront the individual with various concerns about competency and career direction. **Outplacement programs** assist terminated employees in finding suitable employment or in career exploration. For example, a middle manager may decide that starting his or her own business is a more desirable option than working for another company as a manager. The degree of organizational assistance usually depends on the employee's level in the company with higher-level employees usually receiving more support. Outplacement services are usually provided through outside consulting firms that specialize in this activity.

Outplacement programs assist terminated employees in finding employment elsewhere.

To help outplaced employees make the transition, companies may make an offer of cash. This cash, typically called a **severance package**, can be one or two

Severance package is a set of money and benefits offered to employees who leave the company.

MANAGING HUMAN RESOURCES

at the Best Small Companies

G. T. WATER PRODUCTS

- Moorpark, California
- Plumbing products manufacturer
- 28 employees, $3.5 million in sales
- Provides on-site school with extended care before and after; $1,500 adoption assistance; flexible scheduling; benefits for part-timers.

HEMMINGS MOTOR NEWS

- Bennington, Vermont
- Old-car magazine publisher
- 90 employees, $19 million in sales
- Gives six weeks' family leave at two-thirds pay plus six months unpaid leave. Has flexible scheduling; dependent-care assistance plan; benefits for part-timers.

LANCASTER LABORATORIES

- Lancaster, Pennsylvania
- Research-and-analysis lab
- 475 employees, $25 million in sales
- Provides on-site adult day care and childcare; employee fitness center; program for emergency counseling; dependent-care-assistance plan.

RIDGEVIEW HOSIERY

- Newton, North Carolina
- Sock and hosiery maker
- 275 employees, $35 million in sales
- Offers program to bring school counselors into plant every two months to talk with parents on company time; subsidized on-site daycare; employee-assistance program.

WHITE DOG ENTERPRISES

- Philadelphia
- Restaurant and retail store
- 100 employees, $3.4 million in sales
- Celebrates employees' outside interests; encourages employee participation in social action; offers health insurance and vacations for veteran waiters.

WILTON CONNOR PACKAGING

- Charlotte, North Carolina
- Commercial packaging maker
- 200 employees, $8.6 million in sales
- Offers on-site laundry; English and high-school-equivalency classes; door-to-door transport for workers; children's clothing swap center; flextime.[26]

years of salary. Employees with more time in the organization, may also be given some years of credit to ensure that these employees can collect a full retirement benefit from the company.

Career Counseling

Career counseling typically involves a discussion of an individual's work values, career goals, current job activities and performance, and action plans. Counseling can be formal or informal in nature. Formal career counseling is usually conducted by career counselors and vocational psychologists in individual sessions. On an informal level, discussions with supervisors are very important. Supervisors are considered a primary source of career information and can do a number of things to facilitate the career counseling process. They can:

- Develop a knowledge of occupational information and career source material
- Develop an understanding of career theories and applications
- Subscribe to professional career development journals

- Understand the elements of an effective relationship
- Develop good listening and questioning skills
- Learn to respect the confidentiality of employees[27]

Stress Management

Although individuals experience stress for many reasons, uncertainty and lack of control seem to be the major causes. Many employees in the process of managing their careers encounter much uncertainty about the future and lack of control over career direction, especially promotion. Sources of stress can include lack of challenge on the job, job demands that exceed an individual's skills and/or training, inequity, and lack of career opportunities. It can also arise from too much work, typical of the "workaholic."[28] In addition, many employees find the thought of retirement stressful.

Most employees feel better if they can reduce the uncertainty in their lives.

Stress-management programs help individuals identify sources of stress and develop strategies for coping. It is crucial that organizations offer these programs because the symptoms of stress can result in serious health and safety outcomes. Symptoms may be psychological, such as apathy and dissatisfaction; physiological, such as headaches and backaches; or behavioral, such as absenteeism and accidents. We will discuss these in detail in Chapter 17.

Retirement Planning

Many companies accommodate the career needs of employees who are about to retire. Typically, companies offer seminars that provide information on finances, housing or relocation, family relations, and legal affairs. Since research has shown that retirees also face social and psychological adjustments, many retirement planning programs now include additional components that allow for the sharing of emotional and developmental issues. Some companies have formed **social support groups** for retirees that address the special social and emotional needs of this group. Social support groups can be an important part of a person's successful adjustment to retirement.

Social support groups provide unconditional support and acceptance of others.

In addition to retirement planning seminars, companies offer retirement rehearsal arrangements. For example, employees in Polaroid's retirement rehearsal program can leave the program for three months and then decide whether they want to return to work or to continue the retirement; they can also enter a tapering-off program. In this program, the employees gradually work fewer and fewer hours per week.[29]

Both retiring employees and organizations benefit from retirement planning options and seminars. By encouraging more senior employees to retire, companies open up jobs and promotion opportunities for less senior employees. Because of these mutual benefits and the baby-boom bulge in the workforce, it is likely that companies will continue to offer retirement planning accommodations.

Sharing the Responsibility: Your Career Activities

LEARNING OBJECTIVE 4

Describe what you can do to prevent career obsolescence and ensure your employability.

By actively managing your career, you'll do better than by not managing it. "Better" can be measured by any standard you choose—job security, self-esteem, growth, comfort, success in climbing to the top of the organization, or salary level. By planning and managing, you'll increase your chances of obtaining whatever you realistically identify as most important. Exhibit 6.3 outlines a general strategy for planning and managing your career. Fundamental to this is the personal appraisal. **Personal appraisal** (or career self-appraisal) consists of identifying the strengths and weaknesses you possess.

Personal appraisal consists of identifying strengths and weaknesses in relation to career goals.

EXHIBIT 6.3

Personal Career Planning Activities

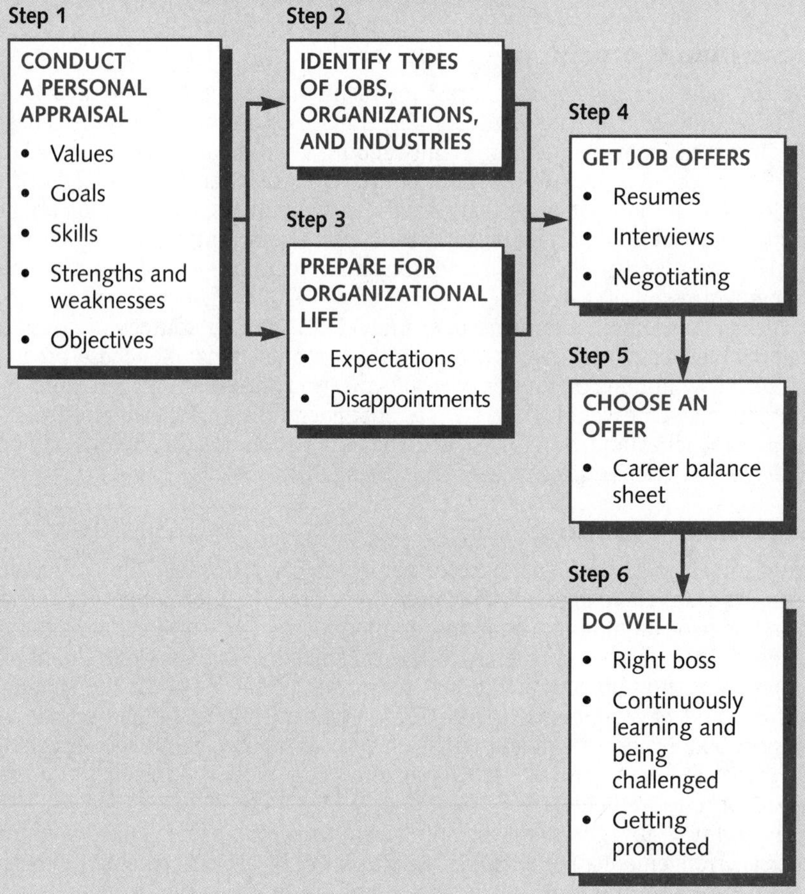

Step 1: Conducting a Personal Appraisal

This step involves taking a personal inventory of the following:

- Values
- Goals
- Skills
- Strengths and weaknesses
- Objectives

Do this step by completing the career self-appraisal exercise shown in Exhibit 6.4.

Step 2: Identifying Types of Jobs, Organizations, and Industries

Because the job or jobs you choose will have such an impact on your life, it is important to carefully analyze what you want from your first job and your first company. You may want to start by first identifying industries in which you may want to work. For example, you may choose to work in an industry with great potential such as those listed on page 200.

EXHIBIT 6.4

Career Self-Appraisal

Steps

1. List five goals you have for each of three categories—career, affiliations, and personal fulfillment (or create other categories).
2. Go back and rate them (1–little importance through 5–great importance). Which list has the most 4s and 5s?
3. Merge the three lists and rank all fifteen goals in order of importance to you.
4. Select your top goal and describe it on the top of the second sheet. Then, discuss it in terms of:
   a. Personal strengths and weaknesses
   b. Obstacles to prevent achieving the goal
   c. Strategies to circumvent obstacles
   d. Are the goals realistic, attainable, and measurable?
   e. What are the rewards for achieving the goal?
   f. Steps for achieving the goal (Do this for all your goals)

	Goal Rating (1, 2, 3, 4, or 5)
Career goals, e.g., become president by 45; become vice-president by 35, etc.	
1. ______	______
2. ______	______
3. ______	______
4. ______	______
5. ______	______
Affiliation/Interpersonal, e.g., family, friends, clubs, group members, etc.	
1. ______	______
2. ______	______
3. ______	______
4. ______	______
5. ______	______
Personal Fulfillment/Achievements, e.g., master the piano, run a marathon, get an MBA degree, etc.	
1. ______	______
2. ______	______
3. ______	______
4. ______	______
5. ______	______
Goal Ranking (Please list in order of importance the fifteen goals from above)	
1. ______	______
2. ______	______
3. ______	______
4. ______	______
5. ______	______
6. ______	______
7. ______	______
8. ______	______
9. ______	______
10. ______	______
11. ______	______
12. ______	______
13. ______	______
14. ______	______
15. (least important) ______	______

Take one important goal, restate it here, and then continue by discussing your personal strengths and weaknesses.

______

______

______

Continued

Personal strengths in relation to attaining the goal
1. ______________________________
2. ______________________________
3. ______________________________
4. ______________________________
5. ______________________________

Personal weaknesses in relation to attaining the goal
1. ______________________________
2. ______________________________
3. ______________________________
4. ______________________________
5. ______________________________

Obstacles in the way to goal attainment	Strategy to overcome obstacles
1. ______________	1. ______________
2. ______________	2. ______________
3. ______________	3. ______________
4. ______________	4. ______________
5. ______________	5. ______________

Rewards for achieving the goal (rank in terms of value)
1. ______________________________
2. ______________________________
3. ______________________________
4. ______________________________
5. ______________________________

Indicators that you have achieved the goal (short and long term)
1. ______________________________
2. ______________________________
3. ______________________________
4. ______________________________
5. ______________________________

Steps for achieving the goal (starting now)	Time deadline
1. ______________	______________
2. ______________	______________
3. ______________	______________
4. ______________	______________
5. ______________	______________

Did You KNOW?

At Bell Labs, researchers studied E-mail patterns to determine why certain scientists under-performed their equally distinguished colleagues. What they found was that scientists who were disliked had been frozen out of the informal E-chat circles that distributed advice, gossip, and other useful information.

- Healthcare
- Telecommunications
- Entrepreneurial firms
- Manufacturing[30]

After identifying a target industry, gather information on a particular company. You can gain direct information through summer work experience, internships, and part-time work; these are valuable ways to gain exposure to new companies.[31] Although some work experiences may be boring, you need to consider them as learning experiences, ways of getting to know yourself better. Other sources of information are newspapers and professional magazines, school placement offices, libraries, the Internet, direct mail, e-mail, job-search firms, friends, and family.

In thinking about the types of jobs, organizations, and industries, weight the relative value to you of such things as more salary and fewer benefits versus less salary and more benefits and more opportunities to learn more skills.[32]

There are many types of jobs to be considered, including self-employment and the more traditional entry-level jobs in larger organizations that are the first step in a series through promotions to senior management positions. Within larger organizations, these traditional paths are available in many functional areas such as human resource management, marketing, manufacturing, and finance. Whatever functional field you may choose, in a larger organization, there is always the possibility for an international assignment as an expatriate.

Expatriate Careers. For many U.S. firms, being competitive now means being globally competitive, and this means developing more **expatriates** (Americans who work in other countries for U.S. companies) to run the businesses overseas. While offering clear career paths for expatriates would seem to be necessary to encourage individuals to become expatriates, it appears that as yet few U.S. firms have done this as indicated in a survey of HR managers in U.S.-based multinational companies.

An expatriate is an employee who works for a domestic company but in its foreign location.

- 56 percent say a foreign assignment is either detrimental to, or immaterial in, one's career.
- 47 percent say their returning expatriates aren't guaranteed jobs with the company upon completion of their foreign assignments.
- 65 percent say their expatriates' foreign assignments are not integrated into their overall career planning.
- 45 percent view returning expatriates as a problem because they are so hard to fit back into the company.
- 20 percent consider their company's repatriation policies adequate to meet the needs of their returning expatriates.[33]

Despite this, it is likely the development of career paths for expatriates will become a trend based upon the increasing international competition described in Chapter 3.

Local-Country National. You may also wish to consider working as a **local-country national** for a foreign-owned firm. While it may be glamorous to work for a British or Japanese firm and travel abroad, there can be some potential drawbacks. They include possible limited promotion opportunities and limited freedom to manage as you would like. As with any decision, it is important to gather as much information as possible before considering this option. However, because of an increase in the number of foreign-owned firms in the U.S., these jobs will be increasingly available.[34]

A local-country national is one working in the United States but for a foreign-owned firm.

Step 3: Preparing for Organizational Life

Some ways to facilitate successful entry into organizational life include:

- **Development of self-awareness.** Individuals must develop an awareness of themselves and their preferred work environment. You can use the self-appraisal form in Exhibit 6.4 for this purpose.
- **Identification of prospective employers.** Because the job or jobs individuals choose have such an impact on their lives, they must analyze carefully what they want from their first job and their first company. (Use all available resources to learn about companies in which you have an interest.)[35]
- **Effective job interview behavior.** "Selling" oneself to prospective employers requires a high degree of self-awareness. The interview is the individual's chance to create a favorable impression, gather additional information about the company, emphasize past accomplishments, demonstrate initiative and leadership through extracurricular activities, and practice interviewing skills (perhaps through information interviews).

Did You KNOW?

The states with the highest percentage of the workers employed by foreign-owned firms are:

Delaware	13.9%
Hawaii	11.4%
South Carolina	8.2%
West Virginia	7.2%
Total for U.S.	5.2%

A career balance sheet lets you list all the good things and bad things about various job choices.

- **Choice of organizations.** Although choosing the best job offer may be more art than science, a **career balance sheet** can help. This involves listing the positive and negative aspects of each offer, making a separate balance sheet for each one. Individuals should consider how each aspect will affect them and others such as their spouse, friends, or family. Balance sheets assist the decision-making by allowing you to organize the information systematically.

It is one thing to know the type of job you might want and the type of industry or organization in which you want to work, but it's an entirely different thing to know the realities of life and work in that organization. Two facets of organizational life that you should be aware of are organizational expectations and disappointment.

Organizational Expectations. Most organizations expect new employees to have certain characteristics:

- Competence to get a job done
- Ability to accept organizational realities
- High personal integrity, strength and ethics
- Capacity to grow
- Willingness to be a team player[36]

Being a team player is a more recent organization expectation.

Organizational Disappointment. Although an organization has high expectations of you, it may not always live up to its end of the bargain. What it does or doesn't do may bring you disappointments (reality shock) such as the following:[37]

- **Low initial job challenge.** Although some findings have indicated the usefulness of giving new recruits a challenging job initially, many organizations continue to ease the new recruit into the organization, thus treating the recruit as a novice.
- **Low self-actualization and need satisfaction.** The new recruit may fail to experience the autonomy and challenge necessary to grow and to develop self-esteem and competency. Some researchers have suggested that an individual may actually lose competency in the job if not given the opportunity to advance and grow in independence.
- **The vanishing performance appraisal, or inability to determine what the real criteria are.** New recruits come on board with the expectation of receiving clear and unambiguous evaluations of their performance. In reality, new recruits report having little feedback on their performance, although their supervisors may claim the opposite.
- **Unrealistically high aspirations.** Most recruits have higher expectations of being able to use their skills and abilities than actually occur. The gap between an individual's skills and the skills actually used on the job is probably increased because of the manager's belief that the new recruit is not capable of assuming responsibility.
- **Source of threat to the boss.** A new recruit's first boss plays a critical role for the recruit's future in the organization. The role tends to be negative, especially if the boss feels threatened by a new recruit who is seen as a "comer" with a great deal more potential than the boss.
- **Amount of conflict and uncertainty in the organization.** New recruits think that rules and procedures, directions, and communications will be clear, crisp, and without conflict. The reality in many situations is just the opposite.[38]

- **Unfair policies and practices.** A survey of women taken in 1995 revealed that while many are better off than they used to be, they continue to face restrictions and discrimination:

Of the 3,000 women polled, 84 percent agreed that regardless of chances that may have occurred, women still face more restrictions in life than men do.[39]

According to the survey, women believe that several factors keep them back, ranging from an old boys' network to the lack of role models and stereotypes.[40]

Furthermore, women do not have as much hope for changing unfair practices as they once had. Only 56 percent see the role of women as continuing to change, down from 73 percent in 1990.[41]

This decline may be a reason so many women are starting their own business.

Step 4: Getting Job Offers

Now that you've narrowed down (but not too much) the types of jobs, organizations, and industries you are interested in and have prepared yourself for organizational life, the next thing to do is get some job offers. Three aspects of getting job offers are as follows:

- Resume writing
- Interviewing
- Negotiating

Resume Writing. The standard resume lists work experience and education in reverse chronological order and includes dates, titles, degrees earned, and responsibilities. Some examples are shown in Appendix D. Include a cover letter tailored to the job and the company with every resume you send. See the "HR Advice and Application: To Fax or Not to Fax" feature for a discussion of the acceptance of resumes by fax.

Start your resume writing now so you have plenty of time to revise it. You may even want to put your resume on your own Home Page on the Internet!

Job Interviewing. Step 1 has great value as preparation for job interviews. If you know yourself inside and out, you will find it easier to "sell" yourself to potential employers. On the next page are six suggestions for participating in job interviews.

HR ADVICE & APPLICATION

To Fax or Not To Fax?

Receiving a resume through the fax machine apparently isn't as taboo as it once was, according to a recent attitude survey of HR professionals. The survey was conducted by an independent research firm for Office Team, a division of Robert Half International, based in Menlo Park, California.

The survey inquired whether it was acceptable for job candidates to fax their resumes to an organization that has advertised a job opening and stated no specific submittal guidelines. Researchers found that 77 percent of the senior managers polled would accept a resume by fax if they hadn't specified otherwise. Although 21 percent of the respondents indicated that they would not consider faxed resumes, 2 percent indicated that they weren't sure whether they would consider such applicants or not. Times have changed. As recently as a few years ago, business etiquette prohibited job seekers from sending resumes to prospective employers by way of facsimile technology.[42]

- Sell yourself to the recruiter with the same determination you would use in selling a product or service to a customer. The interview period is brief, yet a favorable impression of your appearance, sense of purpose, and clarity of self-expression will probably weigh more heavily with the recruiter than your transcript, your resume, or your references.
- Familiarize yourself ahead of time with the employer to be interviewed—know what the company does and what products or service it offers. Ask only pertinent questions during the interview, and suggest how your skills and abilities may benefit the organization.
- Develop your ability to communicate, but do not come on too strong or be overly confident.
- Cite academic achievement, especially if the recruiter appears to relate to the job area you are interested in. Remember that companies often view your college work as a preparatory period. Hence, cite your academic efforts as evidence that you can attain long-range goals and objectives.
- Mention extracurricular activities that demonstrate your leadership or initiative.
- Learn the art of interviewing by accepting as many interview opportunities as you can, even with organizations you think you may not want to join. Interviews can be practiced by role playing.[43]

Negotiating. An important topic that will surely arise in your interviewing is salary. How you handle this topic could make a substantial difference in how much you get paid. Here are a few tips on how to handle this aspect in your job search:

> *It's "dumb" for a job candidate to raise the question of salary early in the hiring process, says Pfizer divisional vice-president Max Hughes. And it is. Until the employer has had time to make up his or her mind to hire you, you aren't worth anything to the employer. To negotiate the highest possible salary, listen and ask questions so that you can identify the other person's needs and communicate how you can help meet them. It's best to delay the subject of salary until later in the interview. Loaded with information about your strengths, the employer should see you as a more valuable asset than when you began to talk.*[44]

Step 5: Choosing an Offer

Get a job you love to do.

George Burns

In the job market today, you may have to exercise your patience! Jobs may not come immediately and you may have to work a bit harder at getting job offers, but offers will come. Once you start receiving job offers, you must be astute in your choice. Although choosing the best offer is really more of an art than a cast-in-concrete method, the career balance sheet described above is a helpful place to start.[45]

Step 6: Doing Well

Doing well involves getting what you want from the organization in which you are working. It means having things go your way. It may mean getting promoted, and it certainly means staying valuable and useful to the organization. As such, it requires that you know about the following:

- Dealing with your boss
- Continuously learning
- Getting promoted
- Being a team player

The Boss. People are more likely to develop strong leadership qualities if they work for a boss who has something to teach, who is on the move, and who is capable of taking others along. The preference for being on a winning team is a survival mechanism. People are less dependent and uncertain if they're allied with bosses who are strong leaders. Consequently, it pays to try to be in a position to select your boss. This is especially true for your first boss. You can enhance your chances of working for the boss of your choice by your own outstanding performance and by being a critical subordinate who is not threatening.[46]

Continuous Learning/Challenging Opportunities. It is important to have the frame of mind to seek new opportunities that are challenging and that require new learning. In the opening feature on employability, Terri Welk is an excellent example of someone who made it her responsibility to go after new learning and new job challenges. This quality will help ensure her long-term employability and self-esteem.[47]

Getting Promoted. Getting promoted is much easier when you:

- **Have credibility with senior managers.** Managers with credibility can take greater risks and make more mistakes because it is known they produce results. You must have credibility with your superiors before you can develop it with subordinates. Take this example: a manager brought in from the outside to run an equipment-design division could barely get the information he needed from headquarters—he had few connections and no clout. Although he had a better idea of what was going on, without the support of top management, his subordinates thought little of him.[48]
- **Have a reputation as being an expert.** When an individual is considered an expert, others tend of defer to that person on issues involving his or her expertise. This is important in large organizations where many people have only secondhand knowledge about one's professional competence.[49]
- **Are the first in a position.** An individual who holds a new position—that is, no one has ever held it before—and who takes risks and succeeds is more likely to be rewarded than one who accomplishes the same thing but who is not the first to hold the position. While excellent performance on routine tasks is usually valued, being innovative is a big plus.[50]
- **Know and use networks.** Knowing about and using networks can be critical to your job success. Essentially a **network** is a collection of friends and acquaintances, both inside and outside one's work place, that can be counted on for some kind of help. Networks can provide many kinds of help including information, services, support, and access.

Excellence is the gradual result of always wanting to do better.

Pat Riley
Coach
Miami Heat Basketball Team

A network is a collection of friends and acquaintances inside and outside one's workplace who can be counted on for some kinds of help.

While getting promoted is certainly still possible, it is becoming more difficult to do it rapidly. The day of the "fast track" appear to be all but over for most employees.[51] Thus you need to prepare yourself for:

- Getting as much out of each job as possible
- Being flexible and open-minded
- Being a team player
- Excelling at your job
- Furthering your own education

For companies such as BMW, Honda, Microsoft, Hewlett-Packard and Steelcase, being able to work well in teams is indispensable.

Being a Team Player. "In an age of teamwork and fluid careers, IQ alone doesn't cut it anymore."[52] Teams and teamwork are major themes of this book because they are reality in companies today. It is becoming rare that the individual superstar prevails. Thus, the more effective you become in working with others, the more likely you will succeed in your career.

Not Going the Big Company Route

You have 4 major choices here:

- Family-owned business
- Small business
- Franchisees
- Entrepreneurial firms

You may decide that for your first job you would rather not go into a large company. If so, you have at least four alternative paths: a) family-owned business, b) small business, c) franchise, or d) entrepreneurial firm. The lists below detail some of the personal characteristics necessary to succeed in each of these environments.

Family-owned Business

- Be able to communicate effectively with other family members, be prepared to set up formal lines of communication.
- Know that you really want to work in your family's business because you want to and NOT because your family has always expected you to.
- To ensure that your decisions are treated with respect by other family members, work out clear lines of authority for decision making BEFORE you enter the business.
- Be accountable for your actions and be honest when dealing with other family members; don't revert to childish behavior if you make mistakes. Be able to objectively evaluate your own performance and the performance of other family members within the business. Be able to compromise at times: a family business means that there will usually be more than one proprietor (and you won't necessarily have the ultimate authority). Be prepared to leave if the relationship between you and your family deteriorates substantially as a result of your being involved with the business.
- Know that one day you will retire—when you leave, stay out.
- Be willing to work long hours.[53]

Small Business

- Be prepared to live with threat and take risks.
- Be able to make decisions on your own without input from others.
- Be able to select staff well: you will only have a small number of staff and each one will be of crucial importance; each will need to be a team player. Ensure that you have ways of objectively measuring your own and others' performance in the business.
- Update your own and your staff's skills on a continual basis.
- Seek feedback from staff on how the business can be improved or adapted to meet a changing business environment.
- Be able to attract and maintain a good customer base against competition from larger firms.
- Be as concerned with the "little things" as the "big things."
- Be comfortable staying small.
- Be willing to work long hours.[54]

Franchisees

- Be energetic and hands on: a well known franchise alone does not automatically succeed.
- Be willing to work long hours.

- Be prepared to work within strict guidelines set out by the franchise (e.g., in recruiting and selecting).
- Be able to train employees in basic skills.
- Be able to motivate staff to work in a particular way, time after time.
- Have a strong service consciousness: be able to create and maintain strong customer links.
- Motivate employees to have a consistent customer focus.
- Be able to discipline employees for not following the rules and procedures of the franchise.[55]

Entrepreneurial Firm

- Have a relentless vision of what you want to do and where you want to go.
- Be innovative.
- Be self-confident.
- Be a risk-taker.
- Be prepared to create, lead, and motivate a team.
- Hire the best people you can find: know that you will need different skills at different stages of your company's development; be prepared to pay them well.
- Be adaptable to constant change and be willing to learn.
- Be willing to work long hours.[56]

Perhaps one item that stands out in all four of these alternatives is "willingness to work long hours." The potential rewards from these hours, however, may be worth it to you: autonomy, freedom from being bossed around, and a nice lifestyle.

Summary

Career planning and management has much to offer individuals and organizations. Because organizations and people are continually changing, career planning and management activities have a dual focus: to help individuals find jobs that are consistent with their personality, interests, and preferences, and to help organizations match available jobs to the skills, knowledge, and abilities of their workforce.

Because organizations are dynamic and present a variety of job transitions (staffing at entry levels, promotions and transfers, layoffs, discharges, retirement), career planning and management activities are relevant to all members of an organization. The different stages of career development (that is, preparation for work, organizational entry, early career, midcareer, and late career) present different issues and problems both to the organization and to the employee. One thing is clear, however: career development is a continuous process. From the organizational perspective, career management activities can contribute to other key human resource functions that enable the company to simultaneously attract and retain the best people. From the individual perspective, each person is responsible for his or her career planning. Career planning enables individuals to proactively manage the numerous transitions that occur during the span of their work lives. Throughout the remaining chapters you will have several opportunities to engage in further career planning activities in the end-of-chapter feature entitled "Career Management Exercises."

Questions to ask throughout your career:

1. **Who are you?**
2. **What do you want?**
3. **Why should I hire you?**
4. **What have you done?**
5. **What do you know?**

Key Concepts

career
career balance sheet
career ladders
career obsolescence
career pathing
career planning
career plateau
continuous learning
expatriate
local-country national
midlife transition
network
outplacement programs
personal appraisal
reality shock
self-assessment
self-management
severance package
social support group
work-family interface program

Review and Discussion Questions

1. With whom do you identify more: Terri Welk or Cary Welk? Why?
2. What is meant by the term career?
3. Responsibility for career planning and management is shouldered by both the individual and the organization. What does each party gain from career planning and management?
4. How might career planning and management from an individual perspective differ today from that of 50 years ago? Is it more difficult today? Why?
5. The organizational entry stage of career development suggests that reality shock is a fact of organizational life. What can human resource managers do to lessen reality shock?
6. What can managers do to motivate employees at each of the five stages of career development? What is your present career development stage?
7. What are some examples of organizational career development programs?
8. Describe the differences in the personnel characteristics necessary to run: a family business; a small business; a franchise; and an entrepreneurial firm.
9. How can you prevent career obsolescence?
10. What will a commitment to continuous learning mean to you?
11. What will you need to do to keep yourself employable?

PROJECTS, EXERCISES & CASES

End-of-Text Projects

Lincoln Electric

1. What does Lincoln Electric do for the career planning and management of its employees?
2. Is there much Lincoln Electric can do for its employees?
3. What would you advise Lincoln Electric to do for the career planning and management activities of its employees?

Nordstrom

1. What does Nordstrom do for the career planning and management of its employees?
2. Is there much Nordstrom can do for its employees?
3. What would you advise Nordstrom to do for the career planning and management activities of its employees?

Field Project

Interview two working people and discuss career planning and management with them. Ask them what career aids their firms offer. Ask them how much they have planned for their own careers, and what they would do differently. Report back to the class and compare results.

Career Management Exercises

1. What Do you Want your First Job To Be?

If you have completed the material presented in Exhibits 6.2 and 6.4, you have begun a very important process that should enable you to place yourself in a life and work situation best suited to your needs. But remember, this is an ongoing process. The following is another task in this process.

Your full-time job after graduation may not be your first job, but it will be a very important one, as you know. Describe the type of job you would like to have and the type of organization you would like to work for after graduation.

Type of Job:

____

____

____

Type (Name) of Organization:

____

____

To provide you with the opportunity to prepare for your career in as much detail as possible, future chapters will ask you to use the job and organization you have indicated here as a basis for further exercises.

2. My Career Objectives

Where are you going with your career? Please complete the following survey.

1. The number of companies you will work for:
   a. 0–3
   b. 4–6
   c. 7–9
   d. 10+

2. The number of times you will need to change cities for work-related reasons:
   a. 0–3
   b. 4–6
   c. 7–9
   d. 10+

3. Do you plan to work closely with individuals from other nationalities?
   a. Yes
   b. No

4. Do you plan to have at least one overseas assignment?
   a. Yes
   b. No

5. Do you have a goal of managing more than 10 individuals?
   a. Yes
   b. No

6. Number of days per week you are willing to travel:
   a. 1
   b. 2
   c. 3
   d. 4
   e. 5

7. Number of hours per week you are willing to work:
   a. 40
   b. 45
   c. 50
   d. 60
   e. 70+

8. The total value of the compensation package (excluding benefits) you expect to receive:
   a. \$20,000–\$30,000
   b. \$30,000–\$40,000
   c. \$40,000–\$50,000
   d. \$50,000 and up

9. The amount of job security you expect to receive:
   a. Low
   b. Medium
   c. High

Case: Are You Staying?

During their traditional reunion on Cape Cod, Bob and Steve are contemplating their futures for the first time. Although only 24 years old, both are already wondering how to better manage their careers. Since graduating together three years ago, they have already attained some success. Both passed the CPA exam the first time through, and both have enjoyed significant pay increases the first two years. Their similarities end here however, for while Bob is contemplating advancement in the same firm he joined two years ago, Steve is contemplating changing firms. They are taking this weekend to reflect on their career experiences thus far.

Bob Lemmon Gets Lucky

Whether or not it was luck, Bob is mighty pleased about working for one of the more successful offices of the "Big Six" accounting firm he joined three years ago. He was excited even before he was hired. During the holiday break in December of his senior year, he remembers going to a party thrown by the firm for accounting students from schools from which the office typically recruited. The party gave the students an informal opportunity to meet several partners, including the managing partner. It also gave the office an information chance to look at the new crop of rookies. Bob couldn't help but be impressed by this party and the chance to meet the managing partner. He also got the chance to meet some of the other students who were eventually hired by the office.

Bob's first two years in the office were extremely gratifying. He worked on a variety of assignments, each one exposing him to different challenges, each one requiring slightly different skills. Any problems, personal or professional, were comfortably discussed with the senior "brother" to whom he was assigned. He would have felt as comfortable, however, talking with a manager or even the managing partner. Managers, partners, and even the managing partner felt it was extremely important to have an open door policy with all employees, especially the new assistants. To facilitate this, the managing partner always made sure they hired for "anticipated growth" rather than as a catch-up mechanism. Although this resulted in "excess hiring" until growth caught up, doing so ensured that managers and partners didn't exceed a 70–75 percent utilization rate. Year-end review time resulted in Bob being told exactly how well he was doing relative to the other assistants. His two pay increases were directly related to the performance appraisal results. As far as the office was concerned, this pay-for-performance policy and candor in telling folks where they stood resulted in enhanced loyalty and a low premature turnover rate. This was reinforced by the "excess hiring" that ensured that assistants were not overutilized, which in turn facilitated good leverage ratios and the manager and partner utilization rate of 70–75 percent. Thus Bob's pressing career question was whether he should stay in audit or transfer to tax in the next year or two.

Steve Luck Gets A Lemon

Steve also works in an office of the same "Big Six" firm, but as far as he is concerned, it is on a different planet from Bob's. Because Steve lived on the West Coast, he wasn't able to attend the party that Bob attended. Talk about being in the wrong place at the wrong time! Subsequently, Steve was hired by another office of the same firm in the following spring by someone he never saw again. Steve's first two years in the office were extremely frustrating and dissatisfying. Although he was given a variety of job assignments, his recollection of the experience was one of exhaustion rather than of the desired variety, growth, and challenge. In each of his first two years, he worked approximately 350 hours of overtime. He knew of three assistants who left because of the excessive overtime (excessive for them at least). What he didn't know, however, was that many of the managers and partners were working as much overtime as he was. Manager utilization rates were reaching as high as 85 percent. Consequently, the managers and partners really didn't have time to sit down and listen to the assistants. While Steve realizes that the "Big Six" accounting firms aren't in business to "coddle" people, he also knows he could have used a pat on the back or an occasional word of encouragement. This environment prevented him from knowing anyone very well, and he has yet to meet the managing partner. This of course makes performance review time one filled with uncertainty. The managers and partners seem to be uncomfortable giving negative feedback and the assistants have no idea where they stand. The assistants thus have only job assignments and pay raises to tell them how the firm thinks they are doing. Thus Steve's pressing career question is whether he should leave the firm now or stay through a third year. He can't think of any reason to stay, but he is hoping discussions with Bob might clarify his options.

Case Questions

1. Does overutilization of assistants result in high levels of premature turnover?
2. Is overutilization the only cause of premature turnover?
3. From an individual point of view, why is Bob's office so satisfying?
4. What would you advise Steve to do?

Case: Career Management for Whom?

Franklin Hudson (FH), a large regional accounting firm in Atlanta, has experienced a smooth growth curve over the past five years.

Although the favorable funding cycle has enabled FH to grow at a steady rate, the firm is finding it increasingly difficult to keep its really good, young assistants. Based on extensive turnover, analyses conducted by Ned Jackson, the human resource planning partner, FH's problem seems to be its inability to keep young assistants beyond the "critical" two-year point. Ned's conclusion is that FH has been essentially serving as an industry college. Many of the assistants who do leave, move over, go into their own practice, join investment banks, or join a small to mid-sized corporation. Such turnover is costly and prevents FH from achieving desired leverage ratios. Their staffing strategy has always been to hire the best and brightest accounting students from the best business schools in the United States.

Ned believes that these young assistants often get lost in the shuffle at the time they join the firm. For example, most (if not all) of the new hires work on numerous projects, and they never really develop a camaraderie with any particular group of assistants. Furthermore, they work in an environment where there traditionally is little feedback given to the new assistants on how well they are doing. Consequently, the new assistants often have difficulty learning the organizational culture—such as who to ask when you have a problem, what the general do's and don'ts are, and why the organization does things in a certain way.

After heading a task force to address this issue, Ned is about to present a proposal to the managing partner designed to reduce turnover among young assistants and recruits. The essence of his plan is to create a mentor program, except that in his plan the mentors will not be the seasoned graybeards of FH, but rather those accountants in the critical two to three-year service window, the period of highest turnover. These accountants will be paired with new recruits before the recruits actually report to FH for work.

According to the task force, the program is twofold: (1) it benefits the newcomer by easing the transition into the firm, and (2) it empowers the two to five-year senior accountants by having them serve in an important role for the firm. In performing this mentor role, these accountants will become more committed and hence less likely to leave. As Ned prepared his fifteen-minute presentation for the managing partner, he wondered whether he had adequately anticipated the possible objections to the program so that he could defend it intelligently.

Case Questions

1. Why is the firm finding it increasingly difficult to keep really good assistants?
2. Should FH change its recruiting strategy?
3. How can FH change its career-related HR practices?
4. What objections is Ned likely to hear from the managing partner?

Chapter 6 Endnotes

1. J. Fierman, "What's Luck Got to Do With It?" *Fortune* (October 16, 1995): 149.
2. P. T. Kilborn, "Job Security Hinges on Skills, Not on an Employer for Life," *New York Times* (March 12, 1994):1, 7. Used by permission.
3. R. Kuttner, "Needed: A Two-Way Social Contract in the Workplace," *Business Week* (July 10, 1995): 22.
4. A. S. Grove, "A High-Tech CEO Updates His Views on Managing and Careers," *Fortune* (September 18, 1995): 229–230; A. Brown, "Career Development 1986," *Personnel Administrator* (March 1986): 45–48; J. Morabito, "Baby Boomers: The Young and the Restless," *Personnel Administrator* (July 1987): 103–108.
5. B. Filipczak, "You're On Your Own," *Training* (January 1995): 32.
6. T. Jackson and A. Vitberg, "Career Development, Part 3: Challenges for the Individual," *Personnel* (April 1987): 54–57; M. London and S. Stumpf, *Managing Careers* (Reading, MA: Addison-Wesley, 1982).
7. J. H. Greenhaus, *Career Management* (Hinsdale, IL: The Dryden Press, 1987); J. H. Greenhaus and N. J. Beautell, "Sources of Conflict Between Work and Family Roles," *Academy of Management Review* (Jan.1985): 76–88.
8. B. Presley Noble, "If Loyalty Is Out, Then What's In?" *New York Times* (January 29, 1995): F21.
9. A. Halcrow, "Voices of HR Experience," *Personnel Journal* (May 1989): 38.
10. J. H. Greenhaus, *Career Management*; D. C. Feldman, *Managing Careers in Organizations* (Glenview, IL: Scott, Foresman, 1988); D. Hellriegel, J. W. Slocum, Jr., and R. W. Woodman, *Organizational Behavior*, 5th ed., (St. Paul, MN: West, 1989), see Chapter 18, 500–531.
11. *Business and Older Workers* (Washington, D.C.: AARP, 1989).

12. B. L. Dilla, "Descriptive Versus Prescriptive Information in a Realistic Job Preview," *Journal of Vocational Behavior* (1987): 33–48.

13. T. A. Stewart, "Looking Out for Number 1: A Complete Guide to Your Career," *Fortune* (January 15, 1996): 5; Caudron, "HR Revamps Career Itineraries," *Personnel Journal* (April 1994): 64B–64P; P. Simonsen and C. Wells, "African Americans Take Control of Their Careers," *Personnel Journal* (April 1994): 99–108.

14. B. Morris, "Executive Women Confront Midlife Crisis," *Fortune* (September 18, 1995): 60–86; "Rethinking Work," *Business Week* (October 17, 1994): 84; J. Fierman, "Beating the Midlife Career Crisis," *Fortune* (Sept. 6, 1993): 52–62; J. Bardwick, *The Plateauing Trap* (New York: AMACOM, 1986); J. Slocum, W. Cron, and L. Yows, "Career Plateauing: Who's Likely to Plateau," *Business Horizons* (1987): 31–38; D. C. Feldman and B. A. Weitz, "Career Plateaus Reconsidered," *Journal of Management* 14 (1988): 69–80; D. T. Hall and M. R. Louis, "When Careers Plateau," *Research-Technology Management* 31, 2 (1989): 41–45.

15. Slocum, Cron, and Yows, "Career Plateauing: Who's Likely to Plateau."

16. Filipczak, "You're On Your Own"; B. Paik Sunoo, "Papa John's Rolls Out Hot HR Menu," *Personnel Journal* (September 1995): 38A7.

17. J. Bardwick, *The Plateauing Trap.*

18. R. Kanter, "Globalism/Localism: A New Human Resources Agenda," *Harvard Business Review* (March–April 1991): 9–10.

19. W. A. Campione, "The Married Woman's Retirement Decision: A Methodological Comparison," *Journal of Gerontology* (1987): 381–386; B. Rosen and T. H. Jerdee, *Older Workers; New Roles for Valued Resources* (Homewood, IL: Dow Jones-Irwin, 1985).

20. N. J. Beautell, "Managing the Older Worker," *Personnel Administrator* (Aug.1983): 31–40; N. J. Beautell and O. C. Brenner, "Employee Retirement Decisions," *Personnel Review* (1987): 31–33; M. Cahill and P. R. Salomone, "Career Counseling and Worklife Extension: Integrating the Older Worker into the Labor Force," *The Career Development Quarterly* (1987): 188–196.

21. M. Hequet, "Flat and Happy?" *Training* (April 1995): 29–34; From D. Kirkpatrick, "Is Your Career On Track?" *Fortune* (July 2, 1990): 38–48; E. Ehrlich, "The Mommy Track," *Business Week* (March 20, 1990): 126–134.

22. D. C. Calabria, "When Companies Give, Employees Give Back," *Personnel Journal* (April 1995): 75–83.

23. "Relocating Dual Career Couples," *Bulletin to Management* (October 4, 1990): 320. See also "Relocating Two-Earner Couples," The Conference Board, 845 Third Avenue, New York, NY 10022; M. Moravec and B. McKee, "Designing Dual-Career Paths and Compensation," *Personnel* (Aug. 1990): 4–9; C. Trost, "How One Bank Is Handling A 'Two Track' Career Plan," *The Wall Street Journal* (March 13, 1989): B1, B8; Z. B. Leibowitz, B. H. Feldman, and S. H. Mosley, "Career Development Works Overtime at Corning, Inc.," *Personnel* (April 1990): 38–46; O. C. Brenner, "Career Reporters To Know Them Could Be to Keep Them," *Personnel* (Nov. 1988): 55–59; J. R. Bratkovich, B. Steele, and T. Rollins, "Develop New Career Management Strategies," *Personnel Journal* (Sept.1990): 98–107.

24. "Relocating Dual Career Couples," 320.

25. R. M. Silberman, "DOL Issues Final FMLA Regulations," *ACA News* (March 1995): 9–12; "Final FMLA Rules Take Effect Feb. 6," *Fair Employment Practices* (January 26, 1995): 7–8; M. Rowland, "A Clearer Picture of Unpaid Leave," *New York Times* (January 29, 1995): F13; "Progress on Family and Medical Leave," *Bulletin to Management* (April 15, 1993): 113–114; "Family and Medical Leave Act," *Fair Employment Practices Guidelines* (March 1993): 1–2.

26. J. Kerr, "The Best Small Companies to Work For in America," *Inc.* (July 1993): 57.

27. J. W. Gilley and H. L. Moore, "Managers as Career Enhancers," *Personnel Administrator* (March 1986): 51–59.

28. J. H. Dobrzynski, "Should I Have Left An Hour Earlier?" *New York Times* (June 18, 1995): Sec. 3, pp.1, 12.

29. Cahill and Salomone, "Career Counseling and Worklife Extension: Integrating the Older Worker into the Labor Force."

30. J. Holusha, "First to College, Then the Mill," *New York Times* (August 22, 1995): Dl, 7.

31. M. Rowland, "Getting Before-the-Job Experience," *New York Times* (June 5, 1994): F15.

32. R. Henkoff, "Winning the New Career Game," *Fortune* (July 12, 1993): 46–64; S. Sherman, "A Brave New Darwinian Workplace," *Fortune* (Jan. 25, 1993): 50–56.

33. M. Loeb, "The Real Fast Track Is Overseas," *Fortune* (August 21, 1995): 129; M. Rowland, "Thriving in a Foreign Environment," *New York Times* (December 5, 1993); "Views on the Expatriate," *The Wall Street Journal* (Dec.11, 1989): B1; C. Reynolds, "Careers in International Human Resources," *The SHRM Student Newsletter* (Jan./Feb. 1992): 1.

34. J. J. Fucini and S. Fucini, *Working for the Japanese* (New York: The Free Press, 1990); S. Moffat, "Should You Work for the Japanese?" *Fortune* (Dec. 3, 1990): 107–108, 112, 116, 120; W. Zeliner, "Help Wanted, Room To Advance-Out the Door," *Business Week* (Oct. 30, 1989): 42.

35. B. Presley Noble, "Stalking the Useful Career Guide," *New York Times* (February 12, 1995): F23; M. Loeb, "Getting Hired By Getting Wired," *Fortune* (November 13, 1995): 252.

36. E. H. Schein, "How to Break in the College Graduate," *Harvard Business Review* (March–April 1964): 70; D. T. Hall and Associates, *Career Development in Organizations* (San Francisco: Jossey-Bass, 1986).

37. D. E. Berlew and D. T. Hall, "Some Determinants of Early Managerial Success," Working paper 81–64 (Cambridge,

MA: Sloan School of Management, MIT, 1964); R. A. Webber, "Career Problems of Young Managers," *California Management Review* (1976): 19–33.

38. D. T. Hall, "Careers and Socialization," *Journal of Management* (1987): 301–321; J. L. Pierce and R. B. Dunham, "Organizational Commitment: Pre-Employment Propensity and Initial Work Experiences," *Journal of Management* (1987): 163–174.

39. J. H. Dobrzynski, "Women Less Optimistic About Work, Poll Says," *New York Times* (September 12, 1995): D5.

40. Ibid.

41. Ibid.

42. "Faxed Resumes Now May Be Considered Proper Etiquette," *Personnel Journal* (Aug. 1993): 16.

43. J. H. Conley, J. M. Hueghi, and R. L. Minter, Perspectives on Administrative Communication (Dubuque, Iowa: Kendall/Hunt, 1976): 172; W. J. Morin, "The Four Interviewer Breeds: How to Tame Them," *New York Times* Recruitment Survey (Oct. 11, 1981): 59, 62; J. T. Yenckel, "Careers: Facing the Interview," *Washington Post* (Oct. 20, 1981): D5.

44. S. Chastain, "On the Job: The Winning Interview," in Winning the Salary Game; Negotiations for Women, eds. D. Littman and C. Stegel (New York: Wiley, 1980); R. H. Frank and P. J. Cook, *The Winner Take-All Society* (New York: The Free Press, 1995).

45. I. Janis and D. Wheeler, "Thinking Clearly about Career Choices," *Psychology Today* (May 1978): 67–76, 121–122.

46. "12 Ways to Negotiate Effectively And Continue to Work Together," *HR Reporter* (December 1995): 1; A. L. Ball, "Mentors & Proteges: Portraits of Success," *Working Woman* (Oct. 1989): 134–142; D. Jacoby "Rewards Make the Mentor," *Personnel* (Dec. 1989): "Faxed Resume's Now May Be Considered Proper Etiquette," *Personnel Journal* (Aug.): 10–14.

47. L. S. Richinan, "How To Get Ahead In America," *Fortune* (May 16, 1994): 46–54; K. Labich, "Kissing Off Corporate America," *Fortune* (February 20, 1995): 44–51.

48. "Living with the New Guidelines on Sexual Harassment," *People and Business* (July 1981): 3.

49. Ibid.

50. Ibid.

51. "Farewell, Fast Track" *Business Week* (Dec. 10, 1990): 192–200; M. Loeb, "The Smart Way to Change Jobs," *Fortune* (September 4, 1995): 139; R. Henkoff, "So, You Want to Change Your Job," *Fortune* (January 15, 1996): 52–56.

52. A. Farnham, "Are You Smart Enough to Keep Your Job?" *Fortune* (January 15, 1996): 34–38.

53. P. S. Estess, "The Parent Trap: The Pros and Cons of Hiring Your Parents," *Entrepreneur* (January 1996): 90–94; P. S. Estess, "Strangers Among Us," *Entrepreneur* (July 1995): 74–77; S. Nelton, "The Agony of Quitting the Family Firm," Part I *Nation's Business* (September 1995): 60, Part II (October 1995): 62.

54. M. Barrier, "Back from the Brink," *Nation's Business* (September 1995): 18–25; L. Brokaw, "The Truth About Start-ups," *Inc.* (March 1993): 56–64; H. Gleckman, "Meet the Giant-killers," *Business Week/Enterprise* (1993): 68–73; J. S. Hornsby and D. F. Kuratko, "Human Resource Management in Small Business: Critical Issues for the 1990s," *Journal of Small Business Management* (July 1990): 9–18.

55. R. Maynard, "Why Franchisors Look Abroad," *Nation's Business* (October 1995): 65–72.

56. A. Bhide, "How Entrepreneurs Craft," *Harvard Business Review* (March–April 1994):150–161; J. H. Eggers and A. Leahy, "Entrepreneurial Leadership," *Business Quarterly* (Summer 1995): 71–76; M. O'Neal, "Just What is an Entrepreneur," *Business Week/Enterprise* (1993): 104–112.

CHAPTER 7

Job Design

Learning Objectives

1. Discuss why job design is so important.
2. Explain the features of the four approaches to job design.
3. Make recommendations concerning different job designs to companies.
4. Describe the process and content models of motivation.
5. Describe the alternative arrangements for employee accommodation.

> *"There isn't any other place to work like Lincoln Electric. They take care of you."*
>
> *Kathleen Hoenigman*
> *Production Worker,*
> *Eighteen-Year Veteran at*
> *Lincoln Electric*[1]

Chapter Outline

Job Design

Approaches to Job Design

Employee Motivation

Alternative Arrangements for Employee Accommodation

Trends in Job Design

International Comparisons

Summary

MANAGING HUMAN RESOURCES

at Lincoln Electric

In 1995, the production workers at Lincoln Electric in Cleveland, Ohio, received bonuses averaging over $50,000. Their total pay, including wages, profit sharing, and bonuses, ranged between $32,000 and more than $100,000! According to Paul Beddia, vice-president of human resources for Lincoln, the company's productivity rate is two to three times that of any other manufacturing operation that uses steel as its raw material and that employs more than 3,400 people in the U.S. While Lincoln is widely cited as an example of a firm with a highly motivated workforce, it is important to keep in mind a few unusual things about this company. First, Lincoln has no paid holidays. Sick days are not paid for by the firm. Workers must accept job reassignment, and overtime is mandatory. There is no seniority and no special parking spaces or special cafeterias. Workers take care of their own retirement needs. Yet, the post-probationary turnover is less than 4 percent per year, and the company receives nearly 1,000 unsolicited job applications or resumes per month!

How does Lincoln do it? This is a question many ask. While its famous piecework system is credited with the high level of employee motivation, it is the company's fundamentally different approach to job design that sets it apart. At Lincoln Electric, the jobs are narrowly and clearly defined and have been so since its inception. Both jobs and the procedures to operate them have been systematically analyzed to gain as much efficiency as possible.

What is seen today at Lincoln reflects its history. Lincoln Electric's famous piecework system was established in 1914, in the heyday of Fredrick W. Taylor and scientific management! Thus the organizational culture is firmly in place. The workers know what to expect, and they are trained to live up to the company's expectations in a broad variety of jobs. Such broad and careful training enables employees to do a variety of jobs at a moment's notice without any loss of quality. With very specific and clear job descriptions, everyone knows what each job is about. Any improvements to the job designs are done through suggestions that are then carefully studied by industrial engineers.

The nature of the jobs further allows Lincoln to motivate employees with *individual* piecework payment systems. Not only are the job designs narrowly defined, they are also defined for the individual, not for a team. Thus, at a time when many organizations are implementing job enrichment and team-based job designs, Lincoln Electric remains an example of the scientific approach to job design, and it demonstrates that this approach can still work. Would it work for you?[2]

This feature on Lincoln Electric illustrates some important ideas about job analysis and job design. Perhaps the most critical one is that the scientific management approach to job design can be very effective. While job enrichment programs are popular today, there are still opportunities to use the more narrowly defined jobs from the days of scientific management. The scientific management approach to job design facilitates the writing of clear and understandable job descriptions; here job descriptions detail how to do the job. Training is made easier with the result being that a number of workers can do any given job, and job assignments can be based on need. Such a flexible system can enable a firm to adapt to a rapidly changing environment.

Did You KNOW?

The productivity level of the Lincoln worker is almost three times as much as the average manufacturing worker!

There are times, however, when the jobs themselves need to be changed. Changes may be needed to provide more motivation, thus making workers more productive, satisfied, involved, and committed. Changes may be needed to accommodate physical capabilities of the workforce or individuals. Companies may need to change the time and location in which the job is performed. These kinds of changes are called alternative arrangements for employee accommodation. We will discuss all of these in this chapter.

In Chapter 8, we will examine the process of analyzing jobs in detail, but to gain an understanding of job design, we will touch on job analysis briefly in this chapter. It is important to keep in mind that job design and job analysis influence everything else in human resource management: recruitment, selection, appraisal, compensation, and training and development. We return to Lincoln Electric in Chapter 14 to discuss its compensation.

Job Design

Job design is the process by which the characteristics and qualities of jobs are determined and created.

Job design is the process by which the characteristics and qualities of jobs are determined and created. Jobs are created in job design, and they are described in job analysis. There are several approaches to job design. We will consider the details of each after we address the importance of job design and the accompanying legal considerations.

LEARNING OBJECTIVE 1

Discuss why job design is so important

Why is Job Design Important?

Since the times of Frederick W. Taylor and the development of scientific management, jobs have been designed for:

- Efficiency, finding the one best way to produce a product
- Productivity, obtaining maximum use of human and physical resources
- Competitive advantage, being better than the competition

Today job design serves as a vital way by which organizations can accommodate a more diverse workforce. Thus, to our list of purposes, we can add:

- Accommodation of a diverse workforce
- Motivation of a diverse workforce
- Fulfillment of individual needs

Together, all these purposes are being served by job design in organizations today. In fact, organizations are emphasizing careful job design more than ever because they recognize that competitive strategies like quality improvement often depend on enriching jobs and creating self-managed teams. Companies know that they must actually accommodate the needs of the diverse workforce in order to attract the best people. Finally, jobs provide meaning and structure to individuals. And through the design of those jobs, workers can experience fulfillment of some of their most important needs.

Because job and job design are so important to companies and their employees, it is not surprising that job design is done through the extensive partnership of line managers, HR professionals, and other employees as shown in "Partnership: Working Together in Job Design." In their working together, they have many choices in how to design jobs for the first time and redesign existing jobs. There are several major approaches to job design from which to choose.

LEARNING OBJECTIVE 2

Explain the features of the four approaches to job design.

Approaches to Job Design

The scientific approach to job design carefully analyzes jobs and breaks them into incremental tasks.

The Scientific Approach

Under the **scientific approach**, job analysts (typically, industrial engineers) take special pains to design jobs so that the tasks performed by employees do not exceed their abilities.[3] The jobs designed this way often result in work being partitioned into small, standardized segments. These tasks lend themselves well to time and motion studies and to incentive pay systems, each for the purpose of

PARTNERSHIP: WORKING TOGETHER IN JOB DESIGN

LINE MANAGERS	HR PROFESSIONALS	EMPLOYEES
Identify job design needs	Identify job design needs	Assist in job design
Assist in job design and redesign	Assist in job design and redesign	Provide feedback about your reactions to job design
Empower employees and facilitate teamwork	Help line managers and employees adjust to empowerment and teamwork	Adopt a positive attitude and be willing to change
Propose accommodations to employees	Monitor and evaluate job design alternatives	Accept responsibility for continually learning new ways to work
Accommodate employees	Develop work place accommodations	Assist your peers throughout the change process
Work with HR professionals to align HR systems with job designs	Work with line managers to align HR systems with job designs	Request job accommodations, if needed

obtaining high productivity. The scientific approach to job design is still an important part of many fine organizations.

Through meticulous human engineering, United Parcel Service (UPS) is highly successful despite stiff competition. In a business where "a package is a package," UPS succeeds through its application of scientifically designed work standards. Their approach has been key to their continuing gains in efficiency and productivity since the privately held company was founded in 1907. In the 1920s, UPS engineers cut away the sides of UPS trucks to study how the drivers performed. The engineers then made appropriate changes in techniques to enhance worker efficiency.

Frederick W. Taylor was the father of the scientific approach to job design.

Time and motion studies enable the company to closely monitor the performance of the workers. At UPS, more than 1,000 industrial engineers use the time study to set standards for a variety of closely supervised tasks. In return, the UPS drivers, all of whom are represented by the Teamsters, earn wages of approximately $17 per hour or $28 with benefits.[4] Because of the company's success in these endeavors, they are able to offer employees better job security.

UPS's scientific approach to job design is, of course, only part of the picture. The company complements this approach with an employee-oriented HR philosophy and modern technology:

> *UPS is the world's largest package distribution company serving a network of more than 185 countries and territories with a daily delivery volume of more than 11.5 million packages.*
>
> *Quality service has been woven into the company since its beginnings in 1907 as a messenger service in Seattle.*
>
> *Throughout its existence, UPS has constantly analyzed its procedures, refined its equipment, and devised new systems to enable employees to provide customers with high-quality service.*
>
> *UPS takes the view there is a direct correlation between quality service and the quality of its people.*

Through the "Delivering Our Future" program, we are gaining further proof of how valuable our drivers and other employees can be in developing our business. This year should present even more opportunities for our people to contribute to the success of their company.

Kent C. Nelson
Chairman and
Chief Executive Officer
UPS

To that end, UPS employs the best people it can find, trains them thoroughly and continuously, rewards them generously, and involves them personally in the business through daily pre-work communication meetings and periodic districtwide service awareness programs.

Succeeding as it does in a highly competitive industry, UPS engineers and fine tunes its service in every way possible. The performance of delivery drivers, for example, is a model of human engineering. Drivers are taught 340 professional, individual methods for delivering and picking up packages.

This "human engineering" approach extends throughout the company. . . from details of sorting packages in the safest, most efficient way possible to teaching methods that result in the successful handling of customer inquiries on the telephone.

Technology too plays an important part in allowing UPS people to work smarter, not harder. Hand-held computers enable delivery drivers to capture signatures and other vital information essential to the tracing of packages. Automated sorting and scanning equipment complement the ability of inside operations to handle the flow of package volume efficiently.

UPS's overall objective is to achieve worldwide leadership in package distribution. To do this, the company will continue to rely on its people, allowing them to develop their individual capabilities that will provide job satisfaction and the opportunity to advance through UPS's policy of promotion from within.[5]

The Individual Contemporary Approach

The individual contemporary design approach enlarges the scope of the job.

Individual contemporary design results in feelings of

- **meaningfulness**
- **responsibility**
- **empowerment**
- **satisfaction in knowing results**

Because the scientific approach is not always effective, organizations began searching for alternative job design approaches. One result is the **individual contemporary design**. As shown in Exhibit 7.1, five positive personal and work outcomes—high motivation, quality work performance, satisfaction, and low absenteeism and turnover—result when people are allowed to function in an environment where work enables the individual to obtain a sense of:

- meaningfulness
- responsibility
- empowerment (not shown in Exhibit 7.1)
- knowing the results

Skill variety is the degree to which tasks require different skills and abilities.

Job significance is the degree to which a job is important.

Job identity is the degree to which a job has a whole and identifiable outcome.

Autonomy is the degree of freedom in deciding how to do the job.

Feedback is the amount of information given about performance effectiveness.

According to researchers, these are critical psychological states that evolve from five core job characteristics: 1) **skill variety** (degree to which tasks are performed that require different abilities and skills); 2) **job significance** (degree to which the job has substantial importance); 3) **job identity** (degree to which a whole and identifiable piece of work with a visible outcome is produced); 4) **autonomy** (degree of freedom and discretion in work scheduling and procedures); and 5) **feedback** (amount of direct and clear information about performance effectiveness). **Job enrichment** results when jobs are high on these core characteristics. When employees value feelings of meaningfulness, responsibility, empowerment, and knowing the results, job enrichment leads to positive personal and work outcomes.[6]

Several different strategies can be used to provide these core job characteristics. For example, job rotation doesn't change the nature of a specific job, but it

EXHIBIT 7.1

The Core Job Characteristics Model

CORE JOB CHARACTERISTICS	CRITICAL PSYCHOLOGICAL STATES	OUTCOMES
Skill variety Job identity Job significance	Meaningfulness of the work	Less absenteeism Less turnover High satisfaction High motivation High-quality work performance
Job autonomy	Responsibility for outcomes of the work	
Feedback from job	Knowing the actual results of the work activities	

does increase the number of duties an employee performs over time. This increases task variety and can also boost job identity and scope of purpose because the employee is performing several jobs. Task identity can also improve when the employee completes a "whole and identifiable piece of work."

Job enlargement is the opposite of the scientific approach, which seeks to increase the number of duties in any given job. Job enlargement can increase skill variety.

Horizontal loading involves adding more duties with the same types of task characteristics; **vertical loading** means creating a job with duties that have many different characteristics. The former approach may increase skill variety, but it's also likely to foster resentment because the employee is expected to do more of the same. Vertical loading is more promising because it closes the gap between planning, doing, and controlling the work. As a result, it affects job autonomy, skill variety, and possible feedback.

The trend in companies today is to provide workers with conditions for more responsibility, empowerment, meaningfulness, and knowledge of results. This can be done with almost any job. As an example, using the core job characteristics model shown in Exhibit 7.1 of a relatively simply job redesign, consider the job of bank tellers. In an effort to improve the jobs of 526 tellers working in 38 banks in the Southwest, the following changes were made:[7]

BEFORE JOB REDESIGN	AFTER JOB REDESIGN
Tellers cashed checks and accepted deposits and payments	Tellers handled all these tasks, increasing *skill variety* and *job identity*
Tellers referred travelers and commercial customers to special clerks; bookkeepers posted checks, deposits, etc.	Tellers were given *autonomy* to handle large, *significant* transactions for local accounts
Feedback on errors was available at the end of the day or the next day	Feedback about errors was available almost *immediately*
No feedback was available about work volume	Feedback about volume was continuously displayed on a computer monitor
Tellers had no signature line to sign off on	Tellers signed their names for each transaction, in recognition of their responsibility for the work

Job enrichment is the experience of having a job high on all five core job characteristics.

Job rotation means the individual moves from job to job.

Horizontal loading means adding more of the same. Vertical loading means adding more variety.

Job enlargement is the result of adding more duties to the job.

The tellers found their new jobs to be more motivating, and, importantly, their job performance improved significantly.

Of course, this is only one example, so you might still wonder, "Does designing jobs according to the model shown in Exhibit 7.1 really work?" Dozens of studies involving thousands of employees in many types of jobs indicate that the answer to this question is yes. Both performance and job satisfaction increase after jobs are redesigned to provide more skill variety, task identity, significance, autonomy, and feedback.[8] These beneficial outcomes are especially likely to be seen among employees with high growth needs. Such people enjoy challenges, like to be creative and innovative, and are comfortable being in positions where they have high levels of responsibility.[9]

Growth needs are those for challenge, creativity, innovation, and responsibility.

Autonomy and Empowerment. But it may not always be possible to change all five core job characteristics. Given the choice of selecting only one to change, which would you select? Today, providing job autonomy appears to be a particularly effective way to obtain high worker commitment and quality. This is because many employees value responsibility and empowerment.[10] Yet providing autonomy depends on more than merely changing the job. In fact, companies with a high level of job autonomy usually have these characteristics:

- They invest a lot of time and effort in hiring, to make sure new recruits can handle workplace freedom.
- Their organizational hierarchy is flat.
- They set loose guidelines, so workers know their decision-making parameters.
- Accountability is paramount. Results matter more than process.
- High-quality performance is always expected.
- Openness and strong communication are encouraged.
- Employee satisfaction is a core value.[11]

Many large companies have been moving to provide these workplace conditions. Jerry Goodman did this at IBAX. He felt strongly that the employees had to be empowered to make a difference in the performance of the company. But he also knew that you can't just empower people and expect positive results. Many employees need support and development to be effectively empowered—in other words, they need to be "enabled." Some employees simply weren't capable of assuming responsibility for important tasks within the organization. Others were capable, but did not have access to the information or resources they needed to do their jobs well. Others lacked the organizational authority to get their jobs done. In all of these cases, Goodman and his leadership team stepped in and provided what was needed. For some employees, that meant additional education and training; in other cases it simply required providing information, resources, or authority. But in virtually all cases, the employees at IBAX were enabled and empowered to do their jobs well.[12]

Small companies by nature are already there. Examples of what can come from small companies who are successfully providing job autonomy are detailed in the feature, "Managing Human Resources in the Best Small Companies: Job Autonomy."

Did You KNOW?

"Managers spend much more time thinking about coaching and building teams . . . .The new game of business is one that requires engaging each individual in personal, intellectual, and emotional excellence, while paradoxically being a superb team player."

Noel Tichy, Professor University of Michigan

The Team Contemporary Approach

Whereas the individual contemporary and scientific approaches design jobs for individuals, the **team contemporary approach** designs jobs for teams of individuals. These designs generally show a concern for the social needs of individuals as well as the constraints of the technology. Here, teams of workers often rotate jobs and may follow the product from start to completion. If the product is large—for example, an automobile—teams may be designed around sections of the final car. Each group then completes only a section and passes its subproduct to the next team.

Team contemporary approach is the design of jobs for teams of employees.

MANAGING HUMAN RESOURCES

in the Best Small Companies
Job Autonomy

ACTION INSTRUMENTS

- San Diego Instrument Manufacturer
- 200 Employees, $25 million in sales
- Urges employees to "make it happen" to solve problems that they discover. Sets loose boundaries to define scope of autonomy. Engenders self-motivation through open-book financial disclosure.

ADVANCED NETWORK DESIGN

- La Mirada, California
- Phone-Service Reseller
- 20 Employees, $3.7 million in sales
- Hires rigorously, trains thoroughly, and then turns employees loose to perform. Provides very little supervision for anyone, including receptionist. Has employees report work progress weekly or monthly.

ALPHATRONIX

- Research Triangle Park, North Carolina
- Optical-Storage-Systems Maker
- 70 Employees, $11.8 million in sales
- Puts recruits through up to five interviews, then assigns them their own projects. Has employees set their own goals and timetables for project completion.

AVID TECHNOLOGY

- Tewksbury, Massachusetts
- Film-Editing-System Maker
- 320 Employees, $50 million in sales
- Screens potential hires based on company's 10 core values, like teamwork, honesty, and passion to win. Lets employees design their own work schedules.

CHILDRESS BUICK

- Phoenix
- Automobile Dealer
- 105 Employees, $30 million in sales
- Empowers salespeople to cut deals on their own. Urges service department teams to boost customer satisfaction. Actively solicits employee ideas.

JOB BOSS SOFTWARE

- Minneapolis Developer of Factory Software
- 40 Employees, $2.3 million in sales
- Encourages employees to take ownership of their jobs. Hires rigorously, trains well, and then grants employees wide latitude. Has managers act more as facilitators than as bosses.[13]

In the team contemporary design, each worker learns to handle several duties, many requiring different skills. When faced with decisions, teams generally try to involve all members. Thus, teams can satisfy preferences for achievement and task accomplishment and some preferences for social interaction. When team members work well together, team decisions and behaviors result in greater output.

Today, teamwork has become so critical for organizations that many are elevating it to a core value.[14] The W. L. Gore & Associates Company, makers of Gore-Tex, certainly embraces teamwork as a fundamental value.[15] As a core value at Weyerhaeuser, it is stated and defined as follows:

> ***Teamwork:*** *Business results are improved by using teams to combine the talents and ideas of people. That means:*

- *People work together and empower each other to be successful.*
- *People have the skills and information that enable them to participate as effective team members and decision makers.*

Did You KNOW?

One survey revealed that most corporations utilize five or six types of teams: functional teams, continuous improvement teams, product teams, project teams, management teams, and problem-solving teams.

Teamwork **means working together to solve problems on the job.**

Clearly, we are looking for attitudes. Today we are operating with teams.

Jack Smith
Chairman and CEO
General Motors

Teamwork is the essence of life.

Pat Riley
Coach
Miami Heat
Basketball Team

Team-based systems give workers more satisfaction.

Self-managed teams are those making many management decisions for their group.

Steelcase, the Grand Rapids, Michigan, office furniture maker, unites all the employees behind the practice of self-managed teams.

- *Diverse work teams, cross-functional and multicultural, are formed where opportunities exist to enhance business results across organizations.*

- *We continuously measure employee involvement and develop action plans to improve.*

- *Where work interdependencies exist, work teams are utilized.*[16]

Although teamwork may be unusual for some employees, it appears that most employees are able to adapt to it. It may take time to install teams and attain high levels of teamwork, but the benefits can be substantial.

Taking Time to Learn Teamwork. Because working in teams is new to many employees and organizations, making the change to teams takes time. Effective teamwork and organizational success do not happen overnight. Typically, teams start out making only a few decisions. After time, training, and familiarity, they begin to make many more decisions. Essentially, the team members pass through stages of greater empowerment (decision-making). In each new stage, they make more decisions, until they can eventually be called **self-managed teams**. IBAX achieved greater productivity and better quality through the use of self-managed teams.

Tasks about which self-managed teams can make decisions are shown in Exhibit 7.2.[17]

Being Successful. Developing self-managed teams capable of making decisions and performing related activities requires change and commitment in several organizational areas. According to one large study, several barriers may inhibit the success of working teams. Wilson Learning Corporation of Eden Prairie, Minnesota, which offers team development training, conducted a large study of team facilitators, administrators, and 25,000 people who work in teams. It concluded that the biggest barriers to effective teams had little to do with the team process itself, but it had a lot to do with organizational barriers. For example, most teams operated in companies that continued to use individual-based compensation and performance appraisal systems.[18] Teams also felt hampered by their inability to access crucial information from their own companies, which were concerned about leakage of proprietary information.[19]

Individual team members also create barriers to effective team designs. It is not enough to change the job design; people need to change, too. The areas in which employees often need individual training, according to Michael Leimbach, director of research for Wilson Learning Corporation, include the following:

- **Advocating.** Team members must learn how to "sell" their point of view to others.

- **Inquiring.** Employees should know how to listen to other team members, as well as to "interview" other employees for needed information.

- **Tension Management.** Instead of avoiding conflict, workers should learn how to create constructive conflict and manage the resulting tension.

- **Sharing Responsibility.** To become a "team player," employees should learn to align personal objectives with the team's objectives and to understand their roles in creating shared outcomes.

- **Leadership.** Employees should understand their roles in leading the team to success.

- **Valuing Diversity**. A team's success results largely from members' differences in expertise, expectations, personalities, and work styles. Therefore,

EXHIBIT 7.2

Task Responsibilities of Self-Managed Teams

The most frequently cited tasks for which work teams take responsibility:

- Perform routine equipment maintenance
- Ensure workplace cleanliness
- Stop production for quality problems
- Assign daily tasks
- Make team-member assignments

The most frequently cited tasks for which work teams share responsibility with the supervisor:

- Identify training needs
- Select team members
- Develop work methods/procedures
- Ensure workplace safety
- Monitor and report on unit performance
- Set team production goals
- Provide training
- Coordinate work with suppliers/vendors

The most frequently cited tasks for which supervisors assume prime responsibility:

- Discipline employees
- Prepare unit budgets
- Conduct performance appraisals

Source: Adapted from S. T. Johnson, "Work Teams: What's Ahead in Work Design and Rewards Management," *Compensation and Benefits Review* (March–April 1993): 37.

team members should learn to value their differences, instead of striving for sameness.

- **Self-Awareness.** Employees must be willing and able to accept constructive criticism from others, and must learn to be self-critical.[20]

Besides these changes in the administrative system and in individual team members, total support must be available from all line managers and union representatives. Ultimately, the success of a team depends on effective partnership.[21]

Human Factors Approach

Human factors to be taken into account in designing jobs include the physical dimensions of the human body, the mechanical principles that govern physical movements, and physiology.[22]

Knowing the physical dimensions of the human body—such as the average width of the palm, the distance between hip and neck or between knee and ankle—aids in the design of equipment used on the job, including tools, machines, furniture, and vehicles. The objective of the human factors approach is to design equipment that fits the full range of physical features found in the population of people likely to be using equipment. The human factors approach is often referred to as **ergonomics.**

Ergonomics is about designing the work place so it is more physically accommodating to employees.

Knowing the biomechanical principles that govern physical movement and muscle functioning helps engineers design equipment that minimizes the amount of stress and fatigue experienced on the job. For example, an understanding of the biomechanics of the wrist, arm, and shoulder allows engineers to design office equipment to minimize the development of carpal tunnel syndrome, which is characterized by numbness, tingling, soreness, and weakness in the hand and wrist.[23]

Did You KNOW?

Eighty percent of us will sustain a back injury during our lifetime.

Human Factors for an Aging Workforce. The human factors approach to job design has proved useful in automobile factories, where the physical capabilities of the workforce have changed. Union members protected from layoffs by their seniority are still at the same jobs, but they are now considerably older. At Chrysler's Jeep plant in Detroit, the average age is 52, about six years above the industry average. Physically, this workforce simply does not perform at the level of a younger workforce. According to industrial relations expert Harley Shaiken: "The traditional way of improving productivity has been to speed up the line, but you can't do that with older workers . . . . you have skill and experience, which can be positive factors if you know how to harness them, [but] you can't rely on 52-year-olds working at the limit to dig you out of a hole."[24] To thrive, the auto industry has had to redesign its plants, installing ergonomic equipment to ease the strain. For example, overhead conveyor belts tilt auto bodies at angles that make assembly work less physically demanding, and the air guns used to drive screws are designed to reduce the stresses that cause carpal tunnel syndrome. Gyms have been installed, and workers have taken "back classes" to learn how to lift without injuring themselves.

LEARNING OBJECTIVE 3

Make recommendations concerning different job designs to companies.

Which Design to Use?

Selection of a job design approach must take into account not only such considerations as the corporate culture, the characteristics of the available workforce, and the environment, but also the advantages and disadvantages of each approach. To help in the selection, Exhibit 7.3 lists advantages and disadvantages of each. The final selection will also be influenced by factors such as cost considerations, technology available, the design used in the rest of the company, and the HR philosophy of the company. For example, when organizations such as UPS and Lincoln Electric value their people and continually demonstrate this, the employees give back more, making the business even more successful. When employees are offered the opportunity to grow with the business and when they know the business goals and concerns of the company, the job designs that result from the increased partnership are sure to be more effective. Perhaps these companies' approaches to job design would be less effective if their HR philosophy was different, but then they have long recognized the importance of people, and their HR philosophies reflect this.

The people we work with deserve the best at all times. We do this by providing opportunities for growth, participation and teamwork. Thus, we strive to create an environment where employees can achieve company goals and personal goals simultaneously.

Paul Beddia, Vice-President Human Resources Lincoln Electric

Employee-Centered Job Redesign. Although the context of the company and its HR philosophy are important determinants of which job design to select, the choices of the employees are also very important.[25] So some companies let the employees do the job redesign.[26] In doing so, however, the companies prepare the employees and offer support along the way. A list of what companies can do for such redesign efforts is shown in Exhibit 7.4.

Major legal considerations for job design are:

- *National Labor Relations Act*
- *Americans with Disabilities Act*

Legal Considerations. Organizations today are not only concerned with creating new job designs but also with creating job designs from existing jobs. Particularly in the latter case—redesigning existing jobs, which many firms find themselves doing when they move to total-quality management—employees are heavily involved in the design decisions. The self-managed team, which is itself a job design where employees make many decisions under the guidance of a supervisor, is often created as a result of the design process. As the team begins to function, the company need to be aware of the *National Labor Relations Act.*

EXHIBIT 7.3

Advantages and Disadvantages of the Four Job Design Approaches

APPROACHES	ADVANTAGES	DISADVANTAGES
Scientific	• Ensures predictability • Provides clarity	• May be boring • May result in absenteeism, sabotage, and turnover
Human Factors (Ergonomics)	• Accommodates jobs to people • Breaks down physical barriers • Makes more jobs accessible to more people	• May be costly to design some jobs • Structural characteristics of the organization may make job change impossible
Motivational		
Individual Contemporary	• Satisfies needs for responsibility, growth, and knowledge of results • Provides growth opportunity • Reduces boredom • Increases performance • Improves morale	• Some people prefer routine • May need to pay more, since it is hard to enrich some jobs • Requires some changes in the total HR system
Team Contemporary	• Provides social interaction • Provides variety • May improve service provided to customers • Reduces absenteeism problem	• Some prefer to work alone • Requires training in interpersonal skills • Major change takes a long time • May require major changes in the structure of the organization and the HR system

National Labor Relations Act. The *National Labor Relations Act* (NLRA) is particularly relevant in job design programs. In cases where a union represents the employees, the employer must consider that almost all issues, including the establishment of programs to change job designs, may need to be negotiated with the union. In many cases, however, employers and unions can cooperatively work together. When this is done, the NLRA requires employers to provide information to the union, when requested, for purposes related to the job design program. In cases where the employees are not represented by a union, employers can implement job design programs unilaterally. There are some limitations, however. For example, employers may not be able to create and dominate employee teams for the sake of modifying job and working conditions because this may constitute behavior that undermines the role of union activity according to the National Labor Relations Board in the cases of *Electromation* (1992) and *DuPont* (1993).

The Principle of Reasonable Accommodation. Today, companies are concerned not only about creating jobs from the beginning, as with small firms just starting, but also with creating new job designs from existing jobs. A job redesign effort at AT&T was an early example of how job redesign can be used to accommodate the physical differences between men and women. In the mid-1970s,

EXHIBIT 7.4

How to Execute an Employee-Centered Work Redesign Program

Employee-centered work redesign programs focus on treating employees as partners rather than subordinates. To execute such a system, the following steps must be taken:

- Teach employees about the mission and goals of the organization and their department.
- Have employees complete a needs-assessment survey to help them identify personal job satisfaction and professional development goals. These should be consistent with the mission and goals of the department and the organization.
- Conduct an exercise to help employees learn to recognize possible obstacles to achieving their goals and identify methods for eliminating or minimizing such barriers.
- Ask employees to prepare an inventory of their existing work responsibilities. This inventory should be broken into three distinct categories: work that will be retained, work that will be modified, and work that will be eliminated. Employees should also identify new work that should be added to their current job.
- Employees should outline methods for accomplishing all modified and new tasks in the inventory. This process increases the employees' sense of accountability for their newly designed jobs.
- Finally, a careful review of the proposal by management should be followed by implementation on a trial basis. This provides for monitoring of the new job design and allows for corrections to be made quickly and easily.

Source: Excerpts from "Employees Redesign Their Jobs," by S. L. Periman, copyright November 1990. Reprinted with the permission of *Personnel Journal*, ACC Communications, Inc., Costa Mesa, California; all rights reserved.

AT&T entered into an agreement with the Equal Employment Opportunity Commission to increase the representation of women in telephone line repair jobs, which had been male-dominated. To achieve this objective, AT&T had to accommodate the physical differences in size between men and women by changing the job design for telephone pole climbers. The telephone line repair workers had to climb up the poles by placing their feet on horizontal bars on either side of the poles. With the old job design, most women were unable to climb the poles simply because the bars were too far apart. AT&T resolved this situation by reducing the distance between the bars. Although this change had to be made on hundreds of thousands of poles, the accommodation was regarded as "reasonable."[27]

Reasonable accommodation is any modification or adjustment that allows qualified applicants or employees with disabilities to participate in the application process or to do the job's essential functions without causing undue hardship to the employer.

Reasonable accommodation is now a common term because of the *Americans with Disabilities Act* of 1990. For organizations with 15 or more employees, the ADA "prohibits bias against qualified individuals with disabilities in all aspects of employment and requires employers to make reasonable accommodations for such individuals so long as the accommodations do not pose an undue hardship to the employer's business."[28] Exactly what this reasonable accommodation means in practice varies with the nature of the company. AT&T had to change the spacing of horizontal bars. Subsequently, bars were replaced by spiked shoes.[29] Because it believed it had found an unusually effective employee, UPS considered it reasonable to spend $11,000 for equipment that enabled a blind man to work as a computer programming instructor.[30] Another employer was told that it was reasonable to supply different gloves to all its medical personnel when one worker developed an allergy to latex and the powder in latex gloves.

Thus, legal considerations in job design influence the nature of job activities and the context in which the job takes place, making more jobs available to more people. The result can be a situation in which the individual, the company, and society all win.

To expand your knowledge about the general coverage of ADA, read the feature, "HR Advice and Application: Allergic to Latex," which describes the emergency medical worker who requested a different type of glove. In this case the

HR ADVICE & APPLICATION

Allergic To Latex

"I have a doctor's note that says I can return to my job, but I have to avoid contact with latex," medical technical Dan Coleman explained.

"I'm truly sorry, but we can't accept this," personnel director Pat Kubricki responded. "All medical technicians have to wear rubber gloves in compliance with safety rules, so there's no way you can come back to work and avoid contact with latex."

Was the employer's action justified?

Facts: An employee whose duties included emergency medical work had been employed more than 10 years without any problems on the job. Due to increasing concerns over bloodborne pathogens such as AIDS, however, new health guidelines required the employee to wear latex gloves on the job whenever there was a chance of contact with bodily fluids. The employee eventually developed an allergy to both the gloves and a powder in the gloves that made them easier to get on and off.

In time, the employee became so highly sensitized that he had an allergic reaction to powder residue on the steering wheel of a vehicle that previously had been operated by another employee wearing the latex gloves. After suffering a series of allergic reactions requiring emergency medical care, a doctor told the employee that in order to be completely risk free, everyone in his workplace would have to stop using the latex gloves.

The employee eventually missed so much work that he used up all his sick leave. When he attempted to return to work, he brought a doctor's note explaining that he must "avoid all contact with latex and latex products." The employer refused to allow his return, saying it would be impossible for the employee to avoid such contact.

The employee objected to the decision, asserting that it amounted to termination. He charged that the employer was obligated to make reasonable accommodations to facilitate his return to work.

Decision: The employer must reinstate the worker and accommodate his disability.

Discussion: The employee's medical records show that he is fully able to perform his job duties as long as he avoids contact with latex gloves and the powder in the gloves, the arbiter notes. Therefore, the arbiter finds, the "entire department would have to be supplied with vinyl or powderfree, hypoallergenic latex gloves" in order for the employee to return to his job.

Supplying different gloves is an "entirely reasonable accommodation" to protect the job of a 10-year employee, the arbiter says. The cost of the accommodation would be "minimal," at about $150 extra per year, he points out. Moreover, medical journals suggest that the prevalence of latex allergies is increasing, and it is likely that other employees would eventually develop allergies to latex as well. Finding the accommodation an appropriate solution to the problem, the arbiter orders the employer to reinstate the employee with back pay and supply new gloves to all employees.

Pointers: Under the *Americans With Disabilities Act,* an employer must make reasonable accommodations for employees with disabilities. However, determining what is "reasonable" is a fact-specific issue that will vary with the employer and individual in question. Under various circumstances, appropriate accommodations might include such things as making existing facilities readily accessible, job restructuring, modifying work schedules, acquiring or modifying equipment or devices, or providing readers or interpreters.

At the same time, an accommodation is not required if it would impose on the employer's business an "undue hardship"—that is, a significant difficulty or expense. Factors that must be considered to ascertain whether an accommodation would impose an undue hardship include:

- The nature and cost of the accommodation
- The size, type, and financial resources of the specific facility where the accommodation would have to be made
- The size, type, and financial resources of the covered employer
- The covered employer's type of operation, including the composition, structure, and functions of its work force, and the geographic separateness and administrative or fiscal relationship between the specific facility and the covered employer.[31]

arbiter, a third party brought in to resolve the dispute, relied upon the ADA and the definition of reasonable accommodation to rule in favor of the worker.

Employee Motivation

Motivation is the process that energizes and directs an individual's behavior toward the fulfillment of the individual's needs and values.

An understanding of employee motivation enables us to see *how* and *why* HR activities such as job design and compensation work. It also enables us to make revisions in HR activities based on the responses and behaviors of employees. **Motivation** is the process that energizes and directs an individual's behavior toward the fulfillment of the individual's needs and values.[32] Individuals are motivated to behave (perform) in particular ways based on their perception of the situation—namely, the intrinsic and extrinsic rewards being offered and the importance of their needs and values that are likely to be fulfilled. This may mean that companies need to determine if there are differences in the needs and values of the workforce and act accordingly. Consider the implications of managing employees of the baby-boom generation versus those from the X-generation, as described in the "HR Advice and Application" feature.

The *quality* and *quantity* of the behavior (performance) depends upon ability and motivation. In other words, individuals perform in ways that will help them satisfy their needs, and they avoid activities that do not satisfy their needs or that

HR ADVICE & APPLICATION

Managing the X Generation

Today's corporation is requiring that the same job performed by two boomers be performed by one Xer. The difference is this: given autonomy in the process, Xers can turn work around faster because they know where the information is and they can find a way to get it.

Throughout this process, though, Xers long for feedback. Their self-esteem training in the third grade and psychological visits in the 10th grade have made them needy for verbal feedback, and they will take it better than most managers are aware.

Autonomy does not mean lack of feedback. Unfortunately, the boomer performance appraisal has actually hindered many employees' growth and development, as evidenced in the recent backlash against formal performance appraisals. Traditional performance appraisals have been compared to a football coach telling a team how well they are performing after the game is already over.

Autonomy also leads to another reward in itself for this generation. It is self-efficacy and the need to do fulfilling work. If they do not like it, they leave. Company loyalty and longevity are not part of this new workforce.

FOCUS ON REWARD

The third step is tying Xer pay into Xer value systems At-risk pay fits well into either an individual- or team-related system. Xers want to be rewarded for their performance with outward, visible rewards. Unlike boomers, Xers need reinforcements with observable results. In an at-risk system, Xers believe they have the potential to earn significantly more or less than their peers based upon the work that they perform. In fact, many surveys and articles report that the top motivator for Xers is free time. Xers will work hard to achieve the time off and the money to use during this time. The important aspect is to tie fair stretch goals into the at-risk and reward positions to pay for that free time.

The efficiencies that Xers achieve to gain more leisure time should not be viewed as "not assigning enough work," but be viewed as efficient working. After all, that is why billions of dollars are spent on technology. However, managers are punishing the effectiveness and efficiencies gained by stacking more work on the Xer, thereby diminishing the desire to improve.[33]

result in punishment. Performance is based on an individual's perception of the situation, as shown in Exhibit 7.5. The individual's perception of the situation includes what is seen as the degree of probability of reaching objectives set by the manager or organization and also the potential for extrinsic and intrinsic rewards.

Extrinsic rewards are rewards given by the organization such as pay, promotion, praise, tenure, and status symbols. When a person acts to receive an extrinsic reward (i.e., money or a better job) or to avoid punishment (i.e., loss of money or criticism), that person is *extrinsically motivated.*

Extrinsic rewards such as pay are given by the organization.

Intrinsic rewards cannot be given by the organization; they originate within the person. Among them are a sense of meaningfulness, a sense of responsibility, and empowerment and satisfaction in knowing the results. The stronger these intrinsic drives are, the more likely job enrichment programs will result in the outcomes shown in Exhibit 7.1. A person who acts for no externally given reward is *intrinsically motivated:* performing the activity well is a reward in itself.

Intrinsic rewards originate within the person.

Extrinsic and intrinsic rewards motivate performance only when the performance appears necessary to obtain them. Organizations can directly control extrinsic rewards such as pay, but their influence on intrinsic rewards is indirect.

Managers cannot change people; they can only change behavior. To do this, they usually must change the work situation—the place and the circumstances of work—so it will allow people to satisfy work-related needs through performance. The balance of our discussion looks at some of the needs people have and examines how work situations can be changed to satisfy these needs. We will look at several different models of motivation.

We will differentiate between content and process models, although basically they differ only in their relative focus, and they overlap considerably. **Content models** focus on the wants and needs that individuals are trying to satisfy (achieve) within the situation. **Process models** focus on how managers can change the situation to better tie need satisfaction to performance. The manager must consider both areas of focus if performance is to be improved.

Content models focus on the wants and needs individuals are trying to satisfy.

Process models focus on how managers can change the situation to better satisfy employee needs.

Content Models of Motivation

LEARNING OBJECTIVE 4

Describe the process and content models of motivation.

Two content models of motivation are discussed in this section. The first, the **need hierarchy model**, describes a hierarchy of needs existing within people. The

EXHIBIT 7.5

The Motivation to Perform

Performance (Effort expended at work) → Depends on employee's perception of: →

1. The probability the performance will meet or exceed manager's objective.
2. The probability that if the objective is met, the manager will give extrinsic rewards.
3. The probability the extrinsic rewards will satisfy some needs.
4. The probability that doing the task will provide intrinsic rewards.
5. The probability the intrinsic rewards will satisfy needs.
6. How much satisfaction of these needs is important or valued.

Need hierarchy model describes a hierarchy of needs existing within people.

Motivation-hygiene model describes factors in the workplace that dissatisfy people and factors that motivate them.

second, the **motivation-hygiene model**, describes factors in the workplace that dissatisfy people and factors that motivate them.

The Need Hierarchy Model. This model, developed by psychologist Abraham Maslow and adapted for use in management by psychologist Douglas McGregor, suggests that:

1. **Adult motives are complex.** No single motive determines behavior; rather, a number of motives operate at the same time.
2. **Needs for a hierarchy.** In general, lower-level needs must be at least partly satisfied before higher-level needs emerge.
3. **A satisfied need is not a motivator.** If a lower-level need is satisfied, a higher-level need emerges. In a sense, humans are always wanting something.
4. **Higher-level needs can be satisfied in many more ways than can lower-level needs.**[34]

Levels of need are identified as physiological, safety (security), social (affiliation), ego (esteem), and self-actualization (or developmental). The sequence and relative importance of these levels are shown in Exhibit 7.6.

The *physiological* level includes the universal needs for food, clothing, and shelter. These needs must be met, at least partly, before higher-level needs emerge. The need for *safety* has been interpreted by recent writers to include more than freedom from physical harm—that is, freedom from job layoffs and loss of income. In most Western countries, basic physiological and safety needs are satisfied for

EXHIBIT 7.6

The Need Hierarchy

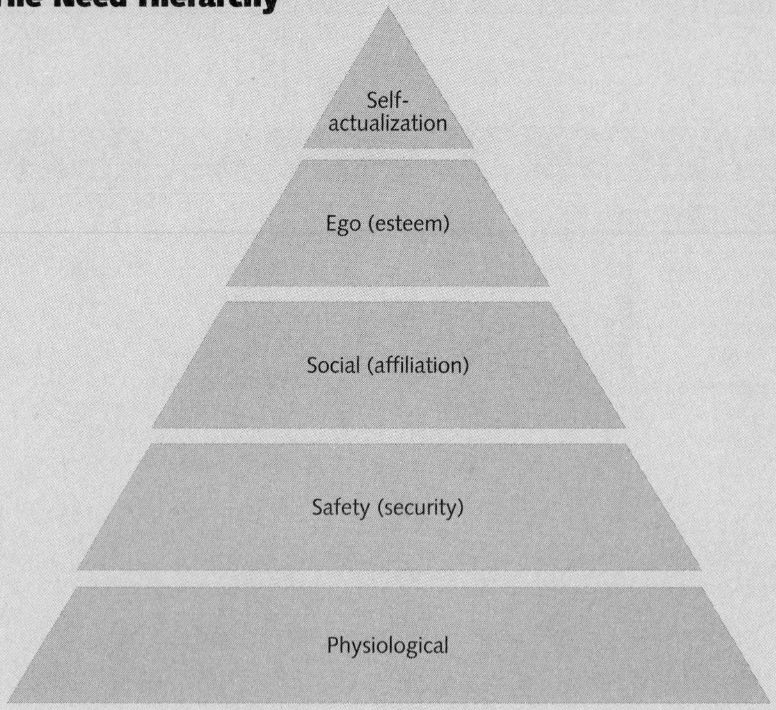

most people. The new emerging definitions of these needs can be seen in the widespread emphasis on job tenure, savings accounts, and various types of insurance.

The *social* level includes the need to belong—to be accepted by others and to give and receive friendship and love. The use of teamwork helps to fulfill social needs.

The *ego* level involves the need to have a firm, stable, and reasonably high evaluation of oneself. This level has both internal and external aspects. The internal aspect is a personal feeling of self-worth, an assurance of one's achievement, knowledge, and competence. The external aspect involves receiving appreciation, recognition, and respect from others. At the *social* level of need, a person wants only to be accepted; at the *ego* level, a person wants to be admired or at least perceived as competent.

At the fifth and highest level, *self-actualization*, individuals are concerned with achieving their full potential through self-development, creativity, and psychological health. The need cannot be completely satisfied by any job. Many people never attempt to satisfy this need, because they remain preoccupied with satisfying the lower-level needs. Maslow estimated some years ago that, in the United States, 85 percent of physiological needs, 70 percent of safety needs, 50 percent of social needs, 40 percent of ego and esteem needs, and only 10 percent of self-actualization needs were being satisfied.[35]

Care should be taken not to overgeneralize from this model.[36] A number of different needs may be in operation at any one time, and not all of them can be satisfied simultaneously. Some aspects of the job may be more satisfying than others, and although some needs are involved only with job behavior or performance, others may be reserved for behavior off the job. For example, as mentioned earlier, it may be impossible for a job to completely satisfy self-actualization or growth needs.

The Motivation–Hygiene Model. About 35 years ago, Frederick Herzberg and his associates asked engineers and accountants what they liked and disliked about their work. After analyzing the data, Herzberg concluded that there were two vital kinds of factors in any job: hygiene and motivation. The motivation-hygiene model is based on the idea that one set of job characteristics determines the degree of worker dissatisfaction (hygiene), and another set determines the degree of positive satisfaction (motivation). In other words, the hygiene factors can be changed to reduce worker dissatisfaction, but these changes are not sufficient to create motivation.

Motivation-hygiene model is based on the ideas of dissatisfaction and satisfaction.

The **hygiene factors** involve the context in which the work is performed. They include company policy and administration; job security; interpersonal relations with supervisors, peers, and subordinates; salary; and working conditions. Herzberg's findings suggested that if these conditions were poor, they could lead to physical or psychological withdrawal from the job. The improvement of conditions is a little like vaccination; it can keep someone from getting sick, but it doesn't make the sick person well—hence the term *hygiene*. The conditions surrounding the job (the hygiene factors) must be adequate before a person is motivated to work, but other factors are necessary to produce that motivation.

Herzberg's hygiene factors:

- **company policy**
- **salary**
- **job security**
- **co-worker relations**
- **working conditions**

The **motivation factors** include a sense of achievement, recognition, advancement, enjoyment of the work itself, the possibility of personal growth, and a sense of responsibility. Increasing job satisfaction and motivation and improving mental health, therefore, tend to increase productivity.

Herzberg's motivation factors:

- **sense of achievement**
- **recognition**
- **advancement**
- **enjoyment of work**
- **personal growth**
- **sense of responsibility**

To summarize Herzberg's findings, what motivates employees toward effective work is a job that is challenging and that encourages feelings of achievement, growth, responsibility, advancement, earned recognition, and enjoyment of the work itself. What dissatisfies them are primarily factors that are not directly part of the job itself, such as poor working conditions, bad lighting, insufficient coffee breaks, lack of opportunity to socialize, unpleasant work rules, unneeded titles, a rigid seniority system, low wages, and a lack of fringe benefits.[37]

The Relationships Between the Content Models. Although the models discussed so for have different sources, they showed marked similarities, as Exhibit 7.7 indicates. The hygiene factors are roughly equivalent to the lower-level hierarchy needs, and the motivational factors are roughly equivalent to the higher-level hierarchy needs.

All the models are slanted toward humanistic concerns; that is, they assume that most people want more self-esteem, which is achieved through greater opportunity for achievement, advancement, and responsibility. This assumption is clearly not true for all people. Thus, the manager using the content approaches should analyze the individuals and the circumstances surrounding the job to determine whether they are satisfactory. If they are, the manager should try to provide opportunities for interesting work, earned recognition, and additional responsibility for those willing to accept it.

Process Models of Motivation

The content models of motivation provide some idea of the needs people try to satisfy. However, they do not show how people attempt to satisfy needs at work or how managers can change the work situation to enable people to satisfy needs through improved job performance. The process models of motivation are more explicit in these areas. We will examine one of them, the expectancy model, in this section. The positive reinforcement model is discussed in Chapter 11, Performance Appraisal and the equity model is discussed in Chapter 13, Compensation.

Expectancy model keys:
- perceptions
- effort-performance relationships
- performance-reward relationships
- performance
- outcomes/preference
- equity
- satisfaction
- choice

The Expectancy Model. The expectancy model of motivation, designed by Victor Vroom, has been the subject of a great deal of research and attention since its development. The **expectancy model** suggests that people are motivated at work to choose among different behaviors or intensities of effort if they believe their efforts will be rewarded and if the rewards they expect to get are important to them. The three primary factors in this model are choice, expectancy, and preference.[38] **Choice** is the freedom to select from among different possibilities or alternatives. People choose from among a wide range of behaviors: they choose to come to work or to call in sick and to work hard on the job or to take it easy. A student may decide to study hard to get a good grade in a particular course (positive outcome) but may have to pass up going to a party (negative outcome). Sometimes the choice is relatively simple, as in these examples. Other times it is more difficult, as in choosing a career.

Choice is the option of selecting events.

EXHIBIT 7.7

A Comparison of the Maslow/McGregor and Herzberg Models

MASLOW/MCGREGOR NEED HIERARCHY	HERZBERG MOTIVATION–HYGIENE MODEL
Physiological needs	Pay; job security; work conditions
Safety needs	Relationships with boss, co-workers
	Company policy; job hazards
Social needs	Recognition from others
Ego needs	Achievement
	Advancement
Self-actualization needs	Growth potential; work itself

Expectancy is the belief, expressed as a subjective estimate or probability (odds), that a particular act will or will not be successful. Individuals who want to attain a particular goal must usually expend some effort to do it. However, people have certain expectations or beliefs about whether their behavior will be successful. If they see the odds as zero, they will not even try.

Expectancy is the estimated probability of an event occurring.

The expectancy model was once explained in the following manner to a group of managers meeting in a conference room A thousand dollars was offered to anyone who could, without special help, kick the ceiling with either foot. When no one even tried, it was pointed out that everyone had subjectively estimated that the odds of kicking the ceiling were zero and, on the basis of this expectancy, had made a choice not to attempt it!

As with positive reinforcement, the standards of an expectancy model should be seen by the employees as challenging but attainable. The probability of accomplishing a task must be low enough that a feeling of achievement can be imparted. **Preferences** involve valuing some rewards more highly than others and avoiding punishment.

Preferences involve the valuing of rewards.

The expectancy model of behavior suggests that people will work (behave) to accomplish goals that satisfy certain needs. The goals may either be ends in themselves or means to an end. For example, an engineer attempting to solve a technical problem worked on Saturdays and Sundays until the problem was solved. Coming to work on the weekend was her *choice*, based on her *preference* for solving the problem rather than enjoying some other activity. Her *expectation* that she would solve the problem was necessary for this choice and preference to operate.

I told them, 'I'll be extremely consistent. I'll treat everybody differently.' I won't treat any one of them the same. The better performer, the harder a guy works, the better I'm going to treat him."

Jimmy Johnson
Coach
Miami Dolphins

The process of choice, expectancy, and preference can be expressed in *five propositions:*

1. Behavior is directed toward satisfying needs by means of achieving certain goals. The goals may be valued for themselves or because they lead to still other goals, such as passing a course to get a diploma to get a better job.
2. The behavior must be seen as a way of making the goal possible, or it will not be chosen. Working on weekends helped the engineer solve a difficult problem. Studying harder usually results in higher grades.
3. In most circumstances, individuals choose among a range of different behaviors to reach certain outcomes. For example, a student who wants high grades can study hard, take easy courses, or join a study group.
4. The more an individual perceives a desired outcome as a direct result of personal behavior, the greater the motivation. For example, if everybody has job security for minimum effort, there is little motivation to work hard for that outcome. However, the motivation to work hard may exist for other outcomes such as a pay increase, promotion, or increased recognition and praise from the boss.
5. Most behaviors have both positive and negative outcomes. Working harder, as in the case of the engineer working weekends, may lead to a quicker solution (positive outcome) but may also lead to fatigue (negative outcome) or loss of social life (negative outcome). However, she clearly felt that the positive outcome was greater than the negative outcomes.

Positive outcomes include:

- **job security**
- **praise**
- **salary**
- **promotion**
- **fairness**
- **freedom**
- **respect**
- **job variety**
- **challenge**
- **participation**

The expectancy model can be summarized as follows: performance at work is a function of the expectation that a desired outcome will be achieved and of a preference for that particular outcome over other desired outcomes. The outcome toward which the performance is directed is also a function of an expectation that it can indeed be achieved.

People are constantly making choices based on the subjective probability that what they do will have a payoff. The situation illustrated in Exhibit 7.8 is that of a married man with two young children who recently graduated from law school.

EXHIBIT 7.8

An Expectancy Model of Motivation

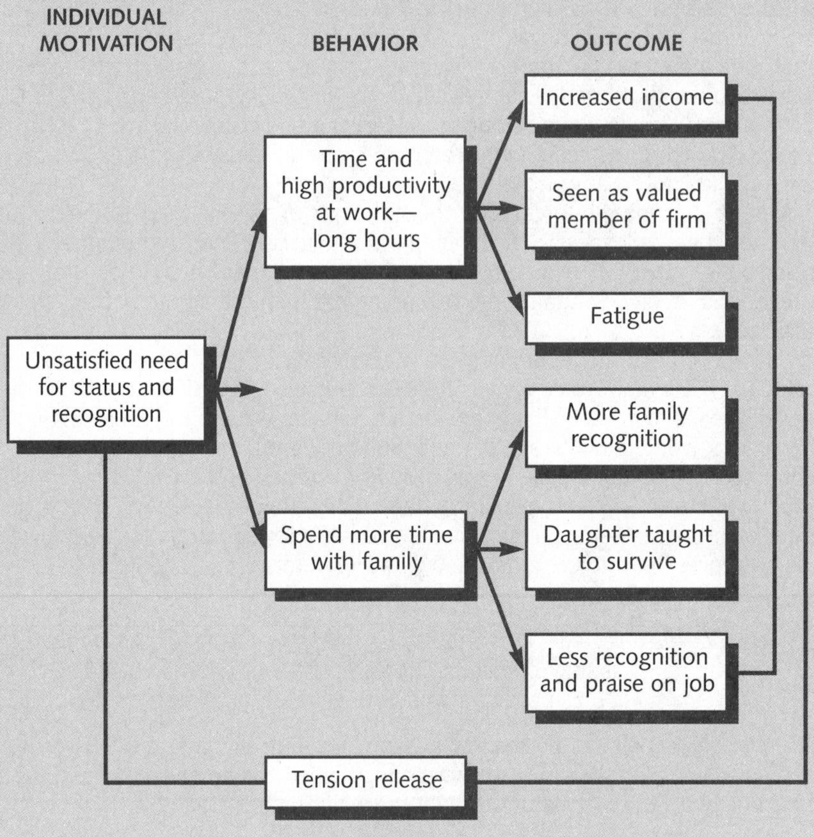

"Success isn't something you chase," says the Chicago Bulls' Michael Jordan. "It's something you have to put forth the effort for constantly."

He has an unsatisfied need for status. This need can be satisfied by obtaining the high regard of those with whom he works in the prestigious law firm or by being seen as an attentive, caring husband and father. He can choose to work harder at the law firm, which may result in the desired outcome of increased status but also may bring negative outcomes of fatigue and emotionally impoverished family life. Or he can choose to spend fewer hours at work and devote more time to his family, which may gain him increased appreciation from family and friends but cause him to lose prestige at work.

Consciously or subconsciously, he will probably subjectively work out answers to a series of expectancy questions before making a choice. What is the probability (expectancy) that harder work will lead to greater status on the job? What is the probability (expectancy) of receiving more recognition from the family by spending more time with them? By teaching his daughter to swim? Although he may not be aware of calculating the relative values of these choices, the calculations nevertheless occur.

In making choices, people constantly ask themselves, "What is the payoff for me?" Exhibit 7.8 is, of course, oversimplified. Our complexity as human beings ensures that a number of needs are usually in operation at the same time. This model effectively shows, however, that we will consider our needs in light of the best known subjective probabilities and that we choose particular behaviors to bring about outcomes to satisfy our needs. Our behavior choices depend on what we perceive to be the greatest reward. Obviously, this perception varies from individual to individual. Some of us occasionally skip an 8:00 or 9:00 A.M. class in order to sleep longer; others of us never do.

The expectancy model forces the manager to focus on a fundamental problem. If workers are to be motivated to perform satisfactorily on the job, they must see a clear-cut payoff. If they do not, it is the manager's responsibility to change the work situation in one of two ways: provide a payoff if none exists or clarify the path to an existing payoff.

This model motivation has significantly influenced the thinking of many managers. Effective managers apply and adapt what is most useful in the model to particular situations with particular employees. In so doing, they serve both the needs of the individuals and the needs of the organization by making individuals more productive, involved, and committed employees. Managers also accomplish these objectives when they consider alternative arrangements for employee accommodation.

Alternative Arrangements for Employee Accommodation

LEARNING OBJECTIVE 5

Describe the alternative arrangements for employee accommodation.

The growing number of single-parent families, the high costs of commuting, the desire for larger blocks of personal time, and the desire of older workers to reduce their hours, all suggest that alternative work arrangements can reduce the stresses caused by the conflicts of juggling job demands, family needs, leisure values, and educational needs. Thus organizations can expect to reduce absenteeism and turnover by offering alternatives to their standard work arrangements. Firms can also increase their attractiveness to a more diverse pool of applicants when they are willing to accommodate individuals. As firms seek to comply with the ADA, they may design jobs to accommodate differently abled people. They can also offer more flexibility in time schedules and job sharing as well as telecommuting arrangements.

Did You KNOW?

Shift workers suffer from:

- **chronic fatigue**
- **higher divorce rates**
- **stomach problems**
- **serious illness**
- **less job satisfaction**
- **impaired social life**

Standard Work Schedules

In the 1860s, the average workweek was 72 hours—12 hours a day, six days a week. It was 58 hours in 1900 and remains approximately 40 hours a week today. Standard work schedules include day, evening, and night sessions as well as overtime, part-time, and shift work over a 40-hour week. A shift worker might report from 7:00 A.M. to 4:00 P.M. one week and from 4:00 PM. to midnight the next. Since the end of World War I, shift work has become more prevalent in industrialized countries. Currently, about 20 percent of all industrial workers in Europe and the United States are on shift work schedules. The percentage of employees on part-time schedules has also increased steadily—from approximately 15 percent in 1954 to more than 25 percent today.

These standard work schedules all have advantages and disadvantages. Initially, employees may select a given schedule, but after that, the days of the week (five) and the hours of the day (eight) are generally fixed. Because employee preferences and interests change over time, what once was an appropriate work schedule may no longer be so. If alternative arrangements are not provided, the employee may leave the organization. Furthermore, the organization may have a difficult time attracting similar types of employees. As a result, it pays to give employees a choice between a nonstandard and standard schedule, as well as a choice of hours, days, and total number of hours to work per week.

Did You KNOW?

Less than half the workforce in the industrial world will be holding conventional full-time jobs in organizations by the beginning of the 21st century. Those full-timers or insiders will be the new minority.

Flextime Schedules

Flextime, a nonstandard work schedule, is popular with organizations because it decreases absenteeism, increases employee morale, induces better labor-management relations, and encourages a high level of employee participation in decision-

Flextime is a nonstandard work schedule giving individuals choices in their working hours.

Band width is the maximum length of the workday—the range of hours during which workers must arrange their schedule.

Core time is the period of time when everyone needs to be at work.

making, control over the job, and discretion. Simply stated, flextime is a schedule that gives employees daily choice in the timing of work and nonwork activities. Consideration is given to **band width**, or maximum length of the workday. This band (often ranging between 10 and 16 hours) is divided into core time and flexible time. **Core time** is the period the employee has to work; flexible time allows the employee to choose the remaining work time. Exhibit 7.9 shows how a 12-hour band width can be divided into blocks of flexible and core times.

Among the advantages of flextime is its ability to increase overall employee productivity. It also enables organizations to accommodate employee preferences, some of which may be legally protected, such as reasonable religious obligations. On the other hand, flextime forces the supervisor to do more planning, sometimes makes communications difficult between employees (especially those with different schedules), and complicates record-keeping. Furthermore, most flextime schedules still require employees to work five days a week.

EXHIBIT 7.9

An Example of Flextime Scheduling

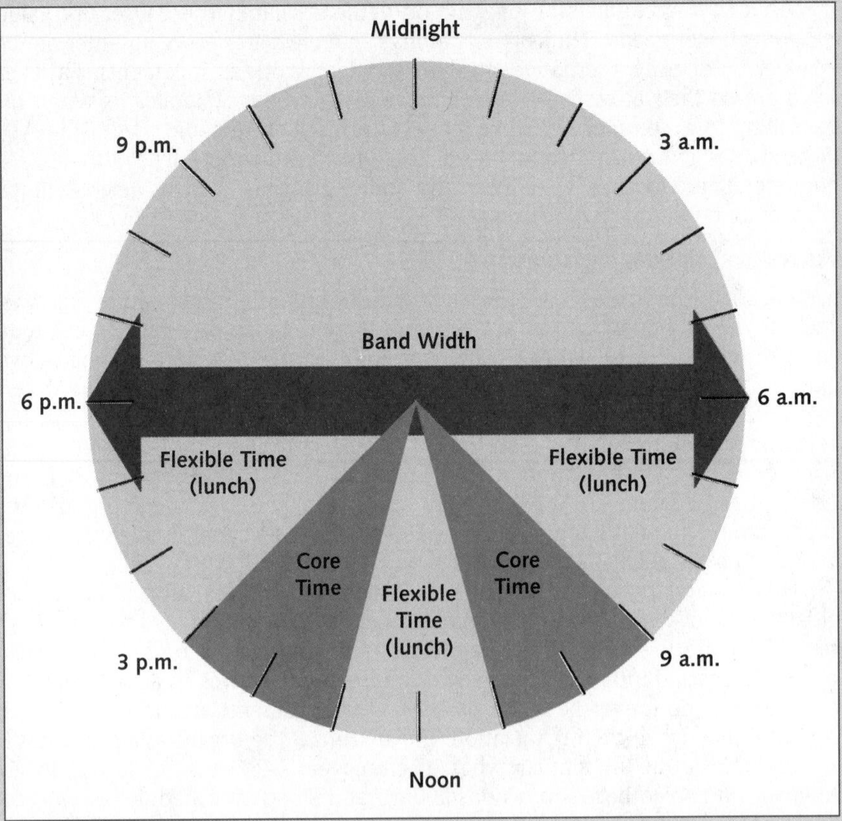

Adapted from A. Cohen and H. Gadon, *Alternative Work Schedules: Integrating Individual and Organizational Needs* © 1978, Addison-Wesley Publishing Company, Inc., Reading, Mass. p. 35 (adapted figure). Reprinted with permission.

Compressed Workweeks

An option for employees who want to work fewer than five days is the **compressed workweek.** By extending the workday beyond the standard eight hours, employees generally need to work only three to four days to equal a standard 40-hour week. For example, at two General Tire and Rubber plants, some employees work only two 12-hour shifts each weekend and yet are considered full-time employees. Compressed workweeks are becoming especially popular for certain occupations such as nursing.

Compressed workweeks are schedules where more time is worked in a shorter time period.

Compressed workweeks permit an organization to make better use of its equipment and to decrease turnover and absenteeism. Scheduling and legal problems may accompany such arrangements, but legal exceptions can be made, and scheduling can become a joint negotiation process between supervisors and employees.

Permanent Part-Time and Job Sharing

Traditionally, part-time work has meant filling positions that lasted only for a short time such as those in retail stores during holiday periods. Now some organizations have designated **permanent part-time** positions. A permanent part-time work schedule may be a shortened daily schedule (for example, from 1:00 to 5:00 PM.) or an odd-hour shift (for example from 5:00 to 9:00 PM.). Organizations can also use part-time schedules to fill in the remainder of a day composed of two 10-hour shifts (representing a compressed workweek).[39]

Permanent part-time is the regular assignment of less than a full week of work.

Job sharing is a special part-time arrangement where two people share one job.

Job sharing is a particular type of part-time work. In job sharing, two people divide the responsibility for a regular full-time job. Both may work half the job, or one person may work more hours than the other. Part-time workers generally receive little or no indirect compensation, but workers on permanent part-time and job-sharing schedules often do. The benefits of these workers are not equal to those of full-time workers but are prorated according to the amount of time they work.

Both permanent part-time and job sharing provide the organization and the individual with opportunities that might not otherwise be available. They offer staffing flexibility that can expand or contract to meet actual demands, using employees who are at least as productive, if not more so, than regular full-time employees. Individuals benefit from being able to enjoy permanent work with less than a full-time commitment to the company.

Combining ergonomic principles with job sharing and team member involvement can enable firms to even accommodate people with life-threatening illnesses such as AIDS. An example of just how this is being done is described in the feature, "Managing Human Resources at Levi Strauss & Co: When AIDS Hits Home."

Contingent Work Arrangements

With the desire for flexibility and the desire to control fixed compensation costs, firms are offering contingent work arrangements. While these can include the traditional part-time work, they often go beyond this. This might include people who work on a temporary assignment—say three to six months. These people may be hired directly by the company or hired through a "temp agency" such as Manpower. Consultants may be hired for special projects. In addition, former employees may serve as a means to outsource work. While generally regarded as a trend to reduce labor costs, outsourcing can also permit a company to have an even staffing level since it only transfers extra work outside the company. If the extra work becomes more predictable, the company may choose to hire workers from its contingent workforce.

Did You KNOW?

The United States' contingent workforce—consisting of roughly 45,000,000 temporaries, self-employed, part-timers, or consultants—has grown 57% since 1980.

Industrial and Electronic Cottages

To provide individuals with even more choices in how to arrange their work and work schedules, some companies are allowing employees to work at home.

MANAGING HUMAN RESOURCES

at Levi Strauss & Co.

When AIDS Hits Home

The Americans with Disabilities Act may he just an abstract concept for companies and employees that have not yet dealt with a seriously ill employee. When a co-worker contracts a life-threatening disease, however, the business and human ramifications hit home.

San Francisco-based Levi Strauss supports employees and work groups that grapple with these situations. Here's how one person's battle with AIDS was handled at the company.

The employee, whom we will call Bill, worked in a nine-person work group and didn't reveal his AIDS diagnosis until his first hospitalization, according to Yvonne Ellison-Sandler, corporate manager for health promotion.

His first step was to inform his manager, and the two decided how to approach the work group with the news. With Bill's consent, the manager explained Bill's condition to his co-workers.

The company had conducted mandatory AIDS education classes several years earlier, so employees possessed some knowledge about HIV, AIDS, and transmission of the virus in the workplace. After Bill's diagnosis, the training was given again. "For most of these people, this was their second hit," Ellison-Sandler says. This time, of course, there was a difference. Now that a co-worker was ill, this was a real-life situation.

During the session, workers shared their reactions to the news, which ranged from sadness to shock to worry. "One of the women in the group was pregnant, and she was worried about her baby," Ellison-Sander says. "There was another person who was very, very angry and felt that he was entitled to know as soon as [Bill had become) HIV-positive. They had drunk off the same glass during the Christmas party." The facilitator maintained the ground rule that no one's reaction be censured or criticized, and the session proved cathartic to most of the group members.

The work-group members met eight times to discuss their reactions to Bill's diagnosis. The man who had become angry in the first session continued to be irate and was finally referred for individual counseling and HIV testing, although he continued to meet with the work group.

Once the group accepted Bill's diagnosis, the members began to attack the problem of how to distribute his work load as his disease progressed. "They had a commitment to Bill, because, I think, they were touched that he would share with them what was going on," says Ellison-Sandler. So when Bill was released from the hospital to continue recovering at home, his co-workers instituted a system for getting the work done, volunteering for extra jobs instead of waiting for them to be assigned.

The work group also came up with a way to communicate with Bill that would minimize the number of telephone calls he would have to answer. Each week, a designated caller would report to the group on the state of Bill's health.

When Bill was able to return to work, the work load had to be redistributed again. The health-promotion department was asked back to help the work group deal with issues such as what co-workers should say to him. Bill told Ellison-Sandler that he encouraged all questions, and he wanted his colleagues to talk to him and not be afraid.

After only three weeks back on the job, Bill became too sick to come into the office, which meant more work shifting. He decided to work from his home, and group members came up with a plan that allowed him to do so. "They worked with him all the way until the day that he died, and they went to the funeral together as a department," says Ellison-Sandler. "It was such an incredible process to observe, and it spoke to the power of dealing with this stuff up front."[40]

Work-at-home arrangements can be made for those with a full-time commitment to the company and for those wanting only part-time employment. Increasingly, individuals are working at home by means of computer terminals linked to the computers at their regular office or plant. In essence, the employee's home then becomes an **electronic cottage**. Individuals can also take home work that involves assembly, such as small toys. After a batch is done, the worker takes it to the regular plant and turns it in for more parts. In this example, the home becomes an **industrial cottage**.[41]

Electronic and industrial cottages are work-at-home arrangements.

The use of industrial and electronic cottages is increasing. These arrangements offer workers yet another choice. One drawback, though, is the difficulty of protecting the health and safety of the employee at home. Another is ensuring that workers are still paid a fair wage for their work. State and federal laws can also restrict home work. One federal law, for example, prohibits commercial knitting at home. The restrictions must be dealt with carefully if expanding cottages are to remain a viable option.

Telecommuting

An extension of the industrial and electronic cottage is **telecommuting**. It allows the employee to interact with the office while working at home or while traveling. You see many people with portable cellular telephones on the street or in their cars conducting business. This is also a form of telecommuting. Cellular or mobile phones, fax machines, and personal computers are making it possible for people to work almost anytime and anywhere. While it may be difficult for a company to monitor the performance of people who telecommute, it is becoming an important way companies can accommodate employees.[42]

Telecommuting is commuting to work by electronic means rather than car, train, or bus.

Because individuals can literally carry around all the things they need to do their work, companies are actually encouraging the development and use of these **virtual offices**.[43] They can reduce the time employees spend commuting, accommodate to the needs of valued employees, and even reduce pollution by eliminating the need for employees to drive to work.

Did You KNOW?

The number of telecommuters in 1995: 10 million. The expected number of telecommuters in 2000: 25 million.

Trends in Job Design

Events of importance for job design occurring today are 1) reengineering and 2) openness and variety.

Reengineering

The need for flexibility and adaptability is associated with reengineering efforts. According to the leading experts in the field, Michael Hammer and James Champy,

> ***Reengineering*** *involves "radical redesign" of existing structures and procedures, not just "fiddling" with what is already in place. Thus, reengineering is not for organizations looking for small, incremental improvements . . . the authors say, but for organizations requiring "dramatic" increases in their performance.*[44]

Reengineering means radical redesign of existing structures and procedures.

Of course, a frequent consequence of reengineering is the need to alter the jobs: not only the content of jobs but also their shape. As a result, employees are typically confronted with the need to adapt to new conditions. Because reengineering efforts can result in such substantial reconfigurations, it is important that they be done right, beginning with systematically collected data. The feature, "HR Application and Advice: Reengineering For Results," describes how IBM and Ford used data to move ahead with reengineering. It also describes some immediate results: the creation of generalists from specialists at IBM and the reduction of employees from 500 to 125 in the accounts payable department. In both cases the need to reengineer comes in part from the desire to serve the customer better, whether the customer is inside or outside. So just as customer needs and desires change, expect the design of jobs to change.

We've changed the job so a waitress can do the job she's supposed to do, provide service to the customer.

Chris Kerbow
Marriott Hotels

HR ADVICE & APPLICATION

Reengineering For Results

REENGINEERING AT IBM

IBM Credit Corp., a subsidiary of IBM that finances the company's computers and services, significantly improved its performance through reengineering, Hammer and Champy say. The company used to handle its credit process through a lengthy, multi-step process that began with a telephone call from a sales representative. When the call was received, information would be written down by one employee, the customer's credit would be checked by another, and their standard contract might be modified by a third person. A fourth person would determine the appropriate interest rate, and a fifth person would create a contract to be delivered to the sales rep. The process took from six days to two weeks.

In examining this routine, IBM executives found that it took only 90 minutes of actual work to process an application, and the remaining time was taken up by moving forms from one department to the next. As part of their reengineering effort, IBM replaced four of the specialist positions with one generalist position to handle the entire process from start to finish. The executives challenged the assumption that each credit application was unique and difficult to process, finding instead that most applications could be handled by one person with access to the appropriate data.

REDESIGN AT FORD

In another reengineering success story, Hammer and Champy describe how Ford Motor Co. was able to reduce dramatically the size of its accounts payable department. The process that Ford reengineered was not "accounts payable," but "procurement," the authors note. Before reengineering, the purchasing department would send a purchase order to a vendor and send a copy of the order to accounts payable. When the vendor delivered the goods, a receiving clerk would fill out another form and send it to accounts payable. Meanwhile, the vendor would send an invoice to accounts payable. When all three documents arrived, an accounting clerk would issue a check. The accounts payable department had 500 employees.

Now, Ford has 125 employees in the accounts payable department. Under the new process, the purchasing department sends a purchase order to a vendor and enters the information into an online data base. When the vendor delivers the goods, the receiving clerk checks the information in the data base against the shipment. If the two match, the clerk accepts the order and enters the information into the computer, which automatically issues a check to the vendor. Executives at Ford challenged the assumption that payment should be made when the company received an invoice, and instead decided to pay when the company received the goods.[45]

Openness and Variety

As companies are restructuring and downsizing, they are changing the workplace, the context of job design:

> *Many employers that undergo restructuring do more than reorganize the work: they also reorganize the workplace into more open and shared configurations to reflect the dynamic changes in their organizational thinking.*
>
> *Some firms are doing away with office space altogether, opting instead for the "open office," which allows no personal space at all. This type of work space configuration relies heavily on technical support—cellular phones, pagers, and laptop computers—which in turn results in employees becoming much more accessible.*[46]

This openness and accessibility, however, may not come without costs. Employees may lose their privacy, and they may lose their ability to focus on their jobs. Such openness raises additional questions, such as:

- How will employees get together to brainstorm in their new work spaces?
- How will noise levels in open work spaces affect concentration and productivity?
- If a previously excellent employee cannot adapt to the new open configuration and is subsequently fired, can he or she then claim wrongful termination, charging a hostile work environment?
- How will employees react over the long-term to the loss of their clearly defined and identifiable personal office space?[47]

At Alcoa in Pittsburgh, everyone, secretary and CEO alike, works in cubicles without permanent doors or walls.

While answers to these questions are largely unknown, companies need to consider them. Working in partnership on job design and spatial design issues will be an effective way to start answering such questions.

In addition to this openness there is variety. In any single work location there may be full-time, part-time, and temporary employees. In addition, some or all of these may be working outside the main work location, perhaps at home, on-the-road, or in the office of a customer or supplier. Added to this is the uncertainty of not knowing if one's employment will change from one day to the next: "Whether you're downsized or outsourced, whether you're fired or continue to work, it'll be under a completely different relationship—the idea of large numbers of white-collar people working in one corporation, moving up and getting a pension is a phenomenon of the 1950s that is drawing to an end."[48]

Individuals desire certainty regarding:
- **What's expected**
- **Employment security**
- **What's rewarded**
- **Being treated fairly**
- **How to do things**

While this new reality provides variety and accommodation to some individuals, it has a tendency to change the work site for others:

> *What's happening now is that people are feeling their way toward a new workplace and a new definition of what the corporation is.*
>
> *The transient nature of work in the new office environment has disrupted the way people make and keep friends. On the other hand, if people no longer envision working together for decades, they do not have the same incentives for cutthroat office politics, since a once-coveted job like a manager's is probably the most tentative now.*
>
> *Where people used to be loyal to a company, now they're loyal to a profession.*
>
> *It's not really a question of coming up through the ranks anymore . . . . In a flattened organization, you jump.*[49]

Thus the variety and uncertainty of the new business realities are making profound changes in the work place.

International Comparisons

In Germany, workers perform in "work islands" where they avoid boredom by rotating jobs, socializing, and working in cycles of up to 20 minutes rather than a few seconds. In assembling electronics products, automobiles, and appliances, the Germans appear to be well ahead of other countries in modifying or reducing the conventional assembly line and its simple, repetitive jobs. This enlightened position in alternative job design is a product of the work humanization movement in Germany, initially funded by the German government in 1974 and maintained by the cooperative relationship between labor and management. Many companies also furnish their own funds for work design innovation projects.

Although each company's project may result in different types of job design, emphasis is commonly placed on enlarging assembly jobs by adding more complex tasks. One goal is to ensure that the job cycle is more than 1.5 minutes, the point below which employees have been found to become dissatisfied with the job. As a consequence of the experiments in various companies, three major ways are being used to modify the traditional assembly line and its jobs. In group assembly, workers rotate jobs as they follow the product from the first to the last step in the assembly process. This is the notion of the work island, where workers have the opportunity to socialize and are tied together by a group incentive pay plan. With individual work stations, work is done by the individual in a cycle time of 10 to 15 minutes. During this time, the worker assembles a major subcomponent of the total product (for example, an electric motor for a washing machine). Finally, assembly lines are being modified to make work easier and lighter. Where the assembly line cannot be easily replaced, as in automotive assembly, the line has been altered so that the worker stands on platforms moving at the same speed as the car.

Summary

The worker-job relationship can be effectively managed with a thorough knowledge of job design. Increasingly, job design is seen as a way to accommodate a diverse work force. This ranges from individuals with preferences for more repetitive tasks to individuals with disabilities that require physical accommodation to perform their jobs.

Legal considerations in job design can heavily influence the nature of job activities and the context in which jobs take place. They also influence the process used to design (and redesign) jobs. In both cases, job design is an important technique companies can use to accommodate the needs of workers. By accommodating workers' needs, more jobs can be made available to more types of people; this can in turn be quite motivational to groups formerly excluded. Such a situation is obviously one in which the individual, the company, and society all win. Besides reasonable accommodation, companies are also offering various forms of alternative work schedules; these also have legal considerations. Further accommodations to the diversity of the workforce are provisions for alternative work arrangements such as telecommuting.

All of these forms of job design and alternative work arrangements enable organizations to more effectively match individuals needs with job demands and conditions. Because predicting exactly who will need or prefer which type of job design and accommodation is critical, HR managers and line managers need to encourage employee input as they diagnose the job situation. One result may be a combination of job designs and alternative work arrangements. The manager is aided in this process by an understanding of employee motivation. While only the basic concepts of motivation are presented in this chapter, you should now have a better framework for understanding why employees do what they do in organizations.

Key Concepts

band width
choice
compressed workweek
core time
content models
electronic cottage
ergonomics
expectancy model
extrinsic rewards
flextime
horizontal loading
human factors
hygiene factors
individual contemporary design approach
industrial cottage
intrinsic rewards
job design

job enlargement
job enrichment
job rotation
job sharing
motivation
motivation factors
motivation-hygiene model
need hierarchy model
permanent part-time
preferences
process models
reasonable accommodation
reengineering
scientific approach
self-managed teams
teamwork
telecommuting
vertical loading
virtual office

Review and Discussion Questions

1. Why does Lincoln Electric have so much success with its operations?
2. How do job enrichment programs differ from job enlargement programs?
3. What are important factors influencing the choice of job design approaches?
4. How can approaches to job design be used to accommodate employees?
5. Describe how the core job characteristics model influences the psychological states of employees.
6. What are process and content models of motivation?
7. Why is it useful to know about various models of motivation?
8. How can alternative work arrangements accommodate employees?
9. How can organizations manage workers who are telecommuters?
10. What impact do telecommuters have on companies' attempts to have teamwork?

Review Questions for the Americans With Disabilities Act of 1990 (ADA)

Questions and Answers for Employers

Q. What does Title I of the *Americans With Disabilities Act* (ADA) do?

A. Title I of the ADA prohibits employers from discriminating against a qualified employee or job applicant with a disability.

Q. Which employers are affected by the ADA, and when does the law take effect?

A. All employers with 15 or more employees are affected; these include private employers, state and local governments, employment agencies, and labor unions. For employers with 25 or more employees, the law took effect on July 26, 1992. For employers with 15–24 employees, the law took effect July 26, 1994.

Q. What employment practices and activities are covered by Title I of the ADA?

A. The ADA prohibits discrimination in all employment practices, including job application procedures, hiring, firing, advancement, compensation, training, and other terms, conditions, and privileges of employment. It applies to recruitment, advertising, tenure, layoff, leave, fringe benefits, and all other employment-related activities.

Q. Who is protected against employment discrimination?

A. Employment discrimination is prohibited against "qualified individuals with disabilities." Persons discriminated against because they have a known association or relationship with a disabled individual are also protected—for example, the wife of a man who is paraplegic would be protected, as would the son of a person with muscular dystrophy or the friend of a person with AIDS.

Q. Who is a person with a disability?

A. A person with a disability is a person who:

1. Has a physical or mental impairment that substantially limits that person in one or more major life activities—for example, caring for oneself, performing manual tasks, walking, seeing, hearing, speaking, breathing, learning, and working;
2. Has a record of such impairment—for example, a person who has recovered from cancer or a recovering alcoholic; or
3. Is *regarded* as having an impairment—for example, a person who is severely scarred, disfigured, or even obese, but who is not actually disabled.

Q. Who is a "qualified" person with a disability?

A. A qualified person with a disability is a person who meets the skill, experience, education, and other job-related requirements for the job and who, with or without "reasonable accommodation," can perform the "essential functions" of the job.

Q. What are a job's "essential functions"?

A. A job's "essential functions" are job functions that are basic, necessary, or vital.

Q. What is a "reasonable accommodation"?

A. A "reasonable accommodation" is any modification or adjustment that allows qualified applicants or employees with disabilities to participate in the application process or to do the job's essential functions. Reasonable accommodation also includes adjustments to assure that a qualified individual with a disability has the same job rights and privileges as nondisabled employees.

Q. What kinds of actions should an employer take to reasonably accommodate applicants and employees?

A. The actions that an employer should take to reasonably accommodate applicants and employees include:

1. Analyzing and describing the job's essential functions.
2. Talking with the person with a disability to discuss what adjustments need to be made to accommodate the employee. Accommodations may include: making existing facilities readily accessible to, and usable by, persons with disabilities; job restructuring; work schedule restructuring; reassignment; acquisition of equipment or devices; providing readers or interpreters; and appropriate modifications of training materials, policies, and examinations.

Q. Are there limits to an employer's obligation to make "reasonable accommodation"?

A. Yes. The person with a disability requiring the accommodation must be otherwise qualified for the job; an employer does not have to hire a person who poses a direct threat to the health and safety of himself or of others; and it is the responsibility of the individual to make his or her disability known to the employer.

Q. Must an employer modify existing facilities to make them accessible?

A. Depending on the nature of the needed modification and the employer's circumstances, an employer may be required to modify facilities to enable an individual to perform essential job functions and to have an equal opportunity to participate in other job-related activities.

Q. Is an employer required to provide a "reasonable accommodation" if it is an undue hardship on the employer?

A. No.

Q. What is an "undue hardship"?

A. An "undue hardship" requires significant difficulty or expense in relation to the size and nature of the business and the type and cost of the accommodation. The employer must prove undue hardship. What may be an undue hardship for one employer may not be an undue hardship for another. Undue hardship will be determined on a case-by-case basis.

Q. May an employer ask if a prospective employee is disabled?

A. An employer may not make a pre-employment inquiry on an application form or in an interview as to whether, or to what extent, an individual is disabled. The employer may ask a job applicant whether he or she can perform the essential functions of the job.

Q. Can employers require pre-employment medical examinations of persons with disabilities?

A. No. An employer cannot require a pre-employment medical examination, but post-job-offer medical examinations are allowed under specific circumstances. A job offer may be conditioned on the results of a job-performance-related medical exam only if it is required of every new employee in the same job category. Medical information obtained from medical exams must be handled according to the ADA's confidentiality requirements.

Q. Are current users of illegal drugs, whether applicants or employees, protected by the ADA?

A. No. However, persons participating in supervised rehabilitation programs (and who are no longer engaging in illegal drug use) are protected.

Source: *Americans with Disabilities Act (ADA) Title 1, Employment* (Washington, D.C.: AARO, 1992). Used by permission.

Review Questions

Please mark which condition(s), under the *Americans with Disabilities Act* is (are) not considered a disability:

___ Severe vision problem
___ Wheelchair confinement
___ Severe hearing problem
___ Mental illness
___ Alcoholism
___ Drug usage
___ Cancer
___ AIDS
___ Diabetes

Answer: All of the above except drug (i.e., illegal) usage.

PROJECTS, EXERCISES & CASES

End-of-Text Projects

Lincoln Electric

1. Describe the following for the Lincoln Electric Company:

   a. The objectives of its job design activities

   b. The degree to which these objectives are serving its business and HR objectives

c. Its job design activities

d. the degree to which these activities are serving its objectives

2. How can the job design activities be improved?

Nordstrom

1. Describe the following for Nordstrom:

a. The objectives of its job design activities

b. The degree to which these objectives are serving its business and HR objectives

c. Its job design activities

d. The degree to which these activities are serving its objectives

2. How can the job design activities be improved?

Field Project

1. Interview one of the overnight delivery carriers (you might have to interview them as they are walking!) and ask them to describe the nature or characteristics of their jobs (number of skills used, degree of freedom, and so forth). Report your findings to the class in terms of the core job characteristics model.

2. Interview several office employees from large and small companies. Ask them their opinion of flexible hours and telecommuting—how does it effect their motivation and productivity? Is there a difference in the perception of the employees of different size companies?

Career Management Exercise

In Chapter 6, you indicated the type of job you want and organization you would like to work for after graduation. Now indicate the amount of the five job core dimensions (low, medium, high) you would like to have on your job:

	Low	Medium	High
Skill variety	______	______	______
Significance	______	______	______
Task identity	______	______	______
Task autonomy	______	______	______
Task feedback	______	______	______

In addition to these job dimensions, are there any other workplace accommodations you would request?

____

____

____

____

____

What are your preferred hours of work (and/or how many days and hours per week/year are you willing to work)?

Preferred weekly schedule: ______________________________

Number of days per week: ______________________________

Weeks per year: ______________________________

We will return to your job requirements again in Chapter 8, Selection and Placement.

Case: Data Entry Operations

Job Objective For Data Entry Employees

To get information from printed or written media entered into computer data files.

Current Situation

There are 15 employees in this unit reporting to one supervisor. They handle a wide variety of data entry work, which is supplied by various departments and groups. Some jobs are small, while others can involve entering up to 100,000 bits of information. Some work comes with a due date, and the remainder has been pre-scheduled on a routine basis.

The work is supplied to the Data Entry employees by an assignment clerk. He attempts to see that each employee gets exactly one-fifteenth of the work. The assignment clerk looks at the work before he assigns it to the data entry employee and makes sure that it is legible. If it is not, he gives it to the supervisor, who returns it to the originating department. Usually, the Data Entry unit has been able to enter about 65,000 data points per employee per day. Because of the exactness of the work and the cost of data entry, the work is sent to verifiers to review, to keep errors to a minimum. However, some errors are not discovered until after the finished job is returned to the client. Turnover is high, and many due dates are not met.

Case Assignment

Listed below are some proposals that might result in improving work performance. Read through the list. Decide which things you would or would not do, and put an X in the appropriate column. Next, rank the items with an X in the Would column, using 1,2,3, etc. The ranking should be in the order of the actions you would take.

		WOULD	WOULD NOT	RANK ORDER
1.	Make sure the forms from which the Data Entry employees get their information are arranged in the best way.	______	______	______
2.	Let some Data Entry employees decide whether their work should be verified.	______	______	______
3.	Tell the Data Entry employees to do the work that has specific due dates first.	______	______	______
4.	Train the assignment clerk so he can help with data entry when the work load is heavy.	______	______	______
5.	Split the group so that fewer Data Entry employees report to a supervisor.	______	______	______
6.	Have the Data Entry employees inspect the media they receive for legibility.	______	______	______
7.	When errors are discovered, feed back the details to the Data Entry employee who made the error.	______	______	______
8.	Have the Data Entry employees verify their own work.	______	______	______
9.	Assign responsibility for entering all of a particular job to an individual.	______	______	______
10.	Arrange for departmental client contacts for certain employees.	______	______	______
11.	Let some Data Entry employees schedule their own day.	______	______	______
12.	Make sure that jobs for a particular group or account always go to the same employee.	______	______	______

VISIT THE LIBRARY

Workforce Oline

Because you are now familiar with getting onto the Internet and the use of HR Headquarters, the following steps are abbreviated.

1. Enter your Web browser.
2. Enter Workforce Online.
3. Review the following article within "Winning Ideas": *Sleep Inn Wakes Up to New Labor*
4. Enter the Research Center.
5. Review the following article under the subheading "Human Resources Management":

Job Sharing: One Job, Double Headache?

Diversity Ignites Effective Work Teams

Employee Team Designs Flexible Benefits Program

Self-directed Work Teams Untax the IRS

Teams Facilitate Change at Turbulent Plant

6. Return to your homepage.

Case: Job Redesign at Aid Association for Lutherans (AAL)

Jerome (Jerry) H. Laubenstein, new vice-president of the insurance department at AAL, is wondering what the best way is to improve the work conditions and performance of his 500 employees. Currently, his employees are divided into three major groups: clerks (the majority), technicians, and managers.

AAL is a nonprofit fraternal society (Mutual benefit association) with 1.5 million members (customers) throughout the United States. AAL has over $6 billion in assets, putting it in the top two percent of life insurers. In the early 1980s, AAL grew dramatically, nearly doubling in size to approximately 2,000 employees. Unfortunately, productivity did not increase at the same rate. It was this latter point that drew the attention of Richard L. Gunderson, the new president and CEO as of 1985. Knowing that AAL, though nonprofit, must still compete with other insurers, Gunderson has established the goals of cutting costs by $50 million over five years and reducing the number of jobs by 250. At the same time, he remains committed to the society's policy of no layoffs or terminations. Thus, workforce reductions will occur only through attrition.

While Gunderson's main concern is productivity, he knows that customer service is an important objective as well. He is aware of the increase in the number of customer complaints over the past 12 months. He is also aware that the service agents (the sales force) are having trouble getting the information they need to service the customers (the policyholders) properly.

Jerry is even more aware than Gunderson of what is going on; after all, it is his department. He also has in his hands the results of a survey done by his five newly appointed regional managers and the 200 employees who volunteered to assist in the efforts to improve the department. They have an interest in improving things, too. In the past few years, as the department has grown, management layers have been added, and the clerks and technicians have been left with less discretion than before. In addition to this, they work on narrowly defined jobs unconnected to other employees' jobs. The work of each employee is passed on to others randomly and very inefficiently. Of course, this situation is compounded by the functional structure of the department. That is, there are three sections, health insurance, life insurance, and support services (shown in Exhibit 1). Typically, if a service agent wants to change a policy, all three sections get involved, but somewhat randomly and very inefficiently. It takes an average of 20 days to get back to the policy-holder. This is also due in part to the climate that has been created over the past few years, described by some as "waiting for marching orders." Jerry is determined to do something. Based on the survey, his basic premises are that the number of separate job titles that exist in the department can be reduced from the current 167 and that the concept of self-directed teams can be put in place. Thus the functional structure is not sacred, and neither are the jobs of the managers.

Case Questions

1. What would you recommend as the final design of the jobs in the insurance department?
2. Who really should decide on the design of the jobs?
3. Will anyone have to be trained or retrained? Will all employees be able to change?
4. How should the changes be made? Should they be done one section at a time or with all 500 employees at once? Again, who should decide?

Case: Redesign or Relocation

During the past five years, productivity and worker satisfaction at the Jackson Toy Company have been declining. Productivity is now so low that Dr. Jackson, the company's founder and president, is seriously considering closing the plant and moving the business south. She wants, however, to retain the company.

When Dr. Jackson, a mechanical engineer, originally founded the toy company in 1965, she installed an assembly line so that workers could become specialized at their jobs and, hence, very productive. Although the employees were very productive during the first 10 years of operation, several of the younger, newly hired employees began complaining about the repetitive, boring nature of the work. It was about that time that Dr. Jackson began to notice a decline in productivity. Her first response was to assume that pay was too low. Whereas many of the original employees were essentially second-income earners, the newly hired employees were sole-income earners. Since pay was only the minimum wage, Jackson assumed that the younger employees were moonlighting in order to earn more money. Then when they came to work, they were too tired to work efficiently. Consequently, she increased everyone's salary by 20 percent. Since there were 75 employees, this represented a substantial increase in payroll expense. Nevertheless, she was concerned about productivity as well as the "plight" of the workers.

About two months after the salary increase, Jackson noted that the level of productivity had not increased. In fact, productivity actually declined slightly. Disappointed, but resolved to do something, Jackson called the local university. Professor Brief, a specialist in job redesign, suggested that Dr. Jackson needed to redesign the jobs for the employees or implement a job rotation program. Although it would be more

CASE EXHIBIT 1

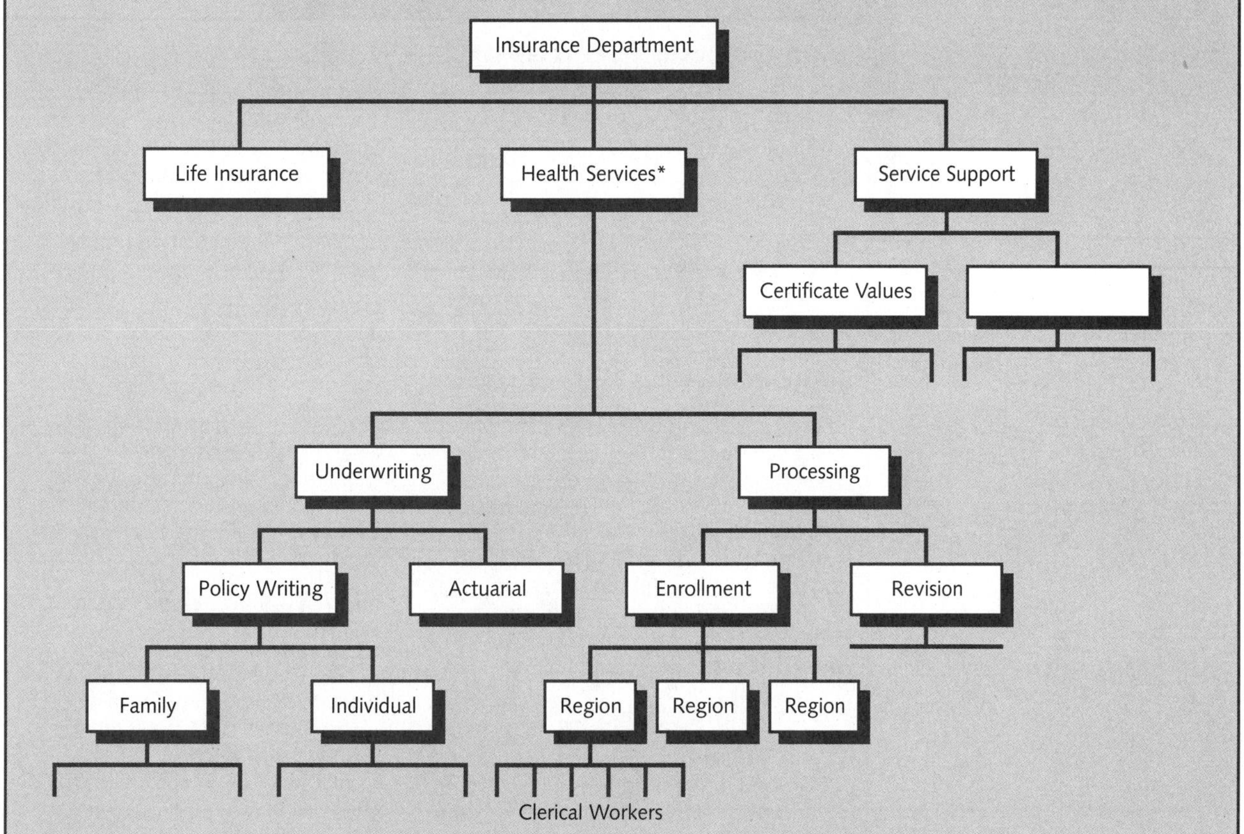

* Structure of life insurance is similar to health services.

costly to redesign the jobs than to implement a rotation program, Professor Brief said that job redesign would more clearly accomplish her objectives. Dr. Jackson, however, wondered if it would be more trouble than it's worth.

Case Questions

1. What is more motivating for the employees: intrinsic or extrinsic rewards?
2. On what basis does Professor Brief claim that job redesign would be worth it?
3. What would you recommend to Dr. Jackson?
4. Was Dr. Jackson's salary increase of 20 percent a valid way to test her assumption? What would you have done?

Chapter 7 Endnotes

1. Z. Schiller, "A Model Incentive Plan Gets Caught in a Vise," *Business Week* (January 22, 1996): 90.

2. T. W. Gerdel, "Lincoln Electric Experiences Season of Worker Discontent," *Plain Dealer* (Cleveland, OH) (December 10, 1995); C. Wiley, "Incentive Plan Pushes Production," *Personnel Journal* (Aug. 1993): 86–91.

3. C. Farrell, "A Wellspring of Innovation," *Business Week/Enterprise* (1993): 57–62.

4. D. Machalaba, "United Parcel Service Gets Deliveries Done by Driving Its Workers," *The Wall Street Journal* (April 22, 1986): 1 and 23; A. Bernstein, "In the Line of Fire at the Teamsters," *Business Week* (August 30, 1993): 39.

5. Personal correspondence with Bob Kenney, UPS, Atlanta, March 1994.

6. Y. Fried and G. R. Ferris, "The Dimensionality of Job Characteristics: Some Neglected Issues," *Journal of Applied*

VISIT THE LIBRARY

End-of-Section Exercise 1

1. Using your web browser, enter Cornell University's Employment Law Documents (see Visit the Internet Library: End-of-Section Exercise 2, at the end of Section 2).
2. Click on the topic "Employment Law" under the heading "Employment Law."
3. Click on the topic "Ch. 24: Technology Related Assistance for Individuals with Disabilities" of "29 US Code—Labor," under the heading "Federal Material."
4. Click on "Findings and purposes."
5. After reading this section, return to your homepage.

End-of-Section Exercise 2

Several sites related to career development can be found on the Internet. The purpose of this exercise is to introduce you to such a site, and also to demonstrate a simple use of a search engine. Search engines on the Internet are powerful tools that can be used to find links to specific topics and sites when you do not have a specific Internet address.

1. Enter SHRM's HR Links site. SHRM includes the Yahoo search engine. Alternatively, you can simply type Yahoo's Internet address in the address field. Yahoo's address is:

   http://www.yahoo.com

2. Assume that what you are looking for is an Internet site about careers called "The Catapult," but that you don't specifically know The Catapult's address. In Yahoo's search field, type "The Catapult" and then click on the "Search" button.
3. Yahoo will locate several Web sites that are related to the search words that you just typed. Look through the list of sites and descriptions to find a listing about a career-related site called "The Catapult." Click on the Keyword accompanying this description. (In case of difficulty, the actual address is:

   http://www.jobweb.org/catapult/catapult.htm)

4. Click on "Career Library Resources" under the heading "Help Guides and Career Library Resources" to browse through some of the career resources that are available.
5. Return to your homepage. Yahoo is but one of several search engines available on the Internet. Each has different capabilities. Some engines allow you to search specific areas of the Internet very thoroughly, while others are more general. Using Yahoo, you can do a search on the words "Search Engines" to locate many search engines on the Internet, as well as sites that provide specific information about search engines and how they compare.

Psychology 71, no. 3 (Aug. 1988): 419–426; J. Thomas and R. Griffin, "The Social Information Processing Model of Task Design: A Review of the Literature," *Academy of Management Review* (Oct. 1983): 672–682; M. A. Campion and P. W. Thayer, "Development and Field Evaluation of an Interdisciplinary Measure of Job Design," *Journal of Applied Psychology* (Feb. 1985): 29–43.

7. B. T. Loher, et al., "A Meta-Analysis of the Relation of Job Characteristics to Job Satisfaction," *Journal of Applied Psychology* 70 (1985): 280–289; L. R. Berlinger, W. H. Glick, and R. C. Rodgers, "Job Enrichment and Performance Improvement," in J. P. Campbell and R. J. Campbell, eds., *Productivity in Organizations* (San Francisco: Jossey-Bass, 1988): 219–254; Y. Fried, "Meta-Analytic Comparison of the Job Diagnostic Survey and Job Characteristics Inventory as Correlates of Work Satisfaction and Performance," *Journal of Applied Psychology* 76 (1991): 690–697.

8. J. R. Hackman and G. R. Oldham, "Development of the Job Diagnostic Survey," *Journal of Applied Psychology* 60 (1975): 159–170; B. Gerhart, "How Important Are

Dispositional Factors as Determinants of Job Satisfaction? Implications for Job Design and Other Personnel Programs," *Journal of Applied Psychology* 72 (1987): 366–373.

9. J. Kerr, "The Best Small Companies to Work for in America," *Inc.* (July 1993): 63.

10. M. Williams, "Back to the Past: Some Plants Tear Out Long Assembly Lines, Switch to Craft Work," *The Wall Street Journal* (October 24, 1994): 10; S. Caudron, "Create an Empowering Environment," *Personnel Journal* (September 1995): 28–36.

11. J. Kerr, "The Best Small Companies to Work For in America."

12. P.S. Lewis, S. H. Goodman, and P. M. Fandt, *Management Challenges in the 21st Century* (St. Paul: West Publishing, 1995).

13. Kerr, "The Best Small Companies to Work For in America."

14. C. Marmer Solomon, "Global Teams: The Ultimate Collaboration," *Personnel Journal* (September 1995): 49–58; K. Sabbagh, *Twenty-First-Century Jet: The Making and Marketing of the Boeing 777* (New York: Scribner, 1996); J. Hoerr, "Work Teams Can Rev Up Paper-Pushers, Too," *Business Week* (November 28, 1988): 64–72; C. Farrell, et al., "Riding High: Corporate America Now Has An Edge Over Its Global Rivals," *Business Week* (October 9, 1995)134–146; M. J. Ferrero, "Self-directed Work Teams Untax the IRS," *Personnel Journal* (July 1994): 66–71; "Teams: Every Team Is a 'Force of Ones'," *HR Reporter* (June 1994)1–2; "Fine-Tuning for Better Teamwork," *Bulletin to Management* (March 10,1994): 80.

15. M. Pacanowsky, "Team Tools for Wicked Problems," *Organizational Dynamics* (Winter 1995): 36–51.

16. Provided by the Weyerhaeuser Company.

17. Adapted from S. T. Johnson, "Work Teams: What's Ahead in Work Design and Rewards Management," *Compensation and Benefits Review* (March–April 1993): 37.

18. "The Problem with Teams: Individuals and Organizations," *HR Reporter* (April 1993): 3–6.

19. J. Gordon, "The Team Troubles That Won't Go Away," *Training* (August 1994): 25–34; A. L. Stern, "Managing by Team Is Not Always as Easy as It Looks," *New York Times* (July 18,1993): F5; J. S. Lublin, "As More Companies Divide Workers into Self-managed Teams, They Try to Link Pay to Team Performance," *The Wall Street Journal* (April 12, 1995): R4; L. Holpp and R. Phillips, "When Is A Team Its Own Worst Enemy?" *Training* (September 1995): 71–82; "Fine-Tuning for Better Teamwork," *Bulletin to Management* (March 10, 1994): 80; S. Caudron, "Diversity Ignites Effective Work Teams," *Personnel Journal* (September 1994): 54–63.

20. "Teamwork: Convenience or Survival?" *Solutions* (February 1994): 42; M. J. Ferrero, "Self-Directed Work Teams Untax the IRS," *Personnel Journal* (July 1994): 66–71; "Teams: Every Team Is a 'Force of Ones'," *HR Reporter* (June 1994): 1–3; C. Lee, "Open-Book Management," *Training* (July 1994): 21–27; R. Henkoff, "S. C. Johnson and Son: When to Take on the Giants," *Fortune* (May 30, 1994): 111–112; B. Dumaine, "The Trouble with Teams," *Fortune* (September 5, 1994): 86–92.

21. B. Dumaine, "Payoff from the New Management," *Fortune* (December 13, 1993): 103–110.

22. M. Hequet, "Ergomania," *Training* (May 1995): 45–50; W. C. Howell, "Human Factors in the Workplace," in M. D. Dunnette and L. M. Hough, *The Handbook of Industrial-Organizational Psychology,* vol. 2 (Palo Alto, CA: Consulting Psychologists Press, 1991): 209–270.

23. S. Lohr, "Waving Goodbye to Ergonomics," *New York Times* (April 16, 1995): Sec. 3, pp. 1,14; Eastman Kodak Company, *Ergonomic Design for People at Work,* vol. 2 (New York: Van Nostrand Reinhold, 1986); D. P. Levin, "The Graying Factory," *New York Times* (February 20, 1994): Sec. 3, p.1.

24. D. P. Levin, "The Graying Factory," *New York Times* (February 20, 1994): Sec. 3, pp.1, 6.

25. R. Henkoff, "Finding, Training, & Keeping the Best Service Workers," *Fortune* (October 3, 1994): 110–122.

26. C. Lee, "Open-Book Management," *Training* (July 1994): 21–27.

27. P. T. Kilborn, "Big Change Likely as Law Bans Bias toward Disabled," *New York Times* (July 19,1992): 1, 24; "Employers' ADA Responses—Concerned but Waiting," *Fair Employment Practices* (July 30, 1992): 87; see also "Discrimination Charges Filed under ADA," *Bulletin to Management* (June 2, 1994): 172–173.

28. Kilborn, "Big Change Likely as Law Bans Bias Toward Disabled"; see also *Fair Employment Practices Guidelines* (November 18, 1993): 136.

29. H. R. Northrup and J. A. Larson, *Impact of the American Telegraph & Telephone–Equal Employment Opportunity Consent Decree* (Philadelphia: University of Pennsylvania Press, 1979).

30. J. G. Frierson, "A Fifty-Question Self-Audit on ADA Compliance," *Employee Relations Today* (Summer 1992): 151–165; "ADA: Understanding the Americans with Disabilities Act," *Bulletin to Management* (April 15, 1993): 1–8.

31. Source: Adapted from "Allergic to Latex," *Bulletin to Management* (October 22, 1992): 331. Reprinted with permission by the Bureau of National Affairs, (Tel. 1-800-372-1033).

32. This discussion is adapted from E. F. Huse, *Management,* 2nd ed. (St. Paul: West, 1982): 383–404; E. Lawler III and J. Rhode, *Information and Control in Organizations* (Pacific Palisades, Calif.: Goodyear, 1976).

33. T. Engle and S. McFather, "Rewards and Recognition for Generation X," *ACA News* (Oct./Nov. 1995). Reprinted from October/November 1995 *ACA News*, with permission from the American Compensation Association (ACA), 14040 N. Northsight Blvd., Scottsdale, Arizona 85260, U.S.A.; Telephone 602/951-9191; fax 602/483-8352. See also A. Farnham, "How to Nurture Creative Sparks," *Fortune* (January 10, 1994): 94–100; and "'Buster' Generation Brings Different Attitudes, Needs," *Bulletin to Management* (April 4, 1996): 105.

34. A. Maslow, *Motivation and Personality* (New York: Harper & Row, 1954); and D. McGregor, *The Human Side of Enterprise* (New York: McGraw-Hill, 1960).

35. Maslow, *Motivation and Personality.*

36. C. Alderfer, *Existence, Relatedness and Growth: Human Needs in Organizational Settings* (New York: Free Press, 1972); L. Waters and D. Roach, "A Factor Analysis of Need Fulfillment Items Designed to Measure Maslow Need Categories," *Personnel Psychology* 26 (Summer 1973): 185–190; and D. Hall and K. Nougaim, "An Examination of Maslow's Need Hierarchy in an Organizational Setting," *Organizational Behavior and Human Performance* 4 (February 1968): 12–35.

37. F. Herzherg, B. Mausner, and B. Snyderman, *The Motivation to Work* (New York: Wiley, 1959); and F. Herzberg, "One More Time: How Do You Motivate Employees?" *Harvard Business Review* 46 (Jan.–Feb. 1968): 53–62.

38. V. Vroom, *Work and Motivation* (New York: Wiley, 1964); and L. Porter and E. Lawler III, *Managerial Attitudes and Performance* (Homewood, IL: Dorsey Press, 1968).

39. C. Marmer Solomon, "Job Sharing: One Job, Double Headache?" *Personnel Journal* (September 1994): 88–96; "Answering the Call for Alternative Work Options," *Bulletin to Management* (August 18, 1994): 257; "More Employers Are Providing Flexibility Through Job Restructuring," *Personnel Journal* (March 1994): 16–17; S. J. Mahun, "Peak-Time Pay for Part-Time Work," *Personnel Journal* (Nov. 1984): 60–65; 5. R. Sacco, "Are In-House Temporaries Really an Option?" *Personnel Administrator* (May 1985): 20–24.

40. P. Froiland, "Managing the Walking Wounded," *Training* (Aug. 1993): 39. Used by permission. Reprinted with permission from the Aug. 1993 issue of *TRAINING* Magazine. Copyright 1993. Lakewood Publications, Minneapolis, MN. All rights reserved. Not for resale.

41. M. Hequet, "How Telecommuting Transforms Work," *Training* (November 1994): 56–61; B. Presley Noble, "Nudging Workers From Comfy Nests: AT&T Pushes for Telecommuting," *New York Times* (July 30, 1995): F10; D. Kroll, "Telecommuting: A Revealing Peek Inside Some of the Industry's First Electronic Cottages," *Management Review* (Nov. 1984): 18–23.

42. "Drawbacks of Telecommuting," *Bulletin to Management* (May 20,1993): 153; "Ask the Experts: Managing Telecommuters," *Fair Employment Practices Guidelines* (June 10, 1993): 8.

43. J. 0. Hamilton, "The New Workplace," *Business Week* (April 29, 1996): 106–117; S. Greengard, "Going Mobile," *Personnel Journal* (March 1996): 128–132; S. Greengard, "Making the Virtual Office A Reality," *Personnel Journal* (September 1994): 66–79; N. F. Crandall and M. J. Wallace, Jr., "The Virtual Workplace: Work and Rewards in the 21st Century," *ACA Journal* (Spring 1995): 6–23; "Virtual Office Redefines Workplace," *Bulletin to Management* (May 19, 1994): 160; S. Ditlea, "Home Is Where The Office Is," *Nation's Business* (November 1995): 41–44; S. Caudron, "Working at Home Pays Off," *Personnel Journal* (November 1992): 40–49.

44. M. Hammer and J. Champy, "Beating the Risks of Reengineering," *Fortune* (May 15, 1995): 105–114; "Reengineering the Organization," *Bulletin to Management* (November 11, 1993): 360; see also M. Hammer and J. Champy, *Reengineering the Corporation: A Manifesto for Business Revolution* (New York: HarperCollins Publishers, Inc., 1993).

45. "Reengineering the Organization," *Bulletin to Management* (November 11, 1993): 360. Reprinted with permission by the Bureau of National Affairs, (Tel. 1-800-372-1033).

46. "When the Walls Come Down," *Bulletin to Management* (January 4, 1996): 8.

47. Ibid.

48. K. Johnson, "Evolution of the Workplace Alters Office Relationships," *New York Times* (October 5, 1994): B1, 8.

49. Ibid.

SECTION 4

Staffing

With an understanding of the environments of HR management and the development of the ability to change and adapt to these environments, companies need to be concerned with more specific HR activities, activities that help staff the organization with people who can perform effectively.

Of course, getting the people we need in order to run the company as effectively as possible is a key task of HR management. The competition for qualified people is so stiff that companies find they must market themselves as top notch career opportunities. If a company has a great reputation in this area, more and better qualified people will apply at the company, and this increases the chances that selected applicants will perform well once hired.

Ensuring that applicants are likely to perform effectively begins with the determination of the duties and purposes of jobs and the skills, knowledge, and abilities needed to perform them. A precise knowledge of the organization's jobs can indicate present and future needs regarding numbers and types of employees. It can help determine how the employees will be obtained (from outside recruiting or internal transfers) and what training needs the organization will have. We will look at these activities in Chapters 8, 9, and 10. In these chapters you will be asked to describe your desired job/career in more detail.

Getting people interested in working for a company is the essence of recruitment. The needs of potential employees and the needs of the organization must be balanced during the recruitment process. When labor supply is high and demand is low, a buyer's market exists, and the needs of the business tend to prevail. When demand for labor is high and supply is low, a seller's market exists, and the needs of applicants tend to prevail.

Because conditions vary, effective firms find that it pays to be consistent—to develop a great set of recruitment procedures and use them consistently. While this may result in more worker accommodation than some firms might initially desire, such approaches can pay off in the long run since reputations take time to establish, and good reputations result in a company being more attractive to candidates during both good and bad employment and economic conditions. We will discuss these issues and ideas associated with recruitment in Chapter 9.

After recruitment has taken place, the organization must decide whether to offer the job, and the applicant must decide whether to accept the offer. The HR department is key in developing and utilizing procedures for selecting the best recruits. Organizations have found that it pays to develop selection procedures that are as job-related as possible, while meeting all requirements. When deciding whether to accept the offer, the recruit should consider the following types of questions: Is this the right organization? Will I be happy with the job and the opportunities to work here? Will my career be advanced if I accept the job offer? The various Career Management Exercises found in Chapters 6, 7, and 8 will help you address such questions.

Throughout this section, you will see once again how many opportunities there are for partnership among line managers, HR professionals, and employees. You will also see how the themes of diversity, globalization, ethics, and total quality management impact recruitment, selection, and placement.

CHAPTER 8

Job Analysis

Learning Objectives

1. Discuss the purposes and importance of doing job analysis.
2. Describe the ways to collect job analysis information.
3. Write job descriptions and job specifications.
4. List the reasons companies develop job families.
5. Describe the trends in job analysis and their impact on your career.

> *"With the job families, we're trying to get rid of all the extraneous details and allow managers and their employees to do what is needed to serve their customers extremely well."*
>
> *Mary Fitzer*
> *Director of Base Salary Development, Aetna*[1]

Chapter Outline

MANAGING HUMAN RESOURCES

Job Description for Senior Vice President, Human Resources

JOB PROFILE

This job represents the personnel point of view in the strategic and operational direction of the business. The incumbent is expected to provide, with the support and concurrence of the President, a philosophy and guiding principles for managing the human resources of the company.

This job requires an incumbent with broad managerial and professional knowledge and experience. From the managerial standpoint, the Human Resources group comprises ten interrelated yet disparate fictional areas: personnel relations, compensation, benefits, training, organization development, recruiting, personnel administration, field personnel services, communications, and home office personnel services. The current staff consists of 75 people, including 42 professionals: The incumbent also has functional responsibility for personnel services to four distribution centers. Budget administration responsibilities approximate $29.7 million.

On the professional side, with the exception of the directors of compensation and staffing and of HR development and the managers of benefits and of media projects, virtually all staff members have been developed inside the company. Technical and professional direction and training rest with the incumbent. The incumbent is expected to provide the company with systems, programs, and processes that effectively support business goals and organization values. The company's principal executives rely on the incumbent's personal experience, skills, and resources to bring the company to current "State-of-the-Art" status.

Although the incumbent is not expected to create or invent systems and programs, he/she is expected to introduce successful practices and adapt them to the company's particular needs. The incumbent must be able to judge when to act and when not to act with patience and persistence. He/she must be able and willing to modify actions to gain agreement and consensus. The incumbent must be able to place the priorities of the company over those of the personnel function. At the same time, the incumbent is expected to be a strong advocate for employee interests and well-being.

CANDIDATE QUALIFICATIONS

Broad experience is required in the following areas:

- Personnel labor relations in both organized and unorganized situations, including union-free policies and practices, organizing campaigns, unfair labor practice charges, arbitrations, labor contract negotiation, and administration.
- Personnel policy formulation, communication, and administration.
- Corporate culture change, including the facilitation of improved organizational effectiveness.
- HR development with special emphasis on all facets of training but also including: organization planning, succession and staff planning, performance standard/expectations, performance review, personal/management development, assessment of management potential, organization development, career pathing, and recruitment/selection process.
- Compensation programs, including job evaluations, wage and salary plan design and administration, short- and long-term incentive plan design and administration, bonus and gain-sharing plans.
- Benefit programs, including the design and administration of health care, dental, life and disability insurance and of defined benefit/contribution plans, vacation, sick pay, holiday, and other policies.
- Human resource information systems, including the development and utilization of cost/time effective reports and analyses.
- Departmental direction, management and administration, including staff selection, training/development and deployment; short- and long-term departmental planning, project management, program development and execution, delivery of HR services, budget development and administration.[2]

The preceding feature is, of course, an official job description that could have come from any number of organizations today. It gives an indication of just how complex and significant the job of a senior vice president of human resources can be. As noted in the description, this is a large HR department: 75 individuals in the HR staff and a budget of $29.7 million. The job description, also called the position profile, states that the job entails responsibility for all the HR activities to be discussed in this book. The candidate qualifications, or job specifications, needed to adequately perform the duties in this position profile are thus rather extensive. How many years do you think it would take to acquire these qualifications? Perhaps 20–25 years? Probably, but maybe this is something to aim for if you want to have a significant position of HR responsibility and challenge someday! You might want to go back to your career planning activity in Chapter 6 and revise your goals accordingly!

While you may not be an HR professional, it's good to know what is expected of the best ones.

Job descriptions and job specifications convey to others what is expected from a person in a job or position. They also help in the recruitment and selection process.

We take a detailed look at job analysis in this chapter. Along with the design of jobs, job analysis is an essential building block for all the other HR management activities. As we proceed, you will see the various ways of performing job analysis and why it is so important.

Job Analysis

Job analysis is the process of describing and recording aspects of jobs.

Job descriptions describe the purposes, duties, and conditions of a job.

Job specifications indicate the skills, knowledge, and abilities needed to do the job.

Job analysis is the process of describing and recording aspects of jobs and specifying the skills and other requirements necessary to perform the job. During the analysis, the purposes of a job, its major duties or activities, and the conditions under which the job is performed are described. These three components form the essential parts of a **job description**. **Job specifications** are based on the job description. They detail the skills, knowledge, and abilities that individuals need to perform a job.[3] They may also detail the personality, interests, and preferences that best fit the job.

LEARNING OBJECTIVE 1

Discuss the purposes and importance of doing job analysis.

Why Is Job Analysis Important?

Job analysis is the basis of job descriptions and specifications. These result from several factors including a company's top management values, assumptions about people, products, customers, technology, and HR philosophy. Together these factors determine how the company will produce and deliver its products and services. Job design creates and shapes the characteristics of jobs that need to be performed to produce and deliver those products and services. Job analysis then describes those jobs and determines the skills, knowledge, and objectives people need to have to perform those jobs. In doing so, job analysis serves many purposes:

- Aids the supervisor and employee in defining each employee's duties and related tasks
- Serves as a reference guide to move employees in the correct work-related direction
- Prescribes the importance and time requirements for a worker's effort
- Provides job applicants with realistic job information regarding duties, working conditions, and job requirements
- Identifies reporting relationships for supervisors and subordinates
- Guides change in work design and task management
- Determines a job's relative worth to maintain external and internal pay equity

- Ensures that companies do not violate the *Equal Pay Act* of 1963
- Provides selection information necessary to make employment decisions consistent with the *Civil Rights Act* of 1964 and 1991, and the *Americans with Disabilities Act* of 1990
- Serves as a basis for establishing career development programs and paths for employees
- Identifies worker redundancies during mergers, acquisitions, and down sizing
- Guides supervisors and incumbents in respectively writing references and preparing resumes for employees leaving and seeking new employment.[4]

These purposes are attained in the process of job analysis that reflects several legal considerations.

These purposes are more thoroughly and accurately accomplished when line managers, HR professionals, and other employees work in partnership. A description of what they can do is outlined in the feature "Partnership: Working Together in Job Analysis." This partnership helps ensure that all aspects of job analysis are addressed.

Aspects of Job Analysis

The renewed interest in job analysis has been spurred in part by organizational efforts to comply with the *Uniform Guidelines and Employee Selection Procedures (Uniform Guidelines)* and numerous court decisions, but it is also a result of the fact that job analysis serves so many purposes and has such an extensive set of relationships with other HR activities. As a consequence, organizations are now engaged in all aspects of job analysis, starting with collecting the information for it.

Uniform Guidelines **are policies and practices for selecting employees in compliance with the law and developed by several federal agencies.**

PARTNERSHIP: WORKING TOGETHER IN JOB ANALYSIS (JA)

LINE MANAGERS

Work with HR managers to determine whether jobs need to be analyzed or reanalyzed.

Help decide who should conduct the JA and for what purposes.

Help identify incumbents to participate in JA.

Provide technical documents to job analyst.

Participate in JA through interviews and questionnaires.

Facilitate job incumbents' participation in JA.

HR PROFESSIONALS

Communicate with line managers and employees about the importance of JA.

Work with line managers to determine whether jobs need to be analyzed/reanalyzed and for what purposes.

Serve as a JA expert, or help select an external vendor to conduct JA.

Ensure line managers and employees are aware of legal considerations.

Prepare job descriptions with line managers.

EMPLOYEES

Understand the purposes and importance of JA.

Help line managers recognize when major changes in your job indicate the need for job analysis or reanalysis.

Provide accurate information for JA process.

Adapt to the changing nature of job and be willing to show flexibility in performing new job tasks.

LEARNING OBJECTIVE 2

Describe the ways to collect job analysis information.

Collecting Information for the Analysis

As defined earlier, job analysis entails both the process of job description and job specification. The attributes of both the job and the person needed to perform the job vary greatly. Possible attributes are listed in Exhibit 8.1. Since the information gathered on these attributes must comply with the *Uniform Guidelines,* it is important to know who collects the information as well as how it is collected.

Incumbents are the current employees in a job.

Job analysis information is collected by:

- **the HR department**
- **department supervisor**
- **job incumbent**

Who Collects the Information? Typically, someone in the HR department, backed up by a supervisor, collects the job information. The **incumbents**, or the persons performing the job, also provide information. Obtaining information from as many sources as possible leads to a greater understanding of the job's particular duties and the skills, knowledge, and abilities needed to perform

EXHIBIT 8.1

Job Analysis Attributes

Job Description

Work Activities

Job-oriented activities (usually expressed in terms of what is accomplished; sometimes indicating how, why, and when a worker performs the activity)
- Work activities/processes
- Procedures used
- Activity records (films, etc.)
- Personal accountability/responsibility

Worker-oriented activities
- Human behaviors performed in work (sensing, decision making, performing physical actions, communicating, etc.)
- Elemental motions (such as those used in methods analysis)

Personal job demands (energy expenditures, etc.)

Machines, Tools, Equipment, and Work Aids Used

Job-Related Tangibles and Intangibles

Materials processed
Products made
Knowledge dealt with or applied (such as law or chemistry)
Services rendered (such as laundering or repairing)

Work Performance

Work measurement (time taken)
Work standards
Error analysis
Other aspects

Job context

Physical working conditions
Work schedule
Organizational context
Social context
Incentives (financial and nonfinancial)

Job Specifications

Personal Requirements

Job-related knowledge/skills (education, training, work experience, etc.)
Personal attributes (aptitudes, physical characteristics, personality, interests, etc.)

Source: Adapted from E. J. McCormick, "Job and Task Analysis," in M.D. Dunnette, ed., *Handbook of Industrial and Organizational Psychology*, copyright©1976 by Rand McNally College Publishing Company, p. 653.

those duties. Because of the legal considerations and the importance of careful job design (the result, after all, of this process) to the organization, the data collector should be trained and then allowed to practice the steps in gathering the information so that the data fulfills a number of important requirements. Not only must the information be accurate, detailed, and complete, it must also be collected in a manner that is in legal compliance and that has not "ruffled any feathers" of either the workers or the supervisors. *Remember, job analysis information is some of the most valuable information:*

> *The data generated by job analyses have significant use in nearly every phase of HR administration: designing jobs and reward systems, staffing and training, performance control and more. Few other processes executed by organizations have the* potential *for being such a powerful aid to management decision making.*
>
> *But the word* potential *must be emphasized. The typical manner in which job analyses are conducted leaves much to be desired because the data tend to be incomplete, inaccurate, and inappropriate. Indeed, using job analysis information as it is commonly collected can create as many problems for an organization as it helps resolve.*
>
> *One reason the analyses tend to be highly flawed is that the data are often gathered by novices or employees who lack appreciation and understanding of the final use of the facts. Too frequently management delegates the task to a new employee or to someone with little experience, assuming that the procedure is routine and elementary. In reality, data collection for job analyses requires practice and considerable human relations skills.*[5]

Communication About Job Analyses. The launching of a job analysis program can be unpopular. It is not only time-consuming, but also potentially threatening to incumbents who perceive that it can lead to changes in job responsibilities, compensation, and training. To defuse potential resentment and misunderstanding, the HR department needs to convey to all employees the purpose of the program, who will be involved, and exactly what will happen as a result of the program. Involving the incumbent and supervisor increases the perceptions of procedural fairness and reduces resistance to change.

Methods for collecting job analysis information include:

- **observations**
- **interview (incumbent)**
- **conference (with analyst/expert)**
- **diaries**
- **questionnaires**
- **critical incidents**
- **mechanical devices**
- **software programs**

Methods of Gathering Information. Methods of collecting information include: 1) observation; 2) interviews with the job incumbents; 3) conferences with job analysts and experts; 4) observations by job analysts; 5) diaries kept by the job incumbents; 6) questionnaires (see Exhibit 8.2 for an example) filled out by the incumbents or observers such as the supervisor or job analyst; 7) critical incidents written by incumbents or others who know the jobs; 8) mechanical devices such as stopwatches, counters, and films; and 9) software programs that produce generic job descriptions with only job description information.[6]

Job Descriptions

LEARNING OBJECTIVE 3

Write job descriptions and job specifications.

Job descriptions and specifications are generated from the data gathered in job analysis. On the basis of job descriptions, performance appraisal forms can be developed and job classification systems established for job evaluation and compensation purposes. Because job specifications identify the education and training needed to perform a job, appropriate recruitment, selection, and training and development programs depend on this process. Typically, a single document is written to describe job duties and underlying tasks.[7]

EXHIBIT 8.2

Sample Questionnaire (Exempt Positions)

Instructions: This is a preliminary step in the preparation of a position description for your job. Complete the questionnaire carefully and give it to your immediate supervisor to review. He or she will then pass it on to the analyst responsible for your area. Use the back of the page if there is not sufficient space for your answers, but try to keep them as concise and relevant as possible.

Your Name: ______________________ Date: ______________________

Job Title: ______________________ Department: ______________________

Immediate Superior: ______________________ His/Her Title: ______________________

1. How would you describe the primary purpose of your job? (i.e., why does it exist?)
2. What is the position immediately superior to yours?
3. List the titles of the jobs you supervise or direct and the number of incumbents in each. Briefly describe the nature of your supervisory activities.
4. What kind of supervision or direction do you receive (if any)? (e.g., to whom do you report, from whom do you receive assignments)
5. What procedural controls are you subject to? (e.g., sales goals, budgets, cost standards)
6. What are the positions or departments with which you have close working relationships and frequent contacts? What is the nature of these contacts?
7. Describe your major job activities (include planning, scheduling, coordinating, etc.)

Source: *How to Analyze Jobs: A Step-by-Step Approach* (1982), 72–73. Reprinted by permission of the publisher, Bureau of Law & Business, Inc., 64 Wall Street, Madison, Conn. 06443.

The Written Document. The final job analysis document should include:

Position description is a collection of duties performed by a single person.

- **Job Title** refers to a group of positions that are identical in regard to their significant duties. In contrast, a **position description** refers to a collection of duties performed by a single person. A company with 50 accounting assistants has 50 accounting positions but probably fewer than five discernible job titles. Differentiating these terms as they apply to particular jobs can be deceptive because jobs in different departments or in different organizations can have the same title yet be quite different in their duties. Thus, to determine whether jobs are similar for purposes of pay or selection procedures, an analyst needs to focus on the degree of overlap in job duties rather than the similarity in job titles.
- **Department** or **division** refers to where the job is located.
- **Date** identifies when the job was analyzed. This will cue job analysts as to when the description should be updated.

The Dictionary of Occupational Titles (DOT) is a valuable source of job analysis information.

- **DOT Code** is a standard job code published in the **Dictionary of Occupational Titles** by the Department of Labor. It provides some desirable but not essential information for validation reports pertaining to the job.
- **EEO-1/AAP Categories** are the reporting categories for annual equal employment opportunity reporting and affirmative action plans.
- **Job Summary** is an abstract of the job. It can be used for job posting, recruitment advertisements, and salary surveys.
- **Supervision Received and Given** identifies reporting relationships. If the job is supervised, the duties associated with the supervision should be detailed under work performed.

- **Work Performed** identifies the duties and underlying tasks that make up a job. A task is something that workers perform or an action they take to produce a product or service. Duties are a collection of tasks that recur and are not trivial. For maximum information use, duties should be prioritized in terms of the time spent as well as importance. A duty may take little time to complete but be critical to job success. Weighted duty statements that prioritize work for incumbents are useful in establishing performance standards and may be important in determining whether job accommodations for individuals protected under the *ADA* are reasonable. A weighted listing of job duties is also important to determine whether jobs are exempt from overtime provisions of the *Fair Labor Standards Act* and whether two jobs with different titles are similar in skill, effort, responsibility, and working conditions as provided under the *Equal Pay Act.*[8]

- How work is performed has become rather important in both service and manufacturing companies. The success of companies such as Southwest Airlines and Wal-Mart depends upon their employees performing their jobs with friendliness to and helpfulness toward the customer. Telemarketing representatives need to be friendly and convince you to buy their products![9] In addition to being friendly and helpful, customer service representatives who answer the phone when you call in your orders at L. L. Bean or Lands End sometimes serve as problem solvers. For example, if a product isn't in stock, they must determine what other product might be an acceptable substitute. At Ford and Chrysler, where total quality management is practiced, employees perform their jobs by cooperating with other workers, solving problems, and getting feedback from customers to improve their products. And increasingly, managers are evaluated on their behaviors toward their employers.

- **Job Requirements** (specifications) delineate the experience, education, training, licensure and specific knowledge, skills, and abilities needed to perform a job. **Knowledge** relates to a body of information in a particular subject area that, if applied, makes adequate performance of the job possible (for example, knowledge of Windows 95 or OSHA regulations). The terms **skill** and **ability** are often used interchangeably and relate to observable capabilities to perform a learned behavior (operate a drill press, for example).

  Job requirements should be limited to the **minimum qualifications** that a new employee can be expected to bring to the job. Minimum qualifications are likely to be the prime focal point for EEO investigations because of potential abuses and the potential for disparate impact are present. For example, a high school diploma is unnecessary for the position of janitor, but the janitor may need basic reading skills to identify cleaning agents. Thus an appropriate requirement would be the ability to read labels and instructions—not a high school diploma. Similarly, an M.S. degree in social work may be an inappropriate qualification for the position of child-welfare worker if individuals without the degree have been shown to perform the job as well. An M.S. degree may be necessary, however, if required by state law.

  Job requirements are also controversial when employers impose artificially high minimum standards to reduce the number of applicants to be processed, to justify high salaries, or to enhance the prestige of the job or organization. High minimums may result in disparate impact. Acceptable minimum qualifications should be the least necessary to do the job: if an incumbent has a college degree, yet the job requires only a high school diploma, only the high school diploma should be listed as required.

- **Job Context** deals with the environment in which the job is performed. For example, work may be conducted outdoors (construction worker), in close quarters (film editor), in remote areas (forest ranger), in high temperatures

Knowledge is the body of information related to a job; skill or ability is a person's observable capability to perform a job.

Minimum qualifications are the least amount of skills necessary to do a job.

Did You KNOW?

"The auto worker is almost a scientist in a technical way. He's required to know so many trades, he's required to know so much."

Joe Lo Galbo
a Ford Motor Co. machinery repairman turned trainer

"At one point, we were hiring hands and arms and legs, and now we are hiring total people—with minds more important than the other."

Robert J. Eaton
Chairman and Chief Executive of Chrysler

Disney chooses language for use in its theme parks that reinforces its employees' understanding that they are in show business and terminology that helps them deliver high-quality service. There is no personnel department—employees are hired by "Central Casting."

(chef), or low temperatures (meat cutter). The job may involve extensive standing (sales clerk), sitting (data entry clerk), exposure to fumes (fiberglass fabricator), noise (drill press operator), electrical shocks (electrician), exposure to diseases (laboratory technician), or stress (pension fund manager). Such details provide an understanding of the setting in which the job is conducted.

Writing Style. An important aspects not to be forgotten in creating job descriptions is the writing style. The *Handbook for Analyzing Jobs* suggests the following:

- A terse, direct style should be used.
- The present tense should be used throughout.
- Each sentence should begin with an active verb.
- Each sentence must reflect an objective, either specifically stated or implied in such a manner as to be obvious to the reader. A single verb may sometimes reflect both objective and worker action.
- All words should impart necessary information; any others should be omitted. Every precaution should be taken to use words that have only one possible connotation and specifically describe the manner in which the work is accomplished.
- The description of tasks should reflect the assigned work performed and, where possible, worker performance ratings.

Keep in mind that the job should be described in enough detail that the reader can understand: 1) what is to be done and how (the domains, behaviors, results, and duties); 2) what products are to be generated (the job's purposes); 3) what work standards are applied (for example, quality and quantity); 4) under what conditions the job is performed; and 5) the job's design characteristics. Design characteristics are included so that individuals can select and be placed on jobs that match or suit their personalities, interests, and preferences and/or be physically accommodated to the job. Job design characteristics are described in Chapter 7.

Exhibit 8.3 is an example of a job description. It does not specifically provide information on performance standards or design characteristics. Performance standards are not typically specified in job descriptions because organizations prefer to retain flexibility and thus include them in the performance appraisal form.

Techniques of Job Analysis

In this section we will discuss the most common techniques of job analysis. Motion studies focus on job efficiency. Task listings and inventories, the Position Analysis Questionnaire, and Job Element Inventory are structured questionnaires that can be computer analyzed. Three other methods (Functional Job Analysis, Critical Incident Technique, and Guidelines-Oriented Job Analysis) are designed to meet specific HR information needs. Finally, three methods (Hay Plan, Management Position Description Questionnaire, Supervisor Task Description Questionnaire), which focus specifically on managerial work, are examined.

Methods Analysis

Methods analysis focuses on analyzing job elements

Job elements are the smallest identifiable components of a job.

Methods analysis focuses on analyzing **job elements**, the smallest identifiable component of a job. The need for methods analysis often comes from: 1) changes in tools and equipment; 2) changes in product design; 3) changes in materials; 4) modifications of equipment and procedures to accommodate handicapped workers; and 5) health and safety concerns.

While HR managers have downplayed the importance of methods analysis in recent years, it is still widely used in manufacturing settings. In fact, the use of new

EXHIBIT 8.3

Position Description (Exempt)

Functional Title: Corporate Loan Assistant
Department: Corporate Banking
Function Code:
Division:
Location: Head Office
Incumbent:
Date: June 1997

Note: Statements included in this description are intended to reflect in general the duties and responsibilities of this classification and are not to be interpreted as being all-inclusive.

Relationships
Reports to: Corporate Account Office A or AA; or Sr. Corporate Account Officer B or BB
Subordinate staff: None
Other internal contacts: Various level of management within the Corporate Banking Department
External contacts: Major bank customers

Summary Statement
Assist in the administration of commercial accounts, to ensure maintenance of profitable Bank relationships.

Domains

A. Credit Analysis (Weekly)
Under the direction of a supervising loan officer: Analyze a customer company's history, industry position, present condition, accounting procedures, and debt requirements. Review credit reports, summarizing analysis and recommending course of action for potential borrowers; review and summarize performance of existing borrowers. Prepare and follow-up on credit communications and reports and Loan Agreement Compliance sheets.

B. Operations (Weekly)
Help customers with banking problems and needs. Give out customer credit information to valid inquirers. Analyze account profitability and compliance with balance arrangements; distribute to customer. Direct Corporate Loan Note Department in receiving and disbursing funds and in booking loans. Correct internal errors.

C. Loan Documentation (Weekly)
Develop required loan documentation. Help customer complete loan documents. Review loan documents immediately after a loan closing for completeness and accuracy.

D. Report/Information System (Weekly)
Prepare credit reports, describing and analyzing customer relationship and loan commitments; prepare for input into Information System. Monitor credit reports for accuracy.

E. Customer/Internal Relations (Weekly)
Build rapport with customers by becoming familiar with their products, facilities, and industry. Communicate with customers and other banks to obtain loan-related information and answer questions. Prepare reports on customer and prospect contacts and follow-up. Write memos on significant events affecting customers and prospects.

F. Assistance to Officers (Monthly)
Assist assigned officers by preparing credit support information, summarizing customer relationship, and accompanying on calls or making independent calls. Monitor accounts and review and maintain credit files. Coordinate paper flow to banks participating in loans. Respond to customer questions or requests in absence of assigned officer.

G. Assistance to Division (Monthly)
Represent bank at industry activities. Follow industry/area developments. Help Division Manager plan division approach and prospect for new business. Interview loan assistant applicants. Provide divisional back-up in absence of assigned officer.

H. Knowledges and Skills (Any item with an asterisk will be taught on the job.)
Oral communications skills, including listening and questioning. Intermediate accounting skills. Writing skills. Researching/reading skills to understand legal financial documents. Organizational/analytical skills. Social skills to represent the Bank and strengthen its image. Sales skills. Knowledge of Bank credit policy and services.* Skill to use Bank computer terminal.* Knowledge of bank-related legal terminology. Independent work skills. Work efficiently under pressure. Courtesy and tactfulness. Interfacing skills. Knowledge of basic business (corporate) finance. Skill to interpret economic/political issues.

I. Physical Characteristics
See to read fine print and numbers. Hear speaker twenty feet away. Speak to address a group of five. Mobility to tour customer facilities (may include climbing stairs). Use of hands and fingers to write, operate a calculator.

J. Other Characteristics
Driver's license. Willing to: work overtime and weekends occasionally; travel out of state every three months/locally weekly; attend activities after work hours; wear clean, neat businesslike attire.

Source: Used by permission of Biddle and Associates, 2100 Northrop Avenue, Sacramento, CA 95825-3937

technologies, collectively referred to as programmable automation, has increased the need for methods analysis. These new processes include computer-aided design (CAD), computer-aided manufacturing (CAM), computer-aided engineering (CAE), flexible manufacturing systems (FMS), group technology, robotics, and computer-integrated manufacturing (CIM).

These new manufacturing technologies can create shock waves in an organization because they require a quantum jump in precision and integration. Automated machine tools can produce parts to more exacting specifications than can the most skilled human machinist, but to do so they need explicit, unambiguous instructions in the form of computer programs.

The new hardware provides added freedom, but it also multiplies the ways to succeed or fail. It therefore requires new skills on the part of managers—for example, *an integrative imagination* and *a passion for detail.* To prevent process contamination, for example, it is no longer possible to rely on people who have a "feel" for their machines, or to merely note on a blueprint that operators should remove iron filings from the part." When using the new automated machine tools, everything must be stated with mathematical precision: "where is the blower that removes the filings, and what's the orientation of the part during operation of the blower?[10]

Because of the advanced technologies, used by such companies as Saturn, Nissan, Corning, Eaton, and Honda, industrial engineers play an important role in job design and methods analysis.

Thus it is increasingly important to study and document work processes. A variety of techniques are available for conducting methods analysis.

Flow Process Charts. These are used to examine the overall sequence of an operation by focusing on either the movement of an operator or the flow of materials. For example, flow charts have been used in hospitals to track patient movements, in grocery stores to analyze the checkout process, in small-batch manufacturing facilities to track material flows from machine to machine, in banks to examine the sequence associated with document processing, and in supervisor-incumbent interactions during performance appraisal interviews.

Worker-Machine Charts. These are useful for envisioning the segments of a work cycle in which equipment and operator are busy or idle. The analyst can easily see when the operator and machine are working jointly or independently. One use of this type of chart is to determine how many machines or how much equipment an operator can manage. A team process chart is an extension of worker-machine charts. Rather than focusing on the operations of a single operator and machine, this chart simultaneously plots the worker-machine interfaces for a team of workers. Such charts are particularly useful for identifying equipment utilization as well as for pinpointing bottlenecks in interdependent tasks.

Time and motion study measures times for units of work.

Time and Motion Study. Also called motion study, this technique has its origins in industrial engineering and the work of Frederick W. Taylor and Frank and Lillian Gilbreth. In essence, work measurement determines times for all units of work activity in a given task or job. Combining these times gives a standard time for the entire job. Observed time is simply the average of recorded times. Normal time is the observed time adjusted for worker performance. This is accomplished by determining a performance rating for observed performance. The performance rating is an estimation of the difference between the normal rate at which a worker can be expected to perform and the observed rate. The adjustment is necessary because workers may deliberately slow down or speed up the processes when observed. For instance, a performance rating of 1.20 indicates that an observed pace is much faster than normal. By comparison, a performance rating of 0.80 assumes that observed performance is slower than normal (a possible occurrence if the job is being studied to set rates of pay).

Standard time is the normal time adjusted for routine work interruptions. These delays may include personal delays (getting a drink of water, going to the washroom) as well as variable allowances specific to the job (mental or physical effort, lighting, atmospheric conditions, monotony, and detail). Industrial engineers have developed tables listing the allowances for different work delays.

These standard times can be used as a basis for wage incentive plans (incentives are generally given for work performance that takes less than the standard time), cost determination, cost estimates for new products, and balancing production lines and work crews.[11] Establishing standard times is challenging since the time it takes to do a job can be influenced as much by the individual doing the job as by the nature of the job itself. Consequently, determining standard times often requires measurement of the "actual effort" the individual is exerting and the "real effort" required. This process may involve trying to outguess someone else.

Work sampling is not only a technique for determining standard times, but also a form of methods analysis. **Work sampling** is the process of taking instantaneous samples of the work activities of individuals or a group of individuals.[12] The activities are timed and classified into predetermined categories. The result is an activity description by classification and the percentage of time required.

Work sampling is the process of taking samples from work activities to measure and analyze them.

Work sampling can be done in several ways: 1) the job analyst can observe the incumbent at predetermined times; 2) a camera can be set to take photographs at predetermined times; or 3) at a given signal, all incumbents can record their activity at that moment.

Work sampling was utilized in a recent study to examine the differences between successful managers and effective managers. **Successful managers** are those who move up formal hierarchies quickly, while **effective managers** are those who have achieved high levels of quality and quantity of work performance and satisfaction. Effective managers, in general, were found to spend their time in the following activities: traditional management (32 percent), routine communication (29 percent), HR management (20 percent), and networking (19 percent). Successful managers spent more time on networking activities and less on HR management activities than did effective managers. The latter spent additional time on routine communication and management.[13]

Successful managers are those who climb the hierarchy fast, and effective managers are those who are great performers.

Structured Questionnaires

In addition to the various methods analyses used for gathering data for job analysis, any of several paper-and-pencil questionnaire methods may also be used.

Task Inventories. In contrast to the multiple methods used in work sampling to gather data, the task inventories method of job analysis is based solely on a structured questionnaire. As such, **task inventories** are a listing of tasks for the job being analyzed, with a provision for some type of response scale for each task. The incumbent, supervisor, or analyst performs the job analysis by checking the appropriate responses.

Task inventories are a job analysis method done by questionnaire.

Suppose an analyst wanted to study three tasks of a specific secretarial job using a task inventory. Part of the questionnaire might look like Exhibit 8.4. Because the development of task inventories requires large samples of employees and complex statistical analysis, their use is usually limited to organizations that employ many people in the same occupation (police, fire fighter, data entry). As a consequence, the use of task inventories is fairly widespread in city and state governments and the military, which typically have many people performing the same job.[14]

Position Analysis Questionnaire (PAQ). This is a structured questionnaire used for research purposes that contain 187 job elements and 7 additional items relating to amount of pay. The **Position Analysis Questionnaire (PAQ)** is organized into six divisions; each division contains some of the job elements. The divisions and a sample of elements include the following:

The PAQ is a structured questionnaire to analyze jobs.

1. **Information input:** Where and how does the worker get the information used in performing the job? Examples are the use of written materials and near-visual differentiation.
2. **Mental processes (information processing activities):** What reasoning, decision-making, planning, and information-processing activities are

EXHIBIT 8.4

Sample of a Task Inventory Questionnaire

	IS TASK DONE?	IMPORTANCE	TIME SPENT
	1. Yes	1. Extremely unimportant	1. Very much below average
	2. No	2. Very unimportant	2. Below average
		3. Unimportant	3. Slightly below average
		4. About medium importance	4. About average
		5. Important	5. Slightly above average
		6. Very important	6. Above average
		7. Extremely important	7. Very much above average
Prioritize typing requirements	① ②	① ② ③ ④ ⑤ ⑥ ⑦	① ② ③ ④ ⑤ ⑥ ⑦
Type address labels	① ②	① ② ③ ④ ⑤ ⑥ ⑦	① ② ③ ④ ⑤ ⑥ ⑦
Type business correspondence	① ②	① ② ③ ④ ⑤ ⑥ ⑦	① ② ③ ④ ⑤ ⑥ ⑦

involved in performing the job? Examples are the level of reasoning in problem solving and coding/decoding (see in Exhibit 8.5).

3. **Work output:** What physical activities does the worker perform, and what tools or devices are used? Examples are the use of keyboard devices and assembling/disassembling.

4. **Relationships with other people:** What relationships with other people are required in performing the job? Examples are instructing and contacting the public or customers.

5. **Job context:** In what physical or social contexts is the work performed? Examples are high temperature and interpersonal conflict situations.

6. **Other job characteristics:** What other activities, conditions, or characteristics are relevant to the job.[15]

Each job element is also rated on one of six rating scales: 1) extent of use; 2) importance of the job; 3) amount of time; 4) possibility of occurrence; 5) applicability; and 6) other.

Using these job elements and rating scales, the nature of the job is essentially determined in terms of communication, decision making and social responsibilities, performance of skilled activities, physical activity and related environmental conditions, operation of vehicles and equipment, and processing of information. With these six dimensions determined, jobs with similar specifications can be compared and placed into families.

While task inventories limit comparisons of jobs within occupations, the PAQ is more general and can be applied to a variety of jobs and organizations without modification. Responses to the items are computer analyzed to produce a job profile that indicates how a particular job compares with other jobs in regard to the six job elements detailed above. The PAQ database also contains information about the relationship between PAQ responses, job aptitudes, and labor market pay rates. These scores can then be used to set qualification or compensation levels for jobs.

EXHIBIT 8.5

Sample PAQ Item Mental Processes

INFORMATION PROCESSING ACTIVITIES	CODE	IMPORTANCE TO THIS JOB
In this section are various human operations involving the "processing" of information or data. Rate each of the following items in terms of how *important* the activity is to the completion of the job.	N	Does not apply
	1	Very minor
	2	Low
	3	Average
	4	High
	5	Extreme

39. ____ Combining information (combining, synthesizing, or integrating information or data from two or more sources to establish new facts, hypotheses, theories, or a more complete body of related information, for example, an economist using information from various sources to predict future economic conditions, a pilot flying aircraft, a judge trying a case, etc.)

40. ____ Analyzing information or data (for the purpose of identifying underlying principles or facts by breaking down information into component parts, for example, interpreting financial reports, diagnosing mechanical disorders or medical symptoms, etc.)

41. ____ Compiling (gathering, grouping, classifying, or in some other way arranging information or data in some meaningful order or form, for example, preparing reports of various kinds, filing correspondence on the basis of content, selecting particular data to be gathered, etc.)

42. ____ Coding/decoding (coding information or converting coded information back to its original form, for example, "reading" Morse code, translating foreign languages, or using other coding systems such as shorthand, mathematical symbols, computer languages, drafting symbols, replacement part numbers, etc.)

43. ____ Transcribing (copying or posting data or information for later use, for example, copying meter readings in a record book, entering transactions in a ledger, etc.)

44. ____ Other information processing activities (specify)

Source: E. J. McCormick, P. R. Jeanneret, and R. C. Mecham, *Position Analysis Questionnaire*, Occupational Research Center, Dept. of Psychological Sciences, Purdue University, West Lafayette, IN 47907. Copyright © 1969 by Purdue Research Foundation.

Thus, the PAQ is a potential selection and job evaluation tool as well as a job analysis tool.

Using the PAQ to set qualification levels is less subjective than a supervisors' opinion. However, there is no direct evidence that obtaining a given test score makes an applicant more likely to perform well on the job. Care is also needed in using the PAQ to set compensation rates since the worth of jobs is not determined independently of the labor market. Thus, jobs highly valued by an organization but less valued in a labor market would be paid the lower market rate. Another concern with the PAQ is that it must be bought from a consulting firm. Consequently, direct costs appear to be high. Finally, it requires a postcollege reading comprehension level to respond to the items. Thus, the PAQ is not well suited to job analysis situations in which job incumbents or supervisors serve as raters.[16]

Job Element Inventory is a more basic form of a structured questionnaire.

Job Element Inventory. Closely modeled after the PAQ, the 153-item **Job Element Inventory** has a readability index estimated to be at the tenth grade level and is explicitly designed for completion by incumbents. The dimensional structure of the job element inventory is similar to that of the PAQ. The advantage of this instrument lies in the cost savings associated with the fact that incumbents rather than trained analysts can complete the instrument.[17]

Functional Job Analysis from the federal government describes job concerns about people, data, and things.

Functional Job Analysis. The U.S. Training and Employment Service developed functional job analysis to describe concerns (people, data, and things) and to develop job summaries, job descriptions, and employee specifications. **Functional**

Job Analysis was designed to improve job placement and counseling for workers registering at local state employment offices.[18]

The functional job analysis is both a conceptual system for defining worker activities and a method of measuring activity levels. Its fundamental premises are as follows:

- A fundamental distinction must be made between what gets done and what workers do to get things done. Bus drivers do not carry passengers; they drive vehicles and collect fares.
- Jobs are concerned with data, people, and things.
- In relation to things, workers draw on physical resources; in relation to data, on mental resources; and in relation to people, on interpersonal resources.
- All jobs require workers to relate to data, people, and things to some degree.
- Although workers' behavior or the tasks they perform can apparently be described in an infinite number of ways, Only a few definitive functions are involved. Thus, in interacting with machines, workers feed, tend, operate, and set up; in the case of vehicles, functions vary in difficulty and content. Each behavior draws on a relatively narrow and specific range of worker characteristics and qualifications for effective performance.
- The functions appropriate to dealing with data, people, or things are hierarchical and ordinal, proceeding from the complex to the simple. Thus, to indicate that a particular function—say, compiling data—reflects the job requirements is to say that it also includes lower-function requirements, such as comparing, and excludes higher-function requirements, such as analyzing.[19]

Exhibit 8.6 lists the worker functions associated with data, people, and things. These worker functions have been used as a basis for describing over 30,000 job titles in the *Dictionary of Occupational Titles* (DOT) and for creating job families (groupings of jobs) based on similar data, people, and things.

It even provides a simple job description for most job titles. Thus, the HR manager who has to prepare job descriptions and specifications might start with the DOT to determine general job analysis information.

EXHIBIT 8.6

Functional Job Analysis Functional Level Rating Scales

DATA	PEOPLE	THINGS
0 synthesizing	0 mentoring	0 setting up
1 coordinating	1 negotiating	1 precision working
2 analyzing	2 instructing	2 operating-controlling
3 compiling	3 supervising	3 driving-operating
4 computing	4 diverting	4 manipulating
5 copying	5 persuading	5 tending
6 comparing	6 speaking-signaling	6 feeding-offbearing
	7 serving	7 handling
	8 taking instructions-helping	

Source: Adapted from U.S. Department of Labor, Employment Service, Training and Development Administration, *Handbook for Analyzing Jobs* (Washington, D.C.: Government Printing Office, 1972), 73.

Dictionary of Occupational Titles (DOT). The U. S. Department of Labor has used functional job analysis (FJA) as a basis for describing thousands of jobs. These results are made available to the public in the *Dictionary of Occupational Titles* (DOT). An example of a DOT entry appears in Exhibit 8.7.

In Exhibit 8.7, the identification code for job analyst (166.267-018) can be used to give a brief description of how the DOT is used. The first three digits (166) indicate the occupational code, which in this case falls within "Professional, Technical, and Managerial Occupations." The next three digits (267) represent the degree to which a job analyst typically has responsibility and judgment over data (2: Analyzing), people (6: Speaking-Signaling) and things (7: Handling). The final three digits (018) are used to indicate the alphabetical order of titles within the occupational group having the same degree of responsibility and judgment.

In addition to describing jobs, the DOT classifies jobs into families of related jobs. In the current version of the DOT (4th edition) jobs are classified into nine major categories. These are:

- Professional, technical, and managerial
- Clerical and sales
- Service
- Agricultural, fishery, forestry, and related occupations
- Processing
- Machine trades
- Bench work
- Structural work
- Miscellaneous

This system is likely to change in the near future, however. The Department of Labor's Bureau of Labor Statistics has been charged with revising the current Standard Occupational Classifications for the 21st century in recognition of the growth that has occurred in the number and diversity of service sector jobs since the current system was developed.[20]

EXHIBIT 8.7

DOT Identification Code for Job Analyst

166.267-018 JOB ANALYST (profess. & kin.) alternate titles: personnel analyst.

Collects, analyzes, and prepares occupational information to facilitate personnel, administration, and management functions of organization: Consults with management to determine type, scope, and purpose of study. Studies current organizational occupational data and compiles distribution reports, organization and flow charts, and other background information required for study. Observes jobs and interviews workers and supervisory personnel to determine job and worker requirements. Analyzes occupational data, such as physical, mental, and training requirements of jobs and workers and develops written summaries, such as job descriptions, job specifications, and lines of career movement. Utilizes developed occupational data to evaluate or improve methods and techniques for recruiting, selecting, promoting, evaluating, and training workers, and administration of related personnel programs. May specialize in classifying positions according to regulated guidelines to meet job classification requirements of civil service system and be known as Position Classifier.

Source: U.S. Department of Labor, *Dictionary of Occupational Titles*, 4th ed. (Washington, D.C.: Government Printing Office, 1991).

Today, a number of private and public organizations use many aspects of FJA. A line manager in a small business, for example, who has to prepare job descriptions and specifications, might start with the DOT to determine general job analysis information, and to find a job description that can be adapted to the specific conditions in the company. The DOT can also be helpful to companies as they expand and create jobs they have never had before, in part because it provides a job description that can be used for recruitment of new talent.

In the future, employers can expect even more help from the Department of Labor. By the 21st century, the Department of Labor hopes to shift the emphasis from job tasks to skill requirements. This is clearly consistent with the types of organizational changes occurring as companies strive to become flatter and more flexible in the ability to use human resources effectively.

Critical Incidents Technique develops a list of effective and ineffective job performance behaviors.

Critical Incidents Technique. A frequently used technique for developing behavioral criteria is the **Critical Incidents Technique**. This technique requires that those knowledgeable about a job describe it to a job analyst. What they describe are called the critical job incidents (that is, those incidents observed over the past six to twelve months that represent effective and ineffective performance). Sometimes the job analyst needs to prompt the person describing the incidents by asking them to write down key things the incumbent must be good at or to identify the most effective job incumbent and then describe that person's behaviors.[21]

Those describing the incidents are also asked to describe what led up to the incidents, what the consequences of the behavior were, and whether the behavior was under the incumbent's control. After the critical incidents (often several hundred for each job) have been gathered and described, they are rated by frequency of occurrence, importance, and the extent of ability required to perform them. The critical incidents and their characteristics can be clustered into job dimensions. These dimensions, which may often use only a subset of all the critical incidents obtained, can then be used to describe the job.

They can also be used to develop performance appraisal forms, particularly Behavioral Anchored Rating Scales and Behavioral Observation Scales (described in Chapter 12). Additionally, critical incidents can be used to develop job-specific situational questions for selection purposes (described in Chapter 10).

As with this technique and those that follow, the major disadvantages are the time required to gather the incidents and the difficulty of identifying average performance. The latter disadvantage, however, can be overcome by obtaining examples of multiple levels of performance.

Guidelines-Oriented Job Analysis is an approach to job analysis based upon the Uniform Guidelines.

Job domain is a category of related duties.

Guidelines-Oriented Job Analysis. This was developed in response to the *Uniform Guidelines*—hence its name. The steps in the **Guidelines-Oriented Job Analysis** each involve the job incumbents. Before any of these steps begin, the incumbents indicate their names, length of time on the job, experience, and the location of the current job.

In the first step, incumbents list their **job domain**, which is a category with related duties. Related duties in a job often fall into broad categories. For example, a secretary may type letters, contracts, and memos. Since these duties are related, they are put into the same domain—in this instance, typing. Jobs typically have several domains.

Duties are observable work behaviors to be performed as part of the job.

Second, after the domains are identified, the incumbents list the critical duties typically performed in each domain. **Duties** are observable work behaviors and something that incumbents are expected to perform. Often each domain contains several duties. Third, once the critical duties are identified, the incumbents indicate how frequently the duties are performed. Then each duty's degree of importance is determined. The fourth step is the incumbents' determination of the skills and knowledge required to perform each duty. Only those skills and knowledge that cannot be learned or acquired in eight hours or less are included. This is consistent with the *Uniform Guidelines*. Failure to select an applicant who could have learned the necessary skills in less than eight hours is not a defensible (job-related) practice.

The fifth step is determining the physical characteristics that incumbents need to perform their job duties. Here the incumbents respond to five open-ended statements, each related to a physical characteristic.

The results of these steps are a job description, similar to the one in Exhibit 8.3 for the Corporate Loan Assistant; a set of individual skills, knowledge, and abilities needed to perform the job; and a basis for developing job-related selection procedures and performance appraisal forms.

Both the critical incidents technique and the guidelines-oriented job analysis, because they focus on behaviors, are useful for developing performance appraisal forms and spotting training needs. In addition, since skills (physical and mental) and knowledge are identified, selection procedures can also be developed, as described in Chapter 10. Both techniques also enhance employee understanding and validity of job analysis since job incumbents are involved in the process. This involvement, however, takes time.[22]

Managerial Jobs

There are a number of special concerns in the analysis of managerial jobs. One is that managers adjust job duties to fit their work style rather than adjust their work style to fit the job. Another concern is that it is difficult to identify what a manager does over time because activities vary from hour to hour or day to day. As immediate situations or exceptions arise, the content of a manager's job changes. Despite these complications, several methods have been developed to analyze managerial jobs.

Management Position Description Questionnaire. Although the functional job analysis approach is thorough, using it well requires considerable training, and its nature is quite narrative. The narrative portions tend to be less reliable than more quantitative techniques such as the **Management Position Description Questionnaire (MPDQ)**.[23] This questionnaire relies on the checklist method to analyze jobs. It contains 197 items related to managers concerns, responsibilities, demands, restrictions, and competencies. The items have been condensed into the following thirteen job factors:

- Product, market, and financial planning
- Coordination of other organizational units and personnel
- Internal business control
- Products and services responsibility
- Public and customer relations
- Advanced consulting
- Autonomous consulting
- Approval of financial commitments
- Staff service
- Supervision
- Complexity and stress
- Advanced financial responsibility
- Broad HR responsibility

"We no longer look at a job as a function or a certain kind of work. Instead, we see it as a set of skills and competencies."

Marile Robinson
Redeployment Manager
Intel Corporation

Responses to the items vary by managerial level in any organization and also in different organizations. It is appropriate for determining the training needs of employees moving into managerial jobs, evaluating managerial jobs, creating job families and placing new managerial jobs into the right job family, compensating managerial jobs, and developing selection procedures and performance appraisal forms.

The Behavioral Job Description uses three categories of behaviors.

Behavioral Job Description. The **Behavioral Job Description (BJD)** builds on the work of the management position description questionnaire (MPDQ). The BJD uses three categories of behaviors to distinguish how managerial jobs at the same level in the organization may differ. The BJD recognizes that managerial jobs differ by function (e.g., marketing, manufacturing, human resources) and by organizational level (e.g., executive vice president, middle manager, supervisor). The main focus of the BJD is to differentiate jobs by behaviors regarding:

- Impact of the managers' activities
- Type of interpersonal contacts
- The managers' approaches to accomplishing work

An example of how two similar product managers' jobs could vary on these three behaviors is shown in Exhibit 8.8. These two jobs represent product managers in two different departments of the same company. Combined results based on the MPDQ and the BJD can illustrate differences in responsibilities, concerns, demands, restrictions, and behaviors by levels within the organization and within the same levels. Such information can be used to tailor recruitment methods and selection strategies for various positions that may seem similar at first glance.

Supervisor Task Description Questionnaire is a systematic way to analyze the supervisor's job.

Supervisor Task Description Questionnaire. While the management position description questionnaire can be used to describe, compare, classify, and evaluate management jobs at all levels, the **Supervisor Task Description Questionnaire** is limited to the work of first-line supervisors. The questionnaire describes 100 work activities of first-line supervisors in these areas:

- Working with subordinates
- Planning subordinates' work
- Maintaining efficient production and quality
- Maintaining safe and clean work areas
- Maintaining equipment and machinery
- Compiling records and reports

A study of more than 250 first-line supervisors in 40 plants showed that job responsibilities are universal regardless of technology or product type.[24]

LEARNING OBJECTIVE 4

List the reasons companies develop job families.

Development of Job Families

The initial results of job analyses are typically many separate and unique job descriptions and employee specifications—as many descriptions as there are jobs. Often, however, these jobs are not greatly different from each other. That is, employees who perform one job can most likely easily perform several others. Those jobs are also likely to be of similar value to the organization. This is why organizations group jobs into **job families** or classes. Jobs are placed in the same family to the extent that they require similar job specifications or have similar tasks and are of similar value to the organization (as determined by a job evaluation study as described in Chapter 13).[25]

Job families are groups of related jobs.

There is no one best way to construct job families. A recently developed method is through the job competency framework, which is based on identifying the **competencies** (knowledge, skills, abilities, attitudes, and personality) that individuals need to perform jobs. Jobs requiring similar competencies for excellent

Competencies are more than knowledge, skills, and abilities.

EXHIBIT 8.8

Profiles of Two Product Manager Jobs

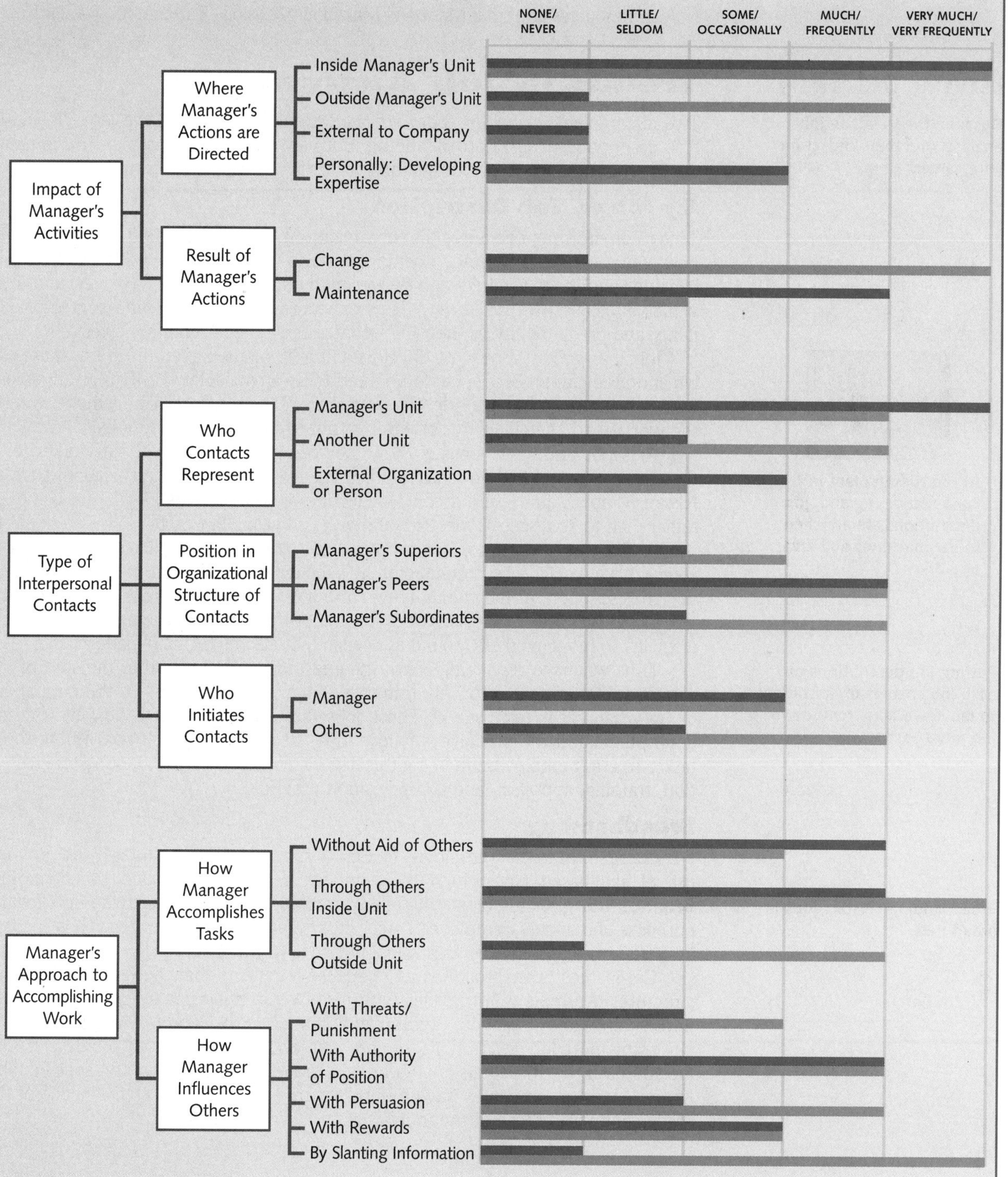

Source: N. Fondas, "A Behavioral Job Description for Managers," *Organizational Dynamics* (Summer 1992): 50. Reprinted by permission of the publisher, from ORGANIZATIONAL DYNAMICS SUMMER 1992 © 1992. American Management Association, New York. All rights reserved.

performance can be grouped into the same job family. The methods of job analysis described in this chapter can also be used to construct families. The use of job families gives companies a lot more flexibility in dealing with changes in job conditions and even in making pay decisions. An excellent description of this is in the feature, "Managing Human Resources at Aetna: Managers Make Pay Decisions Through Job Families."

LEARNING OBJECTIVE 5

Describe the trends in job analysis and their impact on your career.

Trends in Job Analysis

Two major events occurring today are: 1) Rethinking the use of the term "job" and "job description" and 2) broadbanding. Both are largely responses to the changing environment calling for more flexibility.[26]

My Job vs. Job Description

Today's environment requires that organizations be adaptable and that individuals be flexible. At the same time, organizations also need highly repetitive and reliable behavior on jobs to produce and deliver high-quality goods and services, and individuals typically need to know what's expected and to have some degree of certainty and predictability in their life—that is they need a comfort level.

Job analysis methods were developed in a time when everything was more stable and predictable. People could be hired to do a particular job. This arrangement was convenient for management and workers, except when management wanted the workers to change or do something "not in their job descriptions."[27]

Did You KNOW?

At the Nissan plant in Sunderland, England, job descriptions are attached to the machines and areas of work.

Today, organizations focus on how they can get flexibility without worker resistance, yet at the same time satisfy workers' needs for comfort. Organizations such as Nissan Motor Manufacturing and Honda hire applicants to work for the company rather than to do a specific job. At Southwest Airlines, Libby Sartain, vice president of people, likes to say that they hire people to do work, not jobs.[28] These companies, of course, have specific jobs: consequently, it is the job rather than the individual that gets the job description. As the worker moves from job to job, the description stays with the job. In this way, the worker knows what is expected, and management gets not only flexibility to move workers around as needed, but also high-quality performance.

Putting job descriptions on each job enables organizations to move workers from job to job more easily.

Thus what we are seeing is not the end of the job, but rather the shift of the employee's attention from only thinking about doing "my job" to thinking about doing whatever is necessary.[29] Those jobs that are necessary to do have the job descriptions and the employees follow those descriptions when performing those tasks. To assist employees in being this flexible, companies are adapting their selection, training, appraisal, and compensation practices.

Broadbanding

Broadbanding clusters jobs in broad tiers.

For example, increased employee flexibility is coming about through the growing use of skill-based pay, which is described in Chapter 13, and broadbanding. **Broadbanding**, or the clustering of jobs (even job families) into wide tiers for the purposes of managing employee career growth and administering pay, has become an attractive alternative to traditional pay structures.[30]

Companies favor broadbanding because it reflects their flatter organizational structures. Multiple salary grades with narrowly defined pay ranges are collapsed into fewer salary grades with more pay potential. Broadbanding has the impact of clustering more job descriptions into broader job family categories. Job descriptions are still used, but the focus is on a broad class of jobs rather than on specific jobs. Many Japanese companies have found that this approach serves the needs of the organization and those of the individual.

Legal Considerations

These trends might suggest that jobs and job analysis are changing. They, like all aspects of managing human resources and entire companies, are evolving and

MANAGING HUMAN RESOURCES

at Aetna
Managers Make Pay Decisions Through Job Families

Like many large companies, Aetna Life and Casualty Co. in Hartford, Connecticut, always has relied on a highly stratified job-classification system. Everything is connected to job class, from salary levels and promotional opportunities to job descriptions and supervisory responsibility. "You know your job class, you know everything," explains Mary Fitzer, Aetna's director of base-salary development.

But this system no longer is working. As a diversified financial services company, Aetna operates in a fast-moving and increasingly competitive environment. The existing job-classification and compensation system, however, doesn't encourage employees to work any harder or respond any faster to market changes. Why not? Because if a task isn't written into a job description, what incentive is there for an employee to take on added responsibility?

"There's too much work to be done to spend our time continually rewriting 7,000 detailed job descriptions," explains Fitzer. "We need to look at work in a much broader sense."

For this reason, Aetna is in the process of identifying the major skills and competencies that are needed by employees and grouping those skills into a broad job-family structure. "The entire point is to define work, not by what class it's in, but by the actual functions performed," Fitzer says. "Then, we will look at how the market prices that work, give that information to managers, and let them make pay decisions based on an individual's performance." When Aetna completes this process, the company expects to have just 200 job families representing *all* of the company's 42,000 employees.

Managers always have made the pay decisions at Aetna, but through this new structure, the compensation department will be able to provide them with more specific information about what the market is paying for certain jobs. "Instead of saying to them, 'Here's a salary minimum and maximum and you shouldn't pay above or below that,'" says Fitzer, "we'll be able to give them some market guidelines that they can interpret in light of their own budgets and performance levels." This effort in turn will force managers to clearly define employee performance expectations at the start of each business cycle.

With fewer promotional levels, the primary way for employees to get ahead at Aetna will be to earn bonuses by performing better. The company isn't eliminating promotions altogether—there will still be layers, such as entry-level underwriter, underwriter, senior underwriter, and underwriting manager—but compensation decisions will be based on performance and market pricing, not job title.

Aetna realizes that not all employees will do well under the new system. Fitzer explains, "If employees have high security needs and are focusing on the old ways of doing things, it will be difficult for them in the new environment."

Not only will the job-family structure change the ways in which employees are evaluated and managers set salaries, but it also will change the relationship between the HR department and line managers.

"With the job families, we're trying to get rid of all the extraneous details and allow managers and their employees to do what is needed to serve their customers extremely well," says Fitzer.[31]

adapting to the circumstances. They have done so over the years with respect to several legal considerations.

Job analysis faces several legal constraints, largely because it serves as the basis for selection decisions, performance appraisals, compensation, and training determinations. These constraints have been articulated in the *Uniform Guidelines* and several court decisions. For example, Section 14.C.2 of the *Uniform Guidelines* states that "there shall be a job analysis which includes an analysis of the important work behaviors required for successful performance." Any job analysis should thus focus on work behavior(s) and the tasks associated with them.[32]

Where job analysis has not been performed, the validity of selection decisions has been successfully challenged (*Kirkland v. New York Department of Correctional Services,* 1974; *Albemarle Paper Company v. Moody,* 1975). Numerous court decisions regarding job analysis and promotion and performance appraisal also exist. For example, in *Brito v. Zia Company* (1973), the court states that the performance appraisal system of an organization is a selection procedure and therefore must be validated—that is, it must be anchored in job analysis. And in *Rowe v. General Motors* (1972), the court ruled that to prevent discriminatory practices in promotion decisions, a company should have written objective standards for promotion. In *U.S. v. City of Chicago* (1978), the court stated that, in addition to having objective standards for promotion, the standards should describe the job to which the person is being considered for promotion. These objective standards can be determined through job analysis.[33]

Although the *Americans With Disabilities Act* of 1990 (ADA) does not require written job descriptions, employers can conduct analyses to identify essential functions and formulate job descriptions to facilitate compliance with the law.

Written job descriptions may also provide evidence, although not conclusive, of the job's "essential functions" and serve as baselines for performance reviews. It is important, therefore, that written job descriptions be accurate and correspond to the current requirements of the job.[34]

Did You KNOW?

In the first case under ADA, a director of a security firm was awarded $572,000 after being fired when he was diagnosed with terminal brain cancer.

Summary

The creation and maintenance of effective organizations today requires that the worker-job relationship be understood and managed. The way jobs are organized and perceived by job incumbents affect job attitudes and behaviors. Job analysis provides information about what jobs are about and what individuals need to perform them. Job analysis information can be collected by different individuals using several different methods. The result is the information for job descriptions and job specifications. These go a long way in linking the individual to the organization and the job analysis activity to all the other HR activities.

The choice of a job analysis method should be a result of the intended purpose, as defined by the type of HR issue to be served by the analysis. Regardless of the approach, it is important to bear in mind that job analysis serves as the backbone for nearly all the HR activities described in the chapters ahead.

Job analysis is also of value to companies as they seek to adapt to the continuously changing marketplace and heightened levels of competition. These conditions call for rapid changes and responses by companies and by individuals. Newer practices such as job families and broadbanding help companies and individuals change and adapt to the demands of the new workplace.

Key Concepts

ability
broadbanding
Critical Incident Technique
competencies
Dictionary of Occupational Titles (DOT)
duties
Functional Job Analysis
Guidelines-Oriented Job Analysis
incumbent
job analysis
job descriptions
job domain
Job Element Inventory
job elements
job families
job specifications
knowledge
Management Position Description Questionnaire (MPDQ)

methods analysis
minimum qualifications
Position Analysis Questionnaire (PAQ)
position description
skill
successful managers
Supervisor Task Description Questionnaire
task inventories
time and motion study
Uniform Guidelines
work sampling

Review and Discussion Questions

1. List several purposes of job analysis.
2. Describe the partnership in job analysis.
3. How do job descriptions differ from job specifications?
4. Describe the way of gathering job information.
5. Describe the types of method analysis.
6. Describe the types of structured questionnaires.
7. Describe the types of managerial job analysis.
8. How does the use of job families give companies more flexibility with their employees?
9. What are some important legal considerations in job analysis? Refer also to Chapter 7.
10. How can job descriptions give clarity to workers and also flexibility to the organization?

PROJECTS, EXERCISES & CASES

End-of-Text Projects

Lincoln Electric

1. Describe the following for the Lincoln Electric Company:
   - **a.** The objectives of Lincoln's job analysis
   - **b.** The degree to which these objectives are serving the business and HR objectives of Lincoln
   - **c.** Lincoln's job analysis activities
   - **d.** The degree to which these activities are serving Lincoln's objectives
2. How can the job analysis activities at Lincoln be improved?

Nordstrom

1. Describe the following for Nordstrom
   - **a.** The objectives of Nordstrom's job analysis
   - **b.** The degree to which these objectives are serving the business and HR objectives of Nordstrom
   - **c.** Nordstrom's job analysis activities
   - **d.** The degree to which these activities are serving Nordstrom's objectives
2. How can the job analysis activities at Nordstrom be improved?

Field Project

Obtain one or more job descriptions from local companies (e.g., businesses, hospitals, or service organizations) and analyze them in terms of completeness as described in Chapter 8. To what extent do they provide information regarding performance standards, worker activities, equipment used, job context, job characteristics and worker specifications, or personal requirements? Find out what job analysis methods were used by the company to collect the information in the descriptions, who provided the information, and how long ago the information was collected. Suggest specific improvements.

Career Management Exercise

To gain experience in conducting a job analysis and writing a job description, complete the following steps:

1. Select a job that you are interested in knowing more about or might like to perform during some stage of your career. Select a professional job (e.g., manager, financial analyst, chemical engineer, museum curator, dietitian), not skilled job, or semi-skilled job.
2. Select a method to conduct your job analysis.
3. Select a person or persons to interview, observe, etc. Identify and give the telephone number of the individual(s) you interview.
4. Conduct your job analysis.
5. Develop a written job description for the position. Rank the job duties in order of their importance. Indicate the amount of time spent on each task. Also, indicate the criticality of error if this task is performed incorrectly.
6. On a separate typed sheet, explain the method of job analysis you used, why you chose it, and its strengths and weaknesses.
7. Respond to this question: From the perspective of (1) an employee and (2) a manager, why is it important to have an accurate, up-to-date, job description?

Case: Decter Computer Corporation

Cynthia Lee has just been hired as an HR assistant at Decter Computer Corporation (DCC). Cynthia recently finished her bachelor's degree at Northeast University in HR administration, and she is excited about her first HR job. She is eager to apply the skills that she acquired in her undergraduate major. Angela Richards, Cynthia's immediate supervisor, is the HR director at DCC. Cynthia's first major task is to formalize DCC's job descriptions and job specifications based on a job analysis of each position.

DCC is a mid-sized company located in an industrial park in Parsippany, New Jersey. A leading producer of electronic equipment and a major contender in micro-computers and calculators, DCC is one of the leading distributors of micro-computers to large corporations. The company's business has been growing rapidly in recent years despite increased competition. The primary reasons for this are technological advancements DCC has put in place that have increased production capacity, an aggressive marketing strategy, and a reputation for excellent products and service. But the rapid growth has also placed some strain on the HR department and created pressures to formalize work activities and compensation strategies.

Cynthia who joined DCC two months earlier, has been assigned to create job descriptions for positions at DCC, a project that Angela has estimated will take eight weeks to complete. Angela told Cynthia that she would be responsible for the entire project and made it clear that she would be given autonomy to interview both supervisors and employees. Although Angela stressed the significance of the project, Cynthia sensed that Angela had a number of other responsibilities and deadlines to meet and that she did not have much time to spend on job analysis activities. Cynthia viewed the project as a challenge—a chance to prove herself.

Angela sent a memo to all supervisors explaining that Cynthia was responsible for completing a job analysis of each of the positions they supervised. Angela asked for their full cooperation and requested that they call her if they had any questions. After the memo was circulated, Cynthia began lining up interviews with the supervisors. She decided that the supervisors would be the best source of data for job descriptions and specifications, and planned to develop a narrative format similar to a sample job description in one of her personnel texts. As a final step in collecting job information, Cynthia decided to interview at least one employee in each of the positions being studied.

After three weeks, Cynthia became discouraged over the progress she was making on what she believed was a straightforward project. She had managed to interview only 7 of the 20 supervisors. The supervisors seemed unwilling to cooperate with Cynthia. They often missed interview meetings and dragged their feet in rescheduling them. Although Cynthia had originally planned to talk to all of the supervisors first, the delays prompted her to begin interviewing job incumbents.

After only a few interviews with employees, Cynthia became concerned about the quality of information that she was obtaining. The employees appeared to be giving her conflicting information on both their job duties and the skills required to perform their jobs. In general, the employees saw their jobs as more demanding, requiring more duties, and utilizing more skills than the supervisors had indicated. Despite these conflicts, Cynthia decided to push ahead so that she could submit the completed descriptions and specifications to Angela by the agreed-upon deadline.

At the end of the eight weeks and several long nights, Cynthia proudly presented a packet of job descriptions and specifications to Angela. Despite the obstacles, Cynthia believed that she had achieved the major objectives of the project. Angela assigned Cynthia another project. Several weeks later when Cynthia had all but forgotten about the job descriptions and specifications, Angela met with Cynthia to discuss a problem that had developed. It seems that several of the supervisors were annoyed about the difference in opinion with their subordinates over job duties.

Case Questions

1. Was Cynthia's strategy of interviewing one employee in each position a good one?
2. Why were the supervisors unwilling to cooperate with Cynthia?
3. On becoming concerned about the quality of the data, should Cynthia have changed her methods?
4. Do the job descriptions and specifications need to be rewritten? How?

Case: Job Descriptions at HITEK

Jennifer Hill was excited about joining HITEK Information Services after receiving her BA. Her job involved examining compensation practice, and her first assignment was to review HITEK's job descriptions. She was to document her work and make recommended changes, which would include reducing more than six hundred job descriptions to a manageable number.

Background

To its stockholders and the rest of the outside world, HITEK is a highly profitable, highly aggressive company in the computer business. In addition to its numerous government contracts, it provides software and hardware to businesses and individuals. From its inception in the late 1970s, it has maintained its position on the leading edge by remaining flexible and adaptable to the turbulent environment in which it operates. It is a people-intensive organization that relies enormously on its human resources; therefore, it is in HITEK's best interests to establish policies and procedures that nurture productivity and enhance the satisfaction of its employees.

Because the computer industry is growing at an incredible pace, opportunities for placement are abundant, and the competition for high-quality human resources is tremendous. HITEK has grown about 30 percent in the last three years, and its management knows that, as easily as it attracts new employees, it can lose them. However, its turnover rate (14 percent) is about average for its industry.

HITEK remains relatively small at one thousand employees, and it prides itself on its "small team company culture." This culture is maintained partly by the use of a computer mail system that can put any employee in touch with anyone at HITEK and by the utilization of open office spaces. The relatively flat lean organizational structure (See Case Exhibit 1) and the easy accessibility of all corporate levels also promotes an

CASE EXHIBIT 1

HITEK's Organizational Chart

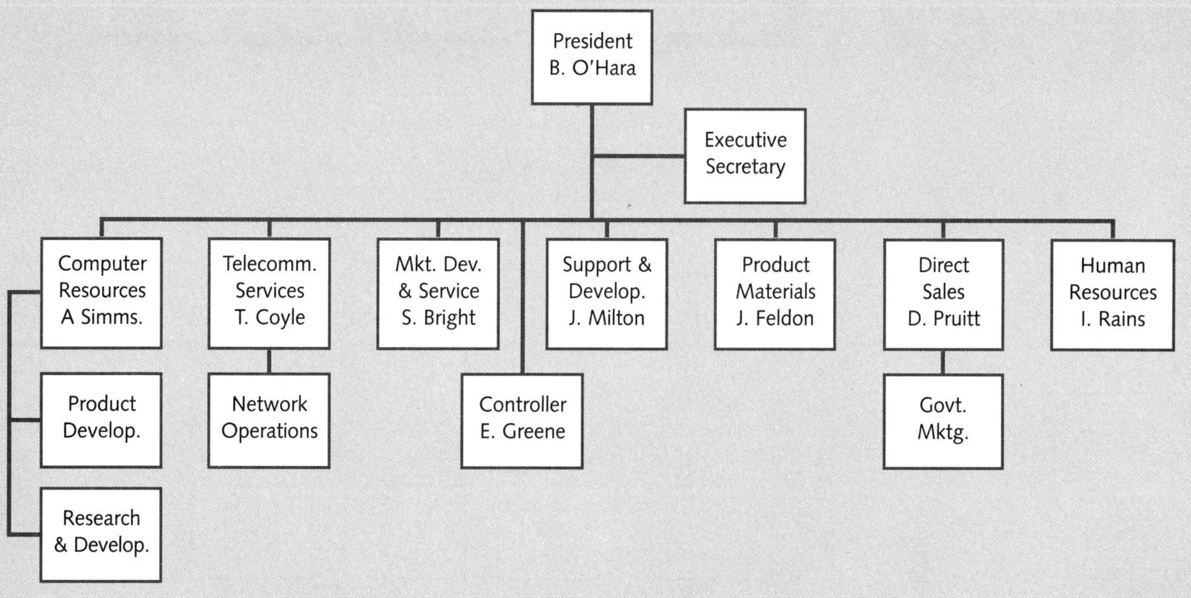

open-door policy. All in all, employees enjoy working for HITEK, and management is in touch with the organization's "pulse."

With the notable exception of the HR department, there are few rules at HITEK. Work in a department is often shared by all levels of employees, and positions are redefined to match the specific skills, abilities, and interests of the incumbent. "Overqualified" and "overachieving" individuals are often hired but are then promoted rapidly. Nothing is written down; and if newcomers want to know why something is done a certain way, they must ask the person(s) who created the procedure. There is extensive horizontal linkage between departments, perpetuating the blurring of distinctions between departments.

The HR Department

The HR department stands in stark contrast to the rest of HITEK. About thirty people are employed in the department, including the support staff members, or about one HR employee per thirty-three HITEK employees. The vice president for human resources, Isabel Rains, rules the department with an "iron fist." Employees are careful to mold their ideas to match Rains perspective. When newcomers suggest changes, they are told that "this is the way things have always been done" because "it's our culture." Most of the HR functions are bound by written rules and standard operating procedures; and, because department employees know their job descriptions well, there is little overlap in duties.

With the exception of one recruiter, all twelve of the incumbents whose positions are represented in Case Exhibit 2 are women. Only half of them have degrees in industrial relations or PHRM, and only one-fourth have related experience with another company. Most of them have been promoted from clerical positions. In fact, some employees view the vice-presidency as a "gift" given to Isabel, a former executive secretary, the day after she received her bachelor's degree at a local college. In other departments, it is widely believed that professional degrees and related experience lead to expertise.

One incident that conveyed the department's image to Jennifer Hill occurred during her second week on the job. While preparing a job description with Dave Pruitt, Jennifer explained that she would submit the job description to Janet Voris for final approval. Dave became confused and asked, "But Janet is only a clerical person; why would she be involved?"

Jennifer Hill's Duties

At HITEK, the pool of job descriptions had grown almost daily as newcomers were hired, but many of the old job descriptions were not discarded, even when obsolete. Other job descriptions needed updating. Jennifer spent some time thinking about how to proceed. She considered the uses of the job descriptions and what steps she would need to take to accomplish all that was expected of her. Support from within the department was scarce because other employees were busy gathering materials for the annual review of HITEK's hiring, promotion, and development practices conducted by the Equal Employment Opportunity Commission.

After six harried months on the job and much frustration, Jennifer had revised all the descriptions that were still needed (examples of "old" and "new" job descriptions appear in Case Exhibits 3 and 4). She was also beginning to develop some strong opinions about how the HR department functioned at HITEK and what needed to be done to improve its

CASE EXHIBIT 2

Structure of HITEK's Human Resource Department

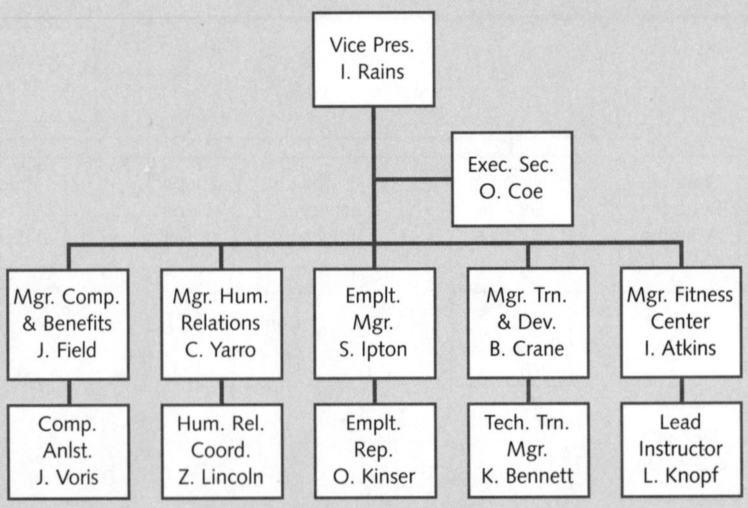

effectiveness and its image. She decided to arrange a confidential lunch with Billy O'Hara.

Case Questions

1. What are the goals of HITEK? Of the HR department? Why does the conflict create problems for HITEK?
2. Organization members can draw from several kinds of power, such as referent power and reward power. Is the HR department powerful? Why is it important for HITEK to maintain a professional, competent HR function?
3. Jobs change frequently at HITEK. Shouldn't the HR department simply discontinue the practice of job analysis and stop writing job descriptions?
4. What steps should Jennifer Hill take in performing the tasks assigned to her? How do your answers to the earlier questions affect your answer?
5. Is the "new" job description (Case Exhibit 4) better than the "old" one (Case Exhibit 3)? Why or why not?
6. What should Jennifer suggest to the president concerning the image and operation of the HR department?

Source: Written by M. P. Miceli, Ohio State University, and Karen Wijta, Macy's.

CASE EXHIBIT 3

An "Old" Job Description

ASSOCIATE PROGRAMMER

Basic Objective	Perform coding, testing, and documentation of programs, under the supervision of a project leader.
Specific Tasks	Perform coding, debugging, and testing of a program when given general program specifications.
	Develop documentation of the program.
	Assist in the implementation and training of the users in the usage of the system.
	Report to the manager, management information services as requested.
Job Qualifications	Minimum: (a) BA/BS degree in relevant field or equivalent experience/knowledge; (b) programming knowledge in FORTRAN; (c) good working knowledge of business and financial applications.
	Desirable: (a) computer programming experience in a time-sharing environment; (b) some training or education in COBOL, PL1, or assembler languages.

CASE EXHIBIT 4

A "New" Job Description

ASSOCIATE PROGRAMMER

General Statement of Duties	Performs coding, debugging, testing, and documentation of software under the supervision of a technical superior. Involves some use of independent judgment.
Supervision Received	Works under close supervision of a technical superior or manager.
Supervision Exercised	No supervisory duties required.
Examples of Duties	(Any one position may not include all the duties listed, nor do listed examples include all duties that may be found in positions of this class.)
	Confers with analysts, supervisors, and/or representatives of the departments to clarify software intent and programming requirements.
	Performs coding, debugging, and testing of software when given program specifications for a particular task or problem.
	Writes documentation for the program.

Continued

Examples of Duties (continued)	Seeks advice and assistance from supervisor when problems outside of realm of understanding arise. Communicates any program specification deficiencies back to supervisor.
	Reports ideas concerning design and development back to supervisor.
	Assists in the implementation of the system and training of end users.
	Provides some support and assistance to users.
	Develops product knowledge and personal expertise and proficiency in system usage.
	Assumes progressively complex and independent duties as experience permits.
	Performs all duties in accordance with corporate and departmental standards.
Minimum Qualifications	Education: BA/BS degree in relevant field or equivalent experience/knowledge in computer science, math, or other closely related field.
	Experience: No prior computer programming work experience necessary.
	Knowledge, Skills, Ability to exercise initiative and sound judgment. Knowledge of a structured language. Working knowledge in operating systems. Ability to maintain open working relationship with supervisor. Logic and problem-solving skills. System flowchart development skills.
Desirable Qualifications	Exposure to FORTRAN, C++ and object-oriented programming languages; some training in general accounting practices and controls; effective written and oral communication skills.

Chapter 8 Endnotes

1. From S. Caudron, "Master the Compensation Maze," *Personnel Journal* (June 1993): 64D; C. Roush, "Aetna's Heavy Ax," *Business Week* (February 14, 1994): 32.

2. Materials adapted from the search firm, Kenny, Kindler, Hunt and Howe, New York City, from *The Changing Human Resources Function* (New York: The Conference Board, 1990): 15. Used by permission.

3. R. Page and D. Van De Voort, "Job Analysis and HR Planning," in *Human Resource Planning, Employment and Placement*, W. F. Cascio. ed. (Washington, D.C.: Bureau of National Affairs, 1989): 2/34–2/72; more traditional definitions of job analyses are found in C. P. Sparks, "Job Analysis," in *Readings in Personnel and Human Resource Management* 3rd ed., R. S. Schuler, S. A. Youngblood, and V. Huber eds. (St. Paul, MN: West, 1988); E. J. McCormick, "Job and Task Analysis," in *Handbook of Industrial and Organizational Psychology*, M. D. Dunnette, ed. (Chicago: Rand McNally, 1979), 651–696; E. J. McCormick, *Job Analysis: Methods and Applications* (New York: AMACOM, 1979).

4. For more discussion on the purpose of job analysis, see R. J. Plachy, "Writing Job Descriptions That Get Results," *Personnel* (Oct. 1987): 56–63.

5. P. C. Grant, "What Use is a Job Description?" *Personnel Journal* (Feb. 1988): 45–49; M. A. Jones, Levine, *Everything You Always Wanted to Know About Job Analysis* (Tampa, FL: Mariner, 1983); R. J. Plachy, "Writing Job Descriptions That Get Results," *Personnel* (Oct.1987): 56–63.

6. "I've used the 'Descriptions Now' [software] program, and am quite enthused about it. It's really pretty easy to use, however like anything, you have to take the time to learn its different aspects...and be ready to use it for its 'templates' as you do custom descriptions...although you get generic job description material with it, you still have to do some basic work in setting minimum requirements, ADA-oriented data for your specific job, etc. All in all, it's the best you can find... especially for the money you'll be spending. Good purchase. Terrific timesaver." Communication from Wilson Gilinksy, (San Diego, CA: VisiCom Laboratories), January 3, 1996.

7. See McCormick, *Job Analysis: Methods and Applications*, and M. A. Jones, "Job Descriptions Made Easy," *Personnel Journal* (May 1984): 31–34.

8. Equal Employment Opportunity Commission. "Uniform Guidelines of Employee Selection Procedures," *Federal Register* 43 (1978): 38290–38315; J. Ledvinka and V. Scarpello, *Federal Regulation of Personnel and Human Resource Management*, 2nd ed. (Boston, MA: Kent, 1990).

9. B. Singer, "It's 7 P.M., And 5 Percent of Omaha is Calling... ," *New York Times Magazine* (December 3, 1995): 68–70.

10. R. H. Hayes and R. Jailkumar, "Manufacturing's Crisis: New Technologies, Obsolete Organizations," *Harvard Business Review* (Sept.–Oct. 1988): 77–85.

11. E. E. Adam Jr. and R. J. Ebert, *Production and Operations Management* (Englewood Cliff, NJ: Prentice Hall,

1986); H. T. Amrine, V. L. Huber, and N. L. Hyer, "The Human Factor in Cellular Manufacturing," *Journal of Operations Management* 5 (1985): 213–228.

12. McCormick, *Job Analysis: Method and Applications.*

13. F. Luthans, R. M. Hodgetts, and S. A. Rosenkrantz, *Real Managers* (Cambridge, MA: Ballinger, 1988).

14. McCormick, *Job Analysis: Methods and Applications.*

15. E. McCormick and J. Tiffin, *Industrial Psychology,* 6th ed. (Englewood Cliffs, NJ: Prentice Hall, 1974). Reprinted by permission of Prentice Hall, Inc. The Position Analysis Questionnaire (PAQ) is copyrighted by the Purdue Research Foundation. The PAQ and related materials are available through the University Book Store, 360 West State Street, West Lafayette, Ind. 47906.

16. For a discussion of the PAQ, see E. T. Cornelius III, A. S. DeNisi, and A. G. Blencoe, "Expert and Naive Raters Using the PAQ: Does It Matter?" *Personnel Psychology* (Autumn 1984): 453–464; J. B. Shaw and J. H. Riskind, "Predicting Job Stress Using Data from the Position Analysis Questionnaire," *Journal of Applied Psychology* (May 1983): 253–261.

17. R. J. Harvery, F. Friedman, M.D. Hakel, and E. T. Cornelius, "Dimensionality of the Job Element Inventory, a Simplified Worker-Oriented Job Analysis Questionnaire," *Journal of Applied Psychology* 73 (1988): 639–646.

18. McCormick, *Job Analysis: Methods and Applications.* See Chapter 30, "Job and Task Analysis."

19. S. A. Fine, "Functional Job Analysis: An Approach to a Technology for Manpower Planning," *Personnel Journal,* 3rd ed. (Washington, D.C.: Government Printing Office, 1965); *Dictionary of Occupational Titles,* 4th ed. (Washington, D.C.: Government Printing Office, 1991); Department of Labor, Manpower Administration, *Handbook for Analyzing Jobs* (Washington, D.C.: Government Printing Office, 1965); Department of Labor, *Task Analysis Inventories: A Method of Collecting Job Information* (Washington, D.C.: Government Printing Office, 1973); J. Markowitz, "Four Methods of Job Analysis," *Training and Development Journal* (Sept. 1981): 112–121.

20. U.S. Department of Labor, Employment and Training Administration, *The New Database of Occupational Titles for the Twenty-First Century,* final report of the Advisory Panel for the *Dictionary of Occupational Titles* (Washington, D.C., 1993).

21. J. C. Flanagan, "The Critical Incident Technique," *Psychology Bulletin* 51(1954): 327–358; G. P. Latham and K. N. Wexley, *Increasing Productivity Through Performance Appraisal* (Reading, MA: Addison-Wesley, 1981).

22. Guidelines-Oriented Job Analysis is a specific technique developed by Biddle and Associates, Sacramento, California, and is described here with their permission.

23. W. W. Tornow and P. R. Pinto, "The Development of Managerial Job Taxonomy: A System for Describing, Classifying, and Evaluating Executive Positions," *Journal of Applied Psychology* 61(1976): 410–418. See also W. F. Cascio, *Applied Psychology in Personnel Management,* 2nd ed., Reston, VA: Reston, 1982).

24. B. C. Dowell and K. N. Wexley, "Development of a Work Behavior Taxonomy for First Line Supervisors," *Journal of Applied Psychology* 63 (1978): 563–572.

25. For an excellent description of issues related to job family or classes, see K. Pearlman, "Job Families: A Review and Discussion of Their Implications for Personnel Selection," *Psychological Bulletin* 87 (1980): 1–28.

26. "The New World of Work," *Business Week* (October 17, 1994): 76–102.

27. A. Downs, "Planned People Obsolescence," *Training* (February 1995): 54–58; M. Moravec and R. Tucker, "Job Descriptions for the 21st Century," *Personnel Journal* (June 1992): 37.

28. See note 1, Chapter 1.

29. W. Bridges, "The End of the Job," *Fortune* (September 19, 1994): 62.

30. W. DeCaporale, "Switching to Broadbanding: One Company's Experience," *ACA News* (April 1996): 8–12; D. Hofrichter, "Broadbanding: A 'Second Generation' Approach," *Compensation & Benefits Review* (September–October 1993): 53–58.

31. Excerpts from "Master the Compensation Maze," by S. Caudron, copyright June 1993.

32. The essence of the *Civil Rights Act* of 1964 and 1991, the *Equal Opportunity in Employment Act* of 1972, and various court decisions is that employment decisions be made on the basis of whether the individual will be able to perform the job. To determine this, organizations should conduct job analyses to determine what skills, knowledge, and abilities individuals need to perform the jobs. Once this is known, selection procedures can be developed. Chapter 8 expands on the job relatedness of selection procedures. For more legal review, see D. E. Thompson and T. A. Thompson, "Court Standards for Job Analysis in Test Validation," *Personnel Psychology* 35 (1982): 865–874.

33. "Objective Employee Appraisals and Discrimination Cases," *Fair Employment Practices* (Dec. 6, 1990): 145–146; R. J. Nobile, "The Law of Performance Appraisals," *Personnel* (January 1991): 7.

34. "Job Analyses and Job Descriptions Under ADA," *Fair Employment Practices* (April 22, 1993): 45.

9

CHAPTER

Recruitment

Learning Objectives

1. Describe why recruitment is so important.
2. Discuss sources and methods for obtaining job applicants.
3. Indicate how organizations can increase their pools of potentially qualified job applicants by methods other than the traditional ones.
4. Describe the impact of workforce diversity on a firm's recruitment policies.
5. Describe the details of affirmative action programs.

Chapter Outline

"If a company depends on employees for a competitive advantage, you've got to create an environment to attract people from all segments of the population."

Jim Porter
Vice President for Human Resources
Honeywell[1]

MANAGING HUMAN RESOURCES

at McDonald's

"Every eight hours, somewhere in the world, another McDonald's restaurant opens its doors. Every eight hours. The ubiquitous quick-service food chain has raised 17,000-plus golden arches in more than 80 countries—its Beijing, China, facility served 50,000 people its first day of business."[2]

As do many service-oriented firms, McDonald's faces problems finding the variety of employees it needs—those who staff its restaurants as well as those intended for management positions, either as restaurant managers or franchise owners.

For its restaurant staff positions, McDonald's has used a variety of recruiting approaches. First, rather than rely on its traditional labor pool, McDonald's has looked to new groups to hire, such as retirees and mothers with young children. To attract these groups, the firm offers flexible working hours. With young people, particularly from inner-city locations, the firm has in the past been able to recruit and hire them but unable to retain them. The company found that inner-city teenagers would often work for a few months and then quit. The teenagers worked just long enough to earn money to buy specific items such as new clothes or a boom box. To retain such employees, McDonald's sought ways to make the jobs more fun. In some parts of the country, for example, the young people are allowed to choose the music played in the restaurant or to wear favorite clothes on particular days, rather than the standard McDonald's uniforms. Such flexibility in company practices has made it a more attractive employer for different groups in the workforce. Finally, to attract employees with potential for restaurant management, McDonald's sponsors summer internships and management training programs for minority students.

Its recruitment of franchise operators, particularly those for overseas restaurants, has been easier because of the opportunities the company offers. In many countries, the franchisees provide a unique and welcome opportunity to be an entrepreneur. Thus, "recruitment" varies greatly depending on the area and type of employee the firm needs.[3]

This feature illustrates several aspects of recruitment today. One is the impact of the declining skilled labor pool. Another is the increasing efforts by organizations to attract and retain workers they have not previously employed. A third aspect is the need for organizations to be systematic in their identification of HR needs and development of recruitment strategies to ensure that their business needs are filled. Another is the impact of the local economy, particularly on the ability of employers to attract sufficient numbers of job applicants. And a final one is the need to recruit and adapt one's recruiting programs to the local environment. These issues, some ongoing and some recent developments, form the subject of this chapter.

Did You KNOW?

McDonald's has more than 200,000 employees worldwide.

Recruitment

Recruitment involves searching for and obtaining qualified job candidates in such numbers that the organization can select the most appropriate person to fill its job needs. In addition to filling job needs, the recruitment activity should be concerned with satisfying the needs of the job candidates.[4] Consequently, recruitment not only attracts individuals to an organization, but also increases the chance of retaining them once they are hired. Of course, the recruitment activity must be done in compliance with legal regulations. Thus **recruitment** is the set of activi-

Recruitment is concerned with searching for and obtaining a pool of qualified job candidates.

ties used to obtain a pool of qualified job applicants. In other words, recruitment finds the organization its most important asset—its human resources.

Recruitment includes several key activities such as: (1) determining the organization's long- and short-range needs; (2) developing effective recruiting materials; (3) developing a systematic and integrated program of recruitment in conjunction with other HR activities and with the cooperation of line managers; (4) obtaining a pool of qualified job applicants; (5) recording the number and quality of job applicants produced by the various sources and methods of recruiting; and (6) following up on applicants, those hired and not hired, in order to evaluate the effectiveness of the recruiting effort. All of these activities must be accomplished within the proper legal context.

LEARNING OBJECTIVE 1

Describe why recruitment is so important.

Why Is Recruitment Important?

Recruiting is important because it can make or break a company. As Jim Porter, vice president for human resources at Honeywell says, some companies depend upon the quality of their people to give them a competitive advantage. Starbucks, the super-successful gourmet coffee shop chain, gets its competitive advantage through people by careful recruitment and training:

> *To maintain quality, Starbucks finds it recruits in colleges and community groups and gives them 24 hours training in coffee making and lore—key to creating the hip image and quality service that build customer loyalty.*[5]

Did You KNOW?

According to a recent Ernst & Young survey, recruiting and retaining key personnel is the biggest concern of the nation's 400 fastest-growing companies.

Increasingly, companies such as McDonald's are recognizing that there is also value in having a workforce that is as diverse as the customers and community served by the company. Many firms have embraced diversity in this way for years. Levi Strauss, for example, is now recognized as among the most culturally and ethnically diverse companies in the U.S., with 56 percent of its 23,000 employees being from backgrounds other than "American-born Caucasian." Fifteen percent of top management are people of color and 30 percent are women. Levi Strauss views this diversity as a way to ensure the company is in touch with the many perspectives of its customers.[6] Deloitte & Touche, a large public accounting firm, says that its campaign to recruit more females has resulted in a new reputation as a women-friendly firm. It now has the greatest number of female employees in the Big Six. According to Jim Wall, national director for HR:

> *It's helping us tremendously in recruiting. The business reasons for doing this are coming home very quickly.*[7]

The general purpose of recruitment—that is providing a pool of potentially qualified job candidates who can make the company as successful as possible—is fulfilled through several more specific purposes, including to:

- Determine the present and future recruitment needs of the organization in conjunction with HR planning and job analysis activities
- Increase the pool of potentially qualified job applicants at minimum cost
- Increase the success rate of the selection process by reducing the number of obviously underqualified job applicants
- Reduce the probability that job applicants, once recruited and selected, will leave the organization after only a short period of time
- Increase organizational and individual effectiveness in the short and long term
- Evaluate the effectiveness of various recruiting techniques and sources for all types of job applicants

- Meet the organization's responsibility for affirmative action programs and other legal and social considerations regarding the composition of its workforce

Because recruiting is so important to companies, it is critical that it be done effectively.[8] Recruitment is particularly effective when a partnership is created among HR professionals, line managers, and current employees.[9] The various activities that can be done in partnership are shown in the feature, "Partnership: Working Together in Recruitment."

Sources and Methods for Obtaining Job Applicants

LEARNING OBJECTIVE 2

Discuss sources and methods for obtaining job applicants.

We now examine the sources where potentially qualified job applicants can be found and the methods used to recruit them. Both sources and methods can be external to the organization as well as internal. A list of both types is shown in Exhibit 9.1.

Internal Sources

Internal sources involve present employees; this recruitment occurs through promotions and transfers, job rotation, and rehires and recalls.

Internal sources include:

- **promotions**
- **transfers**
- **job rotation**
- **rehires and recalls**

Promotion-from-within is the practice of advancing current employees to higher-level jobs.

Promotions. The case for promotion-from-within rests on sound arguments. Internal employees can be better qualified. Even jobs that do not seem unique require familiarity with the people, procedures, policies, and special characteristics of the organization in which they are performed. Employees are likely to feel more secure and therefore identify their long-term interests with an organization that provides them the first choice of job opportunities. Availability of promotions within an organization can also motivate employees to perform.

To assist with maintaining an internal policy, organizations use succession planning and replacement planning charts. Replacement planning charts list the current and potential occupants of positions in the firm. Potential promotions and developmental needs are indicated by the performance levels of employees. Incumbents are listed directly under the job title. Individuals likely to fill potential vacancies are listed next. An example of a replacement chart is shown in Exhibit

PARTNERSHIP: WORKING TOGETHER IN RECRUITMENT

LINE MANAGERS	HR PROFESSIONALS	EMPLOYEES
Identify present and future job openings. Prepare descriptions of job duties and skills needed to fill jobs. Prepare for interviews with job applicants. Work with HR professionals on equal employment and workforce diversity. Help identify potential talent for future promotion and staffing.	Use information from line managers to prepare recruitment activities. Develop sources and methods of recruiting to ensure sufficient number of qualified applicants. Ensure equal employment considerations are met and workforce diversity is effectively managed. Develop and maintain succession plans and replacement charts.	Participate in recruitment efforts such as referring the company to others. Work with HR professionals and line managers in the organization's efforts to effectively manage workforce diversity. Become part of a succession plan or talent pool for further training and development.

EXHIBIT 9.1

Recruitment Sources and Methods Used by Companies (%)

METHOD	ANY JOB CATEGORY*	OFFICE/ CLERICAL	PRODUCTION/ SERVICE	PROFESSIONAL/ TECHNICAL	COMMISSIONED SALES	MANAGERS/ SUPERVISORS
	OCCUPATION					
(Number of companies)	(245)	(245)	(221)	(237)	(96)	(243)
Internal Sources						
Promotion from within	99%	94%	86%	89%	75%	95%
Advertising						
Newspapers	97	84	77	94	84	85
Journals/magazines	64	6	7	54	33	50
Direct mail	17	4	3	16	6	8
Radio/television	9	3	6	3	3	2
Outside Referral Sources						
Colleges/universities	86	24	15	81	38	45
Technical/vocational institutes	78	48	51	47	5	8
High schools/trade schools	68	60	54	16	5	2
Professional societies	55	4	1	51	19	37
Community agencies	39	33	32	20	16	9
Unions	10	1	11	1	—	1
Employee referrals	91	87	83	78	76	64
Walk-in applicants	91	86	87	64	52	46
Employment Services						
State employment services	73	66	68	38	30	23
Private employment agencies	72	28	11	58	44	60
Search firms	67	1	—	36	26	63
U.S. Employment Service	22	19	20	11	7	7
Employee leasing firms	20	16	10	6	2	—
Computerized resume service	4	—	—	4	—	2
Video interviewing service	2	—	—	1	—	1
Special Events						
Career conferences/job fairs	53	20	17	44	19	19
Open house	22	10	8	17	8	7
Other	9	5	5	7	6	7

* Percentages for each job category are based on the number of organizations that provided data for that category, as shown by the number in parentheses.

Source: Reprinted by permission from Personnel Policies Forum, Survey No. 146, Recruiting and Selection Procedures, 4–5 (The Bureau of National Affairs, Inc., Washington, D.C., 1988). Data still accurate as of 1996 according to the Bureau of National Affairs.

9.2. Succession planning is similar to replacement planning except that it is usually longer term and more developmental. With rapidly changing environments, organizations are planning successions more than ever. Realizing that what makes a good manager today may not tomorrow, many companies use HR planning activities to identify what *will* make a good manager in the future. Then, developmental activities, such as job rotations and key task assignments, can be offered as a way to ensure that the right people are available with the right skills at the right time.

EXHIBIT 9.2

Sample Employee Replacement Chart

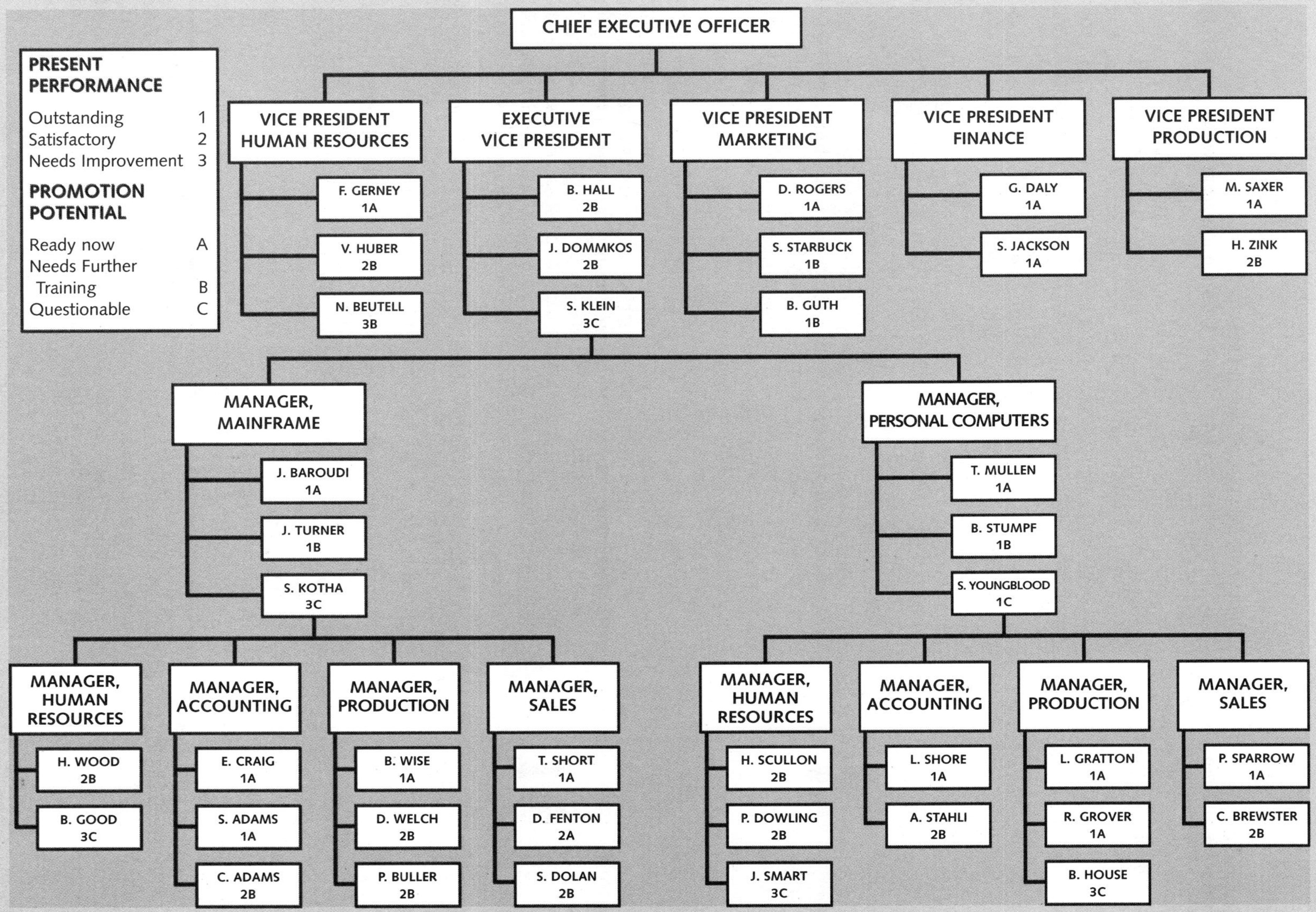

According to Frank Berardi of the corporate HR department at Allstate Insurance: "While there is some concern for numbers, it is primarily the concern for skills that [line managers] are worried about and they want HR to help them develop management education programs and new succession programs. So this is a business issue that is HR in nature."[10]

Talent pools are those employees identified for future development and promotion within the company.

Firms often develop internal **talent pools** from which people can be recruited for new job openings throughout the company. Talent pools give more people a chance for promotion and allow companies to readily replace key individuals who leave the company unexpectedly. If the company in Exhibit 9.2 used a talent pool, the employees would not be stacked in small divisional and functional jobs; instead, all these individuals would be in one job or management grouping, differentiated only in terms of the job *levels* into which each person was ready to be moved. Regardless of whether the company uses replacement charts or the talent pool concept, internal promotion can also be much less expensive to the organization in terms of time and money. By comparison, the outside recruit is often brought in at a higher salary than that earned by people already in similar positions, and the costs to the company of relocating the new recruit and his or her family may range from $50,000 to $500,000. The result, especially if the new recruit fails to contribute as expected, is dissatisfaction among the current employees. In addition, the incentive value of promotions diminishes.[11]

Disadvantages of promotion-from-within include:

- **infighting**
- **inbreeding**
- **lack of varied perspectives**

Disadvantages of a promotion-from-within policy are several. One, there is always the possibility the best-qualified person is not to be found internally. Two, IF the best person is found, he or she may not take the promotion for personal reasons such as a desire to stay in familiar surroundings. Other disadvantages include infighting, inbreeding, and an ensuing lack of varied perspectives and interests. An organization that relies heavily on a promote-from-within policy may end up having to pressure candidates for the promotions.

Given the case for and against the internal promotion policy, it is not surprising that many organizations combine it with obtaining recruits from external sources. The type of employee sought often determines whether the organization looks inside or outside. For example, many organizations are more likely to hire highly trained professionals and high-level managers from the outside. Occasionally, promotions are made on the basis of personal impressions by the organizations. This is particularly true for middle- and upper-level managerial positions. Because it is difficult to defend under current legal guidelines, many organizations have had to reconsider this method of promotion. The use of test results from managerial assessment centers is one alternative to personal impressions. Since assessment centers are used more as a selection than a recruiting device, they are discussed in Chapter 10. Specific applicant sources are discussed later in this chapter.

Did You KNOW?

Eighty-two percent of employees rejected relocation offers in 1994, up from 68% in 1991. The primary reason for rejection was worries about spouses' jobs.

Transfers and Relocations. Another way to recruit internally is by transferring current employees without promotion. Transfers are often important in providing employees with the broad-based view of the organization necessary for future promotions.[12]

Once affirmative action and equal employment concerns are considered, the basis used to select the internal candidates for transfer must be decided. The choice is often seniority versus merit. Unions seem to prefer seniority, while some organizations prefer transfers based on ability. Where seniority systems exist, decisions can be made on that basis even if the results appear contrary to affirmative action and equal employment guidelines (*California Brewers Association v. Bryant,* 1980; *International Brotherhood of Teamsters v. U.S.,* 1977).

Especially when relocation to another part of the country is involved, needs of the candidates are often considered. Some candidates may have personal and family reasons to reject a transfer. Dual-career couples may not be able to find two jobs comparable to their current two jobs. As a consequence, firms are adapting and adjusting to these realities by seeking this information and working with the candidates in order to achieve a mutually beneficial outcome.[13]

Job Rotation. Whereas a transfer is likely to be permanent, job rotations are usually temporary in nature. Job rotation has been used effectively to expose management trainees to various aspects of organizational life. Job rotation has also been used to relieve job burnout for employees in high-stress occupations. For example, the Utah Department of Social Services has a job rotation program in which human service workers swap jobs with workers in other divisions or with employees in federal agencies for periods of up to one year. At the end of the contracted year of service, employees have the opportunity to return to their original positions or remain in the new position. Such programs give employees different perspectives, as well as an opportunity to try out new positions without fear of failure. Management, on the other hand, gets a chance to preview the employee prior to long-term commitment.

A relatively new disadvantage for both job rotation and transfers is the cost of relocation. For the first time at the Mitre Corporation, a Bedford, Massachusetts, systems engineering firm with 6,000 employees, real estate has become a consideration in selecting a candidate to fill a job.[14] This has been largely due to the housing slump in parts of the United States. With housing actually worth less than before, companies have to pay employees for the housing loss they experience when they sell their homes in order to relocate.

Rehires and Recalls. Each week, thousands of employees are temporarily laid off from work, and others are recalled to former jobs. The rehire of former employees or employees temporarily laid off is a relatively inexpensive and effective method of internal recruiting. Unlike new job candidates, the organization already has information about the performance, attendance, and safety records of these employees. Because they are already familiar with job responsibilities, rehires may be better performers than recruits from other sources. Additionally, they tend to stay on the job longer and have better attendance records.

In considering rehiring as a recruitment strategy, organizations need to weigh the costs against the benefits. Rehiring and recalls are particularly beneficial to organizations that have seasonal fluctuations in the demand for workers (for example, department stores, canneries, construction jobs, ski resorts). Canneries in eastern Washington recall large numbers of employees—some who have been employed for more than 20 years—each summer and fall during the apple harvest. This reduces employee costs. The down side of this recruitment approach is that employee commitment may be low. By the time of the recall, a qualified recruit may have found alternative employment—possibly with a major competitor. Finally, because turnover is continual, an organization's contribution to unemployment compensation programs is likely to increase.

Internal Methods

Frequently used internal methods include job posting and skills inventories.

Internal methods:

- **job posting**
- **skills inventories**

Job Postings. Job vacancies can be located by posting a notice on the bulletin board, on Internet, as done at Cisco Systems, the computer networking company in San Jose, California.[15] Job postings prominently display current job openings, thereby extending an open invitation to all employees in an organization. Job postings:

- Provide opportunities for employee growth and development
- Provide equal opportunity for advancement to all employees
- Create a greater openness in the organization by making opportunities known to all employees
- Increase staff awareness of salary grades, job descriptions, general promotion and transfer procedures, and what comprises effective job performance
- Communicate organizational goals and objectives and allow each individual the opportunity to help find a personal fit in the organization's job structure.[16]

AMP, a 25,000-employee manufacturing firm in Harrisburg, Pennsylvania, instituted a telephone-based job posting system in 1992.

Although job postings are usually found on bulletin boards, they also appear in company newsletters, are announced at staff meetings, and may be posted on the Internet. Sometimes specific salary information is included, but job grade and pay range are more typical. Job postings are beneficial for organizations because they improve morale, provide employees opportunity for job variety, facilitate a better matching of employee skills and needs, and fill positions at a low cost.[17]

These benefits, of course, are not always realized. Job posting can create problems such as the following:

- Conflicts may arise if an "heir apparent" in the department is passed over in favor of an outside candidate.
- Conversely, the system may lose credibility if it appears that the successful candidate within the department has been identified in advance and the managers are merely going through the motions in considering outsiders.
- The morale of the unsuccessful candidates may suffer if feedback is not carefully handled.
- Choices can be more difficult for the selecting manager if two or three equally qualified candidates are encountered.

Skills inventories are data files containing information on skills that employees have.

Skills Inventories. Aiding internal job posting and employee recalls are **skills inventories**. Most organizations have skill-related information buried in personnel files. When needed, much time and effort are required to get at it. A formal skills inventory aggregates this information through the use of a human resource information system (HRIS). Any data that can be quantified can be coded and included in a skills inventory.

Common information includes name, employee number, job classification, prior jobs, prior experience, and salary levels. The results of formal assessments, such as those attained in assessment centers, during work sample tests, and with job interest inventories, are usually included. While often overlooked, skill inventories should also include information regarding the employee's job interests, geographical preferences, and career goals. The inclusion of the latter information ensures that potential job assignments will meet individual as well as organizational goals.

Skills inventories are only as good as the data they contain. They are also time-consuming and somewhat costly to maintain. Still, a skills inventory can ensure that any individual who has the necessary qualifications for a position is considered.

External Sources

External sources for obtaining job applicants include:

- **employee referrals**
- **walk-ins**
- **employment agencies**
- **temporary-help agencies**
- **trade associations and unions**
- **schools**
- **foreign nationals**

Recruiting internally does not always produce enough qualified applicants. This is especially true for rapidly growing organizations or those with a large demand for high-talent professional, skilled, and managerial employees. Organizations therefore need external sources. Recruiting from the outside has a number of advantages, including bringing in people with new ideas. It is often cheaper and easier to hire an already-trained professional or skilled employee, particularly when the organization has an immediate demand for scarce labor skills and talents. External sources can also supply temporary employees who provide the organization with flexibility in expanding and contracting.

In general, organizations need to use both internal and external sources of recruitment. A summary of the advantages and disadvantages of each source appears in Exhibit 9.3.

Employee referral programs allow current employees to recommend new job applicants.

Employee Referral Programs. **Employee referral programs** are word-of-mouth advertisements in which current employees refer applicants from outside the organization. Because of the involvement of current employees, this recruiting method blends internal with external recruitment and is a low cost-per-hire means

EXHIBIT 9.3

Sources of Job Applicants

INTERNAL SOURCES

Advantages	Disadvantages
Morale of promotee	Inbreeding
Better assessment of abilities	Possible morale problems of those not promoted
Lower cost for some jobs	"Political" infighting for promotions
Motivator for good performance	Requires strong management development program
Have to hire only at entry level	

EXTERNAL SOURCES

Advantages	Disadvantages
"New blood," new perspectives	May not select someone who will "fit"
Cheaper than training a professional	May cause morale problems for those internal candidates
No group of political supporters in organization already	Longer adjustment or orientation time
May bring competitors' secrets, new insights	May bring in an attitude of "This is the way we used to do it at XYZ Company."
Helps meet equal employment needs	

Source: Adapted from R. L. Mathis and J. H. Jackson, *Personnel: Contemporary Perspectives and Applications*, 8th ed. (St. Paul, MN: West Publishing Co., © 1997). Reproduced by permission. All rights reserved.

of recruiting.[18] Informal referrals consist of informing current employees about job openings and asking them to encourage qualified friends and associates to apply. Formal referral programs, on the other hand, reward employees for referring skilled applicants to organizations. The financial incentive may be as little as $15 or as much as $2,000 for referring someone with a critical skill, such as robotics engineering or specialized nursing care. Financial incentives can be linked to the completion of an application, acceptance of employment, or the completion of work for a specified period of time on the part of the recruit.

Compared to other external recruiting methods, employee referrals for most occupations generally result in the highest one-year survival rates. The findings are less clear regarding performance and attendance by source. One explanation for the success of employee referral programs is that employees provide a balanced view of organizational life. Another explanation is that employees tend to recruit applicants who are similar to them in skills, interests, and abilities. Since the employee is already integrated in the organization culture, this prematching process increases the likelihood that applicants will also fit into the environment. On the surface, referring individuals who are similar in type (age, sex, race, and religion) seems beneficial. However, such referrals—particularly if they are required for employment—may be detrimental to meeting equal employment opportunity obligations.[19]

Walk-ins. As illustrated in Exhibit 9.1, recruitment of walk-ins is especially prevalent for clerical and service-job applicants. Individuals become applicants by walking into an organization's employment office—they have not been referred by anyone. This method, like employee referrals, is informal and relatively inexpensive and is almost as effective as employee referrals in retaining applicants once hired.[20] Unlike referrals, walk-ins know less about the specific jobs available and come without the implicit recommendation of a current employee. This may be a disadvantage compared to referrals since current employees are unlikely to refer or recommend unsatisfactory applicants.

Managerial, professional, and sales applicants, however, are seldom walk-ins, and because this method tends to be a passive source of applicants, it may not provide sufficient numbers to fulfill affirmative action and equal employment requirements. These two problems can be addressed by sponsoring open house events to attract applicants from the nearby community and recruiting at other companies.

Open Houses. An excellent way to introduce individuals to the organization and also attract individuals who might not otherwise apply is the use of open houses. These are events where the firm opens its doors so that individuals can come and take a look at what the company is about and what jobs it might have available. Open houses can give the individual a realistic organizational preview and allow the firm to look at potential applicants in an informal setting. When done during a weekend, the firm might also attract a wider range of applicants—that is, those who work elsewhere during the week.

Other Companies. Companies such as GE and Procter & Gamble are noted for their management development programs and their systematic way of developing people through job assignments. This practice can produce great managers, but it also provides a talented pool of potential candidates for other companies to raid.

Jerry Goodman of IBAX once worked at GE.

> *So many companies have been rejuvenated by the arrival of a new chief executive drawn from the management of the General Electric Company that many investors feel as if they have hit a jackpot when their companies announce such recruiting coups.*
>
> *Companies that hire GE executives usually get managers who have experience running businesses that would be among the nation's largest companies if they were independent. Most have also been through GE's widely admired management training courses and have absorbed GE's global perspective.*[21]

Employees in companies known for their outstanding managers have always been contacted by private employment agencies; increasingly, they are being contacted directly by the company that wants them.

Management development programs are expensive, and some firms do not have them because they think it is foolish to train managers just to be hired by others. This view may be shortsighted for two reasons. First, the developing firm still gets its "pick of the litter," and second, having a good reputation for development serves as a powerful recruiting tool for lower-level jobs.

Employment Agencies. Public and private employment agencies are a good source for temporary employees—and an excellent source for permanent ones. American public employment agencies are under the umbrella of the U.S. Training and Employment Service. The Service sets national policies and oversees the operations of state employment services, which have branch offices in many cities. The *Social Security Act* provides that, in general, any worker who has been laid off from a job must register with the state employment agency to be eligible for unemployment benefits. The agencies then have a roster of potential applicants to assist organizations looking for job candidates.

State employment agencies provide a wide range of services, most of which are supported by employer contributions to state unemployment funds. The agencies offer counseling, testing, and placement services to everyone. They provide special services to individuals, military veterans, minority groups, and college, technical, and professional people. The state agencies also make up a nationwide network of job and applicant information in the form of job banks. These job banks have one drawback, however: the Service and its state agencies do not actually recruit people but only passively assist those who come to them. In addition, those who do come in are often untrained or only marginally qualified for most jobs.

Private employment agencies tend to serve two groups of job applicants—professional and managerial, and unskilled. The agencies dealing with unskilled applicants often provide job candidates that employers would have a difficult time finding otherwise. Many of the employers looking for unskilled workers do not have the resources to do their own recruiting or have only temporary or seasonal demands for them.

Private agencies play a major role in recruiting professional and managerial candidates.[22] These agencies supply services for applicants of all ages; most, however, have had some work experience beyond college. During the past 10 years, the executive recruiting industry has grown phenomenally. The fees charged by these agencies range up to one-third of the first year's total salary and bonus package for the job to be filled.[23]

Even when successful, the cost of using a search firm may be much greater than the fees charged. In the prescreening process, for example, the search firm can err by rejecting a candidate who would do well. These errors pose additional costs to the organization.[24] The organization, however, can minimize these costs by closely monitoring the search firm's activities. Note also that these agencies may prescreen applicants who are already working with other organizations. Consequently, in addition to the expense, this method of dealing with a potential candidate is apt to be secretive and counter to the openness that is desirable in an organization's employment process.[25]

Temporary-Help Agencies. Temporary-help agencies annually employ more than 3 million people.[26] There are over 4,500 of these agencies, and they generate more than $25 billion in annual revenues. Their use is growing as skilled and semiskilled individuals find it preferable to work less than a 40-hour week or on a schedule of their own choosing. Temporary employees (or temps) usually work in a variety of organizations; consequently, they can satisfy preferences for schedule flexibility and workplace variety. Furthermore, temps can receive higher pay than the organization's permanent staff, although they also generally forego benefits.

The use of temps or temporary help is growing rapidly. Manpower, Inc., a temp agency, is one of the largest employers in the U.S. today.

Organizations are using temporary-help agencies more than ever because certain hard-to-get skills are available nowhere else.[27] (This is especially true for small companies that are not highly visible or cannot spend time recruiting.) In addition, many organizations need people for only a short time. Getting them without an extensive search, while retaining the flexibility to reduce their workforce without costly layoffs and potential unemployment compensation payments, is an obvious advantage.

Some firms, especially those just starting up or adding significant numbers of new employees, hire a contract recruiter to run major recruiting operations. **Contract recruiters** are consultants who accept temporary assignments with companies (typically three to six months), become an integral part of the HR staff, and address problems relating to recruitment.

Contract recruiters **are consultants who accept temporary assignments to help companies with their recruiting needs.**

Although employment activity accounts for a majority of their assignments, contract recruiters are increasingly involved in a variety of HR issues, ranging from compensation and benefits to employee relations and to equal access and equal opportunity programs.

Contractors are available immediately, without the expense of employee benefits. Unlike regular employees, a contractor is easily replaced without the trauma of an employee termination. For example, GTE, in Needham, Massachusetts, won a major contract, assuring the government that 1,200 professionals would be on board within 16 months. At the peak of recruiting, 12 recruiting contractors worked full-time as an instant employment staff, establishing a recruiting and selection system. The number diminished to two at the end of the 16 months. Before leaving, the consultants recruited, hired, and trained their own permanent replacements.

Trade Associations and Unions. Unions for the building trades and maritime workers assume responsibility for supplying employers with skilled labor. This practice takes many labor decisions, such as job assignment, out of company hands. The *Taft-Hartley Act,* however, restricts these "hiring hall" practices to a limited number of industries.

Trade and professional associations are important sources for recruiting. Their newsletters and annual conferences often provide notice of employment opportunities. Annual conferences can give employers and potential job applicants an opportunity to meet. Communities and schools have adopted this idea and now bring together large numbers of employers and job seekers at **job fairs.** Of course, with only a limited time for interviews, such fairs or career conferences are only an initial step in the recruitment process. They are, nevertheless, effective for both employers and individuals.

Job fairs **are large, public events where many companies come to look for job applicants.**

Schools. Schools can be categorized into three types—high schools, vocational and technical schools, and colleges and universities. All are important sources of recruits for most organizations, although their importance varies depending on the type of applicant sought. For example, if an organization is recruiting managerial, technical, or professional applicants, then colleges and universities are more important, while high schools and vocational and technical schools become important when an organization is seeking plant/service and clerical employees (see Exhibit 9.1).

Recruiting at colleges and universities is often an expensive process, even if the recruiting visit eventually produces job offers and acceptances. Approximately 30 percent of the applicants hired from college leave the organization within the first five years of their employment. This rate of turnover is even higher for graduate students. Some people attribute this high rate of turnover to the lack of challenge in the initial job assignments. Organizations claim, however, that people just out of college have unrealistic expectations. Partly because of the expense, organizations are now questioning the necessity of hiring college graduates for some of their jobs. Another reason for this re-evaluation is the potential legal burden that an organization must assume if adverse impact results. In this event, the organization may have to show that a college degree is related to the performance of the job.

Nevertheless, college placement services are helpful to a company recruiting in particular fields such as engineering and microelectronics and those seeking highly talented and qualified minorities and women. In addition, organizations make campus visits to recruit college alumni, not just those about to graduate. Outreach programs by college and universities that provide placement services for their alumni enhance the attractiveness of the campus to employers, who benefit by having a broader and more experienced pool of applicants from which to recruit.

Foreign Nationals. As indicated in Chapter 3, certain labor shortages exist; these include professionals such as chemical engineers, nurses, and geologists. As a result, employers sometimes recruit foreign nationals—either overseas or in college placement offices.[28] Organizations use foreign nationals for operations both in the United States and abroad. When they work abroad, foreign nationals can serve as **host-country nationals (HCNs)** (persons working in their own country, which is not the country of the parent company) or **third-country nationals (TCNs)** (persons working in a country that is neither their own country nor the country of the parent company). In either capacity, these employees are critical for any company operating internationally. A novel use of host-country nationals is the recent use of Russian scientists by U.S. firms. This practice not only represents a global solution to a domestic skill shortage, but also an economical way to get highly skilled workers.[29]

Host-country nationals **work for U.S. firms in their own country.**

Foreign nationals have become so critical that U.S. companies have increased efforts to ensure that their foreign employees either are legal or become legal. Under the 1986 *Immigration Reform and Control Act* and the *Immigration Act* of 1990, it is unlawful for employers to hire foreign nationals to work in the U.S. who are illegal aliens.

Third-country nationals **work for U.S. firms in other countries.**

External Methods

Many organizations looking for applicants of all types engage in extensive advertising on radio and television, in the local paper, and in national newspapers such as *The Wall Street Journal.*

Radio and Television. Of the approximately $3 billion spent annually on recruitment advertising, only a tiny percentage is spent on radio and television. Companies are reluctant to use these media because they fear media advertising will be too expensive or that it will make the company look desperate and damage the firm's conservative image.

Yet, organizations are desperate to reach certain types of job applicants, such as skilled workers. In reality, of course, there is nothing inherently desperate about using radio and television advertising. Rather it is the content and delivery that can imply some level of desperation. Recognizing this, organizations are increasing their recruitment expenditures for radio and television advertisements, with favorable results.[30]

Newspapers and Trade Journals. Newspapers have traditionally been the most common method of external recruiting. They reach a large number of potential applicants at a relatively low cost per hire. Newspaper ads are used to recruit for all types of positions, from unskilled to top managerial. The ads range from matter-of-fact to creative.

Trade journals enable organizations to aim at much more specific groups of potential applicants than do the newspapers. Ads in trade journals are often more creative and of a high quality. Unfortunately, long lead times are required, and the ads can thus become dated.

Whatever the medium, preparing ads requires considerable skill. Many organizations hire advertising firms to do this. Selecting an advertising agency must be done with the same care used to select a private recruiting agency.[31] However, for firms that want to prepare the ads themselves, the feature "HR Advice and Application," offers several tips. Because of the cost savings, small firms may write their own ads.

Did You KNOW?

In 1995 the Lincoln Electric Company advertised 800 production openings and received more than 20,000 resumes.

Computerized Services and the Internet. Recent additions to external methods are the computerized recruiting services and the use of the information highway. Cisco Systems uses the Internet both as a place to list job openings and a place to locate job applicants.[32]

Barbara Beck, vice president of HR at Cisco Systems, says Internet recruiting yields high-caliber candidates:

> *It provides a good method of self-selection. We are looking for people who are comfortable with technology, and those people are likely to be found on the Internet. This process is very inexpensive. It's better than a newspaper ad, where you get lots of resumes from people who may or may not have the kind of experience we're looking for.* [33]

Those looking for jobs, the recruitees, are also able to take advantage of computer technology in looking for jobs. There are a number of on-line employment services and bulletin boards that can be a relatively inexpensive and valuable resource. A sample includes:[34]

- **E-Span.** Lists professional and managerial positions.
  http://www.espan.com
- **Help Wanted—USA.** Lists professional jobs.
  http://www.webcom.com/career/icc-employment1.html

HR ADVICE & APPLICATION

Ask the Experts—Winning Help-Wanted Ads

Q-1. How do you make sure that your ad meets equal employment opportunity requirements while accurately describing the position available?

A-1. Before you can begin your search, you'll need to go to your job description. If you don't already have one, bring two or three of your top people from the area you're trying to fill, and with their input, write one. The job description should include all essential and marginal job functions as required by the *Americans with Disabilities Act*. Then you can write a newspaper ad that matches the job description. You must include only objective, job-related requirements.

Q-2. What have you done when an ad didn't work?

A-2. I kept going back to my job description, designing my ad around it. Eventually, I came up with an ad that was very effective and brought in just the type of applicant I was looking for.

Q-3. What should be included in the ad?

A-3. Your recruitment ad—whether it's to be placed in a local paper or a trade magazine—needs to include certain basic elements. The ad should:

- Be descriptive and deal with specific needs. If you're looking for a sales representative, say SALES REPRESENTATIVE in bold type. This will focus attention on the ad by telling the reader exactly what you're looking for.
- Tell the readers exactly what you're selling. Don't make the ad generic or misleading. Give applicants the geographic area of the position you're trying to fill. Does the job require traveling? If so, mention how much travel is required.
- Tell the reader something about your company—and what qualities and qualifications the successful applicant will need. For instance, if the job requires that the applicant have a roadworthy vehicle, say so. Always ask for references. For example, "Applicant must have a reliable auto, strong sales background, and good references."
- Include all essential information. Don't leave anything to the imagination of the applicant. You'll screen out applicants, but that's better than wasting time interviewing people who will only turn you down, anyway, when they find out that no expenses are paid.

Q-4. How do you deal with responses to the ad?

A-4. I have all applicants call a central location and make an appointment for an interview. See them all. Don't screen any applicants over the phone.

A good ad will have done most of your screening for you. For instance, if I ask for good references, a reader who doesn't have them probably isn't going to apply, because he or she doesn't want to be embarrassed when I check them out. My ads usually bring in 15–20 applicants, and most of them are exactly what I'm looking for.

Q-5. Once you've interviewed the applicants, how do you select one?

A-5. First, you have to be sure that the applicant understands the job, the benefits, and what's expected of him or her. Be scrupulously honest about compensation. Don't mislead a candidate for a sales job, for instance, with stories about $100,000 income for hard work when you know your average salesperson makes less than $45,000.

To see if there really is a match, ask a promising candidate to go home and think about the position for a few days. This will give you an additional opportunity to check references—and it will give your prospective hire the opportunity to check references about your company as well.

A careful reference check is time-consuming, but it's essential. To call an applicant's previous employer and ask him or her to be candid is sometimes difficult, but you have to try. In today's litigious society, some companies may be hesitant about giving out any information at all except to confirm that the person was employed there.

Some companies require all applicants to sign release forms noting that former employers will be contacted for references. When you contact a former employer, you may need to do it in writing, on company letterhead, with a copy of the release form enclosed. Even this procedure isn't a guarantee, but you may have better luck getting a more candid reference than you would without it.[35]

- **Online Career Center.** Lists professional jobs.
  http://www.occ.com/occ
- **Academic Position Network.** Lists faculty, staff, administrative and graduate assistantships and fellowships, provided by William C. Norris Institute.
  gopher://wcni.cis.umn.edu:11111/1
- **Career Connections.** Engineering, manufacturing, marketing and computer jobs. Also has service for recent college graduates.
  http://www.acm.org/member_services/career/career_connect.html

Acquisitions and Mergers. Another method of staffing organizations is through mergers and acquisitions. In contrast to the other external methods, this one can facilitate the immediate implementation of an organization's strategic plan by acquiring a company with skilled employees. This ready pool may enable an organization to pursue a business plan, such as developing a new product line, that would otherwise be unfeasible using standard recruiting methods. The need to displace employees and to integrate a large number of them rather quickly into a new organization, however, means that the HR planning and selection process becomes more critical than ever.[36]

Work Flow Management. While you have been reading this chapter you may have said to yourself, "this book keeps talking about organizations having to deal with a labor shortage, yet all I see in the paper are stories about layoffs and the difficulties of getting a job." This is an excellent thought and one that identifies the importance of work flow management, that is, the management of the flow of employees as they join and leave the company.

The demographic data indicate that baby-busters will be in high demand in a growing economy because there are relatively few of them.

Yes, companies in the U. S., Japan, and Europe have been downsizing—at both managerial and nonmanagerial levels.[37] Consequently, organizations have been concerned about outplacement of employees.

But at the same time they have been hiring:

> *Even in tough times, we have to bring some level of entry-level talent into the organization to keep the business revitalized.*
>
> *Andy Esparza*
> *Director of Recruitment and College Relations*
> *AT&T Global Information Solutions*[38]

Lincoln Electric, BMW, and Scott Paper are hiring, but are unable to fill vacancies because of a lack of qualified applicants:

> *More than 20,000 applications have been submitted to Lincoln in the past 18 months, and most were rejected. Yet the maker of motors and welding products says it still has positions to fill and can't find the workers it needs.*
>
> *Around the country, a shortage of skilled labor has created the same paradox: Thousands of people are being turned down for factory work by companies that are actively recruiting. The result: unfilled jobs and very frustrated job seekers.*[39]

The process of recruitment seeks to ensure that the best are attracted to the firm and the best stay. With rapid changes in technology, the need for balancing is even more important. Companies must continually look at their recruitment methods and sources to make sure candidates with the needed skills are available. Likewise, companies must plan to outplace or retain workers whose skills are no longer needed. In this respect, HR planning and recruitment work together. Recruitment is a dynamic activity today, concerned as much about the outflow as the inflow of a company's human resources.

LEARNING OBJECTIVE 3

Indicate how organizations can increase their pools of potentially qualified job applicants by methods other than the traditional ones.

Increasing the Pool of Potentially Qualified Applicants

Although organizations may use many sources of recruitment, they may not always obtain the desired number of applicants nor retain the most valued employees. This is especially true in competitive labor markets. But an organization can enhance its recruitment by offering inducements such as relocation assistance, career development, or child care. Many ideas that organizations are using to increase their pools of qualified job applicants have the added benefit of increasing the probability that once hired, the applicant-employee will stay.

Organizations can become more attractive by conveying job and organizational information realistically.

Conveying Job and Organizational Information

The traditional approach to recruiting matches the applicant's abilities with the skills required on the job. A more recent approach, although still concerned with matching skills and abilities, is also concerned with matching the applicant's personality, interests, and preferences both with the job and with organizational characteristics. Getting new hires to stay is as important as finding applicants who can do the job. Obtaining both is possible by: (1) devoting attention to the job interview, (2) developing policies regarding job offer acceptances, and (3) carefully timing recruitment procedures.

Job Interview. A vital aspect of the recruitment process is the interview. A good interview provides the applicant with a realistic preview of what the job will be like. It can definitely be an enticement to join an organization, just as a bad interview will deter an applicant.

The quality of the interview is, of course, just one aspect of the recruitment process. Other things being equal, however, the chances of a person accepting a job offer increases when interviewers show interest and concern for the applicant. In addition, applicants feel most positive toward the recruitment interview when they can use at least half of the interview to ask questions and when they are not embarrassed or put on the spot by the interviewer.

The content of the recruitment interview is important. Organizations often assume that it is in their best interest to tell a job applicant only the positive aspects of the organization. But studies by the life insurance industry have reported that providing realistic (positive and negative) information actually increases the number of eventual recruits. In addition, those who receive realistic job information are less likely to quit once they accept the job.[40]

Assuming that recruits pass the initial screening (discussed in more detail in (Chapter 10, Selection), they should be given the opportunity to interview with a potential supervisor and even with co-workers. The interview with the potential supervisor is crucial, for this is the person who often makes the final decision.

Policies Regarding Job Offer Acceptance. Employers can influence applicants' selection decisions through the amount of time they allow individuals to ponder the offer. Given unlimited time to ponder their decision, most job seekers will delay decision-making until they have heard from all organizations in the job search net. Thus, setting deadlines is an important detail because the lack of one places the organization at a distinct disadvantage. Unless its job openings are unlimited, it cannot extend an offer to a second-choice candidate until a decision is made by their first choice. Since job markets are dynamic, high-potential candidates may commit elsewhere. Thus, most organizations have recall policies, policies to bring back former employees, and job seekers find themselves in the dilemma of having to decide on a minimally acceptable offer before possibly receiving a preferred offer.

Timing. In markets where recruiting occurs in well-defined cycles (such as college recruiting), organizations can opt to be early participants. Assuming that most individuals evaluate job options sequentially, organizations enhance their chances of obtaining high-potential candidates by participating early in the cycle. For example, high-technology companies involve high-potential juniors in summer internships or cooperative education programs. Progressive organizations are also bypassing traditional second-semester campus interviews and inviting high-potential candidates directly to corporate headquarters early in their senior years. Most major accounting firms have job offers out and accepted by year end. Such strategies are designed to induce commitment from top graduates before exposure to competing firms. Organizations that rely upon traditional second-semester interviews and long, drawn-out selection processes may find themselves in a less competitive position than their proactive recruiting rivals.[41]

Internships can get you to the right place at the right time.

Socialization

Dealing with increased labor shortages of qualified workers can in part be solved by effectively managing the socialization process. **Socialization** is the process that companies use to expose new employees to their culture and ways of doing things. When done successfully, it results in intensely loyal employees who are dedicated to the company. Companies that are excellent at the socialization process include Procter & Gamble, Morgan Guaranty Trust, and Corning Glass.

Socialization is a key HR process in organizations.

Often, the socialization process begins before the employee is hired. At Procter & Gamble (P&G), for example, an elite cadre of line managers trained in interviewing skills probe applicants for entry-level positions in brand management to identify qualities such as the "ability to turn out high volumes of excellent work." Only after successfully completing at least two interviews and a test of general knowledge is the applicant flown to P&G headquarters in Cincinnati, where the applicant is confronted by a day-long series of interviews. If the applicant passes this extensive screening process and is hired, he or she faces a series of rigorous job experiences calculated to induce humility and openness to new ways of doing things. Typically, this phase of socialization involves long hours of work at a pressure cooker pace. Throughout this and other phases of the socialization process, the new employee is constantly made aware of transcendent company values and organizational folklore, including the emphasis on product quality and the dedication and commitment of past employees. This intense socialization results in increased commitment to the success of the company, willingness to work long hours, and decreased absenteeism and turnover.[42]

The intensity of the socialization often depends on employee's backgrounds. Organizations usually recruit from familiar sources that have supplied good applicants in the past. They may also recruit individuals who are already socialized, but by other organizations. Whatever recruitment and selection methods are used, they are not likely to produce new employees who know corporate culture. Thus, socialization is a cost-effective endeavor. Of the possible formalized methods of socialization, two deserve particular attention: job assignments and orientation programs. Job assignments are discussed here, and orientation programs are discussed in the next chapter.

Job Assignments

The aspects of **job assignments** that impart socialization are the characteristics of the initial job, the nature of the early experiences, and the first supervisor. The initial job often determines the new hire's future success. The more challenge and responsibility the job offers, the more likely the person will be successful with the organization.[43] A challenging (but not overwhelming) job assignment implies that

The first job assignment is the first job one gets.

the organization believes the employee can do well and that the organization values him or her. Many times, organizations assign a simple job or rotate the new hire through departments to get a feel for different jobs. But employees may interpret these practices to mean that the organization does not yet trust their abilities or loyalties.

Employees' initial experiences can be heavily influenced by supervisors. These experiences assist new employees in acquiring appropriate values, norms, attitudes, and behaviors. Supervisors serve as role models and set expectations. The positive influence that a supervisor's expectations can have on a new employee is referred to as the **Pygmalion effect**. A supervisor who believes that the new employee will do well conveys this belief to the employee, who then tends to live up to those expectations.[44]

The Pygmalion effect is the impact that the boss's expectations have on the behavior of the worker.

The effectiveness of the socialization process is enhanced when the HR department has actively developed skills in managing workforce diversity. An effective socialization process increases the chances that an employee will stay.

Current Trends

Key trends in recruitment include recruiting in a diverse workforce, and truth-in-hiring.

LEARNING OBJECTIVE 4

Describe the impact of workforce diversity on a firm's recruitment policies.

Recruiting in a Diverse Workforce

As we discussed in Chapter 3, the rapidly changing demographics of the U.S. population has created a mosaic of peoples. Consequently, organizations are looking at a labor force that varies by age, gender, nationality, ethnic and cultural background, and physical abilities. To facilitate the entry of this broad array of people into the world of work, firms are using many recruitment methods. They continually scan the environment, keep themselves well-informed on diversity issues, and look for new ways to recruit populations that may have been overlooked in standard approaches to recruitment. The feature, "Managing Human Resources at Burger King," illustrates a multimethod approach to recruiting in a diverse workforce.

Did You KNOW?

Colorado's highest court upheld a jury's award of $451,600 because a company withheld information about its financial difficulties from a prospective employee. (*Berger v Security Pacific Information Systems*)

Truth-in-Hiring: Ethics in Recruitment

Is it ethical, acceptable behavior for firms to promise something to a job candidate in order to make the firm attractive and then not deliver on the promise? The courts are now saying that if firms do make false promises to job candidates, they can face costly lawsuits (*Stewart v. Jackson & Nash,* 1992). Such truth-in-hiring lawsuits, in which employers are sued for not keeping recruitment promises, have yielded damage awards as high as $10 million! Thus, truth-in-hiring appears to be a legal as well as an ethical issue for the individual and the organization.

The HR department is in a crucial position to ensure that line managers and others involved in recruitment are aware of the law, and that they do not make exorbitant promises. Yes, firms are hiring and they do need good people, but they must look at the short-term and the long-term implications of the contract of trust they hold with job applicants—for ethical and legal considerations.

LEARNING OBJECTIVE 5

Describe the details of affirmative action programs.

Legal Considerations

Legal considerations play a critical role in the recruitment process of most companies in the U.S. Although much of the legal framework facing HR management is directed at employment decisions concerning hiring, firing, health and safety, and compensation, it really begins with the organization's search for job applicants, whether inside or outside the organization. Although the fair employment laws in regard to staffing decisions (hiring, firing, demoting, transferring, and training) specifically apply only to selection, they indirectly affect recruitment. (Some of the

MANAGING HUMAN RESOURCES

at Burger King

In the recruiting area, Burger King managers use many typical tools. They participate in high school job seminars and job fairs, work with local and state agencies to gather referrals, and solicit referrals from politicians who receive work requests from their constituents.

In addition, Burger King has some interesting recruiting programs:

- **Disabilities agencies:** The Florida region is experiencing great success with its "Be Capable" program. More than 100 differently abled young people work in Burger King stores there.

  "Early information indicates that we're experiencing much better retention with this group," said Robert Morrison, director of human resources. "They're more loyal and thankful for the company's efforts in hiring and training them."
- **Senior Citizens:** This growing population is being reached through senior citizens centers. "We're hoping that they will have a positive influence on the young people," said Morrison. "They are a great opportunity for the fast food industry."
- **Operations recruiters:** Three regions—Boston, Atlanta, and Detroit—are experiencing the most severe labor shortages, so Burger King is testing a new position in those areas—operations recruiter. In most regions, recruitment is part of the store manager's job. But in these areas, the operations recruiter is now responsible.
- **Theater commercials:** Recruiting commercials are being aired before the main feature in theaters in Detroit and San Francisco.
- **"Ask me . . . ":** Using employees as recruiters is a proven winner. "Ask me about working for Burger King" buttons, T-shirts, posters, etc., are being used successfully in the Florida region.
- **Crew referral:** Burger King offers cash awards for recruiting. Different regions handle this in different ways. In the areas where young people are exceptionally hard to find, the cash award is simply for bringing in an applicant; in others it is for a new hire.
- **Shift premiums:** Six regions are paying a higher hourly wage for certain, less desirable shifts.
- **Providing transportation:** When a store cannot hire from its own community because it is in an affluent neighborhood where young people don't work or in an industrial area where there are not many young people, Burger King provides transportation or bus fare.
- **Applicant sharing:** Restaurants transfer applications to other stores in the area. "Surprisingly, the restaurant industry hasn't done much of this," said Morrison. "Now we're seeing our managers share their applicants."
- **Ex-employee log:** Some stores call back their good ex-employees to either offer them jobs or ask them to refer their friends.
- **Translates:** Just recently some stores have put recruitment ads in the menu board spot where the pictures of new products are usually placed.
- **TV show:** Burger King is working with an advertising agency to develop a 14-minute television program that will promote the idea of learning through work. It will not focus on Burger King, but on the fast-food industry and the many advantages for young people found there.[45]

laws and acts applicable to selection are discussed in Chapter 10.) Fair employment or equal employment laws most directly relevant to recruitment are those that set out the affirmative action programs. While the *Family and Medical Leave Act* of 1993 can influence recruitment, its major provisions impact benefits, so we will discuss it in Chapter 15.

Affirmative Action Programs

Affirmative action programs (AAPs) are intended to ensure proportional and fair representation of all qualified individuals.

Affirmative action programs (AAPs) are intended to ensure proportional and fair representation of qualified individuals on the basis of race, color, ethnic origin, sex, and disability.[46] As shown in Exhibit 9.4, many firms have AAPs; they generally arise from three different conditions.

Federal Contracts. If a company has a federal contract greater than $50,000 and has 50 or more employees (thereby referred to as a federal contractor), it is required to file, with the Office of Federal Contract Compliance Programs, a written

EXHIBIT 9.4

Corporate Hiring Practices Related to Affirmative Action Programs

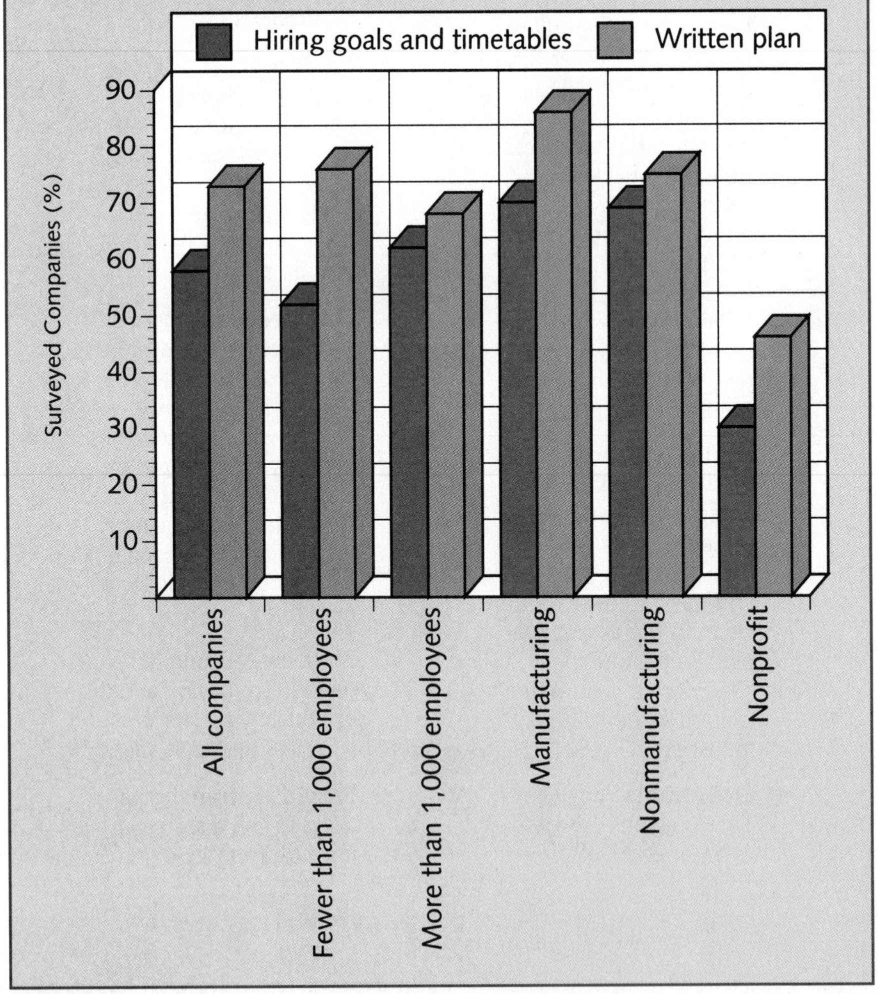

plan outlining steps to be taken for correcting underutilization in places where underutilization has been identified.

Affirmative action programs are designed to facilitate an organization's commitment to provide and achieve proportional representation or parity (or to correct underutilization) in its workforce with the relevant labor market of protected group members. Title VII of the *Civil Rights Act* of 1964 includes women and Americans of African, Hispanic, Native-American, and Asian/Pacific Islands descent.

Did You KNOW?

There are about 65,000 companies that are federal contractors.

The components of AAPs for federal contractors are specified by the Department of Labor in the Office of Federal Contract Compliance Programs (OFCCP). The programs are currently enforced by the OFCCP and the Equal Employment Opportunity Commission (EEOC) through Executive Order 11246.

The components include utilization and availability analyses, goals, and timetables. A **utilization analysis** determines the number of members of minorities and women employed in different jobs within an organization. An **availability analysis** measures how many members of minorities and women are available to work in the relevant labor market. If an organization is employing fewer members of minorities and women than are available, a state of **underutilization** exists. White men are also covered by most equal employment laws, but most examples, except of reverse discrimination, exclude them because they are usually in the majority.

Utilization analysis is the determination of the number of women and minorities currently employed in different jobs.

Availability analysis is the determination of the number of women and minorities in the relevant labor market available to work.

Underutilization exists when the organization uses fewer women and members of minority groups than are available in the relevant labor market.

A **relevant labor market** is generally defined as the geographical area from which come a substantial majority of job applicants and employees. Published population data sources such as the Standard Metropolitan Statistical Analysis can provide initial guidance in determining this defined area. Within a relevant labor market, availability data can be gathered from sources such as the U.S. Census, local and state Chambers of Commerce, and city and state governments. Because organizations may fill certain job openings with applicants in the local area and fill others with applicants from across the nation, organizations may have several relevant labor markets. These markets are important in both AAP development and in defending cases of **prima facie** illegal discrimination. As such, we will discuss them further in the next chapter on selection under "defending against charges of illegal discrimination."

Relevant labor market is the geographical area from which a firm gets most of its employees.

Prima facie means on its face or just as it appears.

After the utilization and availability analyses are completed, goals and timetables are written to specify how an organization plans to correct any underutilization. Because goals and timetables become the organization's commitment to equal employment, they must be realistic and attainable. An example of a utilization plan for one job group in an organization is shown in Exhibit 9.5.[47]

Federal contractors are also required to "take affirmative action to employ and advance in employment qualified handicapped individuals at all levels of employment" (Section 503 of the *Rehabilitation Act* of 1973). The *Rehabilitation Act,* as amended in 1980 and in 1990 by the *Americans with Disabilities Act* of 1990 (ADA), names three categories of disabled persons to be protected against employment discrimination:

- Any individual who has a physical or mental impairment that greatly limits one or more of life's major functions.
- Any individual who has a history of such an impairment.
- Any individual who is perceived as having such an impairment.

The impairments in the first category are usually evident conditions such as amputations, Down's syndrome, paralysis, hearing or visual problems, and so forth. Impairments in the second category can't be readily discerned. Nevertheless, some employers shy away from applicants whose medical histories include cancer, heart disease, diabetes, and similar health problems, perhaps out of fear that a recurrence or other effects of the disease will result in increased insurance costs, a higher rate of absenteeism, and decreased efficiency. In one case, an employer refused

EXHIBIT 9.5

Utilization, Goals, and Timetables

Job Group: ABC
As of: 2/14/97
Availability source: 8-factor analysis

Current Utilization

	MALE	FEMALE	WHITE	BLACK	HISPANIC	ASIAN	NATIVE AMERICAN	MINORITY	TOTAL
Employees (#)	193	7	186	4	3	6	1	14	200
Employees (%)	96.5	3.5	93.0	2.0	1.5	3.0	0.5	7.0	
Availability (%)	88.0	12.0	66.0	15.0	14.0	4.0	1.0	34.0	100.0
Underutilized?	No	Yes	No	Yes	Yes	Yes	Yes	Yes	
Goals									
Based on expansion of 36									
Long-range goal (%)		15.0		15.5	14.5	4.0	1.0	35.0	
Long-range goal (#)		35		37	34	9	2	82	
Annual placement (%)		22.5		21.0	19.7	7.2	1.8	49.7	
Timetables									
If 12 openings (5.1% turnover)—Employment opportunities first year = 48									
Years to goal (#)		14		15	15	1	3		
Hired first year		11		10	9	3	<1		
Hired second year on		3		3	2		<1		
If 24 openings (10.2% turnover)—Employment opportunities first year = 60									
Years to goal (#)		7		11	10	1	2		
Hired first year		14		13	12	4	1		
Hired second year on		5		5	5		<1		
If 47 openings (19.9% turnover)—Employment opportunities first year = 83									
Years to goal (#)		4		5	5	1	1		
Hired first year		19		17	16	6	2		
Hired second year on		11		10	9				
Projected openings 18 (7.6% turnover)—Employment opportunities first year = 54									
Years to goal (#)		10		14	14	1	2		
Hired first year		12		11	11	4	<1		
Hired second year on		4		4	4		<1		

Utilization Analysis

	MALE	FEMALE	WHITE	BLACK	HISPANIC	ASIAN	NATIVE AMERICAN	TOTAL
Employees (#)	193	7	186	4	3	6	1	200
Employees (%)	96.5	3.5	93.0	2.0	1.5	3.0	0.5	
Availability (%)	88.0	12.0	66.0	15.0	14.0	4.0	1.0	100.0
Should have (#)	176	24	132	30	28	8	2	
Underutilized?	No	Yes	No	Yes	Yes	Yes	Yes	
Calculation type		Z		Z	Z	Z	P	
Statistical value		3.59		5.05	4.99	0.54	0.73	
Z or probability		0.00		0.00	0.00	0.59	0.36	
Significant?	No	Yes	No	Yes	Yes	No	No	
Additional needed		8		16	15			

to hire a worker who had leukemia because he was prone to infection from even minor injuries. A Wisconsin circuit court found that the man was qualified to perform his job; therefore, the company could not refuse employment.

Notice that an employer's misconceptions can bring an individual who isn't actually disabled under the coverage of the act or a similar state law. That's what happened, for instance, when an employee was terminated because his employer thought he had epilepsy. The Washington Court of Appeals awarded the worker two years' back pay and ordered him reinstated. Also included are individuals who have suffered from alcoholism and drug abuse and those suffering from AIDS.

Individuals who are HIV positive likely will be covered by the third category of the ADA. This portion of the act protects any individual who is perceived as having a disability.[48]

The ADA permits medical exams only after the job offer has been made. The offer can be made conditional upon the results of the exam, but the employer must make reasonable accommodation. Before the job offer is made, the employer can describe the essential functions to the individual, but the employer cannot inquire about any disabilities the applicant might have.

The rules further state that employers with 50 or more employees who hold federal contracts totaling more than $50,000 must prepare written AAPs for disabled workers in each of their establishments—for example, in each plant or field office. This condition must be met within 120 days after the contractor receives the federal contract. Those who hold contracts or subcontracts of less than $2,500 are not covered by this act. Those with federal contracts that range from $2,500 to $50,000 are required to include an affirmative action clause in their contracts, but they do not need a written AAP.

The HR department should assess current policies, practices, and procedures to ensure that goal attainment is being facilitated. If the policies, practices, and procedures are not facilitating attainment of the goals, they should be modified.

Past Discrimination. This is the second way an affirmative action program may arise. A federal court may require an AAP if a discrimination suit brought against the organization through the Equal Employment Opportunity Commission has found evidence of past discrimination. An AAP under these conditions is generally part of a **consent decree,** a statement indicating specific affirmative action steps to be taken by the organization.

Consent decree is a statement indicating specific affirmative action steps to be taken by a company to remedy past discrimination.

A famous affirmative action program resulting from a consent decree involved American Telephone and Telegraph (AT&T), which the EEOC found to be discriminating against women. Although AT&T did not admit nor was required to admit any act of discrimination, it entered into a consent decree after the EEOC opposed its application for a rate increase.

Although goals set by consent decrees, or as part of the federal contractor's AAP, only specify percentages, they are often seen as establishing quotas. That is, the goals establish that an organization must hire, for example, a certain number of women or African-Americans to correct underutilization or past discrimination in employment. Setting quotas may result in a violation of the Fourteenth Amendment, as well as against Title VII protection against all employment discrimination; for example, white men might not be hired because an organization has a quota to meet. However, the courts have generally held in favor of goals as the only way to reverse previous practices of discrimination *(Detroit Police Officer's Association v. Coleman Young,* 1979; *Charles L. Maehren v. City of Seattle,* 1979; and *City of St. Louis v. U.S.A.,* 1980).

Nevertheless, the issue of reverse discrimination is being heard. For example, the Supreme Court ruled that federal courts could not ignore a seniority-based layoff policy and modify a consent decree to prevent the layoff of black workers (*Firefighter Local Union 1784 v. Stotts,* 1984). In related cases, the Supreme Court has ruled that there are limits to the use of rigid racial and ethnic criteria to accomplish remedial objectives (*Fullilove v. Klutznick,* 1980; *Richmond v. Croson,* 1989).

Voluntary AAPs. In addition to AAPs related to federal contracts and consent decrees, organizations may voluntarily establish goals for hiring and promoting women, members of minority groups, and individuals with disabilities. The exact content of such AAPs depends on the organization and the extent to which various groups are underrepresented.

Organizations often establish voluntary programs without pressure from the EEOC or OFCCP. In fact, organizations can benefit from voluntary AAPs. The key considerations in an organization's establishment of a legal, voluntary AAP are that it be remedial in purpose, limited in its duration, restricted in its reverse discrimination impact—that is, it does not operate as an absolute ban on nonminorities—and flexible in implementation. When an organization's voluntary AAP has these characteristics, the risk of losing a reverse discrimination suit may be minimized. Nonetheless. there is still some risk of being found liable for reverse discrimination (*Martin v. Wilks,* 1989).

International Comparisons

Japan

Japanese firms have traditionally had a very organized system for recruitment.

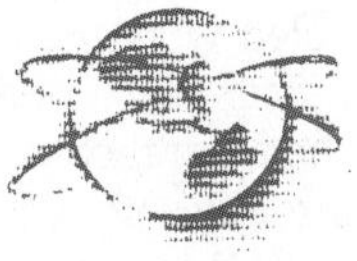

The recruitment of graduates in Japan takes place only once a year, although this is changing somewhat.[49] In a company's direct recruitment, college professors play dominant roles. Company Y asks Professor X to recommend so many students with special qualifications in certain fields. Social sciences, law, and humanities students are considered for administrative jobs such as planning, human resources, sales, or purchasing while technically oriented students are considered for the technical jobs such as engineering, chemistry, and computer science. An example illustrates the process.[50]

The reliance on intermediaries (that is, college professors) for selection decisions serves a number of purposes. First, it is difficult to evaluate a student's technical potential on the basis of a short interview only, when most interviewers have little up-to-date technical background. If a company waited for a written examination, it could not preselect and would risk losing the best candidates to the competition. Second, because of the competition for graduates, recruiters cultivate good relations with college professors, who then recommend individual firms to the students. In this way, the firms get their "fair share" of talent; this prevents a self-defeating bidding war that would raise starting salaries, and—more critically—disrupt the carefully balanced compensation structures of internal labor markets. And last, college grades are not an important selection tool. Specific seminars (courses taken with a professor's permission) are seen as more selective than others and, thus, develop an "elite" reputation for the students taking them. The educational credentials of the school from which the student is graduating are weighted heavily. Given the intense and rigorous competition to enter first-tier schools, companies rely on the university entrance examination as an indicator of the employee's "latent ability."

During the 1970s, many factors in Japanese management practice demanded modification. Economic growth rates were declining and automation was broadly implemented. At this point, Japanese companies began hiring significantly fewer workers in entry-level positions. This resulted in the average age of employees increasing as they moved up the seniority ladder. In turn, pressure was added on average wage costs. The most powerful and negative effect of this era was the low morale caused by few opportunities for real advancement.

Keiretsu is a vertical linkage of companies that are mutual customers and suppliers.

The Japanese responded to these problems quickly instead of ignoring them. They increased their flexibility in employment. This was accomplished with temporary transfers of surplus employees to other companies that are part of the "extended organization." This form of organization, called *keiretsu,* is a vertical linkage of companies that are mutual suppliers and customers. Today, even the concept of lifetime employment is being reduced as firms seek to reduce costs.[51]

Mexico

Mexican employers in the maquiladoras, (border region companies) recruit personnel as the need arises. There is always an abundance of applicants; this allows companies to intensively screen applicants for assembly work. Mexican workers accept this screening because of the relatively good wages and benefits they can get at maquiladoras compared with other employment.

Since the cost of newspapers makes help-wanted advertisements useless, recruitment is done primarily by approaching people and asking them to apply. Therefore, it is common to find many family members working at the same maquiladora. Not surprisingly, traditional Mexican values and social structure are apparent in many organizational programs since workers feel they are part of the organization in a very different way than do American workers. Employers celebrate numerous holidays, and it is common for companies to throw parties for a variety of events to maintain a family atmosphere.[52]

With the passage of the *North American Free Trade Act (NAFTA)* in 1993, economic activity has increased significantly in Mexico. With this likely to continue, companies in Mexico will need to hire workers in greater numbers than family referrals will be able to supply. As this occurs, firms will begin to formalize their recruiting procedures. With the economy and wages increasing, individuals will find the cost of newspapers more accessible to them, thus making the formalized recruiting procedures more effective. And as the recruiting activity increases and formalizes, the selection, performance appraisal, compensation, and training activities will also. Thus, the next several years should see a change in HR management in Mexico.

Summary

Organizations are dynamic, and the need to attract the right number of people at the right time and place is perpetual. Two important HR activities that guide effective recruitment are: (1) HR planning and (2) job analysis. Planning establishes personnel requirements and permits adequate time to anticipate and carry out recruitment activities. Job analysis enables the organization to convey information accurately (via job descriptions and job specifications) to applicants so that both individuals and organizations are well-matched.

Recruitment involves internal and external searches. Although organizations vary considerably in terms of the types of jobs available, both external and internal labor markets exist for the recruitment of suitable applicants. Over time, organizations weigh costs and benefits of internal and external methods in order to choose the most effective ones for a given job. Recruitment is fundamentally the search for information, specifically for a given position. Managing people effectively and efficiently means obtaining this information at the lowest cost possible. Selection is closely connected to recruitment because staffing requires not only the recruitment of the right number of qualified people at the lowest cost, but also the matching of the right person to the right job at the right time.

Legal compliance plays a large role in recruitment, primarily in requiring organizations to meet federal and state fair-employment regulations in their staffing activities. Affirmative action programs, though usually designed explicitly for legal compliance, illustrate how availability and utilization analyses aid organizations in planning for and recruiting human resources.

Key Concepts

affirmative action programs (AAPs)
availability analysis
consent decree
contract recruiters
employee referral programs

host-country nationals (HCNs)
job fairs
keiretsu
prima facie
promotion-from-within
Pygmalion effect
recruitment
relevant labor market
skills inventories
socialization
talent pools
third-country nationals (TCNs)
underutilization
utilization analysis

Review and Discussion Questions

1. Is recruiting more important to a firm like McDonald's than General Motors? Explain.
2. What are the purposes of recruitment? How do these purposes affect other organizational activities?
3. Just-in-time inventory is a concept that enables manufacturers to assemble products from parts that are delivered as needed rather than kept in inventory. Could this concept be applied to recruitment function and the management of human resources? Explain.
4. How does HR planning contribute to effective recruitment? What are the roles of the line manager and HR manager in each of these activities?
5. Why do some organizations use external searches, whereas others use internal searches?
6. The search for job applicants involves finding not only the right number, but also the right kind of applicants. Are some recruitment sources "richer" than others—that is, do they yield more information about the kind of applicant needed? Give examples.
7. How can organizations increase their attractiveness to potential job applicants?
8. How can organizations increase the chances that applicants will stay once hired?
9. What is the impact of workforce diversity on a firm's recruitment policies?
10. What impact has the legal environment had on recruitment? Has this impact been positive or negative for organizations? Explain.

PROJECTS, EXERCISES & CASES

End-of-Text Projects

Lincoln Electric

1. Describe the following:
   a. Lincoln's recruitment objectives
   b. The degree to which these objectives are serving the business and HR objectives of Lincoln
   c. Lincoln's recruitment activities
   d. The degree to which these plans and activities are serving the objectives
2. How can the recruitment activities be improved? How would you evaluate whether the improvements you suggest are effective? Be specific.

Nordstrom

1. Describe the following:
   a. Nordstrom's recruitment objectives
   b. The degree to which these objectives are serving the business and HR objectives of Nordstrom

c. Nordstrom's recruitment activities

d. The degree to which these activities are serving the business and HR objectives

2. How can the recruitment activities be improved? How would you evaluate whether the improvements you suggest are effective? Be specific.

Field Project

1. Outline the information that would be contained in a realistic job preview for prospective college students, and then prepare the preview. This information would be communicated to students in their job interviews. Choose a specific company on which to base your preview.

2. Given that work organizations will be competing for a diverse pool of labor in the near future, it will be critical for organizations to manage diversity effectively. Assume you are in charge of recruiting clerical employees from a labor pool consisting of a large percentage of single parents. What programs might the organization develop and implement to attract qualified single parents to work for your organization? Outline the content of these programs and the rationale for them. Keep in mind the relevant legal constraints that influence managing human resources.

Career Management Exercise

In Chapter 6 you described some career objectives and the types of jobs you want. Now list five companies you would like to interview and work for:

1.

2.

3.

4.

5.

Find out enough about each company to be able to have a good interview—that is, the interviewer is so impressed, you get a job offer on the spot!

Visit the Library

Workforce Online

1. Enter your Web browser.
2. Enter Workforce Online.
3. Find and review the following article: *Contingent Workforce Spurs HR Planning.*
4. Return to your homepage.

Case: Downsizing—Anathema To Corporate Loyalty?

Jim Daniels was unprepared for the dilemma facing Defense Systems, Inc. Jim, vice president of human resources for DSI, joined the company one year ago when he was pirated away from one of the company's major competitors. DSI manufactures electronic components used in weapons supplied to the Air Force and many other firms. In addition, DSI makes semiconductors used in many of the weapons systems as well as in personal computers and automotive computers.

When Jim joined DSI, a major drive to build up the staff in engineering was undertaken in anticipation of a major upturn in the semiconductor market. Unfortunately, industry analysts' projections were optimistic, and the semiconductor market failed to pick up. DSI had recently completed an aggressive hiring policy at the major universities around the U.S. wherein the company had selected 1,000 engineers who were among the cream of the crop with an average GPA of

3.4. Without a pickup in business, however, DSI is confronted with some fairly unpleasant alternatives.

From one point of view, potential cutbacks at DSI fit the overall pattern of cutbacks, restructuring, and downsizing of major U S. companies during the past few years. The motives among firms who have trimmed their workforces vary—some to please Wall Street and the stockholders, others to keep pace with foreign competitors or to shrink an unwieldy organizational structure. To Jim, the DSI layoffs or terminations were poor alternatives to dealing with a turbulent environment.

The major problem, as Jim saw it, was to preserve as many of these jobs as possible until business picked up. To terminate these new hires would irreparably harm DSI's future recruitment efforts. On the other hand, underemploying these talented recruits for very long was bound to lead to major dissatisfaction. Although terminations would improve the balance sheet in the short run, Jim worried about the impact of such a move on corporate loyalty, a fragile and rare commodity at other major firms that have had to cut their white-collar workforce.

Jim is scheduled to meet with the executive committee of DSI in three days to discuss the overstaffing problems and to generate alternatives. In preparation for this meeting, Jim is trying to draw on his experience with his past employer to generate some ideas. A number of differences between DSI and Jim's old employer, though, makes comparisons difficult.

For one, DSI does not employ nearly the number of temporaries or student interns as did his old employer. Nor does DSI rely on subcontractors to produce parts needed in its assembly operation. Because of extra capacity, DSI can currently produce 50 percent of the parts it purchases, whereas Jim's ex-employer could produce only 5 percent.

Another major difference is the degree of training provided by DSI. At Jim's old employer, each employee could expect a minimum of 40 hours of additional training a year; at DSI, however, training consists of about 10 hours per year, much of it orientation training.

Jim wondered whether there might be some additional ways to remove slack from the system and at the same time preserve as many jobs as possible. For example, overtime hours are still paid to quite a few technicians. Would the engineers be willing to assume some of these duties in the interim until business picked up? Some older employees have accumulated several weeks of unused vacation. Could employees be encouraged to take unpaid leaves of absence? Perhaps early retirement incentives could be offered to make room for some of the bright young engineers. DSI also has fourteen other geographic locations, some in need of additional workers.

As Jim thought about these options, one thing was clear: he needs to organize and prioritize these ideas concisely if he is to be prepared for his upcoming meeting.

Case Questions

1. Why is Jim sensitive to DSI's recruitment efforts?
2. What are some potential problems for the current class of engineers recruited at DSI?
3. How could the use of temporaries, student interns, or subcontractors potentially help DSI?
4. Evaluate Jim's alternatives for reducing DSI's labor surplus.

Case: The New Recruit

General Instruments (GI), a defense contractor, employs nearly 1,000 engineers, and designs and manufactures a number of electronic systems for nuclear submarines. Recruiting qualified engineers has been difficult for GI because of the competitive market in Palo Alto and the substantial cost-of-living increase for anyone relocating to the area. Stan Fryer, project leader at GI, knew that today would be one of those proverbial Mondays that managers so often fear. Stan's boss and group manager, Harry Hoskinsson, had left town on business the previous Friday and would not return until the following week.

Stan's problem this morning concerns a new engineer recruit, June Harrison, a single, 25-year-old systems engineer who was hired three weeks ago upon graduation from San Diego State University. Much to Stan's surprise, June has submitted a letter of resignation, stating personal reasons as the cause of her departure. In addition to the letter of resignation, Stan also has a memo from June's supervisor, Lou Snider, describing the events leading up to June's resignation.

As Stan reconstructed these events, it seemed that June was expecting overtime payment in this week's paycheck because of the extra hours she had put in over the previous three weeks. Lou Snider, however, had neglected to file the proper payroll paperwork so that June could receive her overtime in the current pay period. This did not surprise Stan, given Lou's prior history in other supervisory positions. Apparently, Harry Hoskinsson had spoken to Lou about filing so much overtime for his section. So Lou decided to spread out some of the overtime charges over several pay periods.

What Lou hadn't realized was that June had finally secured an apartment in Palo Alto (she had been renting a room in a nearby hotel) and had committed to making a three-month payment and deposit with her paycheck and the additional overtime payment she was expecting. When June realized what was going to happen, she called Harry Hoskinsson to set up a meeting to discuss how she could cover her housing expense. June remembered that when she was being recruited, Harry had emphatically told her to contact him if she ever needed anything or had any problems settling into her new job at GI. Harry was in a bit of a rush to make a staff meeting, so he agreed to see June early the following day. When June reported to Harry's office the next morning, she was understandably upset when Harry's secretary told her that Harry had left town on a business trip. With that, she returned to her office and drafted her resignation letter.

As Stan contemplated how to resolve his "Monday morning" problem, he recalled the speech Harry had given him two years ago when he joined GI. Harry had made clear his distaste for young engineers who tended to live beyond their means and to count on bonuses and overtime as if they were regular and assured components of their paycheck. Nonetheless, Stan decided, despite Harry's speech, that GI must try to arrange for a loan covering June's housing expenses and, more importantly, to persuade her to reconsider her hasty decision.

No sooner had Stan decided on a course of action when June appeared in his doorway. She had done some thinking over the weekend after talking with another GI project engineer, a temporary employee hired only for the duration of his project. It seemed that temporary employees earned about 20 percent more than comparable permanent employees at GI, although they received considerably fewer benefits (such as retirement and health insurance). June made a proposal to Stan: she would retract her resignation letter if GI would permit her, in effect, to quit and be rehired as a temporary project engineer. Otherwise she planned to leave GI and accept a standing offer she had received from an engineering firm in her home city of San Diego. As Stan listened, he wondered how Harry would handle this situation. To Stan, June's proposal sounded like blackmail.

Case Questions

1. Should June have resigned over the overtime issue?
2. Should GI accept June's proposal of rehiring her as a temporary employee?
3. How could the recruiting process for June have been done better?
4. Was the socialization process for June lacking something? What?

Case: Glass Ceilings or Glass Doors?

Southwestern State University prides itself on its rapid growth and expansion of facilities during the decades of the 70s and 80s. Now, in the decade of the 90s, many see Southwestern poised to become, as college presidents are wont to say, a preeminent university. A traditional land grant university with an emphasis on agriculture, Southwestern currently boasts one of the largest schools of business and engineering in the country.

John DeNisi, an employee relations specialist in the personnel department, has witnessed firsthand the rapid growth and transformation of Southwestern during his 11-year tenure in university administration at Southwestern. John is less sanguine about the future, though. Growth will continue, but at a considerably reduced rate given projected population trends for the region. Moreover, John, like others, is worried about Southwestern's stance toward minority recruitment.

Three years ago, John served on a universitywide committee that examined the status of minorities at Southwestern in staff, faculty, and student areas. The final report his committee delivered to the president was not optimistic, to say the least. Southwestern was under-represented in all areas with regard to both blacks and Hispanics. Potentially, Southwestern stands to lose federal funds unless the university undertakes significant moves to attract and retain more minorities in the future. Accordingly, the committee's report recommended renewed efforts to recruit aggressively in all areas, to set aside money for minority recruitment, and to set up minority scholarships to attract more students.

Recently though, John is wondering what impact the current administration policy from Washington would have on Southwestern's steps toward affirmative action. John closely follows reports in the *Chronicle of Higher Education* and the College and University Personnel Association newsletter of the battle in Washington over the status of voluntary affirmative action plans. Although professional groups such as the National Association of Manufacturers and the Society for Human Resource Management support affirmative action as "good business policy," the Department of Justice and the Equal Employment Opportunity Commission (EEOC) seem to have taken a major retreat from earlier administration positions on affirmative action.

The Department of Labor, though, seems to be at odds with the Justice Department and the EEOC because it supports goals and timetables in its enforcement of affirmative action plans for federal contractors. Moreover, the Supreme Court appears to support voluntary affirmative action plans in several recent decisions dealing specifically with such plans. Vocal critics of the new administration stand on affirmative action argue that without affirmative action, minorities will merely bump up against the "invisible ceiling." John wonders what implications these developments could have for Southwestern's stance for the future. If Southwestern initiates such a plan and the Department of Justice then successfully challenges the constitutionality of affirmative action plans, the university could strap itself with discrimination and reverse discrimination suits well into the 21st century.

John's ruminations were abruptly interrupted by a call from the front office informing John that an applicant had requested a meeting. Usually this meant that a disgruntled applicant was unhappy with the impersonal treatment received from the front office. John would then spend a few minutes with the applicant, try to smooth ruffled feathers, and, when necessary, reprimand office staff for rude or discourteous behavior. More often than not, though, John encountered an obnoxious faculty spouse who not only expected immediate employment but also demanded it publicly in a crowded front office.

As John girded himself, he was introduced at the door to Alma Fisher, an African-American woman. Alma did not beat around the bush. "Mr. DeNisi," Alma blurted out, "this university doesn't want to hire blacks, and I want to know what you're going to do about it!" After a few minutes of discussion, John learned that Alma previously worked at the university as a secretary but had left two years ago on maternity leave. Upon reentering the labor force, Alma visited the university employment office, took the clerical tests, and qualified, based on her performance, for a senior secretary position, the highest-paid clerical position at the university.

John's office had matched Alma's qualifications to a position request submitted by the Medical College and referred Alma to the dean of the Medical School for an interview. According to Alma, during the interview the dean asked Alma if she had children and how she supported herself. The straw that broke the camel's back, though, came when the dean asked Alma if she was on welfare. At that point, Alma suggested to the dean that his line of questioning was "inappropriate" and asked the dean to stick to job-related questions concerning her qualifications to do the job. "You know, Mr. DeNisi," asserted Alma, "I did not tell the dean that my previous position with the university was as a secretary to the affirmative action officer. I could sue this university based on his behavior!"

John was struck by the irony of this moment Why worry about glass ceilings at Southwestern, he thought, when the glass doors aren't open?

Case Questions

1. What is the evidence for the existence of glass ceilings or glass doors at Southwestern?
2. As the affirmative action officer for Southwestern, would you be more likely to follow the opinions of the Supreme Court or the current administration?
3. Are the goals and timetables sufficient to achieve racial integration of colleges and universities?
4. Is Alma Fisher a victim of illegal discrimination?

Chapter 9 Endnotes

1. S. Crock and M. Galen, "'A Thunderous Impact' on Equal Opportunity," *Business Week* (June 26, 1995): 37.
2. G. Flynn, "McDonald's Serves Up HR Excellence," *Personnel Journal* (January 1996): 54; C. Marmer Solomon, "Big Mac's McGlobal HR Secrets," *Personnel Journal* (April 1996): 47–54.
3. Information came from P. Sellers, "Look Who Learned About Value," *Fortune* (October, 18, 1993): 75, 78; B. J. Feder, "McDonald's Finds There's Still Plenty of Room to Grow," *New York Times* (January 4, 1994): F5; B. J. Feder, "Dining Out at a Discount Store," *New York Times* (August 16, 1993): Dl, D2.
4. "Employer Recruitment Practices," *Personnel* (May 1988): 63–65; B. Schneider and N. Schmitt, *Staffing Organizations,* 2nd ed. (Glenview, Ill.: Foresman, 1986).
5. "The Starbucks Enterprise Shifts into Warp Speed," *Business Week* (October 24, 1994): 76–78.
6. P. Froiland, "Managing the Walking Wounded," *Training* (August 1993): 36–39; J. J. Laabs, "HR's Vital Role at Levi Strauss," *Personnel Journal* (December 1992): 34–46.
7. "Firm's Diversity Efforts Even the Playing Field," *Personnel Journal* (January 1996): 56.
8. S. Caudron, "Team Staffing Requires New HR Role," *Personnel Journal* (May 1994): 88–93.
9. D. Anfuso, "3M's Staffing Strategy Promotes Productivity and Pride," *Personnel Journal* (February 1995): 28–34; B. Paik Sunoo, "America Online Boots Up for Hypergrowth," *Personnel Journal* (December 1995): 28–38.
10. R. S. Schuler, "Repositioning the Human Resource Function: Transformation or Demise?" *Academy of Management Executive* 4 (3) (1990): 49–59.
11. N. C. Tompkins, "GTE Managers on the Move," *Personnel Journal* (August 1992): 86–91.
12. P. A. Savill, "HR at Inova Reengineers Recruitment Process," *Personnel Journal* (June 1995): 109–114.
13. G. Flynn, "Five Tips to Cut Relocation Costs," *Personnel Journal* (November 1995): 74–78; S. Caudron, "Options Alleviate Employee Qualms About Relocating," *Personnel Journal* (March 1993): 35–40; G. Flynn, "Relocation Has a New Look," *Personnel Journal* (February 1995): 48–60; J. H. Dobrzynski, "For More and More Job Seekers, An Aging Parent Is a Big Factor," *New York Times* (January 1, 1996): 1, 46.
14. A. Swasy, "Housing Slump Boosts Relocation Costs," *The Wall Street Journal* (August 21, 1990): B1.
15. "Cisco Systems' HR is Wired for Success," *Personnel Journal* (January 1996): 59; W. C. DeLone, "Telephone Job Posting Cuts Costs," *Personnel Journal* (April 1993): 115–118.
16. T. Rendero, "Consensus," *Personnel* (Sept.-Oct. 1980): 5.
17. J. R. Garcia, "Job Posting for Professional Staff," *Personnel Journal* (March 1981): 189–192; G. A. Wallrop, "Job Posting for Nonexempt Employees: A Sample Program," *Personnel Journal* (Oct. 1981): 796–798; L. S. Kleiman and K. J. Clark, "An Effective Job Posting System," *Personnel Journal* (Feb. 1984): 20–25.

18. B. Stoops, "Employee Referral Programs" Part I, *Personnel Journal* (Feb. 1981): 98; Stoops, "Employee Referral Programs" Part II, *Personnel Journal* (March 1981): 172–173.

19. Ibid.

20. D. P. Schwab, "Recruiting and Organizational Participation," in *Personnel Management,* K. M. Rowland and G. R. Ferris, eds. (Boston, MA: Allyn and Bacon, 1982): 103–128.

21. B. J. Feder, "Companies Find Rewards in Hiring G.E. Executives," *New York Times* (March 9, 1992): Dl, 4.

22. "Temporary Employment in the U.S.," *Manpower Argus* (December 1995): 2; J. A. Byrne, "Dream Jobs All Over," *Business Week* (April 4, 1994): 34–36; M. S. Taylor and T. J. Bergmann, "Organizational Recruitment Activities and Applicants' Reactions at Different Stages of the Recruitment Process," *Personnel Psychology* (Summer 1987): 265–285.

23. G. McWilliams, "To Have and to Hold," *Business Week* (June 19, 1995): 43.

24. For a detailed discussion of these errors in recruiting decisions, see S. Rubenfeld and M. Crino, "Are Employment Agencies Jeopardizing Your Selection Process?" *Personnel* (Sept.-Oct. 1981): 70–78.

25. McWilliams, "To Have and to Hold."

26. B. Paik Sunoo, "From Santa to CEO—Temps Play All Roles," *Personnel Journal* (April 1996): 34–43; B. J. Feder, "Bigger Roles for Suppliers of Temporary Workers," *New York Times* (April 1, 1995): 37; S. Deisenhouse, "A Temp Firm with a Difference," *New York Times* (Dec. 26, 1993): F3.

27. G. Flynn, "Find the Best Contingent Workers in a Very Tight Market," *Personnel Journal* Supplement (August 1995): 27–30; M. Pandya, "Employee Leasing: The Risks of Swimming in a Big Pool," *New York Times* (June 11, 1995): F10.

28. C. J. Bachler, "Global Inpats—Don't Let Them Surprise You," *Personnel Journal* (June 1996): 54–64.

29. *New York Times* (March 15, 1992): E3. Also see D. Stead and R. D. Hof, "Math Genius with Lab Will Work for Food," *Business Week* (June 14, 1993): 84–86.

30. J. Bredwell, "The Use of Broadcast Advertising for Recruitment," *Personnel Administrator* (Feb. 1981): 45–49; R. Stoops, "Radio Recruitment Advertising: Part II," *Personnel Journal* (July 1981): 532; "Affirmative Action in the 1980's: What Can We Expect?", *Management Review* (May 1981): 4–5; R. Stoops, "Television Advertising," *Personnel Journal* (Nov. 1981): 838; R. Stoops, "Reader Survey Supports Market Approach to Recruitment," *Personnel Journal* (March 1984): 22–24.

31. *FEP Guidelines,* (July 10, 1993): 8. Copyrighted material reprinted with permission of Fair Employment Practices and Bureau of Business Practice, 24 Rope Ferry Road, Waterford, CT 06386.

32. "Cisco Systems' HR is Wired for Success"; "Employers Go On-Line for New Hires," *Bulletin to Management* (June 8, 1995): 184.

33. "Cisco Systems' HR is Wired for Success."

34. P. Kruger, "For Job Seekers, On-Line Options," *New York Times* (August 28, 1994): F21.

35. R. Stoops, "Recruitment Ads that Get Results," *Personnel Journal* (April 1984): 24–26; R. Siedlecki, "Creating A Direct Mail Recruitment Program," *Personnel Journal* (April 1983): 304–307; B. S. Hodes, "Planning for Recruitment Advertising: Part I," *Personnel Journal* (May 1983): 380–384; and J. P. Bucalo, "Good Advertising Can Be More Effective Than Other Tools," *Personnel Administrator* (Nov. 1983): 73–78.

36. D. M. Schweiger, J. M. Ivancevich, and F. R. Power, "Executive Actions for Managing Human Resources Before and After Acquisitions," *Academy of Management Executive* (May 1987): 127–138.

37. "Recruitment in the Age of Downsizing," *New York Times* (March 24, 1994): 96.

38. D. Gunsch, "Comprehensive College Strategy Strengthens NCR's Recruitment," *Personnel Journal* (September 1993): 58–62. Also see B. Smith, "Pinkerton Keeps Its Eye on Recruitment," *HR Focus* (September 1993): 1, 6.

39. R. Narisetti, "Manufacturers Decry A Shortage of Workers While Rejecting Many," *The Wall Street Journal* (September 8, 1995): A4.

40. R. A. Dean and J. P. Wanous, "Effects of Realistic Job Previews on Hiring Bank Tellers," *Journal of Applied Psychology* (Feb. 1984): 61–68; B. M. Meglino and A. S. DeNisi, "Realistic Job Previews: Some Thoughts on Their More Effective Use in Managing the Flow of Human Resources," *Human Resource Planning* (1987) (3): 157–167; and B. M. Meglino, A. S. DeNisi, S. A. Youngblood, and K. J. Williams, "Effects of Realistic Job Previews: A Comparison Using an Enhancement and Reduction Preview," *Journal of Applied Psychology* (May 1988): 259–266.

41. Meglino and DeNisi, "Effects of Realistic Job Previews: A Comparison Using an Enhancement and Reduction Preview." See also S. M. Colarelli, "Methods of Communication and Mediating Processes in Realistic Job Previews," *Journal of Applied Psychology* (August, 1984): 633–642.

42. J. Van Ahn, "The Voice of Experience," Personnel (Jan. 1991): 17; R. Pascale, "Fitting New Employees into the Company Culture," *Fortune* (May 28, 1984): 28–40.

43. D. Berlew and D. T. Hall, "The Socialization of Managers: Effects of Expectations on Performance," *Administration Science Quarterly* (Sept. 1966): 297–323.

44. J. S. Livingston, "Pygmalion in Management," *Harvard Business Review* (July-Aug. 1969): 81–89.

45. *HR Reporter* (June 1988): 1–2. Reprinted by permission of *HR Reporter,* copyright 1988. Updated 1997.

46. G. Flynn, "Deloitte & Touche Changes Women's Minds," *Personnel Journal* (April 1996): 56–66; R. D. Dickson, "The Business of Equal Opportunity," *Harvard Business Review* (Jan.-Feb. 1992): 46–53; P. Gewirtz, "Affirmative Action: Don't Forget the Courts," *The Wall Street Journal* (August 2, 1995): A11; C. Yang, M. Mallory, and A. Cuneo, "A 'Race-Neutral' Helping Hand?" *Business Week* (February 27, 1995): 120–121; J. Kaufman, "How Workplaces May Look Without Affirmative Action," *The Wall Street Journal* (March 20, 1995): B1, 6; S. A. Holmes, "Programs Based On Sex and Race Are Under Attack," *New York Times* (March 16, 1995): C1, 22.

47. The steps in utilization and availability analysis are based on the eight-factor analysis. For a description, see R. H. Faley and L. S. Kleiman, "Misconceptions and Realities in the Implementation of Equal Employment Opportunity," in *Readings in Personnel and Human Resource Management*, 3rd ed., R. S. Schuler, S. A. Youngblood, and V. L. Huber, eds. (St. Paul, MN: West, 1988); and Biddle and Associates, 2100 Northrup Ave., Suite 200A, Sacramento, CA 95825.

48. L. Pechman, "A Level Playing Field or a Quagmire?" *New York Times* (July 30, 1995); J. Bovard, "Get a Whiff of This!" *The Wall Street Journal* (December 27, 1995): 10; C. Yang and S. Anderson, "Business Has to Find a New Meaning for 'Fairness'," *Business Week* (April 12, 1993): 72; "Flexible Policies on Accommodation of Disabilities Recommended," *Fair Employment Practices Guidelines* (December 14, 1995): 148.

49. B. R. Schlender, "Japan's White Collar Blues," *Fortune* (March 21, 1994): 97–104; A. Pollack, "Japanese Graduates Finding Few Jobs," *New York Times* (June 25, 1994): 39.

50. V. Puick, "White-Collar Human Resource Management in Large Japanese Manufacturing Firms," *Human Resource Management* 20, no. 2 (1986): 264; "Learning from Japan," *Business Week* (Jan. 27, 1992): 52–60.

51. K. Lowry Miller, "Land of the Rising Jobless," *Business Week* (January 11, 1993): 47; E. L. Andrews, "Japan's Job Market Shocks Collegians," *New York Times* (September 5, 1995); "Shellshocked by the Yen, Japanese Companies Still Find Ways to Cope," *New York Times* (April 18, 1995): D8; D. Fingleton, "Jobs For Life: Why Japan Won't Give Them Up," *Fortune* (March 20, 1995): 119–125.

52. I. Peritz, "Montreal Firm Found Cheap Labor, Lax Rules in Mexico," *The Gazette* (March 16, 1992): Al, A7.

Selection and Placement

10

CHAPTER

> *"The best thing we can do for our competitors is hire poorly. At Microsoft, we are always looking to hire people who are better than we are."*
>
> *David Pritchard*
> *Director of Recruiting*
> *Microsoft*[1]

Learning Objectives

1. Describe how important selection is to companies.
2. Describe the types of information to gather about job applicants.
3. Discuss several methods of gathering information for selection decisions.
4. Discuss ways the information is used in making selection and placement decisions.
5. Identify legal considerations in selection and placement.
6. Describe how the use of expatriates, third-country nationals, and host-country nationals impact selection and placement.

Chapter Outline

MANAGING HUMAN RESOURCES

at the Walt Disney Company

The next time you visit Walt Disney World in Florida or Disneyland in California, consider the complexity of finding more than 25,000 people needed to fill more than 1,000 types of jobs that make the entertainment complexes so effective. With over 50 million visitors to Disney World and Disneyland yearly, the company is a reigning star in the entertainment business. Since the mid-1980s, when it went through a major change in senior management and strategic direction, the Walt Disney Company has developed a reputation for creativity, strong financial management, and unique—and very effective—approaches to managing people. An example of how that management process works is evident in the approach to staffing—or in Disney parlance, "casting for a role."

The managers and employees of the Walt Disney Company view themselves as part of a large show or production. This is reflected in the way they speak of themselves, their activities, and the process of selecting new members. Eager applicants to the firm are "cast for a role," rather than "hired for a job." Rather than being "employees," applicants who join the firm become "cast members" in a major entertainment production. A "cast director" interviews applicants.

The "casting" process for hourly jobs, for example, reveals a number of effective personnel management practices. A "casting director," or interviewer spends at least eight to ten minutes with every applicant for an hourly job. During that interview, the "casting director" evaluates the applicant in terms of his or her ability to adapt to the firm's very strong culture. This includes, for instance, acceptance of grooming requirements (no facial hair for men, little make up for women) and willingness to work on holidays, since the facilities are open year-round. After the first "screening," the remaining applicants are assessed as they interact with each other and judged as to how well they might fit with the "show."

Once people join the firm, they become "cast members" whose inputs and talents are highly valued by the Walt Disney Company. The company fills 60 to 80 percent of its managerial positions by promoting existing "cast members." In addition, the firm draws on suggested referrals from current "cast members" for help in hiring the 1,500 to 2,000 temporary employees required during particularly busy periods—Easter, Christmas, and summers.

Every newly hired "cast member" participates in an orientation and training program at "Disney University." "Cast members" first receive an overview of Walt Disney Company and learn about its traditions, history, achievements, and philosophy. In addition, "cast members" learn about the key Disney "product"—happiness—and their roles in helping to provide it. Next, each "cast member" learns about the benefits (health, social, recreational) of being part of the Disney "family," gains more direct information about his or her "role" in the production, and has a tour of the complex. Tailored to reflect the needs of each type of cast member and group, the initial orientation and subsequent training has a theme of bringing cast members into the "family" and developing a team sense, as well as a focus on courtesy to "guests," safety, and putting on a good "show" (entertainment).[2]

This feature highlights aspects of selection that we will discuss in this chapter, including: 1) how to collect information on job applicants, 2) how to make selection and placement decisions, 3) how selection can be used to improve the profitability of the company, and 4) how selection ties into the basic philosophy of a company. In addition, we will also look at issues in the selection process such as legal considerations and the selection of international employees. Finally, we will examine the selection process in other countries.

Selection and Placement

Selection is the process of gathering legally defensible information about job applicants in order to determine who should be hired for long- or short-term positions. **Placement** is concerned with matching individual skills, knowledge, abilities, preferences, interests, and personality to a job. Effective selection and placement involve finding the match between organizational needs for qualified and motivated individuals and individuals' needs for jobs in which they are interested and can utilize their skills and abilities.[3]

Selection is the process of gathering legally defensible information about job applicants. Placement is concerned with matching people to jobs.

Partnership in Selection and Placement

Line managers play an important role in the selection and placement activity. They help identify the need for staffing through the organization's HR planning activity, assist with job analysis, and evaluate employee performance. They are typically involved in the interview process. Some CEOs feel that selection is so important that they get involved in selection too:

> *To this day, Bill Gates might call a few people right out of college and say, "Hey, we're interested in having you come to work here, and I just want you to know that we're all aware of your skills and we think you'll have some positive impact on our company."*[4]

The HR department, however, is usually responsible for gathering information and should arrange interviews between job applicants and managers for several reasons:

- Applicants have to go to only one place to apply for a job and have a better chance of being considered for a greater variety of jobs.
- Outside sources of applicants can clear employment issues through one central location.
- Operating managers can concentrate on their operating responsibilities—especially helpful during peak hiring periods.
- Hiring is done by specialists trained in staffing techniques, so selection is often better.
- Costs can be cut because duplication of effort is avoided.
- With increased government regulation of selection, it is important that people who know about these rules handle a major part of the hiring process.

In order for HR professionals to do their job effectively, according to David Pritchard, director of recruiting at Microsoft:

> *Recruiters need to have a very clear idea about the needs of the division they are recruiting for. Though they might report to me, they are truly partners in those organizations. Recruiters attend those business meetings and get feedback from current employees, so they understand the short- and long-term business goals of that particular division. This helps them find the right people and meet hiring needs before they become critical.*[5]

But because it is the line managers and the other employees who may actually be working with the new hire, they are often the ones making the final selection decision. A more extensive listing of the selection and placement activities shared by line managers, HR professionals, and the employees is shown in "Partnership: Working Together in Selection and Placement."

PARTNERSHIP: WORKING TOGETHER IN SELECTION AND PLACEMENT

LINE MANAGERS	HR PROFESSIONALS	EMPLOYEES
Identify staffing needs through articulating business strategies.	Develop/choose selection tests that are reliable and valid.	May interview candidates who may work in their group.
Help HR professionals identify appropriate criteria for evaluating the performance of new hires and new placements.	Coordinate the administrative aspects of the selection process.	May be involved in selecting new group members.
Help HR professionals develop selection tools.	Arrange interviews between applicant and line managers.	May participate as applicants for internal transfers, promotions, etc.
Coordinate selection process with applicant and HR professionals.	Conduct data analyses to establish validity and to determine how to combine results from multiple tests.	May participate by identifying appropriate criteria for evaluating performance.
May administer and score some selection tests.	Provide education and training to all employees involved in the selection process.	
Understand and comply with relevant legal regulations.	Monitor selection outcomes to ensure equal opportunity for all.	
Provide information to other organizations who are conducting reference checks.	Keep complete and accurate records for possible use in defending the organization against lawsuits.	
Facilitate the organization's accommodation to the *Americans with Disabilities Act.*		

LEARNING OBJECTIVE 1

Describe how important selection is to companies.

Why Are Selection and Placement Important?

Selection and placement are critical to any organization; they provide an organization with its core—its human resources. Employees who perform well is, of course, the objective of these two activities. Benefits of core selection and placement include productivity improvements and cost savings. Serving the organization's needs by providing effective selection and placement means attaining several purposes, which are:

- To enable organizations to fulfill their strategies.
- To contribute to the organization's bottom line through efficient and effective production.
- To ensure that an organization's financial investment in employees pays off (for example, hiring an employee with a starting salary of $25,000, annual cost of living adjustments (COLAs) of only 1.5 percent, and no benefits results in an investment of $128,000 in that employee in 5 years and $578,092 in 20 years).
- To evaluate, hire, and place job applicants in the best interests of both the organization and the individual.
- To minimize multimillion-dollar verdicts and settlements in litigation brought by victims of criminal, violent, or negligent acts perpetrated by employees who should not have been hired or kept in their jobs.

Did You KNOW?

A poor hiring decision can cost a firm as much as 5 times the employee's salary. Costs result from lost productivity and company reputation, poor morale amongst existing employees, and increased unemployment insurance costs.

- To fulfill hiring goals and timetables specified in affirmative action programs.[6]

To accomplish the above, selection and placement must be congruent with the needs of the business and integrated with other HR activities.

Linking Selection and Placement with Other HR Practices

Effective firms closely link selection and placement with other HR practices, particularly job analysis, recruitment, and training and development. As firms are required to validate their selection practices, they find that a systematic reliance on job analysis and recruitment facilities shaping their selection criteria and choosing methods of obtaining information. Firms that pursue total quality and customer orientation are also linking selection and placement with training and development. They recognize that the entire process is key to the success of their programs. This is particularly true for "frontline workers," those who directly serve the customers such as the park attendants at Disney and the flight attendants at Southwest Airlines.[7] Of course, these companies try to select individuals who are already motivated to serve the customer:

> *The real key to me is to get the right people into the right jobs.*
>
> *Elizabeth Sartain*
> *Vice President of People*
> *Southwest Airlines*[8]

You cannot expect to delight your customers unless you as an employer delight your employees.

Carla Paonessa
Partner
Andersen Consulting
Chicago

The key then is getting the pool of potentially qualified applicants from the recruitment activity, selecting accurately using the appropriate selection techniques, and then matching the applicants to the jobs. While important for all managers and firms, this process is particularly critical for small businesses as described in the "HR Advice and Application: Workers Are a Small Firm's Most Valuable Asset" feature.

Considerations in the Choice of Selection Techniques

Several technical factors need to be considered, in choosing the right selection techniques, including which predictors and criteria to use.

Predictors

Selection decisions in organizations are generally made on the basis of job applicants' **predictor** scores on various tests. These tests, typically administered to the job applicants sequentially, predict how well applicants, if hired, will perform.

Predictors are used to forecast how well a candidate is likely to perform if hired.

The selection process occurs in steps; Exhibit 10.1 shows a typical process. A wealth of techniques (background information, paper-and-pencil tests, work simulations, physical tests, interviews) can be used to predict job performance, but their usefulness depends on their reliability and validity.

Reliability. The **reliability** of a predictor is the degree to which it produces dependable or consistent results over time. Unreliable predictors produce different results at different times. Tests of physical attributions (height, weight, hearing) tend to be more reliable than tests of personality characteristics (neuroticism, flexible thinking, emotional stability). There are two types of reliability relevant to selection. Consider a cognitive ability test (for example, knowledge of financial principles) administered to 100 job applicants. Its reliability would be high if you retested these job applicants and received similar results the second time. This is called test-retest reliability. Inter-rater reliability focuses on how consistent the ratings of different people are. For example, in unstructured interviews, interviewers will perceive the same job applicant differently; the interviews are thus unreliable.[9]

Reliable and valid predictors do a better job of forecasting success on the job.

HR ADVICE & APPLICATION

Workers Are a Small Firm's Most Valuable Asset

For many small businesses, payroll is easily the single largest expense. Yet business owners often are more knowledgeable about products, plants, equipment and other assets than about their most expensive asset—people.

The reason for this is obvious: people cannot be neatly measured the way raw materials can.

However, an increasingly competitive marketplace is causing many businesses to pay closer attention to this one resource that truly sets them apart from their competition.

The challenge of business today is not simply to find the most qualified worker, but to find a good match between workers and jobs.

The logical approach is to make a concerted effort to get to know employees and candidates—not only their job skills and general intelligence, but their drives, needs, interests and behavioral makeup as well—and then use that information to make a good placement.

Managers must do a number of things both in the hiring process and on the job to understand the people who do the work and manage them accordingly.

- Job candidates should undergo multiple interviews, answering the same questions from different people. This provides an opportunity to compare notes on a given candidate's responses. It also provides a chance for several people to get to know the candidate and to decide how that personality would fit into the department.
- On the job managers should make it their mission to learn more about what motivates employees. They can begin by making themselves more available to employees—at work stations, in the lunchroom, on breaks and during weekly meetings. Keeping the door open to questions and comments tells employees that their contributions are important and gives managers insight into what is happening on the front lines.
- In the planning process, employees should be kept involved and shown that management has an interest in their development on the job. Managers need to define jobs clearly, so employees know what is expected of them. Managers also should discuss individual career plans so people know where they fit into the company's long-term plans and what goals they must achieve. Performance appraisals need to be done in an open, constructive fashion. And efforts to build work teams need to be openly explained and developed with employees.[10]

Validity refers to how well a measure assesses an attribute.

Validity. The term **validity** assesses an attribute. Validity is not absolute but is instead dependent on the situation in which the selection device is being used. For example, a test of aggression may be a valid predictor of police performance yet useless in predicting job success for machinists. Appendix C discusses the different approaches to validating selection devices in more depth.

Mathematically, validity refers to the correlation between the predictor score (selection device) and a criterion (job performance, job rating, number of absences, and so forth). Remember that in basic statistics a correlation coefficient can range from -1.00 to 1.00. The closer the correlation coefficient is to the absolute value of 1.00, the more valid the selection device. For example, work simulation tests have been shown to have average validity coefficients up to 0.47. This is substantially higher than the average validity coefficients of 0.14 for interviews.[11]

Criteria

Criteria are the targets that constitute job performance.

Criteria describe decisive elements of job performance. For example, in a corporate loan assistant's job, being able to document decisions accurately is probably

EXHIBIT 10.1

Possible Steps in the Selection Process

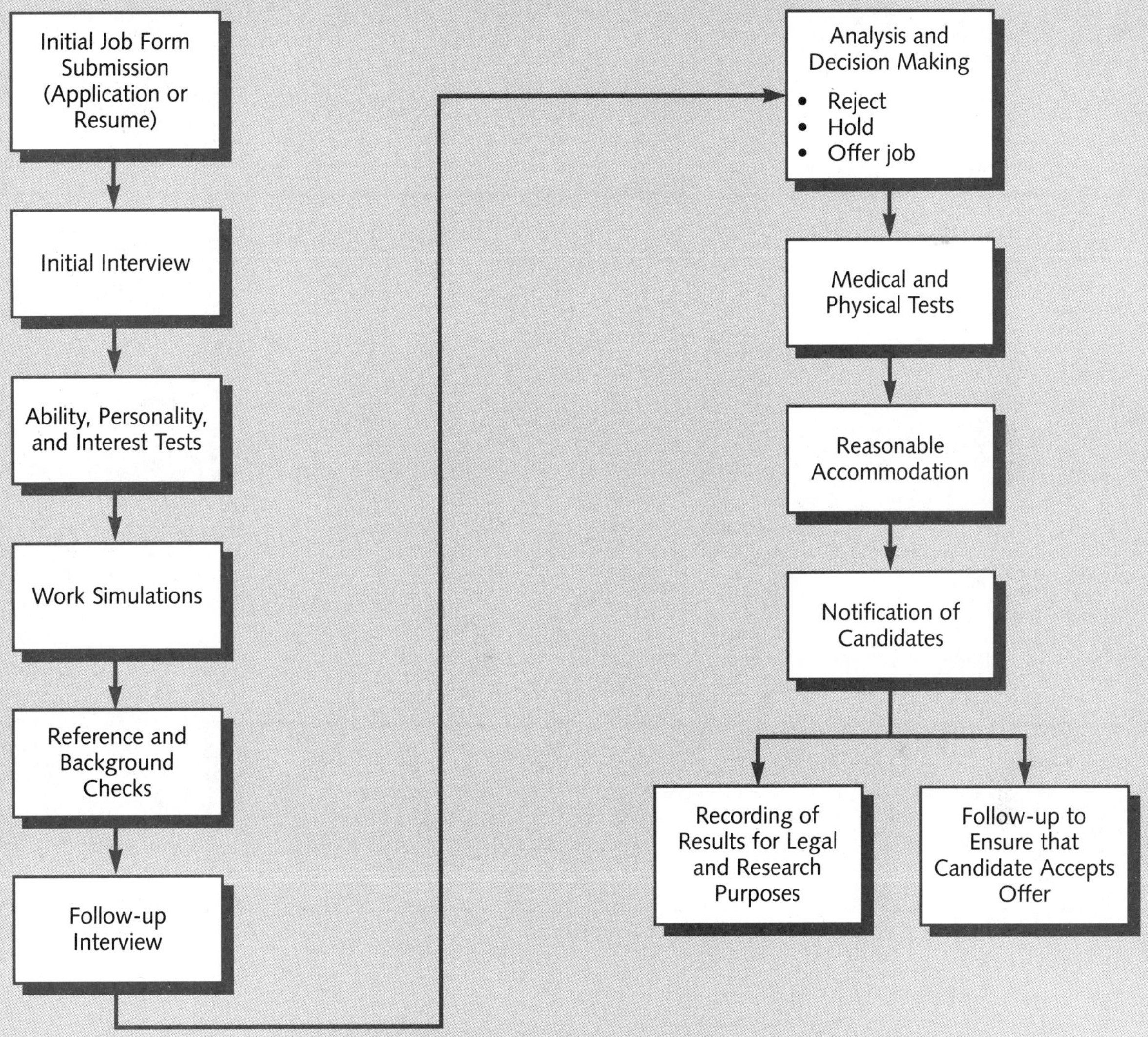

more critical than keeping one's desk clean and organized. Establishing precise criteria and their relative importance facilitates the development of valid predictors.

Performance criteria dictate the type of information to be obtained from job applicants and, to some extent, the method used to gather the information. For example, if absenteeism is an appropriate criterion, a check of references on employment history may be helpful. If level of performance is the criterion, a written test measuring an applicant's skills, knowledge, and abilities may be useful.[12]

It is useful to compare Exhibits 8.3 and 10.2 to see the relationship between the job dimensions (criteria) and the skills, knowledge and abilities required.

As described in Chapter 8, the job analysis provides the basis for determining appropriate, relevant, and important criteria. Compare the relationship between the job dimensions of the corporate loan assistant in Exhibit 8.3 and the skills required to perform the job in Exhibit 10.2. Job incumbents identified both the skills, knowledge, and abilities and the job dimensions as discussed in Chapter 8.

EXHIBIT 10.2

Selection Matrix: Possible Selection Methods for Several Knowledges and Skills

For Job: Corporate Loan Assistant (Internal Hires)
Date: 2/25/97

CODE	QUALIFICATIONS	USED TO RANK?	SAF	WKT	ST	PCD	SOI	DAI	BI/REF	PAF
MQ	1. Communication	Yes	X				X	X	X	X
MQ	2. Math		X		X					
MQ	3. Writing		X							X
MQ	4. Reading		X		X					X
MQ	5. Researching		X							
MQ	6. Organizing	Yes	X							X
MQ	7. Listening	Yes	X				X			X
MQ	8. Social skills		X				X			X
MQ	9. Sales	Yes						X		X
MQ	10. Interpreting	Yes					X			
MQ	11. Bank policy									
MQ	12. Bank services	Yes	X	X				X		X
MQ	13. Computer									

MQ = Is a minimum qualification
MT = May be acquired through training or on the job (desirable); preference may be given to those who possess this knowledge or skill
MA = Can be accommodated within reason
WT = Will be acquired through training or on the job; not evaluated in the selection process. Will applicants be ranked by how much of this knowledge or skill they possess?
SAF = Supplemental Application Form
WKT = Written Knowledge Test
ST = Skills Test
PCD = Physical Capability Demonstration
SOI = Structured Oral Interview
DAI = Departmental Appointment Interview
BI/REF = Background Investigation/Reference Check
PAF = Performance Appraisal Form

Source: Adapted from a form supplied by Biddle & Associates, 2100 Northrop Ave., Sacramento, CA. Used with permission.

The dimensions (domains) were identified as the essence of the job—the job criteria. The method by which the knowledge skills are to be measured is indicated in Exhibit 8.2: they become the predictors of how well the applicant will perform the job criteria. Note that several methods are used for some knowledge skills (for example, bank services [MQ]).

LEARNING OBJECTIVE 2

Describe the types of information to gather about job applicants.

Types of Job Applicant Information

Organizations can gather selection and placement information from job applicants related to the following categories:

- Skills, knowledge, and abilities
- Personality, interests, and preferences
- Other characteristics

Skills, Knowledge, and Abilities

The information gathered on an applicant is generally used to match the applicants skills, knowledge, and abilities (sometimes referred to as competencies) with a suitable job.[13] Such an endeavor is subject to legal constraints and has traditionally been of major interest to organizations because it can predict how well the individual will perform on the job.

Job-relatedness can be demonstrated by this information. However, any skills, knowledge, and abilities that can be learned in fewer than eight hours or taught on the job should not be measured or used in making selection decisions. Furthermore, if job applicants need only a specified minimum level of a skill, knowledge, or ability to perform the job, then the only information that should be obtained is whether or not the applicants meet the minimum levels. If a higher level of skill, knowledge, or ability is likely to result in better performance, then that information should be obtained so that applicants can be ranked and selected. In some companies, workers may be expected to perform a variety of tasks. As we discussed in Chapter 7 on Job Design, firms such as BMW in Spartansburg, South Carolina need the flexibility of assigning workers to a variety of tasks. In this situation the company needs to select applicants with competencies to perform a variety of tasks.[14]

When making decisions in the areas of firing, demotion, layoff (where a bona fide seniority system does not exist) or discipline—all of which are selection decisions under the law—measuring task or job performance rather than skills, knowledge, and abilities is appropriate. If physical abilities are being measured (but only after an offer of employment has been made), consideration must be made for job accommodation. If reasonable accommodation cannot be made for a disability that interferes with performing the essential duties of the job, the applicant can be rejected.

Did You KNOW?

Bill Gates has been quoted as looking for four essential qualities in new hires: ambition, IQ, technical experience, and business judgment, with IQ most important.

Personality, Interests, and Preferences

Information about an individual's personality, interests, and preferences should also be gathered. If used appropriately, this information, in combination with job rewards, culture, and strategy of the firm, can increase employee satisfaction and reduce absenteeism and voluntary turnover. It can also increase job involvement and motivation.[15]

In referring to personality, interests, and preferences, some companies use the term "attitude" or "values." For example, Toyota's mission states that the interests of the firm and its employees are best served by producing high-quality cars efficiently. To meet these goals, employees must value continuous improvement and be committed to Kaizen, the firm's philosophy of continuous improvement.[16] Southwest Airlines seeks candidates who are "self-starters."[17] IBAX looks for individuals who are willing to be "good team players." Regardless of what it is called, the importance of measuring personality, attitude, or values is significant:

> *What are Disney World's 40 interviewers—all of whom started as frontline workers—most interested in? Not cognitive ability. Only applicants seeking a job that involves handling cash take a simple math test. Says Duncan Dickson, director of casting: "We're looking for personality. We can train for skills. We want people who are enthusiastic, who have pride in their work, who can take charge of a situation without supervision."*[18]

An applicant's personality, interests, and preferences can also be useful in placing the individual in a particular part or section of the organization. Should an individual climb the corporate ladder, personality, interests, and preferences will again be relevant.

Did You KNOW?

Rosenbluth International, the nation's fourth-largest travel agency, unabashedly hires people on the basis of "niceness" and then heretically—and successfully—pursues a policy of putting the customer second (and the employee first).

Did You KNOW?

At Lincoln Electric, hiring is done very carefully because employees are expected to make a lifetime commitment to the company. Lincoln selects for both the desire to succeed and the capacity for growth.

Other Characteristics

Employers can gather information about other characteristics such as terms and conditions of employment. These include licenses required by law; willingness to travel or work split shifts, weekends, or under adverse conditions such as confined facilities and high noise levels; uniform requirements; business-related grooming codes; tools required on the job and not provided by the employer; required training to be taken on the job; and driver's licenses. These characteristics can be required as minimum qualifications for a job. Very rarely are they used to rank applicants. Applicants either possess them, or they do not. Although these characteristics offer no indication as to how candidates will do on the job, applicants who are unwilling to comply with them can be disqualified from consideration.

LEARNING OBJECTIVE 3

Discuss several methods of gathering information for selection decisions.

Obtaining the Information

Application

An application is a form seeking information about the job applicant's background and present status.

Methods of obtaining applicant information include:

- **applications**
- **interviews**
- **written tests**
- **reference verification**
- **drug tests**
- **medical and physical tests**

Premised on the assumption that past behavior is a good predictor of future performance, the **application** is a form seeking information about the job applicant's background and present status. Usually this information is used as an initial or pre-employment screen to decide whether the candidate meets the minimum job requirements. Exhibit 10.3 shows an example of an application. While not prohibited per se, many traditional questions are now considered "red flags" of discrimination and should be avoided because of their potential adverse impact, for example:

- **Demographic information.** Questions related to race should be strictly avoided. Since questions regarding age, gender, religion, and national origin are difficult to prove as bona fide occupational qualifications, they should be avoided. Proof of age and citizenship can be required after hiring.
- **Commitment.** Questions over marital status, a spouse's job, dependents, and childcare arrangements need to be asked of both men and women and given equivalent weight if they are asked at all. It is acceptable to ask if applicants have any social, family, or economic responsibilities that would prevent them from performing job duties.
- **Arrests and convictions.** Inquiries on arrest records are not permissible under any conditions. An employer can ask about convictions.
- **Disabilities.** It is acceptable to ask whether there are any disabilities that would interfere with ability to perform a specific job or whether physical accommodations are needed, but only after a job offer is made.
- **Physical requirements.** Height and weight measurements are acceptable for a few jobs. Care needs to be taken to ensure that physical requirements (height and weight) are valid since they tend to discriminate against Hispanics, Asians, and women.
- **Affiliations.** Catchall questions about organization affiliation (for example, list the organizations, country clubs, fraternal orders, lodge memberships), should be avoided. However, it is acceptable to ask about professional organizations that relate to specific jobs.[19]

All our tests have been revised to conform with ADA and the Civil Rights Act of 1991.

Dennis Hathaway
Manager, Business Development
Pinkerton National Detective Agency

The accuracy of applicant-generated information, usually through resumes, is also a concern. Verified Credentials, Inc., reports that almost 30 percent of the resumes they check for employers contain false information. Distortions vary from wrong starting date for a prior job to inflated college grades to downright lies involving education degrees, types of jobs, and former employers. The most common distortions are length of employment and previous salary.[20]

EXHIBIT 10.3

A Typical Application

DATE ______________

NAME ____________________ (LAST) (FIRST) (MIDDLE) TELEPHONE NO. ______________

ADDRESS ____________________ (STREET) (CITY) (STATE) (ZIP)

Position Desired ______________ Are You 18 or Older? ______________ Date You Can Start ______________

Are You Presently Employed? ______________

Is so, where? ______________

FORMER EMPLOYERS (Please list beginning with most recent)

DATE Month & Year	NAME & ADDRESS OF EMPLOYER	Telephone No. May We Call?	SALARY	POSITION	REASON FOR LEAVING

EDUCATION	NAME & LOCATION OF SCHOOL	GRADUATION	SUBJECTS OF SPECIAL INTEREST
HIGH SCHOOL(S)			
COLLEGE(S)			
TRADE, BUSINESS OR CORRESPONDENCE SCHOOLS			

AVAILABILITY

Approximate Total Hours Available: ☐ 15–25 ☐ 35–45

	Weekdays	Weekends			Weekdays	Weekends			Weekdays	Weekends	
Mornings	☐	☐	Yes	**Afternoons**	☐	☐	Yes	**Evenings**	☐	☐	Yes
	☐	☐	No		☐	☐	No		☐	☐	No

Particular hours you will be unavailable to work and the reasons:

____

REFERENCES

Give below names of three persons not related to you, whom you have known at least one year.

NAME	ADDRESS	OCCUPATION	YEARS KNOWN

I authorize investigation of all statements contained in this application. I understand that misrepresentations or omission of facts called for is cause for dismissal. Further, I understand and agree that my employment is for no definite period and may, regardless of the date of payment of my wages and salary, be terminated at any time without any previous notice.

Date ______________ Signature ______________ Interviewed By ______________ Date ______________

Biographical information blanks ask for more information than regular application forms such as Exhibit 10.3.

Biographical Information Blank and Biodata Test. In addition to the application or even as a substitute for it, employers may administer a **biographical information blank**. This form generally requests more information from the applicant than does an application. For example, in addition to the information requested on an application the biographical information blank may request the applicant to indicate a degree of preference for such things as working split shifts, being transferred, working on weekends, or working alone. Exactly which items are asked should be based on the nature of the job. If the job does require working split shifts, for example, indicating preference (or lack thereof) for this may be a good predictor of turnover.[21]

Biodata tests are really records of past achievements and activities such as what you did in high school.

A variation on preference information is information about past achievements and activities. This can be done through **biodata tests**. Biodata tests appear to be good predictors of job success and generally have less adverse impact on minorities than do many traditional tests.[22] Biodata tests ask autobiographical questions on such subjects as academic achievement, work attitudes, physical orientation, and self-perception. According to Frank Erwin, test developer and president of Richardson, Bellows, Henry & Co., biodata tests reduce by more than half the scoring differences that routinely result between applicants on traditional general abilities or intelligence tests.

Education and Experience Evaluations. As part of the initial application process, applicants often complete a form that details their educational achievements and work experience. Validity evidence indicates that education requirements are predictive of job tenure. Like education, experience requirements may be useful in selecting for high-level, complex jobs but not for jobs that require short learning periods.

What is questionable is the *extent* of education and experience that can be required for a specific job. In order to narrow the application pool, some organizations impose inordinately high experience requirements (for example, twenty years or more for) and higher than needed levels of education. These requirements may serve as artificial barriers to those applicants who may have less opportunity to acquire education and experience.[23]

Handwriting analysis is a very popular selection procedure in France.

Handwriting Analysis. In addition to the completed application, an employer may request a special handwriting sample. **Handwriting analysis,** or graphology, is used by 85 percent of all European companies and is catching on in the United States. An estimated 2,000 to 2,500 U.S. employers use graphology as a selection device.[24]

Despite the testimonials, there is no scientific evidence that graphology can predict job performance. In one controlled study of sales success, applicants provided handwriting samples, and graphologists predicted job success. While there was limited evidence of inter-rater agreement on character traits, there was no relationship between the assessments and three measures of job performance (sales productivity and self- and supervisory performance ratings). Graphology is also costly ($50 to $250 per sample), considering its poor predictive ability. Therefore, it is not recommended as a selection device.

References can be very predictive of performance when the information is true.

Reference Verification. Because some job applicants falsify their past and current qualifications, employers are stepping up efforts to check references. Instead of relying on unstructured reference letters (which are always positive), some organizations use outside investigators to verify credentials, others personally contact prior employers to get the information firsthand, and still others have structured the process so that the references provide only job-specific information (goals, accomplishments, degree of supervision).

One reason for the increased rigor in reference checking is that they are quite predictive of performance if done correctly. Another reason revolves around the recent spate of negligent hiring lawsuits. Consider the following typical case:

A woman raped by a cable television installer . . . sued the installer's employers—a cable television franchise and its independent contractor. She claimed that they gave the installer a master key to her apartment, which he used to enter her dwelling on the night of the attack. Because his employers gave him a master key to the apartments, the woman argued that they owed their customers a special duty to ensure that he was not a violent criminal. But they had failed to check his criminal record. The employers settled out of court for $250,000.00.[25]

Unfortunately, it is becoming more difficult to acquire information from former employers because of the potential for negligent referral suits. Previous employers are becoming "street-smart" and are consequently limiting the type of information they give out about former employees. When asked for information, employers options include:

- Getting a legal release of liability
- Not giving any information at all
- Giving only limited information: employee's title, dates of employment, and salary

In giving references, an employer should give only truthful and job related information about an employee, which includes anything in an employee's personnel file that is signed by the employee. Point out that it is the prospective employer's obligation to investigate, not the previous employer's obligation to reveal information.

To get meaningful references:

- Get the basics: verify dates of employment, type of work done, job title, earnings, honesty, who the applicant worked for
- Convince the applicant that references will be checked by stating it in your application and repeating it at the interview. Ask the applicant about his or her eligibility for rehire, quality of work, attendance, and what his or her previous employer will say about the applicant.[26]

Reference checks of prior employment records are not an infringement on privacy if the information provided relates specifically to work behavior and to the reasons an applicant left a previous job. Consequently, employers still routinely verify the accuracy of information on the resume application through reference checking. Suggestions and advice regarding this process are found in the feature, "HR Advice and Application: Ask the Experts—Investigating Application Frauds."

Written Tests

Written testing is another important procedure for gathering information about applicants. The most common types of written tests measure ability (cognitive and psychomotor); personality, interests, and preferences; and achievement.

Written tests can be used to measure:

- **cognitive ability**
- **personality, interests, and preferences**
- **achievement**

Cognitive Ability Tests. Ability tests measure the potential of an individual to perform, given the opportunity. Used in the United States and Europe since the turn of the century, these devices are useful and valid. Recent studies further suggest that they are equally valid for African-American and white applicants and that their use can be generalized to different jobs in different situations. Exhibit 10.4 shows sample items for measuring seven types of cognitive abilities.

HR ADVICE & APPLICATION

Ask the Experts—Investigating Application Frauds

Jeffrey F Robens, manager of government and administrative security for McDonnell Douglas Helicopter Company (Mesa, Arizona).

Q-1. What are the items most likely to be falsified on a resume or employment application?

A-1. Education, work experience, and references. Some people claim to have degrees that they don't have, and some make claims of work experience that are fraudulent. These are just some of the reasons that more and more human resource departments are asking their company's security professionals to screen job applications and make sure that the candidates are what they say they are.

Q-2. How do applicants falsify their education credentials on a resume or application?

A-2. What dishonest applicants exaggerate most often is the amount of their schooling. For example, applicants may indicate that they have a bachelor's or master's degree when, in fact, they don't.

Often, an investigation will reveal that the applicant was enrolled in the degree program at the college or university listed; however, the applicant never actually completed the requirements for the degree. Or applicants will claim to have graduated from an accredited technical institute, but upon investigation, the "institute" turns out to be a bus driver's school.

Q-3. What about work experience?

A-3. The "creative" applicant often counterfeits the length of time on a previous job, the responsibilities held, or the compensation received. On rare occasions, an applicant may list employment that never took place at all, perhaps with a fictitious employer.

Applicants with unsatisfactory employment records attempt to disguise the facts. Sometimes, people will say that they worked from January to December when they actually worked only from January to June and were terminated from a job.

Deceitful applicants also tend to inflate their former salaries in an attempt to make themselves look better than they are.

Q-4. What problems have you found in checking references?

A-4. Unscrupulous applicants may also list fake references to round off their other deceptions. They will list actual people who have never heard of them or fictitious people, hoping that the names and titles will give credence to their claims and that you will not bother to contact the references.

Q-5. How much information on the application or resume should you check?

A-5. You should devise a checklist to clarify what education and experience are essential for any position that needs to be filled. By defining what is essential and what is nonessential, you will not have to verify more information than is required.

Although it is important to confirm applicants' credentials, you may not need to check everything unless you suspect that some information may be false. If a degree is not required for the position, you may not need to contact the school, provided everything else on the application appears satisfactory.

State and federal laws may limit what information is available to you or impose rules on how you should go about obtaining certain information. For instance, credit checks conducted for employment purposes must conform to the guidelines established by the federal *Fair Credit Reporting Act* and any applicable state laws.[27]

Tests have also been developed to measure special abilities. For example, sensory tests measure the acuity of a person's senses such as vision and hearing. These tests may be appropriate for such jobs as wine taster, coffee bean selector, quality control inspector, and piano tuner. Clerical tests focus primarily on perceptual speed. However, specific tests such as the Minnesota Clerical Tests measure these skills in a job-relevant context. Standard Oil developed a cognitive ability test of management reasoning and judgment, while other firms have developed programmer aptitude tests.[28]

These tests can be modified to the candidate for using adaptive testing—that is, making tests increasingly more or less difficult depending on the individual taking the test. Because adaptive testing utilizes computer technology, it is described further in Chapter 19.

EXHIBIT 10.4

Samples of Cognitive Ability and Psychomotor Tests

Verbal Comprehension involves understanding the meaning of words and their relationship to one another. It is measured by such test items as

Which one of the following words means most nearly the same as *dilapidated*:
(1) new (2) injured (3) unresponsive (4) run-down (5) lethargic

Word Fluency involves the ability to name or make words, such as making smaller words from the letters in a large one or playing anagrams. For example,

Using the letters in the word "measurement," write as many three-letter words as you can in the next two minutes.

________ ________ ________ ________

________ ________ ________ ________

Number Aptitude involves speed and accuracy in making simple arithmetic calculations. It is measured by such test items as

Carry out the following calculations:

$$\begin{array}{r} 429 \\ +\,762 \\ \hline \end{array} \qquad \begin{array}{r} 7983 \\ -6479 \\ \hline \end{array} \qquad 721 \times 52 = \_\_\_ \qquad 4920 \div 6 = \_\_\_$$

Inductive Reasoning focuses on the ability to discover a rule or principle and apply it to the solution of a problem. The following is an example:

What number should come next in the sequence of five numbers?
1 3 6 10 15
(1) 22 (2) 21 (3) 25 (4) 18

Memory relates to having the ability to recall pairs of words or lists of numbers. It is measured by such test items as

You have 30 seconds to memorize the following pairs. When the examiner says stop, turn the page and write the appropriate symbols after each of the letters appearing there.

A @ C # E Δ G ?
B > D * F + H $

Perceptual Speed is concerned with the ability to perceive visual details quickly and accurately. Usually these tests are timed and include such items as

Make a check mark in front of each pair below in which the numbers are identical. Work as fast as you can,

___ (1) 755321 753321
___ (2) 966441 966641
___ (3) 334579 334579

Motor Skill—Aiming involves the ability to respond accurately and rapidly to stimuli. For example,

Place three dots in as many circles as you can in 30 seconds.

○ ○ ○ ○ ○ ○○ ○ ○

Source: Modified from M. Dunnette, *Personnel Selection and Placement* (Monterey, CA: Brooks/Cole, 1966), 47–49.

Psychomotor Tests. Many jobs involve a wide range not only of cognitive abilities, but also of psychomotor skills. For example, a bank teller needs certain motor skills to operate a computer or a ten-key calculator and the finger dexterity to manipulate currency.

There are a variety of psychomotor abilities, each of which is highly specific and shows little relationship to other psychomotor abilities or to cognitive abilities. Control precision involves finely controlled muscular adjustments (for example, moving a lever to a precise setting), whereas finger dexterity entails skillful manipulation of small objects (assembling nuts and bolts).

Psychomotor tests are to measure an applicant's physical ability to perform a job.

Psychomotor tests, then, are useful for selecting applicants in many occupations. However, only some categories of these tests may be predictive of job performance in a specific position.

Personality Tests. Personality refers to the unique blend of characteristics that define an individual and determine his or her pattern of interactions with society. While most people believe personality plays an important role in job success or failure, personality tests generally have not been found viable for employee selection. One reason is that personality variables have not been consistently defined. Personality tests are a diverse group of testing devices, each of which was designed to accomplish a different goal, but all of which are called **personality inventories.** The various tests are not equivalent in their construction, measurement goals, or underlying theoretical bases.[29] Consequently, these tests often yield different, incompatible, and even conflicting results.

Personality inventories are tests to measure an applicant's unique characteristics that are personality.

Another problem is that the wrong types of personality measurements have generally been used for selection purposes. The widely used Minnesota Multiphasic Personality Inventory (MMPI) is designed to identify areas of maladjustment. While it is an appropriate selection device for high-stress jobs (for example, police, nuclear power plant employees, air traffic controllers), it is not appropriate for most jobs because the absence of psychopathology does not guarantee the presence of competence: an employee can be both well adjusted *and* hopelessly mediocre in performance.

Finally, in highly structured situations controlled by regulations, rules, and guidelines, an individual's personality is unlikely to have an effect. However, in less structured organizations in which individuality and creativity are encouraged, personality attributes are likely to make the difference between job success and job failure.[30]

While less predictive of job success than cognitive ability tests, carefully developed personality assessments can be inexpensive additions to the selection process for a few jobs. One common multidimensional test of personality that appears useful is the Ghiselli Self-Description Inventory. It includes 64 pairs of trait adjectives.[31] For each pair, a person is asked to choose the most or least descriptive adjective. Responses are then scored across thirteen personality dimensions (for example, supervisory ability, decisiveness, achievement motivation) that relate to managerial competence. The designer of this test, Edwin Ghiselli, was able to show that successful managers perceive themselves quite differently than do unsuccessful managers on these dimensions.

An important legal consideration can arise in the use of personality or "psychological" tests as they are sometimes called. The consideration is invasion of privacy. As the feature "Managing Human Resources: Psychological Testing Leads to Costly Lawsuit," describes, this consideration can be costly.

Interest inventories assess preferences for different types of work and work situations.

Interest Inventories. While applicants may be able to perform in various jobs, **interest inventories** assess their preferences for different types of work and work situations.[32] Such inventories are useful in matching people to jobs they will enjoy. Representative items from an interest inventory include the following:

Do your answers to these items fit your career plans and goals that you wrote in the career planning exercise in Chapter 6?

For each set, write an "M" next to the activity you most like and an "L" next to the item you least prefer.

1. ________ go to a concert	2. ________ work in the garden
________ play tennis	________ go hiking
________ read a book	________ paint a picture

MANAGING HUMAN RESOURCES

Psychological Testing Leads to Costly Lawsuit

An employer that required applicants to answer intimate personal questions in a pre-employment psychological examination agrees to pay more than $2 million to settle a lawsuit over the test.

The employer, which operates a chain of retail stores in California, administered the test to about 2,500 applicants for security jobs. The test's true or false questions included the following:

- I have never indulged in any unusual sex practices.
- I have often wished I were a girl.
- I am very strongly attracted by members of my own sex.
- I believe my sins are unpardonable.
- I feel sure there is only one true religion.
- A minister can cure disease by praying and putting his hand on your head.

Before settling the suit, the employer argued that the test was necessary to screen out applicants who are emotionally unstable, unreliable, undependable, and not inclined to follow directions or established rules, as well as applicants with addictive or violent tendencies who might put customers or other employees at risk.

Under the settlement, the employer admits no wrongdoing, but agrees to set up a $1.3 million fund to be divided among applicants who took the test. Additionally, the employer agrees to pay $60,000 plus attorneys' fees to the four individuals who actually pursued the lawsuit, as well as the costs of notifying the 2,500 applicants.

The case "sends a strong message to other employers that they cannot trample upon the constitutionally protected privacy rights of applicants and employees," according to the applicants' attorney, Brad Seligman of Saperstein, Mayeda, Larkin & Goldstein, Oakland, California. This was the first class-action privacy case in the nation to challenge psychological testing, he adds. (*Saroka v. Dayton Hudson Corp.*, 1993).[33]

Achievement Tests. **Achievement tests** predict an individual's performance on the basis of what he or she knows. Although a test's validity is required, achievement tests may exclude applicants who have not had equal access to the opportunities to acquire the knowledge. Thus, care must be taken to ensure that the skills tested are job-related. Not all achievement tests are actual work samples of the job, and organizations need to be careful in their choice of these tests because some are less job-related than others.

Achievement tests predict an applicant's performance on the basis of what he or she knows.

Paper-and-pencil achievement tests tend to be less job-related because they measure facts and principles, not the practical use of them. For example, you could take a paper-and-pencil test measuring your knowledge of tennis and pass with flying colors and yet play very poorly. However, such tests continue to be used in many areas because they facilitate measuring a large number of people and because they test levels of knowledge presumed to be required. For example, applicants are admitted to the legal profession through bar exams and to the medical profession through medical boards. Paper-and-pencil tests are used in these cases because they are—or are assumed to be—related to performance in the actual job. Job-relatedness is, as with all other tests, a necessary legal defense for the use of paper-and-pencil tests.

Recognition tests, which are examples of past performance, are often used in advertising and modeling to select applicants. The applicants bring portfolios or samples of the work they have done to the job interview. However, portfolios contain no clues as to the conditions or circumstances under which they were done. Some organizations may request written samples from school work for jobs where written expression may be important.

Recognition tests are examples of past performance.

Test Batteries. It is often useful to administer a battery of tests to applicants for vocational counseling or selection. The General Aptitude Test Battery (GATB), which measures cognitive abilities—verbal, numerical, spatial, intelligence form perceptions, clerical perceptions, motor coordination, finger and manual dexterity—is used by U.S. employment offices for counseling purposes.[34]

Alternatively, organizations may use test batteries for selection. For example, Sears has used tests of ability (American Council on Education Psychological Test), values (Allport-Vernon Study of Values), and interest (Kuder Preference Record) since the 1940s to select managers. Similarly, Exxon relied on cognitive ability (Miller Analogies, Nonverbal Reasoning, Management Judgment), personality (MMPI), and an individual's background survey. Because batteries are difficult to develop, they are usually designed under the guidance of industrial psychologists.[35]

Work Simulations

Work simulations or work sample tests assess how applicants can actually do parts of the job.

Work simulations, often referred to as **work sample tests,** require applicants to complete verbal or physical activities under structured "testing" conditions. Rather than measure what an individual knows, they assess the individual's ability to do something. Still, work sample tests are somewhat artificial because the selection process itself tends to promote anxiety and tension.[36] Exhibit 10.5 shows three sets of work sample tests and the jobs for which they are used.

Because they replicate the actual work, work sample tests are not easy to fake. As a result, they tend to be more valid than almost all other types of selection devices. Additionally, they do not have an adverse impact on minority applicants.

EXHIBIT 10.5

Examples of Work Sample Tests and Jobs

JOB	PHYSICAL WORK SAMPLE TESTS
Dental assistants	Carving dexterity
Machine operators	Lathe, drill press, and tool dexterity
Meat scalers	Meat weighing
Mechanics	Belt and pulley installation; gear box repair; motor installation and alignment; sprocket reaming
Miners	Two-hand coordination
Pilots	Rudder control; direction control; complex coordination
Administrative assistants	Word processing on specific equipment; knowledge of Word
	MENTAL WORK SAMPLE TESTS
Magazine editors	Writing skills; page layout; headline writing
Administrators	Judgment and decision making
Engineers	Processing mathematical data
Administrative assistants	Letter composition; proofreading
	VERBAL WORK SAMPLE TESTS
Telephone operators	Role play of telephone contacts
Communication specialists	Oral fact-finding
Construction supervisors	Construction error recognition
Administrative assistants	Telephone screening

Source: Adapted from J. J. Asher and J. A. Sciarrino, "Realistic Work Sample Tests: A Review," *Personnel Psychology* 27 (1974):519-533.

Unfortunately, because simulation tests are job-specific, they are expensive to develop unless large numbers of applicants are to be examined. However, by placing work sample tests at the end of a selection process, the number of applicants tested is smaller and the price lower.

Assessment Center. This selection device evaluates applicants or current employees with regard to how well they might perform in a managerial or higher-level position. More than 20,000 companies now utilize this method, and its use grows each year because of its validity in predicting whether job applicants will be successful or unsuccessful.[37]

An **assessment center** usually involves six to twelve people who have been chosen or who have chosen to attend it. It is most often conducted off-premises by the organization for one to three days. The attendees' performance is usually rated by managers in the organization who are trained assessors. Typically, the purpose is to determine potential promotability of applicants to a first-line supervisor's job.

Assessment centers help identify how well someone might do in a future job.

At a typical assessment center, candidates undergo evaluation using a wide range of techniques. One important activity is the **in-basket exercise,** which creates a realistic situation designed to elicit typical on-the-job behaviors. Situations and problems encountered on the job are written on individual sheets of paper and set in the in-basket. The applicant is then asked to arrange the papers by priority. Occasionally, the applicant may need to write an action response. The problems or situations described to the applicant involve different groups of people—peers, subordinates, and those outside the organization. The applicant is usually given a set time limit to take the test and is often interrupted by phone calls meant to create more tension and pressure.

An in-basket exercise assesses how well a person can (1) identify what's important and (2) organize it accordingly.

Other tests used in managerial selection are the **leaderless group discussion** (LGD) and business games. In the LGD, a group of individuals is asked to discuss a topic for a given period of time. At IBM's assessment center, participants must make a five-minute oral presentation about the qualifications of a candidate for promotion. During the subsequent leaderless group discussion, they must defend their nomination of the candidate with five or more other participants. Participants are rated on their selling ability, oral communication skill, self-confidence, energy level, interpersonal competency, aggressiveness, and tolerance for stress. LGD ratings have been shown to be useful predictors of managerial performance in a wide array of business areas. Additionally, prior experience in LGD does not affect current LGD performance. **Business games** are "living" cases. That is, individuals must make decisions and "live" with them, much as they do in the in-basket exercise.

Leaderless group discussions and business games are often used at an assessment center.

Business games are living cases in which decisions have an immediate impact.

Because in-baskets, LGDs, and business games tend to be useful in managerial selection, they are often used together.[38] As candidates go through these exercises, their performance is observed by a trained team of observers or assessors drawn from the local management group. After the candidates have finished the program, these assessors meet to discuss the candidates and prepare performance evaluations based on their combined judgments of the candidates in such areas as organizing and planning, analyzing, making decisions, controlling oral communications, conducting interpersonal relations, influencing, and exhibiting flexibility. The composite performance on the exercises and tests is then used to determine an assessment center attendee's future promotability. It may also be used to determine the organization's training needs, as well as to make current selection and placement decisions. The composite performance rating is generally given to the attendee, who in turn can use it for his or her own personal career planning purposes.

Assessment centers have been used effectively by manufacturing companies, government, military services, utility companies, oil companies, the foreign service, and educational institutions. They appear to work because they reflect the actual work environment and measure performance in multiple dimensions. Additionally, more than one trained rater with a common frame of reference evaluates each participant's behavior. In terms of cost effectiveness, assessment centers are often criticized as costing too much (from $50 to over $2,000 per applicant). However, annual productivity gains realized by selecting managers via assessment centers average well above administrative costs.[39]

Selection and Placement Interview

The job interview and the perceptions gained from it still comprise the tool most heavily used to determine who gets the job offer.[40] As shown in Exhibit 10.1, the interview is an important part of the selection procedure.

> *At Motorola, every job candidate, even those looking for factory work, goes through three days of interviews. During that time, applicants write a composition and take a 4 1/2-hour test—in math, problem-solving, and ability to work on a team. Only one candidate in 10 makes the cut.*[41]

The reliability and usefulness of the interview depend on several factors.

Degree of Structure. The unstructured interview involves little preparation. The interviewer merely prepares a list of possible topics to cover and, depending on how the conversation proceeds, asks or does not ask them. While this provides for flexibility, the digressions, discontinuity, and lack of focus may be frustrating to the interviewer and interviewee. More important, unstructured interviews result in inconsistencies in the information collected about the candidates.

Patterned or structured interviews are those that ask the same questions in the same order.

Alternatively, in a **patterned** or **structured interview,** all the applicants are asked the same questions in the same order. While structuring the interview restricts the topics that can be covered, it ensures that the same information is collected on all candidates. As a result, managers are less likely to make snap, and possibly erroneous, judgments.

A compromise that still minimizes snap judgments is the semistructured interview. Questions are prepared in advance, and the same questions are asked of all candidates; responses are recorded. However, follow-up questions are allowed to probe specific areas in depth. This approach provides enough flexibility to develop insights, along with the structure needed to acquire comparative information. Regardless of the approach used, companies should focus their questions on job-related experience and education. Legally, employers may not ask questions about:

- Race, religion, age, national origin, disability
- Marital status and spouse's nationality
- Arrest records
- Childbearing plans[42]

Job Relatedness. At one extreme, interviewers focus on generalities about qualifications. Such questions help interviewers form an overall impression of the candidate's competence but are not predictive of success in a specific job. A better approach is to use job analysis to generate questions about job-related experiences and education. This can be aided by knowing the specific job skills and duties.

Because job and job conditions may change quickly and be almost impossible to describe accurately, companies may try to determine how an applicant would perform under these conditions. Microsoft is famous for its "Brainteaser" questions it asks college recruits. For example:

> ***How much water flows through the Mississippi River each day?***
>
> *We're not looking for the "right" answer. We're looking for the method, and we want them to talk about it. We want to see what information they ask for, like the length of the river or the flow rate at certain measuring points. It's a learning process.*[43]

Systematic Scoring. Job interviews vary in the degree to which results are scored. At one extreme, an interviewer merely listens to responses, forms an impression, and makes an accept, reject, or hold decision. Alternatively, raters can be given specific criteria and a scoring key to evaluate responses to each question. This approach is more objective because it helps ensure that applicants are evaluated against the same criteria. Systematic scoring also tends to minimize **halo bias,** in which an interviewer judges an applicant's entire potential on the basis of a single characteristic such as how well the applicant dresses or talks.

Halo bias is a tendency to judge an applicant on just one characteristic.

Number of Interviewers. Typically, applicants are interviewed by one person at a time. Unfortunately, managers sometimes overlap in their coverage of some job-related questions and miss others entirely. An applicant may not have four interviews, but one interview four times. This is a time-consuming process in which the interviewer's and applicant's impressions may vary, depending on what was discussed in one-on-one interviews. This problem can be overcome by using a **panel interview** in which several individuals simultaneously interview one applicant. Because all decision makers hear the same responses, panel interviews produce more consistent results. On the other hand, panel interviews are expensive because many people are involved. However, if applicants are to be interviewed by more than one person anyway, panel interviewing may be more efficient and reliable and as cost effective as individual interviews. A variation of the panel interview is the **team interview.** While several people are used, they are not used simultaneously. The benefits of using the team interview and how to prepare for it are described in the feature, "HR Advice and Application: Expert Opinion—Interviewing Skills: Using Past Performance to Predict the Future."

A panel interview is a series of sequential interviews done by several individuals.

Team interviews improve predictions of an applicant's chances of success.

A further variation on interviews is the use of computers to ask the questions rather than people. For example, Marriott Hotels uses a 15-minute self-administered computer test for certain jobs.[44]

Did You KNOW?

Southwest Airlines worries a lot about hiring the right people. In fact, it flies some of its best customers to Dallas and involves them in the flight attendant hiring process, believing that those who are in contact with the front-line employees probably know best what makes a good employee.

Training. Left on their own, interviewers tend to form impressions based on whatever criteria are most important or salient to them personally. For example, an applicant might be rejected by one interviewer for being "too aggressive" but accepted by another for being "assertive." Consequently, it is important to train interviewers so they interpret information consistently.[45] This can be accomplished by having potential interviewers develop items and scoring approaches such as those in Exhibit 10.6. Alternatively, an interviewer's ratings for "practice" questions can be compared to normative ratings given by other interviewers. Such training brings perceptions into closer congruence with those of the rest of the organization.

Physical Examination

Because of its high cost, the physical examination is often one of the final steps in the selection process. Many employers give common physical exams to all job applicants, whereas special exams are given to only a subset of all applicants.[46] According to the *Uniform Guidelines,* physical examinations should be used to screen out applicants when the results indicate that job performance would be adversely affected. For example, production-job applicants may receive back X-rays, while office-job applicants may not. But this may not be enough, especially for companies trying to prevent or reduce injuries:

> *The Martin-Brower Co. handles more than 100 million boxes per year for McDonald's restaurants—just part of the bargain since Martin-Brower is the major warehouse distributor for McDonald's. A high volume of employee injuries might be considered part of the bargain as well, but the Chicago-based company, which employs 1,750 workers at facilities in 13 states, is working hard to keep that likelihood from becoming a foregone conclusion.*

HR ADVICE & APPLICATION

Expert Opinion—Interviewing Skills: Using Past Performance to Predict the Future

Glenna Sue Davis is human resource and quality control manager at A.E. Staley Manufacturing's potato starch processing facility. In this position, she's responsible for recruiting and hiring engineers, supervisors, and hourly employees.

There are two things that distinguish Davis's approach to hiring: First, she makes an effort to learn what applicants did in past jobs, rather than concentrating solely on what they say they'd accomplish in the positions for which she's interviewing. Second, with hourly positions, she uses a team approach to hiring.

PAST PERFORMANCE

"You really have to be willing to dig a little if you want to get good information," Davis advises. For instance, if you ask a question and the candidate is evasive, restate the question. Davis will sometimes use this technique when she's unsure about the information she's been given.

Hypothetical questions are helpful when trying to explore applicants' backgrounds. "Particularly when I'm hiring engineers, I'll say, 'Tell me about a problem you had (in a certain area) and how you handled it,' or 'How did your past job prepare you to deal with...?'" These types of questions are effective in getting candidates to discuss their experience so that Davis can get the objective information she needs to make informed hiring decisions.

There are three keys, she says, to getting helpful information about past performance and using it to predict future performance:

- **Identify your needs.** Take a good look at the job description and requirements so that you know what the position demands.
- **Identify the behaviors that will lead to successful performance on the job.** For instance, will the candidate need to be self-directed? Assertive? Independent? Cooperative?
- **Develop questions about past behaviors that will provide insights into the future.** For example, "Tell me about a situation in which you had to confront an angry co-worker. How did you handle that situation, and what was the outcome?"

TEAM INTERVIEWS

Davis uses the unusual approach of team interviews to fill hourly positions. "I feel it's important to get a perspective from the people who will be working directly with the new hire," she says. "Team interviewing also provides me with a more in-depth sense of what traits are needed to successfully fill a position."

Davis usually selects a supervisor, an employee from the department whose position she is filling, and a cross section of people from other departments to participate in the interview. She tries to get at least four or five people involved and makes sure there is a mix of male and female interviewers. Another benefit of the team approach to interviewing is that decisions are shared ones and are more likely to be supported by the staff.

Preparation is a critical factor in making this system work, she stresses. "We do a couple of training sessions on our wants, needs, and priorities. Then we put together the questions we'll be asking—of course, every applicant will be asked the same questions."

To make a final selection decision, Staley Manufacturing uses a rating system. "We have a numerical rating system that we use to select the three final candidates. Then the appropriate department head and I will make a final decision from among these three candidates."

Davis's advice to other interviewers is to "hone your skills. Be sure you know what you're going after, and be confident in what you're doing." An excellent way to attain this knowledge and confidence is to adapt Davis's approach to your particular circumstances. Above all, she says, "keep learning. Every time you conduct an interview, you learn something new."[47]

Martin-Brower's early efforts at reducing injuries focused on back problems, according to risk manager Nancy Kusek. The company first implemented a back X-ray requirement for all applicants seeking warehouse or truck driver/loader jobs, but found that X-rays could not adequately gauge the physical ability of workers, she says.

EXHIBIT 10.6

Knowledge, Skills, and Ability Requirements for Teamwork

I. **Communication Skills**
- A. Understand verbal and nonverbal communications
- B. Listen without evaluation
- C. Give feedback to others that can be used
- D. Encourage others to contribute
- E. Facilitate communication across teams

II. **Problem Solving Skills**
- A. Identify problems with others
- B. Gather data to diagnose
- C. Propose and analyze alternative solution
- D. Implement solutions
- E. Evaluate results

III. **Group Member Skills**
- A. Understand group stages of development
- B. Manage group dynamics
- C. Understand social, task, and individual roles
- D. Understand team project planning, goals setting, execution, evaluation, and learning
- E. Manage group conflict
- F. Understand interaction styles of group members
- G. Recognize the variety of types of teams used in organizations

IV. **Performance Management Skills**
- A. Understand need for team mission and objectives
- B. Monitor and measure group performance
- C. Understand self and team management concepts
- D. Have ability to learn from past

Based on M. J. Stevens and M. A. Campion, "The Knowledge, Skill and Ability Requirements for Teamwork: Implications for Human Resource Management," *Journal of Management* 20 (1994): 505–530; B. Dumaine, "The Trouble with Teams," *Fortune* (September 5, 1994): 86–92; and N. R. F. Maier, "Assets and Liabilities in Group Problem Solving: The Need for an Integrative Function," *Psychological Review* (April 1967): 239–249.

According to Kusek, the company now requires new hires to pass a pair of tests: a strength test, where objects with the same weight as the company's shipping cases must be lifted at the frequency required on the job; and an endurance test, where heart rates are recorded after three separate bouts of stair-step exercises. "Bodies can only take so much," she notes, and the tests help the company hire workers who are "more physically fit" than those hired in the past.

Although the strength and endurance tests have been shown to have a disparate impact on women and workers over age 40, the only concern is that "the individual being tested has the strength to perform the job," regardless of other factors. To date, no complaint filed with the Equal Employment Opportunity Commission has succeeded against the company.[48]

Guidelines for assessing physical abilities have been developed that also detail the sensory, perceptual, cognitive, psychomotor, and physical requirements of most jobs (for example, police, firefighters, steel mill laborers, paramedics, and workers in numerous mechanical jobs). When applied carefully, these physical requirements (not physical examinations per se) are extremely useful in predicting job performance, worker's compensation claims, and absenteeism. However, arbitrary physical requirements can screen out women and minorities who could do a job if given the opportunity. To accommodate workers with disabilities, organizations should also explore whether equipment can be "reasonably" adapted. Guidelines on inexpensive adaptations for most types of machinery are available from the federal government.[49]

Genetic screening identifies applicants who may be hypersensitive to pollutants in the workplace.

Genetic Screening. **Genetic screening** identifies individuals who are hypersensitive to harmful pollutants in the workplace. Once identified, these individuals can be screened out of chemically dangerous jobs and placed in positions in which environmental toxins do not present specific hazards.[50]

While cost-effective genetic tests have not yet been developed, 1 percent of major firms already use genetic screening, and 15 percent are considering genetic tests in the future. As scientific research on genetic screening continues, the debate over the ethics of basing employment decisions on immutable traits is likely to grow. It also seems probable that pressure will be exerted on organizations to develop engineering controls that minimize or eliminate workplace pollutants. These controls would be the preferred alternative to genetic screening, a selection criterion over which an individual has no control.[51]

Did You KNOW?

Two of the largest drug testing companies estimate that 15 million employees are tested annually for drug use. Between 6 and 8% test positive.

Drug Testing. Drug abuse is said to cost U.S. industry more than $100 billion annually, and its impact on individuals and society can be significant.[52] Consequently, firms are drug testing.[53] About 70 percent of companies use it in their applicant screening process and about 30 percent use it randomly with current employees.[54] According to the *Drug Free Workplace Act* of 1988, federal contractors, firms that do business with the federal government, must have written drug use policies.

While urine analysis continues to be the most popular method of drug testing, blood samples and hair tests are also used.[55] Regardless of what methods are used for drug testing, a key issue in adopting a drug policy is establishing a disciplinary procedure. "If a drug policy does not state specifically that disciplinary actions will be taken when an employee tests positive for drug use, there's no reason to test. Drug testing doesn't make sense if you're not willing to take disciplinary action based on a confirmed positive test result. A policy calling for discipline in such a circumstance doesn't have to require termination. Rehabilitation can be required as an alternative."[56] Rehabilitation programs, particularly for current employees, are on the rise. Almost 75 percent of companies have employee assistance programs.[57]

Corporate programs make drug use more of a hassle. There's no question they drive down drug use.

Dr. Robert B. Millman
Director
Alcohol and Drug Abuse Programs
New York Hospital—Payne Whitney Psychiatric Clinic

An issue in drug testing is the individual's right of privacy versus legitimate interest of the company to know. It appears that both sides are of concern to the courts. Thus if an employer can show that a random drug test for current employees is necessary for the employer, the court may support it (*Webster v. Motorola,* 1994). The ADA does not consider tests for illegal drug use as medical examinations, therefore, they are not prohibited. Tests to see whether an individual has consumed alcohol, however, are medical and are not allowed.[58]

AIDS Testing. AIDS victims are protected by the *Rehabilitation Act* of 1973 (*Chalf v. U.S. District Court for Central District of California,* 1987). Because AIDS is such a major challenge in today's workplace, organizations are establishing guidelines concerning it. Companies such as IBM, AT&T, and Johnson & Johnson have endorsed these guidelines:

- People with AIDS or who are infected with HIV, the AIDS-causing virus, are entitled to the same rights and opportunities as people with other serious illnesses.
- Employment policies should be based on the scientific evidence that people with AIDS or HIV infection do not pose a risk of transmitting the virus through ordinary workplace contact.
- Employers should provide workers with sensitive and up-to-date educations about AIDS and risk reduction in their personal lives.
- Employers have the duty to protect the confidentiality of employees' medical information.
- Employers should not require HIV screening as part of general pre-employment or workplace physical examinations.[59]

Polygraph Testing. With the passage of the *Employee Polygraph Protection Act* of 1988, employers are restricting their use of **polygraph tests.** In passing the law, supporters of polygraph restriction claimed the tests are accurate only two-thirds of the time and are far more likely to be inaccurate for honest employees. The law restricts pre-employment screening and random use of the device; the law:

Polygraph tests measure an applicant's likelihood of giving false answers.

- Permits private security firms and drug companies to continue to administer polygraph tests to job applicants and employees
- Exempts federal, state, and local government employers from the ban on polygraph testing
- Prohibits employers from disciplining, discharging, discriminating against, or denying employment or promotions to prospective or current workers solely on the basis of polygraph test results
- Provides that employers that violate any provision of the law may be assessed a civil penalty of up to $10,000[60]

Honesty Tests. Partly as a response to regulatory prohibitions on employers' use of polygraphs, the use of paper-and-pencil honesty tests has increased. Paper-and-pencil **honesty tests** attempt to detect the honesty of the respondent by examining how the person responds to such items as, "Did you ever steal?" Despite endorsements from industry, honesty tests have not been subject to extensive validation and therefore caution is recommended in using them as a selection device.[61]

Honesty tests attempt to detect the likelihood an applicant is giving false answers.

Using Information in Selection and Placement Decisions

LEARNING OBJECTIVE 4

Discuss ways the information is used in making selection and placement decisions.

We have discussed the primary techniques for collecting selection and placement information. Now the key questions are: "How can this information be used in making selection decisions? Should just one technique be used (the single-predictor approach), or should several techniques be used (the multiple-predictor approach)?"

Remember, organizations want to make decisions that are correct. In other words, they want to maximize the number of true decisions and minimize the number of false decisions. **True decisions** include rejecting a candidate who would have been a bad performer or hiring a candidate who turns out good. **False**

True decisions are those that are accurate in hiring or rejecting an applicant. False decisions are those that are incorrect in hiring or rejecting an applicant.

decisions include rejecting a good candidate or hiring a bad candidate. For more discussion on this subject, see Appendix C under "Base Rate Versus Predictor Rate."

The Single Predictor Approach

A single predictor approach uses just one piece of information in selecting an applicant.

When managers use only one piece of information or one technique for selecting an applicant, they are employing the **single predictor approach.** Single predictors are used by many organizations to select employees, especially when the predictor can be readily validated. This occurs most frequently when a predictor encompasses the major dimension of the job, thereby making it easy to validate.

> *A few hiring tests are easy enough to validate, especially those in which the candidate actually performs a task he/she will have to perform on the job. It makes obvious good sense, for example, to require a candidate for a secretarial job to pass a typing test.*[62]

The Multiple Predictor Approach

Multiple predictors can be combined in three approaches:

- **multiple hurdles**
- **compensatory**
- **combined**

When there is more than one selection technique being used, the information from all can be combined in one of three ways. This is the essence of the **multiple predictor approach.**

In a compensatory approach, a high score on one test can compensate for a low score on another test.

Compensatory Approach. Since most jobs do not have truly absolute requirements, a **compensatory approach** is more realistic. This approach assumes that good performance on one predictor can compensate for poor performance on another (for example, a low score for a written examination can be compensated for by a high score on an interview). With a compensatory approach, no selection decisions are made until the completion of the entire process. Then, a composite index that considers performance on all predictors is developed.

A combined approach uses parts of the multiple hurdles approach and the compensatory approach.

Combined Approach. Many organizations also use a **combined approach,** in which one or more specific requirements must be met. Once these hurdles are jumped, then the remaining predictor scores are combined into an overall measure of job suitability. Consider college recruiting. Many organizations only interview college students with GPAs that exceed a specific level (first hurdle). To be offered a plant visit, the candidate must first pass a campus interview (second hurdle). At corporate headquarters, the applicant may take aptitude tests, participate in an assessment center, and be interviewed. A composite index that takes into consideration performance in all three areas is used to make the final decision.

In a multiple hurdles approach, an applicant has to score well on all the tests.

Multiple Hurdles. In the **multiple hurdles approach,** an applicant must exceed fixed levels of proficiency on all the predictors in order to be accepted. A score lower than the cutoff score on one predictor (test) cannot be compensated for by a higher-than-necessary score on another predictor. Underlying this approach is the assumption that a specific skill or competency is so critical that inadequacy guarantees the person will be unsuccessful on the job. This assumption legitimately applies for some physical ability requirements (visual acuity for pilots) and for state-mandated licensing requirements (state licensure for nurses).

Example: Selecting for Teamwork. Companies that are trying to enhance their competitiveness by improving quality seem to agree that the employees at the front line—for example, the production workers—are key to improving and delivering quality. Thus, they devote considerable time and effort to selecting production workers. In high quality manufacturing environments, work is now organized around teams, so selecting people who can be effective as team players is essential. Exhibit 10.6 lists several types of knowledge, skills, and abilities that are likely to be needed in team-based organizations. To assess such characteristics, some organizations have developed and use very sophisticated approaches, including those listed for production team workers in Exhibit 10.7. In this exhibit, each box

EXHIBIT 10.7

Methods for Selecting Production Team Workers

Step 1
- Video orientation
- Application

↓

Step 2
- Review of application

↓

Step 3
- General ability test
- Job fit inventory
- Video interpersonal skills exercise
- Math test
- Supplemental background information

↓

Step 4
- Problem-solving and decision-making manufacturing game
- Problem-solving group discussion
- Fact-finding decision making
- Assembly situation

↓

Step 5
- Selection interview

↓

Step 6
- Reference check

↓

Step 7
- Job offer

↓

Step 8
- Health exam

↓

Step 9
- Reasonable accommodation

represents one step in a series of multiple hurdles. A compensatory approach is used to combine the information within each step and decide whether to involve the applicant in the next step. Sophisticated hiring procedures are also recommended for other workers, as described in the feature "HR Advice and Application: Workers Are a Small Firm's Most Valuable Asset," shown earlier in this chapter.

The Decision Itself

Did You KNOW?

Firms having total quality management such as Eaton Corporation, Motorola, Saturn and Honda of America spend up to 20 hours per applicant in selection.

Selection and placement decisions seek to put the right person in the right job. The right person may be from outside or inside the organization. Whether a person is "right" depends on the match between the person's skills, knowledge, and abilities and job-skill demands and between the person's personality, interests, and preferences and job and organizational characteristics. An organization may want applicants to fill newly created jobs or jobs that have become vacant as a result of retirement, transfer, or voluntary termination (turnover). Vacancies can also be created by demotions and layoffs. Remember, however, that as far as equal employment laws are concerned, all decisions about initial hiring, transfer, promotion, demotion, layoff, termination, and admittance to training programs are regarded as selection decisions. The final selection and placement decision may be:

- To hire a new employee
- To transfer an employee from within the organization
- To reject all applicants and do more recruiting
- To "put on hold" some applicants who are qualified but for whom no jobs are currently open
- To demote an existing employee

Promotion Decisions

Did You KNOW?

Disney acquires two-thirds of all salaried employees—such as managers, designers, and marketers—from within the company.

Promotions can be selected from a pool of people within a department, a division, or an entire organization. They occur between two nonmanagerial positions (for example, from Typist I to Typist II), between managerial positions, and between nonmanagerial and managerial positions.

Although promotions generally refer to vertical moves in the organization, promotions may occur when an employee moves to another job at the same level but with more pay or status. However, this type of promotion may violate federal wage guidelines and equal pay regulations, and should be made advisedly.

Many organizations such as Disney have an HR philosophy of promotion-from-within. As you can see from Exhibit 10.8, Disney fills most of its managerial positions by in-house promotions.

Transfer Decisions

A transfer generally refers to a move at the same level and at the same pay. As the 35 to 54 age group increases and organizations continue to reduce the number of middle management positions, transfers may become the alternative to promotions, at least in providing challenge and variety to valued employees. In addition to providing challenge and variety to employees, transfers are also likely to result in employees having a greater understanding of what employees in other parts and functional areas of the organization are doing. Many organizations are using transfers to increase employees awareness of the business and to demonstrate how their work influences the work of others and ultimately the customer. Organizations view these transfers as a vital way to increase the organization's ability to produce high quality products/services and to provide the employees with interesting and challenging work assignments.

EXHIBIT 10.8

The Staffing Process at Disney

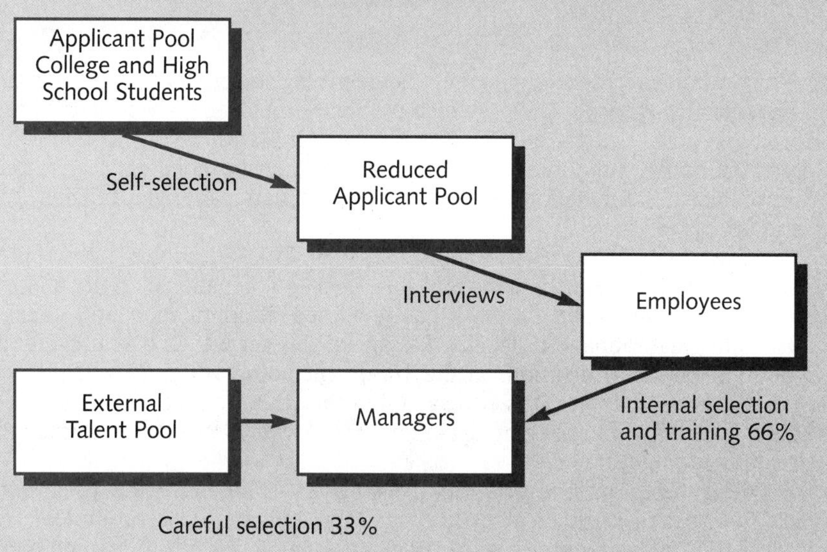

Making Promotion and Transfer Decisions

Immediate supervisors sometimes have significant control over promotion and transfer decisions. When a new job is being created, they can determine exactly who will be promoted by writing the job description to fit only one person. This is not necessarily a fair practice, but it is not uncommon. It is important to remember, however, that promotion decisions are selection decisions and, as such, must be made without illegal discrimination. On the one hand, immediate supervisors may have limited control in deciding who to promote or transfer. Nevertheless, when a vacancy arises, they must search for qualified candidates and assist in the choice. This process is usually carried out in close consultation with one or more higher-level supervisors who ultimately have to approve the choice.

During the past six years, Philadelphia Electric's culture has changed from entitlement-based to skills-based. No longer can employees move up through the company based on seniority alone; now they must prove they have management potential and demonstrate their abilities.

William J. Kaschub
Senior Vice President
Human Resources
Philadelphia Electric

Identifying Candidates for Promotion and Transfer. Candidates may be identified by word of mouth, inspection of the organization's personnel records, promotion lists based on performance or managerial ratings, and formal programs for identifying potential candidates for promotion such as assessment centers. The HRIS (human resource information system) is valuable here because it can store a vast amount of information and speed the process of identifying potential candidates. It can also ensure fairness in the process by giving everyone a chance regardless of where they are currently working or for whom they are working.

Comparing Candidates. The methods that identify candidates can also be used to evaluate and compare them. Although many companies administer a battery of tests to assess mental ability, personality, and interests, one study concluded that tests are ignored more often than not as decision-making aids for internal promotions. Job experience, performance history, and assessment center results are used instead. Interviews are used as well, although more often for candidates from external sources. A powerful **sponsor** (often a manager at a higher level in the organization who "adopts" and looks out for an employee at a lower level) can see that an individual's strengths are noted by others. A final basis for comparing candidates is seniority.

A sponsor is a powerful person in the organization who tries to help you advance.

LEARNING OBJECTIVE 5

Identify legal considerations in selection and placement.

Legal Considerations

Legal considerations are extensive for selection and placement. Numerous acts executive orders, regulations, and agencies have an impact on these activities in all organizations, particularly in cases of illegal discrimination.

Acts

Relevant federal acts include:

- *Civil Rights Act* **of 1866/1871**
- *Civil Rights Act* **of 1964/1991**
- *Age Discrimination in Employment Acts* **of 1967/1978/1986/1990**
- *Vietnam Era Veterans' Readjustment Act* **of 1974**
- *Equal Employment Opportunity Act* **of 1972**
- *Equal Pay Act* **of 1963**
- *Rehabilitation Act* **of 1973**
- *Americans with Disabilities Act* **of 1990**

The historical development of equal employment legislation began with the *Civil Rights Act* of 1866, Section 1981, which prohibits employee discrimination based on race, color, and national origin. The *Civil Rights Act* of 1871, Section 1983, enforces the Fourteenth Amendment to the U.S. Constitution, which has been held to prohibit discrimination based on race, color, national origin, religion, gender, and age.

The *Civil Rights Act* of 1964 and, in particular, Title VII, prohibits discrimination against individuals on the basis of gender, race, color, national origin, and religion. The *Civil Rights Act* of 1991 has redefined discrimination and exposed employers to greater financial liability. Passage of this act was in part triggered by several Supreme Court decisions in the 1980s, including *Wards Cove Packing v. Atonio* (1989). These decisions had, among other things, shifted the burden of proving discrimination to the employee. The *Civil Rights Act* of 1991 returned this burden to the employer.[63]

The *Equal Employment Opportunity Act* of 1972 amended the *Civil Rights Act* of 1964 that had first created the Equal Employment Opportunity Commission. This 1972 amendment expanded the coverage of Title VII to include public and private employers with fifteen or more employees, labor organizations with fifteen or more members, and public and private employment agencies. Elected officials and their appointees are excluded from Title VII coverage but are still covered under the Fourteenth Amendment and the *Civil Rights Acts* of 1866 and 1871. The 1972 amendment also identified exceptions or exemptions to Title VII, including bona fide occupational qualifications, seniority systems, pre-employment inquiries, use of job-related tests for selection, national security interests, and veterans' preference rights. Much of what is discussed under the section below on proving illegal discrimination is based on the *Civil Rights Acts* of 1964 and 1991.

"I will fire you if you discriminate. Anyone who doesn't like the direction this train is moving had better jump off now."

Jim Adamson
CEO
Flagstar, Parent Corporation of Denny's

The *Age Discrimination in Employment Act* of 1967 (ADEA) as amended in 1978, 1986, and 1990, prohibits discrimination against employees and applicants who are more than 40 years old.[64] While age discrimination (bias) has been a significant legal issue in the United States for some time, it is just now becoming an issue in Europe.

> *Rampant job bias against older Europeans is just starting to decline, thanks to a scarcity of young people and the spread of U.S. style advocacy groups. Unlike America, Europe lacks tough laws broadly barring age discrimination. Employers routinely run advertisements seeking workers under 40, force staffers as young as 55 to retire, and fire people simply for being too old.*[65]

As already described, the *Americans with Disabilities Act* of 1990 substantially extends the coverage of the *Rehabilitation Act* to include the same organizations covered by the *Civil Rights Act* of 1991. Coverage began in 1992, with organizations making accommodations for individuals (employees and customers) with disabilities. As defined by the act, an estimated 45 million Americans are classified as disabled. The impact of the act is regarded as the most significant since Title VII. It is likely to supersede both the *Rehabilitation Act* and the *Vietnam Era Veterans' Readjustment Act* of 1974, which protects disabled veterans and veterans of the Vietnam era.[66]

In addition to these major federal acts pertaining to equal employment opportunity, there are state and local government acts and executive orders that employers must follow.

Executive Orders

The equal employment opportunity acts have been supported by a number of **executive orders** (EOs). *EO 11246* of 1965 prohibits discrimination on the basis of race, color, religion, and national origin by federal agencies, contractors, and subcontractors. In 1966, *EO 11375* was signed to prohibit discrimination in these same organizations on the basis of sex. *EO 11478* of 1969 prescribes that employment policies of the federal government be based on merit and that the head of each agency establish and maintain a program of equal employment opportunity.

Executive orders are directives issued by the President of the United States.

Guidelines

While acts and executive orders delineate protected classes, guidelines provide the mechanisms, such as selection tests, by which these acts and orders are implemented. The first set was issued in 1970 by the EEOC and originally intended to provide a workable set of ideal standards for employees, unions, and employment agencies. Those guidelines defined a test as being:

> *. . .all formal, scored, qualified or standardized techniques of assessing job suitability, including . . . background requirements, educational or work history requirements, interviews, biographical information blanks, interview rating scales and scored application blanks.*

Rather than becoming a flexible set of ideal standards (as originally intended), the guidelines became a sort of checklist of *minimum* standards that the courts used for test validation. Concern over this trend prompted the Equal Employment Opportunity Coordinating Council to develop a set of uniform guidelines, to be used by all federal agencies, that were based on sound psychological principles and that were technically feasible. As a result, the *Federal Executive Agency (FEA) Guidelines* were published in 1976 followed by the *Uniform Guidelines on Employee Selection Procedure* in 1978. These *Uniform Guidelines* are a 14,000-word catalog of do's and don'ts and of questions and answers for hiring and promotion (and job analysis as mentioned in Chapter 8). They contain interpretation and guidance not found in earlier EEOC guidelines.

The EEOC has also published other guidelines. On November 10, 1980, the commission issued *Guidelines on Discrimination Because of Sex.* These guidelines are premised on the assumption that sexual harassment is a condition of employment if women are exposed to it more frequently than men (more on this in Chapter 16). Six weeks later, the EEOC issued its *Guidelines on Discrimination Because of National Origin.* The national origin guidelines extended earlier versions of this protection by defining national origin as a *place* rather than a *country* of origin. It also revised the "speak-English-only rules." This means employers can require that English be spoken only if there is a compelling business-related necessity. On September 29, 1981, the EEOC issued guidelines on age discrimination in essence identifying what the *Age Discrimination in Employment Act* meant to do and what it should mean to employers and employees.[67]

Under the *Guidelines on Discrimination Because of Religion,* an employer is obliged to accommodate the religious preferences of current and prospective employees unless the employer demonstrates undue hardship. It appears, however, that if an employer shows "reasonable attempts to accommodate," the courts may be satisfied that no religious discrimination has occurred (*State Division of Human Rights v. Rochester Housing Authority,* 1980; *Philbrook v. Ansonia Board of Education,* 1986).

Professional Standards

Selection processes are also monitored by the American Psychological Association. In 1966 and again in 1974, the American Psychological Association (APA) released its *Standards for Education and Psychological Tests.* These standards were updated in 1985. In 1975 and again in 1987, the Society for Industrial-Organizational Psychology, a division of the APA, published its *Principles for the Validation and Use of Personnel Selection Procedures.* Drawing from relevant research, these standards and principles help clarify issues regarding test fairness and discrimination.

Proving Illegal Discrimination

While the *Civil Rights Act* of 1991 explicitly prohibits discrimination, nowhere in the law is discrimination defined. Essentially, a jury must decide whether or not illegal discrimination has occurred. Broadly speaking, however, the act prohibits differences in the treatment of employees who belong to one of the five protected groups (race, color, religion, gender, and national origin). Discrimination based on age, physical and mental handicaps, or against disabled or Vietnam-era veterans is prohibited by other acts. Discrimination on all other bases or qualifications is untouched by federal law, except when discrimination on nonprohibited factors is disguised as legal discrimination. For example, using minimum height and weight requirements as substitute measures of physical strength may adversely affect women and certain ethnic groups (Asians, Hispanics). When this occurs, the *Civil Rights Act* of 1991 is violated.[68]

Prima Facie Cases. In a typical discrimination suit, a person alleges discrimination due to unlawful employment practices. The person may first go to the Equal Employment Opportunity Commission (EEOC) office. The EEOC may seek out the facts of the case from both sides, attempting a resolution. Failing a resolution, the person may continue the case and file a suit. In the first phase of a discrimination suit, it is the obligation of the plaintiff (the person filing the suit) to establish a *prima facie* case of illegal discrimination by showing disparate impact or disparate treatment.

Disparate treatment refers to an apparent case of illegal discrimination against a person.

Disparate impact is an apparent case of illegal discrimination against a group.

Disparate treatment means there is an apparent case of illegal discrimination against an individual while **disparate impact** is against a group. (Occasionally, the term **adverse impact** is used in making references to the effects of disparate treatment or disparate impact.) The basic criteria for establishing a *prima facie* case of disparate impact were specified by the Supreme Court in *Griggs v. Duke Power* (1974), and those for a disparate treatment case in *McDonnell Douglas Corp. v. Green* (1973). While a charge of disparate treatment has always required evidence of intent to discriminate, only more recently has the Court required the same of some disparate impact cases (*Wards Cove Packing v. Atonio,* 1989). The *Civil Rights Act* of 1991, however, substantially revises the plaintiff's burden of proof responsibility described in the feature, "Managing Human Resources: The Burden of Proof Grows Heavier" in Chapter 4.

Three statistics for disparate impact:

- **comparative**
- **demographic**
- **concentration**

Disparate Impact. Cases of disparate impact rely on three types of statistical evidence.

One approach relies on comparative statistics or comparisons of the rates or ratios of hiring, firing, promoting, transferring, and demoting for protected and nonprotected groups. The *Uniform Guidelines* suggest that disparate impact (adverse impact) has been demonstrated if the selection rate "for any racial, ethnic, or gender subgroup is less than four-fifths or 80 percent of the highest selection rate for any group." This has come to be known as the **four-fifths** or **80% rule.** Originally, this bottom-line criterion was aimed at identifying disparate impact only for an entire set of selection procedures, rather than for any single part. This has now been modified to apply to each part of the procedures as well as to the entire set (*Connecticut v. Teal,* 1982). The EEOC can examine an organization's personnel records and determine the existence of this type of illegal discrimination. The personnel records that employers are required to keep and that the EEOC can examine are called EEO-1 reports.[69]

The four-fifths or 80% rule is a way of determining possible disparate impact in selection.

In contrast, the argument using demographic statistics, a second approach, centers on a comparison of an organization's workforce to the relevant labor market. This argument is rooted in the *Civil Rights Act* of 1964. For example, an employer's selection procedures can be shown to be discriminatory (*prima facie*) if the employer's workforce fails to reflect parity with the race or sex composition of the relevant labor market. Organizations may determine their relevant labor market in several ways. One is by identifying where 85 percent of current employees and job applicants reside. Another is by identifying the labor market from which they generally select applicants. The EEOC, however, may suggest that organizations expand their labor markets; as a consequence, determining relevant labor markets is often an art rather than a science.

Once the relevant labor market has been determined, it is subject to revisions because of changing demographic characteristics in the U.S. labor force. Organizations are witnessing dramatic demographic changes based on comparisons of the 1980 and 1990 national census. As a result of these changes, organizations are having to redetermine their relevant labor markets to defend AAPs and cases of *prima facie* claims of discrimination successfully. *Prima facie* cases of this type are likely to be successfully defended to the extent that parity is attained (that is, the extent to which the proportions of protected group members in an organization's workforce mirror the proportions in the relevant labor market).

The third basis for establishing a case of disparate impact is through the use of concentration statistics. The argument here is that a *prima facie* case of illegal discrimination exists to the extent that protected group members are located in one particular area or job category in the organization. For example, equal numbers of male and female employees may be hired into entry-level jobs in the organization, but the women may be placed predominantly in secretarial jobs. Such a situation provides a case of disparate impact.

Promotion practices can also create unbalanced demographic concentration. For example, in *Wards Cove Packing v. Atonio,* the Wards Cove Packing Company in Alaska was charged by Atonio and other minority workers (primarily Filipinos and Alaska Natives) with illegal discrimination because they were never promoted. Concentration statistics supported this claim. The Court, while not denying the accuracy of the data, stated that Atonio also had the burden of showing intentional discrimination and suggesting alternative procedures that would be equally valid but less discriminatory. This scenario, which was a significant break from past decisions, has been essentially reversed by the *Civil Rights Act* of 1991.

Disparate Treatment. Illegal discrimination against an individual is referred to as disparate treatment. In contrast to the cases of disparate impact, a *prima facie* case of disparate treatment exists to the extent that an individual can demonstrate the following:

- The individual belongs to a minority group.
- The individual applied for a job for which the employer was seeking applicants.
- Despite being qualified, he or she was rejected.
- After the individual's rejection, the employer kept looking for people with the applicant's qualifications.

In disparate treatment, the qualified individual needs to show that someone else was hired instead.

These conditions, which basically present a case of intentional discrimination, were set forth in *McDonnell Douglas Corp. v. Green* (1973). Once a *prima facie* case of disparate treatment has been established by any one of the four ways, the employer must be given the opportunity to defend itself.[70]

Defending Selection Practices

An organization accused of illegal discrimination may be able to successfully defend its employment practices by showing one of the following:

- Job-relatedness
- Business necessity
- Bona fide occupational qualification (BFOQ)
- Bona fide seniority systems (BFSS)
- Voluntary transient affirmative action programs (AAPs)

Job Relatedness. Employee qualifications are necessary for any job. Thus employers are interested in measuring qualifications and establishing predictions on how employees who possess the qualifications will do on the job. To demonstrate **job relatedness,** the company must show that its selection and placement procedures (predictors—tests used for selection decisions) are related to the employee success on the job (*Watson v. Fort Worth Bank and Trust,* 1988). For details, see Appendix C.

Job relatedness is evidence that a selection procedure is related to being able to do the job itself.

It's important to note that any test must be related to important components of the job. For example, a typing test may be an appropriate selection device for clerk-typists who spend 60 percent of their time on data entry. However, it may not be an appropriate selection device for receptionists who spend less than 5 percent of their time typing. Careful job analysis can determine this.

Business Necessity. Although showing the job relatedness of a selection procedure is desirable, it may not always be possible. Some courts, recognizing this situation, have allowed companies to defend their selection procedures by showing business necessity. Whereas the job-relatedness defense often requires a demonstration of actual predictor-criterion relationships, business necessity does not. The case of *Levin v. Delta Air Lines, Inc.* (1984), where the Court decided for the plaintiff who sued because she was dismissed for being pregnant, was decided on the fact that pregnancy was not shown to affect the essence of the business (safe air travel), not on the fact that it failed to affect the ability of a flight attendant to provide service to the air travelers. In cases where business necessity clearly is high, demonstrating that a specific selection procedure is job-related is not necessary (see *Spurlock v. United Airlines,* 1972, and *Hodgson v. Greyhound Lines, Inc.,* 1974, in Appendix A).[71]

Bona Fide Occupational Qualifications. Another defense against a charge of illegal discrimination is **bona fide occupational qualifications (BFOQ).** For example:

BFOQs are the qualifications really necessary to do the job.

> *. . . [T]he EEOC sued the Massachusetts State Registry of Motor Vehicles, charging that denying entry-level jobs to individuals over age 35 violated ADEA. The state argued that the 1986 ADEA amendment exempts all law enforcement officers from the scope of the act for a seven-year period, and that in any event, age is a bona fide occupational qualification for motor vehicle examiners under* Mahoney v. Trabucco, *which upheld an age-50 mandatory retirement rule for Massachusetts state troopers. EEOC countered that few motor vehicle examiners perform active law enforcement duties.*
>
> *Acknowledging that the issue is a close one, the court agrees with the state that motor vehicle examiners, who are authorized to carry weapons, enforce the state's motor-vehicle laws, and perform many of the same duties as state and local police officers, are properly classified as law enforcement personnel and are therefore exempt from ADEA under the 1986 amendment (EEOC v. Commonwealth of Massachusetts, 1987).*[72]

Bona Fide Seniority Systems. Closely related to BFOQs are **bona fide seniority systems (BFSS).** As long as a company has established and maintained a seniority system without the intent to illegally discriminate, it is considered bona fide (*International Brotherhood of Teamsters v. United States,* 1977; *United States v. Trucking Management, Inc.,* 1981; *American Tobacco v. Patterson,* 1982). Thus, promotion and job assignment decisions can be made on the basis of seniority.[73] In a major decision, the Supreme Court ruled that seniority can also be used in the determination of layoffs, even if doing so reverses effects of affirmative action hiring (*Firefighters Local Union 1784 v. Stotts,* 1984).

Bona fide seniority systems (BFSS) are those maintained systematically and accurately on the basis of employee time with the company.

Voluntary Affirmative Action Programs. As described in Chapter 9, organizations may establish affirmative action programs without pressure from the EEOC and OFCCP. For them to be a defense against illegal discrimination, however, the programs need to be remedial in purpose, limited in duration, restricted in impact, flexible in implementation, and minimal in harm to innocent parties. However, there is growing ambiguity as to whether the courts will be sympathetic to these affirmative action programs despite past decisions (*Wygant v. Jackson Board of Education,* 1986; *International Association of Firefighters Local 93 v. City of Cleveland,* 1986).

International Aspects of Employee Selection

LEARNING OBJECTIVE 6

Describe how the use of expatriates, third-country nationals, and host-country nationals impacts selection and placement.

Selecting Expatriate Employees

Although the number of American expatriate employees (Americans who work in other countries for U.S. companies) is small, their importance to companies operating in the international markets is relatively large. Without effective expatriate employees—managers and nonmanagers—U.S. companies would essentially be unable to operate successfully abroad. Nevertheless, ineffective expatriates are alarmingly commonplace. Consequently, American-based multinational companies not only need to obtain candidates for expatriate positions, but must also ensure they are effective on the job.

You could easily be an expatriate some day as discussed in Chapter 6.

A key in selecting any employee is knowing what the job entails. Besides specific job assignments, expatiates are involved in a general way in six major categories of relations: (1) internal relations with their co-workers, (2) relations with their families, (3) relations with the host government, (4) relations with their home government, (5) external relations with the local culture, and (6) relations with the company's headquarters. In addition, expatriates typically work in a culture with a different language—a potential obstacle.

To be successful, then, expatriates need the skills not only to perform a specific job, but also to perform the general duties required by these six categories such as cultural empathy, flexibility, tolerance, and adaptability. Using these criteria for selection, as well as for structuring a preparation process, can go a long way to increase the likelihood of success.[74]

Did You KNOW?

10% of U.S. expatriates get yanked back home because they don't perform well.

Related to the selection of expatriate employees—also called parent-country nationals (PCNs)—is the more general issue of staffing operations abroad. Typically, expatriate employees fill only a few positions. Most of the employees are host-country nationals (HCNs), who are usually selected using host-country practices. The practice of using one's own HR practices abroad is referred to as **ethnocentrism.** Allowing operations in different countries to develop and use their own HR practices is called **polycentrism.** Developing practices that can be applied in all countries, with modest adjustments to local conditions, is called **geocentrism.**[75]

An ethnocentric policy says our way is the best way! Polycentrism says everyone has a best way. Geocentrism says a general way can be adapted.

A growing but still relatively small number of positions are filled by third-country nationals (TCNs), individuals from neither the host country nor the country of the parent firm. They are often selected by the parent firm using practices similar to those used in selecting expatriates. The pros and cons of using these three types of employees are listed in Exhibit 10.9.

Legal Considerations. In the *Civil Rights Act* of 1991, Congress affirmed its policy that American civil rights laws (specifically, Title VII of the *Civil Rights Act* of 1964 and the Americans with Disabilities Act) apply to the employment practices of American multinationals relative to U.S. citizens employed in their foreign operations. (*The Age Discrimination Employment Act* of 1967, ADEA, was amended in 1984 to protect American workers over the age of 40 against discrimination by U.S. companies abroad.) Furthermore, the U.S. District Court in Washington, D.C., ruled that U.S. law can even replace the laws of other nations:

> *A long-standing German labor policy of mandatory retirement at age 65 does not shield an employer from the* Age Discrimination in Employment Act's *protections for American workers in Germany, a federal district court rules.*
>
> *The case involves a nonprofit U.S. corporation well known for two of its broadcast services—Radio Free Europe and Radio Liberty—that employs more than 300 U.S. citizens at its Munich facility. The mandatory retirement policy, contained in the employer's union contract, is found in most collective bargaining agreements in Germany. Two employees discharged because of their age filed a bias suit under ADEA. The employer conceded that the employees had been discharged because of age but argued that ADEA's "foreign laws" exemption—allowing actions taken in order to avoid violating the laws of a foreign country—applied. The "nearly ubiquitous contract terms" are considered to have "legal force" in Germany, the employer contended.*
>
> *Policies and practices, even when embodied in contracts, are not "laws," the court says, distinguishing a country's established "policy" from a foreign law. The former cannot deny Americans working abroad ADEA's protections against age discrimination, the court explains, ruling that "where a foreign labor union policy collides" with a law of the United States, the U.S. law "cannot be expected to bow down." (*Mahoney v. RFE/RL, *1992).*[76]

Some say that this is a rather ethnocentric policy, one that says that U.S. law is best. Conflict with the laws of other nations is bound to occur, according to the critics. What is your opinion of this ruling? Whose law should prevail in a country? Furthering this ethnocentric approach to employment law is the fact that U.S. laws are applicable to foreign firms operating in the U.S. (which currently employ about 5 million American workers):

> *For many reasons having largely to do with significant cultural and managerial differences, Japanese firms have probably received the most attention regarding conflicts between their management and HR practices and those traditionally and legally followed in the U.S. As many as one-third of Japanese firms with operations in the U.S. have been confronted with lawsuits for discrimination in their employment practices relative to their American employees. Part of the problem may be a lack of knowledge about U.S. employment laws But more to the point (and one that must concern all multinational firms) is the conflict between the national culture and employment*

EXHIBIT 10.9

Pros and Cons of PCNs, HCNs, and TCNs

PARENT-COUNTRY NATIONALS (PCNs)

Advantages

- Organizational control and coordination is maintained and facilitated.
- Promising managers are given international experience.
- PCNs are the best people for the job.
- There is assurance that subsidiary will comply with company objectives, policies, etc.

Disadvantages

- The promotional opportunities of HCNs are limited.
- Adaptation to host country may take a long time.
- PCNs may impose an inappropriate headquarter's style.
- Compensation for PCNs and HCNs may differ.

HOST-COUNTRY NATIONALS (HCNs)

Advantages

- Language and other barriers are eliminated.
- Hiring costs are reduced, and no work permit is required.
- Continuity of management improves, since HCNs stay longer in positions.
- Government policy may dictate hiring of HCNs.
- Morale among HCNs may improve as they see the career potential.

Disadvantages

- Control and coordination of headquarters may be impeded.
- HCNs have limited career opportunity outside the subsidiary.
- Hiring HCNs limits opportunities for PCNs to gain overseas experience.
- Hiring HCNs could encourage a federation of national rather than global units.

THIRD-COUNTRY NATIONALS (TCNs)

Advantages

- Salary and benefit requirements may be lower than for PCNs.
- TCNs may be better informed than PCNs about host-country environment.

Disadvantages

- Transfers must consider possible national animosities (e.g., India and Pakistan).
- The host government may resent hiring of TCNs.
- TCNs may want to return to their own countries after assignment.

SOURCE: P. J. Dowling, R. S. Schuler, and D. E. Welch, *International Dimensions of Human Resources Management* 2nd ed. (Belmont, CA.: Wadsworth, 1994): 57. Used by permission.

practices of the parent firm and the employment laws in the overseas locations. As is true with the multinational firms from some other countries as well, Japanese firms tend to use only parent-country (that is, Japanese) executives to run their American subsidiaries, providing few of the perquisites and no opportunities for promotion to the top management slots for their American managers. In addition, all major decision making tends to be made by the Japanese managers, often in consultation with their colleagues back in Japan, rather than in conjunction with their American counterparts. At least three Japanese firms have settled discrimination suits for multimillion dollar figures (Honda of America, Sumitomo Corporation, and Quasar, a division of Matsushita Electric Corporation of America).[77]

The preceding discussion notwithstanding, Japanese firms in the U.S. may be protected in their staffing practices, at least at their top tiers of management. The Seventh Circuit Court of Appeals has ruled that Japanese subsidiaries operating in the United States may legally prefer Japanese citizens over U.S. citizens and that *Civil Rights Act* prohibitions against discrimination on the basis of national origin do not apply. According to the ruling in *Fortino v. Quasar Co.,* 1991, Title VII of the *Civil Rights Act* of 1964 is preempted by a treaty between Japan and the United States that permits companies of either country to prefer their own citizens for executive positions in subsidiaries based in the other country. This ruling clarifies a 1982 Supreme Court decision in *Sumitomo Shoji America Inc. v. Avagliano* and, by extension, applies to both Japanese firms in the United States as well as to American firms in Japan, although U.S. multinationals are less interested in pursuing such "parent company-executive-only" strategies.

International Comparisons

Staffing activities in Japan present alternatives that could be used in the United States. Canada provides a useful comparison with this country in regard to equal employment and human rights legislation.

Japan. Japanese recruitment methods are different from those in the United States, where the emphasis is on skill or job qualifications. In Japan, the emphasis is also on the general attributes of the person being hired. All regular employees of the corporation are hired at one time of the year only (in April, immediately after the end of each academic year). They are recruited during the preceding fall from either the high school level or the college and university level. Employees not hired at this time are considered "nonregular" employees (that is, they may have been employed by other companies earlier in their careers or self-employed; in short, they are hired at times other than the beginning of their careers). In addition to regular and nonregular employees, there are temporary and part-time employees.

For the most part, company employment policies are directed toward regular employees, and a great competition takes place at the time of the April hiring, both among the companies, which seek to attract the best candidates (tests are given on academic and basic aptitudes), and among the graduates, who wish to align themselves with growth companies.

This division between regular employees (estimated to be between 30 and 50 percent of the total national workforce) and the nonregular, part-time, and temporary employees makes the Japanese philosophy of lifetime commitment possible despite economic fluctuations. This, however, is changing today. In times of temporary growth or decline, additional temporary workers may be hired or laid off. Alternative solutions for dealing with down cycles that affect the retention of regular workers include shifting employees to new areas of operations or contracting employees out to other companies in more prosperous industries. The transferred employee continues to remain formally affiliated with the original employer in such cases.

In more serious circumstances, temporary layoffs may be required, though according to Japan's labor standards law, workers receive 60 percent of normal salary during this "vacation." However, because Japanese companies pay close attention to the development of long-term trends, they are generally able to predict a leveling off or decline within an industry and adjust their springtime recruitment efforts accordingly. In addition to the impact of lifetime employment on staffing, Japanese companies also have an extensive commitment to hire and accommodate disabled individuals.

Attention has recently been focused on the issue of equal opportunity for women in the Japanese workforce. Traditionally, many Japanese women leave the labor force when they begin raising families. To ensure opportunities for those wishing to continue working, the Japanese legislature passed the *Equal Employment Opportunity Law,* which went into effect in 1986, however, it has relatively modest sanctions for violators.

For the long term, many Japanese companies see two major trends. One is the need to redeploy and retrain their employees for different industries. For example, Nippon Steel has been shifting employees out of basic steel production and into electronics. The other trend is adjusting the management of employees under economic conditions that, in comparison to the last 20 years, will result in a period of relatively slow growth.

The traditional ways of doing business are changing, even in Japan.

Increasingly, Japanese companies are locating plants and offices in the United States. Selection is viewed by these companies as one of the most critical factors in their success here. Consequently, they put a great deal of time and effort into this activity.[78]

Canada. Most Canadian companies use recruiting and selection techniques similar to those in the United States. At the same time, they face significantly different equal employment legislation or, more broadly, human rights legislation. Relatively comprehensive human rights legislation now exists at the federal level and in each of Canada's ten provinces. This legislation follows a common pattern but has specific deviations in each jurisdiction.

The typical Canadian human rights statute prohibits discrimination based on race, color, religion, ancestry, place of origin, marital status, gender, age, or physical handicap, when such discrimination involves employment or trade union membership services, accommodation that is available to the public, residential, or commercial rentals, or public notices. Some of the statutes also prohibit discrimination by occupational or professional associations, employer or business associations, and employment agencies. The statute is enforced by a human rights commission, whose staff investigates and conciliates complaints successfully, and an *ad hoc* tribunal or board of inquiry of one or more members may be appointed to hold a public hearing.

Civil rights in Canada share similar protections to those in the United States.

In addition to protecting basic human rights, the federal statute prohibits discrimination on the basis of criminal conviction where the person has been pardoned.[79] In the case of the physically handicapped, employment discrimination is prohibited, but other forms of discrimination are not. Employers are not compelled to renovate their premises to accommodate the handicapped. A unique feature of the federal statute in the area of sex discrimination is that employers are required to provide equal pay for work of equal value. This contrasts with the provincial legislation, which does not affect pay differentials between different jobs as long as there is no ongoing practice of denying access to these jobs because of gender.

Summary

This chapter has examined selection and placement procedures, processes, methods, and decisions. To match individual skills, knowledge, and abilities to job demands and individual personalities, interests, and preferences to job and organizational characteristics, organizations need to gather information about job applicants. The three most common methods—interviewing, written testing, and applications—must operate within an extensive framework of legal regulations. These regulations are not intended to discourage the use of these methods but rather to ensure that the information collected, retained, and used respects the individual's right to privacy and an organization's right to select individuals on the basis of legal considerations. Consequently, the types of selection information and the methods used to obtain it vary according to the type of job for which the applicants are being selected. For example, assessment centers are generally used for managerial jobs, and physical tests are used for manufacturing and public health and safety jobs. Exactly how many predictors are used depends on the type of job and the degree of validity and reliability of the predictors being used.

Few organizations, if any, rely on the single-predictor approach to selection and placement. Typically, the selection process is sequential and involves either a multiple hurdles or compensatory approach to decision making. Regardless of the approach, managing human resources effectively involves an assessment of both validity and the potential disparate impact associated with each step as well as with the overall process.

Increasingly, U.S. organizations are operating in other countries. For example, over 40 percent of the 500 restaurants that McDonald's opens each year are overseas. Because the globalization of many U.S. companies is just beginning, increasing expertise in managing expatriates and in how other countries manage their employees are two areas that are likely to be of interest for some time.

Once individuals are selected into an organization, they are typically placed in a job and begin working. It is usual, of course, for some orientation and training to take place. This may last for a few days or several months. It may be a combination of on-the-job instruction and classes at the company's training center.

Key Concepts

achievement tests
application
assessment center
biodata tests
biographical information blank
bona fide occupational qualifications (BFOQ)
bona fide seniority systems (BFSS)
business games
combined approach
compensatory approach
criteria
disparate treatment
disparate impact
ethnocentrism
executive orders
four fifths or 80% rule
genetic screening
geocentrism
halo bias
handwriting analysis
honesty tests
in-basket exercise
interest inventories
job relatedness
leaderless group discussion (LGD)
multiple hurdles approach
multiple predictor approach
panel interview
patterned or structured interview
personality inventories
placement
polycentrism
polygraph test
predictor
psychomotor tests
recognition tests
reference verification
selection
single predictor approach
sponsor
team interview
validity
work sample tests
work simulations

Review and Discussion Questions

1. A frequent diagnosis of an observed performance problem in an organization is "Joe was a selection mistake." What are the short- and long-term consequences of these so-called "selection mistakes"? Relate this question to your own experiences with organizations.

2. Successful selection and placement decisions are dependent on other HR activities. Identify these activities and explain their relationships to selection and placement.
3. Given all of the weaknesses identified with the interview, why is it a popular selection device? How could you improve the interview to overcome some of these weaknesses?
4. What is genetic screening? Is this a means to assess an applicant's skills, knowledge, and abilities or personality, interests, and preferences? How might the rights of the employer conflict with the rights of the individual when genetic screening is used for selection and placement decisions? How would you resolve this conflict?
5. What factors should companies consider when selecting expatriate managers?
6. Explain the difference between single predictor and multiple predictor approaches to validation of selection procedures. What approach does your instructor use in evaluating performance in your human resource management course? Is it compensatory or noncompensatory? Multiple hurdle or multiple cutoff?
7. How do organizations typically make selection, promotion, and transfer decisions?
8. Why are the best people often not the ones hired for the job?
9. Discuss the actual costs of hiring applicants as well as the potential costs that might be incurred if an incorrect selection decision is made.
10. How do the selection and recruitment strategies used in Japan and Canada differ from those used in the United States?

Review: Do's and Don'ts in Job Interviews and On Job Applications

Please indicate what to do and what not to do in interviews and on job applications from the list of items below:

		DO	DON'T
1.	Ask about marital status	______	______
2.	Ask about the number of children	______	______
3.	Ask about skills to do the job	______	______
4.	Ask for a woman's maiden name	______	______
5.	Ask the age of the applicant	______	______
6.	Ask for driver's license	______	______
7.	Ask about race, gender, religious affiliation	______	______
8.	Ask about birthplace of applicant	______	______
9.	Ask about club memberships	______	______
10.	Ask if planning to have children	______	______
11.	Ask about preferred hours of work	______	______
12.	Ask about disabilities	______	______
13.	Ask about other names applicant has used	______	______
14.	Ask about arrest record	______	______

	DO	DON'T
15. Ask about height and weight	______	______
16. Ask about nature of military discharge	______	______
17. Ask about friends or relatives with firm	______	______
18. Ask for clergy as references	______	______
19. Ask about credit questions	______	______
20. Ask if the applicant is willing to travel	______	______

In most situations, it is probably fine to ask questions 3, 6 (when driving is required on the job), 11, and 20 (if job requires travel). Question 12 could be asked in this way, "Is there any condition you have that might make it impossible to perform 'essential job functions' even after some accommodation?" Even here, however, the applicant should be volunteering this information. It is probably best to ask this after a decision to hire has been made. Forget about the rest.

PROJECTS, EXERCISES & CASES

End-of-Text Projects

Lincoln Electric

1. Describe the following for Lincoln Electric:
   a. The objectives of the staffing activities—recruitment and selection
   b. The extent to which these staffing activities are serving the business and its HR objectives
   c. The criteria being used to select applicants
   d. The extent to which these criteria are serving the business and its HR objectives
   e. The specific methods and procedures being used to select applicants
   f. The extent to which these methods and procedures are serving the business and its HR objectives
2. How can the staffing activities at Lincoln Electric be improved?

Nordstrom

1. Describe the following for Nordstrom:
   a. The objectives of the staffing activities—recruitment and selection
   b. The extent to which these staffing activities are serving the business and its HR objectives
   c. The criteria being used to select applicants
   d. The extent to which these criteria are serving the business and its HR objectives
   e. The methods and procedures being used to select applicants
   f. The extent to which these methods and procedures are serving the business and its HR objectives
2. How can the staffing activities at Nordstrom be improved?

Field Projects

1. Prepare a job description for a job you are interested in performing. Detail a selection process for the position. Your report should describe the following:
   a. Selection procedures to be used. If you will use a cognitive ability test, identify which one. If you will use a situational interview, describe the questions that will be asked. If you will use a personality test, identify the specific test.
   b. Provide a rationale for the choice of each selection device.
   c. Outline the order in which the selection devices will be administered and explain the rationale for the ordering.

d. Specify how information will be combined: using a compensatory multiple hurdles or combination approach. Detail how the selection devices will be scored.

e. Finally, specify the costs associated with your selection process.

2. One source of illegal discrimination and waste of human resources comes from worker specifications—minimum ability, experience, or education standards—that are higher than necessary for adequate job performance. To prevent such problems, organizations must establish appropriate specifications and evaluate applicants fairly on how well they meet these specifications. Talk with a human resource manager of a company and ask how she or he arrives at the specifications for various jobs. Report to the class about what you learn. You may wish to invite the manager to class to describe the procedures used by the company to establish worker specifications and selection criteria.

Career Management Exercise

Use your job description from the Career Management Exercise in Chapter 8 to detail a selection process. Your report should describe the following:

1. Selection procedures to be used. If you will use a cognitive ability test, identify which one. If you will use a situational interview, describe the questions that will be asked. If you will use a personality test, identify the specific test.
2. Provide a rationale for the choice of each selection device.
3. Provide the order in which the selection devices will be administered and the rationale for the ordering.
4. Specify how information will be combined (compensatory, multiple hurdles, or a combination). Detail how the selection devices will be scored. Report to the class and compare results.

VISIT THE LIBRARY

Workforce Online

Because you are now familiar with getting onto the Internet, the following steps are abbreviated.

1. Enter your Web browser.
2. Enter Workforce Online.
3. Find and review the following article within "Winning Ideas":

   Disney Helps Keep Kids in School
4. Find and review the following article within the "Research Center":

   Staff Selection Impacts Global Success
5. Return to your homepage.

Case: The Apprentice

Apex Tool Company is a small, family-owned machine shop that has been in business for 47 years. The company was founded by Herbert Shay who, until recently, was active in the shop and was also the company's president. Apex makes fine tools and precision parts for electric motors. The company has 23 full-time employees plus a number of part-timers. Promotions at Apex come slowly and have always been the result of Herb's "eye" and "feel" for the skills and abilities of the employee. All the full-time employees are men, and the majority of the part-timers are married women. All new employees begin by monitoring the machines and turning off the power switch if a problem arises. Employees who show potential are asked to become apprentices where they learn the fine skills of the tool-and-die maker.

When Herbert retired, his son Charles took over the company. Charles's first task was to hire two new employees. He placed an ad in the local newspaper. After interviewing several candidates, Charles hired Heil Burke and Shirley Weeks to monitor machines that are set up by highly skilled mechanics. Neil has had previous machine shop experience, and Charles senses that he will be a prime candidate for a tool-and-die apprenticeship.

Shirley is 41 years old, married, and the mother of two teenagers. She took the job at Apex because the work is easy and the hours of work are flexible. She plans to work part-time and to increase her hours if she likes the job.

Neil is nineteen years old and single. He hopes to demonstrate that he deserves to be an apprentice tool-and-die maker. Neil has been fooling around with machines and building things as long as he can remember. He had several shop classes in high school and excels at "working with his hands." Neil has no interest in college and believes that machine work will be a career.

It has been one year since Neil and Shirley were hired. During this time, Neil has performed many activities in addition to monitoring the machines. For example, when machines break down, Neil helps the mechanic with repairs. He has also assisted with set-ups and retooling activities. Shirley, on the other hand, has monitored the machines exclusively during the year. When her machine breaks down, Shirley waits for a mechanic to fix it. Charles has evaluated his new people in order to select a strong apprentice candidate. Neil's work performance has been excellent, and last week Charles formally offered him the opportunity to become an apprentice tool-and-die maker.

Charles did not really consider Shirley to be a viable candidate for an apprenticeship. Although her work has been good, she has not revealed any particular aptitude for more advanced work. Charles did not think twice about offering Neil the apprenticeship because Neil seemed to be an obvious choice for the position. Shirley, who up to this point has been very mild-mannered, is furious when she finds out that Neil has been offered an apprenticeship. She decides to confront Charles directly about this situation.

Shirley storms into Charles's office and demands to know why Neil was selected for an apprenticeship and she was not. She notes that she and Neil were hired at approximately the same time and that they worked together for the past year. Shirley is visibly upset and angry. She wants specific reasons why she was not given consideration for the higher-level position. Charles, who has never had to deal with a situation like this, really does not know what to say. In the intensity of the moment, he hears himself say something about Neil's range of skills, but he doesn't like the way this is going. In an attempt to bail himself out, Charles offers Shirley a raise to remain at her present job.

Shirley agrees to "think it over" for a couple of days. On Monday morning, she tells Charles point blank that his selection decision was discriminatory and illegal. Shirley told Charles that she does not want a token raise; she wants her apprenticeship. Charles is still quite perplexed as nothing like this has ever happened before at Apex. Charles informs Shirley that he will consider her for an apprenticeship, but he will need a little time to make a decision. When Shirley leaves his office, Charles decides that he may need some legal advice in dealing with this issue.

Case Questions

1. Why didn't Charles consider Shirley for the apprenticeship?
2. Should Shirley expect Charles to give her the reasons he selected Neil?
3. Should Shirley accept the offer of a salary increase or hold out for an apprenticeship?
4. Could Charles change his mind and offer the apprenticeship to Shirley instead of Neil?

Case: False Positive or Positive Step?

Concerns about drug use among transportation personnel (that is, bus drivers, air traffic controllers, train engineers) have captured national headlines. In fact, the Department of Transportation (DOT) has a plan for random drug testing that affects more than half a million airline employees from pilots to mechanics. Under the drug-testing plan, employees are subject to a pre-employment test, periodic testing whenever a physical is taken, post-accident testing, and random testing as well as a test for reasonable cause. An employee is subject to an initial test on a sample of urine and a more sophisticated test if the first test shows the presence of drugs.

Tom Schultz has been a bus driver in New York City for seven years. He is married and the father of three children. His work performance has been above average, and he considers himself a conscientious and dedicated employee. Tom did not give a second thought to a management directive two months ago that stated that all bus drivers would be tested for drug use. In fact, he thought that drug tests for transportation employees were a good idea. Now, however, Tom's life has become a nightmare.

A test on a sample of Tom's urine appeared to have traces of the metabolite for cocaine. He was immediately dismissed from his job and has been unemployed for nearly two months. "I can't understand how something like this could happen," he said. "You know you're innocent, but how do you prove it? I'm guilty until proven innocent. They're out for my job." Tom is appealing his dismissal. As a public employee, he has legal recourse through his union. In the meantime, he is out of work, cannot support his family, and cannot even collect unemployment insurance.

Drug testing also affects many other types of employees in the private sector. Peter Albert was a young successful manager making a good salary in the private sector. Peter's employer tested him for drugs as part of a routine medical checkup. His urine test came back positive. Prior to the test, he had informed the nurse that he had had root canal surgery and was using codeine as prescribed by his doctor. The nurse said that this was no problem and proceeded without so much as noting the information. Peter was fired from his job, and he still does not know what drug he was supposed to have been using. "I've lost my car. My family situation is strained. My bills are piling up. I can't find suitable work paying a suitable salary," said Peter. He has discussed his case with attorneys, but, as a private-sector employee, he does not have any legal recourse at this time.

Consider the following quotations about drug testing in light of the cases of Tom and Peter:

- "If you are not conducting the tests seriously—and I mean watching the urine pass from the body orifice—then you are just playing games.

  Pharmacologist

- "These tests are 100 percent accurate and we'll back that up in court."

  Physician in charge of a drug testing laboratory

- "The false positive rate can be 1 to 2 percent for the most stringent test and as high as 15 to 20 percent for the least expensive test."

  Civil liberties attorney

- "I can beat any Mickey Mouse drug test. I woke my son at 6:00 A.M. and made him urinate in the specimen jar.

  Construction worker who uses marijuana off the job

- "If you don't have a policy, then don't use drug testing. Testing is a tool. No employee has a right to use illegal substances on or off the job."

  Consultant on drug testing to Fortune 500 companies

- "Drug testing is the privacy issue of the decade or perhaps the century. Sifting willy-nilly through people's bodily fluids is an invasion of privacy."

  Civil liberties attorney

- "Drug testing is a witch hunt."

  Peter Albert

Drug testing has already been ruled illegal in several municipalities for police officers and fire fighters, and random drug testing has been declared unconstitutional for civilian Army employees. However, many *Fortune 500* companies continue to include drug testing as a pre-employment hurdle for new employees. Tom Schultz and Peter Albert, however, certainly have their doubts about it.

Case Questions

1. Should Tom and Peter consider drug testing unnecessary?
2. Do you think employers should drug-test all applicants, or only those who work in jobs involving public safety?
3. Can employers supplement their drug tests with other tests to more accurately determine whether employees are really using drugs?
4. Should only job applicants be drug-tested, or should employees be tested also?

Chapter 10 Endnotes

1. "Wired For Hiring: Microsoft's Slick Recruiting Machine," *Fortune* (February 5, 1996): 123.

2. J. Huey, "Eisner Explains Everything," *Fortune* (April 17, 1995): 45–68. Information for the case was taken from R. Cohen, "When You Wish Upon a Deficit," *New York Times* (July 18, 1993): Sec. 2, 1 & 18; G.E. Willigan, "The Value-Adding CFO: An Interview with Disney's Gary Wilson," Harvard Business Review (Jan.-Feb. 1990): 85–93; and S. Greenhouse, "Playing Disney in the Parisian Fields," *New York Times* (Feb. 17, 1991): 1 and 6; J. J. Laabs, "Disney Helps Keep Kids in School," *Personnel Journal* (Nov. 1992): 58–68; "Disney," *Personnel Journal* (Jan. 1992): 58.

3. F. L. Schmidt, D. S. Ones, and J. E. Hunter, "Personnel Selection," *Annual Review of Psychology* 43 (1992): 627–670; A. Tziner, *Organization Staffing and Work Adjustments* (Westport, CT: Praeger, 1990); N. Schmitt and I. Robertson, "Personnel Selection," *Annual Review of Psychology* 41(1990): 289–319; R. D. Gatewood and H. S. Feild, *Human Resource Selection,* 2nd ed. (Hinsdale, IL: Dryden Press, 1990).

4. See note 1.

5. See note 1.

6. D. P. Twomey, *Equal Employment Opportunity Law,* 3rd ed. (Cincinnati, OH: South-Western, 1994); M. Miner, "Legal Concerns Facing Human Resource Managers: An Overview." In *Readings in Personnel and Human Resource Management,* R. S. Schuler, S. A. Youngblood, and V. L. Huber, eds., 3rd ed. (St. Paul, MN: West, 1988), 40–56.

7. R. Henkoff, "Finding, Training & Keeping the Best Service Workers," *Fortune* (October 3, 1994): 110–122; D. Anfuso, "Las Vegas Resort Bets on Training—and Wins," *Personnel Journal* (September 1995): 78–86.

8. B. Paik Sunoo, "How Fun Flies At Southwest Airlines," *Personnel Journal* (June 1995) 62–73.

9. F. N. Kerlinger, *Foundations of Behavioral Research* (New York: Holt, Rinehart and Winston, 1986).

10. R. Sobotka, "Workers Are a Small Firm's Most Valuable Asset," *Plain Dealer* (Cleveland, March 29, 1994): 4C. Used by permission.

11. For an excellent discussion about criteria for selection and placement decisions, see R. D. Arvey and R. H. Faley,

VISIT THE LIBRARY

Exercise 1

1. Using your Web browser, enter Cornell University's Employment Law Documents.
2. Click on the topic "Employment Law," under the heading "Employment Law."
3. Click on the topic "2000e-2000e-17 Equal Employment Opportunity" of "42 US Code-Labor, under the heading "Federal Material."
4. After browsing through this section, return to your homepage.

Exercise 2

Our visit to Microsoft's homepage illustrated that an organization can recruit through its own Web site. Some other organizations recruit through special Internet recruiting services, such as America's Job Bank (AJB). AJB was established by Employment Services, and is owned by the Department of Labor. AJB allows employers to post job openings with detailed job descriptions. Prospective employees can use AJB to search for specific types of jobs in specific areas, to read job descriptions, and to apply for jobs.

1. Enter America's Job Bank **(http://www.ajb.dni.us/index.html)**
2. Within AJB, do an online keyword search for a human resources position in New York. Try using different combinations of keywords (e.g., human resource management, human resource).
3. View at least one of the jobs that comes up, and click on "To Apply" to see how you would apply for the position. (Do not actually complete the application process unless you are currently seeking such a position.)
4. Return to your homepage.

Fairness in Selecting Employees, 2nd ed. (Reading, MA: Addison-Wesley, 1988).

12. For an excellent discussion about criteria for selection and placement decisions, see Schmidt, Ones, and Hunter, op. cit.; see note 3.

13. T. J. Esque and T. F. Gilbert, "Mailing Competencies Pay Off," *Training* (January 1995): 44–50.

14. M. Tennesen, "HR Faces Distinct Issues in Rural Areas," *Personnel Journal* (June 1994): 112–120; E. E. Lawler III, "From Job-based to Competency-based Organizations," *Journal of Organizational Behavior* 15 (1994): 3–15.

15. The basis for the statements and suggestions here include "Educational Requirements," *Fair Employment Practices Guidelines* 186, no. 1(1980); "Experience Required" *Fair Employment Practices Guidelines* 190, no. 5 (1981); "The Importance of Record Keeping," *Fair Employment Practices Guidelines* 185, no. 12 (1980); "Personnel Guidelines for Managers and Supervisors," (1994); Biddle & Associates, Inc., 2100 Northrop Avenue, Sacramento, California, 95825.

16. G. Dessler, "Value-based Hiring Builds Commitment," *Personnel Journal* (November 1993): 98–101; "Screening for Nonunion Workers," *Bulletin to Management* (December 14, 1995): 400.

17. W. Zeliner, "Southwest: Rita Bailey, Manager, Corporate Employment," *Business Week* (February 13, 1995): 69.

18. R. Henkoff, "Finding, Training & Keeping the Best Service Workers."

19. R. S. Lowell and J. A. DeLoach, "Equal Employment Opportunity: Are You Overlooking the Application Form?" *Personnel* 59 (1982): 49–55; E. C. Miller, "An EEO Examination of Employment Applications," *Personnel Administrator* 25 (1980): 63–69.

20. C. J. Bachler, "Resume Fraud: Lies, Omissions and Exaggerations," *Personnel Journal* (June 1995): 51–59; D. G. Lawrence, B. L. Salsburg, J. G. Dawson, and Z. D. Fasmen, "Design and Use of Weighted Application Blanks," *Personnel Administrator* (March 1982): 57–63, 101.

21. A. Childs and R. J. Klimoski, "Successfully Predicting Career Success: An Application of the Biographical Inventory," *Journal of Applied Psychology* (Feb. 1988): 3–8.

22. C. J. Russell, J. Mattson, S. E. Devlin, and D. Atwater, "Predictive Validity of Biodata Items Generated from Retrospective Life Experience Essays," *Journal of Applied*

Psychology 75, no. 5 (1990): 569–580; H. R. Rothstein, F. L. Schmidt, F. W. Erwin, W. A. Owens, and C. P. Sparks, "Biographical Data in Employment Selection: Can Validities be made Generalizable?" *Journal of Applied Psychology* 75, no. 2 (1990): 175–184; M. A. McDaniel, "Biographical Constructs for Predicting Employee Suitability," *Journal of Applied Psychology* 74, no. 6 (1989): 964–970; A. Childs and R. J. Klimoski, "Successfully Predicting Career Success: An Application of the Biographical Inventory," *Journal of Applied Psychology* (Feb. 1988): 3–8.

23. See note 11.

24. K. K. Sackheim, *Handwriting Analysis and the Employee Selection Process* (Westport, CT: Quorum Books, 1990); "Handwriting Analysis," *Bulletin to Management* (May 8, 1986): 152. Reprinted by permission from Bulletin to Management, copyright 1986 by the Bureau of National Affairs, Inc., Washington, D.C. 20037; G. Ben-Shakar et al., "Can Graphology Predict Occupational Success? Two Empirical Studies and Some Methodological Ruminations," *Journal of Applied Psychology* (Nov. 1986): 645–853.

25. "Background Checks," *FEP Guidelines,* no. 266 (1987): 1; "Paper and Pencil Measures of Potential," *Perspectives of Employee Staffing and Selection,*
G. Dreher and P. Sackett, eds. (Homewood, IL: Irwin, 1983): 349–367.

26. "Employment Law Basics: Employees' Rights vs. Employers' Rights," *Fair Employment Practices Guidelines* (October 5, 1995): 117.

27. C. Sparks, "Paper and Pencil Measures of Potential" *Perspectives of Employee Staffing and Selection,* G. Dreher and P. Sackett, eds., 349–367.

28. "Ask the Experts—Investigating Applicant Fraud," *Fair Employment Practice Guidelines* (April 10, 1993): 8. Copyrighted material. Reprinted with permission of *Fair Employment Practices* and Bureau of Business Practice, 24 Rope Ferry Road, Waterford, CT 06386.

29. R. Hogan, B. N. Carpenter, S. R. Briggs, and R. O. Hansen, "Personality Assessment and Personnel Selection," *Perspectives of Employee Staffing and Selection,* 21–51; "The Future of Personality Tests in Employment Settings," *Psychological Science Agenda* (Jan./Feb. 1992): 2–3.

30. M. R. Barrick and M. K. Mount, "The Big Five Personality Dimensions and Job Performance: A Meta-Analysis," *Personnel Psychology* 44 (1991): 1–26; D. V. Day and S. B. Silverman, "Personality and Job Performance: Evidence of Incremental Validity," *Personnel Psychology* 42 (1989): 25–36; T. Newton and T. Keenan; "Further Analyses of the Dispositional Argument in Organizational Behavior," *Journal of Applied Psychology* 76, no. 6 (1991): 781–787.

31. E. E. Ghiselli, *Explorations in Managerial Talent* (Pacific Palisades, CA: Goodyear, 1971); G. S. Taylor and T. W. Zimmer, "Viewpoint: Personality Tests for Potential Employees: More Harm than Good," *Personnel Journal* (Jan. 1988): 60.

32. J. Hogan, "Interests and Competencies: A Strategy for Personnel Selection," *Readings in Personnel and Human Resource Management* (St. Paul, MN: West, 1968): 484–495.

33. "Psychological Testing Leads to Costly Lawsuit," *Bulletin to Management* (July 22, 1993): 226. Reprinted with permission by the Bureau of National Affairs, (Tel. 1-800-372-1033).

34. Conversation with Paul Sackett, March 28, 1994; J. J. Laabs, "Legalities," *Personnel Journal* (Feb. 1992): 109; J. A. Hartigan and A. K. Wigdor, eds., *Fairness in Employment Testing: Validity Generalization, Minority Issues, and the General Aptitude Test Battery* (Washington, D.C.: National Academy Press, 1989).

35. R. T. von Mayrhauser, "The Mental Testing Community and Validity: A Prehistory," *American Psychologist* (Feb. 1992): 244–253; J. P. Guilford and W. S. Zimmerman, *Guilford Zimmerman Temperament Survey* (Orange, CA: Sheridan Psychological Services, 1976); F. L. Schmidt, J. E. Hunt, R. McKenzie, and T. Muldrow, "The Impact of Valid Selection Procedures on Workforce Productivity," *Journal of Applied Psychology* 64 (1979): 609–626.

36. For an extensive review of and guide to these tests, see L. P. Plumke, "A Short Guide to the Development of Work Sample and Performance Tests," 2nd ed. (Washington, D.C.: U.S. Office of Personnel Management, Feb. 1980). Note the interchangeability of the terms work sample and performance tests.

37. S. J. Motowidlo, M. D. Dunnette, and G. W. Carter, "An Alternative Selection Procedure: The Low-Fidelity Simulation," *Journal of Applied Psychology* 75, no. 6 (1990): 640–647; W. Arthur, Jr., G. V. Barrett, and D. Doverspike, "Validation of an Information-Processing-Based Test Battery for the Prediction of Handling Accidents Among Petroleum-Product Transport Drivers," *Journal of Applied Psychology* 75, no. 6 (1990): 656–665.

38. For the LGD, see M. M. Petty, "A Multivariate Analysis of the Effects of Experience and Training upon Performance in a Leaderless Group Discussion," *Personnel Psychology* 27 (1974): 271–282; For business games, see B. M. Bass and G. V. Barnett, *People, Work, and Organizations,* 2nd ed. (Boston: Allyn & Bacon, 1981).

39. B. B. Gaugler, D. B. Rosenthal, G. C. Thornton, and C. Bentson, "Meta-Analysis of Assessment Center Validity," *Journal of Applied Psychology* 72 (1987): 493–511; R. Klimoski and M. Brickner, "Why Do Assessment Centers Work? The Puzzle of Assessment Center Validity," *Personnel Psychology* 40 (1987): 243–260; A. Tziner and S. Dolan, "Validity of an Assessment Center for Identifying Female Officers in the Military," *Journal of Applied Psychology* 67 (1982): 728–736; S. B. Parry, "How to Validate An Assessment Tool," *Training* (April 1993): 37–42.

40. C. L. Martin and D. H. Nagao, "Some Effects of Computerized Interviewing on Job Applicant Responses," *Journal of Applied Psychology* 74, no. 1 (1989): 72–80; W. L. Tullar, "Relational Control in the Employment Interview,"

Journal of Applied Psychology 74, no. 6 (1989): 971–977; A. Peek Phillips and R. L. Dipboye, "Correlational Tests of Predictions from a Process Model of the Interview," *Journal of Applied Psychology* 74, no. 1 (1989): 41–52; T. Hoff Macan and R. L. Dipboye, "The Relationship of Interviewers' Preinterview Impressions to Selection and Recruitment Outcomes," *Personnel Psychology* 43 (1990): 745–768.

41. W. Zeliner et al., "Go-Go Goliaths," *Business Week* (February 13, 1995): 69.

42. "Employment Law Basics: Employees' Rights vs. Employers' Rights"; "Employee Privacy Issues," *Fair Employment Practices Guidelines* (September 8, 1994): 3–5; "Employer Intrusions Shunned," *Bulletin to Management* (September 1, 1994): 280; B. G. Posner, "Hiring the Best," *Inc.* (April 1989): 169.

43. "Microsoft's Brainteasers," *Fortune* (February 5, 1996): 4.

44. Henkoff, "Finding, Training, and Keeping the Best Service Workers" p. 116. Also see D. Stamps, "Cyber-interviews Combat Turnover," *Training* (April 1995): 43.

45. H. J. Bernardin and R. W. Beatty, *Performance Appraisal: Assessing Human Behavior at Work* (Boston: Kent, 1984): 258–260; W. C. Borman, "Format and Training Effects on Rating Accuracy Using Behavior Scales," *Journal of Applied Psychology* 3 (1979): 103–115.

46. The role of the medical doctor in providing the physical exam is an important one. With it, however, is attached responsibility to the employer rather than the employee. See M. S. Novit, "Physical Examinations and Company Liability: A Legal Update," *Personnel Journal* (Jan. 1981): 47–52.

47. FEP Guidelines (May 25, 1993): 8. Copyrighted material reprinted with permission of *Fair Employment Practices and Bureau of Business Practice,* 24 Rope Ferry Road, Waterford, CT, 06386.

48. "Physical-Ability Testing Cuts Injuries, Costs," *Bulletin to Management* (June 22, 1995): 194. Reprinted with permission by the Bureau of National Affairs, (Tel. 1-800-372-1033).

49. E. A. Fleishman, "Some New Frontiers in Personnel Selection Research," *Personnel Psychology* 41, no. 4 (1988): 679–702; E. A. Fleishman, *The Structure and Management of Physical Abilities* (Englewood Cliffs, NJ: Prentice-Hall, 1964); D. L. Gebhardt and C. E. Crump, *Joint Mobility Evaluation Manual for Entry Level Natural Gas Industrial Jobs* (Bethesda, MD: Advanced Research Resources Organization, 1983); D. L. Gebhardt, D. C. Meyers, and E. A. Fleishman, "Development of a Job-Related Medical Evaluation System," *San Bernardino County Medical Standard News* 1 (1984): 1–2; D. C. Meyers, M. C. Jennings, and E. A. Fleishman, *Development of Job-Related Medical Standards and Physical Tests for Court Security Officers,* ARRO Final Report #3062/r81-3 (Bethesda, MD: Advanced Research Resources Organization, 1981).

50. "1995 State Anti-Bias Laws Focus on Genetic Testing and Family Leave," *Fair Employment Practices Guidelines* (January 11, 1996): 3; Olian, "New Approaches to Employment Screening," *Readings in Personnel and Human Resource Management,* 3d ed. (St. Paul, MN: West, 1988): 206–216.

51. R. Cropanzano and K. James, "Some Methodological Considerations for the Behavioral Genetic Analysis of Work Attitudes," *Journal of Applied Psychology* 75, no. 4 (1990): 433–439; Office of Technology and Assessment, *The Role of Genetic Testing in the Prevention of Occupational Disease* (Washington, D.C.: U.S. Government Printing Office, 1983).

52. M. A. Konovsky and R. Cropanzano, "Perceived Fairness of Employee Drug Testing as a Predictor of Employee Attitudes and Job Performance," *Journal of Applied Psychology* 76, no. 5 (1991): 698–707; Drug Testing: Conference Policy Pointers," *Bulletin to Management* (Aug. 7, 1986): 261–262.

53. "Prevalence of Drug Testing Policies Levels Off," *Bulletin to Management* (July 13, 1995): 217; W. L. Holstein, "Finding A Better Way to Test for Drugs," *New York Times* (November 28, 1993): F11.

54. "Prevalence of Drug Testing Policies Levels Off."

55. M. O. Kirk, "At Work, a Different Test for Drugs," *New York Times* (January 21, 1996): F11; "Prevalence of Drug Testing Policies Levels Off."

56. "Drug Policy Pointers," *Bulletin to Management* (Jan. 7, 1988): 8. Used by permission of *Bulletin to Management,* copyright 1988.

57. "Prevalence of Drug Testing Policies Levels Off."

58. "EEOC Issues Final Guidance for Medical Examinations Under ADA," *Fair Employment Practices Guidelines* (January 25, 1996): 5.

59. "The AIDS Epidemic and Business," *Business Week* (March 23, 1987):122; "AIDS Focus: Employee Rights and On-Site Education," *Bulletin to Management* (March 10, 1988): 74.

60. "When Can Workers Refuse Lie Detector Tests?" *Bulletin to Management* (March 9, 1995): 73.

61. H. J. Bernardin and D. K. Cooke, "Validity of an Honesty Test in Predicting Theft Among Convenience Store Employees," *Academy of Management Journal* 36, no. 5 (1993): 1097–1108; B. Kleinmutz, "Lie Detectors Fail the Truth Test," *Harvard Business Review* 63 (1985): 36–42; S. Labato, "Business and the Law: New Rules Limit Lie Detectors' Use," *The New York Times* (Nov. 28, 1988): 22; "Pre–employment Polygraph Testing Restricted," *Bulletin to Management* (June 30, 1988): 201; L. Saxe, D. Dougherty, and T. Cross, "The Validity of Polygraph Testing," *American Psychologist* 40 (1985): 355–365.

62. M.D. Dunnette, *Personnel Selection and Placement* (Monterey, CA: Brooks/Cole, 1966): 174–175.

63. M. Zall, "What to Expect from the Civil Rights Act," *Personnel Journal* (March 1992): 46–50; B. Southard Murphy, W. E. Barlow, and D. D. Hatch, "Manager's Newsfront: Retroactivity of the Civil Rights Act of 1991

Unsettled," *Personnel Journal* (March 1992): 24; "EEOC Issues Policy on Retroactivity of Civil Rights Act of 1991," FEP Guidelines (March 1992): 1–2; "1991 Civil Rights Act Highlights," *FEP Guidelines* (Dec. 1991): 1–2.

64. C. S. Miller, J. A. Kaspin, and M. H. Schuster, "The Impact of Performance Appraisal Methods On Age Discrimination in Employment Act Cases," *Personnel Psychology* 43 (1990): 555–578.

65. J. S. Lublin, "Graying Europeans Battle Age Bias," *The Wall Street Journal* (Aug. 14, 1990): B1.

66. B. Southard Murphy, W. E. Barlow, and D. D. Hatch, "Manager's Newsfront," *Personnel Journal* (August 1994): 26–28; "Americans With Disabilities Act Final Regulations," *Fair Employment Practices* (Aug. 15, 1991); B. Presley Noble, "As Seen from a Wheelchair," *New York Times* (Jan. 26, 1992): F25; J. West, ed., The Americans with Disabilities Act: From Policy to Practice (New York: Milbank Memorial Fund, 1991).

67. "Age Discrimination and Business Justification," *Fair Employment Practices Guidelines* (January 25, 1994): 1–3. For more on age discrimination see A. Zakarian, "Downsizing Defense," *Personnel* (Jan. 1991): 19; P. S. Greenlaw and J. P. Kohn, "Age Discrimination in Employment Guidelines," *Personnel Journal* (March 1982): 224–228; D. H. Weiss, *Fair, Square and Legal: Safe Hiring and Firing Practices to Keep You and Your Company Out of Court* (New York: AMACOM, 1991); A. M. Ryan and M. Lasek, "Negligent Hiring and Defamation: Areas of Liability Related to Pre–Employment Inquiries," *Personnel Psychology* 44 (1991): 293–319.

68. R. D. Arvey and R. H. Faley, *Fairness in Selecting Employees,* (Reading, MA: Addison-Wesley, 1988); R. A. Baysinger, "Disparate Treatment and Disparate Impact Theories of Discrimination," *Readings in Personnel and Human Resource Management,* 3rd ed. (St. Paul, MN: West, 1988): 162–177; P. M. Podsakoff, M. L. Williams, and W. E. Scott, Jr., "Myths of Employee Selection Systems," *Readings in Personnel and Human Resource Management,* 3rd ed. (St. Paul, MN: West, 1988): 178–192.

69. "Go Ahead for AA Data Disclosure," *Fair Employment Practices* (Oct. 29, 1987): 129. Also see R. E. Biddle, "*Ward's Cove Packing v. Atonio* Redefines EEO Analyses," *Personnel Journal* (June 1990): 56, 59–62, 64–65.

70. J. Ledvinka and V. G. Scarpello, *Federal Regulations in Personnel and Human Resource Management* (Boston: PWS-Kent, 1990); R. A. Baysinger, "Disparate Treatment and Disparate Impact Theories of Discrimination," and V. L. Huber, G. B. Northcraft, and M. A. Neale, "Foibles and Fallacies in Organizational Staffing Decisions," in *Readings* (op. cit. see note 5): 162–177; 193–205.

71. For an excellent discussion of the impact and interpretation of the *Uniform Guidelines* and many other issues related to selection and testing, see the special issue of the *American Psychologist* (Oct. 1981).

72. "Age-35 Job Restriction Upheld," *Fair Employment Practices* (Jan. 7, 1988): 2.

73. T. C. McKinney, "The Management of Seniority: The Supreme Court and the California Brewers Case," *Personnel Administration* (Feb. 1984): 8–14.

74. C. Marmer Solomon, "CEO Mom: The Tie That Binds a Global Family," *Personnel Journal* (March 1996): 80–93; C. G. Howard, "Profiles of the 21st Century Expatriate Manager," *HR Magazine* (June 1992): 96; M. Jelinek and N. J. Adler, "Women: World-Class Managers for Global Competition," *Executive* (Feb. 1988): 11–20; P. Dowling and R. S. Schuler, *International Human Resource Management* (Boston: PWS-Kent, 1990); J. S. Black, M. Mendenhall, and G. Oddou, "Toward a Comprehensive Model of International Adjustment: An Integration of Multiple Theoretical Perspectives," *Academy of Management Review* 16, no. 2 (1991): 291–317; H. B. Gregersen and J. S. Black, "Antecedents to Commitment to a Parent Company and a Foreign Operation," *Academy of Management Journal* 35, no. 1(1992): 65–90.

75. D. A. Heenan and H. V. Perlmutter, *Multinational Organization Development* (Reading, MA: Addison-Wesley, 1979); C. M. Solomon, "Staff Selection Impacts Global Success," *Personnel Journal* (Jan. 1994): 88–101.

76. J. Templeman, "A Continent Swarming With Temps," *Business Week* (April 8, 1996): 54; "Age Bias in Germany," *Fair Employment Practices* (December 17, 1992): 145.

77. D. Briscoe, *International Human Resource Management* (Boston: Allyn & Bacon, 1995). This material adapted by permission of the author, Feb. 17, 1994.

78. C. A. Bartlett and H. Yoshihara, "New Challenges for Japanese Multinationals: Is Organization Adaptation Their Achilles Heel?" *Human Resource Management* (Spring 1988): 19-44.

79. This section of human rights in Canada was prepared by Robert J. Kerr, Professor of Law, University of Windsor, for use in this book.

SECTION 5

Training and Appraising

Even with the best staffing procedures, employees may not perform at their highest levels. Such employees can be deficient in one or more skills and abilities that are really needed to do the job. This may have resulted from the employees changing jobs, from their current jobs having changed through new technologies, or simply because their deficiencies weren't picked up by the staffing procedures. Whatever the reason, these skill and ability deficiencies need to be removed. Companies provide training and development as a way to correct these deficiencies.

Chapter 11 covers the many types of training and development activities that companies offer to existing employees. It begins by describing the activity of orientation. New employees need to know where things are, the best procedures to use, and the recommended methods of doing the job. Companies may also have special technology for which new employee training is necessary.

Today, training and development programs encompass a careful discipline that melds the best current knowledge on learning principles and styles with the business and HR needs of any given organization. Not only are the skills and abilities of the entire spectrum of workers—from line workers to people in top management—addressed in the new training and development programs, but company training programs in diversity and ethics are addressing the larger issues facing our society.

While some deficiencies can be corrected in a rather short period of time, others can take much longer. Consequently, we typically find companies offering a variety of training programs (short-term) as well as a variety of development programs (longer-term). These are the subject of our discussion in the first of the three chapters of this section. At the end of Chapter 11, you are asked to describe training and development programs you will expect on your first job.

Employees want to know what they are supposed to do, what's expected of them, what the standards of performance are, and how they're doing. They also want advice for doing even better in the future. This is where performance appraisals in HR management enter the picture. During the recruiting and selection activities, individuals get information on what job they are supposed to do. They may even begin to understand what standards of performance will be expected of them. Companies that do a great job in their staffing activities are increasingly conveying some information to potential employees. However, even in these companies, the newly recruited and selected applicants—and, in some cases, even the current employees—may not know exactly what's expected of them.

In contrast with the training and staffing activities where the HR department and line management may work closely together, line managers are often on their own when it comes to employee appraisal. The HR department may contribute to the design of performance appraisal forms and attempt to impose a schedule on appraisal periods. For the most part, however, line managers convey what's expected to employees, telling them what the standards of performance are and what they can do to improve their performance. A trend that is gaining acceptance gets everyone involved in the appraisal and feedback process. Thus it is likely that at some point you will be asked to appraise your own performance, that of your colleagues, and even that of your boss! Consequently, it is useful to know as much as possible about the activity of performance appraisal.

We split the discussion of performance appraisal into two chapters. Chapter 12 covers the issues involved in gathering the information used for appraisals. We discuss the importance of performance appraisal in organizations that plan to increase the performance and productivity of employees. The many processes and procedures in performance are described next. Ethical and legal issues related to performance appraisals are examined. We conclude by identifying the trend of 360 degree feedback in organizations. At the end of Chapter 12 is another "Career Management Exercise" asking you to apply the material in the chapter to your future job.

Chapter 13 addresses the issues associated with using all the performance appraisal information that has been gathered. We begin by discussing the inherent conflicts in performance appraisal that make the process of using the information so difficult. Then we discuss the processes that organizations can use to help minimize these conflicts so that the valuable process of feedback can take place. Once an organization has accurate, useful feedback, it must understand why each employee is performing at a particular level. Based upon this diagnosis of performance, an organization implements strategies for performance improvement when necessary. To give perspective to this entire activity, some international comparisons will be offered. As with Chapter 12, you will find a "Career Management Exercise" asking you to apply the Chapter 13 material to your future job.

11

CHAPTER

Training and Development

Learning Objectives

1. Describe the purposes and importance of training and development.
2. Determine training and development needs.
3. Answer questions about setting up training and development programs.
4. Describe the different types of training and development programs.
5. Describe how to maximize learning.
6. Indicate how to select a training program.
7. Discuss the many trends in training and development.

There's no magic. What will make all the difference in business will be how well you train your workforce, how well you motivate—and how well you empower.

Robert Eaton
CEO
Chrysler Corporation[1]

Chapter Outline

MANAGING HUMAN RESOURCES

at the Ritz-Carlton Hotel Company

The Ritz-Carlton Hotel Company's pervasive training approach is based on its rallying phrase "We Are Ladies and Gentlemen Serving Ladies and Gentlemen."

If a Ritz-Carlton hotel can't be more truly elegant and service-oriented than the other hospitality choices in the marketplace, its very name is in trouble. So the Ritz-Carlton Hotel Company (Atlanta, Georgia), operator of 28 luxury hotels, makes a priority of its own distinctive brand of training. Every one of the company's 14,000 employees receives not only orientation and training, but also certification in his or her position, according to Mary Anne Ollman, corporate director of training.

Certification for a maid? "Absolutely," explains Debra Phillips, training manager and quality adviser for the Ritz-Carlton New York. "'Room attendants,' as we call them, have a most important job in our organization."

ORIENT, TRAIN, CERTIFY

"Taking a room attendant as an example, first employees must understand the overall company gold standards, allowing us to set up the employee to succeed. The new room attendant would have been selected carefully for certain basic talents and strengths. Then it's our job to train to meet Ritz-Carlton standards," Phillips says. (See the insert on their development formula that builds on employee selection.)

"For the first 60 days on the job, through orientation and training, we make certain that the employee has a thorough understanding of the technical tasks and responsibilities our guests and organization expect them to perform on the job. We repeat our gold standards to them over and over in training, even though they have heard it all in orientation. And they hear it again in the certification process."

Phillips says the training philosophy allows for individual differences in learning, so employees are allowed to choose when they take their tests for certification, as long as it's within the first 60 days of employment. "For a room attendant, as with other positions, the test would include an inspection," says Phillips. "For example, for a duty such as the turn-down service, the second guest room service of the evening, a trainer would go back to a guest room after the new room attendant performed the service to inspect it, ensure mastery, and see that it has been done as the employee has been trained."

In other cases, according to Phillips, inspection is not possible, and observation substitutes for it. A new telephone operator's work is observed until mastery is obtained and signed off by the departmental trainer.

"Certification also includes a test," Phillips adds. "It can be done in written form, or as verbal questions and answers, taking into account individual differences among employees with regard to reading, writing and languages."

What about someone like a payroll clerk, who does not connect with hotel guests? Phillips says it makes no difference. The motto, "We Are Ladies and

---

Ritz-Carlton Hotels Employee Development Formula: (T + F) × I = G

"One of the most critical elements in the HR process at the Ritz-Carlton Hotels is getting the correct employees in here in the first place," said Mary Anne Ollman. "We've identified that the natural abilities we look for in a new employee are things like caring, empathy, high work ethic. And of course job-specific abilities such as math proficiency for an accounting function. We believe that everyone has a gift—that everyone has strengths, which, if identified and brought out, make any weaknesses irrelevant. People have an intrinsic satisfaction in their work when their strengths are used. So we have a formula for helping employees grow, taking into account people's gifts or talent, their fit with the organization, our investment in developing them."

$$(T + F) \times I = G$$

where:

T = Talent I = Investment
F = Fit G = Growth

Gentlemen Serving Ladies and Gentlemen" still applies. In these internal jobs, other employees are the customers, and all the same standards are reinforced through training.

"One thing that is unique about our training and certification standards and process is that we went to the experts to develop them—and I don't mean consultants," says Ollman, the corporate training director.

She means the employees. "In constructing our training programs, we held focus groups with employees, and our training managers worked with employees, so they would help us know how learning best takes place for our organization, as well as to understand what skills are necessary to perform in each job to near perfection," Ollman says.

QUALITY LEADERS AT EACH HOTEL

It seems clear that the training function in Ritz-Carlton Hotels has earned a healthy respect as the major force in quality improvement. While this may be partly—or even mostly—a result of being in the hospitality industry, the company still serves as an interesting model for close quality/training interface.

"In 1984, we did not have training positions in the hotels," Ollman related. "Then one of the regional vice presidents implemented a training position and presented the plan for it to the president of the company. Training has been a critical part of the organization ever since, with a training manager in each hotel."

The Ritz-Carlton's training program has undergone changes as a result of the company's journey into quality management, according to Ollman. It was at that time that the company decided to go for the Baldrige Award for Quality.

"The Baldrige application forced us to take a look at business process design in a way that we had never really done before," she says.

"Right now we are looking at cycle time, such as how long it takes from the moment guests walk in, until they are in their rooms. We've done customer surveys and are studying eighteen cycle times throughout our systems to see where we are as an organization. Then we will be able to judge how to decrease cycle times by taking out the nonvalued elements from jobs. Using the check-in example, if we want to reduce cycle time to two minutes, we may discover we can have the desk receptionists skip an explanation of the in-room bar service, and have the bell staff do that job. Of course, then we must retrain."

Another way that the quality initiatives feed into training is through the hotels' feedback forms. Internal Defect Reports are to be completed by any employee when systems go wrong.

"When the information is compiled and supplied to the hotel's general manager (gm) on a daily basis, it gives the manager a valuable look at what actually went on in the hotel that day. Otherwise a gm might look at the dollar and guest numbers and think, 'Well, we had a bang up day.'"

"This way, the gm can get all the information about the hotel. And the beauty of the system is that it is tracked over time. 'So, something like the problem of the availability of nonsmoking rooms could be pinpointed to a certain pattern. Maybe there's a shortage only on Sundays because that's when the rooms are taken out for deep cleaning."

"The objective in all our work with the defect reports is to better serve guests and internal customers. The more problems we can detect, the fewer there are to be seen by guests."

STANDARDIZED, BUT CUSTOMIZED TRAINING

"We have a number of standards that must be upheld," Ollman said, "so there are corporate-wide core courses taught in each hotel."

"We have a corporate training managers' manual, which works in conjunction with the employee handbook. Then, individual training managers may develop their own courses to suit the particular needs of their hotels. For example, one hotel found that it needed diversity training, since it had an unusually diverse employee population as well as a diverse guest population.

Ollman said successful programs adopted for one hotel often get presented to headquarters and are incorporated into the general course offerings. Training managers meet regularly in both regional and chain-wide gatherings.[2]

This feature is representative of what many outstanding organizations are doing today with training and development.[3] Namely, these firms are using training and development to make their firms more productive and more in line with their overall strategy, in this case high quality, customer satisfaction. The Ritz-Carlton feature also highlights the relationship that training and development has with other HR activities, particularly selection. For training to be effective, it is necessary to understand the employee's level of ability and those personality characteristics and values that might influence how the person will perform in different situations. Finally, the feature indicates how important it is for companies to allow room for local differences. That is, it is important for the corporate offices of the firm not to impose a rigid and fixed program of training on all units of the organization. Individual units always have special needs to be considered, and their participation in final decisions can consider these needs and increase their feelings of participation and empowerment.

Did You KNOW?

The Baldrige Award is named for Malcolm Baldrige, who served as Secretary of Commerce from 1981 until his tragic death in a rodeo accident in 1987. His managerial excellence contributed to long-term improvement in efficiency and effectiveness of government.

Training and development obviously serve many purposes. This chapter examines those purposes in detail. It discusses the types of needs analysis that must be conducted to determine who should receive training, what skills are necessary, and at what level they should be taught. Implementing a successful training and development program involves creating appropriate conditions for training to occur and selecting the type of program that matches needed skills and skill levels. These are described, along with techniques by which to assess training programs. International issues and comparisons in training and development conclude the chapter.

Training and Development

Employee **training and development** is any attempt to improve current or future employee performance by increasing an employee's ability to perform.[4] The need for training and development can arise for many reasons. Job applicants with insufficient skills may be hired; technological changes that result in new job skills can occur; organizations can redesign jobs and also decide to develop a new product requiring technologies not used before. In some of these cases, the need for training and development can be immediate and unplanned or can be anticipated and planned for in the future.

Training and development is any attempt to improve current or future performance by increasing employee ability.

Increasingly, employers are realizing how important it is to provide training and development if they are to stay competitive and profitable. For example, top management at PepsiCo began to emphasize training and development when they recognized that they had to develop their people and businesses in order to be effective.[5]

The development of our best people is the personal responsibility of management.

Roberto C. Goizueta
CEO
Coca-Cola

Today, more organizations than ever are attempting to identify current and future training and development needs and to develop programs that enable employees to perform at the desired level. Also, top management is increasing its support for training and development programs, recognizing them as critical to their companies strategic goals. Without top management support and commitment to training, an organization is likely to concentrate on activities other than training. This is particularly true when the focus is on short-term goals and immediate results. Such a focus allows too little time for the benefits of training and development to accrue.

Why Is Training and Development Important?

LEARNING OBJECTIVE 1

Describe the purposes and importance of training and development.

A major purpose of training and development is to remove performance deficiencies, whether current or anticipated:

> *A majority of respondents (68 percent) agree that lagging skill levels have hurt their organizations, and 53 percent report increased expenditures—primarily in the areas of training and hiring. In terms of organizational impact, the survey notes, low skill levels take their toll in the form of communication problems (cited by 31 percent of respondents), production and quality prob-*

lems (26 percent), difficulties implementing reengineering and reorganization initiatives (21 percent), increased error rates (17 percent), difficulties expanding (17 percent), and decreased customer service (13 percent).[6]

Training to increase productivity is another important purpose. Companies find that by training employees, productivity gains more than offset the costs of training:

Motorola calculates that every $1 it spends on training delivers $30 in productivity gains within three years. Since 1987, the company has cut costs by $3.3 billion—not by the normal expedient of firing workers, but by training them to simplify processes and reduce waste. Sales per employee have doubled in the past five years, and profits have increased 47 percent.[7]

Did You KNOW?

Intel, which makes computer chips, spends more than $120 million a year on training, an average of $3,000 per worker, more than double the national average.

Training is important to organizations that are rapidly incorporating new technologies and consequently increasing the likelihood of employee obsolescence. Such organizations use training and development programs as tools to make the current workforce more flexible and adaptable. If an organization can increase its adaptability, it can enhance its chances for survival and profitability.

Training and development can increase employees' commitment to the organization, and it can strengthen their perceptions that the organization is a good place to work. Greater commitment results in less turnover and absenteeism, giving another boost in productivity. Commenting on this at McDonald's is Stanley Stein, senior vice president of HR and labor relations:

First, thanks to its intense training efforts—it surpasses even the U.S. Army as the nation's largest training organization—the company gives employees ample means for self-advancement. When we hire someone, we put in such an investment that we want them to stay with us for their careers. Proof: More than 60% of McDonald's restaurant managers started as crew.[8]

Did You KNOW?

No nation can thrive in the modern world without investing in its people. This is why national statistics on savings should include the cost of investing in human capital.

Gary S. Becker
The 1992 Nobel Laureate teaches at the University of Chicago

"If you're not thinking all the time about making every person more valuable, you don't have a chance."

Jack Welch
CEO
General Electric

Society at large benefits when individuals are productive and contributing members of organizations. Expanding this idea of community involvement, United Parcel Service trains its managers by, among other things, actually requiring them to serve in the community. A description of this program is found in the feature, "Managing Human Resources at UPS: Listening to the Other America."

Training is also key in implementing a company's strategy. This is exactly how the people at Ritz-Carlton see their investment in training. Indeed, for companies such as Ritz-Carlton, Granite Rock Company, Intel, Motorola, General Electric and Ford, training is an absolute necessity in successfully implementing a quality improvement strategy.[9]

As a consequence of all of these important purposes of training and development, it is not surprising to see a real partnership among line managers, HR professionals, and the other employees in doing training and development. Today, most training and development is done on the job by line managers and the other employees. HR professionals are responsible for training trainers and may participate in portions of the training, especially in their areas of expertise. The feature, "Partnership: Working Together in Training and Development," explores how this partnership works.

LEARNING OBJECTIVE 2

Determine training and development needs.

Determining Training and Development Needs

Training and development is not only important, it is also complex. Thus the success of any training and development program cannot be left to chance. It must begin with a determination of what is needed.

MANAGING HUMAN RESOURCES

at UPS
Listening to the Other America

In four years as a manager at United Parcel Service (UPS), Nelson Whitlow has helped build up the company airline, talked the Federal Aviation Administration into letting UPS have its own weather information system and managed a staff of 40.

But none of that prepared him to work with Miguel DeLeon, a 17-year-old migrant worker who lives with his family in a flimsy paperboard shack in the Rio Grande Valley. When Mr. Whitlow met Miguel recently, the boy had dropped out of high school and didn't want to go back. Was he unintelligent? Unmotivated? No. He needed clothing.

"The kids in his family had nothing to wear, and that's why they had stopped going to school," said Mr. Whitlow. "So we took them to get clothing and shoes. It was a humbling experience.

Helping keep children in school is just one facet of what Mr. Whitlow did recently when UPS sent him to McAllen, Texas. Working 60-hour weeks, he and eight colleagues set up a mobile library for migrant children, laid the plans for a sewing shop to provide jobs and developed a video at a local clinic to educate indigent patients about health and nutrition.

It's all part of an unconventional training program sponsored by the $20 billion Atlanta-based freight company. Each year UPS assigns 40 middle- and upper-level supervisors to month-long community internships. The thought is that living and working in poor communities will help managers better understand employees and customers from diverse backgrounds.

The program was the brainchild of James E. Casey, founder and longtime president of UPS. After the passage of the 1964 *Civil Rights Act,* he knew the company would have to hire more women and minorities. He began sending mobile hiring vans into poor and inner-city neighborhoods. But Mr. Casey quickly realized that bringing these people on board wouldn't work if the company's white male managers were not sensitive to their needs and background.

So he turned to Walter Hooke, a UPS senior manager, who at the time was living in a poor neighborhood in San Francisco and spending his off hours working with the Urban League. In 1968, Mr. Hooke began the companywide internships, which early on were more like extended field trips.

Since then, more than 850 UPS managers have done stints in nineteen cities. Employees today receive full salaries while spending 30 days in one of four communities. In McAllen, they assist poor Mexican-Americans and Latin American refugees. In Chicago, interns live at St. Margaret's Church of Scotland and work with young people and their families.

"Our founder believed you couldn't understand someone's problems unless you were in their shoes," said Dan Preble, the UPS manager who coordinates the program.

UPS employees weren't always as enthusiastic. Early on, the internships were more punitive than a sign that a manager was on the fast track. The most likely candidates were managers who had uttered racial slurs or had a bad record working with minorities. Even today, some of that apprehension lingers. Lou Bennefield, a regional manager in Atlanta, remembers how he tried to get out of going to New York in 1991. "I kept trying to figure out what I'd done wrong," he said.

Shortly after he arrived in New York, Mr. Bennefield got a firsthand view of crime in the streets, riding along with a police officer; he helped serve meals in a soup kitchen and accompanied 40 schoolchildren on the subway for a field trip.

"Before I went, I thought I knew all about the problems in the big city," he said. "But I didn't know anything at all."

The program's results are hard to measure. Mr. Preble points to an employee turnover rate under 2 percent and a solid affirmative action record, but adds that much of the change is personal. The hope is that this will translate into better management.[10]

PARTNERSHIP: WORKING TOGETHER IN TRAINING AND DEVELOPMENT

LINE MANAGERS	HR PROFESSIONALS	EMPLOYEES
Cooperate with HR professionals in identifying training needs.	Coordinate with line managers in linking training to the needs of the business.	Identify their own training needs with HR professionals and line managers.
May participate in the delivery of training programs.	Identify training needs in cooperation with line managers.	Actively participate in training programs.
Give management commitment and support.	Develop the training programs.	Do some of on-the-job training of each other.
Do much of on-the-job training.	Train the line managers and employees in how to train.	

The three major phases of any training and development program are:

1. Assessment, which determines the training and development needs of the organization
2. Implementation (actual training and development), in which certain programs and learning methods are used to impart new attitudes, skills, and abilities
3. Evaluation[11]

The relationships among these phases are shown in Exhibit 11.1. We will focus on the assessment and implementation phases in this chapter and leave the evaluation phase for Chapter 20.

Organizational Needs Analysis

Organizational needs analysis begins with an assessment of the short- and long-term strategy and objectives of the business.

Organizational needs analysis begins with an examination of the short- and long-term strategies and objectives of the organization and the trends likely to affect these objectives. An organization's strategy should be a major concern of any training and development effort.[12] This is where expectations of the employees are shaped. Let's consider the case of the Grand Union, a large grocery store chain in the Northeast. Faced with intense competition from big commodity grocery stores that compete on the basis of low costs and low prices, the top team at Grand Union asked:

> *What business are we in? Who are our competitors? Given that we aren't moving the stores, what do our customers want?*
>
> *Once they answered these questions, the team members decided to embrace a new definition of grocery store: a customer-driven, service-oriented store with an expanded selection of items. From an individual store perspective, this would mean the elimination of many of the current items to make room for more brand items and higher-margin items. The latter meant having a deli section (with the smells of barbecued chicken), an expanded fresh fruit section (more tropical fruits), a variety of small, ethnic food booths (for eating in or taking home), and, yes, a pastry shop.*
>
> *All this sounded great to Bill Reffett, senior vice president of human resources for Grand Union's 20,000 employees. Asked by the others on the*

EXHIBIT 11.1

Model for an Instructional System

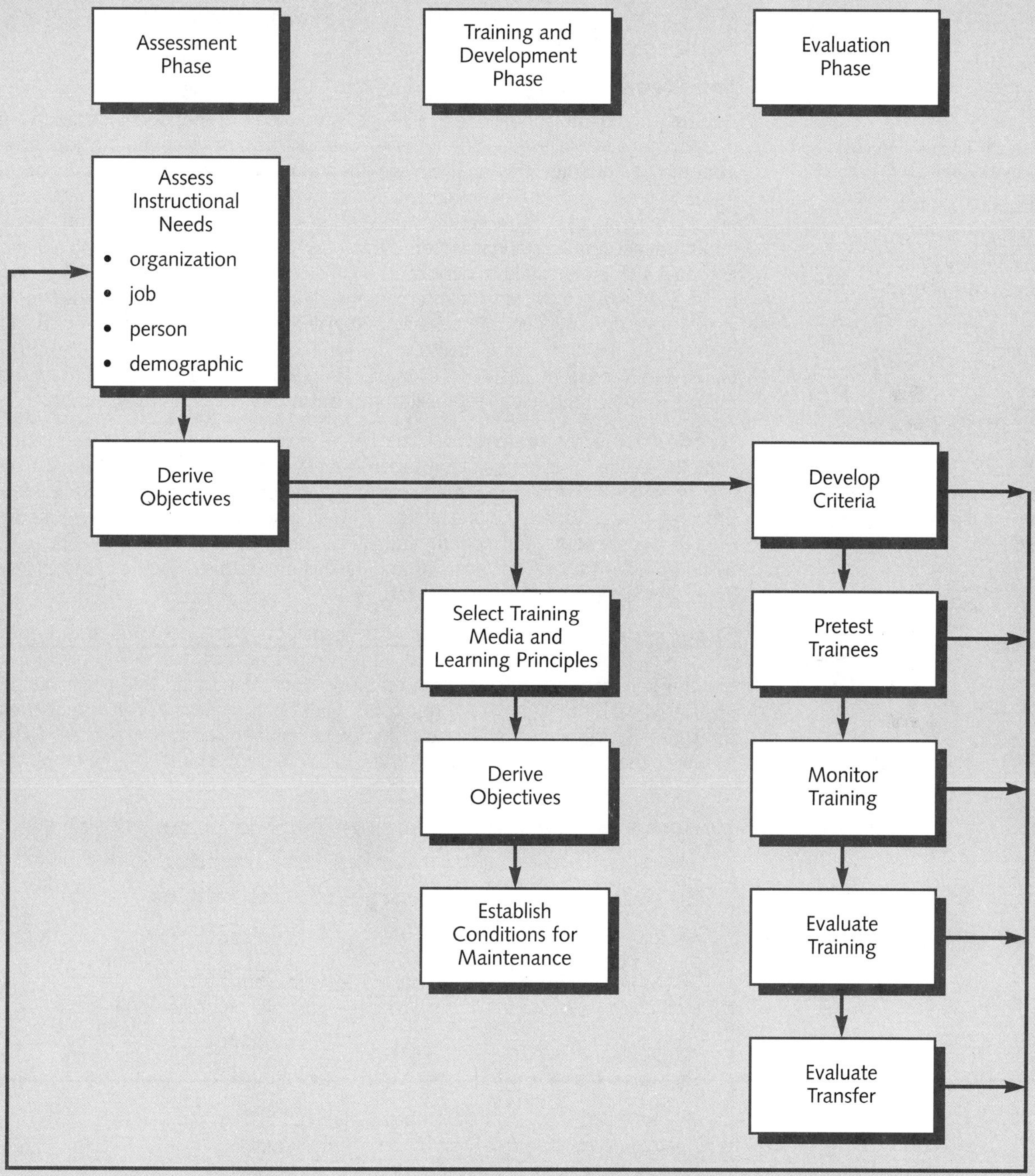

Note: Many other models for instructional systems are used by the military, business, and education. Some of the components of this model were suggested by these other systems.

Source: Adapted from I.L. Goldstein, *Training: Program Development and Evaluation*, 8. Copyright © 1974 Wadsworth, Inc. Reprinted by permission of the publisher. Brooks/Cole Publishing Company, Monterey, Calif.

top team if he could "deliver the people on this one," he answered, "no problem." Bill knew the success of the store's new quality strategy depended on changing employee skills and behaviors.[13]

The organization recognized its need to change. Then this change is defined in terms of how peoples' jobs will change. The specific impact on the employees was determined through a job needs analysis.

Job Needs Analysis

Job needs analysis provides information on:

- **tasks performed**
- **skills needed**
- **acceptable standards**
- **behaviors needed**

Because the organizational needs analysis is too broad to spot detailed training and development needs for specific jobs, it is also necessary to conduct a **job needs analysis**. Essentially, this analysis provides information on the tasks to be performed on each job (the basic information contained in job descriptions), the skills necessary to perform those tasks (from the job specifications or qualifications), the minimum acceptable standards (sometimes excluded from traditional job analysis), and the behaviors needed to perform the job or role. For example if teams are used in the company, a variety of interpersonal behaviors, such as cooperativeness, would constitute needed role behaviors. Increasingly, role behaviors are critical for high quality service. These pieces of information may be gathered from current employees, the HR department, or current supervisors. Grand Union gathered the information through teams representing different areas of the organization.

Success depends on people behaving in new ways in their roles (jobs).

Needed Role Behaviors. Grand Union directed major effort toward identifying the needed role behaviors of supervisors and the remaining staff in the stores. The HR process required the intense involvement of the employees, with guidance provided by the senior vice president of human resources. Together, they identified needed supervisory (department and store managers) and staff role behaviors based on what they saw as characterizing a customer-driven, service grocery store. Then they compared these to the status quo.

Supervisory Roles. Supervisory role behaviors were identified and redistributed. What occurred here was very important. The firm decided to make a distinction between supervisors as an employee job category and tie responsibilities associated with the supervisory role. This distinction made it easier to redistribute the supervisory responsibilities to enhance the level of customer service. Exhibit 11.2 lists the supervisory responsibilities that were redistributed to the employees.

EXHIBIT 11.2

Redistributed Supervisory Responsibilities

Absence control	Personnel recordkeeping
Performance appraisal	Quality circle leadership
Staff deployment	Work planning/allocation
Discipline	Quality control
Shift rotation planning	Recruitment
Employee welfare	Team briefing
Grievance handling	Team building
Health and safety	Communicating
Induction training	

Source: Adapted from R. Schuler, "Strategic Human Resource Management: Linking the People with the Strategic Needs of the Business," *Organizational Dynamics* (AMACOM: New York, Summer 1992): 26.

Staff Roles. The nonsupervisory employees also addressed the question, "What does this new business orientation mean for us at the store?" Because the focus was on the customer, they first asked, "How do we currently interact with the customers?" The analysis resulted in the following list:

- We do not know customer desires.
- We make limited use of customers.
- We are space-driven, not customer-driven.
- We have traditional departments, low margins, high quit rates.
- We feel no ownership of service.
- We lack management skills.

To move to a more customer-driven approach, the employees felt that they would require:

- Having focus groups with customers
- Being customer-driven
- Including service as part of the product
- Adding high-margin departments
- Having stores coordinate efforts, exchange best practices
- Expanding management skills

In addition, these employees asked, "From the broader store viewpoint, what characteristics reflect a solutions-oriented, customer-driven, service operation?" Their answers are listed in Exhibit 11.3. They used this list to analyze the needed role behaviors toward the customer and concluded that substantial changes were in order. The before-and-after role behaviors for the major job categories in a store are listed in Exhibit 11.4.

EXHIBIT 11.3

Organizational Characteristics of a Customer-Driven, Service Organization

- Just-in-time inventory
- Just-in-time working commitment
- Team-oriented
- Multiskilled—technical, process, interpersonal
- Flexibility
- Trust, harmonious employee relations
- Communications
- Egalitarianism
- Distributed leadership
- Responsibility for customers
- Standard operating procedures
- Continuous improvement
- No-fault policies
- Job grade reduction
- Rewards for small improvements/suggestions
- Supplier and customer involvement
- Site visits, comparisons, benchmarks
- Customer knowledge

Source: Adapted from R. Schuler, "Strategic Human Resource Management: Linking the People with the Strategic Needs of the Business," *Organizational Dynamics* (AMACOM: New York, Summer 1992): 28.

EXHIBIT 11.4

Customer-Driven Employee Behaviors at Grand Union

BEHAVIORS BEFORE THE CHANGE	BEHAVIORS AFTER THE CHANGE
Bag Packers	
Ignore customers	Greet customers
Lack of packing standards	Respond to customers
	Ask for customers' preferences
Cashiers	
Ignore customers	Greet customers
Lack of eye contact	Respond to customers
	Assist customers
	Speak clearly
	Call customers by name
Shelf Stockers	
Ignore customers	Respond to customers
Don't know store products/location	Help customers with correct information
	Knowledgeable about product location
Department Workers	
Ignore customers	Respond to customers
Limited knowledge	Know products
	Know store
Department Managers	
Ignore customers	Respond to customers
Ignore workers	Reward employees for responding to customers
Store Managers	
Ignore customers	Respond to customers
Stay in booth	Reward employees for service
	Appraise employees on customer service

Source: Adapted from R. Schuler, "Strategic Human Resource Management: Linking the People with the Strategic Needs of the Business," *Organizational Dynamics* (New York: AMACOM, Summer 1992): 29.

Did You KNOW?

The Red Lion Hotel Company gives its employees a four-step checklist to help them remember the needed behaviors.

Person needs analysis identifies possible areas of performance deficiency in current and future jobs and suggests development programs for improvement.

New Human Resource Practices. Finally, the employees identified HR practices that had to be formulated to match the business, based on the role behaviors needed from the employees, especially those in direct contact with customers. The analysis and formulation resulted in several significantly different HR practices; those practices most affected and how they changed are illustrated in Exhibit 11.5. These changes in HR practices were identified as necessary for the business and as critical to performing as needed by the customer.[14]

Person Needs Analysis

After information about the necessary skills, their importance, and the minimal acceptable standards of proficiency have been collected, the analysis shifts to the individual. A **person needs analysis** can be accomplished in two different ways. Employee performance discrepancies may be identified either by comparing actual performance with the minimum acceptable standards of performance or by comparing an evaluation of employee proficiency on each required skill dimension with the proficiency level required for each skill. The first method is based on the actual, current job performance of an employee; it is therefore used to determine

EXHIBIT 11.5

The Changed HR Practices

HUMAN RESOURCE PLANNING
Longer-term focus
Tie to the needs of the business

STAFFING
More socialization
More opportunities

PERFORMANCE APPRAISAL
Customer service measures used
Feedback provided

COMPENSATION
Relates to performance appraisal
Awards and celebration

TRAINING AND DEVELOPMENT
More skill training
Customer service training

Source: Adapted from R. Schuler, "Strategic Human Resource Management: Linking the People with the Strategic Needs of the Business," *Organizational Dynamics* (New York: AMACOM, Summer 1992): 30.

training needs for the current job. The second method is used to identify development needs for future jobs.[15]

Regardless of method, several different approaches can be used to identify the training needs of individuals.

Output Measures. Performance data (for example, productivity, accidents, customer complaints), as well as performance appraisal ratings, can provide evidence of performance deficiencies. Person needs analysis can also consist of work sampling and job knowledge tests that measure performance capability and knowledge.[16]

Self-Assessed Training Needs. The self-assessment of training needs is growing in popularity. A recent study of training practices in major U.S. firms showed that between 50 and 80 percent of all corporations allow managers to nominate themselves to attend short-term or company-sponsored training or education programs. Self-assessment can be as informal as posting a list of company-sponsored courses and asking who wants to attend or as formal as conducting surveys regarding training needs.[17] Exhibit 11.6 shows sample questions from a managerial self-assessment survey.

Self-assessment is premised on the assumption that employees, more than anyone else, are aware of their skill weaknesses and performance deficiencies. Therefore, they are in the best position to identify their own training needs. One drawback of self-assessment is that individuals who are fearful of revealing any weaknesses may not know or be willing to accurately report their training needs. Consequently, these individuals may not receive the education necessary to remain current in their fields. On the other hand, managers forced to attend programs that they believe they do not need or that do not meet their personal training needs can become dissatisfied with training and thus be less motivated to learn and transfer skills.

Attitude Surveys. Attitude surveys completed by a supervisor's subordinates and/or by customers can also provide information on training needs. For example, when one supervisor receives low scores regarding his or her fairness in treatment as compared with other supervisors in the organization, this can indicate that the supervisor needs training in that area.[18] Not only does this format provide information to management about service, but results can also be used to pinpoint employee deficiencies.

People instinctively want to learn. We are introducing new and improved training programs and aids to create additional opportunities to learn, so our people can use what they learn to help us grow. That's what "Delivering Our Future" to all of our constituencies—employees, customers, shareowners, and communities—is all about.

Kent C. Nelson
Chairman and
Chief Executive Officer
UPS

EXHIBIT 11.6

Sample Questions from a Self-Administered Needs Survey

Please indicate in the blanks the extent to which you have a training need in each specific area. Use the scale below.

To what extent do you need training in the following areas?

TO NO EXTENT				TO A VERY LARGE EXTENT
1	2	3	4	5

Basic Management Skills (organizing, planning, delegating, problem solving)

__ 1. Setting goals and objectives

__ 2. Developing realistic time schedules to meet work requirements

__ 3. Identifying and weighing alternative solutions

__ 4. Organizing work activities

Interpersonal Skills

__ 1. Resolving interpersonal conflicts

__ 2. Creating a development plan for employees

__ 3. Identifying and understanding individual employee needs

__ 4. Conducting performance appraisal reviews

__ 5. Conducting a discipline interview

Administrative Skills

__ 1. Maintaining equipment, tools, and safety controls

__ 2. Understanding local agreements and shop rules

__ 3. Preparing work flowcharts

__ 4. Developing department budgets

Quality Control

__ 1. Analyzing and interpreting statistical data

__ 2. Constructing and analyzing charts, tables, and graphics

__ 3. Using statistical software on the computer

Source: Modified from J. K. Ford and R. A. Noe. "Self Assessed Training Needs: The Effects of Attitude Toward Training, Managerial Level and Function," *Personnel Psychology* 40 (1987): 40–53.

Competency-Based Assessment. A type of needs assessment growing in popularity is competency-based assessment. This approach involves five major steps:

Step 1 **Develop broad competency categories.** The initial step is to develop a set of broad competency areas—that is, to determine the critical skills that employees at a given level or job classification in the organization need to be most effective.

Step 2 **Develop specific competencies.** Once broad categories are selected, the next step is to further define each and develop a list of more specific competencies.

Step 3 Develop a resource guide and a competency rating form. The third step involves the development of resource guides or competency manuals that will aid employers and employees in developing skills.

Step 4 Prepare a developmental plan for each employee. Once each employee has been evaluated, the next step would be for the boss to work with each of his or her subordinates to develop a specific improvement plan.

Step 5 Evaluate employee progress and develop a new plan. Periodic assessment of an employee's progress toward skill development is essential.[19]

These broad and specific competencies are the skills, knowledge, and abilities necessary to do a great job.

Demographic Needs Analysis

In addition to organizational, job, and person needs analyses, organizations must conduct demographic studies to determine the training needs of specific populations of workers.[20] For example, Frito Lay conducted a special assessment to determine the training needs of women and minorities in its sales force. According to Dave Knibbe, Frito Lay management development director, the needs assessment was critical to finding ways the organization could facilitate more rapid career advancement for these employees. This is consistent with research that indicates that different groups have different training needs. For example, first-line supervisors need more technical training (record keeping, written communications), while mid-level managers rate HR courses as most important for meeting their needs, and upper-level managers rate conceptual courses (goal setting, planning skills) as critical to their development.[21] In a study of male and female managers, male managers were found to need training in listening, verbal skills, nonverbal communication, empathy, and sensitivity; women managers, on the other hand, needed training in assertiveness, confidence building, public speaking, and dealing with male peers and subordinates.[22]

Demographic needs analysis identifies training needs by groups in the organization.

Setting Up the Programs

LEARNING OBJECTIVE 3

Answer questions about setting up training and development programs.

Successful implementation of training and development programs depends on selecting the right programs for the right people under the right conditions.

Who Participates in Training?

Once a training need has been established, the participants must be selected. If all employees who need the training cannot be immediately accommodated, the decision must be made as to which group will be trained first.

Also the number of employees to be trained simultaneously must be considered. If only one or two employees are to be trained, then on-the-job approaches such as coaching are generally cost-effective. If large numbers of individuals need to be trained in a short period of time, then programmed instruction may be the most viable option.

Setting up programs involves asking:

- **Who participates in training?**
- **Who conducts the training?**
- **What skills are to be acquired?**

Who Conducts the Training?

Training and development programs can be taught by one of several people, including:

- The supervisor
- HR staff
- A co-worker such as a lead worker or a friend
- An internal or external expert
- The employee—that is, self-paced instruction
- Local universities, colleges, or training institutes

Recognizing the need for a more highly trained workforce, employers are rejecting traditional education seminars in favor of on-site accredited degree programs and continuous on-line training courses, Brown notes. By forming long-term partnerships with colleges and universities, he contends, employers are able to provide their employees with training that is accessible, substantive, and useful.[23]

Did You KNOW?

Jack Welch teaches a 3½ hour leadership class five times a year at GE's Crotonville training center.

The skills to be taught often determine who and where they are taught. For example, basic job skills are usually taught by the immediate job supervisor or a co-worker, whereas a basic organizational orientation is usually handled by the HR staff. Interpersonal and conceptual, integrative skills for management are usually taught by university professors or consultants.

A concern with using immediate supervisors or co-workers as trainers is that, while they may perform the work tasks well, they may not be able to instruct anyone in the procedures. It is also possible that they will teach workers their own shortcuts rather than correct procedures. On the other hand, immediate supervisors or co-workers may be more knowledgeable than anyone else about the work procedures. If co-workers or managers are to be used as trainers, they should receive instruction in how to train and be given sufficient time on the job to work with trainees.[24] Look how this process unfolds at the many business locations of the Mirage Hotel and Resorts of Las Vegas:

Each property has a training director, as well as training managers for each division—gaming, hotel, food and beverage, retail, security, entertainment, human resources. In addition, division training managers select and train team leaders who in turn are responsible for a group of approximately 20 employees; the leaders conduct job-specific training for the company's 433 separate identified jobs.

This job-specific training requires that workers learn somewhere between 10 and 15 required tasks before being allowed to do their job. For example, every maid employed by the Mirage Resorts must demonstrate to his or her trainer that he or she is able to make a hospital corner on a bed.

Mirage Resorts also teaches its workers key behaviors and strategies. For example, it doesn't just teach cocktail servers what the various cocktails are and how to serve them, but also teaches them how to help people if they get too intoxicated, and how to stop serving someone without causing a scene.[25]

Experts may have specific knowledge on a technical skill but may not be familiar with the culture of a specific organization. As a result, they may be respected for their expertise but mistrusted because they are not members of the work group. Still, if no one in the immediate work environment possesses the knowledge needed, or if large numbers of individuals need to be trained, the only option may be to hire experts.

Self-paced instruction is also an option. Learning at one's own pace is both an advantage and a disadvantage. Trainees benefit because they learn at a speed that maximizes retention. However, if there are no incentives for the trainee to complete the instruction in a specified period of time, the training may be placed on a back burner.

Without question, TI owes its success to the thousands of TI people who are making the networked society come to life. This is why we will continue to develop our skills, ensure that we have the best tools to do the job, develop our leadership, and make the most of our teams.

Jerry R. Junkins
Chairman, President, and Chief Executive Officer

What Types of Skills Are To Be Acquired?

In addition to using appropriate training techniques, the training program must have content congruent with the types of skills being taught. In general, skills fall into four broad areas, as discussed below.

Basic Literacy Skills. Organizations are increasingly concerned about **basic literacy skills (BLS)**. Consequently, it is estimated that training programs designed to correct basic literacy deficiencies in grammar, mathematics, safety, reading, listening, and writing will increase into the next century. Organizations are also learning that it pays to train customer service representatives in the art of telephone etiquette. The feature, "HR Advice and Application: Telephone Etiquette" discusses just how important this type of training can be.[26]

Basic literacy skills are those in grammar, math, safety, reading, listening and writing necessary to perform entry-level jobs in most companies.

As the total quality management movement spreads through U.S. industry, companies are realizing that almost all employees need statistics as a basic skill. It is fundamental to W. Edwards Deming's approach to quality, which is improvement by the numbers. In total quality management, determining causes of any lack in quality is done by **statistical process control (SPC)**. SPC is the practice of using statistical analysis to improve quality in operating processes. According to Deming, it is important to analyze the system statistically to know when a system is not producing products with acceptable reliability. At a minimum, a knowledge of means, standard deviations, and ranges is required.

Statistical process control is the practice of using statistics to improve quality in operating processes.

Basic Technical Skills. Training that expands or maintains the technical expertise of employees is a subset of **basic technical skills (BTS)** training. Due to rapid changes in technology and the implementation of automated office, technological updating and skill building have become a major thrust in training to keep technical skills current.[27]

Basic technical skills are those necessary to operate basic technologies such as computers and computer controlled machines.

Interpersonal Skills. Increasingly in demand are the **interpersonal skills (IPS)** in communications, human relationships, performance appraisal, leadership, and negotiations. In fact, IPS tops the list of training needs for first- and middle-level managers. The development of IPS is also important for those employees who deal directly with the public (for example, receptionists, sales associates).[28] But increasingly these skills are necessary in all companies where teams and teamwork are used.[29]

Interpersonal skills are those for communications, performance appraisal, leadership, and negotiations.

Conceptual Integrative Skills. Skills in strategic and operational planning, organization design, and policy development, called **conceptual integrative skills (CIS)**, are needed by organizational planners as well as by top management. Adapting to complex and changing environments is often a part of top- and middle-management responsibilities, and CIS helps people enlarge their capacities in these areas. It is at the heart of today's emphasis on creativity and entrepreneurship.

Conceptual integrative skills are strategic and operational planning, organizational design, and policy development.

Where and How Is the Training Conducted?

LEARNING OBJECTIVE 4

Describe the different types of training and development programs.

A careful choice in location of training programs can enhance their success. Such decisions are constrained by the type of learning that is to occur (basic, technical, interpersonal, or conceptual), as well as by cost and time considerations. Exhibit 11.7 summarizes the various approaches to training according to the locale of the training.

On the Job

On-The-Job Training. A frequently used approach is to train workers on the job. **On-the-job training (OJT)** occurs when an employee is taught a new job or skill under the direct supervision of an experienced worker or trainer. The trainee is expected to learn the job by observing the experienced employee and by working with the actual materials, personnel, and/or machinery that comprise the job. The experienced employee/trainer is expected to provide a favorable role model and to take time from regular job responsibilities to provide the instruction and guidance.

On-the-job training occurs under the direct supervision of another person on the job.

One advantage of OJT is that transfer of training is high. Because trainees learn job skills in the environment in which they will actually work, they are more apt

HR ADVICE & APPLICATION

Telephone Etiquette

The following describes the option of an arbitrator who listened to the facts in this case where an employee was suspended.

"The customer was rude to me first," snapped operator Lucy Lipps. "I tried to be nice, but she was so snotty that I had to stand up to her."

"There is never a reason to be rude to a customer," argued supervisor Alex Bell. "A three-day suspension ought to convince you we're serious about customer service."

Was the suspension for just cause?

Facts: The employee worked as a telephone operator in the company's service center, answering customer questions and providing assistance. A customer contacted the employee and, feeling that she had been treated rudely, asked for the employee's name. The employee would not give her name and instead asked the customer for her name and address. The customer immediately contacted the employee's supervisor and reported the incident. When a follow-up call by the service center manager two days later corroborated the supervisor's record of the incident, the employee was suspended for three days for misconduct.

The employee protested the suspension, claiming that she had encountered a difficult customer but did her best to respond to the customer's needs. The customer was already frustrated before talking with her, she said, and therefore she should not be blamed for making the customer upset.

The company, however, contended that the employee had improperly handled the situation by not giving her name when the customer requested it and improperly asking the customer for her name and address. Further, the company argued. the customer immediately reported the incident to the supervisor on duty and also gave a consistent account of the incident two days later. Because the company's business depended on good service, it maintained, the three-day suspension was appropriate to impress upon the employee the seriousness of the offense.

Award: The suspension is upheld.

Discussion: If the customer had claimed only that the employee used a rude tone of voice and failed to give her name when asked, it might have been possible that the customer was mistaken and "was just upset already" and took her frustration out on the employee, the arbiter concedes. However, there was no explanation offered or a possible explanation as to why the customer would concoct the part of her complaint that the employee asked for her name and address, the arbiter finds. Further, the arbiter points out, even though the employee maintained that the customer was rude to her, the employee knows that rudeness on the part of the customer does not excuse rudeness on the part of a company representative.

The arbiter also notes that the employee had received counseling for similar misconduct less than two years earlier. Although the company initially issued a warning and reduced the warning to counseling, the -employer may consider the incident in determining the appropriate penalty for subsequent similar offenses, the arbiter decides. While the employee has also received commendations for excellent customer service in the past, they do not excuse her rudeness, even if the customer was being difficult, the arbiter declares, upholding the three-day suspension.

Pointers: Employees who staff first-line telephone positions and toll-free lines are an organization's opportunity to make a good first impression, says Nancy Friedman, president of Telephone Doctor, a St. Louis-based consulting firm. A poorly trained employee, however, can damage a company's reputation by not knowing how to handle a telephone call.

By not training employees in proper telephone techniques, employers risk customer dissatisfaction as employees claim they are not able to help callers, as telephones ring endlessly, and as callers are put on hold or transferred to the wrong person. If a caller is already upset, Friedman recommends employees use a four-step process, including:

- **Apologize.** Callers need to hear an apology.
- **Sympathize.** Empathize with callers for the difficulties they are feeling.
- **Accept responsibility.** Take responsibility for the difficulty on behalf of the company, regardless of whether the employee had anything to do with the matter.
- **Take action.** Prepare to solve the customer's problem.[30]

EXHIBIT 11.7

Advantages and Disadvantages of On-the-Job, On-Site, and Off-the-Job Training Programs

TYPE OF PROGRAM	ADVANTAGES	DISADVANTAGES
On the Job		
Orientation	Provides socialization to the company Conveys expectations of the company about acceptable behaviors and performance	Too dominated by the company's views May be too short to be effective
Job instruction training	Facilitates transfer of learning No need for separate facilities	Interferes with performance Damages equipment
Apprenticeship	No interference with real job performance Provides extensive training	Takes a long time Expensive May not be related to job
Internships or assistantships	Facilitates transfer of learning Gives exposure to real job	Not really a full job Learning is vicarious
Job rotation	Exposure to many jobs Real learning	No sense of full responsibility Too short a stay in a job
Supervisory assistance	Informal Integrated into job Inexpensive	Effectiveness rests with supervisor Not all supervisors may do it
On Site But Not On The Job		
Programmed instruction	Provides for individualized learning and feedback Faster learning	Time-consuming to develop Cost-effective only for large groups
Videotapes	Convey consistent information to employees in diverse locations	Costly to develop Don't provide for individual feedback
Videodisks	Store more information than tapes Allow for fast forward Portable	Extremely costly to develop Courseware is limited
Interactive	Training draws on more senses Self-paced learning and feedback	Costly to develop and implement Requires diverse staff to develop
Telecommunications training	Provides for latest insights and knowledge Speeds up communications Standardized	Costly and difficult to set up Not feasible for small firms
Off The Job		
Formal courses	Inexpensive for many No interference with job	Requires verbal skills Inhibits transfer of learning
Assessment centers	Helps learning transfer Realistic preview	Expensive to develop Takes time to administer
Simulation	Helps transfer Creates lifelike situations	Can't always duplicate real situations exactly
Role-playing	Good for interpersonal skills Gives insights into others	Can't create real situations exactly; still playing
Sensitivity training	Good for self-awareness Gives insights into others	May not transfer to job May not relate to job
Wilderness trips; outdoor exercises	Build teams Build self-esteem	Costly to administer Physically challenging

to apply these skills on the job. Assuming the trainer works in the same area, the trainee receives immediate feedback about performance. However, such on-site training is appropriate only when a small number of individuals need to be trained and when the consequence of error is low. The quality of the training also hinges on the skill of the manager or person conducting the training.[31]

Orientation Programs

Orientation programs welcome new employees and inform them about the company.

Orientation programs are frequently used to brief new employees on benefit programs and options, to advise them of rules and regulations, and to provide them with a folder or handbook of the policies and practices of the organization.[32]

The handbooks usually contain information about equal employment opportunity practices, safety regulations, work times, coffee breaks, the structure and history of organization, and perhaps the products or services of the organization.[33]

Although the orientation program conveys some information about the norms, values, attitudes, and behaviors appropriate for new employees, the majority of socialization is left to informal day-to-day interactions among employees.

Orientation programs are almost always coordinated by the HR director. The program itself is usually run by HR staff, with some participation by line managers and other employees, depending on the design of the program.

Once employees are hired, they should immediately begin formal orientation programs.

Arthur Nathan
Vice President
Human Resources
Mirage Casino Hotel

In large organizations, orientation programs are often conducted every week. Some programs have two orientation sessions one week apart, which are typically presented to groups of new hires. Although efficient, this approach tends to negate each employee's sense of identity and importance. To counterbalance this, each employee is often assigned to a trainer or "buddy" (sometimes the immediate supervisor) who can answer further questions and introduce the new hire to other employees in the work unit or department.

Orientation programs can last longer than one or two days. The orientation program at Corning Glass Works, for example, lasts 15 months. The critical components of the program at Corning include:

- Pre-arrival period—the supervisor gets the office ready and, based on discussions with the new hire, creates a preliminary management-by-objectives (MBO) list.
- First day—following breakfast with the supervisor, the new hire goes through personnel processing, attends a half-day "Corning and You" seminar, tours the facility, and meets co-workers.
- First week—this time is set aside for getting settled in the department or office and for one-on-one discussions with the supervisor and co-workers. Performance expectations arid other general job-related matters are discussed, and details of the MBO plan are formalized.
- Second through fourth weeks—regular assignments begin. The new hire also attends a special employee benefits seminar.
- Second through fifth months—assignments increase and progress is reviewed biweekly with the supervisor. The employee also attends six two-and-one-half-hour seminars on such topics as quality and productivity and reviews these with the supervisor.
- Sixth month—the new employee reviews the MBO list with the supervisor and receives a performance review.
- Fifteenth month—MBO and performance and salary reviews are conducted.[34]

In contrast to this lengthy process, most orientation programs last only a few hours, though, and are done within the first week or two of employment. Occasionally, an orientation follow-up takes place a year or so later.

Job Instruction Training. The disadvantages of on-the-job training can be minimized by making the training program as systematic and complete as possible. **Job instruction training (JIT)** represents such a technique. It was developed as a guide for giving on-the-job training to white- and blue-collar employees.[35] Because JIT is a technique rather than a program, it can be adapted to training efforts for all employees in off-the-job and on-the-job programs.

JIT consists of four steps: (1) careful selection and preparation of the trainer and the trainee for the learning experience to follow; (2) a full explanation and demonstration by the trainer of the job to be done by the trainee; (3) a trial on-the-job performance by the trainee; and (4) a thorough feedback session between the trainer and the trainee to discuss the trainee's performance and the job requirements.[36]

Job instruction training (JIT) is a systematic approach to the development and delivery of a training program.

Apprenticeship Training. Another method for minimizing the disadvantages of on-the-job training is combining it with off-the-job training. Apprenticeship training, internships, and assistantships are based on this combination. **Apprenticeship training** is mandatory for admission to many of the skilled trades such as plumbing, electronics, and carpentry. These programs are formally defined by the U.S. Department of Labor's Bureau of Apprenticeship and Training and involve a written agreement "providing for not less than 4,000 hours of reasonably continuous employment... and supplemented by a recommended minimum of 144 hours per year of related classroom instruction." The Equal Employment Opportunity Commission allows the nation's 48,000 skilled trade (apprentice) training programs to exclude anyone over 40 years of age because apprenticeship programs are part of the educational system aimed at youth.[37] To be most effective, the on- and off-the-job components of the apprenticeship program must be well integrated and appropriately planned, and they must recognize individual differences.

Apprenticeship training is a formal program of training that combines on-the-job and off-the-job training.

Internships. Somewhat less formalized and extensive than apprenticeship training are the internship and assistantship programs. **Internships** are often part of an agreement between schools and colleges and local organizations. As with apprenticeship training, individuals in these programs "earn while they learn," but at a rate that is less than that paid to full-time employees or master crafts workers. The internships, however, function as a source not only of training, but also of realistic exposure to job and organizational conditions. **Assistantships** involve full-time employment and expose an individual to a wide range of jobs. However, because the individual only assists other workers, the learning experience is often vicarious. This disadvantage is eliminated by programs using actual job rotation.[38]

Internships offer you a great way to see a company without any commitments. Internships are "earn while you learn" programs of training.

Assistantship is a full-time employment as an assistant.

Job Rotation. **Job rotation programs** are used to train and expose employees to a variety of jobs and decision-making situations. Although job rotation does provide exposure, the extent of training and long-run benefits it provides may be overstated. This is because the employees are not in a single job for a long enough period to learn very much and are not motivated to work hard because they know that they will move on in the near future. As a personal career planning strategy, you may want to avoid job rotation and opt instead for job assignments that are fixed and provide a greater challenge.

Job rotation programs offer exposure to a wide variety of jobs in a short time.

Mentoring. The final and most informal program of training and development involves **supervisory assistance** and **mentoring.**[39] Assisting employees is a regular part of a supervisor's job. It includes day-to-day coaching, counseling, and monitoring workers on how to do the job and how to get along in the organization. The effectiveness of supervisory assistance depends in part on whether the supervisor creates a climate where mutual confidence can flourish, provides opportunities for growth, and effectively delegates tasks. Mentoring programs, in which an established employee guides the development of a less-experienced worker or protégé can increase an employee's skills, achievement, and understanding of the organization.

Supervisory assistance is advice given by the supervisor on a daily basis. Mentoring is advice given for career development over a long period of time.

Did You KNOW?

The best managed firms make use of a broad array of better developmental experiences, "including adding responsibilities to jobs, creating special jobs, using inside and outside training, transferring people between functions and divisions, mentoring and coaching employees, giving those people feedback on progress, and giving them instruction in how to manage their own development."

John Kotter
The Leadership Factor

On Site But Not On The Job

Another option is to conduct the training at the work site but not on the job. On-site training is appropriate for required after-hours training programs and for training programs in which contact needs to be maintained with work units but OJT would be too distracting or harmful. On-site training is also appropriate for voluntary after-hours training programs and for programs that update employees' skills while allowing them to attend to their regular duties.

For example, when a major northeastern grocery store chain switched to computerized scanners, it faced the problem of training thousands of checkers spread out across three states. The cost of training them off site was prohibitive. Yet management was fearful that training employees on the job would slow down service and offend customers. To solve the problem, the grocery chain developed a mobile training van that included a vestibule model of the latest scanning equipment. Checkers were trained on site but off the job in the mobile unit. Once the basic skill of scanning was mastered, employees returned to the store, and the trainer remained on site as a resource person. According to one store manager, the program was effective because employees could be trained rapidly and efficiently. Yet, because the training was not conducted on the job, no customers were lost due to checker errors or slowness.

Programmed instruction (PI) is training given in small pieces which must be learned in a systematic order.

Programmed Instruction. New technologies have rapidly increased the options available to organizations that want to provide on-site training. **Programmed instruction (PI)** is one of the oldest on-site training methods. Here, the instructional material is broken down into frames. Each frame represents a small component of the entire subject to be learned, and each frame must be learned successfully before going on to the next one.

An advantage of PI is that large numbers of employees can be trained simultaneously, with the learner free to explore the material at his or her own pace. Additionally, PI includes immediate and individualized feedback. The downside is that programming computers for PI is involved and time-consuming. It is estimated that 1 hour of programmed instruction requires 50 hours of developmental work. Consequently, this approach is cost effective only if "canned" programs (for example, word processing and database tutorials) are used or if large numbers of employees are to be trained.

Videotaped presentations are those that are made on tape and played back at any time.

Videos. **Videotaped presentations** can be used on site or off site. At its most basic level, video training includes taped instruction that can be stopped and started at any point.

An advantage of videotape instruction is that it can be standardized. When Pizza Hut faced the burden of training 10,000 employees in various locales on such matters as competing with Domino's Pizza in the home delivery market, new products, safe driving, and customer service, it turned to video. Professionally prepared video presentations were mailed out to its individual locations, and the training was then provided on site to each shift of workers. Cost savings over traditional off-site or on-site training were substantial.

Videodisks are large disks that are played with a laser beam and contain large amounts of information.

Videodisks. Organizations with large budgets for training are replacing videotapes with **videodisks**. A videodisk relies on a laser beam to pick up images and project them on a television screen. While more expensive to produce than simple videotape programs, videodisks provide higher-quality images, quicker starts and stops, and greater durability than do tapes. Corporations such as Kodak are relying on videodisks for training in business, computer logic, mechanics, and new technology. Kodak uses videodisks to keep its scientists and engineers updated on technological advances.

Interactive video training combines programmed instruction with video presentation that can be controlled by the learner.

IVT. **Interactive video training (IVT)** combines the best features of programmed instruction with those of videotape and/or videodisk instruction.

Interactive video programs present a short video and narrative presentation (via tape or disk) and then require the trainee to respond to it. Usually, the IVT is attached to a personal computer, and the learner responds to video cues by using the keyboard or by touching the screen. This sequence—packaged program, learner response, and more programmed instruction—provides for individualized learning.

Interactive video training has been used to train 400,000 General Motors workers in occupational health and safety procedures, and it has been used to train Dow Chemical employees in how to deal with petrochemical hazards. Electrical workers have learned how to solve complex wiring problems by tracing patterns on touch-sensitive screens.

Telecommunications. Another innovation for on-site training involves **telecommunications training** using video satellite networks. In 1987, the Public Broadcasting System (PBS) entered the field of satellite training with the establishment of the National Narrowcast System (NNS). Produced in cooperation with the American Society for Training and Development (ASTD), the network offers more than five hours of daily programming via microwave to subscribing businesses, public agencies, and colleges and universities. Contractors are free to tape programs for six months to one year, and the system has nine training tracks targeted for specific groups (for example, sales, supervision, computer literacy, effective communications).

Telecommunications training is based on broadcasts transmitted by satellite networks.

The major advantage of telecommunications training is its potential for speeding up communications within large corporations. A cost study conducted by Kodak estimates that a new product training program beamed via satellite to three cities costs $20,000. However, Kodak also estimates that it would cost five to six times that amount to send engineers and managers on the road to do the same training. More important, six weeks of training time was saved, which is invaluable in a competitive industry.[40]

Off the Job

When the consequence of error is high, it is usually more appropriate to conduct training off the job. For example, most airline passengers would readily agree that it is preferable to train pilots in flight simulators than have them apprentice in the cockpit of a plane. Similarly, it is equally useful to have a bus driver practice on an obstacle course before taking to the roads with a load of school children.

Off-the-job training is also appropriate when complex skills need to be mastered or when the focus is on specific interpersonal skills. For example, it is difficult to build a cohesive work team when members of management are constantly interrupted by telephone calls and subordinate inquiries. Team building is more likely to occur during a management retreat when there is time to focus on establishing relationships.

However, the costs of off-the job training are high. There also is concern over transfer of knowledge to the workplace. As research has shown, the more dissimilar the training environment is from the actual work environment, the more likely it is that trainees *will* not be able to apply knowledge learned to their jobs. For example, the transfer-of-knowledge problem is minimal for vestibule training, in which trainees work in an environment that is comparable to the actual work environment. However, it may be difficult to apply teamwork skills learned during a wilderness survival program to a job because the training environment is so different from work environment.

Did You KNOW?

Ameritech Corporation, putting its top 1,000 managers through intense off-site workshops, even sends executives to work for an afternoon in soup kitchens, housing projects, and AIDS clinics, all as team-building exercises.

Formal Courses. The **formal course method** of training and development can be accomplished either by oneself—using programmed instruction, computer-assisted instruction, reading, and correspondence courses—or with teachers, as in formal classroom courses and lectures. Although many training programs use the lecture method because it efficiently and simultaneously conveys large amounts of information to large groups of people, it does have several drawbacks:

Formal course method is done off the job by the individual alone or in the classroom.

- It perpetuates the authority structure of traditional organizations and hinders performance because the learning process is not self-controlled.
- Except in the area of cognitive knowledge and conceptual principles, there is probably limited transfer of the actual skills and abilities required to do the job.
- The high verbal and symbolic requirements of the lecture method may be threatening to people with low verbal or symbolic aptitude.
- The lecture method does not permit individualized training based on individual differences in ability, interests, and personality.

Because of these drawbacks, the lecture method is often complemented by other training methods.

Simulation is training that is done by creating an artificial or simulated environment.

Simulation. **Simulation,** a training and development technique that presents participants with situations that are similar to actual job conditions, is used for both managers and nonmanagers.[41] A common technique for nonmanagers is the **vestibule method,** which simulates the environment of the individual's actual job. Because the environment is not real, it is generally less hectic and more safe than the actual environment; as a consequence, the potential exists for adjustment difficulties in going from the simulated training environment to the actual environment. However, the arguments for using the simulated environment are compelling: it reduces the possibility of customer dissatisfaction that can result from on-the-job training; it can reduce the frustration of the trainee; and it can save the organization a great deal of money because fewer training accidents occur. Even though these arguments may seem compelling, not all organizations, even in the same industry, see the situation the same way. Some banks, for example, train their tellers on the job, whereas others train them in a simulated bank environment.

Vestibule method is a simulated training experience for nonmanagers.

Flight simulators allow companies to train pilots for less cost and danger than actual flight training.

Assessment Centers. An increasingly popular simulation technique for managers is the **assessment center method.** This is discussed in Chapter 10 as a device for selecting managers. Assessment centers are also useful for identifying potential training needs. Whether used for training or selection, they appear to be a valid way to make employment decisions.[42] In fact, certain aspects of the assessment center, such as the management games and in-basket exercises, are excellent for training and need not be confined to these programs.

Assessment center method is a simulation for managers that combines many job-like experiences and tests. Assessment centers can be used for selection, performance appraisal, and training.

Regardless of where they are used, **management** or **business games** almost always entail various degrees of competition between teams or trainees. In contrast, the **in-basket exercise** is more solitary. The trainee sits at a desk and works through a pile of papers found in the in-basket of a typical manager, prioritizing, recommending solutions to problems, and taking any necessary action in response to the contents.[43]

Management or business games are those that involve competition with others.

In-basket exercise is a training method done alone.

Although the in-basket exercise tends to be an enjoyable and challenging experience, the extent to which it improves a manager's ability depends in part on what takes place after the exercise. The analysis of what happened and what should have happened in both the business games and the in-basket exercise, when done by upper-level managers in the organization, should help trainees learn how to perform like managers. The opportunity for improvement may be drastically reduced if the trainees are left to decide what to transfer from the game or exercise to the job.

Whereas the simulation exercises may be useful for developing conceptual and problem-solving skills, two types of human relations or process-oriented training are used by organizations. Role-playing and sensitivity training develop managers' interpersonal insights—awareness of self and of others—for changing attitudes and for practices in human relations skills such as leadership or interviewing.

Role-playing involves individuals assuming roles that are given to them.

Role-Playing. **Role-playing** generally focuses on emotional (that is, human relations) issues rather than on factual situations. The essence of role-playing is to create a realistic situation, and then have the trainees assume the parts of specific personalities in the situation. The usefulness of role-playing depends heavily on the extent to which the trainees get into the parts they are playing. If you have done any of the role-playing, you know how difficult this can be and how much easier it is to simply read the part. However, when the trainee does get into the role, the result is a greater sensitivity to the feelings and insights that are presented by the role.

Sensitivity Training. Another method of training and development is **sensitivity training.** Individuals in an unstructured group exchange thoughts and feelings on the "here and now" rather than the "there and then." Although the experience of being in a sensitivity group often gives individuals insight into how and why they and others feel and act the way they do, critics claim that these results may not be beneficial because they are not directly transferable to the job.[44]

Sensitivity training provides individuals a situation for an unstructured group exchange of thoughts and feelings.

Wilderness Trips and Other Outdoor Exercises. Other methods organizations use to increase employees' feelings about the here and now and their own self-esteem include programs that involve physical feats of strength, endurance, and cooperation. These can be done on wilderness trips to various destinations.

Did You KNOW?

Organizations such as Outward Bound and the Pecos River Learning Center have been offering wilderness trips and other forms of outdoor activities such as rock climbing and rope courses since the late 1970s.

> *Everyone goes overboard during strategic planning meetings of the Meridian Group. But that doesn't bother Harvey Kinzelberg, 43, chairman of the $250-million-a-year Illinois computer-leasing firm, the nation's third largest. On the contrary, he requires it. Twice a year Kinzelberg charters a boat in the Caribbean, puts his top executives aboard, and leads them in a five-day brainstorming session cum scuba-diving expedition. . . . As often as three times a day, the company's managers pause from strategizing, strap on air tanks and face masks, and go for a plunge in the briny.*
>
> *Kinzelberg claims the downward-bound excursions focus his executives' attention on business by eliminating the . . . distractions of the office. More important, he says, they foster team spirit. "In the potentially life-threatening environment underwater," he explains, "you realize that you depend on everyone else in the company not just for your livelihood in business but for your life as well."*
>
> *Excursions in the deep also provide the benefits of a different perspective, says Kinzelberg. . . . After spearing and killing a large barracuda, as he did on a recent dive, Kinzelberg finds that the sharks he faces in business seem like small fries.*[45]

Wilderness training is used to build team cohesiveness.

Maximizing Learning

LEARNING OBJECTIVE 5

Describe how to maximize learning.

However appropriate and effective a training technique may be, learning will not take place if the training is not structured properly. Exhibit 11.8 details learning factors that increase the success rates of training. As shown, prior to training, the environment must be made ready for learning to occur. During training, steps need to be taken to increase self-efficacy and retention of knowledge. After training, the work environment must be monitored to ensure that what was learned is retained.

Setting the Stage for Learning

Prior to launching the program, the trainer needs to consider how information will be presented. Additionally, he or she must consider the beliefs of trainees regarding task-specific competencies.

EXHIBIT 11.8

Learning Principles that Increase Training Effectiveness

SETTING THE STAGE FOR LEARNING

1. Provide clear task instructions.
2. Model appropriate behavior.

INCREASING LEARNING DURING TRAINING

1. Provide for active participation.
2. Increase self-efficacy.
3. Match training techniques to trainees self-efficacy.
4. Provide opportunities for enactive mastery.
5. Ensure specific, timely, diagnostic, and practical feedback.
6. Provide opportunities for trainees to practice new behaviors.

MAINTAINING PERFORMANCE AFTER TRAINING

1. Develop learning points to assist in knowledge retention.
2. Set specific goals.
3. Identify appropriate reinforcers.
4. Train significant others in how to reinforce behavior.
5. Teach trainees self-management skills.

Did You KNOW?

Many line managers spend up to fifty percent of their time giving and clarifying instructions to new employees.

Clarity of Instructions. Research has demonstrated that learning will not occur unless task instructions are clear and precise. As noted when discussing performance standards (Chapters 12 and 13), an employee must know what is expected in order to perform as desired. Giving clear instructions includes establishing appropriate behavioral expectations. As with performance standards (see Chapter 12), statements of training expectations should be specific, and conditions under which performance is or is not expected should be identified, along with the behavior to be demonstrated.

To set the stage for desired performance, it is also useful to specify up front what the reward will be for performing as desired. A trainee is more likely to be motivated if he or she knows that successful performance can lead to positive reinforcement (promotion, pay raise, recognition) or can block the administration of negative reinforcement (for example, supervisory criticism, firing).[46]

Behavioral modeling **is a visual demonstration of desired behavior.**

In behavioral modeling, the manager says, "Just watch me do it" or "Here, I'll show you."

Use of Behavioral Models. Even when instructions are clear, desired behavior still may not occur if the trainee does not know how to perform as desired. This problem can be overcome through behavioral modeling. **Behavioral modeling** is a visual demonstration of desired behavior. The model can be a supervisor, co-worker, or expert, and the demonstration can be live or videotaped. The important thing is to show employees what needs to be done *prior* to their attempting the behavior.[47]

Care is needed in choosing an appropriate behavioral model. If the model makes the task look too simple, trainees may lose confidence or quit the first time they encounter a difficulty. Thus, models should show not only how to achieve desired outcomes, but also how to overcome performance obstacles.

Increasing Learning During Training

While employees should be responsible for their own learning, organizations can do much to facilitate this.

Active Participation. Individuals learn better when they are actively involved in the learning process. Participation may be direct (hands on) or indirect (role plays and simulations). The important point is to hook the trainee on learning. Through active participation, trainees stay more alert and are more likely to gain confidence.

Self-Efficacy. Even with behavioral modeling, learning may not occur if people judge themselves low in self-efficacy. **Self-efficacy** is defined as a trainee's beliefs about a task-specific ability. If individuals dwell on their personal deficiencies relative to the task, potential difficulties may seem more formidable than they really are. On the other hand, people who have a strong sense of self-efficacy are more likely to be motivated to overcome obstacles.

Self-efficacy is an individual's beliefs about a task-specific ability.

The choice of an appropriate training method is critical to self-efficacy. In a recent study, a group of trainees was taught how to use computer spreadsheets. People low in self-efficacy performed better when one-on-one tutorials were conducted; individuals with high self-efficacy (they believed they could easily learn how to use spreadsheets) performed better when appropriate behavior was merely modeled. Consequently, before choosing training techniques, the level of self-efficacy for each trainee should be determined.[48]

Did You KNOW?

Being able to teach new employees correctly can be critical to the success of a small business.

Enactive Mastery. Self-efficacy increases when experiences fail to validate fears and when skills acquired allow for mastery of once-threatening situations. This process is called enactive mastery. To facilitate task mastery, trainers should arrange the subject matter so that trainees experience success. While this may be easy when tasks are simple, it can be quite difficult when tasks are complex.

Solutions include segmenting the task, shaping behavior, and/or setting proximal goals. Task segmentation involves breaking a complex task into smaller or simpler components. For some jobs (for example, laboratory technician), the components (drawing blood, culturing a specimen, running a blood chemistry machine) can be taught individually and in any order. In others, segments must be taught sequentially because task B builds on task A and task C builds on task B (using mathematics, driving a car, conducting an effective interview.)[49]

Shaping includes rewarding closer and closer approximations to desired behavior. For example, in teaching managers how to conduct a selection interview, trainees can be reinforced for making eye contact and for developing situational questions.

Shaping includes rewarding closer and closer approximations to desired behavior.

The setting of proximal or intermediary goals also increases mastery perceptions. Consider a software developer with an overall objective of developing a new word processing package. Proximal goals might include meeting a project specifications deadline, developing algorithms for fonts by a set deadline, developing an algorithm for formatting paragraphs, and so on. These proximal goals all lead to the attainment of the distal or overall objective.[50]

Plenty of Feedback. In order for individuals to master new concepts and acquire new skills, they must receive accurate diagnostic feedback about their performance. When feedback is either not received or inaccurate, the wrong behaviors may be practiced. While feedback can be provided by a supervisor, co-workers, customers, computers, or the individual performing the task, it must be specific, timely, behaviorally and not personally based, and practical. If a performance discrepancy exists, the feedback should also be diagnostic and include instructions or modeling of how to perform better.[51] Of course individual differences such as the person's readiness for feedback and learning must be considered.

Practice, Practice, Practice. While an individual may be able to perform as desired one time, the goal of training is to ensure that desired behavior occurs con-

The manager must give employees time to practice so it becomes routine.

sistently. This is most likely to occur when trainees are able to practice and internalize standards of performance. Practicing the wrong behaviors is detrimental. Therefore, practice must follow specific feedback.

It should be stressed that, for some jobs, tasks must be overlearned. Overlearning includes the internalization of responses so that the trainee doesn't have to consciously think about behavior before responding. For example, if a plane is losing altitude rapidly, a pilot must know how to respond immediately. There isn't time to think about what should be done! The emergency routine must be second nature and totally internalized.

Maintaining Performance After Training

Once training is completed, the employee needs to be monitored to ensure that newly acquired behaviors will continue. Several steps can be taken to ensure this.

Development of Learning Points. First, new skills and information are more likely to be retained when learning points are developed. Learning points summarize key behaviors—particularly those that are not obvious—and serve as cognitive cues back on the job. While learning points can be written by trainers, trainee-generated learning points—even if they are of lower quality—enhance recall and lead to better skill acquisition and retention.[52]

Reinforcement is positive or negative feedback given after a behavior.

Reinforcement. Learning new behaviors is difficult and threatening. To ensure that trainees continue to demonstrate the skill they have learned, behavior must be reinforced. **Reinforcement** can be positive (praise, financial rewards) or negative (if you perform as desired, I will quit screaming at you), but it must be performance contingent.[53] See Chapter 12 for a more detailed presentation of reinforcement theory.

Train Significant Others. To ensure that reinforcers are appropriately administered, trainers must also train significant others to look for and reinforce desired changes. If a person who has been labeled a troubled employee continues to be viewed as a problem employee, there is no incentive for the person to display new behavior. If, however, a supervisor or co-worker responds positively to behavior changes, the frequency with which the new behavior will be displayed is likely to increase.

Set Specific Goals. It is also useful to set specific goals for subsequent performance. These goals should be challenging but not so difficult as to be perceived as impossible. Without goals, people have little basis for judging how they are doing.[54]

Self-Reinforcement. Because it is not always possible for significant others to reinforce an individual worker, a long-term objective should be to teach employees how to set their own goals and administer their own reinforcement. When people create self-incentives for their efforts, they are capable of making self-satisfaction contingent on their own performance. Obviously, the challenge is to ensure that personal goals are congruent with organizational goals. As noted in previous chapters, this leads to self-management.[55]

Follow-up is a principle of getting back to the person after the training is completed.

Contract plan is a formal agreement by the individual agreeing to perform at a certain level over time.

Follow-Up. A final principle to remember is **follow-up.** Once a participant leaves the training program, the manager should provide a means of follow-up to ensure that the participant is doing what was taught. All too often, participants who want to change their current behavior get back to work and slip into the old patterns. This in turn results in a significant loss of effectiveness of the training program. One approach to preventing this from happening is the **contract plan.** Its simplicity is a key factor in its success. Each participant writes an informal agreement near the end of a training program, stating which aspects of the program he or she believes will have the most beneficial effect back on the job and then agreeing to apply those aspects. Each participant is also asked to choose another participant from the program to whom a copy of the contract is given and who agrees to check up on the participant's progress every few weeks.

Follow-up is critical for a line manager to do in developing employees.

Although incorporating these principles of learning is desirable. Many training and development programs do not have them or are designed without considering reinforcement, feedback, goal setting, and follow-up. Nevertheless, application of these learning principles can increase the chances of successfully implementing a training and development program

Selecting an Appropriate Program

LEARNING OBJECTIVE 6

Indicate how to select a training program.

A knowledge of the principles of learning, the four categories of skills needed by individuals in organizations, and the methods of training and development available (including their advantages and disadvantages), form the basis for selecting the most appropriate training and development programs for a specific organization. This selection is based on the answers to the following questions:

- What skills do the employees need to learn?
- At what level do these skills need to be learned?
- What training and development programs are most appropriate for the required skills and level?

Selection of a training and development program is a result of matching needed skills with the needed level of training.

The Skills Needed

The answers to the first two questions are determined by the results of the needs analyses. Referring to Exhibit 11.1, you can see that the question of what skills employees need to learn can be answered in part by knowing what types of employees need training. For example, if performance deficiencies exist among the supervisory and rank-and-file employees, the training should be aimed at increasing technical skills. Knowledge of the type of employee and the type of skills needed are useful guides to training employees for current and future jobs.

The Level of Skills Needed

The results of the job and person needs analyses determine the levels of skills required, particularly for current job training. The levels needed for future job training are determined by the organizational, job, and person needs analyses.

Program Selection

Finally, organizations must determine the type of programs that are most appropriate for the skill and level of training needed. A guide for making this choice is shown in Exhibit 11.9. For example, apprenticeship training is appropriate for those who need to increase their basic literacy and technical skills, whereas the case discussion method is appropriate for conceptual/integrative skill training at all three levels.

Often, organizations select not just one program but several. Since most jobs involve numerous skills, several training and development programs may be required. For example, today's HR managers need to perform several roles (presented in Chapter 2) that previously were not necessarily required:

- Businessperson
- Shaper of organizational change
- Consultant and partner to line managers
- Strategy formulator and implementor
- Talent manager
- People manager

EXHIBIT 11.9

Selecting a Training and Development Program

SKILL LEVEL REQUIRED	BASIC LITERACY AND TECHNICAL SKILLS	INTERPERSONAL SKILLS	CONCEPTUAL/ INTEGRATIVE SKILLS
Fundamental knowledge	Job rotation Apprenticeship training Job instruction training	Role-playing Sensitivity training Formal courses	Job rotation Simulation Case discussion
Skill development	Job rotation Simulation Supervisory assistance	Role-playing Sensitivity training Job rotation Simulation Wilderness trips	Job rotation Simulation Case discussion
Operational efficiency	Job rotation Apprenticeship training Job instruction training Simulation Internship and assistantship Supervisory assistance	Role-playing Job rotation Apprenticeship training Job instruction training Simulation	Job rotation Simulation Case discussion

Source: Adapted from T. J. Von der Embse, "Choosing a Management Development Program: A Decision Model," *Personnel Journal* (Oct. 1973): 911.

Training and development activities for HR managers that develop the skills, knowledge, and abilities to play these roles are shown in Exhibit 11.10.

There is a growing need for many line managers to develop leadership skills. Good leaders facilitate organizational changes, employee participation, and teamwork. Facilitating teamwork is particularly important and challenging when bringing together employees who generally haven't worked together. Team-building exercises are critical in developing teamwork skills in managers.

Training managers in ethics is also important. Increasingly, firms are actively developing an ethical culture. WMX Technologies is described in Chapter 3. The training they are providing to support this culture is described on page 398 in the feature, "Managing Human Resources at WMX Technologies."

Finally, the effectiveness of a training and development program must be carefully assessed. This is an important component in attaining the goal of a technologically competent and adaptable workforce, and we will discuss this extensively in Chapter 20.

LEARNING OBJECTIVE 7

Discuss the many trends in training and development.

Current Trends

Trends in training and development are mushrooming as world competitiveness, workforce diversity, and total quality management demand fundamental changes in business practices. The trends of particular importance are:

- Managing for globalization
- Training customers
- Training in business ethics
- Training in diversity management
- Managing the change process
- Company schools

EXHIBIT 11.10

Training and Development Activities for Human Resource Managers

BUSINESSPERSON

- Participates in courses on marketing and finance for nonfinancial executives
- Seeks exposure to marketing organization
- Participates in task forces, business planning teams, acquisition/divestiture teams

SHAPER OF CHANGE

- Participates in team-building exercises
- Engages in formalized mentor relationships
- Researches the change process

CONSULTANT AND PARTNER TO LINE MANAGERS

- Does volunteer work in professional organizations, healthcare coalitions, charities, or company consortiums
- Coaches and evaluates performance
- Pairs junior with senior staffers and consults with internal staff

STRATEGY FORMULATOR AND IMPLEMENTOR

- Learns content of business strategy
- Becomes knowledgeable in the strategies of all the businesses or divisions
- Describes the HR implications of these various strategies

TALENT MANAGER

- Talks constantly to all line managers
- Monitors what the competition is doing
- Attends conferences to develop a network
- People manager
- Talks constantly with all employees
- Takes courses in finance and accounting
- Attends HR conferences
- Reads journals on people management

Source: Adapted from *HR Reporter* (July 1987): 3–4. Used by permission.

Managing for Globalization

A few things seem certain, and one is that "globalization" will continue to be an inescapable buzzword. Businesses will operate in an ever more interconnected world. With continuing advances in computers and communications, world financial markets will meld. Manufacturing prowess will appear almost suddenly in new Taiwans and South Koreas.

MANAGING HUMAN RESOURCES

at WMX Technologies

According to Jodie Bernstein vice president of environmental policy, WMX Technologies (formerly Waste Management) is doing ethics training in a variety of ways. One is through management training. A few years ago, we developed a pilot program with the help of consultants, Barbara Tofler and Chuck Powers of Resources for Responsible Management. Through an interview process that identified what issues were most troubling to our managers, they developed a series of case studies that were used in three-and-a-half-hour sessions with managers in our North American and Chemical Waste Management operating groups. The cases dealt with environmental and health and safety issues and also with conventional business ethics: getting and using competitive information, for example."

After some fine tuning, the program is now being incorporated into the existing corporate-wide management training program under the direction of Ron White, director of HR development. "We now offer a four-hour module that explores issues in making ethical business decisions for all levels of management," said White.

"Our top and regional managers have all been through the program, and we're now working with the mid-level managers. Next on the schedule is adapting the program to the supervisory level. Feedback on the program has been good. We can tell there's a higher level of awareness because we hear managers discussing these issues informally now, too."

"Most of the cases we're using now are not related specifically to our business, but involve situations that could occur in any business. One, for example, deals with how to handle a long-service, top-performing salesperson who lied on his resume when he was hired. There aren't any easy answers to problems like these, and people have to learn to use their best business judgment while being mindful of the ethical issues."

"If we get any complaints from the program, it is that people get frustrated by not having black-and-white answers. We've got a pragmatic bunch of people around here, and this program is really pushing them to explore options before making a decision. It's also resulting in more collaboration. People are finding that rather than making a snap decision on the spot, they are better off discussing it with others, even taking the problem to the boss if it's a big one."

"By building the module into our existing training programs, we will be able to get down into the entire organization of 60,000 employees. Right now I'm doing the management training with people on my staff who are regular trainers. But we are also training facilitators at the local level who will be able to run programs as needed in every location. We're not being naive about this. We know that one supervisory training session isn't going to make someone ethically aware forever. We have to keep working on it and reinforcing the message."[56]

A shrinking world will mean an expanding clock. Managers will have to shape organizations that can respond quickly to developments abroad. As speed and agility become paramount virtues, we will see even more decentralization, with responsibility closer to the operating level.[57]

Organizations are having to develop a world or global structure, perspective, and strategy. Human resource policies need to mirror the necessary organizational characteristics. According to Gillette's CEO, Alfred Zeien, doing this takes a great deal of time. Gillette's approach to training for globalization is highlighted in the feature, "Managing Global Human Resources at Gillette: Building a Global Management Team."

MANAGING HUMAN RESOURCES

at Gillette
Building a Global Management Team

Rome wasn't built in a day. Neither was Gillette's international management team. According to Gillette Chairman and CEO Alfred M. Zeien, it takes at least 25 years to build an international management corps that possesses the skills, experience, and abilities to take a global organization from one level of success to the next.

Gillette, through its senior management team, has learned that developing managers through international assignments helps the business grow. The firm's International Trainee Program for new recruits is one of the company's key strategies for building its worldwide management corps. Its other key international staffing strategy is hiring and developing foreign nationals to staff its operations globally. Many of these individuals have become part of Gillette's growing international corps.

Interestingly, fewer than 15 percent of the company's international corps are expatriates—natives of the United States. At least 85 percent of Gillette's international managers come from one of the other 27 countries in which it has operations.

For the most part, Gillette hires foreign nationals to staff management positions in countries other than the United States. Often, however, the organization first identifies these individuals while they're studying at U.S. universities for their MBAs. The new hires typically work at Gillette's Boston headquarters for a year, then return to their home countries, much like trainees in the International Trainee Program.

After working in their home countries for about four years, Gillette typically moves managers on to other countries and other assignments. As Gillette managers build their international experience, they also teach and develop other potential managers within the organization.

Often these managers with international experience are prime candidates for positions that open up when the company enters into new markets or into joint ventures. Such was the case with its new joint venture last fall with a company in China. Because Gillette first started planning the joint venture in China more than four years ago, it began identifying individual managers then who would be right for assignments in that new business.

As Gillette expatriate Bob McCusker puts it, "Gillette has a lot of resources that we can apply to our new ventures." McCusker, currently on assignment in Pakistan, says that he finds it gratifying when individuals who work in a new Gillette venture in one area go on to help develop new ventures in other areas.

Gillette's policy of giving its managers international experience attracts individuals seeking international careers. Gillette managers are constantly on the lookout for individuals who show interest and promise in moving through the Gillette organization worldwide. "One of my responsibilities is to look for people who are promotable internationally," says Jorgen Wedel, president of Braun USA, a subsidiary of Gillette, and a native of Denmark. "We need people who have a global understanding of the business, and we need managers who can manage that business. I think it's one of the key responsibilities of management today."

Dieu Eng Seng agrees. Seng is the area vice president of Oral-B, another Gillette company, Asia Pacific. A native of Singapore, Seng's past service with Gillette has included assignments in Australia, Singapore, China, Hong Kong, Malaysia, and the United States. "One of my key objectives is to identify, recruit, and develop competent managers. I'm confident that from these good people will generate a flow of business growth and profits into the future."

International management teams clearly aren't built in a day. They aren't even built in a year. In Gillette's case, careful planning and constant attention to international development, however, can yield employees that support and grow a business successfully from one decade to the next.[58]

There need to be expatriate, third/country, and host/country HR policies to create an effective worldwide workforce. The expatriate assignment increasingly needs to be made an attractive one in order to attract the best employees, and assignments anywhere have to be seen as vital components of the whole. According to Jerry Junkins, of Texas Instruments, overseas managers need to look beyond their own "fiefdoms" to consider the capabilities and needs of the company as a whole. Junkins now has all the members of the company's worldwide management group working together.[59]

Training is important for expatriates and families in order to increase their success rate.

U.S. Expatriates. The training and development of expatriates (U.S. citizens working abroad for a U.S. company) presents special challenges. Management development of expatriates should take up where selection leaves off. Although only a few companies provide expatriate training, it is critical. The basic aspects of expatriate development include the following:

- Development of expatriates before, during, and after foreign assignments
- Orientation and training of expatriate families before, during, and after foreign assignments
- Development of the headquarters staff responsible for the planning, organization, and control of overseas operations[60]

This range of training is aimed at bringing about attitudinal and behavioral changes in the expatriates, their families, and the staff (here and abroad) responsible for multinational operations.

Did You KNOW?

Procter & Gamble offers overseas employees:

- **Country-specific information**
- **Language and cross-cultural training**
- **Corporate culture training**

Once an employee has been selected for an expatriate position, cross-cultural training becomes the next critical step in ensuring the expatriate's effectiveness and success abroad. Depending on the assigned country, the employee and his or her family may be confronted with a culture markedly different from their own. These contrasts can extend beyond the language barrier and encompass aspects of social life, political climate, and religious differences.[61]

Studies indicate that there are three areas that contribute to a smooth transition to a foreign post: cultural training, language instruction, and assistance with practical, day-to-day matters.[62] The first two phases necessarily begin prior to the international assignment. Because these phases take time, the notification of posting should be done well in advance of the departure. Business conditions, however, cannot always be planned so precisely. Recognizing this, HR specialists must nevertheless encourage line managers to plan for their global needs. The last category, practical assistance, begins once the employee arrives in the host country.

Training Customers

Organizations can use their training and development activities to notify customers. For example,

> *. . . designing, manufacturing, and operating increasingly complex high-technology systems demands advanced knowledge and hands-on expertise. That's why Siemens—one of the world's leading manufacturers of high-technology equipment—conducts a variety of training programs for many of its 27,000 employees, as well as for its customers, all across America.*
>
> *Siemens USA courses are designed to meet the special needs of customers and their markets. For example, on-the-job training for customers ensures that all the capabilities of the company's technologically advanced systems are fully utilized, and all their benefits are fully realized. Similarly, the special classes for Siemens engineering, manufacturing, service, and administrative*

personnel are designed to sharpen skills, enhance professional knowledge, and improve service expertise and effectiveness.

Constant, specialized training is one of the ways Siemens is fulfilling their commitment to keep customers and employees ahead of the competition in a fiercely changing, tough, and complex high-technology marketplace.[63]

Training in Business Ethics

Although becoming increasingly important due to legal considerations, training in business ethics has been low on the priority list of much of U.S. business; witness the results of a recent survey of more than 1,000 members of the American Management Association:

Seventy-three percent of managers surveyed said they probably would resign if their boss insisted that they carry out some action they strongly believed was unethical. This percentage is a decrease from the almost 80 percent of managers who responded the same way in 1981.

Most of the recent participants agreed that corporate codes of ethics and ethics workshops were helpful to understand issues and help guide them through their daily decision making. However, more than three-quarters of these managers noted that their companies did not offer such workshops. Almost half said that their firms did not have a written code of ethics.[64]

As more companies such as WMX Technologies recognize the need for promoting moral excellence, however, they are beginning to provide training in ethical behavior. For example, Chemical Bank has included ethics discussions in its training programs. According to Karen Alphin, employee communications director, Chase Bank's "Decision Making and Corporate Values" program addresses issues that are of interest not just to bankers, but also to ethical individuals. Convinced of the need for "a conversation about ethics," Polaroid Corporation set up a major internal conference that brought philosophers, ethicists, and business professors to the company for lectures and discussions of ethical concepts.[65]

Big Six public accounting firm, Arthur Andersen, also runs several programs on ethical behavior for its employees.[66]

Training in Diversity Management

As indicated in Chapter 5, workforce diversity encompasses race, gender, religion, age, disability, language differences, and cultural differences. HR and line managers are already dealing with these differences through a variety of diversity management programs (a few of which are referred to in Chapter 5). But there are also many other differences in people that are elements of workforce diversity. For example, people differ on their problem-solving and decision-making styles; conflict resolution modes; preferences for different types of leadership; preferences for different degrees of empowerment and participation; and comfort with different types of job design. Knowing how to deal with these differences takes knowledge and a company position of adaptability.

Consequently, organizations are developing and delivering diversity programs.[67] By analyzing its needs for diversity training, the firm can match the content of its diversity program with the particular type of diversity that needs addressing. This approach also makes it easier to measure and monitor progress.

Managing the Change Process

Diversity management, downsizing, and mergers and alliances represent important changes for most organizations, and their success depends on knowledgeable management. As Linda Ackerman, president of Linda S. Ackerman, Inc., in Oakland, California, says:

> *Managing change is "one of the cutting-edge areas" for HR managers today. Most employees are traumatized by complex change, and managers have a responsibility to guide the change process and minimize its effects on employees.*[68]

The change process occurs more smoothly when employees communicate their needs and participate in the process and when top management supports the process and is willing to modify the corporate culture as needed. But top management needs to know how to do this. The more extensive the change—the more people and more parts of the organization significantly changing—the more likely it is that top management needs to know a great deal.

Did You KNOW?

By developing its people through continual learning, J. P. Morgan has transformed itself from a traditional bank into a multiproduct, multimarket, financial services institution.

Executive Education. Top management in many companies are constantly learning about organizational change and how to make change. Organizations such as Xerox, Weyerhaeuser, Northern Telecom, and General Foods implement programs of major change through management and executive education programs. Here the top management teams identify what needs to be done to be more competitive. As introduced in Chapter 5, executive education was critical to the Weyerhaeuser Company as it restructured itself in order to survive the precipitous downturn in the forest products industry in the early 1980s.[69] Action was not only fast, it had a major impact on how the entire company was structured.[70]

Within FPC, chief executive Charles Bingham, and his executive team, along with the director of strategic education, Horace Parker, decided that a major strategic repositioning was going to be made using executive development.[71]

As a result, FPC established extensive executive development program and its own leadership institute.[72] As envisioned, the Leadership Institute has become a place where managers come to discuss the new strategy and its implications for them. The institute has expanded to offer training to managers in needed skills, knowledge, and leadership styles. Success clearly has been due in large measure to the quality of the HR management activities and to the skilled leadership of those at the company.[73]

Company Schools

Company schools focus on the education of employees and sometimes customers. McDonald's Hamburger University, which was begun in 1961, is among the oldest corporate universities. Started in a basement, the center now trains more than 2,500 students annually in the fine details of restaurant and franchise operations. General Electric, which has been an advocate of training and development for years, has an up-to-date facility in Croton-on-Hudson, New York, that it uses for divisional and group training. Corporate schools have also been developed by such diverse firms as AT&T, Ford Motor Company, United Airlines, Chase Manhattan, Kodak, and Digital Equipment.

What sets us apart is that we train people to be merchants. We let them see all the numbers so they know exactly how they're doing within the store and within the company; they know their cost, their markup, their overhead, and their profit. It's a big responsibility and a big opportunity.

Sam Walton
past chairman
Wal-Mart

Motorola dedicated its $10-million Galvin Center for Continuing Education in 1986. The facility contains 88,000 square feet of classrooms, individual instruction centers, an auditorium, lounges, dining facilities, and a fitness center. Affiliated with the National Technological Union, a consortium that teaches by satellite, Motorola offers courses leading to three master's degrees.

More recently, Motorola opened Motorola University, where it spends millions a year to teach total quality management to its own employees and to faculty from business and engineering schools.[74] Like a growing number of corporations, Motorola is committed to company-based education. Motorola is even pushing its training methods in public schools to prepare the next generation of employees.[75]

Many firms are now affiliated with the National Technological Institute of Fort Collins, Colorado, which provides training for engineers via satellite transmission.

Professionals from leading universities, such as Georgia Tech, Boston University, and MIT, teach classes at 24 cooperating colleges of engineering. The companies involved provide courses both live and on tape to suit the convenience of the students. Students interact with instructors via teleconferencing and electronic mail.

In summing up the future in corporate education, some business educators speculate that advanced and specialized training will be a way of life for the foreseeable future. While some company schools will concentrate on the operational mechanics of the business they operate, others will provide more general management education, even global education. Almost without exception, the charges for training will be paid for by the home organization of the trainees, making corporate education a business within a business.

Legal Considerations

Legal considerations are relevant to several aspects of training and development. One aspect is the determination of the training and development needs of an applicant for a job. Legally, an applicant cannot be eliminated from the selection pool just because he or she lacks a skill that can be learned in eight hours. It is thus important to determine what skills an individual needs to perform a job, what skills an applicant possesses, what training programs can remove the deficiencies, and what amount of time is necessary to complete these programs.

Discriminatory Training Practices

Legal considerations increasingly impact the ways in which companies go about providing training and development opportunities for current employees. Bans on discrimination extend to on-the-job training and one-day introductions to new jobs or equipment as well as to affirmative action and formal apprenticeship/training programs. Admission to formal training programs, however, can be limited to those under a certain age, as long as those passed over for the program are not women and minorities who have previously been denied training opportunities. Specific discriminatory training practices can often be determined by the responses to the following questions:

- Are minorities and/or women given the same training opportunities as white men? Be careful! Advertising and recruiting practices come into play here.
- Are requirements for entry into a training program (that is, tests, education, or experience) job-related, or are they arbitrary?
- Are nearly all machine functions or other specialized duties that require training performed by white or male workers?
- Does one class of trainees tend to get more challenging assignments or other special training opportunities?
- Do supervisors know what constitutes training? It could be almost any learning experience, from how to fit a drill bit to a two-week seminar on complex sales procedures.
- Who evaluates the results of instruction or training—only white men?
- Are all trainees given equal facilities for instruction? Are they segregated in any way?
- Do a disproportionate number of women and/or minorities fail to pass training courses? If so, find out whether it is because they are more often unqualified or because they receive inferior instruction.

There are several important questions to ask in offering training and development to employees.

Defenses Against Charges of Discrimination

Organizations can provide a reasonable defense by showing that their training programs were conceived and administered without bias. This, however, is exceedingly difficult to demonstrate unless companies have the foresight to document their training practices. Thus they should follow these guidelines:

- Register affirmative action training and apprenticeship programs with the Department of Labor. This must be done in writing. Include the goals, timetables, and criteria for selection and evaluation of trainees. Such a record will help prove job-relatedness and that there was no intent to discriminate. It can also be valuable in proving that an organization's program was not used as a pretext to discriminate.
- Keep a record of all employees who wish to enroll in your training program. Detail how each trainee was selected. Keep application forms, tests, questionnaires, records of preliminary interviews, and anything else that bears on an employee's selection or rejection for at least two years or as long as training continues.
- Document all management decisions and actions that relate to the administration of training policies.
- Monitor each trainee's progress. Provide progress evaluations, and make sure counseling is available.
- Continue to evaluate the results even after completion of training.

Did You KNOW?

It was the perceived lack of training of a sales clerk that convinced jurors to make K-mart pay $12.5 million to Deborah Kitchen, a victim of a gun bought from K-mart by a drunk customer.

Another avenue toward ensuring that training and development programs are nondiscriminatory is through federal and state government programs. Through careful use of these programs, organizations can sometimes also defray training costs and receive already trained employees. Some programs enable current employees to obtain training. Currently, support from the federal government is funneled through block grants to states and through the Office of Federal Contract Compliance Programs under provisions in the *Job Training Partnership Act* of 1982. Under this act, grants are provided to states that in turn use the money to train economically disadvantaged youths and adults as well as workers whose jobs have been eliminated.[76]

The Role of the Supervisor

Because both individual supervisors (and all managers and executives) and their employers can be sued for violations of fair and equal employment laws, training is strongly recommended as prevention. According to Lucille E. Brown, a partner at the law firm of Schatz & Schatz, Ribicoff & Kotkin:

Line managers need to be aware of the legal considerations in training.

> *The best protection against liability for personnel-related actions is better training for managers and supervisors as to the consequences of their actions. Many employers promote people to supervisory levels based on their expertise and their performance as individual contributors to the company, not on their managerial abilities. Employers need to train these employees in the "science of people management," in Brown's words. "This is absolutely necessary both for the employer and for the supervisor's self-development." Employers should encourage and train supervisors and managers to:*
>
> - ***Document personnel issues*** *such as performance and conduct at the time the performance or conduct becomes a problem.*
> - ***Assess objectively*** *employee performance and conduct.*
> - ***Review carefully*** *communications concerning or directed to employees.*[77]

International Comparisons

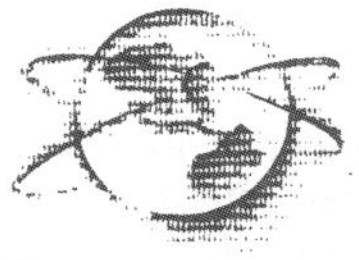

In contrast to companies in the United States, Japanese companies appear to offer far more extensive training for their employees. This also appears to be the case in Germany, particularly regarding apprenticeship training.

Japan. According to studies of vocational training in Japan as many as 80 percent of all business enterprises conduct in-company job training. Broken down according to employee classification, job training is made available to new regular employees in 75 percent of all companies, and to nonregular employees in 52 percent of them.[78]

If classified according to the size of the firm, training increases with organizational size. Every firm with more than 5,000 employees provides its own training. Vocational training in small- to medium-sized companies depends to a greater extent on cooperative centers established through the effort of the government's employment promotion agency, aided by state, municipal, and town agencies.

The in-company form of training is looked upon as the key to each company's productivity and managerial control. Regular employees generally have academic training but few, if any, vocational skills. Training is thus the means by which an employee is shaped to the company's needs. It is not unusual for new employees to have anywhere from one to six months of training before being integrated into the workforce. Supplemental training usually continues throughout the first three years of an employee's career, with additional training provided as needed.

Did You KNOW?

For Honda and other Japanese automakers in the United States, constant training has been a major tactic in their battle against the U.S. car companies.

Descriptions of training programs generally reveal a greater emphasis on the company as a whole—its role in society (including the community, the nation, and the world), its relationship to the competition, its marketing goals and objectives. In short, training constantly seeks to develop the individual worker as a fully rounded worker who not only sees the whole picture, but is also able to respond to it. The payoffs of this philosophy are minimal levels of turnover and absenteeism.[79]

Actual job training teaches workers to apply skills to a variety of situations, thereby permitting worker rotation. All blue-collar workers are expected to be multiskilled within four or five years after joining the company. Many believe that this orientation toward skills enrichment and labor mobility is a crucial factor in the rapid growth of the Japanese economy.

The Japanese also differ substantially in the way they train today's college graduate to become tomorrow's manager. The two major aspects of this training are pre-employment education, or socialization and training given before the first day on the job, and initial managerial education. This training has the following general aims:

- To educate new graduates regarding discipline and the transition from student to company life
- To teach professionalism and the significance and meaning of work
- To provide background information about the company and to familiarize employees with distinctive management trends, rules, and etiquette
- To cultivate a spirit of harmony and teamwork among employees[80]

Pre-employment education consists of communication between the company and the future employees who are still in school. Future employees are frequently sent a directory of all new recruits, an employee handbook, a booklet on health and nutrition, and even words of encouragement from senior employees. Many companies provide an opportunity for future employees to get to know one another by holding meetings that

> *. . .afford an opportunity . . . to learn the company song, to meet senior employees who are graduates of the same university, to visit the factories and*

see exhibitions of the company's products, and to become familiar with the company's various departments and divisions.[81]

Initial managerial education involves starting from the ground up. For example, the current president of Matsushita Electronic Works spent his first six months carrying and shifting goods in the company's storage area. During orientation and the work experience program, new employees live together in company residences. Here they learn social rules, etiquette, human relations, and punctuality—all considered necessary for an effective manager.

An important aspect of this training and development is the evaluation of how well the new employees have done. Mitsubishi, for example, administers a quiz, which the recruits must pass, on the knowledge essential for handling the companies products.

Germany. Germany's economy is based on providing high-priced, high-quality goods. German executives say a key factor in their industrial success is a sophisticated workforce. You need highly qualified people when you produce high-quality goods," says Hans-Peter Kassai, chief economist with Daimler-Benz.[82]

A relatively unique feature of training and development employees in Germany is an extensive and successful apprenticeship system. The three-and-a-half-year apprenticeship program gives employees wide expertise on many machines. The program costs about $5,000 per apprentice, and each year German companies spend about $20 billion on their programs. Apprenticeship training for almost a half million German students begins at age 15 when compulsory schooling ends. At that point, youths select one of several programs. By comparison, in the United States, many machine operators receive just a week or two of training.[83]

Even though apprenticeship programs are costly, German firms believe it pays off because workers end up being more loyal and more willing to stay. Once the companies take on apprentices as permanent employees, they often stay for years, giving a stability and maturity to the workforce that many countries lack. However, demographic shifts are impacting the future supply of skilled workers. In 1993, for the first time, the number of students entering university in Germany exceeded those entering apprentice programs. As a consequence, a number of apprentice slots went unfilled.

Summary

The training and development of employees is becoming an increasingly important and necessary activity of HR management. Rapidly changing technologies make employees obsolete more quickly today than ever before. As employee training and development becomes more important, it must also be more effective. This requires careful attention to the three phases of training and development: assessment or needs analysis, program development and implementation, and evaluation. The three types of needs analysis discussed in this chapter are a careful and systematic diagnosis of the short- and long-range HR needs of the organization; a determination of the skills and abilities necessary for specific jobs in the organization; and an analysis of the current and expected performance levels of employees in the organization compared with the performance levels desired of them. The difference between actual and desired employee performance defines a training and development need.

Effective training and development depends on a sound needs analysis and on careful selection and implementation of training programs. There is no one best way to train employees, since program effectiveness depends in part on the skills to be learned and the level at which they need to be learned. However, several learning principles can make any program better. Those qualities include providing feedback, reinforcement, follow-up, practice, goals, sufficient employee motivation, and consideration for individual differences. Making sure that these are a part of the program can help ensure changes in employee behavior.

The final question then remaining is who should be trained. In general, anyone with an important performance discrepancy should be trained. A program is then chosen that matches skills needed with the type of employee or group to be trained.

The last major phase of training and development is the evaluation phase. This phase compares data to see whether a change has occurred and to determine whether the change is due to the training and development program. This is described in detail in Chapter 20.

Key Concepts

apprenticeship training
assessment center method
assistantships
basic literacy skills (BLS)
basic technical skills (BTS)
behavioral modeling
business games
conceptual integrative skills (CIS)
contract plan
follow-up
formal course method
in-basket exercise
interactive video training (IVT)
internships
interpersonal skills (IPS)
job instruction training (JIT)
job needs analysis
job rotation
management games
mentoring
on-the-job training programs (OJT)
orientation programs
organizational needs analysis
person needs analysis
programmed instruction (PI)
reinforcement
role-playing
self-efficacy
sensitivity training
shaping
simulation
statistical process control (SPC)
supervisory assistance
telecommunications training
training and development
vestibule method
videodisks
videotaped presentations

Review and Discussion Questions

1. Describe and explain the three major phases of any training and development program.
2. How do companies decide whether to invest in training? What factors would influence a company not to invest in training?
3. Reflect for a moment on your own work experience. What benefits did your former (or present) employer receive by training you? Why didn't your employer just hire someone who could perform the job without training?
4. What legal considerations influence training and development decisions? How can training and development programs avoid potential legal problems?
5. What relationship does training and development have with other activities of HR management?
6. What are some design principles that can enhance the learning that takes place in training and development programs?
7. Discuss the strategic involvement of training and development.
8. You have been asked to train employees to use personal computers. What factors would you consider in designing the program?

9. How can training programs in diversity management help organizations?

10. Describe the executive education program and the Leadership Institute at Weyerhaeuser.

PROJECTS, EXERCISES & CASES

End-of-Text Projects

Lincoln Electric

1. Describe the following for Lincoln Electric:
   a. The socialization, training, and development objectives
   b. The degree to which these objectives are serving the business objectives of Lincoln
   c. The socialization, training, and development programs and activities
   d. The degree to which each of these serves the business objectives of Lincoln
2. How can the socialization, training, and development programs and activities at Lincoln be improved?

Nordstrom

1. Describe the following for Nordstrom:
   a. The socialization, training, and development objectives
   b. The degree to which these objectives are serving the business objectives of Nordstrom
   c. The socialization, training, and development programs and activities
   d. The degree to which each of these serves the business objectives of Nordstrom
2. How can the socialization, training, and development programs and activities at Nordstrom be improved?

Field Projects

1. Visit a local business and ask the store manager to describe what training (if any) is offered to new and current employees. Ask who does the training and what the benefits are. Learn about their thoughts on their future needs for training. Report to the class and compare results.
2. Compare the training programs of two companies in same industry. Learn how their training changes the companies' productivity. Compare the effectiveness of their on-job training. Which one of these two companies put more emphasis on on-job training?

Career Management Exercise:
So What Are Your Training Needs and Desires?

One of the trends in companies today is to empower workers, to give them the opportunity and responsibility to guide their own progress and career development. Beginning in Chapter 6, you have been doing many of these activities. In this exercise, you will identify key training programs that could aid your career development.

As an exercise in HR management (your own!), indicate what types of training programs you would like to have over your first five years of work. Whether you expect to change jobs and companies may have a big impact on how you answer this. Refer to Exhibit 11.9 and select those programs from those in on-the-job, on-site but not on-the-job, and off-the-job categories that you think would be most interesting and useful to you.

On-the-Job:

___

On-Site but Not On-the-Job:

___

Off-the-Job:

___

VISIT THE LIBRARY

Workforce Online

Because you are now familiar with getting onto the Internet and the use of HR Headquarters, the following steps are abbreviated.

1. Enter your Web browser.
2. Enter HR Headquarters.
3. Review the following articles within "Winning Ideas":

   How Federal Express Makes Your Package Its Most Important.

   Las Vegas Resort Bets on Training—and Wins.

   Whirlpool Managers Become Global Architects.

   How Gillette Grooms Global Talent.
4. Return to your homepage.

Case: A Training Misdiagnosis or a Mistake

Sue Campbell, the training rep for the regional office of a large service organization, is excited about a new training program. The HR department at the headquarters office had informed her six months ago that it had purchased a speed-reading training program from a reputable firm and that statistics showed that the program had indeed proven to be very effective in other companies.

Sue knew that most individuals in the regional office were faced, on a daily basis, with a sizable amount of incoming correspondence, including internal memoranda, announcements of new and revised policies and procedures, reports of federal legislation, and letters from customers. So, a course in speed reading should certainly help most employees.

The headquarters office had flown regional training reps in for a special session on how to conduct the training, and Sue therefore began the program in her regional office with great confidence. She led five groups (30 employees each) through the program, which consisted of nine two-hour sessions. Sessions were conducted in the on-site training facilities. Altogether, 1,200 employees in the organization participated in the training, at an approximate cost to the company of $110 per participant (including training materials and time away from work). The program was well received by the participants, and speed tests administered before and after training showed that, on average, reading speed increased 250 percent with no loss in comprehension.

A couple of months after the last session, Sue informally asked a couple of employees who went through the training whether speed reading was easing their work load. They said they were not using it at work but did use it in their off-the-job reading. Sue checked with several other participants and heard the same story. Although they were using speed-reading techniques at home and for school courses, they were not using it on the job. When Sue asked them about all the reading material that crossed their desks daily, the typical response was, never read those memos and policy announcements anyway!" Sue is concerned about this information but didn't know what to do with it.

Case Questions

1. Did Sue really waste valuable training funds?
2. Should Sue now start a program to get the employees to read the memos and policy announcements?
3. How could Sue have avoided the situation she now faces?
4. Should organizations provide training programs to improve skills that will not be used on the job?

Case: A Broader View Seizes More Opportunities

Don English, corporate vice president in charge of human resources, is now finally able to take a pause from the stream of "fire fighting" he has been engaged in since he came to Bancroft ten years ago! Like many of his colleagues in other firms, Don's knowledge of HR management came as much from doing it as from formal education.

Because of his workload, Don tended to keep pretty narrowly focused, and he rarely read personnel journals or attended professional conferences. However, recently, things have been easing up. He has been able to recruit and train almost all the division managers in charge of human resources. Now they can do most of the fire fighting, at least that's what Don is planning on. And he has been doing more reading than ever before. Of course, Don has not been totally out of touch with the rest of the world or the growing importance of HR management planning. When he started filling the slots for division personnel managers, he made sure that it was a learning experience for him. Don always required job candidates to prepare a one-hour talk on the state of research and practice in different areas of personnel, for example, selection, appraisal, compensation, or training. He would even invite MBA candidates who had no course work in personnel and ask them to relate their field of interest to HR management.

Don is planning to become the chief executive officer of Bancroft or some other firm of similar or larger size within the next five to seven years. He thinks he can achieve this if he remains in human resources and does an outstanding job. He will have to be outstanding by all standards, both internal and external to the firm. From his interviews during the past three years, Don knows that it is imperative to move human resources in a strategic direction while at the same time doing the best possible job with the "nuts and bolts" activities.

During a moment of reflection, Don begins to scribble some notes on his large white desk pad. In the middle is Bancroft. To its left are its suppliers and to its right are its customers. In his head are all the HR practices he is so familiar with. He has a hunch that there must be a way to use the firm's expertise in performance appraisal and training to help Bancroft be more effective. Bancroft has been learning tremendously from its five-year drive to improve quality, but during the past year, quality gains have slowed. Bancroft must continue to improve its quality, but large internal quality gains are becoming more and more difficult as Bancroft climbs the learning curve. Don wonders, "How can he help Bancroft experience the excitement of seeing large gains in quality improvement again?" Don circles the list of suppliers and begins to formulate a plan that will improve his chances of becoming CEO. He now seeks your advice in exactly what to do and how to go about doing it.

(Yes, this is our case from Chapter 2. There we discussed whether Don really had a place in helping his company gain competitive advantage.)

Case Questions

1. Let's assume that Don has gotten the approval from his boss to help Bancroft's suppliers. Should he work with them all or decide to just start with one or two and see how it goes?
2. If Don can do anything to help his suppliers with their HR management activities, what should he focus on?
3. Should Don actually go into the suppliers and do their HR work, or should he train the suppliers' HR professionals at Bancroft?

Chapter 11 Endnotes

1. K. Labich, "Is Herb Kelleher America's Best CEO?" *Fortune* (May 2, 1994): 50.

2. "Ritz-Carlton Certifies Ladies and Gentlemen," *HR Reporter* (Aug. 1993): 1–4. Reprinted from *HR Reporter* with the permission of the publisher, Buroff Publications, 1350 Connecticut Ave., N.W., Suite 1000, Washington, D.C. 20036.

3. R. Henkoff, "Companies That Train Best," *Fortune* (March 22, 1993): 62–75; R. Henkoff, "Inside Andersen's Army of Advice," *Fortune* (October 4, 1993): 78–86.

4. I. L. Goldstein, "Training in Work Organizations," *Annual Review in Psychology* 31 (1980): 229–272; O. P. Latham, "Human Resource Training and Development," *Annual Review of Psychology* 39 (1988).

5. P. Sellers, "Pepsi Opens A Second Front," *Fortune* (August 8, 1994): 70–76.

6. "Special Survey Report: Human Resources Outlook," *Bulletin to Management* (January 4, 1996): 1; "Skill Deficiencies Pose Increasing Problems," *Bulletin to Management* (October 26, 1995): 337.

7. See note 3.

8. G. Flynn, "McDonald's Serves Up HR Excellence," *Personnel Journal* (January 1996): 54–55.

9. D. Anfuso, "Self-directed Skills Building Drives Quality," *Personnel Journal* (April 1994): 84–93.

10. K. Murray, "Listening to the Other America," *New York Times* (April 25, 1993): F25. Used by permission.

11. L. L. Goldstein, *Training: Program Development and Evaluation,* 2nd ed. (Monterey, CA: Brooks/Cole, 1986).

12. J. W. Walker, "Training and Development," *Human Resource Management in the 1980s,* R. Schuler and S. Carroll, eds. (Washington, D.C.: Bureau of National Affairs, 1983); Goldstein, "Training in Work Organizations"; Wexley and Latham, *Developing and Training.*

13. R. S. Schuler, "Strategic Human Resource Management," *Organizational Dynamics* (Summer 1992): 18–32.

14. For more detail on using HR management in service organizations, see V. Johnston and H. Moore, "Pride Drives Wal-Mart to Service Excellence," *HR Magazine* (Oct. 1991): 79–80, 82; J. E. Santora, "Pacific Bell Primes the Quality Pump," *Personnel Journal* (Oct. 1991): 63–66; D. E. Bowen, R. B. Chase, and T. G. Cummings & Associates, *Service*

Management Effectiveness (San Francisco: Jossey-Bass, 1990).

15. J. W. Walker, "Training and Development," *Human Resource Management in the 1980s,* R. Schuler and S. Carroll, eds. (Washington, D.C.: Bureau of National Affairs, 1983); Goldstein (op. cit., see Note 10); Wexley and Latham, *Developing and Training.*

16. M. Messmer, "Steer Clear of the Skills Gap," *Personnel Journal* (March 1996): 44–49; L. A. Berger, "A DEW Line for Training and Development: The Needs Analysis Survey," *Personnel Administrator* (Nov. 1976): 51–55.

17. R. B. McAfee and P. J. Champagne, "Employee Development: Discovering Who Needs What," *Personnel Administrator* (Feb. 1988): 92–93.

18. Latham, "Human Resource Training and Development."

19. E. L. Bernick, R. Kindley, and K. Petit, "The Structure of Training Courses and the Effects of Hierarchy," *Public Personnel Journal* 13 (1984): 109–119.

20. W. Hardman and J. Heidelberg, "Under Fire at the LAPD," *Personnel Journal* (April 1996): 98–103; C. Berryman-Fink, "Male and Female Managers' View of the Communication Skills and Training Needs of Women in Management," *Public Personnel Management* 14 (1985): 307–314; Latham, (op. cit., see Note 14); F. D. Tucker, "A Study of Training Needs of Older Workers: Implications for Human Resources Development Planning," *Public Personnel Management* 14 (1985): 85–95.

21. M. E. Gist, A. G. Bavetta, and C. K. Stevens, "Transfer Training Method: Its Influence on Skill Generalization, Skill Repetition, and Performance Level," *Personnel Psychology* 43 (1990): 501–523; N. Schmitt, J. R. Schneider, and S. A. Cohen, "Factors Affecting Validity of a Regionally Administered Assessment Center," *Personnel Psychology* 43 (1990): 1–12.

22. J. Main, "The Executive Yearn to Learn," *Fortune* (May 3, 1982): 234–248; M. M. Starcevich and J. A. Sykes, "Internal Advanced Management Programs for Executive Development," *Personnel Administrator* (June 1982): 27–28.

23. "Education Partnerships Create On-Site Universities," *Bulletin to Management* (October 26, 1995): 337.

24. M. Kaeter, "Basic Self-Esteem," *Training* (Aug. 1993): 31–35; M. E. Gist, C. Schwoerer, and B. Rosen, "Effects of Alternative Training Methods on Self-Efficacy and Performance in Computer Software Training," *Journal of Applied Psychology* 74, no. 6 (1989): 884–891.

25. D. Anfuso, "Las Vegas Resort Bets on Training—and Wins," *Personnel Journal* (September 1995): 78–86.

26. C. H. Deutsch, "Vocational Schools in a Comeback," *New York Times* (July 21, 1991): F21; "Training Bosses," Time (June 7, 1982): 61.

27. K. H. Cowdery, "Training Inner-City Youth to Work," *Personnel Journal* (Oct. 1991): 45–48; C. Marmer Solomon, "New Partners in Business," *Personnel Journal* (April 1991): 57–67.

28. R. Henkoff, "Finding, Training & Keeping the Best Service Workers," *Fortune* (October 3, 1994): 110–122.

29. S. N. Phillips, "Team Training Puts Fizz in Coke Plant's Future," *Personnel Journal* (January 1996): 87–92.

30. "Telephone Etiquette," *Bulletin to Management* (June 11, 1992): 179. Reprinted with permission by the Bureau of National Affairs, (Tel. 1-800-372-1033).

31. B. M. Bass and J. A. Vaughan, *Training in Industry: The Management of Learning* (Belmont, CA: Wadsworth, 1966): 88.

32. "1994 Industry Report," *Training* (October 1994): 49.

33. P. Popovich and J. Wanous, "The Realistic Job Preview as a Persuasive Communication," *Academy of Management Review* 7 (1982): 570–578; M. R. Louis, "Managing Career Transitions: A Missing Link in Career Development," *Organizational Dynamics* (Spring 1982): 68–78.

34. *Bulletin to Management* (May 9, 1985): 1, 2.

35. L. A. Ferman, M. Hoyman, J. Cutcher-Gershenfeld, and E. J. Enfeld, *Worker Training: A Legacy for the 1990s* Madison, WI: Industrial Relations Research Association, 1990); A. P. Carnevale, L. J. Gainer, and A. S. Meltzer, *Workplace Basics Training Manual* (San Francisco: Jossey-Bass, 1990); T. T. Baldwin, R. J. Magiuka, and B. T. Loher, "The Perils of Participation: Effects of Choice of Training on Trainee Motivation and Learning," *Personnel Psychology* 44 (1991): 51–65; A. P. Carnevale, L. J. Gainer, and E. Schulz, *Training the Technical Work Force* (San Francisco: Jossey-Bass, 1990); see also Goldstein, note 10.

36. "Planning the Training Program," *Personnel Management,* BNA Policy and Practice Series, no. 41 (Washington, D.C.: Bureau of National Affairs, 1975): 205; see also Bass and Vaughan (op. cit., see Note 25): 89–90; and J. M. Geddes, "Germany Profits by Apprentice System," *The Wall Street Journal* (Sept. 15, 1981): 33.

37. S. Overman, "Apprenticeships Smooth School to Work Transitions," *HR Magazine* (Dec. 1990): 40–43; K. Matthes, "Apprenticeships Can Support the 'Forgotten Youth,'" HR Focus (Dec. 1991): 19; "Focus at Ford Is Education for the Sake of Education," *GED on TV* (July-Aug. 1993): 3; E. Kiester, "Germany Prepares Kids for Good Jobs; We Are Preparing Ours for Wendy's," *Smithsonian* (March 1993): 44–55.

38. M. W. McCall, Jr., M. M. Lombardo, and A. M. Morrison, *The Lessons of Experience: How Successful Executives Develop on the* Job (Lexington, MA: Lexington Books, 1989).

39. R. F. Morrison and Adams, eds., *Contemporary Career Development Issues* (Hillsdale, NJ: Eribaum, 1991); A. Saltzman, Down-Shifting: *Reinventing Success—on a Slower Track* (New York: Harper Collins, 1991); S. L. Willis and S. S. Dubin, eds., *Maintaining Professional Competence: Approaches to Career Enhancement, Vitality and Success Throughout a Work Life* (San Francisco: Jossey-Bass, 1990);

J. A. Scimeer and F. Reitman, "Effects of Employment Gaps on the Careers of M.B.A.'s: More Damaging for Men than for Women?" *Academy of Management Journal* 33, no. 2 (1990): 391–406.

40. G. S. Odiorne and G. A. Rummler, *Training and Development: A Guide for Professionals* (Chicago: Commerce Clearing House, 1988).

41. G. C. Thornton III and J. N. Cleveland, "Developing Managerial Talent through Simulation," *American Psychologist* (Feb. 1990): 190–199; G. Waddell, "Simulations: Balancing the Pros and Cons," *Training and Development Journal* (Jan. 1982): 75–80.

42. For an excellent discussion of assessment centers, see G. C. Thornton III, *Assessment Centers* (Reading, MA: Addison-Wesley, 1992).

43. D. Gunsch, "Games Augment Diversity Training," *Personnel Journal* (June 1993): 78–83.

44. J. P. Campbell, M.D. Dunnette, E. E. Lawler III, and K. E. Weick, Jr., *Managerial Behavior, Performance, and Effectiveness* (New York: McGraw-Hill, 1970); B. Mezoff, "Human Relations Training: The Tailored Approach," *Personnel* (March-April 1981): 21–27.

45. "Downward Bound," *Fortune* (Aug. 15, 1988): 83; H. Campbell, "Adventures in Teamland," *Personnel Journal* (May 1996): 56–62.

46. V. L. Huber, "A Comparison of Goal Setting and Pay as Learning Incentives," *Psychological Reports* 56, (1985): 223–235; V. L. Huber, "Interplay between Goal Setting and Promises of Pay-for-Performance on Individual and Group Performance: An Operant Interpretation," *Journal of Organizational Behavior Management* 7, no. 3/4 (1986): 45–64.

47. Latham (op. cit., see Note 15); C. A. Frayne, *Reducing Employee Absenteeism Through Self-Management Training: A Research-Based Analysis and Guide* (Westport, CT: Quorum Books, 1991).

48. S. J. Ashford and A. S. Tsui, "Self-Regulation for Managerial Effectiveness: The Role of Active Feedback Seeking," *Academy of Management Journal* 34, no. 2 (1991): 251–280; S. I. Tannenbaum, J. E. Mathieu, E. Salas, and J. A. Cannon-Bowers, "Meeting Trainees' Expectations: The Influence of Training Fulfillment on the Development of Commitment, Self-Efficacy and Motivation," *Journal of Applied Psychology* 76, no. 6 (1991): 759–769; M. E. Gist, "The Influence of Training Method on Self-Efficacy and Idea Generation among Managers," *Personnel Psychology* 42 (1989): 787–805.

49. Huber, "Interplay between Goal Setting and Promises of Pay-for-Performance."

50. V. L. Huber, G. P. Latham, and E. A. Locke, "The Management of Impressions through Goal Setting," *Impression Management in the Organization,* R. A. Giacalone and P. Rosenfield, eds. (Hillsdale, NJ: Erlhaun, 1989).

51. P. Hogan, M. Hakel, and P. Decker, "Effects of Trainee-Generated vs. Trainer-Provided Rule Codes on Generalization in Behavioral Modeling Training," *Journal of Applied Psychology* 71(1986): 469–473.

52. W. Honig, *Operant Behavior* (New York: Appleton-Century-Crofts, 1966); Huber, "Interplay between Goal Setting and Promises of Pay-for-Performance;" J. S. Russel, K. Wexley, and J. Hunter, "Questioning the Effectiveness of Behavior Modeling Training in an Industrial Setting," *Personnel Psychology* 34 (1984): 465–482.

53. "A Comparison of Goal Setting and Pay"; V. L. Huber, E. Locke, and G. Latham, *Goal Setting: A Motivational Technique that Works,* (Englewood Cliffs, NJ: Prentice-Hall, 1984).

54. C. Frayne and G. Latham, "The Application of Social Learning Theory to Employee Self-Management of Attendance," *Journal of Applied Psychology* 72 (1987): 387–392; Latham, "Human Resource Training and Development."

55. J. Fierman, "Shaking the Blue-Collar Blues," *Fortune* (April 22, 1991): 209–210, 214, 216, 218; S. R. Siegel, "Improving the Effectiveness of Management Development Programs," *Personnel Journal* (Oct. 1981): 770–773.

56. "Training at Waste Management," *HR Reporter* (April 1991): 1–3. Reprinted from *HR Reporter* with the permission of the publisher, Buroff Publications, 1350 Connecticut Ave., N.W., Washington, D.C. 20036.

57. J. W. Walker, "Managing Human Resources in Flat, Lean and Flexible Organizations: Trends for the 1990s," *Human Resource Planning* 11, no. 2 (1988), 124–132.

58. J. J. Laabs, "How Gillette Grooms Global Talent," *Personnel Journal* (August 1993): 70. Used by permission.

59. K. Labich, "The Innovators," *Fortune* (June 6, 1988) 50–64.

60. A. Rahim, "A Model for Developing Key Expatriate Executives," *Personnel Journal* (April 1983): 315.

61. M. Mendenhall and G. Oddou, "Acculturation Profiles of Expatriate Managers: Implications for Cross-Cultural Training Programs," *Columbia Journal of World Business,* (Winter 1986): 73–79.

62. J. S. Black and M. Mendenhall, "Cross-Cultural Training Effectiveness: A Review and a Theoretical Framework for Future Research," *Academy of Management Review,* vol. 15, no. 1 (1990): 113–136.

63. Used by permission of Siemens, Siemens, USA, New Brunswick, New Jersey.

64. B. Z. Posner and W. H. Schmidt, "Values of American Managers: Then and Now," *HR Focus* (March 1992): 13.

65. "Ethics Exams: Focus for Too Few?" *Bulletin to Management* (Feb. 19, 1987): 64; R. W. Goodard, "Are You an Ethical Manager?" *Personnel Journal* (March 1988): 38–47; "Policy Guide," *Bulletin to Management* (Dec. 18, 1986): 420; "Values and Ethics," *HR Reporter* (March 1987): 3.

66. Arthur Andersen has an extensive set of training materials including written cases, lectures, role plays and video tapes that they use in their ethics training.

67. S. Caudron, "Training Can Damage Diversity Efforts," *Personnel Journal* (April 1993): 51–60; H. B. Karp and N. Sutton, "Where Diversity Training Goes Wrong," *Training* (July 1993): 30–34.

68. *Bulletin to Management* (July 14, 1988): 3.

69. J. Bolt, *Executive Development* (New York: Harper & Row, 1989); A. A. Vicere and K. R. Graham, "Crafting Competitiveness: Toward a New Paradigm for Executive Development," *Human Resource Planning* 13, no. 4 (1990): 281–296; J. K. Berry, "Linking Management Development to Business Strategies," *Training and Development Journal* (Aug. 1990): 20–22.

70. Ibid.

71. Ibid.

72. Ibid.

73. Author's personal conversations with Bill Maki, director of human resources at Weyerhaeuser, Feb. 1994.

74. "B–School Faculty Quality Training," *Fortune* (Jan. 13, 1992): 14. Also see W. Wiggenhorn, "Motorola U: When Training Becomes an Education," *Harvard Business Review* (July-Aug. 1990): 71–83.

75. K. Kelly and P. Burrows, "Motorola: Training for the Millenium," *Business Week,* (March 28, 1994): 158–162.

76. The Job Training Partnership Act," *Bulletin to Management* (April 23, 1992): 124–125.

77. "Personal Supervisory Liability," *Fair Employment Practice Guidelines* (May 25, 1993): 5–6.

78. P. J. Dowling and R. S. Schuler, *International Dimensions of Human Resource Management* (Boston, MA: PWS-Kent, 1990). See also J. S. Black and M. Mendenhall, "Cross-Cultural Training Effectiveness: A Review and a Theoretical Framework for Future Research," *Academy of Management Review* 15, no. 1 (1990): 113–136.

79. "How Japan Inc. Profits from Low Wage Turnover," *Business Week* (December 7, 1987): 24; used by permission of *Business Week,* copyright 1987.

80. M. McComas, "Cutting Costs Without Killing the Business," *Fortune* (October 13, 1986): 76.

81. S. E. Prokesch, "Bean Meshes Man, Machine," *New York Times* (December 23, 1985): 19, 21.

82. *Bulletin to Management* (July 14, 1988): 3.

83. S. Greenhouse, "An Unstoppable Export Machine," *New York Times* (October 6, 1988): D7.

CHAPTER 12

Performance Appraisal: Gathering the Information

Learning Objectives

1. Describe the processes and procedures in performance appraisal.
2. Identify the many approaches and forms that companies use in gathering appraisal information.
3. Describe the advantages and disadvantages of using different raters.
4. Describe the biases in appraisal and how they can be reduced.
5. Describe the current trends in performance appraisal.
6. Describe the legal considerations in performance appraisal.

> *"The company views each employee's performance strategically as a means to help Chaparral gain competitive advantage."*
>
> *Gordon E. Forward*
> *President,*
> *Chaparral Steel Company*[1]

Chapter Outline

MANAGING HUMAN RESOURCES

at the Chrysler Corporation

In the early 1980s, the Chrysler Corporation was about at the end of its rope, but through the coordinated efforts of Lee Iaccoca, his management team, the employees, the United Automobile Workers (UAW) union, and a little help from the federal government, Chrysler staged a rather dramatic turnaround. Today, worldwide sales of $55 billion make it the world's 11th largest manufacturing organization. Chrysler is again able to call itself one of the big three U.S. automakers. As with any successful turnaround, the workforce had to be dedicated to survival and committed to improvement. It has helped a great deal that employees at Chrysler feel that they are part of the team. Here's where performance appraisal comes in! In late 1988, Chrysler began a reverse-appraisal process. It formed a steering committee in which top management and union (UAW) leadership were represented. This was done to ensure that both parties (management and nonmanagement) were involved from the beginning—it wasn't to be seen as a "program imposed by management."

Because this program was new, Chrysler decided to initially develop and test the program in two units of the Vehicle Engineering Division. In this way, the program could be worked out, perfected, and then used in other areas. To ensure that this process of change was as objective as possible (and run as effectively as possible), Debra Dubow, management development specialist in another Chrysler division, was brought in to manage the program, which included developing the new appraisal instrument (remember, this was intended to be used by employees to appraise the performance of their bosses, not the other way around). Involved in this process was the gathering of data that would determine what criteria should be used; later on would come training in how to use the new appraisals. Here's how it got started:

> *Dubow first pulled together a cross-section of employees from the two pilot groups, ranging from vice presidents and union management to first-time supervisors and mechanics. Through this sample of approximately 50 persons, she was able to gather valuable input from different levels of managers and employees, as well as recognize and head off resistance to the new project that might be encountered along the way.*[2]

The decision resulting from these discussions was that Chrysler would develop its own performance appraisal form, not buy an existing one from another organization. The criteria that Dubow and her team initially decided to consider using were those already being used on the employees in the traditional boss-subordinate appraisal process. The final appraisal form developed by the Chrysler team (after many rounds of discussions and revisions!) included many criteria with which the employees were already familiar. The team simply reconfigured the criteria to fit appraising the boss. Examples included:

- Teamwork: "My supervisor promotes cooperation and teamwork within our work group."
- Communication: "My supervisor learns current business information and communicates it to our work group."
- Quality: "My supervisor demonstrates meaningful commitment to our quality efforts."
- Leadership: "My supervisor demonstrates consistency through both words and actions."
- Planning: "My supervisor provides reasonable schedules so that my commitments can be met."
- Development of the workforce: "My supervisor delegates responsibilities and gives me the authority to carry out my job."[3]

It was determined that each of these would be evaluated on a 1 to 5 scale ("almost never" to "almost always").

By the summer of 1989, two pilot groups from top management volunteered to be the first to have their employees appraise their performance.

Continued

Managers were provided with individual reports; they then met with their employees to discuss the results and develop an action plan for improvement. This entire process focused on behaviors that managers could change. Once the top management went through this first round, the process cascaded down, reflecting the philosophy "do as I do," rather than "do as I say." At each level, the action plans for improvement became the measure of accountability: next time around, the managers were asked to discuss how well they had done on their plans with their employees.[4]

This feature illustrates several aspects of performance appraisal. One is that performance appraisal is important enough for all employees in the organization to be involved, from top management to the union workers in production plants. Second, creating a new performance appraisal form and process take time; it needs to be done systematically and with the involvement of all parties. Third, implementing reverse appraisals sends a strong signal to all employees: you have the right to also appraise the boss, the person who traditionally appraises your performance. This opens the process up, making appraisal more egalitarian (a we're-all-in-this-together attitude). And finally, revising an appraisal system takes time, especially in a large organization with a long history of doing things one way. Not only does change take time, but so does its impact. In this chapter, however, we will look at what types of impacts might be expected to occur.

Performance Appraisal

Performance appraisal is a formal, structured way of measuring, evaluating, and influencing an employee.

A performance appraisal system involves the performance appraisal and the entire setting in which the appraisal takes place.

Although employees may learn about how well they are performing through informal means such as favorable comments from co-workers or superiors, **performance appraisal** is defined here as a formal, structured system of measuring, evaluating, and influencing an employee's job-related attributes, behaviors, and outcomes, as well as level of absenteeism, to discover how productive the employee is and whether he or she can perform as or more effectively in the future, so that the employee and the organization and society all benefit.[5]

To account for all the factors that affect this formal, structured system of measuring and evaluating performance, the term **performance appraisal system (PAS)** is used.[6] In essence, the PAS requires the organization to:

- Identify the needs of the business and the implications for managing human resources
- Conduct a job analysis to identify job duties and responsibilities for which criteria need to be developed
- Choose an appropriate and valid performance appraisal method to assess job behaviors or outcomes
- Develop a process for conveying job expectations to employees prior to the appraisal period
- Establish a feedback system relating to job performance
- Evaluate how well the PAS is doing in relation to its stated objectives and make necessary revisions

Factors affecting how well the system works include the characteristics of the organization, characteristics of the rater, the pool of employees being rated, and the individual employee. Because of the importance of this process, we devote two chapters to this topic. This chapter focuses on the gathering of performance information; Chapter 13 focuses on using appraisal information to help employees improve their performance.

Why Employee Performance and Performance Appraisal Are Important

Productivity improvement concerns almost all companies, especially during periods when the environment is highly competitive and the rates of productivity increases are relatively small. The productivity of most organizations is a function of three areas—technology, capital, and human resources. Many organizations have focused on the first two and have consequently overlooked the third one, human resources. Perhaps this reflects managers' greater level of comfort with managing technology and capital. It also reflects a lack of systematic thinking and development of skills to manage human resources.

Did You KNOW?

The best performing employees can produce up to three times as much as the worst performing employees.

Productivity and Competitiveness

Employee performance, (what an employee does or does not do) influences an organization's productivity and its competitiveness. Fortunately, what employees do can be measured and evaluated, particularly their job performance and absenteeism. Job performance describes how well an employee performs his or her job, while absenteeism refers to whether the employee is there to do the work. Performance can be measured by an employee's job-related: 1) *output* (for example, the number of shelves stocked by the shelf stockers at the Grand Union grocery stores, or the number of welding machines assembled by Lincoln Electric workers); 2) *behaviors* (for example, meetings with the workers that the supervisors at Chrysler or Grand Union organize; or pilots working together cooperatively in teams); and 3) *attitudes* (for example, the willingness on the part of the workers at GE to be flexible and adaptable; or the friendliness and high energy level of the flight attendants at Southwest Airlines).

The impact that job performance and absenteeism can have on productivity and the competitive strategy of an organization is now widely recognized. Major quality improvement and quality of work life programs at many large corporations, such as Chrysler, General Electric, Weyerhaeuser, Motorola, and Xerox, have aimed at increasing productivity and achieving improved quality through reducing absenteeism and improving employee performance.[7]

Dysfunctional Activities

Organizations have recently started to focus on how employees impact the operation, image, and profitability of the organization in dysfunctional ways. These behaviors include employee theft, alcohol and drug use, and unethical conduct. Concern over these behaviors is generated by estimates that workplace theft and pilferage of goods cost U.S. businesses more than $40 billion a year, workplace theft of time (employees leaving early, for example) costs employers $170 billion a year, and alcohol and drug use costs employers $99 billion and $67 billion per year, respectively.[8] Although these behaviors have not typically been part of performance appraisal, they certainly can significantly impact productivity and an organization's competitiveness. Consequently, organizations are now including these behaviors in the performance appraisal process.

Upon opening the assembly line 80 years ago, Henry Ford issued a booklet "Helpful Hints and Advice to Employees" warning against drinking, gambling, and borrowing money.

Performance Appraisal Helps Manage Employee Performance

Companies use performance appraisal to serve two major purposes: *evaluative* and *developmental*.[9] The evaluative category includes:

- **Performance measurement**, which establishes the relative value of an individual's contribution to the company and thus provides information that can be used in decisions on layoffs, terminations, and promotions
- **Compensation**, which determines appropriate pay for performance and equitable salary and bonus incentives based on merit or results
- **Motivation**, which is the end result of an effective evaluation

The developmental category includes:

- **Management development**, which identifies and prepares individuals for increased responsibilities and thus provides a framework for future employee development
- **Identification of potential**, which identifies candidates for promotion
- **Feedback**, which informs employees of the organization's standards and how their performance measures up
- **Human resource planning**, which audits management talent and evaluates the present supply of human resources for replacement planning
- **Communications**, which provides a format for dialogue between superior and subordinate and improves understanding of personal goals and concerns
- **Performance improvement**, which encourages continued successful performance and strengthens individual weaknesses to make employees more effective in serving all the organization's stockholders
- **Research on legal compliance**, which establishes the validity of employment decisions made on the basis of performance-based information and provides a defense for management actions such as selection, demotion, or termination

Managers are solely responsible for evaluating their employees. No specific, company-side evaluation forms are used for salespeople and managers. Rather, each manager designs his or her own evaluation system.

Mary Kim Stuart
HR Manager
Nordstrom's

Because of the importance of employee performance and performance appraisal, we typically find an extensive partnership in performance appraisal. As indicated in the feature, "Partnership: Working Together in Performance Appraisal," line managers and other employees are often the ones actually doing the appraisal using procedures and processes developed and administered with and by the HR professionals.

LEARNING OBJECTIVE 1

Describe the processes and procedures in performance appraisal.

Performance Appraisal as a System of Processes and Procedures

In establishing a performance appraisal system, decisions regarding the criteria to measure, the period for the appraisal, and the choice of rater should be made very early in the development of the system.

Identifying Criteria

Criteria are targets constituting job performance.

A valid PAS grows out of an analysis of the needs of the business and a job analysis that has identified important job duties and tasks. Performance criteria can then be developed. **Criteria** are evaluative dimensions against which the employee is measured. They are also performance expectations the employee strives to attain. If, for example, a bank decides that the criterion against which it will evaluate the corporate loan assistant's position described in Chapter 8 (see Exhibit 8.3) is a specific level of customer satisfaction resulting from loan transactions, then the corporate loan assistant should see this specific level as a numerical goal and concentrate on meeting this criterion.[10] At Chrysler, the criteria established for managers included teamwork, communication, and quality. These are all central to meeting the needs of the businesses.

PARTNERSHIP:

WORKING TOGETHER IN PERFORMANCE APPRAISAL

LINE MANAGERS

Work with HR professionals and employees to develop business-relevant criteria for appraisals.

Develop an understanding of how common appraisal errors can be avoided.

Fill out appraisal forms carefully and conscientiously.

Give constructive and honest feedback to the employees.

Seek and accept constructive feedback about own performance.

Use performance information for decision-making.

HR PROFESSIONALS

Work with line managers and employees to develop the criteria for appraisals.

Coordinate the administrative aspects of the appraisal process.

Train everyone who provides appraisal information (e.g., peers, subordinates, supervisors) how to avoid errors in appraisal.

Train line managers to give feedback.

Support line managers in their efforts to keep the performance management system going.

See and accept constructive feedback about own performance.

EMPLOYEES

Work with line managers and HR professionals to develop criteria for appraisals.

May appraise the work of other employees.

May appraise their own performance.

May appraise the performance of the boss.

See and accept constructive and honest feedback.

Strive to improve own performance.

Outcomes and Organizational Effectiveness. Depending on the organization's strategy and its ability to measure performance, criteria that relate to individual or group job behavior or outcomes, or overall organizational effectiveness (for example, profitability, having high quality, and meeting customer service goals) can be developed. Consider the corporate loan assistant's job. Behavioral criteria for this job may include such things as "prepares follow-up documentation in a timely manner." By comparison, outcome criteria refer to the product or output produced (such as "helps generate $5 million in loans each month"). Organizational effectiveness involves an inferential leap. It entails aggregating individual and group outcomes in order to determine how well the organization is functioning. For example, an organizational effectiveness criterion for a vice president of fixed assets might relate to total profitability of the bank for a specific quarter.

A four-step hospitality checklist gives Red Lion Hotel employees a way to remember their company's customer-service goals:

1. **Greet the guest.**
2. **Show the guest that you care.**
3. **Show the guest that you can help (by going out of your way to accommodate the guest's needs).**
4. **Appreciate the guest's business.**

Single or Multiple Criteria. If coordinating market activities is the only job duty, then only the criteria that relate to this single duty are needed. More often, however, jobs are multidimensional, composed of numerous duties and related tasks. For the corporate loan assistant's job described in Chapter 8, the duty, "helps customers with bank problems," is accompanied by other duties such as "develops required loan documentation" or "builds rapport with customers." If job analysis identifies all of these duties as important, all should be measured by a performance appraisal instrument.

If the form or approach used to appraise employee performance lacks the job behaviors and the important and relevant results, the form is said to be **deficient**. If the form includes appraisal of anything unimportant or irrelevant to the job, it is **contaminated**. Many performance appraisal forms actually used in organizations measure some attributes and behaviors of employees unrelated to the employee's job. These forms are contaminated and are in many cases also deficient.[11]

Deficient means the form fails to measure all behaviors or results. Contamination implies the inclusion of non-job-related criteria and standards.

Weighting of Criteria. For jobs involving more than one duty, there is another decision to be made. How should these separate aspects of performance be combined into a composite score or criterion that will facilitate comparisons between employees? One way is to weight each criterion equally, but the most accurate approach is to weight the criteria differently based on the results of a job analysis. Criteria can also be weighted relative to their ability to predict overall performance. Estimates made by HR managers, line managers, and employees can be used to determine appropriate weights for each job dimension.

Performance standards tell how well the employee hits the targets.

In addition to determining the performance criteria and deciding how they are to be weighted, **performance standards** must be identified. These standards measure how well employees are performing. With the use standards, performance criteria take on a range of values. For example, selling 100 units per month may be defined as excellent performance, and selling 80 units may be defined as average. Organizations often use historical records of how well employees have done in the past (to determine what is actually possible) to establish standards. Time and motion studies and work samples can also be used. Whereas these methods are often used for blue-collar and other nonmanagerial jobs, different methods are used for managers. Many organizations evaluate their managers by how well goals are attained. Increasingly, managers are also evaluated by standards of profitability, revenues, costs, increases in customer satisfaction, and even national measures of excellence such as the Baldrige Award for Quality.

The Baldrige Award is the major prize in America for TQM Achievement. The Baldrige winners consistently communicate both good and bad news and make sure that employees find out things before the public does.

Matching the Purpose to the Period

In addition to identifying appropriate criteria, consideration should be given to the period for which performance is to be assessed. On average, most organizations require formal performance review sessions at six-month to one-year intervals. For some jobs, this may be an appropriate interval. For other jobs, performance should be evaluated more frequently. For example, a carpet layer's performance might need to be evaluated at the end of each one- or two-day job rather than annually. At least, the customers may prefer it this way because better installation would probably result.

The evaluation period can also vary depending on the purpose of the appraisal. For communication and clarity, the focus should be on current employee performance during a single performance period. For promotion and training decisions, an examination of performance across multiple appraisal periods may be more useful. If performance is steadily increasing or is consistently high, a promotion or some form of recognition may be justified. If, however, performance remains consistently low, then performance improvement programs may be necessary.

LEARNING OBJECTIVE 2

Describe the advantages and disadvantages of using different raters.

Choice of Raters

While many different sources can be used to gather performance data, the relevance of these sources needs to be considered prior to the choice of rating method. Appraisal sources include supervisors, peers, subordinates, self-appraisal, customers, and computer monitoring.

Appraisal by Superiors. The superior is the immediate boss of the subordinate being evaluated. The assumption is that the superior knows the subordinate's job and performance better than anyone else. But appraisal by the superior has drawbacks. First, since the superior may have reward and punishment power, the subordinate may feel threatened. Second, evaluation is often a one-way process that makes the subordinate feel defensive. Thus, little coaching takes place; justification of action prevails. Third, the superior may not have the necessary interpersonal skills to give good feedback. Fourth, the superior may have an ethical bias against "playing God." Finally, the superior, by giving punishments, may alienate the subordinate.

Nonetheless, as a manager you need to conduct successful performance appraisals. Review and study the insert, "HR Advice and Application," to see the qualities of successful and unsuccessful performance appraisals. These are the responses of employees to the question: What is an example of a good/bad performance appraisal you had with your supervisor?

HR ADVICE & APPLICATION

Successful Performance Appraisals

- We were both prepared.
- Employer backed up all negative and positive feedback with examples. . . made me feel she really understood and thought about my work.
- The feedback was supported by narratives and a review of goals and objectives.
- It gave me developmental feedback that I learned from.
- It provided freedom of debate without retribution.
- It provided real, honest, open communication and sharing of experiences and expectations.
- My supervisor was open to clarifying statements that were ambiguous. We had a very honest exchange and I had a clear understanding.
- The process gave me an opportunity to highlight contributions, an opportunity to make suggestions.

Unsuccessful Performance Appraisals

- Unprepared and preoccupied employer gave me only praise.
- My supervisor did not take my worksheet input seriously.
- There was no elaboration on expectations and no real details about my accomplishments.
- Criticism was personal and not objective.
- Supervisor showed fear and lack of comfort with giving me feedback.
- General feedback did not seem unique to me and was therefore not meaningful.
- One supervisor told me, "I'll let you know when you are not doing a good job," and that was the entire appraisal.

Self-Appraisal. The use of self-appraisal, particularly through subordinate participation in setting goals, was made popular as an important component in management by objectives. Subordinates who participate in the evaluation process may become more involved and committed to the goals. Subordinate participation can also clarify employees' roles and reduce the uncertainty about what to do. This happened at IBAX, when Jerry Goodman changed the strategy of the company and empowered the workers to assume more responsibility for their performance. IBAX employees then become engaged in what Goodman called "covenant defining." As he explains it, "when one has a job to do, they should build a covenant with the person to whom they report. This covenant should define their responsibilities and how they will be measured and evaluated in light of those responsibilities. This covenant becomes a binding agreement between the parties involved as to their commitment to one another." The performance standards that resulted from this process of covenant defining provided the measures by which employees were evaluated and rewarded.[12]

It is very likely that you will appraise your own job performance.

Did You KNOW?

L. L. Bean sold his first pair of hunting boots in 1912. Ninety of his first 1000 pairs fell apart and were returned!

Self-appraisals are also effective tools for programs focusing on self-development, personal growth, and goal commitment. However, self-appraisals are subject to systematic biases and distortions when used for evaluations. There is evidence that self-ratings are more lenient or higher than those obtained from supervisors. Self-ratings will correspond more closely to supervisory ratings when extensive performance feedback is given and when employees know that their performance ratings will be checked against objective criteria.[13]

According to Roger Flax, president of Motivational Systems, a New Jersey management and sales training company, self-appraisals are particularly useful in small companies:

> *There's a lot of assuming that in small companies employees are motivated, so there's not a lot of formal appraisal. One answer may be the employee-*

> *initiated appraisal in which employees are told they can ask for a review from their manager. The on-demand appraisal doesn't replace a conventional semi-annual review, but it promotes an attitude of self-management among workers and often makes critiques more honest.*[14]

Flax suggests employees ask for as many reviews as they feel they need. Listed below are seven questions he believes employees should ask themselves and their managers in their self-initiated appraisals.

- On a scale of 1 to 10, how does my performance rate?
- What are the strongest elements of my work?
- What are the weakest elements?
- Why didn't I get a 10 (highest rating)?
- Where can I go in my job or career in the next eighteen months to four years?
- What skills, training, or education do I need to get to that point?
- What specifically can we agree on that I can do beginning tomorrow?

Team performance and appraisal are important in organizations pursuing total quality management and in serving their customers with fast and friendly service.

Team-Member Appraisal. Team member involvement in the appraisal process can take many different forms.[15] Jamestown Advanced Products, Inc., a small metal fabrication firm, recently had to deal with the issue of employee tardiness. According to team members' assessment of the problem, one person's late arrival disrupted everyone else's schedule, reduced team performance, and consequently lowered financial bonuses. Traditionally, a tardy employee lost some wages but could still receive a quarterly performance bonus. Team members thought this wasn't fair. The work team was encouraged to set performance standards for themselves and to identify consequences for low performance. After the team batted around the issue of how much lateness or absenteeism employees could tolerate and how punitive they should be, the team reached agreement. Employees could be tardy—defined as one minute late—or absent without notice no more than five times a quarter. Beyond that, they would lose their entire bonus.

In addition to defining performance expectations, Jamestown team members commonly serve as evaluators; the co-worker who is at an individual's side all day has an excellent opportunity to observe that individual's behavior. Common performance dimensions on which team members have evaluation expertise include:

1. Attendance and timeliness: attends scheduled group meetings.
2. Interpersonal skills: willing to give and take on issues; not unreasonably stubborn.
3. Group supportiveness: offers ideas/suggestions for the group to use on the project, supports group decisions.
4. Planning and coordination: contributes input to assist other team members in performing their assignments.[16]

Productivity is the output of the team. Cohesiveness is the extent of working and thinking like a team. Motivation is the level of effort and energy of the team.

Firms such as Jamestown have learned that team members can also provide useful information for evaluating how well the team as a whole is functioning. Exhibit 12.1 contains questions that firms can use to assess overall team **productivity**, **cohesiveness**, and **motivation** (drive).

Using this instrument, comparisons between groups can be made to determine the relative degree of productivity, cohesiveness, and drive. Comparisons can also be made within groups by examining group ratings at specific intervals to determine which ones perform effectively and which ones are dysfunctional.

EXHIBIT 12.1

Representative Appraisal Questions to Measure Team or Work Group Cohesiveness, Drive, and Productivity

COHESIVENESS

1. People in this work group pitch in to help one another.
2. People in the work group don't get along with one another. (R)
3. People in this work group take an interest in one another.
4. There is a lot of team spirit among members of my work group.
5. The members of my work group regard each other as friends.
6. The members of my group are very cooperative with one another.
7. My group's members know that they can depend on each other.
8. Group members stand up for one another.
9. Members of my group work together as a team.

DRIVE

10. My group tackles a job with enthusiasm.
11. The group I work with has quit trying. (R)
12. The group is full of vim and vigor.
13. The work of my group seems to drag. (R)
14. My group works hard on any job it undertakes.
15. The group shows a lot of pep and enthusiasm.

PRODUCTIVITY

16. My group turns out more work than most groups in the company.
17. My group turns out as much work as our supervisor expects.
18. My group has an excellent production record.
19. My group gets a job done on time.
20. This work group has an excellent production record.

Items are scored on a 1–7 scale with "1" being strongly disagree and "7" being strongly agree. Items ranked with an (R) should be reverse-scored.

Source: Based on R. M Stogdill; *Group Productivity, Drive and Cohesiveness.* (Columbus, Ohio: Bureau of Business Research. 1965).

Did You KNOW?

Cohesiveness, drive, and productivity are team qualities managers need to influence in a very positive way.

Upward or Reverse Appraisals. While some organizations such as Johnson & Johnson and Sears have been surveying employees for their opinions of management for years, upward appraisals have recently become a new tool among companies seriously focusing on the new environment. Major firms, including Chrysler, AT&T, GE, and DuPont, use subordinates' ratings of how their bosses manage to improve operations to make their organizations less hierarchical, and to develop better managers.[17] While subordinates often do not have access to information about all dimensions of supervisory performance, they do have access to information about supervisor-subordinate interactions. When asked, subordinates usually complain that they do not get enough feedback. They want a pat on the back for doing well and honest criticism—even when it "hurts"—when they haven't performed well. Employees also complain that their supervisors pay only

Did You KNOW?

The upward appraisal process at Chrysler is now used in many of the Fortune 500 companies.

lip service to their input—that suggestions are not taken seriously and are seldom acted upon. Subordinates want their supervisor to go to bat for them more particularly when it comes to salary, promotion, or assignments. A fourth common complaint is that their supervisors don't delegate and give them enough responsibility.

One drawback is that subordinates may not always evaluate performance objectively or honestly. This is particularly likely if subordinates feel threatened (for example, "If I give my boss a low rating, she will reciprocate and give me a low rating, too"). To protect anonymity, evaluations need to be made by at least three or four subordinates and turned in to someone other than the supervisor being evaluated. Alternatively, the evaluations can be scored by a computer, as at Chrysler.

Did You KNOW?

In a survey of executives of the nation's 1,000 largest companies, 60% said employees should be allowed to participate in a formal review of the boss.

Appraisal by Customers. Another source of appraisal information comes from customers or clients of the employee. For example, a medical clinic in Billings, Montana, routinely has patients rate desk attendants and nursing personnel on such features as courtesy, promptness, and quality of care. Domino's Pizza hires mystery customers who order pizzas and then evaluate the performance of the telephone operator and the pizza delivery person.

Computer Monitoring. A more recent event in performance appraisal is the gathering of performance data by computers. Advances in computer technology make it possible for employers to continuously collect and analyze information about work performance and equipment. More and more managers are using this type of data to plan workloads, reduce costs, and find new ways to organize work.[18] Although this method may be fast and seemingly objective, it has raised a number of critical issues in the management and use of human resources. One of the most critical is the employees' right to privacy. Nevertheless, according to the U.S. Office of Technology Assessment:

> *Computer-generated statistics form the basis for the work evaluations of up to 6 million office workers, mostly in clerical occupations or jobs whose duties are largely repetitive. Similarly, some employers are using "service observations"—the practice of listening in on telephone conversations between employees and customers—to ensure that customers receive correct and courteous service.*[19]

Computer monitoring raises several ethical issues.

How would your performance be affected if you knew your boss was monitoring your performance with a computer? Many employees have become concerned enough with it to raise several legal and ethical questions. These include, "Do we have a right to privacy?" and "Is it ethical to monitor employee whereabouts constantly?"[20]

LEARNING OBJECTIVE 3

Identify the many approaches and forms that companies use in gathering appraisal information.

Norm-referenced appraisals evaluate the performance of one employee against that of another. Behavioral appraisals evaluate the performance of an employee against fixed standards. Output-based appraisals evaluate the performance of an employee against numerical output measures.

Approaches to Performance Appraisal

At the outset of this discussion, it should be emphasized that rating forms are not to be equated with appraisal forms. Forms are, however, one very important part of the system. The development of a rating form comes only after systematic job analysis, the identification of criteria and appropriate raters, and decisions about the timing of appraisals. While direct output measures of performance are available for some jobs, by far the most widely-used performance measurement systems are judgmental. The simplest classification of performance appraisal approaches include **norm-referenced**, **behavioral**, and **output-based**. These approaches can be supplemented by narrative essays.

Norm-Referenced Appraisals

For many types of HR decisions, the fundamental question is often, "who is the best performer in the group, or who should be retained, given we have to cut our workforce," or "who should be assigned a specific task?" For these types of decisions, norm-referenced performance formats are appropriate. They result in a listing of employees, starting with the best.

Approaches to performance appraisal are

- **norm-referenced**
- **behavioral**
- **output-based**

Rankings. In **straight ranking**, the superior lists the employees in order from best to worst, usually on the basis of overall performance. Employees can also be ranked by their performance of specific duties. Rankings such as this are appropriate only in small organizations. As the number of employees increases, it becomes difficult to discern differences in their performance—particularly in average performance. Alternative ranking can help. The first step in **alternative ranking** is to put the best subordinate at the head of the list and the worst subordinate at the bottom. The superior then selects the best and worst from the remaining subordinates; the best is placed second on the list, the worst next to last. The superior continues to choose the best and worst until all subordinates are ranked. The middle position on the list is the last to be filled.

Rankings compare each person against the other people.

Paired Comparisons. The **paired-comparison method** involves comparing each employee to every other employee, two at a time, on a single standard to determine who is "better." A rank order is obtained by counting the number of times each individual is selected as being the better of a pair. An advantage of this approach over straight ranking is that it overcomes the problem of an "evaluation set." That is, it forces the rater to consider the performance of each employee to all other employees, one at a time.

Paired comparisons and forced distributions also compare people against each other.

There are several potential problems with paired comparisons. If the number to be ranked is large, the number of comparisons may be unmanageable. [There are $N(N-1)/2$ total comparisons where N is the number of individuals. Thus, for 25 incumbents, there are 300 comparisons if only overall performance is evaluated.] Multiple comparisons may also present another problem. It occurs if employee A is rated better than B, B is rated better than C, but C is rated better than A.

A problem with the ranking and paired comparisons methods is that each person is assigned a unique rank. This suggests that no two subordinates perform exactly alike. Although this may be technically true, many supervisors have observed that some employees perform so similarly that individual differences cannot be discerned.

Forced-Distribution Method. The fourth method, forced distribution, was designed to overcome this complaint and to incorporate several factors or dimensions (rather than a single factor) into the rankings of subordinates. The term **forced distribution** is used because the superior must assign only a certain proportion of subordinates to each of several categories on each factor. A common forced-distribution scale is divided into five categories. A fixed percentage of all subordinates in the group fall within each of these categories. Typically, the distribution follows a normal distribution such as the following:

NUMBER OF EMPLOYEES	LOWEST 10%	NEXT 20%	MIDDLE 40%	NEXT 20%	HIGHEST 10%
50	5	10	20	10	5

A problem with this method is that a group of subordinates may not conform to the fixed percentage. A majority of them may appear to be all good or a majority may appear to be all bad. In these cases, the manager may want to proactively try to change the appraisal process. In many cases, however, the performance of employees can be differentiated, but it requires that the manager do a better job in the appraisal process.

Concerns with Norm-Referenced Appraisals. All three comparative methods assume that good and bad performers are in all groups. You may know from experience, however, of situations in which all the people in a group perform identically. If you encountered such a situation, how would you evaluate these people?[21] Regardless of the appraisal method, they are all based on the assumption that performance is best captured or measured by one criterion: overall performance. Since this single criterion is a global measure and is not anchored in any objective index, such as units sold, the results can be influenced by rater bias or favoritism. As a consequence, the rankings lack behavioral specificity and may be subject to legal challenge.[22]

Another critical problem facing the rater is that no information regarding the absolute level of performance is available. All levels of performance are relative—one employee to the other, thus, managers do not know whether the best performer in a group is actually outstanding, average, or poor, or whether two individuals with adjacent ranks are quite similar or quite different. Using such information for promotion decisions may also be inappropriate since an average performance could be ranked high in a low-performing group but low in comparison to high performers.

Behavioral Appraisals

With norm-referenced appraisals, the supervisor is forced to evaluate each employee relative to other employees. In contrast, behavioral appraisals allow supervisors to evaluate each person's performance independent of other employees but relative to behavioral criteria.

Graphic Rating Scales. The **graphic rating scale** (form) is the most widely-used performance evaluation (see Exhibit 12.2). Graphic rating forms vary in the number of performance dimensions they measure. Many rating forms use indicators of output such as quantity and quality of performance. The term performance is used advisedly here because many of these forms use what some call personality attributes or traits rather than job-related attributes. Care should be taken in defining actual behaviors since some of them may be vulnerable to legal challenges, including terms such as aggressiveness, maturity, and reliability. Use of all attributes should be related to the job and the needs of the business.

Graphic forms are used extensively because they are relatively easy to develop, permit quantitative results that allow comparisons across ratees and departments, and include several dimensions or criteria of performance. But because the rater has complete control in the use of the forms, they are subject to several types of error, including leniency, strictness, central tendency, and halo bias. Nevertheless, they have been shown to be as reliable and valid as more complicated forms, such as forced-distribution forms.[23] Clearly, graphic forms should be developed with an understanding of the business needs and the specific jobs for which the appraisal form is being designed.

In addition to their potential for errors, graphic forms are criticized because they cannot be used for developmental purposes. For example, they fail to tell a subordinate how to improve and are not useful for the subordinate's career development needs. Consequently, organizations often modify the form and add space for short essays so that the appraisal results can be used for developmental as well as evaluative purposes. Exhibit 12.3 shows an example of how one company modified the graphic form in Exhibit 12.2. Even when essays supplement the graphic rating form, the results are still subject to errors.

Consequently, comparisons of ratees within a department or across departments in a company are difficult. Furthermore, the essay form provides only qualitative data. Thus, these appraisals are not easily used in making zero-sum decisions (for example, salary increases, promotions, and layoffs). This also applies to several other qualitative forms of appraisal, including critical incidents, behavioral checklists, and forced-choice forms.

Critical incidents are records of important job performance, good and bad.

Critical Incidents. Dissatisfaction with graphic rating scales has led to the development of other types of behavior rating scales. The most systematic of these approaches relies on **critical incidents** to replace ambiguous graphic scale

EXHIBIT 12.2

Graphic Rating Form for Employee Performance Appraisal

Date Completed

Name	Date of Birth	Date of Employment	Office Location	Department
			Branch Departmental	
Present Job Title	Conversion Code	Years in Present Position	Soc. Sec. No.	Education

	❐	❐	❐	❐	❐
QUALITY OF WORK General excellence of output with consideration to accuracy, thoroughness, dependability, without close supervision.	Exceptionally high quality. Consistently accurate, precise, quick to detect errors in own and others' work.	Work sometimes superior but usually accurate. Negligible amount needs to be redone. Work regularly meets standards.	A careful worker. A small amount of work needs to be redone. Corrections made in reasonable time. Usually meets normal standards.	Work frequently below acceptable quality. Inclined to be careless. Moderate amount of work needs to be redone. Excessive time to correct.	Work often almost worthless. Seldom meets normal standards. Excessive amount needs to be redone.
QUANTITY OF WORK Consider the amount of useful work over the period of time since the last appraisal. Compare the output of work to the standard you have set for the job.	Output consistently exceeds standard. Unusually fast worker. Exceptional amount of output.	Maintains a high rate of production. Frequently exceeds standard. More than normal effort.	Output is regular. Meets standard consistently. Works at steady average speed.	Frequently turns out less than normal amount of work. A low producer.	A consistent low producer. Excessively slow worker. Unacceptable output.
COOPERATION Consider the employee's attitude towards the work, fellow workers, and supervisors. Does the employee appreciate the need to understand and help solve problems of others?	Always congenial and cooperative. Enthusiastic and cheerfully helpful in emergencies. Well-liked by associates.	Cooperates well. Understands and complies with all rules. Usually demonstrates a good attitude. Liked by associates.	Usually courteous and cooperative. Follows orders but at times needs reminding. Gets along well with associates.	Does only what is specifically requested. Sometimes complains about following instructions. Reluctant to help others.	Unfriendly and uncooperative. Refuses to help others.
KNOWLEDGE OF THE JOB The degree to which the employee has learned and understands the various procedures of the job and their objectives.	Exceptional understanding of all phases. Demonstrates unusual desire to acquire information.	Thorough knowledge in most phases. Has interest and potential toward personal growth.	Adequate knowledge for normal performance. Will not voluntarily seek development.	Insufficient knowledge of job. Resists criticism and instruction.	No comprehension of the requirements of job.

Continued

EXHIBIT 12.2 (CONT.)

Assumptions About People At Work

	❐	❐	❐	❐	❐
DEPENDABILITY The reliability of the employee in performing assigned tasks accurately and within the allotted time.	Exceptional. Can be left on own and will establish priorities to meet deadlines.	Very reliable. Minimal supervision required to complete assignments.	Dependable in most assignments. Normal supervision required. A profitable worker.	Needs frequent follow-up. Excessive prodding necessary.	Chronic procrastinator. Control required is out of all proportions.
ATTENDANCE AND PUNCTUALITY Consider the employee's record, reliability, and ability to conduct the job within the unit's work rules.	Unusual compliance and understanding of work discipline. Routine usually exceeds normal.	Excellent. Complete conformity with rules but cheerfully volunteers time during peak loads.	Normally dependable. Rarely needs reminding of accepted rules.	Needs close supervision in this area. Inclined to backslide without strict discipline.	Unreliable. Resists normal rules. Frequently wants special privileges.
KNOWLEDGE OF COMPANY POLICY AND OBJECTIVES Acceptance, understanding, and promotion of company policies and objectives in the area of the employee's job responsibilities.	Thorough appreciation and implementation of all policies. Extraordinary ability to project objectively.	Reflects knowledge of almost all policies related to this position.	Acceptable but fairly superficial understanding of job objectives.	Limited insight into job or company goals. Mentally restricted.	Not enough information or understanding to permit minimum efficiency.

anchors. At its most basic level, the critical incident approach requires supervisors to observe and record employee behaviors that are particularly effective or ineffective in accomplishing their jobs.[24] These incidents generally provide descriptions of the ratee's behaviors and the situation in which those behaviors occurred. Then, the superior's feedback is based on specific behaviors rather than on personal characteristics or traits such as dependability, forcefulness, or loyalty. This feature of the critical incidents technique can increase the chances that the subordinate will improve, since he or she learns more specifically what is expected.

Drawbacks of the critical incidents technique are that 1) keeping records on each subordinate is time-consuming for the superior; 2) the technique is nonquantitative; 3) the incidents are not differentiated in their importance to job performance; and 4) comparing subordinates is difficult because the incidents recorded for each one can be quite different.

Behaviorally anchored rating scales focus appraisal on behaviors that can be changed.

Behaviorally Anchored Rating Scales. A major breakthrough in utilizing critical incidents to evaluate performance was the development of **behaviorally anchored rating scales**. These scales were developed to provide results that subordinates could use to improve performance. They were also designed to make feedback more comfortable.

The development of a behaviorally anchored rating scale generally corresponds to the first steps in the critical incidents method of job analysis (that is, collecting incidents describing competent, average, and incompetent behavior for each job category). These incidents are then placed in broad overall categories or dimensions of performance (for example, administrative ability, interpersonal skill). Each dimension serves as one criterion in evaluating subordinates. Using these

EXHIBIT 12.3

Modification of the Graphic Rating Form Shown in Exhibit 12.2

A. Summary of Current Performance:

1. Employee's strongest points
2. Employee's weakest points
3. What steps have been taken to modify weak points?
4. Is employee properly placed in present job? Explain.

B. Employee's Potential:

1. In what significant ways has this employee demonstrated improvement in the last twelve months?
2. Have you made any suggestions for the employee's self-development?
   Yes ❒ No ❒
   (a) If yes, (1) What was the suggestion?
   (2) How did the employee react?
   (b) If no, what was your reasoning?
3. In your opinion, is the employee limited to the work in the present job?
   Yes ❒ No ❒
4. (a) If your answer to 3 is no, what have you considered as a possibility to improve the employee's position in our company?
   (b) What has been done about it?
5. If your answer to 3 is yes, please explain.

C. Employee's Reactions:

Enter reactions or comments after you have discussed this appraisal with the employee. Are there any changes in your evaluation as a result of your interview?

Supervisor's Signature		Date
	Reviewed	
Department Head	❒	Date
Supv. Officer	❒	Date
HR Dept.	❒	Date

categories, another group of individuals lists the critical incidents pertinent to each category. Exhibit 12.4 shows an example of one such dimension or category, transacting loans, and the critical incidents listed as pertinent to it.[25] This exhibit also shows the next step: the assignment of a numerical value (weight) to each incident in relation to its contribution to the criterion.

Armed with a set of criteria with behaviorally anchored and weighted choices, the superiors rate their subordinates with a form that is relatively unambiguous in meaning, understandable, justifiable, and relatively easy to use. Yet the form has

EXHIBIT 12.4

A Behaviorally Anchored Rating Scale for One Dimension of the Corporate Loan Assistant Job

TRANSACTING LOANS

Anchor	Scale	Anchor
	10	Credit reports are always completed without error
Prepares follow-up documentation in a timely manner.	9	
	8	Provides services desired but not asked for by customer.
Customers praise the help of the assistant.	7	
	6	Assists customers with loan applications.
Develops loan documentation accurately.	5	
	4	Prepares credit reports without having to be told.
Provides information to customers even if not asked.	3	
	2	Fails to help other banks participating in loans.
Loan applicants complain about the loan interview.	1	

its limitations. Since most forms use a limited number of performance criteria, many of the critical incidents generated in the job analysis stage may not be used. Thus, the raters may not find appropriate categories to describe the behaviors—the critical incidents—of their subordinates.[26] Similarly, even if the relevant incidents are observed, they may not be worded in exactly the same way on the form; the rater may thus be unable to match the observed behaviors with the dimension and anchors.

Another concern with behaviorally anchored rating scales is that it is possible for an employee to simultaneously display behavior associated with high and low performance. For example, the corporate loan assistant (see job description in Exhibit 8.3) could prepare follow-up documentation in a timely manner and also receive complaints from loan applicants about rudeness and inappropriate questioning. In a situation such as this, it is difficult for the rater to determine whether the ratings should be high or low.

The trend is to develop forms based on what can make the company most successful.

Strategic Behaviorally Based Rating Scales. An extension of the above approach is the development of criteria that are specifically linked with the strategy of the organization. For example, it is popular for organizations to have a market-driven, customer-oriented strategy (the terms often used for service firms seeking to improve quality). Our description of the Grand Union grocery store in Chapter 11 is an example of this. For the strategy to be implemented successfully, all employees may need to change their performance. National Rental Car implemented such a strategy to serve their customers better and hopefully increase market share. A key to the success of the strategy was the development of strategic behaviorally based rating scales for the customer service representatives (CSR). Shown in Exhibit

12.5 is one dimension of this job, the task of customer service. You can see how much detail is provided; the customer service representative knows exactly what to do and what behaviors are aligned with the company's strategy.[27]

Firms realize that to get quality service from employees, service has to be a part of the appraisal and compensation process.

Mixed-Standard Scales. Mixed-standard rating scales were designed to eliminate some of the problems associated with behaviorally anchored scales. Critical incidents underscore the development of this scale. The format consists of sets of three statements that describe high, medium, and low levels of performance for a specific performance dimension. These items have been scaled using a process similar to that employed in the development of the behaviorally anchored rating scales. The three levels of performance of each dimension are arranged randomly on the rating sheet. Unlike behaviorally anchored scales, where scale values are known, no values are attached to the behavioral incidents. Instead, the rater makes one of three responses to each example.

A score on each performance dimension is calculated on the basis of the pattern of results.[28] The advantage of the mixed-standard format is that the rater is not dealing with any numbers. Consequently, some of the most common errors associated with rating are overcome. Additionally, analysis of rater response patterns can identify raters whose use of the scales is haphazard. A drawback of mixed-standard scales is that scale values are not known. Consequently, developmental information is lost. Still, once developed, mixed-standards scales are relatively easy to use.

Behavioral Observation Scales. Another development in behavioral scales is called the **behavioral observation scale**. Like the behavioral methods already discussed, these scales are derived from critical incidents of job behavior. Behavioral observation scales differ, however, in that job experts are *not* asked to what degree or level of performance they illustrate. Instead, job experts are asked to indicate the frequency with which employees engage in the behaviors. Scores are obtained for each behavior by assigning a numerical value to the frequency judgment. For example, a score of "2" may be assigned if it is almost always observed. These scores can be summed to get an overall rating. Alternatively, scale items relating to a particular performance dimension can be summed and then multiplied by an importance weight. Behavioral items are eliminated if the observed frequency is too high or too low. In either case, the item does not discriminate well between high and low performers.

Behavioral observation scales measure how frequently behaviors are observed.

Exhibit 12.6 includes examples of effective and ineffective job behaviors and the resulting behavioral observation scales. Note that the examples of ineffective performance are reverse-scored.

The advantages of this form include: 1) its basis on a systematic job analysis; 2) clearly stated items and behavioral anchors, 3) employee participation in the development of the dimensions (through the identification of critical incidents in the job analysis), which facilitates understanding and acceptance; 4) its usefulness for performance feedback and improvement, since specific goals can be tied to numerical scores (ratings) on the relevant behavioral anchor (critical incident) for a performance criterion or dimension; and 5) its ability to satisfy the *Uniform Guidelines* for validity (relevance) and reliability.

Scales with detailed behaviors tell an employee exactly how to do things.

The limitations of this form are connected with some of its advantages, especially the time and cost for its development as compared with forms such as conventional rating. Furthermore, several dimensions that are essentially behaviors and not duties may miss the real essence of many jobs, especially managerial, where the job's essence may be the actual outputs produced regardless of the behaviors used to obtain them. When these conditions exist, some argue that a better method is one that is goal oriented or that appraises performance against output measures. Additionally, it requires more observation of performance than other types of behavior scales. If the span of control is large, this may be an impossible task for the supervisor.[29]

EXHIBIT 12.5

National Rental Car's Strategic Behaviorally Based Rating Scale for CSR

Job Title: Office Representative Appraisal Dealing with Customers (CSR)
Task: Customer Service

In the space provided below, please describe your observations of the CSR you are evaluating.

Rating

[ ]	[ ]	[ ]	[ ]	[ ]
Well Below	Below	Standard	Above	Well Above

5. WELL ABOVE STANDARD: Greets customers with a smile while making eye contact, anticipates customer's problems and provides whatever is necessary to make customers become more comfortable and co-workers more effective, asks customers what they need and tells them that we are there to serve them, checks with customers to determine if the car was satisfactory and makes notes of problems with the car to give to service, makes best presentations of self—uniform is neat, clean, and tidy, explains in detail to customers rental processing procedures, quickly communicates positive feedback to co-workers and discusses concerns in private. Keeps composure even when customers are irate with the CSR and the Company, tells customers about the organization and what makes it a good place to work.
4. ABOVE STANDARD: Acknowledges customers by using a greeting when they are standing in line behind the customer being serviced, makes eye contact with greeting, recognizes changes and/or contributions of co-workers and follows up with specific compliments, checks to be certain that customers have been heard accurately by saying "Did I understand you to say that . . . ?", makes positive comments about the organization and its employees to customers, tells people over the phone what they are going to do for them before putting them on "hold," makes certain customers understand what is expected before an activity/procedure is to begin by asking the customers if they fully understand before proceeding, makes suggestions or initiates methods to improve organizational performance, encourages the work of co-workers by letting them know when they have done a good job, works to ensure cooperative, not competitive, efforts with co-workers, makes time to help train new CSRs in rental processing.
3. STANDARD: Listens to customer's needs, apologizes for car problems, and lets them know that she/he will do the best to respond to their needs, greets customers over the phone by telling them who they are talking to and asking how they may be of help, says please and thank you when interacting with customers, grooming is well-maintained, wears clean clothing, is careful with personal hygiene, meets dress code standards, gives directions by showing on the map how to get to where the customer wishes to go, explains to customer specifically what is in the rental agreement in ways the customer can understand, uses name when addressing them such as Mr., Mrs., or Ms., demonstrates respect for property and equipment by ensuring that proper care is given to equipment and appearance of public areas are clean and tidy, greets customers before customer greets them, asks customer what problems they may have had with the car, makes suggestions about ways to improve customer and service performance, tells coworkers when they have done a good job.
2. BELOW STANDARD: Does not greet others or attempt to make them feel good about our organization, does not ask how they may be of help or service to the organization, does not use customer's name when addressing them, hair is not clean nor well-groomed, does not tell others when they have done exceptional work, is not specific with customers in explaining the cost of coverages or what effect waivers have and their coverages, does not use a greeting when answering the phone, puts customers on hold without telling them that they will be on hold or why they are on hold.
1. WELL BELOW STANDARD: Does not listen to others—interrupts customers, closes the station with customers waiting, does not greet others with a smile, or make eye contact, hair and dress are not clean, uniform is soiled or does not meet the dress code, makes unfavorable comments about the organization to customers or co-workers, does not support the efforts of co-workers, does not monitor work area to ensure counter is clean and equipment is well-maintained, does not explain rental procedures to customers or call them by name, discusses customers' problems in public, puts people on "hold" on the phone without telling them what is happening or hangs up on customers, complains about the organization to improve the situation, makeup is overdone, does not make positive comments when possible, discusses co-workers problems with customers, takes credit for others' work, uses abusive language with customers, criticizes co-workers for providing excellent customer service.

Source: From R. W. Beatty, "Competitive Human Resource Advantage Through the Strategic Management of Performance," *Human Resource Planning*, 3 (1989):184–185.

Output-Based Appraisals

While the methods described above focus on job behaviors or processes, output-based appraisals focus on job products as the primary criteria. There are four variants of output-based approaches: 1) management by objectives, 2) performance standards, 3) the direct index measure, and 4) accomplishment records.

Management by objectives uses attainment of objectives to indicate level of performance.

Management By Objectives. **Management by objectives** (MBO) uses successful attainment of objectives to indicate quality of performance. Its application

EXHIBIT 12.6

Behavioral Observation Scales for Effective and Ineffective Performance for the Corporate Loan Assistant Job

EFFECTIVE PERFORMANCE

1. The corporate loan assistant prepares credit reports accurately.

Almost Never				Almost Always
1	2	3	4	5

2. The corporate loan assistant is friendly when interviewing loan applicants.

Almost Never				Almost Always
1	2	3	4	5

3. The corporate loan assistant is effective when interviewing job applicants.

Almost Never				Almost Always
1	2	3	4	5

INEFFECTIVE PERFORMANCE

1. The corporate loan assistant fails to prepare follow-up documentation.

Almost Never				Almost Always
1	2	3	4	5

2. The corporate loan assistant does not help customers with loan applications.

Almost Never				Almost Always
1	2	3	4	5

3. The corporate loan assistant needs to be told to prepare credit reports.

Almost Never				Almost Always
1	2	3	4	5

Note: On an actual form, the items would neither be grouped nor identified as effective and ineffective performance.

and acceptance results in part from its identity with commonly held personal values, especially the philosophy that rewarding people for what they accomplish is important. MBO can attain greater individual-organizational goals congruence and reduce the likelihood that employees are working in directions unrelated to the objectives and purposes of the organization (goal displacement).[30]

Management by objectives is premised on the assumption that an organization's objectives for a specific period should cascade down through the organization. Once goals are established, they are distributed to divisions or responsibility centers and eventually to individual employees. Central to this approach is the issue of **goal congruence**: an individual's goals must be in harmony with those of the department and organization.

Goal congruence is the overlap between an individual's goals and those of the company. Goals are desired objectives or targets.

In some organizations, supervisors and managers work together to establish goals; in others, supervisors establish goals for their managers. The goals can refer to a desired outcome, the means (activities) for achieving the outcome, or both. Goals can also relate to routine activities that comprise day-to-day duties, the identification and solution of problems that hamper individual and organizational effectiveness, or they can be innovative and have a special purpose. Regardless of their focus, the objectives are more effective if they include the following characteristics:

- **Specificity.** Objectives must identify how well the behavior must be performed or how high the output must be to be considered acceptable. Specificity reduces variability in performance and in ratings.
- **Timeliness.** The deadline for completion of the task or the attainment of the output level must be identified.
- **Conditions.** Any qualifications associated with attaining the objective (for example, if the production schedule is adhered to) need to be detailed since many factors beyond the control of the employee may hamper goal attainment.
- **Prioritization.** For behavior to be directed toward desired ends, employees need to understand which objectives are most important. Supervisors and employees can weight them, or weights can be derived from the job description.
- **Consequences.** The consequences for attaining or not attaining the specified level of performance must be spelled out.
- **Goal congruence.** It is important for managers performing similar jobs to assign comparable goals. Individual goals must be congruent with department goals.

Although the use of goals in evaluating managers is effective in motivating their performance, capturing all the important job dimensions in terms of output is not always possible. How the job is done, (that is, job behaviors) may be as critical as the outcomes. For example, it may be detrimental to an organization if a manager meets a personal selling goal by unethical or illegal means.

Situations of potential unethical behavior may require more frequent monitoring of the manager by the company. Also, a rigorous effort should be made from the top down to assure a satisfactory balance between long- and short-term objectives. At Alcan, the Canadian aluminum company, management compensates for the ramifications of including longer-term objectives in an individual's annual performance evaluation by limiting attainment of objectives to 50 percent of a person's annual rating. The other half depends on how the person has carried out his or her principal duties or performed overall.[31]

Companies are now recognizing that the use of goals can be a great way of improving productivity. In particular, companies such as GE, AT&T, and Procter & Gamble are using the term "stretch goals" to encourage employees to really see how much they can do.[32] Under the traditional MBO method, managers are likely to set objectives they think they can attain. Using "stretch goals," managers set goals that they might not think attainable, yet the company encourages them to go for it! An obvious downside here is that individuals may find themselves working long hours to reach those "stretch goals." These issues can be addressed, however, if they involve both the company and the individual. Here's one person's story:

> *As a rather new employee of Procter & Gamble in the Netherlands, I find myself, a middle manager, facing immense stretch goals. Indeed, I regularly say, "You've got to be kidding." But the concept works! Even though I might not reach a specific goal, I do get near it, and that is a greater achievement than I would ever have expected. Furthermore, I don't see failure punished, and I do see gain sharing when goals are attained.*
>
> *I also see colleagues working 16 hours a day. Your article implicitly blames the employer for this, but I believe it is the employee's task to find the right balance between his personal life and work. Inducing a high achiever to*

reach stretch goals is the company's goal; finding the right balance between personal life and work should be the employee's.

Herman W. Mentink
Assistant Brand Manager
Procter & Gamble, Rotterdam[33]

Performance Standards Appraisal. The **performance standards appraisal**, while similar to MBO, uses more direct measures of performance and is usually applied to nonmanagerial employees. Standards, like objectives, need to be specific, time-bound, conditional, prioritized, and congruent with organizational objectives. Compared to objectives, there are generally more standards, and each is more detailed. Generally, the format specifies average expected behavior as well as the level of performance that would be considered exceptional. Each standard is rated separately and multiplied by an importance weight. Scored in this manner, performance standards are compensatory in that high performance in one area can counteract deficiencies in other areas. When only one level of performance (which meets the standard) is specified, low performance cannot compensate for other areas, and the system is noncompensatory.

Performance standards can be used quite nicely with jobs designed by the scientific method.

The major advantage of performance standards is that they provide clear, unambiguous direction to employees regarding desired job outcomes. When exceptional performance is also specified, these scales can motivate the average as well as the exceptional employee. A recent study found that when standards were specific, extraneous factors such as the ratee's prior evaluation, the order of evaluation, and current salary level did not affect judgment. When standards were vague, these same items biased performance ratings.

The disadvantages of these work standards are that they require time, money, and cooperation to develop. As with MBO, the essence of job performance may not be captured entirely by set standards. Consequently, important job behaviors may be ignored in the evaluation process. And although set standards may provide clear direction to the employees and the goals may be motivating, they can also induce undesirable competition among employees. If this competition does not lead to undesirable consequences and if the employees want to participate in the standard- and goal-setting processes, this method can be highly motivating.[34]

Direct Index Appraisal. The direct index approach differs from the other approaches primarily in how performance is measured. The **direct index appraisal** measures subordinate performance by objective, impersonal criteria such as productivity, absenteeism, and turnover. For example, a manager's performance may be evaluated by the number of manager's employees who quit or by the employees' absenteeism rate. For nonmanagers, measures of productivity may be more appropriate. Measures of productivity can be broken into measures of quality and measures of quantity. Quality measures include scrap rates, customer complaints, and number of defective units or parts produced. Quantity measures include units of output per hour, new customer order, and sales volume.

Direct index appraisals are those that measure performance directly, such as number of pieces produced.

Exhibit 12.7 provides an illustration of a direct index for the director of occupational safety. This exhibit includes two direct indices (the quantitative standard for worker's compensations cost reduction and the reports produced). It also has a behavioral standard. Thus, both the outcome and the behavior are important in the overall performance rating for the director's job and are combined into a single format.

Accomplishment Records. A relatively new type of output-based appraisal is called an **accomplishment record**. It is suitable for professionals who claim "my record speaks for itself" or who claim they can't write standards for their job because every day is different. For this approach, professionals describe their

Accomplishment records for a professional writer might include articles and books written.

EXHIBIT 12.7

A Direct Index Appraisal with Unit Outcome, Individual Outcome, and Individual Behavior Measures

Job Title:	Director of occupational safety
Outcome Desired:	Reduce workers' compensation cost
Quantitative standard:	Compensation cost: Present = $475,000: target = $380,000; actual $
Outcome/Task Desired:	Reviews plant facilities for violations and reports to plant manager.
Quantitative standard:	Conducts reviews and issues reports. Reports produced on time for each plant. Present = 85%; target = 92%; actual = %.
Behavioral standard:	After preparing the safety report, this director meets with each plant manager and praises reduction of possible violation incidents and warns of consequences if compliance is not met; goes over the report with each manager in detail; and returns to meet with managers and report progress every two weeks.

Overall Performance Rating:

Well Below Standard	Below Standard	Meets Standard	Exceeds Standard	Well Above Standard
❐	❐	❐	❐	❐

Source: From R. W. Beatty and C. E. Schneier, "Strategic Performance Appraisal Issues," in *Readings in Personnel and Human Resource Management*, 4th ed., R. S. Schuler, S. A. Youngblood, and V. L. Huber, eds., (St. Paul, MN.: West, 1988): 260.

achievements relative to appropriate job dimensions on an accomplishment record form. The professional's supervisor verifies the accuracy of the accomplishments. Then, a team of outside experts evaluates the accomplishments to determine their overall value. While time-consuming and potentially costly because outside evaluators are used, this approach has been shown to be predictive of job success for lawyers. It also has face validity because professionals believe it is appropriate and valid.[35]

Which Approach Is Best?

Research on this question is limited. It does, however, reinforce the necessity of first identifying the purposes to be served with performance appraisal. Each approach can then be assessed in relation to the following criteria:

- **Strategic:** Related to the needs of the business (if customer service is important, does it appraise customer service behavior?)
- **Developmental:** Motivating subordinates to do well, providing feedback, and aiding in HR planning and career development
- **Evaluational:** Promotion, discharge, layoff, pay, and transfer decisions and, therefore, the ability to make comparisons across subordinates and departments
- **Economical:** Cost in the development, implementation, and use

- **Freedom from error:** Halo, leniency, and central tendency and the extent of reliability and validity (described in the following section)
- **Interpersonal:** The extent to which superiors can gather useful and valid appraisal data that facilitate the appraisal interview
- **Practicality:** The ease with which the system can be developed or implemented
- **User acceptance:** The degree to which users accept the appraisal format as being reliable, valid, and useful

Because organizational conditions influence these criteria, it is impossible to identify which approach is really best. The HR manager, however, should be able to evaluate any approach based on these criteria in his or her organization.

Biases in Appraisal and Approaches to Appraisal Training

LEARNING OBJECTIVE 4

Describe the biases in appraisal and how they can be reduced.

Despite the prevalence of performance appraisal systems, many people are dissatisfied with them. Their disillusionment centers on the vulnerability of these measures to intentional as well as unforeseen bias on the part of the rater and ratee.

The Rating Process

The rating process in the PAS is made more complex because it requires the condensation and analysis of large amounts of information. First, employees' behavior or outcomes must be observed. This information must be aggregated and stored in the rater's short-term memory. Because of long appraisal periods, information must be condensed further and stored in long-term memory. When a judgment needs to be made, information relevant to the category to be rated must be retrieved from memory and a comparison made between observed behaviors and the rater's standards. Finally, a rating must be made based on aggregated data retrieved from memory and any additional information the rater intentionally or unintentionally chooses to include. Ratings at this point may be revised depending on the reaction of the employee or higher-level managers. Unfortunately, raters' memories are fallible. Consequently, they fall prey to a variety of rating errors or deviations between the "true" rating an employee deserves and the actual rating assigned.[36]

Rating Errors

When criteria are not clearly specified and there are no incentives associated with rating accuracy, a variety of errors may occur during the rating process.[37]

Halo and Horn. Frequently, a rater will evaluate an employee similarly on all dimensions of performance. Performance on a single dimension will be so outstanding or so important that it influences the rating of other tasks. This effect is called a **halo error**. The opposite of a halo error is a **horn error**, where negative performance in one dimension influences any positive performance.[38]

Halo error is where a good evaluation on one dimension influences evaluation on all the others.

Horn error is where negative evaluation on one dimension influences evaluation on all the others.

Leniency. A second common and often intentional rating error is called **leniency error**, or the process of being too easy. In order to avoid conflict, a manager rates all employees in a particular work group higher than they should be rated. This is particularly likely when there are no organizational sanctions against high ratings, when rewards are not part of a fixed and limited pot, and when dimensional ratings are not required.

Leniency error is the process of evaluating someone too easily.

Strictness. At the opposite extreme of leniency is the **error of strictness** in which ratees are given unfavorable ratings regardless of performance level. Inexperienced raters who are unfamiliar with environmental constraints on performance, raters with low self-esteem, or raters who have personally received a

Error of strictness is the process of evaluating someone too harshly.

low rating are most likely to rate strictly. Rater training, which includes reversal of supervisor subordinate roles and confidence building, will reduce this error.

Halo, horn, leniency, and strictness errors can be further minimized by establishing specific criteria for all performance dimensions, requiring raters to rate each performance dimension separately and then summing these ratings to attain an overall rating. Additionally, raters should receive normative information about their rating patterns.

Error of central tendency is the process of evaluating someone about average on all dimensions.

Central Tendency. Rather than using extremes in ratings, there is a tendency on the part of some raters to evaluate all ratees as average even when performance actually varies. This bias is referred to as the **error of central tendency**. Raters with large spans of control and little opportunity to observe behavior are likely to rate the majority of employees in the middle of the scale, rather than too high or too low. This is a "play-it-safe" strategy. Central tendency can also be a by-product of the rating method. The forced-distribution format requires that most employees be rated average.

Primacy bias is the bias of giving the first information greater weight. Recency of events error gives more weight to the last information.

Primacy and Recency. As noted earlier, the typical appraisal period (six months to a year) is far too long for any rater to adequately remember all performance-relevant information. As explained in Chapter 10, raters may use initial information to categorize a ratee as either a good or bad performer. Subsequently, information that supports the initial judgments is amassed, and disconfirming information is ignored. Thus, the information initially collected is given more weight. This bias is referred to as the **primacy bias**.

Conversely, a rater may not pay attention to employee performance throughout the appraisal period. As the appraisal interview draws near, the rater searches for information cues as to the value of performance. Unfortunately, recent behaviors or outputs are most salient. As a result, recent events are weighted more heavily than they should be. Called the **recency of events error**, this bias can have serious consequences for a ratee who performs well for six months or a year but then makes a serious or costly error in the last week or two before evaluations are made.

Employees and managers can minimize these two errors by keeping ongoing behavioral or critical incident files in which good and poor behaviors and outputs are recorded. Although time-consuming, they ensure that information for the entire period is incorporated into the appraisal.

Contrast Effects. If a criterion is not clear or a ranking system is used, **contrast effects** will occur. An average employee compared to a weak employee will appear outstanding; when evaluated against outstanding employees, the average employee will be perceived as a low performer. Again, the solution is to have specific performance criteria established prior to the evaluation period. Then, an employee with adequate performance receives an acceptable rating.

Minimizing Bias

Even the most valid and reliable appraisal forms are minimally effective when too many extraneous factors impinge on the process. However, as previously noted, many of these errors can be minimized if the following steps are taken:

- Each performance dimension addresses a single job activity rather than a group of activities.
- Overall ratings are not used. Instead, ratings are made on a dimension-by-dimension basis and summed to determine the overall rating.
- The rater can on a regular basis observe on-the-job behavior.
- Terms like average are not used on a rating scale, since different raters have various reactions to such a term.
- The rater does not have to evaluate large groups of employees

- Raters are trained to avoid errors such as leniency, strictness, halo and horn, central tendency, and recency of events.
- Raters are trained to share a common frame of reference.[39]

In addition to the above suggestions, rating accuracy can be improved through careful training that focuses on improving the observation skills of raters and on providing feedback and coaching. Frame-of-reference training, which was discussed in Chapter 10 as a method of increasing selection decision-making accuracy, is also useful here. A comprehensive rater training program might include the following:

1. Raters are given a job description and instructed to identify appropriate criteria for evaluating the job.
2. When agreement is reached, raters view a tape of an employee performing a job.
3. Independently, they evaluate the videotaped employee's performance using the organization's appraisal system.
4. The ratings of participants are compared to those of job experts and to one another.
5. With a trainer as a facilitator, the raters present the rationale for their ratings and challenge ratings and the rationale of other raters.
6. The trainer then helps raters to reach consensus regarding the value of specific job behaviors and overall performance.
7. A new videotape is shown followed by independent ratings.
8. The process continues until consensus is easily achieved.[40]

Organizations that cannot afford to develop videotapes or who use MBO performance standards can accomplish similar results using written-performance profiles instead of videotapes of behavior.

Analysis of Future Performance

The performance appraisal approaches discussed so far appraise past and current performance. Occasionally, it is useful to evaluate an employee's future potential. The **assessment center** method, discussed in Chapter 10, which is used to determine the managerial potential of employees, evaluates individuals as they take part in a large number of activities conducted in a relatively isolated environment. In a typical assessment center, an employee may spend two or three days going through a series of activities, including management games, leaderless group discussions, peer evaluations, and in-basket exercises.

The assessment center helps determine how well someone will do on another job.

Advantages of the assessment center include its validity and its ability to open up the process by which an organization identifies future managers, giving more employees a chance to be recognized. Occasionally, employees find themselves placed in jobs or parts of the organization that are less visible to top management. This, combined with having a supervisor who fails to make fair evaluations of present performance, may "bury" some employees in the organization. An assessment center program that employees can volunteer to attend can reduce this potential for early "burial."

Potential limitations of the assessment center method are its cost, its focus on competition rather than cooperation, and its creation of "crown princes and princesses." The creation of a special class of employees is less likely, however, under a program where participants are either nominated by their supervisors or volunteer on their own initiative. The nature of the activities in the center, including the degree of cooperation or competitiveness, can be regulated to match the needs of the organization and its environment. The relatively high cost of the assessment center approach is justified when the organization benefits from a better and bigger pool of potential managers.

Once performance potential is identified, organizations can establish management inventory systems to facilitate HR planning. Using the same information, organizations can also establish career planning and training programs to eliminate any gaps between current and needed skills. However, organizations need to develop programs that meet legal requirements.

LEARNING OBJECTIVE 5

Describe the current trends in performance appraisal.

Current Trends

Three major trends in performance appraisal are likely to affect you as you proceed in your career.

The Strategically Aligned Performance Appraisal

Much of what has been described in this chapter can be used in either traditional approaches or in the strategic approach. Although both are used in firms today, the strategic approach is gaining in popularity as firms see performance appraisal as an important way to achieve organizational goals. Yes, employees do tend to do what is expected (as generally defined by the performance appraisal system). Therefore, if firms incorporate such company strategies as teamwork and customer satisfaction into performance appraisal criteria, they are more likely to get teamwork and customer satisfaction from their employees, as done at Chrysler. Thus, firms wanting to produce total quality and/or total customer satisfaction need these criteria to be present in the performance appraisal of all employees.

Whether done traditionally or strategically, performance appraisal always involves several components. What these components are and how they get played out under the traditional and strategic approaches are illustrated in Exhibit 12.8.[41]

Is Performance Appraisal On the Way Out?

If companies want employees to work together in teams in their pursuit of strategies such as total quality and customer focus, they must adjust several HR activities. One of the important ones is the performance appraisal system. Typically, the basis for appraisal begins to reflect team-oriented criteria rather than solely individual-oriented criteria. Longer-term criteria become included with more traditional, shorter-term criteria. Peer review is incorporated, along with the traditional supervisory review.

As is usually the case, these changes do not take place overnight; they take place gradually. People need to get comfortable with the new ways. Just as important, organizations need to experiment with what they are doing. New ways of doing things generally have to be adapted to specific conditions facing a given company. In the instance of performance appraisal, companies may continue to make the types of changes described in the above paragraph. At some point, they may ask, Do we even need performance appraisal?

Firms have used performance appraisal systems for a long time now. It is unlikely that they will abandon them wholesale, but some are starting to ask, Why do we do appraisals? As firms address these questions, they may see that they do it more to control than to develop or improve employee performance—and they do it because they assume they need to. [If employee goals are different from organizational goals, then—the assumption goes—firms have to monitor and control what employees do. In some cases, firms are finding that this assumption is wrong: employees can have goals that coincide with the organization's.] W. Edwards Deming, a father in the field of quality management and statistical process control, acted on the assumption that employees will do their best when managers treat them accordingly. In fact, he argued that, in terms of performance problems,

Did You KNOW?

Deming first went to Japan in 1950 to improve their quality. Japan's top prize for quality is named for him. Can one person make a difference? The answer is, yes!

EXHIBIT 12.8

Two Approaches to Performance Appraisal

COMPONENTS	APPROACH: TRADITIONAL	APPROACH: STRATEGIC
Goal	Evaluation	Achievement
Manager	Controls program	Partnership
Employee	Passive	Initiator
View	Review mirror	Prospective
Outcome	Performance Rating	Improved performance
Timing	Once a year	Ongoing
Links	None	Corporate goals
Rewards	Based on rating	Based on contribution
Theme	Control	Sharing
Criteria	Determined by manager	Suggested by and mutually determined employee
Customer	No input	Provides input
Development plan	No input	Essential element
Individual vision	Not discussed	Basis for the plan
Atmosphere	Often confrontational	Supportive

Adaptation from "A New Focus on Achievement," by J. P. McCarthy, copyright February 1991.

managers—not the employees—are largely responsible for the problems. This questioning could eventually result in the disappearance of performance appraisal as most organizations use it today, at least as a method for evaluating employees. Deming strongly maintained that appraisal can be useful, but only to help an employee develop and improve.

Did You KNOW?

Deming believed that managers are responsible for most people performance problems because management created the system.

Performance Management

Based, in part, upon the thinking of Deming, companies now think of employee performance in terms of **performance management.** This thinking reflects the reality that the performance of employees is dependent upon many factors in addition to the employee's skills and abilities. These factors are part of the "system" that Deming talked about. These factors include the reward structure of the company, the availability of resources to do the job, time pressures, quality of supervision, and clarity of communication about expectations. They are important in understanding why employees may perform at the levels they do, in describing employees' ability and motivation, and, therefore, in helping to find ways to improve employee performance. As such, these ideas are discussed in the next chapter, particularly in our discussion of performance deficiencies.

Performance management is the reality that many factors influence an individual's performance in addition to the individual's skills and abilities.

Legal Considerations

LEARNING OBJECTIVE 6

Describe the legal considerations in performance appraisal.

Organizations must pay careful attention to legal considerations in the process of employee performance appraisal, as shown in Exhibit 12.9.[42]

Establishing Valid Criteria and Standards

Developing appraisals that reflect important performance criteria (job components for the appraisal) is necessary if the appraisals are to be considered valid. The U.S. Circuit Court in *Brito v. Zia Company* (1973) found that Zia Company was in violation of Title VII when a disproportionate number of employees of a protected group were laid off because of low performance scores. The critical point was that the performance scores were based on the supervisor's best judgments and opinions, not on important components of doing the job. When companies make performance-based decisions on the basis of appraisals, they are using the appraisals as employment tests; thus, the appraisals must be based on identifiable job-related criteria (*Stringfellow v. Monsanto Corp.*, 1970; *U.S. v. City of Chicago*, 1978). The best way to determine whether the appraisal criteria are job-related is to do a job analysis (*Albemarle Paper Company v. Moody*, 1975).[43]

Once the appropriate performance criteria are established, levels or standards marking the degree of desirability or acceptability of each job criterion can be established. To ensure that a realistic view of job performance is captured, several criteria may be required, and a standard established for each criterion. Having these criteria and standards is necessary, not just for legal considerations, but also for job performance reasons. Consequently, *how* they are established is important.

EXHIBIT 12.9

Prescriptions for Legally Defensible Appraisal Systems

1 Job analysis to identify important duties and tasks should precede development of a performance appraisal system.
2. The performance appraisal system should be standardized and formal.
3 Specific performance standards should be communicated to employees in advance of the appraisal period.
4. Objective and uncontaminated data should be used whenever possible.
5. Ratings on traits such as dependability, drive, or attitude should be avoided.
6. Employees should be evaluated on specific work dimensions rather than on a single global or overall measure.
7. If work behaviors rather than outcomes are to be evaluated, evaluators should have ample opportunity to observe ratee performance.
8 To increase the reliability of ratings, more than one independent evaluator should be used whenever possible.
9. Behavioral documentation should be prepared for ratings.
10. Employees should be given an opportunity to review their appraisals.
11. A formal system of appeal should be available for appraisal disagreements.
12. Raters should be trained to prevent discrimination and to evaluate performance consistently.
13. Appraisals should be frequent, offered at least annually.

Source: Adapted from H. J. Bernardin and W F. Cascio, "Performance Appraisal and the Law," in *Readings in Personnel and Human Resource Management*, 3rd ed., R. S. Schuler, S. A. Youngblood. and V. L. Huber, eds. (St. Paul. MN.: West, 1988): 239.

Using Valid Performance Appraisal Forms

Once the critical job components (criteria) are established, forms based on those components must be used. For example, if quantity of output is a criterion, appraisal forms that ask supervisors their general impressions on how personable and valuable the employees are may lead to an inappropriate appraisal, and, if used for an employment decision, such an appraisal could lead to a *prima facie* case of illegal discrimination. Appraisal forms in which the raters evaluate an employee on attributes such as leadership, attitude toward people, or loyalty are referred to as **subjective forms**. In contrast, appraisals where the evaluation involves specifically-defined behaviors or outcomes—such as level of output, level of specific goal attainment, or number of days absent—are called **objective forms**.

Subjective forms are appraisal forms that lack specific measures of behaviors and output. **Objective forms** are appraisal forms that have specific measures of behaviors and output.

Although the courts will allow a company to use subjective forms (*Roger v. International Paper Co.*, 1975), they generally frown on their use (*Albemarle Paper Company v. Moody*, 1975; *Oshiver v. Court of Common Pleas*, 1979; *Baxter v. Savannah Sugar Refining Corp.*, 1974; and *Rowe v. General Motors*, 1972) because they may not produce fair or accurate evaluations. Consequently, the courts have ruled that when disparate impact is found, all performance appraisal procedures—objective or subjective—must be shown to be job-related (*Watson v. Forth Worth Bank and Trust*, 1988).

It is also important to communicate these expectations to employees in advance of the evaluating period. In *Donaldson v. Pillsbury Company* (1977), a female employee who was dismissed was granted relief because she had never been shown her job description (which would have specified performance criteria).[44]

Summary

Human variability is a fact of organizational life. From the point of view of HR management, it is in an organization's best interest to attempt to select and control individual variability. Chapter 10 addressed how selection and placement decisions enable organizations to staff positions for effective performance. This chapter discusses how organizations control variability in the performance appraisal system itself, and Chapter 13 will discuss how the PAS can control performance variability on the job.

Performance appraisal is not a single act or a particular format used to evaluate job behavior. Rather, it is a system or a set of processes and procedures that evolve over time. A performance appraisal system is premised on the beliefs that individuals will vary in performance over time and that individuals can exert some influence over their performance.

Thus, an effective PAS must generally serve two purposes: 1) an evaluative role to let people know where they stand, and 2) a developmental role to provide specific information and direction so individuals can change (improve) their performance. Performance appraisal is therefore linked to other important HR activities such as compensation, promotion decisions, HR planning, development and training, and validation of selection systems for legal compliance.

Appraisal data are gathered for several reasons: 1) to make the process as objective and fair as possible, and 2) to comply with increasing legal considerations. In general, the more subjective the performance appraisal approach, the less likely the organization is effectively using its people and the more vulnerable the organization is to legal challenge. Although a variety of approaches to performance appraisal exist, they can be classified in three broad approaches: norm-referenced, behavioral, and output approaches. The choice of the best approach is really a function of several criteria: the purpose of the performance appraisal system (evaluation versus development), the costs of development and implementation of the system, the degree to which rater errors are minimized, and user acceptance of the system. Job analysis is an important means of developing job-related performance criteria.

Despite the best-laid plans for a performance appraisal system, HR professionals are often frustrated by the failure of line managers to apply and use the systems consistently. A number of obstacles can contribute to rater resistance: raters may not have the opportunity to observe subordinates' performance, raters may not have performance standards, raters as human judges are prone to error, or raters may view performance appraisal as a conflict-producing activity and therefore avoid it. For these reasons and others, it is important to examine not only why and how appraisal data are gathered, but also, as the next chapter explores, how they are used.

Key Concepts

accomplishment record
alternative ranking
assessment center
behaviorally anchored rating scale
behavioral approach
behavioral observation scales
cohesiveness
contaminated
contrast effects
criteria
critical incidents
deficient
direct index appraisal
error of central tendency
error of strictness
evaluative
forced-distribution method
goal congruence
goals
graphic rating scale
halo error
horn error
leniency error
management by objectives (MBO)
motivation
norm-referenced approach
objective forms
output-based approach
paired-comparison method
performance appraisal system (PAS)
performance management
performance standards appraisal
primacy bias
productivity
rankings
recency of events error
straight ranking
subjective forms

Review and Discussion Questions

1. Are the purposes served by a performance appraisal system the same for a superior, a subordinate, and a HR manager? Explain.
2. Why is job analysis essential to the development of a performance appraisal system?
3. How can companies enhance the legal defensibility of their performance appraisal system?
4. Why does employee performance vary even after employees have successfully passed rigorous organizational selection and placement procedures? How can a performance appraisal system address this performance variability?
5. How is performance appraisal related to the internal and external environments? Discuss.
6. What are the three major approaches to performance appraisal? Give an example of each approach.
7. What is a behaviorally anchored rating scale? What advantages and disadvantages does each appraisal method offer?
8. Performance appraisal approaches differ according to whether behavior or results are evaluated. Can you cite organizational examples where one approach might be preferred over the other? Explain the reasons for the preferences.
9. Explain how an assessment center can be used to evaluate future performance.

PROJECTS, EXERCISES & CASES

End-of-Text Projects

Lincoln Electric

1. Describe the following for Lincoln Electric:
   a. The objectives of its performance appraisals
   b. The extent to which these objectives are serving the business and HR objectives of Lincoln
   c. The performance appraisal criteria
   d. The extent to which these criteria are serving the business and HR objectives of Lincoln
2. How can the performance appraisal activities at Lincoln be improved?

Nordstrom

1. Describe the following for Nordstrom:
   a. The objectives of its performance appraisals
   b. The extent to which these objectives are serving the business and HR objectives of Nordstrom
   c. The performance appraisal criteria
   d. The extent to which these criteria are serving the business and HR objectives of Nordstrom
2. How can the performance appraisal activities at Nordstrom be improved?

Field Project

Since many students start their career after graduation in large companies, it would be interesting to find out what their appraisal procedures are like. The idea of researching the appraisal procedures in small local businesses, however, is no less important for a general understanding.

Divide into groups of four with each group exploring one of the following:

1. Compare the appraisal procedures of two companies—a large corporation and a small proprietorship.
2. Compare the appraisal procedures of two companies from different industries.
3. Compare the appraisal procedures of two companies of about the same sizes and in the same industry (e.g., Burger King and McDonald's, Coca Cola and PepsiCo).

After the groups have presented their findings, discuss the findings as a class. What kind of appraisals are more effective for an employee's satisfaction and motivation? Discuss the differences in appraisals of white-collar and blue-collar employees, and of managers and non-managers.

Career Management Exercise: How Shall We Appraise You?

You have indicated the type of job and organization you would like (Chapter 6), the type of job characteristics most desired (Chapter 7), and the selection procedures that should be used (Chapter 10). Let's assume you are on the job: what type of performance appraisal system would you prefer?

1. Would you like a formal performance appraisal process?
2. What purposes do you want it to serve for you?
3. What form would you like your performance appraisal to take?
4. What people/groups do you want to rate your performance?
5. How frequently do you want to be appraised?
6. Whose performance would you like to appraise?
7. Do you want to have a due process system so you can appeal your appraisal if needed?

VISIT THE LIBRARY

Workforce Online

Because you are now familiar with getting onto the Internet and the use of HR Headquarters, the following steps are abbreviated.

1. Enter your Web browser.
2. Enter Workforce Online.
3. Find and review the following article within the "Research Center":

   Peer Review Drives Compensation at Johnsonville.
4. Return to your homepage.

Case: The Pain of Performance Appraisal

Joe Miller sat at his desk, looking over the performance appraisal form that he had just completed on Bill Cox, one of his insurance underwriters. Bill was on his way to Joe's office for their annual review session. Joe dreaded these appraisal meetings, even when he did not have to confront employees with negative feedback.

A couple of years before, Essex Insurance Company, which had experienced very rapid growth, decided to implement a formal appraisal system. All supervisors were presented with the new appraisal form, which included five different subcategories in addition to an overall rating. They were asked to rate employees on each dimension, using a scale from 1 (unacceptable) to 5 (exceptional). They were also advised to maintain a file on each employee into which they could drop notes on specific incidents of good or poor performance during the year to use as "documentation" when completing the appraisal form. The supervisors were then told that they could only give a rating of 1 or 5 if they had "substantial" documentation to back it up.

Joe had never given ratings of 1 or 5 because he was not diligent about recording specific incidents for employee files; he believed that writing up all of the documentation necessary to justify such a rating was too time-consuming. In Joe's opinion, a couple of employees in his department deserved a 5 rating, but so far none of them had complained about his appraisals.

Bill was one of Joe's "exceptional" workers. Joe had three or four specific examples of exceptional performance in Bill's file, but in looking over the form he could not clearly identify the category in which they belonged. "Oh well," Joe said to himself, "I'll just give him 3s and 4s. I don't have to justify those, and Bill has never complained before." One of the categories was "Analyzing Work Materials." Joe had never understood what that meant or whether it was relevant to the job of insurance underwriter. He checked 3 (satisfactory) for Bill, as he did on all the evaluations he did. He understood the meaning of the other categories—Quality of Work, Quantity of Work, Improved Work Methods, and Relationships with Co-workers—although he was confused as to what a 3 or 4 indicated about each category.

Bill knocked on Joe's door and came in. Joe looked up and smiled. "Hi, Bill. Sit down. Let's get through this thing so we can get back to work, OK?"

Case Questions

1. What problems do you see with the appraisal system Joe is using?
2. What are Bill's likely reactions to being told by Joe that he scored 35 and 45 even though he is one of Joe's exceptional workers?
3. What suggestions do you have for improving the performance appraisal system?

Case: Improving Performance Appraisal

A large automobile engine plant in Saginaw, Michigan, has been having difficulty with its performance evaluation program. The organization has a program by which all operating employees and clerical employees are evaluated semiannually by their supervisors. Their evaluation form (shown in Exhibit 1) has been in use for ten years. It is scored as follows: excellent = 5, above average = 4, average = 3, below average = 2, and poor = 1. The scores for each question are entered in the right-hand column and totaled for an overall evaluation score.

The procedure used has been as follows: each supervisor rates each employee on June 1 and February 1. The supervisor discusses the rating with the employee, then sends it to the personnel department. Each rating is placed in the employee's personnel file. If promotions come up, the cumulative ratings are considered at that time. The ratings are also supposed to be used when raises are given.

The system was designed by the personnel manager who retired two years ago, Mary Bensko. She was replaced by Lillian Meyer, who graduated fifteen years ago with a degree in business from the University of Michigan. Since then, she's had a variety of work experiences, mostly in the automobile industry, and she has done personnel work for about five years.

Lillian has been reviewing the evaluation system. Employees have a mixture of indifferent and negative feelings about it. An informal survey has shown that about half of the supervisors fill out the forms, give about three minutes to each form, and send them to personnel without discussing them with the employees. The rest spend more time completing the forms but communicate the results only briefly and superficially with their employees.

Lillian has found out that the forms are rarely retrieved for promotion or pay-raise analyses. Because of this, most supervisors feel the evaluation program is a useless ritual.

Lillian had seen performance evaluation in her previous employment as a much more useful experience; it included giving positive feedback to employees, improving future employee performance, developing employee capabilities, and providing data for promotion and compensation.

Lillian has not had much experience with design of performance evaluation systems. She feels she should seek your advice on what to do.

Case Questions

1. Write a report summarizing your evaluation of the strengths and weaknesses of the present appraisal system.
2. Recommend some specific improvements or data-gathering activities to develop a better system for Meyer.

CASE EXHIBIT 1

Performance Evaluation Form of Automobile Engine Plant

PERFORMANCE EVALUATION

SUPERVISORS: When you are asked to do so by the HR department, please complete this form on each of your employees. The supervisor who is responsible for 75 percent or more of an employee's work should complete this form on him or her. Please evaluate each facet of the employee separately.

Quality of Work	Excellent	Above Average	Average	Below Average	Poor	Score
Quantity of Work	Poor	Below Average	Average	Above Average	Excellent	
Dependability	Excellent	Above Average	Average	Below Average	Poor	
Initiative at Work	Poor	Below Average	Average	Above Average	Excellent	
Cooperativeness	Excellent	Above Average	Average	Below Average	Poor	
Getting Along with Co-Workers	Poor	Below Average	Average	Above Average	Excellent	

Total ____________

Supervisor's Signature ____________________

Employee Name ____________________

Employee Number ____________________

Chapter 12 Endnotes

1. G. E. Forward, "Mentofacturing: A Vision for American Industrial Excellence," *The Executive* 5 (1991): 32–44.
2. J. E. Santora, "Rating the Boss at Chrysler," *Personnel Journal* (May 1992): 42.
3. Ibid., 42.
4. Ibid., 45. See also A. Taylor III, "Will Success Spoil Chrysler," *Fortune* (Jan. 10, 1994): 88–92.
5. H. S. Field and W. H. Holley, "The Relationship of Performance Appraisal System Characteristics to Verdicts in Selected Employment Discrimination Cases," *Academy of*

Management Journal 25 (1982): 392–406; D. L. DeVries, A. M. Morrison, S. L. Shullman, and M. L. Gerlach, *Performance Appraisal on the Line* (Greensboro, N.C.: Center for Creative Leadership, 1986).

6. A. Mohrman, S. M. Resnick-West, and E. E. Lawler III, *Designing Performance Appraisal Systems* (San Francisco: Jossey-Bass, 1990).

7. J. Pfeffer, *Competitive Advantage Through People* (Boston: Harvard Business School Press, 1995).

8. Alcoholism Has a High Cost," *HR Focus* (Aug. 1993): 8; S. Greengard, "Theft Control Starts with HR Strategies," *Personnel Journal* (April 1993): 81–92.

9. M. Beer, "Performance Appraisal: Dilemmas and Possibilities," *Organizational Dynamics* (Winter 1981): 24–36; See also the entire issue of *Personnel Administrator* (March 1984). For a description of how appraisals can be linked with strategy, see R. W. Beatty, "Competitive Human Resource Advantage Through Strategic Management of Performance," *Human Resource Planning* (Summer 1989): 179–194.

10. F. J. Landy and J. L. Farr, *The Measurement of Work Performance: Methods, Theory and Applications* (New York: Academic Press, 1983), P.C. Smith, "Behaviors, Results and Organizational Effectiveness: The Problem of Criteria." In *Handbook of Industrial Psychology*, M. D. Dunnette, ed. (Chicago: Rand McNally, 1976).

11. S. Carroll and C. E. Schneier, *Performance Appraisal and Review Systems* (Glenview, IL: Scott, Foresman, 1982); G. V. Barrett and M. C. Kernan, "Performance Appraisal and Terminations: A Review of Court Decisions Since *Brito v. Zia* with Implications for Personnel Practices," *Personnel Journal* (Autumn 1987): 489.

12. P. S. Lewis, S. H. Goodman, and P. M. Fandt, *Management: Challenges in the 21st Century* (St. Paul, MN: West Publishing Co., 1995).

13. J. L. Farr and J. Werbel, "Effects of Purpose of the Appraisal and Expectation of Validation on Self Appraisal Leniency," *Journal of Applied Psychology* 71 (1986): 527–529; R. P. Steel and N. K. Ovalle, "Self-Appraisal Based on Supervisory Feedback," *Personnel Psychology* 37 (1984): 667–685; P. R. Sackett, C. L. Z. DuBois, and A. Wiggins Noe, "Tokenism in Performance Evaluation: The Effects of Work Group Representation on Male–Female and White–Black Differences in Performance Ratings," *Journal of Applied Psychology* 76, no. 2 (1991): 263–267; D. A. Waldman and B. J. Avolio, "Race Effects in Performance Evaluations: Controlling for Ability, Education and Experience," *Journal of Applied Psychology* 76, no. 6 (1991): 897–901; P. R. Sacken and C. L. Z. DuBois, "Rater–Ratee Race Effects on Performance Evaluation: Challenging Meta-Analytic Conclusions," *Journal of Applied Psychology* 76, no. 6 (1991): 873–877.

14. "Measuring Performance: Employee Initiated Reviews," *Inc.* (July 1991): 80. See also P. Lanza, "Team Appraisals," *Personnel Journal* (March 1985): 50; J. D. Coombe, "Peer Review: The Emerging Successful Application," *Employee Relations Law Journal* (Spring 1984): 659–671; J. S. Kane and E. E. Lawler III, "Methods of Peer Assessment," *Psychological Bulletin* 3 (1978): 555–586.

15. J. Zigon, "Making Performance Appraisal Work For Teams," *Training* (June 1994): 58–63.

16. Discussions between company officials and Vandra Huber. See also C. A. Norman and R. A. Zawacki, "Team Appraisals–Team Approach," *Personnel Journal* (Sept. 1991): 101–104; J. Fitz-Enz and J. Rodgers, "Get Quality Performance from Professional Staff," *Personnel Journal* (May 1991): 22–24; L. Thornburg, "Performance Measures that Work," *HR Magazine* (May 1991): 35–38; T. Slater, "Get it Right the First Time," *Personnel Journal* (Sept. 1991): 35–40.

17. "Upward Appraisals Rate Highly," *Bulletin to Management* (March 31, 1994): 104; W. Kiechel III, "When Subordinates Evaluate the Boss," *Fortune* (June 19, 1989): 201. See also G. M. McEvoy, "Evaluating the Boss," *Personnel Administrator* (Sept. 1988): 115–120.

18. P. T. Kilborn, "The Boss Only Wants What's Best for You," *New York Times* (May 8, 1994): E3.

19. *Bulletin to Management* (October 8, 1987): 322, 327. See also J. S. Kane, "Measure for Measure in Performance Appraisal," *Computers in Personnel* (Fall 1987): 31–39.

20. "Whose Office Is This Anyhow?" *Fortune* (August 9, 1993): 93.

21. Landy and Farr, *The Measurement of Work.* To be fair, all individuals performing identically should receive the same performance evaluation.

22. P. S. Eyres, "Assessment: Legally Defensible Performance Appraisal Systems," *Personnel Journal* (July 1989): 58–62.

23. L. M. King, J. E. Hunter, and F. L. Schmidt, "Halo in a Multidimensional Forced Choice Performance Evaluation Scale," *Journal of Applied Psychology* 65 (1980): 507–516; R. Jacobs and S. Kozlowski, "A Closer Look at Halo Error in Performance Ratings." *Academy of Management Journal* (March 1985): 201–212.

24. J. C. Flanagan, "The Critical Incident Technique," *Psychological Bulletin* 51 (1954): 327–358.

25. F. J. Landy and J. L. Farr, "Performance Rating," *Psychological Bulletin* (January 1980): 72–107; S. Zedeck, "Behavioral-Based Performance Appraisals," *Aging and Work* 4 (1981): 89–100; K. R. Murphy and J. I. Constans, "Behavioral Anchors as a Source of Bias in Rating," *Journal of Applied Psychology* (Nov. 1987): 573.

26. K. N. Wexley and G. P. Latham, *Improving Productivity Through Performance Appraisal* (Reading, MA: Addison-Wesley, 1981).

27. See Beatty, "Competitive Human Resource Advantage Through Strategic Management of Performance."

28. H. J. Bernardin and R. W. Beatty, *Performance Appraisal: Assessing Human Behavior at Work* (Boston, MA: Kent, 1984); Landy and Farr, *The Measurement of Work.*

29. G. Latham and K. Wexley, "Behavioral Observation Scales for Performance Appraisal Purposes," *Personnel Psychology* 30 (1977): 255–268; M. Loar, S. Mohrman, and J. R. Stock, "Development of a Behaviorally Based Performance Appraisal System," *Personnel Psychology* (Spring 1982): 75–88; Latham and Wexley, *Improving Productivity* (1981): 63.

30. J. S. Kane and K. A. Freeman, "MBO and Performance Appraisal: A Mixture That's Not a Solution, Part 1," *Personnel* (Dec. 1986): 26–36. J. S. Kane and K. A. Freeman, "MBO and Performance Appraisal: A Mixture That's Not a Solution, Part 2," *Personnel* (Feb. 1987): 26–32.

31. R. A. Gentles, "Alcan's Integration of Management Techniques Raises Their Effectiveness," *Management Review,* AMA Forum (April 1984): 31.

32. S. Sherman, "How Tomorrow's Best Leaders Are Learning Their Stuff," *Fortune* (November 27, 1995): 90–102.

33. Letter of H. W. Mentik, "Letters to Fortune," *Fortune* (February 5, 1996): 26.

34. L. Baird, *Managing Performance* (New York: Wiley, 1986).

35. L. Hugh, "Development of the Accomplishment Record Method of Selecting and Promoting Professionals," *Journal of Applied Psychology* 69 (1984): 135–146.

36. D. R. Ilgen and J. M. Feldman, "Performance Appraisal: A Process Focus," in *Research in Organizational Behavior,* B. Staw and L. Cummings, eds. (Greenwich, CT.: JAI Press, 1983): 141–197; A. DeNisi and K. J. Williams, "Cognitive Approaches to Performance Appraisal," *Readings in Personnel and Human Resource Management,* J. Ferris and K. Rowland, eds., (Greenwich, CT: JAI Press, 1988): 109–156.

37. Bernardin and Beatty, *Performance Appraisal*; Landy and Farr, *The Measurement of Work.*

38. M. E. Heilman and M. H. Stopeck, "Being Attractive, Advantage or Disadvantage: Performance-Based Evaluations and Recommended Personnel Actions as a Function of Appearance, Sex, and Job Type," *Organizational Behavior and Human Decision Processes* 35 (1985): 202–215; B. E. Becker and R. L. Cardy, "Influence of Halo Error on Appraisal Effectiveness: A Conceptual and Empirical Reconsideration," *Journal of Applied Psychology* (Nov. 1986): 662.

39. R. L. Dipboye, "Some Neglected Variables in Research on Discrimination in Appraisals," *Academy of Management Review* (Jan. 1985): 118–125; M. R. Edwards and J. R. Sproull, "Rating the Raters Improves Performance Appraisals," *Personnel Administrator* (Aug. 1983): 77–82; R. M. McIntyre, D. E. Smith, and C. E. Hassett, "Accuracy of Performance Ratings as Affected by Rater Training and Perceived Purpose of Rating," *Journal of Applied Psychology* (Feb. 1984): 147–156.

40. B. W. Armentrout, "Eight Keys to Effective Performance Appraisals," *HR Focus* (April 1993): 13; R. I. Henderson, *Performance Appraisal* (Reston, VA: Reston, 1984).

41. "A New Focus on Achievement," *Personnel Journal* (Feb. 1991): 73–75.

42. The importance of this is further emphasized by the ADA; see "Problem of the Month: Performance Appraisals and the ADA," *Fair Employment Practices Guidelines* (September 1992): 3–5.

43. D. I. Rosen, "Appraisals Can Make-or-Break Your Court Case," *Personnel Journal* (November 1992): 113–118.

44. H. J. Bernardin and W. F. Cascio, "Performance Appraisal and the Law," in *Readings in Personnel and Human Resource Management* 3rd ed., R. S. Schuler, S. A. Youngblood, and V. L. Huber, eds. (St. Paul, MN: West Publishing Co., 1988): 239; G. V. Barrett and M. C. Kernan, "Performance Appraisal and Terminations: A Review of Court Decisions Since *Brito v. Zia* with Implications for Personnel Practices," *Personnel Journal* (Autumn 1987): 489.

13

CHAPTER

Utilizing Performance Appraisal Information: Improving Employee Performance

Learning Objectives

1. Describe the conflicts typically involved in performance appraisal feedback.
2. Design appraisal processes for maximum results.
3. Tell why employees do not always perform well even when they have the ability.
4. Identify strategies to improve performance.

Chapter Outline

"Feedback delivers its wallop and generates changes depending on what a person and the organization value. If they care about relationships with others, it will have an effect in that area. If they emphasize management planning, it will have an impact there."

Susan Gebelein
Vice President
Personnel Decisions, Inc.
Minneapolis, Minnesota[1]

MANAGING HUMAN RESOURCES

at Intel
Manager as Judge and Jury

Why are performance reviews part of the management system of most organizations? And why do we review the performance of our subordinates? Andrew Grove, founder and chairman of Intel, posed both questions to a group of middle managers and got the following responses:

- To assess the subordinate's work
- To improve performance
- To motivate
- To provide feedback to a subordinate
- To justify raises
- To reward performance
- To provide discipline
- To provide work direction
- To reinforce the company culture

Next, I (Andrew Grove) asked the group to imagine themselves to be a supervisor giving a review to a subordinate, and asked them what their feelings were. Some of the answers:

- Pride
- Anger
- Anxiety
- Discomfort
- Guilt
- Empathy/concern
- Embarrassment
- Frustration

Finally, I asked the same group to think back to some of the performance reviews they had received and asked what, if anything, was wrong with them. Their answers were quick and many:

- Review comments too general
- Mixed messages (inconsistent with rating or dollar raise)
- No indication of how to improve
- Negatives avoided
- Supervisor didn't know my work
- Only recent performance considered
- Surprises

This should tell you that giving performance reviews is a very complicated and difficult business and that we managers don't do an especially good job at it.

The fact is that giving such reviews is the single most important form of task-relevant feedback we as supervisors can provide. It is how we assess our subordinates' level of performance and how we deliver that assessment to them individually. It is also how we allocate the rewards—promotions, dollars, stock options, or whatever we may use. The review will influence a subordinate's performance—positively or negatively—for a long time, which makes the appraisal one of the manager's highest-leverage activities. In short, the review is an extremely powerful mechanism, and it is little wonder that opinions and feelings about it are strong and diverse.

But what is its fundamental purpose? Though all of the responses given to my questions are correct, there is one that is more important than any of the others: it is to improve the subordinate's performance. The review is usually dedicated to two things: first, the skill level of the subordinate, to determine what skills are missing and to find ways to remedy that lack; and second, to intensify the subordinate's motivation in order to get him or her on a higher performance curve for the same skill level.[2]

More and more attention is being focused on improving employee performance. Firms that want to survive and remain competitive are attempting to do as much as possible to assist their employees, both managers and non-managers, to improve. Giving feedback to employees based on their performance appraisal is one way to improve performance. Two key activities in this process are identifying performance

Intel is the number 1 maker of integrated circuits and has almost $25 billion in sales.

deficiencies and developing strategies and plans to remove them. Unfortunately, this is easier said than done for many reasons. The conflicts inherent in performance appraisal create certain dilemmas.

LEARNING OBJECTIVE 1

Describe the conflicts typically involved in performance appraisal feedback.

Inherent Conflicts in Performance Appraisal

Performance appraisal touches on one of the most emotionally charged activities in business life—the assessment of a person's contribution and ability. The signals a person receives about this assessment have a strong impact on self-esteem and on subsequent performance. Unfortunately, the performance appraisal experience draws poor reviews from employees, employers, and experts alike. Many employees believe that their performance appraisals are often ineffective, biased, and poorly done.

Inherent conflicts occur in performance appraisal because:

- **Most people think they are good performers.**
- **People want to maintain their self-esteem (self-image).**
- **People tend to attribute poor performance to others.**

Managers seem equally disgruntled with the appraisal process. In one survey, managers generally agreed that a performance appraisal should serve as a basis for determining pay increases, developing team players, and improving performance, but that it often falls short of these goals. In fact, only 10 percent of all managers believe that production increases are a result of the appraisal process.[3]

In another survey, the majority of appraisers saw little or no practical value in conducting performance appraisals. Whether the feedback they gave was positive or negative, supervisors felt that at best the status quo was maintained; at worst, the perceived outcome of giving negative feedback was viewed as so aversive that managers preferred not to conduct appraisals at all. This reaction was typical since, as the study found, positive organizational consequences seldom followed accurate appraisals, and negative consequences (confrontation, "bad mouthing," more meetings and memoranda) are assured after negative appraisals. The study concluded that managers also feared the organizational consequences of "making waves" with their subordinates.[4]

High Performers All

One key reason that performance appraisal is viewed negatively centers on the self-evaluation of employees: the overwhelming majority believe they perform better than 75 percent of their peers. Thus, when confronted with information suggesting they performed adequately, but not outstandingly, subordinates perceive that the evaluation is unfair and that the rewards are not equivalent to their contributions. As a result, organizational commitment and job satisfaction drop and remain low for as long as a year after the evaluation.

While one would expect positive feedback to increase job satisfaction, this doesn't occur either. Because employees believe their performance is high, receiving positive feedback merely maintains their current level of satisfaction and commitment. Thus, no matter what a supervisor does, the best he or she can accomplish is to maintain the status quo.

Perceptual Focus

Another reason that performance appraisals are problematic is that supervisors and subordinates view the process from different perspectives. For the subordinate, the perceptual focus is outward, keying in on the environmental factors (the supervisor, lack of supplies, co-workers) that impinge on his or her performance. The perceptual focus of the supervisor is on the subordinate and his or her motivation and ability. These perceptual differences are called *actor* and *observer* differences and can lead to conflict when it comes to identifying the causes of poor or good performance. This perceptual problem is accentuated by the tendency to account for performance in a self-serving manner. In order to protect one's ego, a subordinate is likely to attribute the causes of poor performance to external factors (difficult task, unclear instructions, lack of necessary equipment) and attribute successful performance to one's motivation and ability. Supervisors may respond similarly.

Conflicts in Goals

Goal conflict can also be the problem. Inherent in organizational and individual goals are three sets of conflict; these are the dilemmas in the appraisal process. One is between the organization's evaluative and developmental goals. When pursuing the evaluative goal, superiors make judgments affecting their subordinates' careers and immediate rewards. Many managers feel uncomfortable with this process because it requires them to be both judge and jury, as described by Andrew Grove, chairman at Intel Corporation in the "Managing Human Resources at Intel." Communicating these judgments can lead to the creation of an adversarial, low-trust relationship between superior and subordinate. This in turn precludes the superior from performing the problem-solving, helper role that is essential if the organization wants to serve the developmental goal.

A second set of conflicts arises from the evaluation of various goals of the individual. On the one hand, individuals want valid feedback that gives them information about how to improve and where they stand in the organization. On the other hand, they want to verify their self-image (self-esteem) and obtain valued rewards. In essence, the goals of the individual imply a necessity to be open (that is, welcome feedback for improvement) yet protective (maintain a positive self-image and obtain rewards).

The third set of conflicts arises between the individual's goals and those of the organization. One conflict is between the organization's evaluation goal and the individual's goal of obtaining rewards. Another conflict is between the organization's developmental goal and the individual's goal of maintaining self-image. Exhibit 13.1 shows the nature of these conflicts.[5]

EXHIBIT 13.1

Conflicts in Goals

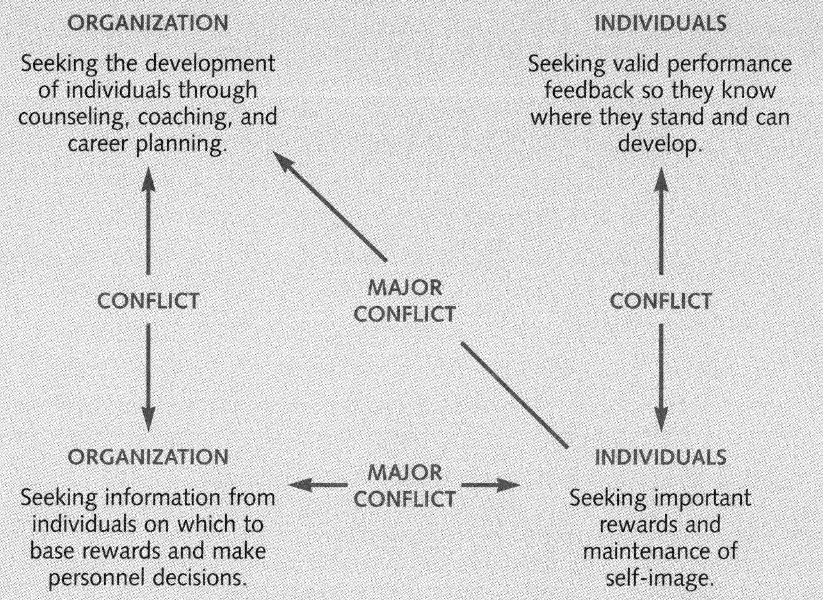

Source: Reprinted, by permission of the author, from "Performance Appraisal: Dilemmas and Possibilities," by M. Beer, *Organizational Dynamics* (Winter 1981): 27 © 1981.

Consequences of Inherent Conflicts

Consequences of inherent conflicts are:

- **Ambivalence**
- **Avoidance**
- **Defensiveness**
- **Resistance**

Among the several consequences of the conflicts just described are ambivalence, avoidance, defensiveness, and resistance. Some of these consequences and conflicts cannot be avoided in gathering performance data and conducting performance appraisals, particularly as it relates to the superior-subordinate relationship described in Chapter 12.

Ambivalence is a consequence for both superiors and subordinates. Superiors are ambivalent because they must act as judge and jury in telling subordinates where they stand, both because the organization demands it and because the subordinates want it. Yet, superiors are uncertain about their judgments and how subordinates will react to negative feedback. This feeling is intensified when superiors are not trained in feedback techniques. Subordinates are equally ambivalent because they want honest feedback, yet want to receive rewards and maintain their self-image (that is, they really want only positive feedback). Additionally, if they are open with their superiors in identifying undeveloped potential, they risk the chance that the superiors may use this to evaluate them unfavorably.[6]

Subordinates and superiors can both be defensive in performance appraisals, particularly when feedback is negative. A classic study at General Electric made the following discoveries:

- Criticism has a negative effect on goal achievement.
- Praise has little effect one way or the other.
- The average subordinate reacts defensively to criticism during the appraisal interview.
- Defensiveness resulting from critical appraisal produces inferior performance. The disruptive effect of repeated criticism on subsequent performance is greater among those who already have low self-esteem.[7]

Accordingly, subordinates attempt to blame others for their performance, challenge the appraisal form, and demand that their superiors justify their appraisals. Initially at least, subordinates are not inclined to apologize for their behavior and seek ways to improve; in fact, they resist superiors' efforts to engage in problem-solving. Consequently, superiors spend most of their time defending their appraisals and resisting subordinates' efforts to have their appraisals altered.

> *"It's a tough job, the equivalent of walking up to a person and saying, 'Here's what I think of your baby'," says Robert Lefton, president of Psychological Associates, a consulting company that has provided training on how to give reviews to over 100 large companies. "It requires knowing how to handle fear and anger and a gamut of other emotions, which a lot of managers aren't comfortable with," he adds.*
>
> *Increasingly, managers must do a better job of appraising employees—not only to help employees mature, but also to increase productivity and company loyalty. Comprehensive performance reviews also reduce the chances that a terminated employee who has been warned of unsatisfactory performance will sue the company.*[8]

Even when good performance is involved, however, superiors still have to make evaluation decisions, and somebody may still end up looking like a poor performer. Because appraisals are uncomfortable yet necessary, seeking ways to make the process better is important. The areas of opportunity include the design of the appraisal system and modifying the characteristics of the performance appraisal interview.

Designing Appraisal Processes for Maximum Results

LEARNING OBJECTIVE 2

Design appraisal processes for maximum results.

Several features can be incorporated into the design of the appraisal system to minimize appraisal conflicts and maximize perceptual congruence.

Use Appropriate Performance Data

The first step in reducing conflict and perceptual difference is to use performance data that focuses on specific behaviors or goals. As noted previously, these performance expectations need to be communicated at the beginning of the appraisal period. Performance data that focus on personal attributes or characteristics are likely to prompt more defensiveness because they are difficult for the superior to justify and because more of the subordinate's self-image is at stake:

> *As Marilyn Moats Kennedy, managing partner of Career Strategies, a management-consulting company in Wilmette, Illinois, says "It's important to critique the* behavior *of an employee, not the employee himself."*
>
> *"If you bark, 'You have a bad attitude,' to your receptionists, for example, you'll likely find yourself facing a very defensive employee. You'll probably get better results if you say, 'When someone steps up to the desk, I'd like them to get the distinct impression that you're delighted to see them.'"*[9]

As shown in Chapter 12, superiors can facilitate specific performance feedback through their selection and use of the appropriate appraisal forms. Specifically, if superiors want to use performance data on behaviors, they can use a critical incident form or a behavioral observation method with specific numerical goals. Using these appraisal formats together would allow the supervisor to manage *what* subordinates are doing as well as *how* they are doing. On the other hand, if supervisors want to focus on goals, then an MBO format would be more appropriate.

- **Focus on facts and figures**
- **Link facts and figures to the performance dimensions**
- **Be sure the facts support your ratings**
- **Keep a running log of performance events for each employee**

Separate Current and Potential Performance During Appraisal

Current performance may have little to do with a subordinate's performance potential, and the two should be separated in an evaluation. Supervisors, however, may unconsciously incorporate evaluations of potential into evaluations of current performance. Conversely, they may incorporate past performance into the evaluation of present performance. In either event, the appraisal of current performance is inappropriately an amalgamation of past, current, and/or potential performance.[10]

As a result, it is likely the appraisal will be unfair. Consider people with high potential. They may receive a lower and possibly unfair evaluation than equivalent performing peers because their supervisors have higher expectations of them. Conversely, adequate performers with low potential may be evaluated adversely because they don't have the ability of the high-potential people, which is unfair to employees who may have no interest in being promoted, yet perform adequately in their current job.

Part of the solution is to use **job-specific criteria** to evaluate current performance and then conduct a separate appraisal on potential. As discussed in the last chapter, the criteria for each job need to be based on job analysis.

Job-specific criteria are dimensions of performance that are related to the specific job.

Separating the two processes allows supervisors to avoid appraising the potential performance of employees not interested in promotion. And for those interested, volunteering to participate in an assessment center or other promotional process cues management that a person is interested in moving up in the organization. In fact, one study of assessment centers found that participation, rather than the evaluation rating received, was the single most important determinant of who did or did not get promoted. By separating the evaluation of current and potential performance and by allowing employees to self-nominate, individual differences are recognized and incorporated in the appraisal process.[11]

Ensure Procedural and Distributive Fairness

To minimize the emotionally charged atmosphere that surrounds the performance appraisal process, managers also need to take steps to ensure that the process is perceived as fair and equitable, as discussed in Chapter 4. Performance appraisal procedures are viewed as fair to the extent that there is:

- **Consistency.** Performance standards are applied consistently to all employees. Allowances are not made for workers with special problems, nor are high performers expected to carry more than their weight.
- **Familiarity.** The use of diaries to record worker outputs, frequent observation of performance, and management by "wandering around" increases a supervisor's job knowledge and consequently creates the impression that the manager and the appraisals are fair.
- **Input Solicitation.** Information regarding performance standards as well as strategies to attain them need to be solicited *prior* to evaluation. More important, this information should be applied at appropriate times.
- **Challenge/Rebut Evaluation.** Consistent with the problem-solving interview to be discussed in the next section, employees need to be able to challenge or rebut evaluations.

The outcome of performance appraisals is viewed as fair when outputs of the appraisal process are distributed fairly. For example, ratings need to be based on performance attained, and recommendations for salary and promotion need to be based on these ratings.[12]

Empower Employees

Part of the difficulty in managing the appraisal system is collecting and maintaining information on all employees. As the span of control increases in size, this task grows to unmanageable levels. One way to resolve this problem and simultaneously increase perceptions of fairness is to shift the responsibility for performance recordkeeping to the subordinate, as in the case of Chaparral Steel—in other words, empower the employee as described in the feature "Managing Human Resources at Chaparral Steel." To enact this process, employees first need training in writing performance standards and in collecting and documenting performance information. In addition, the two-way communication process discussed above needs to operate effectively so employees feel free to renegotiate performance standards that have become obsolete or unattainable due to constraints.

Chaparral Steel trusts its employees and they respond with superior levels of performance!

There are several advantages to delegating responsibility for performance planning, goal setting, and recordkeeping to subordinates. First, they are no longer passive participants reacting to supervisor directives. Second, since it's their responsibility to identify performance hurdles and bring them to the attention of their manager, defensiveness is reduced. Third, the supervisor is free to manage and coach rather than police. Finally, the subordinate feels ownership over the process.

Encourage Appropriate Degree of Participation

Recently, many companies have viewed worker participation as a performance elixir. Some managers that believed allowing workers the opportunity to set or participate in the development of their own goals would result in higher commitment and performance. Research, however, has shown that participation, in and of itself, does *not* lead to higher performance.

More important than the worker participation is the development of specific performance standards and an explanation for their existence. Participation is only

MANAGING HUMAN RESOURCES

at Chaparral Steel

"I have seen the future and it [Chaparral Steel] works." So commented a senior executive from a large U.S. firm who listened to Gordon Forward, president of Chaparral Steel, Midlothian, Texas. In an industry with a history of high costs (requiring an average of six labor hours per ton in 1985), low performance ($70 million loss in 1985), and crushing competition from Japanese steel makers, Chaparral continues to thwart "averages." In the mid-1980s, the "mini-mill" steel company posted an 18 percent sales gain and produced at an average of 1.7 labor hours per ton (compared to 2.3 labor hours per ton by the best equivalent steel firm in Japan). How has the firm done it?

First, the company views each employee's performance strategically as a means to help Chaparral gain competitive advantage. To accomplish this, the company links careful selection and training programs with performance expectations. In addition, Chaparral's basic philosophy of pushing decision-making to the lowest level in the company has resulted in employees taking responsibility for self-management.

Self-management depends on groups of people with different perspectives solving problems. An example of Chaparral's success with this approach dates from the early 1980s when the company needed new mill stands, the equipment that flattens and shapes steel as it goes through the mill. A four-person team, including three mill workers, visited vendors worldwide, reported findings to workers and senior managers, and participated in selecting the equipment. The team then oversaw the equipment purchase (including contract negotiation) and installation. In an industry where such a major capital expenditure typically takes several years to complete, Chaparral did it in under a year.

Gordon Forward captures the basic philosophy with his comment, "It's really amazing what people can do when you let them." Supervisors have responsibility for their own hiring, training, safety programs, and deciding—with workers in their units—how to socialize and train new people. In examining performance expectations for ways that their jobs can "add more value" to the company, Chaparral's security guards have taken on new responsibilities. In addition to monitoring mills at night, security guards also do such tasks as data entry, act as paramedics, and fill up fire extinguishers.

Rather than viewing performance appraisal as a way to monitor performance, firms such as Chaparral use it to examine how to do jobs more effectively and, ultimately, how to turn them completely over to employees. The employees respond with vastly improved performance.[13]

useful if it helps employees identify an appropriate strategy to attain performance. That is, as long as performance standards are specific, time-bound, job relevant, and communicated, motivated employees will perform well.[14]

Did You KNOW?

Managers are more likely to change their behavior if they get evidence from their employees on what should be different.

Engage in Reciprocal Appraisals

To encourage openness in the performance appraisal and to improve superior subordinate relationships, subordinates can engage in appraisals of their superiors as well as themselves. Upward or reverse appraisals can help put into better balance, if not equalize, the power of the superior *vis-a-vis* the subordinate. Such a balance reduces the authoritarian character of the superior-subordinate relationship that contributes to defensiveness and avoidance in the appraisal.[15]

Organizations and superiors facilitate the upward appraisal process by providing forms for subordinates to use and by engaging in other HR policies and procedures indicative of openness (for example, allowing employees to participate in decisions about their own pay increases or in analyzing their own jobs). Furthering this openness and power equalization in performance appraisal is a policy of self-appraisal. Self-appraisal is likely to result in more information for the superior, a more realistic appraisal of the subordinate's performance, and a greater acceptance of the final appraisal by subordinates and superiors.

The Performance Appraisal Interview

The interview style and the level of preparation can enhance the effectiveness of the appraisal interview.

Before the Interview

As emphasized throughout Chapter 12, performance appraisal is an ongoing process of which the interview is only one component. Prior to the interview, the supervisor and subordinate need to prepare. A list of tips on how to prepare is in the "HR Advice and Application" feature.

Schedule in Advance. A week or two prior to the scheduled performance review, the supervisor should personally notify the ratee of the time, date, and place of the interview. Having a secretary schedule the interview increases the likelihood that the purpose and content of the session will be misunderstood. Sending a formal notice builds unneeded formality into the process and immediately shrouds the interview in ambiguity and mistrust. But most importantly, the interview will be more constructive if both parties have time to do their homework.

In setting up the interview, both parties should agree on the purpose and content of the interview. For example, will the subordinate have an opportunity to evaluate the performance of the supervisor, or will the evaluation be one-way? It

HR ADVICE & APPLICATION

Tips on How to Prepare

- Plan the meeting time and location.
- Inform employee of the meeting and its objectives.
- Ask employee to prepare self-appraisal.
- Review your notes about the employee's skills and accomplishments.
- Gather information about the employee from others.
- Review the employee's job description.
- Review last year's appraisal.
- Prepare a *draft* appraisal and plan.
- List your key objectives and prepare the agenda.
- Confer with your manager.
- Think through the employee's likely expectations and reactions.
- Conduct a mental rehearsal.

Tips for Managing the Process of the Appraisal Interview

- Set a positive, cooperative tone.
- Ensure there are no surprises (deal with problems when they arise).
- But if you didn't deal with problems when they occurred, do it now.
- Use the notes you made throughout the year during the interview.
- Focus on what people *do,* not who they *are.*
- The emphasis is on apPRAISE.
- But, constructive criticism prepares the way for improving.
- Ask for self-appraisals to get employees to identify areas for improvement.

is also useful, although possibly inconvenient, to select and use a neutral location for the interview. By holding the session in a neutral location, neither the supervisor nor the subordinate has a power advantage.

Self-Review. If subordinates are empowered, advance notice will give them sufficient time to update their performance records and do a self-review. In situations where employees formally review their own performance, comparisons of self-ratings with ratings by the supervisor can actually be made by each party to the session and then used for subsequent discussion in the interview.

Gather Relevant Information. In preparing for the interview, the rater and ratee must gather all information that has any bearing on the discussions. Here, critical incident files of behavioral diaries can be reviewed. It's also important to review the employee's job description. An agenda can be developed to allow the ratee to study it and make additions or deletions.[16]

Choose an Interview Style

An effective interview session requires both coaching and counseling skills. Additionally, a supervisor needs to be able to listen and reflect on what his or her subordinates are saying about their performance, its causes, and its outcomes. Further tips on managing the appraisal process are shown in "HR Advice and Application".

Tell-and-Sell. The **tell-and-sell interview** lets subordinates know how well they are doing and sells them on the merits of setting specific goals for improvement (if needed). This interview is effective in improving performance, especially for subordinates with little desire for participation.[17] It may be most appropriate in providing evaluation; however, subordinates may become frustrated in trying to convince their superiors to listen to justifications for their performance levels.

Tell-and-sell interview lets subordinates know where they stand and sells them on the merits of improving.

Tell-and-Listen. This approach follows no rigid format but requires question-asking and listening skills on the rater's part. The **tell-and-listen interview** provides subordinates with the chance to participate and establish a dialogue with their superiors. Its purpose is to communicate supervisor's perceptions of subordinate's strengths and weaknesses and to let subordinates respond to those perceptions. Superiors summarize and paraphrase subordinates' responses but generally fail to establish goals for performance improvement. Consequently, the subordinates may feel better, but their performance may not change.

Tell-and-listen interview lets subordinates know where they stand and allows them to participate in setting a future course.

Problem-Solving. Because of the weaknesses of the approaches described above, it is often better for the rater to view the appraisal interview as a **problem-solving interview.** Here, an active and open dialogue is established between superior and subordinate. Perceptions are shared, and solutions to problems or differences are presented, discussed, and sought. Goals for improvement are also established mutually by superior and subordinate. Because this type of interview is generally more difficult for most superiors to do, training in problem-solving is usually necessary and beneficial. Problem-solving is also inappropriate when subordinates are performing adequately. The focus in that case should be on maintaining current performance and/or developing the employee for additional responsibilities.

Problem-solving interview is an open two-way dialogue between supervisor and subordinate about performance matters.

Did You KNOW?

As a manager you really need to know how to problem-solve so you can help improve your employees' performance.

Mixed Interview. In reality, supervisors should be adaptive during the appraisal interview, and the **mixed interview** allows this. Skills are needed for the tell-and-sell and problem-solving interviews, and to make the transition from one to the other. A desirable approach is to use the tell-and-sell interview for evaluation and the problem-solving interview for development. Separate interviews for each purpose, however, may not be feasible. Since corporate policies, time, and expectations may prevent separation of purposes, a single interview must often accomplish both purposes. In this single interview, the subordinate may start out listening to the superior provide an appraisal of performance but then take a more

Mixed interview is a combination of the other types of interviews.

active role in determining what and how performance improvements can be made (problem-solving). Before leaving, the superior needs to conclude with an agreement for improvement, an action plan.[18] Tips for the development of an action plan include:

- Stay focused; avoid irrelevant discussions.
- Discuss objective performance indicators (precision).
- Focus on things the employee can control.
- Ask employee to identify barriers to excellence.
- Offer your support in removing barriers.
- Have employee suggest solutions to problems.
- Be open to suggestions for improving your own effectiveness.
- Work out defined and measurable targets.
- Get employee's commitment to strive for new targets.
- Set review dates and follow through.

Effective Feedback

Effective feedback is information on performance that is understandable, accepted, and invited.

Whether negative or positive, feedback is not always easy to provide. Fortunately, several characteristics of **effective feedback** have been determined.[19]

First, effective feedback is specific rather than general. Telling someone that he or she is dominating is probably not as useful as saying, "Just now you were not listening to what I said, but I felt I either had to agree with your arguments or face attack from you."

Second, effective feedback is focused on behavior rather than on the person. Referring to what a person does is more important than referring to what that person seems to be. A superior might say that a person talked more than anyone else at a meeting rather than that he or she is a loudmouth. The former allows for the possibility of change; the latter implies a fixed personality trait. Frustration only increases when people are reminded of shortcomings or physical characteristics they can do nothing about. At an extreme, workers may experience learned helplessness in which they give up trying to perform well because they know of no way to perform adequately.

Effective feedback also takes the receiver's needs into account. Feedback can be destructive when it serves only the evaluator's needs and fails to consider the needs of the person on the receiving end. It should be given to help, not to hurt.

Effective feedback is well-timed. In general, immediate feedback is most useful—depending on the person's readiness to hear it, the support available from others, and so on. Feedback is probably most effective when it is solicited rather than imposed. To get the most benefit, receivers should formulate questions for the evaluator to answer and actively seek feedback.

Sharing information rather than giving advice provides more effective feedback. In this way, receivers are free to decide for themselves on the changes to make in accordance with their own needs.

At Federal Express, employees are told what's expected, what's rewarded, and how to do things.

Providing only the amount of information the receiver can use, rather than the amount the evaluator would like to give, is also a part of effective feedback. Overloading a person with feedback reduces the possibility that he or she will use it effectively. An evaluator who gives more feedback than can be used is most likely satisfying a personal need rather than helping the other person.

Effective feedback concerns what is said or done and how—not why. Telling people what their motivations or intentions are tends to alienate them and contributes to a climate of resentment, suspicion, and distrust; it does not contribute to learning or development. Assuming knowledge of why a person says or does something is dangerous. If evaluators are uncertain of receivers' motives or intent, the uncertainty itself is feedback and should be revealed.

Finally, effective feedback is checked to ensure clear communication. One way is to have the receiver try to rephrase the feedback to see if it corresponds to what the evaluator had in mind. No matter what the intent, feedback is often threatening and thus subject to considerable distortion or misinterpretation.

Of course, the whole process of feedback is easier if you are comfortable giving feedback. Complete the following survey in Exhibit 13.2 to determine your comfort level. The lower your score, the more comfortable you are.

EXHIBIT 13.2

Performance Appraisal Discomfort Scale

Indicate the degree of discomfort you would feel in the following situations. Answer as candidly as possible by indicating what is true for you. Use the following scale to write in one number in the blank to the left of each item.

5 = High discomfort

4 = Some discomfort

3 = Undecided

2 = Very little discomfort

1 = No discomfort

___ 1. Telling an employee who is also a friend that he or she must stop coming to work late.

___ 2. Telling an employee that his or her work is only satisfactory, when you know that he or she expects an above-satisfactory rating.

___ 3. Talking to an employee about his or her performance on the job.

___ 4. Conducting a formal performance appraisal interview with an ineffective employee.

___ 5. Asking an employee if he or she has any comments about your rating of his or her performance.

___ 6. Telling an employee who has problems in dealing with other employees that he or she should do something about it (e.g., take a course, read a book).

___ 7. Telling a male subordinate that his performance must improve.

___ 8. Responding to an employee who is upset over your rating of his or her performance.

___ 9. Having to terminate someone for poor performance.

___ 10. Letting an employee give his or her point of view regarding a problem with performance.

___ 11. Giving a satisfactory rating to an employee who has done a satisfactory (but not exceptional) job.

___ 12. Letting a subordinate talk during an appraisal interview.

___ 13. Being challenged to justify an evaluation in the middle of an appraisal interview.

___ 14. Being accused of playing favorites in the rating of your staff.

___ 15. Recommending that an employee be discharged.

___ 16. Telling an employee that his or her performance can be improved.

___ 17. Telling an employee that you will not tolerate his or her taking extended coffee breaks.

___ 18. Warning an ineffective employee that unless performance improves, he or she will be discharged.

___ 19. Telling a female subordinate that her performance must improve.

___ 20. Encouraging an employee to evaluate his or her own performance.

Source: J. R. Abbott & H. J. Bernardin, "The Development of a Scale of Self-Efficacy," Working paper, Florida Atlantic University, 1994. Based on P. Villanova, H. J. Bernardin, S. A. Dahmus, and R. L. Sims, "Rater Leniency and Performance Appraisal Discomfort," *Educational and Psychological Measurement* 53 (1993) 789–799.

Interview Follow-Up

Action plan is an agreement regarding future performance improvement.

Even with the most useful feedback, follow-up is essential to ensure that the **action plan** negotiated during the interview is fulfilled. Because changing behavior is hard work, supervisors and subordinates both tend to put the action plan on the back burner. Consequently, a supervisor should verify that the subordinate knows what's expected, has a strategy to perform as desired, and realizes the consequences of good or bad behavior (all parts of the action plan).

Additionally, immediate reinforcement for any new behavior on the job that matches desired objectives is important. If reinforcement is delayed, new behavior is less likely to become a habit. Reinforcement can be as simple as a pat on the back or a nice comment ("That was nice work, George"), or as tangible as a note placed in the employee's file indicating performance improvement.

Did You KNOW?

Lack of follow-up indicates no interest and no importance. Things don't change under these conditions!

Diagnosing Performance Deficiencies

While the interview provides a mechanism by which performance information can be exchanged, it is only one component of an effective behavioral change process. For the appraisal to work well in the process of improving performance, the information on which the interview is based must be accurate. This means that performance gaps or deficiencies need to be identified as soon as possible and the cause of the deficiency accurately pinpointed.

Identifying Gaps in Performance

As discussed in Chapter 12, job performance is appraised in terms of attributes, behaviors, and outcomes and goals. These factors determine performance and identify any gaps. For example, outcomes and goals can identify deficiencies by showing how well an employee does in relation to the goals set. If an employee had a performance goal of reducing the scrap rate by 10 percent but actually reduced it by only 5 percent, a performance gap exists. The discrepancy between set goals and actual outcomes can thus be used to spot gaps. This method is valid as long as the goals are not contradictory and can be quantified in measurable terms *and* the subordinate's performance can be measured in the terms in which the goals are set.[20] Exhibit 13.3 is a checklist of symptoms associated with performance problems: more than one "yes" indicates a need to probe deeper.

In addition to comparing performance to relevant standards, the performance of employees, units, or departments can be compared with one another. For example, organizations with several divisions often measure the overall performance of each division by comparing it with all other divisions. The divisions that are ranked on the bottom become identified as problem areas (that is, they have performance gaps). Efforts to improve performance can then be expected from these divisions.

The final method by which gaps can be identified is by comparison over time. For example, a manager who sold 1,000 record albums last month but only 800 albums this month appears to have a performance gap. Although performance has declined, the supervisor needs to determine whether this gap represents a deficiency that should be or can be corrected or a normal fluctuation. The month in which 1,000 albums were sold may have been the peak of the buying season. During the second month, the employee may have had to attend an important conference vital to longer-run record sales.

Regardless of the method used to discover whether a performance deficiency exists, once detected, managers want to remove it. If they hope to improve their employees' performance, however, they must begin by examining the causes underlying any actual gaps.

LEARNING OBJECTIVE 3

Tell why employees do not always perform well even when they have the ability.

Identifying the Causes of Deficiencies

To uncover the reasons for performance deficiencies, a number of questions can be asked, based on a model of the determinants of employee behavior in organizations.[21]

EXHIBIT 13.3

Checklist for Identifying Performance Problems

Read the following questions about an employee's performance. If you are thinking "yes" in response to a question, place a check mark next to that item. If not, leave it blank.

DO PEERS COMPLAIN THAT

__ 1. She is not treating them fairly?

__ 2. He is not carrying his own weight?

__ 3. She is rude?

__ 4. He is argumentative and confrontational?

__ 5. She is all talk and no action?

DO CUSTOMERS

__ 1. Always ask for someone else to help them?

__ 2. Complain about her attitude?

__ 3. Complain that he has made promises to them that he's never fulfilled?

__ 4. Say she is bad-mouthing you, the organization, or its products?

__ 5. Complain that he is too pushy?

DO YOU

__ 1. Find it difficult to get your own work done because you spend so much time with him on his problems and mistakes?

__ 2. Worry about what she will say to customers and clients?

__ 3. Check his work often because you are afraid of mistakes?

__ 4. Do work yourself that you should have delegated to her?

__ 5. Assign work to others because they can do it faster or better than he can?

__ 6. Hear about her mistakes from your boss or others?

__ 7. Sometimes find out that he has lied to you or stretched the truth?

__ 8. Seldom think of her when you're deciding who should get an important assignment?

DOES HE/SHE

__ 1. Infrequently complete assignments on time?

__ 2. Often show up to work late or not at all?

__ 3. Always have an excuse for poor performance?

__ 4. Wait to be assigned additional work rather than asking for more work when an assignment is completed?

__ 5. Rarely complete assignments in the way you want?

This model enables the HR manager to diagnose deficiencies and correct them in a systematic way. In general, the model says that employees perform well if the following determinants are present:

- Ability
- Interest in doing the job

- Opportunity to grow and advance
- Clearly defined goals
- Feedback on how well they are doing
- Rewards for performing well
- Punishments for performing poorly
- Power to get resources to do the job

As a manager, you need to be very familiar with these possible causes of deficiencies: it's your responsibility!

Exhibit 13.4 more fully describes these determinants and the specific questions to ask in locating causes. Negative responses indicate that the item is probably a cause, and based on a series of such responses, the likely causes for a performance deficiency begin to take shape.

The Attribution Process

The process people use to explain their behavior and the behavior of others is called an **attribution process.** Individuals attribute their and others' behavior to various causes. Understanding the attribution processes that individuals use facilitates predicting what causes and responses managers are likely to attach to the performance deficiencies they see in their subordinates.

Internal attribution is the belief that one's self is the cause.

External attribution is the belief that others are the cause.

In relation to performance, managers attribute causes of subordinates' deficiencies to either the subordinates themselves, **internal attribution,** or to the subordinates' environment, **external attribution.** Internal attributions include low effort (motivation) or low ability; external attributions include task interference, lack of organizational rewards, and poor supervision. Managers are more likely to make internal attributions to the extent that the employee: 1) does not perform poorly on other tasks, 2) performs poorly when other employees perform well on the same task, and 3) has performed poorly on the same task in the past. Managers are also likely to focus on motivation over ability if an employee has performed the task adequately in the past but isn't performing adequately now.[22]

Whether the manager makes internal or external attributions influences the strategy for performance improvement likely to be selected by the manager.[23] If internal attributions are made, the manager is more likely to select strategies aimed at changing the subordinate, such as retraining, termination, or reprimands. If external attributions are made, the manager will likely select strategies that modify the environment, such as job redesign or rewards and punishments.

LEARNING OBJECTIVE 4

Identify strategies to improve performance.

Strategies for Improvement

When deficiencies are found, companies can do many things to facilitate improved employee performance.

Positive Reinforcement System

The positive reinforcement system is based on reinforcement theory in employee motivation and performance.[24] The following is an illustration of the positive reinforcement system.[25]

Positive reinforcement is the use of positive rewards to increase the occurrence of desired performance.

Law of effect states that positively rewarded behavior will be repeated and negatively rewarded behavior will not.

Positive reinforcement system involves the use of positive rewards to increase the occurrence of the desired performance. It is based on two fundamental principles: 1) people perform in ways that they find most rewarding to them; and 2) by providing the proper rewards, it is possible to improve performance. A positive reinforcement (PR) system or program focuses on the behavior that leads to desired results rather than on the results. It uses rewards rather than punishment or the threat of punishment to influence that behavior and attempts to link specific behaviors to specific rewards. This model operates according to the **law of effect,** which states that behavior that leads to a positive result tends to be

EXHIBIT 13.4

Diagnosing Performance Deficiencies

Check which of the following factors affecting an individual's performance or behavior apply to the situation you are analyzing.

	YES	NO
I. Skills, Knowledge, and Abilities of the Individual		
A. Does the individual have the skills to do as expected?	______	______
B. Has the individual performed as expected before?	______	______
II. Personality, Interests, and Preferences of the Individual		
A. Does the individual have the personality or interest to perform as expected?	______	______
B. Does the individual clearly perceive what's actually involved in performing as expected?	______	______
III. Opportunity for the Individual		
A. Does the individual have a chance to grow and use valued skills and abilities?	______	______
B. Does the organization offer career paths to the individual?	______	______
IV. Goals for the Individual		
A. Are there goals established?	______	______
B. Are the goals very specific?	______	______
C. Are the goals clear?	______	______
D. Are the goals difficult?	______	______
V. Uncertainty for the Individual		
A. Is the individual certain about what rewards are available?	______	______
B. Is the individual certain about what to do?	______	______
C. Is the individual certain about what others expect?	______	______
D. Is the individual certain about job responsibilities and levels of authority?	______	______
VI. Feedback to the Individual		
A. Does the employee get information about what is right and wrong (quality or quantity) with performance?	______	______
B. Does the information received tell the employee how to improve performance?	______	______
C. Does the employee get information frequently?	______	______
D. Is there a delay between the time the employee performs and receiving information on that performance?	______	______
E. Can the information be easily interpreted by the employee?	______	______
VII. Consequences to the Individual		
A. Is it punishing to do as expected (immediate)?	______	______
B. Is it punishing to do as expected (long-term)?	______	______
C. Do more positive consequences result from taking alternative action (immediate)?	______	______
D. Do more positive consequences result from taking alternative action (long-term)?	______	______
E. Are there no apparent consequences for performing as desired?	______	______
F. Are there no positive consequences for performing as desired?	______	______
VIII. Power for the Individual		
A. Can the individual mobilize resources to get the job done?	______	______
B. Can the individual influence others to get them to do what is needed?	______	______
C. Is the individual highly visible to others higher up in the organization?	______	______

Source: This format is based on R. F. Mager and P. Pipe, *Analyzing Performance Problems* or *"You Really Oughta Wanna"* (Belmont, CA: Fearon Pittman, 1970).

repeated, while behavior that leads to a neutral or negative result tends not to be repeated. Thus, an effort is made to link behavior to its consequences.

A PR system is installed by four basic steps, as shown in Exhibit 13.5: 1) conducting a performance audit, 2) establishing performance standards or goals, 3) giving feedback to employees about their performance, and 4) offering employees praise or other rewards tied directly to performance.[26]

EXHIBIT 13.5

Steps in a Positive Reinforcement System

This is a linear diagram. From a systems point of view, each step may have unintended consequences.

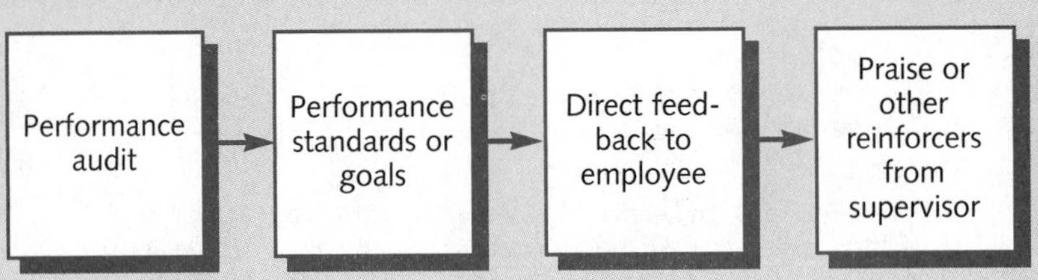

Conducting a Performance Audit. Performance audits examine how well jobs are being performed. Without audits, many managers believe that their operations are going better than they actually are. Emery Air Freight Corporation conducted a performance audit on the way it was shipping packages. The cost of freight is considerably reduced if all the small packages going to a particular city are put in large containers. The managers involved in this part of the operation estimated that large containers were used in shipping about 90 percent of the time. The audit showed, however, that the actual figure was only 45 percent.[27] If possible, workers should be involved in performance audits, since they often know more about the job than anyone else.

Establishing Performance Standards or Goals. Standards are the minimum levels of performance accepted. They should be set after a performance audit and tied directly to the job. The goals should be measurable and attainable, and the standards should be challenging but not impossible to reach—perfection is never possible. Standards are best formed on the basis of observation and common sense, and they should be precise. "Better identification with the organization" and "increased job satisfaction" are too general to be standards. Where possible, the workers should participate in establishing standards.

At Emery Air Freight, the employees in the Chicago customer service department set and reached a standard higher than the one management would have set for giving customer answers within a specified period.[28] However, time limitations can preclude giving employees all the information they need to establish a reasonable standard.

Giving Feedback to Employees about Their Performance. The third step in a positive reinforcement program is to give workers the basic data they need in order to keep track of their own work. The standards of performance for many jobs are not clearly stated; even when clearly stated, they are seldom available to the worker. A woman in an insurance company described her routine as follows: "I glance through the form to see if it is completely filled out. Then I separate the blue copies from the yellow copies and put them in different piles." When asked the purpose of the form, how it was used, and where the different copies went, she reported that she did not know. She had no idea if the information on the form was accurate, and she did not know the consequences for incomplete or incorrectly filled out forms. All she knew was that each line of the form had to have something on it or be returned to another department.

Performance should be measured against standards, and an employee should be given direct feedback.

Performance standards are ineffective without constant measurement and feedback. The feedback should be neutral rather than evaluative or judgmental and, if possible, should come directly to the worker rather than to the supervisor.

Prompt, direct feedback refers, of course, to knowledge of results, an important learning tool. Feedback allows the worker to know whether performance is improving, remaining the same, or getting worse.

Offering Employees Praise or Other Rewards Tied Directly to Performance. As explained earlier, positive reinforcement involves the use of positive rewards to increase the occurrence of the desired performance. The fourth step in a positive reinforcement program—offering employees praise or other rewards tied to performance—is the most important one. If the reward is praise, it should be expressed in specific quantitative terms. "Keep up the good work, Chris" is too general. A better form of praise is "Chris, I liked the imagination you used in getting the product packed. You are running fairly consistently at 97 percent of standard. After watching you, I can understand why."

Nobody knows better than Mary Kay Ash, Chairman Emeritus of Mary Kay Cosmetics, how to motivate a sales force. She has mastered the true power of employee praise and recognition!

One of the most common rewards is money. Although money is very effective as a motivator, many organizations cannot afford to use it that way often. Other rewards can be just as effective, though. They include praise and recognition tied to the specific job behavior, the opportunity to choose activities, the opportunity to personally measure work improvement, and the opportunity to influence both co-workers and management.

Rewards for specific performance should be given as soon as possible after the behavior has taken place. Reinforcement should be more frequent at the beginning but can become less frequent and more unpredictable after the desired performance level is reached.

There are several different types of reward schedules, among them continuous reinforcement and partial reinforcement. Under **continuous reinforcement,** the employee is reinforced every time the correct performance occurs. When this schedule is used, performance improves rapidly but can regress just as rapidly when the reinforcement is removed. In addition, managers find it difficult or impossible to continuously reward performance. Therefore, managers should use **partial reinforcement,** rewarding correct behavior only part of the time. There are a number of partial reinforcement schedules, perhaps the most effective being the variable ratio schedule. Under this schedule, reinforcement is given after an average number of desired responses but not precisely at that average point; rather, the time of dispensation varies somewhere around the average point so that it cannot be predicted exactly.[29] In most organizations, pay occurs on a fixed-interval schedule such as once a week or once a month; pay increases and promotions occur on a variable-interval schedule; and praise, recognition, and similar rewards occur on a partial reinforcement schedule.

Reward

Desired behavior
Continuous reinforcement

More frequent rewards at first | Less frequent later

Partial reinforcement

The six basic rules for using reinforcement are as follows:

1. **Do not reward everyone the same way.** Using a defined objective or standard, give more rewards to the better performers.
2. **Recognize that failure to respond also has reinforcing consequences.** Managers influence subordinates by what they don't do as well as by what they do; lack of reward can thus influence behavior. Managers frequently find the job of differentiating among workers unpleasant but necessary. One way to differentiate is to reward some and withhold rewards from others.
3. **Tell people what they must do to be rewarded.** If employees have standards against which to measure the job, they can arrange their own feedback system to let them make self-judgments about their work. They can then adjust their work patterns accordingly.
4. **Tell people what they are doing wrong.** Few people like to fail; most want to get positive rewards. A manager who withholds rewards from subordinates should give them a clear idea of why the rewards are not forthcoming. The employees can then adjust their behavior accordingly rather than waste time trying to discover what behavior will be rewarded.

5. **Do not punish anyone in front of others.** Constructive criticism is useful in eliminating undesired behavior; so also is punishment, when necessary. However, criticizing or punishing anyone in front of others lowers the individual's self-respect and self-esteem. Furthermore, other members of the work group may sympathize with the punished employee and resent the supervisor.
6. **Be fair.** Make the consequences equal to the behavior. Do not cheat an employee out of just rewards; if someone is a good worker, say so. Some managers find it difficult to praise; others find it difficult to counsel or tell an employee about what is being done wrong. A person who is overrewarded may feel guilty, and one who is underrewarded may become angry.[30]

When the managers and employees at Emery Air Freight understood that only 45 percent of the packages were being shipped in containers, and feedback and positive reinforcement were given, the workers soon hit the standard of 95 percent. The change resulted in savings of about $65,000 per year.[31]

In summary, the manager using the positive reinforcement model should first examine the job (audit the performance) to determine standards, preferably with the assistance of the employees. Then the manager should establish methods of getting direct feedback to employees about individual or group performance. Finally, the manager should provide positive reinforcement as employees come closer to the standard, shifting perhaps from a continuous to a partial reinforcement schedule as they get very close to the standard. At the beginning, the manager might have to look carefully for even small changes in behavior in order to give positive reinforcement; otherwise, behavior might not improve.

Positive Discipline Programs

Some organizations improve performance through their use of positive discipline or nonpunitive discipline.[32] The essential aspects of positive discipline programs include the following:

> *When disciplinary discussions have failed to produce the desired changes, management places the individual on a one-day, "decision-making leave." The company pays the employee for the day to demonstrate the organization's desire to see him or her remain a member of the organization and to eliminate the resentment and hostility that punitive actions usually produce. But tenure with the organization is conditional on the individual's decision to solve the immediate problem and make a "total performance commitment" to good performance on the job. The employee is instructed to return on the day following the leave with a decision either to change and stay or to quit and find more satisfying work elsewhere.*[33]

This program really puts the responsibility for the employee's behavior into the hands of the employee. It tells the employee, however, that the company cares and will keep the employee as long as he or she makes a commitment to do well. If the employee makes the commitment, the company has a good employee. If the employee decides to leave, he or she is not really able to blame the company. Thus far, this type of program appears to work.[34]

Employee Assistance Programs

Employee assistance programs (EAPs) offer help to employees who have chronic problems requiring major attention. EAPs give employees a second chance.

Employee Assistance Programs (EAPs) are specifically designed to assist employees with chronic personal problems that hinder their job performance and attendance. EAPs are often used with employees who are alcoholics or who have severe domestic problems. Since the job may be partly responsible for these problems, some employers are taking the lead in establishing EAPs to help affected workers.[35]

A company that establishes an employee assistance program generally thinks that it has a responsibility toward employees and that employees should be given a chance to correct any undesirable job behavior. Helping alcoholic employees also makes good economic sense, because the average cost to the employer in absenteeism, reduced productivity, accidents in the workplace, and use of the company medical plan is enormous—about 25 percent of the alcoholic's salary. Furthermore, about 65 to 80 percent of those who receive treatment for chemical dependency return to the workforce and do what their supervisors consider a satisfactory job. Nevertheless, employees must also help themselves. If they fail to participate in an EAP or recover through other means, employers may have no choice but to dismiss them. The philosophy of most EAPs is to help individuals help themselves within a context of fairness yet firmness.

Did You KNOW?

Some 20 million Americans abuse alcohol and more than 100,000 die prematurely from alcohol-related causes.

While EAPs providing assistance in alcohol and drug abuse are most common, organizations also establish EAPs for marital and family problems, mental disorders, financial problems, stress, dependent-care programs, bereavement counseling, eating disorders, weight control, smoking cessation, and AIDS support.[36]

To be successful, an employee assistance program should possess the following attributes:

- A policy statement (see the feature, "Managing Human Resources: A Drug-Free Workplace Policy")
- Top management backing
- Union or employee support
- Confidentiality
- Easy access
- Trained supervisors
- Trained union steward, if in a union setting
- Insurance
- Availability of numerous services for assistance and referral
- Skilled, professional leadership
- Systems for monitoring, assessing, and revising

Even though EAPs provide valuable assistance, many employees in need fail to use the programs unless faced with the alternative of being terminated. When so confronted, however, the success rate of those attending EAPs is high. The results can mean substantial gains in employee job performance and reductions in absenteeism and insurance claims. For the 67 employees receiving EAP treatment in one study, the total number of lost work days dropped 29 percent, from 476 days before treatment to 341 days following treatment. The study also found that after EAP participation:

- Combined lost work time was reduced by 18 percent—from 117 instances to 97 instances.
- The cost of health insurance claims declined 26 percent—from a total $36,472 to $27,122.
- Work suspensions dropped from five to three; written warnings decreased from eight to seven; and the number of job-related accidents went from seven to three.[37]

MANAGING HUMAN RESOURCES

A Drug-Free Workplace Policy

It is the policy of XYZ, Inc., to create and maintain a drug free environment in the workplace, as required by the *Drug-Free Workplace Act* of 1988. The use of controlled substances* is inconsistent with the professional and responsible behavior we expect of employees, subjects all employees and visitors to our facilities to unacceptable safety risks, and undermines XYZ's ability to operate effectively and efficiently. Therefore, the employees of XYZ are strictly prohibited from engaging in the unlawful manufacture, distribution, dispensation, possession, sale, or use of a controlled substance at the workplace or while conducting XYZ business off the company's premises. Such unlawful conduct is also prohibited during non-working time to the extent that it 1) impairs, in the opinion of the management of XYZ, the employee's ability to perform his or her job, and 2) affects the company's reputation or threatens its integrity, also in the opinion of XYZ's management.

In order to educate the employees about the dangers of drug abuse, the company has established a drug free awareness program. Periodically, employees will be required to attend informational sessions during which the dangers of drug abuse, XYZ's policy regarding drugs, and the availability of counseling and the company's employee assistance plan will be discussed.

Employees who are convicted of offenses involving controlled substances in the workplace (including employees who plead "nolo contendere"—that is, no contest) must inform the human resources department within five days of the conviction or plea. Employees who violate any aspect of this policy are subject to disciplinary action, up to and including termination from the company. They may be required, at the company's discretion, to participate in and successfully complete a drug-abuse treatment or rehabilitation program as a condition of continued employment.[38]

*Controlled substances are identified in Schedules I through V of Section 202 of the *Federal Controlled Substances Act.* They include marijuana, cocaine, heroin and morphine, as well as barbiturates and amphetamines.

Employee assistance programs can position the organization and the employee on the same side of this difficult issue. Organizations are finding that effective EAPs can make drug testing, which has been controversial among the work force, a nonevent:

> *Both Mobil and Campbell Soup strongly emphasize counseling for drug users, but insist they're not doing so in order to sell testing. Mobil is moving more vigorously to use its plan to stop and treat drug abuse. Valley Bank says its supportive get-help policy has made drug testing a nonevent with employees. American Airlines says assistance plans are more effective than testing in attempts to curb drug abuse.*[39]

Employee Counseling

To change the habits of chronically absent employees, McGraw Edison has devised an innovative counseling program that stresses problem-solving and goal-setting techniques. This individual approach focuses on the "5 to 10 percent of the workforce" that has a history of absenteeism. Before beginning the actual counseling with individual employees, supervisors take the following steps:

- **Identify the consistently worst offenders.** Make a list of all employees who have a record of repeated absences, regardless of the "presumed legitimacy or the underlying reasons" for missing work.

- **Centralize the absenteeism data.** Records and information should be accumulated, analyzed, and maintained in one central location.
- **Collect long-term data.** Absenteeism records on individuals should be kept for a sufficiently long period to show that a clear pattern exists.

Once the decision is made to meet with the employee, supervisors then do the following:

- Examine the attendance record with the employee.
- Make sure the employee is aware of the severity of the problem, as well as the organization's attendance standards.
- Prepare a brief, accurate memo at the session's end outlining the problem, noting the reasons given by the employee, and specifying whether or not the employee responded with a desire to improve.

If the first session has not produced a significant change, a second counseling session should be scheduled. Participants in this session should include the worker's supervisor, the employee, a union representative (if applicable), and higher management officials. An upper-level manager should be present to ensure that due process protection (Chapter 4) is provided for the employee. Results of the second counseling session should also be documented.

Helping employees improve may not always work, but it can provide support for dismissal decisions.

If the employee shows no improvement after the second session, another session can be held, which should again include an upper-level manager. At this stage, the "decision to meet the expected standard of attendance and continuity of employment" should be placed directly on the employee. To dramatize the importance and seriousness of the situation, the employee might be requested to take one-day decision-making leave to decide whether he or she wishes to resign or to commit to a long-term program of positive improvement. If no sign of improvement is shown after this step, discharging the employee may be necessary.

Negative Behavioral Strategies

While most employees want to conduct themselves in a manner that is acceptable to the organization and their co-workers, problems of absenteeism, poor work performance, and rule violation do arise.

Punishment is commonly used in many organizations because of its perceived ability to correct these problems. Discipline or punishment is an effective management tool for the following reasons:

- Discipline alerts the marginal employee that his or her low performance is unacceptable and a change in behavior is warranted.
- Discipline has vicarious reinforcing power. When one person is punished, it signals other employees regarding expected performance and behavioral conduct.
- If the discipline is viewed as appropriate by other employees, it may increase their motivation, morale, and performance.[40]

A recent study in a retail store showed that managers who used the organization's disciplinary system more frequently than their peers had higher department performance ratings.[41] The reason is that individuals in a group rely on one another to learn appropriate behavior. As a result, employees model the behaviors of successful peers and impose group norms on low performers.[42]

Punishment, however, may not always be effective. Employees can resent the punishment and become angry. Their performance may get even worse. The negative effects of punishment can be reduced by incorporating several **hot-stove principles,** including the following:

Hot-stove principles state that discipline is most effective when it is clear, quick, impersonal, and not surprising.

- **Provide ample and clear warning.** Many organizations have clearly defined disciplinary steps. For example, the first offense might elicit an oral warning; the second offense, a written warning; the third offense, a disciplinary layoff; the fourth offense, discharge.
- **Administer the discipline as quickly as possible.** If a long time elapses between the ineffective behavior and the discipline, the employee may not know what the discipline is for.
- **Administer the same discipline for the same behavior for everyone, every time.** Discipline has to be administered fully and consistently.
- **Administer the discipline impersonally.** Discipline should be based on a specific behavior.

Because the immediate supervisor or manager plays the integral role in administering discipline, the HR department and the organization should do the following to increase the discipline's effectiveness:

- Involve managers and supervisors in the selection of their employees.
- Educate managers and supervisors about the organization's disciplinary policies and train them to administer the policies.
- Set up standards that are equitable to employees and that managers and supervisors can easily and consistently implement.

Taking these steps not only reduces the likely negative effects generally associated with disciplines, but also helps ensure that employee rights are respected (discussed further in Chapter 4). This is further guaranteed with the establishment of fair work rules and policies that are consistently applied and enforced.

When Nothing Else Works

Helping employees—especially the problem ones—improve their work performance is a tough job. It's easy to get frustrated and to wonder if you're not just spinning your wheels. Even when we want it to work, it sometimes doesn't work. Still, when you conclude that "nothing works," you're really saying that it's no longer worth your time and energy to help the employee improve. This conclusion should not be made in haste since the organization has already invested a great deal of time and money in the selection and training of this employee. However, there are some situations where more drastic steps may be needed.

- Performance actually gets worse.
- There's a little change but not enough.
- There is no change in the problem behavior.
- Drastic changes in behavior occur immediately but improvements don't last.

If, after repeated warnings and counseling, performance does not improve, there are four last recourses.

Transfers. Sometimes there is just not a good match between an employee and a job. If, however, the employee has useful skills and abilities, it may be beneficial to transfer the employee. Transferring is appropriate if the employee's skill deficiency would have little or no impact on the new position. The concern with transfers is that there must be a job available for which the problem employee is qualified.

Restructuring. Some jobs are particularly unpleasant or onerous. For these positions, the solution may be redesigning the job, rather than replacing the employee. It may also make sense to redesign a position to take advantage of an employee's special strengths. If an employee has extraordinary technical expertise, it may be advantageous to utilize this expertise instead of having the employee perform routine tasks.

Termination. While HR policies vary across organizations and industries, termination is generally warranted for dishonesty, habitual absenteeism, substance abuse, and insubordination, including flatly refusing to do certain things requested and consistently low productivity that cannot be corrected through training. Unfortunately, termination, even for legitimate reasons, is unpleasant. In addition to the administrative hassles, documentation, and paper work involved, supervisors often feel guilty about being the "bad guy." And the thought of sitting down with an employee and delivering the bad news makes most supervisors anxious. As a result, they continue to put off the action and justify this by saying they won't be able to find a "better" replacement. Still, when one considers the consequences of job errors, drunkenness, or "being high" on the job, termination may be cost-effective. Employee rights regarding termination were discussed in Chapters 4 and 5.

Neutralizing. **Neutralizing** problem employee situations involves restructuring an employee's job in such a way that it is easy for the employee to do well. Because group morale may suffer when an ineffective employee is given special treatment, neutralizing should be avoided whenever possible.

Neutralizing gives special accommodation to a problem employee by making it easy for the person to do well.

However, it is a fact of organizational life that neutralizing may be practical when a terminating process is time-consuming and cumbersome, or when an employee is close to retiring. In neutralizing the employee, a manager shouldn't harass the employee, hoping that he or she will quit or transfer, but should assign the employee tasks that are not critical, but in which he or she can be productive.

Current Trends

360-Degree Feedback. A major trend in performance appraisal is **360-degree feedback,** or multisource feedback. A more complete picture is developed when an individual (for example, a manager) receives performance appraisals from subordinates, peers, boss, self, and even customers—hence the name. For example,

360-degree feedback is appraisal information from all directions.

At Warner Lambert Co., a health care products manufacturer in Morris Plains, New Jersey, employees are evaluated by their peers, supervisors, and subordinates, as well as external customers or clients, according to Stella Estevez, manager for global organization and leadership development. Results of the feedback are looked at not just for what they mean to the individual, but also to the company. "Otherwise, you'll be taking care of career development without taking care of business needs," Estevez says.

The "360-degree" appraisal system is more than a mechanism to gain feedback on employees, it is a response to the changing business environment, Estevez adds. The goal is to find the behavioral and people skills that add value and make an employee a top performer, and then train the rest of the workers in those skills, she explains.[43]

Novartis, a large multinational pharmaceutical maker in Basel, Switzerland, uses 360-degree feedback as a way of helping managers understand how they are seen by others. Data are gathered in much the same way as they are at Warner Lambert. Based upon the results, managers construct "action plans" that they will use in the coming year to help improve their leadership skills as seen by others and themselves. At both Novartis and Warner Lambert, managers are given feedback regarding behaviors the companies have identified as consistent with their values and

To embed our values, we give our people 360-degree evaluations, with input from superiors, peers, and subordinates. These are the roughest evaluations you can get, because people hear things about themselves they've never heard before. But they get the input they need, and then the chance to improve. If they don't improve, they have to go.

Jack Welch
CEO
General Electric Company

necessary for their strategies. Thus, the feedback is helpful for the company and the individual. Getting agreement on these behaviors, however, takes time because in multinational companies many national cultures are represented. Frequently, multinational companies end up developing general feedback forms representing the corporate culture. Managers then develop action plans that are most appropriate for their local conditions. A detailed description of 360-degree feedback is presented in HR Advice and Application: Performance Management in the Round."

International Comparisons

To understand what is distinctive about the U.S. culture, 40 international managers (all non-U.S. nationals who were familiar with the U.S. business culture) were interviewed and asked to identify cultural aspects that underlie the U.S. system of management. Of the 40 participants, 36 felt that a strong commitment to the philosophy of meritocracy is a distinctively American societal value. **Meritocracy** emphasizes fairness in evaluating people on their work-related contributions. The managers also noted the short-term orientation in America as emphasized by annual appraisals based solely on current performance.

In other cultures, meritocracy is not so firmly established as a guiding principle. In its place one finds more concern for status, family ties, and loyalty to one's supervisor or organization. In other cultures, recent performance is not always the most important criteria. Behavior over time, loyalty, and the potential for the future are emphasized much more.[44]

There is also evidence that U.S. managers believe in a "Master of Destiny" viewpoint where, if a person works hard and has the ability and motivation to perform, he or she will be able to advance in a company. A more fatalistic view predominates in many other countries. That is, people are born into a certain class, and they are not able, no matter what they do, to improve their standing. In such a culture, there may be no need for a performance management system.[45]

Americans also have very specific ideas about performance appraisal criteria. For example, management guru Peter Drucker writes that "An employer has no business with a man's personality. Employment is a specific contract calling for specific performance and for nothing else."[46] As will be discussed in the following sections, other societies base performance judgments much more on the "whole man or woman" than on actual job performance.

The Pacific Rim Countries

While actual practices vary by country, most Pacific Rim countries use informal and formal appraisal processes to develop and reward employee performance. However, there appears to be less reliance on sophisticated formal systems than in U.S. companies. That is, most dialogue on performance occurs informally on either a one-on-one or group basis, rather than in a formal review session.

Korea. In Korea, performance appraisal systems are in place in almost all large and most small companies. Since promotions are based primarily on seniority, performance appraisal is conducted primarily for purposes of counseling and development. The scope of the appraisal varies with the organization, with some firms approaching the process formally, almost ritualistically, and others approaching it very informally.

Many Koreans believe the cooperative nature of work makes it impossible to differentiate performance levels among employees with any degree of accuracy. As a result, factors such as seniority, loyalty, proper attitude, and initiative are at least as important as actual job performance.

Practices at the Sunkyong Company are representative of the more formalized approach to appraisal in Korea. The appraisal process begins with an extensive

HR ADVICE & APPLICATION

Performance Management "In the Round"

"Employers can better manage the performance of their workers if they replace traditional employee evaluations with 360-degree feedback systems," asserts Mark R. Edwards, president of consulting firm TEAMS Inc. of Tempe, Arizona. In the next 10 years, he predicts, these multiple-source assessment systems will become the most powerful human resource management tool available in motivating productive change.

A DIAGNOSTIC TOOL

In contrast to the traditional approach, where a single supervisor rates employee performance, multiple-source systems allow evaluations to be conducted by a group of colleagues and internal customers who form a circle around the employee. According to Edwards, employees are much more likely to respond constructively to a group's suggestions on how to improve their performance. As a result, the evaluation process becomes more of a diagnostic tool for employee development and less of an instrument to judge and discipline employees.

DESIGNING AN EVALUATION SYSTEM

"As organizations become flatter and move toward team-based management structures, multiple-source evaluation systems can play an integral role in facilitating participation and enhancing productivity," Edwards notes. The essential elements of an effective 360-degree feedback system include the following:

- **Establish feedback criteria.** The first step in designing a multiple-source assessment system is selecting evaluation criteria and developing a behavior profile, so employees can be assessed relative to a model and not relative to co-workers. The process of defining evaluation criteria should be participative. For the system to work effectively, stakeholders in the organization must be given the opportunity to get involved up front.
- **Select evaluation teams.** Do not limit evaluation teams to the employee's closest colleagues. To get the most out of multiple-source assessments, the group should reflect the employee's internal customers. Teams should consist of five to eight members, including the employee being evaluated. Employees then have the opportunity to compare their self-evaluations with the group's assessments.
- **Conduct the evaluations.** Evaluation forms can be distributed in hard copy or electronically. Using an electronic mail system is one very efficient method for carrying out this process. It is important, however, to establish procedures for ensuring the anonymity of evaluators and the confidentiality of their responses.
- **Create summary reports.** After the evaluation forms are collected, summary data should be tabulated and put into a format that is easily understood by employees. Various software packages are available, including one designed by TEAMS Inc., that make it easier to generate tables and graphs from questionnaire responses.
- **Analyze results.** Along with the raw results of the evaluations, provide employees with an analysis of the data that will clarify and focus areas of strength and weakness in their performance.
- **Intervene to improve behavior.** The final step is to use evaluation results to improve employee performance. Instead of focusing only on problems, seek to identify structural constraints to improvement, and attempt to change those factors. For example, does the employee have the necessary training and tools to perform the job, and are internal procedures clearly communicated?

"Organizations will increasingly adopt multiple-source systems as the total-quality movement gains momentum and the technology to do 360-degree feedback improves," Edwards says. He predicts that while less than one percent of employers currently use the systems, that figure will jump to over fifty percent in the next 10 years. In conclusion, there are four basic criteria employers should look for in a multiple-source evaluation system: fairness, accuracy, simplicity, and trustworthiness.[47]

self-assessment inventory that is completed by the employee. Results are discussed with the employee's immediate supervisor and later with the supervisor's supervisor. Extensive peer assessments are also used. In other companies, however, the appraisal review consists of nothing more than informal individual counseling sessions.[48]

People's Republic of China (PRC). Since the end of the Cultural Revolution in 1978, management practices in China have undergone significant changes. Most notable is the shift from a Stalinist system of industrial management (centralization, detailed plans, standard operating procedures) to a new motivational system that emphasizes responsibility and performance. Since 1984, the imperative has been to calculate profit prior to action rather than action before calculation.

At the enterprise level, these changes have been accompanied by a move from participatory management in the *Yan'an* tradition (pluralistic decision-making and tight control) to a new structure of collective leadership. According to a PRC Decision Document, "Modern enterprises must have a minute division of labor, a high degree of continuity in production, strict technological requirements, and a high degree of cooperation." This document also prescribes that enterprises must specify in explicit terms the requirements for each work post and the duties of each worker and staff.

As a result of these reforms, there is an increasing emphasis on performance in Chinese enterprises. In the past, profits reverted directly to the state. Since the Cultural Revolution, a portion of profits can be held out and distributed to employees. Even by Western standards, performance bonuses—even for low-level workers—are high, averaging as much as one-third of one's annual salary. Still, the allocation of these rewards is based on organizational rather than individual performance.

Regarding a shift in values, a recent study found that objective performance is the most important determinant of performance ratings of both U.S. and Chinese decision-makers. However, unlike Americans, Chinese are significantly influenced by employee loyalty/dependability when making performance judgments. Apparently, traditional Chinese cultural values of defining performance in broad terms still remain.[49]

Performance evaluation in China also includes one unique facet: self-criticism. The format of these meetings, called *Hsiao-tsu* sessions, are advocated by the central committee of the national government. The official objective is to create more cohesive groups through identifying insensitive and other dysfunctional behaviors. As operationalized, they appear to serve as reverse appraisal sessions in which lower-ranking employees can make perceived or real mistreatments known to management.[50]

Japan. On first blush, performance appraisal would seem to be an unnecessary control mechanism for the Japanese organization, which emphasizes job rotation, slow promotion, and group, rather than individual, loyalty. As William Ouchi, a cross-cultural management expert notes, "Japanese employees are controlled in a subtle, indirect manner that contrasts greatly with the explicit formal control system used in the United States."[51]

Still, an increasing number of Japanese firms are using formal appraisals to evaluate the contribution of employees and to develop them into better employees. However, the concept of performance has a different meaning in Japan than in Western countries. For example, merit ratings are based on educational attainment and job ability factors such as communication skills, cooperativeness, and sense of responsibility, rather than on work results. The Japanese concept of performance includes not only the achievement of results, but also the expenditure of a good-faith effort.[52]

Summary

Ineffective employee performance, whether anyone wants to admit it or not, plagues all organizations at least some of the time. For a performance appraisal system to be effective, not only must it permit the gathering of performance appraisal data, it must also enable the manager to use this information. Organizations that have developed an effective performance appraisal system, therefore, directly influence productivity, quality of work life, legal compliance, competitive advantage, and flexibility through the gathering and use of performance appraisal data.

Because of the dual purposes of evaluation and development, conflicts are inherent and inevitable. These conflicts, if unaddressed, will cripple the effectiveness of any performance appraisal system. Recognition of their sources, however, suggests how performance feedback can be given to reduce them. From a design perspective, an effective performance appraisal system can avoid inherent conflicts by separating evaluation from development, focusing on behavior rather than subjective traits, distinguishing evaluation of current from future performance, and using multiple appraisals to improve reliability and validity.

If managers are to facilitate improved employee performance, they must learn how to conduct a performance appraisal interview. Feedback can be given through a tell-and-sell, tell-and-listen, problem-solving, or mixed interview. Whereas Chapter 12 emphasized the content of performance appraisal, this chapter considered the process of giving feedback.

Although numerous motivation theories exist to explain human performance in organizations, a single diagnostic model has been provided to help you, the appraiser, get at the "root cause" of the performance problem. Using this model to understand performance gaps forms a basis for choosing different strategies for improvement. From a developmental perspective, strategies that involve participation and job clarification encourage self-directed improvement. Ultimately, problem employees may require outside assistance through counseling or employment assistance programs. Control of behavior can also be achieved by linking rewards to behavior or by using group or organizational norms (as suggested by the discussion of socialization in Chapter 8). Because all organizations experience performance problems, it is crucial that the performance appraisal system, the process of gathering and feeding back appraisal data, functions to improve individual and group performance.

Key Concepts

360-degree feedback
action plan
continuous reinforcement
effective feedback
employee assistance programs (EAPs)
external attribution
hot-stove principles
internal attribution
job-specific criteria
law of effect
meritocracy
mixed interview
neutralizing
partial reinforcement
positive reinforcement
problem-solving interview
tell-and-listen interview
tell-and-sell interview

Review and Discussion Questions

1. What are the inherent conflicts in a performance appraisal system? How can such conflicts be reduced?
2. Suppose you have decided that an employee is not "working out" and must be terminated. What performance appraisal approach would you use to support this decision? Why?

3. It has been argued that from a reward perspective, effective superiors should only spend appraisal time with their effective performers. What is the rationale for this strategy? Do you see any potential problems with this strategy? Explain.
4. What are typical reasons used to explain performance deficiencies?
5. What are the characteristics of effective feedback? What factors might prevent supervisors from giving effective feedback to subordinates?
6. How can an organization recognize and reward superiors for conducting performance appraisals?
7. Using negative behavioral strategies, what steps could a superior take to discourage unwanted subordinate behavior?
8. Assume that you are a professor counseling a student with a grade complaint. Describe how you would conduct this session using the 1) tell-and-sell approach, 2) tell-and-listen approach, and 3) problem-solving approach. As a professor, which approach would you feel most comfortable using? Why? As a student, which would you prefer? Why?
9. Formal performance appraisal usually takes place once or twice a year. What does this suggest about the relative use of the performance appraisal system for evaluation versus development decisions?
10. Discuss the uses of 360-degree feedback.

PROJECTS, EXERCISES & CASES

End-of-Text Projects

Lincoln Electric

1. What level of conflict is inherent in its performance appraisal system?
2. What are the most likely sources of performance appraisal deficiencies?
3. What strategies are used to improve employee performance?
4. How could you improve the organization's feedback and improvement programs?

Nordstrom

1. What level of conflict is inherent in its performance appraisal system?
2. What are the most likely sources of performance appraisal deficiencies?
3. What strategies are used to improve employee performance?
4. How could you improve the organization's feedback and improvement programs?

Field Project

1. Visit some local companies, and ask them how they treat employees who have performance or attendance problems. Do they have an EAP? Compare your findings with those of the class to see how many firms have these programs.
2. Call 1-800-WORKPLACE to learn about the drug-free environment information available.

Career Management Exercise: Do You Want the Bad News or the Good News First?

In Chapter 12, you indicated the type of performance appraisal system components you would like on your job. Because a system isn't really complete without feedback, you need to describe what type of feedback you would prefer.

1. First, do you want to have regular, formal feedback on your job?
2. How often do you want it?
3. From whom do you want it?
4. To whom do you want to give feedback?
5. Describe the feedback characteristics you would find most useful and acceptable to you. For example, does it have to have specific behavioral examples; do you need to have more than one example to illustrate a pattern of behavior?
6. Would you want your organization to offer an EAP? (While you may not personally use one, your co-workers might, you never know.)
7. Do you want your organization to have a formal discipline process beginning with a warning, etc.?
8. Are you willing to be responsible for your own performance appraisal? This includes making sure you ask for it, telling your boss and others when they should review you, and even scheduling the time they should give you the feedback.

Case: So You Want to Be a Manager?

Wally Reibstein was beginning to get the hang of his job, having survived a grueling six months as a newly appointed division engineering manager for a large aerospace firm located on the West Coast. Wally graduated with a degree in engineering from Rensselaer Polytechnic Institute in the early 1980s. He worked first for an industrial fan manufacturer located in the Midwest, the closest job he could find related to his aeronautical engineering training. When his wife decided to pursue an advanced degree in economics at a prestigious West Coast university, Wally found employment with his current employer, and they moved.

During the first five years, Wally demonstrated considerable skill in working with others and successfully completed three different projects on time. One year ago, he was promoted to project engineering manager. Within six months, his immediate boss, a division head, was selected for promotion and recommended Wally to fill his position. Because of his past successes, he got the job, and as division manager he is in charge of a staff of over 50 professional and technical personnel. Five of these professionals are designated as project engineers responsible for specific contracts. The remaining staff of engineers and technicians are about equally distributed over five projects.

Wally has a challenging week ahead of him. He has decided that this is the week for the "rubber to meet the road" in his performance as a division manager. He has scheduled two performance appraisal interviews that promise to challenge his human relation skills. The first review is scheduled on Tuesday with Jerry Masters, a 52-year-old project engineering manager with a Ph.D. in electrical engineering and two masters degrees in computer science and business administration. In Wally's estimation, Jerry is a degree collector and a poor manager. Jerry's project has fallen far behind schedule and is headed for disaster. After reading performance reviews from Jerry's personnel folder, Wally has decided that Jerry must be reassigned. Jerry's past reviews indicate that he seldom met stated objectives despite repeated verbal counseling. Wally's former boss confided that he would have reassigned Jerry himself, but his head count was frozen and he had no one readily available to replace him. Wally has no such constraints. His overhead budget has been increased 10 percent as a result of three consecutive successful quarters of billings for his division. He has also recently interviewed a 45-year-old engineer who, in his judgment, possesses all the qualities needed to succeed where Jerry is failing.

Wally agrees with his former boss's counsel that Jerry is a valued citizen but terribly mismatched in his job; he simply cannot manage a project. Tuesday morning arrives, and Wally decides to level with Jerry and tell him that he is not working out and that he will be reassigned to another project. When Wally informs Jerry of his reassignment, he reacts by launching into a protracted emotional outburst accusing Wally of violating the trust he (Jerry) had placed in him to support his efforts. Jerry reminds Wally of his twelve years of service and the considerable influence he wields. Storming out, Jerry informs Wally that he intends to write a letter to the division president detailing the shoddy treatment he has received. Great, thought Wally, just what he needs to make an impression on the top brass.

Case Questions

1. Is Jerry justified in his emotional outburst?
2. How should Wally have told Jerry about the re-assignment?
3. Where did Wally go wrong?
4. What would you have done if you were in Jerry's shoes?

VISIT THE LIBRARY

Workforce Online

Because you are now familiar with getting onto the Internet and the use of HR Headquarters, the following steps are abbreviated.

1. Enter your Web browser.
2. Enter Workforce Online.
3. Find and review the following article within the "Research Center": *Companies Evaluate Employees From All Perspectives.*
4. Return to your homepage.

Case: Retired on the Job: Career Burnout or the Nonmotivated Employee?

George Benson, the newly appointed manager of Pentarecon Corporation's Production Control and Methods Improvement Division, faces a rather perplexing personnel problem. One of the long-time employees of his division, Harry Norton, isn't performing his job properly. In questioning subordinates, Benson learned that Norton has not performed any real or substantive work for years. Furthermore, his current job actions are a source of embarrassment to the entire division. "Hangover Harry" arrives at work approximately 45 minutes late each morning and proceeds to begin the work day by attempting to recover from the previous evening's outing with his "Scotch friends." Norton's method of recovery appears to involve: 1) reading the paper for about an hour while smoking and drinking coffee; 2) "office hopping" with his coffee cup in order to visit, talk, and interact with his many friends who are employed within the division; 3) a two-hour, three-martini lunch break; and 4) an afternoon nap while secluded back in his office. Benson had expected the employees of his division to resent Norton's behavior and obvious poor or nonperformance. Thus, he was quite surprised when he learned that Norton is almost universally liked and considered somewhat of a folk hero among nonsupervisory employees. Therefore, Benson decided to thoroughly investigate Norton's case before taking any type of personnel action.

From company records, Benson learned that Norton has been employed by Pentarecon Corporation for twelve years. He began his employment with the firm as an internal management specialist. The duties of this position involved the development of methods improvements to facilitate both management and manufacturing operations. Initially, Norton was quite successful in this position. His performance appraisals routinely cited him for both his ingenuity and complete understanding of the complex production control systems used by the firm. Norton was credited with the introduction of new work procedures that lessened both worker fatigue and industrial accidents. Additionally, several of his suggestions resulted in substantial improvements in product quality within the manufacturing department. Recognizing this performance excellence, the firm promoted Norton once and rewarded him with several cash bonuses during his first five years of employment.

During his seventh year of employment, Norton was considered for a supervisory position within the division. Everyone was surprised when Pentarecon's top management finally decided to fill this supervisory vacancy with another employee from the Research and Development Group. Norton appeared to accept this career setback with some degree of indifference. He still exhibited his friendly and engaging interpersonal style that had won him many friends within the division. Yet six months later, a project he was assigned to direct seemed to "never get off the ground" because of his failure to exhibit proper levels of leadership and enthusiasm when dealing with other project analysts. Subsequent job assignments also revealed a substantial deterioration in performance. Norton's failure to consider a variety of relevant variables in his work assignments resulted in the development of nonusable work methods and production control techniques. Norton's supervisor noted that Harry appeared to be drinking heavily during this period of time and was said to be experiencing marital difficulties. This pattern of poor performance, tardiness, and alcohol abuse continued to the point where Norton's supervisor was afraid to assign him projects of any real significance. Therefore, Harry has recently been given either small, noncritical work assignments or no work at all.

Case Questions

1. What are the underlying causes of Norton's performance?
2. Who's responsible for the current state of Norton's performance?
3. Should a) the department management, b) Norton's supervisor, c) the company, have taken action much earlier?
4. What should Benson do now? Should Benson terminate Norton?

VISIT THE LIBRARY

This exercise will introduce you to the American Society for Training and Development. ASTD is the leading society for training and development professionals, and is headquartered in Alexandria, Virginia.

1. Go to the homepage for the American Society for Training and Development:

   http://www.astd.org

2. Select "Who We Are," and then select and read ASTD's mission statement.
3. From ASTD's homepage, select "Shifting Paradigms from Training to Performance," and read the sections therein.
4. From ASTD's homepage, select "Training and Information Sources." From here, find and select an index of World Wide Web sites related to training and performance.
5. Return to your homepage.

Chapter 13 Endnotes

1. B. O'Reilly, "360 Feedback Can Change Your Life," *Fortune* (October 17, 1994): 100.

2. A. S. Grove, *High Output Management* (New York: Random House, 1983): 181–183.

3. *The Wall Street Journal,* (August 28, 1984): 1.

4. N. Napier and G. Latham, "Outcome Expectancies of People Who Conduct Appraisals," *Personnel Psychology* 39 (1986): 827–839.

5. M. Beer, "Performance Appraisal: Dilemmas and Possibilities," *Organizational Dynamics* (Winter 1981): 26.

6. D. T. Hall, *Careers in Organizations* (Pacific Palisades, CA: Goodyear, 1976); D. Feldman, *Managing Careers in Organizations* (Glenview, IL: Scott, Foresman, 1988).

7. H. H. Meyer, E. Kay, and J. R. P. French, Jr., "Split Roles in Performance Appraisal," *Harvard Business Review* (Jan./Feb. 1965): 125.

8. C. Hymowitz, *The Wall Street Journal* (Jan. 17, 1985): 35.

9. Ibid.

10. C. Carr, "The Ingredients of Good Performance," *Training* (Aug. 1993): 51–54; P. Froiland, "Reproducing Star Performers," *Training* (Sept. 1993): 33–38; W. Weitzel, "How to Improve Performance Through Successful Appraisals," *Personnel* (Oct. 1987): 18–23.

11. Separating the review of past performance and future performance is described by Beer, "Performance Appraisal"; S. J. Carroll and C. E. Schneider, *Performance Appraisal and Review Systems* (Glenview, IL: Scott, Foresman, 1982). For a presentation on separating development and evaluation appraisal, see E. E. Lawler, III, A. M. Mohrman, Jr., and S. M. Resnick, "Performance Appraisal Revisited," *Organizational Dynamics* (Summer 1984): 20–42.

12. J. Greenberg, "The Distributive Justice of Organizational Performance Evaluation," *Research in Negotiations in Organizations,* M. Bazerman, R. Lewicki, and B. Sheppard, eds. (Greenwich, CT: JAI Press, 1986): 26–41; J. Greenberg, "Using Diaries to Promote Procedural Justice in Performance Appraisal," *Social Justice Review* (1987): 20–37.

13. B. Dumaine, "Who Needs a Boss?" *Fortune* (May 7, 1990): 52–60; A. M. Kantrow, "Wide-Open Management at Chaparral Steel: Interview with Gordon E. Forward," *Harvard Business Review* (May-June 1986): 96–102; R. Karlin, "Chaparral Beats the Odds," *New Management* (Winter 1987): 15–18.

14. G. Latham, M. Erez, and E. Locke, "Resolving Scientific Disputes by the Joint Design of Crucial Experiments by the Antagonists: Application to the Erez-Latham Dispute Regarding Participation in Goal Setting," *Journal of Applied Psychology* 73 (1988): 753–772.

15. G. P. Nicholas, "Upward Trend Continues in Appraisal Process," *HR Focus* (Sept. 1992): 17; J. S. Russel and D. L. Goode, "An Analysis of Managers' Reactions to Their Own Performance Appraisal Feedback," *Journal of Applied Psychology* (Feb. 1988): 63; F. L. Schmidt, J. E. Hunter, A. N. Outerbridge, and S. Goff, "Joint Relation of Experience and Ability with Job Performance: Test of Three Hypotheses," *Journal of Applied Psychology* (Feb. 1988): 46.

16. For a discussion of these characteristics for an effective appraisal interview, see Beer, "Performance Appraisal," 34–35 and *Bulletin to Management,* (Oct. 1984): 2, 7; P. Wylie and M. Grothe, *Problem Employees: How to Improve Their*

Performance (Belmont, CA: Pitman Learning, Inc., 1981). See also J. Beilinson, "Communicating Bad News," *Personnel* (Jan. 1991): 15.

17. G. P. Latham and L. M. Saari, "The Importance of Supportive Relationships in Goal Setting," *Journal of Applied Psychology* 64 (1979): 163–168.

18. N. R. F. Maier, *The Appraisal Interview* (New York: Wiley, 1958); G. P. Latham and K. N. Wexley, *Increasing Productivity through Performance Appraisal* (Reading, MA: Addison-Wesley, 1981): 152–154; Carroll and Schneider, *Performance Appraisal*: 160–189.

19. M. Hequet, "Giving Good Feedback," *Training* (September 1994): 72–77; D. R. Ilgen and C. F. Moore, "Types and Choices of Performance Feedbacks," *Journal of Psychology* (Aug. 1987): 401.

20. G. P. Latham, L. L. Cummings, and T. R. Mitchell, "Behavioral Strategies to Improve Productivity," *Organizational Dynamics* (Winter 1981): 4–23; S. Greengard, "Theft Control Starts with HR Strategies," *Personnel Journal* (April 1993): 81–91.

21. This section is adapted in part from R. F. Mager and P. Pipe, *Analyzing Performance Problems or "You Really Oughta Wanna"* (Belmont, CA: Fearon Pitman, 1970).

22. M. J. Markinko and W. L. Garner, "Learned Helplessness: An Alternative Explanation for Performance Deficits," *Academy of Management Review* 1 (1982): 195–204; M. E. and F. H. Kanfer, "The Role of Goal Acceptance on Goal Setting and Task Performance," *Academy of Management Review* (July 1983): 454–463; J. C. Naylor and D. R. Ilgen, "Goal Setting: A Theoretical Analysis in Motivation Technology," *Research in Organizational Behavior,* B. M. Shaw and L. L. Cummings, eds., Vol. 6 (Greenwich, CT: JAI Press, 1984): 95–101; S. E. Jackson and R. S. Schuler, "A Meta-Analysis and Conceptual Critique of Research on Role Ambiguity and Role Conflict in Work Settings," *Organizational Behavior and Human Decision Processes* 36 (1985): 16–78; J. L. Pearce and L. W. Porter, "Employee Responses to Formal Performance Appraisal Feedback," *Journal of Applied Psychology* (May 1986): 211.

23. V. Huber, P. Podsakoff, and W. Todor, "An Investigation of Biasing Factors in the Attributions of Subordinates and Their Supervisors," *Journal of Business Research* 4 (1986): 83–97.

24. L. F. McGee, "Keeping Up the Good Work," *Personnel Administrator* (June 1988): 68–72; S. O'Neal and M. Palladino, "Revamp Ineffective Performance Management," *Personnel Journal* (Feb. 1992): 93–102; M. H. Yarborough, "Warning! Negative Influences at Work," *HR Focus* (Sept. 1993): 23.

25. Adapted from E. F. Huse, *Management,* 2nd ed. (St. Paul, MN: West, 1982): 390–391.

26. A. Bandura, *Principles of Behavior Modification* (New York: Holt, Rinehart and Winston, 1969); W. Nord, "Beyond the Teaching Machine: The Neglected Area of Operant Conditioning in the Theory and Practice of Management," *Organizational Behavior and Human Performance* 4 (Nov. 1969): 375–401; W. Hamner, "Worker Motivation Programs: Importance of Climate, Structure and Performance Consequences," in *Contemporary Problems in Personnel: Readings for the Seventies,* W. C. Hamner and F. Schmidt, eds. (Chicago: St. Clair Press, 1974): 280–401.

27. E. Feeney, "At Emery Air Freight: Positive Reinforcement Boosts Performance," *Organizational Dynamics 1* (Winter 1973): 41–50.

28. Ibid., 47–48.

29. W. C. Hamner, "Reinforcement Theory and Contingency Management in Organizational Settings," in *Organizational Behavior and Management: A Contingency Approach,* H. Tosi and W. C. Hamner, eds. (Chicago: St. Clair Press, 1974): 86–111.

30. Ibid.

31. Feeney, "At Emery Air Freight": 42.

32. R. D. Arvey, G. A. Davis, and S. M. Nelson, "Use of Discipline in an Organization: A Field Study," *Journal of Applied Psychology* (Aug. 1984): 448–460; J. Brockner and J. Guare, "Improving the Performance of Low Self-Esteem Individuals: An Attributional Approach," *Academy of Management Journal* (Dec. 1983): 642–656; D. N. Campbell, R. L. Fleming, and R. C. Grote, "Discipline Without Punishment at Last," *Harvard Business Review* (July/Aug. 1985): 162–178; D. Cameron, "The When, Why, and How of Discipline," *Personnel Journal* (July 1984): 37–39.

33. D. A. Nadler and E. E. Lawler, "Motivation—A Diagnostic Approach," *Perspectives on Behavior in Organizations,* J. R. Hackman, E. E. Lawler, and L. W. Porter, eds., (New York: McGraw-Hill, 1977).

34. D. N. Campbell, R. L. Fleming, and R. C. Grote, "Discipline Without Punishment at Last," *Harvard Business Review* (July/August 1985): 162–178.

35. R. W. Hollman, "Beyond Contemporary Employee Assistance Programs," *Personnel Administrator* (Sept. 1981): 37–41; D. Masi and S. J. Freidland, "EAP Actions & Options," *Personnel Journal* (June 1988): 61–67.

36. S. H. Appelbaum and B. T. Shapiro, "The ABCs of EAPs," *Personnel* (July 1989): 39–46; S. J. Smits, L. A. Pace, and W. J. Perryman, "EAPs Are Big Business," *Personnel Journal* 96 (June 1989): 99–106; J. L. Goff, "Diagnose Alcoholism" *Personnel Journal* (May 1990): 107–116.

37. "Productivity and Performance: EAP Improved," *Bulletin to Management* (July 23, 1987): 1. For an excellent discussion of the application of discipline in organizations, see R. D. Arvey and J. M. Ivancevich, "Punishment in Organizations: A Review, Propositions, and Research Suggestions," *Academy of Management Review* 5 (1980): 123–132; W. Kiechel III, "How to Discipline in the Modern Age," *Fortune* (May 7, 1990): 179–180.

38. R. J. Nobile, "The Drug-Free Workplace: Act on It!" *Personnel* (Feb. 1990): 22.

39. "Labor Letter," *The Wall Street Journal* (August 21, 1990): 1. See also J. Beilinson, "Are EAPs the Answer?" *Personnel* (Jan. 1991): 3.

40. D. Grote, *Discipline Without Punishment* (New York: AMACOM, 1996); P. Wylie and M. Grothe, *Problem Employees: How to Improve Their Performance* (Belmont, CA: Pitman Learning, 1981).

41. C. O'Reilly and B. Weitz, "Managing Marginal Employees: The Use of Warnings and Dismissals," *Administrative Science Quarterly* 25 (1980): 467–484.

42. M. Bazerman, *Judgment in Managerial Decision Making* (New York: Wiley, 1986); V. Huber, "Managerial Applications of Decision Theory Concepts and Heuristics," *Organizational Behavior Teaching Review* 10 (1986): 1–24; G. Northcraft, M. Neale, and V. Huber, "The Effects of Cognitive Bias and Social Influence on Human Resource Management Decisions," *Research in Personnel and Human Resource Management,* G. Ferris and K. Rowland, eds., (Greenwich, CT: JAI Press, 1988).

43. "Despite Hitches, Multisource Feedback Moves Ahead," *Bulletin to Management* (January 18, 1996): 17–18; B. O'Reilly, "360 Feedback Can Change Your Life," *Fortune* (October 17, 1994): 93–100.

44. J. R. Fulkerson and R. S. Schuler, "Managing Worldwide Diversity at Pepsi-Cola International." *Diversity in the Workplace: Human Resources Initiatives,* S. E. Jackson, et al., eds. (New York: Guilford Press, 1992): 248–276.

45. N. Adler, *International Dimensions of Organizational Behavior,* 2nd ed. (Boston, MA: PWS-Kent, 1991); W. H. Newman, "Cultural Assumptions Underlying U.S. Management Concepts," *Management in an International Context* (New York: Harper & Row, 1972).

46. P. Drucker, *Management: Tasks, Responsibilities and Practices* (New York: Harper & Row, 1973): 424–425.

47. "Performance Management in the Round," *Bulletin to Management* (August 12, 1993): 256. Reprinted with permission by the Bureau of National Affairs, (Tel. 1-800-372-1033).

48. R. Steers, Y. K. Shin, and G. Ungson, *The Chaebol: Korea's New Industrial Might* (New York: Harper & Row, 1990): 121–122.

49. Based on J. Farh, G. H. Dobbins, and B. S. Cheng, "Cultural Relativity in Action: A Comparison of Self-Ratings Made by Chinese and U. S. Workers," *Personnel Psychology* 44 (1991): 129–147.

50. S. Carroll, "Asian HRM Philosophies and Systems: Can They Meet Our Changing HRM Needs," *Readings in Personnel and Human Resource Management,* R. Schuler, S. Youngblood, and V. Huber, eds., (St. Paul, MN: West, 1988): 442–455.

51. W. Ouchi, *The M-Form Society* (Reading, MA: Addison-Wesley, 1984).

52. T. Mroczkowski and M. Hanaoka, "Continuity and Change in Japanese Management," *California Management Review* (Winter 1989): 39–52.

Compensating

For most people, work is a central activity in their lives. It provides structure, meaning, and purpose. Although work is important, they are unlikely to be satisfied if their employer doesn't pay them well enough, and they will strive to work for a company that pays more than other companies, all other things being equal.

Once on the job, employees generally want to work hard, do a good job, want fair pay, and expect feedback from the boss. Consequently, companies and their HR managers usually try to ensure that their employees are paid fairly, both in terms of what others in the company are being paid and what others with similar jobs in other organizations are being paid. In the first chapter of this three-chapter section on employee compensation, we will discuss issues associated with establishing pay plans to attract, retain, and motivate individuals.

Employees will also work more if they are paid more for their additional work; thus, organizations are increasingly establishing compensation plans that tie additional compensation to additional work. For fairness and equity, companies design performance-based pay plans around performance appraisal systems that are valid and accepted by the employees. These plans can be designed for individuals, teams, or even organizational performance achievements. Because of the growing use of these plans, they are discussed extensively in Chapter 15.

Although employees certainly are concerned with getting paid regularly, and with keeping their jobs, they are also increasingly concerned with the "not so little things": health insurance coverage, disability coverage, unemployment compensation, retirement and pension benefits, vacations, wellness programs, and elder- and child-care opportunities. These programs are valuable, but costly. Consequently, organizations continually evaluate their indirect compensation programs in order to manage their total compensation costs. We will spend Chapter 16 discussing the aspects of indirect compensation. And you will have the opportunity to continue to expand on your planning for a future job with the "Career Management" exercises in Chapters 15 and 16.

14

CHAPTER

Total Monetary Compensation

> *"I was one of the thousands who have been downsized by IBM. I did not have a great deal of trouble getting a new job, but it pays half what I was paid before, and I have absolutely no benefits. Who am I working for? IBM. In other words, 'we need you but not at the salary you were earning after 21 years.'"*
>
> *Raymon Kent*
> *Employee*
> *Apex, NC*[1]

Learning Objectives

1. Identify different methods of job evaluation.
2. Describe how wage and salary levels for jobs are determined.
3. Explain issues in wage and salary administration such as employee participation, pay satisfaction, pay secrecy, and salary versus pay.
4. Describe international compensation.

Chapter Outline

MANAGING HUMAN RESOURCES

at Microsoft

One of the wonder firms of the 1980s and 1990s, Microsoft Corporation, continues to dazzle customers with innovative software programs. Although the company has faced frustration in sometimes bringing a product to market before it is ready, interestingly, the firm's overall performance has not been harmed. As a former Microsoft vice president comments, "(Microsoft has) never shipped a good product in its first version...but they never give up and eventually they get it right."

"Getting it right" demands that the firm has top-notch, creative programmers. Finding such talent is difficult given the lack of programmers nationwide and given Microsoft's stringent recruiting and selection practices. The firm typically hires fewer than one percent of those applying for programmer slots, partly because the company's founder, Bill Gates, insists that the ranks stay lean (to hold down costs). Because Microsoft is such an attractive employer, it can have its pick of the best programmers. Contributing to its attractiveness are its compensation policies and practices.

Once the firm finds its programmers, it rewards their performance in unique ways. Rather than high salaries or perks (no company cars), the company offers generous stock options. Programmers who were on staff prior to the firm's public stock offering in 1986, for example, received options that have made them "paper millionaires."

Since then, the firm has begun a promotion and compensation plan similar to that of law firms. Programmers are evaluated yearly and placed on one of six levels. Their incentive pay and options derive from that evaluation. As a programmer reaches the top two levels, the equivalent of becoming a "partner" in a law firm, there is a big celebration, and the employee receives more stock options. Further, the firm provides multiple career paths, with comparable rewards for programmers who stay in the technical side of software development, as well as those who choose to go into management. Such compensation policies and practices, coupled with an exciting work environment, have created tremendous loyalty among Microsoft employees.[2]

Compared to other companies in the industry, Microsoft does not pay high salaries. Recent hires are paid $35,000 for developers; $45,000 with a master's degree; and $30,000 for testers and other specialists.

This feature illustrates several aspects of compensation. One is that money isn't the only thing that attracts great employees to firms and causes them to stay and perform well. Offering alternate career paths and celebrating important events can be powerful motivating forces for individuals. While money is important, the absolute level of direct compensation need not be extremely high. Bill Gates' salary is certainly low for the CEO of a very successful firm. The attractiveness, however, of stock options (especially with a successful firm) can be a substantial force in motivating individuals to join a firm, work hard, and remain committed to the firm. In turn, this helps make the firm successful. And, this is why the area of total compensation is such an important one to organizational strategy.

Total compensation involves the assessment of employee contributions in order to distribute fairly and equitably both direct and indirect organizational rewards in exchange for these contributions.

Total Monetary Compensation

Total compensation involves the assessment of employee contributions in order to distribute fairly and equitably both direct and indirect organizational rewards in exchange for those contributions. As Exhibit 14.1 shows, monetary rewards can be categorized as direct or indirect compensation. **Direct compensation** includes an employee's **base salary** and **performance-based pay. Indirect compensation**

EXHIBIT 14.1

Components of a Total Reward System

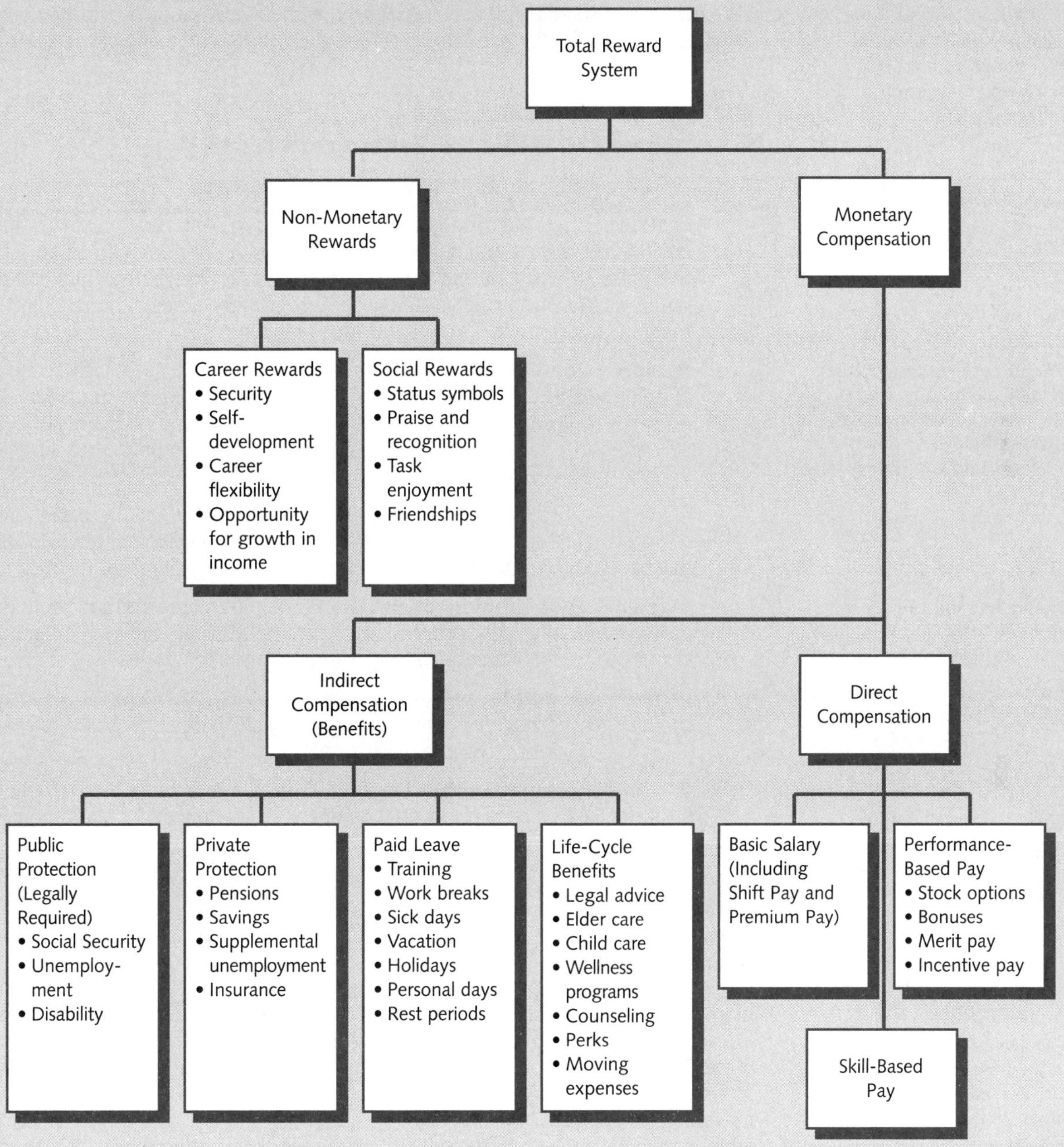

consists of federally and publicly mandated protection programs, private protection programs, health-care benefits, paid leave, and life-cycle benefits. Nonmonetary rewards can be very important to employees.[3] For example, job security has become important in this era of substantial and continuous layoffs by large employers.[4] Recognizing this, some employers offer job security in exchange for no increase in monetary rewards.

With this in mind, however, we will focus our discussion on monetary rewards. We begin with a discussion of compensation's purposes and importance, and then examine its overall role in developing and linking human resource management to the organization's strategy. Next, we present various ways to attain internal and external pay equity. We also examine issues associated with compensation administration (for example, resolving equity imbalances, participation, pay secrecy, and pay satisfaction).

Did You KNOW?

Income growth for adults over the past 20 years has been greatest for college graduates.

Why Is Monetary Compensation Important?

Total compensation serves the following major purposes:

- **It attains business needs and objectives.** An organization may want to create a rewarding and supportive climate, or it may want to be an attractive place to work so that it can attract the best applicants. Total compensation can assist these plans and also further other organizational objectives such as rapid growth, survival, or innovation.[5]

Major purposes of total compensation are to attract applicants, retain good employees, motivate employees, administer pay legally, and attain HR/business plans.

- **It gains a competitive edge.** Total compensation can be a significant cost of doing business. Depending on the industry, labor costs range from 10 to 80 percent of total costs. To gain a competitive advantage, an organization may choose to relocate to areas where labor is cheaper and more interested in performance-based pay.
- **It attracts potential job applicants.** In conjunction with the organization's recruitment and selection efforts, the total compensation program can help assure that pay is sufficient to attract the right people at the right time for the right jobs.
- **It retains good employees.** Unless a monetary compensation program is perceived as internally equitable and externally competitive, good employees (those the organization wants to retain) are likely to leave.

There are two things people want more than sex and money...recognition and praise.

Mary Kay Ash
Chairman Emeritus
Mary Kay Cosmetics

- **It motivates employees.** Many employers, such as Microsoft, seek to be productive and have a motivated workforce. Total compensation can help achieve this goal by tying rewards to performance.
- **It administers pay within the law.** Organizations must be aware of the legal regulations relevant to total compensation and avoid violating them in their pay programs.[6]

Obviously, these objectives are interrelated. When employees are motivated, the organization is more likely to achieve its strategic business objectives. When pay is based on the value of the job, the organization is more likely to attract, motivate, and retain its employees.

As a consequence of effectively serving all these purposes, companies are much more likely to be profitable and competitive, both in the short run and long run. They are also more likely to serve the interests of all the stakeholders of the company. Being so important, it is not surprising to find an extensive partnership in monetary compensation as detailed in the feature, "Partnership: Working Together in Monetary Compensation." As shown in that feature, one of the aspects of monetary compensation that is shared is determining the relative worth of jobs. This determination is the foundation of all other compensation decisions.

Did You KNOW?

The average hourly wage in the movie business is $32.70 and in the missile production business it is $20.60.

Relative job worth can be determined by market survey or job evaluation.

Determining the Relative Worth of Jobs

Market Surveys

Perhaps the fastest and easiest way for a company to decide how much it will pay a person to do a job is to ask others. A small business owner is likely to pay an

PARTNERSHIP: WORKING TOGETHER IN MONETARY COMPENSATION

LINE MANAGERS

With HR, assure alignment of pay system with business.

Participate with HR professionals to determine how to value jobs and people.

Work with HR to communicate pay system.

Make and communicate pay decisions.

Make decisions on direct pay packages.

Make decisions on benefits to offer.

HR PROFESSIONALS

With line managers, assure alignment of pay system with business.

Design process for job evaluation to involve line managers and job incumbents.

Analyze external market.

Develop processes to measure performances and/or skills.

Assess employees' preferences.

Work closely with line managers to finalize pay.

Work with line managers to communicate pay system.

ALL EMPLOYEES

Take responsibility for understanding pay system.

May participate in job evaluation.

Indicate preferences for pay.

May assess the levels of performance and/or skill of self and others.

Indicate preferences for indirect pay.

Manage retirement accounts.

office assistant what others in the same town are paying. This information is available by asking others or by market surveys. Market surveys assess the pay rates for different jobs by the various companies surveyed. The information is used to determine the relative worth of the jobs to companies. However, these market survey rates may reflect factors other than the actual relative worth of a job, including labor market conditions (the number of people out of work and looking for work), traditions and past history of the organization's wage structure, indices of productivity, company profit figures or sales data, and the Consumer Price Index. To avoid these possible distortions in determining the relative worth of jobs, companies use a more systematic approach: job evaluation.

Did You KNOW?

Electricians in San Antonio, Texas, make $12.31 per hour, while their counterparts in San Francisco make $25.28 per hour.

Job Evaluation

LEARNING OBJECTIVE 1

Identify different methods of job evaluation.

Job evaluation emphasizes a systematic, rational assessment of jobs to establish internal equity among different jobs in an organization. While the amount paid for a job can be based on a manager's impression of what the job is worth or on what the external market is paying, more formal methods are often used, including:[7]

- Job ranking
- Job classification
- Factor comparison
- Point rating
- Hay method

Ranking Method. The least specific job evaluation method is **job ranking.** Jobs can be ranked on the basis of such factors as difficulty, criticality to organizational success, or skill required. This method is convenient when there are only a few jobs to evaluate and when one person is familiar with them all. As the number of jobs increases and the likelihood of one individual knowing all jobs declines, detailed job analysis information becomes more important, and ranking is often

The job ranking method involves comparing jobs in a hierarchical fashion.

Benchmark jobs are jobs against which other jobs are compared to determine relative value.

done by committee. Key or **benchmark jobs** are used for comparison when a large number of jobs are to be ranked. These are jobs that most employees both are familiar with and have a similar understanding of their value.

One difficulty in the job ranking method is that all jobs are forced to be different from each other. Making fine distinctions between similar jobs is often difficult, and disagreements thus arise.

Job classification means putting jobs into families or classes.

Job Classification Method. The **job classification method** is similar to the ranking method, except that classes or grades are established and the jobs are then placed into the classes. Jobs are usually evaluated on the basis of the whole job, often using one factor such as difficulty or an intuitive summary of factors. Again, job analysis information is useful in the classification, and benchmark jobs are frequently established for each class. Within each class or grade, there is no further ranking of the jobs.

While the point evaluation system differs from traditional job classification methods, it may produce a similar product. That is, when jobs are assigned to pay grades, jobs are essentially classified according to their worth, and similar rates of pay are issued for jobs in the same pay grade or classification.

A particular advantage of this method is that it can be applied to a large number and wide variety of jobs. As the number and variety of jobs in an organization increase, however, the classification of jobs tends to become more subjective. This is particularly true when an organization has a large number of plant or office locations, and thus jobs with the same title may differ in content. Because evaluating each job separately in such cases is difficult, the job title becomes a more important guide to job classification than job content.

A major disadvantage of the job classification method is that the basis of the job evaluation is either one factor or an intuitive summary of many factors. The problem with using one factor, such as difficulty (skill), is that it may not be important in all jobs. Some jobs require a great deal of skill, but others require a great deal of responsibility. Should these jobs be placed in a lower classification than jobs requiring much skill? Not necessarily. Perhaps both factors could be considered together. Thus, each factor becomes a compensable factor, one that is valued by the organization and something worth paying for. Jobs would then be evaluated and classified on the basis of both factors. However, this balancing of the compensable factors to determine the relative equality of jobs often causes misunderstandings with the employees and the labor leaders.[8] To deal with this disadvantage, many organizations use more quantified methods of evaluation.

In **factor comparisons**, jobs are broken down into factors in order to determine the value of the job.

Factor Comparison. Approximately 10 percent of employers evaluate jobs using the **factor comparison method.** This approach to job evaluation represents a significant change over ranking and classification because **compensable factors** are utilized to determine job worth. Second, the method systematically links external rates of pay with internal, work-related compensable factors.

The factor comparison method of job evaluation consists of several steps:

- **Select compensable factors.** While any number of compensable factors can be used, mental requirements, skill, and physical and working conditions are universally used.
- **Conduct job analysis.** Once the compensable factors are chosen, jobs should be evaluated in relationship to the compensable factors and job specifications that relate to each factor written.
- **Pick benchmark jobs.** Benchmark jobs serve as reference points and consequently should be chosen with care, just as in the ranking method. The content of benchmark jobs should be well known and stable with consistent pay rates in the external market. Benchmark jobs should also cover the entire range of jobs being evaluated.

- **Allocate benchmark wages across factors.** Using a compensation committee, wage rates for each job are allocated to each compensable factor.
- **Slot nonbenchmark jobs.** Other jobs are then slotted into each factor scale based on the amount of pay assigned to each factor. In doing this, jobs are compared against each benchmark job to determine whether they are of greater or lesser value.

Factor comparison assigns monetary value directly to benchmark jobs.

The "price" or wage rates for the benchmark jobs are determined by the market. Although this is a quick method by which to set wage rates, it has the potential to perpetuate traditional pay differentials because the wage rates for other jobs are determined against these jobs. Because the process of determining the rates of other jobs is in the hands of the wage and salary analyst, it can be subjective, furthering the potential for wage discrimination.[9] As such, it has come under attack from the job comparability advocates for claims of pay discrimination. Another concern is that the relationships among jobs may change as external rates of pay or benchmark jobs shift.

In spite of these limitations, the factor comparison method of job evaluation is a definite improvement over ranking and classification. Additionally, it has been found to be acceptable to management, unions, and rank-and-file employees. Because jobs are ranked directly in dollar value, internal and external equity are integrally linked.

Point Rating Method. The most widely used method of job evaluation is the **point rating** or **point factor method,** which consists of assigning point values for previously determined compensable factors and adding them to arrive at a total. Like the factor comparison method, compensable factors play the central role in the point system. Factors are weighted relative to their importance to the firm. A job's total point value and location in the pay structure is the sum of the numerical values for each degree of each compensable factor that the job possesses. The point evaluation system detailed in Exhibit 14.2 has six compensable factors. Five factors are used to evaluate all jobs; supervisory jobs are evaluated on one additional dimension. As shown, problem solving is weighted heaviest (260/1,000 points) while working conditions is the least important (50/1,000 points). The factors also differ in the number and point value of degrees associated with them.

In point rating, factors are given points, and jobs get different point values to indicate their relative worth.

Once factors are identified and weighted, scale anchors reflecting the different degrees within each factor are developed. Exhibit 14.3 shows the degree statements developed by a broadcast company to describe problem solving. In establishing factor scales, an organization can choose to use an existing system or develop compensable factors that are specifically tailored to their needs. In either event, the factors need to be written in clear language. Once the basic system is set up, each job is rated on all compensable factors. The more points assigned to a job, the more valuable it is to the organization.

EXHIBIT 14.2

Sample Point Evaluation System

COMPENSABLE FACTOR	FIRST DEGREE	SECOND DEGREE	THIRD DEGREE	FOURTH DEGREE	FIFTH DEGREE
Job knowledge	50	100	150	200	
Problem solving	50	100	150	205	260
Impact	60	120	180	240	
Working conditions	10	30	50		
Supervision needed	25	50	75	100	
Supervision given	30	60	90	120	150

EXHIBIT 14.3

Compensable Factor and Related Degree Statements

2. Problem solving:
This factor examines the types of problems dealt with in your job. Indicate the one level that is most representative of the majority of your job responsibilities:

Degree 1: Actions are performed in a set order per written or verbal instruction. Problems are referred to supervisor.

Degree 2: Solves routine problems and makes various choices regarding the order in which the work is performed within standard practices. May obtain information from varied sources.

Degree 3: Solves varied problems that require general knowledge of company policies and procedures applicable within area of responsibility. Decisions made based on a choice from established alternatives. Expected to act within standards and established procedures.

Degree 4: Requires analytical judgment, initiative, or innovation in dealing with complex problems or situations. Evaluation not easy because there is little precedent or information may be incomplete.

Degree 5: Plans, delegates, coordinates, and/or implements complex tasks involving new or constantly changing problems or situations. Involves the origination of new technologies or policies for programs or projects. Actions limited only by company policies and budgets.

Advantages of the method are that:

- It is widely used throughout industry, permitting comparisons on a similar basis with other firms.
- It is relatively simple to understand and is the simplest of quantitative methods of job evaluation.
- A well-conceived system has considerable stability: it is applicable to a wide range of jobs over an extended period of time. The greatest assets here are consistency and uniformity and its widespread use throughout industry.
- It is a definitive approach requiring several separate and distinct judgment decisions.

The limitations of the point rating method are few, but an especially critical one is the assumption that all jobs can be described with the same factors. Many organizations avoid this limitation by developing separate factors and point rating methods for different groups of employees.

Exhibit 14.2 shows six compensable factors used by one organization to evaluate the jobs in supervisory, nonsupervisory, and clerical categories. Some factors are more important than others, as shown by the different point values. For example, the second degree of problem solving is worth approximately three times as much as the second degree of working conditions. Each job is evaluated only on its compensable factors. The HR department determines which degree of a factor is appropriate for the job. Then, the points assigned to each degree of each factor are totaled. Levels of compensation are determined on the basis of the point totals.

As with other job evaluation plans, the point factor method incorporates the potential subjectivity of the job analyst. As such, it can potentially be discriminatory. Bias or subjectivity can enter in the selection of the factors, in the relative weights (degrees) assigned to the factors, and in the assignment of degrees to the jobs being evaluated.[10] At stake here are equal pay and job comparability. To make sure its point factor evaluation system is free from potential bias and is implemented as objectively as possible, an organization can solicit the input of the job incumbent, the supervisor, and job evaluation experts as well as its HR department.

Hay Method. A widely used job evaluation system that combines the best characteristics of point evaluation and factor comparison methods of job evaluation is the **Hay Method**. Used worldwide, this method is particularly popular for evaluating executive, managerial, and professional positions, but is becoming more widely used for many others, including technical, clerical, and manufacturing positions.

The Hay Method focuses on three factors:

- **Problem solving**
- **Know-how**
- **Accountability**

Operationally, the Hay Method or plan traditionally relies on three primary compensable factors—know-how, problem solving, and accountability (see Exhibit 14.4 for definitions). Point values are determined for each job using the three factors and their subfactors. Additionally, jobs are compared to one another on each factor. The former approach parallels traditional point evaluation processes, and the latter parallels factor comparison methods.

According to Hay Associates (the consulting firm that installs the Hay Method), a major advantage of their system centers on the wide acceptance of the system. Because organizations worldwide use the system, Hay can provide clients with comparative pay data by industry or locale. Another advantage of the system is that it has been legally challenged and found acceptable by the courts.

EXHIBIT 14.4

Compensable Factors in the Hay Method

PROBLEM SOLVING (MENTAL ACTIVITY)

The amount of original, self-starting thought required by the job for analysis, evaluation, creation, reasoning, and arriving at conclusions.

Problem solving has two dimensions:

- The degree of freedom with which the thinking process is used to achieve job objectives without the guidance of standards, precedents, or direction from others
- The type of mental activity involved; the complexity, abstractness, or originality of thought required

Problem solving is expressed as a percentage of know-how for the obvious reason that people think with what they know. The percentage judged to be correct for a job is applied to the know-how point value; the result is the point value given to problem solving.

KNOW-HOW

The sum total of all knowledge and skills, however acquired, needed for satisfactory job performance (evaluates the job, not the person).

Know-how has three dimensions:

- The amount of practical, specialized, or technical knowledge required
- Breadth of management, or the ability to make many activities and functions work well together; the job of company president, for example, has greater breadth than that of a department supervisor
- Requirement for skill in motivating people

Using a chart, a number can be assigned to the level of know-how needed in a job. This number—or point value—indicates the relative importance of know-how in the job being evaluated.

ACCOUNTABILITY

The measured effect of the job on company goals.

Accountability has three dimensions:

- Freedom to act, or relative presence of personal or procedural control and guidance; determined by answering the question, "How much freedom has the job holder to act independently?"—for example, a plant manager has more freedom than a supervisor under his or her control
- Dollar magnitude, a measure of the sales, budget, dollar value of purchases, value added, or any other significant annual dollar figure related to the job
- Impact of the job on dollar magnitude, a determination of whether the job has a primary effect on end results or has instead a sharing, contributory, or remote effect

Accountability is given a point value independent of the other two factors.

Note: The total evaluation of any job is arrived at by adding the points for problem solving, know-how, and accountability. The points are not shown here.

Still, the Hay Method, like many standardized systems, may not reflect an organization's true needs. In response to this, Hay Associates have been modifying their traditional plan to be more flexible and adaptable to the needs of companies.

Choosing a Job Evaluation Method

Job evaluation methods differ in several respects. Some methods evaluate the whole job, while others evaluate jobs using compensable factors. Job evaluation approaches also vary in the type of output produced. For example, the factor comparison method evaluates jobs directly in dollar worth, while the point evaluation system requires conversion of points to dollars.

An organization's choice of method depends on several factors:

- **Legal and social background.** The job evaluation methods that can be used may be limited by collective bargaining arrangements or by what is legally acceptable.
- **Organizational structure.** In small firms, simple systems such as ranking may be appropriate. However, in a multiplant enterprise, plans may be more complex.
- **Management style.** Management style can vary from autocratic to democratic. Management style will primarily affect the scope of worker participation in the design and application of a job evaluation scheme.
- **Labor-management relations.** No job evaluation scheme can succeed unless the workers accept it. Indeed, the results of many job evaluation programs have been totally rejected because of union opposition. To prevent this, organizations may choose a plan that provides for participation.
- **Cost in time and money.** Job evaluation, like other HR activities, costs time and money. There is up-front cost in developing a tailor-made plan. Canned programs (programs that can be bought off the shelf and used just as they are) may be costly in terms of purchase price and user acceptance. Usually, a job evaluation system takes between six to twelve months for firms employing more than 500 employees.[11]

Single Versus Multiple Plans. Another decision that needs to be made is whether one or several job evaluation plans should be used. Traditionally, job evaluation plans have varied depending on the job family (for example, clerical, skilled-craft, professional). This approach is premised on the assumption that work content of various jobs may vary in terms of working conditions and physical effort while professional jobs may not differ in terms of these compensable factors. Proponents of multiple plans contend that multiple plans are necessary to capture the unique and different job characteristics of job families.

Proponents of comparable worth and those favoring pay equity advocate a single pay plan. Their argument is premised on the assumption that there are universal compensable factors that relate to all jobs. Only when jobs are evaluated using the same criteria can the relative value of all jobs be determined. When separate plans are used, it is much easier to discriminate against specific classes of jobs (for example, clerical versus skilled). To prevent this, universal factors needs to be utilized. The Hay Method is one standardized evaluation system with universal factors. It is also possible, but difficult, to develop firm-specific job evaluation systems with universal factors. Some companies such as Hewlett-Packard use a core set of factors and another set of factors unique to particular occupation groups. However many plans are involved, the results are used to establish job classes and then pay levels.

Skill-Based Evaluation

Skill-based evaluation pays for skills or the worker—not the job.

Whereas the previously mentioned job evaluation plans "pay for the job," **skill-based evaluation** is based on the idea of "paying for the person." As such, this type of evaluation, also called "pay for knowledge," is concerned with employee skills and in developing training programs to facilitate employee skill acquisition.[12]

Skill-based evaluation plans begin with a starting rate given to all new employees. After coming on board, employees are advanced one pay grade for each job skill they learn. Members of each employee's team ensure that the skills are learned correctly. They decide when the employee has mastered a job. Employees reach the top pay grade in the plant after learning all skills. The positive impact of skill-based plans on organizational objectives such as customer service is described in the feature, "Managing Human Resources at Northern Telecom: Skill-Based Program Improves Customer Service."

Skill-based evaluation promotes multiple skills and worker flexibility.

The idea of paying for the person, or at least the person-job combination, rather than just the job, is not new. Many professional organizations such as universities, law offices, and research and development labs have been doing this for a long time. Determining pay rates using **maturity curves** (that combine the job with the employee's years of experience) is a method organizations sometimes use for their scientific and engineering employees. What is new, however, is paying for the person (as determined by skills possessed) in blue-collar jobs. Examples of skill-based evaluation for blue-collar jobs include some of the plants at Honeywell, Westinghouse, Steelcase, and Polaroid. Skill-based evaluation is compared with conventional job evaluation methods in Exhibit 14.5.

Maturity curves determine pay levels by combining the value of the job and the employee's years of experience.

Because skill-based pay results in paying the person rather than the job, it reduces the concern of conventional job evaluation of establishing job classes in order to determine pay levels for jobs. Since many companies still use conventional job evaluation, however, it is useful to discuss job classes and attach pay rates to them.

EXHIBIT 14.5

Comparison of Skill-Based Evaluation and Conventional Job Evaluation

COMPONENT	SKILL-BASED EVALUATION	JOB-BASED EVALUATION
1. Determination of worth	Tied to evaluation of skill blocks	Tied to evaluation of total job
2. Pricing	Difficult because the overall pay system is tied to the market	Easier because wages are tied to benchmark jobs in the labor market
3. Pay ranges	Extremely broad; one pay range for entire cluster of skills	Variable depending on type of job and pay-grade width
4. Evaluation of performance	Competency tests	Job performance measures
5. Salary increases	Tied to skill acquisition as measured by competency testing	Tied to seniority, performance appraisal ratings, or actual output
6. Role of training	Essential to attain job flexibility and pay increases for all employees	Necessitated by need rather than desire
7. Pay growth opportunities	Greater opportunities; anyone who passes competency test advances	Fewer opportunities; no advancement unless there is a job opening
8. Effect of job change	Pay remains constant unless skill proficiency increases	Pay changes immediately to level associated with new job
9. Pay administration	Difficult because many aspects of pay plan (training, certification) demand attention	Contingent upon the complexity of job evaluation and pay allocation plan

Source: Adapted from G.E. Ledford, "Three Case Studies on Skill-Based Pay: An Overview," *Compensation and Benefits Review* (April 1990): 11–23; H. Tosi and L. Tosi "What Managers Need to Know about Knowledge-Based Pay," *Organizational Dynamics* (Winter, 1986).

MANAGING HUMAN RESOURCES

at Northern Telecom

Skill-Based Pay Program Improves Customer Service

As a supplier of products to the telecommunications industry, Northern Telecom serves a constantly changing marketplace. Customer demands are high, the pace is rapid, and the products made by the company are evolving continually. This constant change puts pressure on all Northern Telecom employees to stay abreast of new product technologies, but the product installers feel the pressure most of all.

To encourage field technicians to keep their skills current and to ensure that they're adequately compensated for their increasing skill levels, Northern Telecom established a skill-based pay program in 1991 for the 1,200 installation-department employees. This program is called *Fast Forward.*

"This is a true pay-for-skills program," explains Dennis Garfield, director of installation at the company's Technical Installation Center in Raleigh, North Carolina. "The only way our field technicians can receive an increase in their base pay is through the attainment of new skills."

All of the installation skills that Northern Telecom employees need are listed on a document called the *Skills Capability Record* (SCR). Each skill on the SCR is assigned a point value, based on the difficulty of attaining that skill as well as on how important that skill is to the installation department. Skills range in value from 2 to 40 points, with the high-point skills considered to be the most important.

These points correspond to salary zones that are divided into 100-point increments. As field technicians earn additional points, they move into higher salary zones. "Now there's no such thing as a dollar per point," Garfield emphasizes. "For field technicians to receive an increase in base salary, they must move into a new zone—into another 100-point increment. In other words, someone could go from 699 to 700 points and be eligible for a pay increase."

Employees receive these points when they demonstrate that they can perform a particular skill on a job site without supervision. When this is done, they are *certified* in that skill by a certification committee that includes:

- The district manager
- The employee's immediate supervisor
- A representative from human resources
- A peer

In Fast Forward's first 18 months, close to 90 percent of Northern Telecom's field technicians received some sort of skill-based pay increase. What impact has this had on customer service? "We've heard many positive remarks from customers about our technician's ability to answer their questions about our products," Garfield explains. "Additionally, we have a formal survey that's completed after every job, geared specifically to the installation activity. The surveys are coming back with much higher ratings today than they did two years ago."[13]

Determining Job Classes

Job classes or job families involve grouping together jobs of similar value.

Job families make it easier to administer the compensation program.

Before salaries are determined, job classes or families are created from the results of the job evaluation. Determining **job classes** or **job families** means grouping together all jobs that are similar in value based on job evaluation; for example, grouping all clerical or all managerial jobs together. Jobs within the same class may be quite different, but they are about equal in value to the organization according to the job evaluation. All the jobs in each class or family are assigned one salary or range of salaries. (See our discussion in Chapter 8 on job analysis.)

Why group jobs into classes? One reason is the efficiency gained in salary administration. Also, it can be hard to justify the small differences in pay that might exist between jobs in which job classes do not exist. Finally, small errors that occur in evaluating the jobs can be eliminated in the classification process. Of course, employees can also find fault with the classification results if the jobs are grouped with those they feel are less important. Sometimes the jobs grouped together are too dissimilar because there are too few classes. Using only a few classes is appropriate, however, if many of the jobs in the organization are of similar value.

Establishing the Pay Structure

LEARNING OBJECTIVE 2

Describe how wage and salary levels for jobs are determined.

Once jobs are evaluated and the job classes determined, wage rates or ranges need to be established. Although job classes are determined for the purpose of developing wage rates, job classes are often based on wage rates that already exist. This practice may seem somewhat bizarre, but it is commonly done. Most organizations are already paying their employees and thus need to determine job classes only when many new jobs are introduced, or if they have never really had a sound job analysis program. In addition, if the organization has grown and incorporated many more jobs, it may need to group them into classes for purposes of salary administration. On the other hand, an organization that is just being established is most likely small and will determine the price of its jobs by surveys of what other organizations are paying. Regardless, conducting a wage survey is a critical component in establishing the pay structure.

Wage and Salary Surveys

Wage and salary surveys **provide information on external equity.**

As discussed already, the market, along with other factors, can influence the wage rates established by the organization. This influence occurs whenever the organization conducts wage and salary surveys.

Wage and salary surveys can be used to develop compensation levels, wage structures, and even payment plans (the amount and kind of direct and indirect compensation). Whereas job evaluation helps ensure **internal equity,** wage surveys help ensure **external equity.** Both types of equity are important if an organization is to be successful in attracting, retaining, and motivating employees.[14]

To the extent that auto insurance is a commodity, our biggest differentiator is our people. We want the best people at every level of the company, and we pay at the top of the market.

Peter B. Lewis
Chairman
Progressive Corporation

Organizations use information from and contribute information to wage surveys. Separate surveys are published for different occupational groupings; thus, many larger organizations subscribe to several surveys. For example, surveys exist for clerical workers, professional workers, managers, and executives. Separate surveys are conducted not only because of wide differences in skill levels, but also because labor markets are so different. An organization surveying clerical workers may need to survey companies only within a 10-mile radius, whereas a survey of managerial salaries may cover the entire country.

Grade Structure

Grade structures **put all jobs in pay boxes in order to organize them, as shown in Exhibit 14.6.**

After deciding on the wage and salary information it wants, the organization develops a **grade structure** with pay rates for job categories. A typical grade structure is show in Exhibit 14.6; it is based on job evaluation points associated with a point factor evaluation.

The boxes shown are associated with a range of job evaluation points (the job class) and a range of pay (the pay grade). In essence, these **pay grades** are the job families or classes. Consequently, there may be several different jobs within one box, but they are very similar in job evaluation points, if not in content. The boxes vary in shape but generally ascend from left to right. This reflects increased job worth and associated higher pay levels (shown on the vertical axis) for more valued jobs. The pay levels are established using market information (to ensure external equity).[15]

The wage rate for each job is then determined by locating its grade and moving over to a point on the vertical axis, as done for job A in grade II. A pay limit exists for the jobs in each grade. Staying within those limits (the range) is essential

EXHIBIT 14.6

Establishing a Grade Structure Based on Job Evaluation

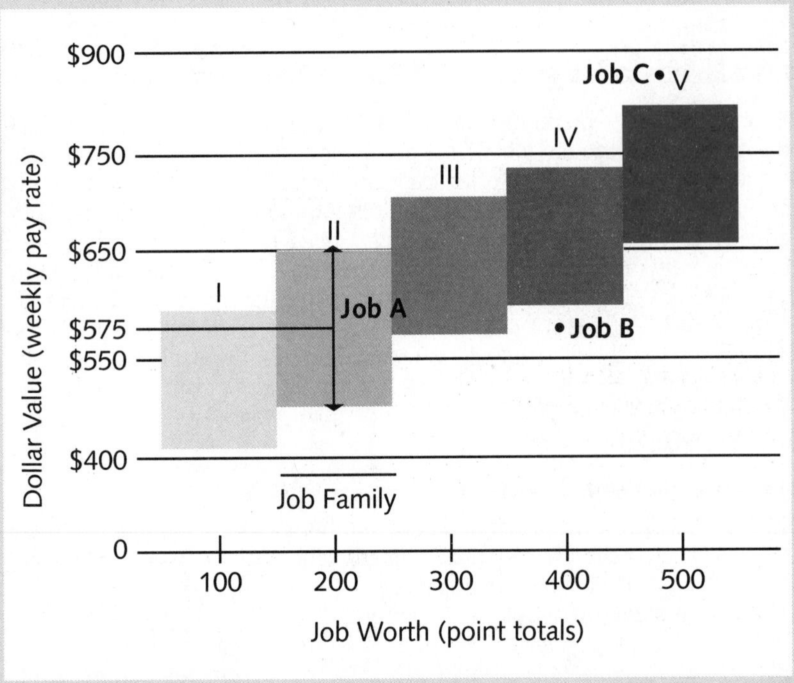

to maintaining internal equity, assuming the job evaluation is valid.[16] For employees to obtain a significant salary increase, they must move into a job in the next higher grade. Generally, each job has a rate range. As shown, job A has a range from $500 per week to $650 per week. The midpoint of this range is $575. These numbers can become critical. Many organizations would like to have the average salary of employees in a job equal the midpoint. If the average is higher than the midpoint, many employees might not receive significant salary increases unless they are promoted.

To circle a job means to highlight it so action will be taken to realign the job with its pay grade.

Occasionally, jobs fall outside the established pay grades (jobs B and C in Exhibit 14.6). When a job falls below the established pay grade, it is circled, and usually a wage adjustment (sweetener) is made to bring the job within the established pay grade. Sometimes, after periods of high inflation rates, the entire salary structure has to be adjusted upward to bring jobs within established pay grades, thereby moving the midpoints up for all pay grades. This ensures external equity and that employees' salaries do not decline in real terms. Sometimes, though, a job will be overpaid (job C in pay grade V). One means of dealing with this is to circle the job, which, in this instance, means adjusting the rate downward after the incumbent leaves.

Broadbanding reduces the opportunities for promotions with pay.

As discussed in Chapter 8, some companies are combining job families to create larger families through broadbanding.[17] In the process of **broadbanding,** the traditional job ladder climbing and promotion-seeking are thus less available. Companies hope that employees will turn their attention to seeking intrinsic satisfaction from the greater ability to move from job to job, a process made easier because more jobs pay the same rates. When this results, companies get greater flexibility in the assignment of employees, and employees become more flexible and adaptable to changing conditions. This also helps teamwork because employees are more likely to be in the same pay grade; thus, there is a greater feeling of fair treatment of all members.[18] Nonetheless, even with broadbanding, employees may still seek promotions, although more limited, and the higher wages that go along with them.

Pay Grades for Skill-Based Pay. The establishment of external equity is more complex with skill-based pay systems than with job-based pay systems. As experienced at Northern Telecom, it was simply not possible to directly compare any particular pay levels in the firm's skill-based pay plan with pay levels of other firms using job-based pay. While organizations using skilled-based pay rely on the market to set levels, the data is used to set minimum, maximum, and average pay levels for the *entire job family,* not to peg each particular skill step in the pay system to jobs found in the outside markets. Exhibit 14.7 depicts the salary guidelines for Northern Telecom's field technician job family. Notice there are five competency levels with an overall pay range of 270 percent. Target high rates are suggested maximum rates of pay for employees at a specific competency level.

Job-based pay describes the others we have discussed.

Skill-based pay is the newer method of evaluating jobs.

EXHIBIT 14.7

Salary Administration Guidelines for a Sample Skill-Based Pay Job Family at Northern Telecom

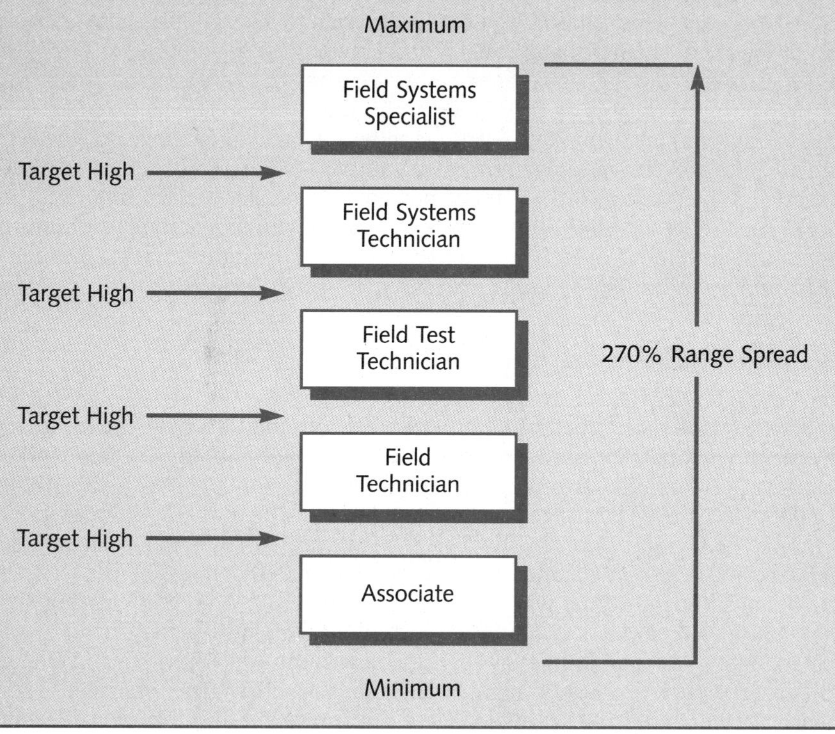

As with job-based pay, organizations employing skill-based pay differ in their pay policies relative to the external market. According to Peter LeBlanc, director of compensation, Northern Telecom matched the market by setting the minimum of the salary range at the labor market entry rate. The maximum was established on the basis of the average rate of pay for the senior job in the firm's traditional benchmark ladder.

Labor Unions

Did You KNOW?

Benefit and direct pay costs per hour of GM union workers is $43.00. For the Bosch nonunion workers it is $16.00 to $23.00.

The presence of a union in a private-sector firm is established to increase wages by 10 to 15 percent. Union presence also adds about 20 to 30 percent to the cost of employee benefits.[19]

> *Pay at Southwest is dictated by any of nine different labor unions—to which about 90% of employees belong. The company just can't get too creative with compensation.*[20]

Cost-of-living adjustments (COLAs) are payments made to account for the changes in the cost of living.

Unions also have pushed for wage escalation clauses that are designed to increase wages automatically during the life of a contract. One way unions have accomplished this is to tie wage increases to changes in the Consumer Price Index. **Cost-of-living adjustments (COLAs)** were popular in the 1960s and 1970s; however, the number of workers covered by COLAs declined during the 1980s and 1990s—primarily because the Consumer Price Index has decelerated in recent years, but also because of growing wage competition from other countries such as Taiwan, South Korea, China, India, and Mexico.

Labor Market

Did You KNOW?

Nobel Prize winner Dr. Kevin Murphy at the University of Chicago proved that a major cause of rising inequality in pay has been the growing demand for sophisticated skills and training.

The labor market influences the wage and salary structure basically through the supply of labor. Shortages in the labor market (internal or external) provide those who are qualified to fill the jobs an opportunity to negotiate better terms of employment. The juggling act between labor supply and demand has ramifications for internal as well as external pay equity. Internally, this can mean pay increases that are relatively higher than those of workers not in short supply. Externally, the firm must also pay a higher rate to attract new hires who are in short supply.

In a country as large as the United States, most organizations experience not one, but several, labor markets. Workers move around. They move to where the jobs are, and they move to where they might want to live. This influences cost-of-living conditions in states throughout our country, which in turn influences pay levels. Such differences influence where companies set up operations and can also prompt them to move operations—for example, J.C. Penney moved its headquarters from New York City to Dallas, Texas.[21]

Individual Wage Determination

Did You KNOW?

In 1971 the hourly pay (1991 dollars) for a high school dropout and a college graduate was $9.59 and $14.72, respectively. In 1991 it was $7.67 and $14.77, respectively.

Once the job analysis and evaluation have been completed, the job classes established, and the wage structure determined, the question becomes how much to pay each individual. For example, consider Ann and John, both of whom work on the same job. The rate range is $3,000 to $4,000 per month; Ann is paid $4,000 and John $3,500. What might account for the pay differential? Although performance contribution is perhaps the logical answer, seniority, market demand, age, and experience (personal contributions) also influence individual wages.

In actuality, individual wage determinations are based on both personal contributions and performance. Thus, age and seniority as well as performance probably influence Ann and John's pay (performance-based pay is discussed in Chapter 15). Even though managers might argue that pay differences based on performance are more equitable, many Japanese companies, for example, reward seniority more than performance. This seems to result in more cooperation and teamwork from employees and a willingness to remain with the same firm for a long time. Southwest Airlines uses seniority for the same reason:

> *The compensation structure weights on the side of seniority, and Southwest emphasizes that good things come to those who wait. (This keeps turnover down around 4%.)*[22]

Issues in Wage and Salary Administration

LEARNING OBJECTIVE 3

Explain issues in wage and salary administration such as employee participation, pay satisfaction, pay secrecy, and salary versus hourly pay.

The following issues in wage and salary administration have particular importance in compensation:

1. To what extent should employees be able to participate in choosing their forms of pay and in setting their own wages?
2. What are the advantages and disadvantages of pay secrecy?
3. What makes employees satisfied with their pay?

Employee Participation

Job evaluation judgments, like other human resource decisions, can be made by a variety of raters including compensation professionals, managers, and job incumbents. Traditionally, compensation professionals and line managers had the most involvement in the design of compensation systems. Now, with the theme of partnership there is an emphasis on employee involvement in job evaluation. Employees are involved in the job evaluation process to broaden their understanding of the process by which job value is established.

One of the most common ways to increase involvement is to establish a job evaluation committee composed of management, nonmanagement, and union representatives. Individuals on such a committee should be knowledgeable about a wide range of jobs. It may also be useful to co-opt antagonists. By involving representatives from all areas, communication is improved, and the likelihood that the organization's values are reflected in the job evaluation system are increased. The involvement of multiple parties does, however, increase the potential for conflict. For example, managers may try to distort job evaluation ratings of a favorite or superstar employee so pay can exceed the maximum permitted for a job of that value. Conversely, compensation professionals will want to preserve pay equity at all costs and thus try to block the efforts of managers to get special pay increases. The process of negotiation and give-and-take is usually worth it because managers and employees are less likely to accept and/or understand the results of a job evaluation study when they were not consulted.

Bonneville International, a broadcast group, has employees update their job descriptions and their supervisors sign off on the descriptions. Using the job description as a common frame of reference, supervisors and employees independently complete the firm's point evaluation instrument. Next, the ratings for the two groups are compared. When rating differences are found, the supervisor meets with employees to reach a consensus on the point value of the job. Because employees are personally involved, there are no job classification appeals, and the system is perceived as procedurally fair. These results indicate that employee participation is well worth the additional time involved.

This example shows the power of partnership between the line manager and employees in creating fairness in pay issues.

Pay Secrecy

According to organizational etiquette, asking others their salaries is generally considered inappropriate. Managers favor **pay secrecy** because it makes their lives

Pay secrecy **refers to the policy of having no public disclosure of employee salaries.**

easier. Without knowledge of pay differentials, employees are less likely to confront their supervisor about inequitable pay. Consequently, managers do not have to defend or justify their actions.

Despite these common perceptions, there are several reasons to have open communication about pay practices. First, certain research indicates that employees misperceive the pay level of other employees. They tend to overestimate the pay of those with lower-level jobs and to underestimate the pay of those with higher-level jobs. Since pay differentials are designed to motivate employees to seek promotion, this misperception may be detrimental to employee motivation. After all, why should an employee gain the experience and accept greater responsibility for only meager salary increases? A second, more practical, reason for an open pay policy is that considerable resources have been devoted to developing a fair and equitable system. For managers and employees to gain an accurate view of the system, they must be informed.

Finally, and potentially most important, pay is a powerful motivator only when its linkage to performance is explicitly stated and known to employees. For an employee to perform well, they must know what performance is desired and what the reward will be for performing well and what the consequence is for performing poorly.

Regarding what should be communicated, many employers specify the range for jobs in a typical career path. In addition to ranges, some organizations detail the typical increases associated with low, average, and top performance. A concern in communicating the latter is that the organization may not be able to maintain the same pay schedule in the future. If increases are lower in subsequent years, there is a risk that employees will become dissatisfied. Still, if it is made clear that the size of the salary increase pool is contingent on the profitability of the organization, this problem can be avoided.[23]

Satisfaction with Pay

If organizations want to minimize absenteeism and turnover as well as maximize motivation through compensation, they must make sure that employees are satisfied with their pay. Since satisfaction with pay and motivation to perform are not necessarily closely related, organizations must know the determinants of pay satisfaction. With this knowledge organizations can develop pay practices more likely to result in satisfaction with pay and motivation to perform. Three major determinants of satisfaction with pay are pay fairness, pay level, and pay administration practices.[24]

People want pay fairness—that is, they look at themselves and others when judging the fairness of their pay. This is the essence of equity theory.

Pay Fairness. **Pay fairness** refers to what people believe they deserve to be paid in relation to what others deserve to be paid. The tendency is for people to determine what they and others deserve to be paid by comparing what they give to the organization with what they get out of the organization. In comparing themselves with others, people may decide whether they are being paid fairly. If they regard this comparison as fair or equitable, they are more likely to be satisfied. If they see this comparison as unfair, they will likely be dissatisfied. This is referred to as **equity theory.**

In addition to absolute levels of pay, people are interested in equity—how they are paid, how they are graded and how they are evaluated relative to other employees.

Herb Kelleher
CEO
Southwest Airlines

Fairness can be increased by giving employees a voice in compensation and also by providing due process. Thus, it is important for organizations to establish formal appeals procedures. Appeals procedures vary in the degree of formality and in how independent the process is from traditional lines of authority. Union contracts often prescribe a formal system where complaints are first filed with the immediate supervisor. If a satisfactory resolution is not attained, the appeal moves forward to a higher level of management until a final decision is reached.[25]

Pay level refers to the actual amount of pay an employee receives.

Pay Level. **Pay level** is an important determinant of the perceived amount of pay satisfaction. People compare actual pay with what they believe they should receive. The result of the comparison is satisfaction with pay if "should" equals "actual." Dissatisfaction results if the actual level is less than the "should" level.

Increasingly, pay-level satisfaction is being related to differences in pay for employees at different levels (especially in comparing nonmanagers to managers) in the organization. U.S. salary survey data show that the average hourly total compensation for all managers is about $25.00 and, for nonmanagerial service workers, it is $7.25. The average differential between the highest and lowest paid employees in large U.S. organizations is about 160:1.[26] In Japan, this same difference is less than 10:1. This is caused in large part by the relatively high level of total CEO compensation. According to Exhibit 14.8, the total compensation for U.S. CEOs is substantially greater than for CEOs in 20 other countries. Of course, there are some variations within the United States. For example, Bill Gates' salary is less than $1 million a year, but the average CEO receives $2 million annually.[27] However:

> *Certain perquisites offered outside the United States balance the scales a bit. The United States is the only one of 20 major countries surveyed by Towers Perrin, an international HR consulting firm, where a car (often with a driver) is not usually provided to the CEO of a $100-million-a-year company. And in many countries with confiscatory tax policies, companies offer tax-favored perks such as club memberships, augmented pensions, and entertainment and housing allowances. But, says Michael Emig, a principal with Wyatt Company, "the order of magnitude of these perks is nothing compared with how much wealth U.S. executives can accumulate over a period of time."*

Did You KNOW?

Adding the value of stock options, total average CEO compensation was $5 million yearly.

EXHIBIT 14.8

Relative Average CEO Total Cash Compensation (for firms with annual sales greater than $100 million U.S.)

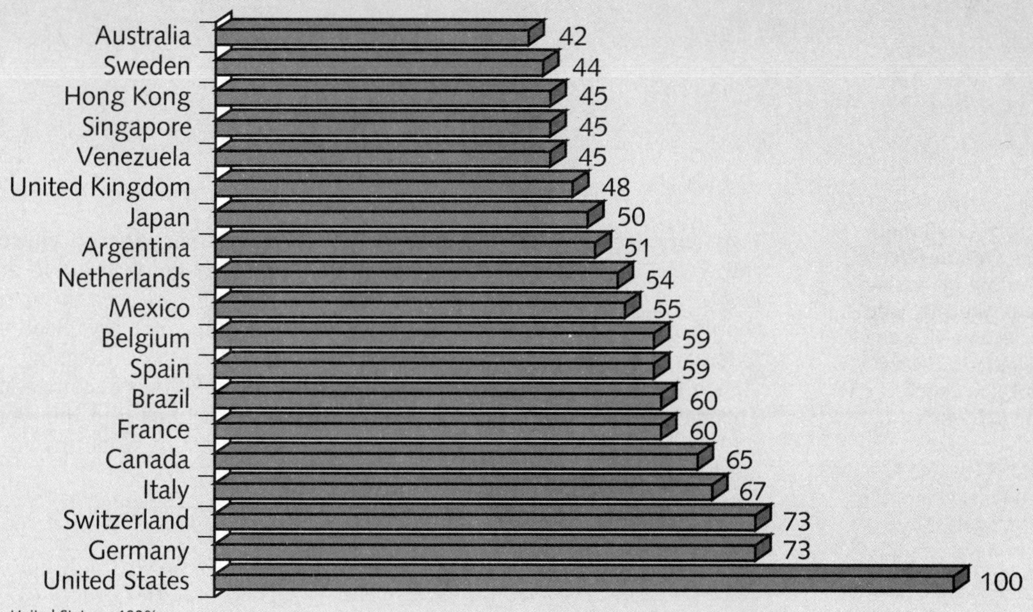

Note: Basis United States = 100%

Source: *International Compensation Report* (New York: Towers Perrin, 1996). Used by permission.

> *The American obsession with superstars also helps drive up the chief's pay. Says Tower Perrin's David Swinford: "In Europe and Japan they still reward longevity and loyalty by promoting from within, whereas we find a home-run hitter and pay to get him as a free agent." Adds Lance Berger of Philadelphia's Hay group: "Each time a CEO changes jobs, it cranks the whole market up a notch."*[28]

Regardless of the reasons for these high levels of CEO pay, employees perceive them as too high. Especially irksome is the CEO practice of asking employees to take pay cuts, while actually increasing their own pay![29] The result of this over the years has been a stagnation and even loss in the real wages of workers. The same is true for benefits.[30] As a consequence, the cost of manufacturing workers in the United States is substantially less than for our major competitors:

Germany	$27.37
Belgium	22.91
Japan	21.38
Sweden	18.81
U.S.	17.10
France	17.10
Italy	16.25
Canada	15.73
Britain	13.68
Australia	13.68
Spain	11.48
Israel	9.06
Korea	6.33
Taiwan	5.47
Hong Kong	4.79
Mexico	2.57[31]

Did You KNOW?

"The pay that the vice presidents get isn't motivating the vice presidents. It's motivating the assistant vice presidents, who want to become vice presidents. Similarly, the CEO's pay is not motivating the CEO so much—he's already there. Rather, it's serving to motivate the vice presidents who are competing against one another to become CEO."

Edward P. Lazear
Professor
Stanford Business School

Pay Administration Practices. What do pay fairness and pay-level issues suggest for pay administration practices? First, if the employer is to attract new employees and keep them satisfied with their pay, the wages and salaries offered should approximate those of other employees in comparable organizations (that is, external equity must exist).[32] Second, the pricing of jobs can enhance pay satisfaction when it is based on a philosophy of equal pay for jobs of comparable worth. This determination can be aided by sound job evaluations. But the worth of jobs must be evaluated according to the factors considered important by both employees and the organizations (so that internal equity exists).

Third, pay-for-performance systems must be accompanied by a method for accurately measuring the performance of employees. They must also be open enough so employees can clearly see the performance-pay relationship. This is discussed further in Chapter 15. Fourth, compensation rates and pay structures should be continually reviewed and revised if necessary. Over time the content of a job may change, distorting the relationship between its actual and its job-evaluated worth.

A final pay administration practice concerns trust and consistency. Employees need to perceive that the organization is looking out for their interests as well as for its own. They want to know that they are being trusted in the same way as the top managers of the organization. Without this knowledge and understanding, not only is the level of trust and pay satisfaction low, but pay also becomes a target for complaints regardless of the real issues. Going a long way to ensure that trust and pay satisfaction do not erode are examples set by the CEO:

> *Some companies have awakened to the hidden costs of the trust gap and are experimenting with ingenious ways of sewing corporate top and bottom back together. Few CEOs have mastered the aristo-bypass, but those who have offer the following advice.*
>
> *Start with the obvious. Tie the financial interests of higher-ups and lower-downs closer together by making exposure to risk and to reward more equitable. When Nucor, a steel company in Charlotte, North Carolina, with $1.1 billion in sales, went through tough times, President Ken Iverson took a 60 percent cut in pay. "How often do you see that?" asks Jude Rich, president of Sibson & Co., a compensation consulting firm. "It makes a real difference if employees see that their CEO is willing to take it in the shorts along with them."*[33]

Legal Considerations

An entire range of environmental concerns affect compensation practices. For example, while organizations use wage survey results to set pay levels for jobs, organizations need to be aware that paying what the market will bear, perhaps paying women and minorities less because they are willing to accept less, is no excuse for wage discrimination. Organizations also need to be concerned over the issue of price fixing. If organizations exchange market data on their own and set pay rates based on this information, the organizations can be charged with price fixing and collusion.

Davis–Bason and Walsh–Healey

The federal government has enacted several laws influencing the level of wages employers may pay, pay structures, and individual wage determinations. The first federal law to protect the amount of pay employees receive for their work was the *Davis-Bacon Act* of 1931; this act required organizations holding federal construction contracts to pay laborers and mechanics the prevailing wages of the majority of the employees in the locality where the work was performed. The *Walsh-Healey Public Contracts Act* of 1936 extended the *Davis-Bacon Act* to include all federal contracts exceeding $10,000 and specified that pay levels conform to the industry minimum rather than the area minimum, as specified in *Davis-Bacon.* The *Walsh-Healey Act* also established overtime pay at one and one-half times the hourly rate. These wage provisions, however, did not include administrative, professional, office, custodial, or maintenance employees, or beginners, or disabled persons.

Wage Deduction Laws

Three federal laws influence how much employers may deduct from employee paychecks. The *Copeland Act* of 1934 authorized the secretary of labor to regulate wage deductions for contractors and subcontractors doing work financed in whole or in part by a federal contract. Essentially, the *Copeland Act* was aimed at illegal deductions. Protection against a more severe threat from an employer with federal contracts was provided in the *Anti-Kickback Law* of 1948. The *Federal Wage Garnishment Law* of 1980 also protects employees against deductions from pay for indebtedness. It provides that only 25 percent of one's disposable weekly earnings or 30 times the minimum wage, whichever is less, can be deducted for debt repayment.

Did You KNOW?

With the poverty line set at $15,600 for a family of four, one full-time worker needs $7.80 per hour to climb above that level.

Did You KNOW?

The city of Baltimore has established a "living wage." With this, companies that do business with the city must pay their workers at least $6.10 per hour.

Fair Labor Standards Act

Partially because *Davis-Bacon* and *Walsh-Healey* were limited in their coverage to employees on construction projects, the *Fair Labor Standards Act* of 1938 (or the Wage and Hour Law) was enacted. This set minimum wages, maximum hours, child labor standards, and overtime pay provisions for all workers except domestic and government employees. The Supreme Court extended the coverage to include state and local government employees in 1985 (*Garcia v. San Antonio Metropolitan Transit Authority*).

1. **Minimum Wage:** The minimum wage began at 25 cents an hour and has reach $5.15. Still, subminimum wages are permitted for learners in semi-skilled occupations, apprentices, handicapped persons working in sheltered workshops, and employees who receive more than $30 per month in tips (up to 40 percent of the minimum requirement may be covered by tips).

2. **Child Labor:** In order to prevent abuses regarding children, the Act also prohibits minors under the age of 18 from working in hazardous occupations. For nonhazardous positions, the minimum age ranges from 14 to 16, depending on the type of work to be performed and whether the employer is a child's parent.

3. **Overtime Provisions:** The overtime provisions of the Act establishes who is to be paid overtime for work and who is not. Most employees covered must be paid time and a half for all work exceeding 40 hours per week. These are called **nonexempt employees.** Several groups of individuals are exempt from both overtime and minimum wage provisions. The **exempt employees** include employees of firms not involved in interstate commerce, employees in season industries, and outside salespeople. Three other employee groups—executives, administrators, and professionals—are also exempt from overtime pay and minimum wage laws in most organizations. Trainee managers and assistant managers, however, are excluded and should thus be paid overtime.[34]

Exempt employees are not covered by overtime or minimum wage provisions. Nonexempt employees are entitled to receive overtime pay.

To be exempt, professionals must spend 80 percent of their work in the following tasks:

- Doing work requiring knowledge acquired through specialized, prolonged training.
- Exercising discretion or judgment.
- Doing work that is primarily intellectual and nonroutine.

The criteria for exempt status as an executive or administrator include spending at least 80 percent of work time in the following tasks:

- Undertaking management duties.
- Supervising two or more employees.
- Controlling or greatly influencing hiring, firing, and promotion decisions.
- Exercising discretion.

In both cases, a comprehensive job analysis is necessary to determine whether a job is exempt. To illustrate how alive and well the Fair Labor Standards Act is, read the feature, "Managing Human Resources at Food Lion, Inc.: Record Settlement Under Fair Labor Standards Act."

Antidiscrimination Laws

Equal Pay Act. While not covered in the original 1938 law, the fourth provision of the *Fair Labor Standards Act* was added as an amendment in

MANAGING HUMAN RESOURCES

at Food Lion, Inc.

Record Settlement Under Fair Labor Standards Act

A record settlement of the *Fair Labor Standards Act* (FLSA) charges will require Food Lion, Inc., to pay more than $16 million in back pay and civil penalties, the Department of Labor announces.

The settlement between the Salisbury, North Carolina, supermarket chain and the Labor Department calls for Food Lion to pay $16.2 million: $13.2 million for back wages to current and former Food Lion employees, $2 million for civil penalties arising from overtime and minimum wage violations, and $1 million for civil penalties for child labor violations. According to DOL, these amounts individually are the highest ever paid by a private employer in each category.

The charges stem from a complaint filed by the United Food and Commercial Workers on behalf of some 330 current and former Food Lion employees. The union alleged that the company's "effective scheduling" policy had resulted in employees working thousands of hours of overtime for which they were not paid. Under the policy, Food Lion would allocate a set number of hours for employees to complete assigned tasks. According to UFCW, the time allocated was often inadequate, and employees would have to work overtime, without compensation, to complete the tasks.

Food Lion consistently denied the allegations, citing an internal policy that prohibits employees from working off the clock. However, the Labor Department proceeded with an investigation of the overtime allegations, and uncovered some 1,300 violations of FLSA's child labor provisions in the process. Subsequently, DOL threatened to take Food Lion to court if it would not agree to settle the charges.

In addition to paying $16.2 million, Food Lion agrees to post copies of the settlement agreement at all of its more than 1,000 stores, train its management staff on compliance with FLSA regulations, and file quarterly reports with the Labor Department on compliance with FLSA regulations and the implementation of a compliance plan. Among other things, the compliance plan calls for the company to conduct periodic audits of its FLSA compliance, to designate a labor standards ombudsman to oversee and coordinate companywide compliance, and to provide an internal dispute resolution procedure for employees to complain about alleged FLSA violations in the future. In agreeing to the settlement, Food Lion does not admit to committing any FLSA violations.[35]

1963. Called the *Equal Pay Act,* this extension prohibits an employer from discriminating

> *...between employees on the basis of sex by paying wages to employees...at a rate less than the rate at which he pays wages to employees of the opposite sex...for equal work on jobs the performance of which requires equal skill, effort, and responsibility, and which are performed under similar working conditions.*

To establish a *prima facie* case of wage discrimination, the plaintiff needs to establish that a disparity in pay exists for men and women performing substantially equal, not necessarily identical, jobs. To determine this, the amount of skill, effort, responsibility, and working conditions required by each job must be assessed through careful job analysis. In making this judgment, job content should be examined, rather than merely job title. If jobs are found to be substantially equal, wages for the lowest paid job must be raised to match those of the higher-paying position.

Freezing or lowering pay of the higher-paid job is unacceptable. Yet even with the same jobs, pay differences between males and females remain:

> *Women who are midlevel managers at hospitals earned only 68% as much as men did, according to a new salary survey published today in* Working Woman *magazine. That's even worse than they fared in the survey last year, when they earned 79% as much as men. Also doing poorly were women selling securities. They made just 55% as much as men. Female obstetrician-gynecologists earn $189,956 yearly vs. $222,454 for males, according to the survey.*
>
> *But there is some good news:*
>
> *The survey finds women in 28 fields earn 85% to 95% of what men in similar jobs get, better than Labor Department statistics that show women get about 74 cents to every dollar men earn.*[36]

Four exceptions can be used to legally defend unequal pay for equal work. They are the existence and use of: 1) a seniority system, 2) a merit system, 3) a system that measures earnings or quality of production, or 4) any additional factor other than gender. To establish a *prima facie* case of discrimination, the plaintiff needs to establish that a disparity in pay exists for employees on equal jobs. If the employer can show the existence of one or more of the four exceptions, however, the differential may be found to be justified.

Civil Rights Acts. Note that the *Equal Pay Act* provides legal coverage only for equal pay for equal work. Only when men and women are performing jobs requiring equivalent skills, effort, and responsibility are they entitled to identical pay (unless there are differences in performance, seniority, or other conditions). Title VII of the *Civil Rights Act* of 1964 and the *Civil Rights Act* of 1991, however, provide broader legal coverage for pay discrimination. While these acts apply to equal pay for equal work, they also apply to compensation where the jobs, though not identical, are comparable.

Comparable worth means that different jobs may still have comparable value and should therefore be paid the same.

Comparable Worth. An important concept in compensation is comparable worth. The heart of the **comparable worth** theory is the contention that, while the "true worth" of nonidentical jobs may be similar, some jobs (often held by women) are paid a lower rate than others (often held by men). Resulting differences in pay that are disproportionate to the differences in the "true worth" of jobs amount to wage discrimination. Consequently, according to the comparable-worth advocates, legal protection should be provided to ensure pay equity.

Several state and local governments have passed comparable-worth or pay-equity legislation. And many businesses have also taken action on pay-equity issues. Exactly what the issues are and how they can be addressed are described in the feature, "HR Advice and Application: Achieving Pay Equity—Not Simple, but Not So Costly."

Internationally, comparable worth is an idea that has been around for some time.

> *The International Labor Organization (ILO), the Geneva-based agency of the United Nations and United States joined in 1934, adopted an international convention on comparable worth almost 35 years ago. And what the ILO's experience shows is that while comparable worth may have helped reduce the gap between male and female wages in some countries that have tried it, it hasn't eliminated the gap. But neither has it led to the major economic or bureaucratic headaches that its critics prophesied.*[37]

HR ADVICE & APPLICATION

Achieving Pay Equity—Not Simple, But Not So Costly

Pay equity is a policy that provides businesses the competitive edge to meet the challenges of the next century, declares the National Committee on Pay Equity. A consistent, fair pay policy whereby all workers are paid equally for work of equal value produces a more productive and better-motivated workforce, which, in turn, promotes recruitment and retention of good workers...

"Smart employers recognize that future profits depend on current investment in their most vital resource: their people,"...says the coalition of labor, women's, and civil rights groups in its report, "Pay Equity Makes Good Business Sense."

Women and men of color are concentrated in lower-paying jobs. Additionally, when women and men of color occupy traditionally white-male-dominated positions—even after accounting for legitimate reasons for pay differences such as differing skills, work experience, and seniority—women and men of color are still paid less, contends the pay-equity committee's publication.

On the basis of every dollar paid to white men in 1988, white women were paid 65 cents, black women were paid 61 cents, and Hispanic women were paid 55 cents, the report notes. Black men were paid 75 cents, and Hispanic men were paid 65 cents for every dollar paid to white men.

Discriminatory wage practices account for between one-quarter and one-half of this disparity in wages, says the report.

WHAT IS PAY EQUITY?

Pay equity, also known in the United States, Canada, and Europe as equal pay for work of equal value, is broader than "equal pay for equal work." Pay equity is a means of eliminating race, ethnicity, and gender as wage determinants within job categories and between job categories, the report says.

Many businesses pay women and men of color less than white males. This result is often unintentional and due in part to personnel systems and wage structures that retain historical biases and inconsistencies that are, in fact, discriminatory, explains the report.

A pay-equity policy examines existing pay policies that underpay women and men of color and activates steps to correct the discrimination.

HOW TO ACHIEVE PAY EQUITY

A comprehensive audit is the first step in implementing a pay-equity policy, explains the committee's report. The audit should examine the following areas for inequities and needed changes:

- Job evaluation
- Market pricing
- Pay administration
- Recruitment

In the area of pay administration, the audit should scrutinize each individual component of a business's system including: salary-range design, salary grades, pay differentials, and the determination of hiring rates. Additional items to be examined for inequities include promotion rates, merit increases, incentive programs, and performance and seniority factors in the pay system.

PAY EQUITY IS NOT COSTLY

Following the lead of public employers, many private-sector businesses are already incorporating pay-equity analyses in their annual budget proposals. "The cost of pay equity adjustments," reports the committee, usually has been "between 2 and 5 percent of payroll."

In no cases have the wages of any workers been lowered in order to achieve pay equity, reports the committee, because the objective of pay equity is to remedy wage inequities for underpaid workers, not to penalize another group of employees.[38]

Since its adoption, more than 100 governments—but not the United States—have ratified the convention. These include most of the nations of Western Europe, Canada, Australia, New Zealand, Japan, and more than 70 developing countries.[39]

International Compensation

LEARNING OBJECTIVE 4

Describe international compensation.

As the environment for many business firms in the United States becomes more global, international compensation becomes a more significant part of total compensation.[40]

Objectives

When developing international compensation policies, a multinational corporation (MNC) seeks to satisfy several objectives. First, the policy should be consistent and fair in its treatment of all categories of international employees. The interests of the MNC are best served if all international employees are relatively satisfied with their compensation package and perceive that they are treated equitably. Second, the policy must work to attract and retain personnel in areas of greatest need and opportunity. Third, the policy should facilitate the transfer of international employees in the most cost-effective manner. Fourth, the policy should be consistent with the firm's overall strategy and structure. Finally, compensation should serve to motivate employees. Some professional international HR managers would say that motivation is the major objective of their compensation programs.[41]

Designing International Compensation Packages

In general, the first issue facing MNCs when designing international compensation policies is whether to establish an overall policy for all employees or to distinguish between PCNs and TCNs. This differentiation may diminish in the future, but it is currently common for MNCs to distinguish between these two distinct groups.

Reminder:

- **PCN = parent-country national or expatriate**
- **TCN = third-country national**
- **HCN = host-country national**

There is even a tendency for MNCs to differentiate among types of PCNs. Separate types of policies may be established based on the length of assignment (temporary transfer, permanent transfer, or continual relocation) or on the type of employee. Cash remuneration, special allowances, benefits, and pensions are determined in part by such classification. Short-term PCNs, for example, whose two- or three-year tours of duty abroad are interspersed with long periods at home, may be treated differently from career PCNs who spend most of their time working in various locations abroad. Both of these groups are different from TCNs, who often move from country to country in the employ of one MNC (or several) headquartered in a country other than their own (for example, a Swiss banker may be in charge of a German branch of a British bank). In effect, these are the real global employees, the ones who can weave together the far-flung parts of a MNC. As the global MNC increases in importance, it is likely that the TCNs will become more valuable and thus able to command levels of compensation equivalent to PCNs.

For PCNs, the most widely used policy emphasizes "keeping the expatriate whole" (that is, maintaining salary level relative to the PCN's colleagues plus compensating for the costs of international service).[42] The basis of this policy implies that foreign assignees should not suffer a material loss due to their transfer. This can be accomplished through the utilization of what is known as the balance-sheet approach. This approach to international compensation is a system designed to equalize the purchasing power of employees at comparable position levels living overseas and in the home country, and to provide incentives to offset qualitative differences between assignment locations.[43]

There are five major categories of outlays that cover all the types of expenses incurred by PCNs and their families:

1. **Goods and services:** home-country outlays for items such as food, personal care, clothing, household furnishings, recreation, transportation, and medical care.
2. **Housing:** the major costs associated with the employee's principal residence.
3. **Income taxes:** payments to federal and local governments for personal income taxes.
4. **Reserve:** contributions to savings, payments for benefits, pension contributions, investments, education expenses, social security taxes, and so forth.
5. **Shipment and storage:** the major costs associated with shipping and storing personal and household effects.

Thus, MNCs seek to develop international packages that are competitive in all of the following aspects of compensation:

Base Salary

- Home rate/home currency
- Local rate/local currency
- Salary adjustments or promotions—home or local standard
- Bonus—home or local currency, home or local standard
- Stock options
- Inducement payment/hardship premium—percent of salary or lump sum payment, home or local currency
- Currency protection—discretion or split basis
- Global salary and performance structure

Taxation Services

- Tax protection
- Tax equalization
- Other services

Benefits

- Home-country program
- Local program
- Social security program
- Car

Allowances

- Cost-of-living allowances
- Housing standard
- Education
- Relocation
- Perquisites
- Home leave
- Shipping and storage

While not all these aspects of international compensation are likely to come into play for every expatriate, it is still rather expensive to have expatriates. Expatriates may be three to six times as much as a non-expatriate. Thus, global firms face rather high compensation bills if they need to staff with expatriates. Although some of these aspects of international compensation may not apply to TCNs or HCNs, all do apply to PCNs.

Base Salary. The term **base salary** acquires a somewhat different meaning when employees go abroad. At home, base salary denotes the amount of cash compensation that serves as a benchmark for other compensation elements (for example, bonuses and benefits). For PCNs, it is the primary component of a package of allowances, many of which are directly related to base salary (foreign service premium, cost-of-living allowances, housing allowances, and tax protection, for example) as well as the basis for in-service benefits and pension contributions.

Did You KNOW?

General Motors spends between $750,000 and $1 million (besides salary) on an executive and his or her family during a three-year overseas posting.

International compensation packages include:

- **Base salary**
- **Taxation services**
- **Benefits**
- **Allowances**

Base salary is the amount of cash compensation that serves as the basis for determining bonuses and benefits.

International compensation is a critical and complex topic. There are many consulting firms that specialize in this area.

When applied to TCNs, base salary may mean the prevailing rate paid for a specific skill in the employee's home country. Typically, companies use local compensation levels as guidelines when developing HCN compensation policies. Conditions that force compensation policies to differ from those in the United States include inflation and cost of living, housing, security, school costs, and taxation. For example, it is far less costly to recruit a construction engineer from Spain or Taiwan to work in the Middle East than from the United Kingdom or the United States.

> *More than half of American companies now tie base salaries to the home countries of the third-country national they employ, rather than to U.S. or host-country salary structures, according to a survey of 117 international companies by Organization Resources Counselors, Inc. The number of companies doing this has risen from 38 percent to more than 52 percent in just two years, and the trend includes those with small as well as large PCN populations. The primary objective is cost saving, since base pay levels of most other countries are below those of the U.S.*[44]

The base salary of a PCN is usually paid either in the home currency at the home rate or in the local currency at a rate equivalent to the rate paid locally for the same job. Similarly, salary adjustments and promotional practices may be fashioned according to either home-country or local standards. In some select cases, global salary and performance structures have been implemented.

Strategic Imperatives

To succeed in an ever-changing international environment, MNCs must look beyond next year's goals and develop clear but flexible long-term compensation strategies.

For a pair of running shoes costing $80 in the U.S., labor costs account for $2.60 of the total cost.

Donna Gibbs
Spokeswoman
NIKE

> *An effective managerial reward system should be linked to long-term corporate strategy and should anticipate changes in employees' valence of different organizational rewards. On the one hand, multinational settings make the complex task of developing such a system even more difficult; on the other hand, the fact that the corporation operates in many different environments permits the establishment of unique reward programs, unavailable in more conventional environments.*[45]

In addition, MNCs need to match their compensation policies with both their staffing policies and general philosophies. If, for example, as discussed in Chapter 8, an MNC has an ethnocentric staffing policy (that is, staffing with an expert chosen by headquarters), its compensation policy should be one of keeping the PCN whole. If, however, the staffing policy follows a geocentric approach (that is, staffing a position with the "best person," regardless of nationality), there may be no clear "home" for the TCN, and the MNC will need to consider establishing a system of international base pay for key managers paid in a major reserve currency such as the U.S. dollar or the Deutschmark. This system allows MNCs to deal with considerable variations in base salaries for managers, such as that noted in the following report:

> *In Switzerland, a department head working for a medium-sized company earns $78,000. The same executive in Germany earns only $64,000. But in the U.S., the equivalent job pays only $54,000, a figure seen as surprisingly low. However, the gap increases as U.S. executives climb the corporate lad-*

der. At the highest levels, CEOs in the U.S. average $2.0 million while those in Switzerland average only $284,000 and in Germany only $275,000.[46]

These actual values have changed with time, but the relative values have not. Further evidence of the disparity between management compensation across countries is shown in Exhibit 14.8, which compares relative compensation for CEOs in 19 countries.

Compensation Practices in Other Countries

Japan. The Japanese are fond of saying there are three sacred treasures of the Imperial House. The first of these is lifetime employment. The second, which stems from lifetime employment, is the traditional seniority system that determines not only wages, but also the timing of promotions. Under this system, an employee rarely works under someone with less seniority in service length, assuming both have similar educational backgrounds. This system has its roots in the traditional *Oyabun-Kobun,* or parent-child relationship, which attaches great respect to the older or senior member of the family (company). The third treasure of the Imperial House is the enterprise (or company) union.

Initially, individual companies pay almost the same starting salary for new employees hired upon graduation from either high school or college. After that, an employee's annual earnings increase according to the merit rating system. In addition, earnings will increase annually by seniority, even if an employee's job responsibilities remain unchanged, until the age of mandatory retirement, now commonly 60 years of age.

As Japan changes, the seniority system is coming under attack as being too expensive.

A distinguishing feature of the Japanese wage system is the provision for a semiannual bonus or wage allowance, separate from the annual incremental rate. Usually paid without exception, even in times of recession, the bonus amount is closely related to both the general economy and the profitability of the company.

In addition to basic salary, Japanese workers customarily receive compensation in the form of housing or a housing allowance, daily living support (including transportation, meals, and workers' uniforms), cultural and recreational benefits, and medical and health care.[47]

Europe. With the development of the European Community (or European Union), there is greater use of the common currency called the **ECU** (European Currency Unit) within business. This currency, already being used by some European firms, will facilitate the mobility of workers across nations. Having a similar impact is the movement toward Europay. **Europay** is a practice of developing a common policy and common set of pay practices regardless of location throughout Europe. This practice, primarily targeted for top management, recognizes the need to treat European operations as truly one market and their employees as truly European.[48]

Did You KNOW?

In 1980 the U.S. surpassed Britain as the nation with the largest gap in income between the rich and poor.

Summary

Organizations are being forced to develop strategic compensation practices in light of a cost-conscious, competitive environment that demands high quality and a continuous flow of new products. Compensation programs must be consistent with the organization's culture and strategic objectives.

Job evaluation is a systematic, rational assessment of the value of jobs that is designed to establish internal equity in jobs. Ranking and job classification methods focus on evaluating the whole job. These methods are premised on intuitive judgments about job worth. Preferable methods include point evaluation and factor comparison systems, both of which evaluate jobs using compensable factors.

In conducting a job evaluation study, a decision needs to be made regarding custom designing or buying a system. While it may be expedient to buy a standardized system, such a system may not reflect organizational needs and values. To ensure systemwide equity, a single job evaluation plan is usually preferred over multiple plans. Another important decision is who should evaluate the worth of jobs. The greater the involvement of employees, the more likely they are to accept the results of the job evaluation study. Alternatively, an organization can choose a pay-for-knowledge system in which pay increases with job skill or flexibility.

Once the worth is determined, jobs must still be priced. Although job evaluation procedures are important in establishing worth, they are more relevant to establishing relative job prices than absolute job prices. To help establish absolute job prices, organizations often use market survey data, especially for those jobs that have identical or nearly identical counterparts in the marketplace. Market surveys for pricing jobs that are not found in other organizations should be done with caution. Such surveys involve subjectivity and are therefore open to potential wage discrimination charges. Organizations should be careful in using market rates to perpetuate wage differentials that are obviously discriminatory. Fair evaluations should be conducted to reduce that likelihood.

In establishing wages, organizations can rely on job evaluations and market surveys, and can use inputs from the employees themselves. Employees can responsibly set their own wages. In the few companies that have tried it, employees have set their own wages without management altering the procedures or changing decisions. The method is most successful, however, in organizations where employees and management have mutual trust and employees are provided with information to help them understand the financial status of the company.

Establishing wages and determining which job evaluation method to use, though important, are only two components of compensation. Other components include selecting the best performance-based pay plan and obtaining benefit from indirect compensation.

In addition, compensation practices must adhere to many legal requirements. The most significant legislation related to compensation are the *Fair Labor Standards Act* and *Equal Pay Act.* Concern over discrimination in pay also causes organizations to consider the manner in which rates of pay are determined.

Key Concepts

base salary
benchmark jobs
broadbanding
comparable worth
compensable factors
cost-of-living adjustments (COLAs)
direct compensation
ECU (European Currency Unit)
equity theory
Europay
exempt employees
external equity
factor comparison method
grade structure
Hay method
indirect compensation
internal equity
job-based pay
job classes
job classification method
job evaluation
job families
job ranking method
maturity curves
nonexempt employees
pay fairness
pay level
pay secrecy
performance-based pay
point factor method
point rating method
skill-based evaluation
skill-based pay
total compensation
wage and salary surveys

Review and Discussion Questions

1. What purposes can total monetary compensation serve?
2. What forms of pay and rewards make up total compensation?
3. What are four basic wage issues that any job evaluation system must address?

4. Describe the basic mechanics of the common job evaluation methods.
5. How do firms establish the actual pay levels for each job?
6. Describe the major issues in wage and salary administration.
7. What are the components of the typical expatriate's compensation package?
8. How do the base salaries of expatriates differ from the base salaries of employees in the United States?
9. What are the advantages of skill-based evaluation over traditional evaluation methods?
10. What is the relationship between total compensation and organizational life-cycle?

PROJECTS, EXERCISES & CASES

End-of-Text Projects

Lincoln Electric

1. Describe the following for Lincoln Electric:
   - **a.** Lincoln's total compensation plan objectives
   - **b.** The degree to which these objectives are serving the business and HR objectives of Lincoln
   - **c.** Lincoln's total compensation plans and activities
   - **d.** The degree to which these plans and activities are serving Lincoln's objectives.
2. How can the compensation activities at Lincoln Electric be improved?

Nordstrom

1. Describe the following for Nordstrom:
   - **a.** Nordstrom's total compensation plan objectives
   - **b.** The degree to which these objectives are serving the business and HR objectives of Nordstrom
   - **c.** Nordstrom's total compensation plans and activities
   - **d.** The degree to which these plans and activities are serving Nordstrom's objectives.
2. How can the compensation activities at Nordstrom be improved?

Field Project

Interview at least five people, and ask them how important pay is to them and what it means to them. Ask them what things they value other than money. Report to the class, and compare your findings with the results of others.

Career Management Exercise

Indicate the relative importance (1 = highest, 12 = lowest; use each number only once) of the following in your job choice:

___ a. company culture

___ b. salary

___ c. signing bonus

___ d. vacation time

___ e. health benefits

___ f. quality of people

___ g. job content

___ h. location

___ i. company reputation

___ j. job security

___ k. degree of autonomy

___ l. technology available

Case: Motivation and Pay Raise Allocation

STEP ONE: PRE-GROUP MEETING PREPARATION

Read the instructions to the "Employee Profile Sheet" and then decide on a pay increase for each of the eight employees. Write your decision in money and percentage amounts. Be prepared to explain your decisions in class.

STEP TWO: GROUP MEETING

Each member should share the recommendations he or she made in Step One and explain his or her reasons for them. After all members have reported, the group should analyze and try to explain differences among everyone's recommendations. The group should then develop a common set of recommendations.

The group may also decide to totally re-vamp the current pay system, e.g., make it more incentive-based. Describe what changes you recommend here. A spokesperson should be appointed to present the group's recommendations to the class.

CASE EXHIBIT 1

Employee Profile Sheet

You must make salary increase recommendations for eight individuals whom you supervise. They have just completed their first year with the company and are now to be considered for their first annual raise. Keep in mind that you may be setting precedents that will shape future expectations and that you must stay within your salary budget. Otherwise, there are no formal company policies to restrict you as you decide how to allocate raises. Write the raise you would give each person in the space to the left of each name. You have a total of $50,000 in your budget for pay raises.

$____ %____ **Arnold J. Adams.** Adams is not, as far as you can tell, a good performer. You have discussed your opinion with others and they agree completely. However, you know that Adams has one of the toughest work groups to manage. Adams' subordinates have low skill levels and the work is dirty and hard. If you lose Adams, you are not sure that you could find an adequate replacement. Current salary: $60,000.

$____ %____ **Bruce K. Berger.** Berger is single and seems to lead the life of a carefree swinger. In general, you feel that Berger's job performance is not up to par, and some of Berger's "goofs" are well-known to other employees. Current salary: $63,750.

$____ %____ **Carol C. Carter.** You consider Carter to be one of your best subordinates. However, it is quite apparent that other people don't agree. Carter has married into wealth and, as far as you know, doesn't need any more money. Current salary: $67,000.

$____ %____ **Daniel Davis.** You happen to know from your personal relationship that Davis badly needs more money because of certain personal problems. Davis also happens to be one of your best managers. For some reason, your enthusiasm is not shared by your other subordinates and you have heard them make joking remarks about Davis' performance. Current salary: $64,000.

$____ %____ **Ellen J. Ellis.** Your opinion is that Ellis just isn't cutting the mustard. Surprisingly enough, however, when you check with others to see how they feel you find that Ellis is very highly regarded. You also know that Ellis badly needs a raise. Ellis was recently divorced and is finding it extremely difficult to support a young family of four as a single parent. Current salary: $60,750.

$____ %____ **Fred M. Foster.** Foster has turned out to be a very pleasant surprise, has done an excellent job, and is seen by peers as one of the best people in your group of managers. This surprises you because Foster is generally carefree and doesn't seem to care very much about money or promotions. Current salary: $62,700.

$____ %____ **Gloria K. Gomez.** Gomez has been very successful thus far. You are particularly impressed by this because Gomez has one of the hardest jobs in the company. Gomez needs money more than many of your other subordinates and is respected for good performance. Current salary: $65,250.

$____ %____ **Harriet A. Hunt.** You know Hunt personally. This employee seems to squander money continually. Hunt has a fairly easy job assignment, and your own view is that Hunt doesn't do it especially well. You are thus surprised to find that several of the other new managers think that Hunt is the best of the new group. Current salary: $61,500.

VISIT THE LIBRARY

Workforce Online

1. Enter your Web browser.
2. Enter Workforce Online.
3. Find and review the following article within "Winning Ideas":

   Ben & Jerry's Caring Capitalism
4. Enter the HR Library.
5. Find and review the following article within the "Research Center":

   HR in Mexico: What You Should Know
6. Return to your homepage.

Case: Pacific Coast Electric Company

Pacific Coast Electric Company (PCEC) is a public utility company located in San Francisco. The company is so successful that it is considered a model for other utility companies. Over the past two years, however, PCEC management has become concerned with increasing payroll costs. Cost containment and a "lean and mean" structure are key ingredients in the company's success. Management wants to study this problem and, if warranted, take corrective action.

Roger Waters is a compensation specialist with PCEC. Roger has been assigned to study PCEC's compensation practices and determine whether any action is required. He decides to compile compensation data for the past five years by using the company's human resource information system (HRIS). Five years will reveal any trends, and the HRIS allows him to break down the data by department, length of service, gender, exempt versus nonexempt employees, and the like.

Roger has uncovered a startling situation. The data indicate that certain nonexempt employees are receiving compensation far in excess of their base pay rate. It seems that these employees are working excessive overtime because of the specific expertise they possess. Overtime rates are one-and-one-half times through 48 hours and double time after that. Employees who work overtime also receive additional compensation, including meal and travel allowances. The base salary for these employees averages $25,000 per year. With overtime, these employees make between $35,000 and $39,000 a year. This situation would be less of a concern if it involved only a few individuals, but hundreds of employees are in this situation. It should be noted that PCEC initiated the overtime policy because of the high cost of consultants—besides, the company feels that its own employees are better skilled and more capable than most consultants.

The employees in question make more than their superiors. First-line supervisors, for example, make approximately 15 percent more than the base compensation of the top craft employees. In other words, supervisors are making approximately $28,750 on the average. Supervisors can receive merit pay, but only a small number of supervisors are eligible for merit awards. Further, supervisors are not paid overtime and receive no meal allowances. Fortunately for PCEC, thinks Roger, our supervisors are not aware of the extent of the pay inequities.

Aside from the obvious problem of employees making a great deal more money than their supervisors, another problem becomes apparent. Examination of the internal labor market reveals that all of the first-line supervisors have come from outside the company. The qualified employees are not accepting "promotions" because they do not want to take a cut in pay. The long-term consequences of this situation could be very serious.

Then Roger looks at a breakdown of the data by gender for the nonexempt employees in question. Women have an average base salary of $23,500 while the average base salary for men is $25,900. Furthermore, not one of the employees receiving high salaries resulting from overtime is female. Roger is very concerned about the differences in compensation for men and women, especially because PCEC prides itself on its equal employment/affirmative action reputation. Men and women are doing essentially the same jobs.

Roger becomes lost in thought as he contemplates his findings. He knows that it will be difficult to frame a report around the compensation issues that he has uncovered. He suspects that it will be even more difficult to recommend changes that will resolve these thorny issues.

Case Questions

1. Are there cases in which employees should be paid more than their supervisors?
2. Does PCEC have a pay-equity problem?
3. What recommendations should Roger make?
4. How should he make compensation changes?

Case: Comparable Worth Finds Rockdale

Bill Starbuck was proud to be assigned to the city beat of *The Rockdale Times*. Bill, a newspaper reporter for two years now, was paying his dues at a small-town newspaper, hoping to work his way up to a larger circulation daily. The city beat would mean that Bill could draw on his background in journalism and political science at Wabash College to write news stories with substance. His prior assignment to the features section of *The Rockdale Times* was interesting but not intellectually stimulating.

Bill's first major assignment was coming up in two days with an invitation to cover a breakfast meeting with the city council. Clyde Langston, Rockdale city manager, was scheduled to present the revised city budget. Bill prepared for the meeting by calling one of his contacts in the city office for some "inside" information. Bill had been dating Jill Bateman, a secretary to the personnel executive director, and he was confident he could learn something about the breakfast meeting agenda.

As Bill hung up from his call to Jill, he wondered what the rumor of a pay raise for some city employees could mean. If anything, the city was expected to trim its budget because of a slowdown in the local economy and loss of revenues due to the shutdown of two plants in the community within the past year. According to Jill, the rumor was that some of the clerical and administrative staff employees were scheduled for midyear pay adjustments. The figure working the hallways was a three percent pay raise, which would come as a pleasant surprise to the 95 employees in the administrative-office clerical positions.

As Bill arrived at the Wednesday morning breakfast meeting, he quickly scanned the room to identify the four city councilmen and one councilwoman. Bill wanted to interview at least three of the members for his story, which was due by 1:00 p.m. After Mayor Jim Earnie arrived, the city council, city manager, and local news reporters finished a quick and cordial breakfast.

Clyde Langston called the group to attention with a rap on his water goblet, and the cordial bantering quickly subsided. Clyde distributed a five-page report of the preliminary budget. Bill quickly scanned the report and noted that the $13.7 million total was considerably trimmed down from last year's budget of $16.4 million. Then, as Bill anticipated, Clyde pointed out a $41,000 line item increase in salaries within the pared-down budget.

Clyde proceeded to explain that the city had done an analysis of their 95 administrative-office clerical positions and their 350 technical-craft positions and decided to make some pay adjustments. All but one of the administrative-office clerks are women, while only 27 of the technical-craft workers are women. The pay range for office workers ranges from a low of $5.19 per hour to a high of $11.17 per hour, with an average of $6.30 per hour. The technical-craft jobs begin at $4.83 per hour and max out at $13.85 per hour, with an average of $9.69 per hour. The net effect of the $41,000 increase was to provide about a three percent increase to the administrative-office clerical workers.

Clyde pointed out that a recently conducted job evaluation study had resulted in the merger of the previously separated job families, such that all jobs were to be evaluated on a common set of attributes. Clyde elaborated further that the impetus of this change was to avoid any litigation over the comparable-worth issue. After completing the budget review briefing, Clyde offered to answer questions. When the council members sat quietly, Jim Earnie thanked the council for their time and adjourned the meeting.

Bill scurried to the door to intercept the council members as they prepared to leave, hoping to get a few reactions to this surprise comparable-worth initiative by the city government. Bill caught all five of the city council members and the mayor and proceeded to ask them what they thought of Clyde's proposal for the pay adjustments. Mayor Jim Earnie, along with three of the council members, indicated that they did not understand the rationale for the raises. After Bill questioned them, they even agreed that they thought that the issue deserved some further discussion.

"I did not know we were using that standard," Councilman Jim Maloney said. "If we're applying comparable worth throughout the system, it would be good to know that, and on what basis it's being done."

Councilwoman Marcie Rivera said she was in accord with the approach. "I'm inclined to agree with the way Clyde put it out," she said, "to avoid any problems in discrimination. If that's the concern here, I feel like it's a step in the right direction."

Amazing, thought Bill as he headed to his car with notes in hand. I just attended a city council breakfast meeting to review the upcoming city budget, and comparable worth is proposed by the city manager. And the mayor and city council hardly noticed until after the meeting was adjourned!

Case Questions

1. Has Rockdale really implemented a comparable-worth standard?
2. How do you think the technical-craft workers will react to the announced pay raise?
3. What other approaches are available for achieving pay equity between men and women?
4. Why have state and local governments shown more interest in comparable worth than have private employers?

Chapter 14 Endnotes

1. Letter of Raymon Kent, "Readers Report," *Business Week* (August 14, 1995): 10. See also S. Tully, "Are You Paid Enough," *Fortune* (June 26, 1995): 66–76.

2. B. Schlender, "What Bill Gates Really Wants," *Fortune* (January 16, 1995): 34–63; T. Engle and S. McFather, "Rewards and Recognition for Generation X," *ACA News* (October/November 1995); S. Manes and P. Andrews, *Gates* (New York: Doubleday, 1993); B. Schlender, "How Bill Gates Keeps the Magic Going," *Fortune* (June 18, 1990): 82–89.

3. B. Nelson, *1001 Ways to Reward Employees* (New York: Workman, 1995); M. Leibman and H. P. Weinstein, "Money Isn't Everything," *HR Magazine* (Nov. 1990): 48–51; R. E. Sibson, *Compensation,* rev. ed. (New York: AMACOM, 1990); G. T. Milkovich and J. M. Newman, *Compensation,* 2nd ed. (Plano, Tex.: Business Publications, 1989); *New Perspectives on Compensation,* D. B. Balkin and L. R. Gomez–Mejia, eds. (Englewood Cliffs, NJ: Prentice-Hall, 1987). The use of divisions is practical because it is then easier to discuss compensation. This is just one way to divide up the components of compensation. For an alternative way, see R. I. Henderson, "Designing a Reward System for Today's Employee," *Business* (July-Sept. 1982): 2–12.

4. L. S. Richman, "CEOs To Workers: Help Not Wanted," *Fortune* (July 12, 1993): 42–43; R. Jacob, The Economy: Girding for Worse," *Fortune* (October 18, 1993): 10; "Employees' Views on Work," *Bulletin to Management* (Sept. 16, 1993): 289.

5. "Southwest Airlines Won't Be Grounded by a Strict Compensation Structure," *Personnel Journal* (March 1995): 23.

6. See J. Kerr and J. Slocum, Jr., "Linking Reward Systems and Organizational Cultures," in *Readings in Personnel and Human Resource Management,* 3rd ed., R. S. Schuler, S. A. Youngblood, and V. L. Huber, eds. (St. Paul, MN: West, 1988); E. E. Lawler III, "The Strategic Design of Reward Systems" in *Readings in Personnel and Human Resources Management,* 2nd ed., R. S. Schuler and S. A. Youngblood, eds. (St. Paul, MN: West, 1984): 253–269; L. L. Cummings, "Compensation, Culture and Motivation: A Systems Perspective," *Organizational Dynamics* (Winter 1984): 33–44.

7. G. Milkovich and J. Newman, *Compensation,* 5th ed. (Chicago: Irwin, 1996).

8. S. M. Emerson, "Job Evaluation: A Barrier to Excellence?" *Compensation and Benefits Review* (Jan.-Feb. 1991): 39–51; C. L. Hughes and W. L. Wright, "Make Pay Plans Work For the People They Pay," *Personnel Journal* (May 1989): 54–63.

9. R. D. Arvey, "Sex Bias in Job Evaluation Procedures," *Personnel Psychology* 39 (1986): 315–335; D. Doverspike, B. Racicot, and C. Albertson, *The Role of Information Processing Variables in the Decision-Making Process in Job Evaluation: Results of Empirical Studies on Sex Prototypes, Person Prototypes and the Effects of Training* (Buffalo, NY: First Annual Conference on HRM Decision Making, Oct. 1986); M. K. Mount and R. A. Ellis, "Investigation of Bias in Job Evaluation Rating of Comparable Worth Study Participants," *Personnel Psychology* 40 (1987): 85–96.

10. "Use Broadbanding to Support Change by Streamlining Salary Ranges," *HR Reporter* (October 1995); "Reports From the Broadbanding Bandwagon," *Bulletin to Management* (March 17, 1994).

11. Milkovich and Newman, *Compensation.*

12. J. Gordon, "Into the Dark: Rough Ride Ahead for American Workers," *Training* (July 1993): 21–30; N. Gupta, G. E. Ledford, D. Jenkins, and D. Doty, "Survey-Based Prescriptions for Skilled-Based Pay," *ACA Journal* (Autumn 1992): 48–58; M. Rowland, "For Each New Skill, More Money," *New York Times* (June 13, 1993): F16.

13. Excerpts from "Master the Compensation Maze," by S. Caudron, copyright June 1993.

14. J. Domat-Connell, "A New Look at the Foundation of Compensation Program Design," *Compensation and Benefits Review* (Mar.-Apr. 1994): 38–46. R. J. Sokol, "Seven Rules of Salary Surveys," *Personnel Journal* (April 1990): 83–87. See also Sibson, *Compensation,* 17–19.

15. Sibson, *Compensation.*

16. For a discussion on the validity of job evaluation systems, see T. Patten, "How Do You Know If Your Job Evaluation System Is Working?" in Balkin and Gomez-Mejia, *New Perspectives on Compensation.*

17. D. Hofrichter, "Broadbanding: A 'Second Generation' Approach," *Compensation & Benefits Review* (September-October 1993): 53–58.

18. P. V. LeBlanc and M. McInerney, "Need a Change? Jump on the Banding Wagon," *Personnel Journal* (January 1994): 72–78.

19. Milkovich and Newman, *Compensation.*

20. "Southwest Airlines Won't Be Grounded by a Strict Compensation Structure."

21. "Annual Pay Levels and Growth in Pay by State," *Bulletin to Management* (Nov. 19, 1992): 365.

22. "Southwest Airlines Won't Be Grounded by Strict Compensation Structure."

23. A. Markels and L. Berton, "Executive Pay: Something to Talk About," *The Wall Street Journal* (April 11, 1996); E. E. Lawler, *Pay and Organization Development* (Reading, MA: Addison-Wesley, 1981).

24. V. Scarpello, V. Huber, and R. J. Vanderberg, "Compensation Satisfaction: Its Measurement and Dimensionality," *Journal of Applied Psychology* (May 1988): 163–171.

25. A. Bernstein, "Is America Becoming More of a Class Society?" *Business Week* (February 26, 1996): 86–91; J. Fierman, "The Perilous New World of Fair Pay," *Fortune* (June 13, 1994): 57–64.

26. E. S. Hardy, "America's Highest-Paid Bosses," *Forbes* (May 22, 1995): 180–228.

27. L. Uchitelle, "1995 Was Good for Companies, And Better for a Lot of C.E.O.s," *New York Times* (March 29, 1996): 1, D8; J. A. Byrne, "How High Can CEO Pay Go?" *Business Week* (April 22, 1996): 100–106; J. A. Byrne, "Gross Compensation?" *Business Week* (March 18, 1996): 32–34; Hardy, "America's Highest-Paid Bosses"; R. J. Dowling, "Downsizing America's Expectations," Review of R. J. Samuelson, *The Good Life and Its Discontents* (New York: Time Books, 1996), *Business Week* (February 5, 1996): 18; A. Bernstein, "Is America Becoming More of a Class Society?" *Business Week* (February 26, 1996): 86–91; R. Norton, "Making Sense of the Boss's Pay," *Fortune* (October 3, 1994): 89.

28. "Abroad, It's Another World," *Fortune,* (June 6, 1988): 78.

29. P. H. Lewis, "Sears Moves to Shed Stake in Prodigy: The On-Line Business is Taking a New Shape," *New York Times* (February 22, 1996): D1, 7; R. Moss Kanter, "The Attack on Pay," *Harvard Business Review* (March-April 1987): 60–67; A. E. Serwer, "Payday! Payday!" *Fortune* (June 14, 1993): 102–111; "Executive Pay Doesn't Add Up," *Business Week* (April 26, 1993): 122; J. Byrne, "That Eye-Popping Executive Pay," *Business Week* (April 25, 1994): 52–58.

30. M. J. Mandel, "Plumper Profits, Skimpier Paychecks," *Business Week* (January 30, 1995): 86–87; K. Bradsher, "Productivity Is All, But It Doesn't Pay Well," *New York Times* (June 25, 1995): E4; A. Bernstein, "The Wage Squeeze," *Business Week* (July 17, 1995): 54–61; C. Duff, "Wages, Benefits Continue Slow Growth," *The Wall Street Journal* (November 1, 1995): A2; J. Spiers, "Why the Income Gap Won't Go Away," *Fortune* (December 11, 1995): 65–70; G. Koretz, "Economic Trends: Was the Last Decade Really So Cruel? Yes," *Business Week* (January 17, 1994): 20; R. B. Reich, "On Jobs and Work: Robert Reich Replies," *Business Week* (November 21, 1994): 12; A. Bernstein, "Inequality: How the Gap Between Rich and Poor Hurts the Economy," *Business Week* (August 15, 1994): 78–83; P. Krugman, "Long-Term Riches, Short-Term Pain," *New York Times* (September 25, 1994): F9; R. B. Freeman, ed., *Working Under Different Rules* (New York: Russell Sage Foundation, 1995); G. S. Becker, "Maybe the Earnings Gap Isn't Such A Bad Thing," *Business Week* (February 6, 1995): 24; M. Mandel et al., "Workers Finally Get Theirs," *Business Week* (November 27, 1995): 36–37.

31. G. Koretz, "Economic Trends: America's Edge In Factory Pay," *Business Week* (November 20, 1995): 38.

32. A. Farnham, "The Trust Gap," *Fortune* (Dec. 4, 1989): 56–78; G. S. Crystal and F. T. Vincent, Jr., "Take the Mystery Out of CEO Pay," *Fortune* (April 24, 1989): 217–220; "Current Issues: A Survey," *HR Reporter* (July 1990); G. S. Crystal, "Executive Compensation: Challenges in the Year Ahead," *Personnel* (Jan. 1988): 33–36; A. R. Karr, "Labor Letter," *The Wall Street Journal* (July 17, 1990): A1.

33. Farnham, "The Trust Gap."

34. G. Flynn, "Overtime Compensation Isn't as Simple as It Seems," *Personnel Journal* (December 1995): 104–109; "Ask the Experts—Questions and-Answers on Classifying White Collar Employees as Exempt From Overtime Regulations," *Fair Employment Practices Guidelines* (April 10, 1994): 8; "Professional Employees: White-Collar Exemption Test," *Bulletin to Management* (February 13, 1992): 45; W. Ringle, "Why the IRS Eyes Executive Pay," *Nation's Business* (October 1995): 32–34; "Most Voluntary Work Must Be Paid," *Bulletin to Management* (September 21, 1995): 304; G. Ameci, "Overtime Pay: Avoiding FLSA Violations," *Personnel Administrator* (Feb. 1987): 117–118; H. Stout, "Propping Up Payments at the Bottom," *New York Times* (Jan. 24, 1988): 4.

35. Record Settlement Under Fair Labor Standards Act," *Bulletin to Management* (August 12, 1993): 249. Reprinted with permission by the Bureau of National Affairs, (Tel. 1-800-372-1033).

36. A. Q. Nomani and R. Sharpe, "Work Week: Women Beware," *The Wall Street Journal* (January 16, 1996): 1; "The Pay Gap Narrows, But," *Fortune* (September 19, 1994): 32.

37. T. Linesenmayer, "Comparable Worth Abroad: Mixed Evidence," *The Wall Street Journal* (May 27, 1986): 26.

38. "Pay Equity Makes Good Business Sense," *Fair Employment Practices* (Aug. 30, 1990): 103; A. Bernstein, "What's Dragging Productivity Down? Women's Low Wages," *Business Week* (Nov. 27, 1989): 171; "Comparable Worth Policies that Work: The Minnesota Case," *The Urban Institute/Policy and Research Report* (Summer 1990): 10–12; G. J. Meng, "All the Parts of Comparable Worth" *Personnel Journal* (Nov. 1990): 99–104.

39. See Lawler, *Pay and Organization Development.*

40. The following materials are adapted from P. Dowling and R. S. Schuler, *International Dimensions of Human Resource Management* (Boston, MA: PWS-Kent, 1990): 117–135. See also three excellent articles entitled, "Compensating Your Overseas Executives," Part 1 (May-June 1990); Part 2 (July-Aug. 1990); and Part 3 (Jan.-Feb. 1991), *Compensation Review.*

41. C. Reynolds, "High Motivation and Low Cost Through Innovative International Compensation," *Proceedings of ASPA's 40th National Conference* (Boston, MA, 1989).

42. C. Reynolds, *Compensation Basics for North American Expatriates* (Scottsdale, AZ: ACA, 1994). See B. W. Teague, "Compensating Key Personnel Overseas" (New York: The Conference Board, 1972), for a discussion of the concept of keeping the expatriate "whole."

43. This discussion of the "balance sheet" approach is based on C. Reynolds, "Compensation of Overseas Personnel," in *Handbook of Human Resources Administration,* 2nd ed., J. J. Famularo, ed. (New York: McGraw-Hill, 1986).

44. HR Reporter Update, 3, no. 2 (Feb. 1987): 2. Also see C. Reynolds, *Compensating Globally Mobile Employees: Approaches to Developing Expatriate Pay Strategies for the Evolving International Corporation* (Scottsdale, AZ: ACA, 1995).

45. V. Pucik, "Strategic HRM in Multinational Corporations," in *Strategic Management of Multinational Corporations,* H. V. Wortzel and L. H. Wortzel, eds. (New York: Wiley, 1985): 430.

46. *HR Reporter Update,* 3, no. 1 (Jan. 1987): 5. Updated in 1994 by 30% to reflect salary increases.

47. M. S. O'Connor, *Report on Japanese Employee Relation Practices and Their Relationship to Worker Productivity,* a report prepared for the study mission to Japan, November 8–23, 1980. Her permission to reproduce this material is appreciated. See also *Employment and Employment Policy* (Tokyo, Japan: Japan Institute of Labor, 1988).

48. P. Sparrow and J. M. Hiltrop, *European Human Resource Management in Transition* (London: Prentice-Hall, 1995).

15

CHAPTER

Performance-Based Pay

Learning Objectives

1. Describe the available merit pay and incentive plans that companies use to motivate employee performance.
2. Describe the incentive plans at Lincoln Electric.
3. Identify obstacles to effectively implementing performance-based pay.
4. Discuss the areas where compensation can be linked to an organization's strategy.

> *One of the issues with Lincoln Electric is how its pay plan can survive rapid growth and globalization.*
>
> *Edward E. Lawler, III*
> *Director, Center for Effective Organizations*
> *University of Southern California*[1]

Chapter Outline

MANAGING HUMAN RESOURCES

at Lincoln Electric

In 1987, when Donald Hastings became president of Lincoln Electric Co., he brought with him total quality management. His goal was to build quality into the process rather than test it at the end of the production line (primarily for electric motors and arc welders). Lincoln's efforts under Donald Hastings have paid off: 25 percent fewer inspectors are needed (the employees assume the responsibility for quality) and 50 percent fewer employee-caused errors show up during testing (testing was used until management was sure that the new efforts were working effectively).

Quality is such an important part of Lincoln's strategy that they include it in their famous incentive plan. It, however, is just one piece of the incentive plan. A closer look reveals a significant number of components, and it is within one of those components, the merit-rating system, that a worker's quality is specifically evaluated and compensated. Workers receive merit ratings or "report cards" twice a year, and these determine the amount of bonus they receive at year-end. The four criteria in the merit rating include: output, quality, dependability, and personal characteristics. Incentives that go hand in hand with this are a base wage, piecework pay, profit-sharing, job security, and an employee stock-ownership plan. Do these work?

As indicated in the feature in Chapter 7 on Lincoln Electric on job design, Lincoln's productivity level is two to three times that of comparable organizations. Average employee compensation is $55,000. Due to the incentive pay plan, production worker pay ranges from $32,000 to more than $100,000. In 1995, however, even these wages did not produce total happiness for all the workforce. The main reason is summed up by one Lincoln worker: "Overall, our wages have been going down for the past 15 years. We're working more hours, and probably getting less than we got 15 years ago, including the bonuses." Information provided by Lincoln support this claim in part. In 1981, the average bonus was $22,000 and in 1995 it was $21,168, despite the 40% profit increase from 1994 to 1995. The reduction in the average bonus, according to the company, is explained by the reality of costs due to plant expansion and an increase in the workforce. This has caused some dissatisfaction and comment by compensation experts like Edward Lawler. Donald Hastings, however, suggests that any discontent is due to the fact that workers have been working too much overtime the past few years. This has resulted from good business conditions and Lincoln's philosophy of employment security. Because it provides this security it must be careful not to hire too many workers. When business activity exceeds the number of workers, the incentive system encourages workers to work harder and longer. The question some ask is, "How long can this continue?"[2]

This feature complements the one in Chapter 7. Together they present a broad overview of this very successful firm. Certainly, the importance of performance-based pay in achieving worker productivity and company success becomes apparent on a perusal of various human resource practices at Lincoln Electric. An array of programs are involved: it is not just one performance-based pay plan that motivates employees, but several. And some analysts say that, without job security (a no-layoff policy was adopted in 1959), the entire incentive system would be far less effective. Thus it is important to keep in mind as you think about the uses of performance-based pay, that it takes several HR practices working together to achieve highly effective employee behavior.[3] And performance-based pay is a powerful cornerstone in all of this.

Did You KNOW?

The average Lincoln factory worker earns $16.54 an hour vs. the $14.25 average manufacturing wage in the Cleveland area.

Performance-Based Pay

Performance-based pay motivates employees through linking pay with performance.

In this chapter we discuss **performance-based pay,** the aspect of total compensation related to motivating employees through linking pay to performance.

Performance-based pay systems relate pay to performance in one of two ways. **Incentive pay plans** measure performance output of individuals, groups, or organizations directly. Incentive pay accounts for a large portion of the individual" total compensation. For example, salespersons may be assured a small base salary, but the majority of compensation is earned through commissions.[4] By contrast, **merit pay plans** generally rely on indirect measures of performance (ratings or rankings). Because the measure of performance is indirect, merit pay plans typically affect a small percentage of an individual's total compensation.

In general, incentive pay plans appear to have substantially more motivational value, but merit pay plans remain much more frequent because they tend to be easier to set up and administer. Whereas there is essentially one type of merit plan, a wide variety of incentive plans exists. An overview of both types is shown in Exhibit 15.1.

Did You KNOW?

Lincoln Electric has paid out more than $700 million in year-end profit-sharing bonuses to employees since it began its bonus program in 1934.

Why Is Performance-Based Pay Important?

Employee Performance and Organizational Competitiveness

Money can be an extremely powerful motivator of performance. Studies of performance-based pay systems have shown that individual incentive plans can improve performance on an average of almost 30 percent over non-performance-based pay systems. Team-based incentive plans can increase performance 15 to 20 percent.[5]

As the feature on Lincoln Electric at the beginning of the chapter illustrates, pay is also important in enhancing organizational quality and competitiveness.[6] This is true even in industries where performance-based pay has traditionally not been used such as healthcare.[7]

Benefits of performance-based pay are enhanced:

- **performance**
- **motivation**
- **quality**
- **competitiveness**

Although effective in positively influencing the bottom line, performance-based pay systems have some disadvantages. One is that they take time to administer. Others include the fact that employees have to work exceptionally hard to earn large incentive bonuses, and occasionally, conflicts arise from rewarding only certain behaviors:

EXHIBIT 15.1

Performance-Based Pay Systems

MERIT PAY PLANS	INCENTIVE PAY PLANS	
	INDIVIDUAL	GROUP/ ORGANIZATION
Typical merit	Piecework plan	Team-based incentive
Lump-sum bonus	Standard hour plan	Scanlon plan
	Measured day work	Rucker plan
	Sales incentive plan	Improshare
	Managerial incentive plan	Profit-sharing plans
	Suggestion systems	Games, awards
		Stock ownership
		Stock options

A costly example of an incentive plan gone awry was when Sears Auto Centers in California were nailed for making unnecessary repairs on customers' cars. The reward system in question based both pay and incentives on the number of parts service managers sold. The service managers allegedly pressured mechanics to install unneeded parts, and the company was charged with defrauding its customers by California investigators. Sears' final settlement reportedly was in the neighborhood of $15 million.[8]

Thus the advantages of performance-based pay apply only when the appropriate conditions exist for its implementation. When there are obstacles in the way of these conditions, the disadvantages far outweigh the advantages. The conditions and obstacles are critical in knowing when to use performance-based pay and are described later in this chapter under "Obstacles to Effectiveness."

Recognizing Employee Contributions

The difference in performance between a peak- and low-performing employee averages 3 to 1 and can be as much as 20 to 1.[9] Thus, another purpose of performance-based pay is to recognize and reinforce the differential contribution of high versus low performance. Good pay and larger increases retain employees, and good performers are the ones managers most want to keep. Additionally, it has been shown that an employee who is rewarded for good performance will be more likely to continue performing well than one who is not appropriately rewarded.[10]

Still, few employees—particularly middle managers—ever see performance really pay. While (most managers believe) the best way to allocate scarce payroll dollars is to provide significant rewards to their top performers, only one-third of employees believe their pay is related to their performance.[11] The problem is that many plans are ill-conceived. Bonuses are not large enough nor sufficiently linked to performance to be motivational.[12] Consequently, performance-based pay plans need to be carefully conceived, implemented systematically, and clearly communicated. As we discuss later in this chapter, several obstacles also have to be removed.[13]

Did You KNOW?

Lincoln has huge variations in worker pay, from $32,000 to more than $100,000.

Merit Pay Plans

LEARNING OBJECTIVE 1

Describe the available merit pay and incentive plans that companies use to motivate employee performance.

Although most managers would agree that the best ways to allocate scarce payroll dollars is to provide significant rewards to their top performers, most would reluctantly admit that they really do not end up paying their top performers much differently from the rest when using merit pay plans. Two principal reasons emerge:

- The typical pay system does not provide enough leeway to reward the really good performers without unfairly penalizing the satisfactory but unexceptional workers who also must be retained and kept motivated.
- Managers are not comfortable with basing large pay distinctions on the often-hazy performance information that they are able to develop.[14]

Merit plans are based on less direct performance measures than incentive plans.

Consequently, merit pay plans had been the plan of choice for rewarding employees at the end of each year's work.[15] Today they are still used in many companies, but less so than even five years ago. Two major reasons for this are: 1) companies need more performance from each employee and some incentive pay like that used at Lincoln Electric can get higher performance; and 2) companies want to control their costs more, therefore using an incentive pay system that does not increase the employee's base salary each year is preferred to a merit pay system that does this.

In merit pay plans, it is necessary to establish guidelines for determining the size of the raises, the timing of when they are given, and the relationship between the merit increments and their place in the salary range. Especially during times of high inflation rates, organizations have to address the general relationship between merit pay and cost-of-living adjustments.

Merit Pay Guidelines

Because most large private organizations have some type of merit plan, it is useful to examine a typical plan. As Exhibit 15.2 shows, pay increments depend not only on employee performance, but also on the employee's position in the salary range.[16] This position is determined by expressing the employee's current salary as a percentage of the midpoint of the salary range for that job. The lower the position in the range (the first quartile is the lowest), the larger the percentage of the merit raise.

Merit Versus Cost-of-Living Adjustments

COLAs became important during the inflationary 1970s and 1980s.

Many large organizations grant **cost-of-living adjustments (COLAs)** or general (non-performance-related) increases to their employees, especially where unions have written COLAs into their contracts. Neither COLAs nor general increases are based on performance, yet they can take the lion's share of money available for compensation increases. And where unionized workers have COLA guarantees, the pressures are great to provide the same benefits to non-union, often white-collar, employees.

Given the choice of merit pay or COLA, many organizations would prefer to eliminate their COLAs in favor of merit pay plans, primarily because COLAs have no relationship to performance yet can be expensive.[17] In addition to not relating performance to pay, COLAs often take salary control out of the hands of the organization and the compensation manager. Since most COLAs are tied to the Consumer Price Index (CPI), all the organization can do is watch salaries increase as the CPI goes up. This can leave so little for merit increases that they are ineffective. In times of high inflation, the issue may be whether to use the entire salary budget for COLAs or for merit increases rather than attempting to divide it up.

But even when the rate of inflation is low and merit raises are given, the incentive value of the raises tends to be modest. This is because of the relatively small amount that merit increases generally represent and the even smaller differences (in absolute dollars) between getting the top increase and an average one. Consequently, organizations are using a modified version of the traditional, yearly merit plan increase: the performance bonus.

Performance Bonuses Rather Than Merit Raises

With increased emphasis on cost-effective HR practices, firms are questioning the traditional practice of granting annual salary or merit increases.[18] Consider an employee who performs excellently one year and is given a 15 percent merit pay increase. The next year, for whatever reason, the employee may not perform as

EXHIBIT 15.2

Typical Merit Pay Guidelines

	INCREASES BY EMPLOYEE'S POSITION IN SALARY RANGE			
PERFORMANCE RATING	FIRST QUARTILE	SECOND QUARTILE	THIRD QUARTILE	FOURTH QUARTILE
Truly outstanding	8-10%	7-8%	5-6%	2-4%
Above average	8-10%	6-7%	4-5%	2% or less
Good	7-8%	5-6%	4% or less	delayed
Satisfactory	2-4%	2% or less	delayed	none
Unsatisfactory	none	none	none	none

well or even adequately. While subsequent performance may decrease, the cost of the original salary increase is a permanent cost for the organization. Merit increases administered in this way may also demotivate other employees because the employee who performed well previously may have a higher base pay than an employee who is currently performing well. As a result, the low performer may receive a larger increase than the better performing employee whose pay is lower.

To rectify this situation, firms such as Whirlpool and Westinghouse replaced merit increases with one-time, semiannual, or quarterly **performance bonuses**. These bonuses may be distributed in one lump sum or in the traditional way (divided up into parts for each check). Bonuses are also popular in competitive high-technology firms. A recent survey showed that 7 percent of managerial, professional, and technical employees were eligible for bonuses in large high-tech firms. In smaller high-tech firms with sales less than $1 billion, almost half of all technical employees receive bonuses. These may be tied to meeting product development deadlines or to the profitability of product lines.[19]

Performance bonuses or lump-sum bonuses are one-time rewards of money tied to performance.

Lump-sum bonuses, as they are also called, are also in union contracts. Common forms of bonuses in union contracts include flat amounts, a percentage of the preceding year's pay or a specified dollar amount multiplied by the number of hours worked.

There are several advantages to bonuses instead of salary increases. First, the bonuses increase the meaning of pay. The lump-sum payment of $5,000 is more striking than a before-tax increase of $100 a week. A wise employee can leverage the value of the bonus further by investing it carefully. This is not possible when increases are spread throughout the year. Second, bonuses maximize the relationship between pay and performance. Unlike permanent salary increases, an employee must perform above average year in and year out to continue receiving bonuses.

A current trend is the use of these bonuses combined with a lower base salary. At Whirlpool Corporation in Benton Harbor, Michigan, workers who had been making $60,000 yearly in base pay were reduced to $54,000. The incentive for the employees to work hard was the opportunity to make a bonus of $12,000 for a total year's pay of $66,000. The size of bonuses can vary and is based upon the employee's success in meeting performance goals that are closely tied to strategy and competitiveness of the company.[20] Nucor Corporation, the highly efficient mini-mill steel maker based in Charlotte, North Carolina does something very similar according to James M. Coblin, Manager of Personnel Services:

> *At Nucor, everything takes a back seat to production, says Coblin. Other than "making a 25 percent return" on operating costs, plant managers have very few requirements. In general, he says, managers are expected to lead by getting out of workers' way.*
>
> *To ensure high production rates, Nucor offers both managers and workers substantial bonuses based on their production. Hourly employees that produce steel bars, for example, receive a 5 percent bonus for every ton of straightened steel they can turn out in an hour over eight tons an hour. The production baseline is slightly below the industry average of 10 tons per hour, but it enables workers to "experience some success right away," notes Coblin. The bonuses have motivated some work groups to turn out between 35 and 42 tons of straightened steel per hour.*[21]

When applied to managerial employees, these bonus plans are referred to as **variable-pay plans**. The feature, "Managing Human Resources at Taco Bell" illustrates this type of pay plan.

Performance-bonus plans for managerial employees are called variable-pay plans.

Occasionally, traditional merit pay and performance-bonus plans are combined. For example, reasoning that excellence is the standard, not the exception,

MANAGING HUMAN RESOURCES

at Taco Bell

Taco Bell Corporation's upbeat advertisements have been so successful that the Irvine, California-based company has opened more than 500 new restaurants in the last five years. Although this is great news for hungry consumers, it was a challenge for the company's HR department to find managers for these restaurants.

"We didn't think we could find all the talent we needed to run those stores," explains Michael J. Rowe, Taco Bell's director of compensation and benefits. "So we decided to ask existing restaurant managers to start supervising two units instead of one."

Instead of increasing the managers' salaries to correlate to their added responsibilities, Taco Bell did something very interesting. The company kept the managers' base salaries the same but allowed them to earn twice as much in bonus pay through a variable-pay program.

"To continue to make a profit, we can't have pay programs that are inefficient," Rowe explains. "We can't afford to give $50,000 in base pay with no performance guarantees. We can, however, afford to pay $30,000 and give managers a $20,000 bonus if they drive profits to the bottom line. The way we do this is through a variable-pay program that funds incremental pay out of incremental profits."

Today the restaurant managers are evaluated and given bonuses based on three objectives:

1. Targeted profit, which relates to bottom-line results
2. Customer service, which is evaluated by an independent marketing-research firm
3. Actual store sales

On average, managers receive a bonus worth about 30 percent of their base pay. But payments that double the base amount aren't uncommon. However, Rowe is quick to emphasize that not all managers earn a bonus all the time. "It isn't an entitlement," he says. "Between 60 percent and 70 percent of managers earn a bonus that's paid every six months. But that means 30 percent of managers don't get anything in their variable pay for six month's work. Believe me, a person who misses a $5,000 bonus payment twice a year will pay attention to the things that drive profitability: sales and customer service."

Although Taco Bell's program isn't punitive in nature, it is high risk. Under the company's previous merit pay system, about 85 percent of restaurant managers received $1,000 bonuses four times each year. "They really had to be bad not to get that money," Rowe explains, "whereas under this system, they really have to be good."

When asked how the variable-pay program fits into Taco Bell's overall strategy, Rowe says that the relationship between both may be irrelevant. "A bonus program at that level should be reflective of what you want to get out of people in that job," he says. "I think it's a mistake for every bonus program in the company to have the same objectives. You have to ask yourself what kind of results you're attempting to obtain from restaurant managers. Hopefully, the answer isn't too different from what you want to get out of your president, but clearly I'm not going to expect my president to do customer service at the unit level."

Taco Bell's program seems to be working. Food costs as a percentage of sales continue to decrease, customer service scores and profit records continue to be broken.[22]

a broadcast firm set its pay policy line at 105 percent of the external market. Pay grade minimums were also established so entry-level trainees with no experience could be paid less. Merit increases were awarded until the employee's base salary reached the pay grade midpoint. Then, annual salary increases were replaced with an annual performance bonus for all excellent or above average employees. Depending on the employee's base salary, these bonuses ranged from $1,000 to $5,000.

Whether combined or used singly, however, some organizations such as Taco Bell and Lincoln Electric think they get more out of their compensation dollars using incentive pay plans.

Did You KNOW?

Variable-pay plans reduce a company's total fixed costs.

Incentive Pay Plans

While individual incentive programs are the tried-and-true form of this pay system, group incentive plans such as Improshare are making waves as the newest form of performance-based pay. Incentive plans can best be classified according to the level at which they are applied: individual or group.

Individual Incentive Plans

LEARNING OBJECTIVE 2

Describe the incentive plans at Lincoln Electric.

Individual incentives remain the most popular form of incentive plan: each person's output is measured, and subsequent rewards are based on the output. The utilization of these plans varies with the type of job. Very few office workers work under these plans, but textile, clothing, cigar, and steel industries rely extensively on them.

While a variety of individual incentive plans exist, they differ in terms of the method of rate determination. When the work cycle is short, units of production generally serve as the method of rate determination. For longer-cycle jobs, the standard is typically based on the time required to complete a unit. Individual incentive systems also vary in regards to the constancy with which pay is a function of production level. One option is to pay a consistent amount at all production levels (for example, 25 cents per carton). Alternatively, pay may vary as a function of production level. For example, employees may be paid 25 cents a carton up to 1,000 units a day. When this threshold is passed, the incentive rises to 27 cents a carton.

Individual incentive plans also share a common job analysis foundation. As discussed in Chapter 8, time and motion studies are often employed to determine how wages are tied to output. The challenge is to identify a "normal" rate of production.[23]

Piecework Plan. Piecework such as Lincoln Electric uses is the most common type of incentive pay plan. Under the **straight piecework plan,** employees are guaranteed a standard rate for each unit of production. For example, if the base pay of a job is $40 per day and the employee can produce 20 units a day at a normal rate, the piece rate may be established at $2 per unit. The incentive pay rate is based on the standard output and the base wage rate. The "normal" rate is more than what the time and motion studies indicate but is supposed to represent 100 percent efficiency. The final rate also reflects the bargaining power of the employees, economic conditions of the organization and industry, and what the competition is paying (See Exhibit 15.3 to see how Lincoln calculates the piecework).

Incentive plans can be based on productivity standards and direct indexes such as straight piecework plans or differential piece rate plans.

In a **differential piece rate plan**, there is more than one rate of pay for the same job. This plan can be operationalized in different ways. Named for its developer, the Taylor Differential plan consists of a higher rate of pay for work completed in a set period. For production per unit that takes longer than the established time to complete the job, the rate of pay is lower. Merrill Lynch, one of the largest stock brokerage firms in the world, instituted a commission plan similar to Taylor's plan, but this, as applied to brokerage firms, has some potentially bad side effects, which we will discuss in the section on straight commission. Sales personnel having higher sales volumes receive higher rates of commission than sales personnel with lower volumes.

Also named for its developer, the Merrick's Multiple-Wage plan operates in the same way except three piece rates are established. Workers receive a 10 percent bonus when they reach 83 percent of standard and an additional 10 percent when they achieve the standard.

The success of any piece rate system depends on more than merely paying individuals for more work. Its success is dependent on how employees are treated

EXHIBIT 15.3

Components of Lincoln Electric's Incentive Plan

Lincoln's incentive plan combines job security with a lucrative compensation program. Below is a summary of the plan's elements.

FEATURES	DESCRIPTION	CRITERIA
Job Security	Guaranteed 30-hour workweek.	Employees are eligible after three years of service and • Pay rates aren't guaranteed. • Job transfers may be necessary. • Overtime is required during peak demand. • Guaranteed hours may be terminated by the company with a six-month notice.
Base Wage	Standard job evaluation procedures are used to set the base wage. However, job evaluation and market requirements determine the actual dollar value of jobs.	Job evaluation compensable factors include skill, responsibility, mental aptitude, physical application, and working conditions.
Piecework	For every job that can be standardized, normal time-study procedures are employed to establish piece rates.	Piece rates are based on the following calculation for consistency and to eliminate constant revisions: 1934 wage rates times cost of living, which fluctuates with the index (Bureau of Labor Statistics). This product is then compared with the area average skilled hourly rate to determine the adjustments to the piece rate.
Advisory Board	Employees elect representatives to an Advisory Board. All employees, except department heads and members of the engineering and time-study departments, are eligible.	The Advisory Board analyzes suggestions that lead to organizational progress. Implemented suggestions have ranged from a savings of $2,400 to over $200,000.
Merit Ratings	Twice a year, managers appraise employee performance through a merit-rating program.	This program uses four report cards. Each card rates work performance on one of the following: output, quality, dependability, and personal characteristics, such as the ability to come up with ideas, and cooperation.
Profit Sharing	All business profits are split three ways: among the company, the shareholders, and the employees as a year-end bonus.	The company receives seed money; the shareholders receive a dividend; and the employees receive a year-end, profit-sharing bonus.
Year-End Profit-Sharing Bonus	The year-end bonus closely approximates the employee's annual earnings.	An employee's bonus is a function of his total annual earnings, biannual merit ratings, and company profits.
Employee Stock-Ownership Plan	Each employee has the opportunity to purchase a limited number of shares of company stock per year.	Employees are eligible after one year of service. On retirement or termination of employment, the company has the option to repurchase the stock.

and the level of employment security provided. These two items have high priority at Lincoln Electric. But to be fair, even at Lincoln Electric there is more to their incentive system than piecework, employee treatment, and security. As shown in Exhibit 15.3, many financial incentives are offered to employees, but it is the final profit-sharing bonus figure that makes the news and makes employees wealthy. To see how this bonus is calculated, see the feature, "Managing Human Resources at Lincoln Electric."

The company is by no means ready to ditch the incentive plan, which once paid employees up to 100% of their wages in annual performance-linked bonuses. But executives are now considering ways to move toward a more traditional pay scheme and away from the flat percentage-bonus formula. "The bonus is a good program, and it has worked well, but it's got to be modified some."

Director David C. Lincoln, whose father John C. Lincoln founded the company in 1895.

Standard Hour Plan. The standard hour plan is the second most common incentive plan. The **standard hour plan** is a piecework plan, except that standards are denominated in time per unit of output rather than money per unit of output. Tasks are broken down by the amount of time it takes to complete them. This can be determined by historical records, time and motion studies, or a combination of both. The time to perform each task then becomes a "standard."

Consider a standard time of two hours and a rate of pay of $12 an hour. If a worker completes six units in an eight-hour day, the worker would receive 6 × $24, or $144. This is substantially more than the standard rate of pay for eight hours of $96.

Rewarding Indirect Labor. While individual piece rate systems work well for the direct laborers, it is more difficult to reward personnel who support and make possible the productivity improvements of the direct laborers. The problem is that these workers often assist a number of direct laborers. They may sort, feed, and prepare raw materials or remove and inspect finished materials. One approach is to provide the same percent increase above normal as is earned by the average direct laborer.

Suggestion Systems. **Suggestion systems** reward employees for money-saving or money-producing ideas and are used extensively. They are perhaps unique in that they attempt to increase the number of good ideas rather than output directly. Yet they are similar to other plans in that the rewards are monetary. Approximately 80 percent of the nation's 500 largest corporations have suggestion systems.[24]

Suggestion systems are activities that are used to gather the ideas for improvements from employees.

Suggestion systems are also important because they can bestow substantial sums of money. Some organizations allow employees as much as 30 percent of the first year's savings.

Suggestion systems, however, generally do not have a favorable reputation because individual awards are too small. Also, employees sometimes never learn the results of their ideas, and companies often save more than the individual receives.

Team-Based Incentives

Team incentives fall somewhere between individual-incentive and whole-organizational plans such as gain sharing and profit sharing (to be discussed next). The goals are tailored specifically to what the team needs to accomplish. Strategically, the goals of individuals are linked to those of the work group (typically ten people or fewer) to achieve financial goals.[26] According to Judy Huret, at the consulting firm of Towers Perrin in San Francisco, team incentives improve employees' "line of sight" regarding what they need to do as a group to enhance profits. For example:

> *An insurance company was encountering friction between two different departments—data processing and claims. The claims people said the data processing staff never met its deadlines. The data processing people said the claims people kept changing their minds and made unreasonable demands. When the company instituted a team incentive plan, senior management facilitated a discussion between the two departments and informed them that their incentive award would be linked to how well they worked together to meet customer needs.*

MANAGING HUMAN RESOURCES

at Lincoln Electric

Under the Lincoln Electric Incentive Plan, employees at Cleveland-based Lincoln Electric Co. receive bonuses based on their productivity. The bonus is determined by a simple bonus-factor formula.

First, the board of directors sets the amount of the year's bonus pool, based on a recommendation by the chairman. The chairman looks at such factors as how much money the company has made, how much seed money is needed, and how much money is needed for taxes and dividends. The average bonus pool during a recent ten-year period was 10.6 percent of sales revenue.

The company then divides this bonus pool amount by the total wages paid. This quotient is the bonus factor. A bonus factor of 1.00 means that the bonus pool is the same as the total companywide wages. Typically, the bonus pool is approximately 75 percent of wages paid.

Once the bonus factor has been determined, the company calculates bonuses by multiplying the bonus factor by individual earnings and merit ratings. Here's an example. A production worker earned \$35,000. His merit rating was 100 percent, or 1.00. The bonus factor is 0.75. The formula for determining his bonus would be as follows:

\$35,000	(earnings)
× 1.00	(merit rating)
\$35,000	
× .75	(bonus factor)
\$26,250	(bonus)

This employee's full bonus would be \$26,250. However, according to Paul Beddia, vice president of human resources at Lincoln, employees must pay for their own hospitalization insurance, which costs approximately \$3,000. The company deducts this money from employees' year-end bonuses. Thus, this production worker would receive a bonus of \$23,250 (before taxes), bringing his annual salary to \$58,250.[25]

The claims group then clearly outlined the specifications and timetable necessary to meet customer service needs and discussed them with data processing. Data processing developed a detailed project plan and shared it with claims. Now that both groups understand the ultimate objective, they can work together to achieve a common goal. The amount of their incentive award will depend on how quickly and how well the team goal is met.[27]

Individuals don't accomplish anything, teams do.

W. Edwards Deming

Given that the prerequisites listed in Exhibit 15.4 are met, team-based incentives offer five major advantages compared with individual incentive systems. First, the mere presence of team members who have some control over rewards evokes more vigorous and persistent behavior than when individuals work alone. Second, the likelihood that conflicting contingencies (peer pressure) will evoke counterproductive control over behavior is reduced. Third, the strength of the rewards is increased since they are now paired with group-administered rewards (praise, camaraderie). Research also suggests that the performance of a group is higher than that attained by individual group members (although not as high as the best person in the group). Fourth, the performance of one group member (usually the high performer) can serve as a model, encouraging other members to imitate successful behavior. Finally, team-based compensation reinforces a corporate culture that emphasizes the importance of teamwork.[28]

But just as Lincoln Electric's success is a sum of more than its piecework plan, meeting performance or productivity goals usually takes more than a team-based incentive plan. For example, in the case of the Aid Association to Lutherans (the

EXHIBIT 15.4

Prerequisites for the Effective Administration of Team Incentives

1. Everyone who's on the team, including indirect laborers and support staff members, is eligible.
2. Team-performance is measurable.
3. Performance standards are communicated to team members in advance of the performance period.
4. The incentive system is easy to understand.
5. Team members receive regular feedback on their progress towards performance targets. "War rooms," including graphs, charts, and statistical analyses, provide ongoing useful feedback.
6. Team members must believe they can affect performance outcomes.
7. Corporate culture must be congruent with team problem solving and participation.

AAL case in Chapter 7), a team-based incentive plan is used along with an individual incentive program, market survey data, and a skill-based pay plan. This is described in the feature, "Managing Human Resources at AAL".

While **team-based incentives** are promising, administrative responsibilities are as great as those associated with individual incentive plans. Job analysis is still necessary to identify how to structure the teams and to ensure that workloads are equivalent between teams. There may also be unintended side effects, including competition between groups, that may or may not complement goal attainment. A second concern is **social loafing**, where group performance declines because team members (consciously or subconsciously) lower their inputs, believing that others in the group will pick up the slack.[29] This is less likely to happen, however, in cases where there is broad-based employee participation and involvement such as in the Scanlon plan.

Did You KNOW?

AAL gets hundreds of requests from other companies to visit their office at Appleton, Wisconsin, and learn how they do it.

Social loafing is where a member of the team fails to pull his own weight.

Cost Reduction Plans

While a variety of cost reduction programs exists, the Scanlon plan developed in the late 1930s is among the oldest. It relies on a ratio between labor costs and sales value of production as the measure for judging business performance. A newer approach, which focuses on an engineering-based productivity measurement, is called **Improshare** (IMproved PROductivity through SHARing).

Scanlon and Rucker Plans. These two plans—Scanlon and Rucker—were developed in the Depression Era. Both focus on cost savings relative to historical standards. The Scanlon and Rucker Plans are built around the following four principles:

- A management philosophy emphasizing employee participation
- A formula to share the benefits of productivity-generated savings among employee and employer
- Employee committees to evaluate ideas
- A formal system for gathering and implementing employee suggestions on ways to increase productivity or reduce costs

The Scanlon and Rucker plans stress sharing and participation in company operations and profitability.

Even though the Scanlon and Rucker plans share a common philosophy, they differ in one important aspect: the Scanlon plan focuses only on labor cost savings.

MANAGING HUMAN RESOURCES

at AAL

Aid Association for Lutherans (AAL), a fraternal-benefits society, leaves nothing to chance when it comes to compensating members of its insurance-service teams. The company, which is based in Appleton, Wisconsin, has devised a four-legged compensation stool, which allows the company to:

- Recognize individual achievements
- Reward team productivity
- Compensate employees for the acquisition of new skills
- Remain competitive with its salary structure

AAL has 15 service teams, organized geographically, that perform all services necessary for the company's insurance products. For example, a team, comprising 25 employees, can underwrite a policy, pay a claim, change beneficiaries, and modify coverage levels. Furthermore, team members can provide these services for any product, be it life insurance, health, or disability insurance.

Before developing the team structure in 1987, the company organized these services functionally, according to the type of product. Service requests traveled from unit to unit, increasing the amount of time needed to service a customer, and boosting the chance for errors.

"By moving to teams, we were challenging employees to see the whole job, rather than just the piece they performed individually," explains Jerry Laubenstein, vice president of insurance services. "But we also wanted them to learn additional jobs that could help the team as a whole, and we wanted the team to find ways to boost its overall performance."

To promote all of these changes, AAL revamped its compensation structure completely to include four main elements.

1. *A skill-based pay program.* The company has implemented a skill-based pay system that compensates individuals for each additional skill they acquire in an effort to help the team. As one of the first organizations to implement skill-based pay for white-collar workers, AAL developed a dictionary that describes all the services performed by team members and lists their associated dollar value. Employees are paid a base wage for the primary service they perform, and they can receive incremental pay increases for each service added to their repertoire of skills.

2. *A team-incentive program.* AAL has implemented a team incentive program through which the entire team is awarded an annual bonus based on three factors:

   - Productivity
   - Customer satisfaction
   - Quality of work

   This team incentive can be worth as much as 10 percent of an employee's annual compensation.

3. *The use of market data.* The company now relies heavily on market data to ensure that employees are paid competitive wages.

4. *An individual incentive program.* AAL has added an incentive component that recognizes outstanding achievements by individual employees. This lump-sum incentive is paid once a year only to those employees who are already paid at market value. This incentive is worth as much as 6 percent of an individual's compensation.

AAL's compensation structure didn't change all at once, Laubenstein says, and there were several problems along the way. "We went to teams in 1987 and didn't put any incentives in place until 1989. Then we moved entirely to team incentives, where we didn't recognize individuals at all. This caused a lot of problems with employees who were used to being recognized individually. In 1991, we modified the program to recognize both individual and team achievements. In 1993 it was modified again."

Is the program working? "We're on a journey, and we haven't reached the destination yet," Laubenstein cautions. "But in the five years that we've been in teams, we've increased our productivity by 40 percent. Surveys reveal that more than 90 percent of our customers are satisfied with the level of service they're receiving. I'd say things are coming along well."[32]

Suppose that the historical costs of labor for your firm are $1 million a year. If actual labor costs are less than anticipated costs ($800,000), a portion ($50,000) of the money saved is placed in a set-aside in case labor costs soar in subsequent quarters. The remaining savings ($150,000) are split among the company and the employees. In contrast, the Rucker plan ties incentives to a wide variety of savings. A ratio is calculated that expresses the value of production required for each dollar of total wages.

Both plans are appropriate in small, mature firms employing fewer than five hundred workers. Since standards are based on past performance, simple and accurate measures of performance are needed. Because of the heavy involvement of all employees, the culture must be open, trusting, and participative.[31]

Improshare. Developed in the mid-1970s by Mitchell Fein, Improshare uses easy-to-obtain past production records to establish base performance standards. Any savings arising from production of agreed-upon output in fewer than expected hours are shared by the firm and the employees. As a percentage of pay, Scanlon plans average 5 percent payouts, whereas Improshare plans provide 10 percent.

Improshare rewards employees for the savings that accrue from reaching performance targets.

Three controls in the Improshare plan permit changes in the measurement standards. The maximum employee gainshare is 30 percent of base wages. Gains above this amount are "banked" and added to the next payout below 30 percent. If production continues to be high, management can buy back the gain over 160 percent. Consider an employee who earns $10 an hour and worked 2,500 hours. If the gain for the year rests at 180 percent, employees receive 50 percent of the difference between 160 percent and 180 percent or $2,500 [20% (buyback) × 50% (division) × $10 (hourly rate) x 2,500 (hours worked) = $2,500.] The base for future calculations would be increased by 1.8/1.6 = 1.125.

Did You KNOW?

Thanks to gain sharing, operators of Chick-Fil-A fast-food chicken outlets made more than $100,000 a year.

Productivity Improvement Plans

In comparison to the Scanlon plan and Improshare, that share cost savings with employees, productivity improvement plans reward employees based upon gains in productivity levels. That is why they are often referred to as **gainsharing plans.**[32]

Gainsharing plans reward employees for gains based on productivity improvement.

Gainsharing payouts are based largely on production levels that are adjusted upward as productivity improves.[33] Basing monetary rewards upon improvements in productivity reflects the goals of many companies to do more with less. It also reflects a reality that productivity is something over which the employees have control, just as they do in cost savings plans. Nevertheless, productivity gains do not always result in increased profits for the company. Consequently, some companies prefer to use plans to share profits as opposed to plans to reward productivity improvements.[34]

Profit-Sharing Plans

Introduced first in the Gallatin glassworks factory in New Geneva, Pennsylvania, in 1794, approximately 430,000 **profit-sharing plans** now exist in American businesses. As defined by the Council of Profit Sharing, these plans include any procedure under which an employer pays or makes available to regular employees, special current or deferred sums based on the profits of the business in addition to their regular pay.

Profit-sharing plans enable employees to share in the profits.

Did You KNOW?

Levi Strauss will pay its workforce a bonus of $750 million if it has a cumulative cash flow of $7.6 billion between 1996 and 2001. This is roughly equal to the 1996 salaries of all employees.

Profit-sharing plans fall into one of three categories. *Current distribution plans* provide for a percentage of profits to be distributed quarterly or annually to employees. *Deferred plans* are the fastest growing type of plan due to tax advantages. Earnings are placed in an escrow fund for distribution upon retirement, termination, death, or disability. About 20 percent of firms with profit-sharing programs have *combined plans* in which a portion of profits is currently distributed to employees with the remaining amount set aside in a designated account.

Like cost reduction plans, profit-sharing plans are designed to pay out incentives when the organization is most able to afford them. They differ in that employee involvement is not an important component of the plan. The motivational potential of deferred plans is also questionable since employees are unlikely to see the relationship between their performance and profitability of the firm.[35] Examples such as Lincoln Electric, Wal-Mart, Nucor Steel, and Hallmark, however, suggest that profit sharing can be very motivational, especially when it is accompanied by employee participation and feelings of involvement.[36]

> *"Profit sharing is an important reward for the associates who have made Wal-Mart successful," said David Poneman, a retail analyst with Sanford C. Bernstein & Co. in New York.*[37]

Did You KNOW?

The top 5% of all households own 77% of the stock. The bottom 80% own about 2%.

Stock Ownership Plans

While cost-sharing, productivity-improvement, and profit-sharing plans all help direct the attention of workers to success at the department or company level, they do not reflect what the investment firms on Wall Street think about the value of the company. Stock ownership plans, however, do exactly this. By awarding employees with stock or options to buy stock, the employees focus their attention on the stock price of the firm.

The deal is good for Philip Morris. Employees' base pay won't rise. Nor will benefits, such as pension and life insurance, which are tied to annual wages and total 29% of pay. And current stockholders' shares won't be diluted, since workers probably will get less than 500,000 shares out of 850 million outstanding.

Stock for Pay. Workers can get stock in many ways. At Philip Morris Company, an agreement between the company and International Association of Machinists representing the workers gives them stock in lieu of pay hikes during the next two years. The novel trade-off is part of a larger trend by companies to tie pay to company performance. And while it leaves Philip Morris workers less certain about how much they'll make, union leaders plan to pursue the concept at other companies.

> *"It's a gamble, but it's one we're willing to take," says Steven Spain, the chief negotiator for the International Association of Machinists (IAM).*[38]

Employees at United Airlines went even further than those at Philip Morris, by taking stock in exchange for wage concessions and work rule changes. In the process of taking 55 percent of ownership in United Airlines for these concessions, United Airlines became the largest employee-owned company in the U.S.[39]

Employee stock ownership plans (ESOPs) grant shares of stock to employees as a means of long-term savings and retirement.

Stocks for Savings. Rather than using stock as a form of immediate pay, some companies enable employees to accumulate the stock of the company toward longer term savings and retirement. This can be done through special stock ownership plans set up by the company. These plans, referred to as **employee stock ownership plans (ESOPs)**, grant shares of the company stock to employees (described further in Chapter 16). Some companies believe that stock ownership plans are effective for all workers because they increase the employee's identification with and commitment to the company:

> *A stock ownership plan for employees for the United Parcel Service (UPS) is being expanded beyond the ranks of management to include all full-time workers. The change comes at a time when UPS is trying to increase employee awareness and responsibility related to customer service.*

According to UPS Chairman and CEO Kent C. Nelson, now is an appropriate time to give non-management employees the opportunity to have a personal stake in the company's performance as well. "Today, more than ever, we are calling on our people at all levels to take direct responsibility for the customer's satisfaction," Nelson says. "We are creating an environment of continuous improvement at UPS. To achieve this, all of our people must be totally focused and totally committed," he asserts.

With the company's marketplace changing rapidly and customer expectations increasing, everyone at UPS has to be ready to accept a heightened role in the business, according to Nelson. The hourly workers at UPS have shown that they are ready to help transform the company by identifying and implementing innovative solutions to customer needs, he contends, and the offer of stock ownership shows that the company recognizes their contributions and wants them to share in the results of their efforts.[40]

Did You KNOW?

There are about 10,000 ESOPs in the U.S. that cover about 10% of the workforce.

Each year, 15 percent of UPS's pretax profit is used to buy company stock that is distributed to entry-level supervisors on up. "We have 25,000 owner-managers who have virtually every cent they own invested in stock of this company."

Companies can also provide employees with stock purchase arrangements. Through these arrangements, employees may purchase company shares at a discount to the market price. If used as a 401(k) retirement plan (described in Chapter 16), the company may even share the cost of these purchases with the employees.

Stock Options. Rather than provide employees with the stock directly, companies may choose to set up **stock option** plans for workers. PepsiCo, with its 450,000 employees in 166 countries, gives stock options instead of providing an ESOP. PepsiCo believes that their stock option plan is more consistent with its performance-oriented culture than is an ESOP.

A stock option is an opportunity for an employee to buy the company's stock at a later date but at a price established when the option is granted.

Here's how the plan works. The company grants stock options each July to all full-time employees. The amount each person receives is based on 10% of his or her total compensation the prior year. The stocks are 20% exercisable each year, meaning that workers are fully vested after 5 years. They have 10 years to exercise their options.

That can mean a sizeable nest egg for a long-term employee. Assuming a constant annual salary of $30,000 during a 30-year period and a starting price of $30 a share, the gains would be $205,000. If a 6% salary growth is assumed, the value after 30 years would be $357,000.

Says a PepsiCo corporate representative: "People make a real difference at PepsiCo in the creation of shareholder value. Our corporate success is tied very closely to individual achievement, and this program provides a strong incentive for every employee to act like an entrepreneur."[41]

Did You KNOW?

PepsiCo's stock option plan can make its employees wealthy by retirement if the stock does well.

Recently, the two thousand pilots at Southwest Airlines agreed to receive stock options on almost 1.5 shares of stock for no wage increases in the first five years of their ten year contract with the company.[42]

Microsoft Corporation is famous for its stock option plan. While stock option plans are typical in entrepreneurial firms. They have not made so many millionaires as they have at Microsoft:

...[A]s the rule of thumb, Microsoft employees with more than six years' seniority have a shot of becoming independently wealthy. A typical salaried

employee's option grant of 1,500 shares in 1982, plus regular additions, compounded and untouched, is worth over $5 million pretax today.[43]

If there are so many employees in the company who have become millionaires because of the stock option, they why don't they just quit? Obviously, these Microsoft millionaires do not view their jobs only in terms of their paycheck. Mike Maples, of Microsoft's office of the president, calls these people his "volunteers." Says Maples:

"We're able to keep them because their jobs are meaningful, not because they need more money. That really makes you think about how we manage here."[44]

Did You KNOW?

IBAX found the Best Demonstrated Practices Award very motivational for teams.

Games and Awards

As competition increases, companies are turning to novel ways to motivate employees. Domino's Pizza spends a million dollars holding its "Distribution Olympics." Top employees from across the country are identified, flown to the national headquarters, and paid to spend three days playing job-related games. Winners of the games garner substantial cash prizes. According to a Domino's spokesperson, the games encourage employees to hone their job skills and produce a better product. They also enhance Domino's fundamental belief that the contribution of every employee matters.[45]

Beyond the formal monetary reward system, IBAX implemented an awards program that was based on both individual and team performance. For example, one award, the Best Demonstrated Practices Awards, recognized work teams that showed substantial creativity or significant performance improvements.

Other companies are using on-the-job lotteries as a way to spark high productivity. Employees with performance above a specified threshold participate in the lottery. Even bigger than games and awards for motivating employees are apartments and cars. However, smaller gifts such as a class ring can also be motivating. This and other forms of nonfinancial recognition are described in the feature "Managing Human Resources at Appleton Papers".

Compensation for Special Groups

The performance-based systems described so far share an important characteristic: they are usually applied to employees who are covered under the *Fair Labor Standards Act (FLSA).* There are other groups, however, for which there are special compensation concerns. This section will discuss the special compensation concerns of sales personnel, executives, and international employees.

Sales Personnel

Because a large part of a salesperson's job is unsupervised, performance-based compensation programs are useful in directing sales activities. Still, only 20 percent of all sales personnel are paid by straight incentives. More than half of all sales plans use a combination of salary and individual or group incentives.[46]

Straight Salary. Approximately 30 percent of all sales personnel are paid a straight salary. The latter is appropriate when the major function of the sales person is providing customer service or "prospecting new accounts under low success conditions." Straight salary plans are also appropriate in jobs demanding high technical expertise but little ability to close sales. Consider the job of a product engineer for a software publishing house. Duties of this job might include developing and executing sales and product training programs, participating in trade shows, promoting new products, and meeting with distributors to encourage pushing product lines. In such jobs, a high salary to attract technically competent individuals is more critical than incentives to close the sale.

MANAGING HUMAN RESOURCES

at Appleton Papers

The quality-improvement process at Appleton Papers in West Carrollton, Ohio, began in 1988. Three years into the process, the effort had created no discernible improvements in customer satisfaction, morale, safety records, or profitability.

"Quality had become more of a program than a process," explains Wayne Reveal, the organization's manager of organizational services. Why? "Because there was an obvious lack of recognition of employee behavior."

Among other things, Reveal says, quality is an attempt to create or change *behavior* sets, yet Appleton workers who performed good work went unrecognized, and employees who performed poorly escaped disciplinary action.

In an attempt to reshape and reinforce its quality effort, Appleton implemented a comprehensive worker-recognition process in 1991. Today, each line manager receives a recognition budget from which he or she can buy gifts to reward employees for good behaviors.

The company's basic rule is that recognition gifts must be personal in nature and something that the employees wouldn't buy for themselves. The organization encourages managers to use the gifts as surprise rewards for good work, as well as incentives for special achievement.

Recently, for example, a department manager wanted to offer an incentive for several of the employees on his crew to acquire their GEDs. Thinking about other important aspects of high school, he realized that he couldn't offer them the opportunity to attend the senior proms they had missed, nor could he give them an actual high-school diploma. What he could do—and did—was to give each worker who completed his or her GED successfully a class ring from the high school from which the person would have graduated.

There are no guidelines attached to the recognition process. Appleton simply encourages employees to recognize others when and where it's appropriate.

"This isn't a one-size-fits-all program," Reveal says. Instead the company encourages managers to think about what the individual being recognized would value most. Some employees favor public recognition, for example, whereas others find such accolades embarrassing.

Managers aren't the only ones charged with the responsibility for recognizing good deeds. All employees are encouraged to give quality thank-you notes to co-workers, supervisors, and subordinates in recognition of good work. Furthermore, the organization's CEO recognizes individual and team achievement on an annual basis with lucrative, high-profile recognition items. "Employees used to think that recognition was only the job of human resources," Reveal says. "Now they realize that it's everyone's job."

In addition to recognizing good deeds, Appleton's managers must take the time to deal with inappropriate behavior as well. "We can't just reinforce positive behavior without also letting the employees know what negative behavior looks like," Reveal explains. This kind of response can range from brief verbal warnings to initiation of the progressive discipline process.

Before implementing the new recognition system, Appleton trained its managers in how both to give and to receive recognition effectively. "We didn't want an employee to recognize his or her manager for a job well done and have that manager shrug off the compliment," Reveal says. "We had to make sure that managers knew how to receive recognition gracefully as a way to reinforce the importance of it."

Is the company's quality effort more successful now because of its recognition process? Yes, according to Reveal.

Appleton has moved from an *unfavorable* to a *favorable* financial position, 75 percent less time is lost due to on-the-job accidents, and, though it's hard to measure, morale has improved. As Reveal says, "Let's just say it feels better around here."[47]

The advantages of a straight salary program are several. From the salesperson's viewpoint, it takes the ambiguity out of the salary process. It's also simpler to administer. If nonsales functions (for example, paperwork and customer support) are important, salaried sales personnel are more willing to perform these functions. The drawback is that straight salaries reduce the connection between performance and pay.

The commission is equivalent to Lincoln's piece rate system.

Straight Commission. In theory, a **commission** is simply a percentage of the sales price of the product. The exact percentage depends on the product being sold, industry practices, the organization's economic conditions, and special pricing during sales promotions. In establishing a sales commission program, the following questions need answering:

- What criteria will be used to measure performance?
- Are territories equivalent in sales potential?
- Will commission rates vary by product or vary depending on sales level?
- Will there be a cap on earnings?
- Will credit for a sale be given at point of sale, at delivery, or at receipt of payment?
- What will be the timing of commission payments (monthly, quarterly)?

Once these questions are answered, a program can be set up. The success of commission-only plans rests directly on the salesperson. The more sales, the greater the earnings; no sales means no income. The success also rests on whether the salespeople will even accept the incentive pay program.

The power of such incentives can be so high that it elicits unintended behaviors.[48] Churning among stockbrokers is one example. As a federal judge said recently, "As long as investment brokers are paid on straight commission, the potential exists for brokers to excessively trade accounts in an effort to generate fees without regard to the customers' financial needs and investment objectives." Commission-only plans also make it difficult to direct the efforts of salespeople toward activities (paperwork) that do not have an immediate influence on obtaining additional sales.

As companies rethink their strategic objectives, they often evaluate their current pay system for salespeople who represent the company to their valued customers. IBM's recent restructuring provides a vivid example. IBM has approximately 30,000 employees who sell their products and services around the world. According to one general manager, "In the old days, we'd give a branch manager a revenue quota, and that would be it. We'd see him at year end and he'd tell us how he did."

But IBM's new strategy is to focus much more on customer satisfaction and profits. To implement this strategy, CEO Louis Gerstner wants to be sure salespeople think about the implications for IBM of the deals they cut with customers. To achieve the appropriate focus within the salesforce, he dramatically restructured their commission system. In 1993, only 6% of commission pay was tied to profits, but in 1994, 60% was tied to profits (not overall revenue). And, the other 40% is tied to customer satisfaction, in order to reduce the temptation to simply push fast-turnover, high profit products. Supporting the new pay system, salespeople now also have access to information that had been closely guarded before—the margins for the products they sell. So far, IBM's major competitors haven't followed in IBM's footsteps, and it remains to be seen how well this new system will serve IBM's new strategy. But the example clearly illustrates the powerful role sales commissions are believed to exert over behavior.[49]

Did You KNOW?

Nordstrom is famous for its great service and its great commission pay plan.

Combined Plans. Because of these concerns, more than half of all sales compensation plans combine base salary and incentives. Exhibit 15.5 shows the

EXHIBIT 15.5

Basis for Incentive Pay for Field Sales Personnel

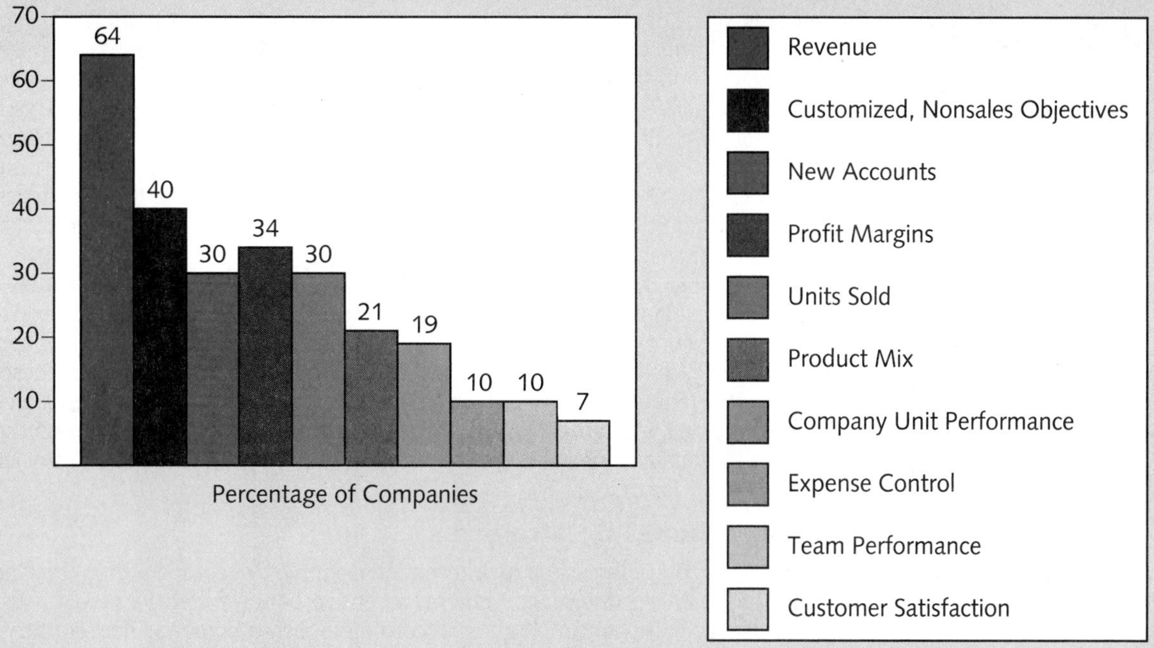

Source: Based on a survey conducted by Hewitt Associates, as represented in G. Fuchsberg, "Selling Isn't Everything," *The Wall Street Journal* (April 13, 1994): R8.

components most commonly found in pay plans for salespeople. In setting up a combined plan, the critical question is what percentage of total compensation should be salary and what percentage should be commission. The answer to this question depends on the availability of sales criteria (sales volume, units sold, product mix, retention of accounts, number of new accounts), and the number of nonsales duties in the job. Commonly, these plans are based on an 80/20 salary to commission mix. However, organizations wishing to push sales over customer service functions may utilize different ratios (60/40 or even 50/50).

The commission portion of the sales compensation can be established in one of two ways. The simplest is to use a commission combined with a *draw.* The salesperson receives a specific salary each payday. Quarterly or monthly, the total commission due the salesperson is calculated. The amount taken as a draw is deducted with the salesperson receiving the remainder. Alternatively, bonuses can be given when sales reach a specific level.[50]

Sales plans often include contests to direct sales activities to certain products or outcomes. Vacations as well as goods such as golf clubs are commonly rewarded. These contests provide very visible rewards. Records of who is winning can be placed on the bulletin board and in company newsletters.

Did You KNOW?

Pat McCarthy sells in the men's clothing department at Nordstrom. With commissions, McCarthy can earn upwards of $90,000 plus profit sharing and other benefits.

Executive Compensation

Annual bonuses ranging from 20 to 45 percent of base salary are used by companies to reward their executives, according to a Conference Board survey of 580 large U.S. firms. Annual bonus plans are nearly universal in energy (97 percent), manufacturing (92 percent), service firms (92 percent), and banking (81 percent), but less prevalent in public utilities. Because base salaries are considerably lower in companies with bonus plans, they provide a strong incentive for executives to perform well in the short run. However, they do not work well in companies with one or more of the following characteristics: 1) tight control of stock ownership, 2) not-for-profit institutions, and 3) firms operating in regulated industries.[51]

Did You KNOW?

These companies offer stock option plans to most of their employees:

- **DuPont**
- **PepsiCo**
- **Pfizer**
- **Microsoft**
- **Toys 'R' Us**
- **Southwest Airlines**

Stock Options. The next most frequently used method of rewarding executives is stock options. Approximately 75 percent of energy, manufacturing, and insurance firms provide such plans. The awarding of stock options is premised on the assumption that managers will work harder to increase their performance and the performance of the firm if they share in the firm's long-run profits. This focus on long-term incentives reflects a concern by boards of directors for long-term achievement over short-run profits. Of course, this same logic applies to firms offering stock options to their nonmanagerial workers as well. While this practice is limited, companies like PepsiCo show that it has as positive an effect on employees as it does on managers!

Following the *Economic Recovery Tax Act* of 1981, most companies with stock option plans use **incentive stock options (ISO).** When an ISO is exercised, the executive pays only 20 percent capital gains on the first $100,000 of appreciated value. While this is far less than the previous 50 percent tax rate, these programs still require a large cash investment. Consequently, some companies are experimenting with **stock appreciation rights (SAR),** which allow executives to realize capital gains of stock options without requiring the purchase of stocks.[52]

International Employees

Expatriates typically get paid in dollars and the local currency.

Continuing our discussion of international employee compensation in Chapter 11,[53] if the MNC utilizes any type of incentive bonus system, a policy is usually established. Bonuses can be given according to either home- or host-country policies. Actual payments can be made in either local or foreign currency and will often be a combination of the two or at the discretion of the recipient. For example, the majority of U.S. financial services companies have an overall policy of paying PCNs according to the U.S. salary structure (this includes bonus programs and salary increase practices). Most often, this compensation is paid partly in U.S. dollars and partly in the local currency. While the local currency portion is generally pegged to pay ordinary living expenses, bonuses are typically paid in U.S. dollars. Salary practices for TCNs tend to vary more widely and may be paid according to the home structure, a U.S. structure, or the host-country structure.

Reminder:

MNC = multinational corporation

PCN = parent-country nationals

TCN = third-country nationals

Questions that MNCs generally address when planning for their incentive bonuses include:

- What techniques can be used to provide management incentives abroad?
- Incentive bonuses help many companies achieve their objectives at home, but can they be used as effectively in subsidiary operations?
- How can companies design appropriate incentive bonuses for managers in an area suffering from rapid inflation?[54]

American MNCs frequently link stock opportunities to executive performance. Consider, however, the situation in other countries:

Belgium	Problematic. Some stock plans conflict with a government-imposed wage freeze.
Brazil	Impossible. Foreign-exchange controls prohibit out-of-country stock investment; phantom stock plans are a headache.
Britain	Easy. But sometimes labor unions can get in the way.
Eastern Europe	Forget it. Even if you get government permission, chances are you've talked to the wrong bureaucrat.

Germany	Can I get that in deutsche marks? U.S. plans suffer when the dollar is weak.
Israel	Difficult. Exchange controls forced National Semiconductor to a third-party system, but plan has only scant participation.
Luxembourg	Tax haven. Great place to set up a trust to administer stock plans.
Mexico	May regret it. Labor laws can force a one-time stock grant into an annual event.
Netherlands	No thanks. Employees may like the stock options, but they won't appreciate a hefty tax bill upfront.
Philippines	Time-consuming. Requires government approval and lots of worker education.[55]

Parent-country nationals often receive a salary premium as an inducement to accept a foreign assignment or to compensate for any hardship suffered due to the transfer. Under such circumstances, the definition of hardship, eligibility for the premium, and amount and timing of payment must be addressed. For cases in which hardship is determined, MNCs often refer to the U.S. Department of State's Hardship Post Differentials Guidelines to determine an appropriate level of payment. As others have noted, however, there are many problems involved with international comparisons of the cost of living.[56] It is important to note that TCNs do not receive these payments as often as PCNs. Foreign service inducements, if used, are most commonly made in the form of a percentage of salary, usually 5 to 40 percent of base pay. Such payments vary depending on the assignment, actual hardship, tax consequences, and length of assignment. In addition, differentials may be considered; for example, a host country's workweek may be longer than that of the home country, and a differential payment may be made in lieu of overtime, which is not normally paid to PCNs or TCNs.

Currency protection is also an issue affecting compensation. Several alternatives for this protection exist. Employees may have discretion over the currency used in payments, or a standard split basis for all PCNs may exist. A split basis may be applied on a case-by-case basis, depending on the particular assignment. With regard to local currency payments, a policy concerning exchange rate adjustments is necessary to assure that all employees are treated fairly.

Administrative Issues

LEARNING OBJECTIVE 3

Identify obstacles to effectively implementing performance-based pay.

Although performance-based pay systems are capable of substantially improving productivity, many obstacles in their design and implementation may suppress their potential effectiveness. Organizations can identify these obstacles and remove them. The following discussion of the obstacles pertains equally to merit pay and incentive pay; the second and third administrative issues apply primarily to merit pay.

Obstacles to Effectiveness

Obstacles encountered in the design and implementation of performance-based pay systems can be grouped into three general categories: 1) specifying and measuring job performance, 2) identifying valued rewards (pay being just one of many rewards), and 3) linking rewards to job performance.[57]

A prerequisite to rewarding job performance is specifying what job performance is, determining the relationships between levels of job performance and rewards, and accurately measuring job performance. These steps are often difficult because of the changing nature of work, its multidimensional nature, technological developments, lack of supervisory training, and the manager's value system.

These problems are detailed in Exhibit 15.6 along with their implications for management.

A second set of obstacles involves identifying rewards for desired behaviors. Rewards other than pay may have more motivational value, especially for employees whose pay increments may be largely consumed by increased taxes. Some employees, even those at Lincoln Electric, may begin to value time-off as much as overtime.[58] Consequently, the manager must discover the rewards most valued by the employees and contingently administer those that are most reinforcing.

The third category of obstacles involves the difficulties in linking rewards to job performance. The causes of these problems include inappropriate contingencies, inaccurate performance appraisal measures, and existing employee opposition. Often employee opposition is a major obstacle in successfully implementing performance-based pay, especially incentive plans. This opposition originates in employee beliefs about incentive plans, particularly the belief that management cannot be trusted.[59]

Did You KNOW?

Both UPS and Lincoln Electric believe that their success is not possible without the workers' trust in management.

This lack of trust has immediate implications for the establishment of rates and standards that form the basis of incentive systems. Workers may play elaborate charades for the benefit of time-study engineers doing the work measurement described in Chapters 7 and 8, but these maneuvers do not entirely fool the engineers who know workers might try to be misleading. Therefore, the engineers plug in estimates of how much they are being fooled, turning scientific observation and measurement into a guessing game.[60] The result may be inaccurate or unfair rates, which reduce the incentive value of the system, the profitability of the company, or both. Even assuming these obstacles are removed, the organization still must select the pay plan that best fits the needs of the company and then audit it to make sure that it is effective.

Auditing the Merit Pay System

For any merit pay system to be successful, it must be administered accurately across employees, fairly across all units or divisions in a company, and within the pay structure for all salary grades. That is, employees have to know that their merit raise is determined in the same way throughout the company regardless of the supervisor and that it is based on an accurate measure of job performance. While the accuracy of performance appraisals may be ensured by using a behavioral-based appraisal method (see Chapter 12), fair and consistent administration (within the pay structure) is accomplished by means of compa-ratios and performance ratios.

Compa-ratio is the measure of the average salary in relation to the midpoint of the range.

Performance ratios indicate where the performance rating of any employee stands in relation to others.

These ratios help companies manage their pay levels. They are also used to help ensure that employees throughout the company are treated fairly.

Compa-ratios and performance ratios used together can highlight pay and job performance relationships by individual employee, by salary grade, by level in the organization, or by department or division in the company. The **compa-ratio** is the measure of the average salary in relation to the midpoint of the range for a given salary grade. It is determined by dividing the average salary for the grade by the midpoint for that grade and multiplying by 100. A compa-ratio of 110, for example, means that as a group, individuals are being paid 10 percent over the midpoint for the given salary grade. Assuming a normal distribution of job performance and experience levels, the average compa-ratio in any department or division should be close to 100. Ratios higher than 100 may suggest leniency (therefore inaccuracy) in pay decisions, while ratios less than 100 may mean the opposite. If allowed to exist, ratio differentials across departments or divisions can indicate inconsistent merit pay administration.

Similar conclusions can be drawn from the use of **performance ratios.** These ratios indicate where the performance rating of any employee stands relative to other employees. This is done by determining the midpoint of a performance range, dividing that into each employee's performance rating, and multiplying that figure by 100. This process can be facilitated by choosing a performance appraisal method that uses points rather than relative rankings. Most methods discussed in Chapter 12, except the ranking method, can effectively measure performance ratios.[61]

EXHIBIT 15.6

Obstacles to the Design of Effective Reward Systems and Their Implications for Management

OBSTACLES	CAUSES	IMPLICATIONS FOR MANAGEMENT
A. Difficulties in specifying and measuring performance	1. Changes in the nature of work • Increase in service-oriented jobs • Increase in white-collar, managerial, and professional jobs • Increases in the interdependencies and complexity of work	1. Develop techniques for specifying desirable behaviors and clarifying the objectives of the organization.
	2. Multidimensional nature of work • Single-item measures of performance are often inadequate • In many jobs today, multiple criteria are necessary to assess performance.	2. Utilize evaluation procedures that recognize the multidimensional nature of performance.
	3. Technological developments • Technological developments often result in new and untested methods of work. • Machine-paced jobs permit little variation in performance	3. Develop a reliable and valid performance appraisal system based on results and/or behavioral standards.
	4. Lack of supervisory training • Use of untrained, inexperienced supervisors in the evaluation process • Perceptual biases	4. Train supervisors to use the PA system appropriately and to understand potential sources of bias.
	5. The manager's value system • Lack of interest in or inability to differentiate among high and low performers • Failure to see long-range outcomes of differential rewarding	5. Clearly define long-term consequences of performance-contingent and noncontingent reward practices.
B. Problems in identifying valued rewards	1. Choice of rewards • Choosing a reward that is not reinforcing	1. Make managers aware of the effects of rewards on employee performance and satisfaction
	2. Utilizing rewards of insufficient size or magnitude • Lack of resources • Company policy	2. Train managers to identify rewards for their subordinates
	3. Poor timing of rewards • Size of organization: bureaucracy • Standardization/formalization of feedback mechanisms • Complexity of feedback system	3. Administer rewards of sufficient magnitude. 4. Administer rewards as quickly after desirable responses as possible.
C. Difficulties in linking rewards to performance	1. Failure to create appropriate contingencies between rewards and performance • Lack of knowledge, skill, experience • Belief system • Difficulty of administration	1. Train manager to establish appropriate contingencies between rewards and performance.
	2. Creating inappropriate contingencies • Rewarding behavior that does not increase performance • Rewarding behavior A, but hoping for B	2. Use information obtained from appraisals of employee performance as basis for reward allocation decisions.
	3. Nullifying intended contingencies • Using improper PA instrument • Improper use of PA instrument • Failure to use information obtained • Inconsistently applied	3. Administer the reward system consistently across employees.
	4. Employee opposition • Individually: mistrust, lack of fairness, inequity • Socially: restrictions due to fear of loss of work • Outside intervention: union	4. Obtain employee participation in the design and administration of the pay plan.

Source: P. M. Podsakoff, C. N. Greene, and J. M. McFillen, "Obstacles to the Effective Use of Reward Systems," in *Readings in Personnel and Human Resource Management*, 3rd ed., R. S. Schuler, S. A. Youngblood, and V. L. Huber, eds (St. Paul, MN: West, 1988): 284–285.

Participation in Performance-Based Pay Systems

Employee participation can take place at two critical points in performance-based pay systems: 1) in the design stage and 2) in the administration stage.

Design Stage. Many pay plans are designed by top management and installed in a fairly authoritative fashion. Often employees can do the same things even more effectively. That is, employees can be responsible for designing the pay plan, as suggested in the previous chapter. Furthermore, they understand and accept the plan more readily if they are involved. Participation in plan design can also reduce the potential resistance to change that accompanies almost any change in an organization. Consequently, employees are more motivated to increase performance.

These potential advantages of employee participation in pay plan design may not always materialize. For example, they fail to occur when management is not truly participative but rather tries to manipulate employees into participation. They also will not occur when employees prefer not to participate. These reasons also apply to employee participation in the administration of the pay plan.

Administration Stage. As indicated in Chapter 14, employees can responsibly determine when and if other workers should receive pay increases. This also appears to be true for individuals determining their own pay increases. Nevertheless, employee participation may not work in all cases, nor is it necessarily appropriate under all circumstances.[62]

LEARNING OBJECTIVE 4

Discuss the areas where compensation can be linked to quality.

Current Trends

Perhaps not surprisingly by this time, an important trend here is linking performance-based pay to the strategy of the organization. Another trend is putting pay into perspective.

Linking to Organizational Strategy

Pay can be very important when getting employees to go along with a total quality management strategy.

As with total compensation, pay is, or can be, a powerful motivator in shaping employees' behaviors. Organizations are using pay as a way to implement such programs as total quality management. As described in Chapters 3 and 12, employee behaviors are critical in getting high quality in service firms or manufacturing firms. Do you regard a smile on the face of a store clerk and a "thank you for shopping" comment from the cashier of the local store as examples of quality customer-oriented service? Many people do and are in fact willing to pay more for the goods in stores such as Nordstrom that have salespeople like these.

How do stores get people who are willing to commit to customer service? Among other things, organizations clearly have to pay people for these behaviors. If companies want to have a strategy of total quality, they need to identify the behaviors necessary and then pay people for those behaviors. This is in fact what organizations are doing, according to a report published by the Hay Group consulting firm:

> *Organizations that institute quality programs should structure their compensation practices to reward quality, concludes a report by the Hay Group. Compensation practices alone cannot make quality initiatives succeed, the report says, but they can help motivate employees to take responsibility, find innovation, and reduce costs.*
>
> *The shift to quality often requires fundamental organizational change, the report warns. Additionally, most organizations try several approaches to quality before they find the system that works best for them. Whatever the new quality process entails, however, the following elements must be present to ensure its success:*

- *Management must be committed to the quality movement and not be looking for a "quick fix."*
- *Management must define quality outcomes and have measurement systems to gauge progress toward those outcomes.*
- *Management must empower the workforce and shift the focus from individual effort to teamwork.*
- *Management must link pay to quality-improvement goals.*[63]

Pay in Perspective

Another important trend is that both individuals and organizations are putting pay into perspective. While pay certainly remains important because it buys us goods and services and tells us how well we are doing, many people are also concluding that pay is not everything! Having good colleagues, good working conditions and opportunities for job growth are also very important.[64] This comes at a time when organizations are faced with tremendous global competition that makes it more and more difficult to automatically pass on higher costs to the customer. This is not to say that incentive pay is likely to die on the vine because of cost pressures, but it does say that companies will likely use a combination of pay and non-pay rewards to motivate employees. And because we are now in a period of lower inflation, smaller pay increases are likely to be seen as more motivational than they were during the higher inflationary period of the early 1980s.

As the case of Lincoln Electric illustrates, companies that are using incentive pay plans are also putting pay into perspective by considering the entire needs of employees. Thus when trying to understand why Lincoln Electric employees work so hard, we must look at the human resource philosophy of the company as well as the incentive pay plans. Their HR philosophy is built on care and concern for the employee and the employee's family as described in Chapter 7. From it come many HR practices such as family benefits for education and health, training opportunities, and safety programs. Together, these all convey to the employee a sense of caring and belonging. They help put pay and its motivational value into perspective. In turn, they help make the incentive pay plans at Lincoln Electric successful.

We increasingly demand that our workers take on responsibility and risk, yet their pay is falling. Will $8-an-hour machinists do high-performance work? "The real answer is, we don't know yet. But you can't expect workers to keep contributing their ideas when they don't get rewarded for them."

Paul Osterman
Professor of Management
MIT

Legal Considerations

By definition, pay discrimination based on performance (not job status) is an inevitable and appropriate outcome of a properly administered performance-based pay system. Performance-based compensation is intended to create behaviors that lead to the accomplishment of organizational goals. Rewards that are administered contingently (that is, according to performance) cause increases in subsequent employee performance and expressions of satisfaction among high performers. They encourage low performers to either perform at a higher rate or exit the organization. The legal issue, then, is not whether to discriminate in pay but how to administer performance-based pay so it does not unfairly discriminate against protected-group members.

As indicated in Chapter 14, the *Civil Rights Acts* of 1964 and 1991 apply not only to selection decisions, but also to pay decisions. Under both laws, a supervisor may be charged with unlawful discrimination by an employee (in a protected group) who believes that a pay raise was denied on the basis of factors unrelated to performance. Raises not related to performance, however, are legal. Defensible factors (when they are equally applied to all employees) include the following:

- Position in salary range
- Time since last increase

- Size of last increase
- Pay relationships within the company or department
- Pay levels of jobs in other companies
- Salaries of newly hired employees
- Budgetary limits

What is critical for all pay plans is that the same rules are used to give raises fairly and consistently among all employees.

Summary

Performance-based pay systems continue to attract the attention of many HR managers, and line managers continue to ask whether pay can be used as a motivator with their employees. Yet their experiences with merit pay convince them that pay does not necessarily do a good job of motivating. The success of many incentive plans, however, indicates that pay can motivate job performance, although many problems can arise because of the many obstacles associated with the implementation of incentive plans.

Which incentive pay plan is appropriate must be determined by several factors such as the level at which job performance can accurately measure performance (individual, team, or organization) for given individuals, the extent of cooperation needed between individuals, and the level of trust between management and nonmanagement. Several plans can be used together to reward different teams of employees for good job performance. However, there may be limits on a specific organization's decision to use performance-based pay; these can include management's desire to have incentive pay, management's commitment to design and implement one or several systems, the extent to which employees influence the output, the extent to which a good performance appraisal system exists, the existence of a union, and the degree of trust in the organization. Whether the organization is public or private also influences the decision. Generally, only private organizations utilize incentive systems. Both types, however, can and do use merit pay systems.

Key Concepts

commission
compa-ratio
cost-of-living adjustments (COLAs)
differential piece rate plan
employee stock ownership plan (ESOP)
gainsharing plans
Improshare
incentive pay plans
incentive stock options (ISO)
lump-sum bonuses
merit pay plans
performance-based pay
performance bonuses
performance ratios
profit-sharing plans
Scanlon and Rucker plans
social loafing
standard hour plan
stock appreciation rights (SAR)
stock option
straight piecework plan
suggestion systems
team-based incentives
variable-pay plans

Review and Discussion Questions

1. Do you believe that an employee's behavior is always influenced by the reward expected? Is this true for your behavior in this course?

2. Suppose that people do not always do things because of the tangible rewards they can receive. Does this invalidate the theory of performance-based pay? Explain.
3. What conditions are necessary for effective performance-based pay systems?
4. What are the most common performance-based pay systems? How do you account for their popularity?
5. What obstacles arise in specifying and measuring job performance?
6. How can an organization determine whether merit pay is administered accurately across all employees or across all its units and divisions?
7. Describe a performance-based pay system that you have directly experienced. Did the system work? If not, why not?
8. Debate the following assertion: If selection and placement decisions are done effectively, individual performance should not vary a great deal; therefore, a performance-based pay system is not needed.
9. How can employees participate in both the design and administration of a performance-based pay system? In general, will employee participation have positive or negative consequences for the operation of the system?
10. Explain how a pay system can be linked to an organization's strategy.

PROJECTS, EXERCISES & CASES

End-of-Text Projects

Lincoln Electric

1. Describe the following for Lincoln Electric:
   a. Lincoln's incentive plan objectives
   b. The degree to which these objectives are serving the business and HR objectives of Lincoln
   c. Lincoln's incentive plans and activities
   d. The degree to which these plans and activities are serving the objectives of Lincoln
2. How can Lincoln's incentive compensation activities be improved?

Nordstrom

1. Describe the following for Nordstrom:
   a. Nordstrom's incentive plan objectives
   b. The degree to which these objectives are serving the business and HR objectives of Nordstrom
   c. Nordstrom's incentive plans and activities
   d. The degree to which these plans and activities are serving the objectives of Nordstrom
2. How can Nordstrom's incentive compensation activities be improved?

Field Projects

1. Interview two or three employees of a local company to learn whether they are paid on the basis of their performance and, if so, on what basis. If they are not paid for performance, find out whether they would like to be and, if so, under what type—merit or incentive-based plans. Identify the type of person who prefers performance-based pay and the type who does not.
2. To intensify the comparison of people and their priorities of compensation, compare employees from private with public companies, managers with non-managers, white-collar with blue-collar employees, men with women, teenagers with adults.

Career Management Exercise: So Tell Me, "What Will It Take to Get You?"

Refer to previous Career Management exercises in Chapters 6, 8, and 9. There you described a job you might want and developed some selection procedures for it. Now let's take this a step further: Tell me what it will take to get you to join my firm. (Assume I have the job you want!) That is tell me how your direct compensation should be structured. (Use any of the materials from Chapters 14 and 15.)

1. First, provide some percent breakdowns of the various parts of your direct compensation package. For example:
   ________ % Base salary
   ________ % Performance-based
      ________ % Merit
      ________ % Incentive
         ________ % Individual
         ________ % Team
2. What is the total dollar value of your first year's direct compensation?
3. To make this a bit more challenging, assume that you want to take an overseas assignment for your first three years! Now indicate percents and dollars.
4. Refer to Chapter 6 and review the discussion of career stages. Then complete the parts in items 1 and 2 again for each career stage!

VISIT THE LIBRARY

Workforce Online

1. Enter your Web browser.
2. Enter Workforce Online.
3. Find and review the following article within "Winning Ideas": *PepsiCo Shares Power and Wealth with Workers.*
4. Enter the HR Library.
5. Find and review the following article under the keyword "Research Center": *Tie Individual Pay to Team Success.*
6. Return to your homepage.

Case: The Time Clock

Susan Crandall was feeling good about her new position at Western National Bank. Susan, a seven-year employee at Western, had come a long way from her starting position as a teller to her present position as human resource manager, thanks in many respects to her predecessor, Anna Bavetti.

Anna had recently resigned from the bank to take a position with a local computer software company, which was experiencing explosive growth. This company recognized they needed to systematize their staffing practices, so when Anna learned of the opportunity, she jumped. Anna was frustrated by what she considered conservative and stodgy management at the bank, so a change in scenery was a welcome relief.

Anna had begun at Western as an assistant to the then HR manager Nancy Hyer. Anna had an MBA degree from North Carolina and an undergraduate degree from Grinnell College. Anna quickly realized that her technical skills were superior to Nancy's, but she admired Nancy's street smarts and willingness to battle the CEO of the bank over new initiatives in the HR area. Nancy had put in a performance appraisal plan and an absenteeism plan before transferring to the trust department with what was touted as a promotion.

Anna, though, did not see the move as a promotion. In her estimation, Nancy had gotten too strong and was creating a lot of waves for the top brass at the bank, who were unwilling to move at the pace that Nancy had set. When the president of Western, Larry Wilson, asked Anna to assume the role of assistant vice president of personnel, Anna welcomed the opportunity to continue the initiatives begun by Nancy.

Anna decided that she was going to undertake two goals immediately. First, she was going to begin developing Susan. Nancy was too hard on Susan in Anna's estimation. Although Susan didn't have a college degree (she had had to drop out because her mother was ill), she had common sense and extremely good people skills. Over the next year, Anna progressively increased Susan's responsibilities by involving her in applicant screening and interviewing and including her on project assignments. Over time, Susan and Anna developed a teamlike approach to their work and learned to rely on each other to keep the HR management office functioning smoothly.

When Susan learned of Anna's departure, she was saddened but not surprised. Anna always seemed too liberal and progressive for upper management of the bank. Anna valued people and looked for the best in them. Anna, more than the other officers at the bank, seemed genuinely concerned about the welfare of the employees, especially the mostly nonexempt employee workforce. Susan was flabbergasted, though, when Larry Wilson called her into his office and asked her to assume Anna's job. Her pay would increase by 150 percent. Although the job would mean longer hours and more responsibilities, under Anna's tutelage, Susan felt confident that she could rise to the occasion.

Susan wanted more than anything to carry through on Anna's second goal, which was to link the performance evaluation system developed by Nancy to the annual pay increases. The bank had entered an era of competition with other banks and savings and loans, so productivity was a major concern for the bank. Besides cutting staff to the minimum, Susan believed that in the long run, linking pay to effort and performance would encourage productivity among all employees. Susan believed that Western's staff were hard working and would welcome the opportunity to see their pay linked to their performance.

Susan noticed it was almost 5 P.M. and she needed to speak with Gerry Latham, vice president for operations, regarding her proposed merit plan, which would influence his group the most. As she passed by the elevators, she noticed several employees waiting beside the time clock. It was common practice for the nonexempts to wait for a seemingly inordinate amount of time for the elevator to arrive on the fifth floor of the bank building. A common practice was to wait until the elevator bell chimed and the doors began to open before clocking out.

As several of the employees hurriedly punched the clock and dashed to the elevator, Larry Wilson appeared behind Susan. Larry called out to Susan, who was deep in thought about how to present her merit plan to Gerry Latham. "Susan, did you see that?" questioned Larry. "I'm sorry, Larry, I was lost in thought. What are you talking about?" replied Susan. As the elevator doors closed, Larry picked up his voice in obvious irritation. "I think those employees would just as soon cheat us if they are charging their wait time on the elevators. How do we know that they're not trying to cheat us in the morning when they clock in or when they return from lunch late and have a co-worker punch them in? Susan, I want you to investigate this tomorrow, first thing. This kind of fraud has got to stop immediately." Oh boy, thought Susan. How am I going to defuse this bomb? As Susan started back down the hall toward Gerry Latham's office, she began to understand the frustration that occasionally leaked through Anna's otherwise calm exterior when she occupied Susan's job.

Case Questions

1. What strategic considerations support the concept of a performance-based pay plan in banking?
2. At a minimum, what HR activities must exist prior to implementing a performance-based pay plan in a bank or elsewhere?
3. Does the culture at Western support a performance-based pay plan?
4. How should Susan respond to Larry's directive to investigate the time clock fraud?

Case: Merit or Demerit?

BLTC is a firm engaged in the manufacture and distribution of chemicals. Because many of the manufacturing, storage, and distribution processes of BLTC are monitored and controlled by computer technology, the firm's computer operations expenditures are substantial. Tod Jenkins, the director of the firm's computer operations division, estimated that the projected annual budget for his division would be in the neighborhood of $2,500,000. The comptroller of BLTC felt that this amount was excessive and directed Jenkins to reduce costs wherever possible. To accomplish this objective, Jenkins assigned a number of systems analysts to review the current level and type of computer services provided to the organization. These analysts were instructed to streamline operations and eliminate unnecessary or infrequently used management reports and computer equipment.

Stan Cook is one of the best and brightest systems analysts who works for Jenkins. After weeks of intensive investigation, Cook submitted a proposal that permitted a $450,000 reduction in the computer operations budget. These budgetary reductions were accomplished by:

1. Consolidating the existing elements of the management/production control monitoring system
2. Eliminating redundant reporting and data collection procedures
3. Utilizing less expensive "batch" computer processing where possible
4. Eliminating unnecessary or infrequently used computer equipment

5. Increasing utilization and coordination of existing computer resources

Thus, Cook was able to reduce operational costs without reducing the level or quality of services provided to management.

Jenkins was greatly impressed by Cook's activities and felt that he deserved some special form of recognition. Therefore, he informed Cook that he was recommending him for a special merit award (SMA). These SMAs, which are administered by the comptroller's office, constitute an important part of the firm's motivational program. Under this program, the employee's supervisor makes a recommendation as to the amount of the cash award to be received by the employee. In general, the dollar value of the SMA is a percentage of the amount of the cost savings for which the employee was responsible. Jenkins recommended that Cook receive a monetary bonus equivalent to three percent of the cost savings he generated, or $13,500.

Two months after Jenkins recommended Cook for the SMA, Jenkins received a letter from the comptroller indicating that Cook did not qualify for an award. The comptroller justified his decision by stating that the development of plans to reduce computer operation costs was an integral part of Cook's job and, therefore, did not warrant additional compensation. Jenkins felt that this decision was both unjustified and characteristic of an "accounting mentality." For the next several months, he and the comptroller exchanged letters and telephone calls arguing for their respective viewpoints. When Cook inquired as the status of his SMA, Jenkins was forced to tell him of the long-running dispute with the comptroller. However, Jenkins assured Cook that the SMA would be awarded even if the firm's president had to be brought in to settle the dispute.

Approximately sixteen months after Jenkins submitted the original SMA recommendation, a compromise agreement was worked out with the comptroller. According to this agreement, Cook was to receive $250 and a printed certificate of achievement. At the awards ceremony, Cook accepted the monetary award and certificate from the comptroller. The following day, Cook informed Jenkins that he was submitting his resignation in order to accept a job offered to him by another firm.

Case Questions

1. Was the bonus of three percent a fair amount?
2. What are the real problems with BLTC's suggestion system?
3. Was Cook's response justified?
4. What would you do if you were Cook?

Chapter 15 Endnotes

1. Z. Schiller, "A Model Incentive Plan Gets Caught in a Vise," *Business Week* (January 22, 1996): 89.

2. Z. Schiller, "A Model Incentive Plan Gets Caught in a Vise," *Business Week* (January 22, 1996): 89–90; T. W. Gerdel, Lincoln Electric Experiences Season of Worker Discontent," *Plain Dealer* [Cleveland] (December 10, 1995); C. Wiley, "Incentive Plan Pushes Production," *Personnel Journal* (Aug. 1993): 86–92; K. Chilton, "Lincoln Electric's Incentive System: Can It Be Transferred Overseas?" *Compensation and Benefits Review* (Nov.-Dec. 1993): 21–30; R. Hodgetts, "A Conversation with Donald F. Hastings of the Lincoln Electric Company," *Organizational Dynamics* (Winter, 1997): 68–74.

3. A. Farnham, "Mary Kay's Lessons in Leadership," *Fortune* (Sept. 20, 1993): 68–77.

4. E. E. Lawler III, "Pay for Performance: A Motivational Analysis," *Readings in Personnel and Human Resource Management* 2nd ed., R. S. Schuler, S. A. Youngblood, and V. Huber, eds. (St. Paul, MN: West, 1984).

5. Wiley, "Incentive Plan Pushes Production"; J. McAdams and E. Hawk, "Capitalizing on Human Assets Through Performance-based Rewards," *ACA Journal* (Autumn 1992): 60–72.

6. "Productivity Boosters in Employee-Owned Firms," *Bulletin to Management* (May 5, 1994): 137–138; "Pay Plans Can Drive Performance," *Bulletin to Management* (October 20, 1994): 336; "Aligning Compensation with Quality," *Bulletin to Management* (April 1, 1993): 97.

7. *The Wall Street Journal* (July 1, 1985): 1; "Compensation: Growth Bonuses," *Inc.* (Feb. 1988): 100.

8. B. Filipczak, "Why No One Likes Your Incentive Program," *Training* (Aug. 1993): 21.

9. N. H. Mackworth, "High Incentives Versus Hot and Humid Atmospheres in a Physical Effort Task," *British Journal of Psychology* (1947): 90–102; P. M. Podsakoff, M. L. Williams, and W. E. Scott, Jr., "Myths of Employee Selection Systems," *Readings in Personnel and Human Resource Management* 3rd ed., R. S. Schuler, S. A. Youngblood, and V. Huber, eds. (St. Paul, MN: West, 1988): 178–192.

10. L. C. Cumming, "Linking Pay to Performance: Why Is It So Difficult?" *Personnel Administrator* (May 1988): 47–52; T. Rollins, "Pay for Performance: Is it Worth the Trouble?" *Personnel Administrator* (May 1988): 42–46.

11. D. Filipowski, "Perspectives: Is Pay Linked to Performance?" *Personnel Journal* (May 1991): 39.

12. See note 8.

13. P. M. Podsakoff, C. N. Greene, and J. M. McFillen, "Obstacles to the Effective Use of Reward Systems," *Readings in Personnel and Human Resource Management, R. S. Schuler, S. A. Youngblood, and V. L. Huber, eds. (St. Paul, MN: West, 1988):* 275–904.

14. D. Q. Mills, *The New Competitors* (New York: Wiley, 1985); G. Milkovich and J. Newman, *Compensation* (Plano, TX: Business Publications, 1984); C. Cumming, "Linking Pay to Performance," *Personnel Administrator* (May 1988): 47–52; T. Rollins, "Pay for Performance: Is It Worth the Trouble?" *Personnel Administrator* (May 1988): 42–46.

15. G. E. Ledford, Jr., "Merit Pay System is Fatally Flawed," *ACA News* (May 1995): 2; B. P. MacLean, "Value-Added Pay Beats Traditional Merit Programs," *Personnel Journal* (Sept. 1990): 46–51; J. L. Pearce, "Why Merit Pay Doesn't Work," *New Perspectives*; R. E. Kopelman, "The Case for Merit Rewards," *Personnel Administrator* (Oct. 1983): 60–68.

16. See note 10.

17. For a discussion of these and other aspects of merit pay administration, see E. J. Brennan, "Merit Pay: Balance the Old Rich and the New Poor," *Personnel Journal* (May 1985): 82–85.

18. "Creative Compensation Strategies: Reasons for Implementation," *Solutions* (January 1994): 24; R. B. Hill, "A Two-Component Approach to Compensation," *Personnel Journal* (May 1993): 154–161.

19. L. Uchitelle, "Boeing's Fight Over Bonuses," *New York Times* (October 12, 1989): Dl, D6; "Number of Lump-Sum Bonuses Escalating," *Bulletin to Management* (April 9, 1987): 113; L. Uchitelle, "Bonuses Replace Wage Raises and Workers Are the Losers," *New York Times* (June 26, 1987): 1, 31; G. S. Crystal, "Executive Compensation: Challenges in the Year Ahead," *Personnel* (Jan. 1988): 33–36; S. L. Minken, "Does Lump-Sum Pay Merit Attention?" *Personnel Journal* (June 1988): 77–83; A. Bernstein, "How'd You Like A Big Fat Bonus—And No Raise?" *Business Week* (November 3, 1986): 30–31; E. E. Lawler III, "Gainsharing," *New Perspectives on Compensation,* D. B. Balkin and L. R. Gomez Mejia, eds. (Englewood Cliffs, NJ: Prentice-Hall, 1987): 225–230.

20. M. Rowland, "Taking Care of Labor at Whirlpool," *New York Times* (March 5, 1995): F15; S. Greengard, "Leveraging a Low-Wage Work Force," *Personnel Journal* (January 1995): 90–102.

21. "Personnel Shop Talk," *Bulletin to Management* (August 4, 1994): 242; S. Baker, "From Blueprints to Grand Design," *Business Week* (January 8, 1996): 34; "Taco Bell: A Highly Leveraged Rewards System," *ACA Journal* (Spring 1995): 21.

22. Adapted from "Master the Compensation Maze," by S. Caudron, copyright June 1993.

23. D. W. Belcher and T. J. Achison, *Compensation Administration* (Englewood Cliffs, NJ: Prentice-Hall, 1977); R. I. Henderson, *Compensation Management: Rewarding Performance* (Reston, VA: Reston, 1985); G. Milkovich and J. Newman, *Compensation,* 2nd ed. (Plano, TX: Business Publications, 1989).

24. M. A. Tather, "Turning Ideas into Gold," *Management Review* (March 1985): 4–10.

25. Excerpts from "Incentive Plan Pushes Production," by C. Wiley, copyright August 1993. Reprinted with the permission of *Personnel Journal,* ACC Communications Inc., Costa Mesa, CA. All rights reserved.

26. E. Lawler and D. Cohen, "Designing Pay Systems to Fit Teams," *ACA Journal* (Autumn 1992): 6–18.

27. B. Geber, "The Bugaboo of Team Pay," *Training* (August 1995): 25–34; J. S. Lublin, "As More Companies Divide Workers into Self-managed Teams, They try to Link Pay to Team Performance," *The Wall Street Journal* (April 12, 1995): R4; J. Huret, "Paying for Team Results," *HR Magazine* (May 1991): 39–43.

28. "Emphasize Teamwork, Not Pay," Letter of C. J. Carter, *Personnel Journal* (January 1995): 13; P. Barton, "Paying Teams," *ACA News* (September 1995): 1, 18–19.

29. "Compensating Teams: A Conundrum," *HR Reporter* (September 1993): 3; S. Caudron, "Tie Individual Pay to Team Success," *Personnel Journal* (October 1994): 40–45; C. Meyer, "How the Right Measures Help Teams Excel," *Harvard Business Review* (May-June 1994): 95–103.

30. Excerpts from "Master the Compensation Maze," by S. Caudron, copyright June 1993.

31. R. I. Henderson, *Compensation Management: Rewarding Performance* (Reston, VA: Reston, 1985).

32. "Gain-Sharing Plan Pointers," *Bulletin to Management* (April 16, 1987): 128; B. W. Thomas and M. Hess Olson, "Gain Sharing: The Design Guarantees Success," *Personnel Journal* (May 1988): 73–79; C. S. Miller and M. H. Schuster, "Gainsharing Plans: A Comparative Analysis," *Organizational Dynamics* (Summer 1987): 44–67; T. L. Ross, R. A. Ross, and L. Hatcher, "Communication: The Multiple Benefits of Gainsharing," *Personnel Journal* (Oct. 1986): 14–25; R. C. Scott, "Test Your Gain Sharing Potential," *Personnel Journal* (May 1988): 82–84; J. C. Horn, "Bigger Pay for Better Work," *Psychology Today* (July 1987): 54–57.

33. R. L. Masternak, "Gainsharing Boosts Quality and Productivity at a BFGoodrich Plant," *National Productivity Review* 1994;12(2): 225–238.

34. D. O'Neill, "Blending the Best of Profit Sharing and Gainsharing," *HR Magazine* 1993;39(3): 66–70.

35. G. W. Florkowski, "The Organizational Impact of Profit Sharing," *Academy of Management Review* (Oct. 1987): 622–636.

36. "Profit Sharing Plans Scarce but Successful," *Bulletin to Management* (June 2, 1994): 169; L. Uchitelle, "Good Jobs in Hard Times," *New York Times* (October 3, 1993): 1, 6; K. Matthes, "Greetings from Hallmark," *HR Focus* (Aug. 1993): 12–13; J. Labate, "Deal Those Workers In," *Fortune* (April 19, 1993): 63.

37. K. Helliker and B. Ortega, "Falling Profit Marks End of Era at Wal-Mart," *The Wall Street Journal* (January 18, 1996): B1.

38. A. Bernstein, "At Philip Morris, Blue Chips for Blue Collars," *Business Week* (March 27, 1995): 38.

39. A. Bernstein, "United We Own," *Business Week* (March 18, 1996): 96–102; A. Bryant, "A Down-to-Earth View at United," *New York Times* (October 28, 1994): D1, 2; S. Chandler, "A United United is Still a Ways Off," *Business Week* (May 23, 1994): 32; A. Bryant, "United's Chief Finds USAir A Hard Sell," *New York Times* (November 2, 1995): D1, 7; A. Bryant, "After 7 Years, Employees Win United Airlines," *New York Times* (July 13, 1994): A1, D13; A. Bryant, "A Peek at New Directions at United," *New York Times* (April 14, 1994): D4.

40. "Personnel Shop Talk," *Bulletin to Management* (September 21, 1995): 298.

41. "PepsiCo Shares Power and Stock with Workers," *Personnel Journal* (January 1995): 79.

42. "Newsfile: Southwest Airlines Expected to Reach Ground Breaking Wage Agreement with Pilots," *Personnel Journal* (February 1995): 12.

43. "Millionaires at Work," *Fortune* (April 3, 1995): 20.

44. Ibid., p. 21.

45. K. M. Evans, "On-the-Job Lotteries: A Low-Cost Incentive That Sparks Higher Productivity," *Personnel* (April 1988): 20–26; "Recognizing Reward Programs," *Personnel Journal* (Dec. 1986): 66–78; W. S. Humphrey, *Managing for Innovation: Leading Technical People* (Englewood Cliffs, NJ: Prentice-Hall, 1987): 128–133; K. Troy, "Recognize Quality Achievement with Noncash Awards," *Personnel Journal* (October 1993): 111–117; G. Flynn, "Non-sales Staffs Respond to Incentives," *Personnel Journal* (July 1994): 33–37; S. Caudron, "Are Your Temps Doing Their Best?" *Personnel Journal* (November 1995): 32–38.

46. C. F. Schultz, "Compensating the Sales Professional," in *New Perspectives on Compensation,* D. B. Balkin and L. R. Gomez-Mejia, eds. (Englewood Cliffs, NJ: Prentice Hall, 1987): 250–258; J. O. Steinbrink, *Sales Force Compensation: Dartnell's 22nd Biennial Survey* (Chicago: Dartnell Corporation, 1984): 47.

47. Excerpts from "Master the Compensation Maze," by S. Caudron, copyright June 1993.

48. A. Kohn, "Why Incentive Plans Cannot Work," *Harvard Business Review* (Sept.-Oct. 1993): 54–63.

49. Ibid., p. 60.

50. F. Schwadel, "Chain Finds Incentives a Hard Sell," *The Wall Street Journal* (July 5, 1990): 3. See also C. H. Deutsch, "Avon Keeps Ringing, but Wall Street Won't Answer," *New York Times* (July 15, 1990): F7.

51. J. Byrne, et al., "That Eye-Popping Executive Pay: Is Anybody Worth This Much?" *Business Week* (April 25, 1994): 52–58; T. Egan, "Strikers at Boeing Point to Top Management's Stock Option," *New York Times* (November 25, 1995): 6; J. R. Deckop, "Top Executive Compensation and the Pay-for-Performance Issue," in *New Perspectives on Compensation,* D. B. Balkin and L. R. Gomez-Mejia, eds. (Englewood Cliffs, NJ: Prentice Hall, 1987): 285–293.

52. P. Chingos, "Executive Compensation in the 1990s: The Challenges Ahead," *Compensation and Benefits Review* (Nov.-Dec. 1990): 20–31; M. J. Mandel, "Those Fat Bonuses Don't Seem to Boost Performance," *Business Week* (Jan. 8, 1990): 26; B. A. Stertz, "Chrysler Urges Its 100 Top Executives To Bet More of Their Pay on Firm's Fate," *The Wall Street Journal* (April 2, 1990): A4; G. S. Crystal, "Incentive Pay That Doesn't Work," *Fortune* (Aug. 28, 1989): 101, 104; G. S. Crystal, "Rendering Long-Term Incentives Less Risky For Executives," *Personnel* (Sept. 1988): 80–84; M. A. Mazer, "An End to Stock Appreciation Rights?" *Personnel Journal* (Nov. 1990): 53–57; G. S. Crystal, "Handling Underwater Stock Option Grants," *Personnel* (Feb. 1988): 12–15; M. A. Mazer, "Benefits: Are Stock Option Plans Still Viable?" *Personnel Journal* (July 1988): 48–50.

53. The following material is adapted from P. Dowling, R. S. Schuler and D. Welch, *International Dimensions of Human Resource Management* (Belmont, CA: Wadsworth, 1994): 154–161; A. V. Phatak, R. Chandram, and R. A. Ajayi, "International Executive Compensation," in *New Perspectives on Compensation,* D. B. Balkin and L. R. Gomez-Mejia, eds. (Englewood Cliffs, NJ: Prentice-Hall, 1987): 315–327.

54. The following material is adapted from P. Dowling, R. S. Schuler and D. Welch, *International Dimensions of Human Resource Management* (Belmont, CA: Wadsworth, 1994): 154–161; A. V. Phatak, R. Chandram, and R. A. Ajayi, "International Executive Compensation," *New Perspectives on Compensation,* D. B. Balkin and L. R. Gomez-Mejia, eds. (Englewood Cliffs, NJ: Prentice-Hall, 1987): 315–327.

55. T. Parker-Pope, "Culture Clash," *The Wall Street Journal* (April 12, 1995): R7.

56. M. J. Bishko, "Compensating Your Overseas Executives, Part 1: Strategies for the 1990s," *Compensation and Benefits Review* (May-June 1990): 33–43; "Compensating Your Overseas Executives, Part 2: Europe 1992," *Compensation and Benefits Review* (July-Aug. 1990): 25–35.

57. These have been identified by Podsakoff, Greene, and McFillen. See also P. Nulty, "Incentive Pay Can Be Crippling," *Fortune* (November 13, 1995): 235.

58. Z. Schiller, "A Model Incentive Plan Gets Caught in a Vise," *Business Week* (January 22, 1996): 89–90.

59. Lawler, *Pay and Organizational Effectiveness;* Lawler, *Pay and Organizational Development;* R. B. Goettinger, "Why Isn't Incentive Compensation Working?" *Personnel Journal* (June 1982): 436–442; S. R. Collins, "Incentive Programs: Pros and Cons," *Personnel Journal* (July 1981): 571–576.

60. W. F. Whyte, "Skinnerian Theory in Organizations," *Psychology Today* (April 1972): 67–68, 96, 98, 100.

61. J. D. McMillan and V. C. Williams, "The Elements of Effective Salary Administration Programs," *Personnel Journal*

(Nov. 1982): 832–838; T. A. Mahoney, "Compensating for Work," in *Personnel Management,* K. N. Rowland and G. R. Ferris, eds. (Boston, MA: Allyn-Bacon, 1982): 227–262. For a case study of merit pay assessment issues, see S. C. Freedman, "Performance-Based Pay: A Convenience Store Case Study," *Personnel Journal* (July 1985): 30–34; J. R. Terborg and G. R. Ungson, "Group Administered Bonus Pay and Retail Store Performance: A Two Year Study of Management Compensation," *Journal of Retailing* (Spring 1985): 63–77.

62. See note 6.

63. "Aligning Compensation with Quality," *Bulletin to Management* (April 1, 1993): 97.

64. T. Engle and S. McFather, "Rewards and Recognition for Generation X," *ACA News* (October/November 1995).

16

CHAPTER

Indirect Compensation

Learning Objectives

1. Describe why the area of indirect compensation is so important to U.S. corporations.
2. Describe the various public and private protection programs.
3. Thoroughly discuss healthcare benefits.
4. Discuss the alternative life-cycle benefits.
5. Describe the numerous legal considerations in indirect compensation.

> *"People come here for the benefits, and they stay for them. . . . Turnover is very expensive, and our benefits keep our rate down."*
>
> *Bradley Honeycut*
> *Director of Compensation and Benefits*
> *Starbuck's Coffee Company*[1]

Chapter Outline

MANAGING HUMAN RESOURCES

at Steelcase

Steelcase, headquartered in Grand Rapids, Michigan, is the world's leading designer and manufacturer of office furniture. It serves virtually every country of the world through 900 independently-owned dealers. Its own workforce of almost 20,000 employees is also spread throughout the world. It has over 25 manufacturing plants in the United States, six in France, three in the United Kingdom and one each in seven other countries, including Mexico, Japan, and Germany.

Steelcase is a business totally focused on the customer, quality improvement, and continuous innovation. This focus translates into their mission: "We are committed to helping your people work more effectively. How? By integrating the goals of your organization, the technology you use, and how your people work in the space they occupy. This focus governs all our research efforts and the products, services, and expertise we provide through our independent, worldwide dealer network."

Although Steelcase is a big operation with about $2.5 billion in sales, it has many competitors. One of its most significant competitors is another Michigan-based firm, Herman Miller. Others include Haworth, Inc., and Hon, Inc. Consequently, Steelcase is very concerned about managing and reducing its costs. For example, in 1986 it focused on reducing the costs of workers' compensation, essentially the costs associated with having people hurt, injured, and out-of-work. Under medical services, Steelcase developed and implemented a "return-to-work" program that has reduced the average cost per claim.

The plan has two major concepts:

1. A medical review board that systematically examines the injured person and the injury situation to make the correct diagnosis of the claim. The intent here is to uncover all the facts and build an atmosphere of trust and understanding between worker and company.
2. A return-to-work component that enables workers to get back to work as soon as possible: once the injury has been diagnosed, the biggest manageable expense is the time in getting the worker back to work. By setting up therapy centers and accommodating working conditions, Steelcase reduced time away from work for most injuries by 50 percent in six years. Their average cost per claim went from $1,552 in 1983 to $1,213 in 1996.

This program has resulted in cost savings of over $4 million per year, or over $40 million since the program's inception. Little wonder it has received the strong support of the former and current presidents and CEOs, Jerry K. Myers and Jim Hackett respectively.

Cost reduction in this area is a crucial issue for most companies because workers' comp costs have risen dramatically. Payouts in the United States have climbed from $22 billion in 1980 to $70 billion in 1996! While this is smaller than the $250 billion that employers currently pay for healthcare costs, workers' comp is rising faster.

State governments are concerned about the issue as well. Because worker claims and healthcare costs vary by state, companies in different states pay different rates for their workers' compensation insurance. In California, workers' comp claims have risen so high that firms are leaving the state, taking valuable jobs with them. (In California, the average cost per claim rose from $6,000 in 1980 to $20,000 in 1992).[2]

This feature addresses a mounting crisis in cost containment for American business. As international competition increases, U.S. firms struggle to contain their costs. For many firms, total compensation costs are a significant part of the problem. But as many firms are discovering, these costs, although significant, are manageable. Steelcase's approach is an excellent example of what firms can do to reduce their workers' comp costs. Firms are also attempting to reduce other compensation costs by asking workers to contribute to some of the expenses—for example, to pay for some of their healthcare. In some cases, firms are just cutting back on what they are willing to offer employees. Because these events are likely to continue and affect you directly (at work) or indirectly (through the price of goods and services that you buy), we devote this chapter to indirect compensation.

Indirect Compensation

Indirect compensation is in-kind payments employees receive for their being members of the company.

Indirect compensation is an issue that is garnering much attention today from organizations, workers, politicians, and the media. The changes occurring in our society—and the world—ensure that this will be a hot issue well into the twenty-first century. While specific elements of plans vary, employee benefits and services, **indirect compensation**, is generally defined as in-kind payments employees receive for their membership and/or participation in the organization. It includes such items as:

- Public protection programs
- Private protection programs
- Healthcare benefits
- Paid leave
- Life-cycle benefits

Several of these categories are mandated by federal and state governments and must therefore be administered within the boundaries of laws and regulations. Many others are provided voluntarily by organizations and vary with the organization.

Indirect compensation provides protection against health- and accident-related problems and ensure income at the end of one's work cycle. Legally required payments include Social Security, unemployment compensation, and workers' compensation; private protection programs include healthcare, life insurance, and disability insurance. Retirement income is provided through pensions and savings plans. Benefits programs also include pay for time not at work (for example, vacations, holidays, sick leave and absence pay, breaks, and wash-up and clean-up time). A growing category of benefits relates to changing lifestyles. These benefits enable an employee to enjoy a better lifestyle or to meet social or personal obligations while minimizing employment-related costs. Discounts, education assistance, and childcare and eldercare fall into this category.

LEARNING OBJECTIVE 1

Describe why the area of indirect compensation is so important to U.S. corporations.

Why Is Indirect Compensation Important?

Indirect compensation (also referred to as benefits) is provided by firms to attract and retain valued employees. Until recently, employers provided relatively generous benefits, but the tide has shifted for several reasons. First, it is a major, increasingly costly part of total compensation. In 1929, total benefits payments were 5 percent of total pay. By 1995, benefits had risen to 40 percent of wages and salaries, or roughly \$7 per payroll hour or \$14,678 per year per employee.[3] While these numbers are large and represent substantial dollars for employers, there are major differences across industries. Indirect compensation tends to be a bit greater on average in the manufacturing industries than in the nonmanufacturing industries, and it's greater for blue-collar workers than for white-collar and service workers.[4] Benefits are also higher in mature companies compared to start-up companies, and in companies with union representation.[5]

Regardless of the type of worker or sector of the economy, the cost of benefits to organizations is enormous. While wages and salaries have increased forty-fold over the past 50 years, indirect compensation has increased even more—500 times.[6]

There are several reasons why organizations pump so much money into benefits programs. They believe that benefits help by:

- Attracting good employees
- Increasing employee morale
- Reducing turnover
- Increasing job satisfaction
- Motivating employees
- Enhancing the organization's image among employees and in the business community
- Making better use of compensation dollars

Did You KNOW?

Concerns about wage and benefit costs make small firms reluctant to hire more employees.

Unfortunately, there is ample research to demonstrate that these purposes are not always attained, largely because of inadequate communication. As a consequence, firms are now sending their employees more information about their benefits.[7]

Another important reason some of the purposes of indirect compensation are not attained is that employees often regard compensation benefits, not as rewards, but as conditions (rights) of employment. They also think of indirect benefits as safeguards provided by the organization as a social responsibility because they are not provided by society.[8]

Even when indirect compensation is regarded as a reward, its importance from the viewpoint of employees relative to other aspects of the organization (for example, opportunity for advancement, salary, geographic location, job responsibilities, and prestige of the job) can be low, therefore, making its motivational value less than it otherwise could be. Offering flexibility to employees in choice of indirect compensation packages tends to increase the motivational value.[9]

The perception that the benefits firms provide are very costly also increases motivational value. This perception is growing as some firms reduce or even eliminate benefits and ask workers to share the costs of providing them. This is called **cost sharing**. In the process workers learn, not only the costs, but also the range of benefits.

Cost sharing **means that companies ask employees to pay some of the costs of their benefits.**

External Influences

The skyrocketing growth in the type and cost of employee benefits can be traced to several environmental trends.

- **Wage controls.** The imposition of wage controls during World War II and the Korean War forced organizations to offer more and greater benefits in lieu of wage increases to attract new employees.
- **Healthcare costs.** Healthcare costs have been increasing at an alarming rate. In 1940, U.S. healthcare expenses were $4 billion, about 4 percent of GDP. In 1995, they were more than $900 billion, or 15 percent of GDP. For employers, the average health-benefit cost per employee was almost $4,000 in 1995. Although these costs had been rising faster than inflation, they appear to be under control today.[10] The same appears to be the case, although less so for workers' compensation.[11]
- **Union bargaining.** From 1935 into the 1980s, unions were able to gain steady increases in wages and benefits for their members. As currently conceptualized, practically all benefits are mandatory bargaining items that require an employer to bargain in good faith at union proposals to add benefits.[12]

Through more aggressive use of managed healthcare, companies have been able to slow the growth of healthcare costs dramatically since 1994.

General Motors (UAW)

Benefits

- **Full healthcare coverage with no deductibles or copayments, vision and dental care**
- **Full pension after 30 years**
- **Life insurance; disability benefits**
- **Legal services**
- **Supplemental unemployment benefits**

Cost Per Hour Of Labor: $43.00

Quaker grants bonuses of as much as $500 for families who exercise, shun smoking, and wear seat belts. Employees can keep the money or invest in added benefits.

- **Federal tax policies.** Income tax legislation has had, and continues to have, a critical influence on the design of benefits packages. Employers are interested in benefits expenses that include pretax business costs; employees want to receive benefits without the burden of increased taxation.
- **Inflation.** Benefits managers, more so than compensation managers, must anticipate the effects of inflation on medical service, education, and pension benefits. For example, double-digit inflation in the 1980s eroded the purchasing power of some retirees and resulted in adjustments in the level of benefits.
- **Competition.** Most companies label their benefit packages as "competitive." Due to increased competition, many companies are going beyond mere statements and developing innovative packages of benefits to attract and retain employees. Wellness programs, health screenings, and employee assistance programs are examples of new benefits options. Flexible benefit plans or cash options instead of benefits are new responses to external competitive pressures.
- **Social Legislation.** A variety of laws including the *Family Leave and Medical Act* of 1993, the *Americans with Disabilities Act* of 1990 (ADA), the *Age Discrimination in Employment Act,* the *Health Maintenance Organization Act* of 1973, and the *Employee Retirement Income Security Act* (ERISA) have been passed that significantly affect the administration and offering of indirect compensation.
- **Expansion of Social Security.** In 1935, the *Social Security Act* covered 60 percent of all workers. Subsequently, the scope of benefits and the percentage of eligible workers has increased substantially. Now 95 percent of all workers are covered and receive disability and health benefits in addition to retirement pay.

LEARNING OBJECTIVE 2

Describe the various public and private protection programs.

Protection programs assist employees and their families if and when their direct pay is stopped to help pay for healthcare expenses.

Public protection programs are those provided by the government to assist employees and their families.

Public Protection Programs

Protection programs are designed to assist the employee and his or her family if and when the employee's income (direct compensation) is terminated and to alleviate the burden of healthcare expenses. Protection programs required by federal and state government are referred to as public programs, and those voluntarily offered by organizations are called private programs. The various programs in each are listed in Exhibit 16.1.

The Social Security System

Public protection programs are the outgrowth of the *Social Security Act.* The act initially set up systems for retirement benefits, disability, and unemployment insurance. Health insurance, particularly Medicare, was added in 1966 to provide hospital insurance to almost everyone age 65 and older.

Funding of the Social Security system is provided by equal contributions from the employer and employee under terms of the *Federal Insurance Contribution Act* (FICA). Initially, employee and employer paid 1 percent of the employee's income up to $3,000. Currently, they pay Social Security tax on the first $62,700 of the employee's income at the rate of 6.2 percent (for retirement and disability) and total of income at the rate of 1.45 percent (for hospital insurance via Medicare).

Did You KNOW?

Today, only about 65% of men aged 55-64 are in the labor force, down from 83% in 1970.

The average Social Security benefit for a single person is about $8,640; for a married couple it is about $15,000 per year, with adjustments made for increases in the Consumer Price Index. The maximum benefits from Social Security are now around $1,248 a month for a person aged 65 who retired in 1996. Retired people aged 65 to 69 can earn about $11,000 annually without sacrificing benefits;

EXHIBIT 16.1

Protection Programs

COVERAGE	PRIVATE PLANS	PUBLIC PLANS
Retirement	• Defined-benefit pensions • Defined-contribution pensions • Money purchase and thrift plans (401(k)s and ESOPs)	• Social Security old age benefits
Death	• Group term-life insurance (including accidental death and travel insurance) • Payouts from profit-sharing pension, and/or thrift plans • Dependent survivors' benefits	• Social Security survivors' benefits • Workers' compensation
Disability	• Short-term accident and sickness insurance • Long-term disability insurance	• Workers' compensation • Social Security disability benefits • State disability benefits
Unemployment	• Supplemental unemployment benefits and/or severance pay	• Unemployment benefits
Medical/dental expenses	• Hospital/surgical insurance • Other medical insurance • Dental insurance	• Workers' compensation • Medicare

beneficiaries under age 65 can earn about $8,000. Recipients aged 70 or older may earn any amount without a reduction in benefits.[13]

Did You KNOW?

Almost all economists agree that businesses pass along the cost of Social Security in the form of lower wages.

Unemployment Compensation Benefits

To control costs, the *Social Security Act* dictates that unemployment compensation programs be jointly administered through the federal and state governments. Because income levels vary from state to state, unemployment compensation also varies by state, although the federal rate is the same for all states ($133.00). Consequently, the total tax liability to a company varies greatly across the country as shown in Exhibit 16.2.

All profit-making organizations pay a tax on the first $7,000 to $10,000 of wages paid to each employee. The state contribution rate for employers, however, varies according to the number of unemployed people drawing from the fund.[14] Consequently, during periods of high unemployment, employers make larger contributions than they do during periods of stable employment.

To be eligible for benefits, an employee must:

- Have worked a specified number of weeks (set by the state)
- Be able and available to work
- Be actively looking for work
- Not be unemployed due to a labor dispute (except in Rhode Island and New York)
- Not have been terminated for gross misconduct
- Not have terminated voluntarily

EXHIBIT 16.2

Employer's Tax Liability for Unemployment Insurance, 1995

Total Tax Liability per Employee, by State

RANK	STATE	TOTAL TAX	RANK	STATE	TOTAL TAX
1	Rhode Island	$660.80	27	Arkansas	$254.00
2	Hawaii	540.40	28	Wyoming	234.50
3	Alaska	534.00	29	Missouri	226.00
4	Connecticut	496.00	30	Kentucky	224.00
5	Michigan	474.00	31	Mississippi	210.00
6	Massachusetts	466.40	32	Louisiana	209.00
7	Washington	454.00	33	Utah	204.50
8	Pennsylvania	448.00	34	North Dakota	203.40
9	District of Columbia	416.00	35	New Hampshire	200.00
10	New York	371.00	36	Iowa	198.00
11	Illinois	362.00	37	Arizona	189.00
12	Idaho	350.00	37	South Carolina	189.00
13	New Jersey	337.60	37	Tennessee	189.00
14	Maryland	328.00	40	Florida	182.00
15	Oregon	322.00	41	Colorado	176.00
16	California	308.00	42	Georgia	175.00
16	Maine	308.00	42	Oklahoma	173.70
16	Ohio	308.00	44	Texas	173.00
19	West Virginia	304.00	45	Virginia	168.00
20	Delaware	302.50	46	Indiana	154.00
21	Nevada	302.00	47	Alabama	144.00
22	Minnesota	300.80	48	North Carolina	135.80
23	Wisconsin	287.00	49	Kansas	112.00
24	New Mexico	272.00	49	Nebraska	112.00
25	Montana	257.50	51	South Dakota	98.00
26	Vermont	256.00			

Source: *Bulletin to Management* (August 17, 1995): 261. Reprinted with permission by the Bureau of National Affairs, (Tel. 1-800-372-1033).

The length of time an employee may receive benefits is a function of how long the employee worked prior to termination, but the standard maximum is 26 weeks. Extended benefits of up to 13 weeks are provided during periods of high unemployment or when jobs are lost due to foreign competition. The level of benefits ranges from 50 to 70 percent of base salary up to a maximum weekly amount that varies by state (around $225). With the passage of the *Tax Reform Act* of 1986, unemployment compensation became fully taxable, making actual benefit levels much lower.[15]

Medicare

When Medicare became operational in 1966, benefits managers felt this program would be a cure-all, satisfying the healthcare needs of older Americans. Managers anticipated significant cost savings by coordinating private medical programs with Medicare. Unfortunately, this has not proved to be true. In the era of early retirements to reduce staffing levels, organizations have discovered that the assurance of continuing health coverage is a critical factor in an individual's decision to elect retirement. Because a majority of retirements occur before the age of 65 (the age for Medicare eligibility), there is a gap in healthcare coverage that must be subsumed by organizations. Medicare has progressively shifted cost responsibility to subscribers and, as a result, retirees over age 65 are demanding supplemental health benefits from their former employers.

Because employers' liabilities for post-retirement health benefits are estimated in the billions of dollars, the Financial Accounting Standards Board (FASB) has specified that these liabilities be included in corporate financial statements. A partial consequence is that organizations have begun avoiding promises of specific levels of benefits for future retirees. They have also started to reduce their liabilities by making big payments.

Workers' Compensation

As described in the opening feature on Steelcase, Inc., workers' compensation costs are of major concern to organizations. Of the more than 6.4 million job-related injuries reported annually in the private sector, about half are serious enough for the injured worker to lose work time, experience restricted work activity, or both. Almost 60 percent of these injuries are associated with repetitive motions such as vibration, repeated pressure, and carpal tunnel syndrome, and a majority require medical care and result in lost work time.[16]

Did You KNOW?

Steelcase is rated four times safer than the national average for the light-metal industry by the National Safety Council.

When such injuries or illnesses occur as a result of on-the-job concerns, workers may be eligible for **workers' compensation insurance.** Administered at the state level and fully financed by employers, workers' compensation benefits are provided for temporary and permanent disability, disfigurement, medical expenses, and medical rehabilitation. Survival benefits are provided following fatal injuries.[17]

Workers' compensation insurance provides coverage to workers who are injured on the job.

While specific terms and conditions vary by state, a job-related workers' compensation benefits are provided regardless of fault in accident. Awards can consist of lump-sum monetary benefits (for example, $10,000 for the loss of an eye), the payment of medical benefits, or long-term payments tied to the worker's income level. Currently, most states award employees who are unable to work at least two-thirds of their gross, before-injury, salary. Employer contributions to the state-managed programs are contingent on their accident rates. For many companies, these costs are growing faster than any other benefit.

There are several reasons for the increase. Even though the economy has been moving from manufacturing to service, the number of claims has doubled in the past decade. Some of the increase is due to real and debilitating diseases that science recently has linked to the workplace (for example, carpal tunnel syndrome, asbestosis). Increases are also due to fraud; a recent study estimates that 20 percent of all workers' comp claims are fraudulent.[17] To deal with phony claims, state-owned or state-managed workers' comp insurers are utilizing a variety of strategies including case monitoring, videotaping, media blitzes, and prosecution.

Did You KNOW?

Workers' compensation costs vary by state and the record of the firm. Firms in New York pay 57% more than the national average.

Proactive workers' compensation administrators such as Gil Fry at Lincoln Electric and Libby Child at Steelcase, apply a variety of healthcare cost-containment strategies to workers' comp such as:

- Developing networks of preferred provider organizations
- Specifying fees for treating workers' comp claimants
- Limiting payments to medically necessary or reasonable procedures

- Requiring precertification of hospital admissions
- Establishing concurrent review of inpatient hospital stays
- Routinely auditing hospital and healthcare bills[18]

Did You KNOW?

Illegal drug users have more on-the-job accidents and file twice as many workers comp claims.

Employers also are jumping on the cost-containment bandwagon. For example, Sprague Electric Co. in Concord, New Hampshire, assembles a team consisting of the worker's supervisor, a rehabilitation counselor, and the firm's human resource manager. Using videotaped demonstrations of the employee's job and physician input, the team identifies components of the jobs the worker can still perform, as well as appropriate accommodations that need to be made.[19]

To assertively manage workers' compensation costs, Burns of Boston, a Rhode Island-based photo frame and album manufacturer, recommends four things:

Dow's "Backs in Action" program encourages exercise, dieting, and ergonomics. The company has decreased on-the-job strains and sprains up to 90%.

1. Actively manage your workers' comp insurance carrier by using all of the services it can provide.
2. Aggressively review cases each quarter until you're satisfied that open cases are being resolved and closed appropriately.
3. Request that your carrier's loss control representative visit your office or plant location to evaluate your safety awareness program.
4. Ensure that a company representative attends every workers' comp hearing. Your presence gives incredible weight to any claims challenge and shows the hearing officer the company's concern for speedy case resolution.[20]

Did You KNOW?

At Sky Chefs Kitchen in El Paso, Texas, each morning begins with an employee-led stretching session designed to curb back injuries.

To reduce workers' compensation costs, Sky Chefs, the Arlington, Texas-based company that prepares in-flight meals for many airlines, offered its supervisors an incentive to improve the safety of their employees: 25% of their bonuses are tied to their safety records. Employees are also more responsible for training and instruction in safe handling and lifting procedures. Because of their program, lost work days have declined more than 50 percent. So instead of 8,000 employees having 1,000 injuries per year and losing 18,000 workdays, Sky Chefs is down to less than 8,500 lost workdays. With back strain their most common injury costing about $25,000 per claim, you can see how much money this can save everyone.[21]

Regardless of the fact that the costs of disability and the associated cost of workers' compensation, many companies still supplement the coverage of workers' compensation with private short-term and long-term disability insurance. This insurance pays workers unable to work because of injuries incurred off the job. In addition, they may also provide group life insurance and accidental death insurance for their employees.[22]

Private Protection Programs

Private protection programs are those provided by companies to assist employees and their families.

Private protection programs are offered by organizations but are not required by law. They include retirement income plans, capital accumulation plans, savings and thrift plans, and supplemental unemployment benefits, and guaranteed pay. Some firms also are offering work options for retirees including temporary full-time and part-time employment.

A qualified plan is a pension plan covered by the Internal Revenue Code requirements. A nonqualified plan is a pension plan not covered by the Internal Revenue Code.

The various retirement income plans can be classified in terms of whether they will be qualified or nonqualified. A **qualified plan** means that the pension plan covers a broad, nondiscriminatory class of employees, meets Internal Revenue Code requirements, and consequently receives favorable tax treatment. For example, the employer's contributions to the plan are tax deductible for the current year, and employees pay no taxes until retirement. **Nonqualified plans** do not adhere to the strict tax regulations and cover only select groups of employees. They are often utilized to provide supplemental retirement benefits for key executives.

Pension Plans

The largest category of private protection plans is pensions. Four out of five employees in medium and large firms are covered by some type of private pension or capital accumulation plan and rely on these plans to provide future security. A less-known fact is that the 20 largest pension funds (13 of them funds of public employees) hold one-tenth of the equity capital of America's publicly owned companies. All told, institutional investors—primarily pension funds—control close to 40 percent of the common stock of the country's largest businesses. Pension funds also hold 40 percent or more of the medium- and long-term debt of the country's bigger companies. Thus, employees, via their pension funds, have become one of America's largest lenders as well as business owners.[23]

Each year more and more workers become owners of companies through investments of their pension money.

Defined-Benefit Plans. With a **defined-benefit plan,** the actual benefits received on retirement vary by age and length of service of the employee. For example, an employee may receive $50 a month for each year of company service. As described in Exhibit 16.3, defined plans are preferred by paternalistic employers and unions because they produce predictable, secure, and continuing income. Another advantage of defined-benefit plans is that they are carefully regulated by the *Employees' Retirement Income Security Act.* In addition to the reporting,

In defined-benefits plans, employees know exactly what monthly pay they get during retirement.

EXHIBIT 16.3

Comparison of Defined-Benefit and Defined-Contribution Pension Funds

ASPECT	DEFINED-BENEFIT PLAN	DEFINED-CONTRIBUTION PLAN
1. Definition	Benefits vary by age and length of service according to a formula. Set amount received.	Each employee has an account to which personal, and/or corporate contributions are made.
2. Source of funding	Majority funded entirely by company contributions. Some public-sector funds require employee participation.	Employer and employee both contribute to the plan. Formulas are 50-50 or higher employer to employee contribution.
3. Prevalence	20 percent of new plans. Majority of existing plans.	80 percent of new plans. Minority of existing plans.
4. Supporting culture	Paternalistic, mature, union.	Competitive, participative, start-up.
5. ERISA control	Must meet ERISA funding requirements. Must have termination insurance. Excise tax on asset reversions.	No set funding requirement. No plan termination insurance.
6. Advantages to employee	Guaranteed level of retirement income.	No set retirement income. Based on profitability of investments.
7. Disadvantages to employee	Pension may not be enough to maintain standard of living.	Contributions restricted, early withdrawals penalized, loans limited. Must contribute funds to activate.
8. Advantages to employer	Contributions are tax deductible. Rewards long-term employee.	Less costly. Less risky.
9. Disadvantages to employer	Difficult to determine how to credit employees before fund was started. May be underfunded.	Contributions increase as employees' income goes up.

Source: Adapted from R M. McCaffery, *Employee Benefit Programs. A Total Compensation Perspective* (Boston, MA: PWS-Kent, 1992).

disclosure, fiduciary standard, plan participation rules, and vesting standards, defined-benefit plans must adhere to specific funding-level requirements and be insured against plan termination due to economic hardship, misfunding, or corporate buyouts.

The Pension Benefit Guaranty Corporation (PBGC) administers a required insurance program and guarantees the payment of basic retirement benefits if a pension plan is terminated.

The **Pension Benefit Guaranty Corporation (PBGC)** administers the required insurance program and guarantees the payment of basic retirement benefits to participants if a plan is terminated. The PBGC can also terminate pension funds that are seriously underfunded. In July, 1991, they moved to do exactly that with Pan Am's pension fund. The airline had missed three required funding contributions over the past year. According to James Lockhart, executive director for PBGC, "We had to act immediately to keep the pension insurance safety net strong for workers and retirees and stem the rising costs for companies with well-funded pension plans."

When a plan is terminated, employees who participated in the plan are guaranteed to receive what they contributed. In the case of Pan Am, this covered 34,000 participants, including 11,000 retirees enrolled in Pan Am's Cooperative Retirement Income Plan and 750 participants in the Defined-Benefit Plan for Flight Engineers. According to Lockhart, PBGC lost more than $600 million due to the mismanagement of this plan alone. Losses like this explain why PBGC's long-term deficit now tops more than $2 billion and why retirement programs are feared to be the next "savings and loan crisis" of the 1990s.[24]

In defined-contribution plans, usually both the employer and employee contribute. This is in the spirit of cost-sharing.

In defined-contribution plans, employees know exactly what is put in, but they don't know what the payments will be during retirement.

Defined-Contribution Plans. Eighty percent of new plans are **defined-contribution plans.** With this type of plan, each employee has a separate account to which employee and employer contributions are added. Typically, the employee must activate the plan by agreeing to contribute a set amount of money the employer then matches the percentage contribution to a specific level. Defined-contribution plans are more prevalent in competitive, participative organizations.

Money-purchase plans are defined-contribution pension plans to which the employer makes fixed contributions.

The two most common types of defined-contribution plans are money-purchase and tax-deferred profit-sharing plans. With **money purchase plans**, the employer makes fixed, regular contributions for participants, usually a percentage of total pay, to a fund. Employees may also make voluntary contributions. The maximum amount is equal to 25 percent of earned income, up to a maximum of $30,000 for all defined-contribution plans. Monies are held in trust funds; and the employee is given several investment options that differ in terms of the degree of risk and growth potential. At retirement, accumulated funds are used to provide annuities. In some cases, lump-sum distributions are made.

Tax-deferred profit-sharing plans are those to which contributions are made tax-deferred until withdrawal.

Tax-deferred profit-sharing plans provide for employee participation in profit sharing using a predetermined formula. Monies contributed to these plans are set aside until retirement when the employees can cash in their profits. From the employer's perspective, tax-deferred profit-sharing plans are useful because they deduct up to 15 percent of participants' compensation (up to an income level of $200,000) for profit-sharing contributions. Additionally, they pass on the investment risk to the employee.[25]

Supplemental Plans

Did You KNOW?

401(k) plans are becoming very popular because employer and employee both contribute and the employee is responsible for the investment decisions.

In addition to Social Security and standard pension plans, large firms often offer a supplemental defined-contribution plan or savings plan. Currently, 30 percent of all employees participate in supplemental plans. Such plans serve as the third leg of the retirement income stool: they provide additional retirement income or serve as a source for accumulating funds to meet short-term needs and goals. These plans take one of two forms: savings plans that work as defined-contribution plans [called 401(k) plans], and employee stock ownership plans (ESOPs) described in Chapter 15.[26]

As provided in the Internal Revenue Code, a key feature of a savings plan is that the employee must elect to participate in the program by setting aside a small percentage of pay. Other features of the plan include loan provisions and limited in-service withdrawal for hardship or for employment termination. Participants can elect to receive their entire contribution in a lump sum upon retirement or termination. ESOPs have the feature of giving employees a sense of ownership in the firm through stock ownership.[27]

Individual Retirement Accounts

Under current jaw, an employee who is not an active participant in an employer-sponsored pension plan during any part of a year may contribute up to $2,000 unconditionally to an **Individual Retirement Account (IRA).** The latter provision applies only if a joint tax return is filed. Employees who are involved in employer-sponsored pension plans also may participate, providing their income does not surpass limits set by the IRS.

An Individual Retirement Account (IRA) is a tax-favored retirement plan for employees who are not covered by an employer sponsored plan.

Guaranteed Pay Plans

A relatively new type of income guarantee involves providing guaranteed pay to nonexempt employees who are laid off. Such plans protect employee income during periods of involuntary unemployment. In automotive, steel and related industries, the protection project is in the form of **supplemental unemployment benefits** plans. Such plans provide income safety nets by providing corporate-financed unemployment benefits—up to 85 percent of regular take-home pay for up to three years.[28]

Supplemental unemployment benefits are those given to some employees as a safety net during times of unemployment.

Healthcare Benefits

LEARNING OBJECTIVE 3

Thoroughly discuss healthcare benefits.

Coverage for medical expenses including hospital charges, physician charges, and other medical services is the core of a group health plan and will be discussed first. Organizations may also provide wellness programs, employee assistance programs, and short- and long-term disability insurance. Because the cost is far below what employees would pay on their own, health benefits—particularly medical insurance—represent an important, although costly, benefit. Unfortunately, most employees underestimate the cost of health benefits to the organization and view coverage as an entitlement rather than a costly benefit. In a recent study, more than 80 percent of all workers said their employers are obligated to provide healthcare for them, but almost half of the employees did not know what their health insurance cost their employer.[29]

In reality, healthcare costs more than $900 billion or 15 percent of the nation's gross domestic product (GDP). Employer-funded healthcare costs, like workers' compensation, double every five years. To fund the rising healthcare costs, businesses are passing the burden on to consumers. For example, Detroit automakers estimate that $500 to $700 is added to the retail price of each automobile to pay for employee healthcare costs.[30]

Did You KNOW?

41% of full-time workers are without health insurance?

Medical Care Approaches

Employers can finance and provide medical expense benefits to employees and their dependents in different ways. The most widely used source for financing group medical benefits involves insurance companies. However, a variety of other approaches are gaining in popularity as businesses attempt to thwart rising costs.

Lincoln Electric offers its employees one of four healthcare plans that the employees can buy.

Insurance Companies. Insurance carriers offer a broad range of healthcare services from which employers can select coverage. Premiums are set and adjusted depending on usage rates and increases in healthcare costs. The insurance company administers the plan, handling all the paperwork, approvals, and problems. Proponents of this approach argue that insurers protect the plan sponsor against wide fluctuations in claims experience and costs and offer opportunities for participation in larger risk pools. Insurance companies also have administrative expertise related to certification reviews, claim audits, coordination of benefits, and other cost containment services.

Did You KNOW?

Fewer employees are joining traditional healthcare plans.

Did You KNOW?

More employees are joining managed care programs . . .

- **48% in 1992**
- **52% in 1993**
- **63% in 1994**
- **71% in 1995**

Provider Organizations. Blue Cross/Blue Shield associations are nonprofit organizations that operate within defined geographic areas. While Blue Cross plans cover hospital expenses, Blue Shield plans provide benefits for charges by physicians and other medical providers. Typically, these associations negotiate arrangements with their member hospitals and physicians to reimburse the hospital or physician at a discounted rate when a subscriber incurs a charge. As originally established, the rate represents full payment for the service, and there is no additional charge. However, recently skyrocketing costs in healthcare have resulted in deductibles ($50 to 250 per year per person) and cost-sharing (10 to 20 percent) on the part of employees.

Health Maintenance Organizations. A survey of almost 2,000 firms found that 80 percent of all organizations now offer healthcare through **health maintenance organizations (HMOs)**.[31]

Health Maintenance Organizations **(HMOs) offer health insurance as an alternative to regular group healthcare coverage.**

The growth in HMOs was stimulated by the passage of the *Health Maintenance Organization Act* of 1973 (HMO). This act requires that companies with at least 25 employees living in an HMO service area must offer membership in that organization to employees as an alternative to regular group health coverage, provided the HMO meets federal qualification requirements. HMO amendments of 1988 relaxed many of the federal rules governing HMOs and specifically repealed the dual-choice alternative, effective in October 1995. This shift in legislative direction is designed to make the HMO field more competitive and, as a result, employers more receptive to using HMOs.

Preferred-Provider Networks. Preferred-provider organizations (PPOs) are a relatively new option in healthcare delivery. Introduced in the 1980s, these plans cover 55 to 60 million participants. With these programs employers contract directly—or indirectly through an insurance company—with a provider organization to secure agreements from healthcare providers (physicians, dentists, laboratories, hospitals) to deliver services to group health plan participants on a discounted basis. Because these plans are relatively unregulated with respect to rate setting and requirements, employers have a great deal of flexibility in structuring an arrangement.

Preferred-Provider Organization **(PPOs) are those that have agreements with companies to provide healthcare to their employees at a discount.**

Unlike HMOs, employees are not required to use PPO providers exclusively. However, there are usually incentives (lower deductibles or cost-sharing) when a PPO is utilized. For example, the employer may cover all healthcare costs provided by a PPO but only 80 percent of the cost of care provided by physicians outside of the PPO network.[32]

Did You KNOW?

The Camberley Hotel in Atlanta reduced healthcare costs and employee turnover when it became self-insured.

Self-Funded Plans. A growing number of companies are opting for self-insured or self-funded plans as a way to control medical plan costs and gain relief from state insurance regulations. By eliminating or reducing insurance protection, the employer saves on carrier retention charges (the amount of money not utilized to pay claims). This includes such things as state premium taxes, administrative costs, risk and contingency expenses, and reserve requirements. Typically, the employer creates a voluntary employee beneficiary association and establishes a tax-exempt trust. The trust's investment income is tax-exempt as long as it is used to provide benefits to employees and their dependents.

Cost Containment Strategies. To further control costs, firms are also employing a variety of cost containment strategies. While no strategy can hold the line on soaring medical costs, these strategies represent employers' best efforts to date to control costs. Some of the more common strategies include:

- **Hospital utilization programs** that review the necessity and appropriateness of hospitalization prior to admission and/or during a stay
- **Coordination of benefits** with other providers to prevent duplicate payment for the same healthcare service

- **Data analysis** to determine the most viable cost management approach. Simulations and experience-based utilization assumptions are used to develop models.
- **Managed care** with many employers active participants in case management, especially through working with HMOs. Interventions include requirements for second opinions and peer reviews.[33]
- **Cost-sharing with employees** by raising deductibles and contribution levels. Employers thus hold the line on overall expenses.
- **Incentives** that some firms hope will change employees' behaviors so they are healthier. While this may have substantial merit, it can also have substantial risks.[34] In the worst case, companies may be in violation of the *Americans with Disabilities Act* if individuals with specific disabilities are treated differently than employees without the disability. There are also ethical dilemmas. While employees may consider it fair to give premium rebates for healthy lifestyles, most would not tolerate raises in premiums for genetically linked conditions. To stimulate your own debate and discussion, the issues here are discussed further in the feature, "HR Advice and Application: Ethics and Lifestyle."

Wellness Programs

Frustrated with efforts to manage healthcare costs for employees who are already sick, a growing number of employers are taking proactive steps to prevent healthcare problems. Moving beyond employee exercise classes and stress management classes, a handful of firms are implementing carefully designed wellness programs, which are producing significant savings on the bottom line.[35]

For example, the Adolph Coors Company based in Golden, Colorado, has spent the past ten years fine-tuning its wellness program. For every dollar spent on wellness, Coors sees a return of $6.15, including $1.9 million annually in decreased medical costs, reduced sick leave, and increased productivity. According to William Coors, chairman and CEO, the secret to Coors' success is really no secret. "Wellness is an integral part of the corporate culture."[36]

Steelcase tested 4,000 workers for everything from seat-belt use to cholesterol. By promoting healthy lifestyles, the furniture maker should save $20 million over ten years.

The commitment at Coors to wellness includes a health-risk assessment, nutritional counseling, stress management, and programs for smoking cessation, weight loss, and orthopedic rehabilitation. "When employees hear health warnings and statistics on the television, the warnings are always about someone else. When they read a personalized assessment that indicates a genuine risk of heart attack based on heredity, cholesterol, and high blood pressure, the warnings take on new significance," says D. W Edmonton, Ph.D., director of the University of Michigan Fitness Research Center.

Overweight Coors' employees learn about the long-term risks associated with obesity through a health hazard survey. They're educated about the effect of excess weight on the cardiovascular, endocrine, and musculoskeletal systems. Then an individual plan is developed. The individualized program may include individual counseling, group classes, and medical programs such as Optifast. The company even gives employees a financial incentive if they participate in the program and achieve and maintain their weight loss goal during a twelve-month period. To further encourage involvement, classes are held at the company.

Coors pays bonuses for healthy habits. Employees can use the award—a maximum of $500 per family—to buy extra holidays or pay for financial planning.

Coors has been sensitive to the ADA requirements that employers cannot make entry into a wellness program conditioned on the passage of a medical exam and that facilities be accessible to all:

> *At Adolph Coors Company, in Golden, Colorado persons with disabilities have complete access to all of the company's facilities and its wellness center, says corporate communications manager, Joe Fuentes. Part of the*

HR ADVICE & APPLICATION

Ethics and Lifestyle

Just taking in a movie with someone else's wife? Laural Allen, 23, and Sam Johnson, 20, had been working for Wal-Mart in Gloversville, New York, for several months when they began dating. Neither was a supervisor, and they were employed in different departments. Says Johnson: "One day the store manager called Laural in and fired her. Later she fired me. The reason she gave is that although Laural is legally separated from her husband, she's not divorced. They didn't tell us there's a rule like that." The couple has sued for $4 million, plus back pay and reinstatement on grounds of wrongful discharge. Wal-Mart declines to comment while the case is being litigated.

Assuming Johnson's story is true, Wal-Mart's action seems such an outrageous breach of privacy that it must be illegal. But maybe not. Employers can fire employees or reject job candidates for any reason that a contract or law doesn't specifically forbid. Federal and state laws prohibit discrimination based on race, religion. age, and gender, but Washington does not protect jobs for those who tango, motorcycle, tease pit bulls, play bridge, or otherwise amuse themselves during off hours. And only a handful of states do.

The Wal-Mart case, where morality seems the issue, is unusual. More commonly, employers try to control workers' physical well-being. Why? Cautious, healthy workers cost less. A late 1980s study of 46,000 DuPont employees showed that each year the average smoker cost the company an additional $960 in medical claims and sick days; the overweight person, $401; the alcohol abuser, $369; a worker with elevated cholesterol, $370; one with high blood pressure, $343. Turner Broadcasting has refused to hire smokers since 1986. North Miami requires applicants to sign an affidavit that they have not used tobacco products for the previous year. Arlene Kurtz, a clerk typist denied a city job because she smokes, has sued, but Florida has no statute protecting smokers.

Twenty-eight other states, including Illinois, New Jersey, and New York, have passed laws shielding smokers from such discrimination, urged on by the strange bedfellowship of the tobacco industry and the American Civil Liberties Union. Eight of those states protect a range of activities. New York, for example, makes it illegal to fire an employee who during off-hours engages in sports, games, hobbies, exercise, reading, or watching TV or movies. Lewis Maltby, an ACLU attorney, argues that all legal activities that are not directly related to work should be protected. Says he: "We all do something dangerous, whether it's scuba diving or eating red meat."

He has a point. Firing an employee for having a couple of drinks after his shift is heavy-handed. An Indianapolis manufacturing company, Best Lock Corporation, did just that when it discharged Daniel Winn, a machine operator, several years ago. An alternative might be charging workers for bad habits that ultimately take money from colleagues' pockets. General Mills lowers workers' insurance premiums by as much as 20 percent if they live healthfully. Among the - half-dozen measurements: wearing seat belts, not smoking; drinking moderately or not at all, and controlling weight and blood pressure.

Beginning next year, Butterworth Hospital of Grand Rapids, Michigan, will offer its 5,000 employees financial incentives to live healthfully—and will punish those who don't. Staffers who hew to the proper lifestyle will find up to $25 extra in each biweekly paycheck. Employees who do poorly on tests or who refuse to cooperate will be docked up to $25 every two weeks. Some employees consider the policy overbearing. Says one nurse, Julie Ostrander: "I resent someone else trying to control my behavior."

Genes determine weight and cholesterol levels as much as diet does. Should workers be penalized for their parentage? And how does the employer find out whether a worker gets tipsy on a Saturday night? Before adopting such programs, companies ought to consider the consequences thoroughly.[37]

wellness program includes a medical questionnaire that determines employees' "health age" in relation to their "chronological age," Fuentes says. The program is totally voluntary for employees, he adds.

The questionnaire asks employees whether they smoke, wear a seat belt, have high blood pressure, and exercise, and also includes questions about the employees' medical history, Fuentes says. All Coors employees are cov-

ered by their health insurance at 85 percent, he notes. Employees that pass the questionnaire are then covered at 90 percent. If employees fail the test, they can have a plan of action recommended by the community outreach person who runs the program, he explains.

Test results are confidential and made available only to the community outreach person who administers the survey, Fuentes notes. In addition, employees can choose not to follow up on the test results. Thus far, he says, there have been no legal conflicts with ADA.[38]

Employee Assistance Programs

Whereas wellness programs attempt to prevent healthcare problems, **employee assistance programs (EAPs)** are specifically designed to assist employees with chronic personal problems that hinder their job performance and attendance as presented in Chapter 13. EAPs are often used with employees who are alcoholics, have drug dependencies, or who have severe domestic problems that interfere with competency on the job. EAPs also assist employees in coping with mental disorders, financial problems, stress, eating disorders, and smoking cessation. They provide dependent-care programs, bereavement counseling, and AIDS support group meetings.[39] Because the job may be partly responsible for these problems, some employers are taking the lead in establishing EAPs to help affected workers.[40] Thus EAPs serve as an important form of indirect compensation that benefits the individual and the firm.

Employee Assistance Programs (EAPs) assist employees with chronic personal problems that hinder their performance and attendance.

Paid Leave

Paid leave is not as complex to administer as benefits from protection programs, but it is certainly the more costly, accounting for more than 10 percent of the total payroll. If absenteeism policies are not designed correctly, costs can escalate even further. The two major categories are time not worked off the job (holidays, vacations, sick days) and time not worked on the job (rest periods, wash-up times, lunches).[41]

Off-the-Job

The most common paid off-the-job components are vacations, sick leave, holidays, and personal days. The challenge in administering these benefits is to contain the costs of these programs while seeking better ways to package them.

Vacations. Vacations are granted because employees need time to recuperate away from the physical and mental demands of work. It is also believed that vacation time is an appropriate reward for service and commitment to the organization. Recently, a small number of firms have granted sabbaticals to employees (similar to those in academia), which after a stated period of service can be used for self-improvement, community work, or teaching. Tandem Computers, which has been granting six-week sabbaticals plus normal vacation time at full pay, claims that in the short term such programs have a negative impact on productivity, but in the long term they enhance productivity.

Length of vacations tend to vary by industry, locale, company size, and profession. Some firms believe that longer vacations for more senior employees help to counterbalance salary compression problems. However, there are no hard data to suggest that employees view this as a fair exchange.[42]

Starbucks' employees, part-timers included, get paid vacations plus stock options. Given the company's astounding growth, a typical employee who bought into the stock plan in 1991 could now enjoy a whopping $15,840 in net profits on a $2,160 investment.

In setting up vacation programs, several issues need to be addressed: 1) Will vacation pay be based on scheduled hours or on hours actually worked? 2) Under what circumstances can an employee be paid in lieu of a vacation? 3) Can vacations be deferred, or will they be lost if not taken? 4) What pay rate applies if an employee works during a vacation? The trend is toward vacation "banking," with employees able to roll over a specified period of unused vacation days into a savings investment plan.[43]

Holidays. Employees in the United States average about ten paid holidays a year. However, the actual days vary by industry and locale. For example, in some southern states, the birthdays of Jefferson Davis and Robert B. Lee are observed, in Utah there is Mormon Pioneer Day, and in Alaska there is Steward's Day.

Trends in union contract negotiations include floater holidays that meet employee preferences, as well as personal holidays in recognition of the employee's birthday. Conversely, other organizations are cutting back on the number of paid holidays because they are an investment with marginal return. Companies are also moving toward established holiday pay policies such as "In order to be eligible for holiday pay, an employee must perform work on the day before and the day after the holiday." Obviously, these policies are intended to deter absenteeism They are also intended to reduce costs. According to the data shown in Exhibit 16.4, the employers spend about $3,500 for vacations and holidays for the average worker.

EXHIBIT 16.4

Average Annual Employee Benefits and Earnings

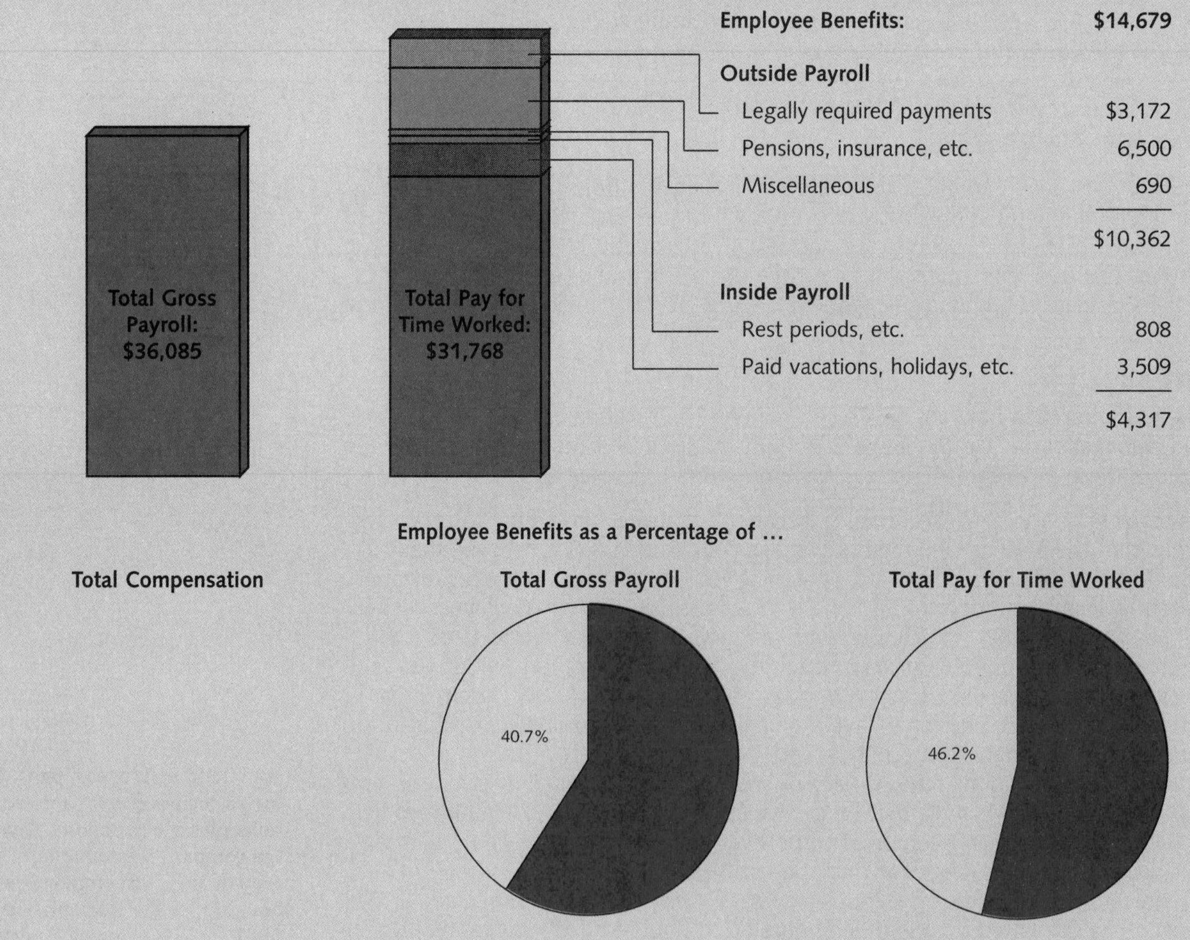

Source: *Bulletin to Management* (December 21, 1995): 405. Reprinted with permission by the Bureau of National Affairs (Tel. 1-800-372-1033).

Paid Absences. On any given day, 1 million American workers who are otherwise employed will be absent from work. In the United States, the absenteeism rate ranges from 2 to 3 percent of total payroll. However, some organizations report absenteeism in excess of 20 percent. An estimated 400 million person days are lost each year as a result of employee absenteeism. This is almost ten times the number of person days lost to strikes over a ten-year period.[44]

In comparison with other countries, the United States is midrange. Japan and Switzerland have lower absenteeism rates; Italy, France, and Sweden report substantially higher rates. The problem in Italy became so severe at one point that police began arresting some of the habitual absentees, charging them with fraud.[45]

What makes absenteeism so problematic is the cost of employee replacement. It has been estimated that for every 1 percent change in the national absentee rates, the gross national product goes down by $20 billion. Absenteeism at General Motors has been estimated to cost $1 billion annually.[46]

While there are many reasons employees do not attend work (health, family problems, transportation difficulties), there is evidence that absences are proportional to the number of paid days off offered by an organization. That is, as the number of paid days off increases, the number of days of actual absence increases proportionally. As pay rates rise, absenteeism also increases, with employees potentially "buying" time off. Consequently, because of lax policies, many organizations unwittingly not only tolerate or accept absenteeism, but actually reward it. Their policies make it easier to be absent than to come to work.[47]

Negative strategies to control absenteeism include disciplinary procedures against employees who are absent weekly, once every two weeks, without a physician's excuse, before or after a holiday, after payday, without calling in, or for personal business. Absences for these reasons are subject to employee discipline ranging from oral warnings for first offenses to discharge. Unfortunately, these policies appear to be generally ineffective in controlling absenteeism among habitual offenders.

Programs that reward attendance—cash prizes, bonuses, conversion of a proportion of unused absence days to vacation days—appear more promising. To prevent unscheduled absenteeism, organizations have also moved toward a policy of paid leave for "personal days off." The logic here is that employees must notify officials in advance that they will be absent. As discussed in Chapter 10, self-management programs for habitual offenders also offer some hope to controlling excessive absenteeism.[48]

On-the-Job

Paid benefits for time not worked on-the-job include rest periods, lunch periods, wash-up time, and clothes-change and get-ready times. Together these benefits are the fifth most expensive indirect compensation benefit.

Another benefit that is growing in popularity is paid time for physical fitness. This is clearly pay for time not worked, but organizations often offer it because of its benefit—healthy workers.

Life-Cycle Benefits

LEARNING OBJECTIVE 4

Discuss the alternative life-cycle benefits.

In response to a growing number of single parents, two-earner families, employees with aging parents in need of care, and nontraditional families, employers are expanding their benefits packages to address new priorities.[49] As shown in Exhibit 16.5, only a handful of firms currently offer these benefits. However, employers realize that a failure to address these needs in the near future will restrict their ability to compete. Three categories of life-cycle-related benefits—childcare, eldercare, changing lifestyle—will be discussed in greater detail below.

Childcare Services

Recognizing that childcare is a shared responsibility, more and more employers are providing childcare assistance to their employees. In fact, a survey of more than

EXHIBIT 16.5

Prevalence of Selected Life-Cycle Benefits for 1990 and Projected for Year 2000

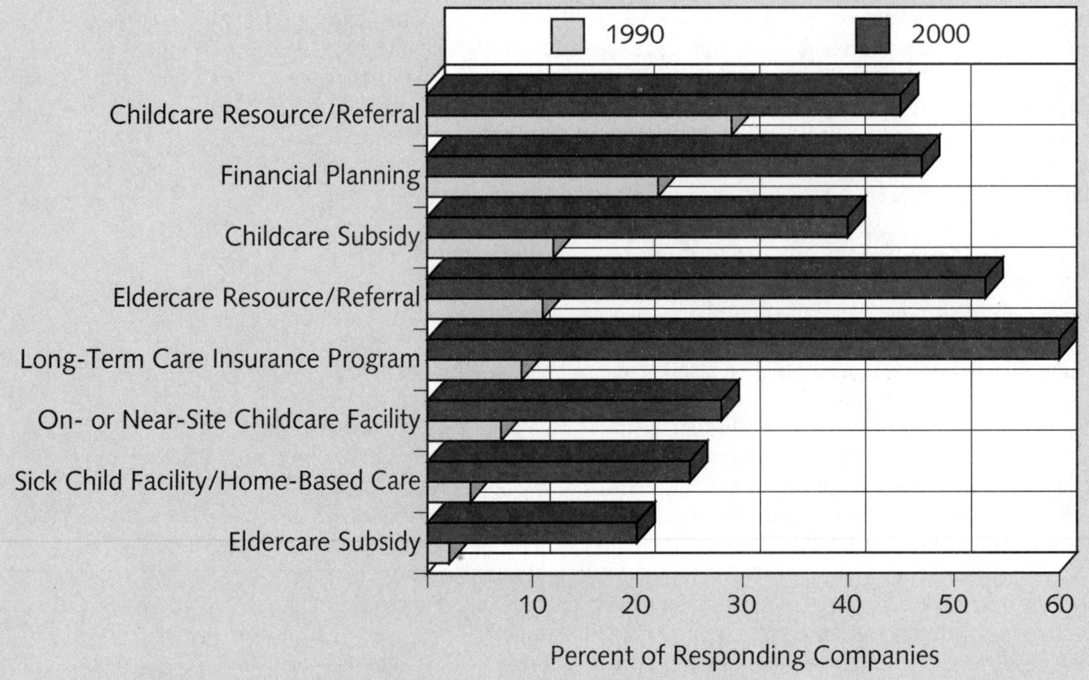

Source: International Foundation of Employee Benefit Plans

Being family-friendly means the employee offers many life-cycle benefits.

At J&J, employees can bring their infants in for free tests and checkups six times annually. Prevention saves $13 million a year.

10,000 firms employing ten or more workers showed that 63 percent of all employers offer some benefits, schedule help, or services relating to childcare. Employee preferences for various childcare options vary. Thus, in order to remain competitive, firms need, at a minimum, to survey their employees to find out their preferences, and they may need to offer a variety of options to meet employee needs. Exhibit 16.6 shows a possible list of options that employers can provide. By providing options such as these, employers such as Ben & Jerry's, develop an image of being family-friendly. The benefits of having such an image are described in "Managing Human Resources at Johnson & Johnson and Fel-Pro." While the family-friendly benefits are provided at some cost, employees can share in these costs through dependent-care reimbursement accounts.

EXHIBIT 16.6

Family-Friendly Benefits

Summer day camp	On-site childcare	Childcare referrals
Scholarships	Eldercare	Familycare leave
Summer employment	Flexible schedules	Eldercare referrals
Emergency care for adults	Familycare absence	Spouse relocation
Subsidized tutoring	Relocation planning	Adoption benefits
Sick child care	Assistance plans	Reimbursement accounts

Source: Adapted from B. P. Noble, "Making a Case for Family Friendly Programs," *The New York Times* (May 2, 1993): F25.

MANAGING HUMAN RESOURCES

at Johnson & Johnson and Fel-Pro

It is hard-sell gospel among advocates of "family-friendly" or "family-supportive" corporate policies that helping employees helps the bottom line. But gospel doesn't crunch as well as numbers, and the unsentimental, lynx-eyed financial types who prowl the balance sheets of corporate America in these lean times tend to be nonbelievers.

Researchers are beginning to accumulate the systematic, hard evidence that advocates need to make their case. According to two studies, companies that make it easier for employees to juggle their work and family responsibilities do reap gains in greater loyalty, increased job satisfaction, and lower turnover. The benefits of the policies also seem to reverberate beyond the companies' HR departments.

"Lavish claims for all the wonderful things work-family programs do always made us nervous because they used an untested hypothesis," said Ellen Galinsky, co-president of the Families and Work Institute, the New York research group that did one of the studies. "We knew lots of studies that showed the cost of not providing programs. Finally we have two studies that begin to address the benefits," she told an audience of HR executives at the Conference Board's annual family and work conference last week in New York.

The studies were in essence evaluations of work-family programs at Johnson & Johnson (J & J), the consumer and pharmaceuticals giant based in New Brunswick, New Jersey, and Fel-Pro, Inc., a medium-size maker of automotive sealing products based in Skokie, Illinois.

J & J and Fel-Pro both offer an extensive menu of family programs, including on-site childcare as well as dependent and eldercare resources and flexible schedules.

The Families and Work Institute found that four years after the J & J "Balancing Work and Family" program began, 38 percent of the employees who responded to the survey said they "strongly agreed" that they felt more comfortable raising personal issues at work. That was up from 18 percent in 1990, when the base-line evaluation was done. And slightly more than half the employees said they strongly agreed that supervisors—who are critical to the success of work-family programs—were responsive to their personal and family needs, up from 36 percent in 1990.

One important consequence of the changes since 1990, said Chris Kjeldsen, a J & J vice president, is that employees no longer feel they have to lie to get permission to take time off if a child is sick or for some other family emergency. "It's bringing about a positive cultural change at J & J," he said.

Nearly three-quarters of the employees who responded to the survey said the family policies were "very important" in deciding whether to stay at the company.

At Fel-Pro, researchers from the University of Chicago found that employees who took advantage of work-family programs were more likely to participate in total quality management and other programs companies consider critical to their competitiveness. They were also more likely to be "good corporate citizens" who pitched in to help other employees, the researchers said.

Susan Lambert, the Fel-Pro study's principal investigator, said family policies are often seen primarily as a way to attract women to a company. "They have additional benefits," she said. "They can help lay the groundwork for other major cultural changes."

Neither study found evidence to support a fear common among managers that employees will exploit and abuse company programs. At J & J, Mr. Kjeldsen said, there was no increase in absenteeism or tardiness or decrease in productivity even though, because of the economy, people were working longer and had more responsibility.

In both studies, the employees who used and liked family programs most were the highest performers, the least inclined to leave the company, and the least likely to have disciplinary problems. Since the J & J program began, employees seem to take their job troubles home less. Given the difficult economic times and the pressure on employees, Ms. Galinsky said, "that is an astonishing finding."[50]

Dependentcare Reimbursement Accounts. Dependentcare reimbursement accounts, a form of flexible spending accounts, have become the most prevalent type of childcare benefit in the 1990s. These accounts allow employees to pay for qualified expenses with pretax dollars subject to a use-it-or-lose-it rule. They benefit employees greatly, and they entail minimal administrative costs for the sponsoring organization. The maximum amount an employee can channel into one of these accounts is $5,000 a year. For an employee to participate in a reimbursement account, the child must be under the age of thirteen. Additionally, the expense must be necessary to permit an employee to work, both husband and wife to work, or a spouse to attend school full-time.

For the employee, these accounts offer potential tax advantages. Consider a single parent with a four-year-old daughter. He anticipates childcare expenses of $5,000 in the next year. His projected salary for the next year is $35,000. Listed below is the employee's disposable income without and with an employee-financed dependentcare reimbursement account.

	Without Account	With Account
Gross salary	$35,000	$35,000
Pre-elected payroll deduction	– 0	– 5,000
	$35,000	$30,000
Estimated taxes (federal income tax and Social Security)	– 3,115	– 2,670
Net salary	31,885	27,330
Payment from account		+ 5,000
Available income	31,885	32,330
Payment to childcare center	– 5,000	– 5,000
Disposable income	$26,885	$27,330

As shown, the employee has $445 more in disposable income using a dependentcare reimbursement account.[51]

Resource and Referral Programs. Childcare information and referral assistance is offered by 29 percent of U.S. firms. These company-sponsored programs counsel employees about daycare options and refer them to prescreened local providers. Prescreening ensures the centers in the network meet minimum care standards and are financially responsible.

Serving a largely female workforce, First Chicago pays for about 800 deliveries a year. Coaching pregnant women has drastically reduced C-sections and underweight babies.

The program offered by the Kodak Company is typical. The leading manufacturer of photographic products and healthcare products contracted with Work/Family Directions, Inc., a national organization that specialized in childcare resources and issues to maintain its Childcare Resource and Referral Program. To provide Kodak employees with detailed information and referrals, Work/Family directors established contracts with community-based childcare agencies throughout the country. Because not all areas have sufficient childcare services, Kodak also has provided start-up costs to develop childcare programs in areas of short supply. During the program's first eighteen months, Kodak's funding resulted in the addition of 650 family daycare homes in communities where Kodak employees live.

Steelcase employs a childcare administrator whose staff evaluates daycare centers and familycare homes. An employee survey of users indicates that more than 90 percent of the employees who use the Steelcase program feel more relaxed and productive at work.[52]

At the 3M Company in St. Paul, Minnesota, Working Parent Resource Fairs are held biannually to give employees the chance to peruse a range of parent or child-related services. "In the spring, parents look for what to do with kids during the summer," Suzanne T. Osten, childcare administrator, noted. "We hold the fair early to give them time to plan ahead." Typically, more than 600 employees attend the four-hour fair (total cost to 3M is only $2,000), which features exhibitors from

67 organizations. Exhibitors include church social services, Parents Without Partners, the Minnesota Council for the Gifted and Talented, Minnesota Safe Kids Project, and Science Museum of Minnesota. Employers are given time off from work to attend the fair and shop for service.[53]

On-Site Care Facilities. By 1994, there were more than 2,500 employer-sponsored on-site or near-site care centers in operation. In San Francisco, office and hotel complexes with more than 50,000 square feet must either provide an on-site facility or pay into a city childcare fund. Although the operation of such centers can be costly, a growing number of employers now accept the burden of operating and funding such centers as a social and business necessity.

Consider the comments of Dick Parker, director of administrative services for Merck & Co., at groundbreaking ceremonies for its $8 million childcare center:

> *You don't provide childcare just because you want to be a good guy. You do it for business reasons, Merck decided to build the center for three reasons: retention, recruitment. and productivity. Child care will become more and more of a recruitment issue in the future. If employees are worried about their childcare services, that will affect their productivity and retention.*[54]

Linda Fitzpatrick, director of human resources for Gentech, a pharmaceutical company in the San Francisco area, makes a similar point noting that, "Providing a near-site center makes good business sense. Not only is the center a great recruiting tool, but we've found that employees come back to work sooner after maternity leave because they know that their child is receiving quality, nearby care." Gentech's center is open from 6:45 A.M. to 7:00 P.M. and accepts children from six weeks to six years of age. The building is maintained by Gentech, but the program is operated by an independent childcare group.

Employees pay between $390 and $490 per month (depending on age). The company offers a 50 percent scholarship to employees who earn less than $25,000.

Campbell Soup Company's childcare center is located across the street from its corporate headquarters and cares for 110 children. Contending that on-site care cuts absenteeism, reduces distractions for employees, and helps with hiring, the company picks up 40 percent of the weekly expense for each child. The Hacienda Child Development Center in Pleasanton, California, serves multiple employers (for example, Hewlett-Packard, Computerland, Prudential Insurance Company). Operating costs are funded from parent fees and business fees. Employees working in the Hacienda Business Park receive a discount on monthly rates.

Eldercare

Of employees over the age of 30, 28 percent currently spend an average of ten hours a week giving care to an older relative. For a significant portion, this commitment equals a second job. Some 12 percent of workers who care for aging parents are forced to quit their jobs to do so. With the continued aging of the baby-boomers, more and more employers are considering ways to assist workers who are caring for elderly relatives. Assistance ranges from information and referral programs to specialized care insurance. As described later, the *Family and Medical Leave Act* of 1993 supports employee time off for both childcare and eldercare.

Information and Referral Programs. In 1990, only 11 percent of employers offered eldercare information and referral programs to link employees with community resources that already exist; by the year 2000, the number could exceed 50 percent. Like the dependentcare programs discussed previously, company-operated eldercare referral programs are designed to assist the care giver in identifying appropriate community resources.

To address the need for eldercare assistance and stay within the budget, First Interstate Bank of California has entered into a public-private partnership with the County Division on Aging. The agency is a member of a nationwide eldercare resource and referral system. Linked into the system, First Interstate employees call a toll-free number and talk to a counselor about what resources they need and in what city they're needed. The counselor calls back with a list of potential resources including at-home care for the elderly, daycare centers, and support groups for the caregiver.[55]

Eldercare Centers. Recognizing that eldercare is not always available, a small but growing number of firms are offering on-site or corporate-financed eldercare centers. The Stride Rite Corporation, a leading marketer of high-quality footwear for children and adults, is a leader in this venture. Stride Rite has had an on-site childcare center since 1971. In 1990, the firm opened the Stride Rite Intergenerational DayCare Center, which houses 55 children between the ages of 15 months and 6 years and 24 elders who are over the age of 60. Group activities that routinely bring elders and children together, include reading and writing stories, cooking and eating, card games, and field trips. Employees pay a percentage of their annual household income through payroll deduction.[56]

Long-Term Care Insurance. One of the newest and fastest growing options is long-term care insurance. While only 8 percent of firms currently offer this benefit, nearly 70 percent of companies are expected to offer this eldercare option by the year 2000. This type of insurance covers medical, social, custodial, and personal services for people who suffer from chronic physical or mental illnesses or disabling injury or disease over an extended period of time. Typically, coverage is offered to employees on an employee-pay-all basis. Premium rates are age-based, and in some plans there is a maximum age (typically 79) for participation. Benefit maximums are related to care site (nursing home versus daycare center) and include lifetime limits.[57]

Changing Lifestyles

With demographic and value shifts, there is not a wider array of lifestyles than ever before in our country. As a consequence, a rising percentage of workers—unmarried couples, divorced people, same sex domestic partners, single parents—do not fit into conventional benefits packages. Recognizing that people are assets to the organization and that the world of work can never be fully separated from the rest of one's life, cutting-edge companies are redesigning their benefits packages to address the needs of all employees.

Adoption Benefits. In 1989, the Communications Workers of America negotiated a benefit plan with AT&T that provides a $2,000 allowance per adoption. That agreement is expected to serve as a model for other unions to follow as part of their bargaining strategy for the 1990s. An adoption benefit plan is a company-sponsored program that financially assists or reimburses employees for the costs associated with the adoption of a child. The most frequently covered benefits include adoption agency fees, attorney fees, and court costs. Some plans also include paid or unpaid leave, and a handful cover pregnancy care expenses for the birth mother.

Benefits for Spousal Equivalents. The Lotus Development Corporation, now a division of the IBM Corporation, modified its insurance and benefits policy to offer the partners of homosexual employees the same benefits accorded heterosexual spouses. According to Russell J. Campanello, vice president for human resources, "This is fair and equal." Lotus's decision did not come easily. In 1989, three workers began petitioning Lotus for spousal benefits. Even after Lotus agreed, it took the company and the three employees two years to develop a workable policy. The insurance carrier that pays Lotus's claims above $140,000 was reluctant to take on more homosexual enrollees, largely because of potential AIDS-related bills. After researching the actual costs carefully, Lotus convinced the carrier that the cost was not a seven-digit dollar issue but about the same as treating a coronary patient, Campanello said.

Premiums for the 12 "spousal equivalents" currently enrolled in the program cost Lotus about $30,000, none of which is tax deductible because the IRS doesn't recognize unmarried partners. Participating employees pay about $1,350 in taxes a year on the premium's benefits. To be eligible, a couple must live together and share financial obligations. If they break up, the employee must wait one year before registering a new partner. In addition to healthcare, the plan includes life insurance, relocation expenses, bereavement leave, and a death benefit.[58]

Educational Expense Allowances. Faced with skill obsolescence, downsizing, and retraining demands, almost 75 percent of all medium and large firms provided some form of educational expense assistance. Most plans covet registration fees, and some assist with graduation fees, laboratory expenses, entrance examinations, professional certification, and activity fees. Typically, these programs require a relationship between the course and some phase of company operations. For example, National Healthcorp, which is headquartered in Murfreesboro, Tennessee, offers tuition assistance to any aide who wishes to become a nurse. The company will pay for up to two years of school in exchange for the aide's promise to stay on staff that long after graduation.[59]

Administrative Issues

Although organizations tend to view indirect compensation as a reward, recipients do not always see it that way. This causes organizations to become concerned with their package of indirect compensation benefits and how they are administered.

Determining the Benefits Package

The benefits package should be selected on the basis of what is good for the employee as well as for the employer. Often, knowing employee preferences can determine which benefits should be offered. For example, employees may have a strong preference for dental insurance over life insurance, even though dental insurance may be only one-fourth the cost to the company. As workers get older, their desire for higher pension benefits increases steadily. This is also the case for employees with rising incomes. Employees with children prefer greater hospitalization benefits than those without.[60]

Organizations are constrained, however, by their size in the feasibility of what they can offer. According to Jordan Shields, owner of a consulting firm specializing in benefits:

> *Companies that have fewer than ten employees may have difficulty finding an insurance carrier, even for basic medical. Dental and vision care insurance options aren't very good. Disability plans for these small companies will be either very restrictive or very expensive.*
>
> *"If there are between 10 and 24 employees," says Shields, "vision, dental and disability options are OK. Medical options are a bit easier to find than for the smallest firms, but it still isn't a breeze. At that size, there's no flexibility to offer more than one medical plan." Only after a company has at least 25 employees can it begin to offer a choice of medical plans. In fact, Shields says, federal law requires that companies that have 25 employees or more may be obligated to offer more than one plan—an HMO and an indemnity plan.*
>
> *Companies having more than 50 employees, and certainly those with more than 100, have more options and can even participate in partial self-insurance programs. "If you self-insure, then you, as the employer, retain part*

Did You KNOW?

Only 51% of the 37 million workers in companies with fewer than 25 employees have company-paid health insurance.

of the risk for the health of the employee," says Shields. "You're acting partially as the insurance company, which means that if your employees stay fairly healthy and don't file a lot of claims, you won't pay as much in premiums."

As companies grow, they encounter fewer limitations. A firm that has 300 to 400 employees can choose from among many options and carriers and can establish a large plan that can be modified easily. However, a firm that grows from 10 to 150 employees within a year or two will have major changes to make. Unfortunately, like many other functions at young, fast-growing firms, benefits management tends to lag behind the more urgent line functions.[61]

Providing Benefit Flexibility

When employees can design their own benefits package, both they and the company profit.[62] At least that is the experience at companies such as IBM, Ford Motor Company, TRW, the Educational Testing Service (ETS), and Morgan Stanley. At ETS, the company provides a core package of benefits to all employees covering basic needs such as personal medical care, dental care, disability, vacation, and retirement. In addition, each individual can choose, cafeteria-style, from optional benefits or increase those in the core package. Employees are allowed to change their packages once a year. At Morgan Stanley, about two-thirds of its eligible employees elected their own benefit package over the standard no-choice plan. The options themselves were developed by the employees working in small group discussions.

Communicating the Benefits Package

Providing benefit flexibility is good not only because it gives employees what they are more likely to want, but also because it makes them aware of the benefits they are gaining and thereby not only increase their morale (because they feel well protected), but also increases their commitment to the organization.[63] Many employees are unaware of the costs of benefits and even of which benefits they are receiving. If employees have no knowledge of their benefits, there is little reason to believe the organization's benefit program objectives will be attained. Many organizations indicate that they assign a high priority to telling employees about their benefits. However, a majority spend only $10 per employee per year doing this, while the average benefits package costs over $13,000 per employee! Communicating the benefits package and providing employees with benefit flexibility increase the positive impact of indirect compensation. This impact and the process of communicating the benefits package at Hewlett-Packard are described in the feature, "Managing Human Resources at Hewlett-Packard."

Current Trends

The trends discussed in the previous two chapters also relate to and are likely to influence the administration of indirect compensation during the remainder of the 1990s.[64] These trends include the linking of compensation to organizational strategy and to the organization's life cycle. But one that is uniquely related to indirect compensation is the trend to manage and reduce costs.

Managing and Reducing Indirect Compensation Costs

As stated earlier, the costs of indirect compensation have been rising rapidly during the past decade. Today, the average is almost $14,000 per employee, almost 50 percent of the cost of the total pay for time worked! Healthcare costs alone

MANAGING HUMAN RESOURCES

at Hewlett-Packard

Employee satisfaction rises when workers receive greater information about the benefit packages available to them, reports Arthur J. Young, manager of corporate benefits for Hewlett-Packard Co.

Based on attitude surveys involving several thousand of Hewlett-Packard's 56,000 U.S. workers, Young found a significant improvement in employees' perceptions about their benefits after they participated in an eight-hour workshop on financial planning and company benefits. Interestingly, he notes that the employees who took the workshop started out slightly more negative than the overall workforce in their views about the adequacy of company-provided benefits.

Before they attended the workshop, 62 percent of the participating employees said they felt their benefit needs were met by the benefit packages provided by the company, says Young. Afterward, 93 percent of the employees said they felt their needs were met.

The survey also revealed improved understanding of Hewlett-Packard's 401(k) retirement plan and better comprehension of traditional pension benefits, Young says. Initially, 55 percent of the participating employees said they understood the company's retirement programs, while 97 percent indicated that they understood the programs following the workshop.

A separate employee survey addressing work and family issues has already produced some changes at Hewlett-Packard, Young continues. When asked about their priorities for assistance from the company, employees indicated a desire to have more flexible work hours, work-at-home opportunities, and a more liberal leave-of-absence policy, he notes. In response to those results, the company has changed its rehire policy and increased its support for telecommuting.

Hewlett-Packard, which spends $2.5 billion annually on benefits for workers across 45 countries, tries to survey 10 percent of the workforce in each of its 100 entities at least every three years, Young points out. Employees are the company's most important asset, "and we want to continue to remind them that we're paying attention to them," he contends.[65]

account for almost $4,000 of this total, and they are increasing at a rate of 10 percent yearly. This is at the same time that global competition is increasing, particularly from nations whose direct and indirect compensation costs are one-tenth that of those in the United States.

While the role of the federal government in healthcare may level the playing field for competitors within the United States and is likely to provide healthcare benefits to more Americans, U.S. employers will still continue to pay significantly for healthcare for their own workers.

Thus the trend is clear: manage and reduce benefit costs. Managing costs means having second opinions and fewer choices in healthcare coverage. It means making sure that a disability is really a disability and that workers get back to work as soon as possible. It means being proactive and seeking ways to prevent sickness and injury (in this respect, the HR professionals in compensation need to work closely with those in health and safety). These all represent programs that a few companies are already doing—for example, Steelcase with disability and workers' compensation. Many more are likely to start such programs before the year 2000.

Firms are asking workers to participate in their own healthcare and retirement costs. This approach is consistent with employee empowerment and self-management. By providing workers with benefit information, they may be able to assist in the cost-reduction process without we eliminating benefits. Win-win situations can be created where costs are reduced and coverage is maintained. When these ben-

Did You KNOW?

The Bureau of Labor Statistics reports that while 82% of full-time employees working for medium-sized and large companies get healthcare, in small businesses (defined as those with fewer than 100 employees), just 71% do.

The story is the same with retirement plans. In big businesses, 78% of employees get them; in small businesses, only 45% do. Part-timers in small businesses fare even worse—only 5% have medical coverage, for instance.

Did You KNOW?

The cost of healthcare for each citizen in the United States is $2,668. In Great Britain, it is $1,043, and in Canada, it is $1,915.

efits also meet individual needs, the employer is likely not only to reduce costs, but also to maintain employee commitment. Experiences at Steelcase, Johnson & Johnson, Lincoln Electric, Coors, and Fel-Pro all indicate that win-win situations, with extensive employee involvement and understanding, are possible.

Employers in the United States are not the only ones dealing with benefit costs. In Canada and Europe, where most of the healthcare and pensions are provided by the government, these governments in seeking ways to balance their budgets, are moving to reduce costs for healthcare and pensions. If European governments do this, both employees and the governments are expecting employers to absorb some of the costs. This comes at a time when many European employers are already providing generous vacations and paying some of the highest wages in the world. Thus the pressure to manage and reduce benefit costs is likely to be even greater in Europe than it is in the United States.

LEARNING OBJECTIVE 5

Describe the numerous legal considerations in indirect compensation.

Legal Considerations

Indirect compensation grew rapidly during the Great Depression of the 1930s, which produced the first major legislation involving benefits. The *Social Security Act*, passed in 1935, provided old age, disability, survivor's, and health benefits and established the basis for federal and state unemployment programs. The *Wagner Act*, or the *National Labor Relations Act* (NLRA) of 1935, ensured the growth of benefits packages by strengthening the union movement in the United States. Both the *Social Security Act* and the *Wagner Act* continue to play significant roles in the administration of benefits.

After World War II, the legal environment further stimulated indirect compensation. Two court cases expanded benefits coverage by declaring that pension and insurance provisions were bargainable issues in union and management relations. The right to bargain over pensions was established in *Inland Steel v. National Labor Relations Board* (1948), and the right to bargain over insurance was upheld in *W. W. Cross v. National Labor Relations Board* (1949).

Equal Pay Act of 1963

This act, described in Chapter 15, mandates that employees on the same jobs be paid equally, except for differences in seniority, merit, or other conditions unrelated to gender. Direct as well as indirect compensation are included in the term *paid equally*. Thus, for example, women and men on the same job, other factors being equal, must receive the same level of direct and indirect compensation. Actuarial data, however, indicated that women live approximately seven years longer than men. Therefore, on the average, women will receive a greater total level of retirement benefits than men. Is this equal indirect compensation? Would it be equal if women contributed more? In *Los Angeles Department of Water v. Manhart* (1981), the court ruled against the department's policy of having female employees contribute more to their retirement than males. Furthermore, when men and women make equal contributions to their pensions, their pension benefits must be equal (*Arizona Governing Committee v. Norris,* 1983). Additional guarantees for equal pension-benefit treatment to surviving spouses, male and female, are contained in the *Retirement Equity Act* of 1984.

Pregnancy Discrimination Act of 1978

Prior to this act, many companies viewed pregnancy as a voluntary condition, not an involuntary sickness, that should therefore not be covered by disability benefits. The *Pregnancy Discrimination Act* of 1978, however, states that pregnancy is a disability and qualifies a person to receive the same benefits as any other disability. Applying this statute, a state appeals court in Michigan ruled that a labor contract between General Motors and United Auto Workers that provided sickness and accident benefits of up to 52 weeks but that limited childbearing disability to 6 weeks was illegal.[66]

Another issue in this area, which is not covered by the *Pregnancy Discrimination Act,* is whether companies must offer the same pregnancy benefit program to wives of male employees and to husbands of female employees. The Supreme Court ruled in the *Newport News Shipbuilding and Dry Dock Co. v. EEOC* (1983), that employers who provide healthcare insurance to spouses of employees that includes complete coverage for all disabilities except pregnancy are violating Title VII of the *Civil Rights Act* of 1964. In essence, employers must provide equal benefit coverage for all spouses.

Americans with Disabilities Act of 1990

The Equal Employment Opportunity Commission (EEOC) enforces the *Americans with Disabilities Act* described in Chapters 5 and 8. Related to the selection of employees, the EEOC in 1993 issued a policy declaring that employers may not refuse to hire people with disabilities because of concern about their effect on healthcare costs. In addition, disabled employees must be given "equal access" to any health insurance provided to other employees:

> *The EEOC policy statement gives many examples. It suggests that an employer may not set a lower level of benefits for a specific disability like deafness, AIDS, or schizophrenia or for "a discrete group of disabilities" like cancers, kidney diseases, or various forms of muscular dystrophy.*
>
> *But under the policy, an employer could make very broad distinctions and could, for example, provide a lower level of benefits for eye care than for the treatment of other physical conditions. "Such broad distinctions, which apply to the treatment of a multitude of dissimilar condition do not necessarily violate the Americans with Disabilities Act," the policy says.*[67]

Thus, especially in terms of the numbers of individuals impacted, this policy ruling on the ADA has enormous implications in terms of costs:

> *Millions of people may be affected by the new policy. The Census Bureau reports that 77 million Americans have difficulty hearing what is said in normal conversations, while more than 13 million have impaired eyesight and 8 million have severe difficulty walking. At least 1.3 million people use wheelchairs or walkers.*[68]

The ruling also impacts many businesses and health insurers (who provide health insurance to the businesses). The EEOC has recognized the impact on both sides but comes down strongly on the side of the disabled.

Family and Medical Leave Act of 1993

The Family and Medical Leave Act requires employers with 50 or more employees to grant up to twelve weeks unpaid leave annually:

> *...for the birth or adoption of a child, to care for a spouse or an immediate family member with a serious health condition, or when unable to work because of a serious health condition. Employers covered by the law are required to maintain any pre-existing health coverage during the leave period and, once the leave period is concluded, to reinstate the employee to the same or an equivalent job.*[69]

The definition of "serious health condition" includes pregnancy, chronic conditions such as asthma, long-term conditions such as Alzheimer's, and serious conditions that would result in incapacitation without multiple treatments, such as cancer requiring chemotherapy or radiation treatments.

Although employees are required to give advance notice of the need for leave—at least thirty days' or as much notice as is practicable—and to explain the reasons for requesting leave, employers are responsible for designating any qualifying leave taken by employees as FMLA leave and notifying employees in writing of the designation. Leave taken for a serious health condition pursuant to a workers' compensation benefit plan may be charged concurrently against an employee's FMLA leave entitlement. However, accrued paid leave may not be substituted for FMLA leave at the same time the employee is collecting workers' compensation benefits. Medical records created for purposes of FMLA and ADA must be maintained in accordance with ADA's confidentiality requirements.[70]

To be eligible for FMLA provisions, employees must have worked at a company for at least twelve months and have put in at least 1,250 hours in the year before the leave. This act is entirely consistent with what some companies have been doing for some time in their efforts to accommodate to an increasingly diverse workforce and make their firms "family-friendly."

Age Discrimination in Employment Act of 1967

This act essentially prohibits the forced retirement of employees on the basis of age if they are working for a private business with at least 20 people on the payroll. One exception to this is top-level executives, who can be retired at age 70. These provisions are contained in a 1986 amendment to the act, which took effect on January 1, 1987. Employees can still choose to retire voluntarily at 65 and receive full benefits, however.

Some members of Congress seek to increase to 68 the age at which full Social Security benefits can start. Although this has not been done yet, Congress has attempted to reduce some of the burden on Social Security through a provision in the *Tax Equity and Fiscal Responsibility Act* of 1982. According to that act, employers with 20 or more workers must include those between the ages of 65 and 69 in their group health plans unless the employees specifically choose Medicare, funded by Social Security, as their primary coverage. Nonetheless, employers may still freeze pension contributions and plans for employees at age 65.

Amending ADEA is the *Older Workers Benefit Protection Act* of 1990. This prohibits discrimination in employee benefits. As a result of this act, Congress amended ADEA by defining the term "compensation, terms, conditions, or privileges of employment" to encompass all employee benefits, including benefits provided under a bona fide employee benefit plan.

ERISA and Private Employers' Pensions

Building on the foundation of the *Revenue Act* of 1942, the *Employees' Retirement Income Security Act* (ERISA) was enacted to protect employees covered by private pension programs. While ERISA does not require an employer to offer a pension fund, it is designed to protect the interests of workers covered by private retirement plans. Employees are eligible for private pension fund participation after one year of service or at age 25.[71]

Vesting means conveying full ownership of the employer's pension contributions to the employee; the ownership at vesting remains with employee even if the employee leaves the company.

Because of problems over ownership of pension funds, ERISA also established provisions regarding vesting. **Vesting** refers to the time when the employer's contribution belongs to the employee. There are three basic options:

1. Full vesting after 10 years of service
2. Twenty-five percent vesting after 5 years, with 5 percent additional vesting until 10 years of service, and then 10 percent vesting for years 10 through 15
3. Fifty percent vesting when the employee has worked 5 years and when age and service equal 45; each additional year of service increases vesting by 10 percent

Because companies in the past have used pension funds for operating expenses, ERISA also prohibits the use of unfunded pension programs that rely on the goodwill of the employer to pay retirement benefits out of current operating funds when needed. Money paid into a pension fund must be earmarked for retirees whether paid in part by the employee, as in contributory programs, or paid solely by the employer, as in noncontributory programs.

In a defined-benefit plan, the actual benefits received upon retirement vary by age and length of service of the employee. One concern with such plans is overfunding, or having more money in the account than is needed to meet future funding requirements. Overfunding increases the likelihood of takeover bids because an acquiring company can terminate the pension program, retrieve the excess funding, and then start a new pension fund. To resolve this problem, organizations are reducing their contributions to defined-budget plans or are switching to defined-contribution plans.

Under ERISA, employers are not required to accommodate new or transferred employees who wish to deposit funds into their retirement plans. Employers can allow employees to transfer money on a voluntary basis to individual retirement accounts. When this occurs, the pension funds are said to be **portable**. Increasingly, employers are making it possible for employees to transfer their retirement funds to another firm.

Because the ERISA only covered single-employer firms, the *Multi-Employer Pension Plan Amendment Act* of 1980 was passed to broaden the definition of defined-benefit plans to include multi-employer plans. If any employer withdraws from multi-employer plans, they, rather than the employees, face liability for doing so and must reimburse employees for money lost.[72] Congress also has passed several tax acts that influence the administration or level of indirect compensation programs.

Economic Recovery Tax Act of 1981

A major provision of this act is that employees can make tax-deductible contributions of up to $2,000 to an employer-sponsored pension, profit-sharing, or savings account, or to an individual retirement account. The act also made it possible for employers to provide company stock to employees and pay for it with tax credits or to establish a payroll-based stock ownership plan that facilitates employee stock ownership (ESOPs) of organizations.[73]

ESOPs enable employees to become owners of the firm they work for.

Because these plans are so attractive to organizations, millions of employees have gained direct ownership of stock in their own companies. By the year 2000, 25 percent or more of all U.S. workers may own part or all of their companies.

> *The appeal of ownership programs goes far beyond the tax breaks available to ESOPs. At a time when competitive pressures are forcing companies to keep a lid on labor costs, many are using stock plans as a substitute for cash compensation. Stock is being used to fund bonuses, pension and savings plans, and even retiree medical benefits.*
>
> *Such programs are not without risk, particularly if corporate sponsors go belly-up in future years. But they can help make companies more competitive, enhance productivity, and bolster morale when wage hikes need to be deferred. Because workers are concerned with job security, they represent a source of patient capital that is likely to value long-term performance over short-term profits.*
>
> *The most intriguing aspect of this trend is the possibility that workers who own a significant share of their companies will want a voice in corporate governance, as has already happened in the case of several companies contem-*

Did You KNOW?

In 1994, United Airlines formed an ESOP. Eighteen months later, labor costs were down 7%, revenue was up 15% and the stock price was up 120%. It hired 7,000 employees.

plating mergers. Employers who prepare for this development by setting up mechanisms for dialogue can lay the groundwork for productive cooperation between labor and management in future decision making. Those who don't may find worker ownership a mixed blessing.[74]

Tax Equity and Fiscal Responsibility Act of 1982

This act sharply cut the maximum benefit and contribution limits for qualified pension plans (legally covered) and set limits for loans from such plans. The maximum individual yearly retirement benefit now stands at $94,023, and the maximum employer contribution per employee per year is $30,000. As an outgrowth of the act, some organizations have established nonqualified pension plans (not legally protected) for high-income employees. Contributions to these plans are taxable, while contributions to qualified plans are not.

Deficit Reduction Act of 1984

Along with several IRS rulings, this act makes some benefits—particularly **flexible spending plans**—taxable. In one form, employees are given the choice between several nontaxable benefits in return for reduced pay. In another, money is set aside initially and, if employees don't use the benefits, they receive the money. In still another, no money is set aside, but employees are reimbursed for some expenses.

Consolidated Omnibus Budget Reconciliation Act of 1985

This act assures that terminated or laid-off employees have the option to maintain their healthcare insurance by personally paying for the premiums. The option must also be extended to employees who lose their health benefits eligibility because their work hours have been reduced to the point where they no longer are eligible for coverage.

Tax Reform Act of 1986

Two provisions of this act affect indirect compensation. Essentially, the act caps at $9,500 the amount of tax-exempt deferred contribution employees can make to a deferred pay plan. Effective January, 1989, the act also put into force provisions to reduce the disparity of benefits provided high- and low-income employees. Because of the difficulty of implementing this provision, it has been modified substantially.[75]

Revenue Reconciliation Act of 1993

This act further limits the amount of money employers may contribute to qualified retirement plans. Now the percentage of salary an employer contributes is based on a maximum of $150,000 rather than $250,000.

International Comparisons

Canada

In Canada, the sharpest contrasts with the United States concerning compensation are found in indirect compensation, particularly pensions and healthcare.[76] For example, Canada has the Canada Pension Plan (CPP) and the Quebec Pension Plan in the province of Quebec, both of which are similar to the U.S. Social Security system. CPP is a mandatory plan for all employees except government workers. Like the Social Security system, CPP pays retirement benefits, disability pensions, benefits for children of disabled contributors, orphans' benefits, and pension benefits to survivors' spouses. Canada also has private pension plans, although fewer than 40 percent of all employees are covered by these plans. The administration of these plans is governed by the Pension Benefits Act, which is less extensive in its regulation of private pension plans than the U.S. *Employees' Retirement Income Security Act* (ERISA).

Canada has a national healthcare system that covers virtually the entire population. This system is called a "single-payer" plan because the government pays for the healthcare costs. As a consequence of this, employers do not contribute to employee healthcare as they do in the U.S. This system, rather than having employers offer healthcare benefits directly to their employees, has employers contribute to the national healthcare fund. The result is that all employees are covered rather than only those employees who happen to work for employers who provide the coverage for their workers.

Reports published by the Canadian National Bureau of Economic Research, indicate that since the inception of national healthcare (in the late 1960s), employment levels and wages levels have risen rather than fallen (this was the prediction because the system required employers to pay based upon the number of employees). The explanation for the finding was that the national healthcare system raises labor productivity by improving employee health and by making it easier for employees to change jobs. The result is that employers are more willing to hire workers.

Mexico

The Mexican Federal Labor Law governs all benefits matters in Mexico. The state labor boards oversee the enforcement of the law.[77] These boards have representatives from the government, labor, and management. The law states that full-time employees should get certain fringe benefits, including six days paid vacation yearly, a minimum wage (about $15 a day), a 25 percent vacation pay premium, seven paid federal holidays, a profit-sharing plan, social security, and an employer-paid payroll tax that funds employee daycare centers.[78]

The employer has twenty-eight days to evaluate the employees' work ethics. After that period, the worker is granted job security and termination becomes difficult. This is especially true in terms of financial liability. For example, an employer that decides to fire a worker who has been with the company for six months could be charged for an additional six weeks, plus vacation pay and bonuses accordingly. It is therefore worthwhile to screen employees before hiring.

An employee is considered tenured after one year of employment. A tenured worker may be dismissed only for causes specifically set out in the Mexican Federal Labor Law—for example, falsifying employment documents, or committing dishonest or violent acts during working hours. For a dismissal to be valid, a written notice of the firing and complete documentation of the offenses must be given.

Upon leaving a firm, employees may receive benefits from three sources:

- Social security is mandatory and covers old-age, survivors', and disability pensions, and medical and maternity benefits.
- Retirement savings systems require employees to pay into a retirement fund two percent of base pay.
- Severance pay is a major part of company retirement plans. There are two types: *antiguedad* and *cesantia*. *Antiguedad* is paid upon an employees' voluntary resignation after fifteen years of service, an employee's death, or an employee's disability. Compensation is twelve days' pay for each year of service, with a maximum of two times the minimum wage. *Cesantia* is severance paid upon termination without just cause. Just cause is limited to gross misconduct—poor performance is not considered just cause. Severance is not necessary upon retirement. This sets up a problem because employees are often significantly better off being dismissed than voluntarily retiring. To remedy this, some companies establish informal voluntary retirement programs with pension plans to allow retiring employees to receive severance pay.

Individual operations can give their own benefits to entice workers, above and beyond the legal requirements. Some of these benefits include transportation, showers at the plant, wages double the minimum wage, subsidized or in some cases free lunches, on-site education, athletic activities, and cosmetics for female workers.

Certain border plants, *maquiladoras*, are short of good workers because of housing shortages and transportation difficulties in many of the northern towns. The solution for some maquiladoras is to locate in a central area so that most employees are within walking distance.

Most maquiladoras pay the Mexican legal minimum wage, which varies about 10 percent throughout the country. Since the wage is relatively low, turnover may range from 30 percent to 100 percent a year in major cities. To avoid problems associated with high turnover, some maquiladoras pay their employees above minimum wage. Others prevent high turnover by making employees feel that they can move up in the company, and offer an increase in salary after a certain amount of service time given to the company.[79]

Hours of Work

There are major differences within the industrialized countries in the hours worked by employees. These differences typically result from the variation in the number of vacation days and holidays granted to employees. And while you might think that more time off would result in less absenteeism once back on the job, this is not always the case. Exhibit 16.7 shows the variation in hours of work per week and absenteeism rates for several nations.

Life may appear pretty comfortable in the four European nations. But with the worldwide competition, there is tremendous pressure to reduce paid vacation and holidays in these countries. Of course, this is not easy, because of social customs,

EXHIBIT 16.7

Hours of Work, Vacation, Holidays, and Absenteeism

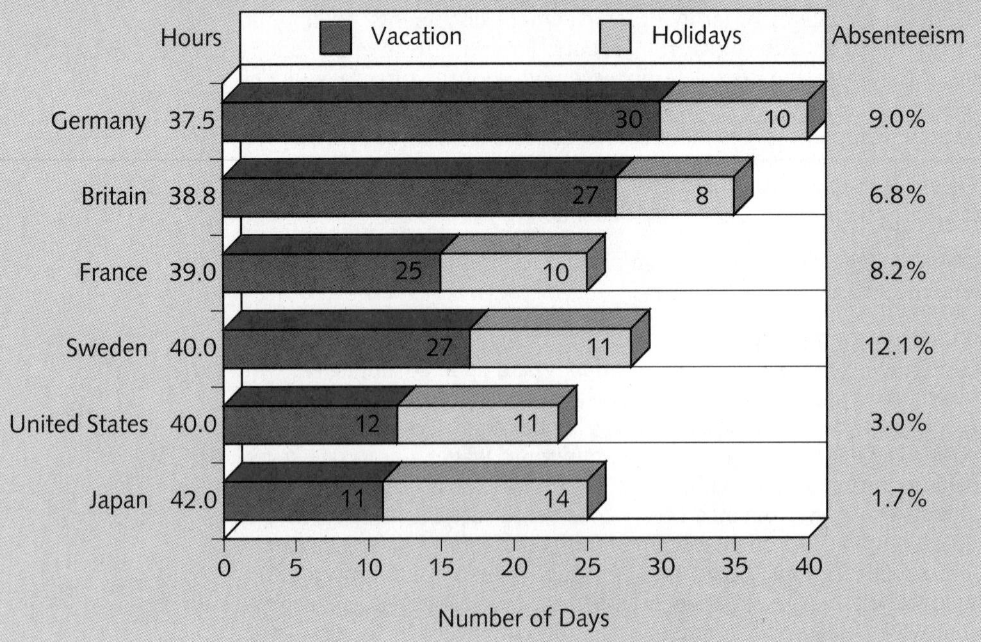

the union movement, and an unemployment rate above 10%. The unemployment rate is a major social concern of the European Union, and one way to deal with it is to reduce the work week for each worker! This results in a clash between the needs of society for less unemployment and the needs of companies to reduce their labor costs by reducing paid vacations and holidays![80]

Summary

Chapters 14, 15, and 16 have addressed frequently asked questions in organization orientation programs such as, "How much do I get paid?" and "When and how long is my vacation?" Organizations have traditionally responded to both questions with, "More than ever before." This has occurred despite the lack of evidence that indirect compensation attains the purposes of total compensation. Money, job challenge, and opportunities for advancement appear to serve the purposes of compensation as much as, if not more than, pension benefits, disability provisions, and services, especially for employees aspiring to managerial careers.

This is not to say, however, that employees do not desire indirect benefits; they can be motivational under the right conditions. Organizations have offered indirect benefits at such a rapid rate in part because employees desired them. The specific benefits offered by an organization have not always been valued, however, nor have employees necessarily known what benefits were offered. As a result of the existence now of the "right conditions" detailed above, some organizations are soliciting employee opinions about their preferences for compensation programs. Organizations are communicating their benefits programs more clearly today. Current evidence suggests that employees' lack of awareness of the contents and value of their benefit programs may partially explain why the programs were not perceived more favorably. Increased communication and more employee participation in the benefits packages will increase the likelihood that the organization benefits from providing indirect compensation; indirect benefits are motivational under the right conditions. And those conditions exist now: 1) The media blitz on the healthcare crisis has probably made more workers aware of their coverage, or lack thereof, than all the company education programs combined. Workers are starting to say, "Wow. I've got a good deal here." 2) Our aging population—the baby-boomers are on the brink of mid-life—is about to start focusing more than ever before on pension funds and the like, especially with the coming crisis in Social Security. Now that the two-income family is the rule and not the exception, parents of young children and children of aging parents are looking to the workplace for solutions as to how to juggle these demands that often conflict with the demands of a job.

These benefits do not come without costs, although some benefits may be gained at less cost than others. To ensure that an organization is getting the most from its indirect compensation, thorough assessments must be made of what the organization is doing, what other organizations are doing, and what employees prefer to see the organization doing.

To improve the motivational value of indirect compensation, organizations should try to provide what employees want. As with direct compensation, employees, being human, will continue to want more benefits. However, not all employees will want the same benefits. For example, younger employees may have a stronger preference for insurance benefits, time off, childcare assistance, and educational benefits, while older employees may have a greater interest in eldercare referrals, retirement benefits, and preretirement counseling opportunities.

In addition to providing a wide range of benefits to employees, numerous federal and state laws must be considered. Federal laws, such as the Family and Medical Leave Act, the Equal Pay Act, and the Americans with Disabilities Act, have a significant influence on indirect compensation. Ignoring these federal laws and various state laws will result in fines and penalties, thus reducing the effectiveness of indirect compensation.

As more U.S. firms move into international markets, the need to understand international compensation increases in importance. As U.S. multinational corporations send more expatriates abroad, they will need to weigh costs against benefits.

Key Concepts

cost-sharing
defined-benefit plan
defined-contribution plan
employee assistance programs (EAPs)
flexible spending plans
health maintenance organizations (HMOs)
indirect compensation
Individual Retirement Account (IRA)
money purchase plans
noncontributory programs
nonqualified plan
Pension Benefit Guaranty Corporation (PBGC)
portable
Preferred-Provider Organization (PPOs)
private protection programs
protection programs
public protection programs
qualified plan
supplemental unemployment benefits
tax-deferred profit-sharing plans
vesting
workers' compensation insurance

Review and Discussion Questions

1. What are the purposes of indirect compensation? How can these purposes best be met?
2. In what sense is indirect compensation "indirect"?
3. What are some of the historical and legislative events that have shaped the growth of indirect compensation?
4. Describe the problems that could be encountered in administering a flexible, or cafeteria-style, indirect compensation program.
5. Distinguish between public and private protection programs, and give examples of each.
6. How would you rationalize the benefit to the organization of providing a physical fitness facility and program for the workforce? How would you assess and compare benefits and costs?
7. For each broad category of indirect compensation, describe the incentives that the employer and the employee have for minimizing the cost of this benefit.
8. Explain how the hours of work vary from country to country.
9. Describe compensation aspects of a family-friendly company.
10. Can small firms offer much indirect compensation?

PROJECTS, EXERCISES & CASES

End-of-Text Projects

Lincoln Electric

1. Describe the following for Lincoln Electric:
   a. Lincoln's indirect compensation plan objectives
   b. The degree to which these objectives are serving the business and HR objectives of Lincoln
   c. Lincoln's indirect compensation plans and activities

d. The degree to which these plans and activities are serving Lincoln's objectives

2. How can Lincoln's indirect compensation activities be improved?

Nordstrom

1. Describe the following for Nordstrom:

   a. Nordstrom's indirect compensation plan objectives

   b. The degree to which these objectives are serving the business and HR objectives of Nordstrom

   c. Nordstrom's indirect compensation plans and activities

   d. The degree to which these plans and activities are serving Nordstrom's objectives

2. How can Nordstrom's indirect compensation activities be improved?

Note: For these projects, use your "best guesses," because the cases do not cover indirect compensation extensively. Your responses here might reflect what effective companies in general do with respect to indirect compensation.

Field Project

Interview an HR manager in a local company and ask about their benefits program. How has it changed in the past several years? What methods are used to communicate the program to employees? How do they measure the effectiveness of the benefits? How do they know what the employees want, and what are the future of benefits in the company?

Career Management Exercise: Speaking of Benefits

In the Career Management Exercise in Chapter 15, you provided a list of what it would take to get you to work at my firm (direct compensation). Your request there totaled 100 percent. But we now know that total compensation is composed of important indirect components, as well as the direct ones. So, in this exercise, you need to first indicate how much of your total compensation (percentage) you want (are willing) to have in direct and indirect compensation. Then you will go on and provide breakdowns for the other areas. Remember, this is what you are asking the employer to pay (give you). Indirect compensation for you in the form of legal payments (such as Social Security and worker's compensation) by the employer costs approximately 22% (Exhibit 16.4) of total compensation. These should therefore be included in your calculations. Therefore, if you want your total compensation to be 60% direct and 40% indirect, 22% of the indirect is already taken care of with the legal payments.

1. Indicate the percentages of total compensation:

   _______ % Direct compensation

   _______ % Base

   _______ % Performance-based

   _______ % Indirect compensation

2. This part is a bit more challenging because you must estimate what each benefit costs and calculate its percentage of indirect compensation. Use the dollar estimates of your direct compensation from Chapter 15. Try to make your estimates as realistic and detailed as possible by referring to Exhibit 16.4 and discussions throughout the chapter. Begin by using these general categories and expand as needed.

   $ ______; ______ % Health and medical insurance

   $ ______; ______ % Dental care

   $ ______; ______ % Eyecare

   $ ______; ______ % Retirement/pension contributions

   $ ______; ______ % Disability, short and long term

   $ ______; ______ % Wellness, exercise programs

   $ ______; ______ % Vacation days; holidays
   # of days each: ______ / ______

   $ ______; ______ % Family-friendly benefits
   Enter choices from Exhibit 16.6

   $ ______; ______ % Stock ownership plan

   $ ______; ______ % Other? Describe and indicate percentage.

3. Of these items you have indicated you want the company to pay for (give you), list the ones you would be willing to pay for and indicate the percentage after the items:

   ______________________________ %

   ______________________________ %

   ______________________________ %

   ______________________________ %

   ______________________________ %

   ______________________________ %

4. In summary, what is the dollar value of your year's total compensation.

   $ __________ Direct

   $ __________ Indirect

   $ __________ Total

VISIT THE LIBRARY

Workforce Online

1. Enter your Web browser.
2. Enter Workforce Online.
3. Read and review the following articles within "Winning Ideas":

   Deer's HMO Turns Crisis into Profit

   Steelcase Slashes Workers' Comp Costs

   HR's Role in Creating Mexico's First HMO
4. Return to your homepage.

Case: Who's Benefiting?

Jack Parks is a benefits manager in the auto electronics division of USA Motors, a major manufacturer of audio systems and auto electronic ignition systems. He is very concerned after analyzing the impact of absenteeism on the division's staffing costs for the previous quarter. What troubles Jack is an agreement that the national union negotiated with USA Motors ten years ago that, in effect, paid workers for being absent. Of course, the "paid absence" agreement was not supposed to work quite that way. In theory, workers were given one week of paid absence against which they could charge their personal absences. Presumably, this system would encourage workers to notify their supervisors so that staffing arrangements could be made and production maintained.

In practice, workers discovered that by not charging off any "paid absences," they could receive a full week's pay in June when the company paid off the balance of the unused paid absences for the previous year. This cash bonus, as workers had come to think of it, often coincides with the summer vacation taken by many of the 8,000 hourly employees when USA Motors shuts down for inventory.

As Jack learned, employees with chronic absentee records had figured out how to charge off absences using the regular categories, which permits sick days, excused, and unexcused absences. In Jack's mind, USA Motors might just as well have negotiated a cash bonus for hourly workers or given them another 10 to 15 cents per hour.

After reviewing the division's absenteeism rates for controllable absences—that is, those categories of absences believed to be of the employee's own choice—Jack concludes that the company could reduce this rate from the previous year's figure of 11 percent. And then Jack has a brainstorm: what USA Motors needs to negotiate is an incentive plan for reducing absenteeism. The plan Jack has in mind entails a standard for the amount of controllable absence deemed acceptable. If a chronically absent employee exceeds the standard, then vacation, holiday, and sickness/accident pay would be cut by 10 percent during the next six months. If worker absence continues to exceed the allowable limits, then vacation, holiday, and sickness pay would be cut during the next six months by the actual percentage of absent days incurred by the chronic absentee. Hence, if a worker misses 15 percent of scheduled work days during the first six-month period, vacation pay for the next six-month period would be reduced by 10 percent. If the employee continues to be absent at the 15 percent rate, then vacation pay would be reduced by 15 percent during the next six months.

Jack immediately drafted a memorandum outlining the program and submitted it to the corporate HR manager of USA Motors for inclusion in the upcoming bargaining session. To Jack's surprise and delight, the memorandum received strong corporate support and is scheduled as a high priority bargaining topic for the fall negotiations.

Case Questions

1. Will the incentive plan to reduce absenteeism succeed?
2. How much absenteeism is really under the employee's control?
3. Why didn't the "paid absence" plan work?
4. What plan would you suggest to USA Motors?

Case: Flowers or Fiasco?

Although secretaries, like any group of good employees, should be complimented and recognized for good work throughout the year, many organizations save their plaudits for secretaries' week. Generally, secretaries' week occurs in the spring, just at the time the doldrums of winter are leaving and the fragrances of the new season are most inviting. Thus, the secretaries of a particular university were especially delighted to be given a day off during secretaries' week last year. Like the students and faculty, they were able to enjoy a beautiful, sunny spring day. Though this fringe benefit of a day off was not planned nor formally agreed to, the secretaries were looking forward to the same thing this year. This was especially true because the winter was a severe one and many of the secretaries had put in extra hours without pay during the year.

Consequently, the secretaries were extremely displeased, some even angry, when, on the first day of secretaries' week, the dean of the school sent them flowers. Since last year they received a day off, but no flowers, they assumed that this gesture meant they would not get a day off. And they were right! Offended and angered, they "forgot" to send the dean a note thanking him for the flowers. Several weeks passed, and the dean realized he had not received the traditional thank-you note. Puzzled, the dean related what had happened to Professor Freedman, a human relations specialist on the faculty. Professor Freedman, sensitive to the needs of both the dean and the secretaries, later that day asked the head secretary to tell him about secretaries' week. After learning the secretaries' interpretation of what had happened, Professor Freedman shared this with the dean. After the professor left, the dean muttered to himself, "It doesn't pay to try to be nice to people nowadays."

Case Questions

1. Do you agree with the dean's final statement?
2. Where did the dean go wrong?
3. Do you think the secretaries should have been happy with the flowers? Were they ungrateful?
4. What should the dean do next year? Is there anything he should do now?

VISIT THE LIBRARY

Exercise 1, Section 6

1. Using your Web browser, enter Cornell University's Employment Law Documents. (See Visit the Internet Library, Exercise 2 at the end of the Section 2.)
2. Click on the topic "Employment Discrimination," under the heading "Employment Law."
3. Click on the topic *Equal Pay Act of 1963,* and scroll down to the section labeled "(d) Prohibition of sex discrimination."
4. After reading this section, return to your homepage.

Exercise 2, Section 6

The National Center for Employee Ownership (NCEO) is a private, non-profit membership organization that disseminates information on employee stock ownership plans. This exercise will introduce you to NCEO's Web site.

1. Go to NCEO's homepage **(http://www.nceo.org)**
2. Select "About the NCEO" and read this section.
3. Go back to NCEO's homepage and select NCEO's Library.
4. Select "Library" for a general overview of ESOPs.
5. Go back to NCEO's homepage and select "Internet Resources."
6. Return to your homepage.

Chapter 16 Endnotes

1. R. McGarvey, "Something Extra," *Entrepreneur* (May 1995): 70.

2. J. J. Laabs, "Steelcase Slashes Workers' Comp Costs," *Personnel Journal* (Feb. 1993): 72–87; "Workers' Comp Strategy Saves $4 Million Yearly," *Personnel Journal* (Jan. 1993): 55; B. Croft, "Wiring Up Workers' Comp Claims," *Personnel Journal* (April 1996): 153–157.

3. "Employee Benefits—March 1995," *Bulletin to Management* (July 20, 1995): 228–229; "Not So Fringe Anymore," *The Wall Street Journal* (December 18, 1995): R 18, insert; *U. S. Chamber of Commerce's 27th Survey of Employee Benefits* (U.S. Chamber of Commerce, 1615 H St. N.W., Washington, D.C. 20062); ERISA: *The Law and the Code*, D. J. Domone and D. A. Sayre, eds., (Edison, NJ: BNA Books, 1990); "Fringe Benefits in Medium and Large Firms," *Bulletin to Management Datagraph* (Sept. 6, 1990): 284–286. Employers, however, may still provide benefits, see B. J. Coleman, *Primer on Employee Retirement Income Security Act*, 3rd ed. (Washington, D.C.: Bureau of National Affairs, 1989).

4. "Employee Benefits—March 1995"; "Not So Fringe Anymore"; L. Uchitelle, "For Employee Benefits, It Pays to Wear the Union Label," *New York Times* (July 16, 1995): F10.

5. "Employee Benefits—March 1995"; "Not So Fringe Anymore"; Uchitelle, "For Employee Benefits, It Pays to Wear the Union Label"; R. Brookler, "HR in Growing Companies," *Personnel Journal* (November 1992): 80B–O.

6. G. Flynn, "Hallmark Cares," *Personnel Journal* (March 1996): 50–61; S. Caudron, "Andersen Is at Employees' Service," *Personnel Journal* (September 1995): 88–96; "Amenities Help Workers Simplify Life," *Bulletin to Management* (July 20, 1995): 232.

7. "Personnel Shop Talk," *Bulletin to Management* (July 6, 1995): 210; J. Birnbaum, "Goodbye Corporation, Farewell Benefits," *New York Times* (December 17, 1994): 36; T. Chauran, "Benefits Communication," *Personnel Journal* (Jan. 1989): 70–77.

8. T. J. Bergmann and M. A. Bergmann, "How Important Are Fringe Benefits to Employees?" *Personnel* (Dec. 1987): 59–64; R. M. McCaffery, *Employee Benefit Programs: A Total Compensation Perspective* (Boston, MA: PWS-Kent, 1988).

9. For an excellent discussion of what attracts individuals to organizations, see D. P. Schwab, "Recruiting and Organizational Participation," *Personnel Management*, K. M. Rowland and G. R. Ferris, eds., (Boston, MA: Allyn and Bacon, 1982): 103–128.

10. R. D. Hershey, Jr., "Only a Scant Increase in Employee-Benefit Costs," *New York Times* (April 26, 1995): D1.

11. Freudenheim, "The Price of Worker Health Care."

12. Uchitelle, "For Employee Benefits, It Pays to Wear the Union Label."

13. B. Norton, "The Evils of Social Security," *Fortune* (April 15, 1996): 65; "Survey Gauges Managerial Performance," *Bulletin to Management* (October 19, 1995): 329; R. Kuttner, "Why Are We So Insecure About Social Security?" *Business Week* (July 4, 1994): 16; P. Magnusson, "Commentary: Social Security: Apocalypse Soon—Or Sooner," *Business Week* (May 1, 1995): 138; "Social Security and Employees," *Bulletin to Management* (March 16, 1995): 84–85.

14. "State Unemployment Insurance Funds," *Bulletin to Management* (August 17, 1995): 260–261.

15. R. M. McCaffery, *Employee Benefit Programs: A Total Compensation Perspective* (Boston, MA: PWS-Kent, 1988); B. S. Murphy, W. E. Barlow, and D. D. Hatch, "Unemployment Compensation and Religious Beliefs," *Personnel Journal* (June 1987): 36–43; L. Uchitelle, "Jobless Insurance System Aids Reduced Number of Workers," *New York Times* (July 26, 1988): 1.

16. S. Lohr, "A Compromise Plan to Address Workplace Ergonomics Stays on the Shelf," *New York Times* (April 8, 1996): D5; "Crackdown on Job-Injury Costs," *New York Times* (March 16, 1995): C1; M. D. Fefer, "Taking Control of Your Workers' Comp Costs," *Fortune* (October 3, 1994): 131–136; R. Shafer Bruce, "Workers' Comp: Ripe for Cost-Cutting," *New York Times* (March 12, 1995): F13; "Workers' Compensation Benefits," *Bulletin to Management* (November 16, 1995): 364–365.

17. T. Smart, "First Aid for Workers' Comp," *Business Week* (March 18, 1996): 106; "Benefits Policies," *Bulletin to Management* (November 30, 1995): 383; "Checklist for Workers' Compensation Fraud," *Bulletin to Management* (December 9, 1993): 385; "Frahm Says 'Decade of Dread' In Workers Comp is Finished," *HR Reporter* (November 1994): 1–2; P. Kerr, "Fraud Pushes Worker's Comp. Near Crisis," *Seattle Times* (Dec. 29, 1991): A4.

18. *Managing Workers' Compensation Costs* (New York: William M. Mercer Company, 1991); A Tramposh, *Avoiding the Cracks: A Guide to the Workers' Compensation System* (New York: Praeger, 1991).

19. "Injured Workers: Cost-Cutting Rehabilitation Option," *Bulletin to Management* (Oct. 15, 1987): 330, 335.

20. M. W. Fitzgerald, "How to Take on Workers' Compensation and Win," *Personnel Journal* (July 1991); 31–33.

21. Fefer, "Taking Control of Your Workers' Comp Costs."

22. "Life, Accident, and Disability Insurance," *Bulletin to Management* (January 21, 1993): 24.

23. S. Woolley, "Corporate America's Clean Little Secret," *Business Week* (March 18, 1996): 104; P. F. Drucker, "Reckoning with the Pension Fund Revolution," *Harvard Business Review* (March–April 1991): 106–114; "Americans on Benefits: Keep Them Coming," 4–5; McCaffery, *Employee Benefit Programs: A Total Compensation Perspective.*

24. M. Rowland, "A Threat to Defined-Benefit Plans," *Nation's Business* (June 1995): 64–65; F. R. Bowen and C. F. Schultz, "Performance-Based Executive Pensions," *Solutions* (January 1994): 38–39; M. Rowland, "Pension Shift for Small Business," *New York Times* (February 26, 1995): F27; D. C. Johnson, "From Washington, The Fading Pension," *New York Times* (May 4, 1995): D1; B. Leonard, "Agency Protects Pan Am Pension Benefits," *HR News* (Sept. 1991): A1, 10.

25. "Pension Issues: A 50 Year History and Outlook," *Newsletter 33*, no. 3 (Martin E. Segal Company, New York, February 1990); T. F. Duzak, "Defined Benefit and Defined Contribution Plans: A Labor Perspective," in *Economic Survival in Retirement* (New York: Salisbury, 1990): 69; U.S. Department of Labor, Bureau of Labor Statistics, *Employee Benefits in Medium and Large Firms*, 1989 (Washington, D.C.: U.S. Government Printing Office, June 1990).

26. "Employee Savings Plans," *Bulletin to Management* (December 14, 1995): 396–397; T. P. Pare, "Everything You Ever Wanted to Know About 401(k)s, But Were Afraid to Ask," *Fortune* (December 25, 1995): 176–184; D. C. Johnston, "Who's Been Eating My Nest Egg?" *New York Times* (November 26, 1995): Sec. 3, p.1; "Building a Better 401(k)," *The New York Times* (October 22, 1995): Sec. 3, p.1; J. M. Laderman, "The Smart 401(k)," *Business Week* (July 3, 1995): 58–67.

27. C. H. Farnsworth, "Experiment in Worker Ownership Shows a Profit," *New York Times* (Aug. 14, 1993): L33 and 46; "New Developments in Global Stock Plans," *HR Focus* (Nov. 1992): 19.

28. G. A. Patterson, "Hourly Auto Workers Now on Layoff Have a Sturdy Safety Net," *The Wall Street Journal* (Jan. 29, 1991): A1, A2.

29. M. Rowland, "A Health Benefit Often Overlooked," *New York Times* (April 24, 1994): F17; "Perspectives: Health Care Costs," *Personnel Journal* (July 1990): 12.

30. "New Survey Tracks Health Care Costs," *Bulletin to Management* (February 8, 1996): 48; "Health Cost Increases in Single Digits," *Bulletin to Management* (February 24, 1994): 64; "Health Insurance Coverage," *Bulletin to Management* (March 31, 1994): 100–101.

31. R. D. Hershey, Jr., "Only a Scant Increase in Employee-Benefit Costs," *New York Times* (April 26, 1995): D1; M. Freudenheim, "10 Companies Join in Effort to Lower Bids by H.M.O.s," *New York Times* (May 23, 1995): D2; E. Faltermayer, "Why Health Costs Can Keep Slowing," *Fortune* (January 24, 1994): 76–79; K. Matthes, "Healthcare Checkup: How to Evaluate an HMO," *HR Focus* (Sept.1993): 3A; "Monitoring Performance," *Bulletin to Management* (April 8, 1993): 106; J. J. Laabs, "Deere's HMO Turns Crisis Into Profit," *Personnel Journal* (Oct. 1992): 82–89; J. J. Laabs, "How Campbell Manages Its Rural Health Care Dollars," *Personnel Journal* (May 1992): 74–81.

32. M. McNamee, J. Weber, and R. Mitchell, "Healthcare Reform: It's Already Here," *Business Week* (June 14, 1993): 114–121.

33. "Computer Giants Target Health Benefits," *Bulletin to Management* (August 31, 1995): 280; S. Caudron, "Carving Out Healthcare Savings," *Personnel Journal* (April 1995): 38–48; P. Kerr, "Betting the Farm on Managed Care," *New York Times* (June 27, 1993): 1, 6.

34. "An Incentive a Day Can Keep Doctor Bills at Bay," *Business Week* (April 29, 1991): 22.

35. "Wellness Programs Offer Healthy Returns," *Bulletin to Management* (March 7, 1996): 80; S. Tully, "America's Healthiest Companies," *Fortune* (June 12, 1995): 98–106; G. Flynn, "Companies Make Wellness Work," *Personnel Journal* (February 1995): 63–66; J. E. Santora, "Sony Promotes Wellness to Stabilize Health Care Costs," *Personnel Journal* (Sept. 1992): 40–44.

36. S. Caudron, "The Wellness Pay Off," *Personnel Journal* (July 1990): 55–60; "How Healthy are Corporate Fitness Programs?" *The Physician and Sports Medicine* (March 1989). Also contact Wellness Councils of America (WELCOA), 1823 Harney St., Ste. 201, Omaha, NE 68102, (402) 444–1711.

37. "Whose Office Is It Anyhow?" *Fortune* (August 9, 1993): 92. ©1993 Time Inc. All Rights Reserved.

38. "Wellness Plans and the Disabilities Act," *Bulletin to Management* (May 27, 1993): 168.

39. "Be Careful What Your Employees Think You'll Never Find Out About," *HR Reporter* (May 1994): 1–3; D. L. Jacobs, "Can a Visit to the Company Doc Help a Cold but Hurt a Career?" *New York Times* (May 21, 1995): F10, 11.

40. P. Stuart, "Investments in EAPs Pay Off," *Personnel Journal* (Feb. 1993): 43–54.

41. G. Flynn, "Benefits That Work Against You," *Personnel Journal* (October 1995): 77–96.

42. A. Markels, "Use It or Lose It: Vacation Time Expires Now," *The Wall Street Journal* (December 28, 1995): B1, 5.

43. McCaffery, *Employee Benefit Programs: A Total Compensation Perspective.*

44. G. Latham and N. Napier, "Practical Ways to Increase Employee Attendance," *Absenteeism: New Approaches to Understanding, Measuring and Managing Employee Absence*, P. Goodman and R. Atkins, eds., (San Francisco: Jossey-Bass, 1984); R. Steers and S. Rhodes, "Major Influences on Employee Attendance: A Process Model," *Journal of Applied Psychology* 63 (1978): 391–407.

45. D. Scott and S. Markham, "Absenteeism Control Methods: A Survey of Practices and Results," *Personnel Administrator* 27 (1982): 73–86.

46. D. R. Dalton and W. D. Todor, "Turnover, Transfer and Absenteeism: An Interdepartment Perspective," *Journal of Management* (Summer 1993): 193–220.

47. J. Chadwick-Jones, N. Nicholson, and C. Brown, *Social Psychology of Absenteeism* (New York: Praeger, 1982).

48. Scott and Markham, "Absenteeism Control Methods: A Survey of Practices and Results."

49. "'Lifecycle' Support for Work and Family," *Bulletin to Management* (November 24, 1995): 376; "Personnel Shop Talk," *Bulletin to Management* (May 11, 1995): 146.

50. Noble, "Making a Case for Family Friendly Programs"; "Family Friendly Benefits Have Spread Greatly," *Bulletin to Management* (March 7, 1996): 73–74, 79. Also read J. J. Laabs, "HR's Vital Role at Levi Strauss," *Personnel Journal* (Dec. 1992): 34–46.

51. "Flexible Spending Accounts," *Bulletin to Management* (June 22, 1995): 1–8; M. B. Scott, "How Companies Help with Family Care," *Employee Benefit Plan Review* (May 1990): 12.

52. "International Foundation of Employee Benefits Plans," *Nontraditional Benefits for the Work Force of 2000: A Special Report* (Brookfield, WI: IFEBP, 1990).

53. S. Overman, "3M Arranges Summer Child Care," *HR Magazine* (March 1991): 46–47.

54. C. M. Loder, "Merck and Co. Breaks New Ground for Employee Child Care Centers," *The Star Ledger* (May 1990): 12; "Companies Cited for Supporting Working Mothers," *HR Focus* (Dec. 1991): 13; S. J. Goff, M. K. Mount, and R. L. Jamison, "Employer Supported Child Care, Work/Family Conflict, and Absenteeism: A Field Study," *Personnel Psychology* 43 (1990): 793–809; S. Zedeck and K. L. Mosier, "Work in the Family and Employing Organization," *American Psychologist* (Feb. 1990): 240–251.

55. E. Smith, "First Interstate Finds an Eldercare Solution," *HR Magazine* (July 1991): 152; A. E. Scharlach, B. F. Lowe, and E. L. Schneider, *Elder Care and the Work Force* (Lexington, MA: Lexington Books, 1991); L. Crawford, *Dependent Care and the Employee Benefits Package* (Westport, CT: Quorum Books, 1990).

56. "International Foundation of Employee Benefits Plans," *Nontraditional Benefits for the Work Force of 2000: A Special Report*, p.150.

57. Ibid.

58. "Lotus Opens a Door for Gay Partners," *Business Week* (Nov. 4, 1991): 80–81; "Domestic Partner Benefits Gain Foothold," *Bulletin to Management* (June 15, 1995): 192.

59. "National Healthcorp," *Fortune* (July 29, 1991): 110; L. A. Ferman, M. Hoyman, J. Cutcher-Gershenfeld, and E. Savoie, *Joint Training Programs: A Union–Management Approach to Preparing Workers for the Future* (Ithaca, NY: ILR Press, 1991).

60. K. P. Shapiro and J. A. Sherman, "Employee Attitudes Benefit Plan Designs," *Personnel Journal* (July 1987): 49–53.

61. R. Brookler, "HR in Growing Companies," *Personnel Journal* (Nov. 1992): 802.

62. B. Olmsted and S. Smith, "Flex for Success!" *Personnel* (June 1989): 50–54; M. E. Grossman and M. Magnus, "The Boom in Benefits," *Personnel Journal* (Nov. 1988): 51–55; W. Wendling, "Responses to a Changing Work Force," *Personnel Administrator* (Nov. 1988): 50–54; C. A. Baker, "Flex Your Benefits," *Personnel Journal* (May 1988): 54–60; J. E. Santora, "American Opts For Flex," *Personnel Journal* (Nov. 1990): 32–34.

63. G. Flynn, "Build the Wow-factor into Pension Training," *Personnel Journal* (April 1996): 70–77; C. Murino, "What Benefit Is Communication?" *Personnel Journal* (February 1990): 64–68; Bureau of National Affairs, "Cost, Communication and Compliance Concerns," *Bulletin to Management* (March 21, 1985): 7; "Pay off," *The Wall Street Journal* (July 8, 1982): 1; R. Foltz, "Communique," *Personnel Administrator* (May 1981): 8.

64. G. Flynn, "Hannaford Bros. Makes Health Care A Maine Event," *Personnel Journal* (May 1996): 48–55; "A New Age in Employee Benefits: Report on the 7th Annual Corporate Benefits Conference," *Bulletin to Management* (November 9, 1995): 14.

65. "Personnel Shop Talk," *Bulletin to Management* (July 6, 1995): 210. Reprinted with permission by the Bureau of National Affairs, (Tel. 1-800-372-1033).

66. "Permissible Pregnancy Practices," *Fair Employment Practices* (Dec., 1983): 3. The Pregnancy Disability Amendment also has other provisions; for a description of them, see S. R. Zacur and W. Greenwood, "The Pregnancy Disability Amendment: What the Law Provides, Part II," *Personnel Administrator* (March 1982): 55–58.

67. R. Pear, "Disabled and Chronically Ill Gain Health Coverage and Job Rights," *New York Times* (June 9, 1991): A15.

68. Ibid.

69. B. P. Noble, "Interpreting the Family Leave Act," *New York Times* (August 1, 1993): F24. See also D. Gunsch, "The Family Leave Act: A Financial Burden?" *Personnel Journal* (Sept.1993): 48–57.

70. "Important Changes in Final Family and Medical Leave Rules," *Fair Employment Practices* (February 23, 1995): 21; "DOL Extends FMLA Deadline For Final Regulation Compliance," *HR Reporter* (February 1995): 1–2; B. Presley Noble, "Making Family Leave a Reality," *New York Times* (July 31, 1994): F19; "Enforcement of Family and Medical Leave Act," *Fair Employment Practices* (June 16, 1994): 70; G. Flynn, "HR Must Take Proactive Steps to Curb FMLA Misuse," *Personnel Journal* (September 1994): 36–45.

71. The Bureau of National Affairs, "ERISA's Effects on Pension Plan Administration," *Bulletin to Management* (Aug. 9, 1984): 1–2; K. D. Gill, ed., *ERISA: The Law and the Code*, 1985 ed. (Washington, D.C.: Bureau of National Affairs, 1985); B. J. Coleman, *Primer on Employee Retirement Income Security Act* (Washington, D.C.: The Bureau of National Affairs, 1985).

72. J. A. LoCicero, "How to Cope with the Multi-Employer Pension Plan Amendments Act of 1980," *Personnel Administrator* (May 1981): 51–54, 68; J. A. LoCicero, "Multi-Employer Pension Plans: A Time Bomb for Employers?" *Personnel Journal* (Nov. 1980): 922–932.

73. S. Chandler, "United We Own," *Business Week* (March 18, 1996): 96–100; A. Bernstein, "Why ESOP Deals Have Slowed to a Crawl," *Business Week* (March 18, 1996): 101–102.

74. "The Real Strengths of Employee Stock Ownership," *Business Week* (July 15, 1991): 156.

75. D. Schwartz, "The Last Word on Section 89," *Personnel Journal* (Jan. 1989): 48–57; R. E. Johnson and S. J. Velleman, "Section 89: Close the New Pandora's Box," *Personnel Journal* (Nov. 1988): 70–78; J. Ortman. "Section 89: Why You Should Act Now," *Personnel Journal* (Nov. 1988): 78–79.

76. S. L. Dolan and R. S. Schuler, *Human Resource Management: The Canadian Dynamic* (Ontario, Canada: Nelson, 1994).

77. This section is adapted from G. Flynn, "HR in Mexico: What You Should Know," *Personnel Journal* (August 1994): 34–44. See also A. Winsor, *The Complete Guide to Doing Business in Mexico* (New York: AMACOM, 1994).

78. "Tips to Succeed South of the Border," *Bulletin to Management* (April 28, 1994): 129–130. For more discussion on pensions in Latin America, see J. Brooke, "Quiet Revolution in Latin Pensions," *New York Times* (September 10, 1994): 37.

79. G. Smith, S. Baker, and W. Glasgall, "Mexico: Will Economic Reform Survive the Turmoil?" *Business Week* (April 11, 1994): 24–27; S. Baker, G. Smith, and E. Weiner, "The Mexican Worker," *Business Week* (April 19, 1993): 84–92.

80. M. J. Mandel, "Canada's Health Plan Gives Employment Figures a Rosy Glow," *Business Week* (Feb. 28, 1994): 22.

SECTION 7

Establishing and Improving Work Environments and Relationships

Safe and healthy working conditions are important to us all. Most of us would not take a job if we thought the conditions unsafe or unhealthy. Most companies would not knowingly design a job to be unsafe and unhealthy. Not only would such an action be highly illegal, it would be against the value system of the people in the organization. In fact, most companies find that having an outstanding record of safety and health enhances their ability to attract and retain a competent workforce. Consequently, in Chapter 17, we discuss how companies can be made safe and healthy for employees, if they are not already. We will also discuss the significance of poor safety and health conditions. High technology brings with it a potential for unforeseen side effects on health that only time and the application of more technology will reveal. This is important for you as an individual, regardless of whether you will be working at home, in a factory, in an office, or on the road, because your long-term health and the quality of your life may depend on it.

Unionization is an interesting process with strong historical, cultural, and legal roots in this country. Union organizing activities are often emotionally charged, and even if unsuccessful can have lasting ramifications on an organization and its HR philosophy. When faced with unionization efforts, a company must decide whether or not unionization is in its best interests. The answer to this question is not always predictable. Then the organization must formulate a strategy to affect the outcome of potential unionization efforts, and it must eventually deal with the outcome.

Once in place, unions represent the interests of the employees in discussions with the company. Contracts are established between the workers' union and the management of the company. These two parties negotiate and bargain over working conditions, wages, and benefits. Longtime adversaries with fundamentally conflicting goals, today unions and management are discovering that there is little room for conflict if organizations are to remain competitive in the global economy. Thus, establishing and maintaining effective work relationships is such an important topic that it is the focus of the remaining two chapters of this section. Chapter 18 describes the history of the union movement, why unions are attractive to individuals, the structure of today's union movement, and aspects associated with the formation of the unions. Chapter 19 describes collective bargaining, the process by which wages and working conditions are established.

In Chapter 20, we discuss the system that can facilitate the efforts of organizations in their quest to be better places to work—an organization's information system. We address issues surrounding data information and assessment systems. To manage human resources effectively today requires systematic and scientific tools and techniques. Some of these tools and techniques are associated with the Internet, the World Wide Web, computer technology, automation, and HR information and data systems. The computer has become a major tool in the repertoire of organizations as they seek to manage their human resources ever more effectively. The use of HR information systems (HRIS) can ease and speed HR decisions. The system can identify qualified individuals for job openings, quantify the effectiveness of diversity programs, and track absentee rates over several years. For the HR department to be world-class, to link more effectively with the business, and to better serve the needs of the line manager and the business, it must use the best, most up-to-date technology possible. The increasing importance of this area has changed the role of the HRIS manager from that of a project manager to that of a strategic partner. Organizations can no longer assume that their HR activities are working or that improvements are not necessary. Continual assessment is another way HR professionals can demonstrate not only to the organization, but also to line managers and employees, that what the HR department is doing is working effectively in partnership with the organization's stockholders.

Occupational Safety and Health

17

CHAPTER

"As Rosendin Electric, Inc.'s benefits administrator, I'm a crusader for safety—especially if it slashes workers' compensation costs by $350,000. That's just what my safety program did last year."

Linda Johnson,
San Jose, California[1]

Learning Objectives

1. Describe the benefits and costs of safety and health in organizations.
2. Explain the model of occupational safety and health.
3. Discuss the legal considerations.
4. Describe the common hazards.
5. Describe what organizations are doing and can do to improve occupational safety and health.
6. Describe some safety and health issues in other countries.

Chapter Outline

MANAGING HUMAN RESOURCES

at ACI America

Here's what William M. Minderman, vice president of human resources, had to say when asked about occupational safety and health at his company, ACI America in Memphis, Tennessee. "You often hear, 'Our industry is different—you can't avoid safety problems.' But you can. We are in industries noted for high accident rates—we own glass companies in the construction industry. We have seven divisions in 110 locations in about 17 states, and we are the largest purchasers of flat glass outside General Motors. Our environments for safety are quite diverse—from retail stores to construction sites or large plants.

"Our country has increased its emphasis on safety in the last 10 years, and our efforts have really come together. Most states charge a percentage of payroll for workers' compensation—a percentage that's dependent on the industry. For example, for construction workers in California, the rate is $15 for every $100 of payroll. In Texas, the rate is $14 for every $100 of payroll. Typically, most employers pay those rates. We pay about 40 percent of those rates, and some of our competitors pay 120 percent of those rates. Our accident frequency is significantly lower than is typical in our industries, as shown by SIC coded data published by the National Safety Council.

PERFORMANCE COUNTS

"You can't just give lip service to safety. The managers of our location have five or six key responsibilities they are accountable for on their performance appraisals—and safety is one of them. In the performance appraisal, we measure accident rates for each manager at each location and how well the manager conforms with corporate policy. Conformance with corporate policy is audited by our insurance carrier on a yearly basis, and we do our own audits as well. If the manager is having safety problems, he is given an incentive opportunity to improve his performance.

"We set annual safety goals for each division, and we have good historic performance data by location. We know our higher risk areas and seasons; for example, more construction in summer causes more injuries.

"We have fairly rigid company policies for managers. For example, they must hold monthly meetings on safety (covering types of accidents, why they happen, and how to avoid them), and report accidents to both the insurance company to process the claim, and to the division HR manager. Through the insurer, we have an on-line system, and we know our daily accident rate. We get monthly and year-to-date reports, and these reports are shared with our president. The vice-president and general managers of each division also get their division's performance summarized, as does each operation within each division.

"We provide support at a corporate level—a safety orientation, including a videotape, and some general information applicable across the company. Our divisions do things on their own, as well.

HR'S ROLE

"HR managers can't do the job themselves—but they can encourage conformance to policies and procedures and reporting guidelines. Our division HR managers check reports and make sure that investigations are held and that managers have a plan on what to do.

"Our HR managers help with orientations, seeing that we have company physicians and appropriate incentive programs. They provide a key focus for our safety programs.

"But the most important aspect of safety is interest and commitment from the top. It doesn't take people long to separate what's said from what's meant. There have to be lots of pushes. It's critical that management keep the pressure on—day to day, year to year. Then, employees buy in because it's expected. You have to show you mean it—monitor results, and pay for performance."[2]

This feature illustrates some crucial issues about occupational safety and health. One is the increased emphasis firms are putting on safety programs. Another is the benefits associated with workplace safety: a safe work environment keeps employees healthy and productive, and it reduces the workers' compensation costs that firms pay to the state in which they do business. A third issue is the importance of making line managers and employees responsible for safety through policies, goals, performance appraisal, and compensation. Finally, note the central role of the HR manager. While not out on the line themselves, they can still do much to assist line managers and employees in making conditions safer and healthier.

Of course, to do this effectively, HR managers need to know the issues of occupational safety and health in organizations. Workplace hazards are divided into the accidents and diseases that produce physiological and physical conditions, and the stress and low quality of working life that result when psychological conditions are not optimal. We will look at strategies to improve employee safety and health, including such measures as improved record-keeping, job redesign, ergonomics, and educational programs.[3] Then we will briefly examine the role of the federal government in establishing and enforcing safety standards.

Did You KNOW?

Tyson Foods, the poultry producer in Springdale, Arkansas, estimates that up to 95% of its 81 plants in 18 states have some sort of safety contest or awareness program for its 51,000 employees.

Occupational Safety and Health

Occupational safety and health refers to the physiological/physical and psychological conditions of an organization's workforce that results from the work environment provided by the organization.

If an organization takes effective safety and health measures, fewer of its employees have short- or long-term ill effects as a result of being employed at that organization.

Physiological/physical conditions include occupational diseases and accidents such as actual loss of life or limb; cardiovascular diseases; various forms of cancer such as lung cancer and leukemia; emphysema; and arthritis. Other conditions that are known to result from an unhealthy work environment include white lung disease, brown lung disease, black lung disease, sterility, central nervous system damage, and chronic bronchitis.

Psychological conditions refer to organizational stress and low quality of working life. These encompass dissatisfaction, apathy, withdrawal, projection, tunnel vision, forgetfulness, inner confusion about roles and duties, mistrust of others, vacillation in decision-making, inattentiveness, irritability, procrastination, and a tendency to become distraught over trifles.

Occupational safety and health refers to the physiological/ physical and psychological conditions of the workforce.

Physiological /physical conditions include many occupational diseases and accidents. Psychological conditions refer to organizational stress and low quality of working life.

Why Is It Important to Improve Occupational Safety and Health?

LEARNING OBJECTIVE 1

Describe the benefits and costs of safety and health in organizations.

Improving safety and health conditions can reduce the symptoms and costs of poor safety and health. Certain groups of employees appear to be more affected than others and perhaps should be targeted for more intensive efforts.

> *We've reached an accommodation with blue-collar death. Forget that a U. S. worker is five times more likely to die than a Swede. . . Forget that a U. S. worker is three times more likely to die than a Japanese.*
>
> *The sad reality is that blue-collar blood pours too easily. [Occupational Safety and Health Administration] fines amount to mere traffic tickets for those who run our companies. The small fines are simply buried in the cost of production. Blood can be cash accounted, given a number, and factored with other costs . . .*[4] *This has tremendous implications for the union-man-*

agement relationship, not to mention costs from poor worker morale, lower productivity and mounting litigation.

Blue-collar workers are not the only ones to suffer from workplace hazards. White-collar workers, including managers, also encounter workplace hazards:

"Stress is the most pervasive and potent toxin in the workplace," says Leon J. Warshaw, executive director of the New York Business Group on Health, a coalition of businesses concerned about health care. In California, mental stress claims are the most rapidly increasing type of workers' compensation cases, having risen 700 percent in the last decade. And a poll earlier this year found that 25 percent of the employees surveyed at New Jersey businesses suffered from stress-induced ailments.[5]

A safe and healthy workplace is a corporate value at Weyerhaeuser. They say that "All employees are accountable for a safe, clean workplace and are empowered to challenge any activity that compromises safety and/or cleanliness."

Although the traditional ill effects on the white-collar workforce have been those related to psychological conditions, there is growing concern today over physical conditions relating to the unforeseen effects of the computer terminal (eyestrain, miscarriages, carpal tunnel syndrome) and closed office buildings, where chemical components from sources such as carpeting and building construction build up and are circulated through the ventilation system.

As a consequence of the importance of safety and health, everyone in the company is concerned. The feature, "Partnership: Working Together in Safety and Health" illustrates some health and safety activities for line managers, HR professionals, and all other employees. The importance of these activities is even more evident in our discussion of the benefits and costs of safety and health.

The Benefits of a Safe and Healthy Work Environment

If organizations can reduce the rates and severity of their occupational accidents, diseases, and work-related stress levels and improve the quality of work life for their employees, they can only become more effective. Such an improvement can result in 1) more productivity due to fewer lost workdays, 2) increased efficiency from a more committed workforce, 3) reduced medical and insurance costs, 4) lower workers' compensation rates and direct payments because fewer claims are filed, 5) greater flexibility and adaptability in the workforce as a result of increased participation and an increased sense of ownership, and 6) better selection ratios because of the enhanced image of the organization.[6] Companies can thus increase their profits substantially.

PARTNERSHIP:

WORKING TOGETHER IN SAFETY AND HEALTH

LINE MANAGERS	HR PROFESSIONALS	EMPLOYEES
Make safety and health a major objective of the firm.	Work with other professionals such as medical doctors and industrial engineers to develop new programs.	Participate in the development and administration of safety and health programs.
Support the HR professionals' efforts to train all employees in safety and health.	Create HR programs that train employees for safe and healthy behaviors and reward them for their success.	Perform in accordance with established safety and health guidelines.

The Costs of an Unsafe and Unhealthy Work Environment

Back injuries are the most prevalent of all workplace injuries. Every year an estimated 10 million employees in the United States encounter back pain that impairs their job performance. Approximately 1 million employees file workers' compensation claims for back injuries and lose 75 million work days. Billions of dollars are spent each year to treat back pain—perhaps $25 billion in workers' compensation payments alone.[7]

Did You KNOW?

Each year there are about 500,000 cases of job-related illnesses and 6 million injuries.

Estimates of workplace deaths range from 2,800 (Bureau of Labor Statistics) to around 10,000 yearly (National Safety Council). In either case, the numbers are significant.[8]

Of course, there are differences in these rates depending on job type, and sometimes even on the state. For example, the accidental death rate for 100,000 workers in the United States is seven, but for the workers in Alaska's fishing industry, it is nearly 100 times this figure.[9]

Construction is one of the most dangerous jobs in America, placing workers in a constantly changing raw environment where one misstep or forgetful moment can snuff out a life or crush a limb. Pressures to finish a job quickly often push foremen and workers to take risks, industry experts say, amid a macho culture of muscle, sweat, and swagger that tends to belittle safety measures and confuse caution with timidity.

The new push for safety, the experts say, is being led by large companies forced by the recession to try to save money and become more competitive by taking advantage of revised insurance industry policies that reward good safety records.

"When companies understand that safety saves them money and increases productivity, they become believers," says Mr. Steven Thies, corporate safety manager for Henkels & McCoy, a 5,000-worker utility construction company based in Blue Bell, Pennsylvania.[10]

Did You KNOW?

About 220,000 workers die around the world every year in work accidents or from illness contracted at work.

Construction, along with mining and agriculture, are typically the three most dangerous industries nationwide, with deaths per 100,000 employees yearly being around 32, 43, and 40, respectively. Regardless of industry, vehicle accidents and homicide are the biggest sources of work-related death.[11]

While it is impossible to obtain precise information, the costs of workplace deaths and injuries are estimated to be more than $50 billion. Similar cost estimates are made for the more than 500,000 workers who annually succumb to occupational diseases.

Did You KNOW?

Of the 6 million injuries, about half result in lost work time.

In addition to the costs of the physical/physiological conditions are the enormous costs associated with the psychological conditions that include organizational stress and a low quality of working life. For example, alcoholism, often the result of attempts to cope with job pressures, costs organizations and society over $65 billion annually. Of this, $20 billion is attributed to lost productivity and the remainder to the direct costs of insurance, hospitalization, and other medical costs.[12] Perhaps more difficult to quantify, but just as symptomatic of stress and poor quality of working life, are workers' feelings of lack of meaning and involvement in their work and loss of importance as individuals.

A Model of Occupational Safety and Health

LEARNING OBJECTIVE 2

Explain the model of occupational safety and health.

The sources of safety and health conditions in organizations can be labeled as workplace environment hazards; these are comprised of two components: the

Physical work environment reflects the tangible aspects of the work place that can cause occupational accidents and diseases. Sociopsychological work environment reflects the social, emotional, interpersonal, and personal aspects of the workplace that can cause low quality of working life and stress.

physical work environment and the **sociopsychological work environment.** Together, these sources, the physical/physiological and psychological conditions, and their outcomes constitute a model of occupational health and safety in organizations (Exhibit 17.1).

Legal Considerations

There are four major categories into which the legal framework for occupational safety and health can be divided: the **Occupational Safety and Health Administration (OSHA),** workers' compensation programs, the common-law doctrine of torts, and local initiatives.

LEARNING OBJECTIVE 3

Discuss the legal considerations.

The Occupational Safety and Health Administration (OSHA)

The federal government's primary response to the issue of safety and health in the workplace has been the *Occupational Safety and Health Act* of 1970, which created OSHA and which calls for safety and health inspectors of organizations regardless of size, reporting by employers, and investigations of accidents and allegations of hazards. The other two organizations are the **National Institute for Occupational Safety and Health (NIOSH)** and the Occupational Safety and Health Review Commission. The Commission reviews appeals made by organizations that received citations from OSHA inspectors for alleged safety and health violations.[13] OSHA is responsible for establishing and enforcing occupational safety and health standards and for inspecting and issuing citations to organizations that violate these standards.

Occupational Safety and Health Administration (OSHA) is the office of the Federal Government concerned with occupational safety and health.

OSHA is the major federal agency watching out for occupational health and safety. OSHA requires organizations to:

- **allow inspections**
- **keep records**
- **disclose medical records**

Regardless of whether organizations are inspected, they are required to keep safety and health records so that OSHA can compile accurate statistics on work injuries and illnesses. These include all disabling, serious, or significant injuries and illnesses, whether or not they involve loss of time from work. Excluded are minor injuries that require only first aid treatment and do not involve medical treatment, loss of consciousness, restriction of work or motion, or transfer to another job. Falsification of records or failure to keep adequate records can result in some rather substantial fines. The record keeping requirement was recently qualified, however:

EXHIBIT 17.1

Model of Occupational Safety and Health in Organizations

SOURCES OF HAZARDS IN THE WORKPLACE	SAFETY AND HEALTH CONDITIONS	OUTCOMES
Physical work environment →	Physiological/physical: • occupational accidents • occupational diseases	High turnover/absenteeism Dissatisfaction Medical claims Low productivity Low efficiency High workers' compensation costs Low job involvement Low quality
Sociopsychological work environment →	Psychological: • low quality of working life • organizational stress	

> *An employer may withhold injury and illness records from federal safety investigators if it has a legitimate need to keep the records private, and the Occupational Safety and Health Administration has failed to obtain a warrant granting it access to such documents, the Occupational Safety and Health Review Commission (OSHRC) rules. Rejecting the principle that OSHA compliance officers have unlimited rights to make warrantless examinations of an employer's records, the commission holds that the employer had a reasonable expectation of privacy in safeguarding the information in its injury records. Such documents, OSHRC points out, may contain proprietary information on operations and manufacturing processes that employers may want to keep confidential.* (Kings Island Division of Taft Broadcasting Co., 1987).[14]

Did You KNOW?

OSHA estimates that more than 100,000 lives have been saved since OSHA was established in 1970.

In addition to keeping records, the *Access to Employee Exposure and Medical Records Regulation* of 1980 requires organizations to show or give to employees, their designated representatives, and OSHA, their on-the-job medical records. This regulation also requires employers to provide access to records of measurements of employee exposure to toxic substances.

The employee's right to know has been further strengthened by the *Hazard Communication Standard* that went into effect in 1986.[15] Under this standard, employers are required to provide workers with information and training on hazardous chemicals in their work area at the time of their initial assignment and whenever a new hazard is introduced. According to OSHA, effective communication is the real key and should include information for employees on the following:

- The standard's requirements and operations in the workplace that use hazardous chemicals
- Proper procedures for determining the presence of chemicals and detecting hazardous releases
- Protective measures and equipment that should be used
- Location of the written hazard communication programs[16]

Whereas OSHA was established to provide workers protection against accidents and diseases, workers' compensation was established to provide financial aid for those unable to work because of accidents and diseases, as described in Chapter 16.[17]

Workers' Compensation Claims

For many years, workers' compensation awards were granted only to workers unable to work because of physical injury or damage (that is, due to accidents and diseases). Since 1955, however, court decisions have either caused or enticed 15 states to allow workers' compensation payment in job-related cases of anxiety, depression, and mental disorders.[18]

That year, the Texas Supreme Court charted this new direction in workers' compensation claims by stating that an employee who became terrified, highly anxious, and unable to work because of a job-related accident had a compensable claim even though he had no physical injury (*Bailey v. American General Insurance Company,* 1955). In another court ruling (*James v. State Accident Insurance Fund,* 1980), an Oregon court ruled in favor of a worker's claim for compensation for inability to work due to job stress resulting from conflicting work assignments.[19]

The Common-Law Doctrine of Torts

Much of the legal consideration discussion we have had in this book is based upon statutory law, that is, laws passed by legislative bodies at the federal and state levels. For example, the *Civil Rights Act* of 1991 and the *Americans with Disabilities Act* of 1990 and *Occupational Safety and Health Act* of 1970 are statutory law. But there is also the **common-law doctrine of torts**. This refers to decisions made in court cases regarding wrongful acts such as personal injuries committed by an employee on another employee or even a customer which results in a lawsuit against the employer. Employees can obtain damage awards by suing employers. However, employees must demonstrate that the employer engaged in reckless or intentional infliction designed to degrade or humiliate. A few such cases have been successfully brought against employers, but they appear to be the exception, in part because workers' compensation programs were designed to remove workplace accidents and injury from litigation.[20] However, the cases successfully brought against employers are notable because of the costs involved. Some notable cases are detailed in the feature, "Managing Human Resources and Workplace Torts: Who's Responsible?" In a more recent case, the Oregon Circuit Court of Appeals stated that:

Common-law doctrine of torts refers to decisions made in court cases regarding wrongful acts such as personal injury.

> *McDonald's Corp. is liable for $400,000 in damages related to an accident caused by a teenaged employee who fell asleep while driving home from work. . . .The employee worked until 11:30 p.m. on a Sunday night, then slept for seven hours before going to school, working from 3:30 p.m. until 7:30 p.m., and returning at midnight to work until 8:20 a.m. Tuesday. The employee died in the crash, and the driver of the car he struck sued for negligence. Upholding the claim, the court finds that McDonald's continued to work the employee after he reached a visibly fatigued state (Faverty v. McDonald's Restaurants of Oregon, Inc., 1995).*[21]

Local Initiatives

State, municipal, and city governments may pass their own safety and health laws and regulations that go beyond the coverage of OSHA. Consequently, employers need to be aware of local regulations. Sometimes these local initiatives offer a glimpse as to what other areas or even the federal government might do in the future. This seems to be the case with the law passed in San Francisco imposing safeguards on workers using video display terminals. The law requires the use of adjustable chairs and tables, angle-adjustable screens and keyboards, work time at tasks away from the computer, training of workers and supervisors, and the use of printer covers to reduce office noise. The local labor unions heralded the San Francisco law as a model for other cities and municipalities.

The ADA has applications here just as it does in job design, selection, training, employee rights, and compensation.

Americans with Disabilities Act (ADA)

As defined in Chapter 10, the ADA applies to disabled individuals; this covers applicants for jobs and treatment of current employees, including layoff and discharge. Here is where the relationship between the ADA and occupational health and safety kick in: employee layoffs and discharges (terminations) are constituting 50 percent of all claims filed under the ADA. And 15 percent of these are for back pain. Because victims are entitled to sue for up to $300,000, lots of employers are tempted to settle before going to trial.[22] Organizations are therefore actively seeking ways to remove hazardous conditions from the work environment.

LEARNING OBJECTIVE 4

Describe the common hazards.

Hazards in Occupational Safety and Health

As Exhibit 17.1 shows, both the physical and the sociopsychological aspects of the workplace environment are important components of occupational safety and

MANAGING HUMAN RESOURCES

and Workplace Torts Who's Responsible?

Employers may be held liable for the negligent acts of employees committed within the scope of their employment. On this basis, employers are paying huge damages claims in lawsuits for negligent hiring, retention, and supervision, say Ronald Green and Richard Rubenstein, authors of a book on workplace torts.

CASES IN POINT

Recent years have seen a proliferation of lawsuits against employers resulting from employees' illegal acts. Litigation is often the resort of individuals injured or damaged by incompetent, unsafe, or dangerous employees. Some employees should not have been hired initially or retained once their dangerous proclivities were discovered, the authors conclude. Cases that illustrate this point include:

- **Incompetent employees.** A retired police officer with no medical training and cataracts was hired by a hospital to coordinate its kidney transport unit. A patient was given a transplant of a cancerous kidney, causing the death of the patient. The donor's medical chart revealed that the kidney was cancerous. A $3.5 million suit was settled by the hospital for the negligent hiring of the kidney transport coordinator, who was unskilled in reading medical charts and unable to read in any event due to his cataracts. (*Kolator v. State,* 1988)
- **Unsafe employees.** An airline passenger was arguing with a boarding agent and grabbed his arm. The agent kicked the passenger in the shins and bit her hand. On request, the airline tested the agent for AIDS, and the test was positive. The passenger then charged the airline with negligent hiring, seeking $12 million in damages. The case is pending in federal court. (*Doe v. American Airlines,* 1986)
- **Dangerous employees.** A supermarket providing home delivery hired an applicant after a 20-minute job interview. While making a delivery on his fourth day of employment, he raped and robbed a customer in her home. The court ruled that when a firm provides delivery services, it has a duty to its customers to employ safe help. In this case, since the personnel director conducted "a cursory" interview and failed to check employment references, a jury could infer that the supermarket failed to exercise due care and caution. The negligent hiring suit reportedly was settled for a six-figure amount. (*Rosen-House v. Sloan's Supermarket,* 1988)
- **Violent employees.** After a customer in a car rental office argued with the rental agent, the employee struck him with a blow to the head, knocking him to the floor. As the customer lay on the floor, the employee repeatedly kicked him and pummeled him with "judo chops." In the customer's civil action for negligent retention, the evidence showed that the employee had a history of blowing up at and threatening customers. Moreover, the rental company had not disciplined the employee either before or after the incident. A jury awarded the customer $350,000 in compensatory damages and $400,000 in punitive damages. (*Greenfield v. Spectrum Inv. Group,* 1985)[23]

health. Each aspect impacts health and safety. Traditionally, hazards in the physical environment have received greater attention. Increasingly, however, both OSHA and companies themselves admit that sociopsychological conditions greatly impact health and safety, and they are doing something about it. For example, in combating stress and its symptoms:

Coors, the Colorado-based brewery, has a stress management program that features more than 20 courses which address family and personal issues as well as workplace issues.

> *. . .at Hoffman-LaRoche Inc., the Nutley, New Jersey-based subsidiary of the Swiss pharmaceutical concern, employees receive after-hours instruction in a variety of stress-management methods. They include meditation, breathing exercises, and a technique called 'dot stopping." A form of biofeedback, the technique teaches employees to control their stress by recalling a wonderful moment and focusing on the feelings and sensations they had then.*[24]

Today, efforts to improve occupational safety and health are not complete without a strategy for reducing psychological work-related stress. Developing effective strategies begins with an understanding of the factors in the workplace environment that affect these two aspects of safety and health.

Occupational Accidents

Occupational accidents are those injuries sustained on the job from physical conditions in the workplace.

Certain organizations, and certain departments within an organization, always have higher **occupational accident** rates than others. Several factors can explain this difference.

Organizational Qualities. Accident rates vary substantially by industry. For example, firms in the construction and manufacturing industries have higher incidence rates than firms in services, finance, insurance, and real estate. When employees believe this, they tend to think things just can't be changed. According to Donald Brush, vice president and general manager at the Barden Corporation, Danbury, Connecticut:

> *Over the years, Barden employees assumed that, because we are a metal working shop, people were just going to get hurt. Several years ago, we created a Safety and Health Committee that meets monthly to consider our safety and health performance and to effect improvements. More recently, we created a Safety Development Committee whose members included a line superintendent as chairman, the safety engineer, the plant chemist, the occupational health nurse, and the training coordinator—a nice mix of line, staff, and human resource representation. This committee reports to the Safety and Health Committee. Its objective is to develop programs that strengthen safety awareness and performance. While it is too early to prepare a report card, early indications are that results will be favorably impressive. At about the same time, it became clear that the safety engineer was not producing the same results we wanted. After weighing the facts, we created something new and promising. We eliminated the safety engineering position as such and transferred its accountabilities to the Medical Department. The occupational health nurse had previously shown considerable knowledge about safety matters, and her aggressive investigation of accidents and near-misses prompted us to create a new position encompassing both the safety and the medical functions. The occupational health nurse has thus been promoted to a new position entitled Manager of Employee Health and Safety. We believe that this position is unique for a small company, and we are optimistic about results.*[25]

Interestingly, small and large organizations (those with fewer than a hundred employees or more than a thousand) have lower incidence rates than medium-sized organizations. This may be because supervisors in small organizations are better able to detect safety hazards and prevent accidents than those in medium-size ones. And larger organizations have more resources to hire staff specialists who can devote all their efforts to safety and accident prevention.

In general, however, it is the working conditions (outdoors versus indoors), and the tools and technology available to do the job (for example, heavy machinery versus personal computers) that most impact occupational accidents. Next in line are the workers themselves.

The Unsafe Employee? Although organizational factors certainly play an important role in occupational safety, some experts point to the employee as the pivotal cause of accidents. Accidents depend on the behavior of the person, the degree of hazard in the work environment, and pure chance. The degree to which the person contributes to the accident can be an indication of an individual's proneness to accidents. Accident proneness cannot be considered a stable set of personal traits that always contribute to accidents. Nevertheless, certain psychological and physical characteristics seem to make some people more susceptible to accidents.

For example, employees who are emotionally "low" have more accidents that those who are emotionally "high," while employees who have had fewer accidents have been found to be more optimistic, trusting, and concerned for others than those who have had more accidents. Employees under greater stress are likely to have more accidents than those with poorer vision. Older workers are likely to be hurt less than younger workers. People who are quicker at recognizing visual patterns than at making muscular manipulations are less likely to have accidents than those who are just the opposite. Many psychological conditions probably related to accident proneness—for instance, hostility and emotional immaturity—may be temporary states. Thus, they are difficult to detect until at least one accident has occurred. Because none of these characteristics is related to accidents in all work environments and because they are not always present in employees, selecting and screening job applicants on the basis of accident proneness is difficult.

The Violent Employee? Workplace violence is growing rapidly and employers are being held responsible, as described in the feature "Managing Human Resource and Workplace Torts: Who's Responsible?" Death by homicide is the second biggest cause of death in the workplace today.[26] While it may be difficult to

Did You KNOW?

Small firms cannot afford lost time from accidents: Each employee represents a larger percentage of the workforce than in larger firms.

Did You KNOW?

Each year nearly 1 million workers become victims of workplace violence, resulting in almost 2 million days of lost work.

HR ADVICE & APPLICATION

The Violent Employee—Warning Signs

If any of the following warning signs are present, employers should consult resource specialists to determine whether monitoring is sufficient or whether immediate action is warranted. Possible resources include a company physician, an employee assistance provider, law enforcement officials, an attorney, or a violence-assessment specialist.

- **Verbal threats.** Individuals often talk about what they may do. An employee might say, "Bad things are going to happen to so-and-so," or "That propane tank in the back could blow up easily."
- **Physical actions.** Troubled employees may try to intimidate others, gain access to places they do not belong, or flash a concealed weapon in the workplace to test reactions.
- **Frustration.** Most cases do not involve a panicked individual who perceives the world as falling apart. A more likely scenario involves an employee who has a frustrated sense of entitlement to a promotion, for example.
- **Obsession.** An employee may hold a grudge against a co-worker or supervisor, and some cases stem from romantic interest.[27]

identify the violent employee before the fact, there are some common signs that employers are urged to watch for. These are described in the feature "HR Advice and Application: The Violent Employee—Warning Signs."

Occupational Diseases

Potential sources of work-related diseases are as distressingly varied as their symptoms. Several federal agencies have systematically studied the workplace environment, and they have identified the following hazards: arsenic, asbestos, benzene, bichloromethylether, coal dust, coke-oven emissions, cotton dust, lead, radiation, and vinyl chloride. Workers likely to be exposed to those hazards include chemical and oil refinery workers, miners, textile workers, steelworkers, lead-smelters, medical technicians, painters, shoemakers, and plastics- industry workers.

The long-term consequences of these hazards have been linked to thyroid, liver, lung, brain, and kidney cancer; white, brown, and black lung disease; leukemia; bronchitis; emphysema; lymphoma; aplastic anemia; central nervous system damage; and reproductive disorders (for example, sterility, genetic damage, abortions, and birth defects). Continued research will no doubt uncover additional hazards that firms will want to diagnose and remedy for the future well-being of their workforces.[28]

Occupational diseases are diseases that are contracted from workplace conditions.

Categories of Occupational Diseases. A major category of **occupational disease** involves illnesses of the respiratory system. Chronic bronchitis and emphysema are among the fastest growing diseases in the country, doubling every five years since World War II; they account for the second highest number of disabilities under Social Security.[29] Cancer, however, tends to receive the most attention, since it is a leading cause of death in the United States (second after heart disease). Many of the known causes of cancer are physical and chemical agents in the environment. And because these agents are theoretically more controllable than human behavior, OSHA's emphasis is on eliminating them from the workplace.

OSHA's emphasis on health is not aimed solely at eliminating cancer and respiratory diseases, however. OSHA is also concerned with the following categories of occupational diseases and illnesses: 1) occupation-related skin diseases and disorders, 2) dust diseases of the lungs, 3) respiratory conditions due to toxic agents, 4) poisoning (systematic effects of toxic materials), 5) disorders due to physical agents, 6) disorders associated with repeated trauma, and 7) all other occupational illnesses.[30] OSHA requires employers to keep records on all of these diseases.

Occupational Groups at Risk. Taxi drivers, miners, construction and transportation workers, firefighters, and police officers experience the bulk of both occupational disease and injury. The least safe occupations are firefighters, police officers, and construction. In addition, large numbers of petrochemical and oil refinery workers, dye workers, dye users, textile workers, plastic-industry workers, painters, and industrial chemical workers are also particularly susceptible to some of the most dangerous health hazards. Interestingly, skin diseases are the most common of all reported occupational diseases, with leather workers being the group most affected.

Of course, occupational diseases are not exclusive to the blue-collar workers and manufacturing industries. The "cushy office job" has evolved into a veritable nightmare of physical and psychological ills. Among the common ailments are varicose veins, bad backs, deteriorating eyesight, repetitive motion syndrome, migraine headaches, hypertension, coronary heart disorders, and respiratory and digestive problems. The causes of these in an office environment include the following:

Did You KNOW?

Repetitive movements, both in the office and factory, result in almost two-thirds of the workplace illnesses.

- Too much noise
- Interior air pollutants such as cigarette smoke and chemical fumes—for example, from the copy machine
- Uncomfortable chairs

- Poor office design
- New office technology such as video display terminals
- Repetitive movements.[31]

In addition, dentists are routinely exposed to radiation, mercury, and anesthetics, and cosmetologists suffer from high rates of cancer and respiratory and cardiac diseases connected with their frequent use of chemicals.

When the Quality of Working Life Is Low

For many workers, a **low quality of working life** is associated with workplace conditions that fail to satisfy important needs and interests such as a sense of responsibility, challenge, meaningfulness, self-control, recognition, achievement, fairness or justice, security, and certainty.[32] Organizational structures that contribute to a low quality of working life include:

Low quality of working life is a workplace condition that fails to satisfy needs and interest such as a sense of responsibility, fairness and certainty.

- Jobs with low task significance, variety, identity, autonomy, feedback, and qualitative underload.
- Minimal involvement of employees in decision-making and a great deal of one-way communication with employees
- Pay systems not based on performance or based on performance not objectively measured or under employee control
- Supervisors, job descriptions, and organizational policies that fail to convey to the employee what is expected and what is rewarded
- Human resource policies and practices that are discriminatory and of low validity
- Temporary employment conditions where employees are dismissed at will (employee rights do not exist)

Many conditions in organizations are associated with a low quality of working life. The same is true of organizational stress. Remember, however, that a condition causing stress or low quality of working life for one individual may not cause it in another individual because of differences in preferences, interests, and perceptions of uncertainty in the environment.

Organizational Stress

Prevalent forms of **organizational stress** include the four S's. Other major factors include change, work pace, the physical environment, and job burnout. With these factors or sources of stress we extend the discussion of career stress in Chapter 6, where three classes of symptoms were presented: physiological, psychological, and behavioral.

Organizational stress is a condition of uncertainty and anxiety resulting from workplace conditions.

The Four S's. Common stressors for many employees include the following: 1) supervisor, 2) salary, 3) security, and 4) safety.[33] Petty work rules and relentless pressure for more production are major stressors that employees associate with supervisors. Both deny worker needs to control the work situation and to be recognized and accepted.

Salary is a stressor when it is perceived as being distributed unfairly. Many blue-collar workers feel they are underpaid relative to their white-collar counterparts in the office. Teachers think they are underpaid relative to people with similar education who work in private industry.

Employees experience stress when they are not sure whether they will have their jobs next month, next week, or even the next day. For many employees, lack of job security is even more stressful than holding jobs that are generally unsafe. At least the employees know the job risks, whereas the lack of job security creates a continued state of uncertainty.

Fear of workplace accidents and the resulting injuries or death can be stressful for many workers. When pressure for production is increased, this fear over workplace safety can increase to a point that production may decrease rather than increase. This result, in turn, may lead to a vicious cycle that is counterproductive for the workers and the organization.

Organizational Change. Changes made by organizations are often stressful, because they usually involve something important and are accompanied by uncertainty. Many changes are made without advance warning. Although rumors often circulate that a change is coming, the exact nature of the change is left to speculation. People become concerned about whether the change will affect them, perhaps by displacing them or by causing them to be transferred. The result is that the uncertainty surrounding a change yet to come causes many employees to suffer stress symptoms.

Companies have been finding that downsizing is a legitimate reason many employees are stressful. Downsizing for those who stay and for the employees who go is a major change. What one company is doing about this is described in the feature, "Managing Human Resources at Adolph Coors Company."

Work pacing refers to who or what controls the flow of an employee's work.

Machine pacing gives control over the work pace to something other than the employee.

Work Pacing. **Work pacing,** particularly who or what controls the pace of the work, is an important potential stressor in organizations. **Machine pacing** gives control over the speed of the operation and the work output to something other than the individual. Employee pacing gives the individual control of the operations. The effects of machine pacing are severe, because the individual is unable to satisfy a crucial need for control of the situation. It has been reported that workers on machine-paced jobs feel exhausted at the end of the shift and are unable to relax soon after work because of increased adrenaline secretion on the job. In a study of 23 white- and blue-collar occupations, assembly workers reported the highest level of severe stress symptoms.

Physical Environment. Although office automation is a way to improve productivity, it has stress-related drawbacks. One aspect of office automation with a specific stress-related drawback is the video display terminal (VDT). Other aspects of the work environment associated with stress are crowding, lack of privacy, and lack of control over aspects of the environment that the employee would like to change (for example, moving a desk or chairs or even hanging pictures in a work area in an effort to personalize it). Another aspect is the sheer weight of items, for example boxes that workers are expected to lift as a regular part of the job. In its efforts to improve productivity in the highly competitive package delivery business, UPS raised the weight limit on lifting from 70 pounds to 150 pounds. OSHA officials contend that this requirement may be a source of UPS's higher-than-industry-average injury rate.[34]

Like many companies, UPS has to deal with the issues associated with productivity improvements and worker safety.

The Stress-Prone Employee? Yes, there are individual differences in how people respond to the conditions just described. A classic difference used in stress work is referred to as Type A or Type B behavior. Type A people like to do things their way and are willing to exert a lot of effort to ensure that even trivial tasks are performed in the manner they prefer. They often fail to distinguish between important and unimportant situations. They are upset, for instance, when they have to wait 15 minutes to be seated in a restaurant, since this is not in compliance with their idea of responsive service. In short, the Type A person spends much of his or her time directing energy toward the noncompliances in the environment. Still, Type A people are "movers and shakers." They enjoy acting on their environment and enjoy modifying the behavior of other people. They are primarily rewarded by compliance and punished by noncompliance. Type B people, then, are generally much more tolerant. They are not easily frustrated, easily angered, nor do they expend a lot of energy in response to noncompliance. Type B people may be excellent supervisors to work for—that is, until you need them to push upward in the

MANAGING HUMAN RESOURCES

at Adolph Coors Co.

A stress management program at Adolph Coors Co., a Golden, Colorado-based brewery, has expanded to help workers cope with increasing work-force changes. A 1993 downsizing of 643 employees through voluntary separations, followed by corporate reorganization, has led to a rethinking throughout the company on Coors' direction, says Bob Tank Jr., manager of counseling services.

Originally, the stress management program included only a course on anger management and an exercise component. Now, both group programs and individualized help in managing stress are offered through the employee assistance plan, says Tank. He notes that group programs help employees see that they are "not alone" in their need to reduce stress.

Coors' stress management program currently features 27 different courses which address family and personal concerns as well as workplace issues such as communication, self-esteem, and how to work together. The program also can be "customized" to address specific problems. For example, a work group requested training because it had been struggling with bickering, strife, and management/worker dysfunction, says Tank. Instruction was aimed at clarifying roles and redirecting energies. Feedback following the classes showed success in deflating the dysfunctional processes and clarifying team operations.

With so much going on in the company this year, employee participation in the stress management program has dropped off in every area except for a tremendously popular course on dealing with corporate change, Tank notes. To boost participation, Coors integrates more programs into the workplace, makes programs user-friendly, and makes them available to production areas. In addition, information on stress reduction is made available through open houses and notices in cafeterias and individual worksites.

Outreach programs can be an effective, less formal way to help employees deal with change, Tank adds. Companies today need to stay flexible to adapt and do what is necessary to thrive, he says. Coors wants its employees to be able to do the same.[35]

organization on your behalf. They probably would permit you and other subordinates a lot of freedom, but also might not provide the types of upward support necessary for effective leadership.[36]

Job Burnout. A special type of organizational stress is called **job burnout**. This condition happens when people work in situations in which they have little control over the quality of their performance but feel personally responsible for their success or lack of it. People most susceptible to burnout include police officers, nurses, social workers, and teachers. When people begin to show burnout, they reveal three symptoms: 1) emotional exhaustion, 2) depersonalization, and 3) a sense of low personal accomplishment. Since this condition benefits neither the individual nor the organization, many programs have been designed to help people deal with burnout.

Strategies for Improvement

LEARNING OBJECTIVE 5

Describe what organizations are doing and can do to improve occupational safety and health.

Once the cause of stress is identified, strategies can be developed for eliminating or reducing it (see Exhibit 17.2). To determine whether the strategy is effective, organizations can compare the incidence, severity, and frequency of illness and accidents before and after the intervention. There are OSHA-approved methods for establishing safety and health rates; we will describe these first, and then we will present strategies for accident control and for reducing occupational disease and improving the sociopsychological work environment.

EXHIBIT 17.2

Sources and Strategies for Improving Occupational Safety and Health

SOURCE	STRATEGY
Physical Work Environment	Record the accident
Occupational accidents	Redesign the work environment
	Set goals and objectives
	Establish safety committees
	Provide training and financial incentives
Occupational diseases	Record the disease
	Measure the work environment
	Communicate information
	Set goals and objectives
Sociopsychological Work Environment	
Stress and burnout	Establish organizational stress programs
	Increase employees' participation in decision-making
	Establish individual stress programs
	Ensure adequate staffing
	Provide adequate leave and vacation benefits
	Encourage employees to adopt healthy lifestyles

Safety and health rates are described in terms of

- **incidence**
- **frequency**
- **severity**

Safety and Health Rates

OSHA requires organizations to maintain records of the incidence of injuries and illnesses. Some organizations also record the frequency and severity of each.

Incidence Rate. The most explicit index of industrial safety is the **incidence rate**. It is calculated by the following formula:

$$\text{Incidence rate} = \frac{\text{Number of injuries and illnesses} \times 200{,}000}{\text{Number of employee hours worked}}$$

Incidence rate is the number of recorded injuries or illnesses per 100 workers per year.

200,000 is the base for 100 full-time workers (40 hours per week, 50 weeks). Suppose an organization had 10 recorded injuries and illnesses and 500 employees. To calculate the number of yearly hours worked, multiply the number of employees by 40 hours and by 50 work weeks: 500 × 40 × 50 = 1 million. The incidence rate thus would be 2 per 100 workers per year.

Severity rate reflects the actual hours lost due to injury or illness.

Severity Rate. The **severity rate** reflects the hours actually lost due to injury or illness. It recognizes that not all injuries and illnesses are equal. Four categories of injuries and illnesses have been established: deaths, permanent total disabilities, permanent partial disabilities, and temporary total disabilities. An organization with the same number of injuries and illnesses as another but with more deaths would have a higher severity rate. The severity rate is calculated as follows:

$$\text{Severity rate} = \frac{\text{Total hours charged} \times 1 \text{ million (hours)}}{\text{Number of employee hours worked}}$$

Frequency Rate. The **frequency rate** reflects the number of injuries and illnesses per million hours worked rather than per year as in the incidence rate. It is calculated as follows:

Frequency rate reflects the number of injuries and illnesses per million hours worked.

$$\text{Frequency rate} = \frac{\text{Number of injuries and illnesses} \times 1 \text{ million (hours)}}{\text{Number of employee hours worked}}$$

Accident Control

Designing the work environment to make accidents unlikely is perhaps the best way to prevent accidents and increase safety. Among the safety features that can be designed into the physical environment are guards on machines, handrails in stairways, safety goggles and helmets, warning lights, self-correcting mechanisms, and automatic shutoffs. The extent to which these features will actually reduce accidents depends on employee acceptance and use. For example, eye injuries will be reduced by the availability of safety goggles only if employees wear the goggles correctly.

If employees are involved in the decision to make some physical change to improve safety, they are more likely to accept the decision than if they are not part of the decision-making process. Thus the safety programs most likely to succeed are those that have the greatest support of all the employees. These programs are the ones likely to be the most thorough. Of course, the involvement of the supervisors is also very critical for the success of safety programs. The American Building Maintenance Industries, based in San Francisco, whose employees clean office windows in high-rise buildings, has several safety programs involving a partnership among the employees, supervisors, and the company. For example:

American Building Maintenance Industries has a real concern for the safety of its employees, who are often working 50 stories above street-level.

- Supervisors are required to make safety reports, and timeliness is emphasized. When an injury or problem occurs, detailed reports including witnesses, pictures, and a description of what occurred are required within 24 hours. The emphasis is on fact-finding, not fault-finding.
- When a pattern of certain injuries in a particular location is revealed through report analysis (for example, back injuries may be occurring frequently at one building site), the company brings the supervisors in and reviews the safety measures they take. The company then reviews what the supervisor can do to improve safety in the area.
- Supervisors are responsible for training. They use training films and direct interaction to show employees the right way to do their jobs safely.
- Supervisors give employees five-minute safety talks every month, and employees must sign to show they've attended. Topics include vacation safety, lifting trash, wearing rubber gloves, handling cords, and handling hazardous materials safely. Employees are urged to read rating sheets on chemicals used, and every effort is made to see that chemicals are as safe as possible.
- Inspections are held to identify hazards. One gets so used to seeing something that it's ignored. Sometimes it takes fresh eyes to see danger, such as extension cords or newspapers stacking up.[37]

Ergonomics. Another way to improve safety is to make the job itself more comfortable and less fatiguing through ergonomics. Ergonomics considers changes

Ergonomics is an approach to job design concerned about worker safety and health.

in the job environment in conjunction with the physical and physiological capabilities and limitations of the employees.[38] See Chapter 7 for an extended discussion of ergonomics.

Ergonomics can help reduce the 75 million lost workdays due to back injuries.

In an effort to reduce the number of back injuries, the Ford Motor Company redesigns work stations and tasks that may be causing musculoskeletal problems for workers. For instance, lifting devices are being introduced on the assembly line to reduce back strain, and walking and working surfaces are being studied to see if floor mats can reduce body fatigue. Videotapes that feature Ford employees performing their jobs both before and after ergonomic redesign are used in training.[39]

> *A three-pronged prevention program stressing education, exercise, and the use of back belts is helping thousands of Federal Express package handlers avoid back injuries.*
>
> *The first component of the program raises overall awareness about back injuries through safety training, tips in employee newsletters, and weekly group meetings to discuss safe lifting techniques. The second component prepares workers physically through a pre-shift stretching routine designed to limber muscles. This 10-minute exercise is mandatory for all workers whose jobs involve lifting. The third component—the use of flexible back supports by all package handlers at the company—not only helps physically, but also serves as a constant reminder for employees to lift safely.*[40]

In an effort to reduce repetitive motion injuries, Zeneca Pharmaceuticals uses a variety of techniques. Their efforts have been so successful that their workforce had no such injuries in 1994. The techniques they used to achieve this success are described in the feature, "Managing Human Resources at Zeneca."

At Subaru-Izuzu Automotive's plant in Lafayette, Indiana, workers try to prevent injuries from occurring by doing aerobic and stretching exercises before their work day begins and once during the day for five minutes.[41]

Safety Committees. Another strategy for accident prevention is the use of **safety committees**. The HR department can serve as the coordinator of a committee composed of several employee representatives. Where unions exist, the committees should have union representation as well. Often, organizations have several safety committees at the department level for implementation and administration purposes and one larger committee at the organizational level for policy formulation.

The HR department can be instrumental in accident prevention by assisting supervisors in their training efforts and by implementing safety motivation programs such as contests and in-house communications. Many organizations display signs indicating the number of days or hours worked without an accident. Many organizations display posters saying "Safety First." In safety contests, prizes or awards are given to individuals or departments with the best safety record. These programs seem to work best when employees are already safety conscious and when physical conditions of the work environment pose no extreme hazards.

Bank One, headquartered in Columbus, Ohio, reminds workers to wear seat belts when traveling on company business.

Behavior Modification. Reinforcing behaviors that reduce the likelihood of accidents can be highly successful. Reinforcers can range from nonmonetary reinforcers, such as feedback, to activity reinforcers, such as time off, to material reinforcers, such as company-purchased doughnuts during the coffee break, to financial rewards for attaining desired levels of safety.

The behavioral approach relies on measuring performance before and after the intervention, specifying and communicating the desired performance to employees, monitoring performance at unannounced intervals several times a week, and reinforcing desired behavior several times a week with performance feedback.

MANAGING HUMAN RESOURCES

at Zeneca

An ergonomics program that makes use of rubber exercise strips and an interior decorator has helped eliminate repetitive motion injuries at Zeneca Pharmaceuticals in Wilmington, Del.

Zeneca became concerned about ergonomics after its 1991 safety logs indicated an increase of more than 50 percent in the number of repetitive motion injuries suffered by its employees since the year before, says David Irwin, supervisor of safety and environmental operations at the 2,400-employee firm. Zeneca instituted a program to address the problem in 1993.

At a cost of $10,000, the program relies on one-hour sessions in which small groups of employees gather to learn about ergonomics issues. In addition to ensuring that departments are not depleted of staff, the limited size encourages participation, Irwin says. For example, employees are quizzed to determine their general knowledge about ergonomics, and are asked about specific tasks and body parts, such as tendons, that might be involved in repetitive motion injuries.

The program includes a 10-minute video on ergonomics for computer users, as well as a slide presentation that demonstrates various tasks that place employees at risk. Zeneca's fitness manager then leads employees through a number of exercises—using a three-foot by one-foot rubber strip—to strengthen shoulder muscles and other parts of the body that tire during long periods of keystroking.

Zeneca also brings in a furniture specialist—who spent her time solely on interior decorating before the program—to instruct employees on posture and equipment use. She explains the best way to set up adjustable work stations and demonstrates ergonomic solutions such as raising a computer monitor, removing overhead lighting, and adding a task lamp to block headache-producing window glare. She also teaches employees to arrange their desks so that frequently used items are close at hand, because constant upward reaching can cause strain.

Noting that Zeneca experienced no repetitive motion injuries in 1994, Irwin says the program has clearly demonstrated to management that ergonomic problems can be controlled.[42]

Management by Objectives Programs. Behavior modification programs are often linked successfully to management-by-objectives programs that deal with occupational health. The seven basic steps of these programs are as follows:

1. Identify hazards and obtain information about the frequency of accidents.
2. Based on this information, evaluate the severity and risk of the hazards.
3. Formulate and implement programs to control, prevent, or reduce the possibility of accidents.
4. Set specific, difficult, but attainable goals regarding the reduction of accidents or safety problems.
5. Consistently monitor results.
6. Provide positive feedback for correct safety procedures.
7. Monitor and evaluate the program against the goals.[43]

Reducing Occupational Diseases

By far, more costly and harmful overall to organizations and employees than occupational accidents are occupational diseases. Because the causal relationship between the physical environment and occupational diseases is often subtle, developing strategies to reduce their incidence is generally difficult.

Record Keeping. At a minimum, OSHA requires that organizations measure the chemicals in the work environment and keep records on these measurements. Their records must also include precise information about ailments and exposures. Such information must be kept for as long a period as is associated with the incubation period of the specific disease—even as long as 40 years. If the organization is sold, the new owner must assume responsibility for storing the old records and continuing to gather the required data. If the organization goes out of business, the administrative director of OSHA must be informed of the whereabouts of the records. Guidelines for record keeping are given in Exhibit 17.3.

Communicating Health and Safety Information. In addition to keeping records, the *Access to Employee Exposure and Medical Records* (AEEMR) regulation of 1980 requires organizations to show or give to employees, their designated

EXHIBIT 17.3

OSHA Guidelines for Recording Cases

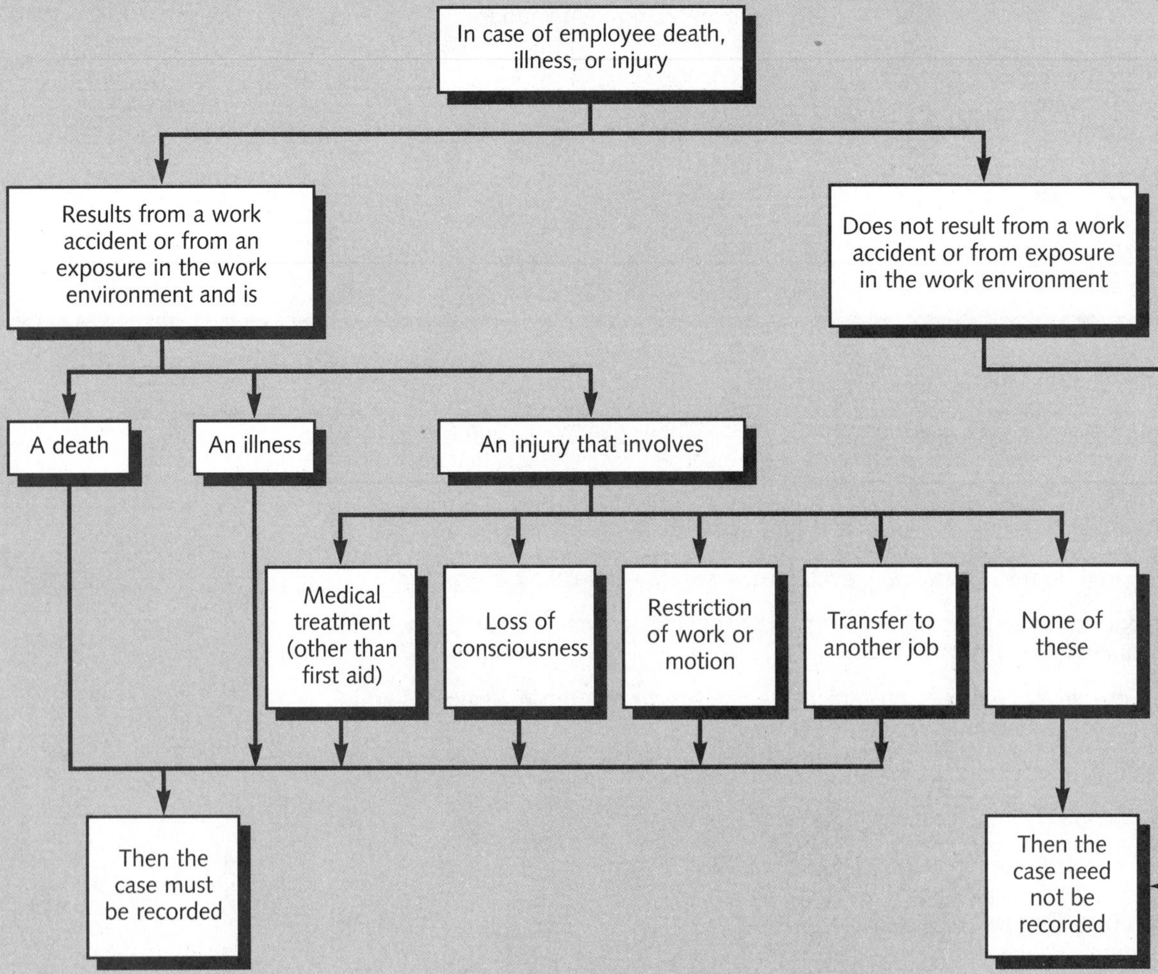

representatives, and OSHA their on-the-job medical records of measurements of employee exposure to toxic substances. The employee's right to know has been further strengthened by the *Hazard Communication Standard* that went into effect in 1986. This law requires that employees be trained prior to job assignment and retrained any time a new hazard is introduced into the work environment.

Monitoring Exposure. While the obvious approach to controlling occupational illnesses is to rid the workplace of chemical agents or toxins, an alternative approach is to monitor and limit exposure to hazardous substances For example, the nuclear industry recruits hundreds of "jumpers" who fix the aging innards of the nation's nuclear generating stations. The atmosphere is so radioactive that jumpers can stay in only about ten minutes before they "burn out." Their exposure has to be closely monitored to ensure that it does not exceed more than 5,000 millirems (roughly 250 chest X-rays) annually.

Company reward and compensation practices can make it tempting for workers to put themselves at risk. In this case, who's responsible for injury?

Unfortunately, jumpers get rewarded for absorbing the maximum rather than a safe limit of radiation on any given job. Rather than 12 hours of pay for their 10 minutes of work, jumpers get a bonus of several hundred dollars each time they "burn out" between jobs. Even with monitoring, it is estimated that 3 to 8 out of every 10,000 jumpers will eventually die as a result of the exposure.[44]

In addition to monitoring for radioactivity, some organizations now monitor genetic changes due to exposure to carcinogens (for example, benzene, arsenic, ether, and vinyl chloride). Samples of blood are obtained from employees at fixed intervals to determine whether the employee's chromosomes have been damaged. If damage has occurred, the employee is placed into a different job.

Genetic Screening. Genetic screening is the most extreme, and consequently the most controversial, approach to controlling occupational disease. As noted in Chapter 10, the genetic makeup of individuals may make them more or less predisposed to specific occupational diseases. By genetically screening out individuals who are susceptible to certain ailments, organizations lower their vulnerability to workers' compensation claims and problems. Opponents of genetic screening contend that genetic screening measures one's predisposition to disease, not the actual presence of disease; therefore, such testing violates an individual's rights.[45]

Work Environment

Increasingly, organizations are offering training programs designed to help employees deal with work-related stress. For example, J. P. Morgan offers stress management programs as part of a larger supervisory and management development curriculum. Offered to supervisors, professional staff, and officers, these courses provide supervisory and management material, specific technical supervisory/management information skills, and a developmental program designed to give experienced nonofficer managers and professionals some perspective on their roles within the bank. The emphasis here is on providing workers with concrete information to reduce the ambiguity associated with fast-paced, rapidly changing work roles.[46] Other potential remedies for workplace stress are described in the feature, "HR Advice and Application: Solutions to Workplace Stress."

Organizations can offer many activities or programs to improve physical and sociopsychological work conditions. Selecting the most appropriate activity should be based on a thorough analysis of existing safety and health hazards. It also depends on an assessment of past activities and strategies used by other organizations.

Individual Stress Management Strategies. Time management can be an effective individual strategy to deal with organizational stress. It is based in large part on an initial identification of an individual's personal goals. Other strategies that should be part of individual stress management include good diets, regular exercise, monitoring physical health, and building social support groups. Many large organizations such as Xerox encourage employees to enroll in regular exercise programs where their fitness and health are carefully monitored.[47]

HR ADVICE & APPLICATION

Solutions to Workplace Stress

When stress invades the workplace, both employers and employees pay dearly. For employers, the costs include high turnover, stress-related health claims, and reduced productivity. For employees, stress takes its toll on health and well-being, work performance, and morale.

STRESS EFFECTS

Four in ten American workers say their jobs are "very" or "extremely" stressful, while 39 percent say they often think about quitting their job, according to a survey of 1,299 employees by Northwestern National Life Insurance Company (NWNL). Half of the surveyed employees say job stress reduces their productivity, and a third say they experience frequent stress-related illnesses. Of employees who say they have high-stress jobs, 65 percent suffer from exhaustion, and 44 percent report headaches or migraines. Also, employees in high-stress jobs are nearly three times as likely to experience anxiety, ulcers, anger, or depression, the survey concludes.

Based on the survey findings, NWNL researchers suggest the following steps to reduce tension and stress in the workplace:

- **Allow employees to talk freely with one another.** Employees thrive in an atmosphere where they can consult with colleagues about work issues. Moreover, in organizations where employees talk freely with one another, productivity and problem-solving are usually enhanced.
- **Reduce personal conflicts on the job.** Employers can reduce stress by training managers and employees on how to resolve conflicts through open communication, negotiation, and respect. Managers can minimize conflicts by treating employees fairly and clearly defining job expectations.
- **Give employees adequate control over how they do their work.** Employees take greater pride in their work, are more productive, and are better able to deal with stress if they have some control over how they perform their work. Managers who let employees make decisions create an atmosphere that reduces stress and increases job satisfaction.
- **Ensure adequate staffing and expense budgets.** Staff reductions and budget cuts usually increase stress in the long run. Overburdened employees frequently suffer high stress levels that cause lower productivity, illness, turnover, and accidents.
- **Talk openly with employees.** Open communication between management and employees reduces job stress and helps employees cope with the challenges of the workplace.
- **Support employees' efforts.** When employers show their support of employees' contributions to the organization, stress levels are significantly lower. Managers can show support by regularly asking employees how their work is going, listening to them, and addressing issues that are raised.
- **Provide competitive personal leave and vacation benefits.** Workers who have time to relax and recharge after working hard are less likely to develop stress-related illnesses.
- **Maintain current levels of employee benefits.** Workers' stress levels increase when their benefits are reduced. Employers should determine whether the savings from reduced benefits are worth the risk of employee burnout.
- **Reduce the amount of red tape for employees.** When employees must deal with too much bureaucracy, they become discouraged and demoralized. Employers should ensure that employees' time is not wasted on unnecessary procedures.
- **Recognize and reward employees for their accomplishments and contributions.** A pat on the back, public praise, or a bonus or raise can result in significant increases in employee morale and productivity.[48]

Current Trends

Companies are combating rising costs stemming from work-related injuries and disease with occupational health policies and wellness programs. These have, however, served to open up complex ethical issues.

Occupational Health Policies

As scientific knowledge accumulates and liabilities rise, more and more organizations are developing policy statements regarding occupational hazards. These policy statements grow out of concern that organizations should be proactive in dealing with this problem. For example, Dow Chemical's policy states that "No employee, male or female, will knowingly be exposed to hazardous levels of materials known to cause cancer or genetic mutations in humans."[49]

An example of the growing complexity of this problem has been the debate over whether women of child-bearing age should be allowed to hold jobs in settings that could endanger fetuses. Johnson Controls in Milwaukee, Wisconsin, which makes lead automobile batteries for such customers as Sears and Goodyear, had restricted women's access to jobs in its Bennington, Vermont, plant. Johnson's management claimed that the factory's air contained traces of lead and lead oxide. While presumably not high enough to harm adults, these toxin levels were high enough to endanger children and fetuses. Thus, women were allowed to work in the plant, but only if they were unable to bear children (either because of surgery to prevent pregnancies or because they were too old to have children). According to the company, "the issue was protecting the health of unborn children."

As you can see, companies face serious issues in health and safety that are not always easy to resolve.

Women's advocates and union leaders argued that the firm was guilty of sex discrimination. Specifically, they claimed that lead levels were too high for men as well, that the firm was making a decision for women rather than allowing women to decide whether to take the risk, that such rules invade women's privacy, and, finally, that the restrictions denied women access to high-paying jobs. A typical factory job in Bennington paid $6.35/hour versus $15.00/hour in the Johnson Controls plant.[50]

What made the situation more complex was that many workers were reluctant to leave jobs to avoid occupational exposure unless they were guaranteed that their income would not suffer. Some workers went so far as to have themselves sterilized to protect their jobs. When the Supreme Court heard this case, they ruled in favor of the workers, thus striking down the company's fetal protection policy (*United Auto Workers v. Johnson Controls,* 1991).

The policies of AT&T and Digital Equipment illustrate alternative strategies. Their policies provide income protection for pregnant production workers who might be exposed to the toxic gases and liquids used to etch microscopic circuits onto silicon wafers. Other companies are obtaining voluntary consent agreements from employees who choose to stay on hazardous jobs. While these agreements may absolve employers from punitive damages in civil court, they do not alleviate liability under workers' compensation laws and civil disability suits.

Ethics in Shaping Behavior

Employers have known for a long time that a small percentage of their workforce is responsible for the bulk of the health insurance claims. Originally, they tried to encourage their employees to be healthy by offering to subsidize health club memberships and building exercise facilities and jogging trails, but the results were disappointing. Now it appears that many companies are implementing incentive-based healthcare programs and non-smoking campaigns.[51]

While no one denies that healthcare costs in the United States are very high, some question just how far companies should be allowed to go in "encouraging" their employees to shape up. How much should employers be allowed to know about what the employees do in their spare time? Is it possible that company policies and practices will become so financially attractive to employees that they will do things that they would not otherwise have done?

The potential for creating situations involving ethical or unethical behavior needs to be watched closely. It is too early to tell just how this situation will unfold. Doubtless, employers and employees are concerned about costs and health; perhaps creative solutions will save the day.[52] Such solutions will also have an impact not only on occupational safety and health, but also on employee rights (Chapter 4) and indirect compensation (Chapter 16).

LEARNING OBJECTIVE 6

Describe some safety and health issues in other countries.

International Safety and Health Issues

As consciousness of health and well-being has risen worldwide, pressures to improve health care in work environments have increased in some countries. In other countries, however, health hazards are still ignored; by having lax safety standards, developing countries can lure large multinational firms to their shores.

Monitoring in Other Countries

Following the leakage of lethal methyl isocyanate gas at Union Carbide's pesticide plant in Bhopal, India in 1986, which killed more than 2,000 people, India formed committees in every state to identify potential hazards in factories. While foreign investments and technology are still welcome, the government now insists on knowing more about potential risks as well as identified existing risks. New regulations in India require environmental impact studies for all new plants.[53]

By comparison, some countries have had workers' compensation programs and monitoring systems for years. For example, in 1972, New Zealand introduced a no-fault insurance program that covers job injuries. That same year, Finland passed an accident insurance act making it possible to receive workers' compensation for muscular pain and tendonitis caused by one's work. In 1977, Sweden passed a law requiring employers to modify the work environment to meet the physical and psychological makeup of workers.

The response to health hazards has been quite different in Mexico. A disaster that killed more than 500 people and wounded thousands at Pemex, a state-owned gas monopoly in Mexico, has had no noticeable effect on regulations. This is a common situation in developing countries. These countries are often so in need of economic development that they may accept any industry—even those that have the potential for significant harm. This, of course, presents serious ethical questions for firms operating in the developing nations.

Did You KNOW?

According to the International Labor Organization, the number of work-related accidents worldwide each year is about 125 million.

Summary

Employees' health will become increasingly important in the years ahead. Employers are becoming more aware of the cost of ill health and the benefits of having a healthy workforce. The federal government, through OSHA, is also making it more necessary for employers to be concerned with employee health. The government's current concern is primarily with employee health as related to occupational accidents and diseases, both aspects of the physical environment. However, organizations can choose to become involved in programs dealing with employee health and the workers' sociopsychological environment as well. If organizations choose not be become involved with improving the sociopsychological environment, the government may prescribe mandatory regulations. Thus, it pays for organizations to be concerned with both aspects of the work environment now. Effective programs for both environments can significantly improve both employee health and the effectiveness of an organization.

When the adoption of improvement programs is being considered, employee involvement is crucial. As with many quality-of-working-life programs, employee involvement in improving safety and health is not only a good idea, but also one likely to be desired by employees. Many things can be done to make work environments better, but it is important to distinguish two types of environments: the physical and the sociopsychological. Each is different and has its own unique components. Although some improvement strategies may work well for one component of the work environment, they will not work in others. Again, a careful diagnosis is required before programs are selected and implemented.

Assuming that a careful diagnosis indicates the need for a stress management program, the challenge is in deciding which program or strategy to select from the many organizational and individual stress management strategies currently available. Programs such as time management or physical exercise could be set up so employees could help themselves cope, or the organization could alter the conditions within the organization that are associated with stress. The latter requires a diagnosis of what is happening, where, and to whom before deciding how to proceed. Because so many possible sources of stress exist, and because not all people react the same way to them, implementing individual stress management strategies may be more efficient. However, if many people are suffering similar stress symptoms in a specific part of the organization, an organizational strategy is more appropriate.

Information regarding many aspects of safety and health is insufficient either because it does not exist (for example, knowledge of causes and effect) or because organizations are unwilling to gather or provide it. From a legal as well as a humane viewpoint, it is in the best interests of organizations to seek and provide more information so that more effective strategies for improving safety and health can be developed and implemented. Failure to do so may result in costly legal settlements against organizations or further governmental regulation of workplace safety and health.

Key Concepts

common law
doctrine of torts
employee pacing
ergonomics
frequency rate
incidence rate
job burnout
low quality of working life
machine pacing
National Institute of Occupational Safety and Health (NIOSH)
occupational accidents
occupational disease
occupational safety and health
Occupational Safety and Health Administration (OSHA)
organizational stress
physical work environment
physical/physiological conditions
safety committees
severity rate
psychological conditions
sociopsychological work environment
work pacing

Review and Discussion Questions

1. How are physical hazards distinct from sociopsychological hazards? What implications does this distinction have for programs to deal with these hazards?
2. Is there such a thing as an unsafe worker? Assuming that accident-prone workers exist, how can HR managers address this problem?
3. Who is responsible for workplace safety and health? The employer? The employee? The federal government? Judges and juries?

4. What requirements does OSHA impose on the employer for promoting workplace safety?
5. Identify four sources of work stress. Why are claims relating to worker stress on the rise? How can organizations manage work stress?
6. What can employees do for themselves to manage work stress?
7. How might a company's strategy to prevent occupational accidents differ from a program to prevent occupational disease? In what ways might the programs be similar?
8. The United States prides itself on freedom, democracy, and a free market economy. If this is true, why not make the employee responsible for health and safety? In other words, employers who offer riskier employment will simply pay workers more for bearing that risk (a wage premium), and the workers, in turn, can buy more insurance to cover the additional cost.
9. In what ways can an organization prevent occupational accidents?
10. What are some ethical issues in safety and health?

PROJECTS, EXERCISES & CASES

End-of-Text Project

Lincoln Electric

Answer the following for Lincoln Electric:

1. How important are safety and health issues at Lincoln Electric? Explain.
2. What are the most likely types of safety and health issues at Lincoln Electric?
3. What safety and health programs should be in place at Lincoln Electric? Who should be responsible for them?

Nordstrom

Answer the following for Nordstrom:

1. How important are safety and health issues at Nordstrom? Explain.
2. What are the most likely types of safety and health issues at Nordstrom?
3. What safety and health programs should be in place at Nordstrom? Who should be responsible for them?

Field Projects

1. Conduct research by comparing two companies within the same industry. Distinguish them by the level of care they put to the safety of their employees in the workplace. Find out whether the costs incurred in safety procedures create bigger return in overall revenue of the companies. (Hint: Compare fiscal year periods before and after safety procedures were increased. Which period saved more overhead costs? Legal expenses and health expenses? Safety procedure expenses?
2. Interview a small business owner and discuss health and safety. Cover topics such as importance, frequency, costs, and solutions.

VISIT THE LIBRARY

Exercise 1, Section 7

1. Enter your Web browser.
2. Enter HR Headquarters.
3. Enter the HR Library.
4. Find and review the following article within the "Research Center": *Deflecting Workplace Violence*
5. Return to your homepage.

Case: Safety Net or Death Trap?

Appliance Park is located in Henderson, a small city in western Kentucky next to the Ohio River. Appliance Park is aptly named for its major employer, Appliance House, which created 800 manufacturing jobs for this small community. Appliance House manufactures washing machines, dryers, and dishwashers at its Appliance Park location.

Two weeks ago, a tragedy occurred at Appliance Park that was felt throughout the community. Joe Kitner fell to his death at the east plant, where washing machines are assembled. Joe, 24 years old, was a local football star in high school and had worked at Appliance Park full-time since his graduation from Henderson Central High School. An investigation of the accident was conducted by representatives of the corporate safety staff and Teamster local officials, who represent the nonexempt workers at Appliance Park. Although not widely reported, a curious set of factors contributed to Joe's death.

The assembly line at the washing machine division occupies two stories within a large prefab building on the east side of the park. A rope net or mesh is suspended about 30 feet above the groundlevel floor to catch accessories and parts that drop from the upper conveyor system where some of the assembly of the washing machines is conducted. Periodically, when model changeovers are scheduled on the line, a changeover crew is assigned to switch the setup of the various machines throughout the assembly line. One of Joe's jobs on the changeover crew was to climb out on the net and retrieve the parts that had dropped from the previous production run. The net, though tightly strung across the ceiling, did have a tear on one side where a bracket that had fallen previously had cut part of the mesh. Although the changeover crew was responsible for inspecting and repairing the net, they often overlooked minor rips because of the production time lost in making repairs to the mesh net.

An autopsy of Joe Kitner revealed that he died of a brain hemorrhage suffered in the fall to the concrete floor below. The autopsy also revealed that Joe had a small but malignant brain tumor located near the part of the brain that controls the central nervous system. The medical examiner did not discuss whether the tumor was far enough along to affect Joe's judgment or motor abilities. But the other test result from the autopsy indicated that Joe had consumed alcohol a few hours before his death, probably at lunch. His blood alcohol level, however, was not high enough for him to have been ruled intoxicated using the state DWI standard.

The changeover crew experienced some difficulty in replacing Joe Kitner. Because the plant was unionized, his job was open to bid, but no one would bid for the job. Under these circumstances, the company used seniority to determine who would work the job among the assemblers. Luther Duncan was selected, and he really had little choice because he was low man on the totem pole with only seven years' seniority at the plant. Although the changeover job involved several duties, Luther knew that inevitably he would be asked to climb out on the net.

Luther had been on the job for only eight days when his foreman ordered the assembly line shut down for a model changeover for the next production run. At first, Luther decided not to think about what he eventually would have to do. But when his time came to scale the utility ladder to the rope net, Luther balked. No amount of encouragement, cajoling, or threatening would change Luther's mind; he simply was not going up that ladder with the memory of Joe's death fresh in his mind.

Alex Stearns, the Teamster steward, pulled Luther aside and pleaded with him to obey his foreman's order to complete the job. Alex even promised to file a grievance concerning the rip on the side of the net, which still had not been repaired. Luther stood firm and adamantly refused to proceed. Despite Alex's intervention, Luther's foreman suspended him for the remainder of the day and told him to report, along with Alex Stearns, to the plant superintendent's office early the next morning. When Luther reported to the superintendent's office the next day, he was informed of his dismissal for insubordination.

Case Questions

1. Do you agree with the decision to fire Luther?
2. Who was really at fault in Joe's death?
3. How could Joe's death have been prevented?
4. Why did Alex encourage Luther to obey his foreman?

Case: Who's There on the Line?

The telecommunications field is changing very rapidly. In perhaps no other field has the impact of technology had such a significant effect on the jobs of so many workers. Mitch Fields, for example, still remembers that tragic day in November 1963 when President Kennedy was assassinated while Mitch was pulling the afternoon shift as a switchman for Midwest Telephone Company (MTC). As Mitch described it, it sounded like 30 locomotives hammering their way through a large room filled with walls of mechanical switches putting phone calls through to their destination. Today, that room of switches has been replaced by a microchip. Mitch himself has undergone extensive training to operate a computer console used to monitor and diagnose switching problems.

The job of operator has changed from sitting in long rows operating equipment attached to walls of jacks and cords to individual work stations that look like command centers out of a Star Trek spaceship. In addition, the competitive environment of telephone services has changed dramatically because of deregulation and competition from other phone companies offering similar services. The new thrust now is to shift operator performance from being not just fast and friendly but profitable as well, by marketing the company ("Thank you for using MTC") and selling high-profit-margin services ("Is there someone else you would like to talk to? The person-to-person rate is only additional for the first minute").

The operator's job at MTC remains unchanged in two respects: operators will talk to nearly 600 people in a typical day, some of whom are still abusive. Operator job performance is monitored by both supervisors and the computer. Technological innovation has enabled MTC to monitor each operator by computer to produce statistics on numbers of calls handled per shift, speed of the call, and amount of revenue generated by the calls. In addition to computer monitoring, supervisors may also listen in on operators to ensure that proper operator protocol is followed. For example, customers are never told they dialed the "wrong" number, obscene calls are routed to supervisors, and one learns to say "hold the line" or "one moment please" instead of "hang on."

Meeting performance standards based on these criteria does not typically lead to large rewards. A beginning operator usually earns about $12,000 a year working swing shifts that may begin at 8:30 A.M., noon, 2:00 P.M., 4:30 P.M., 8:30 P.M., or 2:00 A.M. Only the highest rated operators have the opportunity to be transferred, promoted, or receive educational benefits.

Steve Buckley, training and development manager for MTC, knows that to change the fast and friendly MTC operator of the past to one who is fast, friendly, and profitable as well is going to be a real challenge. Steve has not figured out yet how to get the operators to conclude each transaction by saying "thank you for using MTC." A recent clandestine supervisor survey revealed that fewer than 20 percent of the operators were using the requested reply. Steve is also being pressured by the local union leaders who represent the telephone operators to reduce the job stress brought on by the high volume of people transactions and the constant, computer-assisted surveillance. One thing is for sure, however: Steve must implement a plan for improvement.

Case Questions

1. Can Steve really change the behavior of the operators?
2. How can Steve succeed in getting the operators to say "thank you for using MTC"?
3. Is computer monitoring the answer?
4. Should the operators really decide on the change?

Chapter 17 Endnotes

1. L. Johnson, "Preventing Injuries: The Big Payoff," *Personnel Journal* (April 1994): 61.
2. "A Proud Record at ACI American," *HR Reporter* (Oct. 1990): 5. Reprinted from *HR Reporter* with the permission of the publisher, Buroff Publications, 1350 Connecticut Ave., N.W., Suite 1000, Washington, D.C. 20036.
3. R. S. Schuler, "Occupational Health in Organizations: A Measure of Personnel Effectiveness," *Readings in Personnel and Human Resource Management,* 2nd ed., R. S. Schuler and S. A. Youngblood, eds., (St. Paul, MN: West, 1984).
4. J. A. Kinney, "Why Did Paul Die?" *Newsweek* (Sept. 10, 1990): 11.
5. T. F. O'Boyle, "Fear and Stress in the Office Take Toll," *The Wall Street Journal* (Nov. 6, 1990): B1, B2.
6. K. Matthes, "A Prescription for Healthier Offices," *HR Focus* (April, 1992): 4–5; "Indoor Air Issues Confront Employers," *Bulletin to Management* (Oct. 22, 1992): 329.
7. V. Frazee, "Benefit from Ergonomics Assessment," *Personnel Journal* (March 1996): 133; "Back Injuries," *Bulletin to Management* (Jan. 9, 1992): 396.
8. "Occupational Injuries and Illnesses," *Bulletin to Management* (January 18, 1996): 20-21.
9. B. Saporito, "The Most Dangerous Jobs in America," *Fortune* (May 31, 1993): 131–140; "Occupational Injuries and Illnesses," *Bulletin to Management* (Jan. 6, 1994): 4–6.
10. "Occupational Injuries and Illnesses," *Bulletin to Management* (January 18, 1996): 20–21; J. Nordheimer, "Pressures of Costs Drive Some Contractors to Stress Worker Safety," *New York Times* (Aug. 21, 1993): 25.

11. "Workplace Fatalities—1994," *Bulletin to Management* (August 24, 1995): 268–269.

12. These estimates should be regarded as conservative because they do not include the costs due to stress and health and accident costs associated with (caused by) low quality of working life.

13. B. Presley Noble, "Breathing New Life Into OSHA," *New York Times* (January 23, 1994): F25; "OSHA: Reforms and Penalties," *Bulletin to Management* (Jan. 28, 1993): 25; D. Foust, "Stepping into the Middle of OSHA's Muddle," *Business Week* (Aug. 2, 1993): 53.

14. "On the Safety and Health Scene," *Bulletin to Management* (April 2, 1987): 105.

15. B. Meir, "Use of Right-To-Know Rules Is Increasing Public's Scrutiny of Chemical Companies," *The Wall Street Journal* (May 23, 1985): 10; Bureau of National Affairs, "OSHA's Final Labeling Standard," *Bulletin to Management* (Dec. 1, 1983): 1.

16. P. A. Susser, "Update on Hazard Communication," *Personnel Administrator* (Oct. 1985): 57–61; M. G. Miner, "Legal Concerns Facing Human Resource Managers: An Overview," *Readings in Personnel and Human Resource Management,* 3rd ed., R. S. Schuler, A. Youngblood, and V. Huber, eds. (St. Paul, MN: West, 1988). "Hazard Communication Training: Compliance Cues," *Bulletin to Management* (March 13, 1986): 81.

17. *The Wall Street Journal* (Oct. 2, 1984) 1; Bureau of National Affairs, "State Right-To-Know Laws: Toxic Substances," *Bulletin to Management* (Nov. 22, 1984): 4–5; "Worker Right to Know," *Chemical Work* (April 18, 1984): 38–44.

18. M. Novit, "Mental Distress: Possible Implications for the Future," *Personnel Administrator* (Aug. 1982): 47–54. The *Civil Rights Act* of 1971, Section 1983, enforces the 14th Amendment providing for "equal protection of the laws" and prohibits employment discrimination on the basis of race, color, national origin, religion, sex, or age.

19. Determining responsibility is sometimes difficult because determining cause-and-effect relationships is difficult, especially when reactions such as asbestosis or hypertension take so long to develop or occur only in some people working under the same conditions as others. For a discussion, see A. D. Marcus, "Fearful of Future, Plaintiffs Are Suing Firms for What Hasn't Happened Yet," *The Wall Street Journal* (July 11, 1990): B1, B8.

20. "Cutting Workers' Compensation Costs," *Bulletin to Management* (April 22, 1993): 122.

21. "Trends," *Bulletin to Management* (May 11, 1995): 151.

22. D. Frum, "Oh My Aching . . . You Name It," *Forbes* (April 26, 1993): 53. See also A. Farnham, "Back Ache," *Fortune* (Dec. 14, 1992): 132–140.

23. "Workplace Torts," *Bulletin to Management* (Oct. 1, 1992): 312. Reprinted with permission by the Bureau of National Affairs, (Tel.1-800-372-1033).

24. O'Boyle, "Fear and Stress in the Office Take Toll."

25. From personal correspondence with Donald Brush, President, Bearings Division, Barden Corporation, March 8, 1989.

26. B. Meier, "When Abuse Follows Women to Work," *New York Times* (March 10, 1996): F11; G. Flynn, "What You Can Do About Weapons in the Workplace," *Personnel Journal* (March 1996): 122–126; "Workplace Violence Risks and Responses," *Bulletin to Management* (September 7, 1995): 288; "Victims of Workplace Violence Number in Thousands," *Bulletin to Management* (June 1, 1995): 169; "Workplace Violence," *Bulletin to Management* (February 23, 1995): 64; D. Anfuso, "Deflecting Workplace Violence," *Personnel Journal* (October 1994): 66–75; "Workplace Violence: When Dissatisfaction Turns To Fury," *HR Reporter* (March 1994): 1–2; "Preventing Liability for Violence," *Fair Employment Practices Guidelines* (August 25, 1994): 6–8; C. Marmer Solomon, "Talking Frankly About Domestic Violence," *Personnel Journal* (April 1995): 62–72; B. Filipczak, "Armed and Dangerous at Work," *Training* (July 1993): 39–43.

27. "Preventing Workplace Violence," *Bulletin to Management* (June 10, 1993): 177. Reprinted by permission. Copyright 1993 by The Bureau of National Affairs, Inc. (800-372-1033).

28. C. S. Weaver, "Understanding Occupational Disease," *Personnel Journal* (June 1989): 86–94.

29. Ibid.

30. C. L. Wang, "Occupational Skin Disease Continues to Plague Industry," *Monthly Labor Review* (Feb. 1979): 17–22.

31. "A Spreading Pain, and Cries for Justice," *New York Times* (June 5, 1994): Sec. 3, 1, 6; K. R. Pelletier, "The Hidden Hazards of the Modern Office," *New York Times* (Sept. 8, 1985): F3; J. Hyatt, "Hazardous Effects of VDT Legislation," *Inc.* (March 1985): 27; W. L. Weis, "No Smoking," *Personnel Journal* (Sept. 1984): 53–58; "VDT Study: Safety Charges, Design Changes," *Bulletin to Management* (July 21, 1983): 285; "Office Hazard: Factor Environment Can Boomerang," *Impact* (June 22, 1983): 1.

32. "Charges of Emotional Distress: A Growing Trend," *FEP Guidelines* (Dec. 1989): 1–4. See also a set of references identifying and discussing each preference or interest listed here in R. S. Schuler, "Definition and Conceptualization of Stress in Organizations," *Organizational Behavior and Human Performance* 23 (1980): 184–215; R. S. Schuler, "An Integrative Transactional Process Model of Stress in Organizations," *Journal of Occupational Behavior* 3 (1982): 3–19. C. S. Weaver, "Understanding Occupational Disease," *Personnel Journal* (June 1989): 3–19.

33. A. B. Shostak, *Blue-Collar Stress* (Reading, MA: Addison-Wesley, 1980).

34. C. Drew, "In The Productivity Push, How Much Is Too Much?" *New York Times* (December 17, 1995): Sec. 3, 1 and 12.

35. "Personnel Shop Talk," *Bulletin to Management* (September 8, 1994): 282. Reprinted with permission by the Bureau of National Affairs, (Tel. 1-800-372-1033).

36. M. Friedman and R. Roseman, *Type A Behavior and Your Heart* (New York: Alfred A. Knopf, 1974).

37. Safety: A Quick Pay-Off, A Long-Term Commitment," *HR Reporter* (Oct. 1990): 6; see also "Safety Programs and Accident Reduction," *Bulletin to Management* (October 6, 1994): 320; "A Life for Back Injury Prevention," *Bulletin to Management* (November 30, 1995): 383.

38. D. P. Levin, "The Graying Factory," *New York Times* (Feb. 20, 1994): Sec 3, 1, 3; For extensive discussion of office space and physical design issues, see L. Altman, "Some Who Use VDTs Miscarried, Study Says," *New York Times* (June 5, 1988): 22; "Reproductive Hazards—How Employers Are Responding," *Fair Employment Practices* (Oct. 29, 1987): 132; R. S. Schuler, L. R. Ritzman, and V. Davis, "Merging Prescriptive and Behavioral Approaches for Office Layout," *Production and Inventory Management Journal* 3 (1981): 131–142.

39. "National ASPA Conference Highlights," *Bulletin to Management* (July 28, 1988): 239. See also J. R. Hollenbeck, D. R. Ilgen, and S. M. Crampton, "Lower Back Disability in Occupational Settings: A Review of the Literature from a Human Resource Management View," *Personnel Psychology* 45, no. 2(1992): 247–278.

40. "Personnel Shop Talk," *Bulletin to Management* (August 25, 1994): 266.

41. D. Gunsch, "Employees Exercise to Prevent Injuries," *Personnel Journal* (July 1993): 59–62.

42. "Personnel Shop Talk," *Bulletin to Management* (November 30, 1995): 378. Reprinted with permission by the Bureau of National Affairs, (Tel.1-800-372-1033).

43. H. M. Taylor, "Occupational Health Management-by-Objectives," *Personnel* (Jan-Feb. 1980): 58–64.

44. M. Williams, "Ten Minutes Work for 12 Hours Pay? What's the Catch?" *The Wall Street Journal* (Oct. 12, 1983): 19.

45. L. Johnson, "Preventing Injuries: The Big Payoff," *Personnel Journal* (April 1994): 61–64; J. Olin, "New Approaches to Employment Screening," *Readings in Personnel and Human Resource Management,* 3rd ed., R. Schuler and S. A. Youngblood, eds., (St. Paul, MN: West, 1988).

46. J. C. Erfurt, A. Foote, and M. A. Heirich, "The Cost-Effectiveness of Worksite Wellness Programs for Hypertension Control, Weight Loss, Smoking Cessation and Exercise," *Personnel Psychology* 45 (1992): 5–27; D. L. Bebhardt and C. E. Crump, "Employee Fitness and Wellness Programs in the Workplace," *American Psychologist* (Feb. 1990): 262–272.

47. O'Boyle, "Fear and Stress in the Office Take Toll."

48. "Solutions to Workplace Stress," *Bulletin to Management* (Feb. 11, 1993): 48. Reprinted by permission. Reprinted with permission by the Bureau of National Affairs, (Tel. 1-800-372-1033). For more on employee burnout see "Employee Burnout: Causes and Cures, Part 2," NWNL, P.O. Box 20, Minneapolis, MN 55440, (612) 342-7137; S. E. Jackson and R. S. Schuler, "Preventing Employee Burnout," *Personnel* (March-April 1983): 58–68; B. Dumaine, "Cool Cures for Burnout," *Fortune* (June 20, 1986): 78–84.

49. "Fetal Protection Policy Struck Down," *FEP Guidelines* (May 1991): 1–2; "Fetal Protection Ruling," *Fair Employment Practices* (March 28, 1991): 31; S. Wermiel, "Justices Bar 'Fetal Protection' Policies," *The Wall Street Journal* (March 21, 1991): B1; C. Trost, "Workplace Debate," *The Wall Street Journal* (Oct. 8, 1990): 1; B. Meier, "Companies Wrestle with Threats to Workers' Reproductive Health," *The Wall Street Journal* (Feb. 5, 1987): 25; L. Altman, "Some Who Use VDTs Miscarried, Study Says," *New York Times* (June 5, 1988): 22; "Reproductive Hazards—How Employers Are Responding," *Fair Employment Practices* (Oct. 29, 1987): 132.

50. From S. B. Garland, "A New Chief has OSHA Growing Again," *Business Week* (Aug. 20, 1990): 57; P. T. Kilborn, "Who Decides Who Works at Jobs Imperiling Fetuses?" *New York Times* (Sept. 2, 1990): A1, 12; R. Winslow, "Air Polluted by Carbon Monoxide Poses Risk to Heart Patients, Study Shows," *The Wall Street Journal* (Sept. 4, 1990): B4; R. Winslow, "Safety Group Cites Fatalities Linked to Work," *The Wall Street Journal* (Aug. 31, 1990): B8; and C. Trost, "Business and Women Anxiously Watch Suit on 'Fetal Protection'," *The Wall Street Journal* (Oct. 8, 1990): 1.

51. R. A. Mamis, "The Environment: He Pays Them to Quit Puffing," *Inc.* (August 1994): 108.

52. M. Rowland, "Matching Life-Styles to Benefits," *New York Times* (March 1, 1992).

53. P. R. Balgopal, C. Ramanathan, and M. Patchner, "Employee Assistance Programs: A Cross-Cultural Perspective," paper presented at the Conference on International Personnel and Human Resource Management (Dec. 1987, Singapore); "Foreign Firms Feel the Impact of Bhopal Most," *The Wall Street Journal* (Nov. 26, 1986): 24.

Unionization

18

CHAPTER

> *"Labor's victories can be yours too. With decent paychecks, we can buy your products and services."*
>
> *John J. Sweeney*
> *President*
> *AFL-CIO*
> *Addressing Business Leaders*[1]

Learning Objectives

1. Identify why unionization is important.
2. Explain the attraction the unions have for workers.
3. Explain the historical development and the current state of the union movement.
4. Describe the union organizing campaign.
5. Describe the legal context of the union movement.
6. Recommend what unions should do.
7. Describe the international union movement.

Chapter Outline

MANAGING HUMAN RESOURCES

at Federal Express

The Air Line Pilots Association, the largest pilot union in the airline industry, won a major victory in January 1993, when pilots at the Federal Express Corporation voted to be represented by them.

The move was a defeat for Federal Express, the nation's largest air carrier of documents, packages, and heavy air freight. The company had worked hard to keep its workforce non-union. Federal Express charged that the election had been "tainted" and that the company's position had been misrepresented. It said some pilots who did not want union representation had voted for one union out of fear that another union would be elected and asked the National Mediation Board to investigate its objections.

TERMED COUP FOR UNIONS

Joseph Blasi, an expert on labor in the airline industry and a professor at Rutgers University, called the vote a major coup for unions, which have been on the defensive in the airline industry, where companies have sought concessions and have cut back employees to cope with declining passenger traffic.

"Federal Express prided itself on being a progressive non-union company whose workers did not need union representation," he said.

The breakthrough for the union was aided, he said, when Federal Express acquired Flying Tiger Line in 1989 for $880 million. Though the company gained many valuable rights to fly on international routes by buying Flying Tiger, it also inherited about 1,000 pilots who belonged to the Pilots Association.

Mr. Blasi said that there had been tension between the union and non-union pilots at Federal Express and that the union vote indicated a willingness to work together to improve compensation and benefits.

The Pilots Association was chartered by the AFL-CIO in 1931 and represents 41,000 pilots at 45 U.S. airlines. It is generally the most powerful union at any airline even though it may not be the one with the most members. A pilot strike can quickly shut down a carrier.

In the vote at Federal Express, which was monitored by the National Mediation Board, of the 2,279 pilots eligible to vote, 1,015 cast their vote for ALPA while 271 voted for the United States Pilot Association.

FIRST EFFORT FAILED

"Once the dust settles, I think that both Federal Express management and the pilots who didn't vote for ALPA will see that union representation for our pilots will make our company a better airline in the long run," said Captain Don Wilson, a member of the Federal Express Pilots Organizing Committee.

He said that an effort to unionize in 1989, led largely by pilots from Flying Tiger, had failed. This time, he said, a group of Federal Express pilots approached ALPA to help organize the company "We wanted a voice on the issues that shape our careers," he said.

He said that the company had fought back with its own group of pilots opposing the union and with a literature, video, and billboard campaign.[2]

This feature highlights several points about unionization today. First, it is not necessarily dying out in the United States. While the overall percentage of Americans belonging to unions has declined over the years, there are pockets of membership gain such as with the Airline Pilots Association (ALPA) at Federal Express. ALPA, has however, been taking losses at other airlines such as United, Delta, and American as these carriers have been forced to downsize substantially. A second point is that union membership is not always built on the backs of workers in the lowest paid or least desirable jobs. For example, Don Wilson, the 20-year captain and pilot at Federal Express who was behind the organizing drive, makes more than $175,000 yearly! Another point is that union-representation elections are monitored by an outside federal organization called the National Mediation Board in the transportation industry. The Board's mission is to make elections as open and fair as possible. It is up to the Board to make the final certification of the ALPA as the bargaining agent for all the pilots of Federal Express. And a final point is that even the best managed companies cannot assume that they can maintain a non-union status forever.

Federal Express, under the leadership of Fred Smith, has been one of the outstanding companies in terms of customer satisfaction and growth. But several changes lead to the unionization drive. First, there was the merger with the Flying Tiger line and its unionized pilots. Then came the slowdown in the airline industry, the demise of Pan Am and Eastern Airlines, and the layoffs at United and American; as a result, the younger pilots at Federal Express saw their chances of making captain decline dramatically. Finally, more senior pilots saw their pension benefits falling behind those at unionized carriers.

UPS has 170,000 employees who are members of the International Brotherhood of Teamsters.

Because the conditions making unionization attractive at Federal Express can occur at almost any firm, it is important to be knowledgeable and current on unionization activities. While you may not ever become a union member, you may be influenced by others who are or have been union members. Thus it is important to know the facts behind unionization and the activity of collective bargaining, and we begin in this chapter where we examine unionization.

Unionization

Unionization is the effort by employees and outside agencies (unions or associations) to act as a single unit when dealing with management over issues relating to their work.

When recognized by the National Mediation Board or the National Labor Relations Board, a **union** has the legal authority to negotiate with the employer on behalf of employees—to improve wages, hours, and conditions of employment—and to administer the ensuing agreement. The process of unionization is illustrated in Exhibit 18.1.

Unionization is the effort by employees to act as a single unit in dealing with managements over their work.

A union is a legal body that has authority to negotiate with an employer on behalf of the employee over wages and working condition.

Why Is Unionization Important?

LEARNING OBJECTIVE 1

Identify why unionization is important.

Unionization is important for both employers and employees. To employers, the existence of a union—or even the possibility of one—can significantly influence the ability of an organization to manage its vital human resources. To employees, unions can help them get what they want (for example, high wages and job security) from their employers.[3]

Understanding the unionizing process, its causes, and its consequences is an important part of managing human resources effectively. Unionization can result in less flexibility in hiring, job assignments, and in slowing the introduction of new work methods such as automation; it can also result in a loss of management control, inefficient work practices, and an inflexible job structure. Unions obtain rights for their members that employees without unions do not legally have. This, of course, forces non-unionized companies to consider their employees' reactions to many more decisions. In some cases, however, employers who are non-union and want to remain that way give more consideration and benefits to their employees. Consequently, the claim that it is more expensive for a company to operate with unionized rather than non-unionized employees is not always true.

Unions can also assist employers through wage concessions or cooperation in joint workplace efforts, such as teamwork programs or Scanlon plans, allowing employers to survive particularly difficult times and even remain profitable and competitive during those times. This has been particularly true in the automobile and airline industries. Unions can also identify workplace hazards and improve the quality of working life for employees.

Unions can help managers manage the company.

EXHIBIT 18.1

The Process of Unionization

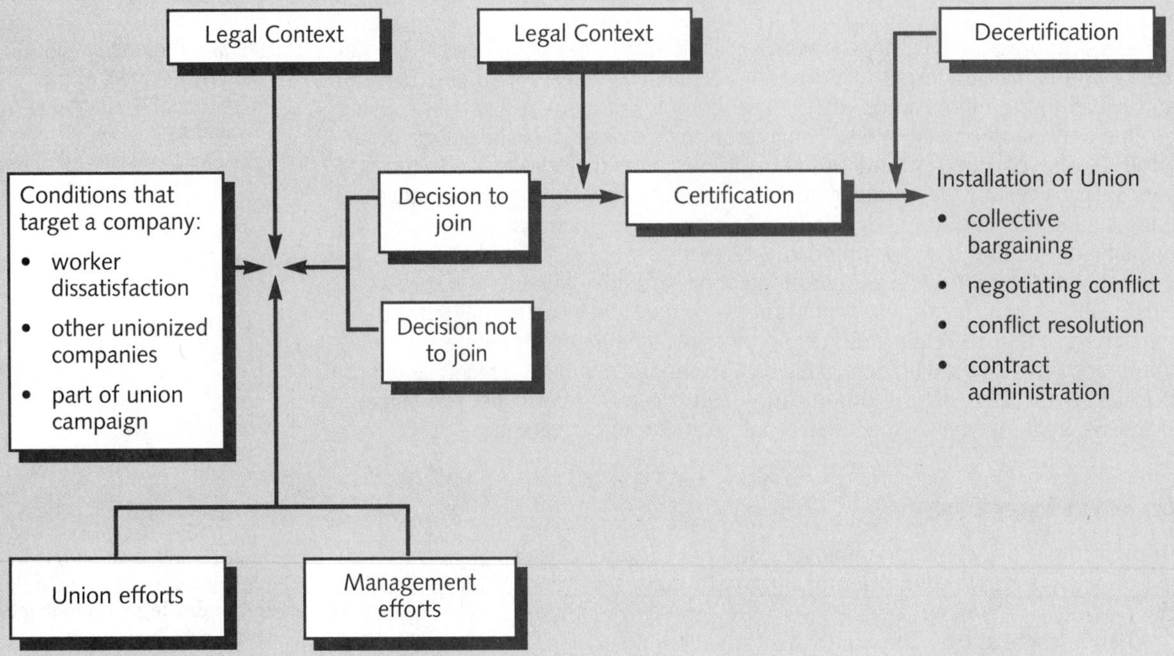

Unionization is not only important, it is also a process that is shared by four groups. While not always working in harmony, these four groups can work in partnership for everyone's benefit. The various roles that these four groups can play are listed in the feature, "Partnership: Working Together in Unionization."

LEARNING OBJECTIVE 2

Explain the attraction the unions have for workers.

What Is the Attraction of Unionization?

Unions were originally formed in response to the exploitation and abuse of employees by management. To understand the union movement today, however, we need to examine what makes employees decide to join or not join unions.

The Decision to Join

Three separate conditions that strongly influence an employee's decision to join a union are dissatisfaction, lack of power, and union instrumentality.

A psychological contract is an unwritten understanding between employee and employer about mutual expectations.

Dissatisfaction can result from a broken psychological contract.

Dissatisfaction. When an individual takes a job, certain conditions of employment (wages, hours, and type of work) are specified in the employment contract. A **psychological contract** also exists between employer and employee, consisting of the unspecified expectation of the employee about reasonable working conditions, requirements of the work itself, the level of effort that should be expended on the job, and the nature of the authority the employer should have in directing the employee's work.[4] These expectations are related to the employee's desire to satisfy certain personal preferences in the workplace. The degree to which the organization fulfills these preferences determines the employee's level of satisfaction.

PARTNERSHIP: WORKING TOGETHER IN UNIONIZATION

LINE MANAGERS	HR PROFESSIONALS	EMPLOYEES	UNIONS
Know and appreciate the historical context of union-management relations.	Train line managers in the legal considerations protecting the unionization rights of employees.	Present their views about working conditions to HR professionals and line managers.	Seek to represent the employees' views to the company.
Understand why employees are likely to join a union.	Develop HR policies and programs that make for good working conditions.	Desire to have a voice and influence on work place conditions, wages, and working hours.	Offer to improve wages and working conditions for their members.
Support the efforts of HR professionals in making policies and programs for good working conditions.	Continually survey employees' attitudes so that management knows employees' views and opinions.		Offer to work with management to improve company profitability and survival.
Manage employees with respect and equality.			
Know what can and cannot be said to employees regarding unionization during an organizing campaign.			

Dissatisfaction with the implicit terms and conditions of employment (the psychological contract) will lead employees to attempt to improve the work situation, often through unionization. A major study found a very strong relationship between the level of satisfaction and the proportion of workers voting for a union. Almost all the workers who were satisfied voted against the union.[5]

Thus, if management wants to make unionization less attractive to employees, it must consider making work conditions more satisfying. Management and the HR department often contribute to the level of work dissatisfaction by:

- Giving unrealistic job previews that create expectations that cannot be fulfilled
- Designing jobs that fail to use the skills, knowledge, and abilities of employees and fail to satisfy their personalities, interests, and preferences
- Practicing poor day-to-day HR management and supervisory practices, including unfair treatment and one-way downward communication
- Failing to tell employees that management would prefer to operate without unions and that the organization is committed to treating employees with respect.[6]

Lack of Power. Unionization is seldom the first recourse of employees who are dissatisfied with some aspect of their job. The first attempt to improve the work situation is usually made by an individual acting alone. Someone who has enough power or influence can affect the necessary changes without collaborating with others. The features of a job that determine the amount of power the job holder has in the organization are **essentiality**, or how important or critical the job is to the overall success of the organization, and **exclusivity**, or how difficult it is to replace the person. An employee with an essential task who is difficult to replace

Essentiality asks how important the job is, and exclusivity asks how difficult it is to replace the person.

may be able to force the employer to make a change. If, however, the individual task is not critical and the employee can easily be replaced, other means, including collective action, must be considered in order to influence the organization.[7]

In considering whether collective action is appropriate, employees are also likely to consider whether a union could obtain the aspects of the work environment not now provided by the employer and to weigh those benefits against the costs of unionization. In other words, the employees would determine union instrumentality.[8]

Instrumentality indicates how likely is it that the union can help.

Union Instrumentality. Just as employees can be dissatisfied with many aspects of a work environment such as pay, promotion opportunity, treatment by supervisor, the job itself, and work rules, employees can also perceive a union as being **instrumental** in removing these causes of dissatisfaction. The more that employees believe that a union can obtain positive work aspects, the more instrumental the union is for the employees. The employees then weigh the value of the benefits to be obtained through unionization against its costs such as the lengthy organizing campaign and the bad feelings among supervisors, managers, and other employees who may not want a union. Finally, the employees weigh the costs and benefits against the likelihood of a union being able to obtain the benefits: the perceived union instrumentality. When the benefits exceed the costs and union instrumentality is high, employees will be more willing to support a union.

Exhibit 18.2 summarizes the reasons for deciding to join a union. In general, the expectation that work will satisfy personal preferences induces satisfaction or dissatisfaction with work. As the level of dissatisfaction increases, individual workers seek to change their work situation If they fail and if the positive consequences of unionization seem to outweigh the negative ones, individuals will be inclined to join the union.

The Decision Not to Join

Deciding whether to join a union involves an assessment of the negative consequences of unionization. Employees may have misgivings about how effectively a union can improve unsatisfactory work conditions. Collective bargaining is not always successful; if the union is not strong, it will be unable to make an employer meet its demands. And even if an employer does respond to union demands, the workers can still be affected adversely. The employer may not be able to survive when the demands of the unions are met, and thus the company may close down, costing employees their jobs. The organization may force the union to strike, inflicting economic hardship on employees who may not be able to afford being out of work, or it may in some cases attempt reprisals against pro-union employees, although this is illegal.[9]

Beyond perceptions of unions as ineffective in the pursuit of personal goals, employees may also resist unionization because of general attitudes toward unions. Employees may identify strongly with the company and have a high level of commitment to it. They would therefore tend to view the union as an adversary, and they would be receptive to company arguments against unions.

Identification with a profession makes union membership unattractive.

Employees may also perceive the goals of the union as objectionable and likely to harm the company and the free enterprise system in general. They may object to the concept of seniority or even to the political activities of the unions. Moreover, certain employees—for example, engineers or scientists—view themselves as professionals and find collective action to be contrary to such professional ideals as independence and self-control.

The decision not to unionize can be influenced by management as well. Employers can influence the employees' decision by establishing good management practices: fostering employee participation in planning and decision making, opening channels of communication, setting up processes for handling employee problems and grievances, developing employee trust, and offering competitive wages.[10]

EXHIBIT 18.2

Processes in the Decision to Organize

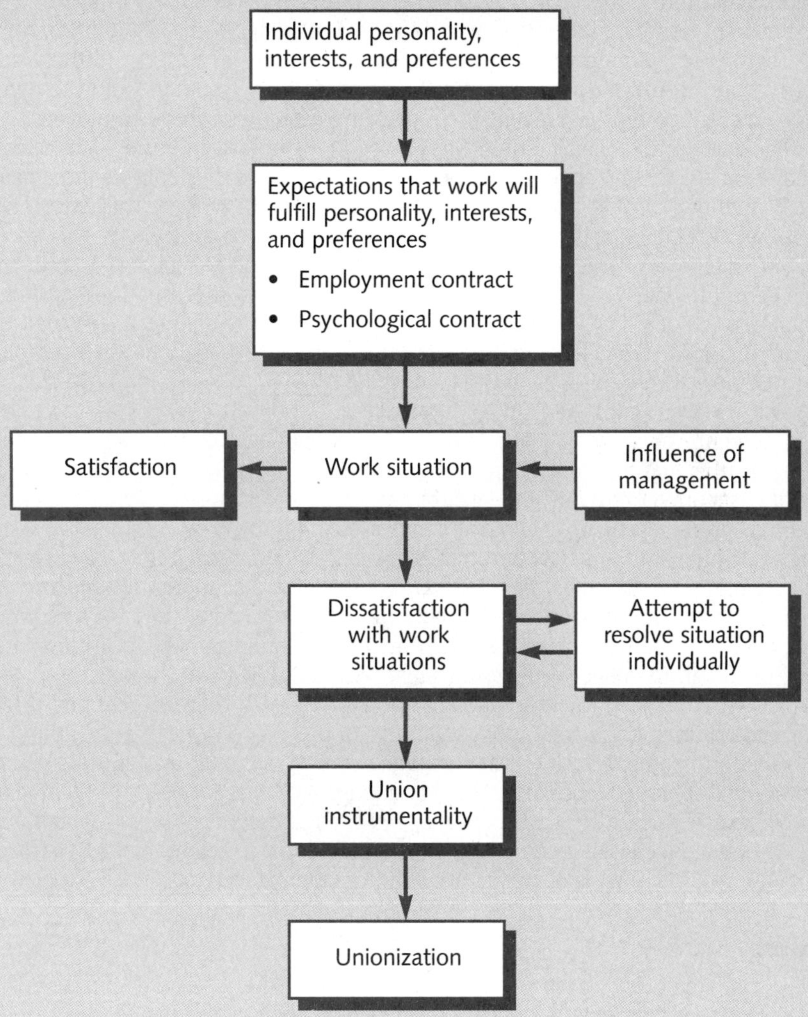

It should be noted that some employers perceive that they may benefit from their employees unionizing. This is especially so when the union brings some certainty and discipline to the workforce. In essence, a union can help manage the workforce.[11] Organizations have seldom seen unions in this way, however. In fact, the history of unionization in the United States suggests exactly the opposite.

The Historical Context and Unions Today

LEARNING OBJECTIVE 3

Explain the historical development and the current state of the union movement.

A better understanding of the attitudes and behaviors of both unions and management can be gained through a knowledge of past union-management relations. The legal considerations discussed earlier form part of this historical context.

The Early Days

The beginning of the labor union movement in the United States can be traced back to the successful attempt of journeymen printers to win a wage increase in 1778. By the 1790s, unions of shoemakers, carpenters, and printers had appeared in Boston, Baltimore, New York, and other cities. The Federal Society of Journeymen Cordwainers, for example, was organized in Philadelphia in 1794, primarily to resist employers' attempts to reduce wages. Other issues of concern to these early unions were **union shops** (companies using only union members) and the regulation of apprenticeships to prevent the replacement of journeymen employees.

Union shops are firms using only union members.

The early unions had methods and objectives that are still in evidence today. Although there was no collective bargaining, the unions did establish a price below which members would not work. Strikes were used to enforce this rate. These strikes were relatively peaceful and for the most part successful.

One negative characteristic of early unions was their susceptibility to depressions. Until the late 1800s, most unions thrived in times of prosperity but died off during depressions. Part of this problem may have been related to the insularity of the unions. Aside from sharing information on strikebreakers or scabs, the unions operated independently of each other.

The work situation had undergone several important changes by the end of the nineteenth century. Transportation systems (canals, railroads, and turnpikes) expanded the markets for products and increased worker mobility. Increases in capital costs prevented journeymen from reaching the status of master craftworker (that is, from setting up their own businesses), thereby creating a class of skilled workers. Unionism found its start in these skilled occupations, largely because "the skilled worker . . . had mastered his craft through years of apprenticeship and was no longer occupationally mobile" and the alternatives were "to passively accept wage cuts, the competition of non-apprentice labor, and the harsh working conditions, or to join in collective action against such employer innovations."[12]

Unions continued to experience ups and downs that were largely tied to economic conditions. Employers took advantage of the depressions to combat unions: In "an all out frontal attack . . they engaged in frequent lockouts, hired spies . . . summarily discharged labor 'agitators,' and [engaged] the services of strikebreakers on a widespread scale."[13] These actions, and the retaliations of unions, established a tenor of violence and lent a strong adversarial nature to union-management relations; the residual effects of which are still in evidence today.

Unions Today

Today the adversarial nature of the union-management relationship has been replaced to a certain extent by a more cooperative one. This change (discussed in collective bargaining) has been dictated in part by current trends in union membership, including the decline in membership.[14]

Decline in Membership. The proportion of the labor force represented by unions has been declining steadily since the mid-1960s. In 1995, approximately 16 percent of all workers were represented by unions. This is down from its high of 35 percent in 1945 and down from 23 percent in 1980.[15]

Factors contributing to the percentage decline include the increase in public-sector employment and white-collar jobs—both of which have historically had a low proportion of union members. Other contributing factors are the decline in employment in industries that are highly unionized, the high levels of unemployment, the increased decertification of unions, union leadership, union responsiveness to membership, and management initiatives.[16]

In the future, however, economic conditions and legislation may make unionization more feasible in white-collar and public-sector jobs. Indeed, most organizing activities today are focused on the public-sector services and healthcare as described in the feature, "Managing Human Resources in Hospitals."[17]

MANAGING HUMAN RESOURCES in Hospitals

Union organizing activity in the healthcare industry is expected to increase during the next few years, according to a report by the American Hospital Association (AHA) and BNA (Bureau of National Affairs) interviews with healthcare labor relations officials. Structural changes in the industry have increased employees' job-security concerns and work-related stress levels, management and union officials note, adding that unions are expected to step up their organizing efforts in the healthcare sector—proven over the past decade to be susceptible to union overtures.

AHA'S ANALYSIS

Following passage of the Taft-Hartley's 1974 healthcare amendments . . . , hospital-organizing activity mushroomed. Healthcare representation elections rose from 3.2 percent of the total number of elections conducted in 1974 to 11.8 percent in 1975. Since 1980, the union representation rate among healthcare employees has risen some 6 percent, to an estimated 20 percent, while the overall private-sector rate has steadily declined from 23 percent of the organizable workforce in 1980 to 18 percent in 1985.

The healthcare industry has become an increasingly attractive target for union organizers for a number of reasons, AHA says. Widespread layoffs—the result of federal regulations and healthcare cost-containment efforts—have made job security a priority issue for employees and given union-organizing drives a major boost. Moreover, while many healthcare workers traditionally have viewed themselves as white-collar professionals and rejected collective bargaining, AHA says, "as professional concerns with issues such as compensation, job security, equitable policy administration, and meaningful work involvement expand, identification with unionized segments of the workforce also is expanding."

CAMPAIGN CONCERNS

Employees of hospitals feel more insecure than ever before, viewing top management as less interested in them than it was several years ago, declares James Velghe, president of Management Science Associates, Kansas City, Missouri. Noting that hospitals are particularly vulnerable to unionization threats from all-professional bargaining units that include registered nurses, Velghe warns that unions are conducting more sophisticated and selective organizing campaigns.

Management's failure to respond to employees' needs accounts for the recent increase in union activity in the healthcare industry, says K. Bruck Stickler, labor counsel for the American Hospital Association. As hospitals downsize, merge, and consolidate, many healthcare workers feel threatened by job loss, Stickler notes, and see union representation as a way to gain clout. Employees who think they are being treated unfairly—for example, laid off without relation to seniority—are more likely to look to unions for help.[18]

To gain more organizational ability, power, and financial strength, several unions merged. Although mergers may not automatically increase membership, they can mean more efficiency in union-organizing efforts and an end to costly jurisdictional disputes among unions. The increased organizational strength resulting from mergers may also enable unions to expand the coverage of their membership into industries and occupations previously underrepresented.

Distribution of Membership. Historically, membership has been concentrated in a small number of large unions. In 1976, 16 unions represented 60 percent of union membership, and 85 unions represented just 2.4 percent. Similarly, the National Education Association accounted for 62 percent of all association members. Many employee associations are small because they are state organizations; their membership potential is therefore limited.

Did You KNOW?

New York and Hawaii have the highest percent of unionization: about 28%. South Carolina is the lowest at 3.8%.

Unions today are exhibiting a substantial and increasing amount of diversification in their membership. For example, in 1958, 73 percent of the unions had at least four-fifths of their members in a single industry; this figure dropped to 55 percent in 1976. The most pronounced diversification has occurred in manufacturing. For example, of the 29 unions that represent workers in chemicals and allied products, 26 presently have less than 20 percent of their membership in a single industry.[19]

How American Unions Are Structured

The basic unit of labor unions in the United States is the national union (or international union), a body that organizes, charters, and controls member union locals. The national union develops the general policies and procedures by which locals operate and provides assistance to the locals in areas such as collective bargaining. National unions give the locals clout because they control a large number of employees and can influence large organizations through national strikes or slowdown activities.[20]

The AFL-CIO is the dominant organization for the union movement.

The major umbrella organization for national unions is the American Federation of Labor and Congress of Industrial Organizations (**AFL-CIO**). It represents about 85 percent of the total union membership and contains 81 national unions. The AFL-CIO is an important and powerful body with 13 million members.[21]

Every two years the AFL-CIO holds a convention to develop policy and amend its constitution. Each national union is represented in proportion to its membership. Between conventions, an executive council (the governing body) and a general board direct the organization's affairs; a president is in charge of day-to-day operations.

The executive council's activities include evaluating legislation that affects labor and watching for corruption within the AFL-CIO. Standing committees are appointed to deal with executive, legislative, political, educational, organizing, and other activities. The department of organization and field services, for instance, focuses its attention on organizing activities Outside of headquarters, three structures exist to organize the local unions. Many of the craft unions are organized into the trade department and the industrial department, which represent them in the national union. The remaining locals are organized directly as part of the national unions. They are affiliated with headquarters but retain independence in dealing with their own union matters.

Did You KNOW?

The two largest unions in the AFL-CIO are the:

- **Teamsters (1.3 million)**
- **American Federation of State, County and Municipal Employees (1.2 million)**

Besides the 81 national unions within the AFL-CIO, about 60 national unions, representing less than 4 million workers, operate independently. Although this separation is not considered desirable by the AFL-CIO, its impact has been diminished substantially since the Teamsters re-affiliated with the AFL-CIO in 1987.

At the heart of the labor movement are the 70,000 or so local unions, varying in size up to 40,000 members. The locals represent the workers at the workplace, where much of the day-to-day contact with management and the HR department takes place. Most locals elect a president, a secretary-treasurer, and perhaps one or two other officers from the membership. In the larger locals, a business representative is hired as a full-time employee to handle grievances and contract negotiation. The other important member of the union local is the **steward**, an employee elected by his or her work unit to act as the union representative at the workplace and to respond to company actions against employees that may violate the labor agreement. The steward protects the rights of the worker by filing grievances when the employer has acted improperly.

A steward serves as the union representative at the workplace.

How Unions Operate

Activities of union locals revolve around collective bargaining and handling grievances. In addition, locals hold general meetings, publish newsletters, and otherwise keep their members informed. Typically, however, the membership is apathetic about union activities. Unless a serious problem exists, attendance at meetings is usually low, and even the election of officers often draws votes from less than one-fourth of the membership.

At headquarters, the AFL-CIO staff and committees work on a wide range of issues, including civil rights, community service, economic policy, education, ethical practices, housing, international affairs, legislation, public relations, research, safety, Social Security, and veterans' affairs. A publications department also produces a variety of literature for the membership and outsiders. National union headquarters provide specialized services to regional and local bodies. People trained in organizing, strikes, legal matters, public relations, and negotiations are available to individual unions.

National unions and the AFL-CIO are active in the political arena. Labor maintains a strong lobbying force in Washington and is involved in political action committees and also at the state and local government level. A recent development has been the international political activities of some of the large national unions. For example, the United Auto Workers have held discussions with Japanese car manufacturers concerning levels of imports and the construction of assembly plants here. They have also lobbied Washington to restrict car imports in an attempt to bolster U.S. automakers and to increase jobs. Their highly publicized lobbying effort against NAFTA was unsuccessful. Thus, to help their membership, unions are expanding their activities on all levels and, in some cases, working with other organizations to attain mutual goals.

Union activities include involvement in:

- **civil rights**
- **community service**
- **economic policy**
- **education**
- **ethical practices**
- **housing**
- **international affairs**
- **legislation**
- **public relations**
- **research safety**
- **Social Security**
- **veterans' affairs**
- **publications**
- **special services to locals**
- **national politics**

The Organizing Campaign

LEARNING OBJECTIVE 4

Describe the union organizing campaign.

One of the major functions of the National Labor Relations Board (NLRB) is to conduct the election of unions to represent nongovernment employees. This is accomplished through a certification election to determine whether the majority of employees want the union. Under U.S. labor law, the union certified to represent a group of employees has sole and exclusive right to bargain for that group:

> *The process by which a single union is selected to represent all employees in a particular unit is crucial to the American system of collective bargaining. If a majority of those voting opt for union representation, all employees are bound by that choice and the employer is obligated to recognize and bargain with the chosen union.*[22]

Because unions can acquire significant power, employers may be anxious to keep them out. Adding to this potential union-management conflict is the possibility of competition and conflict between unions if more than one union is attempting to win certification as the representative of a group of employees.

Several stages in the certification process can be identified: 1) a campaign to solicit employee support for union representation, 2) the determination of the appropriate group the union will represent, 3) the pre-election campaign by unions and employers, 4) the election itself, and 5) the certification of a union.[23] These steps are outlined in Exhibit 18.3. The next stage of the organizing process—negotiation of a collective bargaining agreement—is discussed in Chapter 19.

Soliciting Employee Support

In the campaign to solicit employee support, unions generally attempt to contact the employees and obtain a sufficient number of authorization cards to enable them to request an election from the NLRB.

Establishing Contact Between the Union and Employees. Contact between the union and employees can be initiated by either party. National unions usually contact employees in industries or occupations in which they have an interest or are traditionally involved. The United Auto Workers, for example, would be likely to contact non-union employees in automobile plants, as they have done for the new plants that have been built in the South. Another prominent

EXHIBIT 18.3

The Certification Process

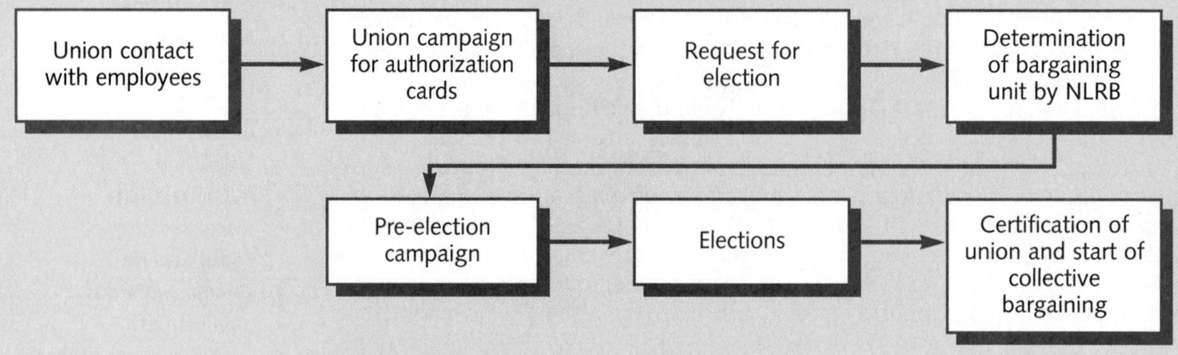

Source: William D. Todor, Professor of Human Resource Management, The Ohio State University.

example of union initiative was the attempt of two competing unions—the United Farm Workers and the Teamsters—to organize the agricultural workers in California in the 1960s and 1970s. These unions were often aggressive, even violent, during their campaigns for worker support. One consequence of their precertification activities, which included national boycott of grapes and lettuce, was the *California Agricultural Relations Act* of 1975, which regulates union-management relations in the agriculture industry.

In many cases, the union is approached by employees interested in union representation, and the union is happy to oblige. Employees may have strong reasons for desiring this affiliation—low pay, poor working conditions, and other factors relating to dissatisfaction. Because workers generally tend to be apathetic toward unions, however, their concern must become quite serious before they will take any action. At this point, the company must be careful and avoid committing unfair labor practices. Accordingly, employers *should not*:

- *Misrepresent the facts.* Any information management provides about a union or its officers must be factual and truthful.

- *Threaten employees.* It is unlawful to threaten employees with loss of their jobs or transfers to less desirable positions, income reductions, or loss or reduction of benefits and privileges. Use of intimidating language to dissuade employees from joining or supporting a union also is forbidden. In addition, supervisors may not blacklist, lay off, discipline, or discharge any employee because of union activity.

- *Promise benefits or reward.* Supervisors may not promise a pay raise, additional overtime or time off, promotions, or other favorable considerations in exchange for an employee's agreement to refrain from joining a union or signing a union card, to vote against union representation, or otherwise to oppose union activity.

- *Make unscheduled changes in wages, hours, benefits, or working conditions.* Any such changes are unlawful unless the employer can prove they were initiated before union activity began.

- *Conduct surveillance activities.* Management is forbidden to spy on or request anti-union workers to spy on employees' union activities, or to make any statements that give workers the impression they are being watched.

Supervisors may not attend union meetings or question employees about a union's internal affairs, nor may they ask employees for their opinions of a union or its officers.

- *Interrogate workers.* Managers may not require employees to tell them who has signed a union card, voted for union representation, attended a union meeting, or instigated an organization drive.
- *Prohibit solicitation.* Employees have the right to solicit members on company property during their nonworking hours, provided this activity does not interfere with work being performed, and to distribute union literature in nonwork areas during their free time.[24]

Employers *can,* however,

- Discuss the history of unions and make factual statements about strikes, violence, or the loss of jobs at plants that have unionized.
- Discuss their own experiences with unions.
- Advise workers about the costs of joining and belonging to unions.
- Remind employees of the company benefits and wages they receive without having to pay union dues.
- Explain that union representation will not protect workers against discharge for cause.
- Point out that the company prefers to deal directly with employees, and not through a third party, in settling complaints about wages, hours, and other employment conditions.
- Tell workers that in negotiating with the union, the company is not obligated to sign a contract or accept all the union's demands, especially those that aren't in its economic interests.
- Advise employees that unions often resort to work stoppages to press their demands and that such tactics can cost them money.
- Inform employees of the company's legal right to hire replacements for workers who go out on strike for economic reasons.[25]

Authorization Cards and the Request for Elections. Once contact has been made, the union begins the campaign to collect sufficient **authorization cards**, or signatures of employees interested in having union representation. This campaign must be carried out within the constraints set by law. If the union obtains cards from 30 percent of an organization's employees, it can petition the NLRB for an election. (Procedures in the public sector are similar.) If the NLRB determines there is indeed sufficient interest, it will schedule an election. If the union gets more than 50 percent of the employees to sign authorization cards, it may petition the employer as the bargaining representative. Usually employers refuse, whereupon the union petitions the NLRB for an election.

Authorization cards are those indicating employees are interested in having union representation.

Employees interested in unionization sign authorization cards.

The employer usually resists the union's card-signing campaign. For instance, companies often prohibit solicitation on the premises. However, employers are legally constrained from interfering with an employee's freedom of choice. Union representatives have argued that employers ignore this law because the consequences are minimal—and by doing so, they can effectively discourage unionism.

During the union campaign and election process, it is important that the HR manager caution the company against engaging in unfair labor practices. Unfair labor practices, when identified, generally cause the election to be set aside. Severe violations by the employer can result in certification of the union as the bargaining representative, even if it has lost the election.

Determination of the Bargaining Unit

Employees to be represented by a union are called a bargaining unit.

When the union has gathered sufficient signatures to petition for an election, the NLRB will make a determination of the **bargaining unit**, the group of employees that will be represented by the union. This is a crucial process, for it can determine the quality of labor-management relations in the future.

> *At the heart of labor-management relations is the bargaining unit. It is all important that the bargaining unit be truly appropriate and not contain a mix of antagonistic interests or submerge the legitimate interests of a small group of employees in the interest of a larger group.*[26]

In order to assure the fullest freedom of collective bargaining, legal constraints and guidelines exist for the unit. Professional and nonprofessional groups cannot be included in the same unit, and a craft unit cannot be placed in a larger unit unless both groups agree to it. Physical location, skill levels, degree of ownership, collective bargaining history, and extent of organization of employees are also considered.

From the union's perspective, the most desirable bargaining unit is one whose members are pro-union and will help win certification. The unit must also have sufficient influence in the organization to give the union some power once it wins representation. Employers generally want a bargaining unit that is least beneficial to the union; this will help to maximize the likelihood of failure in the election and to minimize the power of the unit.[27]

Pre-Election Campaign

Pre-election campaign is one conducted before the vote to see who wins: union or employer.

After the bargaining unit has been determined, both union and employer embark on a **pre-election campaign**. Unions claim to provide a strong voice for employees, emphasizing improvement in wages and working conditions and the establishment of a grievance process to ensure fairness. Employers emphasize the costs of unionization—union dues, strikes, and loss of jobs.

The impact of pre-election campaigns is not clear. A study of 31 elections showed very little change in attitude and voting propensity after the campaign. People who will vote for or against a union before the election campaign generally vote the same way after. Severe violations of the legal constraints on behavior, such as using threats or coercion, are prevented by the NLRB, which watches the pre-election activity carefully.

Election, Certification, and Decertification

Generally, elections are associated with the process of determining whether the union will win the right to represent workers. Elections can also determine whether the union will continue to have the right to represent a group of employees.

Certification election occurs when a union obtains a majority vote.

Election and Certification. The NLRB conducts the **certification election**. If a majority votes for union representation, the union will be certified. If the union does not get a majority, another election will not be held for at least a year. Generally, about one-third to one-half of the elections certify a union, with less union success in larger organizations. Once a union has been certified, the employer is required to bargain with that union.

Decertification election votes to remove a union from representation.

Decertification Elections. The NLRB also conducts **decertification elections**, which remove a union from representation. If 30 percent or more of the employees request such an election, it will be held. Decertification elections most frequently occur in the first year of a union's representation, when the union is negotiating its first contract. Union strength has not yet been established, and employees are easily discouraged about union behavior.

Legal Considerations

LEARNING OBJECTIVE 5

Describe the legal context of the union movement.

The federal government entered the labor scene in an attempt to stabilize the violent and disruptive labor situation in the 1920s and the 1930s. Court actions and efforts by employers prior to this time generally suppressed the rights of workers to act collectively to protect their interests. This was consistent with classical economic theory in which the free operation of the law of supply and demand was considered essential.

> *According to this theory, control of wage rates by workers artificially inflated prices, ultimately harming commerce, the community, and even workers themselves, because higher prices discouraged consumption and created unemployment. Therefore, according to many observers, the best prescription for a healthy economy was one free of either government regulation or private regulation via collective action of workers.*
>
> *Until 1935, application of these restrictive theories of law inherited from England reflected the political assumption that free competition and the sanctity of contract and property rights of individuals were fundamental values of society that must be protected.*[28]

The courts protected these "fundamental values of society" by declaring that attempts by workers to band together to increase wages (that is, form a union) were conspiracies condemned by law (*Commonwealth v. Pullis, Philadelphia Cordwainers, Pennsylvania,* 1806). Later this outright condemnation was modified to include the necessity of applying a "means test" before condemning the union as an illegal conspiracy (*Commonwealth v. Hunt,* 1842). The courts then used the means test to hamper efforts at unionization.

By the 1880s, the conspiracy doctrine was reinforced by civil law, particularly civil injunctions. Civil injunctions maintained the status quo until the legal issues could be resolved, and they are still used for this purpose. Thus, if workers attempt to join together and strike for the purpose of attaining higher wages, an injunction can be granted by the courts forcing the workers to return to work until the legality of the strike is decided. The injunction can also be granted quickly (in order to provide an equitable remedy) without the use of juries and other time-consuming legal proceedings. The impact of injunctions on unionization was particularly evident when the Supreme Court ruled that injunctions could be used to enforce **yellow-dog contracts**—that is, contracts signed by employees agreeing not to join a union (*Hitchman Coal & Coke v. Mitchell,* 1917).

Yellow-dog contracts are contracts signed by employees agreeing not to join a union.

Further protection for the "fundamental values of society" was provided by the *Sherman Antitrust Act,* which was passed by Congress in 1890 to limit the ability of organizations (for example, unions) to engage in acts (such as union mergers) that lessened competition. This act, as applied to unions, was upheld by the Supreme Court in *Loewe v. Lawlor* (The Danbury Hatters case), 1908. The application of the *Sherman Antitrust Act* to unions was reinforced by the *Clayton Antitrust Act* of 1914 and subsequent court decisions (*Duplex Printing Co. v. Deering,* 1921; *United Mine Workers of America v. Coronado Coal Company,* 1922).

Although this supposed protection of society was largely maintained throughout the 1920s, early legislation in the railway industry (because of the industry's impact on the public welfare) suggested it was not sacrosanct. Union activities derived support from the *Arbitration Act* of 1888; the *Erdman Act* of 1898, which outlawed yellow-dog contracts in the railway industry; and *Adair v. United States* (1921), which upheld the unconstitutionality of the yellow-dog contract.

Railway Labor Act

The Railway Labor Act sanctioned unionization in railways.

These events in the railway industry culminated in the *Railway Labor Act* of 1926, which brought about the demise of the "fundamental values of society" doctrine for all other industries. This act was passed by Congress in 1926 to prevent labor unrest in the railway industry from having serious economic consequences. It has since been expanded to include air carrier employees as well. It was the first act to protect "the fundamental right of workers to engage in labor organizing actively without fear of employer retaliation and discrimination.[29] Other objectives of the act were to avoid service interruption, to eliminate any restrictions in joining a union, and to provide for prompt settlement of disputes and grievances.

The act specified that employers and employees would maintain an agreement over pay, rules, working conditions, dispute settlement, representation, and grievance settlement. A board of mediation (later called the National Mediation Board) was created to settle disputes by encouraging, as necessary, negotiation, then arbitration, and finally emergency intervention by the president. A second board—the National Railway Adjustment Board—was created in 1934 to deal with grievances. This board has exclusive jurisdiction over questions relating to grievances or the interpretation of agreements concerning pay, rules, or working conditions; it makes decisions and awards binding on both parties.

National Labor Relations Act

The National Labor Relations Act sanctioned unionization throughout industry.

The success of the *Railway Labor Act* led Congress to enact a comprehensive labor code in 1935. The purpose of the *National Labor Relations Act* (or *Wagner Act*) was to restore the equality to bargain collectively with employees and employers.

The act affirmed employees' rights to form, join, or assist labor organizations to bargain collectively, and to choose their own bargaining representative through majority rule. As stated in Section 8, the second significant portion of the act identified the following unfair labor practices on the part of the employers:

- Interference with the efforts of employees to organize
- Domination of the labor organization by the employer
- Discrimination in the hiring or tenure of employees in order to discourage union affiliation
- Discrimination for filing charges or giving testimony under the act
- Refusal to bargain collectively with a representative of the employees

Court interpretation of these unfair labor practices has made it clear that bribing, spying, blacklisting union sympathizers, moving a business to avoid union activities, and other such employer actions are illegal.

Employer groups criticized the *Wagner Act* on several grounds. They argued that the act, in addition to being biased toward unions, limited the constitutional right of free speech of employers, did not consider unfair labor practices on the part of unions, and caused employers serious damage when there were jurisdictional disputes.

The National Labor Relations Board (NLRB) was established to administer this act. Its major function is to decide all union-organizing efforts and unfair labor practice suits except in areas such as transportation, which are covered by the National Mediation Board. Recent rulings by the Board have focused on the second practice listed above. The rulings in the cases of Electromation (1992) and E. I. DuPont de Nemours & Co. (1993) essentially reaffirmed that some employee committees may be unlawful because of involvement or domination by the employer. These decisions caution employers about their involvement or control over employee teams, and even their efforts to encourage employee participation.[30]

Labor-Management Relations Act

The Taft-Hartley Act balances union-management power and protects the public interest.

Congress responded to these criticisms in 1947 by enacting the *Labor-Management Relations Act,* often called the *Taft-Hartley Act.* This act revised and expanded the *Wagner Act* in order to establish a balance between union and management power and to protect the public interest. It introduced the following changes:

- Employees were allowed to refrain from union activity as well as to engage in it.
- The closed shop was outlawed, and employees were required to agree in writing before union dues could be deducted from their paychecks.
- Employers were ensured of their right to free speech, and they were given the right to file charges against unfair labor practices such as coercing workers to join the unions, causing employers to discriminate against those who do not join, refusing to bargain in good faith, requiring excessive or discriminatory fees, and engaging in featherbedding activities.
- Certification elections (voting for union representation) could not be held more frequently than once a year.
- Employees were given the right to initiate decertification elections.

These provisions indicated the philosophy behind the act—as Senator Robert Taft put it—"simply to reduce the special privileges granted labor leaders."

From time to time, amendments have been added to the *Taft-Hartley Act.* For example, the 1980 amendments to the act provide for an identical accommodation for employees with religious objections to union membership or support. Thus employers and unions must respect (within reason) the religious beliefs of employees as protected by Title VII. For example, an employee may, on religious grounds, contribute to a charity in lieu of paying union dues (*Tooley v. Martin-Marietta Corp.* 1981).

Labor-Management Reporting and Disclosure Act

Although the *Taft-Hartley Act* included some regulation of internal union activities, continuing abuses of power and the corruption of some union officials led to the passage of a "bill of rights" for union members in 1959. The *Labor-Management Reporting and Disclosure Act,* or the *Landrum-Griffin Act,* provided a detailed regulation of internal union affairs. Its provisions include the following:

The Landrum-Griffin Act regulates internal union affairs.

- Equality of rights for union members in nominating and voting in elections
- Controls on increases in dues
- Controls on suspension and firing of union members
- Elections every three years for local offices and every five years for national or international offices
- Restriction of the use of trusteeships to take control of a member group's autonomy for political reasons
- Definition of the type of person who can hold union office
- Filing of yearly reports with the secretary of labor

The intention of this act was to protect employees from corruption or discriminatory labor unions. By providing standards for union conduct, the act eliminated much of the flagrant abuse of power and protected the democratic rights of employees to some degree. The United Mine Workers, for example, held their first election of international officers in 1969 as a result of the *Landrum-Griffin Act.*

Court Decisions and Congressional Acts

One of the most significant court decisions of the 1980s is *First National Maintenance Corp. v. NLRB.* In this case, the Supreme Court held that an employer is not obligated to bargain with the union about a decision to close a portion of its business. In addition, the NLRB ruled that labor law is not necessarily violated when supervisors who support union activities are fired along with workers as part of an employer plan to discourage unions. In this particular case, however, the board ruled that the employer must rehire the workers fired for union activities.

The cornerstone of labor relations, the grievance-arbitration process, was established in *Textile Workers Union v. Lincoln Mills* (1957). In that case, the Supreme Court held that the agreement to arbitrate grievances is the *quid pro quo* for an agreement not to strike through the years. This agreement, however, has led to the problem of unfair representation by the union of its members. Over the past ten years, cases filed by employees with the NLRB against their unions for unfair representation (breach of duty) have risen to several thousand annually. Although the union's obligation of fair representation is clear, the specific duties involved have been left unclear by numerous court decisions, including *Ford Motor Co. v. Huffman* (1953) and *Hines v. Anchor Motor Freight Co.* (1976).

Finally, the Supreme Court has ruled that bona fide seniority systems are protected under Section 703(h) of Title VII of the *Civil Rights Act* of 1964. Thus, equal employment considerations in general do not overrule seniority systems in employment decisions where a seniority system has been in existence for some time or where its intention is not discriminatory (*California Brewers Association v. Bryant,* 1980; *International Brotherhood of Teamsters v. United States,* 1977; *American Tobacco v. Patterson,* 1982). The importance given to seniority is also reflected in cases involving the *Rehabilitation Act* and the *Americans with Disabilities Act*:

> *For example, in a layoff where the employer had two workers in light-duty positions, the law would not require the employer to retain the less senior employee with a disability over the more senior workers.*[31]

Federal Employee Regulations

These labor laws just described were enacted to govern labor relations in the private sector. In fact, the *Wagner Act* specifically excludes the U.S. government, government corporations, states, and municipal corporations in its definition of employer, and for a long time, government employees lacked the legislative protection afforded private-sector workers until a series of key executive orders were put in place. Federal employee labor relations were, until recently, exclusively controlled by executive orders issued by the president.

The government's view of its employees differs from its view of private-sector employees. Several of the rights of unions in the private sector are not included in public sector regulations, although the content of these regulations often is lifted from private sector acts.

Did You KNOW?

Executive Order 12954 (1995) barred most federal contractors from hiring permanent replacement workers. A U.S. Court of Appeals, however, overturned this Executive Order.

Executive Orders. The first set of regulations for federal employee labor relations was Executive Order 10988 introduced by President John Kennedy in 1962. This order forbade federal agencies from interfering with employee organizing or unlawful union activity and provided for recognition of employee organizations. Employee organizations were denied the right to strike, however, and economic issues were not part of the bargaining process, since these are fixed by the civil service classification system. Agency heads were made the ultimate authority on grievances, and managers were excluded from the bargaining units.

Executive Order 11491, issued in 1970 and amended in 1971 (EO 11616) and 1975 (EO 11838), addressed some of the difficulties presented by the first executive order. It created the Federal Labor Relations Council to hear appeals from the decisions of agency heads, prescribed regulations and policies, and created a Federal Services Impasses Panel to act on negotiation impasses. The Council and the employee representatives could meet and discuss personnel practices and working conditions, but all agreements had to be approved by the Council head.

Unfair labor practices by both agency management and labor organizations were delineated. The Council was restricted from interference, discrimination, and sponsorship of union discipline against an employee for filing a complaint and was required to recognize or deal with a qualified union. Labor organizations were also restrained from interfering, coercing management or employees, discriminating against employees, calling for or engaging in a strike, or denying membership to an employee.

These controls on employers and labor organizations are similar to those found in private sector legislation. Yet federal employees do not have the same bargaining rights. They lack rights in four areas:

- No provision is made for bargaining on economic issues.
- Although the parties can meet and confer, there is no obligation to do so.
- The ultimate authority is the agency head rather than a neutral party.
- There is no provision for union security through the agency shop, which requires all employees to pay dues but not to join the union.

Civil Service Reform Act. In 1978, the *Federal Service Labor-Management Relations Statute* was passed as Title VII of the *Civil Service Reform Act*, which has been referred to as "the most significant change in federal personnel administration since the passage of the *Civil Service Act* in 1883.[32] Several significant changes were made by the statute, including:

- Passage of the statute removed the president's ability to change the act through executive order and, in general, made it more difficult to change the legislation.
- It established the Federal Labor Relations Authority (FLRA), modeled after the NLRB, as an "independent, neutral, full-time, bipartisan agency"[33] created, as President Jimmy Carter said, "to remedy unfair labor practices within the Government." Interpretation of the act is the province of the FLRA and the courts. Agency heads, including the president, cannot define the meaning of the act.
- An aggrieved person may now seek judicial review of a final order of the FLRA. The FLRA may also seek judicial enforcement of its order.
- Negotiated grievance procedures, which must be included in all agreements, must provide for arbitration as the final step.

State and Local Employee Regulations

Employee relations regulations at the state and local level are varied. Not all states have legislation governing their employees, but some states have legislation covering municipal employees as well. One widespread regulation can be noted: collective bargaining is permitted in most states, and it covers wages, hours, and other terms and conditions of employment. The "other terms and conditions" have caused the most difficulty in interpretation. Managerial prerogatives are usually quite strong, especially for firefighters, police, and teachers. The requirement to bargain over certain issues in the private sector is not so stringent as the state or local level. In addition, some 20 states have passed **right-to-work laws**, which prohibit union membership as a condition of employment.

Right-to-work laws prohibit union membership as a condition of employment.

Although the rights and privileges of public sector labor organizations are not as extensive as those in the private sector, the greatest growth in unionization in recent years has come in the public sector. Indeed, union representation is substantially higher in the public sector than in the private sector, approximately 35 percent versus 11 percent.

LEARNING OBJECTIVE 6

Recommend what unions should do.

Current Trends

What Should Unions Do?

The future role of the union is generating a great deal of discussion and speculation these days.[34] Some foresee a halt to the decline in union membership in the private sector. This is expected to follow from the decline in the numbers entering the workforce and a subsequent tighter labor market; from more sophisticated and efficient organizing activities; from the rising appeal of unions among less skilled workers; and from the increasing ability and willingness of unions to offer a broader array of consumer benefits and new forms of membership; and by merging with other unions and becoming stronger.[35]

All this needs to be put in the perspective of the environment. The U.S. economy will continue to globalize, and firms will continue to find high-quality, low-wage workers.[36] The decline in mass production will continue at the same time as the skill levels of the workforce increase. As Ray Marshall, former Secretary of Labor, describes it "[E]conomic success will require new policies and high-performance systems more appropriate for a global, knowledge-intensive economic environment."[37] A description of what this means for employees and companies is described in the feature, "HR Advice and Application." In addition to Marshall, others have called for creating a new labor policy that involves changing the laws, attitudes, and behaviors of government, employees, and employers.[38]

A final perspective needs to be included here as well: the union movement will continue to be heterogenous. There will be differences within the movement, with some unions—such as the UAW—being more willing to enter into collaborative agreements and others less willing.[39] Thus we are likely to see several answers to the question, "What should unions do?"

HR ADVICE & APPLICATION

One Employer's Experience

Through workplace cooperation, employees are empowered to make meaningful decisions at Electro-Galvanizing Co. in Cleveland, according to Cal Tinsley, plant manager, and Thomas Zidek, process technician and president of Steelworkers Local 9126. The company, commonly referred to as L-SE, was created in 1985 as a joint venture between LTV Corp. and Sumitomi Metals of Japan.

With the agreement of the union, L-SE was designed to provide a work environment in which "respect, dignity, and cooperation were to be the way of life," Zidek explains. Adversarial relationships were typical in the steel industry at the time, Zidek notes, but workers still supported the new environment. Most of the individuals hired were laid-off steelworkers who realized they wanted something new for the future.

Before startup, workers received technical training as well as extensive training in problem-solving skills and how to deal with people. Workers then chose their positions based on the skills they brought to the company. That level of involvement continues at L-SE through problem-solving teams and committees on hiring, safety, gain-sharing, skill-based pay, training, and customer concerns.

According to Tinsley, L-SE has tried to promote equality by eliminating traditional barriers between labor and management, whether they are physical or psychological. For example, there is no traditional personnel department at L-SE. Also, similar uniforms are worn by workers and managers, making it hard to distinguish between them, and the company has a common locker room, no assigned parking places, and no time clocks.

As part of the company's normal operations, employees hold weekly workshops that focus on quality, notes Zidek. "We are continuously improving our processes that way," he says. Moreover, he points out, employees have the power to stop production or shipments if quality is not high.

The most important innovation at L-SE, says Tinsley, is the creation of an environment where employees want to make participation work. The proof that it works, he says, is that L-SE has gained a reputation as the premium supplier of electrogalvanized material in the automotive industry.[40]

International Comparisons

LEARNING OBJECTIVE 7

Describe the international movement.

Germany

The belief that workers' interests are best served if employees have a direct say in the management of the company is called **codetermination**. The original ideas about codetermination, called *mitbestimmung*, were conceived in Germany and are now spreading into many other European countries.

Codetermination gives workers the feeling that they are represented in major decisions.

Under codetermination, unions are often given seats on the boards of directors of corporations. Managers are encouraged to consult with unions before making major organizational changes, including mergers, investments, plant closings, or relocations. If management disagrees with the union position, management prevails. However, unions can veto subcontracts by the company, and they have access to all company records.

Under the political leadership of the Social-Democratic government in Germany, consensus was reached during the early 1980s to promote international competitiveness through technological superiority and to overcome barriers to innovation by integrating the trade unions into the process of change. The German system of labor relations, with its key features of centralization, jurisdiction, and participation, seem to be functioning well, even in the face of changed socioeconomic conditions. The efficiency and legitimacy of collective bargaining seem also to hold given the codetermination practice and similar system flexibility. Low levels of conflict and commitment to cooperation characterize the labor relations system in Germany. As German firms layoff workers in the recessionary times of the 1990s, this cooperative relationship is being tested.

Since the unions' defeat in the 1930s, the German labor movement has consisted of unions with structures that are a synthesis of traditional elements of the socialist and the Catholic labor movement. Although labor is dominated by the Social Democrats, the Catholic influence on the development of such concepts as codetermination, social partnership, or capital formation for employees has become an integral part of the German trade unions' ideology. A second principle of the trade unions in Germany is that they are organized on an industrial basis. The dominant labor organizations are the seventeen trade unions affiliated with the DGB (Confederation of Trade Unions). The DGB sets the pattern in negotiating for the majority of the workers. The other trade union federations—the DBB (Association of Civil Servants), DAG (White-Collar Association), and the CGB (Christian Trade Unions) lack significant bargaining power; hence civil servants are not allowed to strike.

In the 1980s, unionized employees who were members of DGB affiliates made up a third of the labor force. Nonetheless, their power and influence stretches significantly beyond their numbers. For example, employee support for unions far exceeds their readiness for unionization. In fact, during elections of workplace representatives, about 80 percent of all employees vote regularly for candidates who have been nominated by DGB unions. Another feature of the German unions is their centralized authority. Most of the internal decision-making takes place in the upper echelons of union bureaucracy.

Did You KNOW?

German workers have it good: average wages and benefits in manufacturing average $30 per hour. However, the rate of unemployment is 10%.

German employers are also organized and centralized. There are employers' associations in several industries, often dominated by large-scale companies. The largest employers' umbrella organization is the BDA (Federation of German Employers' Association). The BDA coordinates various kinds of legally binding agreements for its members. For example, in 1978, it published a "taboo catalog" containing rules and provisions of the association designed to strengthen its bargaining power. It limited management compromise in bargaining; among its provisions was an instruction that Saturday, usually not a working day, should remain a working day in order to maximize the use of labor and machinery. Although this instruction was reversed in 1984, it illustrates the strategy of the employers' association to establish common policies. The notable efficiency of German human resource practices can be explained by the convictions of labor and management to the labor relations system and the cultural predisposition of the Germans to adhere to discipline, rules, and regulations.[41]

Great Britain

The industrial relations system in Great Britain differs markedly from those in both the United States and other European countries. Traditionally, the framework of labor law in Britain has been noninterventionist, fostering an essentially voluntary system of industrial relations. Under this system, employers have had no general legal duty to recognize and bargain with their employees, while employees have had no legally protected rights to organize themselves in unions. Also, negotiated agreements signed between unions and employers are not enforceable as legal contracts. The collective agreements familiar to U.S. managers are more akin to "gentlemen's agreements" in Britain and are based on social rather than on legal sanctions.[42]

As with so many aspects of life in Britain, the explanation for this state of affairs is largely historical. The development of British labor law has progressed via the granting of immunities from existing restrictive statutes—such as immunity from prosecution for criminal conspiracy—rather than through the legislation of positive rights. Unlike their U.S. counterparts, British unions have not viewed the law as a positive and protective force guaranteeing their right to existence.

The full, long-run consequences of these changes are difficult to predict with any certainty. Managers in Britain still face a workforce that is highly unionized compared with that in the United States, where less than 16 percent of the labor force is currently in unions. Managers in many parts of British industry must also negotiate with a multiplicity of unions, the representational boundaries of which often owe more to craft tradition and the accidents of history than they do to the logic of efficient production. They must also operate on a day-to-day basis without the support of legally enforceable collective agreements. Important developments at the shop-floor level do, however, offer some clues to a changed future. On the union side, both the engineering and the electricians unions have been willing to sign single-union agreements that include no-strike clauses. They have also shown a preference for cooperative over confrontational relations with management. Perhaps significantly, the key movers on the management side of these innovative agreements have often been overseas companies setting up operations in Britain. Japanese companies such as Nissan, Hitachi, and Toshiba are notable examples, but innovative agreements have also been signed with some U.S. firms. This is a useful reminder that the behavior and attitudes of both sides determine the quality of labor-management relationships.

Did You KNOW?

The Amalgamated Engineering and Electrical Union has a single union deal with Nissan in Sunderland, England. By comparison, U.K. firms typically deal with multiple unions in one location.

Canada

Approximately one-third of the Canadian labor force is unionized. About three-fourths of the union members are affiliated with the Canadian Labor Congress (CLC). As in the United States, the union local is the basic local unit. The CLC is the dominant labor group at the federal level. Its political influence may be compared with that of the AFL-CIO.

Although the labor laws in Canada are similar to those in the United States, noteworthy differences do exist. Since 1925, the majority of Canadian workers have been covered by provincial, not federal, labor laws, whereas in the United States over 90 percent of the workers are covered by the *National Labor Relations Act.* The Canadian *Industrial Relations Disputes and Investigations Act* of 1973, on the other hand, covers less than 10 percent of the labor force.

Canadian labor laws require frequent interventions by government bodies before a strike can take place. In the United States, such intervention is largely voluntary. Compulsory arbitration in Canada is governed by the *Public Service Staff Relations Act* of 1967. This law also allows nonmanagerial government employees to join unions and bargain collectively.

This history of labor relations in Canada and the United States is similar because both nations follow British common law, except that provincial governments, rather than the national government, have developed most of the Canadian labor laws. Since the decision in *Toronto Electric Commissioners v. Snider* (1925), Canadian workers have been governed primarily by provincial laws (except for employees working for the national government and industries under national coverage, as defined by amendments to the 1973 industrial relations act—for instance long-shoring, seafaring, provincial railroads, Crown corporations, and airlines). Many of the features of the *Taft-Hartley Act* have been incorporated into the labor laws of the Canadian provinces. For the union movement as a whole, the trend toward concessionary bargaining to avoid layoffs and plant closings appears to be less evident than it is in the United States.[43]

Japan

The third sacred treasure of the Imperial House of Japan (we discussed the first two in Chapter 14) is what is known as the enterprise union. Unlike in the United States and Europe, where unions are organized horizontally and industrywide, almost all trade unions in Japan are formed on a company-by-company, or enterprise, basis. Enterprise unions today account for nearly 90 percent of all Japanese union organizations. Four principal industrywide federations of workers serve as coordinators and formulators of unified and reliable standards, and sources of information.

Although the enterprise concept received a fair amount of attention in the United States during the 1920s and 1930s, such unions collapsed, primarily as a result of excessive management involvement and their narrow field of interest. The success of the enterprise union in Japan is attributed to two major differences. First, the allocation of financial responsibility between the enterprise union and the trade or regional organizations reflects a difference in the organizational roles of Japanese labor unions. In Western countries, where centralized union control and authority are predominant, the national union receives union dues, decides how they are to be used, and returns a portion to the local unions for expenses. In Japan, the enterprise union controls the dues, passing on 10 to 20 percent to the federation.[44]

As a result of the enterprise union's role, problems in labor-management relationships can be dealt with more directly, without necessarily involving an outside body. The "mixed" union representation of all blue-collar and some white-collar workers has also proved valuable in determining more representative concerns. As a result of greater union participation by employees of a given company, some of Japan's current top management were once active labor union leaders.

The second difference that accounts for the success of the enterprise union system in Japan is cultural: the greater company and national loyalty shown by each worker. Accordingly, workers do not look on the union solely as a negotiating body but use its structure to deal with such issues as industry and technical reforms new plant and equipment investments, and matters of personnel and productivity development.

Australia

It is interesting to note that the institutional framework of both U.S. and Australian industrial relations evolved from similar historical circumstances: the need to compel strong employers to meet and deal with a weak labor union movement for collective bargaining purpose.[45] The legislative solutions to this situation that were enacted in each country were, however, quite different.

American legislation in the 1930s carefully avoided imposing the decisions of a third party on labor and management by providing a detailed legal framework within which the parties were compelled to bargain in good faith with each other. In contrast, Australian legislation at the turn of the century provided centralized government machinery for the establishing and enforcing of industrial awards.[46]

Did You KNOW?

Harry Bridges, leader of the International Longshoremen in the 1930s, came from Melbourne, Australia.

In 1983, the national government commissioned a committee of inquiry on industrial relations in Australia (generally referred to as the Hancock Committee in recognition of the chair, Professor Hancock).[47] The Hancock Committee recommended a number of changes in the system, such as the establishment of a new labor court and the extension of grievance procedures, but it did not recommend total deregulation of the centralized system.[48]

After much debate and delay, the national government's response to the recommendations of the Hancock Report was presented in the *Industrial Relations Bill* of 1988. Although the bill supports the need for increased flexibility in the industrial relations system, it presents a much diluted version of the original reforms recommended. The main elements of this bill include an updated name for the ACAC (to be known as the Industrial Relations Commission), which now has the power to hear unfair dismissal cases, and provisions for greater opportunities for enterprise-level negotiations. Despite the different approaches of labor unions and employer associations to industrial relations, both groups have advocated reforms that allow for decentralization and greater flexibility within the present system.[49]

Given the collectivist and centralist traditions of Australian labor relations, dramatic changes are unlikely, and any assumption of convergence over time to a system based solely on plant or enterprise collective bargaining, as in the United States, would be unwarranted. Foreign companies doing business in Australia still need to analyze the industrial relations implications of their business strategies in considerable detail.

Mexico

The Mexican *Federal Labor Law* governs all labor matters, and the state labor boards oversee its enforcement. Labor relations in Mexico are somewhat different in custom and in practice than in the United States. The employee-employer relationship is somewhat closer and more in terms of a family. When a labor union declares a strike, all employees, including management, must leave the plant. If the strike is legal, the workers receive pay for the duration of the strike.

The industrial relations function of a maquiladora company is very important in its day-to-day operation. As a group, the maquiladora companies have done an effective job in administering the labor laws of Mexico.[50] For the most part, maquiladoras have operated without unions. However, if a company is not operated effectively and not in accordance with good HR management, there is always the potential attraction of unionization.

Summary

Employees are generally attracted to unionization because they are dissatisfied with work conditions and because they feel powerless to change those conditions. Some major sources of dissatisfaction are inequity in pay administration, poor communications, and poor supervisory practices. By correcting these, or not allowing them to occur in the first place, organizations can help prevent unions from being attractive. However, once a union-organizing campaign begins, a company can't legally stop it unless an unfair labor practice is committed by the union. At this point, it may be best to hire a labor attorney familiar with the NLRB and labor law to monitor the practices of the union. Should a charge be filed with the NLRB it is important to remember that it takes a long time for the charge to be heard. There are, however, other ways to delay the organizing campaign, such as challenging the bargaining unit, challenging the election procedures, and even conducting a campaign touting company-provided benefits.

Organizations can also establish initial conditions that makes unionization a less attractive alternative. For example, organizations can make sure their compensation package is in good order. Pay should be competitive, and the principles of equal pay for equal work and equal pay for comparable worth should be observed. Supervisors should be trained in effective communication styles and methods. Employee rights must be recognized and observed. Participation and employee involvement programs and safety programs are also helpful in establishing a positive, attractive organizational climate.

Some organizations may not bother with defensive maneuvering because they may decide that unions are useful to them. Unions can bring an element of peace and stability among the workers and actually help organizations manage. At the same time, unions can also cause inflexibility and block attempts to make improvements where needed—for example, by blocking a change to total-quality management. Thus, it's also possible that an organization may prefer to help the employees decertify an unwanted union.

Historically, unions and management have operated as adversaries because many of their goals are in conflict. But since conflict is ultimately detrimental to both management and unions, labor relations have gradually changed, thereby reducing this conflict. For instance, unions and management have begun to cooperate to achieve mutual goals. Although cooperation is not widespread, it may be the style of union-management relations in the future.

Key Concepts

AFL-CIO
authorization cards
bargaining unit
certification election
codetermination
decertification
essentiality
exclusivity
instrumental
pre-election campaign
psychological contract
right-to-work laws
steward
union
unionization
union shops
yellow-dog contracts

Review and Discussion Questions

1. Identify and discuss the factors that make unionization attractive to employees. Are these factors different today than they were 50 years ago?
2. Briefly describe the history of the union movement.
3. What is a certification election? A decertification election? Who do you suppose wins the majority of certification elections today? Why has the rate changed over time?
4. What is the structure of unionization in the United States today?
5. What are the important legal considerations related to activities like TQM and employee participation?
6. What is a company permitted to do during a union organization campaign?
7. Describe the important legal considerations in unionization.
8. What should unions do?
9. What is codetermination? Would it work in the United States?
10. Compare and contrast union-management conditions in the United States, Japan, Mexico, and Canada.

PROJECTS, EXERCISES & CASES

End-of-Text Projects

Lincoln Electric

Answer the following for Lincoln Electric:

1. What are the views of management at Lincoln Electric regarding union representation of their workers?
2. Why does the management at Lincoln Electric hold these views?
3. Why have the workers at Lincoln Electric not sought representation?
4. What change could cause the workers at Lincoln Electric to seek union representation?

Nordstrom

Answer the following for Nordstrom:

1. What are the view of management at Nordstrom regarding union representation of their workers?
2. Why does the management at Nordstrom hold these views?
3. Why have the workers at Nordstrom not sought representation?
4. What change could cause the workers at Nordstrom to seek union representation?

Field Project

Interview human resource managers on their views of unions. Visit union companies and non-union companies. Interview union members, non-union members, and union officers to learn their views on unions. Present your findings to the class.

Career Management Exercise

During your career, you 1) may have to decide whether you will join a union or 2) may be required to discourage your employees (within the guidelines of the law) from forming a union.

1. Explain why you would decide to join a union or why you would refuse to join. Indicate conditions under which you would or would not join.
2. Now explain why you have decided to discourage your employees from forming a union (or why you have decided not to fight unionization efforts at your company).

Case: A Bad Place To Work

Brenda C. is a nursing aide at a nursing home. She has been a diligent employee there for two and a half years, and she enjoys her work. She is considered a good worker by her supervisor. Recently, she has become increasingly concerned with the pay and the working conditions at the home.

Although the nursing aides often do extra work to help a resident, and as a group are dedicated to their work, the pay scale is significantly below that of other homes in the area. In addition, the nursing aides and other nursing home staff have no area where they can get away from the residents for a break; in fact, the nursing home does not provide for a coffee break at all. The nursing staff do, however, take informal breaks whenever they can get a few minutes, and Brenda has found that these help her function better in the sometimes hectic work situation. Since the staff are not allowed to eat in the cafeteria, they must provide for their lunch by eating out or bringing a bag lunch. Occasionally, the staff are delayed at the restaurant and are late returning to work.

It seems to Brenda that providing a lounge area for coffee and lunch breaks would make the job much easier and would result in better care for the residents. She approached her supervisor about the matter, but he was not receptive and suggested that she concentrate on her job. Brenda persisted and was told that the budget is too tight and space too limited.

Brenda knows that her nursing aide friends in other homes have such facilities, and she is fairly certain that those homes are financially no better off than hers. She feels she can get no further on her own, so she contacts the union that represents nursing aides in some of the other homes and arranges for a meeting after work on Friday, expecting a good turnout. She discusses the situation with her co-workers, and many of them are very interested.

On Friday afternoon, the manager of the nursing home calls her into his office and tells her that her performance has recently been inadequate (although her last review was good), that her attitude toward the residents has changed, and that he is terminating her employment as of that day. Brenda is shocked. She tells her co-workers what has happened, and they are also very surprised. Four people attend the union meeting that night. They soon leave expressing fear for their jobs.

Case Questions

1. Why is Brenda interested in getting a union involved in her situation?
2. What are the major aspects of the nursing home that you find objectionable and would prefer not to have?
3. Can unionization help Brenda and her co-workers? How?
4. What can the nursing home do to change Brenda's mind?

Case: That's Hard To Say

Western Manufacturing is a moderately sized (110 employees) assembly plant in the Midwest. Until recently, the employees have expressed little interest in being unionized. Their pay and fringe benefits are competitive with comparable unionized plants in the vicinity. Moreover, Western Manufacturing has a well-defined grievance process that has been relatively successful in resolving employee problems.

However, several employees have suggested to their friends at the plant that a labor union might be a good idea. In fact, these employees have begun a drive to unionize. They have been campaigning rather strongly, and they will soon begin collecting authorization cards and then make a formal request for election.

Management of Western Manufacturing is not pleased with these recent developments and has begun a fairly active campaign against unionizing. They have pointed out in several meetings between the shift supervisors and their employees that the wages, benefits, and working conditions are at least on a par with comparable union plants and maybe slightly better. Within six weeks, three such meetings have been called to explain the company's position to the employees.

The employees who are most active in the campaign to have union representation have complained bitterly that these meetings called by management during company time are a clear case of unfair labor practices. Not surprisingly, the company disagrees.

Case Questions

1. Comment on the union representatives position with respect to the meetings.
2. Comment on the management's position with respect to the meetings.
3. Is this an unfair labor practice? Why or why not?
4. What is the fundamental, central issue involved here?

Chapter 18 Endnotes

1. S. Greenhouse, "Labor Chief Asks Business For a New 'Social Compact'," *New York Times* (December 7, 1995).

2. A. Salpukas, "Federal Express Pilots Vote for Union," *New York Times* (Jan. 15, 1993): D4. Used by permission. See also A. Salpukas, "Labor's Showdown at Federal Express," *New York Times* (Feb. 7, 1993): Sec. 3, 1 and 6. Although the union was voted by the pilots, the contract negotiations for the first contract between the company and union went on for a couple of years. For more details, see D. Greising, "Fedex May Get A Christmas Rift," *Business Week* (November 20, 1995): 92; "Federal Express Pilots Union Threatens Work Slowdown During Holiday Rush," *Personnel Journal* (January 1995): 12; D. Greising, "Watch Out For Flying Packages," *Business Week* (November 14, 1995): 40; S. Strom, "A Wild Sleigh Ride at Federal Express," *New York Times* (December 20, 1994): Dl, 2.

3. For a more extensive discussion of unionization and the entire union-management relationship, see H. J. Anderson, *Primer of Labor Relations,* 21st ed. (Washington, D.C.: Bureau of National Affairs, 1980); B. W. Justice, *Unions, Workers, and the Law* (Washington, D.C.: Bureau of National Affairs, 1983). See also "Union Membership and Earnings," *Bulletin to Management* (March 2, 1995): 68–69; P. Hamill, "In Defense of Honor," *New York Times Magazine* (December 31, 1995): 18–19.

4. E. H. Schein, Organizational Psychology (Englewood Cliffs, NJ: Prentice-Hall, 1965).

5. J. G. Getman, S. B. Goldberg, and J. B. Herman, *Union Representation Elections: Law and Reality* (New York: Russell Sage Foundation, 1976); "Employee Survey: Unionization and Attitude Measure," *Bulletin to Management* (April 24, 1986): 133–134.

6. "The UAW vs. Japan: Its Showdown Time in Tennessee," *Business Week* (July 24, 1989): 64–65; K. B. Noble, "Union Organizers' Task Is Uphill at Nissan Point," *New York Times* (April 3, 1988): 18; D. P. Levin, "Nissan Workers in U.S. Test Union and Industry," *New York Times* (Aug. 12, 1989): 8; R. Kuttner, "A Beachhead for the Beleaguered Labor Movement," *Business Week* (July 17, 1989): 14–15.

7. A. Ritter, "Are Unions Worth the Bargain?" *Personnel* (Feb. 1990): 12–14; Brett "Behavioral Research on Unions," and Brett, "Why Employees Want Unions," 47–59.

8. S. A. Youngblood, A. D. DeNisi, J. Molleston, and W. H. Mobley, "The Impact of Work Attachment, Instrumentality Beliefs, Perceived Labor Union Image, and Subjective Norms on Union Voting Intentions and Union Membership," *Academy of Management Journal* (1984): 576–590.

9. Getman, et al., *Union Representation Elections: Law and Reality.*

10. J. H. Hopkins and R. D. Binderup, "Employee Relations and Union Organizing Campaigns," *Personnel Administrator* (March 1980): 57–61.

11. Pro-union legislation in the 1920s and 1930s was favored by some pro-management groups because it was seen as a way to bring some degree of certainty and peace to union-management relationships. See B. E. Kaufman, *Industrial Relations* (Ithaca, NY: Cornell, 1993).

12. A. A. Sloane and F. Witney, *Labor Relations,* 5th ed. (Englewood Cliffs, NJ: Prentice-Hall, Inc., 1985): 57.

13. Ibid., 62.

14. For an extensive presentation of union membership data, see C. D. Gifford, ed., *Directory of U.S. Labor Organizations, 1995-96 Edition* (Washington, D.C.: BNA, 1996); and B. T. Hirsch and D. A. Macpherson, *Union Membership and Earnings Data Book, 1996 Edition* (Washington, D.C.: The Bureau of National Affairs, 1996).

15. "Union Membership and Earnings," *Bulletin to Management* (March 2, 1995): 68–69; "Union Membership," *Bulletin to Management* (March 17, 1994): 84–86.

16. L. Uchitelle, "Survey Points to a Cause of Union Decline," *New York Times* (June 2, 1995): D16.

17. "Health Care Organizing," *Bulletin to Management* (June 3, 1993): 172–173.

18. Health Care Industry: Prime Organizing Target," *Bulletin to Management* (Feb. 12, 1987): 49. Reprinted with permission by the Bureau of National Affairs, (Tel. 1-800-372-1033).

19. Gifford, ed., *Directory of U.S. Labor Organizations.*

20. L. Balliet, *Survey of Labor Relations* (Washington, D.C.: Bureau of National Affairs, 1981): 72–105.

21. "AFL-CIO Membership," *Bulletin to Management* (October 26, 1995): 340–341.

22. Getman et al., *Union Representation Elections: Law and Reality.*

23. For an extensive discussion of the organizing campaign, see J. A. Fossum, "Union-Management Relations," in *Personnel Management,* K. M. Rowland and G. R. Ferris, eds., (Boston, MA: Allyn and Bacon, 1982); W. E. Fulmer, "Step by Step Through a Union Campaign," *Harvard Business Review* (July-Aug. 1981): 94–102.

24. "Dealing with Organizing: Do's and Don'ts," *Bulletin to Management* (March 7, 1985): 8.

25. Ibid.

26. D. P. Twomey, *Labor Law and Legislation,* 6th ed. (Cincinnati, OH: South-Western, 1990).

27. Getman et al., *Union Representation Elections: Law and Reality.*

28. A good discussion of earlier contributions to labor law can be found in Twomey, *Labor Law and Legislation;* R. C. Trussell, ed., *U.S. Labor and Employment Laws* (Washington, D.C.: Bureau of National Affairs, Cambridge University Press, 1987).

29. Balliet, *Survey of Labor,* p.44.

30. M. Booth, "Outdated Laws Foil Worker Participation," *New York Times* (June 18, 1995): F13; "Joint Committees Found Unlawful," *Bulletin to Management* (June 24, 1993): 200.

31. "Do Union Contracts Conflict with ADA?" *Bulletin to Management* (Dec. 9, 1991): 400.

32. H. B. Frazier III, "Labor Management Relations in the Federal Government," *Labor Law Journal* (March 1979): 131.

33. Ibid.

34. T. Kochan and P. Osterman, *The Mutual Gains Enterprise* (Boston: Harvard, 1995); A. Bernstein, "A New Deal At the AFL-CIO?" *Business Week* (October 30, 1995): 119–120; S. Greenhouse, "Labor Chief Asks Business For a New 'Social Contract'," *New York Times* (December 7, 1995); C. McDonald, "U.S. Union Membership in Future Decades: A Trade Unionist's Perspective," *Industrial Relations* (Winter 1992): 13–30; eds. A. Gladstone et al., *Labour Relations in a Changing Environment* (New York: Walter de Gruyter, 1992); M. Bognanno and M. Kleiner, "Introduction: Labor Market Institutions and the Future Role of Unions," *Industrial Relations* (Winter 1992): 1–12.

35. S. B. Garland et al., "Breath of Fire or Last Gasp?" *Business Week* (August 14, 1995): 42; A. Bernstein et al., "Rubber Workers With Nerves of Steel," *Business Week* (December 18, 1995): 44; R. Marshall, "The Future Role of Government in Industrial Relations," *Industrial Relations* (Winter 1992): 31–49.

36. D. Moberg, "Like Business, Unions Must Go Global," *New York Times* (December 19, 1993): F13.

37. M. Hequet, "Whither Labor?" *Training* (April 1996): 28–36; J. Reid, Jr., "Future Unions," *Industrial Relations* (Winter 1992): 122–136.

38. T. Kochan, "Creating a Labor Policy for the 1990s," *Boston Globe* (September 12, 1995): 40.

39. Kochan, *The Mutual Gains Enterprise;* "Cooperation Emerges in the Workplace", *Bulletin to Management* (May 25, 1995): 168.

40. "High-Performance Workplaces Highlighted," *Bulletin to Management* (Aug. 5, 1993): 248. Reprinted by permission, The Bureau of National Affairs, Inc. (Tel. 1-800-372-1033).

41. K. Lowry Miller, "Are the Easy Times Gone for Good?" *Business Week* (January 29, 1996): 48–49; M. Markham, "German Workers Watch the Clock," *New York Times* (May 13, 1984); P. Revzin, "Swedes Gain Leisure, Not Jobs, by Cutting Hours," *The Wall Street Journal* (Jan. 7, 1985): 10.

42. P. Sparrow and J. M. Hiltrop, *European Human Resource Management in Transition* (London: Prentice-Hall, 1995).

43. D. J. Schneider, "Canadian and U.S. Brands of Unionism Have Distinctly Different Nationalities," *Management Review* (Oct. 1983): 31–32.

44. M. S. O'Connor, *Report on Japanese Employee Relations Practices and Their Relation to Worker Productivity, a report prepared for the Study Mission to Japan,* (Nov. 1980): 8–23.

45. K. F. Walker, "The Development of Australian Industrial Relations in International Perspective," in *Perspectives on Australian Industrial Relations,* W. A. Howard, ed. (Melbourne: Longman Cheshire, 1984).

46. For a comparison of laws governing union security in Australia and the United States, see B. Aaron, "Union Security in Australia and the United States," *Comparative Labor Law* 6 (1984): 415–441.

47. "Management Pressures for Change and the Industrial Relations System," *Business Council of Australia submission to the Alternatives to the Present Arbitration System conference,* Oct. 1984, Sydney.

48. Report of the Committee of Review: Australia Industrial Relations Law and Systems (Canberra: Australian Government Publishing Service, 1985). For an analysis of these changes, see "Australia Vaults Ahead with Free Banking," *The Wall Street Journal* (Nov. 4, 1985): 10, 26.

49. P. Dowling, R. Schuler, and D. Welch, *International Dimensions of Human Resource Management,* 2nd ed. (Belmont, CA: Wadsworth, 1994).

50. *Maquiladora Program Overview,* (Newport Beach, CA: 1988): 10.

19

CHAPTER

Collective Bargaining

Learning Objectives

1. Describe the different relationships in collective bargaining.
2. Describe the process of collective bargaining.
3. Describe the elements of agreement negotiation.
4. Discuss forms of conflict resolution.
5. Explain the elements of contract administration.
6. Discuss the current trends in collective bargaining.

"In some cases, [the union] was absolutely right. The protests refocused everyone to the sense of urgency to get the quality problems fixed."

Richard G. (Skip) LeFauve
President
Saturn[1]

Chapter Outline

MANAGING HUMAN RESOURCES

at Saturn

In some cases, [the union] was absolutely right," concedes Richard G. (Skip) LeFauve, President of Saturn, who adds that the protests ["refocused everyone to the urgency of the quality problems"]. Skip LeFauve is referring to the protests by the union workers at the General Motors Saturn plant in Spring Hill, Tennessee. When GM's then chairman, Robert Stempel, paid a visit to the plant in the autumn of 1991, the workers, wearing black and orange armbands, launched a work slowdown. Another one of those strikes to get higher wages? No, this was a protest against the higher production quotas GM was trying to impose on the plant. While high quality and high quantity can go hand in hand when everything is working right, it can be too much to expect in the early stages of operation. Since production at the plant was in the early stages, the workers were more concerned about quality—about the car and the customer's satisfaction with the product—than they were with quantity of output. It could be argued that the workers basically had no reason to go for quantity, since they get paid by the hour and not for the number of cars that go out the door (at least not in the short run). However, the same could be said for the workers' interest in quality.

Quality takes commitment, dedication, and training, and the United Automobile Workers (UAW) have not been known for their concerns over quality or quantity. However, the Spring Hill plant workers staged the slowdown because of concerns about quality! They believed quality was more critical than quantity for the longer term success of the company!

Why were the union workers at the Saturn plant behaving contrary to the traditional stereotype? Because management was behaving contrary to its stereotype. Management was giving workers more say in production and was treating workers as co-owners and as valued members of the team. Any employee who didn't want to fit into this new scheme of labor-management relationship in the auto business could collect a generous severance package ($15,000 to $50,000, depending on length of service), but few did. This new scheme excited the entire workforce.

Reflecting upon their original agreement, GM management heard the concerns of the workers at the plant and gave them the benefit of the doubt. They knew Saturn was the real test case for whether or not GM could build cars to compete directly with the top-selling Japanese cars, and they needed the total commitment of the workforce to succeed in this effort.[2]

These events at the Saturn plant highlight several important aspects of collective bargaining. One is that union workers can be as concerned about quality as anyone else. Another is that cooperation is possible between unions and management. Cooperation between UAW and GM has not only been high at the Spring Hill plant, it has also been high at GM plants in Flint, Michigan (Buick City); the NUMMI joint venture in Fremont, California; and those in the Cadillac Division, winner of the prestigious Baldrige Award for quality. The total quality management program at Saturn shows that union-management cooperation can result in benefits both to the workers and to the company. At Saturn, these have included improved quality, lower absenteeism, increased satisfaction, more employment security and training, and increased profitability. An important aspect of collective bargaining relationships—and one that should never be underestimated—is that they are dynamic. By early 1993, pressures at the Spring Hill plant caused severe strains on its cooperative spirit; these pressures included:

Did You KNOW?

During 1985, Saturn's HR function formed a proactive partnership with the United Auto Workers. This was a clear statement that people issues and participative, collaborative team behavior would be considered equally important to engineering, manufacturing, and finance.

- Less commitment from recent hires to Saturn's employee-participation ideals
- Burnout from 50-hour-and-up workweeks
- Growing distrust of the union's close ties with Saturn's management
- Anger at lack of elections for key union posts on the shop floor
- A reduction of training for new workers.[3]

Through extensive discussions and agreements to hire and train more workers and reduce the workweek, cooperative and harmonious union-management relations returned.

Collective Bargaining

Collective bargaining is a complex process in which union and management negotiators maneuver to win the most advantageous contract.

Collective bargaining is a complex process in which union and management negotiators maneuver to win the most advantageous contract. Reaching agreement on the variety of issues involved depends on the following:

- Quality of the union-management relationship
- Processes of bargaining used by labor and management
- Management's strategies
- Union's strategies
- Joint strategies

These critical determinants of the collective bargaining process are described in detail here prior to our examination of the bargaining process.

LEARNING OBJECTIVE 1

Describe the different relationships in collective bargaining.

Union–Management Relationships

To understand the union-management relationship it is critical to view it within the context of the labor relations system.[4] This system is composed of three groups—employees, management (line managers and HR professionals), and the union—with the government influencing interactions among the three. Employees may be managers or union members, and some of the union members may be part of the union management system (local union leaders). Each of the relationships is regulated by specific federal statutes as discussed in the previous chapter.

Each group in the labor relations system traditionally has different goals. Workers are interested in improved working conditions, wages, and opportunities. Unions are interested in their own survival, growth, and acquisition of power, all of which depends on their ability to maintain the support of the employees by providing for their needs. Management has overall organizational goals (such as profit, market share, and growth) and also seeks to preserve managerial prerogatives to direct the workforce and to attain the personal goals of the managers (promotion or achievement). Government is interested in a stable and healthy economy, protection of individual rights, and safety and fairness in the workplace. All of these factors influence the roles that these groups play. The possible roles are shown in the feature, "Partnership: Working Together in Collective Bargaining."

The adversarial system is a competitive situation in union-management relationships.

Adversarial Relationships. The goals of the various groups in the labor relations system are not always seen as compatible. Thus an adversarial system has emerged, with labor and management attempting to get a bigger cut of the "pie" while government oversees its own interest. In an **adversarial system** of union-management relations, the union's role is to gain concessions from management during collective bargaining and to preserve those concessions through the grievance procedure. The union is thus an outsider and a critic.[5]

PARTNERSHIP: WORKING TOGETHER IN COLLECTIVE BARGAINING

LINE MANAGERS	HR PROFESSIONALS	EMPLOYEES	UNIONS
Work with HR professionals in developing an effective relationship with union representatives. Work with HR professionals and union representatives in resolving grievances. Engage in cooperative relations with the union and employees. Know and work with the union-management contract.	Work with line managers in dealing effectively with union representatives. Develop mechanisms for effective grievance resolution. Move along such issues as total quality management and quality of work life programs.	Bargain in good faith through their union representatives with line manager and HR professionals. Fulfill their rights and responsibilities in the union contract.	Bargain with line managers and HR professionals. Seek improvements in conditions and wages. Be willing to adapt to local conditions and changes in technology and economic conditions.

Historically, unions have adopted an adversarial role in their interactions with management. Their focus has been on wages, hours, and working conditions as they attempted to get "more and better" from management. This approach works well in economic boom times but encounters difficulties when the economy is not healthy. High unemployment and the threat of continued job losses induced unions to expand their role, especially since many of their traditional goals—better pay, hours, and working conditions—have already been achieved. Many unions have begun to enter into new, collaborative efforts with employers. The result of this can be described as a cooperative relationship.

The cooperative system is a problem-solving situation in union–management relationships.

Cooperative Relationships. In a **cooperative system**, the union's role is that of a partner, not a critic, and the union and management are jointly responsible for reaching a cooperative solution. Thus union and management must engage in problem solving, information sharing, and integration of outcomes.[6]

Cooperative systems have not been a major component of labor relations in the United States. Other countries—Sweden and Germany, for example—have built cooperative mechanisms into their labor system. But increasingly, U.S. management and labor are evolving a cooperative relationship. Management recognizes that most organization improvement programs need the acceptance of the union to be successful, and active involvement of the union is one of the best ways to gain this acceptance.[7]

While the switch from an adversarial to a cooperative relationship is not easy, it is occurring more and more frequently. The feature, "Managing Human Resources at AT&T," illustrates just such a change.

As we discussed in Chapter 7, teamwork is a critical component in the efforts of firms to improve quality. Unions such as the UAW and the CWA and firms such as Ford Motor and AT&T recognize how important quality is to survival. Consequently, they are working together to ensure that teamwork programs succeed. Of course, not all unions or firms are in favor of these "workplace reforms."[8]

"Today, our union is facing up to the tough task of rebuilding the nation and getting Americans back to work. Our priority is figuring out how to compete in the global economy."

"What's good for working people is good for America." We all know the middle class is the source of our country's economic strength. So we're fighting for good jobs and seeking pragmatic solutions at the bargaining tables. We're asking business and government to join us in pursuing this distinctly American strategy.

Ron Carey
President
Teamsters Union

In all fairness, it should be noted how difficult the transition from an adversarial to a cooperative relationship is for most unions as well as firms. The

MANAGING HUMAN RESOURCES

at AT&T

When AT&T and its unions settled their differences and signed a contract in 1992, the talk afterward was of mutual interests, shared goals, and cooperation in the service of the common goal—that of global competition. Conspicuously absent was the rowdy language associated in the public's imagination with collective bargaining.

Worker participation is not entirely new at AT&T. Almost 10 years ago, the union tried to improve its members' lot with a "quality of life" proposal. The company experimented with labor-management projects. Some of the programs continue, but some failed, victims of labor upheavals, personnel departures, or restructurings.

The new contract calls for an unusual degree of labor-management cooperation that only can be achieved by a huge change in culture. This cultural change came at a time when the telecommunications industry was experiencing significant upheaval. AT&T recognized that a shift in management paradigms was inevitable. "It's a bread-and-butter issue," said Burke Stinson, an AT&T spokesman.

In 1984, when its monopoly protection vanished, AT&T faced fierce new competition from companies like MCI and Sprint. Hence, the company began exploring strategies to assure its dominant position in the marketplace.

Why did the union decide to cooperate? Why give up the pleasure of the barricades for collaboration? In the years before 1992, the union was in a reactive mode," said Morton Bahr, Communication Workers of America (CWA) president. "We had no role in the decision-making process. Everything that was negotiated took place essentially after decisions were made. This contract guarantees us, in writing, to be involved in the information-sharing process that's so necessary before decisions are made."

The appropriate buzz phrase for what Mr. Bahr is talking about is "worker empowerment". Theoretically, at least, the contract could lead to the quality-of-worklife improvements the CWA has sought before. Theoretically, it could also institutionalize something unions have been trying to tell management, at different volumes, for years a happy worker is a more productive worker.

In return for flexibility, the unions get a voice and a company commitment to, among other things, employment security, education, and training or retraining.

AT&T seems genuinely intent on reconfiguring its corporate culture, a task likened by one conference participant to "turning an aircraft carrier around." There is agreement between the parties that the workplace of the future will have four components: "workplace models" as strategies for promoting change; business unit" division planning councils to improve customer satisfaction; the constructive relationship council, a remnant of the 1989 contract agreement that will review contract-related issues; and a human resources board whose scope will include external issues like health care that have an impact on AT&T employees.[9]

recent decision General Motors made to continue its Arlington, Texas plant and close its Willow Run, Michigan plant illustrated that unions also may have their hands full dealing with locals that experiment more than the parent organization wants them to. For example, Stephen Yokich, a UAW vice president, assailed the union local at Arlington for its willingness to adjust its work schedule.[10]

Regardless of whether union and management share an adversarial or cooperative relationship, they still must engage in bargaining to arrive at a union-management contract. This process is often influenced by the type of union-management relationship that exists.

Processes of Bargaining

The most widely used description of bargaining identifies five types of processes in contract negotiations: distributive bargaining, integrative bargaining, concessionary bargaining, continuous bargaining, and intraorganizational bargaining.

Distributive Bargaining. **Distributive bargaining** takes place when the parties are in conflict over the issue, and the outcome represents a gain for one party and a loss for the other. Each party tries to negotiate for the best possible outcome. This process is outlined in Exhibit 19.1.

On any particular issue, union and management negotiators each have three identifiable positions. The union has an **initial demand point**, which is generally more than it expects to get; a **target point**, which is its realistic assessment of what it may be able to get; and a **resistance point**, which is the lowest acceptable level for the issue. Management has three similar points: an **initial offer**, which is usually lower than the expected settlement; a **target point**, at which it would like to reach agreement; and a **resistance point**, which is its upper acceptable limit. If, as shown in Exhibit 19.1 management's resistance point is greater than the union's, a **positive settlement range** exists where negotiations can take place. The exact agreement within this range depends on the bargaining behavior of the negotiators. If, however, management's resistance point is below the union's, there is no common ground for negotiation. In such a situation, a **negative settlement range**, or bargaining impasse, exists.[11]

Using wages as an example, the union may have a resistance point of $8.40 per hour, a target of $8.60, and an initial demand point of $8.75. Management may offer $8.20 but have a target of $8.45 and a resistance point of $8.55. The

LEARNING OBJECTIVE 2

Describe the process of collective bargaining.

Distributive bargaining provides a win-lose resolution in union-management relations.

Initial demand point is a demand by the union for a wage settlement that is higher than what is expected to be granted.

Target point is a realistic assessment of the wage and condition the union is likely to get from management.

Resistance point is the lowest acceptable level that the union can take or the highest acceptable offer by management.

Target point is a desired settlement point on the part of management.

Positive settlement range is an area where negotiations can take place successfully.

Negative settlement range is an area where negotiations cannot take place successfully.

EXHIBIT 19.1

The Negotiating Process

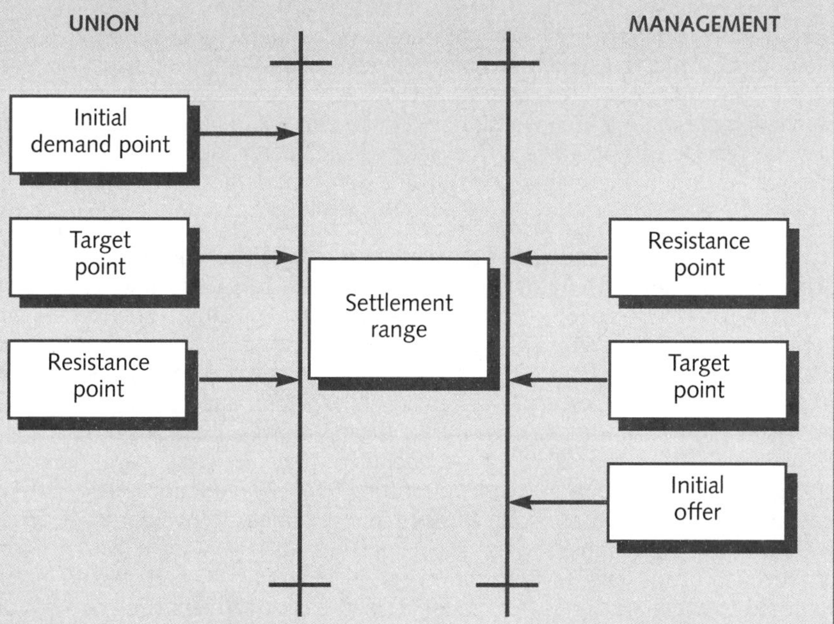

Source: Adapted from R. Walton and R. B. McKersie, *A Behavioral Theory of Labor Negotiations* (New York: McGraw-Hill Book Company, 1965): 43.

positive settlement range is between $8.40 and $8.55, and this is where the settlement will likely be. Recognize that only the initial wage demand and offer are made public at the beginning of negotiations.

Because many issues are involved in a bargaining session, the actual process is much more complicated. Although each issue can be described by the above model, in actual negotiations, an interaction occurs among issues. Union concessions on one issue may be traded for management concessions on another. Thus the total process is dynamic.

The ritual of the distributive bargaining process is well established, and deviations are often met with suspicion. The following story illustrates this point, in which a labor lawyer tells of

> *. . . a young executive who had just taken over the helm of a company. Imbued with idealism, he wanted to end the bickering he had seen take place during past negotiations with labor. To do this, he was ready to give workers as much as his company could afford. Consequently, he asked some members of his staff to study his firm's own wage structure and decide how it compared with other companies, as well as a host of other related matters. He approached the collective bargaining table with a halo of goodness surrounding him. Asking for the floor, he proceeded to describe what he had done and with a big smile on his face made the offer.*
>
> *Throughout his entire presentation, the union officials stared at him in amazement. He had offered more than they had expected to secure. But no matter, as soon as he finished, they proceeded to lambaste him, denouncing him for trying to destroy collective bargaining and for attempting to buy off labor. They announced that they would not stand for any such unethical maneuvering, and immediately asked for 5 cents more than the idealistic executive had offered.*[12]

Integrative bargaining **focuses on creative solutions.**

Integrative Bargaining. When there is more than one issue to be resolved, the potential exists to make trade-offs between the issues or to pursue integrative agreements. **Integrative bargaining** focuses on creative solutions to conflicts that reconcile (integrate) the parties' interests and yield high joint benefit. It can only occur when negotiators have an "expanding pie" perception—that is, when the two parties (union and management) value particular issues differently.[13]

Concessionary bargaining **means having to give back.**

Concessionary Bargaining. While distributive and integrative bargaining represent die primary approaches to bargaining, **concessionary bargaining** often occurs within these two frameworks. Concessionary bargaining may be prompted by severe economic conditions faced by employers. Seeking to survive and prosper, employers seek givebacks or concessions from the unions, giving promises of job security in return. During die past few years, this type of bargaining has been particularly prevalent, especially in automobiles, steel, and rubber, and to some extent in the transportation industry. In these industries, concessions sought by management from the unions have included wage freezes; wage reductions; change in, or elimination of, work rules; fringe benefit reductions; delay or elimination of COLAs; and more hours of work for the same pay. Two-tier wage systems were tried in some industries, but problems of inequity and lower worker morale offset much of the savings from the lower labor costs.[14] Nonetheless, they have returned in some situations, for example, in the contract between the UAW and Caterpillar.[15] Lincoln Electric tried the approach of bringing in new workers at a lower wage rate until they became fully productive. Because of employee dissatisfaction, this was dropped in 1995.

Continuous Bargaining. As affirmative action, safety and health requirements, and other government regulations continue to complicate the situation for both unions and employers, and as the rate of change in the environment continues to increase, some labor and management negotiators are turning to **continuous bargaining**. A joint committee meets on a regular basis to explore issues and solve problems of common interest. These committees have appeared in the retail food, over-the-road trucking, nuclear power, and men's garment industries.[16]

Continuous bargaining means the discussions are always going on.

Several characteristics of continuous bargaining have been identified:

- Frequent meetings during the life of the contract
- Focus on external events and problem areas rather than on internal problems
- Use of outside experts in decision making
- Use of a problem-solving (integrative) approach[17]

The intention is to develop a union-management structure that is capable of adapting positively and productively to sudden changes in the environment. This continuous bargaining approach is different from, but an extension of, the emergency negotiations that unions have insisted on when inflation or other factors have substantially changed the acceptability of the existing agreement. Continuous bargaining is a permanent arrangement intended to avoid the crises that often occur under traditional collective bargaining systems.

Intraorganizational Bargaining. During negotiations, the bargaining teams from both sides may have to engage in **intraorganizational bargaining**—that is, conferring with their constituents over changes in bargaining positions. Management negotiators may have to convince management to change its position on an issue—for instance, to agree to a higher wage settlement. Union negotiators must eventually convince their members to accept the negotiated contract, so they must be sensitive to and realistic about the demands of the membership. When the membership votes on the proposed package, it will be strongly influenced by the opinions of the union negotiators.

Intraorganizational bargaining means that the union leaders may need to confer and bargain with the membership.

Negotiating the Agreement

LEARNING OBJECTIVE 3

Describe the elements of agreement negotiation.

Once a union is certified as the representative of a bargaining unit, it becomes the only party that can negotiate an agreement with the employer for all members of that work unit, whether they are union members or not. Thus the union holds an important and potent position and serves as a critical link between employees and employer. The union is responsible to its members to negotiate for what they want, and it has the duty to represent all employees fairly. The quality of its bargaining is an important measure of union effectiveness.

Negotiating Committees

The employer and the union select their own representatives for the **negotiating committee**. Neither party is required to consider the wishes of the other. Management negotiators, for example, cannot refuse to bargain with representatives of the union because they dislike them or do not think they are appropriate.

The negotiating committee conducts the bargaining process.

Union negotiating teams typically include representatives of the union local, often the president and other executive staff members. In addition, the national union may send a negotiating specialist, who is likely to be a labor lawyer, to work with the team. The negotiators selected by the union do not have to be members of the union or employees of the company. The general goal is to balance bargaining skill and experience with knowledge and information about the specific situation.

At the local level, when a single bargaining unit is negotiating a contract, the company is usually represented by the manager and members of the labor relations or human resource staff. Finance and production managers may also be involved. When the negotiations are critical, either because the size of the bargaining unit is large or because the effect on the company is great, specialists such as labor lawyers may be included on the team.

In national negotiations, top industrial relations or personnel executives frequently head a team made up of specialists from corporate headquarters and perhaps managers from critical divisions or plants within the company. Again, the goal is to have expertise along with specific knowledge about critical situations.

The Negotiating Structure

Most contracts are negotiated by a single union and a single employer. In some situations, however, different arrangements can be agreed on. When a single union negotiates with several similar companies—for instance, firms in the construction industry or supermarkets—the employers may bargain as a group with the union. At the local level, this is called **multiemployer bargaining**, but at the national level it is referred to as **industrywide bargaining**. Industrywide bargaining occurs in the railroad, coal, wallpaper, and men's suits industries. National negotiations result in contracts that settle major issues such as compensation, whereas issues relating to working conditions are settled locally. This split bargaining style is common in Great Britain and has been used in the auto industry in the United States. When several unions bargain jointly with a single employer, they engage in **coordinated bargaining**. Although not as common as the others, coordinated bargaining appears to be increasing, especially in the public sector.

Multiemployer bargaining has several companies involved in bargaining. Industrywide bargaining has companies within an industry bargaining.

One consequence of coordinated and industrywide bargaining is often **pattern settlements**, where similar wage rates are imposed on the companies whose employees are represented by the same union within a given industry. Pattern settlements can be detrimental because they ignore differences in the employers' economic condition and ability to pay. The result can be settlements that are tolerable for some companies but cause severe economic trouble for others. As a partial consequence of this, pattern settlements have become less numerous.

Pattern settlements affect many companies at once.

A negotiating structure that exists in the contract construction industry is wide-area and multicraft bargaining. This bargaining structure has arisen in response to the need for unionized employers to be more price competitive and have fewer strikes and in response to the desire by construction trade unions to gain more control at the national level. Consequently, the bargaining is done on a regional (geographic) rather than a local basis. In addition, it covers several construction crafts simultaneously instead of one. The common contract negotiations resulting from **wide-area and multicraft bargaining** lessen the opportunity for unions to whipsaw the employer. This technique uses one contract settlement as a precedent for the next, which then forces the employer to get all contracts settled in order to have all the employees working. Under the threat of **whipsawing**, an employer frequently agrees to more favorable settlements on all contracts regardless of the conditions and merits of each one just to get all employees back to work.[18]

Wide-area and multicraft bargaining aims for price competitiveness and fewer strikes.

Preparation for Bargaining

Prior to the bargaining session, management and union negotiators need to develop strategies and proposals.

Management Strategies. In preparing for negotiations with the union, management needs to concentrate on the following areas:

1. Specific proposals for changes in contract language
2. The general size of the economic package that the company anticipates offering during the negotiations

3. Statistical displays and supportive data that the company will use during negotiations
4. A bargaining book for the use of company negotiators in which information on issues that will be discussed is compiled, giving an analysis of the effect of each clause, its use in other companies, and other facts.[19]

An important part of this preparation is the calculation of the cost of various bargaining issues or demands. The relative cost of pension contributions, pay increases, health benefits, and other provisions should be determined prior to negotiations. Other costs should also be considered. For instance, what is the cost to management, in its ability to do its job, of union demands for changes in grievance and discipline procedures or transfer and promotion provisions? The goal is to be as well prepared as possible by considering the implications and ramifications of each issue and by presenting a strong argument for the management position.

Union Strategies. Like management, unions need to prepare for negotiations by collecting information. Because collective bargaining is the major means by which a union can convince its members that it is effective and valuable, this is a critical activity.

Unions collect information in at least three areas:

1. The financial situation of the company and its ability to pay
2. The attitude of management toward various issues, as reflected in past negotiations or inferred from negotiations in similar companies
3. The attitudes and desires of the employees

The first two areas give the union an idea of what demands management is likely to accept. The third area is important, but it is sometimes overlooked. The union should be aware of the preferences of its membership. For instance, is a pension increase preferred over increased vacation or holiday benefits? The preferences will vary with the characteristics of the workers. Younger workers tend to prefer more holidays, shorter workweeks, and limited overtime, whereas older workers are more interested in pension plans, benefits, and overtime. The union can determine these preferences by surveying its members.

Issues for Negotiation

The issues that can be discussed in collective bargaining sessions are specified by the *Labor-Management Relations Act*. This act has established three categories: 1) mandatory issues, 2) permissive issues, and 3) prohibited issues.[20]

Employers and employee representatives (unions) are obligated to meet and discuss "wages, hours, and other terms and conditions of employment." These are the **mandatory issues**, and include the issues that affect management's ability to run the company efficiently or that clash with the union's desire to protect jobs and workers' standing in their jobs. The specific topics that fall into this category have historically been the subject of considerable debate. The Supreme Court's decision in *Borg Warner Corporation v. NLRB* (1982) suggests that the distinction between mandatory and permissive bargaining issues rests on whether the topic regulates the relations between the employer and its employees. Any issue that changes the nature of the job itself or compensation for work must be discussed in collective bargaining. Mandatory issues therefore include subcontracting work, safety, changes of operations, and other actions management might take that will have an impact on employees' jobs, wages, and economic supplements. With the Supreme Court decision in the *First National Maintenance* case in 1981, management's obligation to bargain over plant closings was substantially reduced.

Mandatory issues **include the conditions of employment.**

Permissive issues are those that are neither mandatory nor illegal. They are issues not specifically related to the nature of the job but still of concern to both parties. For example, issues of price, product design, and decisions about new jobs

Permissive issues **are beneficial to both parties.**

may be subject to bargaining if the parties agree to it. Permissive issues usually develop when both parties see that mutual discussion and agreement will be beneficial, which is more likely when a cooperative relationship exists. Management and union negotiators cannot refuse to agree on a contract if they fail to settle a permissive issue.[21]

Prohibited issues concern illegal activities.

Prohibited issues are those concerning illegal or outlawed activities such as the demand that an employer use only union-produced goods or, where it is illegal, that it employ only union members. Such issues may not be discussed in collective bargaining sessions.

Although the actual issues for negotiation can be expected to vary, they are always far more extensive than those brought out during the initial organizing campaign. In contrast to organizing, where the critical issues are grievances, economics, job security, and supervision, a multitude of mandatory issues exist for negotiation, not to mention the permissive issues. Most of the issues for negotiation are mandatory, including direct compensation.

Did You KNOW?

More employers are seeking to negotiate lump-sum payments in lieu of automatic percentage pay increase.

Direct Compensation. Wage conflicts are the leading cause of strikes. Difficulties arise here because a wage increase is a direct cost to the employer, as is a wage decrease to the employee. As discussed in Chapters 14 and 15, rates of pay are influenced by a variety of factors, including the going rate in an industry, the employer's ability to pay, the cost of living, and productivity. All of these subjects are debated often and discussed extensively in negotiations.

Indirect Compensation. Because the cost of indirect compensation now runs as high as 45 percent of the total cost of wages, it is a major concern in collective bargaining. Such provisions are very difficult to remove once they are in place, so management tends to be cautious about agreeing to them. Some of the most commonly negotiated ones are as follows:

- **Pensions.** Once management has decided to provide a pension plan, the conditions of the plan must be determined (when the benefits will be available, how much will be paid, and whether they become available according to age or years of service). Finally, the organization must decide how long employees must work for the company to receive minimum benefits (vesting) and whether the organization will pay the whole cost or whether the employees or the union will be asked to contribute.

- **Paid vacation.** Most agreements provide for paid vacations. Length of vacation is usually determined by length of service, up to some maximum. The conditions that qualify an individual for a vacation in a given year are also specified. Agreements occasionally specify how the timing of vacations will be determined.

Did You KNOW?

A major issue between the UAW and General Motors is the use of outsourcing work because it means less work for union members and possibly less job security.

- **Paid holidays.** Most agreements provide time off with pay on Independence Day, Labor Day, Thanksgiving, Christmas, New Year's Day, and Memorial Day. Several others may also be included.

- **Sick leave.** Unpaid sick leave allows the employee to take time off for sickness without compensation. Paid sick leave is usually accumulated while working. Typically one-half to one and one-half days of paid sick leave are credited for each month of work.

- **Health and life insurance.** The employer may be required to pay some or all of the costs of health and life insurance plans.

- **Dismissal or severance pay.** Occasionally, employers agree to pay a set amount to any employee who is dismissed or laid off because of technological changes or business difficulties.

- **Supplemental unemployment benefits.** In the mid-1950s, the United Auto Workers negotiated a plan to supplement state unemployment benefits and to make up the difference when these state benefits expired. Most contracts with this provision are found in the auto and steel industries, where layoffs are common, but workers in other industries are beginning to negotiate them as well.

Hours of Employment. Finally, while organizations are required to pay overtime for work in excess of 40 hours, unions continually try to reduce the number of hours worked each week. Negotiations focus on including lunch hours in the 8-hour-day requirement. Additionally, negotiations may focus on providing overtime after any 8-hour shift, rather than after 40 hours.

Institutional Issues. Some issues are not directly related to jobs but are nevertheless important to both employees and management. **Institutional issues** that affect the security and success of both parties include:

- **Union security.** A majority of the major labor contracts stipulate that employees must join the union after being hired into its bargaining unit. However, 20 states that have traditionally had low levels of unionization have passed right-to-work laws outlawing union membership as a condition of employment.
- **Check-off.** Unions have attempted to arrange for payment of dues through deduction from employees' paychecks. By law, employees must agree to dues check-off in writing. Most union contracts contain this provision.
- **Strikes.** The employer may insist that the union agree not to strike during the life of the agreement, typically when a cost-of-hiring clause has been included. The agreement may be unconditional allowing no strikes at all, or it may limit strikes to specific circumstances.
- **Managerial prerogatives.** Over half the agreements today stipulate that certain activities are the right of management. In addition, management in most companies argues that it has "residual rights"—that all rights not specifically limited by the agreement belong to management.

Administrative Issues. The last category of issues is concerned with the treatment of employees at work. **Administrative issues** include:

- **Breaks and cleanup time.** Some contracts specify the time and length of coffee breaks and meal breaks for employees. In addition, jobs requiring cleanup may have a portion of the work period set aside for this procedure.
- **Job security.** This is perhaps the issue of most concern to employees and unions. Employers are concerned with restrictions on their ability to lay off employees. Changes in technology or attempts to subcontract work are issues that impinge on job security. A typical union response to technological change was the reaction of the International Longshoremen's Association in the late 1960s to the introduction of containerized shipping. The union operated exclusive hiring halls, developed complex work rules, and negotiated a guaranteed annual income for its members. Job security continues to be a primary issue for longshoremen, telephone workers, and most other blue-collar occupations as well.
- **Seniority.** Length of service is used as a criterion for many personnel decisions in most collective agreements. Layoffs are usually determined by seniority. "Last hired, first fired" is a common situation. Seniority is also important in transfer and promotion decisions. The method of calculating seniority is usually specified to clarify the relative seniority of employees.

Institutional issues affect the security and success of both the union and management.

Administrative issues are those that address the treatment of employees at work.

Did You KNOW?

Saturn Corporation chose Tennessee even though its employees are members of the UAW and it is a right-to-work state. Reasons why it did include:

- **Attractiveness or livability of the location, in terms of its beauty, terrain, climate, and recreational opportunities.**
- **Business climate, as reflected in the attitudes and interest shown by local communities, the state government, and its congressional delegation.**
- **Proximity to quality higher-education opportunities, including engineering schools.**
- **Availability of well-established employee-training facilities and resources.**
- **An ambiance conducive to creating an innovative business venture.**

Did You KNOW?

Chrysler produces only 30% of its own parts; Ford about 50%; and GM about 70% at its 194 plants.

- **Discharge and discipline.** This is a touchy issue, and even when an agreement addresses these problems, many grievances are filed concerning the way employees are disciplined or discharged.
- **Safety and health.** Although the *Occupational Safety and Health Act* specifically deals with worker safety and health, some contracts have provisions specifying that the company will provide safety equipment, first aid, physical examinations, accident investigations, and safety committees. Hazardous work may be covered by special provisions and pay rates. Often the agreement will contain a general statement that the employer is responsible for the safety of workers so the union can use the grievance process when any safety issues arise.
- **Production standards.** The level of productivity or performance of employees is a concern of both management and unions. Management is concerned with efficiency, but unions are concerned with the fairness and reasonableness of management's demands.
- **Grievance procedures.** This is a significant part of collective bargaining and is discussed in more detail later in this chapter.
- **Training.** The design and administration of training and development programs and the procedure for selecting employees for training may also be bargaining issues.
- **Duration of the agreement.** Agreements can last for one year or longer, with the most common period being three years.

Factors Affecting Bargaining

The preceding discussion suggests that negotiations proceed in a rational manner and end in resolution when a positive contract zone—a set of outcomes that is preferred over the imposition of a strike—exists. Unfortunately, negotiators often fail to reach agreement, even when a positive contract zone exists.

To fully understand the negotiation process, it is important to examine the decision processes of negotiators. If the biases of negotiators can be identified, then prescriptive approaches and training programs can be developed to improve negotiations. The following are common cognitive or mental limitations to negotiator judgments.[22]

The Mythical Fixed Pie. All too frequently, negotiators believe that their interests automatically conflict with the other party's interests. In other words, what one side wins, the other side loses. However, most conflicts usually have more than one issue at stake, with the parties placing different values on the different issues. Consequently, the potential usually exists for integrative agreements. A fundamental task in training negotiators lies in identifying and eliminating this false "fixed pie" assumption and preparing them to look for trade-offs between issues of different value to each side.

Framing refers to how an issue is presented.

Framing. Consider the following bargaining situation. The union claims that its members need a raise to $12 an hour and that anything less will represent a loss due to inflation. Management argues that the company can't pay more than $10 an hour and that anything more would impose an unacceptable loss. If each side had the choice between settling at $11 an hour or going to binding arbitration, they are likely to take the risk and move toward arbitration rather than settlement.

Changing the frame of the situation to a positive one results in a very different outcome. If the union can view anything above $10 an hour as a gain, and if management can view anything under $12 as a gain, then a negotiated settlement is likely—at $11.

As the preceding example emphasizes, the frame (positive or negative) of negotiators can make the difference between settlement and impasse. One solution then to impasses is to alter the frame of references such that it is positive, rather than negative.[23]

Conflict Resolution

LEARNING OBJECTIVE 4

Discuss forms of conflict resolution.

Although the desired outcome of collective bargaining is agreement, there are many occasions where negotiators are unable to reach one. In these situations, several alternatives are used to break the deadlock. The most dramatic response is the strike or lockout, but third-party interventions such as mediation and arbitration are also common.

Strikes and Lockouts

When the union is unable to get management to agree to a demand it feels is critical, it may resort to a strike. A **strike** can be defined as the refusal of employees to work. Alternatively, management may refuse to allow employees to work, which is called a **lockout**.[24]

A strike is a refusal of employees to work. A lockout is a refusal by management to allow employees to work.

To proceed with a strike, the union usually holds a strike vote to gain members' approval. Strong membership support for a strike strengthens the union negotiators' position. If the strike takes place, union members picket the employer, informing the public about the existence of a labor dispute and preferably, from the union's point of view, convincing them to avoid this company during the strike. A common practice is the refusal of union members to cross the picket line of another striking union, which adds support to the striking union.

Employers usually attempt to continue operations while the strike is in effect. They either run the company with supervisory personnel and people not in the bargaining unit or hire replacements for the employees. Although it appears that the company can legally hire replacements, the union reacts strongly to the use of "scabs," as the **replacement workers** are called, and they can be a cause of increasingly belligerent labor relations.[25] The success of a strike depends on its ability to cause economic hardship to the employer. Severe hardship usually causes the employer to concede to the union's demands.[26] Thus, from the union's point of view, it is paramount that the cost of this lack of production be high. The union, therefore, actively tries to prevent replacement employees from working. Some companies have hired replacement workers as permanent workers when a strike cannot be ended through negotiation. This tactic has given employers even more power in the strike situation. Thus, the union movement is seeking legislation to prevent replacement workers from becoming permanent workers.

Replacement workers are non-union workers hired by management to replace striking workers.

The timing of the strike is often critical. The union attempts to hold negotiations just prior to the period when the employer has a peak demand for its product or services, when a strike will have maximum economic impact.

Strikes have been on the decline (see Exhibit 19.2), but when they do occur, they are costly both to the employer, who loses revenue, and to the employees, who face loss of income. If a strike is prolonged, it is likely that the cost to employees will never fully be recovered by the benefits gained. In part because of this, employers seek to avoid strikes, and unions use them only as a last resort. Moreover, the public interest is generally not served by strikes. They are often an inconvenience and can have serious consequences for the economy as a whole.

Slowdowns. Short of an actual strike, unions may invoke a **slowdown**. The impact of slowdowns can be more effective than an actual strike. For example,

> *Until the resistance began at the Caterpillar plant here, Lance Vaughan first installed a set of small hydraulic hoses on the huge off-highway trucks that he helps to assemble, and then a big outside hose. Now he installs the big*

EXHIBIT 19.2

Major Work Stoppages, 1947–1994

STOPPAGES INVOLVING 1,000 OR MORE WORKERS

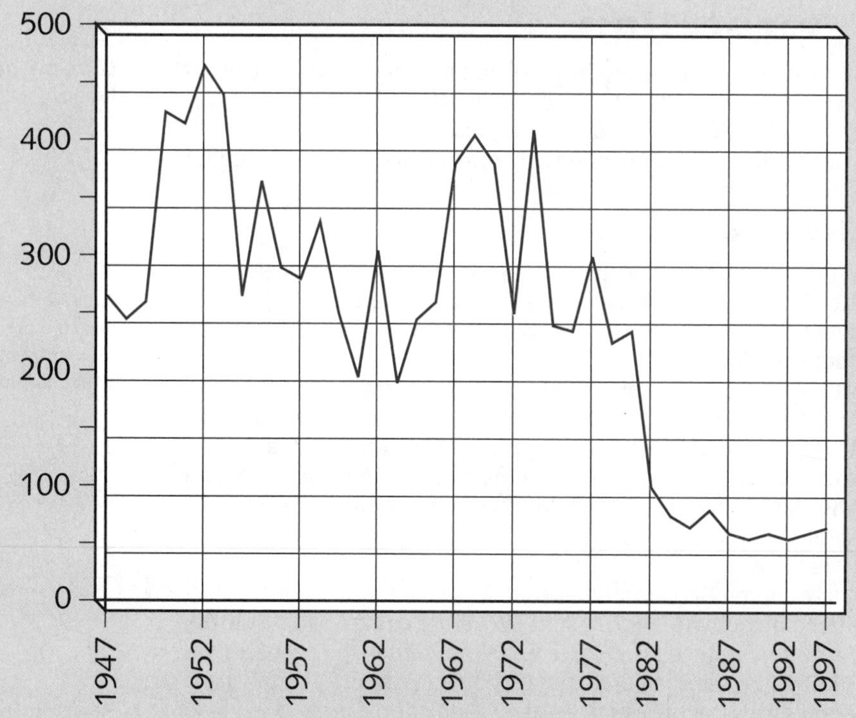

Source: Adapted from "Strike Activity Up in 1994," *Bulletin to Management* (February 23, 1995): 61. Reprinted with permission by the Bureau of National Affairs, (Tel. 1-800-372-1033).

one first, and reaches awkwardly around it to attach the others, losing production time in the process.

This is not sabotage. The instructions furnished by Caterpillar's engineers specify the inefficient procedure, Mr. Vaughan says. Normally, he ignores such instructions and makes a note to himself to tell the engineers to fix the mistake. Now, he no longer speaks up. Withholding initiative, he works "to the rules" furnished by the company.

"I used to give the engineers ideas," said Mr. Vaughan, who is 38 and has worked at Caterpillar for nearly 20 years. "We showed them how to eliminate some hose clips and save money. And I recommended larger bolts that made assembly easier and faster, and were less likely to come loose."[27]

Did You KNOW?

At Caterpillar, workers engaged in a slowdown by just following what was written in their job description.

At Caterpillar, the slowdown was referred to as an "in-plant strategy." Regardless of the name, the impact is the same: a reduction of work output, physically and mentally.

A primary boycott is typically an informational boycott that asks customers not to buy a particular product.

Primary Boycotts. Unions sometimes want to make the public more aware of their cause. As a consequence they may engage in a **primary boycott**. For example, a union that is striking a soda-bottling company may set up an informational picket line at grocery stores that sell the soda-bottling company's products. It has generally been ruled that as long as the picket line focuses on asking customers not to buy its soda, it constitutes a primary boycott and thus is legal. It becomes illegal when the picket line tries to prevent customers from shopping at the grocery store. This action is called **secondary boycott**, and because it can harm an innocent third party, the grocery store here, it is illegal.

A secondary boycott is one that asks customers not to shop at a store that carries a particular product.

Corporate Campaigns. Another indirect tactic in the form of a secondary boycott is called a **corporate campaign**. In the corporate campaign, a union may ask the public and other unions to write letters to a company asking it to change the way it bargains with the union.[28]

A corporate campaign is one where the union asks the public to write the company and tell it to change its relations with the union.

Mediation

Mediation is a procedure in which a neutral third party assists the union and management negotiators in reaching voluntary agreement.[29] Having no power to impose a solution, the mediator attempts to facilitate the negotiations between union and management. The mediator may make suggestions and recommendations and perhaps add objectivity to the often emotional negotiations. To have any success at all, the mediator must have the trust and respect of both parties and have sufficient expertise and neutrality to convince the union and employer that he or she will be fair and equitable.

Mediation is a procedure where a neutral third party assists union and management in reaching a voluntary agreement.

The U.S. government operates the Federal Mediation and Conciliation Service (FMCS) to make experienced mediators available to unions and companies. A program called "Relationships by Objective" is offered by the FMCS to eliminate the causes of recurrent impasses. It uses aspects of attitudinal structuring to increase the likelihood of a cooperative relationship between union and management.

Did You KNOW?

The real power of the arbitrator's decision was established by three Supreme Court decisions (see Appendix A) in 1960 referred to as the Trilogy cases and all involving the United Steelworkers.

Arbitration

Arbitration is a procedure in which a neutral third party studies the bargaining situation, listening to both union and management and gathering information, and then makes recommendations that are binding. The arbitrator, in effect, determines the conditions of the agreement.[30] It involves the arbitrator choosing between the final offer of the union and the final offer of the employer. The arbitrator cannot alter these offers but must choose one as it stands. Since the arbitrator chooses the offer that appears most fair, and since losing the arbitration decision means settling for the other's offer, there is pressure to make as good an offer as possible. The intention of **final-offer arbitration** is to encourage the parties to make their best offer and to reach an agreement before arbitration becomes necessary. This is also true with respect to the use of **closed-offer arbitration**. Here the arbitrator receives information only on the parties' original positions without any information on the bargaining progress up to the time the arbitrator is selected.

Arbitration is a procedure where a neutral third party makes recommendations to union and management that are binding.

Final-offer arbitration encourages union and management to make their best offers before the arbitration decision is made.

Closed-offer arbitration is based on the arbitrator knowing only the original positions of the union and management.

Once the impasse is removed, union and management have a contract agreement. Abiding by it is the essence of contract administration; however, there are times when arbitration is again necessary—namely, when a grievance is filed. This type of arbitration is referred to as rights or **grievance arbitration**. In contrast, the arbitration process that deals with the contract terms and conditions (described previously) is called **interest arbitration**. Although interest arbitration is relatively infrequent in the private sector, it is more common in the public sector, where it becomes a necessary *quid pro quo* for foregoing the strike option.[31] However, only about 20 states have compulsory interest arbitration procedures.

Grievance arbitration is an arbitration over grievance rather than the entire contract.

Interest arbitration is an arbitration that deals with the entire contract.

Contract Administration

LEARNING OBJECTIVE 5

Explain the elements of contract administration.

Once signed, the collective agreement becomes "the basic legislation governing the lives of the workers."[32] That is, the daily operation and activities in the organization are subject to the conditions of the agreement. Because of the difficulty of writing an unambiguous agreement anticipating all the situations that will occur over its life, disputes will inevitably occur over its interpretation and application. The most common method of resolving these disputes is a **grievance procedure**. Virtually all agreements negotiated today provide for a grievance process to handle employee complaints.

Grievance procedures are the steps used in processing a grievance.

Grievance Procedures

A grievance is a charge that the union-management contract has been violated.

Basically a **grievance** is a charge that the union-management contract has been violated.[33] A grievance may be filed by the union for employees or by employers, although management rarely does so. The grievance process is designed to investigate the charges and to resolve the problem.

The following sources of grievances have been identified:

- Outright violation of the agreement
- Disagreement over facts
- Dispute over the meaning of the agreement
- Dispute over the method of applying the agreement
- Argument over the fairness or reasonableness of actions[34]

In resolving these conflicts, the grievance procedure should serve three separate groups: the employers and unions, by interpreting and adjusting the agreement as conditions require; the employees, by protecting their contractual rights and providing a channel of appeal; and society at large, by keeping industrial peace and reducing the number of disputes in the courts.

Grievance procedures typically involve several stages. The collective bargaining agreement specifies the maximum length of time that each step may take. For example, it may require the grievance be filed within five days of the incident that is the subject of dispute. The most common grievance procedure, shown in Exhibit 19.3 involves four steps:

- **Step 1.** An employee who feels that the labor contract has been violated usually contacts the union steward, and together they discuss the problem with the supervisor involved. If the problem is simple and straightforward, it is often resolved at this level. Many contracts require the grievance to be in written form at this first stage. However, cases may be resolved by informal discussion between the supervisor and the employee and, therefore, do not officially enter the grievance process.
- **Step 2.** If agreement cannot be reached at the supervisor level, or if the employee is not satisfied, the complaint can enter the second step of the grievance procedure. Typically, a company HR staff member now seeks to resolve the grievance.
- **Step 3.** If the grievance is sufficiently important or difficult to resolve, it may be taken to the third step. Although contracts vary, top-level management and union executives are usually involved at this stage. These people have the authority to make the decisions that may be required to resolve the grievance.
- **Step 4.** If a grievance cannot be resolved at the third step, most agreements require the use of an arbitrator. The arbitrator is a neutral, mutually acceptable individual who may be provided by the FMCS or some private agency. The arbitrator holds a hearing, reviews the evidence, then rules on the grievance. The decision of the arbitrator is usually binding.

Did You KNOW?

The American Arbitration Association has offered dispute resolution services since 1926.

Since the cost of arbitration is shared by the union and employer, some incentive exists to settle the grievance before it goes to arbitration.[35] An added incentive in some cases is the requirement that the loser pays for the arbitration.[36]

EXHIBIT 19.3

Typical Union–Management Grievance Procedure

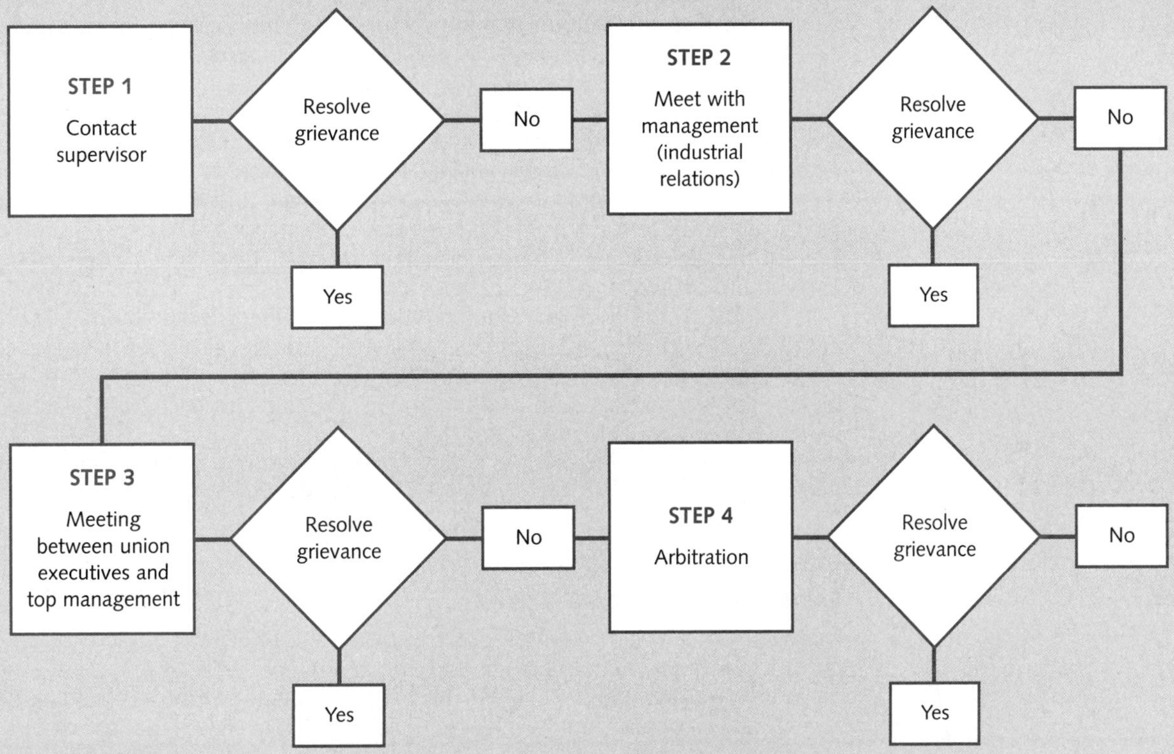

Source: William D. Todor, Professor of Human Resource Management, The Ohio State University

The expectation is that the parties will screen or evaluate grievances more carefully because pursuing a weak grievance to arbitration will be expensive.

Occasionally, the union will call a strike over a grievance in order to resolve it. This may happen when the issue at hand is so important that the union feels it cannot wait for the slower arbitration process.[37] This "employee rights" strike can be legal but not if the contract specifically forbids strikes during the tenure of the agreement; then it is illegal and is called a **wildcat strike**. Wildcat strikes are not common, however, because most grievances are settled through arbitration.

A wildcat strike is illegal and typically violates the contract.

Grievance Issues

Grievances can be filed over any issue relating to the workplace that is subject to the collective agreement, or they can be filed over interpretation and implementation of the agreement itself. The most common type of grievance reaching the arbitration stage involves discipline and discharge.

Although it is accepted that absenteeism can be grounds for discharge, the critical issue is the determination that the absenteeism in question is excessive. Insubordination usually is either failure to do what the supervisor requests or the more serious problem of outright refusal to do it. If the supervisor's orders are clear and explicit and if the employee is warned of the consequences, discipline for refusal to respond is usually acceptable. The exception is when the employee feels that the work endangers health.

Because seniority usually determines who is laid off, bumped from a job to make way for someone else, or rehired, its calculation is of great concern to employees. Seniority is also used as a criterion to determine eligibility for promotions and transfers, so management must be careful to avoid complaints and grievances in this area.

Compensation for time away from work, vacations, holidays, or sick leave is also a common source of grievances. Holidays cause problems because special pay arrangements often exist for people working on those days.

Wage and work schedules can also lead to grievances. Disagreements often arise over interpretation or application of the agreement relating to such issues as overtime pay, pay for reporting, and scheduling. Grievances have been filed over the exercise of management rights—that is, its right to introduce technological changes, use subcontractors, or change jobs in other ways. This type of behavior can also be the source of charges of unfair labor practices, since these activities may require collective bargaining.

The *Taft-Hartley Act* gives unions the right to file grievances on their own behalf if they feel their rights have been violated. This act also gives unions access to the information necessary to process the grievance or to make sure the agreement is not being violated. In addition, unions may file grievances for violations of union shop or check-off provisions.

Occasionally, other activities prompt grievances. Wildcat strikes or behavior that functions as a strike (mass absences from work, for example) can result in a management grievance. Increasingly, outsourcing and replacement workers are issues resulting in grievances.

Management Procedures

Management can significantly affect the grievance rate by adopting proper procedures for taking action against an employee.[38] One of the most important procedures involves that of discipline and discharge. The issue of just cause and fairness is central to most discipline grievances. Employers must ensure that the employee is adequately warned of the consequences, that the rule involved is related to operation of the company, that a thorough investigation is undertaken, and that the penalty is reasonable. The following activities have been identified as being useful in meeting these considerations:

- Explanation of rules to employees
- Consideration of the accusations and facts
- Regular warning procedures, including written reports
- Involvement of the union in the case
- Examination of the employee's motives and reasons
- Consideration of the employee's past record
- Familiarization of all management personnel, especially supervisors, with disciplinary procedure and company rules

In areas outside of discipline and discharge, management can avoid grievance problems by educating supervisors and managers about labor relations and about the conditions of the collective agreement. It has been found that supervisors with labor knowledge are an important factor in the reduction of grievances.

Union Procedures

The union has an obligation to its members to provide them fair and adequate representation and to process and investigate grievances brought by its members speedily (*Vaca v. Sipes,* 1967; *Hines v. Anchor Motor Freight,* 1976; *Smith v. Hussman Refrigerator Co. & Local 13889, United Steel Workers of America,*

1980). Thus it should have a grievance-handling procedure that aids in effectively processing grievances without being guilty of unfair representation.

Unfair representation, according to the NLRB, is usually related to one of four types of union behavior:

Unfair representation is a charge against the union of not fairly representing its members.

- **Improper motives of fraud.** The union cannot refuse to process a grievance because of the employee's race or gender or because of the employee's attitude toward the union.
- **Arbitrary conduct.** Unions cannot dismiss a grievance without investigating its merits.
- **Gross negligence.** The union cannot recklessly disregard the employee's interests.
- **Union conduct after filing the grievance.** The union must process the grievance to a reasonable conclusion.[39]

Because the employer can also be cited for unfair representation, management should attempt to maintain a fair grievance process. Company labor relations managers should avoid taking advantage of union errors in handling grievances so that this action does not affect fair representation.

Another important influence on the grievance process is the union steward. Since the union steward is generally the first person to hear about an employee's grievance, the steward has substantial influence on the grievance process. A steward can either encourage an employee to file a grievance, suggest that the problem is really not a grievance, or informally resolve the problem outside the grievance procedure. The personalities of stewards may, in fact, influence the number of grievances filed.[40] Because stewards are selected from the ranks of employees and may have little knowledge of labor relations, the union should train them to improve their effectiveness. The company can also be liable in a fair-representation suit and therefore should support such training.

Current Trends

Learning Objective 6

Discuss the current trends in collective bargaining.

Strategic Involvement

Management and workers alike are finding that a mutual involvement in the business strategy benefits them both. Strategic involvement is probably key in the transition from the adversarial relationship to one of mutual cooperation and partnership. Several areas stand out as prime examples of what can happen when workers and management alike are involved in business strategy.[41]

Employee Involvement. Ford Motor Company has engaged in a program of increased worker involvement and more cooperative labor relations with the United Auto Workers. The results have been higher product quality than its competitors and a marketing campaign centered on the slogan, "Quality is Job 1." This program has also affected efficiency in a positive way. Similar results have been obtained at Westinghouse Corporation, Saturn, AT&T, Xerox, and the Mass Transportation Authority of Flint, Michigan. In these companies, the gains have been the fruit of the increased employee commitment associated with quality circle programs. In addition to gains in quality and efficiency, these companies have experienced fewer grievances, reduced absenteeism and turnover, lower design costs, higher engineering productivity, and fewer costly changes in design cycles.

Did You KNOW?

United Airlines is one of the largest employee-owned companies.

We will continue to see this strategic involvement into the next century, in forms similar to those taken at Saturn and AT&T. Another form of involvement gaining momentum is the employee takeover (employees assume all or part of the equity ownership). In recent years, the workers at TWA acquired a 45 percent stake in the airline for granting wage concessions. Workers at Northwest Airlines and United Airlines made similar arrangements.[42] This trend of employees giving up wage demands for ownership in the company and the hopes of job security may continue to increase.

Board Membership. Another area in collective bargaining is that of unions gaining a seat on the board of directors. Such membership is similar to the codetermination system of Germany described in Chapter 18. However, in the U.S., membership results from union-management bargaining rather than federal mandate.

> *Giving unions access to the board room is common in Europe, where the unions are stronger, but is still quite novel in the United States. It has generally only been entertained by troubled companies that have had to work closely with their unions to avert bankruptcy or liquidation.*[43]

Unions now hold seats on the boards of National Steel Corporation, Wheeling-Pittsburgh Steel Corporation, and the LTV Corporation. Only the future will tell whether this becomes a major movement where even nontroubled companies elect to make unions bona fide occupants of the boardroom.

International Comparisons

Within North America

We focus our discussion of international comparisons on Mexico, Canada, and the United States. The reason is because of the increased economic activity within this region since the 1993 passage of NAFTA. Although this agreement is limited to the trading relationships among the three countries, it is likely to have major impacts on employment conditions. It is projected that as the amount of trade and economic activity increase among these three nations, conditions such as wages and benefits, health and safety will become more similar. Current differences on many major employment conditions are shown in Exhibit 19.4. As you examine this exhibit, note that there are some employment conditions that exist in Mexico and Canada, for example, healthcare benefits, that do not exist in the United States. And there are also some conditions, such as unemployment insurance and workers' compensation insurance, that exist in Canada and the United States but not in Mexico.

Note that while the minimum wage in the United States and Canada are about equal, Mexico's is much less. This difference, combined with the relatively high quality of workforce in Mexico, makes Mexico attractive to employers. Over the past decade many firms, including those from Japan, the U.S. and Europe, have moved to Mexico to set up operations. Much of this movement can today be found along the U.S.-Mexican border. With the passage of NAFTA it is predicted that there will be less movement of plants from the United States and Canada to Mexico, and more movement of plants from Asia and Europe into Mexico to take advantage of the employment conditions and the free trade within North America. In addition, other countries in Central and South America, for example, Chile, Brazil and Argentina, are interested in joining the NAFTA.

Thus, while the NAFTA is only a trading agreement (in contrast to the European Community (Union) which covers political, cultural, and educational issues in addition to economic trading issues), it is expected to have a major impact on employment conditions within the three countries of North America. In turn this is likely to change the living conditions and purchasing power for its more than three hundred and fifty million inhabitants.

The NAFTA is also likely to have a major impact on the union movement. In fact it has already had the impact of increasing the cooperation between the unions in the U.S. and Mexico:

EXHIBIT 19.4

Comparisons of Private-Sector Labor Law in the North American Trading Block*

EMPLOYMENT CONDITIONS	UNITED STATES	CANADA	MEXICO
Minimum wage (US$)	$4.25/hr	$3.51/hr	$0.46/hr (ave.)
Maximum work week	40 hours (8 × 5)	varies with province	48 hours (8 × 6)
Pensions	optional	required contribution	optional
Social Security (old age)	required contribution	required contribution	required contribution
Social Security (disability)	required contribution	no provision	required contribution
Healthcare benefits	optional	required contribution	required contribution
Unemployment insurance	required contribution	required contribution	no provision
Workers' compensation insurance	required	yes, varies with province	no provision
Pay equity/comparable worth	no provision	in Ontario	no provision
Plant closing notification	60 days	yes, varies with province	yes
Severance pay	optional	varies with province	90 days pay
Housing assistance	optional	optional	5% base salary
Profit sharing	optional	optional	10% net profits
Christmas bonus	optional	optional	15 days pay
Holiday leave	optional	3+ paid holidays	7 paid holidays
Vacation leave	optional	10 paid days	6+ paid days
Sick leave	required	paid by gov't. after 3 weeks	paid by gov't.
Maternity leave	required	17 weeks + 24 weeks	12 weeks
Gender discrimination	prohibited	prohibited	prohibited
Race/color discrimination	prohibited	prohibited	prohibited
Religious discrimination	prohibited	prohibited	prohibited
National origin discrimination	prohibited	prohibited	no provision
Age discrimination	prohibited	prohibited	no provision
Disability discrimination	prohibited	prohibited	no provision
Marital status discrimination	no provision	prohibited	no provision

*In all NAFTA countries, states and provinces also have jurisdiction over labor law and may set additional standards.

Source: Institute for International Human Resources, Society for Human Resource Management, Briefing Paper on the North American Free Trade Agreement, January, 1993.

When the Campbell Soup Company threatened to move some operations to Mexico if Midwestern tomato pickers demanded higher wages, the Farm Labor Organizing Committee, a Midwest union, discouraged the move by helping its Mexican counterpart win a stronger contract.

United States unions are also helping Mexican unions to organize, especially at American-owned factories. For instance, the United Electrical Workers—which has lost nearly one-fifth of its members to factory relocations in Mexico—has begun to subsidize organizers at Mexican plants of the General Electric Company.[44]

Such cooperation has also occurred between unions in the U.S. and Europe. Some observers see more of this cooperation needing to occur for the union movement to survive—as the companies whose workers they represent develop global strategies, so do the unions who want to continue to represent those workers.

Summary

In the U.S., collective bargaining is currently at a critical crossroads. Global competition has brought about a greater emphasis on the mutual survival of both company and union. This has resulted in a shift from the traditional adversarial relationship between union and management to one of cooperation. New bargaining strategies characterize this altered relationship. Productivity bargaining is an attempt to encourage increased effectiveness in the workplace by passing some of the savings of modernization or increased efficiency on to the employees. Another innovation is continuous bargaining, where a joint union-management committee meets on a regular basis to deal with problems.

Although obstacles exist to union-management cooperation—a history of adversarial relations, hesitancy on the part of the union to give up the traditional roles of labor, and both parties' fear of losing power—present economic conditions and the threat of an influx of foreign products are prompting many organizations to act for their mutual benefit.

The quality of the union-management relationship can have a strong influence on contract negotiations. Labor and management each select a bargaining committee to negotiate the new agreement. The negotiations may be between a single union and a single company or multiple companies, or between multiple unions and a single company. Bargaining issues are mandatory, permissive, or prohibited. Mandatory issues must be discussed, permissive issues can be discussed if both parties agree, and prohibited issues cannot be discussed. The issues can be grouped into wage issues, economic supplements issues, institutional issues, and administrative issues.

Almost all labor contracts outline grievance procedures for handling employee complaints. The most common grievance is related to discipline and discharge, although wages, promotions, seniority, vacations, holidays, and management and union rights are also sources of complaints. Management can influence the results of grievances by developing a procedure that ensures their actions are just and fair. Written records of actions taken are useful for potential arbitration. Unions have a legal responsibility to represent the employee fairly in grievances; therefore, they also need a grievance-handling procedure.

Key Concepts

administrative issues
adversarial system
arbitration
closed-offer arbitration
collective bargaining
concessionary bargaining
continuous bargaining
cooperative system
coordinated bargaining
corporate campaign
distributive bargaining
final-offer arbitration
framing
grievance
grievance arbitration
grievance procedure
industrywide bargaining
initial demand point
initial offer
institutional issues
integrative bargaining
interest arbitration
intraorganizational bargaining
lockout
mandatory issues
mediation
multiemployer bargaining
negative settlement range
negotiating committee
pattern settlements
permissive issues
positive settlement range
primary boycott
prohibited issues
replacement workers
resistance point
secondary boycott
slowdown
strike
target point
unfair representation
wide-area and multicraft bargaining
wildcat strike
whipsawing

Review and Discussion Questions

1. What is a bargaining unit? Why is its formation important?
2. Why has there been a recent trend toward cooperation between unions and management?
3. What are the steps in a typical grievance procedure? Is this process formal or informal?
4. Distinguish among mandatory, permissive, and prohibited bargaining issues.
5. Distinguish mediation from arbitration. How does a grievance procedure differ from interest arbitration?
6. How can unions assist organizations in TQM programs?
7. What is likely to be the impact of companies using replacement workers?
8. Describe the strategic involvement of unions.
9. Do you expect more worker slowdowns in this decade? More strikes?
10. Compare and contrast wages and working conditions among the U.S., Canada, and Mexico.

PROJECTS, EXERCISES & CASES

End-of-Text Projects

Lincoln Electric

Answer the following for Lincoln Electric:

1. How do the employees have their grievances heard?
2. How can employees influence their wages and the conditions of work?
3. How does Lincoln Electric convince the employees that they do better than if they had a union to bargain for them?

Nordstrom

Answer the following for Nordstrom:

1. How do the employees have their grievances heard?
2. How can employees influence their wages and the conditions of work?
3. How does Nordstrom convince the employees that they do better than if they had a union to bargain for them?

VISIT THE LIBRARY

Exercise 2, Section 7

1. Enter your Web browser.
2. Enter HR Headquarters.
3. Review the following article within "Winning Ideas:" *Behind the Wheel at Saturn, Coors Taps Employee Judgement*
4. Return to your homepage.

Field Project

Interview a human resource manager in a unionized company. Discuss key bargaining issues and how the company is likely to resolve them. Also discuss the procedures maintained by the HR department to avoid conflicts between their company and unions that might create extra costs, lower morale of management and employees, and consume a great deal of time.

Case: The Union's Strategic Choice

Maria Dennis sat back and thoughtfully read through the list of strategies the union's committee had given her that morning. If her union is to rebuild the power it has lost over the past few years, it is time to take drastic action. If the union continues to decline as it has been, it won't be able to effectively represent its members as their exclusive bargaining agent.

Maria was elected two years before at her union's convention to be the international president of the Newspaper Workers International Union (NWIU). At the time she knew it would not be an easy job, and she had eagerly looked forward to taking on a new challenge. But she had no idea during the election just how difficult it would be to get the union back on its feet again.

The NWIU was founded in the late 1890s by newspaper typographers who were responsible for such tasks as setting type on linotype machines, creating the layout of the newspaper, proofing the articles, and printing the newspaper. Members of the union typically completed a six-year apprenticeship, learning all the different tasks involved in the printing process. At that time, the printing profession was considered to be the elite of the industrial workforce. The craft demanded that typographers be literate at a time when even the middle and upper classes were not. The combination of this historical literacy with proficiency in a highly skilled, highly paid craft gave printers elite status among manual workers.

Since the 1970s, the union had declined in stature. Automation led to a deskilling of the craft. The introduction of video display terminals, optical character recognition scanners, and computerized typesetting eliminated substantial composing room work, and the demand for skilled union workers was reduced. The union experienced its peak membership of 120,000 in 1965. Throughout the 1970s and 1980s membership declined substantially, and in 1988, the total membership was only 40,000.

The union's reduced membership has resulted in other problems for the union. First, there are fewer members to pay dues to the union, which is their main revenue-generating function. Consequently, the union has had some serious financial problems and has been forced to cut some of its services to the members

Second, the union experienced a significant loss in bargaining power with newspaper management. In the past, the printers had been fairly secure in their jobs because there was a good demand in the labor market for individuals who could run the complicated printing equipment. But the switch to automation eliminated many jobs and made it possible for employers to easily replace union employees. Anyone can be trained in a short time to use the new printing equipment. Therefore, if union members decided to strike for better wages, hours, and working conditions, management could easily, and legally, find replacements for them. In essence, the union is increasingly unable to fulfill its main mission to collectively represent those employees who have voted for it. To solve the current crisis, Maria is considering five options.

- Implement an associate member plan through which any individual can join the union for a fee of $50 a year. While these members would not be fully represented on the job, they would get an attractive package of benefits, such as low-cost home, health, and auto insurance.
- Attempt some cooperative labor-management relations programs such as trying to get member representation on newspaper boards of directors or employee participation programs in the work place.
- Put more effort into political action. For example, lobby for labor law reform or for new laws more favorable to unions. Try to initiate action that would result in harsher penalties against employers that practice illegal union-avoidance activities such as threatening to move the business if a union is voted in or firing pro-union employees.
- Appeal to community leaders to speak out in favor of the union in order to improve public relations, to recruit new members, and to encourage employers to bargain fairly when negotiating with the union.
- Search for another union with which they might merge, thus increasing their membership, strengthening their finances, increasing their bargaining power, and obtaining economies of scale.

Maria realizes each of the above options could have both positive and negative results and is unsure which strategy, if any, she should recommend for the union to pursue. In less than three hours, however, she will present the list to the council with her recommendations.

Source: By Kay Stratton-Devine, University of Alberta

Case Questions

1. What are the strengths and weaknesses of each strategy?
2. What strategies could be employed to get new bargaining units?
3. What other types of services could the union offer to its members?
4. What would your recommendation be? Justify your response.

Chapter 19 Endnotes

1. "At Saturn, What Workers Want is . . . Fewer Defects," *Business Week* (Dec. 2, 1991): 117–118. As of October 1994, Mr. LeFauve was given the additional responsibilities of running GM's entire domestic small-car operations. His challenge now is to ensure Saturn's successes are transferred elsewhere.
2. "Goal of Improvement Drives Training at Saturn," *Bulletin to Management* (May 16, 1996): 153–154; D. Woodruff, "Saturn: Labor's Love Lost?" *Business Week* (Feb. 8, 1993): 122–123; D. Woodruff, J. Treece, S. W. Bhargava, and K. Miller, "Saturn," *Business Week* (Aug. 17, 1992): 87–91; J. L. Lewandowski and W. P. MacKinnon, "What We Learned at Saturn," *Personnel Journal* (Dec. 1992): 30–32; and B. P. Noble, "Toward the Factory on a Hill," *New York Times* (Nov. 8, 1992): F25.
3. Woodruff et al., "Saturn: Labor's Love Lost?"
4. J. M. Brett, "Behavioral Research on Unions and Union Management Systems," in *Research in Organization Behavior,* vol. 2, B. M. Straw and L. L. Cummings, eds. (Greenwich, CT: JAI Press 1980).
5. Ibid.
6. D. D. Tippett and J. Costa, "Labor Adversaries Bury the Hatchet," *Personnel Journal* (May 1996): 100–107; P. Stuart, "Labor Union Become Business Partners," *Personnel Journal* (August 1993): 54–63; see J. M. Brett, "Behavioral Research on Unions," J. M. Brett, "Why Employees Want Unions," *Organizational Dynamics* 8 (1980); 45–59; W. C. Hamner and F. J. Smith, "Work Attitudes as Predictors of Unionization Activity," *Journal of Applied Psychology* 63 (1978): 415–421; "Unions Are Turning to Polls to Read the Rank and File," *Business Week* (Oct. 22, 1984): 66–67; W. Serrin, "Unions Are Shifting Gears But Not Goals," *New York Times* (March 31, 1985): 2E.
7. D. Q. Mills, *The New Competitors* (New York: Free Press, 1985): 225–242; M. Schuster, "The Impact of Union-Management Cooperation on Productivity and Employment," *Industrial and Labor Relations Review* (April 1983): 415–430; H. C. Katz, T. A. Kochan, and K. R. Gobeille, "Industrial Relations Performance, Economic Performance, and QWL Programs: An Interplant Analysis," *Industrial and Labor Relations Review* (Oct. 1983): 3–17.
8. J. Hoerr, "The Strange Bedfellows Backing Workplace Reform," *Business Week* (April 20, 1990): 57. See also R. Koenig, "Quality Circles Are Vulnerable to Union Tests," *The Wall Street Journal* (March 28, 1990): B1; L. E. Hazzard, "A Union Says Yes to Attendance," *Personnel Journal* (Nov. 1990): 47–49; B. Filipczak, "Unions: Cooperation or Capitulation in the '90s?" *Training* (May 1993): 25–34.
9. B. P. Noble, "More Than Labor Amity at AT&T," *New York Times* (March 14, 1993): F25. Used by permission.
10. T. Hayes, "Saving 3,727 GM Jobs in Texas," *New York Times* (March 1, 1992): F10.
11. J. A. Fossum, *Labor Relations: Development, Structure, Process,* 4th ed. (Plano, TX: Business Publications Inc., 1988).
12. A. A. Blum, "Collective Bargaining: Ritual or Reality?" *Harvard Business Review* (Nov.-Dec. 1961): 64.
13. M. Bazerman, *Judgement in Managerial Decision Making* (New York: Wiley, 1986); M. Bazerman and J. S. Carroll, "Negotiator Cognition," in *Research in Organizational Behavior,* vol. 9, L. L. Cummings and B. M. Straw, eds. (Greenwich, CT: JAI Press, 1987); M. H. Bazerman, T. Magliozzi, and M. A. Neale, "The Acquisition of an Integrative Response in a Competitive Market," *Organizational Behavior and Human Decision Processes* 34 (1985): 294–313.
14. K. Jennings and E. Traynman, "Two-Tier Plans," *Personnel Journal* (March 1988): 56–58.
15. K. Kelly, "Caught in Cat's Claws," *Business Week* (December 4, 1995): 38; D. Woodruff, "Will Yokich Breathe Fire into the UAW?" *Business Week* (December 5, 1994): 64–66; R. L. Rose, "Caterpillar Continues to Stand Tough as Strikers Return," *The Wall Street Journal* (December 8, 1995): B1, 13.
16. A. A. Sloane and F. Whitney, *Labor Relations,* 5th ed. (Englewood Cliffs, NJ: Prentice-Hall, 1985).
17. Fossum, *Labor Relations: Development, Structure, Process.*
18. P. T. Hartman and W. H. Franke, "The Changing Bargaining Structure in Construction: Wide-Area and Multicraft Bargaining," *Industrial and Labor Relations Review* (Jan. 1980): 170–184.
19. Sloane and F. Whitney, *Labor Relations,* p.59.
20. *1996 Source Book on Collective Bargaining: Wages, Benefits, and Other Contract Issues* (Washington, D.C.: The Bureau of National Affairs, 1996); "1996 Employer Bargaining Objectives," *Bulletin to Management* (October 12, 1995): 324–325; G. P. Zachary, "Unions Talk Tough But Face Big Hurdles," *The Wall Street Journal* (January 22, 1996): 1;

D. Greising, "Pilots to Delta: We May Walk," *Business Week* (February 5, 1996): 6; Hartman and Franke, "The Changing Bargaining Structure in Construction: Wide-Area and Multicraft Bargaining."

21. Fossum, *Labor Relations: Development, Structure, Process.*

22. M. Bazerman and M. A. Neale, "Heuristics in Negotiation: Limitations to Effective Dispute Resolution," in *Negotiating in Organizations,* M. Bazerman and R. Lewick, eds. (Beverly Hills, CA: Sage, 1983): 51–67; M. Gordon et al., "Laboratory Research in Bargaining and Negotiations: An Evaluation," *Industrial Relations* (Spring 1984): 218–223; R. E. Walton and R. B. McKersie, *A Behavioral Theory of Labor Negotiations* (New York: McGraw-Hill, 1965).

23. M. Neale, V. Huber, and G. Northcraft, "The Framing of Negotiations: Contextual versus Task Frame," *Organizational Behavior and Human Decision Processes* 39 (1987): 228–241.

24. "Lockout and Shutdowns," *Labor Relations Reporter* (Washington, D.C.: Bureau of National Affairs, 1985), LRX 688–691, 810.

25. S. Caudron, "The Changing Union Agenda," *Personnel Journal* (March 1995): 42–49; "Bridgestone Plans to Hire Permanent Replacements," *The Blade* (Toledo, OH) (August 20, 1994): 26; R. Narisetti, "Work Week: Rubber Workers Strike Out," *The Wall Street Journal* (March 7, 1995): 1.

26. "Employment Law Changes Expected," *Bulletin to Management* (March 18, 1993): 88; D. J. B. Mitchell, "A Note on Strike Propensities and Wage Developments," *Industrial Relations* 20 (1981): 123–127; J. Kennan, "Pareto Optimality and the Economics of Strike Duration," *Journal of Labor Research* 1(1980): 77–94.

27. L. Uchitelle, "Labor Draws the Line in Decatur," *New York Times* (June 13, 1993): Sec. 3, 1 and 6.

28. J. Tasini, "For the Unions, a New Weapon," *New York Times Magazine* (June 12, 1988): 24–25, 69–71.

29. "Resolving Disputes Through Mediation," *Bulletin to Management* (July 28, 1994): 240; S. Briggs, "Labor/Management Conflict and the Role of the Neutral," in *Personnel and Human Resource Management,* 3rd ed., R. S. Schuler, S. A. Youngblood, and V. L. Huber, eds. (St. Paul, MN: West, 1988).

30. D. E. Feller, "End of the Trilogy: The Declining State of Labor Arbitration," *Arbitration Journal* (Sept. 1993): 18–26; S. L. Hayford, "The Coming Third Era of Labor Arbitration," *Arbitration Journal* (Sept. 1993): 8–17, 77, 78.

31. E. Schine and L. Himelstein, "The Explosion in Private Justice," *Business Week* (June 12, 1995): 88–89; "Judgement Day for Arbitrators," *Business Week* (April 19, 1982): 66; R. Johnson, "Interest Arbitration Examined," *Personnel Administrator* (Jan. 1983): 53–59, 73; P. Compton-Forbes, "Interest Arbitration Hasn't Worked Well in the Public Sector," *Personnel Administrator* (Feb. 1984): 99–104; "Collective Bargaining Through Diplomacy," *Bulletin to Management* (Jan. 25, 1990): 32.

32. R. L. Blevins, "Maximizing Company Rights Under the Contract," *Personnel Administrator* (June 1984): 75–82; and D. A. Hawver, "Plan Before Negotiating . . . and Increase Your Power of Persuasion," *Management Review* (Feb. 1984): 46–48; R. J. Colon, "Grievances Hinge on Poor Contract Language," *Personnel Journal* (Sept. 1990): 32–36.

33. S. H. Slichter, J. J. Healy, and E. R. Livernash, *The Impact of Collective Bargaining on Management* (Washington, D.C.: The Brookings Institution, 1960), 694.

34. Ibid., 694–696.

35. J. N. Draznin, "Labor Relations," *Personnel Journal* (July 1981): 528; J. N. Draznin, "Labor Relations," *Personnel Journal* (Aug. 1980): 625; B. A. Jacobs, "Don't Take 'No' for an Answer," *Industry Week* (Jan. 26, 1981): 38–43; Kochan, Collective Bargaining and Industrial Relations, 385–386; I. Paster, "Collective Bargaining: Warnings for the Novice Negotiator," *Personnel Journal* (March 1981): 203–206.

36. B. R. Skeleton and P. C. Marett, "Loser Pays Arbitration," *Labor Law Journal* (May 1979): 302–309.

37. G. W. Bolander, "Fair Representation: Not Just a Union Problem," *Personnel Administrator* (March 1980): 39.

38. B. Vlasic, "What Labor Problem?" *Business Week* (April 15, 1996): 106–107; B. Vlasic, "Bracing for the Big One," *Business Week* (March 25, 1996): 34–35; M. Maynard, "GM Strike Ends; Production Hurt," *USA Today* (August 26, 1994): B1; "Negotiations That Unite The Parties," *Bulletin to Management* (October 5, 1995): 320.

39. Memorandum 79–55, *National Labor Relations Board* (July 7, 1979).

40. D. R. Dalton and W. D. Todor, "Manifest Needs of Stewards: Propensity to File a Grievance," *Journal of Applied Psychology* (Dec. 1979): 654–659.

41. T. A. Kochan, R. B. McKersie, and P. Cappelli, "Strategic Choice and Industrial Relations Theory," *Industrial Relations* (Winter 1984): 16–38; T. A. Kochan and J. Chalykoff, "Human Resource Management and Business Life Cycles: Some Preliminary Propositions," paper presented at UCLA Conference on Human Resources and Industrial Relations in High Technology Firms (June 21, 1985); Mills, *The New Competitors,* 243–271.

42. A. Bryant, "Labor Desires May Threaten Northwest Air," *New York Times* (April 9, 1996): D1, 12.

43. A. L. Cowan, "Steel Pact Lets Union Name a Board Member," *New York Times* (August 1, 1993): L34.

44. D. Moberg, "Like Business, Unions Must Go Global," *New York Times* (Dec. 9, 1993): F13. See also S. Baker, G. Smith and E. Weiner, "The Mexican Worker," *Business Week* (April 19, 1993): 84–92; and W. C. Symonds, G. Smith and S. Baker, "Border Crossings," *Business Week* (Nov. 22, 1993): 40–42.

20

CHAPTER

Human Resource Data, Information, and Assessment Systems

> *"Going online has provided us with a tremendous boost in productivity."*
>
> *Barbara Beck,*
> *Vice President of Human Resources,*
> *Cisco Systems*[1]

Learning Objectives

1. Describe the purposes and importance of HR data and information systems.
2. Describe computer technology, HR data and information, and their impact on HR.
3. Discuss the ethical implications of computer technology and HRIS.
4. Briefly describe how to assess each HR activity.
5. Describe the current trends in HR data, information, and assessment systems.

Chapter Outline

MANAGING HUMAN RESOURCES

via the Internet

Cyberspace is a new recruitment source. Not surprisingly, many within the HR field are beginning to take notice of the vast online universe. And recruiting is perhaps the hottest area of all. Step inside the Menlo Park, California, headquarters of Cisco Systems, and you're likely to see the HR department of the future. Almost all open positions are posted on the Internet—on the firm's own World Wide Web *homepage* and on various career services. Net browsers can view as many as 400 ads at any given time.

And, apparently, a lot of people like the idea of looking for work online. The company receives as many as 700 resumes electronically every month—approximately 30% of the total it receives overall. Some months the figure has reached 50%. All resumes automatically are routed into a Resumix system, where they can be recalled at a moment's notice—whether at the Bay Area headquarters or across the country at the firm's Boston or Raleigh sites.

"Company recruiters no longer have to spend their time scouring resumes to find the appropriate candidate; they simply can fill the position," says Barbara Beck, vice president of human resources. "Going online has provided us with a tremendous boost in productivity. It's facilitating communication, and it's making it easier for everyone to use HR services. It allows us to add maximum value. We're working very hard to stay ahead of the technology curve and have an extremely sophisticated human resources organization."

Indeed, Cisco's Web site, besides displaying the job listings, contains information about the company's products, its financial data, its culture and history. "And that saves a lot of time for HR, which no longer has to field as many inquiries," Beck says.

Another HR person who finds online recruiting particularly appealing is Elaine Hart, manager of recruitment for Staples, the nation's third largest discount office-products superstore chain. In March, the Framington, Massachusetts-based company joined the Monster Board, a career center and job-placement service on the Internet's World Wide Web. Hart typically posts listings within Staples' homepage; when job seekers browse through, they're able to click on an icon to go to the company, and then search job openings by region, category, and other parameters. They're also able to get information on the company itself.

"It's a way to demonstrate that the company is on the leading edge of technology, and it's a way to make the entire recruiting process more efficient," says Hart. Indeed, when an applicant responds to a posting, the E-mail message is routed directly to Hart's computer. A process that can take weeks using traditional methods—newspapers, trade ads and paper-based resumes—now can take only hours. That allows Staples to find qualified applicants far more quickly. In addition, electronic postings create greater flexibility. Hart can modify or remove an ad if it isn't working or if a position is filled.

Recruiting online saves time, reduces the amount of paper Hart must handle, and lowers administrative costs. But, more importantly, venturing online allows the company to reach an expanded audience. Already, she's receiving as many as a half dozen electronic resumes and applications a day. And virtually all of those who respond to the online ads tend to be highly educated, well trained, and perfectly comfortable with computers and online services—a set of skills that's becoming crucial in the 1990s. Of course, many technical specialists—particularly in computer hardware, software and networking—gravitate to online forums, making the medium a particularly fertile area for mining prospects.[2]

The Internet is a worldwide network that connects computers and allows for transmission of data.

This feature describing how Cisco Systems and Staples use the **Internet** to manage their human resource needs represents a growing trend in companies, large and small. Increasingly, companies are using technology to facilitate the rapid and easy transmission of voice, data, and visual communications. This is not only enabling companies to compete in an environment where speed is critical, but it is also facilitating communication among companies' various locations around the country/world. Great information systems and computer technology facilitate this. Of course, these techniques aren't useful unless the data used is good, so we need to be concerned about the quality of data. Thus, with good data and today's technology, HR professionals can better serve their organizations, the line managers, employees, and themselves! That's why we finish this book talking about information systems in some detail.

Did You KNOW?

The Internet connects more than 40 million people in 4 million host computers in more than 70 countries.

Human Resource Data, Information, and Assessment Systems

Human resource data and information systems are closely linked in discussion and application. Human resource information systems (HRIS), introduced in Chapter 3, generally refer to a database used for managing human resources. For many people, **information** is something that they find useful, that they did not know, and that can be used to solve a problem. **Data,** however, is more specific; it refers to facts—usually in numerical form—about people or things. In this sense, data become information when accessed by people who need it and who can use it to solve problems. And when data and information are organized, systematic, and integrated, we refer to them as **data and information systems.** An example of the type of data and information that can be stored in an HRIS is shown in Exhibit 20.1. In this chapter, we discuss these systems and their characteristics. We also discuss assessment systems.

Information is data that can be used to offer insights and understanding and to solve problems.

Data are numerical facts, about people, or things.

Data and information systems are organized, systematic, and integrated.

Assessment systems are organized approaches to measuring and evaluating.

As with data and information systems, **assessment systems** are organized approaches to measuring and evaluating the success of a human resource activity. Assessment systems enable the HR professional and others to determine whether the data and information are being used as effectively as possible.[3]

Why Are Data, Information, and Assessment Systems Important?

LEARNING OBJECTIVE 1

Describe the purposes and importance of HR data and information systems.

Information is the true capital of business today. Without strong systems of communicating and transferring it, an organization will find itself at an overwhelming competitive disadvantage. Hence the central role of HR data, information, and assessment cannot be overlooked. Together they do many things for an organization. They:

- Enable the organization to do a better job of linking HR planning with business planning.
- Integrate HR data and information from separate parts of the organization into a central location, one that can be accessed and distributed widely.
- Help line managers fulfill their HR responsibilities such as assisting their employees with career planning, performance appraisal, and training needs assessment.
- Facilitate the storage of vast amounts of data and information.
- Help the HR professionals fulfill their responsibilities and more closely link to the needs of the business, line managers, and employees.
- Research HR activities for purposes of validation and improvement.
- Enable organizations to adapt more rapidly and effectively to changes in the environment.
- Enable organizations to serve the broader objectives of decentralization and employee empowerment.
- Facilitate communications with employees through surveys.

EXHIBIT 20.1

Primary Forms of Information Stored in a HRIS

GENERAL DATA

Absenteeism
Attendance
Date of birth
Department code
Disciplinary actions
Employee number
Grievance tracking
Home address
Job level
Job title
Marital status
Office telephone number
Safety/OSHA requirements
Status (full-time, part-time, terminated)
Veteran status
Worker's compensation
Applicant tracking
Attitude surveys
Date of status
Dependents
Emergency contacts
Employment history
Hire date
Home telephone number
Job posting
Location
Office address
Performance appraisal rating
Social Security number
Union code
Work shift

AFFIRMATIVE ACTION/EEOC

ADA status
Citizenship
Gender
Minority status
Availability analysis
EEO code (professional, technical, etc.)
Job group within EEO code
Workforce utilization analysis

BENEFITS

Accidental death and dismemberment coverage*
Company credit union
Flexible or cafeteria benefits plan*
Life insurance coverage*
Savings bonds*
Tuition dollars refunded
401k contribution*
COBRA
Dental*
Health plan coverage (family, single)*
Long-term disability coverage*
Stock plan option*
Vacation and sick leave
*Employee and employer contribution

COMPENSATION

Bonus pay
Merit pay
Payroll planning and implementation
Salary history
Stock purchase plan
Job evaluation
Pay frequency (weekly, biweekly, monthly)
Retiree pension obligations
Salary level & range

EDUCATION

Field of degree
Skills profile (languages, training, licenses, etc.)
Year degree awarded
Highest degree earned
Training received (internal, external)

HUMAN RESOURCE PLANNING

Candidate lists
Labor market analysis
Recruitment source
Succession planning
Turnover analysis
Environmental scanning
Needs assessment
Skills inventory
Supply assessment

Source: Adapted from E.P. Bloom, "Creating an Employee Information System," *Personnel Administrator*, November 1982, page 68, by Mark A. Huselid, Professor of Human Resource Management, Rutgers University, 1997.

All forms of computer and telecommunications hardware and software are making these HR systems faster and easier to use.

We will discuss each of these more extensively in the remainder of this chapter. In attaining the preceding purposes, the data and information systems make their HR department and professionals more effective and, at the same time, make the organization more competitive and successful.

While a manually operated HRIS—where records are in file cabinets and changes are made by typewriter (and white out!)—can be used, most organizations now use computer technology for some or all of the data. Regardless of a company's size, as it uses the power of technology, it develops a greater capacity for success. Such companies find it useful to form a partnership in managing their human resources through data, information, and assessment. An example of the activities that can be shared in this partnership are described in the feature, "Partnership: Working Together in HR Data, Information, and Assessment Systems."

Linking HR Planning with Business Planning

Computers make it ever more feasible to relate HR planning with the planning needs of the business. At the Chevron Corporation in San Francisco, the HR group has been able to do this by decentralizing their HRIS; rather than a single centralized system, the business units each have their own HRIS. Because each unit is

PARTNERSHIP:

WORKING TOGETHER IN HR DATA, INFORMATION, AND ASSESSMENT SYSTEMS

LINE MANAGERS	HR PROFESSIONALS	EMPLOYEES
Provide accurate and current HR data to enable the linkage of HR data and business needs.	Link HR databases to the needs of the business.	Use computer-based HR activities to manage own career.
Help assess the quality of HR activities.	Develop user-friendly HRIS.	Participate in organizational surveys.
Use on-line data accessibility in the daily management of employees.	Continually assess and improve HR activities.	Play an active role in assessing HR activities.
	Link HR databases to the needs of the business.	Use computer-based HR activities to help solve organizational problems.
	Provide timely and usable data.	

different in terms of business needs, planning cycles, and degree of change, decentralization allows the system to be used in a way that is comfortable for each unit. With greater comfort comes greater usage of the system.[4]

Did You KNOW?

Chevron is a heavy user of decentralized HR information and data systems.

Integrating Data and Information

The HRIS at Chevron is designed to be customer-oriented—that is, oriented to the business. It is designed to gather data from several business units. The data is gathered on the terms of the individual unit and then is made accessible again to each unit, on its terms. Of course data can also be integrated by the units directly. Fast and easy-to-use e-mail systems enable companies to link their units together with minimal cost and maximum efficiency. The impact can go far beyond cost and efficiency as described in the feature, "Managing Human Resources at Chevron."

HR data and information need to be related to the business and systematically integrated.

Computer Technology, HRIS, and Human Resources

LEARNING OBJECTIVE 2

Describe computer technology, HR data and information, and their impact on HR.

Managing human resources effectively requires a great deal of data and information. Computer technology enables organizations to combine this data and information in efficiently centralized locations (the databases we call HRIS), and then make it available for use by others regardless of their location. The two major components of computer technology are the hardware and the software.

Computer Hardware and Software

Computer hardware is the equipment, such as the computers, printers, servers, disk drives, scanners, monitors, and keyboards. Computers include mainframes, minicomputers, and microcomputers (PCs). Because the cost of computing has come down and the power of minicomputers and PCs has increased, mainframes are less prominent today (although they still operate as the "garage or attic" where a great deal of data and information can be stored).[6] Instead, minicomputers and PCs used as services for local-area networks (LANs) more easily and readily distribute data (often downloaded from the mainframe) and information. Laptop computers and desk terminals enable more data and information to be put into the hands of more people. This is, of course, consistent with the themes of empowerment, self-management, the virtual office, and partnership that we have been discussing throughout this text.

Computer hardware is the equipment:

- **computers**
- **disk drives**
- **scanners**
- **monitors**
- **keyboards**
- **servers**

MANAGING HUMAN RESOURCES

at Chevron

The phrase "interactive corporation" increasingly applies to Chevron Corp., as employees of the San Francisco-based oil company take advantage of computer technology to communicate ideas and share information.

According to Chevron spokesman Jay Stuller, the company is embracing decentralization and "horizontal communication" among its multinational employees. Technology is helping Chevron blur the lines between employee ranks, operating companies, and professions, he asserts.

Tools employed by Chevron to increase cross-functional information sharing include Lotus Notes, the discussion-type database, and a group problem-solving software program that brings 15 to 20 people together to brainstorm via networked computers.

Lotus Notes helps Chevron's widely dispersed workforce keep up to date on "best practices" for performing various tasks, says Catherine Carr, a Chevron quality consultant. This "groupware" tool allows many people to monitor a single database.

Of Chevron's 45,000 employees worldwide, about 4,000 can read the information in the Lotus Notes database, while about 180 have "write access" that enables them to edit or add information. All users can send messages back and forth via e-mail.

Employees can use the computer system to post informal "scratches and itches," Carr says. A "scratch" might be a notice recommending a particular book or suggesting other helpful resources, she explains, while an "itch" might ask for input on "who out there knows how to best meet customer satisfaction needs?" More formal contributions cover product development, environmental compliance, and corporate planning, she notes.

The brainstorming software, according to Stacy Hunt, a Chevron technology consultant, allows employees to come together, type out their ideas anonymously on separate computers, and view each other's ideas on a large screen at the front of the room. Such sessions enable employees to generate a lot of information in a brief period without the inhibitions that commonly arise when speaking out in front of peers or superiors, she explains.[5]

Computer software is the program instructions that tell the hardware what to do.

Computer software contains program instructions that indicate to the hardware what to do. There are literally hundreds of specialized programs just for HRIS. Specialized software has been designed for functions such as benefit administration, succession planning, and payroll administration. To stay current with what's available, it is necessary to constantly scan the PC magazines and HR professional journals such as *Online Sources for Human Resources.*

A key to the success of an HRIS system is an HR staff that understands each unit's business, business processes, and financial processes. In this way, the HR staff can design activities to better address the needs of each unit. This in turn encourages the units to share their good data with the central system, which makes better use of the central system.

Helping Line Managers and Employees Fulfill Their HR Responsibilities

In companies where the needs of the business are understood by the HR professionals, it is likely that data and information systems exist where managers have on-line access to process pay changes, promotions, transfers; perform candidate searches, and staffing requests; and complete other transactions that traditionally were paper driven. This really enables line managers to fulfill their HR responsibilities much more efficiently and to furnish more useful information to the HRIS.

Portions of HR systems can be designed for employee access. Such systems provide direct access by employees to flexible benefit enrollments, career planning and self-assessment, job posting, and training.

Legal Compliance

The computerized HRIS can facilitate the easy storage of, and access to, human resource records that are vital for organizations.

To comply with federal equal employment laws, organizations must follow several HR record keeping requirements. Title VII of the 1964 *Civil Rights Act* says organizations must keep all employment records for at least six months. The *Equal Pay Act* and the *Age Discrimination in Employment Act* require records to be kept three years. Three years, however, is not always the limit. If an employee or a government agency lodges a charge against a firm (and this could be any number of years), the firm should have all of its records regarding the person making the complaint as well as records on all other employees in similar positions. The organization must also keep records on all other employees in similar positions. The organization must also keep records on seniority, benefits, and merit and incentive plans until at least one year after the plans end.

HR data and information are required by several federal agencies.

Did You KNOW?

The Internet address for the U.S. Department of Labor is http://www.dol.gov

Organizations need records to fill out the numerous reports that are required for legal compliance. Employers of 100 or more workers must annually file EEO-1 reports to comply with Equal Employment Opportunity laws. Multi-establishment employers need only file separate EEO-1 reports for each establishment employing 50 or more workers. Organizations with government contracts must fill out affirmative action reports that the Office of Federal Contract Compliance Programs (OFCCP) sends. Government contractors required to fill out Standardized Affirmative Action Formats (SAAFs) for the OFCCP can propose one SAAF to cover all its establishments as long as its HR activities are the same for each establishment.

As described in Chapter 17, keeping and maintaining safety and health records is a requirement of OSHA. A good database can also be part of a strategy to improve occupational safety and health.

Helping HR Professionals Fulfill Their Responsibilities

Technology and sound data and information systems help HR professionals perform their responsibilities more effectively. Perhaps the areas of greatest application are in planning, recruiting, compensation, and training and development.

HR Planning. While planning is crucial in this fast-paced environment, it must be done more rapidly than ever. And because the demands for quality and effectiveness are so high, companies must utilize all of their human resources effectively. A great HRIS can thus be vital to a company:

> *Information provided by integrated software systems has powerful implications for HR's role in long-term planning. Succession planning is a good example because HR is at the core of determining—and consequently planning—a succession path for both employees and positions. It's here that integrated software provides the quality information that you can incorporate into effective decision-support systems.*
>
> *A solid organization needs a contingency plan for every position. Take a vice president's position, for example. Using a position-control system, you can determine the compensation, skills, education, and experience needed to fill that position. Then you can begin succession planning by grooming candidates for the inevitable vacancy (even if several years in the future). If three people are in line for that position, you can ensure that the candidates gain what they need to eventually fill the position.*

Recruitment. As described in the opening feature, "Managing Human Resources via the Internet," recruiting is a major HR activity that can be done using on-line technology. The advantages are numerous.

> *"Company recruiters no longer have to spend their time scouring resumes to find the appropriate candidate; they simply can fill the position," says Barbara Beck, vice president of human resources at Cisco. "Going online has provided us with a tremendous boost in productivity. It's facilitating communication, and it's making it easier for everyone to use HR services. It allows us to add maximum value. We're working very hard to stay ahead of the technology curve and have an extremely sophisticated human resources organization."*[8]

So recruiting on-line is easy and useful, but it can be costly:

> *The cost of establishing an online presence for recruiting purposes can vary greatly. The least expensive option is simply listing an open job in a professional online forum or an Internet news group. That costs nothing, and thousands of such listings are visible on any day of the week. Turning to an outside agency such as Gonyea and Associates or E-Span, which can ensure that millions of users are exposed to the ads, can cost from $75 an ad to $3,000 or $4,000 a year for unlimited advertising. A few firms charge as much as $20,000 a year. A company that chooses to establish a homepage on the Web's Career Mosaic or Monster Board will likely fork over anywhere from $1,000 to $10,000. An organization intent on setting up their own Web site can spend considerably more. Although a Sun Microsystems or Hewlett-Packard workstation sitting on a desktop can become a server on the Web—thus supplying text and graphics to others on the Internet—it's far more challenging to develop an eye-catching interface and link data effectively. As a result, the expertise of an outside consultant or agency often is required.*[9]

Did You KNOW?

You can find many job openings posted on the homepage of many companies.

Monetary Compensation. A computerized HRIS can be instrumental in managing total compensation and ensuring equity. The four components of monetary compensation are direct monetary, indirect monetary, direct nonmonetary, and indirect nonmonetary rewards. In ledger format, HR specialists can maintain the value (cost) total compensation in several configurations. For example, total compensation can be computed for each employee and the average for each position or department. In addition, specific components of total compensation can be calculated and used for projecting and establishing salary and benefits budgets for appropriate organizational units. In conjunction with job evaluation, the HR department can determine whether compensable factors are being assigned monetary values systematically or randomly. This can serve as an initial step in minimizing inequitable compensation.

Performance appraisal information is closely related to the compensation activity. Computers can link the HR department with other departments and thereby facilitate projecting departmental salary budgets.[10]

Performance-Based Pay. Much of the time spent in compensation planning is lost to pencil pushing and number crunching. The computerized HRIS can accommodate performance-based pay planning and administration in the following ways. First, establishing a merit pay plan grid on a computer system can facilitate administration because the computer can be programmed to post the appropriate percentage increases. Second, budget plans can be made simply by manipulating the percentage values on the grid, automatically changing each individual's pay, and, of course, planning strategies can be considered by department, position, or other meaningful ways. Because time is a cost to any organization, the ability to analyze this information in a minimal amount of time represents a substantial cost efficiency.

A computerized HRIS facilitates the management and manipulation of the data used in projecting salary structure, compa-ratios (compensation cost/amount of revenue generated ratios), total cost of selected configurations of benefits packages and the cost of compensation in the future under different rates of inflation. These calculations can be made on the basis of an individual employee, a group, or the overall organization. Selected information can be further extracted for summary reports and projections for areas other than the HR department such as a budget sheet for the comptroller or the line managers.

Many firms have "benefit-lines" so employees can learn about and change their benefits.

Training and Development. Computer-based training (CBT) is now widely available. A great deal of training for airline pilots is conducted using CBT and flight simulators. While efficient, CBT is, however, not the total solution. SimuFlite Training International, a competitor of FlightSafety International—both offer pilot training—learned through trial and error (and customers' reactions) that CBT needs to be mixed with instructor training to be effective.[11]

At the Hudson's Bay Company, one of Canada's largest retailers, CBT is used to train new sales associates in everything from store procedures to customer-service practices. CBT has replaced the three-day intensive training program that consisted entirely of oral presentations. Because of its successes, CBT is used for training in many topics, including:

- Interviewing techniques
- Effective people management
- Retail method of inventory
- Retail marketing
- Sales promotion
- Professional selling skills
- Line-budget maintenance
- Check authorization
- Inventory systems
- Career planning
- Family budgeting[12]

Did You KNOW?

You can find out about training jobs on the Internet at http://www.astd.org

Overall, the results indicate that CBT is more cost-effective than traditional training because students get to the work situation sooner and end up spending less time in the classroom.

Total quality management and continuous improvement depend on good data, a strong HRIS, and continual assessment. Creating this culture and making it run successfully is a role for which the HR department is especially suited. Quality questions related to HR include: Who are the best performers? Are we selecting the best applicants regarding math skills?

Continuous improvement depends upon targets, measurement, and a willingness to change and learn.

Conducting Research for Validation and Improvement

On any given day, an HR department evaluates a number of candidates for a variety of positions. Deciding which predictors are relevant (valid) for a particular case and administering a multitude of predictors (tests) make this work challenging. Effective management of predictors is critical in the face of extensive laws and regulations. Doing these tasks effectively requires a great deal of information, and computer technology enhances the coordination of scheduling, administration, and evaluation of predictors by processing this information in a variety of ways.

Validation Study. The HR department can quickly do a validation study (described in Appendix C) by correlating the current job performance data with any of several predictors, if these data are stored in an HRIS and analyzed by computer. With a computerized HRIS, the utilization rates for affirmative action programs can also be determined quickly and easily. The results of any kind of test can be stored in an HRIS and used with job analysis data (also in the HRIS) to make better selection and placement decisions. This same information can then be used to plot career paths for employees.

Interviewing. Computers are used to reduce first-impression biases inherent in the interview. Computer-aided interviewing presents a structured interview directly to an applicant, without an interviewer present. Although it does not replace the face-to-face interview, it complements it by providing a base of information about each applicant before the interviewer meets the applicant. This provides a first impression based on information that is job-relevant rather than anecdotal.

Computer interviewing is also faster. An applicant can complete a 100-question computer-aided interview in about 20 minutes. The same information would require a face-to-face interview of more than two hours. In addition to time savings, computer-aided interviewing provides an automatic record of answers that can be compared across applicants. And as mentioned in Chapter 10, applicants are likely to give more candid responses in a computer interview than a personal interview.

Enabling Organizations to Adapt More Quickly and Effectively

At Microsoft, the Redmond, Washington, software company, CEO Bill Gates uses a sophisticated electronic mail system to eliminate bureaucratic bottlenecks, where layers of people wait to get answers.

A host of new technologies are making a difference in business today including information technology, office automation, factory automation, data communications, and voice communications.[13] Described in Chapter 3 as telematics technology, they are revolutionizing the ways we work and the ways we organize. Singly or together, these technologies are facilitating the following capabilities within organizations:

- Networking across organizational units and countries
- Control over time and space
- Higher productivity and amplification of human cognitive functions
- New extensions of human action
- New levels of efficiency and productivity or energy and materials conserving
- New power to centralize and decentralize
- Blurring of organizational distinctions
- Promotion of monitoring, evaluation, and simulation
- Erosion of hierarchical relationships
- Shifting of power
- Shifting of authority
- Integration[14]

The impact of the telematics technology revolution is also being seen in manufacturing advances.[15] The revolution within industrial manufacturing include the emerging of technologies of:

- Robotics and factory automation
- Computer-aided design, manufacturing and engineering

- CAD/CAM/CAE
- Computer integrated manufacturing
- Lasers and optics
- Biotechnologies
- Polymers and alloys
- Advanced ceramics[16]

Accompanying the increased factory automation is an increase in the use of robots. Annual sales of robots are expected to be 20,000 units by the end of the century, compared with the current rate of 5,000 units. Estimates are that today robots have displaced about 5 percent of the workforce. To avoid layoffs, substantial retraining will be required of many employees. The costs of this training will be offset by lower labor costs, enhanced product quality, fewer defects, and a better flow of materials.

The biggest gains in office productivity are expected to come from adapting new technologies such as work stations to the jobs of professionals and managers and making vastly greater use of technology to manage people.[17] Productivity gains are also expected to come from re-engineering programs that streamline work flow and work methods. Eventually, almost a majority of the white-collar jobs in the United States will be touched by re-engineering and the use of technology.

Did You KNOW?

The first practical industrial robot was introduced during the 1960s. Today there are over 20,000,000.

A Big Cultural Impact. Data and information systems, whether in the factory or the office, have had, and will continue to have, an impact on organizational structuring. Because information is instantaneously available, there is little need for layers of management between the top and first-line management. Consequently, organizational culture will change significantly. Top management will, in the future, bypass middle managers on their way to first-line management—in fact, there may be few middle managers left when the transformation is complete. The chain of command will be radically different, and fast and effective communications will be the result. As described in the feature, "Managing Human Resources at Chevron," the company becomes more egalitarian and participative.[18]

Some observers, however, suggest that telematics will be used to redesign jobs à la Frederick Taylor in the name of scientific management.[19] Barbara Garson, in *The Electronic Sweatshop*, however, is concerned that the computer's ability to monitor behavior will lead to oppressive control of employees. She also suggests that what some fast-food restaurants are doing with their computer systems is creating jobs that virtually remove the need for employees to think and, therefore, to grow on the job. In essence, she sees telematics as leading to the deskilling of jobs. And while some may say this is necessary because of the evolving nature of the workforce, others say that it only perpetuates the deskilling of the U.S. workforce and thus the eventual decline of U.S. industry.

Although the challenges HR managers face in the telematics revolution are significant, there are other considerations. For instance, work can now go directly to the worker. The need for more daycare services can be addressed in part by allowing workers to do their work at home, linked the whole time to the company's mainframe computer or local work stations. Not only does this have implications for supervision and training, it also has legal implications. The HR department needs to monitor the legal events regarding the utilization of homework activities and the limits of liability for worker safety and health. The ability to have individuals work at home hastens the trend toward using subcontractors and contingent employees. This can lead to lower labor costs because contingent employees essentially have no benefit packages.

Thus the possibilities for organizational improvements for survival and competitiveness through automation and advanced technology are enormous. And so are the implications for our society.

Did You KNOW?

Development of the integrated circuit (invented in the late 1950s) has permitted an ever-increasing amount of information to be processed or stored on a single microchip. This is what has driven the Information Revolution.

Communicating with Employees Through Surveys

Communication has never been more important.

> *Companies claim they are improving communications with employees in this jittery era of downsizings. But a recent survey shows that they're not doing such a great job. Employees polled say they:*
>
> *Don't believe what management says 64%*
> *Aren't well-informed of company plans 61%*
> *Don't get decisions explained well 54%*[20]

Improving the avenues for communication facilitates the transmission of ideas into product improvements and organizational changes and, at the same time, enhances job involvement, participation, and one's sense of being in control.

Computer technology and an organization's HRIS can not only help organizations perform many tasks more quickly and accurately, but can also help with communications. A good illustration of this is the organizational survey.

Organizational surveys are systematic and scientific ways of gathering information.

Organizational surveys are systematic and scientific ways of gathering information for the purpose of assessing current conditions, seeking areas for improvement, and then developing the programs that will implement the improvement. While this can happen without computer technology, it is certainly much easier with it and therefore more likely to occur.

What Do We Measure? In each of the uses for HR data discussed in the previous chapters, the data gathered have either been measures of job performance or predictors of job performance such as tests and background characteristics. But the HR profession often needs other types of data. For example, to develop ways to improve employee performance, the HR staff needs to measure how employees perceive their environment, including the consequences of job performance, quality of feedback, and aspects of goal setting. It is equally necessary to gather data on employee's perceptions of behaviors of their supervisors, role conflict, and role awareness. This is not to say, however, that the objective qualities of the job are not important. But with these two kinds of data, objective and perceptual, the HR staff can begin to make other changes for organizational improvement.

You can't give 'em what they want without asking.

Wayne Wilson
Corporate Vice President,
Human Resources
Blue Cross,
Western Pennsylvania

It is also important to know how employees react to the environment and job qualities. Many of these reactions, which include physical measures such as blood pressure and heart rate, are symptoms of employee stress. Because one very important criterion for all sorts of goals is employee health, systematically gathering this type of information is imperative. Thus organizational surveys generally attempt to measure the following:

- **Employee perceptions:** role awareness, role conflict, qualities of the job, and interpersonal qualities, such as those of the supervisor and group members.
- **Employee reactions:** feelings, such as satisfaction, and physiological responses, such as heart rate and blood pressure.
- **Behaviors:** employee performance, absenteeism, and turnover.

Conducting an Organizational Survey. Important steps for the HR staff—or an outside consultant—to consider when conducting an organizational survey include planning, actual data collection, and ensuring employee participation.[21] These become necessary, however, only after top management has given its support for the survey.

As the first step, the following must be considered:

- Specific employee perceptions and responses that should be measured.
- Methods that will be used to collect the data, including observations, questionnaires, interviews, and personnel records.
- Reliability and validity of the measures to be used.
- People from whom the data will be collected—all employees, managerial employees only, a sample of employees, or only certain departments within the organization.
- Timing of the survey and whether to make the survey part of a longer-term effort.
- Types of analyses that will be made with the data.
- Specific purposes of the data—for example, to determine reasons for an organization's turnover problem.

This last consideration is important, because by identifying the problem, the HR staff can determine which models or theories will be relevant to the survey. Knowing which model will be used indicates what data are needed and what statistical techniques will be necessary to analyze the data.

The next step is the actual collection of data. Three things are important here. It must be decided who will administer the questionnaire—the line manager, the HR staff, or someone from outside the organization. It must be decided where, when, and in what size groups the data will be collected. Both these considerations are influenced by the method used to gather the data. For example, if a questionnaire is used, larger groups are more feasible than if interviews are conducted. Finally, employee participation in the survey must be ensured. This can be done by gathering the data during company time and by providing feedback—for instance, by promising employees that the results of the survey will be made known to them.

Because it is the line manager whose work and behaviors are often the focus of these surveys, they are directly impacted by the results of these surveys.

The actual feedback process is the third step. As part of this process, the data are analyzed according to the purposes and problems for which they were collected. The results of the analysis can then be presented to line managers, who in turn discuss them with their employees. The feedback sessions can be used to develop solutions to any problems that are identified and to evaluate the effectiveness of programs that may already have been implemented on the basis of an earlier survey.

The extent to which employees actually participate in the development of solutions during the feedback process depends on the philosophy of top management. Organizations willing to survey their employees are also usually willing to invite their participation in deciding to make things better. It is this willingness that allows organizational surveys to be used most effectively.

Are We Important? In the Chapter 2 case, "Bringing the Department to the Business," Mike Mitchell "customized" the HR department at the Swiss Bank of North America. In order to succeed at this, he needed the help of the people in his department: they had to change their ways of behaving—they had to go out and talk with customers and develop new products for them! First Mike had to instill a new confidence in his people and show them that what they were doing was important.

Here is where he relied on a short survey. The survey asked the employees in his department to indicate what impact, if any, the HR department was having in the company. In other words, he asked them to indicate if they worked in a unit that made a difference. Of course, they generally thought they did, but they hadn't really addressed this issue in very specific terms until they participated in Mike's survey, which was something like the one in Exhibit 20.2. He asked them what impact they would have if they made the HR department even better than it was—

if they made it a world-class operation! He and his group discussed the results, which gave everyone an opportunity to really see just how many things in the company they did impact. This process energized the group and got them really believing in what they were doing. They were able to take this newfound confidence out into the company and show their customers all the great things the HR department could do for them!

LEARNING OBJECTIVE 3

Discuss the ethical implications of computer technology and HRIS.

Computer Technology, HRIS, and Ethics

With a computerized HRIS, human resource departments can quickly generate confidential personnel information in a variety of formats. Thus, many copies of confidential information may exist at any one time, increasing the likelihood that some may be misplaced or even stolen. As a result, file security is of concern. Today's HRIS systems include access protectors that limit who can read or write to a file, and they can be designed to allow a single person or a group of individuals access or no access. While these systems reduce the threat of file invasion, most designers of "secure" systems build in back door entries. If discovered by an unauthorized user, such a user can gain access to the program. Thus, company computer security is of great concern and companies are doing everything to deal with it.

Today a computerized HRIS can ensure that employee policies are implemented fairly. Expert systems such as those developed by HumanTek, a San Francisco software company, guide managers with employee problems to solutions. By asking a series of questions, the computer steers the manager to organizational policies and precedents that relate to the specific performance problem. Some of the more sophisticated programs even give managers advice. According to Walter Ratcliff, HumanTek consultant, expert systems will be the best friend of tomorrow's manager. Rather than flipping through a human resource manual, a supervisor will turn on his or her computer for advice.

A computerized HRIS can be used to monitor the performance of employees, as described in Chapter 12. The Office of Technology Assessment in Washington, D.C., estimates that up to 10 million workers are regularly monitored at their computers:

> *At hundreds of companies, the performance of data-entry clerks is judged by the speed of their computer-measured keystrokes. Directory-assistance operators at telephone companies are allotted 25 seconds or less to root out a number, however vague the request, and computers record their times.*
>
> *In supermarkets, computers measure the speed with which the checkout clerks sweep purchases over the optical scanner.*
>
> *In an office building in downtown St. Louis, customer-service representatives at Union Pacific Railroad offices who book shipments for companies that send their goods by rail work at the kind of pace that telephone operators and airline reservation agents do.*
>
> *"A customer calls in and says, 'I need two freezer cars to ship frozen french fries from American Falls, Idaho, to a warehouse in Kentucky,'" says Tracey Young, an official with the transportation and communication workers union. Computers track the origin, duration, and frequency of calls, and supervisors, secretly and at random, listen in.*[22]
>
> *In such situations, employees complain of their rights to privacy being violated while companies state that they need the information to be competitive. Meanwhile, the customer may claim the right to good service, and if computer monitoring is what it takes, then companies may decide in favor*

EXHIBIT 20.2

Impact Criteria

If an organization's HR department goes from being just average to being excellent, what criteria are affected and to what extent? Please check (✔) the criteria affected and circle the extent of impact.

CRITERIA		SMALL EXTENT 1	2	MODERATE EXTENT 3	4	GREAT EXTENT 5
1._____	Market share of firm	1	2	3	4	5
2._____	Sales per employee	1	2	3	4	5
3._____	Line manager satisfaction	1	2	3	4	5
4._____	Employee satisfaction	1	2	3	4	5
5._____	Health and safety rates	1	2	3	4	5
6._____	Grievances filed	1	2	3	4	5
7._____	Profitability of firm	1	2	3	4	5
8._____	Flexibility of workforce	1	2	3	4	5
9._____	Return on assets	1	2	3	4	5
10._____	Productivity	1	2	3	4	5
11._____	Employee stress	1	2	3	4	5
12._____	Absenteeism rates	1	2	3	4	5
13._____	Turnover rates	1	2	3	4	5
14._____	Customer satisfaction	1	2	3	4	5
15._____	Respect from others	1	2	3	4	5
16._____	Visits from outsiders	1	2	3	4	5
17._____	Ease of recruitment	1	2	3	4	5
18._____	Selection ratios	1	2	3	4	5
19._____	Involuntary terminations	1	2	3	4	5
20._____	Strategy implementation	1	2	3	4	5
21._____	Role of HR in the firm	1	2	3	4	5
22._____	Competitiveness of firm	1	2	3	4	5
23._____	Line manager use of HR	1	2	3	4	5
24._____	News stories about the firm	1	2	3	4	5
25._____	HR costs	1	2	3	4	5
26._____	Skill levels of employees	1	2	3	4	5
27._____	Legal claims filed	1	2	3	4	5
28._____	Quality of products/services	1	2	3	4	5
29._____	Innovation rates	1	2	3	4	5
30._____	Others, please describe	1	2	3	4	5
	________________	1	2	3	4	5
	________________	1	2	3	4	5
	________________	1	2	3	4	5
	________________	1	2	3	4	5

of the customer. At this time, regulations on the use of computer monitoring are basically in the development stage. Needless to say, it is an important employee rights issue that is likely to gain increased attention from its increasing use.[23]

While privacy is a big area of concern with computer networks, e-mail, and the Internet, there are two other critical issues: sexual harassment and trade secrets.

In considering the threat of sexual harassment, employers should recognize that the Internet gives employees easy access to sites that contain pornographic materials. If they broadcast these materials, offended co-workers may claim that a hostile work environment exists. Harassment issues may also arise if employees transmit messages that contain profanity or sexual references.

In the realm of trade secrets, employers must confront the fact that computers make it easy for employees, whether inadvertently or intentionally, to transmit confidential employer information. The following steps can help safeguard employers from potential problems:

- Revise restrictions regarding confidentiality and sexual conduct in employee manuals to state that they extend to electronic communications
- Have management information systems personnel install encryption and technical devices to limit transmission of inappropriate information
- Ask MIS to keep an audit log of all inbound and outbound transmissions to create an archive of potential unauthorized transmittals
- Include misinformation and other markers in trade-secret files to make it easier to track any use by pirates
- Review insurance coverage to make sure it extends to risks created by Internet use[24]

LEARNING OBJECTIVE 4

Briefly describe how to assess each HR activity.

Assessment Systems for Human Resource Management

Data and information systems enable the HR department and the organization to perform many functions faster and more efficiently. To know if this is being done, the HR department must assess the effectiveness of HRIS. Assessment systems help the HR department determine what the customer wants, how well the department is doing, and what might be done to improve products and services. As such, assessment systems are an integral part of customerization and partnership attitude. They are also consistent with a total quality management system and the philosophy of continuous, data-based improvement. Let's begin our discussion of assessment systems for HR management by looking at the overall department operation and then at several HR activities.

Assessment is the measurement and evaluation of HR activities and of the HR department itself!

Starting with the Human Resource Department

An HR department can demonstrate its contribution to the organization in many ways. As the staff seek to become partners with the rest of the organization, they must learn to provide evidence of their contributions. While such contributions can be assessed against many criteria or standards, two categories put everything in perspective: doing the right things and doing things right.[25]

Doing the right thing means that the HR department does things that are needed by the organization to be successful.

We operate the HR department so that we save the company more than we cost the company.

Paul Beddia
Vice President of
Human Resources
Lincoln Electric Company

Doing the Right Things. **Doing the right thing** means that the HR department does things that are needed by the organization to be successful. In essence, assessors ask whether the department is enabling the organization to be more successful in areas such as competitiveness, profitability, adaptability, and strategy implementation. Is it facilitating the work of line managers and the employees in their efforts to contribute to the maximum of their potential? More broadly, the HR department can be assessed against all the key stakeholders discussed throughout this text.

HR must also be concerned with certain vendors such as insurance companies, trainers and motivational speakers, and service bureaus. Are you doing all you can to make sure these vendors have what they need to do their jobs? Insurance companies, for example, are vital to many organizations. Are you giving healthcare providers timely and accurate information? Managing vendors as customers allows HR to serve its organization both in long-term strategy and in special situations.[26]

Doing Things Right. **Doing things right** means that the HR department does the right thing as efficiently as possible. Of course, the organization wants to hire the best people, but they want to do it at the least possible cost per hire. The HR department wants to facilitate the work of the line managers, but they want to do it in a way that maximizes the benefit and minimizes the cost.

Doing things right means that the HR department does the right things as efficiently as possible.

Within each of these two categories, many more specific measures can be used. For example, "doing the right things" measures can include: knowledge of the organization's strategy; knowledge of the line managers' HR needs; development of plans that are consistent with the firm's strategy; and degree of involvement in the strategic planning process. Measures of efficiency, perhaps the more traditional way that HR departments have been assessed, are many. For example, just within the recruiting and selecting activity, measures include:

- Number of candidates interviewed per position
- Ratio of offers accepted to offers extended
- Number of good hires (tenure or performance after the first year)
- Distribution of good hires per source
- Average tenure per hire
- Percent of hires who stay for a minimum desired period of time
- Percent of hires who are outstanding second-year performers
- Cost per hire who stays three or more years

Knowing the categories for assessing HR contributions is the first step. Actually doing the assessment is the second step. As implied in the list of efficiency measures for recruiting and selecting, assessment can be made by determining the costs and benefits in dollars and cents; it can be made using measures of timeliness. In other words, assessment uses **quantitative measures.** While measures such as the "cost per hire who stays three or more years" might be regarded as a *specific* quantitative indicator, measures such as firm productivity or profitability might be regarded as *general* quantitative indicators.

Quantitative measures are numerical values and ratios used to assess how well HR is being done.

Assessment also uses **qualitative measures.** For departments that want to be more customer focused, an increasingly important way to make qualitative assessments is to ask line managers or employees their opinions of the quality of service being delivered.

Qualitative measures are opinions and comments used to assess how well HR is being done.

While it may be easy to categorize these measures of assessment here, in reality, they are not always clear-cut. For example, qualitative measures are subjective, and choosing categories here that are important to a specific organization and then framing the questions so that the results are useful is not a small effort. There is an art as well as a science to constructing an effective survey.

There are many quantitative measures from which to choose. These measures must be relevant, and there must be enough of them to give an accurate picture of performance, but not so many as to overwhelm the analyst and the recipients of the results. This too is an art. Sometimes, simple data give a better picture of performance than the latest technical tools, and at other times, only high-tech tools will do the job.

Did You KNOW?

Firms with the best HR practices have a shareholder return of 9.4%. Those with the worst practices have a return of 6.5%.

Human Resource Planning

Planning can make or break an organization especially over the long term. Without effective HR planning, an organization may find itself with a plant or an office and no people to run it. On a broad level, then, planning can be assessed on the basis of whether the organization has the people it needs—the right people, at the right place, at the right time, and at the right salary.

At more specific levels, planning activities can be assessed by how effectively they, along with recruitment, attract new employees, deal with job loss, and adapt to the changing characteristics of the environment. Because an important part of planning is forecasting, HR planning can be assessed by how well its forecasts (whether of specific personnel needs or of specific environmental trends) compare with reality. Several other criteria against which planning can be assessed were presented in Chapter 5 in the section on HR planning control and evaluation.

Career Planning and Management

Assessing the effectiveness of career planning and management must be done from both individual and organizational perspectives. Although the overall purpose of career management is to match individual ability to job demands and individual needs to job rewards, specific purposes relate primarily to either the individual or the organization.[27]

Career planning and management is assessed from both individual and organizational perspectives.

The Individual Perspective. From the individual's perspective, effective career planning should result in the following beneficial outcomes:

- A more realistic awareness of skills, abilities, and weaknesses
- An awareness of needs, values, and goals
- An awareness of realistic job and career opportunities that match abilities and personalities, interests, and preferences
- A greater sense of self-esteem from doing what one wants to do
- A more satisfied and productive individual

Employees are more satisfied as a result of job placement activities that match them on personality, interests, and preferences as well as skills, knowledge, and abilities. Sometimes, however, in the initial stages of gaining self-awareness, an individual may leave an organization in search of better matches. How do organizations respond to this? If they offer career programs for their benefit as well as for that of the individual, organizations often wish the individual well because the program has identified that the optimal match lies outside the company. Or, should the program indicate that the individual is the type of employee the company wants in its pool of assets, interesting possibilities can be offered to encourage the person to stay. Flexible career paths can be a solution here.

Did You KNOW?

"People who don't have high school degrees are falling off the charts—they are falling off the cliffs. Their wages are plummeting. Their benefits are disappearing."

Labor Secretary
Robert B. Reich, 1996

The Organizational Perspective. From the organization's perspective, effective career development programs should result in the following beneficial outcomes:

- More effective use of its current workforce
- Reduced absenteeism because employees are better fitted to their job situation
- Reduced turnover after employees go through career planning and find an appropriate job in the current organization
- Improved morale among employees who decide to remain
- A workforce with lower potential for obsolescence and a higher level of flexibility and adaptability to changing circumstances
- More employees suitable for potential promotion
- A better image as an organization to work for and, as a result, a larger pool of job applicants to select from
- A greater likelihood of fulfilling equal opportunity employment obligations and using the skills of all employees
- Improved performance

Again, the evidence of how well career development programs provide these outcomes is limited. However, those organizations that do have them—for instance, Cisco, Ameritrust, PepsiCo, J.C. Penney, and Procter & Gamble—indicate that they are able to identify more potential promotable employees and that they have an easier time attracting qualified candidates because they are known for offering career development opportunities. Career development is becoming a strategy that enables companies to remain competitive.

Job Analysis

A variety of standards have been proposed for analyzing the usefulness of job analysis methods. These include whether the method 1) is versatile in analyzing a variety of jobs, 2) is standardized in its procedures for data collection and analysis, 3) has user acceptability and involvement, 4) requires training for those involved in using the method, 5) is ready to use, 6) requires a lot of time to complete and obtain results, 7) is reliable and valid, and 8) has overall benefits in relation to other methods and the costs incurred in its use.[28]

Unfortunately, even leading organizations may not always employ elaborate and formalized job analysis processes. The majority of them do, however, rely on a job analysis manual and analyst training to standardize procedures with statistical analyses conducted to assess the reliability of results and user acceptance assessed through surveys. Still, even leading organizations fall short of theoretical recommendations for analyzing job analysis procedures.[29]

Recruitment

The recruitment activity is supposed to attract the right people at the right time within legal limits so that people and organizations can select each other in their best short- and long-term interests. Likewise, this is how recruitment should be assessed. Exhibit 20.3 shows more specific criteria for assessing recruitment, grouped by the stage of the recruitment process in which they are most applicable.

Assessing Costs and Benefits. In addition to assessing each benefit criterion of recruitment, each method or source of recruitment can be evaluated, or "costed out" on its short- and long-term benefit costs. Finally, the utility of each method can be determined by comparing the number of potentially qualified applicants hired by each method and by occupational group. The method resulting in the most qualified applicants at the lowest per-hire cost may be determined most effective in the short-term.

Assessing recruiting can save firms thousands of dollars!

The significant figures to review are the costs associated with hires versus costs associated with nonhires. If an organization is spending more than two-thirds of its recruiting budget on individuals who never join the company, the recruiting program needs revamping. Costs should include salaries of recruiters and line managers involved in interviewing and selection; all mailing, telephone, and recruiting materials; administrative support; and all recruitment advertising including receptions, videos, and programs.

Performance Appraisal

Chapter 12 categorized the importance and purposes of performance appraisal into evaluation and development. Although all organizations may not desire their performance appraisal to serve both purposes, all should be concerned with the legal requirements the appraisal must meet. Assuming an organization desires to serve both purposes and meet the legal requirements, how can it assess how well its performance appraisal systems are doing.[30]

Did You KNOW?

Continuous improvement is difficult without information on how well we are doing now.

Overall Assessment. Before evaluating specific aspects of an organization's performance appraisal system, it may be useful to perform an overall assessment to determine quickly how well the system is doing. This can direct the next level of assessment toward specific areas.[31]

EXHIBIT 20.3

Some Criteria for Assessing Recruitment

STAGE OF ENTRY	TYPE OF CRITERIA
Pre-entry	Total number of applicants Number of minority and female applicants Cost per applicant Time to locate job applicants Time to process job applicants
Offers and hires	Offers extended by source Total number of qualified applicants Number of qualified female, minority group, and disabled applicants Costs of acceptance versus rejection of applicants
Entry	Initial expectations of newcomers Choice of the organization by qualified applicants Cost and time of training new employees Salary levels
Postentry	Attitudes toward job, pay, benefits, supervision, and co-workers Organizational commitment Job performance Tenure of hires Absenteeism Referrals

A fast-start approach for an overall view is for employees, both supervisors and subordinates, to respond to a questionnaire such as the one shown in Exhibit 20.4. As indicated in the scoring instructions, three subcategories (A + B + C) are added for an overall score. The three subcategories correspond to the major purposes of appraisal. Note that the assessment includes administrative features of appraisal—that is, whether performance appraisal records are maintained and how accessible they are. These features facilitate the developmental purpose of performance appraisal.

This questionnaire can give an organization a general picture of how well it is doing with its performance appraisal system. As a guide, scores on the subcategories of 9 or 10 suggest the purpose is being well served. Scores of 4 to 8 suggest average service, while 2 or 3 suggest it is not being served at all. Adding the scores on the three subcategories gives an overall assessment of the purposes of appraisal. Scores of 26-30 suggest the performance appraisal system is doing well, scores 21-25 suggest good, 11-20 average, and less than 11 poor. Average scores or less on the subcategories or overall total indicate room for improvement. They also suggest that specific areas should be assessed in depth to determine the cause of these scores. The HR staff can do this by asking a number of specific questions.

Specific Assessment. The specific assessment of an organization's performance appraisal system requires an examination of the entire system.[32] The following questions can provide an assessment of its specific components:

- What purposes does the organization want its performance appraisal system to serve?
- Do the appraisal forms really get the information to serve these purposes? Are these forms compatible with the jobs for which they are being used—are they job related? That is, are the forms based on behaviors or outcomes that might be included in a critical incidents job analysis?

EXHIBIT 20.4

Organizational Performance Appraisal Questionnaire Evaluation

Respond to the following six statements by indicating the extent to which you agree (or disagree) that the statements accurately describe performance appraisal in your organization. Some statements refer to your experiences in appraising your subordinates' performance; others refer to your experience in being appraised yourself. Try to reflect as accurately as you can the current conditions in your organization based on your experiences.

SA = Strongly Agree A = Agree ? = Neither Agree nor Disagree D = Disagree SD = Strongly Disagree

1. I have found my boss's appraisals to be very helpful in guiding my own career development progress.	SA	A	?	D	SD
2. The appraisal system we have here is of no use to me in my efforts toward developing my subordinates to the fullest extent of their capabilities.	SA	A	?	D	SD
3. Our performance appraisal system generally leaves me even more uncertain about where I stand after my appraisal than beforehand.	SA	A	?	D	SD
4. The appraisal system we use is very useful in helping me to clearly communicate to my subordinates exactly where they stand.	SA	A	?	D	SD
5. When higher levels of management around here are making major decisions about management positions and promotions, they have access to, and make use of, performance appraisal records.	SA	A	?	D	SD
6. In making pay, promotion, transfer, and other administrative personnel decisions, I am not able to obtain past performance appraisal records that could help me to make good decisions.	SA	A	?	D	SD

SCORING

Use the following grid to determine point scores for each item by transferring your responses onto the grid. Place the number in the box at the bottom of each column, then add pairs of columns as indicated.

	Statement Number					
Response	**1**	**2**	**3**	**4**	**5**	**6**
SA	5	1	1	5	5	1
A	4	2	2	4	4	2
?	3	3	3	3	3	3
D	2	4	4	2	2	4
SD	1	5	5	1	1	5

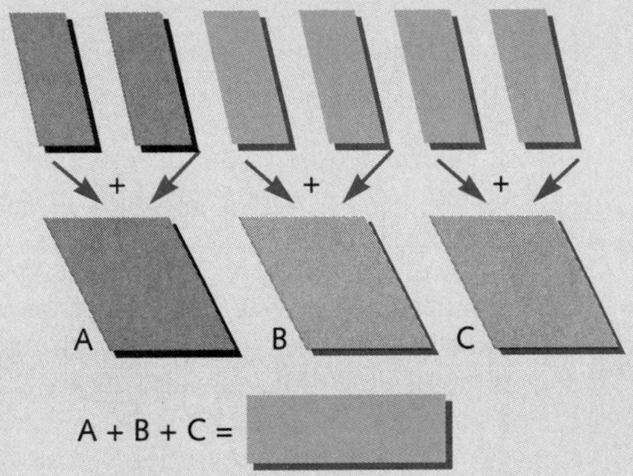

Source: Used by permission of M. Sashkin. Copyright 1981 by M. Sashkin. All rights reserved. See also M. Sashkin, *Assessing Performance Appraisal* (San Diego, CA: University Associates, 1981).

Did You KNOW?

Employees want to:

- **know what is expected**
- **get feedback**
- **be treated fairly**
- **get rewarded**

- Are the appraisal formats designed to minimize errors and ensure consistency?
- Are the processes of the appraisal effective? For example, are the appraisal interviews done effectively? Are goals established? Are they developed jointly? Do superiors and subordinates accept the appraisal process?
- Are superiors rewarded for correctly evaluating and developing their employees? Are they trained in giving feedback, setting goals, and problem-solving techniques? Are they trained to spot performance deficiencies and correctly identify the causes?
- Are the evaluation and developmental components separated? Do the superiors vary their interview styles according to the purpose of the interview?
- Are superiors relatively free from task interference in doing performance appraisal?
- Are the appraisals being implemented correctly? What procedures have been set up to ensure that the appraisals are done correctly? What supporting materials are available to aid superiors in appraising their subordinates?
- Do methods exist for reviewing and evaluating the effectiveness of the total system? Do systematic procedures exist for gathering data to measure how well the goals and objectives are being met?

By addressing these questions and taking corrective action where necessary, an organization's performance appraisal system is more likely to serve its purposes and the broader organizational goals of managing human resources effectively. For an organization just beginning to implement a performance appraisal system, the implications of all these questions should be understood and taken into account in the initial performance appraisal system design.[33]

Monetary Compensation

In assessing how effectively an organization administers its compensation program, the following major purposes of monetary compensation must be kept in mind:

In assessment, it is important to start with the purposes being served.

- Attracting potentially qualified employees
- Motivating employees
- Retaining qualified employees
- Administering pay within legal constraints
- Attaining HR plans and strategic business objectives

If an organization hopes to achieve these purposes, employees generally need to be satisfied with their pay. This means the pay levels should be competitive, employees should perceive internal pay equity, and the compensation program should be properly administered.[34] It also means that compensation practices must adhere to the various state and federal wage and hour laws, including comparable worth considerations.

Consequently, an organization's monetary compensation can be assessed by comparing its pay levels with other organizations, by analyzing the validity of its job evaluation method, by measuring employee perceptions of pay equity and performance-pay linkages, and by determining individual pay levels within job and across jobs.

Monetary compensation can also be assessed by how well it helps attain strategic business objectives. Lincoln Electric has a compensation system tied to the company's profits. In addition to having high motivation to produce, Lincoln Electric workers rarely quit. Their turnover rate is less than 1 percent. The result of Lincoln's compensation system is a cost-efficient competitive advantage that allows it to price its products below competitors, yet maintain equal, if not better, quality. Other companies also use their compensation systems strategically. For example, TRW and Hewlett-Packard use compensation to drive their search for innovative products and services.

Hewlett-Packard stimulates entrepreneurial behavior in its project leaders by tying more rewards to their success. Successful project leaders are given banquets, stock options, and personal computers. At TRW, units or teams are given credit for sales generated in another department in return for helping that department. TRW fosters innovation by stimulating interdependence through its compensation practices. These companies get what they pay for: a steady stream of product and service improvements and enhancements that help them stand alone among their competitors, hence a strong competitive advantage.[35]

Performance-Based Pay Systems

Regardless of organizational conditions and considerations, performance-based pay systems can be assessed on the basis of three criteria: 1) the relationship between performance and pay—that is, the time between performance and the administration of the pay (the actual time and the time as perceived by employees); 2) how well the plan minimizes the perceived negative consequences of good performance, such as social ostracism; and 3) whether it contributes to the perception that rewards other than pay (such as cooperation and recognition) also stem from good performance. The more the plan minimizes the perceived negative consequences and the more it contributes to the perception that other good rewards are also tied to performance, the more motivating it is likely to be. Exhibit 20.5 presents an evaluation of individual, team, and organization-wide plans based on these three criteria.

Exhibit 20.5 uses three objective measures to determine the level of job performance to be rewarded: sales or units made (productivity), cost effectiveness or savings below budget, and traditional superior's ratings. As discussed in Chapter 12, the more objective measures generally have higher credibility, are more valid, and are more visible and verifiable than the traditional supervisor ratings. Consequently, the objective measures (productivity and cost effectiveness) are more likely to link pay to job performance than they are to minimize negative side effects. This evaluation is based on the notion that people do what is rewarded. More objective measures tend to clarify what is rewarded and what is not. This may produce more keen competition with other workers, result in more social ostracism, and lead workers to perceive that good job performance may reduce the work available to them.[36]

Indirect Compensation

Several purposes of indirect compensation were listed in Chapter 16. The impact of the indirect benefits in fulfilling these purposes is half of the equation for measuring the effectiveness of the benefits package. The other half involves determining the costs. Determining the effectiveness of the indirect benefit program also involves a comparison of the costs and benefits.[37]

Assessing the benefits and costs of providing benefits is still a major concern of many companies.

An organization can determine the dollar value of the costs of indirect compensation in the following ways:

- Total costs of benefits annually for all employees
- Cost per employee per year divided by the number of hours worked
- Percentage of payroll divided by annual payroll
- Cost per employee per hour divided by employee hours worked

EXHIBIT 20.5

Effectiveness of Performance-Based Pay Systems

TYPE OF PLAN	PERFORMANCE MEASURE	TIE PAY TO PERFORMANCE	MINIMIZE NEGATIVE SIDE EFFECTS	TIE OTHER REWARDS TO PERFORMANCE
Merit				
Individual	Productivity	+2	0	0
	Cost effectiveness	+1	0	0
	Superior's rating	+1	0	+1
Team	Productivity	+1	0	+1
	Cost effectiveness	+1	0	+1
	Superior's rating	+1	0	+1
Organizational	Productivity	+1	0	+1
	Cost effectiveness	+1	0	+1
	Profit	0	0	+1
Incentive				
Individual	Productivity	+3	−2	0
	Cost effectiveness	+2	−1	0
	Superior's rating	+2	−1	+1
Team	Productivity	+2	0	+1
	Cost effectiveness	+2	0	+1
	Superior's rating	+2	0	+1
Organizational	Productivity	+2	0	+1
	Cost effectiveness	+2	0	+1
	Profit	+1	0	+1

Source: E.E. Lawler, III, *Pay and Organizational Effectiveness*, p. 165. © Copyright 1971 by McGraw-Hill Book Company. Reprinted with permission.

These costs can then be compared with the benefits such as reduced turnover, less absenteeism, or an enhanced company image among employees. The dollar value of these benefits (for example, reduced absenteeism) can then be determined, enabling the organization to compare its benefits costs directly against its benefits savings.

Training and Development Evaluation Methods and Designs

Evaluation Methods. Many ways of evaluating training and development programs have been proposed. Among the many options are changes in productivity, attitude survey results (covering, for example, satisfaction with supervisor, job satisfaction, stress, role conflict, and knowledge of work procedures), cost savings, benefit gains, and attitudes toward training.[38]

While different evaluation methods have been proposed through the years, most training experts agree that evaluation should depend on the criteria to be measured (the questions to be answered):

1. **Reaction to training.** Did the trainees like the program? Was the instruction clear and helpful? Do they believe that they learned the material?
2. **Learning.** Did they acquire the knowledge and skills that were taught? Can they talk about things they couldn't talk about before? Can they demonstrate appropriate behaviors in training (role play)?
3. **Behavior or performance change.** Can trainees now do things they couldn't do before (for example, negotiate, conduct an appraisal interview)? Can they demonstrate new behaviors on the job? Is performance on the job better?

4. **Produce results.** Were there tangible results in terms of productivity, cost savings, response time, quality or quantity of job performance? Did the training program have utility?

The choice of criteria influences the training evaluation method to be used. For example, a short attitude survey could be used to assess the response of trainees to the course. However, such a survey would not provide information regarding learning, behavior, and results. In fact, when learning has been stressful or difficult, the trainees' reaction may even be negative.

If the objective is to assess what was learned, then a paper-and-pencil test may be appropriate. Additionally, it is possible to analyze the content of responses to such training exercises as in-basket tests, role plays, or case analyses. While this may indicate that learning has occurred, it will not reveal whether learning has been transferred to the job.

To assess whether behavior or performance has changed, output measures, performance evaluation reports, and employee attitude surveys provide better information. For example, if employees report more positive attitudes toward supervisory communications *after* they complete an interpersonal skills program, it may be deduced (assuming other hypotheses can be ruled out) that the training resulted in behavioral change. Finally, bottom-line results might be assessed by examining work-group or unit output measures.

Evaluation Designs. Once the criteria for assessing an HR program or activity have been selected, consideration must be given to the manner by which the criteria will be evaluated. The alternatives we have are called **evaluation designs.** There are three major categories of evaluation designs—pre-experimental, quasi-experimental, and experimental—and they each offer advantages and disadvantages in accuracy of information gained, ease of use, and costs in administration.[39] Data collection techniques that can be used include surveys, interviews and organizational records.

Evaluation designs are used to determine the impact of an HR program or activity.

The most rigorous evaluation design is the **experimental design.** As shown in Exhibit 20.6 there are two types of experimental designs. Both of these use the random assignment of individuals to groups to be tested (T_1 = time and T_2 = time two) and not all groups receive a treatment (X = any program being implemented to produce change).[40] Evaluation using the experimental design allows the training manager to be more confident that:

Experimental design is the most rigorous form of evaluation design to determine the impact of an HR program or activity.

- A change has taken place—e.g., that employee productivity has increased
- The change is caused by the program or HR activity
- A similar change could be expected if the program were done again with other employees

Because of many organizational constraints preventing random assignment, however, the training manager is generally not able to use the experimental design and must settle for a moderately rigorous **quasi-experimental design**.

Quasi-experimental design is a less rigorous form of evaluation design to determine the impact of an HR program or activity.

In the quasi-experimental design random assignment is not done. Although using the experimental design is desirable, many organizations find it difficult to randomly assign employees to training programs. Organizations generally want all employees in a section trained, not just a few who are randomly selected. Consequently, the quasi-experimental design is the more likely evaluation that organizations use. In both classes of quasi-experimental design shown in Exhibit 20.6, however, multiple measures (T_S) are taken. In the time-series several measures are taken before the treatment and after. In the nonequivalent control groups, two groups receive multiple measurement, but only one receives a treatment. But again, though to a lesser extent than the experimental design, this design is time consuming and constrained by realities of organizations. Thus the **pre-experimental design** looks most attractive to companies.

Pre-experimental design is the least rigorous form of evaluation design to determine the impact of an HR program or activity.

EXHIBIT 20.6

The Three Major Classes of Evaluation Designs Used to Determine Program Effectiveness

PRE-EXPERIMENTAL	QUASI-EXPERIMENTAL	EXPERIMENTAL
1. One-shot case study design	1. Time-series design	1. Pretest/post-test control group design
X T_2	$T_1T_2T_3$ X $T_4T_5T_6$	T_1 X T_2 T_1 T_2
2. One-group pretest/post-test design	2. Nonequivalent control groups	2. Solomon four-group design
T_1 X T_2	T_1 X T_2 T_1 T_2	T_1 X T_2 T_1 T_2 X T_2 T_2

Source: Based on I. Goldstein, *Training: Program Development and Evaluation*, 2nd ed. (Monterey, CA: Brooks/Cole, 1986), 157–167.

In the pre-experimental designs shown in Exhibit 20.6, the two classes are much simpler and far less costly and far less time consuming than the other two designs. In the one-shot design, measurement is done only once and in the one-group pre-test/post-test only one group is used. But with the ease and low cost come less accuracy and confidence in measuring change that may have been the result of a training program (or any other program to produce change). These, however, are the realities of organizations and reflect the constraints and trade-offs HR professionals face daily. Similar, though unique, realities are evident in collective bargaining.

Collective Bargaining

Because of the unique nature of the collective bargaining process, statistical, hard-number evaluation designs may not be appropriate or easy to use. Rather, the effectiveness of the entire collective bargaining process may better be measured by the extent to which each party attains its goals, but even this approach has its difficulties. Because the two groups' goals are incompatible in many cases and can therefore lead to conflicting estimates of effectiveness, a more useful measure may be the quality of the system used to resolve conflict. Conflict is more apparent in the collective bargaining process, where failure to resolve the issues typically leads to strikes. Another measure of effectiveness is the success of the grievance process, or the ability to resolve issues developing out of the bargaining agreement.

Effectiveness of Negotiations. Because the purpose of negotiations is to achieve an agreement, this agreement becomes an overall measure of bargaining effectiveness. A healthy and effective bargaining process encourages the discussion of issues and problems and their subsequent resolution at the bargaining table. In addition, the effort required to reach agreement is a measure of how well the process is working. Some indications of this effort are the duration of negotiations, the outcome of member ratification votes, the frequency and duration of strikes, the use of mediation and arbitration, the need for government intervention, and the resulting quality of union-management relations (whether conflict or cooperation exists). Certainly joint programs for productivity and quality of working life improvements could be regarded as successes in this venture.

Effectiveness of Grievance Procedures. How successful a grievance procedure is may be assessed from different perspectives. Management may view the number of grievances filed and the number settled in management's favor as measures of effectiveness. Unions may also consider the number of grievances, but from their point of view, a larger rather than a smaller number may be considered more successful.

Although the views of management and the union may differ, an overall set of measures to gauge grievance procedure effectiveness can be related to the disagreements between managers and employees. Measures that might be included are frequency of grievances; the level in the grievance procedure at which grievances are usually settled; the frequency of strikes or slowdowns during the term of the labor agreements; the rates of absenteeism, turnover, and sabotage; and the necessity for government intervention.

The success of arbitration is often judged by the acceptability of the decisions, the satisfaction of the parties, the degree of innovation, and the absence of bias in either direction. The effectiveness of any third-party intervention rests in part on how successfully strikes are avoided because the motivation for such intervention is precisely to avert this extreme form of conflict resolution.

Current Trends

LEARNING OBJECTIVE 5

Describe the current trends in HR data, information, and assessment systems.

The rapid rate of change in this area means that issues come up, get resolved, and the technology moves on, often at a mind-boggling rate. And this becomes an issue itself. Keeping up with the rate of change is an underlying trend that will not itself change or disappear. Another trend is securing the company's HRIS.

HRIS Managerial Competencies

This is a new era for the HRIS manager, the person who runs the department's data and information system. The HRIS manager is now seen not as someone concerned with how efficiently the department can store and retrieve data and information, but as someone who is a strategic partner and who manages organizational change.

Typically, when organizations first created their HRIS, they needed a specialist to manage the area; it eventually became a separate unit within the HR department with its own HRIS manager. Over the years, the role of this manager has changed from a project manager to a systems manager and now a strategic change partner. This evolution is described in the feature, "Managing Human Resources: Change at HRIS," and it parallels that of the HR manager discussed in Chapter 2. Not surprisingly, these role changes have produced the same need for new competencies in both the HR manager and the HRIS manager.

Today's HRIS manager needs a broader strategic understanding of the business. An awareness of the global environment and how the organization can be global and act local is crucial. The HRIS can enable the organization to operate as a global organization and at the same time remain sensitive to local conditions and needs. It can enable managers worldwide to tap into a database with information on potential managers for operations in distant countries, without even knowing the candidates. A database on career information can enable individuals to compete for an organization's jobs worldwide because they can be known to the company's managers all over the world. Thus, in the process of constructing and operating an HRIS, the manager needs to be familiar with the global needs of the business and how an HRIS can assist it in being successful.

Information Security

According to Marc Tanzer, president of BCI/Information Security in Portland, "When corporate spies want confidential information, they often infiltrate HR departments first. A well-structured information-security program can keep spies

MANAGING HUMAN RESOURCES

Change at HRIS

Having an HRIS manager within the organization was a relatively new concept in the early 1970s. The role of this position was largely to capture basic personnel data on homegrown systems. The automation of employee files, basic head-count reports, and such information as EEO compliances represented the HRIS mission and guided internal development projects. As package mainframe-based systems became readily available, the capacity and functional capabilities of the HRIS expanded. The HRIS manager's role shifted from *project manager* (responsible for internal systems development) to *systems manager* (responsible for centralized processing of reports, data integrity, and other administrative functions). Then came the microcomputer revolution of the 1980s, which permitted decentralized access, shared processing, data ownership at the source, and the extension of HRIS data and processes to new constituencies. This revolution turned many HRIS managers into consultants.

Now a new era is at hand, as the human resource department and its systems support have become strategic partners in managing change. With this evolutionary stage, as with the others, comes the need for HRIS management to learn new skills and competencies to remain assets to their organizations.[41]

from obtaining your company's secrets."[42] The names of employees, where they work, and what they do can be valuable information to other companies, especially competitors. Such information can identify employees and what company projects they are working on, and recruiting efforts can then be attempted to lure these people away. This, of course, goes on, and organizations that value openness and access to information are especially vulnerable. If companies are to empower people, they often need to have this type of openness and information accessibility. It is hard to put a limit or restriction on it without changing this culture of openness and trust. Companies such as Tandem Computers in Cupertino, California, handle this concern by:

- Creating an awareness among managers and employees that there is a potential problem with others gaining access to company information and data
- Tightening up telephone security so that callers need to identify themselves and the right screening questions are asked
- Weeding out bogus job candidates (that is, those who are only going through the motions to gain access to information)
- Adding more restrictions in confidentiality agreements (when individuals join the firm, they can be asked to sign agreements not to reveal company secrets to others at any time, even if they leave)
- Classifying and restricting access to information to groups of individuals on a need-to-know basis

Not only can these programs limit information leakage, they can also protect the individual employee from unauthorized people obtaining personal information—not a trivial thing today in light of rising employee violence and credit-card scams.

While some say that restricting the type and amount of information collected reduces the potential for invasion of privacy, this has to be balanced against the HR department's need for information for its various programs. Family-friendly activities such as childcare, eldercare, and employee assistance programs cannot take place without a sound database. Nor can the numerous legal obligations that have to be met be fulfilled without an effective HRIS. Some balance must be struck, the balance must be struck, the latest security must be used, and the environment must be continually scanned for the latest computer hacking scams—the best defense here is a good offense!

Summary

For organizations to succeed today, they need to be managed systematically and scientifically. That is, they need to be managed with the latest, most effective data, information, and assessment tools and techniques. In addition, a culture needs to be created to support the use of these tools and techniques, and employees' skills must be developed so that they are able to use the system. All of this falls within the responsibility of the HR department.

The success of the HR department in developing systems for collecting and utilizing information and data, however, depends on their partnership with line managers and employees. Line managers must be willing to give the data and information and then use it; employees need to be willing to learn how to use it and then be willing to change and adapt; and HR professionals must be willing to build an HRIS that will serve the needs of the organization and accomplish their goals more effectively. The HRIS can be used to develop job-related tests so that only the applicants most likely to be successful are selected. An effective HRIS can assist in training employees so that they are better able to diagnose problems and develop effective solutions.

HR professionals, line managers, and employees can and must work together to effectively assess just how well the organization is managing its human resources. Through systematic approaches to assessment, these groups can carefully evaluate the organization's success in all its HR programs and activities. For example, many companies use annual, confidential surveys to assess how well they are doing regarding job satisfaction, harassment, or diversity. The results of these surveys then establish benchmarks that can assess programs for continual improvements; an HRIS is crucial to this effort.

As organizations build substantial HR databases, the potential for misuse and abuse also increases. Consequently, the HRIS staff has a special responsibility to secure these systems; yet the goal of security must be met without limiting the organization's capacity to rapidly and correctly adapt to changing conditions. A good and successful balancing of these somewhat conflicting needs is beneficial to both the organization and the individual. Thus, as we go forward in our efforts to better manage human resources, we will see HR professionals at the forefront in the development, utilization, and protection of HR data, information, and assessment systems.

Key Concepts

assessment systems
computer hardware
computer software
data
data and information systems
doing the right things
doing things right
experimental design
evaluation designs
information
Internet
organizational surveys
pre-experimental design
qualitative measures
quantitative measures
quasi-experimental design

Review and Discussion Questions

1. What are the purposes of HR data, information, and assessment systems?
2. Describe how computer technology and HRIS help line managers fulfill their HR responsibilities.
3. Describe how a computerized HRIS can be used in the HR research process.
4. Should companies be limited in the amount of personal information they can keep on an HRIS?
5. What are the key steps in conducting an organizational survey?
6. How can performance appraisal systems be assessed?
7. How can performance-based pay systems be assessed?
8. How can the collective bargaining process be assessed?
9. What are the new competencies for the HRIS manager?
10. What is the relationship between computer technology and the HR department's efforts to be more customer-oriented?

PROJECTS, EXERCISES & CASES

End-of-Text Projects

Lincoln Electric

1. Why would Lincoln Electric likely do an assessment of its HR activities?
2. For what HR activities does Lincoln Electric do assessment?
3. For what activities could or should Lincoln Electric do assessment, if it is not already?

Nordstrom

1. Why would Nordstrom likely do an assessment of its HR activities?
2. For what HR activities does Nordstrom do assessment?
3. For what activities could or should Nordstrom do assessment, if it is not already?

Field Projects

1. Interview at least three HR managers, and discuss the extent to which they assess the effectiveness or efficiency of their HR activities. Report to the class and compare results.
2. Conduct a search on the Internet to find the Websites of at least five large companies. Report to the class the types of human resource information provided at these sites.

Case: CompuTest, Inc.: The Case of Alternative Personnel Selection Strategies

In order to answer the case questions on CompuTest, Inc., you will need to refer to the materials in Appendix C where the types of validation studies are discussed.

Fiscal 1995 was a landmark year of development and growth for CompuTest, Inc. As Jerome J. Rosner, president, indicated in a report to the stockholders, "Our company emerged to become a major force in the growing field of computerized testing." It was a year that saw the company grow from 350 to over 460 employees. Although a number of people were added to the marketing, sales, and research opera-

VISIT THE LIBRARY

Workforce Online

1. Enter your Web browser.
2. Enter HR Headquarters.
3. Enter the HR Library.
4. Find and review the following article with the "Research Center":

   A New HRIS in Wake County Streamlines HR
5. Return to your homepage.

tions, the largest numbers were selected for clerical and administrative positions.

To date, the company has principally targeted individual mental health practitioners, psychiatric hospitals, and other medical professionals as the best markets for its products. The company expects these specialized markets to continue to represent a substantial part of their revenue base through 1998. Thereafter, CompuTest expects its sources of revenue to shift as they aggressively enter the vast industrial market. In business and industry, thousands of ability tests are administered annually. In the past, these tests were given to employees and prospective employees by traditional paper-and-pencil methods—a long, cumbersome, and expensive process. As Paul Lefebre, the company's manager of HR research states, "CompuTest's current and future testing products have the capability of revolutionizing the area of employee screening with new technologies never before available in the HR field."

One of the newest products developed for the industrial market is a comprehensive battery of computer-administered clerical tests. The company, however, does not want to introduce these tests into the market prior to gathering evidence concerning the predictive effectiveness of the tests. Paul Lefebre is currently searching for potential sites to conduct criterion-related validity studies. One place to start is his own firm!

Recently, Lane Carpenter, the director of human resources, has brought a troubling problem to the attention of President Rosner; many complaints are being raised about the quality of clerical personnel being selected with the company's verbal ability test. She has informed President Rosner that although 170 clerical and administrative personnel have been selected with this test, the company has not conducted a criterion-related validation study to evaluate its usefulness. President Rosner has therefore called a meeting with Lane Carpenter and Paul Lefebre.

Jerome Rosner: As you both are aware, we are facing a number of complaints about the quality and quantity of clerical job performance throughout our company. I would also like to bring to your attention that we have a projected need for 50 additional clerical personnel in our current job categories by the end of 1998. This situation requires us to closely examine our current clerical selection procedures and possibly consider alternatives. I would also like us to reconsider the performance appraisal form we are currently using. Our performance appraisal system does not seem to incorporate some of the major duties or tasks that our clerical personnel are being asked to perform. Lane, you have expressed some concerns about the currently used verbal ability test for selecting clerical personnel.

Lane Carpenter: Yes, I am concerned not only with how good this test is at screening potentially successful clerical personnel, but also with how we would defend such a test if challenged in court. I assume you are aware that this test was developed and adopted only on the basis of a content-oriented validation study.

Jerome Rosner: Yes, Paul has informed me of the strategy used in developing the verbal ability test. Paul, you also mentioned in a previous discussion that we might be able to conduct another type of validation study for this test.

Paul Lefebre: We currently have a sufficient number of clerical personnel with verbal ability test scores and performance ratings to conduct a criterion-related validation study. And, since we have just completed a comprehensive job analysis of all clerical positions and expected openings, we can now revise our clerical performance appraisal system to more accurately reflect the tasks they perform.

Jerome Rosner: Does this job analysis also indicate the abilities necessary to effectively perform these tasks?

Paul Lefebre: Yes, the job analysis clearly identifies the required abilities, and it indicates that although the major duties differ across some of our clerical jobs, the entry-level ability requirements for all of our clerical jobs are similar.

Lane Carpenter: If the ability requirements are similar, we might be able to conduct a criterion-related validation study for the verbal ability test with our current clerical employees.

Paul Lefebre: That is a definite possibility. It might also be helpful for us to consider validating our newly developed computerized clerical ability test battery. That is, we could gather some evidence for its predictive effectiveness in our own company prior to marketing it. Of course, we would have to determine which tests were appropriate or should be considered for a validation study here.

Jerome Rosner: Paul, that sounds like a good idea. If we are going to successfully market our computerized testing products, we should also be willing to use them. An important question related to your suggestion is how our computer-administered clerical test battery would compare with our currently used verbal ability test. Can we improve our predictions of who will turn out to be successful workers? If we decide to replace our current test with a battery of clerical tests, would it be cost beneficial? Paul, I would appreciate your validating our current verbal ability test and the computer-administered clerical test battery and how we might compare these alternatives.

Case Questions

1. What is the difference between the test being developed on the basis of a content-oriented validation study versus a criterion-related validity study?
2. Does CompuTest first have to change its performance appraisal form before doing a criterion-related validation study?
3. On what basis will Paul Lefebre go about determining the tests that would be appropriate to include in the computerized clerical test battery?
4. How should Paul Lefebre go about validating the firm's verbal ability test and the clerical test battery and comparing them?

VISIT THE LIBRARY

Exercise 1

1. Using your Web browser, enter Cornell University's Employment Law Documents.
2. Click on the topic "Workplace Safety" under the heading "Employment Law."
3. After reading this section, return to your homepage.

Exercise 2

The purpose of this exercise is to introduce you to the Occupational Safety and Health Administration's (OSHA's) homepage, and to some of the programs and services that OSHA provides.

1. Go to OSHA's homepage: **http://www.osha.gov**
2. Select "Information about OSHA."
3. Select "OSHA's Mission" and read this section.
4. Go back to OSHA's homepage and select "Programs and Services."
5. After browsing through the list of OSHA's programs and services, select "OSHA Consultation Service," and read this section.
6. Go back to your homepage.

Exercise 3

The Office of the American Workplace (OAW) is a branch of the Department of Labor that studies and promotes cooperative labor-management relations. OAW provides a list of companies that have adopted innovative workplace practices and cooperative labor management relations. This list, which contains descriptions of the organizations and their practices, is readily accessible through the Internet.

1. Go to OAW's homepage: **http://www.fed.org**
2. Use the alphabetical index to browse through the list of best-practice companies.
3. Select any one of the companies to read a best-practice description.
4. Go back to your homepage.

Chapter 20 Endnotes

1. Excerpt from "Catch the Wave as HR Goes Online," by S. Greengard, copyright July 1995.

2. Ibid.

3. M. Kavanagh, H. G. Guental, and S. I. Tannenbaum, *Human Resource Management Information Systems* (Boston: PWS-Kent, 1990); A. J. Walker, *Handbook of Human Resource Information Systems* (New York: McGraw-Hill, 1993); and V. R. Ceriello, *Human Resource Management Systems: Strategies, Tactics, and Techniques* (Lexington, MA: Lexington Books, 1991).

4. G. Flynn, "A New HRIS in Wake County Streamlines HR," *Personnel Journal* (May 1994): 137–142; S. Greengard, "The Next Generation," *Personnel Journal* (March 1994): 40–46; J. F. Stright, Jr. "Strategic Goals Guide HRMS Development," *Personnel Journal* (Sept. 1993): 68–79.

5. "Personnel Shop Talk," *Bulletin to Management* (October 26, 1995): 338. Reprinted with permission by the Bureau of National Affairs (Tel. 1-800-372-1033).

6. S. Greengard, "Client/Server: HR's Helping Hand?" *Personnel Journal* (May 1996): 90–98; S. Greengard, "Privacy: Entitlement or Illusion?" *Personnel Journal* (May 1996): 74–88; S. Greengard, "When HRMS Goes Global: Managing the Data Highway," *Personnel Journal* (June 1995): 90–106; P. Rosenfield and J. E. Edwards, "Automated System Assesses Equal Opportunity," *Personnel Journal* (September 1994): 99–103; "Mission Impossible: Choosing A New HRIS to Meet Unique and Demanding Business Requirements," *Solutions* (January 1994): 10–11; "Using New Technologies for Innovative Solutions," *Solutions* (February 1994): 28–31; "HRMS Redefines Its Heritage," *Solutions* (February 1994): 20–21; "Technology Solutions: Globalization: A Human Resources Mandate," *Solutions* (January 1994): 62–63; R. J. Thurston and J. R. Jones, "Health-care Reform Warrants HRIS Updates," *Personnel Journal* (May 1994): 43–45; B. Croft, "Use Technology to Manage Your Expats," *Personnel Journal* (December 1995): 113–117; S. Greengard, "How Technology Is Advancing HR," *Personnel Journal* (Sept. 1993): 80–90; M. Alpert, "CD-ROM: The Next PC Revolution," *Fortune* (June 29, 1992): 68–73; E. I. Schwartz, "The Power of Software," *Business Week* (June 14, 1993): 76.

7. Stright, "Strategic Goals Guide HRMS Development" p. 71.

8. Greengard, "Catch the Wave as HR Goes Online."

9. Ibid.

10. J. J. Laabs, "OLIVER: A Twist on Communication," *Personnel Journal* (Sept. 1991): 79–82; "Compensation Advances into a New Decade: Report on 1990 ACA National Conference," *Bulletin to Management* (Nov. 1990): 345; "Computer Use Rising in HR Departments," *Bulletin to Management* (June 15, 1989): 189; R. J. Sahl, "Get it Together! Integrating the HR Department," *Personnel* (Feb. 1989): 39–45.

11. C. Bovier, "How a High-Tech Training System Crashed and Burned," *Training* (Aug. 1993): 26–29.

12. "Employees Need Maps for the Information Highway," *Bulletin to Management* (October 12, 1995): 321; K. Allan, "Computer Courses Ensure Uniform Training," *Personnel Journal* (Jan. 1993): 57; and B. C. Herniter, E. Carmel, and J. Nunamaker, Jr., "Computers Improve the Efficiency of the Negotiation Process," *Personnel Journal* (April 1993): 93–99.

13. M. J. Dreyfuss, "Catching the Computer Wave," *Fortune* (Sept. 26, 1988): 78–82; R. Tetzelli, "The Internet and Your Business," *Fortune* (March 7, 1994): 86–96.

14. J. F. Coates, "An Environmental Scan: Projecting Future Resource Trends," *Human Resource Planning* (Dec. 1987): 219–289.

15. J. Main, "The Winning Corporation," *Fortune* (Sept. 26, 1988): 50–56; S. Tully, "The Modular Corporation," *Fortune* (Feb. 8, 1993): 106–115.

16. Coates, "An Environmental Scan: Projecting Future Human Resource Trends."

17. M. Mandel and C. Farrell, "The Technology Payoff," *Business Week* (June 14, 1993): 57–73; S. Sherman, "The New Computer Revolution," *Fortune* (June 14, 1993): 56–80; J. Byrne, R. Brandt and O. Port, "The Virtual Corporation," *Business Week* (Feb. 8, 1993): 98–102.

18. S. D. Solomon, "Use Technology to Manage People," *Inc.* (May 1990): 124.

19. Main, "The Winning Corporation," 82. See also J. Byrne, "The Horizontal Corporation," *Business Week* (Dec. 20, 1993): 76–81.

20. From *Business Week* (May 16, 1994): 8.

21. R. B. Dunham and F. J. Smith, *Organization Surveys* (Glenview, IL: Scott, Foresman, 1979): 91–97. See also W. H. Read, "Gathering Opinion On-Line," *HR Magazine* (Jan. 1991): 51–53.

22. P. T. Kilborn, "Workers Using Computers Find a Supervisor Inside," *New York Times* (Dec. 23, 1990): 1, 18L. See also "Surveillance and Searches: Reducing the Risks," *Bulletin to Management* (Nov. 7, 1991): 345; *Federal Government Information Technology: Electronic Surveillance and Civil Liberties* (Washington, D.C.: Office of Technology Assessment, OTA-CIT-293, Oct. 1985); *The Electronic Supervisor: New Technology, New Tensions,* OTA-CIT-333 (Washington, D.C.: U.S. Government Printing Office, Sept. 1987).

23. Ibid. See also N. J. Beutell and A. J. Walker, "HR Information Systems," in R. S. Schuler, *Managing HR in the Information Age* (Washington, D.C.: BNA, 1991): 167–203.

24. "Dodging Cyberspace Pitfalls," *Bulletin to Management* (October 12, 1995): 328.

25. M. E. Cashman and J. C. McElroy, "Evaluating the HR Function," *HR Magazine* (Jan. 1991): 70–73; M. Mercer,

Turning Your Human Resources Department into a Profit Center (New York: American Management Association, 1989); B. R. Ellig, "Controlling HR Costs," *Personnel* (April 1990): 20–23; W. F. Cascio, *Costing Human Resources: The Financial Impact of Behavior in Organizations,* 3rd ed. (Boston: PWS-Kent, 1991); D. Ulrich, "Assessing Human Resource Effectiveness: Stakeholder, Utility and Relationship Approaches," *Human Resource Planning* 12:4 (1989): 301–316; L. Dyer, *Human Resource Management: Evolving Roles and Responsibilities* (Washington, D.C.: BNA Books, 1988): 187–227; J. Fitz-enz, *Human Values Management: The Value-Adding Human Resource Management Strategy for the 1990s* (San Francisco: Jossey-Bass, 1990); A. S. Tsui, "A Multiple-Constituency Model of Effectiveness: An Empirical Examination at the Human Resource Subunit Level," *Administrative Science Quarterly 35* (1990): 458–483.

26. Greengard, "Catch the Wave as HR Goes Online."

27. T. Jackson and A. Vitber, "Career Development, Part 1: Career and Entrepreneurship," *Personnel* (Feb. 1987): 12–17.

28. R. A. Ash and E. L. Levine, *Personnel* (Nov.-Dec. 1980): 53–59; E. L. Levine, R. A. Ash, and N. Bennett, "Exploratory Comparative Study of Four Job Analysis Methods," *Journal of Applied Psychology* (1980): 524–535; E. L. Levine, R. A. Ash, and F. Sistrunk, "Evaluation of Job Analysis Methods by Experienced Job Analysts," *Academy of Management Journal* (1983): 339–348.

29. F. Krystofiak, J. M. Newman, and G. Anderson, "A Quantified Approach to Measurement of Job Content: Procedures and Payoffs," *Personnel Psychology* (Summer 1979): 341–357.

30. The following assessment discussion relates to aspects of the total performance appraisal system generally. Specific parts of the performance appraisal system are discussed but not in detail. For a detailed discussion of some parts, see F. Landy and J. Far, "Performance Ratings," *Psychological Bulletin* 87 (1980): 72–107; F. Landy, J. L. Barnes-Farrel, R. J. Vance, and J. W. Steele, "Statistical Control of Halo Error in Performance Ratings," *Journal of Applied Psychology 65* (1980): 501–506.

31. See M. Sashkin, "Appraising Appraisal: Ten Lessons From Research for Practice," *Organizational Dynamics* (Winter 1981): 37–50.

32. M. Beer, "Performance Appraisal: Dilemmas and Possibilities," *Organizational Dynamics* (Winter 1981): 26.

33. R. I. Lazar, "Performance Appraisal: What Does the Future Hold?" *Personnel Administrator* (July 1980): 69–73; A. M. Morrison and M. E. Kranz, "The Shape of Performance Appraisal in the Coming Decade," *Personnel* (July-Aug. 1981): 12–22.

34. A "properly administered" compensation program implies several qualities of total compensation: the job evaluation process is valid; pay is administered in a nondiscriminatory way; compensation policies are communicated to be understood; the administrative costs are contained; it has sufficient motivational value; and it is supported by top management.

35. E. E. Lawler III, "The Strategic Design of Reward Systems," *Readings in Personnel and Human Resources Management,* 2nd ed., R. S. Schuler and S. A. Youngblood, eds. (St. Paul, MN: West, 1984): 253–269; L. L. Cummings, "Compensation, Culture and Motivation: A Systems Perspective," *Organizational Dynamics* (Winter 1984): 33–44.

36. M. Lerner, "Measuring Pay Costs in Your Organization Against Pay in Other Organizations," *Personnel* (Aug. 1988): 70–73.

37. R. B. Dunham and R. A. Formisano, "Designing and Evaluating Employee Benefit Systems," *Personnel Administrator* (April 1982): 29–36.

38. For an extensive description of training and development assessment, see J. Fitz-enz, "Yes...You Can Weigh Training's Value," *Training* (July 1994): 54–58; M. J. Burke and R. R. Day, "A Cumulative Study of the Effectiveness of Managerial Training," *Journal of Applied Psychology* (1986): 232–245; "Cost-Effective Training Techniques," *Bulletin to Management* (Aug. 26, 1986): 284; H. E. Fisher and R. Weinberg, "Make Training Accountable: Assess Its Impact," *Personnel Journal* (Jan. 1988): 73–74; J. Fitz-enz, "Proving the Value of Training," *Personnel* (March 1988): 17–23; J. K. Ford and S. P. Wroten, "Introducing New Methods for Conducting Training Evaluation and for Linking Training Evaluation to Program Redesign," *Personnel Psychology* (Winter 1984): 651–666.

39. F. O. Hoffman, "A Responsive Training Department Cuts Costs," *Personnel Journal* (Feb. 1984): 48–53; D. L. Kirkpatrick, "Four Steps to Measuring Training Effectiveness"; H. W. Smith and C. E. George, "Evaluating Internal Advanced Management Programs"; S. B. Wehrenberg, "Evaluation of Training: Part I," *Personnel Journal* (Aug. 1983): 608–610; S. B. Wehrenberg, "Evaluation of Training: Part II," *Personnel Journal* (Sept. 1983): 698–702.

40. Excerpt from "New Competencies Define the HRIS Manager's Future Role," by J. Pasqualetto, copyright January 1993.

41. Ibid.

42. M. Tanzer, "Keep Spies Out of Your Company," *Personnel Journal* (May 1993): 45–51. See also T. Hunter, "How Client/Server Is Reshaping the HRIS," *Personnel Journal* (July 1992): 38–46; J. J. Laabs, "Electronic Campus Captures Apple's Corporate Memory," *Personnel Journal* (Nov. 1993): 104–109.

THE LINCOLN ELECTRIC COMPANY

This case was written by Arthur Sharplin and appears in R.S. Schuler and P.D. Buller (eds.), *Cases in Management, Organizational Behavior and Human Resource Management* 5e (St. Paul, MN: West Publishing, 1996). It is adapted here by R. S. Schuler and used with the permission of Arthur D. Sharplin.

People are our most valuable asset. They must feel secure, important, challenged, in control of their destiny, confident in their leadership, be responsive to common goals, believe they are being treated fairly, have easy access to authority and open lines of communication in all possible directions. Perhaps the most important task Lincoln employees face today is that of establishing an example for others in the Lincoln organization in other parts of the world. We need to maximize the benefits of cooperation and teamwork, fusing high technology with human talent, so that we here in the USA and all of our subsidiary and joint venture operations will be in a position to realize our full potential.

George Willis, former CEO, The Lincoln Electric Company

Today, the Lincoln Electric Company under the leadership of Donald Hastings, is the world's largest manufacturer of arc welding products and a leading producer of industrial electric motors. The firm employs almost 4,000 workers in three U.S. factories near Cleveland and almost an equal number in factories located in other countries. This does not include the field sales force of more than 200. The company's U.S. market share (for arc-welding products) is estimated at more than 40 percent.[1]

The Lincoln incentive management plan has been well known for many years. Many college management texts make reference to the Lincoln plan as a model for achieving higher worker productivity. Certainly, the firm has been successful according to the usual measures.

James F. Lincoln died in 1965 and there was some concern, even among employees, that the management system would fall into disarray, that profits would decline, and that year-end bonuses might be discontinued. Quite the contrary, since Lincoln's death, the company appears as strong as ever. Each year, except the recession years 1982 and 1983, has seen high profits and bonuses. In 1995, Lincoln Electric's centennial, sales for the first time surpassed $1 billion. While there was some employee discontent about relatively flat bonuses in 1995, employee morale and productivity remain very good.[2] Employee turnover is almost nonexistent except for retirements. Lincoln's market share is stable. The historically high stock dividends continue.

A Historical Sketch

In 1895, after being "frozen out" of the depression-ravaged Elliott-Lincoln Company, a maker of Lincoln-designed electric motors, John C. Lincoln took out his second patent and began to manufacture his improved motor. He opened his new business, unincorporated, with $200 he had earned redesigning a motor for young Herbert Henry Dow, who later founded the Dow Chemical Company.

Started during an economic depression and cursed by a major fire after only one year in business, the company grew, but hardly prospered, through its first quarter century. In 1906, John C. Lincoln incorporated the business and moved from his one-room, fourth-floor factory to a new three-story building he erected in east Cleveland. He expanded his workforce to 30 and sales grew to over $50,000 a year. John preferred being an engineer and inventor rather than a manager, though, and it was to be left to another Lincoln to manage the company through its years of success. In 1907, after a bout with typhoid fever forced him from Ohio State University in his senior year, James F. Lincoln, John's younger brother, joined the fledgling company. In 1914 he became the active head of the firm, with the titles of General Manager and Vice President. John remained president of the company for some years but became more involved in other business ventures and in his work as an inventor.

One of James Lincoln's early actions was to ask the employees to elect representatives to a committee which would advise him on company operations. This "Advisory Board" has met with the chief executive officer every two weeks since that time. This was only the first of a series of innovative personnel policies which have, over the years, distinguished Lincoln Electric from its contemporaries.

The first year the Advisory Board was in existence, working hours were reduced from 55 per week, then standard, to 50 hours a week. In 1915, the company gave each employee a paid-up life insurance policy. A welding school, which continues today, was begun in 1917. In 1918, an employee bonus plan was attempted. It was not continued, but the idea was to resurface later.

The Lincoln Electric Employees Association was formed in 1919 to provide health benefits and social activities. This organization continues today and has assumed several additional functions over the years. In 1923, a piecework pay system was in effect, employees got two weeks paid vacation each year, and wages, were adjusted for changes in the Consumer Price Index. Approximately 30 percent of the common stock was set aside for key employees in 1914. A stock purchase plan for all employees was begun in 1925.

The Board of Directors voted to start a suggestion system in 1929. The program is still in effect, but cash awards, a part of the early program, were discontinued several years ago. Now, suggestions are rewarded by "additional points" which affect year-end bonuses.

The legendary Lincoln bonus plan was proposed by the Advisory Board and accepted on a trial basis in 1934. The first annual bonus amounted to about 25 percent of wages. There has been a bonus every year since then. The bonus plan has been a cornerstone of the Lincoln management system and recent bonuses have approximated annual wages.

By 1944, Lincoln employees enjoyed a pension plan, a policy of promotion from within, and continuous employment. Base pay rates were determined by formal job evaluation and a merit rating system was in effect.

In the prologue of James F. Lincoln's last book, Charles G. Herbruck writes regarding the foregoing personnel innovations:

> *They were not to buy good behavior. They were not efforts to increase profits. They were not antidotes to labor difficulties. They did not constitute a "do-gooder" program. They were expression of mutual respect for each person's importance to the job to be done. All of them reflect the leadership of James Lincoln, under whom they were nurtured and propagated.*

During World War II, Lincoln prospered as never before. By the start of the war, the company was the world's largest manufacturer of arc-welding products. Sales of about $4,000,000 in 1934 grew to $24,000,000 by 1941. Productivity per employee more than doubled during the same period. The Navy's Price Review Board challenged the high profits. And the Internal Revenue Service questioned the tax deductibility of employee bonuses, arguing they were not "ordinary and necessary" costs of doing business. But the forceful and articulate James Lincoln was able to overcome the objections.

Certainly since 1935 and probably for several years before that, Lincoln's productivity has been well above the average for similar companies. The company claims levels of productivity more than twice those for other manufacturers from 1945 onward. Information available from outside sources tends to support these claims.

Company Philosophy

James F. Lincoln was the son of a Congregational minister, and Christian principles were at the center of his business philosophy. The confidence that he had in the efficacy of Christ's teachings is illustrated by the following remark taken from one of his books:

> *The Christian ethic should control our acts. If it did control our acts, the savings in cost of distribution would be tremendous. Advertising would be a contact of the expert consultant with the customer, in order to give the customer the best product available when all of the customers needs are considered. Competition then would be in improving the quality of products and increasing efficiency in producing and distributing them; not in deception, as is now too customary. Pricing would reflect efficiency of production; it would not be a selling dodge that the customer may be sorry he accepted. It would be proper for all concerned and rewarding for the ability used in producing the product.*

There is no indication that Lincoln attempted to evangelize his employees or customers—or the general public for that matter. Neither the former chairman of the board and chief executive, George Willis, nor the current one, Donald F. Hastings, mention the Christian gospel in their recent speeches and interviews. The company motto, "The actual is limited, the possible is immense," is prominently displayed, but there is no display of religious slogans, and there is no company chapel.

Attitude Toward the Customer

James Lincoln saw the customer's needs as the raison d'être for every company. "When any company has achieved success so that it is attractive as an investment:" he wrote, "all money usually needed for expansion is supplied by the customer in retained earnings. It is obvious that the customer's interests, not the stockholder's, should come first." In 1947 he said, "Care should be taken . . . not to rivet attention on profit. Between 'How much do I get?' and 'How do I make this better, cheaper, more useful?' the difference is fundamental and decisive." Willis, too, ranks the customer as management's most important constituency. This is reflected in Lincoln's policy to "at all times price on the basis of cost and at all times keep pressure on our cost. . . ." Lincoln's goal, often stated, is "to build a better and better product at a lower and lower price." James Lincoln said, "It is obvious that the customer's interests should be the first goal of industry."

This priority, and the priority given to other groups, is reflected in the Mission and Values Statement and the set of Goals shown in Appendix A.

Attitude Toward Stockholders

Stockholders are given last priority at Lincoln. This is a continuation of James Lincoln's philosophy: "The last group to be considered is the stockholders who own stock because they think it will be more profitable than investing money in any other way." Concerning division of the largess produced by incentive management, he wrote, "The absentee stockholder also will get his share, even if undeserved, out of the greatly increased profit that the efficiency produces."

Attitude Toward Unionism

There has never been a serious effort to organize Lincoln employees. While James Lincoln criticized the labor movement for "selfishly attempting to better its position at the expense of the people it must serve;" he still had kind words for union members. He excused abuses of union power as "the natural reactions of human beings to the abuses to which management has subjected them." Lincoln's idea of the correct relationship between workers and managers is shown by this comment: "Labor and management are properly not warring camps; they are parts of one organization in which they must, and should, cooperate fully and happily."

Beliefs and Assumptions About Employees

If fulfilling customer needs is the desired goal of business, then employee performance and productivity are the means by which this goal can best be achieved. It is the Lincoln attitude toward employees, reflected in the following comments by James Lincoln, which is credited by many with creating the success the company has experienced:

> *He is just as eager as any manager is to be part of a team that is properly organized and working for the advancement of our economy.... He has no desire to make profits for those who do not hold up their end in production, as is true of absentee stockholders and inactive people in the company.*
>
> *If money is to be used as an incentive, the program must provide that what is paid to the worker is what he has earned. The earnings of each must be in accordance with accomplishment.*
>
> *Status is of great importance in all human relationships. The greatest incentive that money has, usually, is that it is a symbol of success. The resulting status is the real incentive.... Money alone can be an incentive to the miser only.*
>
> *There must be complete honesty and understanding between the hourly worker and management if high efficiency is to be obtained.*

These beliefs and assumptions have helped shaped Lincoln's human resource objectives. These are shown in Appendix B.

Lincoln's Business

Arc-welding has been the standard joining method in shipbuilding for decades. It is the predominant way of connecting steel in the construction industry. Most industrial plants have their own welding shops for maintenance and construction. Manufacturers of tractors and all kinds of heavy equipment use arc-welding extensively in the manufacturing process. Many hobbyists have their own welding machines and use them for making metal items such as patio furniture and barbecue pits. The popularity of welded sculpture as an art form is growing.

While advances in welding technology have been frequent, arc-welding products, in the main, have hardly changed. Lincoln's Innershield process is a notable exception. This process, described later, lowers welding cost and improves quality and speed in many applications. The most widely-used Lincoln electrode, the Fleetweld 5P, has been virtually the same since the 1930s. The most popular engine-driven welder in the world, the Lincoln SA-200, has been a gray-colored assembly including a four-cylinder continental Red Seal engine and a 200 ampere direct-current generator with two current-control knobs for at least four decades. A 1989 model SA-200 even weighs almost the same as the 1950 model, and it certainly is little changed in appearance.

The company's share of the U.S. arc-welding products market appears to have been about 40 percent for many years. The welding products market has grown somewhat faster than the level of industry in general. The market is highly price-competitive, with variations in prices of standard items normally amounting to only a percent or two. Lincoln's products are sold directly by its engineering-oriented sales force and indirectly through its distributor organization. Advertising expenditures amount to less than three-fourths of a percent of sales. Research and development expenditures typically range from $10 million to $12 million, considerably more than competitors.

The other major welding process, flame-welding, has not been competitive with arc-welding since the 1930s. However, plasma-arc-welding, a relatively new process which uses a conducting stream of super heated gas (plasma) to confine the welding current to a small area, has made some inroads, especially in metal tubing manufacturing, in recent years. Major advances in technology which will produce an alternative superior to arc-welding within the next decade or so appear unlikely. Also, it seems likely that changes in the machines and techniques used in arc-welding will be evolutionary rather than revolutionary.

It is also reasonable to observe that Lincoln Electric's business objectives, shown in Appendix C, are likely to change in an evolutionary rather than a revolutionary way.

Products

The company is primarily engaged in the manufacture and sale of arc-welding products—electric welding machines and metal electrodes. Lincoln also produces electric motors ranging from one-half horsepower to 200 horsepower. Motors constitute about eight to ten percent of total sales. Several million dollars have recently been invested in automated equipment that will double Lincoln's manufacturing capacity for one-half to 20 horsepower electric motors. The electric welding machines, some consisting of a transformer or motor and generator arrangement powered by commercial electricity and others consisting of an internal combustion engine and generator, are designed to produce 30 to 1,500 amperes of electrical power. This electrical current is used to melt a consumable metal electrode with the molten metal being transferred in super hot spray to the metal joint being welded. Very high temperatures and hot sparks are produced, and operators usually must wear special eye and face protection and leather gloves, often along with leather aprons and sleeves. Lincoln and its competitors now market a wide range of general purpose and specialty electrodes for welding mild steel, aluminum, cast iron, and stainless and special steels. Most of these electrodes are designed to meet the standards of the American Welding Society, a trade association. They are thus essentially the same as to size and composition from one manufacturer to another. Every electrode manufacturer has a limited number of unique products, but these typically constitute only a small percentage of total sales.

Welding electrodes are of two basic types: coated "stick" electrodes and coiled wire. Coated "stick" electrodes, usually 14 inches long and smaller than a pencil in diameter, which are held in a special insulated holder by the operator, who must manipulate the electrode in order to maintain a proper arc-width and pattern of deposition of the metal being transferred. Stick electrodes are packaged in 6-to 50-pound boxes.

Coiled wired, ranging in diameter from .035′ to 0.219′, is designed to be fed continuously to the welding arc through a "gun" held by the operator or positioned by automatic positioning equipment. The wire is packaged in coils, reels, and drums weighing from 14 to 1,000 pounds and may be solid or flux-cored. For more information on products visit the Web site

http://www.Lincolnelectric.com.

Manufacturing Process

The main plant is in Euclid, Ohio, a suburb on Cleveland's east side. The layout of this plant is shown in Exhibit 1. There are no warehouses. Materials flow from the

EXHIBIT 1

Main Factory Layout

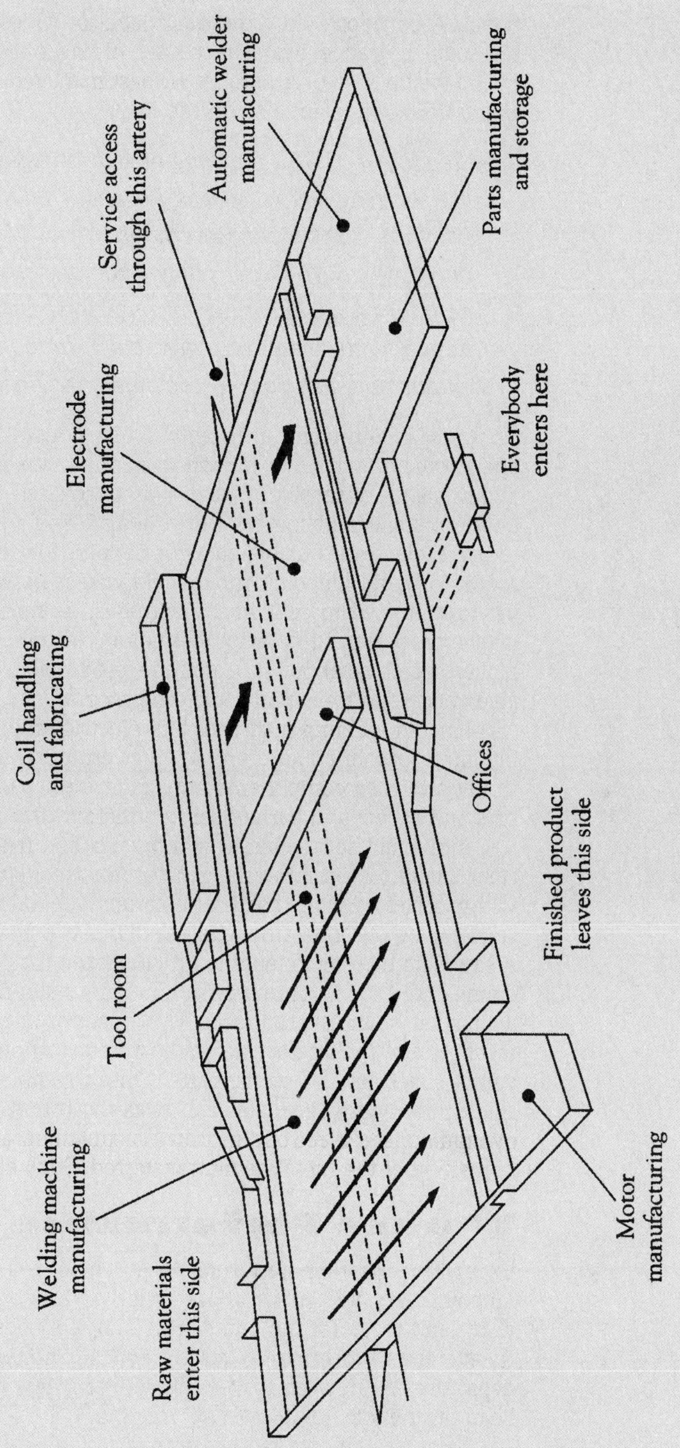

half-mile long dock on the north side of the plant through the production lines to a very limited storage and loading area on the south side.

Materials used on each work station are stored as close as possible to the work station. The administrative offices, near the center of the factory, are entirely functional. A corridor below the main level provides access to the factory floor from the main entrance near the center of the plan. *Fortune* recently declared the Euclid facility one of America's 10 best-managed factories, and compared it with a General Electric plant also on the list:

> *Stepping into GE's spanking new dishwasher plant, an awed supplier said, is like stepping "into the Hyatt Regency." By comparison, stepping into Lincoln Electric's 33-year-old, cavernous, dimly lit factory is like stumbling into a dingy big-city YMCA. It's only when one starts looking at how these factories do things that similarities become apparent. They have found ways to merge design with manufacturing, build in quality, make wise choices about automation, get close to customers, and handle their workforces.*

Another Lincoln plant, in Mentor, Ohio, houses some of the electrode production operations, which were moved from the main plant. Electrode manufacturing is highly capital intensive. Metal rods purchased from steel producers are drawn down to smaller diameters, cut to length and coated with pressed-powder "flux" for stick electrodes or plated with copper (for conductivity) and put into coils or spools for wire. Lincoln's Innershield wire is hollow and filled with a material similar to that used to coat stick electrodes. As mentioned earlier, this represented a major innovation in welding technology when it was introduced. The company is highly secretive about its electrode production processes, and outsiders are not given access to the details of those processes.

Lincoln welding machines and electric motors are made on a series of assembly lines. Gasoline and diesel engines are purchased partially assembled but practically all other components are made from basic industrial products, e.g., steel bars and sheets and bar copper conductor wire.

Individual components, such as gasoline tanks for engine-driven welders and steel shafts for motors and generators, are made by numerous small "factories within a factory." The shaft for a certain generator, for example, is made from raw steel bar by one operator who uses five large machines, all running continuously. A saw cuts the bar to length, a digital lathe machines different sections to varying diameters, a special mining machine cuts a slot for the keyway, and so forth, until a finished shaft is produced. The operator moves the shafts from machine to machine and makes necessary adjustments. Another operator punches, shapes and paints sheetmetal cowling parts. One assembles steel laminations onto a rotor shaft, then winds, insulates and tests the rotors. Finished components are moved by crane operators to the nearby assembly lines.

Worker Performance and Attitude

Exceptional worker performance at Lincoln is a matter of record. The typical Lincoln employee earns about twice as much as other factory workers in the Cleveland area. Yet the company's labor cost per sales dollar is well below industry averages. Worker turnover is practically nonexistent except for retirements and departures by new employees. Turnover is less than 4% for employees who have been on the jobs for at least 18 months.[3]

Sales per Lincoln factory employee currently exceed $150,000. An observer at the factory quickly sees why this figure is so high. Each worker is proceeding busily and thoughtfully about the task at hand. There is no idle chatter. Most workers take no coffee breaks. Many operate several machines and make a substantial component unaided. The supervisors are busy with planning and record keeping duties and hardly glance at the people they "supervise." The manufacturing procedures appear efficient—no unnecessary steps, no wasted motions, no wasted materials. Finished components move smoothly to subsequent work stations. Appendix D includes summaries of interviews with employees.

Organizational Structure

Lincoln has never allowed development of a formal organization chart. The objective of this policy is to insure maximum flexibility. An open door policy is practiced throughout the company, and personnel are encouraged to take problems to the persons most capable of resolving them. Once, Harvard Business School researchers prepared an organization chart reflecting the implied relationships at Lincoln. The chart became available within the company, and present management feels that had a disruptive effect. Therefore, no organizational chart appears in this report.

Perhaps because of the quality and enthusiasm of the Lincoln workforce, routine supervision is almost nonexistent. A typical production foreman, for example, supervises as many as 100 workers, a span-of-control which does not allow more than infrequent worker-supervisor interaction.

Position titles and traditional flows of authority do imply something of an organizational structure, however. For example, the Vice-President, Sales, and the Vice-President, Electrode Division, report to the President, as do various staff assistants such as the Personnel Director and the Director of Purchasing.

Using such implied relationships, it has been determined that production workers have two or, at most, three levels of supervision between themselves and the President.

Human Resource Policies

As mentioned earlier, it is Lincoln's remarkable human resource practices which are credited by many with the company's success.

Recruitment and Selection

Every job opening is advertised internally on company bulletin boards and any employee can apply for any job so advertised. External hiring is permitted only for entry-level positions. Selection for these jobs is done on the basis of personal interviews—there is no aptitude or psychological testing. A committee consisting of vice presidents and supervisors interviews candidates initially cleared by the Personnel Department. Final selection is made by the supervisor who has a job opening. Nonetheless, it is increasingly desirable that factory workers have some advanced math skills and understand the use of computers. Out of over 20,000 applications received by the Personnel Department during a recent period relatively few were hired in 1994-1995. Consequently Lincoln's expansion is becoming increasingly dependent upon getting employees qualified to work in the Lincoln environment, within the famous incentive system.[4]

Job Security

In 1958 Lincoln formalized its guaranteed continuous employment policy, which had already been in effect for many years. There have been no layoffs since World War II. Since 1958, every worker with over two year's longevity has been guaranteed at least 30 hours per week, 49 weeks per year.

The policy has never been so severely tested as during the 1981 to 1983 recession. As a manufacturer of capital goods, Lincoln's business is highly cyclical. In previous recessions the company was able to avoid major sales declines. However, sales plummeted 32 percent in 1982 and another 16 percent the next year. Few companies could withstand such a revenue collapse and remain profitable. Yet, Lincoln not only earned profits, but no employee was laid off and year-end incentive bonuses continued. To weather the storm, management cut most of the nonsalaried workers back to 30 hours a week for varying periods of time. Many employees were reassigned and the total workforce was slightly reduced through normal attrition and restricted hiring. Many employees grumbled at their unexpected misfortune, probably to the surprise and dismay of some Lincoln managers. However, sales and profits—and employee bonuses—soon rebounded and all was well again.

Performance Evaluations

Each supervisor formally evaluates subordinates twice a year using the cards shown in Exhibit 2. The employee performance criteria, "quality," "dependability," "ideas and cooperation," and "output" are considered to be independent of each other. Marks on the cards are converted to numerical scores which are forced to average 100 for each evaluating supervisor. Individual merit rating scores normally range from 80 to 110. Any score over 110 requires a special letter to top management. These scores (over 110) are not considered in computing the required 100 point average for each evaluating supervisor.

Suggestions for improvements often result in recommendations for exceptionally high performance scores. Supervisors discuss individual performance marks with the employees concerned. Each warranty claim is traced to the individual employee whose work caused the defect. The employee's performance score may be reduced, or the worker may be required to repay the cost of servicing the warranty claim by working without pay.

Compensation

Basic wage levels for jobs at Lincoln are determined by a wage survey of similar jobs in the Cleveland area.[5] These rates are adjusted quarterly in accordance with changes in the Cleveland area wage index. Insofar as possible, base wage rates are translated into piece rates. Today the average Lincoln factory worker earns $16.54 an hour vs. the average $14.25 manufacturing wage in the Cleveland area. Practically all production workers and many others—for example, some forklift operators—are paid by piece rate. Once established, piece rates are never changed unless a substantive change in the way a job is done results from a source other than the worker doing the job.

In December of each year, a portion of annual profits is distributed to employees as bonuses. Incentive bonuses since 1934 have averaged about 90 percent of annual wages. The average bonus for 1995 was $18,887. Even for the recession years 1982 and 1983, bonuses had averaged $13,998 and $8,557, respectively. Individual bonuses are proportional to merit-rating scores. For example, assume the amount set aside for bonuses is 80 percent of total wages paid to eligible employees. A person whose performance score is 95 will receive a bonus of 76 percent (0.80 x 0.95) of annual wages. While these percentage have often resulted in high *total* compensation, some employees believe that their bonuses are not rising fast enough, despite rising profits. This reflects the firm's decision to use the money to expand the operations rather than put them into higher bonuses. It also reflects the fact that there are more workers today sharing in a bonus pool which is only a little higher than in many years in the 1980s.[6]

Vacations

The company is shut down for two weeks in August and two weeks during the Christmas season. Vacations are taken during these periods. For employees with over 25 years of service, a fifth week of vacation may be taken at a time acceptable to superiors.

EXHIBIT 2

Merit Rating Cards

QUALITY

This rating has been done jointly by your department head and the Inspection department in the shop and with other department heads in the office and engineering.

→ Increasing Quality →

This card rates the QUALITY of work you do.

It also reflects your success in eliminating errors and in reducing scrap and waste.

DEPENDABILITY

This rating has been done by your department head.

→ Increasing Dependability →

This card rates how well your supervisors have been able to depend on you to do those things that have been expected of you without supervision.

It also reflects your ability to supervise yourself including your work safety performance, your orderliness, care of equipment, and the effective use you make of your skills.

IDEAS & COOPERATION

→ Increasing Output →

This card rates your Cooperation, Ideas, and Initiative.

OUTPUT

This rating has been done jointly by your department head and the Production Control Department in the shop and with other department heads in the office and engineering.

→ Increasing Output → Days Absent

This card rates HOW MUCH PRODUCTIVE WORK you actually turn out. It also reflects your willingness not to hold back and recognizes your attendance record.

New ideas and new methods are important to your company in our continuing effort to reduce costs, increase output, improve quality, work safety and improve our relationship with our customers. This card credits you for your ideas initiative used to help in this direction.

It also rates your cooperation—how you work with others as a team. Such factors as your attitude toward supervision, co-workers and the company, your efforts to share knowledge with others, and your cooperation in installing new methods smoothly, are considered here.

Work Assignment

Management has authority to transfer workers and to switch between overtime and short time as required. Supervisors have undisputed authority to assign specific parts to individual workers, who may have their own preferences due to variations in piece rates. During the 1982-1983 recession, 50 factory workers volunteered to join sales teams and fanned out across the country to sell a new welder designed for automobile body shops and small machine shops. The result: $10 million in sales and a hot new product.

Employee Participation in Decision Making

Thinking of participative management usually evokes a vision of a relaxed, nonauthoritarian atmosphere. This is not the case at Lincoln. Formal authority is quite strong. "We're very authoritarian around here," says Willis. James F. Lincoln placed a good deal of stress on protecting management's authority. "Management in all successful departments of industry must have complete power," he said, "Management is the coach who must be obeyed. The men, however, are the Players who alone can win the game." Despite this attitude, there are several ways in which employees participate in management at Lincoln.

Richard Sabo, Assistant to the Chief Executive Officer, relates job enlargement/enrichment to participation. He said, "The most important participative technique that we use is giving more responsibility to employees. We give a high school graduate more responsibility than other companies give their foremen." Management puts limits on the degree of participation which is allowed, however. In Sabo's words:

> *When you use 'participation,' put quotes around it. Because we believe that each person should participate only in those decisions he is most knowledgeable about. I don't think production employees should control the decisions of the chairman. They don't know as much as he does about the decisions he is involved in.*

The Advisory Board, elected by the workers, meets with the chairman and the president every two weeks to discuss ways of improving operations. As noted earlier, this board has been in existence since 1914 and has contributed to many innovations. The incentive bonuses, for example, were first recommended by this committee. Every employee has access to Advisory Board members, and answers to all Advisory Board suggestions are promised by the following meeting. Both Willis and Hastings are quick to point out, though, that the Advisory Board only recommends actions. "They do not have direct authority," Willis says, "And when they bring up something that management thinks is not to the benefit of the company, it will be rejected."

Under the early suggestion program, employees were awarded one-half of the first year's savings attributable to their suggestions Now, however, the value of suggestions is reflected in performance evaluation scores, which determine individual incentive bonus amounts.

Training and Education

Production workers are given a short period of on-the-job training and then placed on a piecework pay system. Lincoln does not pay for off-site education, unless very specific company needs are identified. The idea behind this latter policy, according to Sabo, is that everyone cannot take advantage of such a program, and it is unfair to expend company funds for an advantage to which there is unequal access. Recruits for sales jobs, already college graduates, are given on-the-job training in the plant followed by a period of work and training at one of the regional sales offices.

Fringe Benefits and Executive Perquisites

A medical plan and a company-paid retirement program have been in effect for many years. A plant cafeteria, operated on a break-even basis, serves meals at about 60 percent of usual costs. The Employee Association, to which the company does not contribute, provides disability insurance and social and athletic activities. The employee stock ownership program has resulted in employee ownership of about 50 percent of the common stock. Under this program, each employee with more than two years of service may purchase stock in the corporation. The price of these shares is established at book value. Stock purchased through this plan may be held by employees only. Dividends and voting rights are the same as for stock which is owned outside the plan. Approximately 75 percent of the employees own Lincoln stock.

As to executive perquisites, there are none—crowded, austere offices, no executive washrooms or lunchrooms, and no reserved parking spaces. Even the top executives pay for their own meals and eat in the employee cafeteria. On one recent day, Willis arrived at work late due to a breakfast speaking engagement and had to park far away from the factory entrance.

Financial Policies

James F. Lincoln felt strongly that financing for company growth should come from within the company—through initial cash investment by the founders, through retention of earnings, and through stock purchases by those who work in the business. He saw the following advantages of this approach:

1. Ownership of stock by employees strengthens team spirit. "If they are mutually anxious to make it succeed, the future of the company is bright."
2. Ownership of stock provides individual incentive because employees feel that they will benefit from company profitability.
3. "Ownership is educational." Owner-employees "will know how profits are made and lost; how success is won and lost....There are few socialists in the list of stockholders of the nation's industries."
4. "Capital available from within controls expansion." Unwarranted expansion would not occur, Lincoln believed, under his financing plan.
5. "The greatest advantage would be the development of the individual worker. Under the incentive of ownership, he would become a greater man."
6. "Stock ownership is one of the steps that can be taken that will make the worker feel that there is less of a gulf between him and the boss....Stock ownership will help the worker to recognize his responsibility in the game and the importance of victory."

Until 1980, Lincoln Electric borrowed no money. Even now, the company's liabilities consist mainly of accounts payable and short-term accruals. The unusual pricing policy at Lincoln is succinctly stated by Willis: "At all times price on the basis of cost and at all times keep pressure on our cost." This policy resulted in the price for the most popular welding electrode then in use going from 16 cents a pound in 1929 to 4.7 cents in 1938. More recently, the SA-200 Welder, Lincoln's largest selling portable machine, decreased in price from 1958 through 1965. According to Dr. C. Jackson Grayson of the American Productivity Center in Houston, Texas, Lincoln's prices increased only one-fifth as fast as the Consumer Price Index from 1934 to about 1970 This resulted in a welding products market in which Lincoln became the undisputed price leader for the products it manufactures. Not even the major Japanese manufacturers, such as Nippon Steel for welding electrodes and Saka Transformer for welding machines, were able to penetrate this market.

Substantial cash balances accumulated each year preparatory to paying the year-end bonuses. Modest success with international expansion put some pressure on what was basically a conservative financial philosophy. However, the company borrowed money in 1992 to pay for employee bonuses in the United States. In 1995 Lincoln issued $119 million of new stock. This sale created greater public ownership. As a consequence, Don Hastings remarked that the company must now consider not only the employees but its shareholders, customers, and suppliers.[7] For more current financial information visit Lincoln's Web site.

How Well Does Lincoln Serve Its Stakeholders?

Lincoln Electric differs from most other companies in the importance it assigns to each of the groups it serves. Hastings identifies these groups, in the order of priority ascribed to them, as: 1) customers, 2) employees, and 3) stockholders. As suggested, the 1995 stock issue increased the salience of the stockholders.

Certainly the firm's customers have fared well over the years. Lincoln prices for welding machines and welding electrodes are acknowledged to be the lowest in the marketplace. Quality has consistently been high. The cost of field failures for Lincoln products was recently determined to be a remarkable 0.04 percent of revenues. The "Fleetweld" electrodes and SA-200 welders have been the standard in the pipeline and refinery construction industry, where price is hardly a criterion, for decades. A Lincoln distributor in Monroe, Louisiana, says that he has sold several hundred of the popular AC-225 welders, which are warranted for one year, but has never handled a warranty claim.

Perhaps best-served of all management constituencies have been the employees. Not the least of their benefits, of course, are the year-end bonuses, which effectively double an already average compensation level. The foregoing description of the personnel program and the comments in Appendix D further illustrate the desirability of a Lincoln job.

While stockholders were relegated to an inferior status by James F. Lincoln, they have done very well indeed. Recent dividends exceeded $11 a share and earnings per share have approached $30. In January 1980, the price of restricted stock, committed to employees, was $117 a share. By 1989, the stated value, at which the company will repurchase the stock if tendered, was $201. A check with the New York office of Merrill Lynch, Pierce, Fenner and Smith at that time revealed an estimated price on Lincoln stock of $270 a share, with none being offered for sale. Technically, this price applies only to the unrestricted stock owned by the Lincoln family, a few other major holders, and employees who have purchased it on the open market. Risk associated with Lincoln stock, a major determinant of stock value, is minimal because of the small amount of debt in the capital structure, because of an extremely stable earnings record, and because of Lincoln's practice of purchasing the restricted stock whenever employees offer it for sale. The 1995 stock sale has changed this situation dramatically. The stock now trades freely on the NASDAQ stock exchange.

A Concluding Comment

It is easy to believe that the reason for Lincoln's success is the excellent attitude of the employees and their willingness to work harder, faster, and more intelligently than other industrial workers. However, Sabo suggests that appropriate credit be given to Lincoln executives, whom he credits with carrying out the following policies:

1. Management has limited research, development, and manufacturing to a standard product line designed to meet the major needs of the welding industry.

2. New products must be reviewed by manufacturing and all producing costs verified before being approved by management.

3. Purchasing is challenged to not only procure materials at the lowest cost, but also to work closely with engineering and manufacturing to assure that the latest innovations are implemented.

4. Manufacturing supervision and all personnel are held accountable for reduction of scrap, energy conservation, and maintenance of product quality.

5. Production control, material handling, and methods engineering are closely supervised by top management.

6. Management has made cost reduction a way of life at Lincoln, and definite programs are established in many areas, including traffic and shipping, where tremendous savings can result.

7. Management has established a sales department that is technically trained to reduce customer welding costs. This sales approach and other real customer services have eliminated nonessential frills and resulted in long-term benefits to all concerned.

8. Management has encouraged education, technical publishing, and long range programs that have resulted in industry growth, thereby assuring market potential for the Lincoln Electric Company.

Sabo writes, "It is in a very real sense a personal and group experience in faith—a belief that together we can achieve results which alone would not be possible. It is not a perfect system and it is not easy. It requires tremendous dedication and hard work. However, it does work and the results are worth the effort."

APPENDIX A

Mission and Values Statement

The mission of The Lincoln Electric Company is to earn and retain global leadership as a total quality supplier of superior products and services.

Our Core Values

As a responsible and successful company in partnership with our customers, distributors, employees, shareholders, suppliers and our host communities, we pledge ourselves to conduct our business in accordance with these core values:

- Respond to our customers' needs and expectations with quality, integrity and value
- Recognize people as our most valuable asset
- Maintain and expand the Lincoln Incentive Management philosophy
- Practice prudent and responsible financial management
- Strive continually to be environmentally responsible
- Support communities where we operate and industries in which we participate

To Realize Our Mission and Support Our Core Values, We Have Established the Following Goals:

Respond to Our Customers' Needs and Expectations With Quality, Integrity and Value

- Assure value through innovative, functional and reliable products and services in all the markets we serve around the world.
- Exceed global standards for products and service quality.
- Provide our customers with personalized technical support that helps them achieve improvements in cost reduction, productivity and quality.
- Lead the industry in aggressive application of advanced technology to meet customer requirements.
- Invest constantly in creative research and development dedicated to maintaining our position of market leadership.
- Achieve and maintain the leading market share position in our major markets around the world.

Recognize People As Our Most Valuable Asset

- Maintain a safe, clean and healthy environment for our employees.
- Promote employee training, education and development, and broaden skills through multi-departmental and international assignments.
- Maintain an affirmative action program and provide all employees with opportunities for advancement commensurate with their abilities and performance regardless of race, religion, national origin, sex, age or disability.
- Maintain an environment that fosters ethical behavior, mutual trust, equal opportunity, open communication, personal growth and creativity.
- Demand integrity, discipline and professional conduct from our employees in every aspect of our business and conduct our operations ethically and in accordance with the law.
- Reward employees through recognition, "pay for performance," and by sharing our profits with incentive bonus compensation based on extraordinary achievement.

Maintain and Expand the Lincoln Incentive Management Philosophy

Promote dynamic teamwork and incentive as the most profitable and cost-effective way of achieving:

- A committed work ethic and positive employee attitudes throughout the Company.
- High quality, low-cost manufacturing.
- Efficient and innovative engineering.
- Customer-oriented operation and administration.
- A dedicated and knowledgeable sales and service force.
- A total organization responsive to the needs of our worldwide customers.

Practice Prudent and Responsible Financial Management

- Establish attainable goals strategic planning and accountability for results that enhance shareholder value.
- Promote the process of employee involvement in cost reductions and quality improvements.
- Recognize profit as the resource that enables our Company to serve our customers.

Strive Continually To Be Environmentally Responsible

- Continue to pursue the most environmentally sound operating practices, processes and products to protect the global environment.
- Maintain a clean and healthy environment in our host communities.

Support Communities Where We Operate and Industries In Which We Participate

- Invest prudently in social, cultural, educational and charitable activities.
- Contribute to the industries we serve and society as a whole by continuing our leadership role in professional organizations and education.
- Encourage and support appropriate employee involvement in community activities.

APPENDIX B

What Are the HR Objectives of Lincoln Electric?

- To "maintain and expand the Lincoln Incentive Management Philosophy"
- To "recognize people as [their] most valuable asset"
- To promote training, education and development that broaden employee skills
- To "maintain an affirmative action program and provide all employees with opportunities for advancement commensurate with their abilities and performance regardless of race, religion, national origin, sex, age or disability"

APPENDIX C

Business Objectives of Lincoln Electric:

- To be a global leader in price and quality and serve the customers first
- To "earn and retain global leadership as a total quality supplier of superior products and services"

- To "respond to [their] customers, integrity and value"
- To "practice prudent and responsible financial management"
- To "strive continually to be environmentally responsible"
- To "support communities where [they] operate and industries in which [they] participate"
- To "maintain an environment that fosters ethical behavior, mutual trust, equal opportunity, open communication, personal growth and creativity."
- To promote feedback
- To "demand integrity, discipline and professional conduct from our employees in every aspect of [their] business and conduct [their] operations ethically and in accordance with the law"
- To "reward employees through recognition, 'pay for performance,' and by sharing [their] profits with incentive bonus compensation based on extraordinary achievement" as a means of motivation
- To "promote dynamic teamwork and incentive"

APPENDIX D

Employee Interviews

Typical questions and answers from employee interviews are presented below. In order to maintain each employee's personal privacy, fictitious names are given to the interviewees.

Interview 1

Betty Stewart, a 52-year-old high school graduate who had been with Lincoln 13 years was working as a cost accounting clerk at the time of the interview.

Q: What jobs have you held here besides the one you have now?

A: I worked in payroll for a while, and then this job came open and I took it.

Q: How much money did you make last year, including your bonus?

A: I would say roughly around $25,000, but I was off for back surgery for a while.

Q: You weren't paid while you were off for back surgery?

A: No.

Q: Did the Employees Association help out?

A: Yes. The company doesn't furnish that, though. We pay $8 a month into the Employee Association. I think my check from them was $130.00 a week.

Q: How was your performance rating last year?

A: It was around 100 points, but I lost some points for attendance for my back problem.

Q: How did you get your job at Lincoln?

A: I was bored silly where I was working, and I had heard that Lincoln kept their people busy. So I applied and got the job the next day.

Q: Do you think you make more money than similar workers in Cleveland?

A: I know I do.

Q: What have you done with your money?

A: We have purchased a better home. Also, my son is going to the University of Chicago, which costs $13,000 a year. I buy the Lincoln stock which is offered each year, and I have a little bit of gold.

Q: Have you ever visited with any of the senior executives, like Mr. Willis or Mr. Hastings?

A: I have known Mr. Willis for a long time.

Q: Does he call you by name?

A: Yes. In fact he was very instrumental in my going to the doctor that I am going to with my back. He knows the director of the clinic.

Q: Do you know Mr. Hastings?

A: I know him to speak to him, and he always speaks, always. But I have known Mr. Willis for a good many years. When I did Plant Two accounting I did not understand how the plant operated. Of course you are not allowed in Plant Two, because that's the Electrode Division. I told my boss about the problem one day and the next thing I knew Mr. Willis came by and said, "Come on, Betty, we're going to Plant Two." He spent an hour and a half showing me the plant.

Q: Do you think Lincoln employees produce more than those in other companies?

A: I think with the incentive program the way that it is, if you want to work and achieve, then you will do it. If you don't want to work and achieve, you will not do it no matter where you are. Just because you are merit rated and have a bonus, if you really don't want to work hard, then you're not going to. You will accept your 90 points or 92 or 85 because, even with that you make more money than people on the outside.

Q: Do you think Lincoln employees will ever join a union?

A: I don't know why they would.

Q: So you say that money is a very major advantage?

A: Money is a major advantage, but it's not just the money. It's the fact that having the incentive, you do wish to work a litter harder. I'm sure that there are a lot of men here who, if they worked some other place, would not work as hard as they do here. Not that they are overworked—I don't mean that—but I'm sure they wouldn't push.

Q: Is there anything that you would like to add?

A: I do like working here. I am better off being pushed mentally. In another company if you pushed too hard you would feel a little bit of pressure, and someone might say, "Hey, slow down, don't try so hard." But here you are encouraged, not discouraged.

Interview 2

Ed Sanderson, a 23-year-old high school graduate who had been with Lincoln four years, was a machine operator in the Electrode Division at the time of the interview.

Q: How did you happen to get this job?

A: My wife was pregnant, and I was making three bucks an hour and one day I came here and applied. That was it. I kept calling to let them know I was still interested.

Q: Roughly what were your earnings last year including your bonus?

A: $45,000.

Q: What have you done with your money since you have been here?

A: Well, we've lived pretty well and we bought a condominium.

Q: Have you paid for the condominium?

A: No, but I could.

Q: Have you bought your Lincoln stock this year?

A: No, I haven't bought any Lincoln stock yet.

Q: Do you get the feeling that the executives here are pretty well thought of?

A: I think they are. To get where they are today, they had to really work.

Q: Wouldn't that be true anywhere?

A: I think more so here because seniority really doesn't mean anything. If you work with a guy who has 20 years here, and you have two months and you're doing a better job, you will get advanced before he will.

Q: Are you paid on a piece rate basis?

A: My gang does. There are nine of us who make the bare electrode, and the whole group gets paid based on how much electrode we make.

Q: Do you think you work harder than workers in other factories in the Cleveland area?

A: Yes, I would say I probably work harder.

Q: Do you think it hurts anybody?

A: No, a little hard work never hurts anybody.

Q: If you could choose, do you think you would be as happy earning a little less money and being able to slow down a little?

A: No, it doesn't bother me. If it bothered me, I wouldn't do it.

Q: Why do you think Lincoln employees produce more than workers in other plants?

A: That's the way the company is set up. The more you put out, the more you're going to make.

Q: Do you think it's the piece rate and bonus together?

A: I don't think people would work here if they didn't know that they would be rewarded at the end of the year.

Q: Do you think Lincoln employees will ever join a union?

A: No.

Q: What are the major advantages of working for Lincoln?

A: Money.

Q: Are there any other advantages?

A: Yes, we don't have a union shop. I don't think I could work in a union shop.

Q: Do you think you are a career man with Lincoln at this time?

A: Yes.

Interview 3

Roger Lewis, a 23-year-old Purdue graduate in mechanical engineering who had been in the Lincoln sales program for 15 months, was working in the Cleveland sales office at the time of the interview.

Q: How did you get your job at Lincoln?

A: I saw that Lincoln was interviewing on campus at Purdue, and I went by. I later came to Cleveland for a plant tour and was offered a job.

Q: Do you know any of the senior executives? Would they know you by name?

A: Yes, I know all of them—Mr. Hastings, Mr. Willis, Mr. Sabo.

Q: Do you think Lincoln sales representatives work harder than those in other companies?

A: Yes. I don't think there are many sales reps for other companies who are putting in 50- to 60-hour weeks. Everybody here works harder. You can go out in the plant, or you can go upstairs, and there's nobody sitting around.

Q: Do you see any real disadvantage of working at Lincoln?

A: I don't know if it's a disadvantage, but Lincoln is a spartan company, a very thrifty company. I like that. The sales offices are functional, not fancy.

Q: Why do you think Lincoln employees have such high productivity?

A: Piecework has a lot to do with it. Lincoln is smaller than many plants, too; you can stand in one place and see the materials come in one side and the product go out the other. You feel a part of the company. The chance to get ahead is important, too. They have a strict policy of promoting from within, so you know you have a chance. I think in a lot of other places you may not get as fair a shake as you do here. The sales offices are on a smaller scale, too. I like that. I tell someone that we have two people in the Baltimore office, and they say "You've got to be kidding." It's smaller and more personal. Pay is the most important thing. I have heard that this is the highest paying factory in the world.

Interview 4

Jimmy Roberts, a 47-year-old high school graduate who had been with Lincoln 17 years, was working as a multiple-drill press operator at the time of the interview.

Q: What jobs have you had at Lincoln?

A: I started out cleaning the men's locker room in 1967. After about a year I got a job in the flux department, where we make the coating for welding rods. I worked there for seven or eight years and then got my present job.

Q: Do you make one particular part?

A: No, there are a variety of parts I make—at least 25.

Q: Each one has a different piece rate attached to it?

A: Yes.

Q: Are some piece rates better than others?

A: Yes.

Q: How do you determine which ones you are going to do?

A: You don't. Your supervisor assigns them.

Q: How much money did you make last year?

A: $53,000.

Q: Have you ever received any kind of award or citation?

A: No.

Q: Was your rating ever over 110?

A: Yes. For the past five years, probably, I made over 110 points.

Q: Is there any attempt to let the others know. . ?

A: The kind of points I get? No.

Q: Do you know what they are making?

A: No. There are some who might not be too happy with their points and they might make it known. The majority, though, do not make it a point of telling other employees.

Q: Would you be just as happy earning a little less money and working a little slower?

A: I don't think I would, not at this point. I have done piecework all these years, and the fast pace doesn't really bother me.

Q: Why do you think Lincoln productivity is so high?

A: The incentive thing—the bonus distribution. I think that would be the main reason. The paycheck you get every two weeks is important too.

Q: Do you think Lincoln employees would ever join a union?

A: I don't think so. I have never heard anyone mention it.

Q: What is the most important advantage of working here?

A: Amount of money you make. I don't think I could make this type of money anywhere else, especially with only a high school education.

Q: As a black person, do you feel that Lincoln discriminates in any way against blacks?

A: No. I do not think any more so than any other job. Naturally, there is a certain amount of discrimination, regardless of where you are.

Interview 5

Joe Trahan, 58-year-old high school graduate who had been with Lincoln 39 years, was employed as a working supervisor in the tool room at the time of the interview.

Q: Roughly what was your pay last year?

A: Over $56,000, salary, bonus, stock dividends.

Q: How much was your bonus?

A: About $26,000.

Q: Have you ever gotten a special award of any kind?

A: Not really.

Q: What have you done with your money?

A: My house is paid for, and my two cars. I also have some bonds and the Lincoln stock.

Q: What do you think of the executives at Lincoln?

A: They're really top notch.

Q: What is the major disadvantage of working at Lincoln Electric?

A: I don't know of any disadvantage at all.

Q: Do you think you produce more than most people in similar jobs with other companies?

A: I do believe that.

Q: Why is that? Why do you believe that?

A: We are on the incentive system. Everything we do, we try to improve to make a better product with a minimum of outlay. We try to improve the bonus.

Q: Would you be just as happy making a little less money and not working quite so hard?

A: I don't think so.

Q: Do you think Lincoln employees would ever join a union?

A: I don't think they would ever consider it.

Q: What is the most important advantage of working at Lincoln?

A: Compensation.

Q: Tell me something about Mr. James Lincoln, who died in 1965.

A: You are talking about Jimmy Sr. He always strolled through the shop in his shirt sleeves. Big fellow. Always looked distinguished. Gray hair. Friendly sort of guy. I was a member of the Advisory Board one year. He was there each time.

Q: Did he strike you as really caring?

A: I think he always cared for people.

Q: Did you get any sensation of a religious nature from him?

A: No, not really.

Q: And religion is not part of the program now?

A: No.

Q: Do you think Mr. Lincoln was a very intelligent man, or was he just a nice guy?

A: I would say he was pretty well educated. A great talker—always right off the top of his head. He knew what he was talking about all the time.

Q: When were bonuses for beneficial suggestions done away with?

A: About 18 years ago.

Q: Did that hurt very much?

A: I do not think so, because suggestions are still rewarded through the merit rating system.

Q: Is there anything you would like to add?

A: It's a good place to work. The union kind of ties other places down. At other places, electricians only do electrical work, carpenters only do carpentry work. At Lincoln Electric we all pitch in and do whatever needs to be done.

Q: So a major advantage is not having a union?

A: That's right.

Letter From the CEO

To Our Shareholders

Each of you is aware that your company faced enormous challenges in 1993. Those challenges required a focused, creative and positive leadership approach on the part of your management team. As I write this, first quarter 1994 results indicate that the domestic economy is continuing its upward surge. Because of the many tough decisions we had to make in 1993, we are now poised to take advantage of an improved economic climate. Even though much of my personal time has been devoted to overseeing the situation in Europe, excellent results are being achieved in the U.S.A. and Canada.

During 1993, a thorough strategic assessment of our foreign operations led to the conclusion that Lincoln Electric lacked the necessary financial resources to continue to support twenty-one manufacturing sites. We did not have the luxury of time to keep those plants operating while working to increase our sales and profitability. As a result, with the endorsement of our financial community, the Board of Directors approved management's recommendation to restructure operations in Europe, Latin America and Japan.

The restructuring included closing the Messer Lincoln operations in Germany, reducing employment throughout Lincoln Norweld, which operates plants in England, France, the Netherlands, Spain and Norway; and closing manufacturing plants in Venezuela, Brazil, and Japan. The result was a workforce reduction totaling some 770 employees worldwide. We are not abandoning these markets by any means. Rather, the restructuring will allow us to retain and increase sales while relieving us of the high costs associated with excess manufacturing capacity. Now that the restructuring has been accomplished, we operate fifteen plants in ten countries. This capacity will be adequate to supply the inventory needed to support our customers and an increasingly aggressive marketing strategy. We are internationally recognized for outstanding products and service, and we have been certified to the international quality standard ISO-9002.

It was not easy for Lincoln Electric to eliminate manufacturing capacity and jobs. However, I must point out that the overseas companies were given repeated opportunities to turn their performance around. In all fairness, no one anticipated the depth of the recession that continues to devastate Europe, and particularly Germany. But we could not in good conscience, risk both the continuous erosion of shareholder value and the jobs of our dedicated U. S. employees, by remaining unprofitable in these manufacturing operations.

For the second year in the history of this company, it was necessary to take restructuring charges that resulted in a consolidated loss. The restructuring charge totaled $70,100,000 ($40,900,000 after tax), and contributed to a consolidated net loss for 1993 of $38,100,000, compared to a $45,800,000 consolidated loss in 1992.

In 1993 our U.S. and Canadian operations achieved outstanding results with increased levels of sales and profitability and a significant gain in market share. We made a huge step forward by concentrating on the "Top Line" to meet one of our major goals—manufacturing and selling $2.1 million worth of product from our Ohio company each billing day from June 1 through the end of the year. Our Canadian company also made significant contributions with a 38 percent increase in sales. The bottom line automatically moved into greater profitability.

These impressive gains were not made without sacrifice. Lincoln manufacturing people voluntarily deferred 614 weeks of vacation, worked holidays, and many employees worked a seven day-a-week schedule to fill the steady stream of orders brought in by the sales department as we capitalized on an emerging domestic economy that we felt was being largely ignored by our major competitors.

This remarkable achievement would never have been possible without the expert management of your President and Chief Operating Officer Frederick W. Mackenbach. His leadership consistently inspired our employees and management team alike. The U. S. company's extraordinary performance encouraged the Board of Directors to approve a gross bonus of $55 million, and to continue the regular quarterly dividend payment throughout the year. As you know, the usual course of action for a company reporting a consolidated loss is to cut or defer bonuses and dividends. That these were paid is a tribute to our Board and their steadfast belief in the long range, proven benefits of the Incentive Management System.

Thinking in the long term is critical to our progress in a world that too often seems to demand instant solutions to complex problems. Your Chairman, your Board, and your management team are determined to resist that impulse. Currently, Lincoln people around the world are working diligently to formulate a Strategic Plan that will carry this company into the next century. An important element of this business plan will be our new state-of-the-art motor manufacturing facility, which is on schedule. Furthermore, we have strengthened our international leadership with the addition of executives experienced in global management to our Board and to key management posts.

While your company is indeed emerging from a very challenging period in its history, we project excellent results for 1994, with strong sales, increased profits, and the benefits of those developments accruing to shareholders, customers and employees. As the year proceeds, we will be looking forward to our Centennial in 1995. I am confident that you and I will enjoy celebrating that event together.

Sincerely,

Donald E. Hastings

Chairman and Chief Executive Officer (Retired May 1997)

Postscript: In Lincoln Electric's centennial year, 1995, sales topped $1 billion for the first time. It was also the year that Hastings eliminated the two-tier wage plan that was instituted in 1993. Under this plan, new hires started at 75% of the normal pay rate. This plan increased the turnover among the new hires and was regarded as unfair by senior workers. According to one of them, "If an individual shows he can handle the workload, he should be rewarded." As of 1997, Lincoln Electric appears to be back on track, committed as ever to its philosophy and values.[8] Although Donald F. Hastings has been replaced by Anthony A. Massaro, he continues to be an inspiration for the direction and spirit of Lincoln Electric.

Endnotes

1. T. W. Gerdel, "Lincoln Electric Experiences Season of Worker Discontent," *Plain Dealer* [Cleveland] (December 10, 1995).

2. Ibid.

3. Z. Schiller, "A Model Incentive Plan Gets Caught in a Vise," *Business Week* (January 22, 1996): 89, 92.

4. R. Narisetti, "Job Paradox Manufacturers Decry A Shortage of Workers While Rejecting Many," *The Wall Street Journal* (September 8, 1995): A4.

5. Schiller, "A Model Incentive Plan Gets Caught in a Vise," *Business Week* (January 22, 1996): 89, 92.

6. Gerdel, "Lincoln Electric Experiences Season of Worker Discontent," *Plain Dealer* [Cleveland] (December 10, 1995).

7. Ibid.

8. R. M. Hodgetts, "A Conversation with Donald F. Hastings of the Lincoln Electric Company," *Organizational Dynamics* (Winter 1997): 68–74; M. Gleisser, "Lincoln CEO's Formula: Mutual Trust and Loyalty," *Plain Dealer* (June 22, 1996): 2-C.

CASES

NORDSTROM

This case was prepared by Richard D. Freedman and Jill Vohr, and appears in R.S. Schuler and P.D. Buller (eds.), *Cases in Management, Organizational Behavior and Human Resource Management* 5e (St. Paul, MN: West Publishing, 1996). Updated by R. S. Schuler for *Managing Human Resources* 6e (Cincinnati, OH: South-Western College Publishing, 1998).

In 1880, John W. Nordstrom left Sweden and sailed to the United States. Twenty-one years later, with a $13,000 fortune struck in Klondike gold, he opened up a shoe store in Seattle. Today that small downtown store is a shoe and apparel empire with almost 100 outlets in more than ten states.

Nordstrom is one of the most successful department stores with 1996 sales of $4.5 billion.[1] During the 1980's and 1990's, the company doubled its size from 29 to 83 stores, opening outlets across California and eastward, in Virginia, Washington, DC, and most recently, in Paramus, New Jersey. Typically, sales and net earnings grew comparably. In 1996, however, profits dipped about 10% due to a slow response to customer trends. Today the company is very optimistic about the future.[2] The number of Nordstrom employees has grown to 35,000.

Despite its recent expansion, Nordstrom has remained a family operation. Grandsons John, Bruce, and Jim are all co-chairmen and Jack McMillan, a Nordstrom by marriage, is the company's president. Nordstrom has no chief executive. The company prides itself on having cultivated a family orientation among its workers. All employees are made to feel like members of a family sharing in "the Nordstrom Way."[3]

The Nordstrom Way is perhaps what has set the department store apart from its competition. It is customer service like no one else offers, service above and beyond the call of duty. At Nordstrom, service is an art form. The store hosts gala dinners and fashion shows, has valet parking, concierges for special requests stationed near every store's entrance and soothing ballads played on Steinways at every store accompanying eager smiles from salespeople ready and willing to go to great lengths to please the Nordstrom customer. Such amenities have won Nordstrom customer loyalty and affection. In Seattle, it is common to see bumper stickers that proclaim: "I'd rather be shopping at Nordstrom's." Bruce Nordstrom says of the company's customer service tradition: "We were raised sitting on a shoe stool on our knees in front of a customer. And that is both a literal and figurative posture....A born servant, if you will. There's nothing wrong with that. We' re proud of it....and I think our people know that that's what we do."[4] Nordstrom employees, 'Nordies,' all have similar characteristics. They are upbeat, ambitious but, at the same time, selfless. The Nordstrom store directory describes the Nordie service expectation:

> *"Our staff is genuinely interested in seeing that all your needs are met. They are professionals—will help you with everything from gift suggestions to wardrobe planning. They will even accompany you from department to department until you find exactly what you're looking for."*[5]

Nordies keep personal books listing each of their customers and record every activity and correspondence. Thank you letters are sent to customers for purchases regardless of size. One man was sent a thank you note for buying only a pair of socks.[6] Nordies will personally deliver purchases as well; outside of work time and even on holidays, all to cultivate that special relationship and trust that has resulted in Nordstrom's faithful customer base and glowing sales record.

Thank you letters and personal deliveries only barely suggest what the Nordstrom Way entails. One employee spent over three hours on Easter Sunday finding a customer's house so he could deliver a stuffed rabbit to the customer's wife in person.[7] Another employee searched every store in the company to find a blue shirt with a white cuff and white collar that a customer had seen in an ad. Although the employee never found the shirt in his size, she personally delivered one to him at work the next morning. She had sewn a blue and white shirt together.[8]

What motivates Nordstrom employees to go to such personal trouble for their customers? High salaries for one. Nordstrom employees earn some of the highest salaries in the retail business. Pat McCarthy, a longtime Nordie, is one of them. Twenty years at Nordstrom has enabled him to cultivate a strong, loyal customer base that has brought him commissions of $80,000 plus a year.[9] "It's really a people job, which I love," says McCarthy. "Every year my sales have gotten progressively better.[10] Base pay rates are also high—between $5 and $11 an hour, which is well above the industry standard of $6 to $7.[11] High salaries have given Nordstrom a reputation that attracts good salespeople. Company officials say as many as 2,000 employment applications are received when 100 new entry level openings are announced.[12]

All salespeople start "on the floor," and the company has a strict policy of promoting only from within. Potential managers are required to have at least two years experience selling, and are promoted after less time only under special circumstances. Promotions for all Nordies are based on three criteria: customer service, productivity, and teamwork. If a salesperson has good team spirit, a solid record of fine customer service, and high sales per hour (SPH), after an appropriate length of time with the company, that employee will likely be promoted to department manager. Similarly, a manager whose department goals have been successively reached or surpassed over his or her length of employment, has fine customer service skills and good relations with employees will rise to buyer or store manager positions.

Employees receive little formal training when they are hired or promoted to a new position. Most of the training is informally provided through on the job communication. What formal training they do receive is of a practical nature, e.g. scheduling procedures, salary and commission determinations, benefit opportunities. The three Nordstrom performance criteria (customer service, productivity, and teamwork) are emphasized, although trainees are not told how these criteria are evaluated. Trainees are encouraged to seek information from co-workers and superiors who are described as friendly and accessible. Personal books are provided for use in keeping records of customers, sales, thank you letters, and letters from customers. New employees are also given their own set of business cards to emphasize entrepreneurial opportunities and to encourage them to develop a solid customer base.

Not long ago, Nordstrom replaced its 20-page rule book with a one page sheet and a few words of wisdom: "Use your best judgment in all situations." and "Do whatever it takes to make the customer happy."[13] Nordstrom gives people the freedom to do whatever it takes to make the customer happy (as long as it's legal). The company maintains a decentralized approach to management. Managers are given significant freedom to operate their departments in the Nordstrom way. Individual creativity is a by-product of freedom. They are responsible for hiring, scheduling, and evaluating their crew and receive little guidance in the form of written company policies. Nordstrom hires people who will create their own business and strict policy might stifle ingenuity and creativity. Therefore, most of the information guiding salespeople is received from their managers and not dictated from above. As described by regional personnel director, Molly Goe, each department manager runs his or her department like an individual boutique.[14]

Managers are solely responsible for evaluating their employees. According to Personnel Manager, Mary Kim Stuart, no specific, company-wide evaluation forms are used for salespeople and managers.[15] Rather, each manager designs his or her own evaluation system. If the manager considers an aspect of an employee's performance worth noting it is communicated to the store manager. The store manager, in turn, decides whether to note it in the employee's file.

Like their salespeople, managers are "on the floor" selling and receive a commission. However, their base salaries are much higher. Consequently, although commissions provide managers with an incentive to sell they are less critical for their income than for salespeople.

All Nordstrom salespeople are on a commission system called a draw. Hourly rates are determined based on the salesperson's abilities and length of employment with the company. Commission percentages for salespeople are strictly based on

SPH. Employees receive either their commission percentage times their total sales for that pay period or their hourly rate times their total work hours depending on which is higher. For example, Joe Demarte, Nordstrom's vice president of personnel, explains that a salesperson with a *6.75%* commission who works 40 hours for $10 an hour and sells $10,000 worth would earn *$675* rather than $400. If he sold $1,000 worth, he would earn his hourly wage and no commission.[16] Consequently, only if an employee's sales are high relative to the hours they have worked, will they receive a commission. The higher the total dollar sales, the higher the commission. The incentive is to generate high pace and high dollar sales.

Although most of the training is implicit, Nordstrom's expectations of its employees are explicit. "The life of a Nordstrom salesperson is defined by goals. Daily, monthly, quarterly, and annual goals, departmental, storewide, and company goals, qualitative and quantitative."[17] These goals are formulated at the top by senior managers and trickle down through the hierarchy to departmental managers who are responsible for meeting designated sales quotas for their departments. Managers' salaries, commissions, and bonuses depend on whether or not they attain these goals. Successive failure to reach targets can lead to dismissal. The same is true for salespeople. Managers encourage salespeople to reach high SPH levels. Some even set specific targets for their employees to ensure the attainment of their departments' sales quotas. Managers are free to implement their own approach to productivity as long as it achieves set targets and is consistent with the Nordstrom Way.

SPHs must be kept above a specified minimum level or a salesperson will not receive commission. Low SPHs reflect poor performance and can therefore be grounds for dismissal. Charts are displayed on bulletin boards in back rooms that rank employees by SPH. Ranking reflects an employee's sales ability on the floor. A red line across the chart designates the minimum SPH level necessary to receive a commission. Employees use these charts to keep tabs on their performance and see themselves in relation to their coworkers.

Everyone is formally and informally aware of their sales performance. In addition to the SPH chart, employees can keep track of their performance on computer printouts available in back offices that list their sales by employee identification number. Salespeople often know each other's number and can see how they stand in relation to one another. To keep it that way, some store managers broadcast the prior days top 20 salespeople over a loudspeaker each morning. Numerous sales contests operate as incentives. For example, free dinners are given to employees who make the most multiple-item sales to individual customers. Often, within a department, a $20 bill is passed around throughout the day to the salesperson who has rung up the highest single sale. At the end of the day, the winner gets to keep the $20 bill. Top salespeople are named "Pacesetters", which carries with it roughly the status of a varsity letter on a high school athlete's jacket. Motivational skits are used to generate sales enthusiasm. Managers dress up as Kermit the Frog to get employees whipped into a selling frenzy, or a department's staff performs the Michael Jackson song "Beat it" with the words, "Charge it."[18] Nordstrom also offers a course on self-motivation encouraging salespeople to ask themselves what they want to accomplish each day to spur them to take responsibility for their own future. Many do, especially the successful ones. Employees seem to know precisely what they want and need to achieve. One top saleswomen stated, "The first year I consciously set quarterly goals to achieve the Pacesetter requirement. My second year my personal goal was $500,000, and I paced myself accordingly. My third year I wanted to achieve $1 million in total sales. To accomplish this I set monthly and quarterly quotas and closely monitored my progress."[19] Clearly, the best salespeople are entrepreneurial self-starters.

Managers are also encouraged to be self-motivated. "Every year the company's managers gather in meetings where they publicly state their store or departmental goals for the next 12 months. Then their bosses will reveal their own goals for the

same manager, sometimes with a dramatic flourish."[20] Working at Nordstrom is not for everybody. The company has very high expectations. If you don't meet them, you're gone.

Good customer relations the Nordstrom Way are also important. Employees buzz with tales of extraordinary efforts made by salespeople. Peer competition and pressures to be a member of "the Nordstrom family" keep salespeople striving for a popularity that is based on their sales ability. Rewards for customer satisfaction are high. Bonuses up to $100 are awarded to salespeople with the best customer relations. Managers read letters received from pleased customers aloud at company meetings and over the loudspeaker. Whoops and cheers are heard from listeners. The salespeople who received the letters are honored as "Customer Service All Stars".[21] Their pictures are hung on the wall next to the customer service desk. They receive extra discounts on store merchandise and commendations on their personal records.

To check on the customer service provided by their employees, Nordstrom periodically dispatches "secret shoppers," people who pretend to be shoppers.[22] Salespeople are encouraged to be friendly and warm. Nordstrom does not tolerate rude behavior towards its customers. Smile contests are conducted to motivate courteous behavior. Pictures of smiling employees are taken and displayed in the lunchroom. Those that smile the most on the job receive the highest praise. "Recognition is the number one motivation," says Demarte with respect to Nordstrom contests. "We recognize our top performers constantly, as well as our customer service heroics."[23]

Most Nordstrom employees strongly uphold the Nordstrom philosophy of service. Some are almost religious about it, happily dedicating their lives to master "The Nordstrom Way". Yet, other employees feel the customers are catered to at the expense of their own working conditions, that systems meant to encourage employees actually oppress them, placing them in an environment of constant pressure, harassment, and competition. Some employees began to accuse Nordstrom of unfair labor practices. The United Food and Commercial Workers Union, of which only 2,000 of the 30,000 Nordstrom workforce are members, became involved.[24] Accusations of "off the clock" work and overbearing work pressures dominated complaints.

All employees are expected to contribute to stocking, delivering, and picking up merchandise. Much of this work is done off the clock, past the end of a shift, on the weekends or through breaks and lunches. Also employees are expected to maintain close relations with their customers which implicitly entails thank you notes and sometimes personal deliveries. The Nordstrom practice is not to include the hours spent at these activities in the total hours worked for each employee's pay period. Union leader, Joe Peterson, in his fight against Nordstrom and what he feels is grossly unfair treatment of employees, continues to search for and encourage employees to hop on the bandwagon. Over 500 complaints were filed with the workers' union and as more complaints poured in, the union set up an 800 hotline to handle them. An article in *The Wall Street Journal* included several stories told by Nordstrom employees themselves.

Taking Out the Trash

A divorced California homemaker who returned to the job market at 40, Patty Bemis joined Nordstrom in 1981, lured by the promise of a bigger income and the "status" of induction in the Nordie elite. She stayed for eight years. "They came to me," she recalls of the Nordstrom recruiters. "I was working at The Broadway as Estee Lauder's counter manager and they said they had heard I had wonderful sales figures." Ms. Bemis was thrilled. "We'd all heard Nordstrom was the place to work. They painted a great picture and I fell right into it." She found herself working progressively harder for less money and amid more fear. "The managers were these little tin gods, always grilling you about your sales," she recalls. "You feel like your job was constantly in jeopardy. They'd write you up for anything, being sick, the way you dressed." Once, she had to get a doctor's note so she wouldn't get in trouble for wearing low-heel shoes to work. Sufficiently cowed, she reported to work even when she had strep throat. Worn down by pressure, "the girls around me were dropping like flies," she says. "Everyone was always in tears. You feel like an absolute nothing working for them."

Ms. Bemis was consistently one of her department's top sellers, but some years she only made $18,000, far below what she had expected she would earn. She won a company-wide sales contest, and received "a pair of PJs," she recalls. "Whoopiedoo!" And she logged many unpaid hours, delivering cosmetics to customers and unpacking hundreds of boxes of makeup.... "Working off the clock was standard," crucial to elevating sales per hour. "In the end, really serving the customer, being an All-Star, meant nothing; if you had low sales per hour, you were forced out."

During a big Clinique sale, Ms. Bemis says she worked 12 to 15 hours shifts for a number of days without overtime pay or a day off. On the drive home at 10:30 on the tenth night, she passed out at the wheel and slammed into the freeway's center divider, she says. While she was at home recovering from head injuries, she recalls, "The manager kept calling me and saying, 'Patty, we can't hold your job much longer.'" Her doctor told her she should stay out a few weeks but she didn't dare. "Now, I know I have all these rights. But at the time all I knew was I had to have that job."

She finally left last spring. "I just couldn't take it anymore—the constant demands, the grueling hours. I just said one day, life's too short." She took a sales post at Scandia Down Shops, where she says she makes $400 more a month than at Nordstrom. "And I can sleep at night."[25]

A Broken Clock

The first time Lori Lucas came to one of the many "mandatory" Saturday morning department meetings and saw the sign: "Do Not Punch the Clock." She assumed the managers were telling the truth when they said the clock was temporarily out of order. But as weeks went by, she discovered the clock was always "broken" or the timecards were just missing.

Finally she, and several other employees just marked the hours down on their timecard manually. She and another employee recall that their manager whited-out the hours and accused the two of not being "team players."

The department meetings "were unbelievable," Ms. Lucas recalls. "There you'd be at seven in the morning and they had all these security guards dressed up like the California Raisins, with plastic garbage bags stuffed with M&Ms around their midriffs. And all you can hear is people chanting, 'We're number one!' and 'You want to do it for Nordstrom.' Finally I went up to the store manager and said, 'What is this all about?' and she said, 'You are here to learn the Nordstrom Way.'"

The Nordstrom Way involved an endless round of contests ("Who Looks More Nordstrom" was a popular one, intended to encourage employees to shop at the stores) and the daily recital of "affirmations" ("I only sell multiples," was one chanted by salespeople).

And the Nordstrom Way, Ms. Lucas discovered, meant working for free. "My manager would say, 'You go clock out and come down and we'll talk.' That was her little trick way of saying there's nonsell work to do."

Like most salesclerks at Nordstrom, Ms. Lucas also had daily quotas of thank you letters to write, and monthly customer-service "books" to generate photo albums that are supposed to be filled with letters from grateful customers. ("People would get so desperate they would have their friends and relatives write fake letters for them." Petra Rousu, a 10-year salesclerk veteran, recalls.) Such duties, Ms. Lucas says, were supposed to be tackled only after hours. "I'd be up till 3 a.m., doing my letters, and doing my manager's books" she says. "Before you know it, your whole life is Nordstrom. But you couldn't complain, because then your manager would schedule you for the bad hours, your sales per hour would fall and next thing you know, you're out the door."

The pressure eventually gave Ms. Lucas an ulcer, she says. One day after working 22 days without a day off, she demanded a lunch break. On her hour off, she applied for and got a new job elsewhere and gave notice as soon as she returned. "I remember thinking, I'm making less than $20,000 a year. Why am I killing myself? Nordstrom was the most unfair place I ever worked."[26]

Staying On Top

For nearly two years, Cindy Nelson had stayed on top of the chart in one of the Bellevue, Washington, stores. She was on her way to making "Pacesetter" again.... A clique of sales clerks on the floor, led by numbers two and three on the charts, held a pow-wow one day, decided that Ms. Nelson must be stealing their sales and vowed to have her "watched," according to court depositions that later became part of a suit filed by Ms. Nelson against Nordstrom.

On September 29, 1986, Cindy Nelson reported for work and was immediately whisked into the personnel office. The department manager had before her five notes of complaint from the salesclerks, all unsigned, which claimed Ms. Nelson had been stealing sales.

Ms. Nelson asked to inspect the sales receipts in question and confront her accusers, but the manager, Rhonda Eakes, refused. "I just didn't feel that it was any of her business," Ms. Eakes explained later in her deposition. Then she told Ms. Nelson that she was fired. (All of the managers and employees involved in Ms. Nelson's firing declined comment, referring queries to Mr. Nordstrom, who said, "That gal wasn't a good employee.")

"I was totally stunned," recalls Ms. Nelson, who had a stack of customer-service citations in her file and had been told she was about to make manager. She was also, up until then, "your 100-percent gung-ho Nordie. This whole time I thought I was going to be this great Nordstrom person and now I was nothing, a nobody. I became an emotional wreck."[27]

Other criticisms were made of Nordstrom. Allegedly employees were required to purchase and wear Nordstrom clothing while on the job.[28] The company was also accused of having discriminatory practices.[29] Part of becoming a Nordie, employees say, involves acquiring a certain look. Lupe Sakagawa, a top saleswoman, recalls that on her first day on the job, her manager strong-armed her into buying $1,400 of the "right" clothes—all from the department. But that wasn't enough. The store manager then called her in and told her: "Correct your accent." Ms. Sakagawa is Mexican. "It was very hard for me to prove myself" she says, "because of that image of the Nordstrom Girl—blond hair, young, and cute."[30] Nordstrom has since hired a black human resources officer and the company reports that 25.6% of all its employees are minorities.[31]

Other sentiments were brought to the attention of the media through Peterson, who felt employees are being exploited. Peterson specifically criticized the SPH incentive. He believed that in order to keep SPH up, employees were encouraged to keep their work hours down. Consequently, they could not record hours spent doing certain non-selling chores (stock taking, personal deliveries, thank-you notes) on their time sheets. Nordstrom's position was that the employees are compensated by commissions that actually pay them for doing extra tasks. Employees willingly donate their time. It is not explicitly required of them. Peterson argued that "...If one employee is donating a lot of time, it forces others to do the same or it creates an atmosphere where everyone is playing on an unequal playing field."[32] Because employees who log only sales times have higher SPH than coworkers who clock in all other business and support activities, employees are motivated to decrease their nonsales hours. They work off the clock to be awarded better shifts and more hours. In response, Demarte insisted that because

SPH is the objective performance evaluation factor...that's what people focus on.[33] Evaluation is not based just on SPH. People who perform the best are also best in giving the customer service and working as a team. Yet, Demarte does admit there is pressure. "People who perform the most effectively are the ones we need to have on the floor. Therefore, there's this pressure to be better."[34] Middle management encourages workers to get jobs done within certain time frames and if they can't meet the deadlines, exert "implied pressures" on their salespeople to get the job done after work hours. President Jack McMillan insists that "the system is as level a playing field as you can find for people to rise up quickly on their own merit. Everybody starts on the selling floor and the ones that show initiative, creativity, and desire rise up in the system and become department managers. Those department managers that show the ability to make things happen rise up to be buyers or store managers or vice presidents. We think it's a great system, but it's obvious there are some glitches in it. One way to control selling costs—not the right way—is to encourage people to get the work done in a certain time frame. If they can't get it done, then there is implied pressure to work off the clock. We are responsible for the pressure from middle managers. There was no plan or scheme, but it happened. I guess you could say we were negligent for not knowing, but we are responsible for it."[35] Recently Nordstrom set aside $15 million to pay back employees who were victims of management glitches.[36]

Despite Nordstrom's promises' of back pay (in 1993 Nordstrom set aside $15 million in a reserve fund to pay back wages to employees who had performed off-the-clock services), the union still fought them, pointing a finger at Nordstrom's high turnover rates, even for the retail industry. Nordstrom replied that although salespeople who regularly had trouble meeting sales quotas or coping with pressure to improve their performance were dismissed, these employees usually leave of their own volition. Having been made to feel uncomfortable or inadequate in the Nordstrom culture that celebrates accomplishment, they recognize that they do not belong. They leave before the company has cause to dismiss them. Nordstrom compensates by attempting to hire people who are innate Nordies. The company's hiring philosophy supports their decentralized management style. Bruce Nordstrom is quoted as saying, "All we do is hire nice, motivated, hardworking people and then we leave them alone to do what they do best. The system is to have self-empowered people who have an entrepreneurial spirit, who feel that they're in this to better themselves and to feel good about themselves and to make more money and to be successful."[37] Jim Nordstrom adds, "There's expectations on our people. And when people apply for a job anyplace, they want to work hard and they want to do a good job. That's their intention. And our intention is to allow them the freedom to work as hard as they want to work."[38] However, miss your quota three months in a row, and you're out. "If you don't like to win, it's hard to be successful in this company," says Midwestern regional manager Bob Middlemas.[39]

Although there were several complaints, it seemed that most Nordstrom employees also did not support their union leader's accusations. In December 1990, more than half of the 1,850 employees left the union after membership became optional.[40] With continued pressure by Peterson, a former Nordstrom shoe salesperson, Nordstrom responded with an anti-union campaign. And in July of 1991, employees consisting of salespeople, office workers, clerks and display workers at five stores in Seattle voted by more than a 2-to-1 ratio to end union representation altogether.[41] Indeed, several employees speak in favor of Nordstrom stating that they love working for the company and do not want anything changed.[42]

"It's a feeling, it's family," Ms. Sargent says enthusiastically. "Sure, during the busy seasons, you do work six to seven days a week, but being in the store with the Christmas tree here, you create your own memories." Ms. Sargent, who has worked for Nordstrom in Seattle for seven years, says she doesn't mind that she sometimes does work for free. "When I go home and do follow-ups or write thank-yous, I think it's inappropriate to be charging the company for that."

At the San Francisco store, another set of employees testified to the company's virtues. "Here at Nordstrom, I feel I can be the best that I can be," says Doris Quiros, a salesperson in the women's sportswear department. While other retailers "give you a big book of rules, when I came here, Nordstrom gave me one with only one rule: Use you best judgment. That's because they want me to be my own boss." In the women's shoes department, Tim Snow, a former waiter, says people are impressed now when they learn where he works. "You can be at the grocery store and you show them your ID card and they'll start right off on how much they love to shop there."[43]

If happy employees are not enough to justify the existing Nordstrom system, the company's success and their numerous satisfied customers are. "They treat you with the most reverence you can imagine," one customer said after a salesperson offered her the option of either wearing a Nordstrom dress that had a run in it and returning it at her convenience for a full refund or taking $100 off the price. "It's so darn easy to go in there."[44] Betsy Sanders, the head of the company's Southern California division, sometimes stands at the store exit at night as the store closes and says good night to departing customers. One evening, as she bade some shoppers farewell, she heard one say: "What kind of drugs are these people on? Even the doormen are nice."[45]

Looking for ways to attract more customers, Nordstrom introduced a mail-order catalog. In its first year, 1994, it attracted 300,000 shoppers. At the same time Nordstrom introduced a proprietary Visa credit card and went online with its Nordstrom Personal Touch America on marketplace MCI:

- http://www.internetmci.com/marketplace
- 6870401@mcimail.com, or
- http://www.nordstrom-pta.com

Endnotes

1. J. Greenwald, "Losing Its Luster," *Time* (March 24, 1997): 64–65.

2. Ibid.

3. Robert Spector and Patrick D. McCarthy, *The Nordstrom Way* (New York: John Wiley & Sons, Inc., 1995); Charlene Marmer Solomon, "Nightmare At Nordstrom," *Personnel Journal* (September, 1990): 77.

4. Marti Galovic Palmer, Producer, "The Nordstrom Boys," *60 Minutes* Vol. XXII Num.33, May 6, 1990: 8.

5. "How Nordstrom Got There," *Stores* (January 1990): 68.

6. Mary Kim Stuart, Nordstrom Personnel Director (Paramus, New Jersey) telephone conversation with author, November 9, 1990.

7. "The Nordstrom Boys," *60 Minutes*: 8.

8. Ibid.

9. Susan C. Faludi, "At Nordstrom Stores Service Comes First—But at a Big Price," *The Wall Street Journal* (February 20, 1990).

10. Ibid.

11. Seth Lubove, "Don't Listen to the Boss, Listen to the Customer," *Forbes* (December 4, 1995): 45–46; Dori Jones Yang, "Will 'The Nordstrom Way' Travel Well?" *Business Week* (September 3, 1990): 83.

12. Joyce Anne Oliver and Eric J. Johnson, "People Motive Redefines Customer Service," *HR Magazine* Vol. 35 Iss. 6 (June 1990): 120.

13. Mary Kim Stuart interview, November 9, 1990.

14. Solomon, "Nightmare At Nordstrom," p. 77.

15. Mary Kim Stuart interview, November 9, 1990.

16. Solomon, "Nightmare At Nordstrom," p. 79.

17. Richard W. Stevenson, "Watch Out Macy's, Here Comes Nordstrom," *New York Times* (August 27, 1989): 39.

18. Ibid.

19. Ibid.

20. Ibid.

21. Solomon, "Nightmare At Nordstrom," p. 83.

22. Faludi, "At Nordstrom Stores, Service Comes First—But at a Big Price."

23. Solomon, "Nightmare At Nordstrom," p. 77.

24. Ibid., 78.

25. Faludi, "At Nordstrom Stores, Service Comes First—But at a Big Price"; Robert Spector and Patrick D. McCarthy, *The Nordstrom Way* (New York: John Wiley, 1995).

26. Ibid.

27. Ibid.

28. Solomon, "Nightmare At Nordstrom," p. 78.

29. Faludi, "At Nordstrom Stores, Service Comes First—But at a Big Price."

30. Ibid.

31. Solomon, "Nightmare At Nordstrom," p. 78.

32. Ibid., 80.

33. Ibid., 81.

34. Ibid.

35. Robert Spector, "Nordstrom Discusses Its Problems," *Women's Wear Daily* (March 27, 1990): 18.

36. Solomon, "Nightmare At Nordstrom," p. 80.

37. "The Nordstrom Boys," *60 Minutes*: 10.

38. Ibid.

39. Lubove, "Don't Listen to the Boss, Listen to the Customer," p. 46.

40. "Nordstrom Workers in Seattle Reject Union," *New York Times* (July 20, 1991).

41. Ibid.

42. Solomon, "Nightmare At Nordstrom," p. 77.

43. Faludi, "At Nordstrom Stores, Service Comes First—But at a Big Price."

44. Richard W. Stevenson, "Watch Out Macy's, Here Comes Nordstrom," *New York Times* (August 27, 1989): 38.

45. Ibid., 40.

APPENDICES

APPENDIX A
Legislation, Court, and NLRB Decisions Affecting Human Resource Management

APPENDIX B
Information for Managing Human Resources

APPENDIX C
The Validation Process

APPENDIX D
The Resume

APPENDIX A

Legislation, Court, and NRLB Decisions Affecting Human Resource Management

Employment Legislation/Basic Provisions

Act	Jurisdiction	Basic Provisions
Fair Labor Standards Act (1938) and subsequent amendments—FLSA	Most interstate employers, certain types of employees, are exempt from overtime provisions—executive, administrative, and professional employees and outside salespeople	Establishes a minimum wage; controls hours through premium pay for overtime; controls working hours for children
Minimum Wage Law (1977)	Small businesses	Sets graduated increases in minimum wage rates
Equal Pay Act (1963 amendment to the FLSA)	Same as FLSA except no employees are exempt	Prohibits unequal pay for males and females with equal skill, effort, and responsibility working under similar working conditions
Civil Rights Act (1964) (amended by EEOA 1972)	Employers with fifteen or more employees, employment agencies, and labor unions	Prevents discrimination on the basis of race, color, religion, sex, or national origin; establishes EEOC
Civil Rights Act of 1991	Same as the Civil Rights Act of 1964	Protects groups against discrimination (as does the 1964 act), but makes provision for jury trials and punitive compensation
Equal Employment Opportunity Act (1972)—EEOA	Adds employees of state and local government and educational institutions, reduced number of employees required to fifteen	Amends Title VII, increases enforcement powers of EEOC
Executive Order 11246 (1965) as amended by Executive Order 11375(1966)	Federal contractors and subcontractors with contracts over $50,000 and fifty or more employees	Prevents discrimination on the basis of race, color, religion, sex, or national origin, establishes Office of Federal Contract Compliance (OFCC)
Revised Order Number 4 (1971)	Federal contractors	Defines acceptable affirmative action program
Executive Order 11478 (1969)	Federal agencies	Prevents discrimination on the basis of race, color, religion, sex, or national origin
Age Discrimination in Employment Act (1967)—revised 1978; 1986	Employers with more than twenty employees	Prevents discrimination against persons age forty and over, and states compulsory retirement for some workers
Rehabilitation Act (1973) as amended 1980	Government contractors and federal agencies	Prevents discrimination against persons with physical and/or mental handicaps and provides for affirmative action
Americans with Disabilities Act (1990)	15 or more employees	Protects against discrimination of individuals with disabilities
Older Worker Benefit Protection Act of 1990	Same as the Age Discrimination in Employment Act as amended	Employers are prohibited from discriminating with regard to benefits on the basis of age

Act	**Jurisdiction**	**Basic Provisions**
Immigration Act of 1990	*Immigration Reform and Control Act* of 1986—IRCA	Amends the employer-verification and unfair-immigration—related employment practices as defined by the IRCA
The Family and Medical Leave Act of 1993	Employers with 50 or more employees	Allows workers to take up to 12 weeks unpaid leave for pregnancy or illness of close family member
Glass Ceiling Act of 1991	Same as the 1991 *Civil Rights Act*	Empowers the Glass Ceiling Commission to focus greater attention on eliminating artificial barriers for advancement of women and minorities
Prevailing wage laws—1. *Davis-Bacon Act* (1931) and 2. *Walsh-Healey Act* (1935)	Employers with government construction projects of $2,000 (Davis-Bacon) and government contracts of $10,000 or more	Guarantees prevailing wages to employees of government contractors
Legally required fringe benefits— 1. OASDHI (1935 and amendments)	Virtually all employers	Provides income and healthcare to all retired employees and income to the survivors of employees who have died
2. Unemployment compensation (1935)	Virtually all employers	Provides income to employees who are laid off or fired
3. Workers' compensation (dates differ from state to state)	Virtually all employers	Provides benefits to employees who are injured on the job and to the survivors of employees who are killed on the job
Occupational Safety and Health Act (1970)—OSHA	Most interstate employers	Assures as far as possible—safe and healthy working conditions and the preservation of our human resources
Employee Retirement Income Security Act (1974)—ERISA	Most interstate employers with pension plans (no employer is required to have such a plan)	Protects employees covered by a pension plan from losses in benefits due to: • mismanagement • plant closings and bankruptcies • job changes
Freedom of Information Act (1966)	Federal agencies only	Allows individuals to review employers' records on them and bring civil damages
The Pregnancy Discrimination Act of 1978	Same as *Civil Rights Act* (1964)	Identifies pregnancy as a disability and entitles the woman to the same benefits as any other disability
Privacy Act of 1974 (Public Law 93-579)	Federal agencies only	Allows individuals to review employer's records on them and sue for civil damages
Uniform Guidelines on Employee Selection Procedures (1978)	Same as EEOA (1972)	Updates EEOC 1970 guidelines to more clearly define adverse impact and test validation
Guidelines on Sexual Harassment (1980)	Same as EEOA (1972)	Defines standards for what constitutes harassment
Vietnam Era Veterans Readjustment Act (1974)	Government contractors with contracts in excess of $10,000	Provides for affirmative action in the employment of Vietnam era veterans

Act	Jurisdiction	Basic Provisions
Civil Rights Act of 1866, Section 1981	All citizens	Gives all persons, regardless of race, age, and national origin, the same contractual rights as "white citizens." Does not apply to sex-based discrimination.
Civil Rights Act of 1871, Section 1983	All citizens	Applies to sex-based discrimination
The First Amendment, U.S. Constitution	All citizens	Guarantees freedom of speech and religion
The Fifth Amendment	All citizens	Guarantees due process of law
The Fourteenth Amendment	All citizens	Prohibits abridgment of federally conferred privileges by actions of the state
Employee Polygraph Protection Act (1988)	Private employers	Prohibits most employees from polygraph testing without reasonable suspicion
Drug-Free Workplace Act (1988)	Federal contractors with contracts exceeding $25,000	Requires employers to maintain drug-free workplace
Worker Adjustment and Retraining Notification Act of 1988	Employers with more than 100 employees	Requires 60 days notice of plant or office closing

Labor Relations Legislation: Private Sector

Act	Jurisdiction	Basic Provisions
Railway Labor Act (1926)—RLA	Railroad workers and airline employees	Provides right to organize, provides majority choice of representatives, prohibits "yellow dog" contracts, outlines dispute settlement procedures
Norris-LaGuardia Act (1932)	All employers and labor organizations	Prohibits yellow dog contracts, injunctions for nonviolent activity of unions (strikes, picketing, and boycotts), provides limited union liability
National Labor Relations Act (1935)—*Wagner Act*	Nonmanagerial employees in private industry not covered by *Railway Labor Act* (RLA)	Provides right to organize, provides for collective bargaining, requires employers to bargain, unions must represent all members equally
Labor Management Relations Act (1947)—*Taft-Hartley Act*	Nonmanagerial employees in private industry not covered by RLA	Prohibits unfair labor practices of unions; outlaws closed shop; prohibits strikes in national emergencies; requires both parties to bargain in good faith
Labor Management Reporting and Disclosure Act (1959)—*Landrum-Griffin Act*	Labor organizations	Outlines procedures for redressing internal union problems
Amendments to *Taft-Hartley Act* (1974)	Labor organizations	Specifies illegal activities within union

Labor Relations Legislation: Public Sector

Act	Jurisdiction	Basic Provisions
Executive Order 10988 (1962)	Federal employees	Recognizes employee's right to join unions and bargain collectively; prohibits strikes. Requires agency to meet and confer with union on policy practices and working conditions

Act	Jurisdiction	Basic Provisions
Executive Orders 11616 (1971) and 11838 (1975)	Federal employees	Expand EG 11491 to cover labor-management relations: addresses disputes of bargaining rights; orders elections; consolidates units, limits scope of grievance and arbitration procedures
Civil Service Reform Act (1978)	Federal employees	Defines grievance procedure and requirements for goal-type performance appraisals; establishes Senior Executive Service (SES)

Court and NLRB Decisions Provisions

United Steelworkers of America v. Warrior & Gulf Navigation Co. (1960); *United Steelworkers of America v. American Manufacturing Co.* (1960), and *United Steelworkers of America v. Enterprise Wheel & Car Corp.* (1960)
Referred to as the "Trilogy" cases, these three cases upheld the arbitrator's authority to remedy violations of collective bargaining agreements. The court, however, could decide the question of arbitrability. If the court determines that a collectively bargained contract calls for arbitration, then the arbitrator can arbitrate it. This was further upheld in *AT&T Technologies, Inc. v. Communications Workers of America* (1986).

Stringfellow v. Monsanto Corporation (1970)
Established the precedent for giving credit to the employer for making performance appraisal-based decisions on the basis of evidence that the appraisal uses definite identifiable criteria based on the quality and quantity of an employee's work.

Phillips v. Martin Marietta Corp. (1971)
Whether a BFOQ exists depends on whether it can be shown that the qualification is demonstrably more relevant to job performance for a woman than a man.

Diaz v. Pan American World Airways, Inc. (1971)
The primary function of an airline is to transport passengers safely from one point to another Therefore, not hiring males for flight attendants is discriminatory. Business necessity is established.

Griggs v. Duke Power (1971)
Test for hiring cannot be used unless job related. Organizations must show evidence of job relatedness. Not necessary to establish intent to discriminate.

Board of Regents of State Colleges v. Roth (1972)
Protects workers from discharge when due process hasn't been given.

Richardson v. Hotel Corporation of America (1972)
Dismissal on grounds of conviction record resulted in adverse impact; but since conviction record argued (not shown) to be related to business necessity (not job performance), dismissal is okay.

Spurlock v. United Airlines (1972)
Use of college degree as a selection criterion valid because job related, even though no performance data provided.

Rowe v. General Motors Corporation (1972)
All white supervisory recommendations were based on subjective and vague standards which led to a lack of promotions for black employees. Identified five discriminatory factors.

Hodgson v. Robert Hall Clothes, Inc. (1973)
Pay differentials between salesmen and saleswomen justified on the basis of profitability of area in which employees work.

McDonnell Douglas Corporation v. Green (1973)
Employer's test device constitutes prima facie case of racial discrimination under four different criteria (see Chapter 7).

Brito v. Zia Company (1973)
Zia violated Title VII because they laid off a disproportionate number of a protected group on the basis of low performance scores on measures that were not validated.

Sugarman v. Dougal (1973)
The due process and equal protection clauses of the Fifth Amendment also apply to aliens in public employment.

Hodgson v. Greyhound Lines, Inc. (1974)
Could discriminate without empirical evidence on basis of age. Good faith used to show older people would make less safe drivers.

Corning Glass Works v. Brennan (1974)
The Equal Pay Act is violated by paying male inspectors on the night shift a higher base wage than female inspectors on the day shift.

Baxter v. Savannah Sugar Refining Co. (1974)
Subjective appraisal form is viewed as discriminatory.

Green v. Missouri Pacific R. R. Co. (1975)
Applying the lessons from Griggs v. Duke Power, the court and the EEOC have found it unlawful to refuse to hire job applicants because of their arrest record except for certain circumstances *(Richardson v. Hotel Corporation of America)*.

Kirkland v. New York Department of Correctional Services (1975)
The use of quotas was rejected as a method of determining promotions except as an interim measure to be used until nondiscriminatory procedures to determine promotion are established.

Stamps (EEOC) v. Detroit Edison (1975)
Title VII does not provide for an award of punitive damages. Back pay and attorney fees are the explicit provisions of Title VII.

Rogers v. International Paper Company (1975)
Subjective criteria are not to be condemned as unlawful per se because some decisions about hiring and promotions in supervisory and managerial jobs cannot be made using objective standards alone. This opinion, however, is somewhat contrary to those in *Albemarle Paper Company v. Moody* (1973); *Baxter v. Savannah Sugar Refining Corporation* (1974); and *Rowe v. General Motors* (1972).

Albemarle v. Moody (1975)
Need to establish evidence that test is related to content of job. Could use job analysis to do so, but not evidence from global performance ratings made by supervisors.

McDonnald v. Santa Fe Trail Transportation Co. (1976)
Requires consistency in dismissal policies due to absenteeism.

Mastie v. Great Lakes Steel Corporation (1976)
As with *Stringfellow*, the court said that the objectivity of evaluation can be established by demonstrating that the company performed and relied on a thorough evaluation process intended to be used fairly and accurately.

Smith v. Mutual Benefit Life Insurance Company (1976)
Employer is not discriminating if refusing to hire male appearing to be effeminate.

Chrysler Outboard v. Dept. of Industry (1976)
Employer refuses to hire a worker who had leukemia because he was prone to infection. Court said he had to be hired because he was qualified.

Watkins v. Scott Paper Company (1976)
Performance data to validate tests that are derived from graphic scales are too vague and easily subject to discrimination.

Robinson v. Union Carbide Corporation (1976)
These two require written standards for promotion to help prevent discrimination.

Wade v. Mississippi Cooperative Extension Service (1976)
Performance scores used to decide promotions and salary issues not valid because no job analysis.

Washington v. Davis (1976)
When a test procedure is challenged under constitutional law, intent to discriminate must be established. No need to establish intent if filed under Title VII, just show effects. Could use communication test to select applicants for police force.

Castaneda v. Partida (1977)
Prima facie evidence of discrimination established when evidence of both statistical disparity and discriminatory selection procedures vis-a-vis the gross population figures.

General Foods Corp. (1977)
Corporatewide team program of employee-employer cooperation does not violate the *National Labor Relations Act* because program established to promote efficiency, not forestall unionization.

James v. Stockham Values and Fitting Company (1977)
An apprenticeship program was viewed as discriminatory since selections were made by supervisors who were given guidelines.

Barnes v. Costle (1977)
Sexual harassment is a form of sex discrimination under Title VII, and employer is responsible if takes no action on learning of events.

Mistretta v. Sandia Corporation (1977)
Employment decisions suspect when based on evaluations that reflect only best judgments and opinions of evaluators rather than identifiable criteria based on quality or quantity of work or specific performances that are supported by some kind of record.

Hazelwood School District v. U.S. (1977)
Labor market comparisons must be based on relevant labor market and not general labor market.

International Brotherhood of Teamsters v. United States (1977)
Bona fide seniority systems maintained without discriminatory intent are exempt from Title VII liability if established before 1964.

United Air Lines, Inc. v. McMann (1977)
Employer can force retirement before age of sixty-five if it has bona fide retirement plan.

Yukas v. Libbey-Owens-Ford (1977)
All practices against nepotism, especially close relatives and spouses, are nondiscriminators, especially in same department and/or as in supervisor-subordinate relationship.

Flowers v. Crouch-Walter Corporation (1977)
Plaintiff established *prima facie* evidence that a discharge was discriminatory and not based on performance.

Donaldson v. Pillsbury Company (1977)
Requires clear establishment and communication of job requirements and performance standards.

James v. Stockman Values and Fittings Company (1977)
White supervisors without formal guidelines selecting applicants to apprenticeship program is discriminatory. Need more discrete performance appraisal.

Dothard v. Rawlinson (1977)
Height requirements not valid, therefore constitutes discriminatory practice.

Bakke v. Regents of the University of California (1978)
Reverse discrimination not allowed. Race, however, can be used in selection decisions. Affirmative action programs permissible when prior discrimination established.

United States v. City of Chicago (1978)
Specific promotion criteria must be used that are related to the job to which being promoted.

Detroit Police Officers Association v. Coleman Young (1979)
Court holds in favor of goals and quotas to reverse previous discrimination.

NLRB v. Wright Line, Inc. (1981)
In cases where an employee is fired for what may appear to be union-related activities, the employer must show (to be vindicated in the dismissal) that the discipline imposed is the same as in other cases where union activity was not an issue.

American Textile Manufacturers Institute v. Donovan (1981)
OSHA need not do cost-benefit analyses before issuing working health standards.

Tooley v. Martin-Marietta Corporation (1981)
Must be religious accommodation for employees who object to union membership or support (as long as no undue hardship on union).

Los Angeles Dept. of Water v. Manhard (1981)
Rules against department rule of having female employees contribute more to a retirement plan than men.

Clayton v. United Auto Workers (1981)
When a union member feels unfairly represented and only the employer can grant the relief requested, the employee need not exhaust internal union remedies before suing the employer.

Lehman v. Yellow Freight System (1981)
Informal affirmative action not permissible although formal voluntary one such as Weber is okay.

Northwest Airlines, Inc. v. Transport Workers (1981)
An employer found guilty of job discrimination cannot force an employee's union to contribute to the damages, even though the union may have negotiated the unequal terms.

County of Washington, Oregon v. Gunther (1981)
It can be illegal (under Title VII and EPA 1963) to pay women unfairly low wages even if not doing same work as men (not a comparable worth case).

First National Maintenance v. NLRB (1981)
Management does not have to negotiate with unions in advance over closing plants or dropping lines.

Texas Department of Community Affairs v. Joyce Ann Burdine (1981)
A defendant in a job discrimination case need only provide a legitimate, nondiscriminatory explanation for not hiring or promoting a woman or minority, and need not prove that the white man hired was better qualified. The burden of proving intentional discrimination rests with the plaintiff.

Fernandez v. Wynn Oil Company (1981)
Title VII does not permit employers to use stereotypic impressions of male and female roles as a BFOQ defense to sex discrimination. Employer can't use customer preferences for working with male employees as a defense of discrimination.

Connecticut v. Teal (1982)
Employers must defend each part of a selection process against adverse impact and not just the end result of the entire process (the bottom line).

Spirit v. TIAA/CREF (1982)
Retirement annuities must be equal, regardless of sex.

Borg Wartier Corp. v. NLRB (1982)
Distinction between mandatory and permissible. Terms depend on whether topic regulates the employer-employee relation.

American Tobacco v. Patterson (1982)
Bona fide seniority systems without discriminating intent are exempt from Title VII liability.

Newport News Shipbuilding and Dry Dock Co. v. EEOC (1983)
If an employer supplies any level of health benefits to female workers' husbands, the employer must also supply the same level of benefits to male workers' wives, and that includes pregnancy benefits. This, in effect, reverses the Supreme Court's ruling in *General Electric v. Gilbert*, where the court said that pregnancy benefits need not be given the same treatment by employers as other health and disability programs.

Arizona Governing Committee v. Norris (1983)
Pension payouts by employers should be equal for women and men, and past unequal treatment of women must be cured by retroactive funding of pensions. This decision is in essence the other half of the issue. The first half was rendered in the Supreme Court decision of *Los Angeles Department of Water and Power v. Manhart,* where the decision was made that requiring larger contributions by females than males into pension programs is discriminatory.

NLRB v. Transportation Management (1983)
Employees are protected by the NLRA when helping organize employees. If an employee claims to be fired for trying to organize a union but the employer claims it was poor performance, the employer has the burden of proof. In cases where such "mixed" motives for employer action may exist, the employer must prove the case.

Firefighters Local Union No 1784 v. Stotts (1984)
In this decision, the Supreme Court upheld the bona fide seniority system over an affirmative action consent decree in a situation of layoffs. Thus, the employees most recently hired could be subject to layoff even though this action could compromise the affirmative action efforts.

Otis Elevator v. NLRB (1984)
Employees need not bargain over a transfer of operation if move is based on economics, not labor cost consideration.

AFSCME v. State of Washington (1985)
State had systematically paid jobs dominated by women less than their value according to job evaluation. Court of appeals overturned this decision saying state could not be forced "to eliminate an economic inequality that it did not create."

Pattern Makers' League v. NLRB (1985)
Employees may resign from a union at any time, even during a strike or when one is imminent.

Garcia v. San Antonio Transit Authority (1985)
Extends coverage of FLSA to state and local governments.

Scott v. Sears Roebuck (1985)
Woman unsuccessful in sex harassment suit based on acts by coworkers. Woman did not complain to supervisors. Court ruled only responsible for acts of coworkers if they knew or should have known of acts and took no action.

Horn v. Duke Homes (1985)
Court endorsed principle that employers have strict liability for sexual harassment by supervisors (company claimed that it was not liable because it was not aware of the behavior). Court supported full back pay (plaintiff had been terminated).

Glasgow v. Georgia Pacific Corp. (1985)
Court accepts sexual harassment argument on basis of creating hostile work environment (no quid pro quo). Company was found by Court to have made sexually harassing environment a condition of employment because harassment went on for a long period of time with organization doing nothing. Court outlined four-point test for sexually harassing work environment.

1. Harassment was unwelcome
2. Harassment was because of sex
3. Harassment affected terms and conditions of employment
4. Knowledge of harassment is "imputed" to employer

Wygant v. Jackson Board of Education (1986)
The Court ruled that white teachers were illegally dismissed in order to hire minority teachers in the School Board's efforts to fulfill a voluntary affirmative action program.

Barns v. Washington Natural Gas (1986)
Employer fires an employee because he was believed to have epilepsy. Awarded two years back pay and reinstatement.

Local 28 of the Sheet Metal Workers v. Equal Employment Opportunity Commission (1986)
The Court approved a lower court order requiring a New York City sheet metal workers' local to meet a 29 percent minority membership goal by 1987. The Court also held that judges may order racial preferences in union membership and other context if necessary to rectify especially "egregious" discrimination.

Local 93 of the International Association of Firefighters v. City of Cleveland (1986)
The Court held that lower Federal courts have broad discretion to approve decrees in which employers, over the objections of white employees, settle discrimination suits by agreeing to preferential hiring or promotion of minority-group members. It upheld a decree in which Cleveland agreed to settle a job discrimination suit by African-American and Hispanic firefighters by temporarily promoting African-American and Hispanic workers ahead of whites who had more seniority and higher test scores.

Meritor Savings Bank v. Vinson (1986)
The Court held that sexual harassment is a form of sex discrimination prohibited by Title VII of the Civil Rights Act and that employers may be liable for condoning a hostile work environment. However, the Court made it clear that employers will not be automatically liable for sexual harassment by supervisors or employees.

Philbrook v. Ansonta Board of Education (1986)
An employer may choose its own method of religious accommodation over a plan suggested by the worker as long as the employer's plan is reasonable.

Johnson v. Transportation Agency, Santa Clara County (1987)
The U.S. Supreme Court ruled that the county was justified in giving a job to a woman who scored two points less on an exam than a man. The county had an affirmative action plan that was flexible, temporary, and designed to correct the imbalance of white males in the workforce.

School Board of Nassau County, Fla. v. Airline (1987)
The U.S. Supreme Court ruled that contagious diseases are not automatically excluded from coverage of the handicap provisions of Section 504 of the 1973 Rehabilitation Act.

Luck v. Southern Pacific Transportation Company (1987)
The court ruled that the company wrongfully discharged Barbara Luck for refusing a drug test on the grounds that it violated her rights to privacy. Subsequently, the company stopped its random drug-testing program.

U.S. v. Paradise (1987)
The U.S. Supreme Court affirmed the affirmative action plan for the state troopers at Alabama in which promotion and hiring quotas were established in order to correct racial imbalances even though it may result in discrimination against an individual because of race or color.

Chalk v. U.S. District Court for Central District of California (1987)
Although handicapped because of AIDS, the teacher was otherwise able to perform his job within the meaning of the *Rehabilitation Act* of 1973 and, therefore, should be allowed to teach.

O'Connor v. Ortega (1987)
Supreme Court recognized workplace privacy for the first time.

EEOC v. Commonwealth of Massachusetts (1987)
A Massachusetts law requiring entry-level motor vehicle examiners to be aged 35 or younger does not violate *Age Discrimination in Employment Act* because it is a bona fide occupational qualification (BFOQ).

Watson v. Fort Worth Bank and Trust (1988)
The U.S. Supreme Court held that all selection procedures—objective or subjective, scored or unscored—should be subject to adverse impact analysis, compelling a demonstration by the employer that the procedure is job related if adverse impact is shown.

Kraszewski v. State Farm (1988)
Out of court settlement firm agrees to set aside half of its new sales jobs to women for ten years and to pay damages and back pay.

Arrow Automotive Industries v. NLRB (1988)
Company does not have to bargain on plant closings even if based on labor-cost considerations.

Wards' Cove Packing v. Atomo (1989)
Concentration statistics were used to prove adverse impact. Court ruled that burden of proof should not shift to employer unless it can be proved that a specific policy created the disparity.

Hopkins v. Price Waterhouse (1989)
The court upheld the award of a partnership to the female accountant who successfully claimed that sexual stereotyping prevented her promotion.

Dimaranan v. Pomona Valley Hospital (1991)
The court essentially ruled that employers can restrict the use of foreign languages only when there is a compelling business-related necessity to do so.

EEOC v. Arabian American Oil Co. (1991)
The U.S. Supreme Court decided that Title VII has no application to U.S. employers employing U. S. citizens to work abroad. ADEA and the *Civil Rights Act* of 1991, however, have application.

Gilmer v. Interstate/Johnson Lane Corp. (1991)
The Supreme Court ruled in favor of alternative dispute resolution (ADR) by stating that employees can be required to go to arbitration before pursuing litigation.

Electromation Inc. v. NLRB (1992)
The Board held that 'action committees' at Electromation were illegal "labor organizations" because management created and controlled the groups and used them to deal with employees on working conditions in violation of Section 8 (a) 2 of the NLRA.

Stewart v. Jackson & Nash (1992)
A truth-in-hiring lawsuit in which the appeals court declared that the law firm's misrepresentations caused Stewart to join a firm in which her skills as an environmental lawyer were not used although promised to be so.

Soroka v. Dayton Hudson Corporation (1991)
A California court ruled against the use of pre-employment psychological tests by Target Stores (a division of Dayton Hudson). The company had been using the tests to screen retail store security officers for emotional stability. The court found that the tests represented an invasion of privacy under California law.

Stender v. Lucky Stores (1992)
The court ruled that the use of interest surveys as a defense in disparate treatment and disparate impact cases by Lucky Stores is permitted. "Even in a situation where gender stereotypes about work interest patterns reflect reality, it is unlawful for an employer to discriminate against those whose work interests deviate from the stereotype," the court decides.

E. I. DuPont de Nemours and Company v. NLRB (1993)
The Board concluded that DuPont's six safety committees and fitness committee were employer-dominated labor organizations and that DuPont dominated the formation and administration of one of them in violation of Section 8 (a) 2 of the NLRA.

St. Mary's Honor Center v. Hicks (1993)
The Supreme Court ruled in this disparate treatment case, that the suing employee has to produce evidence that the employer's true motive is not a discriminatory one. This increases the burden of proof on the employee to demonstrate that the employer intentionally discriminated.

EEOC v. AIC Security Investigations (1993)
The court ruled in favor of a director of a security firm who was discharged after he was diagnosed with terminal brain cancer and awarded the individual $572,000. The first case under ADA.

Harris v. Forklift Systems (1993)
The Supreme Court affirmed the "reasonable women" standard by sending the case back to the appeals court stating that Harris did not have to prove that she was psychologically damaged for her boss' behavior to claim sexual harassment.

Electromation Inc. v. NLRB (1994)
The court upheld the NLRB's ruling in the 1992 decision of the same case.

Black Fire Fighters Association of Dallas v. City of Dallas (1994)
Race-conscious promotion remedies must be narrowly tailored to remedy past discrimination, the appeals court explains. Finding that the 28 blacks are slated for promotion without regard to whether anyone is the victim of past discrimination, that the city is not the type of "particularly egregious" employer that a court must force to promote minorities through broad, race-conscious remedies, and that the benefits of having more minority supervisors does not justify imposing racial classifications with such loose connections to remedying past discrimination, the court concludes that the remedy unnecessarily harms other firefighters.

Ensley Branch, NAACP v. Seibels (1994)
"The goal of eliminating discrimination may justify some interim use of affirmative action, but affirmative action selection provisions are themselves a form of discrimination that cannot continue forever. "An end to racial discrimination demands the development of valid, nondiscriminatory selection procedures to replace race-conscious selection procedures," the court rules.

Grant v. Lone Star Co. (1994)
The court held that private employees are exempt from personal liability under suits brought under Title VII. This extends the exemption that had been given earlier to public employees. The reasoning here was that Congress probably did not want to impose the burden of costly litigation upon individuals nor businesses with fewer than 15 employees.

Dirschel v. Speck (1994)

The court held that individual employees may be personally liable under suits brought under Title VII when they act as agents of the employer and when they possess independent authority to make employment decisions regarding the employee who claims bias. Thus a CEO (Speck) had independent authority over the female executive (Dirschel) and was acting as the hospital's agent when allegedly making offensive and hostile remarks.

This set of court cases is meant to provide a sampling of those mentioned in the text. For descriptions of these and other cases, see J. Ledvinka, and V.G. Scarpello *Federal Regulation of Personnel and Human Resource Management*, 2nd ed. (Boston: Kent, 1991); J. Bernardin and W. Cascio, *Annotated Bibliography of Court Cases Relevant to Employment Decisions 1980–1984* (Boca Raton: Florida Atlantic University, 1984); M.D. Levin-Epstein, *Primer of Equal Opportunity*, 3rd ed. (Washington, D.C.: NA, 1984); M. McCarthy, ed., *Complete Guide to Employing Persons with Disabilities* (Albertson, NY: National Center on Employment of the Handicapped at Human Resources Center, 1985); M.A. Player, *Federal Law of Employment Discrimination* (St. Paul, MN: West Publishing, 1991); D.P. Twomey, *Equal Opportunity Law* (Cincinnati: South-Western, 1994).

APPENDIX B

Information for Managing Human Resources

Journals, Magazines, and Newspapers

Business Week, published by McGraw-Hill, 1221 Avenue of the Americas, New York, New York 10020.

Employee Relations Law Journal, published by Executive Enterprises, Inc., 33 West 60th Street, New York, New York 10023. Articles on current personnel topics with the related legal considerations are contained in each quarterly issue.

Fair Employment Practices, Bulletin to Management, the Bulletin on Training, published by the Bureau of National Affairs, 1231 25th Street N.W., Washington, D.C. 20037.

FEP Guidelines, published by the Bureau of Business Practices, 24 Rope Ferry Road, Waterford, Connecticut 06386.

Fortune, published by Time-Life, Rockefeller Center, New York, New York 10020.

Human Resource Management, published by the Graduate School of Business, University of Michigan, Ann Arbor, Michigan 48109.

Human Resource Planning, published by the Human Resources Planning Society, 41 E. 42nd Street, New York, New York 10017.

Inc., published by Inc. Business Resources, 38 Commercial Wharf, Boston, Massachusetts 02110-3883.

Industrial and Labor Relations Review, New York State School of Labor and Industrial Relations, Cornell University, Ithaca, New York. Opinions and reports of studies on labor legislation, collective bargaining, and related subjects.

Industrial Medicine and Surgery, Industrial Medicine Publishing Company, 605 North Michigan Avenue, Chicago, Illinois. Emphasizes health programs in industry, with reports on health hazards, occupational diseases, handicapped workers, medical services, and related subjects.

Industrial Relations, Institute of Industrial Relations, University of California, Berkeley and Los Angeles, California. Ideas and opinions as well as reports of research.

International Journal of Human Resource Management, published by Routledge Journals, 11 New Fetterlane, London, England. Focus is international human resource management.

Journal of the American Society of Training Directors, official publication of the American Society of Training Directors, 2020 University Avenue, Madison, Wisconsin. Broad coverage of the personnel field, with a special emphasis on training problems.

Journal of Applied Psychology, American Psychological Association, 1313 16th Street N.W., Washington, D.C. All phases of applied psychology, with numerous reports of personnel research.

Labor Law Journal, Commerce Clearing House, Inc., 214 N. Michigan Avenue, Chicago, Illinois. Generally presents nonlegalistic discussions of legal phases of industrial relations.

Management Record, The Conference Board, 247 Park Avenue, New York, New York. Numerous reports of both experience and research, surveys conducted by the National Industrial Conference Board staff, and digests of symposia.

Management Review, American Management Association, 135 W. 50th Street, New York, New York 10020. General coverage of all phases of management.

Monthly Labor Review, Bureau of Labor Statistics, U.S. Department of Labor, Washington, D.C. Summaries of staff studies on industrial relations; statistical sections include continuing series on industrial disputes, employment, payrolls, and cost of living.

HR Focus, American Management Association, 135 W. 50th Street, New York, New York 10020. Broad interest in entire field of industrial relations, with numerous reports of surveys, studies, and experience.

HR Magazine, published by the Society for Human Resource Management, 606 Washington Street, Alexandria, Virginia 22314.

Personnel Management, formerly the Journal of the Institute of Personnel Management, Institute of Personnel Management, Management House, 80 Fetter Lane, London, England. Theory and practice in both personnel management and labor relations.

Personnel Psychology, 745 Haskins Road, Suite A, Bowling Green, OH 43402. Emphasizes reports on research in psychological aspects of personnel.

Public Personnel Quarterly, published by the International Personnel Management Association, 1859 K. Street N.W., Washington, D.C.

Studies in Personnel Policy, National Industrial Conference Board, 247 Park Avenue, New York, New York. Mainly compares experience and evaluations of programs, with frequent surveys of policy and practice.

Training, published by Lakewood Publications, 50 South Ninth St., Minneapolis, Minnesota 55402.

The Wall Street Journal, published by Dow Jones, P.O. Box 300, Princeton, New Jersey 08543-1818.

Workforce, formerly Personnel Journal, 245 Fischer Ave. B-2, Costa Mesa, California 92626. Covers a broad spectrum of topics in human resource management.

Working Age, published by the AARP, 601 E. Street, N.W., Washington, D.C. 20049.

Associations

AFL-CIO, 815 16th St., N.W., Washington, D.C. 20006, (202) 637-5000.

American Arbitration Association, 140 W. 51st St., New York, NY 10020, (212) 484-4800.

American Association of Retired Persons (AARP), 601 E. Street, N.W., Washington, D.C. 20042, (202) 434-2277.

American Compensation Association, 14040 N. Northsight Blvd., Scottsdale, AZ 85260, (602) 951-9191.

American Management Association, 135 W. 50th St., New York, NY 10020, (212) 586-8100.

American Society for Healthcare Human Resources Administration, 840 N. Lakeshore Dr., Chicago, IL 60611, (312) 280-6111.

American Society for Industrial Security, 1655 N. Fort Meyer Dr., Suite 1200, Arlington, VA 22209, (703) 522-5800.

American Society for Training and Development, 1630 Duke Street, Alexandria, VA 22312, (703) 683-8100.

American Society of Pension Actuaries, 1700 K. St., N.W., Suite 404, Washington, D.C. 20006, (202) 659-3620.

American Society of Safety Engineers, 1800 East Oakton, Des Plaines, IL 60018, (312) 692-4121.

Bureau of Labor Statistics (BLS), Department of Labor, 3rd Street & Constitution Ave , N.W., Washington, D.C. 20210.

Bureau of National Affairs (BNA), 1231 25th Street. N.W., Washington, D.C. 20037.

Commerce Clearing House, Inc., 4025 W. Peterson Avenue, Chicago, Illinois 60646.

Employee Benefit Research Institute, 2121 K. St., N.W., Suite 860, Washington, D.C. 20037, (202) 659-0670.

Employee Relations Council, 1627 K. St., N.W., Washington, D.C. 20006, (202) 857-0857.

Equal Employment Opportunity Commission (EEOC), 1801 L. Street, N.W., Washington, D.C. 20507, (202) 663-4900/1-800-699-EEOC.

Human Resource Certification Institute (HRCI), 606 N. Washington, Alexandria, VA 22314, (703) 548-3440.

Human Resource Planning Society, 41 E. 42nd St., Suite 1509, New York, New York 10017, (212) 490-6387.

Human Resource Systems Professionals, P.O. Box 8040-A202, Walnut Creek, CA 94596, (415) 945-8428.

International Labour Organization (ILO), CH-1211, Geneva, Switzerland, (212) 697-0150.

Industrial Relations Research Association, 7726 Social Science Bldg., Madison, WI 53706, (608) 262-2762.

International Personnel Management Association, 1617 Duke St., Alexandria, VA 22314, (703) 391-7436.

Labor Management Mediation Service, 1620 I. St., N.W., Suite 616, Washington, D.C. 20006.

National Association of Manufacturers (NAM), 1331 Pennsylvania Ave., N.W., Suite 1500N, Washington, D.C., (202) 637-3000.

National Association of Personnel Consultants, 3133 Mt. Vernon Ave., Alexandria, VA 22305, (703) 684-0180.

National Labor Relations Board, 1099 14th St. N.W., Washington, D.C. 20570, (202) 273-1000.

National Mediation Board, 1301 K. Street N.W., Suite 250 E, Washington, D.C. 20572.

National Safety Council, 1121 Spring Lake Drive, Itasca, IL 60143-3201, (708) 285-1121.

Occupational Safety and Health Administration (OSHA), 200 Constitution Ave., N.W., Washington, D.C. 20210, (202) 523-8045.

Office on the Americans with Disabilities Act, Civil Rights Division, U.S. Department of Justice, P.O. Box 66118, Washington, D.C. 20035-6118, (202) 514-0301 (Voice), (202) 514-0381 (TDD), (202) 514-0383 (TDD).

Office of Federal Contract Compliance Programs (OFCCP), 200 Constitution Ave. N.W., Washington, D.C. 20210

Office of the American Workplace, Department of Labor, 200 Constitution Ave. N.W., Washington, D.C. 20210.

Pension Benefit Guaranty Corporation, P.O. Box 7119, Washington, D.C. 20044.

Profit Sharing Council of America, 200 N. Wacker Drive, Suite 1722, Chicago, IL 60606, (312) 372-3411.

Society for Human Resource Management (SHRM), including Institute for International Human Resources, 606 N. Washington, Alexandria, VA 22314, (703) 548-3440.

U.S. Chamber or Commerce, 1615 H. Street, N.W., Washington, D.C. 20062.

U.S. Department of Labor, 200 Constitution Ave N.W., Washington, D.C. 20210, (202) 219-7316.

The specific interpretation and application of the *Americans With Disabilities Act* is certain to be refined and modified as it is put into practice. For the most current information, contact:

The President's Committee on Employment of People with Disabilities 1331 F. Street, N.W., Washington, D.C. 20004-1107, (202) 376-6200 (Voice), (202) 376-6205 (TDD).

For specific information on making reasonable accommodations in the workplace, contact: National Organization on Disability, 910 16th St. N.W., Washington, D.C. 20006, (202) 293-1944.

Job Accommodation Network (JAN), West Virginia University, 809 Allen Hall, P.O. Box 468, Morgantown, WV 26506, 1-800-526-7734.

For specific information on small business, see:

The State of Small Business (1997) A Report to the President: Annual Report on Small Business and Competition, Washington, D.C.: United States Government Printing Office.

The States and Small Businesses (1993) A Directory of Programs and Activities, Washington, D.C.: United States Government Printing Office.

For specific information on unions see: C. D. Gifford, *Directory of U.S. Labor Organizations 1996 Edition* (Washington, D.C.: The Bureau of National Affairs, 1996).

For specific information total quality, see The Malcolm Baldrige National Quality Award managed by United States Department of Commerce, Technology Administration, National Institute of Standards and Technology, Route 270 and Quince Orchard Road, Administration Building, Room A537, Gaithersburg, MD 20899-0001. Administered by American Society for Quality Control, P.O. Box 3005, Milwaukee, WI 53201-3005.

WEB Sites for Business and HR Information

Due to the dynamic nature of the Web, site addresses may change. This listing is current at the time of publication.

Society for Human Resource Management
http://www.shrm.org

Workforce Online
http://www.workforce-online.com

Human Resources Net
<NRNET@cornell.edu>

BenefitsLink
http://www.benefitslink.com

Training and Seminar Locators
http://www.tasl.com/tasl/home.html

Securities and Exchange Commission
http://www.sec.gov

Social Security Administration
http://www.ssa.gov

U.S. Department of Labor; and Bureau of Labor Statistics
http://www.dol.gov

Internal Revenue Service
http://www.ustreas.gov

LABORNEWS (OSHA Web site)
http://www.osha.gov

AMERICA'S JOB BANK (Department of Labor's Job Bank)
http://www.AJB.dni.us

Recruitment Web sites (specializing in high-tech positions)
http://www.chron.com
http://www.rpi.edu/dept/cdc/newsrps.html
http://www.occ.com/occ/ResumesByState.html

Monster's HR Net Page
http://www.monster.com/hrnethome.html

Training and Development Home Page
http://www.tcm.com/trdev/; then click on www homepages

Online Career Center (OCC)
http://www.occ.com/occ

Small Business Administration
http://www.sbaonline.sba.gov

The Bureau of National Affairs
http://www.bna.org

Homepage for Lincoln Electric
http://www.lincolnelectric.com

Home Page for Nordstrom:
http://www.nordstrom-pta.com

The Americans with Disabilities Act Document Center
http://janweb.icdi.wvu.edu/kinder

The BenefitsLink Homepage
http://www.magicnet.net/benefits

Occupational Safety and Health Resources
http://turva.me.tut.fi/~tuusital/oshlinks.html

Office of the American Workplace's Best Practices Clearinghouse
http://www.saic.com/fed/uscompanies/labor

The AFL-CIO's Labor Web
http://www.aflcio.org

American Compensation Association
http://www.ahrm.org/aca/aca.htm

WashLaw Web at Washburn University of Law
http://lawlib.wuacc.edu/washlaw/washlaw.html

The Legal Information Institute of Cornell Law School
http://www.aw.cornell.edu

Job Search
http://www.jobweb.com

Homepages for Companies in Text

WMX Technologies
http://www.wmx.com

Southwest Airlines
http://www.iflyswa.com

General Electric
http://www.ge.com

Levi Strauss & Co.
http://www.levi.com

BMW
http://www.bmwusa.com

Wal-Mart
http://www.wal-mart.com

Pepsi-Cola International
http://www.on.net/clients/pepsi

Hallmark Cards
 http://www.goldcrown.com/index.htm
McDonald's
 http://www.mcdonalds.com
Walt Disney Company
 http://www.disney.com
Ritz-Carlton Hotel Company
 http://ritz-carlton-montreal.com
Chrysler Corporation
 http://www.chryslercorp.com
Intel
 http://www.intel.com
Chaparral Steel
 http://www.steelnet.org/sma/forward.html
Microsoft
 http://www.microsoft.com
Steelcase
 http://www.steelcase.com
Federal Express
 http://www.fedex.com
Saturn
 http://saturncars.com/index.html
AT&T
 http://att.com
Chevron
 http://www.chevron.com

APPENDIX C

The Validation Process

Regardless of the method or site used to study human resource issues, HR professionals need to be concerned about the reliability and validation of measurement devices. **Reliability** refers to the consistency of measurement, whereas **validity** relates to the truth or accuracy of measurement. The concept of a correlation coefficient is important to both reliability and validity.

Validity

As defined in the Principles for the Validation and Use of Personnel Selection Procedures (American Psychological Association), **validity** is the degree to which inferences from scores on tests or assessments are supported by evidence.[1] This definition implies that validity refers to the inferences made from use of a measure, not to the measure itself. Three primary strategies have been identified to gather evidence to support or justify the inferences made from scores on measures: criterion-related, content-oriented, and construct validation strategies.

Criterion-Related Strategy

A **criterion-related** strategy is an assessment of how well a measure (that is, predictor) forecasts a criterion such as job performance. This tends to be the primary validation strategy used in personnel research. The major steps that make up this strategy are shown in Exhibit 1. The two types of criterion-related validation strategies are concurrent and predictive—shown in Exhibit 2.

Concurrent validation evaluates the relationship between a predictor and a job criterion score for all employees in the study at the same time. For example, this strategy could be used to determine the correlation between years of experience and job performance. Data would be collected from each person in the study about years of experience and performance scores. All persons in the study would have to be working in similar jobs, generally in the same job family or classification. Then a correlation would be computed between the predictor scores and criterion scores.

The term **correlation,** or observed **correlation coefficient** (denoted by the symbol r), is the degree to which two or more sets of measurements vary. A positive correlation exists when high values on one variable (for example, job knowledge test) are associated with high values on another variable (for example, high overall ratings of job performance). A negative correlation exists when high values on one variable are associated with low values on another variable. The correlation coefficient, which expresses the degree of linear relationship between two sets of scores, can range from positive to negative. The range is from +1 (a perfect positive correlation coefficient) to −1 (a perfect negative correlation coefficient). Illustrations of several linear relationships represented by plotting actual data of personnel selection test—job performance relationships are shown in Exhibit 3.

The steps in determining predictive validity are similar, except that the predictor is measured sometime before the criterion is measured, as shown in Exhibit 1. Thus, the **predictive validity** of a predictor could be determined by measuring an existing group of employees on a predictor and waiting to gather their criterion measures later, or by hiring a group of job applicants regardless of their scores on the predictor and measuring them on the criterion later. For either type of criterion-related validation strategy, it is important to demonstrate that the predictors and performance criteria are related to the duties of the job.

The classic example of a predictive validation study is AT&T's Management Progress Study.[2] In that study, personnel researchers at AT&T administered an assessment center, similar to the one described in Chapter 8, to 422 male

EXHIBIT 1

Steps for Implementing and Evaluating a Personnel Selection Strategy

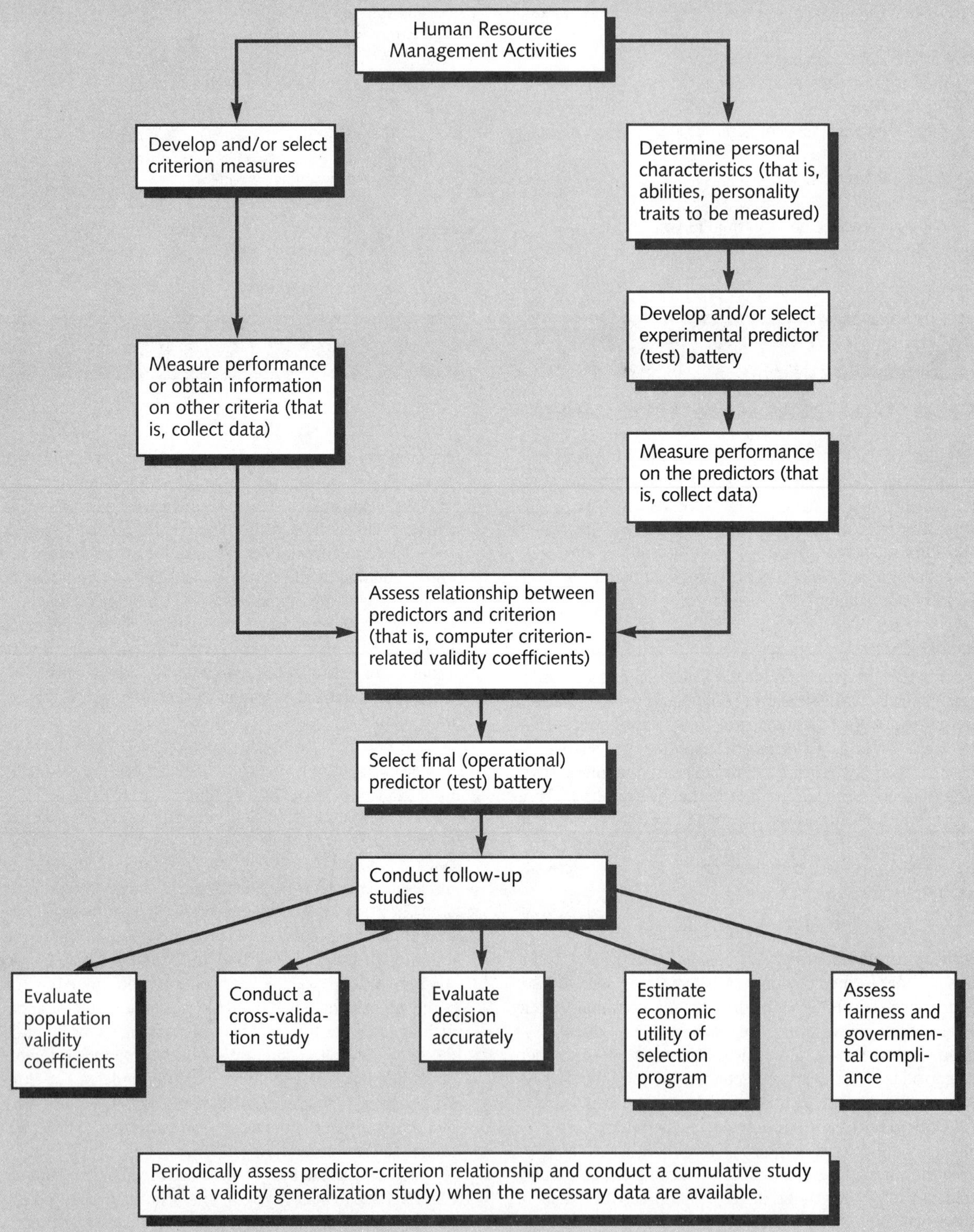

EXHIBIT 2

Criterion-Related Validation Strategies

CONCURRENT STUDY

Test (predictor) scores are gathered	Criterion scores are gathered	Correlation between scores on predictor (*x*) and criterion (*y*), r_{xy}, is calculated

PREDICTIVE STUDY

Test (predictor) scores are gathered	Criterion scores are gathered	Correlation between scores on predictor (*x*) and criterion (*y*), r_{xy}, is calculated

EXHIBIT 3

Scatterplots Indicating Possible Relationships Between Personnel Selection Test Scores and Job Performance Scores

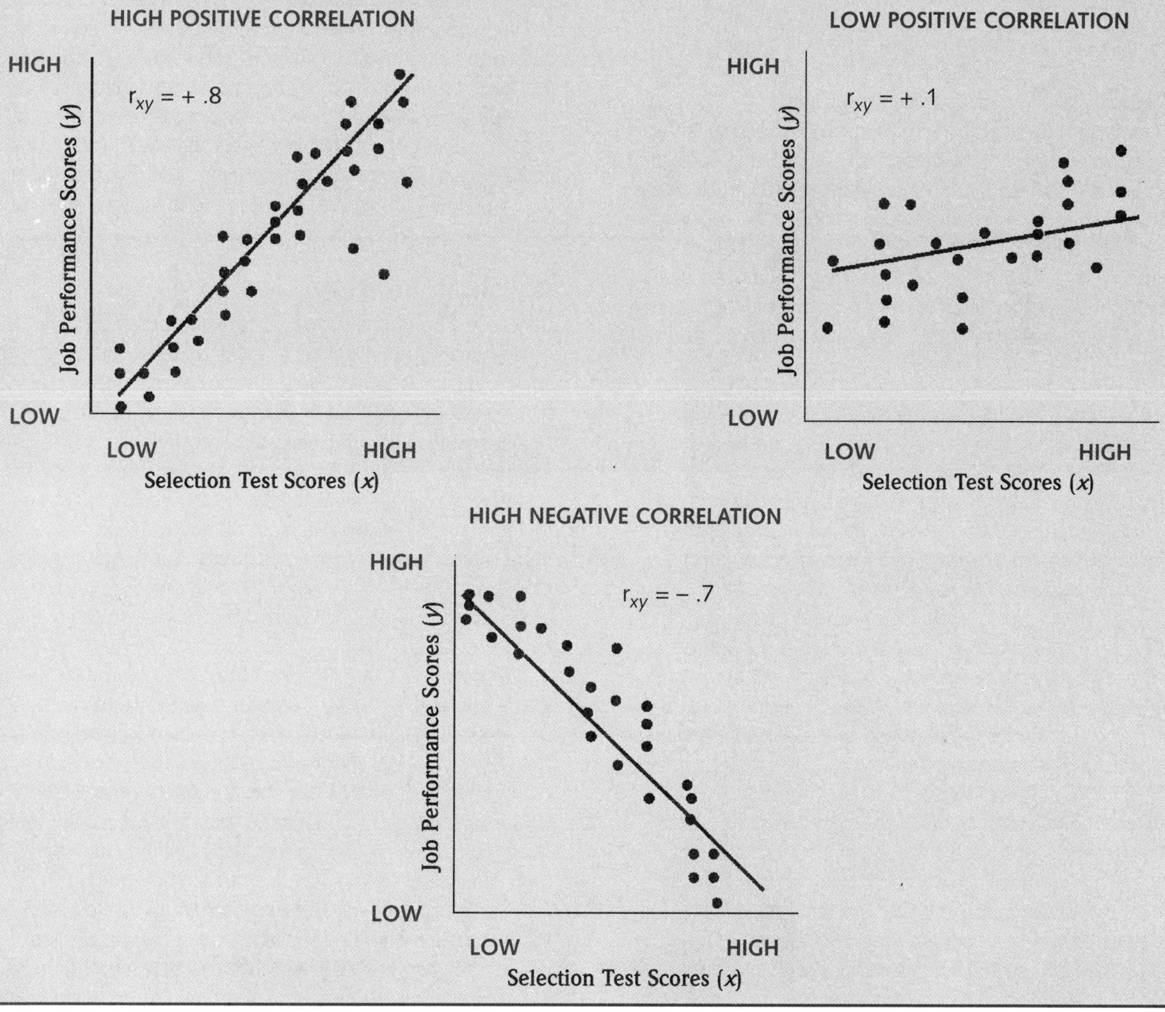

employees, stored the results, and waited eight years before evaluating their predictions of how far these individuals would progress in AT&T's management hierarchy. For a group of college graduates, the predictions were highly accurate; a correlation of .71 was obtained between the assessment center predictions and level of management achieved. In addition, a twenty-year follow-up of the original predictions showed that the assessment center was still useful in predicting who would reach even higher levels in AT&T's management hierarchy.

An assessment of criterion-related validity is often important for many personnel decisions. In fact, it is the heart of most personnel decisions. The greater the validity coefficient for a test, the more efficient selection and placement decisions will be. And the more efficient these decisions, the more productive the workforce will be.

Although the Uniform Guidelines of 1978 require organizations to demonstrate the job-relatedness of a selection procedure, they do not specify the actual degree of job-relatedness. Thus, an organization can claim its selection procedures are job-related or permit valid inferences even though the correlation coefficient between the predictor and criterion is .3 rather than .6 or .7. Although the Uniform Guidelines do not specify the magnitude of the correlation necessary to claim job-relatedness, they do indicate that the correlation should be statistically significant.

An important aspect of criterion-related validity is the relevance or appropriateness of the criterion being correlated with the predictor. In a criterion-related validity study, the predictors should be shown to correlate with the criteria, and the criteria should be shown relevant and important to the jobs in question. Failure to establish these points was the heart of the U.S. Supreme Court's decision in the Albemarle case, in which the Court first looked at a validation study:

> *The study in this case involved no analysis of the attributes of, or the particular skills needed in, the studied job groups. There is accordingly no basis for concluding that "no significant differences" exist among the lines of progression, or among distinct job groupings within the studied lines of progression.*
>
> *Albemarle's supervisors were asked to rank employees by a "standard" that was extremely vague and fatally open to divergent interpretations. . . (T)here simply was no way to determine whether the criteria actually considered were sufficiently related to the Company's legitimate interest in job-specific ability to justify a testing system with a racially discriminatory impact.*
>
> *The fact that the best of those employees working near the top of a line of progression score well on a test does not necessarily mean that that test, or some particular cutoff score on the test, is a permissible measure of the minimal qualifications of new workers entering lower level jobs.*
>
> *Albemarle's validation study dealt only with job-experienced white workers: but the tests themselves are given to new job applicants who are younger, largely inexperienced, and in many instances nonwhite.*

On many occasions, employers are not able to obtain sufficient empirical data for a criterion-related validity study. Consequently, other methods of validation are helpful in determining the validity of measures used in personnel research.

Content-Oriented Strategy

A **content-oriented validation** strategy differs from a criterion-related strategy in that it estimates or judges the relevance of a predictor as a sample of the relevant situations (for example, behaviors or tasks) that make up a job. In essence, job-relatedness here is an estimation or judgment. According to the *Uniform Guidelines* of 1978, "A selection procedure can be supported by a content validity strategy to the extent it is a representative sample of the content of the job." The administration of a typing test (actually, a work sample test if used for typists) as a selection device for hiring typists is a classic example of a predictor judged to be content valid.[3] In this case, the predictor is a skill related to a task that is actually part of the job. Thus, to employ a content validation strategy, one must know the duties of the actual job.[4] As discussed in Chapter 8, information about job tasks and duties can be obtained using one or more job analysis procedures.

Job analysis is discussed here as a critical element in content validation. It should be regarded as the starting point and the thread that ties together any basic personnel selection and validation study. It is also a critical activity in determining construct validity.

Construct Strategy

Instead of showing a direct relationship between a test or other selection information (for example, education or experience levels) and job criteria, selection methods seek to measure (often by tests) the degree to which an applicant possesses abilities and characteristics (psychological traits) that are deemed necessary for successful job performance. These underlying psychological traits are called **constructs** and include, among many others, intelligence, leadership ability, verbal ability, interpersonal sensitivity, and analytical ability. Constructs deemed necessary for doing well on job criteria are inferred from job behaviors and activities (duties) indicated in the job analysis.

A **construct validation** study attempts to demonstrate that a relationship exists between a selection procedure or test (a measure of the construct) and the psychological trait (construct) it seeks to measure. For example, does a reading comprehension test reliably and accurately measure how well people can read and understand what they read? To demonstrate construct validity, one would need data showing that high scorers on the test actually read more difficult material and are better readers than low scorers on the test, and that reading ability is related to the duties shown in the job description. Other evidence that the test is measuring the relevant construct could be obtained based on its relationship to other measures that assess both similar and unrelated constructs. In essence, construct validity is not established with a single study. Rather, it is assessed based on the cumulation of a body of empirical evidence. This evidence is likely to include information gathered from both criterion-related and content-oriented validation studies.

Validity Generalization

The essence of **validity generalization** is that a test or predictor predicts the same way for all individuals in similar jobs in the same or similar organizations. That is, if two similar jobs exist in two parts of an organization or in two different organizations, a given selection test should be equally valid for the two jobs. This assumes, however, that some degree of similarity in jobs and conditions can first be identified. Similarity of jobs and conditions are judged by the results of job analyses. If validity generalization can be successfully established, an organization can save a great deal of time and money in developing valid, job-related predictors. In short, if the validity of a predictor for a job has already been established, it may be utilized as a predictor in another, perhaps newly created, similar job.

Base Rate Versus Predictor Rate

Another big step in finding, developing, and using job-related predictors is showing how beneficial they are, if indeed they are more beneficial than using no predictors at all. In using predictors, an organization is assuming that: 1) some job applicants will perform better than others; 2) they can be spotted (by using predictors) and selected; and 3) the **predictor rate,** that is, the number of true decisions relative to the total number of decisions, exceeds the **base rate,** or the proportion of applicants who would succeed on the job from those randomly selected. The more the predictor rate exceeds the base rate, the more useful the predictor.

The importance of having a higher predictor rate than the base rate can be illustrated with the concepts of **false negatives, false positives, true positives,** and **true negatives.** What an organization wants to do in selecting employees is to make as many true decisions (true positive and negative) as possible and to minimize the number of false decisions (false positive and negative). Using a test with a predictor rate higher than the base rate results does this. For example, if the base rate is .5 (half the applicants randomly hired turn out to be good performers) and the predictor rate is .8 (80 percent of the selection decisions are correct), then using a valid predictor will yield more correct decisions than randomly selecting applicants. This can be illustrated using two scattergrams, each with one hundred applicants hired, one showing low validity and a .5 base rate and the other showing high validity and a .8 predictor rate. A predictor (test) **cutoff score** is used to categorize those who would be hired and predicted to be good performers and those who would be rejected and predicted to be poor performers. The two scattergrams are shown in Exhibit 4.

In scattergram A there is essentially no relationship or validity between the test scores (if one had been used) and the performance scores. Note that an equal number of applicants turned out to be true positive (TP), false positive (FP), true negative (TN), and false negative (FN). (In all quadrants the number of applicants (n)=25.) Note also that the predictor rate does not exceed the base rate.

If the predictor with a .8 rate were used to select the applicants, the results would be substantially different. In scattergram B the number of individuals in the four categories is not equal. In fact, FP and FN are each 10, and TP and TN are each 40. Thus, 80 correct decisions were made. Hence, the predictor rate of .8 exceeds the base rate of .5. Thus, using tests with predictor rates exceeding base rates tends to improve the utility of the selection process. Final evaluation of the real utility of the selection process, however, must incorporate the assessment of several costs, including those from using the test and those resulting from false decisions.

Selection Ratio

An important concept in evaluating selection and placement procedures is the **selection ratio,** which is defined as the proportion of individuals actually hired among those who applied. For example, from 200 applicants, only 10 individuals are hired. This would represent a selection ratio of 10/200 or 5 percent. Generally speaking, managers prefer small selection ratios—that is, when there are many more applicants than jobs, because the organization can raise the predictor cutoff and thus be more selective.

The fewer applicants an organization has, the less sure it can be that it has the best possible applicant. With few applicants, it must be more careful in matching them to the jobs available. If an organization must hire all the applicants because there are so few, the validity of the selection and placement devices becomes irrelevant. This is especially true when there is only one type of job available.

When everyone who applies is hired, chances are slim that all will have the ability to do well. Consequently, the organization may need to establish extensive and perhaps costly training programs. The organization can also try to attract more job applicants by raising wages, but that may only lead to more trouble. For example, raising the wages of new employees may be unfair to the rest of the employees and make them unhappy (pay equity is discussed in Chapter 14). Thus, it pays an organization to attract as many potentially qualified applicants as possible and reduce its selection ratio. Without choice, the utility of selection devices is minimal; with it, their utility may be high and chances are greater the applicants chosen will do well and be satisfied.

Utility and Costs

The value of selection and placement procedures can now be seen to vary as a function of the following basic criteria.

- **Magnitude of the validity (regardless of type) and reliability.** As validity and reliability increase, so does the utility of the procedures.

EXHIBIT 4

Comparison of Predictor and Base Rates for Tests with Low and High Validity

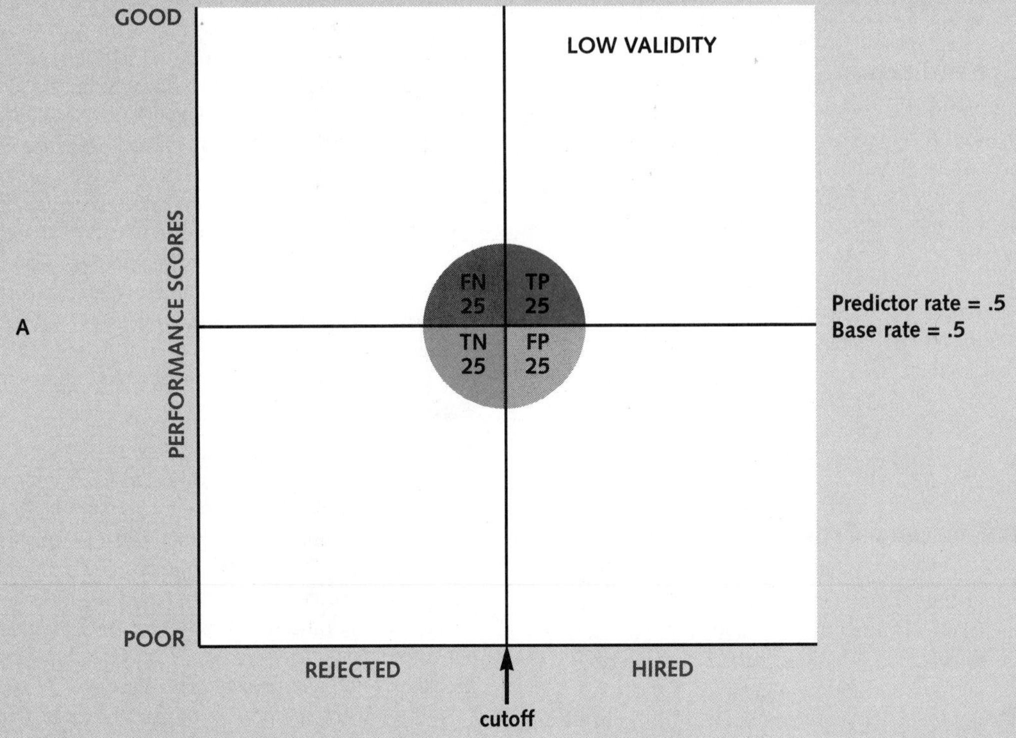

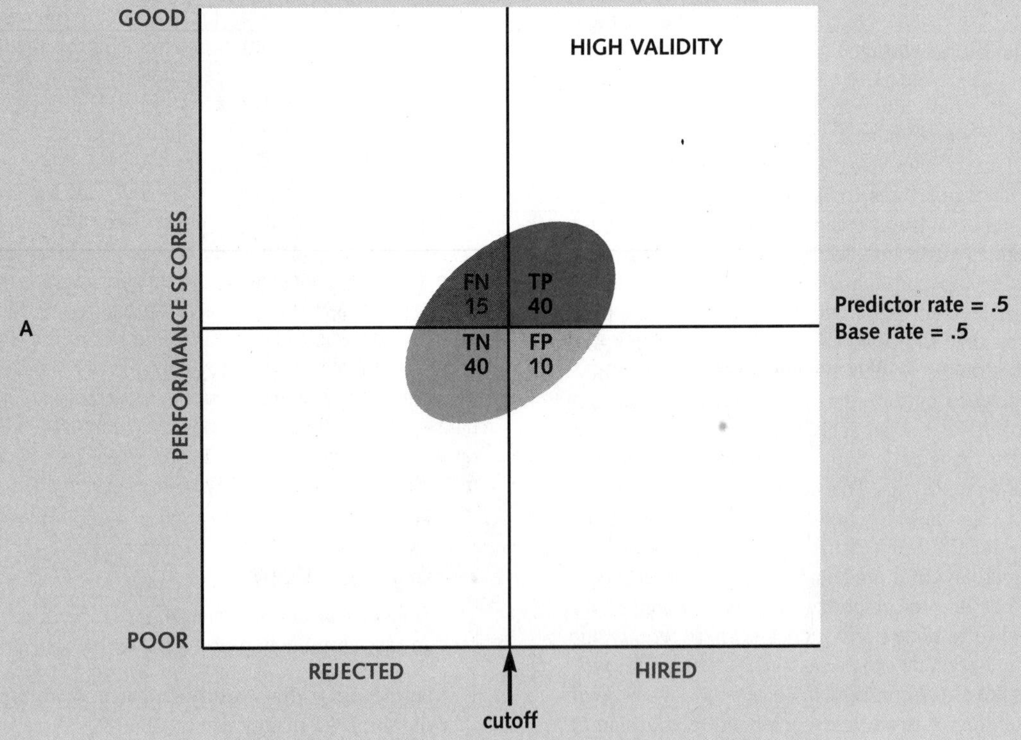

- **Base rate.** As the differential between the base rate and predictor rate increases (assuming the predictor rate is higher than the base rate), the utility of the selection procedures increases.

- **Selection ratio.** As selection ratios become smaller, the cost of testing increases and the utility of the selection procedures increases (assuming other factors, such as the predictor cutoff, remain constant). This is because many applicants must be tested even though only a few will be selected.[5]

The impact and utility of these three criteria may be changed significantly by the costs involved. For example, it may be more useful for an organization to use a particular selection test with a validity of .4 rather than another with a validity of .5 if the costs of developing and using the latter are twice as expensive. Against these relative costs must be compared the relative gains. The test with the higher validity may result in gains large enough to offset its greater implementation expense.

Consequently, organizations should use selection and placement procedures that maximize relative gain as opposed to cost. Generally, those procedures producing potentially greater gains are more job-related and also relatively more costly. Thus, it is necessary to measure both the benefits (of true decisions) and their costs carefully.

Actual costs incurred in hiring applicants include the following:

- Recruiting and assessment costs—salaries of personnel staff, advertising expenses, and travel expenses.

- Costs of personnel testing.

- Induction and orientation costs—administrative costs of adding the employees to the payroll and salaries of the new employees and those responsible for orienting them to their new jobs.

- Training costs—salaries of training and development staff, salary of the new employees during training, and costs of any special materials, instruments, or facilities for training.

Potential costs that might be incurred if a wrong selection decision is made include the following:

- Costs associated with hiring a person who subsequently fails—recordkeeping costs, termination costs: costs of undesirable job behavior; such as materials or equipment damaged; loss of customers, clients, or patients; loss of goodwill; and costs incurred in replacing a failing employee.

- Costs associated with rejecting a person who would have been successful on the job—competitive disadvantage if applicant is hired by another firm (for example, loss of a top sports star to a competing team), and costs of recruiting and assessing an additional applicant to replace the rejectee.[6]

In addition to comparing the costs and benefits of alternative selection and placement procedures, organizations should also compare the costs and benefits of other techniques, such as job design or supervisory training programs, that increase job performance and employee retention. The costs and benefits of alternatives to selection and placement will be influenced by the same basic criteria as well as by several other criteria.

Endnotes

1. American Psychological Association, Division 14, *Principles for the Validation and Use of Personnel Selection Procedures* (Washington, D.C.: APA, 1980).

2. For a discussion of the AT&T Management Progress Study as well as an overview of assessment centers, see A. Howard, "An Assessment of Assessment Centers," *Academy of Management Journal* 17 (1974): 115–134. A twenty-year follow-up study of AT&T's original Management Progress Study predictions was reported in A. Howard. "Cool at the Top Personality Characteristics of Successful Executives," paper presented at the Annual Convention of the American Psychological Association, Toronto, Canada, August 1984.

3. R. S. Barrett, "Is the Test Content-Valid: Or, Who Killed Cock Robin?" *Employee Relations Law Journal* 6 (4) (1981): 584–600; R. S. Barrett, "Is the Test Content-Valid Or, Does It Really Measure Construct?" *Employee Relations Law Journal* 6 (3) (1981): 459–475.

4. For a discussion and reconceptualization of the concept of content validity, see R. M. Guion, "On Trinitarian Doctrines of Validity," *Professional Psychology* 11 (1980): 385–398.

5. R. D. Arvey, *Fairness in Selecting Employees* (Reading, MA: Addison-Wesley, 1979): 35–37. Arvey provides an excellent in-depth discussion of these issues. See also P. M. Podsakoff, M. E. Williams, and W. E. Scott, Jr., "Myths of Employee Selection Systems," in *Readings in Personnel and Human Resource Management*, 3d ed., R. S. Schuler, S. A. Youngblood, and V. L. Huber, eds. (St Paul, MN: West, 1988).

6. Ibid.

APPENDIX D

The Resume

The goal of your resume is to effectively communicate your qualifications to prospective employers. In many cases your resume will determine whether or not you are granted an interview. The resume, by itself, however will not get you a job. If it gets you in the door, then it has served its purpose.

What Do You Have to Offer?

To develop an effective resume you must first have a thorough knowledge of the product you are selling—you! What are the talents, skills, accomplishments, and experiences that you are marketing? To adequately answer this question you may want to sit down with a counselor and have him/her assist you with the self-assessment process.

Targeting

Once you know what skills and knowledge you have to offer, the next step is learning what qualifications are valued by employers in your field. Do different organizations in the same field look for similar or different qualifications? How much do you know about the position for which you are applying? Are any specific skills stressed in the job description? Make sure you emphasize the aspects of your experience which are most relevant to the job.

Assignments

Visit your career resource center and library to research your field(s) of interest. For each occupation try to answer the following questions. What are the typical career paths for this occupation? What are the typical job responsibilities? What skills and training are required?

Talk to at least 3 knowledgeable people in your field to supplement your library research. Suggestions include Career Week speakers, internship supervisors, professors, and members of professional associations.

What Format Should I Choose?

There are basically two resume formats—the Chronological and the Functional.

The **Chronological** resume is by far the most popular and is generally preferred by employers. Chronological resumes are arranged in time order, with one's most recent experience listed first. They work well for students whose work experience is directly related to their professional objective.

The **Functional** resume is organized according to specific skill categories which allow the writer to highlight particular areas of competency that may have been gained through a wide variety of experiences. This style can be beneficial for students whose experience is not directly related to the career field which they have chosen to pursue. The major drawback of the functional resume is that certain information is taken out of context, leaving the reader with the impression that the applicant may be trying to hide something.

How Long Should It Be?

A resume is a summary of your qualifications, not a novel. The most effective resume's are concise and direct. For most fields a one page resume is standard. Consult with a career counselor regarding your particular situation.

What's the Best Way to Say It?

The best resume is clearly written, and speaks the language of the employer. Avoid repetition, wordiness, cryptic abbreviations, and jargon. Start your sentences with action verbs.

Are Looks Important?

Although your resumes content is paramount, its appearance can determine whether or not it gets read. Your resume must look professional. It should be printed on high quality paper of neutral color with high quality print (we recommend laser printing). Make the resume inviting, but not flashy. Day-glo or sheepskin paper may impress your friends but will probably have an adverse effect on the employer.

What Should I Include?

A sample resume is shown in Exhibit 1.

1. **Name, Address and Phone Number** (day and evening)
2. **Objective** (optional)—To formulate a solid objective try to answer the following questions. What is it you really want to do? For whom? Where? At what level of responsibility?
3. **Education**—list the schools you attended (with dates, degrees, honors), classes you've taken that are relevant to your objective (you may want to describe any special projects, papers, or presentations that were a part of your course-work).
4. **Experience**—list all the positions you've ever held (include paid, volunteer, and intern positions). Put these in chronological order and for each position ask yourself:
   - What were my major accomplishments? (quantify, if possible)
   - What were my main responsibilities?
   - What skills did I acquire, improve, utilize?
   - What special knowledge did I gain?

   Now decide which positions are most relevant for your resume. You do not need to list every job you've ever held.
5. **Activities** (optional)—Were you a member of any clubs? What about other on or off-campus organizations? (e.g.,

EXHIBIT 1

Sample Resume

David Job Seeker
40 W. 4th Street, New York, New York 10012
Telephone: 212.998.1212
e-mail: djseeker@Stern.nyu.edu

Education:

New York University, Leonard N. Stern School of Business, New York, NY
Majors: Finance and Management
Minor: Japanese
B.S. expected in the summer of 1997
Major GPA: 3.65
Current GPA: 3.20

Experience:

Profita Development Ltd., Hong Kong, H.K.
Intern - 12/95–1/96 and Summer 95

- Developed and implemented technical solutions for company MIS, and MIS software.
- Assisted in managing the purchase of inventory for the production of pigments and chemicals from China to U.S. and to various European markets.
- Developed, maintained, and updated sales/inventory database.
- Translated sales orders, documents, and letters from English to Chinese and vice versa.
- Communicated extensively with high-level staff of business headquarters in Shanghai, China.

C.S. First Boston, New York, NY
Administrative Assistant - Summer 94

- Worked closely with an independent consultant in the Sales and Trading department.
- Generated charts and data for trading purposes.
- Developed understanding of sales and trading culture and capital market activities.

Computer Skills:

- *Operating Systems*: Mac/OS, MS-DOS, Windows 3.11, and Windows 95.
- Working Knowledge of FTP, Gopher, and Netscape.
- *Applications:* MS Word 6.0, MS PowerPoint, MS Access, MS Excel, WordPerfect 6.0, and Statistix 4.1.

Languages:

Fluent in Mandarin, Cantonese, Taiwanese Chinese, and proficient in Japanese and Spanish.

Activities and Interests:

- Chinese MCI Society, New York University—Head of the Planning Committee
- Finance Society, Lennard N. Stern School of Business–Active member
- International Business Society, Leonard N. Stern School of Business–Active member
- Enjoy reading, badminton, tennis, basketball and crew.

Personal:

Fast learner, and highly motivated.

References furnished upon request

fraternities, student publications, charitable groups, etc.) Were you a member of any athletic teams? Were you elected or appointed as an officer of a club organization? Describe your accomplishments in the above activities.

6. **Skills** (optional)—What hard skills do you possess (e.g., language ability, computer skills, and other technical skills)?

7. **Interests** (optional)—What do you like to do outside of work and school? Are you a weekend athlete or a midnight Mozart? Be specific.

The Cover Letter

The cover letter is probably the most underrated component of the job search. If written well, it can pique the curiosity of the employer and motivate him/her to carefully read your resume. If written poorly, the resume may never get read.

Basic Tips

1. Write to a specific individual—never Dear Sir or Madam.
2. Tailor your letters—don't mass produce them.
3. Keep it brief—3 or 4 paragraphs will suffice.
4. Use stationery and print that match your resume.

How Do I Start?

Your introduction must answer it least the following three questions:

1. What position are you applying for?
2. How did you hear about it (e.g., through a friend, an ad, Career Services, etc.)
3. What is/was your major?
4. When will/did you graduate?

The Body of the Letter—Your Sales Pitch

This is where you need to emphasize your strengths and relate them to the requirements of the position. Tell the employer what you can do for them as opposed to what they can do for you. Stress that you possess certain skills that can help your potential employer solve certain concrete problems.

The Final Paragraph

Close by requesting an interview. Indicate that you will be following up by phone Always, thank the employer for their consideration.

The Thank You Letter

This is your chance to show your appreciation to everyone who has assisted you with your job search, including those who interviewed you. The thank you letter is a nice personal touch that will create a very positive impression of you in the employer's mind. The main goal is to remind the reader of who you are, and to show them how interested you are in the opportunity being offered.

Tips

1. Keep the letter brief—two to three paragraphs should suffice.
2. If you neglected to mention one of your strengths during the interview, here is your opportunity. Also, you may want to remind the reader of an important point that you raised during the interview.

Source: This material is from the New York University Career Guidebook and is used here with the permission of the Office of Career Services, New York University and Future First Publishing under the direction of Trudy Steinfeld, Director OCS.

GLOSSARY

Absolute standards This approach allows superiors to evaluate each subordinate's performance independent of the other subordinates and often on several dimensions of performance.

Accommodation A human resource philosophy and practice that attempts to make workplaces and work schedules more compatible with the individual.

Accomplishment records Historical measures of performance used by professionals and scientists to indicate achievements.

Achievement tests Measures of an individual's performance based on what he or she knows. These may be actual work samples of the job or paper-and-pencil measures.

Action plan Negotiated at the end of the performance appraisal interview, a plan to improve performance going forward.

Administrative issues Issues concerning the treatment of employees at work such as breaks and cleanup time.

Adversarial system A view of labor and management that depicts each of the two parties in conflict over achieving incompatible goals.

Adverse impact A general expression referring to the effects of disparate treatment or disparate impact.

Affirmative action programs Programs that are designed to ensure proportional representation of employees on the basis of race, ethnic origin, sex, or disability. Companies that have federal contracts exceeding $50,000 are required by the federal government to have such programs. They can also be established on a voluntary basis or as part of a consent decree.

AFL-CIO The American Federation of Labor and Congress of Industrial Organizations, a major umbrella for national unions that represents a majority of the union members in the United States.

Alternative dispute resolution (ADR) A term used to describe various methods of settling disputes short of filing a civil lawsuit.

Alternative procedures requirement The need to show that alternative ways or procedures may exist that result in less disparate impact than current out staffing practice. Also known as cosmic search requirement.

Alternative ranking A comparative approach in which the superior alternates between ranking the best and worst until all subordinates are ranked.

Alternative work arrangements Making available hours of work and days of work that differ from the more traditional eight to five, Monday to Friday schedule.

Apprenticeship training A training format based on learning while doing for a long time before being recognized as competent to be a full-fledged employee.

Aptitude tests Measures of an individual's potential to perform. Intelligence tests are aptitude tests.

Arbitration A procedure in which a central third party studies the bargaining situation, listening to both parties and gathering information and then reaches a decision that is usually binding for the parties.

Assessment The process of measuring and comparing the costs and benefits to determine effectiveness or value especially as it relates to each personnel activity in a company and the entire HR department in a company.

Assessment center Used to determine managerial potential of employees; evaluates individuals as they take part in a large number of activities conducted in a relatively isolated environment. It is also useful for identifying potential training needs.

Assistantships A type of on-the-job training that involves full-time employment and exposes the individual to a wide range of jobs through assisting other workers.

Association A formal group of individuals that represents them as employees before the employer in many ways similar to a union except that the association often is involved in fewer functions than a union.

Attitudinal structuring The relationships between labor and management during collective bargaining that result in shaping of attitudes toward one another.

Attribution process The psychological condition of assigning blame or explanation to an event.

Authorization cards After initial contact between unions and employees, the union may begin to obtain signatures of employees; if 30 percent sign the card, it can petition the NLRB for a certification election.

Autonomy Freedom to make decisions in deciding how to do one's job.

Availability analysis Process of determining how many women and minorities are available to work in the relevant labor market of an organization.

Baldrige award The major award in the U.S. for TQM achievement.

Band width The maximum length of work day from which an employee can choose the hours he or she will work.

Bargaining unit The heart of the labor-management relationship A group of employees certified by the NLRB to be able to be included in the union.

Base rate The ratio of applicants who would succeed on the job relative to the total number of applicants when the test is not used for selection.

Base salary The amount of pay which is stable or constant over a period of time and is received regardless of performance level.

Behaviorally anchored rating scale (BARS) A quantitative absolute form that expands upon the conventional rating form by more extensively specifying the anchors on behavioral dimensions used to evaluate the subordinate.

Behavioral approach Evaluating the performance of an employee against specific behavioral statements.

Behavioral observation scale (BOS) Similar to BARS except in development of the dimensions, scale format, and scoring.

Benchmark jobs Jobs against which the worth of other jobs are determined by an analysis of the compensable factors and their dollar values in the benchmark jobs and by extant factors existing in the other jobs.

Benchmarking A structured approach for looking outside an organization and adopting the best practices to complement internal operations with creative, new ones.

Benefit criteria Indicators used to show the positive impact of HR activities.

Biodata test Information on a person's background, such as what he or she did in school and elsewhere before employment, that is used to predict how well the person is likely to perform on the job.

Biographical information A form on which an applicant may indicate information about past accomplishments, interests, and preferences that can be used to supplement an application blank.

Bona fide occupational qualification (BFOQ) A defense for disparate impact. For example, hiring only males to play male roles in theatrical productions is BFOQ.

Bona fide seniority system (BFSS) A formal system of seniority that has been and is maintained with the intent of purpose not to discriminate on the basis of Title VII.

Bottom-line rule The 80 percent rule whereby disparate impact is demonstrated if the hiring rate (after an applicant goes through all selection procedures of a minority or female applicant) is less than 80 percent of the hiring rate for white males.

BSG Basic skills of grammar, math, safety, reading, listening, and writing. These represent one of the four categories of skills and abilities that can be increased by training.

BST Basic skills of a technical nature to do the specific job. These represent one of the four categories of skills and abilities that can be increased by training.

Business games A kind of work sample test used in managerial selection. Business games may be similar to in-basket exercises or simulation tests; but they are called games because there are generally rules for play and a winner.

Business necessity Used as a basis for defending disparate impact. Business necessity suggests that the "essence" of the business operation would be undermined by hiring members of the protected group.

Business values Those ideals and principles held by the company that tell employees how they and the company should behave. To be distinguished from "personal" values.

Candidate profiles A major component of a job matching system that contains the descriptions of the candidates available for jobs.

Career balance sheet A technique where one systematically lists the advantages and disadvantages of each job and compares them to help make a decision among more than one choice.

Career obsolescence A condition or state reached by an employee making his/her skills no longer relevant to the job.

Career pathing Two major activities of identifying employee abilities, values, goals, strengths, and weaknesses (career planning) and providing a set of job experiences that aid the employee in satisfying those attributes (job progression).

Career planning activities Offered by the organization to help individuals identify strengths, weaknesses, specific goals, and jobs they would like to attain.

Career plateau A situation in which career progress slows and the prospects for promotion decrease dramatically.

Carpal tunnel syndrome An illness characterized by numbness, tingling, soreness, and weakness in the hands and wrists often resulting from the job.

Cash-or-deferred arrangements (CODAs) Deferred savings plans for working individuals that generally are not subject to tax.

Centralization A term applied to organizations where essential decision making and policy formulation is done at one location (for example, headquarters).

Certification election An election conducted by the NLRB to determine if a majority of the employees in a bargaining unit want the union to represent them all.

CIS Behavior-based conceptual, integrative skills, such as strategic and operational planning and organizational design and policy skills. These represent one of the four categories of skills and abilities that can be increased by training.

Closed-offer arbitration A type of arbitration in which the arbitrator receives information on only the parties' original positions without any information on the bargaining process up to the time the arbitrator is selected.

Codetermination A system of governing an organization where the employees in addition to management help run the company through union representation on the board of directors.

Cognitive job elements Represent the specific parts of a job such as communicating, decision making, analyzing, and information processing.

Collective bargaining Bargaining or joint discussion over wages, hours, and conditions of employment between management and a formal representative of the employees.

Commissions Individual incentive pay plans for salespeople.

Compa-ratio The measure of the average salary for a given pay grade relative to the midpoint of that pay grade.

Comparable worth Proponents of this compensation issue contend that while the "true worth" (intrinsic value) of jobs may be similar, some jobs (often held by women) are paid at a lower rate than others (often held by men). Resulting differences in pay that are disproportionate to the differences in the "true worth" of jobs amount to wage discrimination.

Comparative standards or Comparative approach In this approach to performance evaluation, subordinates are all compared against each other to determine their relative performance.

Comparative statistics Alleging disparate impact by showing that protected group members are selected at less than 4/5ths the rate of the dominant group.

Compensable factors Yardsticks or factors against which to compare or measure jobs to determine their relative worth.

Compensatory approach In a hiring process, an approach where a weak point on an applicant can be made up for (compensated) by a strong point.

Compressed work weeks Work weeks of fewer than the traditional five days yet equal in time to those of five days.

Computer-assisted instruction (CAI) Training that is accomplished by using computer technology, for example, software designed to teach auto mechanics.

Concentration statistics Alleging disparate impact by showing that protected group members are concentrated in particular sections or jobs of a company.

Concessionaire bargaining Bargaining by unions where they give up or concede issues or positions to management.

Concurrent validation Measuring the relationship between a predictor (test) and a job criterion score (job performance) whereby the predictor and criterion are collected at the same time.

Confirmation approach When a manager "loads the deck" to favor a particular candidate by selecting several candidates for final decision who have far less qualifications.

Consent decree A specific statement by an organization indicating the affirmative action steps it will take in response to an equal employment complaint.

Conspiracy doctrine A major legal tool for employers during the nineteenth century to combat and prosecute workers' organizations as illegal attempts to restrain trade.

Constructs General frames of reference that are used to encompass many specific ideas or topics.

Contaminated The degree to which a measure of performance measures or taps more dimensions of performance that are unrelated to the actual performance of an individual.

Content models Of motivation, focus on the needs and wants individuals are trying to satisfy.

Contingent rewards Extrinsic rewards given to reinforce a particular behavior. Reinforcement is an essential component of the training process.

Contingent workers Employees who work for the firm but on the provision that they may be put on lay-off or temporary suspension on short notice. Also referred to as buffer employees.

Continuous bargaining When unions and management representatives meet on a regularly scheduled basis to review contract issues of common interest.

Continuous learning Always finding new ideas, new ways of doing things, and being willing to change.

Contract plan An informal agreement written by each participant in training specifying one aspect of the training that will be most beneficial when back on the job and agreeing to effect that aspect once back on the job. An important dimension of the contract is selecting a "buddy" to follow-up or check on the trainee's success in implementing that aspect of the training.

Contract employee Employing the services of an individual for a specific period of time and paying only the direct wages of the individual.

Contract recruiting Recruiting and hiring of individuals for a set period of time as spelled out in a contract.

Contrast effect A good person looks even better when placed next to a bad person.

Contributory programs A type of retirement plan in which both the employee and the organization contribute for benefits to be obtained at retirement.

Conventional rating A quantitative absolute form in which a superior evaluates subordinates by checking how well they are doing on a form with several dimensions (traits) and numbers.

Cooperative acceptance Ensuring that employees have a work environment free from sexual harassment.

Cooperative system A view of labor and management that depicts each of the two parties engaging in reciprocal problem solving, information sharing, and integration of goals.

Coordinated bargaining When several unions bargain jointly with a single employer.

Core time The time in which everyone must work; there is no choice about this time.

Corporate campaign A boycott where the union appeals to the public to support its efforts against an employer.

Corporate culture The values, norms, and statements of what is important to a company and how its employees should be treated.

Cost-benefit assessment Process of measuring and comparing the costs of the benefits of doing HR activities.

Cost criteria Indicators used to show the cost of providing a HR activity.

Cost-of-living adjustments (COLAs) Salary or compensation variation that is related to economic conditions (cost of living changes) rather than performance.

Cost-reduction strategy A method of being competitive by reducing the costs of the firm.

Cost-sharing A trend whereby firms are asking their employees to help pay for some of the costs of indirect compensation.

Critical incidents An absolute form in which the superior records the critical or important events exhibited by a subordinate on a predetermined list of critical incidents.

Critical incident technique (CIT) Method of job analysis whereby behavioral descriptions that have a critical or essential impact on the performance of a job (good, average, or bad) are recorded.

Customerization Means viewing everybody, whether internal or external to the organization, as a customer and then putting that customer first.

Cutoff scores Scores on a test or predictor below which one decision is made (not to hire) and above which another decision is made (to hire).

Decentralization A term applied to organizations where essential decision making and policy formulation is done at several locations (for example, in the divisions or departments of the organization).

Decentralizing The process by a company of moving decision making authority to lower managerial and nonmanagerial levels.

Decertification election An election conducted by the NLRB to remove a union from representation if the employees currently represented by the union vote to do so.

Decline stage The final stage of the business when profits and sales are falling.

Deficient The degree to which a measure of performance fails to measure or tap all the essential elements in the actual performance of an individual.

Defined benefit A specific dollar benefit an individual is to receive from the pension plan upon retirement.

Defined contribution An employee pension plan to which a defined or specified contribution is made by the employer.

Delphi technique A number of experts take turns at presenting a forecast statement. As the process continues, the forecast is subject to other members' revisions until a viable forecast emerges.

Demographics Characteristics of a population (for example, ages, sex, race).

Demographic statistics Alleging disparate impact by showing that protected group members are more heavily represented in the labor market than they are in the company.

Department structure An organization that is divided into specialized areas such as finance, marketing, manufacturing and human resources.

Depth interview An interview where the interviewer has only a general set of questions to ask and where the interviewee is asked to go into detail in answering.

Dictionary of Occupational Titles (DOT) Source for obtaining the job descriptions for almost 30,000 different jobs.

Differential piece rate plan An individual incentive pay plan where several rates of pay exist for the same job.

Direct compensation The basic wage and performance-based pay including merit and incentive pay.

Direct index Assessment approach that tends to be more objective because such things as actual units sold, scrap rate, absenteeism, and units produced are used to evaluate performance.

Disparate impact Illegal discrimination in employment practice in the selection of a protected group.

Disparate treatment Illegal discrimination in employment practices in the selection of an individual.

Distributive bargaining A type of collective bargaining where both labor and management try to attain goals that would result in a gain for one party but a loss for the other.

Distributive justice Is actual outcome or resolution of a situation. It affects one's perception of fairness. See Fairness.

Diversity management Management of heterogeneous groups, that is, groups that vary in many characteristics.

Divisional structure An organization that has several units, each with its own departmental structure serving its own customer.

Earned time A positive behavioral control strategy to reduce absenteeism through a "no-fault" approach that provides employees potential days off they use as (if) needed.

Economic supplements A type of compensation for employees including things like pensions, vacations, paid holidays, sick leave, health insurance, and supplemental unemployment benefits.

ECU The common currency unit being adopted in Europe as the nations integrate their economies (European Currency Unit).

Effectiveness indicators Measures HR departments use to demonstrate their effectiveness.

80 percent rule A selection rate for any protected group must be 80 percent of the rate for the group with the highest rate. If, for example, a company hires 50 percent of all white male applicants who apply in a particular job category, then it must hire at least 40 percent (80 percent of 50 percent) of all blacks who apply and 40 percent of all women and other protected groups.

Electronic cottage Homes of employees equipped with computers and means by which they can communicate with the main office or plant.

Employee assistance programs (EAPs) Programs specifically designed to assist employees with chronic personal problems (for example, marital dysfunctions, alcohol abuse) that hinder their job performance, attendance, and corporate citizenship.

Employee pacing Condition in which the pace or rate at which the employee works is determined by the employee and not the machine as under machine pacing.

Employee referral programs (ERPs) Essentially word of mouth advertising involving current employees recruiting (informally) potentially qualified job applicants.

Employee rights Rights desired by employees regarding the security of their jobs and the treatment administered by their employers.

Employee services and perquisites A form of indirect compensation that varies depending on employee type and organization to offset the problems of working (for example, daycare) or used to symbolize a status differential (for example, company-paid memberships to country, athletic, and social clubs).

Employment-at-will A common law doctrine stating that employers may dismiss their employees for any reason. Recently, court decisions and legislation have created some exceptions to this rule.

Employment contract An agreement between the employee and the employer regarding certain conditions of employment (for example, wages, hours, and the type of work).

Employment security The offering of permanent employment status, usually in exchange for a pledge to be retrained, to be productive, and to be assigned to different jobs.

Empower Passing on to employees the freedom and responsibility to make decisions and give them the ability to know how to do so.

Entrepreneurial strategy Where the employees are encouraged to take risks and be innovative.

Environmental scanning A process of continually examining the internal and external environments.

Ergonomics An approach to job design concerned with designing and shaping jobs to fit the physical abilities and characteristics of individual workers.

ERISA The Employees' Retirement Income Security Act, passed to protect employees against their company's retirement fund going bankrupt.

Error of central tendency Type of halo error where all dimensions are rated average or all individuals receive average ratings.

Error of leniency Type of halo error where all dimensions are given a favorable rating or all individuals are given a more lenient rating.

Error of strictness Type of halo error where all dimensions are given an unfavorable rating or all individuals receive a tougher rating.

ERTA The Economic Recovery Tax Act of 1981 that made it possible for employees to establish IRAs (the IRA provisions were modified by the Tax Reform Act of 1986).

Essay method A performance evaluation method in which the superior describes in writing (essay form) the performance of the subordinates.

Essentiality The amount of power a job holder (any employee) has, which is determined by how critical the job is to the organization and by exclusivity.

ESOPs Employee stock ownership plans in which employees can be owners of the firm's stock.

Ethics A set of guiding principles for interactions with others.

Europay The trend to pay employees throughout Europe, especially managers, the same general amount of compensation.

Evaluation design Methods by which training programs can be evaluated to determine how effective the training programs are (that is, how much change is made).

Exclusivity The difficulty in replacing a job holder.

Exempt employees Job incumbents are not paid overtime for working overtime; they are exempt from the wage-hour laws requiring overtime pay.

Expatriate employee An employee of one country who works in another country.

Expectancy model Suggests that people are motivated at work to choose among different behaviors if the result is rewards that are valued.

Experimental design Most rigorous form of design used to assess the impact of training programs.

Extended CIT The application of the critical incident technique to a variety of job domains identified by job incumbents.

Extension of bargaining Where the arbitrator attempts to reach a rational and equitable decision acceptable to both parties in arbitration.

External attribution Assigning the cause of an event to an outside force or person.

External environment Aspects of the external environment such as worldwide and domestic economic conditions, worldwide and domestic population characteristics, labor force educational attainment levels and values, legislative and regulatory conditions, and general economic and organizational trends that influence the nature and quality of HR management activities.

External equity Determining the wage rates for different jobs on the basis of what other companies are paying for those jobs.

Extrinsic rewards Those given by the organization such as pay.

Factor-comparison method Similar to point rating in that it has compensable factors but in factor comparison the factors have dollar not point values.

False decisions Typically in selection of deciding not to hire someone who would have been good or hiring someone who turns out not to be good.

False negatives Incorrect predictions that applicants will perform poorly when in fact applicants will perform successfully.

False positives Incorrect predictions that applicants will perform well when in fact applicants will perform poorly.

Feasibility assessment Estimating the value of using a predictor by examining its costs and benefits and by comparing it against alternative ways.

Federal Labor Relations Authority (FLRA) Modeled after and similar to the NLRB but intended to serve to remedy unfair labor practices in the federal government.

Federal Unemployment Tax Act See FUTA.

Feedback See Job feedback.

FICA The Federal Insurance Contribution Act, passed to establish a way to fund the Social Security system with payments from employee and employer.

Fiduciaries Individuals entrusted with the management of money; for example, those who are responsible for the management of pension fund money as defined by ERISA.

Final-offer arbitration A type of arbitration where the arbitrator chooses between the final offers of either union or management.

Flexible compensation An approach to compensation that gives individuals a chance to choose what types of compensation they prefer as opposed to the organization just handing them a fixed compensation package.

Flexible spending plans Plans that provide some form and level of pay to employees that is nontaxable to some extent.

Flexiyear schedules A work system where employees think and schedule work time in terms of a year rather than a day or week as in the case of flextime schedules.

Flextime A work schedule that gives employees daily choice in the timing of work and nonwork activities.

Forced choice form An absolute form in which the superior evaluates the subordinate by choosing which item in a pair of items better describes the subordinate.

Forced distribution method A comparative approach in which the superiors are forced to place subordinates in ranks that represent groups or percentage clusters.

Formal course method An off-the-job training program that includes self-training program and informal classrooms and lectures.

4/5 rule The bottom-rule or 80 percent rule expressing the percentage used in establishing a *prima facie* case of illegal discrimination.

401(k) plans Cash or deferred arrangements that enable an employee to save money; they are often tax-free and are often contributed to by the employer.

Frame of reference training Training so individuals better understand the scales or standards being used to select or appraise an individual.

Frequency rate A formula to determine amount of accidents and diseases similar to the incidence rate except that it is calculated using the number of hours worked rather than on a per annum basis.

Functional job analysis (FJA) A description of the nature of jobs, job summaries, job descriptions, and employee specifications.

Funded A characteristic of newly created pension programs (that money is earmarked for them) required by ERISA.

FUTA Federal Unemployment Tax Act that requires all profit-making organizations to pay a tax on the first $7,000 of wages paid to each employee. The purpose of unemployment compensation is to provide income to an individual who is employed but not currently working, or who is seeking a job.

Gaining competitive advantage Using HR practices to gain a lasting advantage over the competition.

General labor market The geographical area surrounding a company from which it may or may not obtain its employees.

Genetic screening A process of selecting or not selecting people on the basis of gene tests.

Glass ceiling That invisible barrier that often prevents women and minorities from climbing the corporate ladder.

Goals As used in Affirmative Action Programs, targets to be attained by hiring employees so as to equate availability and utilization determinations.

Goal setting People learn quickly and perform better when specific, hard, and clear objectives are set.

Golden handcuffs Extremely favorable monetary arrangements that build up over time making it more and more costly for an employee to leave an organization.

Golden parachute Extremely large sums of money made available to executives if their jobs are lost due to mergers and acquisitions.

Grade structure An arrangement showing the relationship between pay levels and the value of jobs as determined by a job evaluation method.

Graphic rating A form of performance evaluation involving dimensions of behavior against which employees are appraised.

Grievance arbitration Arbitration that takes place during the life of a contract over a grievance filed by either party.

Grievance procedure The most common method of resolving disputes between union and management over application and interpretation of the agreement or contract.

Growth stage When the profits and sales of the firm are increasing at a rapid rate.

Guidelines oriented job analysis (GOJA) A person-focused job analytic technique based on the Uniform Guidelines. The process involves six steps that produces information helpful for the development of performance appraisal, training, and selection procedures.

Halo error (bias) Where positive performance on one dimension overshadows performance on other dimensions.

Harassment Offensive and hostile behaviors in a work environment that is unwelcomed and prohibits effective work performance.

Hay Plan or Hay Method A structured procedure for analyzing jobs that is systematically tied into a job evaluation and compensation system. The Hay Plan includes information about the nature and scope of a position as well as how to reward that position.

Historical records Organizations often use information on how well employees have done in the past (to determine what is actually possible) to establish what is average performance or excellent performance.

HMOs Health maintenance organizations including hospitals, clinics, doctors, nurses, and technicians that came about as a result of the Health Maintenance Organization Act of 1973.

Honesty tests Paper and pencil tests used to measure the extent to which a job applicant is likely to be honest and not lie or cheat on the job.

Horizontal loading The adding of duties to a job that are similar to those already in the job and that require the same skills, knowledge, and abilities.

Horn error Where negative performance in one dimension supersedes any positive performance.

Host Country National (HCN) An individual working in the branch of a multinational corporation that is the home of the individual.

Hot stove principle A person who has once been hurt or burned severely is not likely to commit the same mistake again.

Human factors An approach to job design that includes the physical dimensions of the human body, its mechanical principles and physiology. Also see Ergonomics.

Human resource generalist HR department staff member knowledgeable about many HR activities.

Human resource management The use of several activities to ensure that human resources are used effectively for the benefit of the individual, the organization, and society.

Human resource practices Refers to all the ways in which the several HR activities can be done or practiced. For organizations these practices are choices in the ways they practice the HR activities and therefore practice managing human resources.

Human resource specialist HR staff with in-depth knowledge about one or two HR activities.

Human resource information system (HRIS) A method that allows more rapid and frequent data collection to back up a forecast of personnel needs.

Hygiene factors For motivation include company policy, salary, and job security.

Illegal discrimination While selection decisions are discriminatory, the basis for some are prohibited by legal or regulatory provisions.

Improshare Improved productivity through sharing, a gain-sharing incentive pay program for employees based on improved productivity.

In-basket exercise A simulation training technique in which the trainee sits at a desk and works through a pile of papers found in the in-basket of a typical manager, prioritizing, recommending solutions to problems, and taking any necessary action.

Incentive pay plan Method of monetary and non-monetary compensation related to direct indexes of performance for the individual group or organization. It generally represents a substantial proportion of an individual's direct compensation.

Incentive stock option Individual incentive plan that awards stock such as in stock option plans.

Incidence rate An explicit formula for determining the amount of accidents and diseases per year by the number of employee exposure levels. Required by OSHA.

Indirect compensation Rewards or benefits provided by the organization to employees for their memberships or participation (attendance) in the organization. Also known as fringe benefits or supplemental compensation.

Individual contemporary design Approaches to job design and redesign that enable employees to expand their skills and experience more job activities.

Industrial cottage Small manufacturing operations that are set up in the homes of individuals who then work at home.

Industrywide bargaining Employers bargain as a group with the union at the national level.

Initial demand point A demand by the union for a wage settlement that is higher than what is expected to be granted.

Initial offer Made by the management to represent what wages and conditions it will grant to the union.

Innovation strategy A method to make an organization more competitive by improving its level of creativity and the number of new products and services it offers.

Institutional issues Issues not directly related to the job that affect the security and success of union and management, such as strikes and union security.

Instrumental (also instrumentality) The extent to which workers see the union as able to satisfy their demands and needs.

Integrative bargaining A type of collective bargaining where labor and management work to solve contractual problems to the benefit of both.

Interest arbitration Arbitration that deals with the terms and conditions of the contract.

Interest tests A kind of personality and preferences test of an individual's interests. These tests are not necessarily predictive of job performance, but they can predict which job will be more in line with a person's interests.

Internal attribution Assigning the cause for an event to one's self.

Internal environment Characteristics of the organization such as its culture, size, technology, structure, strategy and top management's goals and values that influence the nature of the HR activities.

Internet A network that links together more than 40 million host computers in more than seventy countries.

Internal equity Determining the wage rates for different jobs within one organization on the basis of the relative worth of those jobs to the organization.

Interrater reliability The consistency or agreement of two or more people (raters) on the evaluation of the same event or person.

Internships Training programs (often part of an agreement between schools, colleges, and universities and organizations) where an individual may work full-time but only for a short while.

Interpersonal competence tests Measures of social intelligence. These include aspects of intelligence related to awareness of nonverbal and social information.

Intraorganizational bargaining The process of negotiating terms influencing their constituents over changes in bargaining positions.

Intrapreneurship Entrepreneurial behavior within an existing organization rather than starting a new business outside an organization.

Intrinsic rewards Those originating from within the person such as a sense of meaningfulness.

IPS A category of learning involved with the acquisition of interpersonal skills including communications, human relations, decision making, leadership, and labor relations.

Job analysis The process of describing or recording the purposes, task characteristics, and task duties of a job in a given organization setting to determine a match for individual skill, experience, knowledge, and needs.

Job banks Places where computerized listings of jobs and their characteristics are maintained These banks are generally associated with public employment agencies.

Job burnout A specific set of symptoms brought on by severe or chronic stress directly related to the career rather than personal difficulties. Related symptoms are chronic fatigue, low energy, irritability, and negative attitude toward job and self.

Job classes Used interchangeably with job families.

Job classification method Similar to ranking except that classes or grades are established and then the jobs are placed into the classes.

Job description A detailed statement of the duties, purposes, and conditions under which a job is to be performed.
Job domain A category of related duties.
Job elements The smallest identifiable components of a job.
Job enlargement An approach to job design that leads a job horizontally, that is, adds more of the same type of duties requiring the same skills.
Job enrichment An approach to job design that loads a job vertically, that is, increases the number of skills needed and the sense of significance.
Job evaluation Comparison of jobs by the use of formal and systematic procedures to determine their relative worth within the organization.
Job fairs Events where many employers gather to talk with potential job applicants, often students, about job opportunities.
Job families Grouping together all jobs of nearly the same value to the organization for the purpose of establishing a wage structure that reflects internal equity.
Job feedback The degree to which the job itself provides the worker with information about how well the job is being performed.
Job identity The degree to which a job requires completion of a "whole" and identifiable piece of work.
Job instruction training (JIT) A systematic technique for on-the-job training consisting of four steps: 1) careful selection and preparation of trainer and trainee for the learning experience to follow, 2) full explanation and demonstration by the trainer, 3) a trial on-the-job performance by the trainee, and 4) a thorough feedback session highlighting job performance and job requirements.
Job matching programs An essential function in effective recruiting that entails fitting the needs of people to the requirements of the job.
Job needs analysis An examination of the organization that provides information on the tasks to be performed on each job, the skills necessary to perform tasks, and the minimum acceptable standards of performance.
Job posting A procedure of posting within the organization a list of jobs that are available.
Job profiles A major component of a job matching system that contains the descriptions of jobs that are available.
Job progression A set of job experiences provided through a series of job assignments.
Job progression program A systematic effort by companies to tie individual career needs to the practical needs of the organization by identifying what individuals want and what organizations need and can offer.
Job ranking method A hierarchy or ladder of jobs constructed from the job analysis to reflect the relative value of jobs to the organization.
Job-relatedness Refers to selection tests and qualifications being related to an employee's being successful on the job. If a test or qualification is shown to be job-related, a disparate impact charge can be defended.
Job rotation An approach to job design that does not change the design of a job, but rather rotates the worker from job to job.
Job sex-role stereotyping The process of associating characteristics of jobs and roles with the incumbents of those jobs and roles.
Job sex-typing Classifying a job according to a male or female suffix (for example, male-foreman, female-seamstress) generally reflecting a traditional sex-role bias.
Job sharing Arrangements for two people or more to share (split) the hours of one job, for example, two people will take one job and each will work four hours daily.
Job significance The degree to which the job has a substantial impact on the lives of other people.
Job specification A detailed statement of the skills, knowledge, and abilities required of a person doing a given job.
Judgmental forecast A personnel planning forecasting technique that relies on the personal judgments of selected experts.
Kaizen The Japanese word meaning continuous improvement.
Keiretsu In Japan, a vertical linkage of companies that are mutual suppliers and customers.
Labor-Management Relations Act See Taft-Hartley Act.
Labor-Management Reporting and Disclosure Act See Landrum-Griffin Act.
Labor market The number and characteristics of the persons in the workforce who are either working or are looking for work.
Labor relations system A conceptual paradigm used to help identify and define the interrelationships among management, union, and employees.
Landrum-Griffin Act Passed in 1959 to regulate the internal affairs of unions, also known as the Labor-Management Reporting and Disclosure Act.
Laws of effect Behavior that results in positive outcomes tends to be repeated.
Lie detector test An increasingly common part of a selection procedure used to predict employees who are likely to lie or steal, also called a polygraph exam.
Line managers Individuals who are responsible for managing employees who are involved in production and delivery of the firm's goods and services.
Liquidation/divestiture strategy Where the firm is pursuing tactics to get out of the business.
Local country national See host country national.
Lockout A refusal of management to allow workers to work.
Low quality of work life A sociopsychological work environment component characterized by oneway communications, lack of respect for employee rights, poor personnel, and policies that produce unfavorable psychological conditions and outcomes.
Lump sum bonuses Salary increases in one payment rather than being divided into several smaller increases.
Machine pacing A condition under which the machine determines how fast the work must be done, therefore, the pace at which the employee works is determined by the machine.
Management by objectives (MBO) This approach evaluates the performance of managers (typically) on the basis of how well they have attained their predetermined goals or objectives.
Management position description questionnaire (MPDQ) A method of job analysis that relies upon the checklist method to analyze jobs, especially management jobs.
Managerial estimate Estimates of staffing needs made by either the top-down version or the bottom-up version.
Managerial level HR activities of a medium-term length to develop and implement that may involve line managers.
Managing diversity Effectively utilizing the talents of all members of a diverse workforce.
Mandatory issues Wages, hours, and other terms and conditions of employment over which management must bargain according to the NRLA.
Matrix structure An organization where employees report to more than one boss, each in a different unit of the company.
Mature stage When profits and sales growth begin to slow and organizations lower costs to increase profit margins.
Maturity curves Compensation determined on the basis of years of experience in a profession such as engineering.
Measured day work An incentive pay plan where production standards are established, although not as precisely as in piecework plans, and employees are paid according to those standards.
Mediation A procedure in which a central third party assists union and management negotiations in reaching a voluntary agreement.
Medicare A federal program that defrays medical costs for senior citizens.
Merit pay plans Methods of monetary compensation (generally related to subjectively evaluated performance) that represents only a small percentage increment in an employee's direct compensation.
Meritocracy Emphasizing fairness in evaluating people on their work-related contributions.
Methods analysis The use of individual activity units to describe the way a job is to be performed and evaluated. Also known as motion study. Best application is to nonmanagerial jobs.
Midlife transition Reexamination of one's accomplishments relative to initial career goals that occurs between the ages of forty and fifty-five.
Mixed interview A performance appraisal interview in which the rater combines the tell-and-sell with the problem-solving types.

Motivation-hygiene model Describes factors in the workplace that dissatisfy people and factors that motivate them.

Multidomestic structure These operations may become so large, or local conditions may require, that they almost operate as independent companies, each responsible for its own major business decisions.

Multiemployer bargaining Employers bargain as a group with the union at the local level.

Multilateral bargaining A type of collective negotiating in which more than two parties are involved in the negotiating and there is no clear union-management dichotomy.

Multinational Corporation (MNC) A firm that operates in several countries of the world.

Multinational structure An organization that has operations in more than one country and whose major business decisions are made at the headquarters.

Multiple cutoff model A hiring process where an applicant must exceed fixed levels of proficiency (do well on all tests) but in no particular sequence.

Multiple hurdle model A hiring process where an applicant must do well on several tests or predictors and must do well in sequence.

Multiple linear regression An extension of simple linear regression where several independent variables (Xs) are used to predict or forecast future events more accurately. For example, productivity is predicted by an equation relating absenteeism (X1), turnover (X2), and waste (X3) to the dependent variable productivity (Y).

Multiple management programs Training programs for managers where lower and middle-level managers get an opportunity to work with top-level managers.

Multiple predictor approach Combining several pieces of information or predictors to make a selection decision.

Narrative essay A written, open-ended statement of evaluation or appraisal of an employee.

National Institute of Occupational Safety and Health (NIOSH) A federal agency created to aid in the research, dissemination, and education of health and safety issues and provide expertise to organizations in need of such services.

National Labor Relations Act (NLRA) See Wagner Act.

National Labor Relations Board (NLRB) Established by the Wagner Act to administer the National Labor Relations Act.

National union A basic unit of labor unions that organizes, charters, and controls member union locals and develops general policies and procedures by which locals operate.

Need hierarchy model Describes a hierarchy of needs existing within people for motivation.

Negative settlement range When there is no overlap between union demands and management's concessions, thus resulting in no grounds for settlement.

Negotiating committee Representatives from the unions and management who meet to negotiate a contract.

Network A collection of friends, acquaintances, and colleagues, both inside and outside one's workplace, that can be summoned to provide some kind of help or support.

Neutralizing The process of putting aside an employee whose performance is marginal at best, in order to prevent influencing others.

New social contract This new relationship between employee and employer centers around immediate work rather than longer-term careers in companies.

Nominal group technique A structured group process where several individuals list and identify their ideas. All ideas are considered by all members and action is decided upon after a structured evaluation is completed.

Noncompensatory approaches Hiring processes in which weak points cannot be made up for by strong points.

Noncontributory programs A type of retirement plan in which the employee is the sole contributor for benefits to be obtained at retirement.

Nonexempt employees Jobs in which the incumbents are paid overtime for working overtime; they are not exempt from wage-hour laws not requiring overtime pay.

Nonqualified pension plans Pension plans that do not come under the purview of ERISA. In addition, under these plans, the employer's contribution is not tax deductible, and the employee is taxed on contributions.

Nonverbal cues Behavior that does not involve words or speech. Examples include body movement, gestures, handshake, eye contact and physical appearance.

Norm-referenced approach (appraisal) A performance appraisal method in which employees are compared to each other in terms of overall performance.

Normal time The observed time adjusted for worker performance in a time study.

No-risk standards An enforcement tool used by OSHA that would require organizations to make their work environments absolutely free of any risks from employee exposure.

Objective forms Appraisals where the evaluation is done against specifically defined behaviors or outcomes such as levels of output, level of specific goal attainment, or number of days absent.

Observed time The average of observed times in a time study.

Occupational accidents Accidents such as loss of limb, loss of hearing, or even loss of life as a consequence of the physical environment of an organization.

Occupational diseases Diseases or illnesses such as cancer and leukemia that result from aspects of the physical work environment.

Occupational safety and health Physical/physiological and psychological conditions of an organization's workforce.

Occupational Safety and Health Administration (OSHA) A Federal agency vested with the power and responsibility for establishing and enforcing occupational safety and health standards and for inspecting and issuing citations to organizations in violation of such standards. Created by the Occupational Safety and Health Act in 1970.

Occupational Safety and Health Review Commission (OSHRC) The reviewer of appeals by organizations that have received citations from OSHA.

Off-the-job training programs (OFFJT) Training programs that are conducted outside the work organization.

On site but not on-the-job programs A set of training programs that are offered at work but not on the job of the employees.

On-the-job-training programs (OJT) A whole set of training programs that are conducted on the job or where the people are working.

Operational level Short-term HR activities typically performed by the HR department.

Organizational life cycle Like product life cycle, this states that organizations go through different stages of development or growth. Each stage has different implications for managing human resources.

Organizational needs analysis An examination of short- and long-term objectives of the organization, personnel resource needs, efficiency indexes, and organizational climate as they relate to the training and development needs of the organization.

Organizational strategy The nature and direction of the businesses that the firm decides in order to compete and survive.

Organizational structure The allocation of tasks and responsibilities among individuals and departments.

Organizational survey Gathering data from individuals in a company to determine how things are going and how workers feel.

Orientation programs Activities used by employers to help familiarize new employees with the work environment and the culture of the firm.

Output approach (Output-based appraisal) A performance appraisal approach using hard or direct measures of output, such as goals, against which to evaluate employees.

Outsourcing The practice of having another company perform an activity once done inside your own company.

Ownership The experience employees have when feeling that they participate in the development and implementation of an idea, service or product, with or without financial stakes.

Paired comparison method A comparative approach in which the superior compares each subordinate with every other subordinate in order to evaluate the subordinate's performance.

Panel interview An interview in which there are several interviewers for just the one interviewee.

Paper-and-pencil achievement tests Measures of job-related knowledge rather than work samples of the job itself.

Parent Country National (PCN) An individual working for a multinational corporation of the same nationality. Also see expatriate employee.

Partial reinforcement Providing immediate reward or follow-up to individuals on an intermittent basis rather than continuous basis.

Patterned or structured interview An interview that has a specific set of questions in a fixed order.

Pattern settlements A settlement between a union and management that is based upon and similar to an agreement made by another company with the union.

Pay fairness Ensuring that what employees are paid is in relationship to what they and others give to the organization.

Pay for time not worked A form of indirect compensation received by an employee for time not spent working. Two categories: off the job (e.g., vacations, sick leave, holidays, personal days, comprising the major portion of costs of indirect benefits) and on the job (e.g., lunch and rest periods, physical fitness facilities).

Pay grades Basically families of jobs that share a similar pay range.

Pay secrecy The issue of whether employees should or should not have access to the organization's compensation schedule.

Performance appraisal A system of measuring, evaluating, and influencing an employee's job-related attributes, behaviors and outcomes, and level of absenteeism to discover at what level the employee is presently performing on the job.

Performance appraisal system (PAS) The entire system that incorporates the following method used to gather the appraisal data; job analysis; establishment of validity and reliability of the method; characteristics of the rater and ratee that influence the process; use of the information for development and evaluation, evaluation of performance appraisal in relation to its stated objectives.

Performance-based pay Pay systems that relate pay to performance including incentive pay plans and merit pay plans.

Performance criteria Dimensions or factors used to judge an individual in performing a particular job.

Performance management A recognition that an employee's performance is often determined by the system (the organization) as much as it is the ability and motivation levels of the employee.

Performance ratios Ratios that indicate where the performance rating of any employee stands relative to the other employees.

Performance shares Under this managerial incentive plan, managers receive shares or stocks in a company as a performance reward based upon how well the company is doing.

Performance standards Indicators or levels attached to the performance criteria to enable a judgment to be made about how well an individual is performing.

Permanent part-time Fixed arrangements for regular employees to work fewer than five days per week or forty hours per week.

Permissive issues Bargaining over these issues is not mandatory but is not specifically illegal.

Person needs analysis An examination of the deficiencies between an employee's actual performance and the desired performance or between an employer's proficiency on critical job dimensions and the desired proficiency required on the job dimensions.

Personal appraisal Identifying your abilities, values, and goals across several life dimensions that are important to you. Strengths and weaknesses are also noted.

Personal competence test A test designed to measure whether individuals know how to make appropriate and timely decisions for themselves and whether they put forth the effort to do so.

Personality inventories Tests that tap individual traits or characteristics, for example, California Psychological Inventory, Minnesota Multiphasic Personality Inventory.

Physical abilities analysis A person-focused method of job analysis that uses nine abilities to analyze the physical requirements of tasks.

Physical abilities test Tests used to measure the physical abilities of job applicants to determine whether they have the necessary strength or other physical abilities needed to do the job.

Physical job elements The specific physical properties of a job such as lifting, lighting, coloring, sound, speed, and positioning.

Physical work environment Composed of the building, chairs, equipment, machines, lights, noise, heat, chemicals, toxins, and the like that are associated with occupational accidents and diseases.

Physiological/physical conditions The conditions of the work environment that lead to occupational diseases and accidents.

Placement An activity concerned with ensuring that job demands are filled and that individual needs and preferences are met.

Point-rating or Point-factor method A job evaluation strategy that assigns point values to previously determined compensable factors and adds them to arrive at a total score used to determine wage levels.

Polygraph Test See Lie Detector Test.

Portable A pension that an employee can take when leaving a company.

Position analysis questionnaire (PAQ) A structured procedure used in job analysis that describes jobs in terms of worker activities, based on a person-oriented trait system that allows it to be applied across a number of jobs and organizations without modification. A salient disadvantage is its length.

Positive reinforcement system An incentive system based on the notion that behavior can be understood and modified by its consequences. The system lets employees know how well they are meeting specific goals and rewards improvements with praise and recognition. No money is involved.

Positive settlement range Overlap area between management's resistance point and the union's resistance point that facilitates an acceptable settlement.

Predictive validity Similar to concurrent validity except that the predictor variable is measured some time before the performance variable.

Predictor rate The proportion of correct decisions (true positive plus true negative) relative to the total number of decisions when a test is used for selection.

Predictors The tests or pieces of information used by HR departments to predict how well an applicant is likely to do if hired.

Pre-election campaign Preliminary efforts by labor and management to persuade employees to vote for or against union certification.

Pre-experimental design Least rigorous form of design used to assess the impact of training programs.

Preference tests A kind of selection test that is used to match employee preferences with job and organizational characteristics.

Preferred provider organization (PPO) Medical care being provided to employees that are preferred by the employer.

Preretirement counseling Counseling given to employees before retiring in order to facilitate their transition from work to nonwork. This may result in early retirement decisions but it need not always.

Prima facie As it appears or "on its face."

Primacy bias A tendency to use information gathered first in making final evaluations.

Primary effect An order effect where first information is given greater weight—the notion of a first impression.

Privacy rights An employee right on the job protected by the Privacy Act of 1974. This act applies only to federal agencies and involves the verification of references in selection and employment decisions.

Private protection programs Programs such as for insurance and retirement that are provided by the employer.

Problem-solving interview A participative performance appraisal interview in which the ratee and rater try to understand and solve performance problems.

Procedural justice The process of reaching a resolution to a situation. See Fairness.

Process models Of motivation, focus on how managers can change the situation to better satisfy employee needs.

Productivity bargaining A special form of integrative bargaining in which labor agrees to scrap old work habits for new and more effective ones desired by management. In exchange, management offers labor the gain of modernization and increased labor efficiency in the form of work incentives.

Profit-sharing plans An organizational-level incentive plan involving the awarding of money to employees if some level of company profit is attained.

Programmed instruction A systematic and stepwise presentation of skills and tasks broken down into "frames" in which each "frame" must be successfully completed before going into the next. Feedback concerning the correctness of response for each "frame" is provided immediately and allows individuals to pace themselves.

Progressive discipline A system whereby employees are increasingly more severely disciplined or punished with the repetition of offenses.

Prohibited issues Bargaining about these issues is illegal for unions and employers.

Protection programs Indirect compensation designed to protect the employee and family if and when the employee's income (direct compensation) is terminated and to protect the employee and family against the burden of healthcare expenses in the event of disability.

Psychological contract An informal and unwritten understanding between employees and employer about what it is reasonable to expect from an employee in exchange for what is in the employment contract.

Psychomotor tests Aptitude tests that combine mental and physical aspects of individual ability, for example, MacQuarrie Test for Mechanical Ability, Tweeser Dexterity Tests.

Public employment agencies An external recruiting source coordinated with the U. S. Training and Employment Service. Such agencies at the state level provide counseling, testing, and placement for everyone. These agencies also have access to a nationwide network of job information and application information.

Public protection programs Programs such as for insurance and retirement that are provided by the government.

Pygmalion effect The self-fulfilling prophesy of telling someone they will succeed and then observing that person succeed.

Qualified pension plans Pension plans covered by and set up as defined by ERISA.

Qualitative measures Measures that are more subjective, less easy to quantify (although some attempts can be made to do so, for example, customer satisfaction is at 90%).

Quality circles An innovative management concept that helps contribute to an organization's growth and well-being, based on the philosophy that a company's workforce participation is its most valuable resource because they are often the most qualified to identify and solve work-related problems.

Quality improvement strategy A plan by which to improve the competitiveness of an organization by improving the quality of its products and services.

Quality of working life (QWL) A process by which all members of the organization, through appropriate channels of communication set up for this purpose, have some say about the design of their jobs in particular and the work environment in general to satisfy their needs.

Quantitative measures Specific, objective indicators or indicies that can be quantified.

Quasi-experimental design A design of moderate rigor to assess the impact of a training program.

Quotas Specific number or percentage goals established by an organization for minority hiring to correct underutilization or past discrimination in employment.

Railway Labor Act (RLA) Passed by Congress in 1926 to prevent serious economic consequences in the railway industry from labor unrest.

Realistic job preview A recruitment technique in which the potential applicant is made aware of the positive and negative aspects of the organization. An applicant is encouraged to approach current employees and the line manager and to ask questions about the appropriate fit between his or her needs and the organization's needs.

Reality shock Career disappointment from having higher expectations of jobs than the jobs can really fulfill.

Recency effect An order effect where the last or most recent information is given greater weight.

Recency-of-events error See Recency effect.

Recognition tests Examples of past behavior or performance that indicate the quality of an individual's work, for example, portfolios.

Recruitment The set of activities and processes used to legally obtain a sufficient number of the right people at the right place and time so that the people and the organization can select in their own best short-run and long-run interests.

Redundancy planning Developing alternative strategies for obsolete employees to acquire skills necessary for other types of work. Planning includes counseling, training, and part-time employment.

Reengineering Taking a look at what the HR department is doing to see if it can be done better. Also meaning a radical redesign of existing structures and procedures, not just fiddling with what is already in place.

Reference verification A method for validating information provided by the application, for example, using school records and transcripts, calling previous employers.

Reinforcement Essentially means giving people immediate follow-up on their performance based on the premise that people will do what is rewarded and avoid doing what is punished.

Relevant labor market The geographical area from which a company obtains a large portion of its workforce for a given occupational group.

Reliability The consistency of a test or test item upon repeated measurement. Also see Test-retest reliability.

Replacement planning Replacement charts to help plan for who will be able to replace whom in the event of a position becoming vacant.

Resistance point The lowest acceptable level that the union can take on behalf of its members or the highest acceptable level for management.

Responsibility centers A method to appraise managers by measuring how well they do in relationship to costs, profits, or revenues for a given unit or division.

Right to plant/office closing or relocation notification The right to be informed before a company closes a plant or office or before it decides to move it.

Right-to-work A Taft-Hartley provision that does not require employees to join a union to work even if a union exists.

Role playing Off-the-job training in which a realistic situation is created and individuals learn by playing roles in the situation.

Rucker plan A group-based incentive pay plan that is similar to the Scanlon plan but is more complex in the determination of the size of incentives.

Safety committee A strategy for accident prevention that involves employees in safety policy formulation and implementation.

Salary compression A decrease in the range of pay between various positions (levels) in the organization.

Sandwich approach Used in performance appraisal feedback to describe the fact that negative feedback is squeezed between positive feedback.

Scanlon plan A type of companywide incentive program emphasizing management-employee relations, especially employee participation, and underscoring efficient operations through cooperation. In effect, employees share in organization profits as a result of contributing and cooperating to attain higher productivity.

Scientific approach An approach to designing jobs that minimize the skills needed by the worker to perform the job. The result is often a job that is simple and repetitive.

Selection The process of gathering information for the purposes of evaluating and deciding who should be hired, under legal guidelines, for the short- and long-term interests of the individual and the organization.

Self-assessment Evaluating one's self in the career planning process.

Self-efficacy An individual's beliefs about a task-specific ability.

Self-fulfilling prophecy Something becomes reality because of the fact it was predicted to occur.

Self-managed teams Those making many management decisions for their group.

Self-management Essentially motivating, managing, and directing one's own behavior rather than having a manager do it.

Sensitivity training A method of training and development conducted in a group setting that aims to give individuals insight into how and why they and others feel and act the way they do.

Severance package Cash and benefits provided to employees who are asked and/or encouraged to leave the company.

Severity rate Reflects the hours actually lost due to injury or illness by differentially weighting categories of injuries and illnesses.

Sex-role stereotyping When roles in society become defined as being or having a sex type; for example, traditionally the role of a housekeeper was defined as being female and the job of breadwinner as being male.

Sexual harassment Physical violation or verbal abuse of employees particularly by managers and supervisors.

Shaping Rewarding closer and closer approximations to desired behaviors.

Significant risks An enforcement tool superseding the no-risk standard as a result of a court decision in Industrial Union Department, *AFL/CIO v. American Petroleum Institute,* 1980. This standard implied that OSHA cannot demand compliance with the no-risk standard if the organization in question can show its existing exposure level to harmful agents is below a threshold assessment as determined by OSHA.

Simple linear regression A quantitative formula used to relate an independent variable (X) to a dependent variable (Y) For example, a forecast of future events such as sales (Y) is predicted by demand (X).

Simulation A training program that presents individuals with situations that are similar to actual job conditions and that are off the job.

Simulation tests A kind of achievement test used in the selection process The applicant is given a task to perform, although the situation in which the task is performed is not necessarily recreated.

Single predictor approach The use of one test or piece of information to choose an applicant for the job.

Skill-based evaluation A job evaluation strategy in which the organization compensates the employee by paying the person for skills and experience relative to the organization's mission.

Skill variety The degree to which a job requires a number of different skills to be performed correctly.

Skills inventories A record or file of the skills possessed by the workforce.

Social loafing An individual in a group or team fails to contribute his/her fair share.

Social Security system A public protection program of the federal government that provides retirement and disability benefits. Funding is provided by equal contributions of employee and employer.

Socialization A process of bringing an individual into an organization and of transmitting norms, values, and skills to that individual.

Sociopsychological work environment The non-physical parts of the work environment including such things as relationships with supervisors, company policies, structure of the organization, organizational changes, uncertainty, conflicts, and relationships with co-workers.

Stakeholders The institution and people who influence and are influenced by how well human resources are managed.

Standard hour plan This second most widely used incentive pay plan pays on the basis of time per unit of output rather than the quantity of output.

Standard resume An organized chronological documentation of work and educational experience relating to one's career and qualifications. Generally prepared by an applicant for a position.

Standard time Is the normal time adjusted for normal work interruptions in a time study.

Start up stage When a company is just beginning and there is high risk.

Statistical process control (SPC) A term used to describe the concept of using the tools of statistics to assist in controlling the quality of operating processes.

Statistical projection A forecasting technique used in HR planning that, for example, uses simple linear regression to predict employment growth as a function of sales growth.

Steward An employee elected by the work unit to act as the union representative on the work site and to respond to company actions against employees that violate the labor agreement.

Stock appreciation rights Generally given to executives who can earn additional income from the gain in the value of the company's stock without buying the stock.

Stock option A managerial incentive plan in which the manager is given an opportunity to buy stocks of the company at a later date, but at a price established at the time the option is given.

Straight piecework plan The most common type of incentive pay plan. Under this plan employees get a standard rate of pay for each unit of output.

Straight ranking A comparative approach in which the superior lists the subordinates from best to worst usually on the basis of overall performance.

Strategic level HR activities that take a longer time to implement and often are for the benefit of the entire firm.

Stress interview An interview in which an applicant may be intentionally annoyed or embarrassed by the interviewer to see how the applicant reacts.

Strictness An error of being too hard when evaluating the performance of employees.

Strike A refusal of employees to work at the company.

Structured job analysis The use of a standard format for job descriptions so that all organizations can use the same job categories.

SUB See Supplemental Unemployment Benefits.

Subjective forms Appraisal forms on which the raters evaluate an employee on the basis of "subjective" attributes such as leadership, attitude toward people, or loyalty.

Subordinate The term used to denote the person whose performance is being appraised.

Succession planning Like replacement planning but tends to be longer term, more developmental, and offer more flexibility.

Suggestion systems A form of incentive compensation paid to employees who are responsible for money-saving or money-producing ideas for the organization.

Supervisor Task Description Questionnaire A structured method of analyzing the jobs of supervisors.

Supervisory assistance An informal method of training, often being discussions between a supervisor and his or her employee.

Supplemental unemployment benefits (SUB) Benefits received by employees who are laid off, from their company until returning to work or until the benefits expire (for example, after twenty-six weeks).

Systematic approach Determining the HR needs of the organization and then putting together HR activities and practices that send the same message to employees consistently.

Taft-Hartley Act Enacted by Congress in 1947 to restore the balance between labor and management and respond to the pro-union bias alleged to have been a part of the Wagner Act.

Talent pools The development of a large number of employees (a pool) who can be picked for promotion and rotation to more challenging jobs.

Tailored, or adaptive, testing Testing that is made to fit with the specific needs or environment of the company using the test.

Target point A realistic assessment of the wage and conditions of employment the union is likely to get from management.

Task inventories A method of job analysis based solely on a structured questionnaire that determines and lists the tasks for the jobs that are being analyzed.

Team contemporary A major classification of approaches to job design that focus on the group-job design interface (or relationships).

Team interviews Conducted by several people, typically not at the same time.

Teamwork Cooperation among individuals in solving problems and in performing their jobs.

Telecommuting A combination of work-at-home and work-while-traveling.

Tell-and-listen interview A performance appraisal interview in which the rater informs the ratee of the evaluation and then listens to the ratee on the evaluation.

Tell-and-sell interview A performance appraisal interview in which the rater informs the ratee of the evaluation and sells the ratee on the evaluation.

Termination-at-will See Employment-at-will.

Termination for good cause The practice or doctrine of firing employees only for a good or reasonable reason.

Termination for just cause The dismissal of an employee for a job performance reason such as poor performance.

Test-retest reliability A process of determining the accuracy of a test or predictor by comparing the results from two separate uses.

Third Country National (TCN) An individual of one nationality working for a company of the different nationality in a branch of the company located in yet another country.

Time Study See Work Measurement.

Timetables Identify specific dates where affirmative action goals and quotas are to be met.

Tin handcuffs Relatively small monetary or stock inducements to entice employees to stay with the company.

Tin parachutes Relatively small amounts of monetary compensation given to employees dismissed as a consequence of a merger or acquisition.

Total compensation The activity by which organizations evaluate the contributions of employees in order to distribute direct and indirect monetary and nonmonetary rewards fairly within the organization's ability to pay and within legal regulations.

Total Quality Management An approach to improving quality that involves the entire organization.

Transnational structure Refers to an organization that also has operations in more than one country but whose major business decisions are likely made throughout the world.

True decisions Typically in selection of deciding to hire someone who performs well and rejecting someone who would have performed poorly.

True negatives Correct predictions that applicants will perform poorly, who in fact do perform poorly.

True positives Correct predictions that applicants will perform well, who in fact perform successfully.

Turnaround strategy Faced with going out of business, a firm may attempt to do things to survive, to turn it around.

Uncertainty A lack of predictability or an inability to tell what things are or will be like; a state of unpredictability.

Underutilization Employing members of minorities groups at less than the rate of their availability in the relevant labor market.

Unfair representation Breach of duty by a union to represent fairly all employees covered by the union-management contract.

Unfunded Pension programs established on the goodwill of the employer rather than on money to be used to pay pension obligations.

Union An organization with the legal authority to negotiate with the employer on behalf of the employees and to administer the ensuing agreement.

Union instrumentality The degree to which union membership can rely on obtaining valued outcomes such as pay raises.

Union locals The grass-roots units of the labor organization that represents the employees who are in the same union unit at a given workplace.

Union shop A provision (in about thirty states) that says that employees must join the union (if the company has one) after a set number of days from initial employment.

Unionization or unionizing The effort by employees and outside agencies (unions and associations) to band together and act as a single unit when dealing with management over issues related to their work.

Unqualified pension plan A plan not set up under the guidelines of ERISA.

Utilization analysis Process of determining the number of women and minorities in different jobs within an organization.

Valid predictor Any test used for staffing that predicts or correlates with actual job performance.

Validity The degree to which a predictor or criterion measures what it purports to measure or demonstrates the job-relatedness of a test by showing how well an applicant will perform based on the test predictions.

Values These communicate how the employees should go about performing their jobs and attaining the company's vision and business objectives. These are personal values.

Vanishing performance appraisal When the giving and receiving of performance appraisal feedback is no longer a pleasant experience, it is avoided and just vanishes.

Vertical loading Adding duties to a job that are different from those already in the job and that require different skills, knowledge, and abilities.

Vesting Pertains to qualifications required to become eligible for an organization's pension benefits.

Virtual corporation It is a temporary network of companies with diverse core competencies who quickly form a collaboration to take advantage of fleeting opportunities.

Virtual office It is an office that is virtually anywhere, largely due to new technologies and ease of communication.

Vision A company's vision states simply what it wants to be.

Voice The ability of employees to have their opinions, views, and grievances heard and considered.

Wage-dividend plans A special type of cash plan where the percentage of profits paid to employees is determined by the amount of dividends paid to stockholders.

Wage surveys Published reports of what several different companies are paying for different types of jobs.

Wagner Act The major comprehensive labor code enacted in 1935 with the intent by Congress to restore equality of bargaining power between labor and management. This is also known as the National Labor Relations Act.

Weighted application An application in which some information is given more importance or weight as a predictor of future success.

Weighted checklist Identical to a critical incidents format but with various points to differentiate the varying importance of different incidents.

Wellness tests Health assessments of employees that include measures of blood pressure, blood cholesterol, high density cholesterol, skin fold evaluation of diet, life-change events, smoking, drinking, and family history of chronic heart disease.

Whipsaw The process by which unions use one contract settlement as a precedent for the next and force the employer to settle all contracts before work is resumed.

Wide-area and multicraft bargaining A negotiating structure that exists in the construction industry in which several separate construction unions may settle with a contractor together.

Wildcat strike A strike that is not legal because the contract forbids it, yet the union strikes anyway.

Work measurement The determination of standard times for all units of work activity in any task. Includes the assessment of "actual effort" exerted and the "real effort" required to accomplish a task.

Work pacing Refers to the rate or flow of work and who controls the rate or flow. See also Machine pacing.

Work sample test A test that consists of an actual simulation of the job or critical tasks associated with the job. An example would be a typing test used to select a secretary.

Work standards approach A type of goal-oriented form of evaluation, similar to management by objectives, except that the predetermined goals are dictated by management and often established by work measurement.

Workers' compensation insurance A health insurance program offered by an employer to cover (compensate for) worker sickness and disability.

INDEX

F

J

K

L

M

N

O

P

T

U

V

W

X

Y

Z